Lecture Notes in Information Systems and Organisation

Volume 47

Lecture Notes in Information Systems and Organization—LNISO—is a series of scientific books that explore the current scenario of information systems, in particular IS and organization. The focus on the relationship between IT, IS and organization is the common thread of this collection, which aspires to provide scholars across the world with a point of reference and comparison in the study and research of information systems and organization. LNISO is the publication forum for the community of scholars investigating behavioral and design aspects of IS and organization. The series offers an integrated publication platform for high-quality conferences, symposia and workshops in this field. Materials are published upon a strictly controlled double blind peer review evaluation made by selected reviewers.

LNISO is abstracted/indexed in Scopus

More information about this series at http://www.springer.com/series/11237

Frederik Ahlemann · Reinhard Schütte ·
Stefan Stieglitz

Editors

Innovation Through Information Systems

Volume II: A Collection of Latest Research
on Technology Issues

 Springer

Editors
Frederik Ahlemann
Faculty of Business Administration
and Economics
University of Duisburg-Essen
Essen, Germany

Reinhard Schütte
Faculty of Business Administration
and Economics
University of Duisburg-Essen
Essen, Germany

Stefan Stieglitz
Department of Computer Science
and Applied Cognitive Science
University of Duisburg-Essen
Duisburg, Germany

ISSN 2195-4968   ISSN 2195-4976 (electronic)
Lecture Notes in Information Systems and Organisation
ISBN 978-3-030-86796-6   ISBN 978-3-030-86797-3 (eBook)
https://doi.org/10.1007/978-3-030-86797-3

This Springer imprint is published by the registered company Springer Nature Switzerland AG
The registered company address is: Gewerbestrasse 11, 6330 Cham, Switzerland

Preface

Business Information Systems Engineering is a vital scientific discipline, which has objects of investigation that can hardly be more timely: the design, use, and management of information systems (IS). The discipline's wide range of topics is impressive, which is also documented through the contributions submitted to the 16th International Conference on Business Information Systems Engineering (WI21). Innovation through IS has been the guiding theme for the conference, representing both the present and the future. The coronavirus pandemic has made it clear to individuals, companies, and society as a whole that the digitalization trend will not lose its power for a long time to come. Areas of society long known for their slowness to adopt digital technologies, such as health, education, and government services, are opening up to the use of modern digital IS. The massive expansion of online shopping and the increased acceptance of digital customer touchpoints will stay even when the pandemic has ended. Moreover, virtual teamwork and working from home concepts are now implemented in many companies that were reluctant to embrace these trends before the pandemic started. Altogether, the past year has enabled a new level of digitalization and is driving companies to take further steps to digitalize products, services, and business models.

Digitalization is changing our world faster than ever, and Business Information Systems Engineering as a discipline has the potential to play a major role in understanding and shaping this development. Not only does Business Information Systems Engineering combine technical and economic knowledge in its origins, but also its intrinsic interdisciplinary nature gives it a great position to continue and extend collaboration with other disciplines, such as business economics, informatics, communication science, and psychology. In recent years, it has become clear that addressing complex organizational and societal problems requires theoretical and methodological approaches used in different disciplines. Making visible how rich, wide-ranging, and practically relevant the outcomes of our discipline are is a major goal besides contributing to the academic discourse of our community.

Business Information Systems Engineering as an established discipline gains its profile from three constituent aspects. *First,* Business Information Systems Engineering research presupposes an *information technology artifact.* This technical artifact is at least fundamentally understood (and not merely represented as a black box). This implies an understanding of the design process as well as the context of use. *Second,* the use of the technical artifact *takes place in a system that has social elements.* The integration of socio-organizational aspects is necessary because the appropriation and use of the artifact by people influences its mode of action. *Third, resource constraints can be observed in all actions in organizations.* Economic considerations are required if an organization's goal is to be achieved in the best possible way. This implies the need for economical design, use, and management of information technology (IT) artifacts as well as the question of added value that arises from their use. For example, Business Information Systems Engineering is not just about the issue of developing software according to user requirements but also about the successful use of software in organizations, which is reflected in economic dimensions.

It is a mark of great success that our discipline actively addresses a wide range of urgent research fields by submitting so many research articles to WI21. In these proceedings, we have structured the accepted papers in the areas of *domain, technology,* and *management* and a *general* area on innovative, emerging, and interdisciplinary topics and methods, theories, and ethics in Business Information Systems Engineering. The high number of papers submitted has made it necessary to publish several volumes. We have used the conference structure to divide the conference proceedings into three volumes. The first volume contains the domain-related tracks, supplemented by the two general tracks. In the second volume, the tracks on technology are summarized, and the third volume contains the management tracks. A total of 267 full papers and 80 short papers were submitted for the conference, of which 93 were accepted as full papers and 28 as short papers, resulting in an acceptance rate of 35% for the full papers and for the short papers. All the accepted papers passed a double-blind peer-review process.

The details of the short papers can be found in the table of contents and the brief introductions to the tracks; they are not detailed in this preface. The student track's interesting and diverse contributions, a clear indicator of the discipline's attractiveness for students, have also been included in the conference proceedings.

In the following, we briefly summarize the articles submitted for the different domains. In doing so, we aim to highlight the wide range and diverse nature of the contributions that characterize our academic community.

Volume I: Domain

Domain represents that part of the discourse that is of scientific interest, which has become highly differentiated due to problem specificity in research. This structure largely follows the divisions in management consultancies, standard software manufacturers, the software product-related organization of IT in companies or, in the area of research, also the call for applications-oriented research programs by the Federal Ministry of Economics in Germany. The domains contain their own "language games" with deviating application architectures and economical problem definitions. The five tracks on creating value through digital innovation in healthcare, retail, digital services and smart product service systems, and smart city and e-Government examine a broad spectrum of current technology use in specific domains.

At the time of the conference, hardly any area is more present from the point of view of the digitization discussion than *Digital innovation in healthcare*. This is also documented by the contributions accepted in this track. The role of patients in the value creation of digital innovations often depends on the patients. One paper focuses on their attitudes toward apps for chronic disease management and another discusses in an empirical study how satisfied elderly people are with telemedical remote diagnostic applications. In the third paper, the evidence about patient engagement tools and their integration in patient pathways is analyzed. The transformation path from research to clinical practice for data-driven services is the subject of the last paper in this section, which analyzes how a third party can take part in less digitalized domains like health care.

The *Retail* domain is subject to two requirements as a result of digitalization: the improvement of internal and network-like value creation processes and the implementation of omnichannel customer requirements, including diverse customer touchpoints. The customer interface capabilities are essential for companies, especially after the pandemic experiences of the past year. The three selected contributions are dedicated to this topic. In the first contribution, the impact of the coronavirus pandemic on local retailers and local retailer shopping platforms was investigated with interviews. The role of personality traits and gender roles in choosing a consumer channel was investigated in a laboratory experiment with the result of significant differences in channel evaluation. The third paper discusses digitalization of luxury retail by assessing customers' quality perception of a digital sales desk for jewelry stores.

In a sense, a symbiosis of old material and new informational worlds is explored in the track *Digital services and smart product service systems*: A maturity model for manufacturers with five areas (strategy, culture, structure, practice, and IT) is used to show the stages from a pure product to a product service system provider, existing methods for the design of a digital service in operational practice are evaluated, a conceptual framework for tools for the development of digital services is designed, and requirements for augmented reality solutions for safety-critical services are formulated.

The *Digitalization and society—even in times of corona* track discusses societal challenges and the role and usage of information technologies. An empirical paper on an online survey conducted in March 2020 examines if willingness to release private data increases if fear of the crisis exists. The role of trust in government also has an impact on voluntary data provision, as shown in the paper. The perceived stress of knowledge workers working at home in COVID-19 times is investigated in another empirical study. The third paper reviews online platforms for cultural participation and education and develops a taxonomy. The differences in the challenges of digital transformations between industrial and non-profit organizations in the areas of business processes, business models, and customer experience are investigated using a grounded theory approach. The fourth paper discusses the success factors of pandemic dashboards and the development of dashboards for the specific requirements of COVID-19 data. The last paper in this section discusses the impact of digitizing social networks on refugee decision making in Germany.

The *Smart city and government track* contains both conceptual and empirical contributions. An empirical paper on competence requirements for the digitalization of public administration analyzes job advertisements, while a literature review on requirements for blockchain-based e-government services represents the status of the scientific debate on e-government blockchain approaches. The future of cities in the South Westphalia region in Germany is the subject of a scenario-based paper that examines how we can prepare cities against uncertain future circumstances. The potential uses of smart city data in smart city projects are explored through a taxonomy of such projects that provides guidance for real-world projects. The focus on sustainable urban logistic operations is directed in a contribution that offers a design-oriented strategic decision support approach. In the last contribution of the track, an explicable artificial intelligence approach is demonstrated as a support for public administration processes.

The two general tracks on innovative, emerging, and interdisciplinary topics and methods, theories, and ethics in Business Information Systems Engineering and the students' track conclude the first volume.

The track *Innovative, emerging, and interdisciplinary topics* includes five papers that address the influence of organizational culture on idea platform implementation, a taxonomy for data strategy tools and methodologies in the economy, the design of an adaptive empathy learning tool, an empirical study of secondary school students' openness to study Business Information Systems Engineering, and the altered role of 3D models in the product development process for physical and virtual consumer goods.

The track *Methods, theories, and ethics in Business Information Systems Engineering* includes three full papers on ethical design of conversational agents, a framework for structuring literature search strategies in information systems, and the design of goal-oriented artifacts from morphological taxonomies.

The *Student* track, which has been part of WI conferences since 2016, comprises 16 selected full papers and another 13 contributions accepted for the poster session. These contributions are listed in the table of contents. The program chairs consider the strong involvement of students as a distinguishing feature of Business Information Systems Engineering. For this reason, the student challenge became part of the WI2021 in Essen to bring students and companies together and to emphasize the application orientation as a further strength of Business Information Systems Engineering.

Volume II: Technology

The second volume is dedicated to the core of change in organizations, information *technology*. The five tracks of the second volume are data science and business analytics, design, management, and impact of AI-based systems, human–computer interaction, information security, privacy, and blockchain, and social media and digital work, which represent the wide range of technologies investigated in Business Information Systems Engineering.

The first track in the technology section is dedicated to the perspectives of *Data science and business analytics*. Hardly any area is associated with as much expectation in operational practice as the possibilities for using as much data as possible. A wide variety of contributions were selected that report on managing bias in machine learning projects and the design of hybrid recommender systems for next purchase prediction based on optimal combination weights, present a holistic framework for AI systems in industrial applications, use natural language processing to analyze scientific content and knowledge sharing in digital platform ecosystems demonstrated for the SAP developer community, and realize information extraction from invoices based on a graph neural network approach for datasets with high layout variety.

The second technology track, *Design, management, and impact of AI-based systems,* also covered a wide range of topics. The first paper presents a socio-technical analysis of predictive maintenance. The evaluation of the black box problem for AI-based recommendations is empirically investigated on the basis of interviews in the second paper, and the role of influencing factors and the challenges of chatbots at digital workplaces is the subject of the third contribution. Another empirical work examines the relationships of AI characteristics, project management challenges, and organizational change. The challenges for conversational agent usage through user-specific determinants and the potential for future research are the subject of the fourth paper in this track. A design science perspective is used for an augmented reality object labeling application for crowdsourcing communities and also to construct an artificial neural network-based approach to predict traffic volume. A hybrid approach is used at a German bank by combining leveraging text classification with co-training with bidirectional language models. The eighth and final paper in this track contributes to explaining suspicion by designing an XAI-based user-focused anti-phishing measure.

One research direction that has been established in Computer Science longer than in Business Information Systems Engineering is *Human–computer interaction*. Four contributions were accepted, which deal with the influence of the human-like design of conversational agents on donation behavior, state-of-the-art research on persuasive design for smart personal assistants, a conversational agent for adaptive argumentation feedback, and insights from an experiment with conversational agents on the relation of anthropomorphic design and dialog support.

The five papers accepted in the *Information security, privacy, and blockchain* track consider data protection challenges and their solutions with regard to blockchain technologies from the perspective of German companies and organizations, a survey of private German users about the relationship between IT privacy and security behavior, cyber security challenges for software developer awareness training in industrial environments, the hidden value of using design patterns to whitebox technology development in legal assessments, and an analysis of the user motivations driving peer-to-peer personal data exchange.

The last technology track focuses on *Social media and digital work*. In the first accepted contribution, the design principles for digital upskilling in organizations are analyzed. A comparative study on content and analyst opinion, crowd- or institutionally oriented, is the subject of the second contribution. The third paper is dedicated to a no-code platform for tie prediction analysis in social media networks. The track on social media and digital work is rounded off with problems and solutions in digital work, exploring measures for team identification in virtual teams.

Volume III: Management

The third volume of the conference covers *Management* aspects and has the largest number of tracks. The volume includes tracks on data management and data ecosystems, digital education and capabilities, digital transformation and business models, digital innovations and entrepreneurship, enterprise modeling and information systems development, the future of digital markets and platforms, IT strategy, management, and transformation and, finally, management of digital processes and architecture.

Data management and data ecosystems form the starting point for value creation processes, which are expressed, among other things, in data-as-a-service considerations. In the first paper of this track, the authors design a data provenance system supporting e-science workflows. A taxonomy for assessing and selecting data sources is designed in the second paper, which also discusses aspects of the efforts for data integration in a big data context. Another literature-based paper develops four types of hybrid sensing systems as a combination of high-quality and mobile crowd sensing systems.

The *Digital education and capabilities* track includes four papers. In the first paper, a literature review about digital credentials in higher education institutions is presented. The interplay between digital workplace and organizational culture is investigated using a multi-case study in the second paper. The current performance of digital study assistants and future research fields are subject to state-of-the-art investigations in the last paper of this track.

The track *Digital transformation and business models* has been particularly topical and not only since the coronavirus pandemic. The first article takes a long-term look at which strategic orientations are identifiable, and digital business model patterns are investigated. In the second article, digital leadership is analyzed through a literature review. The path from the producer to the holistic solutions provider is an empirically oriented investigation of digital service development in an automotive environment, while the fourth contribution focuses on the success of digital transformation and asks, using the notion in IS literature, what is meant by digital transformation success. The last article in this track explores IT artifacts in people analytics and reviews tools to understand this emerging topic.

Digital innovation and entrepreneurship, the fourth management track, comprises four papers, which deal with the impact of business models on early stage financing, structuring the different capabilities in the field of digital innovation, structuring the digital innovation culture using a systematic literature review, and the question of how to recombine layers of digital technology to create digital innovation.

The track *Enterprise modeling and information systems development* as a traditional research field of our community includes three papers this year. The first is devoted to language-independent modeling of subprocesses for adaptive case management. Challenges of reference modeling are investigated in the second contribution by comparing conventional and multi-level language architectures. The last contribution is dedicated to how dimensions of supply chains are represented in digital twins by presenting a state-of-the-art survey.

With eight contributions, the *Future of digital markets and platforms* track indicates the enormous interest that our community is showing in this topic. This track also presents systematizing literature work in the form of literature reviews, taxonomies, and empirical work. The first paper undertakes a literature-based review of 23 digital platform concepts, leading to eight research focus areas. The second paper develops a taxonomy of industrial Internet of Things (IIoT) platforms with architectural features and archetypes. The third paper explains that existing reviews matter for future reviewing efforts. The reviewing effort, measured by the willingness to write an evaluation and how long the textual explanations are, is negatively correlated to the number of existing reviews. In an experiment with 339 participants, it was investigated how different evaluations are between anonymous crowds and student crowds in terms of their information processing, attention, and selection performance. The role of complementors in platform ecosystems is the subject of a literature-based review. In another paper, an empirical examination from social media analytics about IIoT platforms describes currently discussed topics regarding IIoT platforms. The principles for designing IIoT platforms are presented, analyzing an emerging platform and its ecosystem of stakeholders with a focus on their requirements. The track is rounded off with a contribution on how data-driven competitive advantages can be achieved in digital markets, which provides an overview of data value and facilitating factors.

Strategic IT management, which forms the core of the *Information technology strategy, management, and transformation* track, is also one of the traditional pillars of Business Information Systems Engineering at the interface with business administration. The first contribution considers the problem of how the design of IS for the future of leadership should be structured. The role of open source software in respect to how to govern open-source contributions is a case study-oriented research contribution of the second paper. The third paper analyzes feedback exchange in an organization and discusses the question of whether more feedback is

always better. The impacts of obsolescence in IT work and the causes, consequences, and counter-measures of obsolescence are the subject of the fourth paper
in this track. Chief digital officers, a significant role in the organization in times of
digitalization, are reviewed, and a suggestion for a research agenda is presented in
the fifth contribution. An empirical investigation of the relationship between digital
business strategy and firm performance is presented in paper six, and the role of IT
outside the IT department is discussed in paper seven of the track. The last paper
analyzes the requirements for performance measurement systems in digital innovation units.

The final track, *Management of digital processes and architectures*, concerns the
connection of digital processes and architectures. Consequently, the first contribution to the track asks the empirically motivated question: How does enterprise
architecture support the design and realization of data-driven business models?
Event-driven process controls, which are important in business reality, are related to
the Internet of Things (IoT) in the second contribution. This combination of the
technical possibilities of IoT systems with the event-driven approach defines the
purpose and attractiveness of IoT architectures and scenarios. Based on a literature
review, an outlook on a future research agenda is given, and the final contribution in
this track is dedicated to the status quo of process mining in the industrial sector and
thus addresses the use of an important method of Business Information Systems
Engineering in industry as a domain.

Due to the restrictions of the coronavirus pandemic, the International Conference
on Wirtschaftsinformatik 2021 will be held as a purely virtual event for the first
time. This is clearly a drawback, because meeting colleagues and getting into
face-to-face discussions is one of the highest benefits of this conference. Also, we
are sadly missing the chance to present the University of Duisburg-Essen and the
vibrant Ruhr area to our community. However, the conference's virtual design has
huge potential for the whole community to use and reflect on digital communication
and collaboration and to invent new concepts of interaction for the future.

The Conference Chairs would like to thank our sponsors who made the WI2021
possible and gave valuable input for innovative ways of virtual interaction and
collaboration. Furthermore, we want to thank the Rectorate of the University of
Duisburg-Essen for supporting the event. Moreover, we want to thank all those
researchers who contributed to WI2021 as authors, those colleagues who organized
conference tracks and workshops, and those who supported the track chairs as
associate editors, session chairs, and reviewers. We are aware that all these services
for the community are time-consuming and mean substantial efforts to make such a
conference a successful event. We are especially grateful for the support of the
scientific staff involved. In particular, we would like to thank Jennifer Fromm,
Dr. Erik Heimann, Lennart Hofeditz, Anika Nissen, Erik Karger, and Anna
Y. Khodijah.

In these special times, we would like to close the preface with the words of Friedrich Schiller (in German):

Einstweilen bis den Bau der Welt
Philosophie zusammenhält
Erhält sich das Getriebe
Durch Hunger und durch Liebe

April 2021

Frederik Ahlemann
Reinhard Schütte
Stefan Stieglitz
Conference Chairs WI 2021

Contents

Human Computer Interaction

Student Track

Data Science and Business Analytics

Introduction to the WI2021 Track: Data Science and Business Analytics

Ivo Blohm[1], Barbara Dinter[1], and Natalia Kliewer[2,3]

[1] University of St.Gallen, Institute for Information Management,
St. Gallen, Switzerland
ivo.blohm@unisg.ch
[2] Chemnitz University of Technology, Chair for Information Systems,
Chemnitz, Germany
barbara.dinter@wirtschaft.tu-chemnitz.de
[3] Freie Universität Berlin, Chair for Information Systems, Berlin, Germany
natalia.kliewer@fu-berlin.de

1 Track Description

The increasing availability of data and advances in data processing and analysis methods have led to a flourishing of data science and business analytics. This not only constitutes new research efforts in information systems research (e.g. artificial intelligence (AI), processing of unstructured data, decision support systems, or visualization), but also has a significant impact on established topics in information systems research such as business intelligence and decision support systems. In this track, we welcomed the entire diversity of information systems research efforts in the fields of data science and business analytics and were open to all methodological approaches.

2 Research Articles

We received 23 submissions out of which we selected 17 for peer review. Finally, we selected seven papers for inclusion into the conference program. We had the broad and extensive support from a very knowledgeable set of associate editors and reviewers. Without their help, compiling the track program would not have been possible!

Across the accepted papers, we found three overarching and recurring themes that were also touched by some of the submissions that were not accepted for publication: (1) applications of text mining and natural language processing, (2) improving recommendation systems for e-commerce, and (3) adoption and management frameworks for machine learning and AI. A common meta-topic across all papers also included the systematic integration of unstructured data sources and extracting information from them in order to create better information systems or managing them more effectively.

2.1   Applications of Text Mining and Natural Language Processing

The first stream of research in this track deals with developing novel applications of text mining and natural language processing. The joint goal of these papers is to distill relevant information from large corpora of text such as invoices (Krieger et al. 2021), discussion topics on digital platforms (Kauschinger et al. 2021), and the scientific computer vision literature (Kortum et al. 2021).

2.2   Recommendation Systems in E-Commerce Applications

The second stream of research proposes novel approaches to improve recommendation systems in e-commerce settings. The work of Haubner and Setzer (2021) evaluates the value of a novel weighting scheme for ensembling the predictions of individual regression-based recommendation systems. Similarly, Meydani et al. (2021) try to increase the performance of graph-based recommendation system by considering the inferred level of trust among users and its evolution.

2.3   Adoption and Management Frameworks for Machine Learning and Artificial Intelligence

The final stream of research deals with presenting novel frameworks for managing AI more effectively. Kaymakci et al. (2021) focus on a generic conceptual model of an AI system for the application in manufacturing and a four-phase model to guide developers and project managers. Similarly, Fahse et al. (2021) introduce a framework for managing bias in machine learning projects that provides an overview of potential biases and corresponding mitigation methods for each phase of the well-established CRISP-DM process model.

3   Associate Editors

- Paul Alpar, University of Marburg
- Rainer Alt, University of Leipzig
- Bastian Amberg, Freie Universität Berlin
- Henning Baars, University of Stuttgart
- Tobias Brandt, Erasmus University of Rotterdam
- Catherine Cleophas, Christian-Albrechts-Universität zu Kiel
- Jan Fabian Ehmke, University of Vienna
- Andreas Fink, Helmut Schmidt University of Hamburg
- Christoph Flath, University of Würzburg
- Burkhard Funk, University of Lüneburg
- Kai Heinrich, Technical University of Dresden
- Sarah Hönigsberg, Chemnitz University of Technology

- Christian Janiesch, University of Würzburg
- Ralf Knackstedt, University of Hildesheim
- Heiner Lasi, Ferdinand-Steinbeis-Institut der Steinbeis-Stiftung
- Stefan Lessmann, Humbold University of Berlin
- Oliver Müller, University of Paderborn
- Boris Otto, Technical University of Dortmund and Fraunhofer-Institut für Software- und Systemtechnik
- Bodo Rieger, University of Osnabrück
- Roman Rietsche, University of St. Gallen
- Christian Schieder, Ostbayerische Technische Hochschule Amberg-Weiden
- Daniel Schnurr, University of Passau
- Guido Schryen, University of Paderborn
- Benjamin Spottke, University of St. Gallen
- Lena Wolbeck, Freie Universität Berlin
- Lin Xie, Leuphana University of Lüneburg

References

Fahse, T., Huber, V., Giffen, B.V.: Managing bias in machine learning projects. In: International Conference on Wirtschaftsinformatik, Essen, Germany (2021)

Haubner, N., Setzer, T.: Hybrid recommender systems for next purchase prediction based on optimal combination weights. In: International Conference on Wirtschaftsinformatik, Essen, Germany (2021)

Kauschinger, M., Schreieck, M., Böhm, M., Krcmar, H.: Knowledge sharing in digital platform ecosystems – a textual analysis of sap's developer community. In: International Conference on Wirtschaftsinformatik, Essen, Germany (2021)

Kaymakci, C., Wenninger, S., Sauer, A.: A holistic framework for ai systems in industrial applications. In: International Conference on Wirtschaftsinformatik, Essen, Germany (2021)

Kortum, H., Leimkühler, M., Thomas, O.: Leveraging natural language processing to analyze scientific content: proposal of an Nlp pipeline for the field of computer vision. In: International Conference on Wirtschaftsinformatik, Essen, Germany (2021)

Krieger, F., Drews, P., Funk, B., Wobbe, T.: Information extraction from invoices: a graph neural network approach for datasets with high layout variety. In: International Conference on Wirtschaftsinformatik, Essen, Germany (2021)

Meydani, E., Düsing, C., Trier, M.: Towards a trust-aware item recommendation system on a graph autoencoder with attention mechanism. In: International Conference on Wirtschaftsinformatik, Essen, Germany (2021)

Information Extraction from Invoices: A Graph Neural Network Approach for Datasets with High Layout Variety

Felix Krieger[1]([✉]), Paul Drews[1], Burkhardt Funk[1], and Till Wobbe[2]

[1] Institute of Information Systems, Leuphana Universität, Lüneburg, Germany
{felix.krieger,paul.drews,burkhardt.funk}@leuphana.de
[2] EY, GSA Assurance Research and Development, Essen, Germany
till.r.wobbe@de.ey.com

Abstract. Extracting information from invoices is a highly structured, recurrent task in auditing. Automating this task would yield efficiency improvements, while simultaneously improving audit quality. The challenge for this endeavor is to account for the text layout on invoices and the high variety of layouts across different issuers. Recent research has proposed graphs to structurally represent the layout on invoices and to apply graph convolutional networks to extract the information pieces of interest. However, the effectiveness of graph-based approaches has so far been shown only on datasets with a low variety of invoice layouts. In this paper, we introduce a graph-based approach to information extraction from invoices and apply it to a dataset of invoices from multiple vendors. We show that our proposed model extracts the specified key items from a highly diverse set of invoices with a macro F_1 score of 0.8753.

Keywords: Graph attention networks · Unstructured data · Audit digitization · Graph-based machine learning

1 Introduction

According to the study conducted by Frey and Osborne [1], auditing is among the professions which are most likely to be impacted by computerization, as they involve a high number of repetitive, structured tasks. One crucial task that fits this description is the extraction of information from invoices (EII), which is performed during tests of details. Tests of details are substantive audit procedures to obtain evidence that the balances and disclosures related to the audited company's financial statement and the corresponding transactions have been recorded and reported correctly [2]. Invoices are used frequently here, as they are the most elemental source of data used in accounting. They hold the details of any commercial exchange of goods or services between companies and/or consumers. Details of interest to the auditor are e.g. invoice numbers, invoice and due dates, total and tax amounts, VAT numbers, and line items. When performing tests of details, auditors draw samples of invoices, which can range from dozens to hundreds of documents in size, depending on the beforehand conducted risk assessment. Reviewing

F. Ahlemann et al. (Eds.): WI 2021, LNISO 47, pp. 5–20, 2021.
https://doi.org/10.1007/978-3-030-86797-3_1

the sampled invoices by hand for tests of details requires many person-hours per audit engagement. Automating EII can thus increase the efficiency of audits, while simultaneously increasing audit quality by allowing auditors to focus on higher value-added tasks, and through the ability to test more invoices by increasing the processing speed. Initially proposed solutions for automating EII employ rules-based processing and template-matching [3–5], which require human input to construct business rules and templates. In an audit context, the scalability of such solutions quickly reaches its limits: Especially bigger audit firms audit a wide range of clients from multiple industries, which receive invoices from a multitude of different business partners. The layouts of invoices can vary highly between issuing companies (hereafter referred to as 'vendors'). The efficiency gains from rules- or template-based automation solutions would soon be canceled out by the effort required for their adaption to individual vendor layouts. For a solution to be employed in audits, it should therefore be able to capture the general patterns prevalent on invoices and generalize to unseen invoice layouts. The applicability of such a solution would also extend beyond auditing and could support administrative processes, especially accounts payable, in public and private organizations. To address the complexity of dealing with a multitude of invoice layouts, recent research in the area of EII has proposed machine learning (ML)-based approaches [6–11]. The challenge for the application of ML to EII is that the text follows a 2-dimensional layout, as opposed to the sequential, unformatted text usually assumed by natural language processing (NLP) methods. Previous studies proposed to employ graphs for representing the text on an invoice document such that the layout is preserved [9, 10]. The key items are extracted from this document graph by using graph convolutional neural networks (GCN) [9, 10]. GCN leverage a context diffusion mechanism, which is functionally similar to the local receptive fields in (grid) convolutional networks used in computer vision (CV) [12]. Graph representations of invoices are albeit less granular than their pixel-based CV counterparts [7, 8], making them more computationally efficient. However, the ability to extract key items from invoices of GCNs has so far only been demonstrated on invoice datasets with minor variations in layouts [10]. In line with the above-mentioned requirements for the audit domain, our research therefore addresses the following research question:

"How can graph-based neural networks be applied to extract key items from invoices with a high variety of layouts?"

The contribution of this paper lies in the introduction of a graph attention-based model to extract information from invoices, and its application on a dataset of invoices sourced from a multitude (277) of vendors.

2   Related Work

Early works concerned with the automation of EII have studied rule- and template-based approaches to automating this task [3–5]. These approaches are able to extract the desired information, albeit only from known invoice templates, and require human input to create new rules or templates. One of the first proposed systems to apply ML was CloudScan [6], which uses an LSTM-based neural network to extract key items via sequence labeling, a common approach to information extraction in NLP. However, such approaches assume the text to be sequential and unformatted and do not account for the 2-dimensional layout of invoices.

Recent studies have proposed different approaches to represent the text on invoices such that the layout is preserved. The approaches can be broadly classified into grid-based [7, 8] and graph-based [9, 10]. In the former, the text is mapped to a grid, as in *Chargrid* [7] and *BERTgrid* [8]. The latter approaches model documents as graphs, in which either words [9] or whole text segments [10] are represented as nodes, and their spatial relationships are represented as edges. In [10], the edges are furthermore weighted with the distances between text segments. As is shown in Table 1, the document representation and the methods used are intertwined. Table 1 summarizes the methodology of previous studies and provides details on the respective data sets and the reported performance metrics: Grid-based approaches lean methodologically more towards CV and define the task of extracting key items as semantic segmentation and/or bounding box regression [7, 8]. The graph-based approaches lean more towards NLP, using word/node classification and sequence labeling to identify key items [9, 10]. Majumder et al. [11] use a different approach. Their work is based on representation learning and leverages prior knowledge about key items which is used to generate prototypical embeddings for each key item. For each field, candidate words are selected based on their inferred data type. To determine whether a candidate is a key item, it is embedded together with its contextual information, and the cosine distance between the candidate's embedding and the respective key item embedding is calculated [11].

While there are different approaches to document representation, a notion common to all mentioned works is the importance of context for the detection of key items. To this end, grid [7, 8] or graph [9, 10] convolutions are employed in the recent litera-ture, as well as the attention mechanism [11], or a combination thereof [10]. Further similarities can be found in the nature of the features used. Usually, some combination of syntactical, positional, and/or semantic features are employed. Syntactical features capture (dis-) similarities in the syntax of words and are obtained via character [7, 8] or byte pair [9] encoding, as well as through the inference of data types (string, date, alphanumeric, etc.) [9, 11]. Positional features are usually bounding box coordinates either used as explicit features [11], implicitly encoded in the document representation [7–10], or Euclidean distances between text boxes [9, 10]. Semantic features are obtained through word embedding layers [11] or from language models such as word2vec [10] or BERT [8]. In addition to semantic, positional, and semantic features, Lohani et al. [9] use external databases to discover known entities (cities, zip codes, etc.). While the general type of features used is similar across approaches, the specific utilization and the respective implementation of the model vary. The works reviewed in this section are difficult to compare in terms of performance, as each work relies on different proprietary invoice datasets. As is shown in table 1, the datasets vary in size and variety; Majumder et al. [11] use the most exhaustive dataset of the works presented in this section, with each invoice coming from a different vendor. The dataset used by Katti et al. [7] and Denk et al. [8] is comparable in size and variety. Liu et al. [10] use a set of Chinese invoices, which all follow the same government-regulated layout. In terms of size, it is comparable to the dataset used by Lohani et al. [9]. The authors however do not provide any further details, such as the number of vendors or templates or the exact distribution of languages.

Table 1. Methodology, dataset details and reported performance measures of related studies

	Document representation structure and granularity	Model type	Information extraction task	Dataset size	Dataset languages	Number of vendors / layouts in dataset	Reported averaged performance over all key items
Denk et al. [7]	Grid; Characters	(Grid) Convolu-tional Neural Network	Semantic segmentation, bounding box regression	12.000	Several, mainly English	Most vendors appear once or twice [7]	61.48% Accuracy measure (as reported in [8])
Katti et al. [8]							65.49% Accuracy measure
Liu et al. [10]	Graph; Text segments	Graph Attention Network, BiLSTM-CRF	Sequence labelling	3.000	Chinese	Single layout	0.881 F_1 score
Lohani et al. [9]	Graph; Words	Graph Convolu-tional Network	Node classification	3.100	English, French	No reference	0.93 F_1 score (Micro) 0.93 Precision (Micro) 0.929 Recall (Micro)
Majumder et al. [11]	Candidate represent-tations; Words	Attention-based Neural Network	Measuring candidate embedding similarity to field embedding	14.327	English	14,327	0.878 F_1 score (Macro)

Apart from the datasets, another difficulty in comparing approaches is given through the different evaluation methodologies and metrics. Katti et al. [7] and Denk et al. [8] evaluate the performance of their models on the character level. To this end, they use a metric similar to the word error rate. As they are based on the same dataset and use the same metric, they are the most comparable works reviewed in this section. Denk et al. [8] show that *BERTgrid* is able to outperform *Chargrid* with 65.49% average accuracy over 61.48%. by extracting BERT features for every word on the invoice from a BERT model trained on invoices. The other works evaluate their models on the word level. Lohani et al. [9] present very detailed results for the most exhaustive list of extracted key items of all works reviewed in this section. They report F_1 scores, precision, and recall for 27 extracted key items, with micro-averages of 0.93, 0.93 and 0.929 respectively. The other graph-based approach presented by Liu et al. [10] achieves an averaged F_1 score of 0.881 on an invoice dataset. No details on the averaging method are provided. They furthermore report F_1 scores for 6 out of 16 extracted key items on the invoice dataset.

Majumder et al. [11] present F_1 scores for 7 extracted key items along with a macro-averaged F_1 score of 0.878. Naively observed, it may seem that the approach introduced by Lohani et al. [9] performs better than the approaches presented by Liu et al. [10] and especially Majumder et al. [11]. Due to the specifics of the datasets, a direct comparison of the presented results is not meaningful. The limited variety of the invoice dataset used by Liu et al. [10] and the incomplete information regarding the variety of the dataset used by Lohani et al. [9] leave doubt as to whether graph-based approaches would perform as well in a setting with a higher variety of layouts. Our work aims to close this research gap by exploring the performance of a graph-based neural network for EII on a dataset with invoices from a multitude of vendors.

3 Methodology

To evaluate the performance of graph-based models in EII, we introduce a graph network model that draws inspiration from the above presented recent research. Figure 1 depicts the document representation and model architecture, and how they are intertwined. The model takes document graphs as input, in which each node represents a word in the document. Syntactic, positional, and semantic features are attached to each node, which are derived from the word the node represents. The edges in the document graphs represent the relative positional relationship between the words. Key items are then extracted via node classification. In this section, we introduce the representation of documents through node features and document graphs and the architecture of the proposed model.

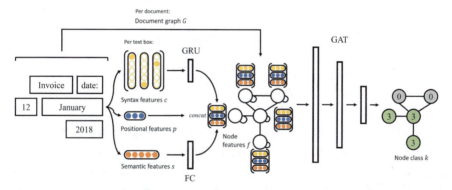

Fig. 1. The node features are embedded using fully connected (FC) and recurrent (GRU) layers and are attached to the document graph, which is passed into graph attention layers (GAT) for node classification

3.1 Document Representation

As mentioned before, we use graphs to represent documents, which are constructed from optical character recognition (OCR) outputs of invoices. We use word-level OCR outputs, such that OCR yields a set of text boxes $\mathcal{D}$, which contains all n recognized words w on the document. Each text box corresponds to a word. We ignore empty and whitespace text boxes. The bounds of the text boxes are described by the cartesian coordinates x_1, y_1, x_2, y_2 of the box' corners, measured in pixels. The width and height of a document are denoted by W, H such that $0 \leq x_{1,2} \leq W$ and $0 \leq y_{1,2} \leq H$. An OCRed document can hence be formally described as a set of n text boxes on a 2-dimensional plane $\mathcal{D} = \left\{ (w^{(j)}, x_1^{(j)}, y_1^{(j)}, x_2^{(j)}, y_2^{(j)}) | j \in \{1, ..., n\} \right\}$, where the superscript refers to a text box. Each text box in $\mathcal{D}$ is represented as node in the document graph $G = (V, E)$. $V = \left\{ v^{(i)} | i \in \{1, ..., n\} \right\}$ is a set of nodes, and $E = \left\{ e_{ij} | i, j \in \{1, ..., n\} \right\}$ a set of edges between nodes $v^{(i)}$ and $v^{(j)}$. Figure 2 depicts an example of the graph representation used in our approach. E is then constructed from the text box coordinates. We use the following algorithm to construct E: Using the bounding box coordinates, each node $v^{(i)}$ is connected through e_{ji} with its neighbors $v^{(j)}$ to the top, bottom, left and right. The neighborhood $\mathcal{N}(i)$ of $v^{(i)}$ are all nodes which are connected to it via an edge: $\mathcal{N}(i) = \{v^{(j)} \in V | e_{ji} \in E\}$. $\mathcal{N}(i)$ can contain more than four elements, as the edges are in rare instances not symmetrical.

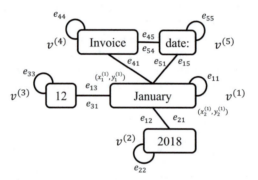

Fig. 2. Example for the constructed document graph, showing the neighborhood $\mathcal{N}(1)$ for the node $v^{(1)}$ representing $w^{(1)}$ "January"

For $v^{(j)} | j \neq i$ to become a candidate for a horizontal neighbor, it must fulfill either $x_2^{(j)} \leq x_1^{(i)}$ (left neighbor) or $x_2^{(j)} \geq x_1^{(i)}$ (right neighbor), while simultaneously fulfilling $y_1^{(i)} \leq y_1^{(j)} \leq y_2^{(i)}, y_1^{(i)} \leq y_2^{(j)} \leq y_2^{(i)}$ or $y_1^{(j)} \leq y_1^{(i)}, y_2^{(i)} \leq y_2^{(j)}$. From these candidates, the candidate with the smallest Euclidean distance between the respective outer coordinates is then selected as neighbor. An example for this heuristic is given in Fig. 3.

Vertical neighbors are determined analogically. In addition to the neighbors, each node includes a self-loop e_{ii}. Through the self-loops, the model proposed in Sect. 3.2 can access the node's own features. The edges in E are unweighted and undirected, the in-degree of $v^{(i)}$ is equal to its out-degree.

For each node in G, word-level features are extracted. We use three types thereof: Syntactic features, positional features, and semantic features. The syntactic features are used to capture the fine-grained syntactical (dis-) similarities between tokens. Character level one-hot representations of $w^{(j)}$ are extracted, using a fixed dictionary of 110 capital and lowercase Western European letters, numbers and special characters. The length of

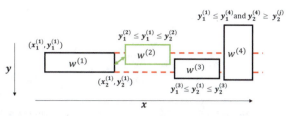

Fig. 3. Valid right neighbor candidates for $v^{(1)}$, with $v^{(2)}$ being selected as neighbor

each token is padded to ten characters. The one-hot encoding process yields a tensor $\mathbf{C} = [c_1, ..., c_n]$ with dimensions $(n \times 110 \times 10)$. The coordinates of the text boxes are used to extract positional features. The $x_{1,2}^{(j)}$ and $y_{1,2}^{(j)}$ coordinates are scaled to W and H respectively. The positional features include the width, height, and area of the text box, and the Euclidean distances to the nearest neighbors. Missing values for distances are imputed using the maximum possible distance 1.0. Missing values appear if a node has no neighbor in one of the directions. In sum, 13 positional features are extracted for each text box, yielding a matrix $\mathbf{P} = [p_1, ..., p_n]$ of shape $(n \times 13)$. The semantic features are supposed to capture the meaning behind a token and its relationship to other tokens. To this end, we extract word embedding vectors for $w^{(j)}$ using a pretrained multilingual BERT [13] base model. To ensure the scalability of the system, we refrain from building dictionaries or embedding tables of a fixed set of words. Another reason for this is the susceptibility of OCR to noise, depending on the quality of the underlying document. For each $w^{(j)}$, BERT outputs a feature vector of length 768. Passing each token into BERT, a feature matrix $\mathbf{S} = [s_1, ..., s_n]$ is obtained. Four model inputs are generated in summary: The document graph G, a feature tensor containing the one-hot encoded tokens $\mathbf{C}$, the positional feature matrix $\mathbf{P}$, and the semantic feature matrix $\mathbf{S}$.

3.2 Model Architecture

We use the document representation described above as input to the model to perform node classification on the document graph G; each node is assigned a corresponding class label. The model proposed in this paper is composed of recurrent, linear, and graph attention layers. Figure 1 shows the model architecture, along with the correspondent in- and outputs. The first layers are designated for feature embedding. The one-hot encoded character sequences $\mathbf{C}$ are passed into a gated recurrent unit (GRU) [14] layer, which extracts syntax-sensitive word embeddings $\mathbf{C}'$. Recurrent layers (such as GRU) have been shown to be useful for character-level language modeling [15]. The semantic features $\mathbf{S}$ are embedded into a lower dimensional vector space using a fully connected layer (FC) with *ReLu* nonlinearity, yielding $\mathbf{S}'$. The embedded syntactic and semantic features are then concatenated with the positional features to form the node features $\mathbf{F} = (\mathbf{C}'||\mathbf{P}||\mathbf{S}')$, where $||$ denotes the concatenation operator. G and $\mathbf{F}$ are passed into the graph attention (GAT) layers [16]. GAT layers perform weighted neighborhood feature aggregation over G, using attention scores as weights. The attention mechanism allows the model to focus on specific neighboring nodes. For a node $v^{(i)}$ and its neighborhood $\mathcal{N}(i)$ of adjacent nodes, which includes its self-loop e_{ii}, the forward propagation rule of a GAT layer l

can be written as.

$$h_i^{(l+1)} = \sigma\left(\sum_{j\in N(i)} \alpha_{ij}^{(l)} z_j^{(l)}\right) \tag{1}$$

where $\alpha_{ij}^{(l)} = softmax\left(w_{ij}^{(l)}\right)$ and $w_{ij}^{(l)}$ are the raw attention scores $w_{ij}^{(l)} = LeakyRelu\left(a^{(l)^T}\left(z_i^{(l)}\|z_j^{(l)}\right)\right)$. $a^{(l)^T}$ is a vector learned by the model and $z_i^{(l)}, z_j^{(l)}$ are the linear activations of layer l. σ denotes the nonlinearity, for which we use *ReLu* on the GAT layers, similar to Lohani et al. [9]. We use multiple GAT layers to extend the context used to classify a node beyond its direct neighborhood $N(i)$ to include the neighborhoods $N(j)$ of the nodes in $N(i)$ [12]. In the first two GAT layers, we additionally employ multi-headed attention. Multi-headed attention has been applied to increase the stability of the learning process in GAT layers [16]. The attention heads compute Eq. (1) independently, their outputs are then concatenated and passed into the next layer. The last layer is a single-headed GAT layer with a *softmax* activation function, which performs the node classification. It returns a probability distribution over the classes for each node in the document graph.

4   Experimental Setup

We test the above-proposed document representation and model using a set of invoices to determine its performance in a realistic setting. For now, we focus on a limited set of key items to be extracted: The *invoice number*, the *invoice date*, and the *total amount*. We define a fourth class, *"unlabeled"*, for all other text on the invoice. Details on the dataset and the model implementation and training are given below.

4.1   Dataset

As of now, there are no publicly available sets of labeled invoices, which are sufficient in size and variety to train sophisticated ML models. For this research, we were provided a set of invoices by an audit firm, in which they are the recipient. The dataset is composed of 1129 English one-page invoices from 277 different vendors. We annotated the invoices ourselves by hand for the key items. Individual key items can be composed of multiple words and appear more than once on one invoice. The classes (i.e. key items) in our dataset are sharply imbalanced: Out of the 243,704 textboxes retrieved in our dataset, only 1427 (~0.58%) contain *invoice numbers,* 2221 (~0.91%) contain *total amounts,* and 2600 (~1.06%) contain *invoice dates*. Table 2 details the split of the dataset into training, validation, and test sets. We chose validation and test set sizes of 10% each, to save as many examples for training as possible. The data splits were stratified across vendors. This way we ensure that both the validation and test splits contain invoices from vendors that remained unseen during training.

Table 2. Details on data splits

	Number of invoices	Number of unique vendors	Number of vendors unique to split
Training set	903	239	178
Validation set	113	58	18
Test set	113	62	18

4.2 Implementation and Training

The model described above is implemented using Pytorch 1.7.0 with CUDA 10.1 and the Deep Graph Library [17] 0.5.2. We use Tesseract 4.0 as OCR engine. Table 3 outlines the chosen model specification in terms of layer sizes (number of hidden nodes) and the number of attention heads in the GAT layers. The size of the GAT 1 layer equals the sum of sizes of the FC and GRU layers and the number of positional features p.

Table 3. Selected model specification

Layer	Size	# Attention heads
FC	256	-
GRU	128	-
GAT 1	397	12
GAT 2	192	8
GAT 3	512	1

The model is trained using the multi-class cross-entropy loss between the predicted and target labels for the nodes, with class weighting to address the class imbalance described above. The 'unlabeled' class is weighted with 0.1112 and the key item classes with 1.0. The weighting increases the misclassification cost for key items compared to the 'unlabeled' class. Training batches are constructed from batches of documents, using 8 invoices per batch. The invoices in the training set are shuffled. ADAM [18] is used as optimizer with the standard configuration $\beta_1 = 0.9, \beta_2 = 0.999, \varepsilon = 1e - 8$. We employ gradient clipping to control for the exploding gradients problem in recurrent layers; all gradients with L^2 norm over 0.5 are clipped. A fixed stepwise learning rate (α) schedule is applied: The model training starts with $\alpha = 5.4452 * 10^{-4}$, and α is decreased by factor 10 every 50 epochs. We furthermore use an early stopping criterion, which aims to maximize the macro F_1 score on the validation set with a patience of 50 epochs.

The above described model specification (layer sizes, number of attention heads per layer) and training hyperparameters (α, batch size, weighting of the "unlabeled" class) were selected using a hyperparameter search with Hyperband [19]. 50 hyperparameter configurations were tried with the objective to maximize the macro F_1 score on the validation set. For each configuration, the model was trained for a minimum of 10 and a maximum of 60 epochs. The best configuration achieved a macro F_1 score (incl. the "unlabeled" class) of 0.8956 after 60 epochs.

5   Results

We report F_1, precision, and recall scores for the extracted key items. We furthermore include their macro averages, both including and excluding the unlabeled class. The scores are calculated by comparing the model outputs with the annotated instances in the test set. The model outputs were generated using the model state after the completion of epoch 64, as the early stopping criterion ended the model training on epoch 115. We furthermore analyze the attention weights inferred on the document graph edges by the model.

5.1   Classification Results

Table 4 shows the classification results on the test set. The model is able to detect all three key items, though performing better on *invoice numbers* and *invoice dates* than *total amounts*. For *total amounts* and *invoice dates*, precision and recall are well balanced, leading to reasonable high F_1 scores. For *invoice numbers*, the spread between precision and recall is higher.

Table 4. Classification results on test set

	Unlabeled	Invoice number	Total amount	Invoice date	Macro avg. incl. unlabeled	Macro avg. excl. unlabeled
Precision	0.9959	0.9391	0.8333	0.9196	0.9220	0.8974
Recall	0.9971	0.8571	0.8072	0.8996	0.8902	0.8546
F_1 Score	0.9965	0.8963	0.8200	0.9095	0.9055	0.8753

This can also be seen in Fig. 4, which shows a plot of the precision and recall scores for different probability thresholds (precision-recall curve), along with isometric lines for several levels of F_1 scores. The curve for *invoice numbers* indicates high trade-off costs between precision and recall if a recall over 0.9 was to be achieved. Generally, the figure shows that higher F_1 scores are attainable through threshold moving; F_1 scores over 0.9 for *invoice numbers* and close to 0.85 for *total amounts* could be achieved.

5.2   Attention Analysis

To classify a node $v^{(i)}$, the model has not only access to the node's own features but to all features of $\mathcal{N}(i)$. The distinguishing ability of GAT is to perform feature aggregation weighted by the attention weights allocated to the connecting edges e_{ij}. Analyzing the

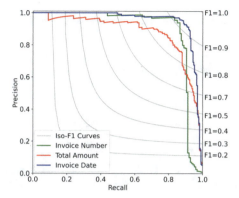

Fig. 4. Precision-recall curves for different probability thresholds for the key items *invoice number*, *total amount,* and *invoice date*

attention weights inferred by the model therefore allows to gain an understanding if and how contextual relationships affect the node classification. To this end, we analyze the attention weights allocated by the model on the edges of the document graphs in the test set.

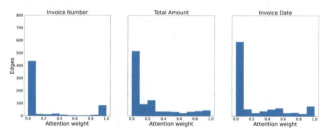

Fig. 5. Distribution of attention weights over all edges on predicted key item nodes

Figure 5 depicts the distributions of attention weights inferred by the last GAT layer on the edges which connect all nodes classified as key items with their surrounding nodes. For *invoice numbers*, the model infers sharp attention weights, i.e. the weights tend to be closer to either 0.0 or 1.0, resembling a bimodal distribution. For *invoice dates* and *total amounts,* this distribution is flatter; weights in between the two extremes are allocated more frequently. As the model allocates weights close to 0.0 very often, we furthermore narrow the analysis down to the attention allocated towards the self-loops. This way, we can analyze whether the model disregards the neighborhood features in favor of the node features or vice versa.

Figure 6 shows the distribution of attention weights on the node's self-loop edges e_{ii}. The model infers primarily very small attention weights for *invoice numbers*, which indicates that the classified node's own features informed the classification not as much as the features of its neighboring nodes $v^{(j)}$. In the case of *total amounts* and *invoice dates*, the self-loop edges received much higher attention weights. In summary, the attention weights on the self-loops imply that *invoice numbers* are rather identified via their context, whereas *total amounts* and *invoice dates* are identified via their own features.

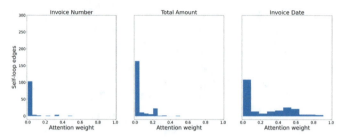

Fig. 6. Distribution of attention weights over self-loop edges on predicted key item nodes

This is also reflected in Fig. 7: The figure depicts graphs that summarize the attention weights inferred on the edges of the 2-hop neighborhood of predicted key items. The attention weights are summed by similar words. The thickness of the edges connecting the tokens reflects the attention placed by the model on the respective relationships, summed across all document graphs in the test set. For each key item, we exemplarily choose the 10 terms which have received the highest attention weights. In the figure, <Key Item> denotes a neighboring token which has also been classified as a key item, <Self> denotes the attention on the self-loop.

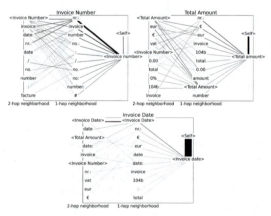

Fig. 7. Attention weights allocated towards the edges of extracted key items, summed across unique words

In the case of *invoice numbers*, the model assigns most attention to combinations of words that form some variation of "invoice number." For the *invoice date*, the model allocates most attention to the self-loop and to neighboring nodes which have also been classified as invoice dates. Similarly, the classification of *total amounts* is mainly based on the node's own features, and the context receives only small attention weights. For these two key items, their context is less important for their classification than their own features.

The analysis of attention weights shows that the model classifies nodes both based on the node's own features, as well as based on the features of neighboring nodes. The weighting hereby varies by key item class. Furthermore, it shows that the model is capable of identifying contextual relationships over multiple hops in the graph. This is highly relevant as discriminative terms such as "invoice number", "total amount" and "invoice date" are usually composed of multiple words.

6 Discussion

Prior research has presented promising results for graph-based approaches to EII. However, these were tested on invoice datasets with a low variety of invoice layouts. The purpose of this research is therefore to evaluate the effectiveness of a graph-based approach on a dataset containing invoices from a multitude of vendors, based on a novel model architecture. Our results show that the model is able to capture the patterns prevalent on invoices to extract the defined key items. They further show that the model emphasizes either the context of a word or the word itself to classify it, depending on the key item class. One interesting finding is that the model identifies relevant context over multiple hops in the graph, thereby combining multiple words.

The intended area of application for the model proposed in this paper is the test of details in audits. The overall goal of the test of details is to see whether the details (key items) from the invoices have been recorded correctly. To this end, the key items extracted by the model are reconciled against other, mostly structured, sources of data. Hereby, false positives and false negatives incur different costs with respect to the overall goal of automating EII: False positives (falsely detected key items) require the active attention of an auditor. False negatives (falsely not detected key items), can be offset by further testing of details until sufficient audit evidence is collected. In that regard, the current performance of the model is adequate, yet offers room for further improvement. The model achieves macro averaged precision and recall of 0.8974 and 0.8546 on the key items. While the current performance of the model would not be enough to fully automate this task, it can still lead to efficiency gains in an audit engagement, as long as the effort to review possible false positives is smaller than the effort to extract all key items from the invoices by hand. The raw outputs of the model could also be further enhanced by heuristics and business rules to reduce false positives, which we did not explore in this paper. For example, rules could be applied which retrieve only the key items with the highest probability per document. Another possibility is to perform logical checks on the data type of a retrieved key item, e.g. evaluating whether retrieved *invoice dates* can be parsed as dates. For full automation of the task, the model should be tunable such that precisions close to 1.0 can be achieved by threshold moving, without sacrificing too much recall. In that case, it could substitute human labor by only requiring limited amounts of additional testing.

In the usage of graphs, our work relates to the approaches by Lohani et al. [9] and Liu et al. [10]. As anticipated, we do not match their respective results. We achieve F_1 scores on the *invoice number*, *total amount*, and *invoice date* of 0.8963, 0.8200, and 0.9095, while Liu et al. [10] report 0.961, 0.910, and 0.963 for the respective key items, and Lohani et al. [9] report 0.90, 0.99, and 0.95. For Liu et al. [10], this gap in performance can be attributed to the much higher layout variety in our dataset. As Lohani et al. [9] do not report in detail on the variety in their dataset, we can only safely attribute this performance gap to the difference in size: Our dataset is smaller than the invoice datasets used in related works. The differences in variety and size render the results hardly comparable. This also applies to a comparison with the results presented by Majumder et al. [11], which use the biggest and most diverse dataset in all of the related research. However, similar to our results and the results of Liu et al. [10], they report worse performance on *total amounts* than the other two key items. They achieve F_1 scores of 0.949 and 0.940 on *invoice numbers* and *invoice dates*, and 0.858 on *total amounts*. A possible explanation for this is that *total amounts* can appear multiple times on one invoice and are difficult to identify by their context.

In general, we see advantages to the graph approach: The model can access an arbitrary number of direct or indirect neighbors of each node, instead of restricting it to a fixed-sized number of neighbors, like in the approach used by Majumder et al. [11]. This advantage is however contrasted by the computational cost of constructing the document graph in the first place. To extract node embeddings from the document graph, we use GAT layers, similar to Liu et al. [10]. This way, edges between nodes can be individually weighted, unlike the graph convolutions used in [9]. GAT networks are also better suited for transductive graph learning tasks [16]. Hence, document graphs can be processed individually instead of requiring one large graph composed of multiple documents for both learning and inference. Our approach deviates from Liu et al. [10] in the granularity of the graph: Similar to [9], we construct the graph from single words instead of using paragraph-like text blocks.

The presented research must be seen in light of some limitations, which are mainly grounded in the dataset. First, multiple recurring vendors are present in the dataset, hence recurring layouts. Though we try to control for this effect by applying stratified sampling in the training, validation, and test splits, overfitting might still be an issue. Furthermore, all invoices in our dataset are addressed to the same recipient. These however are realistic circumstances for the audit domain, where a client might have recurrent business with suppliers, and all invoices are addressed to the client. Second, we only used English invoices. We have yet to assess how the model responds to invoices from several languages. A further limitation is grounded in the size of the dataset; compared to other works in the area, our dataset is quite small. The classification results of our models are therefore not comparable to other research.

7   Conclusion and Outlook

EII is a highly structured, repetitive task in auditing, which can highly benefit from automation. The high variety of invoice layouts faced by auditors calls for approaches that are able to capture the general patterns on invoices. Recent research in this area has proposed graph-based approaches to EII, showing promising results. However, these approaches have been so far applied to datasets with a low variety of invoice layouts. In this paper, we introduce a novel graph-based model architecture, perform an experiment using a dataset from 277 different vendors. The dataset resembles a realistic setting faced by auditors. We show that the model extracts specified key items with high F_1 scores, by leveraging contextual relationships between words on the invoices. While our results do not match the scores achieved by previous works due to the higher variety of invoice layouts in our dataset, they indicate that graph-based models are capable of learning the general patterns prevalent on invoices and extrapolate them.

As of now, we do not see our research on this topic as concluded. As the dataset used in this research is small compared to other related works, further research with bigger datasets and more invoice layouts needs to be conducted to strengthen our results. Complementary to that, we aim to explore more architectural options for the model, such as replacing the GRU with a convolutional layer to extract character-level word embeddings. In our usage of graphs, we further aim to explore edge features. Interesting features could be both continuous, such as the semantic and spatial distance between words, as well as categorical, such as whether words are linked entities or the direction of the edge. Further research should also include more key items to be extracted; especially line items represent an interesting area of investigation. We also plan to extend this model to extract key items from further document types such as receipts, purchase orders, etc.

As pointed out in Sect. 2, the whole research field of EII lacks comparability. Unfortunately, as of now, there are no publicly available labeled sets of invoices that are sufficient in size and variety to train sophisticated ML models. It could therefore vastly benefit from a study that benchmarks different approaches on the same dataset, or from an openly accessible annotated dataset.

References

1. Frey, C.B., Osborne, M.A.: The future of employment: How susceptible are jobs to computerisation? Technol. Forecast. Soc. Chang. **114**, 254–280 (2017)
2. IAASB: International Standard On Auditing 330: The Auditor's Responses To Assessed Risks (2009). https://www.ifac.org/system/files/downloads/a019-2010-iaasb-handbook-isa-330.pdf
3. Esser, D., Schuster, D., Muthmann, K., Berger, M., Schill, A.: Automatic indexing of scanned documents: a layout-based approach. Doc. Recognit. Retr. XIX. **8297**, 82970H (2012)
4. Lopresti, D., Hu, J., Kashi, R. (eds.): DAS 2002. LNCS, vol. 2423. Springer, Heidelberg (2002). https://doi.org/10.1007/3-540-45869-7
5. Schuster, D., et al.: Intellix – End-User trained information extraction for document archiving. In: 2013 12th International Conference on Document Analysis and Recognition. pp. 101–105 (2013)
6. Palm, R.B., Winther, O., Laws, F.: CloudScan - A Configuration-Free Invoice Analysis System Using Recurrent Neural Networks. In: 2017 14th IAPR International Conference on Document Analysis and Recognition (ICDAR). pp. 406–413. IEEE, Kyoto (2017)
7. Katti, A.R.: Chargrid: Towards understanding 2D documents. In: Proceedings of the 2018 Conference on Empirical Methods in Natural Language Processing. pp. 4459–4469. Association for Computational Linguistics, Brussels, Belgium (2018)
8. Denk, T.I., Reisswig, C.: BERTgrid: Contextualized Embedding for 2D Document Representation and Understanding [cs]. arXiv:1909.04948 (2019)
9. Lohani, D., Belaïd, A., Belaïd, Y.: An invoice reading system using a graph convolutional network. In: Carneiro, G., You, S. (eds.) ACCV 2018. LNCS, vol. 11367, pp. 144–158. Springer, Cham (2019). https://doi.org/10.1007/978-3-030-21074-8_12

10. Liu, X., Gao, F., Zhang, Q., Zhao, H.: Graph convolution for multimodal information extraction from visually rich documents. In: Proceedings of the 2019 Conference of the North. pp. 32–39. Association for Computational Linguistics, Minneapolis - Minnesota (2019)

11. Majumder, B.P., Potti, N., Tata, S., Wendt, J.B., Zhao, Q., Najork, M.: Representation learning for information extraction from form-like documents. In: Proceedings of the 58th Annual Meeting of the Association for Computational Linguistics. pp. 6495–6504. Association for Computational Linguistics, Online (2020)

12. Bacciu, D., Errica, F., Micheli, A., Podda, M.: A gentle introduction to deep learning for graphs. Neural Netw. **129**, 203–221 (2020)

13. Devlin, J., Chang, M.W., Lee, K., Toutanova, K.: BERT: Pre-training of deep bidirectional transformers for language understanding. In: Proceedings of the 2019 Conference of the North American Chapter of the Association for Computational Linguistics: Human Language Technologies, Vol. 1. pp. 4171–4186 (2019)

14. Cho, K., van Merrienboer, B., Gulcehre, C., Bahdanau, D., Bougares, F., Schwenk, H., Bengio, Y.: Learning Phrase Representations using RNN Encoder–Decoder for Statistical Machine Translation. In: Proceedings of the 2014 Conference on Empirical Methods in Natural Language Processing (EMNLP). pp. 1724–1734. Association for Computational Linguistics, Doha, (2014)

15. Karpathy, A., Johnson, J., Fei-Fei, L.: Visualizing and Understanding Recurrent Networks [cs]. arXiv:1506.02078 (2015)

16. Veličković, P., Casanova, A., Liò, P., Cucurull, G., Romero, A., Bengio, Y.: Graph attention networks. In: 6th International Conference on Learning Representations, ICLR 2018 - Conference Track Proceedings. pp 1–12 (2018)

17. Wang, M., et. al.: Deep Graph Library: A Graph-Centric, Highly-Performant Package for Graph Neural Networks [cs, stat]. arXiv:1909.01315 (2020)

18. Kingma, D.P., Ba, J.: Adam: A Method for Stochastic Optimization [cs]. arXiv:1412.6980 (2017)

19. Li, L., Jamieson, K., DeSalvo, G., Rostamizadeh, A., Talwalkar, A.: Hyperband: A novel bandit-based approach to hyperparameter optimization. In: The Journal of Machine Learning Research 18, Vol. 1. pp 1–52 (2018)

Knowledge Sharing in Digital Platform Ecosystems – A Textual Analysis of SAP's Developer Community

Martin Kauschinger[✉], Maximilian Schreieck, Markus Boehm, and Helmut Krcmar

Department of Informatics, Technical University of Munich, Munich, Germany
{martin.kauschinger,maximilian.schreieck,markus.boehm,
helmut.krcmar}@tum.de

Abstract. Research on digital platform ecosystems is growing rapidly. While the relevance of third-party applications is commonly known, scholars have made only minor attempts to analyze knowledge sharing between platform owners and third-party developers. We find that third-party application development is a knowledge intensive task that requires knowledge to cross organizational boundaries. In this paper, we use computational analytic methods to analyze knowledge sharing in a digital platform ecosystem. We collected trace data about a third-party developer ecosystem with frequent knowledge exchange between the platform owner and third-party developers. We developed a web scraper and retrieved all 4866 pages of SAP's developer community that were tagged 'SAP Cloud Platform'. Next, we used text mining to render a topic model. Based on the latent dirichlet allocation algorithm, we extracted 25 topics that were frequently discussed in the community. We clustered the topics into the following six meta-topics: User Accounts and Authentication, Connectivity, Cloud Database, Specific Technologies, SAP Resources, and Installation. Platform owners can use our approach to (1) identify frequently discussed topics, (2) generate meta-knowledge in these topics and (3) use the meta-knowledge to improve their platform core and its boundary resources.

Keywords: Platform ecosystem · Enterprise software · Knowledge sharing · Application development · Text mining

1 Introduction

Digital platforms have risen to such prominence in the global economy that they have stimulated a rapidly growing body of scholarly research [1, 2]. By deriving their economic power from the conglomerate of external actors, digital platforms outperform traditional companies across various industries. For example, apple revolutionized the mobile operating systems market by opening application development for third-parties. So far, digital platforms have not only outperformed traditional companies, they have also disrupted several industries by changing the provisioning and consummation of digital services [3]. Economic indicators reveal a similar picture about the economic

© The Author(s), under exclusive license to Springer Nature Switzerland AG 2021
F. Ahlemann et al. (Eds.): WI 2021, LNISO 47, pp. 21–39, 2021.
https://doi.org/10.1007/978-3-030-86797-3_2

power of digital platforms. In 2020, according to market capitalization, seven of the top ten public companies used platform business models [4].

On an abstract level, platforms describe the notion of providing a technological system that acts as a foundation upon which other firms can develop complementary products, technologies or services [5]. Tiwana, Konsynski and Bush [6, p. 675] adapted the notion of platforms to the software context and define a digital platform 'as the extensible codebase of a software-based system that provides core functionality shared by the modules that interoperate with it and the interfaces through which they interoperate'.

As platforms bring together a variety of actors, they depend on so-called network effects [7]. These effects are best described as the increase of utility that a user derives from the consumption of a good or service for every other person consuming the same good or service [8]. In other words, network effects imply that a technology's usefulness increases as the number of user increases [7]. This coherency is often illustrated by using the telephone as an example. The first telephone did not have any value for its owner because other callable telephones did not exist. However, this changes as soon as other telephones enter the network. Then, the value increases for every new telephone [9]. As of now, researchers produced a plethora of scholarly articles that stress the importance of network effects for curating platform ecosystems [e.g. 10, 11]. For example, a big proportion of Amazon's retailing success originates from the large network of independent retailers that sell their products on Amazon's marketplace. Another example are mobile operating systems. The large variety of apps being available on Android's Playstore or Apple's Appstore were significant drivers for their success. On the contrary, Microsoft's Windows Phone failed miserably due to missing third-party applications.

We adopt the view of Hein et al. [3] that 'a digital platform ecosystem comprises a platform owner that implements governance mechanisms to facilitate value-creating mechanisms on a digital platform between the platform owner and an ecosystem of autonomous complementors and consumers'. Besides the widespread success of digital platforms in consumer markets, more and more companies adopt platform-based business models in business-to-business markets. Thereby, the enterprise software market is no exception. In recent years, traditional ERP vendors such as Oracle and SAP have gotten into fierce competition with cloud-native companies such as Salesforce or ServiceNow. While the latter pursued a cloud platform strategy from their beginning, the former transition from on-premises system to cloud-based solutions. Generally speaking, the concept of app stores being implemented in enterprise software platforms (e.g. the SAP Cloud Platform or the Now Platform) is very similar to the ones that are known from mobile operating systems. The central element is the provisioning of a base system that comes with a marketplace that can be used to install and deploy new applications. Furthermore, the majority of applications are developed and maintained by third-parties [12, 13].

The widespread uptake of platform strategies creates several challenges for vendors of enterprise software [14–16]. On the one hand, vendors who previously sold on-premises systems have to cope with the increasingly complex information systems landscape of their customers. Nowadays, many enterprises use a mixture of on-premises and cloud solutions that result in difficulties with respect to technical integration [17]. Usually, the on-premises systems have gone through a long series of update cycles and are inherently associated with legacy issues. Such legacy systems require additional integration tools to be compatible with modern cloud solutions. On the other hand, the uptake of platform strategies turns once product-based vendors of enterprise software into ecosystem curators. This shift requires platform owners to collaboratively develop and commercialize a shared technology with customers, consultants and third-party developers [14]. Consequently, those vendors have to shift their focus from product development to governing partnerships and complementary products [18–20].

To enable the development of third-party applications, platform owners have to share development related knowledge with third-party developers. As of yet, the scholarly discourse on knowledge sharing between platform owners and third-party developers was limited to the concept of boundary resources. Prior research identified three types of boundary resources: Software development kits (SDKs), application programming interfaces (APIs), and technical documentation [3, 19, 21]. These boundary resources ease third-party development by providing information about the platform's functionalities [21, 22]. We identified that platform owners use several additional resources to share knowledge with third-party developers. These resources consist but are not limited to tutorials, code snippets, online communities, trainings, and blogs [14].

In this paper, we study the role of sponsored online communities for knowledge sharing in digital platform ecosystems. In particular, we investigate how platform owners can use online community data to generate insights into their platform ecosystem. We find that this relatively unexplored area is worth investigating for several reasons. First, empirical evidence suggests that developers get a vast amount of knowledge from online communities [23, 24]. In that regard, third-party application development is no different. Second, we explored online communities of leading enterprise software vendors and discovered that these communities accumulated a vast amount of peer reviewed knowledge. In fact, Oracle's developer community consists of 3.7 million users, 2.2 million discussions and 7.8 million comments [25]. Salesforce's developer community features 264,000 discussions, without considering Salesforce's Trailblazer community or questions asked on StackExchange [26]. SAP's online community comprises 2.5 million questions of which 1.0 million have been answered. Additionally, the community has 2.8 million users and 123,000 blog posts [27]. Third, we argue that online communities have decent scaling potentials for platform owners. In such communities, third-party developers can share knowledge among one another with minimum moderation effort required by the platform owner.

For our study, we retrieved all 4866 pages of SAP's developer community that were tagged 'SAP Cloud Platform'. Next, we used text mining and rendered a topic model [28, 29]. Based on the latent dirichlet allocation algorithm [30], the model extracted 25 coherent topics that we clustered into the following six meta-topics: User Accounts and Authentication, Connectivity, Cloud Database, Specific Technologies, SAP Resources, and Installation.

With our findings we contribute to the discourse on digital platform ecosystem by providing researchers and practitioners with an analytic lens to study knowledge sharing between platform owners and third-party developers. Furthermore, we help platform owners to generate insights into their platform ecosystem by analyzing digital trace data. Platform owners can use these insights to improve the platform's attractiveness for third-party developers [22].

The remainder of the paper is structured as follows. In the next chapter, we clarify the theoretical background of the paper. This includes concepts such as modularization, boundary resources, knowledge sharing, and online communities. We conclude this chapter with our research question. In the third chapter, we report our study design. We also cover our case company, our dataset, and our research model and its parameters. In the fourth chapter, we report our results before interpreting them in chapter five. Finally, we summarize the contribution of our paper before we point out limitations and avenues for future research.

2 Theoretical Background

The software industry is currently experiencing several changes that go hand in hand with a concept called software 'platformization'. This concept characterizes the process in which a platform owner creates access and interaction opportunities around the platform core [31]. Besides, software is getting more and more embedded into our daily personal and professional routines [9]. This embeddedness requires software systems which can execute services in a flexible and independent way. The majority of software vendors coped with these changes by transforming their former monolithic architectures into modular designs [16]. Baldwin and Clark [32, p. 1117] describe a system as modular 'if its parts can be designed independently but will work together to support the whole system'.

Platform ecosystem are built upon such modular designs to enable the development and execution of third-party applications. It is through their modularity that they leverage outside innovation and spur ecosystem growth [33]. Compared to traditional business models, this concept offers innovative ways for joint value creation between platform owners and external developers. On the one hand, platform owners can expand their service portfolio by integrating a new group of stakeholders into the value creation process [34]. Furthermore, third-party developers follow a solution-driven development approach, which is often unmatched by large and hierarchical organizations. On the other hand, third-party developers can use the platform's marketplace to distribute and sell their applications to a high number of potential customers [22]. By this means, developers can amortize their development costs significantly faster than by establishing own distribution channels.

Scholars and practitioners stress the relevance of boundary resources for cultivating platform ecosystems through third-party development [14, 35]. In a broad sense, platform boundary resources are any resources that help external developers in their development work [36]. In a more narrow sense, boundary resources can be defined as 'the software tools and regulations that serve as the interface for the arm's-length relationship between the platform owner and the application developer' [21, p. 176]. The boundary resource model by Ghazawneh and Henfridsson [21] describes the usage of boundary resources and the associated interplay between platform owners and third-party developers. According to this model, platform owners craft boundary resources and provide them in a space accessibly by third-party developers. Then, third-party developers use these boundary resources to build complementary applications. Researchers also theorize that platform owners can use boundary resources to govern third-party application development [2].

Prior research was mostly limited to three types of boundary resources: SKDs, APIs [21], and technical documentation [2, 37]. We argue that these resources fall short in explaining knowledge sharing in digital platform ecosystems to its full extent. Although third-party developers acquire a profound amount of knowledge through technical documentation, we find that platform owners maintain a plethora of additional resources to address knowledge boundaries within their ecosystem. Examples for such additional resources are blog posts [19], information portals, online communities, and sample code [14]. All of these examples are designed as self-services. Through this design, third-party developers can use the resources mostly independently. Foerderer, Kude, Schuetz and Heinzl [14] also describe the above-mentioned examples broadcasting approaches because they are accessible by third-party developers without having to interact with the platform owner. Consequently, such resources have efficient scaling potentials compared to helpdesks or account managers.

In this paper, we follow these more recent approaches and investigate the role of online communities for knowledge sharing at the boundary between platform owners and third-party developers. Parnin [23] points out, that software companies invest heavily in creating official documentation for millions of topics concerning their APIs. Thereby, writing technical documentation comes inevitable with the problem that very few experts compose documentation for a large and heterogenous crowd of developers. By doing so, these companies neglect how developers integrate information from the web into their development work. On the contrary, Parnin [23] and Parnin and Treude [24] describe a process called crowd documentation, which characterizes that developers produce a huge amount of indirect documentation by publishing and reading blog posts and question and answer forums [23, 24]. Furthermore, [23] found that developers get as much as 50% of their code from online communities like StackOverflow. Additionally, developers visit online communities up to then ten times more often than the official documentation [23].

Against this background, we explore how platform owners can profit from crowd documentation posted in online communities. Our subsequent argumentation is built upon the work of Fisher [38], who reasons that firms derive competitive advantage when engaging with online communities. More precisely, Fisher [38] claims that firms can profit from three types of benefits: Information benefits, influence benefits, and solidarity benefits. Information benefits arise because members of a firm will most likely be exposed to valuable, novel, and insightful messages that are shared among community members. Examples for information benefits are market insights or user innovations. Influence benefits describe that firms may be able to utilize a sense of obligation and reciprocity when engaging with an online community. Lastly, solidarity benefits characterize loyalty and willingness to do things for one another, without an expectation of getting something in return. In other words, by building rapport, community members might be turned into evangelists for the firm's products and services [38].

In this paper, we focus on information benefits and conceptualize online communities as a key boundary resource for third-party developers. Furthermore, we define online communities as 'open collectives of dispersed individuals with members who share common interests, and these communities attend both their individual and their collective welfare' [39, p. 1224]. Emerging from technology-enabled forums, they facilitate communication and exchange among individuals and entities with shared interest [40]. However, in the information systems field, the role of online communities has mostly been discussed with respect to open source communities being a functional form of organization [41]. Some researchers investigated online communities as a means for knowledge sharing [42] and drivers for user contributions [39, 43–45]. We differentiate between autonomous and sponsored online communities [46, 47]. Whereas autonomous communities are acting mostly independent, sponsored online communities have at least one corporate entity that governs its activities. Due to our focus on digital platform ecosystems, we solely focus on online communities that are sponsored by a platform owner. Examples for such communities are SAP's Developer Community, Salesforce's Trailblazer Community or the Now Community.

While these communities have not received much attention in the platform ecosystem literature yet, they offer the potential to generate significant insights into the work and problems of third-party developers. For example, platform owners can engage in moderating behavior and thereby build relationship and trust with external developers. Some companies even use online communities as a social customer relationship tool (e.g. the Microsoft Office Support Forum) [48]. However, not only platform owners benefit from online communities. As mentioned above, online communities are strongly embedded into the work of software developers. For example, third-party developers can share development related problems and ask for solutions to be provided by the community. Also, when searching the web for potential solutions, online communities provide a vast amount of peer-reviewed knowledge articles. Prior research has shown that platform owner's engagement in sponsored communities has a significant positive effect on member's knowledge contributions [49]. In this paper, we seek to explore the information benefits that platform owners derive when engaging in sponsored communities. Thus, we formulate the following research question:

Research question: How can platform owners generate information benefits when engaging in sponsored online communities?

3   Dataset and Research Method

To answer our research question, we conducted a single case study with SAP being the focal firm of our study [50]. We chose SAP for several reasons. First, SAP has a long history of collaborating with external partners to develop extensions for their ERP system. In other words, the modularity of their systems existed several years before the platform ecosystem literature emerged. For that reason, SAP managed to establish a large and dynamic ecosystem of partners and consulting firms around their technology. Second, we chose the context of enterprise software because the adoption of complex digital platforms requires complementary and specialized knowledge to unlock their productivity [14]. Consequently, frequent knowledge exchange between the platform owner and third-parties is necessary to establish a successful ecosystem. The extensibility of SAP's system has been further increased by the introduction of the SAP Cloud Platform [16]. Third, due to the idiosyncratic and specific needs of customers, SAP's products require customization to fit specific business practices. Therefore, we assume an accumulation of expert knowledge by third-parties. Fourth and most significant, SAP is hosting the SAP Community Network since 2003. Back then, the community was a major knowledge hub for developers of SAP's partner firms. Over the years, the community evolved into a knowledge repository for several other stakeholders such as SAP users, technical architects, consultants and system integrators. Today, the community comprises several areas: A question and answer forum, expert blogs, a technical library, a code-sharing gallery, e-learning catalogues, and wikis [15, 49]. Eight years after its introduction, the SAP community network had more than 2.5 million monthly active users [51].

We developed a web scrapper to extract data from the SAP community network. In particular, we crawled the question and answer forum of the community. In this forum, community members post questions that are answered by SAP employees or by other community members. Once a question has been posted, other members can either answer or comment on the question. Members can use 'likes' to upvote contributions of others. The thread initiator can mark an answer as 'accepted' to indicate that the answer solved his problem. With more than 2.5 million questions, the forum contains a vast amount of knowledge related to SAP's technology. Due to the scope of the paper, we limited ourselves to the topic 'cloud platform', crawling only pages that had the tag 'SAP Cloud Platform'. We collected the data in October 2019 and retrieved a dataset of 4866 pages. For our analysis, we used four data points per page. First, we excerpted the title of each page. Usually, the title describes the respective question in a short sentence (e.g. *'On-Premise connectivity without using cloud connector'*). Second, we extracted the question asked by the thread initiator. Third and fourth, we collected all corresponding answers and comments (see [52] for an example).

Next, we used a text mining approach [53] to analyze the huge amount of digital trace data [54–56]. Text mining is a method for analyzing big chunks of textual data like blog posts, social media data, or online discussion forums [29, 57]. Due to its automated, computationally intensive approach, it is an adequate method for analyzing large data sets such as SAP's developer community. Furthermore, it enables researchers to analyze text collections that are too large to code by hand [54]. Researchers have used several approaches for text mining, for example latent semantic analysis [58], probabilistic latent semantic analysis [59], latent dirichlet allocation [30] and sentiment analysis [60]. We used the latent dirichlet allocation (LDA) algorithm [30] of the python package 'Gensim' [61], because it enables the discovery of latent structures in textual data. With more than 28,000 citations, the LDA algorithm is one of the most frequently used algorithm for text mining [30]. Studies using the LDA algorithm have been published in leading IS journals, such as MIS Quarterly [62].

More precisely, we used topic modeling – an approach that uses the LDA algorithm [29]. Topic models rely on statistical associations of words in a text to generate latent topics. Such models search for clusters of co-occurring words that represent higher order constructs [29, 63]. Compared to traditional research methods like interviews or surveys, topic models provide a computational lens into the structure of large text collections [64]. A disadvantage of the LDA algorithm is that it does not consider how topics are related to one another. We addressed this issue by in-depth sensemaking and content analysis of the topics. Additionally, we clustered semantically related topics into meta-topics.

Before we transformed our data into the required estimation form, we cleaned it from remaining HTML-tags. Then, we followed the steps as outlined in the literature [29, 61, 65]. We started with lowercasing our documents before we tokenized them by splitting them into single words. Thereafter, we lemmatized our tokens by transforming them into their dictionary form. The removal of irrelevant stop words such as 'this' or 'it' was done with the list of stop words from the python package 'nltk'. Where necessary, we manually added stop words during the first iterations of our model estimation. We added bi-grams and tri-grams for tokens that appeared more than 5 times. In the end, the data consist of 35729 unique tokens that we derived from 17058 documents.

We specified our model parameters as follows. First, we had to determine the number of topics to extract. Therefore, we used the number of unique tags as a proxy for the amount of topics [66]. Consequently, we evaluated all 'SAP Cloud Platform' sub-tags (e.g. 'SAP Cloud Platform Integration Suite') and merged similar sub-tags into one topic. For example, the tags 'SAP Cloud Platform Big Data Services' and 'SAP Cloud Platform Big Data Services Tools' were synthesized into a single topic. Once we evaluated the coherence of all tags, we decided to extract 25 topics from the data. Then, we set the chunk size to 17058 to process all our documents at once. Passes specify how often we train the model. We checked when additional passes added only marginal improvements. Consequently, we set this value to 25. Finally, we decided to loop over each document for 100 iterations to reach proper document convergence. Table 1 summarizes the parameters.

Table 1. Model parameters

Parameter	Value
Number of topics	25
Chunk size	17058
Passes	25
Iterations	100
Number of tokens	35729
Number of documents	17058

We trained the model and received 25 topics respectively. More precisely, the model provided us with word combinations that co-occur frequently within the documents. Similar to Shi et al. [62], we focused on the top ten words per topic. Then, we applied qualitative sensemaking as outlined by Lindberg et al. [56] and analyzed the word-topic combinations in-depth. This analysis started with gathering and investigating examples in which the word combinations occur. We followed up with an iterative process of labeling the topics and stopped once we reached saturation. Background research was carried out where necessary. Once we had a clear concept of the topics, we started to developed topic descriptions. Based on the examples gathered in the previous steps, we searched for illustrative examples of the topics. Since the LDA algorithm does not consider relationships between the topics, we clustered our topics into six meta topics to further improve the structure and clarity of our results. Due to space constraints, we only report meta-topic names, topic names, topic descriptions and examples. A list of word-topic combinations, as well as a list of example pages per topic is available from the authors upon request.

4 Results

We report the results of our analysis in Table 2. Based on our findings, we developed the following six meta-topics: User Accounts and Authentication, Connectivity, Cloud Database, Specific Technologies, SAP Resources and Installation. In the following, we describe these meta-topics by using illustrative topic excerpts.

An exemplary topic from the meta topic **User Accounts and Authentication** is Trial Account Privileges. While drilling into the details of the topic, we found that SAP is providing free trial accounts for the SAP Cloud Platform. However, these accounts come with inferior account privileges that result in several unexpected errors. One user reports the following issue: *"Everything goes fine except when doing create table statement, an insufficient privilege error appear[s]"*. The meta-topic **Connectivity** comprises all topics regarding backend connectivity. An exemplary topic is Cloud Connector. This connector was developed by SAP to connect existing on-premises systems with the SAP Cloud Platform. Such integration is – of course – not done on the fly. Another user reveals: *"And after that, whenever I try to open the Cloud Connector, it says 'Could Not open Service manager'"*. The meta topic **Cloud Database** contains all topics related to managing cloud databases and their associated tools. For the topic Database Administration, a user reports: *"The error message is Existence of database user/schema for schema Idf2c could not be checked in the underlying DBMS system due to an error. Contact HCP support if the error persists"*. The meta topic **Specific Technologies** comprises several topics that focus on a single technology such as OSGi, OData or the SAP Document Service. OData is an open communication standard for REST APIs. It is part of the SAP Gateway. An example for this topic is a user who states: *"My team has set up a[n] odata provisioning in Neo environment [...]. However, we have a new requirement to reuse the odata provisioning destination in [the CloudFoundry environment] [...]"*.

The remaining two meta topics consist of one topic each. The meta topic **SAP Resources** covers the topic SAP Help Portal. This portal is a central information hub of SAP's partner and comprises content such as product hierarchies or learning journeys. The contributions from this topic usually reference some parts of the portal. In Table 2 we provide an example in which a SAP employee answers a question by referencing an article on entitlement: *"For more information on managing entitlements, see: [...]"*. The meta topic **Installation** consists of the topic Installing SAP tools for Eclipse. A member reports: *"I had no problems installing the SAP HANA Cloud Platform Tools, but I cannot install SAP HANA Tools. (I am using Eclipse Java EE IDE for Web Developer)"*. In the next step, we discuss how SAP can generate information benefits from the ongoing discourse in the community.

Table 2. Model results

Topic	Description	Example
Meta-Topic: User Accounts and Authentication		
User Authentication	Issues related to accessing restricted applications or systems	*"Need help to register an user for an application in Cloud IDP when I enable the option in User Application Access: Private (Only users registered by the application can log on)"*
Trial Account Privileges	SAP provides free trial accounts for their cloud. Issues due to missing privileges of trial accounts or users	*"I'm creating a JAVA app to create a table and access data within HDI in SCP with trail account. Everything goes fine except when doing create table statement, an insufficient privilege error appear."*
Cloud Platform Account	Issues related to accessing or creating cloud platform (trial) accounts	*"I've verified this behavior with different developers. It's the same and all of them now blocked from accessing their SCP trial accounts."*
Anonymous User and Client	Anonymous logins provide access to SAP systems without any form of authentication. Issues related to such logins	*"I setup the anonymous login according to note: "1828575 - Anonymous login not supported while calling AS2 adapter."*
Meta-Topic: Connectivity		
Cloud Connector	The SAP Cloud Connector connects the cloud platform with on-premises systems	*"I installed SAP Cloud Connector 2.0. It installed without any problem. And after that, whenever I try to open the Cloud Connector, it says 'Could Not open Service manager'."*
Connecting to Apache Server	Connection issues associated with Apache servers	*"sometimes, while deploying a.war file to HCP, the execution fails with an 'internal server error'"*
Apache Catalina	Issues regarding the Catalina Services of Apache Servers	*"java.lang.NullPointerException: Cannot invoke org.apache.catalina.Context.getServletContext() Anyone experienced this error after the server startups?"*
Connecting from SAP Tools for Eclipse	Issues with respect to establishing a connection between SAP Developer Tools for Eclipse and a Back-End system	*"It seems to me that you are trying to add a HANA system on your Eclipse IDE The error: "Connection to host 'hanatrial.ondemand.com' failed" tells me that you have tried to add your Hana Trial Account and while Eclipse tried to connect to that account and retrieve the available schema IDs it failed"*

(continued)

Table 2. (*continued*)

Topic	Description	Example
Accessing Cloud Repository	Issues regarding connections to GIT or ABAP repositories	*"git clone [url of repository in SAP Cloud Platform Git service], I get an error of fatal: Authentication failed for [url of repository in SAP Cloud Platform Git service]'."*
Meta-Topic: Cloud Database		
Database Administration	Issues regarding the management and administration of databases	*"The error message is Existence of database user/schema for schema Id f2c could not be checked in the underlying DBMS system due to an error. Contact HCP support if the error persists."*
Tables and Database Schemas	Issues regarding tables and database schemas of SAP Cloud systems	*"HANA on SCP Neo: How can I create a HANA schema with JPA/Eclipselink?"*
SAP HANA Cockpit	The SAP HANA cockpit provides several tools for administration and monitoring of HANA databases	*"I Tried to access SAP HANA Cockpit (administration tool) after creating MDC database in SAP Cloud trial, I am getting 404 error."*
Mapping Issues	Issues regarding the mapping of values and tables	*"I have requirement in message mapping. I need to map the value dynamically based on following. for example: EN - > ENGLISH"*
Cloud Instances	Issues related to instantiating processes or services in the cloud	*"A week ago I created a HANA Cloud instance on the Cloud Foundry Trial environment. This SAP HANA Instance stops after a certain time of inactivity. However, today I was not able to start the instance at all. It gives a message 'Stopping Failed'."*
Meta-Topic: Specific Technologies		
OSGi	OSGi is a framework for developing and deploying modular java-based applications. It is part of SAP's technology stack	*"I cannot find any good samples showing how to create and deploy a WAB (web application bundle) to HCP Java EE 6 Web Profile Server along with deploying the osgi bundles it requires."*

(*continued*)

Table 2. (*continued*)

Topic	Description	Example
OData	OData (Open Data Protocol) is a communication standard for REST APIs. It is part of the SAP Gateway	*"My team has set up a odata provisioning in Neo environment and the UI5 app is able to query data from it when deploying to Neo. The authentication type is AppToAppSSO. However, we have a new requirement to reuse the odata provisioning destination in CF and build a new UI5 app using that destination which deployed to CF."*
CMIS and SAP Document Service	CMIS is an open standard that allows different content management systems to interoperate. The SAP document service is an implementation of the CMIS standard	*"In the openSAP course we showed the following scenario: The Document Service implements the CMIS protocol but is available only from apps running inside HCP. The CMIS protocol can however be proxied, such a proxy is already preimplemented and you only need to configure & deploy it, see Document Service: Access from External Applications"*
Email Integration	All issues related to Email integration of the SAP Cloud Platform (e.g. for sending notifications)	*"I want to deploy a spring boot application in SAP Cloud Platform Neo environment. It has a endpoint /sendmail which sends a mail to a particular user when called. For now, I have hard coded the credentials in application.properties file and it works."*
Kepler IDE	Kepler is a version of the Eclipse IDE. All issues associated with the Kepler IDE	*"I am getting the following error while installing HANA tools in eclipse: Unable to read repository https://tools.hana.ondemand.com/kepler"*
Mobile Services	All issues related to SAP mobile cards and services	*"My approach: to develop a nodejs app based on SAP Approuter. In my scenario, I was using Mobile Services on Cloud Foundry and we have Application Runtime service quotas, so I decided to build a CAP nodejs app with approuter"*
NetWeaver Technology	SAP NetWeaver is the software stack for many SAP applications. All issues related to the NetWeaver technology	*"There exists a free Gateway Demo system provided by SAP. It provides different example services. Maybe they are useful for your needs. All details are described in post SAP Netweaver Gateway Demo System and the posts linked in that post (e..g what services are provided, how you get access…)"*

(*continued*)

Table 2. (*continued*)

Topic	Description	Example
Application Runtimes	All issues related to runtime environments and deployment of applications	*"I am trying to create a Full Stack Application for Cloud Foundry in WEB IDE Full Stack. Project Structure/modules consists of java cds hdb. Required Project settings done. Not able to find the root cause for the same or not able to debug what could be the issue."*
Interoperability	All issues related to the interoperability of technologies used by the SAP Cloud Platform	*"The error message indicates that you have an issue with your Java truststore. What (Open?)JDK version do you have installed? Do you have the cacert file installed in the Java folder under /lib/security?"*
Meta-Topic: SAP Resources		
SAP Help Portal	Issues related to the SAP Help Portal. This portal is a major information resource for SAP's Partners	*"For more information on managing entitlements, see: https://help.sap.com/viewer/65de2977205c403 bbc107264b8eccf4b/Cloud/enUS/c8248745dde2 4afb91479361de336111.html"*
Meta-Topic: Installation		
Installing SAP Tools for Eclipse	All issues related to installing SAP Developer Tools for Eclipse	*"I had no problems installing the SAP HANA Cloud Platform Tools, but I cannot install SAP HANA Tools. (I am using Eclipse Java EE IDE for Web Developers. Version: Mars.2 Release (4.5.2) Build id: 20160218–0600 with Java Web Server)"*

5   Interpretation

The aim of this paper was to explore the information benefit that platform owners derive from analyzing activities in online communities. We showed that platform owners can use topic modeling to extract latent topics that are frequently discussed in the community. Thereby, we provide them with a means to generate information benefits from digital trace data. Furthermore, by clustering the topics into higher order meta-topics, we added semantic relationships between the topics.

Platform owners can use the aforementioned information benefit in two ways. On the one hand, they can use it to improve the tuning of existing boundary resources. On the other hand, they can use feedback from third-party developers to refine the platform core (e.g. through bug fixes). We structured the remaining discussion along these two avenues. With Fig. 1, we provide a model that illustrates this idea.

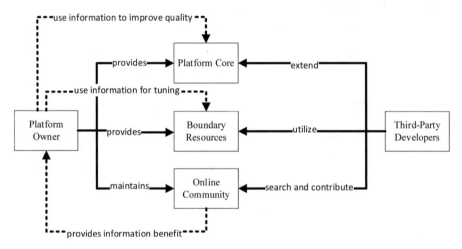

Fig. 1. The role of online communities in third-party application development

Regarding the improvement of the platform core, platform owners can use the topics and meta-topics to prioritize questions and issues of the community. For example, consider the following two topics: 'Trial Account Privileges' and 'Tables and Database Schemas'. The usage of trial accounts is free of charge for community members. Issues from this topic will probably not affect any running systems. However, issues from the topic 'Tables and Database Schemas' might affect a variety of SAP's customers. Consequently, it can directly affect SAP's value delivery in a harmful way. Such prioritization is also relevant because platform owners can adjust the allocation of time and resources to the most relevant topics. Platform owners can drill into more details by comparing total and relative statistics of the topics, for example by using 'term frequency – inverse document frequency' (commonly known as TF-IDF) measures [67]. Additionally, our data-based topic extraction helps platform owners to structure areas without tags (e.g. the topic 'Accessing Cloud Repository').

Furthermore, platform owners generate significant insights into bugs that third-party developers experience. In this regard, we differentiate between actual bugs and errors that arouse from incorrect handling of the technology (e.g. wrong connection settings). For the former, we identified a prime example in the topic 'Cloud Instances'. Thereby, an issue reported by a community member led to a bug fix. After the issue was reported, an SAP employee replied: *"Update: the problem was identified and has been fixed. You should be able to start/stop your instances again. Please let us know if you still encounter problems"*. We identified another fix in the topic 'SAP HANA Cockpit'. After several community members reported an issue regarding the Admin Cockpit, an SAP employee opened a ticket. After the fix he stated: *"Hi All, [i]t should work now. I will close this ticket. If you have another issue then please open a new ticket"*.

We classify the feedback on errors that arose from incorrect handling of the technology as an information benefit. Such errors are indicators for missing, misleading, or outdated information in technical documentation or tutorials. For example, in the topic Mobile Services a user reports: *"I'm trying to follow the tutorial 'Implement Your First Screen in an iOS APP' and at step 5, when the following code has to be added [...] there is an error saying [...]"*. For this particular example, the destination of a controller was not set correct. SAP can use this feedback to update the tutorial. Another user reported: *"I am starting to play with HCP IoT Services and I am hitting a problem following the Starter Kit for SAP HCP IoT Services tutorial/instructions [...]. The problem appears when trying to simulate sending data from a device using the python script provided in the starter kit"*. Besides an information benefit regarding tutorials, we found similar issues regarding the SAP Help Portal. One user reports: *"We have build [a] Proxy Bridge for Document Service. Based on the Help guide [...]* https://help.sap.com/[...]. *But while [we] access the Url for testing the service [...]. [We get the] error message [...]."* All three cases demonstrate how SAP generates an information benefit regarding their boundary resources. In the topic application runtimes, we managed to identify a top contributor because his name appeared as the fifth most frequent word. Consequently, platform owners can identify experts and reward them with badges or titles.

6 Conclusion and Limitations

In this paper, we built upon a new and broader understanding of boundary resources in digital platform ecosystems. More precisely, we emphasized the necessity for extending the threefold differentiation of APIs, SDKs, and technical documentation. By considering new types of boundary resources (e.g. blogs and online communities), we contribute and expand the current discourse on knowledge sharing in digital platform ecosystems. Furthermore, we pursued on investigating how platform owners can generate an information benefit when engaging in sponsored online communities. Based on the LDA-algorithm, we presented a data-driven and text-mining based approach for generating information benefits from online community data. Furthermore, we theorize and show how platform owners can transform the results into competitive advantage.

As any other research, our paper is not without limitations. Firstly, we conducted a single case study [50, 68] with SAP being the focal firm of our study. Therefore, we acknowledge that our results are specific to our case company [69]. Although single case studies are limited with regards to drawing causations and generalizability [69], we see no issues in repeating our study with any other case company. Second, due to using data from a question and answer forum of a third-party developer ecosystem, we approve an overrepresentation of negative feedback about the platform ecosystem due to errors and issues reported in the community. We are currently digging deeper into how platform owners can use information benefits from online communities by conducting interviews.

We suggest that future research addresses the following three areas. First, whilst we focused on sponsored online communities of enterprise software platforms, future research should also investigate the role of autonomous communities for digital platform ecosystem. Therefore, other researchers should shed light onto the role of StackOverflow for digital platform ecosystem. For example, on StackOverflow, more than 1.3 million questions are tagged 'Android'. Second, whilst the research on digital platform ecosystems is still growing, the area of platform evolution remains largely untouched. We identified that gathering longitudinal case data is a major challenge for conducting research on platform evolution. By using trace data from an online community, we can use the evolvement of topics over time as a proxy for platform evolution. Third, as outlined by Gaskin et al. [70], we suggest the analysis of sociomaterial routines in third-party developer communities. Based on a typology of questions, we might derive activity-routine combinations that help platform owners in moderating their community.

References

1. Gawer, A.: What drives shifts in platform boundaries: an organizational perspective. In: DRUID. (2015)
2. Schreieck, M., Wiesche, M., Krcmar, H.: Design and governance of platform ecosystems - key concepts and issues for future research. In: Twenty-Fourth European Conference on Information Systems (ECIS) (2016)
3. Hein, A., et al.: Digital platform ecosystems. Electron. Mark. **30**, 87–98 (2020)
4. Cusumano, M.A., Yoffie, D.B., Gawer, A.: The future of platforms. MITSloan Management Review **61**, 45–54 (2020)
5. Yoo, Y., Boland, R.J., Lyytinen, K., Majchrzak, A.: Organizing for innovation in the digitized world. Organ. Sci. **23**, 1398–1408 (2012)
6. Tiwana, A., Konsynski, B., Bush, A.A.: Platform evolution: coevolution of platform architecture, governance, and environmental dynamics. Inf. Syst. Res. **21**, 675–687 (2010)
7. Reuver, M.D., Sorensen, C., Basole, R.C.: The digital platform: a research agenda. J. Inf. Technol. **33**, 124–135 (2017)
8. Katz, M.L., Shapiro, C.: Network externalities, competition, and compatibility. Am. Econ. Rev. **75**, 424–440 (1985)
9. Tiwana, A.: Platform Ecosystems - Aligning Architecture, Governance, and Strategy. Morgan Kaufmann, Walham (2014)
10. Song, P., Xue, L., Rai, A., Zhang, C.: The ecosystem of software platform: a study of asymmetric cross-side network effects and platform governance. MIS Q. **42**, 121–142 (2018)
11. Weiss, N., Schreieck, M., Wiesche, M., Krcmar, H.: Setting up a platform ecosystem - how to integrate app developer experience. In: 2018 IEEE International Conference on Engineering, Technology and Innovation (2018)
12. SAP SE. https://store.sap.com/en/. Accessed 22 Dec 2020
13. ServiceNow Inc. https://store.servicenow.com/sn_appstore_store.do#!/store/home. Accessed 22 Dec 2020

14. Foerderer, J., Kude, T., Schuetz, S.W., Heinzl, A.: Knowledge boundaries in enterprise software platform development: antecedents and consquences for platform governance. Inf. Syst. J. **29**, 1–26 (2019)
15. Huang, P., Ceccagnoli, M., Forman, C., Wu, D.J.: When do ISVs join a platform ecosystem? evidence from the enterprise software industry. In: Proceedings of the Thirtieth International Conference on Information Systems (2009)
16. Schreieck, M., Wiesche, M., Kude, T., Krcmar, H.: Shifting to the cloud - how SAP's partners cope with the change. In: Proceedings of the 52nd Hawaii International Conference on System Sciences (2019)
17. Amazon Web Services Inc. https://aws.amazon.com/de/blogs/awsforsap/aws-and-sap-announce-iot-interoperability-solution/. Accessed 22 Dec 2019
18. Ceccagnoli, M., Forman, C., Huang, P., Wu, D.J.: Cocreation of value in a platform ecosystem: the case of enterprise software. MIS Q. **36**, 263–290 (2012)
19. Eaton, B., Elaluf-Calderwood, S., Sorensen, C.: Distributed tuning of boundary resources: the case of apple's ios service system. MIS Q. **39**, 217–243 (2015)
20. Sarker, S., Sarker, S., Sahaym, A., Bjorn-Andersen, N.: Exploring value cocreation in relationships between an ERP vendor and its partners: a revelatory case study. MIS Q. **36**, 317–338 (2012)
21. Ghazawneh, A., Henfridsson, O.: Balancing platform control and external contribution in third-party development: the boundary resources model. Inf. Syst. J. **23**, 173–192 (2013)
22. Goldbach, T., Benlian, A.: How informal control modes affect developers' trust in a platform vendor and platform stickiness. In: Proceedings der 12. Internationalen Tagung Wirtschaftsinformatik (2015)
23. Ninlabs Research. http://blog.ninlabs.com/2013/03/api-documentation/. Accessed 2 Dec 2020
24. Parnin, C., Treude, C.: Measuring API documentation on the web. In: Web2SE'11, pp. 25–30 (2011)
25. Oracle Corporation. https://community.oracle.com/tech/developers/categories/. Accessed 22 Dec 2020
26. Salesforce.com Inc. https://developer.salesforce.com/forums/ForumsCategories. Accessed 22 Dec 2020
27. SAP SE. https://community.sap.com/. Accessed 22 Dec 2020
28. Blei, D.M.: Probabilistic topic models. Commun. ACM **55**, 77–84 (2012)
29. Hannigan, T.R., et al.: Topic modeling in management research: rendering new theory from textual data. Acad. Manag. Ann. **13**, 586–632 (2019)
30. Blei, D.M., Ng, A.Y., Jordan, M.I.: Latent dirichlet allocation. J. Mach. Learn. Res. **3**, 993–1022 (2003)
31. Benlian, A., Kettinger, W.K., Sunyaev, A., Winkler, T.J.: Special section: the transformative value of cloud computing: a decoupling, platformization, and recombination theoretical framework. J. Manag. Inf. Syst. **35**, 719–739 (2018)
32. Baldwin, C.Y., Clark, K.B.: The architecture of participation: does code architecture mitigate free riding in the open source development model? Manage. Sci. **52**, 1116–1127 (2006)
33. Boudreau, K., Lakhani, K.R.: How to manage outside innovation. MIT Sloan Manag. Rev. **50**, 69–76 (2009)
34. Schreieck, M., Wiesche, M.: How established companies leverage IT platform for value co-creation - insights from banking. In: Proceedings of the Twenty-Fifth European Conference on Information Systems, pp. 1726–1741 (2017)
35. West, J., Mace, M.: Browsing as the killer app: explaining the rapid success of apple's iPhone. Telecommun. Policy **34**, 270–286 (2010)
36. Pruegl, R., Schreier, M.: Learning from leading-edge customers at the sims: opening the innovation process using toolkits. R&D Manag. **36**, 237–250 (2006)

37. Dal Bianco, V., Myllärniemi, V., Komssi, M., Raatikainen, M.: The role of platform boundary resources in software ecosystems: a case study. In: 11th Working IEEE/IFIP Conference on Software Architecture (WICSA) (2014)
38. Fisher, G.: Online communities and firm advantages. Acad. Manag. Rev. **44**, 279–298 (2019)
39. Faraj, S., Jarvenpaa, S.L., Majchrzak, A.: Knowledge collaboration in online communities. Organ. Sci. **22**, 1224–1239 (2011)
40. Autio, E., Dahlander, L., Frederiksen, L.: Information exposure, opportunity evaluation, and entrepreneurial action: an investigation of an online user community. Acad. Manag. J. **56**, 1348–1371 (2013)
41. Lindberg, A., Berente, N., Gaskin, J., Lyytinen, K.: Coordinating interdependencies in online communities: a study of an open source software project. Inf. Syst. Res. **27**(4), 751–772 (2016)
42. Faraj, S., Johnson, S.L.: Network exchange patterns in online communities. Organ. Sci. **22**, 1464–1480 (2011)
43. Ma, M., Agarwal, R.: Through a glass darkly: information technology design, identity verification, and knowledge contribution in online communities. Inf. Syst. Res. **18**, 42–67 (2007)
44. Ray, S., Kim, S.S., Morris, J.G.: The central role of engagement in online communities. Inf. Syst. Res. **25**, 528–546 (2014)
45. Ahlander, L., Frederiksen, L.: The core and cosmopolitans: a relational view of innovation in user communities. Organ. Sci. **23**(4), 998–1007 (2012)
46. Blohm, I., Kahl, V., Leimeister, J.M., Krcmar, H.: Enhancing absorptive capacity in open innovation communities. In: Leimeister, J.M., Rajagopalan, B. (eds.) Virtual Communities. M.E. Sharpe Publisher, New York (2014)
47. West, J., O'Mahony, S.: The role of participation architecture in growing sponsored open source communities. Ind. Innov. **15**, 145–168 (2008)
48. Lu, Y., Singh, P.V., Sun, B.: Is a core-periphery network good for knowledge sharing? a structural model of endogenous network formation on a crowdsourced customer support forum. MIS Q. **41**, 607–628 (2017)
49. Huang, P., Tafti, A., Mithas, S.: Platform sponsor investments and user contributions in knowledge communities: the role of knowledge seeding. MIS Q. **42**, 213–240 (2018)
50. Yin, R.K.: The case study as a serious research strategy. Comput. Sci. **3**, 97–114 (1981)
51. Hinchcliffe, D., Kim, P.: Social Business By Design: Transformative Social Media Strategies for the Connected Company. Jossey-Bass, San Francisco (2012)
52. SAP SE. https://answers.sap.com/questions/12992903/on-premise-connectivity-without-using-cloud-connec.html. Accessed 22 Dec 2020
53. Bissantz, N., Hagedorn, J.: Data mining. Bus. Inf. Syst. Eng. **1**, 118–122 (2009)
54. Berente, N., Seidel, S., Safadi, H.: Research commentary - data-driver computationally intensive theory development. Inf. Syst. Res. **30**, 50–64 (2018)
55. Cecez-Kecmanovic, D., Davison, R.M., Fernandez, W., Finnegan, P., Pan, S.L., Sarker, S.: Advancing qualitative is research methodologies: expanding horizons and seeking new paths. J. Assoc. Inf. Syst. **20**, 246–263 (2020)
56. Lindberg, A.: Developing theory through integrating human and machine pattern recognition. J. Assoc. Inf. Syst. **21**, 90–116 (2020)
57. Cogburn, D.L., Hine, M.J., Peladeau, N., Yoong, V.Y.: Text mining in big data analytics. In: Proceedings of the 51st Hawaii International Conference on System Sciences (2018)
58. Deerwester, S., Dumais, S.T., Furnas, G.W., Landauer, T.K., Harshman, R.: Indexing by latent semantic analysis. J. Am. Soc. Inf. Sci. **41**, 391–407 (1990)
59. Hofmann, T.: Probabilistic latent semantic analysis. In: Proceedings of the Fifteenth Conference on Uncertainty in Artificial Intelligence (UAI1999) (1999)

60. Pang, B., Lee, L.: Opinion mining and sentiment analysis. Found. Trends Inf. Retr. **2**, 1–135 (2008)
61. Rehurek, R., Sojka, P.: Software framework for topic modelling with large corpora. In: Proceedings of the LREC 2010 Workshop on New Challenges for NLP Frameworks (2010)
62. Shi, Z., Lee, G.M., Whinston, A.B.: Toward a better measure of business proximity: topic modeling for industry intelligence. MIS Q. **40**, 1035–1056 (2016)
63. DiMaggio, P., Nag, M., Blei, D.: Exploiting affinities between topic modeling and the sociological perspective on culture: application to newspaper coverage of U.S. government arts funding. Poetics **41**(6), 570–606 (2013)
64. DiMaggio, P.: Adapting computational text analysis to social science (and vice versa). Big Data and Society July-December **2**(2), 1–5 (2015)
65. Bird, S., Klein, E., Loper, E.: Natural Language Processing with Python Analyzing Text with the Natural Language Toolkit. O'Reilly Media (2009)
66. Safadi, H., Johnson, S.L., Faraj, S.: Core-Periphery Tension in Online Innovation Communities. Organization Science (Forthcoming)
67. Aizawa, A.: An information-theoretic perspective of TF-IDF measures. Inf. Process. Manag. **39**(1), 45–65 (2003)
68. Yin, R.K.: Case Study Research - Design and Methods. Sage, Thousand Oaks (2009)
69. Ruddin, P.L.: You can generalize stupid! social scientists, bent flyvbjerg, and case study methodology. Qual. Inq. **12**, 797–812 (2006)
70. Gaskin, J., Berente, N., Lyytinen, K., Yoo, Y.: Toward generalizable sociomaterial inquiry. MIS Q. **38**, 849–872 (2014)

Leveraging Natural Language Processing to Analyze Scientific Content: Proposal of an NLP Pipeline for the Field of Computer Vision

Henrik Kortum[1]([✉]), Max Leimkühler[1], and Oliver Thomas[1,2]

[1] Smart Enterprise Engineering, German Research Center for Artificial Intelligence, Osnabrück, Germany
{henrik.kortum,max.leimkuehler}@dfki.de
[2] IMWI, Universität Osnabrück, Osnabrück, Germany
oliver.thomas@universität-osnabrueck.de

Abstract. In this paper we elaborate the opportunity of using natural language processing to analyze scientific content both, from a practical as well as a theoretical point of view. Firstly, we conducted a literature review to summarize the status quo of using natural language processing for analyzing scientific content. We could identify different approaches, e.g., with the aim of clustering and tagging publications or to summarize scientific papers. Secondly, we conducted a case study where we used our proposed natural language processing pipeline to analyze scientific content about computer vision available at the database IEEE. Our method helped us to identify emerging trends in the recent years and give an overview of the field of research.

Keywords: Natural language processing · Machine learning · Emerging trends · Computer vision · W2V

1 Introduction

The number of scientific publications is developing rapidly and has been growing in recent years [1–4]. Due to the large number of publications, it is increasingly difficult to gain an overview of complex scientific topics and to derive trends for researchers [5–7]. For example, 23,777 publications on the topic of computer vision exist on the IEEE platform alone. Of these, 2,887 papers were published in 2019[1]. A manual review of the publications is connected with a very high effort and is almost impossible to handle. Nevertheless, researchers have a legitimate interest in gaining an overview of a research topic, e.g. computer vision. This problem has been addressed in various publications. A possible solution scenario for the aggregation of information is the use of natural language processing (NLP) to evaluate scientific content. E.g. NLP is used to summarize scientific papers or to extract key phrases. Based on this motivation and the resulting problems, the following research questions (RQ) are addressed in this paper:

---

[1] See Sect. 3.2 for the derivation of the numbers.

F. Ahlemann et al. (Eds.): WI 2021, LNISO 47, pp. 40–55, 2021.
https://doi.org/10.1007/978-3-030-86797-3_3

RQ1: what is the status quo of using NLP for analyzing scientific content?
RQ2: can NLP be utilized to structure keywords of a scientific text corpus and to identify trends?

To answer the RQ, this paper is structured as follows. First, in Sect. 2 foundations about NLP are presented. This is followed in Sect. 3 by the concretization of the research approach. Sections 4 and 5 present the results, which are critically discussed in Sect. 6. Finally, the paper is completed by the conclusion in Sect. 7.

2   Foundations About Natural Language Processing

Tokenization is used to make a text processable by algorithms. Therefore, the string representing the text itself, should first be broken down into smaller elements, so called tokens. These can be, sentences, words, word pairs (n-grams) or single characters. The process of token generation is not trivial and ranges from a simple separation on the basis of "spaces" between words, over the use of lexicons, to the use of more complex procedures, such as conditional random fields or deep neural networks [8].

Besides tokenization *normalization* is an essential part of the preprocessing of texts and can be carried out by various methods e.g. stemming or lemmatizing. During stemming, words are traced to their word stem by using heuristics. This is often done by removing certain word endings [9]. It should be noted that stemming also inevitably leads to the loss of information and certain errors can occur.

In general, the preprocessing of a corpus also includes a *cleanup* process. Certain words can have a negative influence on NLP tasks, because they do not provide any semantic or contextual value [10]. These words are called stop words. They increase the dimensionality of the data set, which in turn has a negative influence on performance. Stop words can be divided into two categories: general and domain-specific stop words. General stop words occur in all texts and are independent of the subject of a text. Typical examples are articles or prepositions. Domain-specific stop words, on the other hand, have no explanatory value for a specific domain or a concrete analysis objective [11]. To achieve better results with NLP tasks, both general and domain-specific stop words should be removed during preprocessing [11].

In order to make texts or tokens processable by neural networks or other NLP algorithms a conversion into numerical representation is necessary. A widespread problem of many NLP techniques is the lack of the ability to map similarities and relationships between words and to consider contextual information [12]. Word embeddings are a popular and effective way to transform words into a machine-processable format [13]. They are capable of mapping both syntactic and semantic relationships between words by taking into account the context in which a word is mentioned [14]. Word embeddings represent words as vectors of real numbers. The entire vocabulary occurring in the training data set is transferred into a multi-dimensional vector space whose dimensions function as latent, continuous features. The transformation takes place via a flat neural network, which is trained on the basis of a very large text corpus. The words used in the training vocabulary in a similar or identical context are arranged close to each other in the generated vector space [15]. Using similarity measures for vectors – e.g., cosine similarity – the similarity between words can be determined. Word vectors can be used to map semantic and contextual relationships between words [12]. A widely used method for clustering and comparing entire documents of a corpus is topic modeling [16]. In this context, latent dirichlet allocation (LDA) [17] is the most widespread approach. It is based on the assumption that each document can be represented as a probabilistic distribution over latent topics, where a topic in turn is characterized by a distribution over words [16]. Another, comparatively recent method that can be used for different NLP tasks are Bidirectional Encoder Representations from Transformer (BERT). To use BERT for NLP tasks pretraining and finetuning are required. During pretraining on unlabeled texts BERT learns deep bidirectional representations. In the finetuning step an additional layer can be added and BERT can be trained to solve specific tasks, like language inference or question answering. With BERT state of the art results have been archived on several natural language processing tasks [18]. Another approach called ELMo, short for embeddings from language models, can also be used for a variety of natural language processing tasks and is state of the art. In ELMo a deep bidirectional language model pretrained on large text corpus is used. These representations can be added to existing models to improve the performance on different NLP tasks [19].

3   Research Approach

To answer RQ1, first a literature review as described in Sect. 3.2 was performed. The results of the literature review are also included to answer RQ2. Furthermore, a case study was conducted to investigate RQ2. A proposed method based on a NLP-pipeline was tested to structure keywords within a research area and identify emerging trends. The proposed method is described in Sect. 3.3 In this specific case study the research area of computer vision was investigated by the automated processing of *author keywords, abstracts and publication years* of scientific publications. The data collection is described in detail in Sect. 3.2.

3.1   Literature Review

In order to answer RQ1 and to get first insights for RQ2 a structured literature review was conducted in consideration of [20] and [21]. With RQ1 and RQ2 the focus and thus also step 1 of the literature search according to [21], definition of review scope, was concretized firstly. Since the main focus is on the analysis of scientific content using NLP, these two expressions were integrated into the search term. The search string was formulated as followed secondly: "natural language processing" AND "scientific content". According to [21] the third step of the literature review is the literature search. For the literature search the databases AISeL, Ebsco, IEEE, ISI Web of Knowledge, JSTOR, ScienceDirect, SpringerLink and Wiley were considered. The table below gives an overview of the results of the literature search, which was conducted in august 2020 (Table 1).

Table 1. Findings of the initial literature search

Database	Total result	Sorted by title	Sorted by content	Without duplicates
AISeL	2,245	15	3	3
Ebsco	684	11	0	0
IEEE	83	8	4	3
Web of Knowledge	2,028	24	15	14
JSTOR	4	0	0	0
ScienceDirect	28	4	2	2
SpringerLink	78	16	4	4
Wiley	25	9	0	0
Sum	**5,175**	**87**	**28**	**26**

In addition to the initial search, a backward search was conducted to identify further relevant literature. During backward search [7, 22–32] were identified. A total of 38 sources were thus included in the literature analysis and synthesis. In order to ensure the actuality of the review, it was examined when the publications were released. The oldest publication to be considered in the further analysis is from the year 2006. The majority of the selected publications are from 2013 to 2020, which underlines the up-to-datedness of the topic. The fourth step of the literature search is the literature analysis and synthesis. A concept matrix according to [20] was used for the synthesis and content analysis of the literature. As concepts the goals of the NLP workflow of the respective paper were abstracted.

3.2 Data Collection

Computer vision is an established field of research, which has been in existence for many years, but has gained in relevance especially in recent times. For this reason, we have decided to investigate the research field in more detail. Therefore, all publications about computer vision were extracted from IEEE to test our proposed method. The search was limited to the keyword "computer vision" in abstract or title in order to obtain only relevant hits on the topic. The following information was extracted for each publication: *author keywords, abstracts and publication years*. The search was conducted on 13.08.2020. A total of 23,777 publications were identified and the above-mentioned information were extracted. Figure 1 shows the distribution of the publications over the time period.

3.3 Proposed Method: NLP-Pipeline

Our proposed method consists of the five steps: preprocessing, training, prediction, evaluation and trend analysis. Each step of the NLP pipeline is divided into input, action and output as shown in Fig. 2. The key element of our pipeline is the generation of word

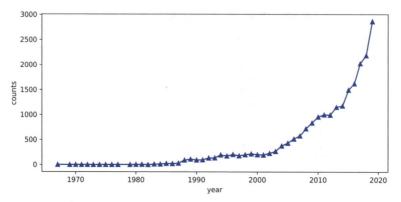

Fig. 1. Distribution of publications about computer vision over time period.

embedding's to represent terms in a vector space. This word-level representation allows us to identify keywords used in similar contexts in order to expand the literature search and identify trends.

	Input	Action	Output	
1. Preprocessing	raw author keywords, raw abstracts	cleanup, stemming, n-gram transformation, tokenizing	keywords, abstracts,	
2. Training	abstracts	train W2V model, generate W2V embeddings	word vectors	
3. Prediction	author keywords, wordvectors	calculate similarity, reduce dimensions, plot graph	most similar words, term scatter plot	optional feedback loop
4. Evaluation	most similar words, term scatter plot	evaluate	evaluated synonyms	
5. Trend analysis	synonyms, author keywords, publication years	detect synonyms in author keywords	trendplots	

Fig. 2. Proposed NLP pipeline for identifying emerging trends.

1. The preprocessing of a raw text corpus is an essential step of every NLP pipeline [33]. Nevertheless, it is important to note that the implementation of preprocessing steps affects the resulting word embeddings and the performance of their calculation [9, 34]. In case of our pipeline the preprocessing consists of the steps, stop word removal stemming, n-gram transformation and tokenizing, which are applied to the data fields *author keywords* and *abstract*. These are normalized by a stemming process using the porter stemmer [35]. The purpose is to merge keywords with identical content (e.g., "*network*" and "*networks*"), so that they are considered the same in the following analysis. Additionally, stop words are removed from title and abstract that do not provide semantic or contextual meaning. The stemming and the cleaning have the purpose to optimize the subsequent training of the word vectors and to minimize the number of data points in the resulting vector space. To include contextually relevant n-grams, we have merged all author keywords that are n-grams with a "_" character (e.g., *deep learning*  *deep_learning*), created a mapping and replaced

matching n-grams in the abstract with these tokens. Finally, the full abstract string was split into lists of tokens by separating between spaces.

2. In the following step, a word vector model is trained, generating a 300-dimensional vector space based on the *preprocessed abstract*, whereby terms used in a similar context are placed close together. In order to learn the relevant contexts for a considered use case, the word vector model must be fitted to the corresponding scientific texts. We use the Python library *gensim* and a Word2Vec (W2V) model to generate the word vectors. The model was trained with the continuous bag of words (CBOW) method, over 500 epochs, with a window size of five. We decided to apply a word vector model because our case study is about identifying synonyms for keywords and therefore requires an approach that allows a calculation of similarities on term level. The strength of word vector models - also compared to more recent approaches, such as BERT - is based on the possibility to simply analyze terms in the spanned vector space using vector geometry. Specifically, W2V was chosen as the underlying calculation method, since it tends to perform well on stemmed corpus [34].

3. Calculating cosine similarity, the most similar terms for given keywords can now be retrieved to find synonyms in vector space. The idea is that through the trained W2V model, the user gets suggestions for synonyms which he might not have found on its own. For further exploration, a visualization of the learned word representations is useful. Since we are particularly interested in maintaining local similarity structures for synonym recognition, we choose UMAP [36] to reduce the dimensionality of our embeddings. The resulting 2D vectors are displayed in a scatterplot to visualize the subject area and provide a starting point for identifying additional keywords.

4. Evaluation: similar terms identified should be treated as suggestions and carefully evaluated by the researchers, since not all terms discovered are necessarily contextual synonyms. The identification of unsuitable terms leads to a feedback into the preprocessing phase, where they can be added as stop words. If necessary, preprocessing steps can be adapted, e.g. to adjust the degree of stemming if terms cannot be interpreted by the researcher or are over/under stemmed [9].

5. Finally, matching synonyms can be included in the search by looking for the corresponding substrings in the *author keywords* data. For each publication year, all papers are selected that contain the keyword to be analyzed or its synonyms as *author keyword* in order to show a trend of the chosen topic. Section 5 shows an instantiation of our proposed method for a scientific text corpus from the field of computer vision.

4 Status Quo of NLP for Analyzing Scientific Content

The structured literature review has shown that NLP is used to analyze scientific content mainly for summarization, clustering and tagging of publications and to optimize as well as simplify a literature search. NLP is also used to create bibliometric networks, to analyze citations and to predict future research trends.

The aim of the summarization is to provide the essential core statements of a scientific publication in a short and succinct manner. One approach of summarization is the processing of citations [5]. This approach is chosen because in citations a high aggregation of the contents has already been done [6]. In the Table 2 the results of the literature analysis and synthesis are summarized.

Table 2. Concept matrix for goals of using NLP for analyzing scientific content (S = Summarization, CT = Clustering and tagging, BN = Bibliometric networks, CS = Citation semantics, SL = Simplify literature search, OF = Overview and future trends)

#	Author and year	S	CT	BN	CS	SL	OF
[37]	Abuhay et al., 2018						X
[24]	Abu-Jbara et al., 2013				X		
[26]	Achakulvisut et al., 2016					X	
[38]	Almeida et al., 2016					X	
[39]	Almugbel et al., 2019	X	X			X	
[40]	Avram et al., 2014			X	X		
[27]	Beltagy et al., 2019		X				
[31]	Chen and Zhuge, 2014	X					
[5]	Cohan and Goharian, 2018	X			X		
[28]	Collins et al., 2017	X					
[41]	Ghosh and Shah, 2020			X	X		
[42]	Giannakopoulos et al., 2013		X				
[43]	Hassan et al., 2018		X				
[44]	Janssens et al., 2006		X				
[32]	Joorabchi and Mahdi, 2013		X				
[3]	Kerzendorf, 2019					X	
[45]	Khan et al., 2016		X			X	
[46]	Koukal et al., 2014					X	
[47]	Krapivin et al., 2008		X			X	
[48]	Krasnov et al., 2019		X	X			X
[1]	La Quatra et al., 2020	X					
[29]	Li et al., 2019	X					
[49]	Li et al., 2018	X	X		X		
[50]	Łopuszyński and Bolikowski, 2015	X	X				
[51]	Łopuszyński and Bolikowski, 2014	X	X				
[6]	Ma et al., 2018	X					
[2]	Mueller and Huettemann, 2018	X	X				
[23]	Nam et al., 2016		X			X	
[52]	Nédey et al., 2018		X				
[53]	Petrus et al., 2019		X				
[22]	Prabhakaran et al., 2016		X				X

(continued)

Table 2. (*continued*)

#	Author and year	S	CT	BN	CS	SL	OF
[25]	Qazvinian et al., 2013	X					
[7]	Qazvinian and Radev, 2008	X	X	X			
[54]	Sateli and Witte, 2014					X	
[55]	Schafer and Spurk, 2010		X	X	X	X	
[30]	Schäfer et al., 2008					X	
[4]	Sergio et al., 2019		X			X	
[56]	Szczuka et al., 2012		X			X	
Sum	38	13	21	5	6	13	3

Related to this is clustering and tagging. In clustering, an attempt is made to combine publications that deals with the same topic. Tagging is close to clustering. In tagging with NLP keywords were automatically assigned to publications by analyzing e.g., title and abstracts. Tagging is often used for organizing digital content [43].

Bibliometric networks are useful for visualizing connections between publications. Indicator for the networks can be e.g., authors, affiliations or keywords as well. In connection with summarization, bibliometric networks can help to give an overview of an entire topic [7]. Another aim is citation semantics. The aim is to predict in what context a citation is used. E.g., a citation can be used to criticize the scientific results of the cited paper, but it could also be used in a neutral and descriptive context. Possible approaches to predict the purpose and polarity of citations are supervised methods [24] as well as unsupervised ones [5].

The identification of relevant literature is important for the researchers [26]. Therefore, researchers are trying to improve the literature search with NLP. All above mentioned concepts are utilized to simplify the literature search. E.g. summarization [5, 39], clustering and tagging [4, 39, 56], bibliometric networks [55] and citation semantics [55] are used to optimize literature search and help researchers to identify relevant literature. NLP is also used to get an overview of a scientific area and to predict future trends. E.g. in [37] a non-negative matrix factorization topic modeling method is used to identify relevant research topics from scientific papers. The results are stored in time series data which is the basis for predicting future research trends with the help of auto-regressive integrated moving averages. A differentiated approach is described in [22]. Relevant topics were identified by using topic modelling. In addition to the pure terms, a classifier is used to examine in which context the extracted terms are used, e.g., as a method or as an objective. According to the authors' argumentation this has an influence on how a topic will develop in the future.

5 Emerging Trends in Computer Vision

In this chapter we operationalized our proposed method. Therefore, we conducted a case study to find synonyms for keywords and identify emerging trends in the field of computer vision. The identification of the trends is not to be understood as a forecast, but serves as an overview for the development of the different topics within the research area computer vision.

5.1 Preprocessing

In our case study the raw abstract contains 115,987 different terms. After a first cleaning process 55,195 terms remain. Table 3 shows the most common keywords for our computer vision corpus.

Table 3. Most relevant keywords (before stemming)

Year	Keyword (counts, relative counts)
Overall	computer vision (1,679, 0.07), deep learning (970, 0.04), image processing (552, 0.02), machine learning (380, 0.02), object detection (342, 0.01), convolutional neural network (325, 0.01), feature extraction (272, 0.01), convolutional neural networks (272, 0.01), image segmentation (247, 0.01), segmentation (228, 0.01), face recognition (221, 0.01)
2019	deep learning (370, 0.13), computer vision (302, 0.11), convolutional neural network (118, 0.04), image processing (99, 0.03), machine learning (95, 0.03), object detection (94, 0.03), convolutional neural networks (92, 0.03), cnn (88, 0.03), segmentation (47, 0.02), image classification (45, 0.02), feature extraction (44, 0.02)
2018	deep learning (219, 0.10), computer vision (204, 0.09), machine learning (72, 0.03), convolutional neural network (69, 0.03), image processing (69, 0.03), convolutional neural networks (64, 0.03), cnn (43, 0.02), object detection (40, 0.02), feature extraction (30, 0.01), recognition (30, 0.01), image classification (27, 0.01)

The table can be explained using the example of "*deep learning*". In 2019 a total of 370 publications were tagged with the keyword "*deep learning*", corresponding to about 10% of the publications in 2019. A look at the previous year 2018 shows a distinct trend.

5.2 Training and Prediction

As you can see in Table 3, there are many synonyms or close related terms in the 10 top words per year, like "*convolutional neural network*" and "*deep neural network*". Therefor a word vector model is used to find similar words (based on cosine similarity) and to aggregate them for further analysis. The example of the keyword "*object detection*" demonstrates how adding synonyms to the keywords can help to provide a more reliable overview of the research area. Here the search for the substrings "*detect*" and "*recognit*" reveals specific use cases of object detection which otherwise would not have been considered (e.g., "*mango species detection*", "*recognition of cars*", "*makeup detection*", "*malaria parasite detection*"). The trained NLP model provides the researcher with knowledge in form of close related terms that he himself might not have known. For further investigation of the word vectors, we have visualized them in a scatterplot in which each term represents a data point as well as implemented a function to display the *n* most similar words to a given keyword. The overall scatterplot and the 10 most similar terms for the keywords *"object detection"*, *"deep learning"* and *"classification"* are shown in Fig. 3.

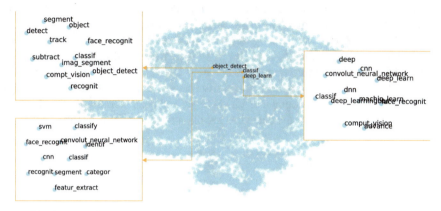

Fig. 3. Visualization of trained word vectors reduced to 2 dimensions using UMAP.

5.3 Evaluation

We treat the most similar words as suggestions and manually remove terms that we do not want to consider for the following trend analysis and therefore not to be added to the corresponding keywords. Similar terms can then be summarized, included in the analysis and help to obtain a better understanding of the subject area. Table 4 shows the 10 most similar terms for *"object detection"*, *"deep learning"* and *"classification"* the removed words for the respective keyword are crossed out.

Table 4. Evaluation of synonym suggestions for relevant keywords

Keyword	Synonyms (similarity score)
Object detection	detect (0.41), object (0,4), subtract (0.37), recognit (0.36), classif (0.34), segment (0.33), ~~compt_vision~~ (0.33), imag_segment (0.32), track (0.32), face_recognit (0.32)
Deep learning	machin_learn (0.53), deep (0.51), cnn (0.49), convolute_neural network (0.47), advance (0.38), dnn (0.37), ~~comput_vision~~ (0.35), ~~face_recognit~~ (0.34), deep_learningbas (0.34), ~~classif~~ (0.33)
Classification	classify (0.59), recognit (0.58), categor (0.44), face_recognit (0.39), feature_extract (0.38), segment (0.36), ~~convolute_neural_network~~ (0.36), identif (0.36), svm (0.35), ~~cnn~~ (0.35)

5.4   Trend Analysis

The synonyms are now used for an investigation of all *author keywords* by searching for matching substrings. If a substring is contained in a keyword, the corresponding paper is considered relevant for our analysis. The following graphs in Fig. 4 show the development over time for three selected computer vision topics (including their synonyms): *"object_detection", "classification", "deep_learning"*. The results of the trend analysis can be confirmed by adding expert knowledge, e.g., for the keyword *"deep learning"*. Since 2000, deep learning has been successfully used for object detection, classification and segmentation. However, the breakthrough did come in 2012, when Krizhevsky et al. won the imagenet classification challenge [57]. They trained large, deep convolutional neural networks to classify images. This was the breakthrough of deep neural networks in the computer vision scene and deep learning has been one of the predominant methods for the detection and classification of objects [58].

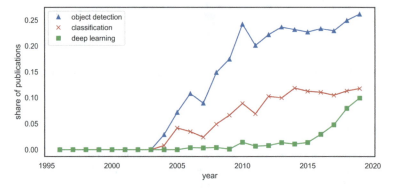

Fig. 4. Emerging trends in computer vision.

6   Discussion

In the following, implications as well as limitations will be discussed. Probably the most important implication of NLP for the analysis of scientific content arises for scientists themselves. Because of the large number of publications, it is difficult to get an overview of research areas [5]. NLP can help to solve exactly this problem with the concepts identified in the literature review. By clustering and summarizing publications, information is made available in an aggregated form. Bibliometric networks as well as the identification of emerging trends help to monitor the development of research. Sentiment analysis of citations provide an indication of the quality of a publication. The method presented in this paper also can be classified into the concept matrix of the conducted literature review: overview and future trends as well as simplify literature search.

There are also implications for practitioners. The identification of emerging trends plays an important role in open innovation. In open innovation, enterprises broaden their perspective and use external sources of information to identify innovations in order to improve their technologies [59]. Science is an established source for innovation in open innovation [60]. Our proposed method can help to optimize the open innovation process and to identify emerging trends early. Furthermore, the defined concepts during literature review can have impact on this. Due to the large number of scientific publications NLP can help in summarizing, clustering and tagging these documents. Thus, methods are made available to open innovation in order to handle the information overload. Related to this another implication can arise for economic planners and training providers. The forecast of manpower requirements and the required skills is of particular importance for this target group [61]. Using the example of design science research, the connection can be illustrated. The goal of design science is the development, improvement and evaluation of powerful IT artifacts to support organizations in achieving their objectives [62]. At least when managers are convinced of the usefulness of an IT artifact, it is necessary to build up know-how in this area. Our method can help to identify these needs in advance. Furthermore, fast response times are a central component of a company's success and require the processing of large amounts of data [63]. As our NLP pipeline is not restricted to scientific texts and can also be transferred to corporate documents, it might be of assistance here. In this sense, our pipeline represents an approach to gain a better overview of large unstructured text sets and is thus a tool for text-dominated data ecosystems.

Our research has some limitations, which we present in the following. In relation to our proposed method, the question of generalizability arises, e.g., for fields with less frequency, because for the training of word-vector-models large data sets are required. Using the example of "Computer Vision", which provides a large data set, we were able to show that our proposed NLP pipeline is capable of structuring key terms of a scientific field and to identify emerging trends. Nevertheless, a case study cannot provide comprehensive evidence [64]. We want to encourage researchers to use our method to investigate other fields to identify emerging trends and to provide expert knowledge to support further evidence. In addition to expert knowledge for the evaluation of the results, other data sources can be used in further research projects, such as google search trends. From a data analysis point of view, it can be assumed that an extension of the text corpus on which the training is based would further improve the quality of the word vectors and learned connections. We therefore suggest connecting additional data sources for further work. The used abstracts provide a good basis, as they summarize the essential statements of a paper. However, an abstract does not reflect the full level of detail of a scientific paper or may even contain non-existent contributions [5, 65]. Due to this fact, further research has to be conducted to extend our method to full text analysis. Our presented NLP pipeline is to be understood as a support system, but not as an approach for a full automation. In addition, it should be verified if transfer learning approaches lead to better results by re-training pre-trained embeddings with the domain texts, instead of learning the word vectors from scratch. Further potential exists with regard to the model for generating word representations. In principle, the W2V model proposed in our pipeline can be substituted by other models as long as they support a vector representation at word level. LDA2Vec [66], for example, enables the joint training of word, topic and document vectors in a common representation space and thus offers a promising approach to combine the strengths of LDA with W2V like vector representations [66].

7 Conclusion

With regard to RQ1, the literature review showed that NLP is used to examine scientific literature. The main focus is the optimization of a literature search. Summarization as well as clustering and tagging are common concepts that are used for this. With respect to RQ2, concepts have been identified during the literature search that address the problem of structuring and deriving research trends. In addition, the case study showed that our proposed NLP pipeline can be used to get a better overview of relevant terms within a research area. Therefore, we trained word-vector-models based on abstracts to find and aggregate most similar words. In the next step, emerging trends could be identified by using the synonyms for a given sets of keywords to search for the corresponding substrings in the Authors keywords. For the present use case we could show that our proposed NLP-pipeline helps to identify trends and to gain a more holistic picture of relevant terms within the topic area. The extent to which these findings can be applied to other fields and text corpus within and beyond the scientific field will have to be examined in further research.

References

1. La Quatra, M., Cagliero, L., Baralis, E.: Exploiting pivot words to classify and summarize discourse facets of scientific papers. Scientometrics **125**(3), 3139–3157 (2020). https://doi.org/10.1007/s11192-020-03532-3
2. Mueller, R.M., Huettemann, S.: Extracting causal claims from information systems papers with natural language processing for theory ontology learning. In: Presented at the Hawaii International Conference on System Sciences (2018)
3. Kerzendorf, W.E.: Knowledge discovery through text-based similarity searches for astronomy literature. J. Astrophys. Astron. **40**(3), 1–7 (2019). https://doi.org/10.1007/s12036-019-9590-5
4. Sergio, M.P., Costa, T. de S., Pessoa, M.S. de P., Pedro, P.S.M.: A semantic approach to support the analysis of abstracts in a bibliographical review. In: 2019 IEEE 28th International Conference on Enabling Technologies: Infrastructure for Collaborative Enterprises (WETICE), Napoli, Italy, pp. 259–264. IEEE (2019)
5. Cohan, A., Goharian, N.: Scientific document summarization via citation contextualization and scientific discourse. Int. J. Digit. Libr. **19**(2–3), 287–303 (2017). https://doi.org/10.1007/s00799-017-0216-8
6. Ma, S., Xu, J., Zhang, C.: Automatic identification of cited text spans: a multi-classifier approach over imbalanced dataset. Scientometrics **116**(2), 1303–1330 (2018). https://doi.org/10.1007/s11192-018-2754-2
7. Qazvinian, V., Radev, D.R.: Scientific paper summarization using citation summary networks. In: Proceedings of the 22nd International Conference on Computational Linguistics, Association for Computational Linguistics, USA, vol. 1, pp. 689–696 (2008)
8. Tomanek, K., Wermter, J., Hahn, U.: Sentence and token splitting based on conditional random fields. In: Presented at the (2007)

9. Jivani, A.: A comparative study of stemming algorithms. Int. J. Comp. Tech. Appl. **2**, 1930–1938 (2011)
10. Mohan, V.: Preprocessing Techniques for Text Mining - An Overview (2015)
11. Makrehchi, M., Kamel, M.S.: Automatic extraction of domain-specific stopwords from labeled documents. In: Macdonald, C., Ounis, I., Plachouras, V., Ruthven, I., White, R.W. (eds.) ECIR 2008. LNCS, vol. 4956, pp. 222–233. Springer, Heidelberg (2008). https://doi.org/10.1007/978-3-540-78646-7_22
12. Mikolov, T., Chen, K., Corrado, G., Dean, J.: Efficient estimation of word representations in vector space (2013)
13. Mikolov, T., Sutskever, I., Chen, K., Corrado, G., Dean, J.: Distributed representations of words and phrases and their compositionality (2013)
14. Turney, P.D., Pantel, P.: From frequency to meaning: vector space models of semantics. JAIR **37**, 141–188 (2010)
15. Levy, O., Goldberg, Y.: Linguistic regularities in sparse and explicit word representations. In: Proceedings of the Eighteenth Conference on Computational Natural Language Learning, pp. 171–180. Association for Computational Linguistics, Ann Arbor (2014)
16. Jelodar, H., et al.: Latent Dirichlet Allocation (LDA) and topic modeling: models, applications, a survey. Multimed. Tools Appl. **78**, 15169–15211 (2019)
17. Blei, D.M., Ng, A.Y., Jordan, M.I.: Latent dirichlet allocation. J. Mach. Learn. Res. **3**, 993–1022 (2003)
18. Devlin, J., Chang, M.-W., Lee, K., Toutanova, K.: BERT: pre-training of deep bidirectional transformers for language understanding [cs]. arXiv:1810.04805 (2019)
19. Peters, M.E., Neumann, M., Iyyer, M., Gardner, M., Clark, C., Lee, K., Zettlemoyer, L.: Deep contextualized word representations (2018)
20. Webster, J., Watson, R.T.: Analyzing the past to prepare for the future: writing a literature review. MIS Q. 26 (2002)
21. Brocke, J., Simons, A., Niehaves, B., Riemer, K., Plattfaut, R., Cleven, A.: Reconstructing the giant: on the importance of rigour in documenting the literature search process. In: ECIS (2009)
22. Prabhakaran, V., Hamilton, W.L., McFarland, D., Jurafsky, D.: Predicting the rise and fall of scientific topics from trends in their rhetorical framing. In: Proceedings of the 54th Annual Meeting of the Association for Computational Linguistics, Association for Computational Linguistics, Berlin, Germany, vol. 1, pp. 1170–1180 (2016)
23. Nam, S., Jeong, S., Kim, S.-K., Kim, H.-G., Ngo, V., Zong, N.: Structuralizing biomedical abstracts with discriminative linguistic features. Comput. Biol. Med. **79**, 276–285 (2016)
24. Abu-Jbara, A., Ezra, J., Radev, D.R.: Purpose and polarity of citation: towards NLP-based bibliometrics. In: HLT-NAACL (2013)
25. Qazvinian, V., et al.: Generating extractive summaries of scientific paradigms. JAIR **46**, 165–201 (2013)
26. Achakulvisut, T., Acuna, D.E., Ruangrong, T., Kording, K.: Science concierge: a fast content-based recommendation system for scientific publications. PLoS ONE **11**, e0158423 (2016)
27. Beltagy, I., Lo, K., Cohan, A.: SciBERT: a pretrained language model for scientific text (2019)
28. Collins, E., Augenstein, I., Riedel, S.: A supervised approach to extractive summarisation of scientific papers. In: Proceedings of the 21st Conference on Computational Natural Language Learning (CoNLL 2017), Association for Computational Linguistics, Vancouver, Canada, pp. 195–205 (2017)
29. Li, L., et al.: CIST@CLSciSumm-19: automatic scientific paper summarization with citances and facets. In: BIRNDL@SIGIR (2019)

30. Schäfer, U., Uszkoreit, H., Federmann, C., Marek, T., Zhang, Y.: Extracting and querying relations in scientific papers. In: Dengel, A.R., Berns, K., Breuel, T.M., Bomarius, F., Roth-Berghofer, T.R. (eds.) KI 2008. LNCS (LNAI), vol. 5243, pp. 127–134. Springer, Heidelberg (2008). https://doi.org/10.1007/978-3-540-85845-4_16
31. Chen, J., Zhuge, H.: Summarization of scientific documents by detecting common facts in citations. Futur. Gener. Comput. Syst. **32**, 246–252 (2014)
32. Joorabchi, A., Mahdi, A.E.: Automatic keyphrase annotation of scientific documents using Wikipedia and genetic algorithms. J. Inf. Sci. **39**, 410–426 (2013)
33. Aklouche, B., Bounhas, I., Slimani, Y.: Query expansion based on NLP and word embeddings. In: TREC (2018)
34. Roy, D., Ganguly, D., Bhatia, S., Bedathur, S., Mitra, M.: Using word embeddings for information retrieval: how collection and term normalization choices affect performance. In: Proceedings of the 27th ACM International Conference on Information and Knowledge Management, pp. 1835–1838. ACM, Torino (2018)
35. Porter, M.F.: An algorithm for suffix stripping. Program **40**, 211–218 (2006)
36. McInnes, L., Healy, J., Melville, J.: Umap: uniform manifold approximation and projection for dimension reduction (2018)
37. Abuhay, T.M., Nigatie, Y.G., Kovalchuk, S.V.: Towards predicting trend of scientific research topics using topic modeling. Procedia Comput. Sci. **136**, 304–310 (2018)
38. Almeida, H., Jean-Louis, L., Meurs, M.-J.: Mining biomedical literature: an open source and modular approach. In: Khoury, R., Drummond, C. (eds.) AI 2016. LNCS (LNAI), vol. 9673, pp. 168–179. Springer, Cham (2016). https://doi.org/10.1007/978-3-319-34111-8_22
39. Almugbel, Z., El, N., Bugshan, N.: Automatic structured abstract for research papers supported by tabular format using NLP. IJACSA 10 (2019)
40. Avram, S., Velter, V., Dumitrache, I.: Semantic analysis applications in computational bibliometrics. Control Eng. Appl. Inform. **16**, 62–69 (2014)
41. Ghosh, S., Shah, C.: Identifying citation sentiment and its influence while indexing scientific papers. In: Presented at the Hawaii International Conference on System Sciences (2020)
42. Giannakopoulos, T., Dimitropoulos, H., Metaxas, O., Manola, N., Ioannidis, Y.: Supervised content visualization of scientific publications: a case study on the arXiv dataset. In: Kłopotek, M.A., Koronacki, J., Marciniak, M., Mykowiecka, A., Wierzchoń, S.T. (eds.) IIS 2013. LNCS, vol. 7912, pp. 206–211. Springer, Heidelberg (2013). https://doi.org/10.1007/978-3-642-38634-3_23
43. Hassan, H.A.M., Sansonetti, G., Gasparetti, F., Micarelli, A.: Semantic-based tag recommendation in scientific bookmarking systems. In: Proceedings of the 12th ACM Conference on Recommender Systems, ACM, Vancouver, British Columbia, Canada, pp. 465–469 (2018)
44. Janssens, F., Leta, J., Glänzel, W., De Moor, B.: Towards mapping library and information science. Inf. Process. Manage. **42**, 1614–1642 (2006)
45. Khan, A., Tiropanis, T., Martin, D.: Exploiting semantic annotation of content with Linked Open Data (LoD) to improve searching performance in web repositories of multi-disciplinary research data. In: Braslavski, P., et al. (eds.) RuSSIR 2015. CCIS, vol. 573, pp. 130–145. Springer, Cham (2016). https://doi.org/10.1007/978-3-319-41718-9_7
46. Koukal, A., Gleue, C., Breitner, M.H.: Enhancing literature review methods - towards more efficient literature research with latent semantic indexing. In: ECIS (2014)
47. Krapivin, M., Marchese, M., Yadrantsau, A., Liang, Y.: Unsupervised key-phrases extraction from scientific papers using domain and linguistic knowledge. In: 2008 Third International Conference on Digital Information Management. pp. 105–112. IEEE, London (2008)
48. Krasnov, F., Dimentov, A., Shvartsman, M.: Comparative analysis of scientific papers collections via topic modeling and co-authorship networks. In: Ustalov, D., Filchenkov, A., Pivovarova, L. (eds.) AINL 2019. CCIS, vol. 1119, pp. 77–98. Springer, Cham (2019). https://doi.org/10.1007/978-3-030-34518-1_6

49. Li, L., et al.: Computational linguistics literature and citations oriented citation linkage, classification and summarization. Int. J. Digit. Libr. **19**(2–3), 173–190 (2017). https://doi.org/10. 1007/s00799-017-0219-5

50. Łopuszyński, M., Bolikowski, Ł: Towards robust tags for scientific publications from natural language processing tools and wikipedia. Int. J. Digit. Libr. **16**(1), 25–36 (2014). https://doi. org/10.1007/s00799-014-0132-0

51. Łopuszyński, M., Bolikowski, Ł: Tagging scientific publications using wikipedia and natural language processing tools. In: Bolikowski, Ł, Casarosa, V., Goodale, P., Houssos, N., Manghi, P., Schirrwagen, J. (eds.) TPDL 2013. CCIS, vol. 416, pp. 16–27. Springer, Cham (2014). https://doi.org/10.1007/978-3-319-08425-1_3

52. Nédey, O., Souili, A., Cavallucci, D.: Automatic extraction of idm-related information in scientific articles and online science news websites. In: Cavallucci, D., De Guio, R., Koziołek, S. (eds.) TFC 2018. IAICT, vol. 541, pp. 213–224. Springer, Cham (2018). https://doi.org/ 10.1007/978-3-030-02456-7_18

53. Petrus, J., Ermatita, Sukemi: Soft and hard clustering for abstract scientific paper in Indonesian. In: 2019 International Conference on Informatics, Multimedia, Cyber and Information System (ICIMCIS), pp. 131–136. IEEE, Jakarta (2019)

54. Sateli, B., Witte, R.: Collaborative semantic management and automated analysis of scientific literature. In: Presutti, V., Blomqvist, E., Troncy, R., Sack, H., Papadakis, I., Tordai, A. (eds.) ESWC 2014. LNCS, vol. 8798, pp. 494–498. Springer, Cham (2014). https://doi.org/10.1007/ 978-3-319-11955-7_73

55. Schafer, U., Spurk, C.: TAKE scientist's workbench: semantic search and citation-based visual navigation in scholar papers. In: 2010 IEEE Fourth International Conference on Semantic Computing, pp. 317–324. IEEE, Pittsburgh (2010)

56. Szczuka, M., Janusz, A., Herba, K.: Semantic clustering of scientific articles with use of DBpedia knowledge base. In: Bembenik, R., Skonieczny, L., Rybiński, H., Niezgodka, M. (eds.) Intelligent Tools for Building a Scientific Information Platform, pp. 61–76. Springer, Berlin Heidelberg, Berlin, Heidelberg (2012)

57. Krizhevsky, A., Sutskever, I., Hinton, G.E.: ImageNet classification with deep convolutional neural networks. Commun. ACM. **60**, 84–90 (2017)

58. LeCun, Y., Bengio, Y., Hinton, G.: Deep learning. Nature **521**, 436–444 (2015)

59. Galbraith, B., McAdam, R.: The promise and problem with open innovation. Technol. Anal. Strateg. Manag. **23**, 1–6 (2011)

60. Cassiman, B., Di Guardo, M.C., Valentini, G.: Organizing links with science: cooperate or contract? Res. Policy **39**, 882–892 (2010)

61. Wong, J., Chan, A., Chiang, Y.H.: A critical review of forecasting models to predict manpower demand. CEB. **4**, 43–56 (2012)

62. Hevner, A.R., March, S.T., Park, J., Ram, S.: Design science in information systems research. MIS Q. **28**, 75 (2004)

63. Thomas, O., Varwig, A., Kammler, F., Zobel, B., Fuchs, A.: DevOps: IT-Entwicklung im Industrie 4.0-Zeitalter: flexibles Reagieren in einem dynamischen Umfeld. HMD. 54, 178–188 (2017)

64. Abercrombie, N., Hill, S., Turner, B.S.: The Penguin Dictionary of Sociology. Penguin Books, London (1986)

65. Atanassova, I., Bertin, M., Larivière, V.: On the composition of scientific abstracts. J. Doc. **72**, 636–647 (2016)

66. Moody, C.E.: Mixing dirichlet topic models and word embeddings to make lda2vec (2016)

Hybrid Recommender Systems for Next Purchase Prediction Based on Optimal Combination Weights

Nicolas Haubner[1]([✉]) and Thomas Setzer[2]

[1] Institute of Information Systems and Marketing,
Karlsruhe Institute of Technology, Karlsruhe, Germany
`nicolas.haubner2@partner.kit.edu`
[2] Ingolstadt School of Management,
Catholic University of Eichstätt-Ingolstadt, Ingolstadt, Germany
`thomas.setzer@ku.de`

Abstract. Recommender systems (RS) play a key role in e-commerce by pre-selecting presumably interesting products for customers. Hybrid RSs using a weighted average of individual RSs' predictions have been widely adopted for improving accuracy and robustness over individual RSs. While for regression tasks, approaches to estimate optimal weighting schemes based on individual RSs' out-of-sample errors exist, there is scant literature in classification settings. Class prediction is important for RSs in e-commerce, as here item purchases are to be predicted. We propose a method for estimating weighting schemes to combine classifying RSs based on the variance-covariance structures of the errors of individual models' probability scores. We evaluate the approach on a large real-world e-commerce data set from a European telecommunications provider, where it shows superior accuracy compared to the best individual model as well as a weighting scheme that averages the predictions using equal weights.

Keywords: Hybrid recommender systems · Forecast combination · Optimal weights · Demographic filtering

1 Introduction

Personalized information systems (IS) are crucial nowadays in the areas of marketing and sales, providing a unique experience to users with the help of dialogues and relevant content. Advances in technology have made it possible to collect and process increasing amounts of data, such as customer profiles, activities and interests. Turning this data into actionable insights is not only key to acquiring and retaining customers, but also to providing suitable purchasing recommendations for up- and cross-selling items relevant to and appreciated by existing customers in order to increase customer lifetime values.

In this spirit, recommender systems (RS) are personalized ISs with the goal of helping customers make better (purchasing) decisions. There are different criteria for measuring the quality of an RS, e.g. serendipity, diversity, and predictive accuracy. In this paper, we

F. Ahlemann et al. (Eds.): WI 2021, LNISO 47, pp. 56–71, 2021.
https://doi.org/10.1007/978-3-030-86797-3_4

focus on the latter aspect. IS research has shown that the accuracy of recommendations, i.e. the perceived personalization, is of key importance for customers to adopt an RS as a decision aid, and thus, purchasing recommended items. More accurate RSs increase decision quality and also help companies retain customers [1].

Increasing the predictive accuracy of an RS can be achieved in several ways, e.g. by applying an improved predictive algorithm, tuning hyper-parameters or collecting additional input data for single RS techniques used. In addition to and independent of the former approaches, accuracy and robustness of RSs can be improved by combining multiple different prediction algorithms. This is called a hybrid RS (HRS). HRSs have been shown in the IS literature to improve decision quality and satisfaction with the system, compared to using only single recommendation methods such as collaborative or content-based approaches [2].

There are different ways of combining RSs into a hybrid, e.g. weighted, switching, mixed, or feature combination. In this study, we focus on weighted HRSs. The literature on how to select combination weights in weighted HRSs is very limited, specifically in the context of purchase predictions. Providing products or product categories of interest to a current user is key to content and affiliate marketing, generating leads and developing existing customers in terms of up- and cross-selling endeavors.

In [3], the authors propose a method of estimating optimal weights (OW) for combining multiple RSs in a rating prediction scenario. Their approach derives in-sample OW that minimize the mean squared error (MSE) of the HRS on the training data given certain assumptions. We transfer the weighting method from regression to a multi-category classification problem, where the goal is to predict the next purchase of a given customer based on the customer profile. For that, we use the Brier score, which quantifies the mean squared deviation of the estimated purchase probability from the true outcome. The Brier score is therefore analogous to the MSE in regression settings and is used in this work to estimate weights for combining probability scores of multiple classifiers.

The approach is evaluated on a labeled real-world data set from a large European telecommunications provider, where it is used to predict purchasing probabilities for three categories of mobile devices. The task is to predict the conditional probability, given that a certain customer is going to buy a mobile device, in which category it will be. Thus, the problem can be regarded as a top-1 recommendation task. Experimental results show that the proposed classifier weighting method leads to significant improvements, both in the Brier score and the accuracy score, compared to both the individual models as well as a combination where all models receive equal weights.

The remainder of this paper is organized as follows. Section 2 provides foundations of HRSs and forecast combination. Section 3 describes the proposed classifier weighting method. Section 4 outlines the experimental design to evaluate the proposed method on a real-world data set. Section 5 reports the experimental results, and Sect. 6 discusses the benefits and shortcomings of the proposed approach. Finally, we conclude and suggest directions for future research in Sect. 7.

2   Related Work

In this section, we review foundations of the proposed weighting approach. Section 2.1 gives an overview of HRSs with a focus on weighted approaches. Section 2.2 provides background on statistical forecast combination. Section 2.3 summarizes the research gap and motivates the novel method.

2.1 Hybrid Recommender Systems

An RS is a software system designed for estimating users' interest for products, based on their past purchases and possibly other inputs, and suggesting them those items with the highest estimated interest. RSs reduce information overload and improve users' decision quality by limiting the number of options. For companies, they increase sales and help market long-tail items which would otherwise be hard to find. RSs are nowadays used by, among others, e-commerce sites, digital marketing systems, social networks, and streaming platforms, where their advantages have been shown extensively [2].

An RS's quality relates to criteria such as serendipity, diversity, and accuracy. Serendipity denotes the ability of an RS to suggest items that a given user was not aware of, but finds interesting. Diversity refers to the composition of recommendations. Instead of suggesting several similar items, a good RS should be able to cater to the different interests of a given user. Finally, an accurate RS makes recommendations which fit user needs, such that the products are then taken by users with high probability, e.g. a customer ultimately purchases suggested products or watches suggested movies (e.g. [4]).

There are several methods for calculating prediction scores from available data, such as collaborative filtering, content-based filtering, demographic filtering, or knowledge-based systems, each using different input data sources and applying different algorithms. Each RS algorithm has certain shortcomings, e.g. the cold-start problem, where collaborative filtering methods are not able to provide recommendations for new users or new items (e.g. [4]).

HRSs combine two or more individual RSs in order to alleviate those problems as well as improve accuracy and robustness. Burke [5] classifies HRSs into seven types: weighted, switching, mixed, feature combination, cascade, feature augmentation, and meta-level. In this study, we focus on weighted HRSs, where several individual RSs calculate predictions independently, and those predictions are then combined using an aggregation function. While it has been shown that using a weighted average of RSs' predictions often leads to increased accuracy due to reduced model variance, published work on the selection of combination weights is scarce. In [6], different supervised models like ridge regression, neural networks, or gradient boosted decision trees for learning weights are compared. In [3], a model to learn weighting schemes from the errors observed for individual models is transferred from the forecasting to the RS domain, using the error covariance structure of the RSs to estimate OW. The model transferred is the one introduced in [7], which will be described in more detail in the next section.

2.2 Statistical Forecast Combination

In statistical forecasting, the combination of multiple prediction models has been subject to a large body of research. In [7], a weighting strategy is introduced which, for two combined models, can be shown to minimize the MSE in-sample, given the individual forecasts are unbiased, i.e. they do not consistently over- or underestimate the true values, and the performance of the individual forecasts is time-invariant. This weighting strategy is coined OW.

OW can generally be calculated for k prediction models (see e.g. [8]): let y be the vector of actual outcomes and $\hat{y}_l$ model l's predictions for the entries in y. Assuming error vectors $e_l = y - \hat{y}_l, l \in \{1, \dots, k\}$ of the individual models are multivariate normal with mean 0, OW can be learned that minimize the MSE over available ratings in y. With Σ_E denoting the variance-covariance matrix of the error matrix $E = (e_1, \dots, e_k)$, and $\vec{1}$ as a k-dimensional column vector with all ones, Eq. (1) derives the OW vector.

$$w = \frac{\Sigma_E^{-1} \vec{1}}{\vec{1}' \Sigma_E^{-1} \vec{1}} \tag{1}$$

Note that Eq. (1) minimizes the sum of squared deviations from zero (as of the unbiasedness assumption) subject to the constraint that the weights sum up to one, i.e. a weighted average. Although optimal in-sample, OW has often been reported to be outperformed on unseen data by more robust weighting strategies such as giving equal weights to all forecasts, i.e. a simple average (SA) (e.g. [9, 10]). This observation is called the "forecast combination puzzle". It can be explained by the fact that learned weights like OW must be estimated from past errors, often with rather small data sets available. Hence, OW can overfit the training data due to high model variance. SA, on the other hand, has no variance as it does not adjust weights to training data and is therefore more robust (e.g. [10]).

Contrary to the forecast combination puzzle, in [3] it is shown that given sufficient amounts of training observations, OW can be learned that are close to the ex-post OW (i.e. the unknown linear weight vector leading to the smallest out-of-sample MSE). The authors analyze this approach on a large publicly available data set with ratings of movies and find that it leads to accuracy improvements over the best individual RS as well as SA.

2.3 Contribution of this Paper

In summary, little research has been published on the selection of combination weights in weighted HRSs. As described above, there exist some weighting strategies for regression scenarios, mainly rating prediction, but for classification tasks, binary or multi-class, we are not aware of analytical methods for weighting different kinds of algorithms.

However, those kinds of problems appear very often in e-commerce, where a company wants to estimate, for a given user, purchasing probabilities of different products or product categories in order to show personalized advertisements or select suitable customers for marketing campaigns. In this paper, we propose an analytical weighting procedure to increase the accuracy and robustness of a multi-class classifier ensemble over the best individual classifier as well as SA. The proposed technique offers a means to increase accuracy and robustness without requiring expensive brute-force search or additional input data.

Commonly, e-commerce companies already test and compare different algorithms with the goal of maximizing predictive accuracy. Depending on the size of a company and its number of customers, an accuracy increase as small as 1% can lead to a significantly higher profit. The proposed approach offers a simple and efficient means to combine their existing methods and thus achieve higher levels of performance and profit.

We adapt the method introduced in [3] of learning combination weights for combining multiple RSs in a rating prediction task. We combine classifying RSs based on the covariance structures of the individual models' probability scores such that the Brier score is minimized in the same fashion as the MSE is minimized in regression settings. Next purchase (class) predictions on unseen data are then derived as the class with the highest probability score.

As described in Sect. 1, both the importance of accurate RSs and the benefits of HRSs have been demonstrated in IS research. The weighting method proposed in this paper therefore provides a relevant contribution both to the existing body of research and to practitioners, mainly large companies with substantial data available and many customers.

3 Methodology

This section introduces the approach to estimate OW for combining predictions of classification algorithms. Section 3.1 considers the assumptions and requirements of the weighting method. Section 3.2 describes the estimation of optimal combination weights in detail.

3.1 Model Assumptions

The classifier weighting is based on statistical forecast combination, as introduced in Sect. 2.2. In regression settings, Eq. (1) ensures a minimal in-sample MSE given that the individual models' errors follow a multivariate normal distribution with mean 0, i.e. the models are unbiased.

Our adapted classifier weighting scheme relies on the Brier score [11] as the classification equivalent of the MSE. For c possible outcomes (classes) and n observations, it calculates as shown in Eq. (2), where y_{ij} represents the actual outcome for observation i and class j, which is either 0 or 1, and $\hat{y}_{ij}$ represents the estimated probability with $0 \leq \hat{y}_{ij} \leq 1$ and $\sum_{j=1}^{c} \hat{y}_{ij} = 1, i \in \{1, \ldots, n\}$.

$$BS = \frac{1}{n} \sum_{i=1}^{n} \sum_{j=1}^{c} (y_{ij} - \hat{y}_{ij})^2 \qquad (2)$$

For each observation and each class label, we calculate the deviation between the predicted probability of the observation pertaining to the class and the true outcome. For each observation, the predicted probabilities sum to 1, and the true outcome is 1 for one class label and 0 for all the other labels. Since the errors are flattened, yielding error vectors of length nc, the deviations between prediction and ground truth sum exactly to 0 for each observation. Consequently, the mean deviation for each flattened error vector is also 0. Regarding the multivariate normality of the error vectors, respective analyses of the data set are provided in Sect. 5.1.

Another assumption of the classifier weighting method is that the minimization of the Brier score of a classifier ensemble results in an accuracy gain over all individual classifiers as well as an equal weights combination. We expect the Brier score to be an appropriate metric due to its interpretation as the MSE in probability estimation.

3.2 Classifier Weighting Method

Input to the method is a labeled classification data set with n observations, and k classification models. The output is $\hat{w}$, the estimate of the out-of-sample OW vector with $\hat{w} \in \mathbb{R}^k$ and $\sum_{l=1}^{k} \hat{w}_l = 1$. The number of classes in the data set is denoted by c. A portion of the input data is held out, resulting in two subsets, the training set with n_t observations and the holdout set with n_h observations. The split is performed stratified, i.e. the class distributions in the training and holdout set are practically equal.

Instance	Class	$\hat{y}_1$	$\hat{y}_2$	y
1	1	0.3343	0.2531	0
	2	0.1396	0.3511	0
	3	0.5261	0.3958	1
2	1	0.0192	0.0982	0
	2	0.4492	0.4895	1
	3	0.5316	0.4123	0
3	1	0.2614	0.1163	0
	2	0.4296	0.4690	1
	3	0.3091	0.4148	0

Fig. 1. Example for prediction vectors and actual outcomes with $n = 3$ instances, $c = 3$ classes, and $k = 2$ classification models

All classifiers are fitted on the training set. Each classifier $l \in \{1, \ldots, k\}$ then makes probability predictions $\hat{Y}_{hl} \in [0, 1]^{n_h \times c}$ on the holdout set. These predictions are flattened into a prediction vector $\hat{y}_{hl}$ of length $n_h c$, which contains predicted probabilities for each instance $i \in \{1, \ldots, n_h\}$ and for each class $j \in \{1, \ldots, c\}$. $y_h = (y_{1,1}, \ldots, y_{n_h,c})'$ denotes the vector of true outcomes in the holdout set. For each instance, y_h contains 1 for the actual class label of the instance, and 0 for all other class labels. Figure 1 shows an example of two prediction vectors and the true outcome. For simplicity, we omit the h subscript in this and the following figures.

For each classifier l, the vector $\hat{y}_{hl}$ of predicted probabilities is then compared to the vector y_h of actual outcomes. The error vector for classifier l is calculated as $e_{hl} = y_h - \hat{y}_{hl}$. For each of the k classifiers, this error vector is computed, yielding an error matrix $E_h = (e_{h1}, \ldots, e_{hk})$. Calculating OW from those error vectors can be shown to minimize the Brier score in-sample, analogous to the MSE in a regression setting. Figure 2 displays the error matrix for the predictions from Fig. 1.

With Σ_h as the variance-covariance matrix of E_h, the OW estimate $\hat{w}$ can be computed using Eq. (1). The variance-covariance matrix of the error matrix from Fig. 2 is given by (Eq. 3)

$$\Sigma_h = \begin{pmatrix} 0.1789 & 0.1730 \\ 0.1730 & 0.1825 \end{pmatrix}. \tag{3}$$

e_1	e_2
-0.3343	-0.2531
-0.1396	-0.3511
0.4739	0.6042
-0.0192	-0.0982
0.5508	0.5105
-0.5316	-0.4123
-0.2614	-0.1163
0.5704	0.5310
-0.3091	-0.4148

Fig. 2. Example for error matrix based on the predictions in Fig. 1

The weight vector estimated in this example is $\hat{w} = (0.6163, 0.3837)'$. Finally, training and holdout set are concatenated again, and all k individual classifiers are re-fitted on all n observations. This is to ensure that all models can process as many observations as possible in the training phase. The classifiers' probability predictions on new, unseen data are subsequently combined using the weight vector $\hat{w}$ estimated on the training set.

Many classification algorithms yield class membership scores that can be used to rank observations based on their likelihood to pertain to a certain class. However, those scores in general cannot be interpreted as proper probability estimates, since they are not well-calibrated, i.e. predicted class membership scores do not match ex-post probabilities [12]. While this is not an issue for class predictions of single classifiers, in classifier ensembles it is important to have reliable probability estimates. Therefore, we compare the OW estimation with and without calibration. For the calibration setting, we use isotonic regression as introduced in [13].

4   Experimental Design

We now describe the experiments conducted to evaluate the proposed weighting approach. Section 4.1 describes the use case and data set used for evaluation. Section 4.2 introduces the individual classifier methods used for the HRS. In Sect. 4.3, details about the experiments and evaluation criteria are given.

4.1 Use Case and Data Set

For the evaluation of the proposed classifier weighting scheme, we used a proprietary real-world data set from a large European telecommunications provider. Figure 3 displays the schema of the data set. It contains several hundred thousand purchases of mobile devices by customers. All purchases occurred in the years 2018 and 2019. In the figure, the last column represents the target variable, the first two columns are metadata for identification, and the columns in between are predictors.

Order date	Customer ID	Socio-demographic variables	Contract properties	Mobile data usage	...	Device type bought (class)
1/1/2018	...	...	...	...	...	1
1/1/2018	...	...	...	...	...	2
...	...	...	...	...	...	...
12/31/2019	...	...	...	...	...	3

Fig. 3. Schematic display of the data set used for evaluation

The mobile devices are divided into three categories. The goal is to predict, for each of the $c = 3$ categories, the conditional probability that the given customer will select the respective category, given a purchase. The category with the highest estimated probability is then recommended. The most frequent of the three class labels occurs in 48% of cases in the data set. Thus, a simple classifier which always predicts that label would already achieve an accuracy score of 48%, which can serve as a lowest bound for more sophisticated models.

The data set contains more than 40 predictor variables, consisting of customer properties such as sociodemographics, characteristics of the customer's contract, and aggregated behavioral information such as mobile data usage. The data types of the predictors are mixed, comprising binary, integer, real-valued as well as categorical variables. All values of the predictors were measured immediately before the respective purchase, representing a snapshot of the respective customer and contract in order to recognize purchasing patterns.

4.2 Individual Classifiers

This section describes the individual models used to test the weighting method. Since the model's inputs are vectors representing customers via their respective properties, the method used here can be classified as demographic filtering (e.g. [14]), although the predictors do not only contain demographic information. In total, $k = 7$ classifying algorithms were combined, which are briefly outlined here. We used the implementations in the Python package *scikit-learn* [15] for the individual classifiers.

- **Logistic regression**: The logistic regression model assumes a linear relationship between the predictor variables and the log-odds of the positive outcome of a binary dependent variable (e.g. [16]). The model can be extended for non-binary classification either fitting a one-vs-all model for each class label or minimizing the multinomial logistic loss. The latter is used here.

- **k-nearest neighbors classifier**[1]: A k-nearest neighbors classifier predicts, for a given instance to classify, the class which most occurs in the k training points with the smallest distance to that instance [17]. For probabilistic predictions, the class distribution of those k instances is predicted. The distance metric used here is the Euclidean distance, and the number of neighbors considered was set to $k = 5$.

- **Multi-layer perceptron**: A multi-layer perceptron is a frequently-used form of neural networks, consisting of an input layer with m nodes (the number of features), an output layer with c nodes (the number of classes), and one or more hidden layers (e.g. [16]). The nodes of the hidden layer use a nonlinear activation function, in our case the rectified linear unit $f(x) = \max\{0, x\}$. The weights between nodes are initialized randomly and then sequentially updated using the back propagation algorithm, which computes the gradient of the loss function with respect to each weight. The weight optimization is done using the efficient stochastic gradient descent method Adam [18], and the maximum number of iterations is set to 1000.

- **Decision tree**: The decision tree algorithm [19] learns simple "if-else" style decision rules by recursively splitting the data set with respect to a certain variable and value in order to create subsets which are more pure in terms of class distribution. We used a maximum depth of 5 in order not to overfit the training set.

- **Random forest**: The random forest algorithm [20] fits an ensemble of decision trees on the training data. By randomly selecting bootstrap samples of data and randomly selecting a subset of variables available for splitting at each node, the trees in the ensemble are partially independent, reducing the model variance and thus alleviating a single decision tree's tendency to overfit the training data. For predicting probabilities on new data, the average of predicted probabilities of all trees in the ensemble is calculated. We chose a number of 100 trees with a maximum depth of 5 for the forest.

- **AdaBoost**: AdaBoost [21] is an ensemble method which fits simple base learners sequentially, where in each iteration, weights for previously misclassified instances are increased such that the next base learner is forced to focus on more difficult cases. For prediction, the outputs of all base learners are aggregated. We used 50 decision trees with a depth of 1, also known as "decision stumps".

- **Gradient boosting**: Gradient boosting [22] sequentially builds an additive model. In each iteration, c (the number of classes) regression trees are fitted on the negative gradient of the loss function, which for probabilistic outputs is the deviance. We chose a value of 100 iterations.

4.3   Evaluation and Benchmarks

As mentioned in Sect. 4.1, the prediction task in this business case was to recommend one of $c = 3$ possible classes of mobile devices to each customer in the test set. Therefore, an ensemble of three-class classifiers was used. In order to evaluate the classifier weighting approach we propose, the following methods were compared:

---

[1] Note that in this bullet point only, k represents the number of neighbors. In the rest of the article, k is used to denote the number of classifiers combined in the HRS.

- **Individual classifiers**: For each of the seven models described in Sect. 4.2, the individual performance on the test set was calculated.
- **SA**: An equal weights average of the predictions of all seven classifiers on the test set was used as a benchmark for the hybrid approach.
- **OW estimate**: This is the approach proposed in this paper (see Sect. 3 for details).
- **Out-of-sample OW**: The linear weight vector with ex-post minimal Brier score, calculated on the test set, serves as an upper performance bound for any linear weight vector. The goal of the OW estimate is to come as close as possible to this performance.

For each of the mentioned methods, there are two treatments: first, the probabilistic predictions are taken as-is. Second, the predicted probabilities are calibrated using isotonic regression before making predictions or combining the probabilistic predictions. The un-calibrated and calibrated treatments are compared.

In order to evaluate the weighting approach and compare it to other strategies, 10% of the data set was used as a test set. Another 10% of the data set was used as a holdout set to calculate out-of-sample errors of the individual classifiers in order to estimate OW, as described in Sect. 3.2. This leaves 80% of the data set as a training set.

We used two evaluation metrics in the experiment: the accuracy score and the Brier score which was also used for weight estimation. Those two metrics were chosen because the proposed weighting approach aims at increasing the accuracy of a classifier ensemble over all individual components as well as an SA combination by minimizing the Brier score. As mentioned in Sect. 3.1, we expect the minimization of the Brier score to result in a significant accuracy gain.

For reasons of robustness, the experiment was repeated ten times with random training-holdout-test allocations. Accuracy and Brier scores were averaged over those runs, and their standard deviations are reported.

5   Empirical Evaluation

This section contains the experimental results of comparing the proposed classifier weighting method to the afore-mentioned benchmarks. Section 5.1 describes the data preparation, i.e. checking the model requirements. Section 5.2 reports the results.

5.1   Data Preparation

As mentioned above, the weighting method requires unbiased individual estimators (mean errors of 0) and multivariate normal error vectors. We described in Sect. 3.1 that the mean errors are 0 when using the flattened deviation between predicted probabilities and true outcomes as error vectors. Now, we inspect the distribution of deviations.

Figure 4 displays, for each individual classifier, a histogram of out-of-sample errors, using ten equal-width bins. The vertical axes are not labeled since the number of observations in the test set would give away the number of observations in the entire data set (see Sect. 4.1). The left part of the figure shows the histograms when feeding error vectors into the weight estimation as-is, i.e. without calibration. It is clear to see that the errors are not normally distributed. Some of the classifiers partially exhibit a bell-shaped

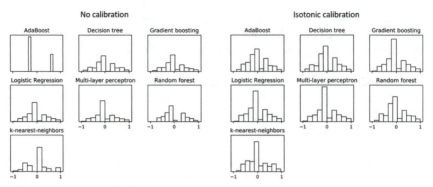

Fig. 4. Histograms of individual classifiers' out-of-sample errors without calibration (left) and with isotonic calibration (right)

distribution, however all with a gap around 0. Others, especially AdaBoost, are nowhere near bell-shaped.

However, applying the mentioned classifier calibration technique using isotonic regression changes the error distribution. The right part of Fig. 4 shows the same plot, but this time after isotonic calibration of each classifier. While there is still a gap near 0, all distributions now exhibit a bell-shaped form. They are still not normally distributed, but the calibration helps to better approach the assumption.

5.2 Results

Table 1 displays the results of comparing the HRS using OW estimation, an HRS using SA combination, and the individual classifiers. Both for the accuracy and the Brier score, the mean and standard deviation over ten runs are reported. For better comparability, the percentage differences between the OW estimation and the other methods is also reported for both metrics (columns "Diff."). As mentioned in Sect. 4.3, in addition to the individual classifiers, the SA combination and the OW estimate, the results using out-of-sample OW are also reported (last row) as an upper bound for the performance of a linear weighting vector.

The table shows that the combination using OW estimation clearly outperforms all individual methods as well as the SA combination. The best-performing individual classifier, which is the neural network with an accuracy of 66.8%, has a 2.4% lower accuracy and a 4.99% higher Brier score than the HRS using the OW estimate. An SA combination using equal weights slightly outperforms the best individual method, but leads to a 2.2% lower accuracy and a 6.25% higher Brier score than estimated OW.

The results also show that the estimated OW vector is very close in both accuracy (0.07% lower) and Brier score (0.07% higher) to the ex-post, out-of-sample OW vector. This indicates that the weighting approach proposed in this study can yield weight vectors that are close to the best possible linear weighting HRS.

Table 2 displays the results when all classifiers' probability estimates are calibrated using isotonic regression before estimating OW. After calibration, all classifiers' Brier

Table 1. Comparison of performance between a hybrid recommender system using optimal weight estimation, a simple average combination, and all individual classifiers

Method	Accuracy (std.)	Diff	Brier score (std.)	Diff
Logistic regression	0.6440 (0.0012)	+6.14%	0.1595 (0.0004)	−10.70%
k-nearest-neighbors	0.6280 (0.0016)	+8.84%	0.1677 (0.0004)	−15.09%
Multi-layer perceptron	0.6675 (0.0015)	+2.40%	0.1499 (0.0005)	−4.99%
Decision tree	0.6463 (0.0013)	+5.76%	0.1600 (0.0003)	−10.98%
Random forest	0.6430 (0.0014)	+6.30%	0.1649 (0.0004)	−13.63%
AdaBoost	0.6503 (0.0012)	+5.10%	0.2187 (0.0000)	−34.88%
Gradient boosting	0.6590 (0.0013)	+3.71%	0.1529 (0.0003)	−6.88%
Simple average	0.6688 (0.0012)	+2.20%	0.1519 (0.0002)	−6.25%
Optimal weight estimate	0.6835 (0.0013)		0.1424 (0.0003)	
Ex-post optimal weights	0.6840 (0.0013)	−0.07%	0.1423 (0.0003)	+0.07%

scores are in a range between 0.15 and 0.16. Their individual accuracies are not significantly affected, with one exception: the calibrated nearest-neighbors classifier has an accuracy of 64.8%, as compared to 62.8% for the non-calibrated version. This indicates that the calibration changed the order of the class ranking for some instances, leading to a higher number of correct class predictions.

Table 2. Results analogous to Table 1 after isotonic calibration of individual classifiers

Method	Accuracy (std.)	Diff	Brier score (std.)	Diff
Logistic regression	0.6440 (0.0014)	+6.40%	0.1593 (0.0004)	−10.83%
k-nearest-neighbors	0.6484 (0.0017)	+5.69%	0.1561 (0.0003)	−9.01%
Multi-layer perceptron	0.6673 (0.0015)	+2.68%	0.1500 (0.0005)	−5.29%
Decision tree	0.6460 (0.0013)	+6.07%	0.1600 (0.0003)	−11.21%
Random forest	0.6461 (0.0018)	+6.05%	0.1593 (0.0003)	−10.80%
AdaBoost	0.6487 (0.0011)	+5.63%	0.1579 (0.0003)	−10.03%
Gradient boosting	0.6590 (0.0012)	+3.97%	0.1528 (0.0003)	−7.03%
Simple average	0.6648 (0.0015)	+3.07%	0.1500 (0.0002)	−5.29%
Optimal weight estimate	0.6852 (0.0013)		0.1421 (0.0003)	
Ex-post optimal weights	0.6861 (0.0013)	−0.12%	0.1419 (0.0003)	+0.12%

As for the weighted HRSs, the SA combination of calibrated classifiers has a slightly better (smaller) Brier score and worse (smaller) accuracy than the non-calibrated SA combination. Now, the best individual classifier, which is again the neural network, slightly outperforms the SA combination in terms of accuracy. For the estimated OW, the Brier score is virtually unchanged, while the accuracy slightly increases when using calibration. This is probably caused by the nearest-neighbors classifier's gain in accuracy. The performance increase of the OW estimation over the best classifier (2.68%) as well as the SA (3.07%) is even higher than in the no-calibration treatment.

6 Discussion

In this section, we discuss and interpret the results obtained from the experimental evaluation in the previous section.

First, as apparent in Table 1, the technique of estimating OW using a subset of the available training data and then applying the learned weighting to the full data set clearly outperforms the SA combination as well as all individual methods. Although seven classification models were combined, meaning a weight vector of length $k = 7$ had to be estimated, the estimated OW comes very close to the ex-post OW, both in terms of accuracy and Brier score. This is probably due to the rather large data set used in the experiments, leading to robust weight estimates. Large e-commerce vendors usually have large data sets available, making the proposed approach a feasible and effective means to boost predictive accuracy.

In the use case of this paper, the proposed classifier weighting approach was able to increase the accuracy over the best individual classifier as well as SA by more than 2%. The impact of such an improvement depends on the business case at hand. For the project partner that provided the data set, this improvement is significant. Due to the high number of customers, being able to predict the right purchase in 2% more of the cases can lead to a considerable profit enhancement. Other large corporations, especially in e-commerce, could benefit in a similar way. On the other hand, for smaller companies with fewer customers as well as smaller data sets, other factors are more important, such as the model interpretability.

The theoretical model requirements were not entirely fulfilled in the use case, since the classifier error vectors were not normally distributed. Real-world use cases often differ substantially from theoretical requirements, which is why many approaches do not work well under those circumstances. However, the proposed approach was still able to reach an accuracy and Brier score very close to the ex-post best possible, and to improve performance over individual classifiers and SA combination. This shows that the classifier weighting is well suited for practitioners, even if the data is messy, as it often is in practice.

The classifier weighting method can be integrated into existing machine learning pipelines rather easily. Due to its analytical nature, it does not require expensive computations, and the weights are readjusted automatically without regular human intervention. Therefore, the cost-benefit ratio calculates favorably. The potential of gaining significant performance was shown in this study, and because of the added robustness, there is minimal risk of losing accuracy given sufficient data.

Second, as can be seen when comparing Table 1 to Table 2, although calibrating the probability estimates of the individual classifiers using isotonic regression led to decreasing Brier scores of the individual models (especially AdaBoost), it did not lead to significant differences in the accuracy of the OW combination. This is probably because almost all classifiers already had mostly well-calibrated scores.

Finally, while in general, a minimal Brier score does not automatically lead to the highest accuracy, in our case, the methods with the lowest Brier score (neural network for the individual methods and OW estimate for the HRSs) did have the highest accuracies as well. Especially the OW estimate, which aims at minimizing the Brier score of an HRS, outperforms all other models by more than 2% in terms of accuracy. This indicates that selecting combination weights based on the Brier score is a good strategy for creating accurate HRSs and therefore confirms our last assumption from Sect. 3.1.

7 Conclusion

In this paper, we presented an approach to estimate optimal combination weights for HRSs in a classification context, e.g. for purchase prediction. The weighting method fits all individual classifiers on a subset of the available training data and calculates out-of-sample errors of probabilistic predictions on the rest of the training data. Using the variance-covariance matrix of those out-of-sample errors, a weight vector is calculated which is optimal on the holdout set. Then, all classifiers are re-fitted on the entire available data set, and the calculated weight vector is used for combining predictions on new, unseen data.

Results on a real-world e-commerce data set show that this approach significantly outperforms both an SA combination, assigning equal weights to all components, as well as all individual classifiers. This is an encouraging finding, indicating that OW estimated using the Brier score is an adequate and simple method for increasing accuracy and robustness of classifiers.

This study contributes to research and practice. First, a novel and accurate analytical weighting scheme for classifiers is proposed. It contributes to the literature on weighted HRSs as well as classifier ensembles in general. For practitioners, especially companies with many customers and large data sets as well as different classifying models in use, the method provides a computationally efficient means of increasing accuracy and robustness, and thus revenue and profit, without requiring great effort to set up or maintain.

As a limiting factor, we did not engage in extensive hyper-parameter tuning for the individual classification algorithms, since the goal of this study was to demonstrate the improvement of a weighted HRS using an OW estimate over all individual models as well as an SA combination. In addition, we did not perform any feature selection or engineering. Performing both of those tasks might have improved the accuracy of the HRS even further.

Future research should investigate how well the OW estimation based on the Brier score performs in settings with fewer training observations or more classifiers. We expect that for smaller data sets, the advantage over SA decreases due to the bias-variance trade-off between those two weighting methods. Shrinking the estimated OW vector toward SA (e.g. [23]) or similar robust weighting strategies with lower variance might be a remedy against this effect.

Another interesting direction for future studies is to test the approach introduced in this paper using other algorithms, e.g. implicit feedback collaborative filtering methods (which would require other data sets), and study whether it is also able to improve an ensemble of RSs in terms of other metrics, such as ranking metrics which are often relevant in a top-N recommendation setting.

References

1. Komiak, S.Y., Benbasat, I.: The effects of personalization and familiarity on trust and adoption of recommendation agents. MIS Q. **30**(4), 941–960 (2006)
2. Xiao, B., Benbasat, I.: E-commerce product recommendation agents: use, characteristics, and impact. MIS Q. **31**, 137–209 (2007)
3. Haubner, N., Setzer, T.: Applying optimal weight combination in hybrid recommender systems. In: Proceedings of the 53rd Hawaii International Conference on System Sciences (2020)
4. Adomavicius, G., Tuzhilin, A.: Toward the next generation of recommender systems: a survey of the state-of-the-art and possible extensions. IEEE Trans. Knowl. Data Eng. **17**, 734–749 (2005). https://doi.org/10.1109/TKDE.2005.99
5. Burke, R.: Hybrid recommender systems: survey and experiments. User Model User-Adapt. Interact. **12**, 331–370 (2002). https://doi.org/10.1023/A:1021240730564
6. Jahrer, M., Töscher, A., Legenstein, R.: Combining predictions for accurate recommender systems. In: Proceedings of the 16th ACM SIGKDD International Conference on Knowledge Discovery and Data Mining, pp. 693–702. ACM, New York (2010). https://doi.org/10.1145/1835804.1835893
7. Bates, J.M., Granger, C.W.J.: The combination of forecasts. OR **20**, 451 (1969). https://doi.org/10.2307/3008764
8. Timmermann, A.: Chapter 4 forecast combinations. In: Elliott, G., Granger, C.W.J., Timmermann, A. (eds.) Handbook of Economic Forecasting, pp. 135–196. Elsevier (2006). https://doi.org/10.1016/S1574-0706(05)01004-9
9. Clemen, R.T.: Combining forecasts: a review and annotated bibliography. Int. J. Forecast. **5**, 559–583 (1989). https://doi.org/10.1016/0169-2070(89)90012-5
10. Smith, J., Wallis, K.F.: A simple explanation of the forecast combination puzzle. Oxford Bull. Econ. Stat. **71**, 331–355 (2009). https://doi.org/10.1111/j.1468-0084.2008.00541.x
11. Brier, G.W.: Verification of forecasts expressed in terms of probability. Mon. Weather Rev. **78**, 1–3 (1950)
12. Niculescu-Mizil, A., Caruana, R.: Predicting good probabilities with supervised learning. In: Proceedings of the 22nd International Conference on Machine Learning, pp. 625–632 (2005)
13. Zadrozny, B., Elkan, C.: Transforming classifier scores into accurate multiclass probability estimates. In: Proceedings of the Eighth ACM SIGKDD International Conference on Knowledge Discovery and Data Mining, pp. 694–699 (2002)
14. Pazzani, M.J.: A framework for collaborative, content-based and demographic filtering. Artif. Intell. Rev. **13**, 393–408 (1999). https://doi.org/10.1023/A:1006544522159
15. Pedregosa, F., et al.: Scikit-learn: Machine Learning in Python [cs]. arXiv:1201.0490 (2012)
16. Hastie, T., Tibshirani, R., Friedman, J.: The Elements of Statistical Learning. Springer New York (2009). https://doi.org/10.1007/b94608
17. Altman, N.S.: An introduction to kernel and nearest-neighbor nonparametric regression. Am. Stat. **46**, 175–185 (1992). https://doi.org/10.1080/00031305.1992.10475879
18. Kingma, D.P., Ba, J.: Adam: a method for stochastic optimization. arXiv preprint arXiv:1412.6980 (2014)
19. Breiman, L., Friedman, J., Stone, C.J., Olshen, R.A.: Classification and Regression Trees. CRC press (1984)

20. Breiman, L.: Random forests. Mach. Learn. **45**, 5–32 (2001). https://doi.org/10.1023/A:101 0933404324
21. Freund, Y., Schapire, R.E.: A decision-theoretic generalization of on-line learning and an application to boosting. In: European Conference on Computational Learning Theory, pp. 23–37. Springer (1995). https://doi.org/10.1007/3-540-59119-2_166
22. Friedman, J.H.: Greedy function approximation: a gradient boosting machine. Ann. Stat. **29**(5), 1189–1232 (2001)
23. Blanc, S.M., Setzer, T.: When to choose the simple average in forecast combination. J. Bus. Res. **69**, 3951–3962 (2016). https://doi.org/10.1016/j.jbusres.2016.05.013

Towards a Trust-Aware Item Recommendation System on a Graph Autoencoder with Attention Mechanism

Elnaz Meydani[1]([⊠]), Christoph Düsing[1], and Matthias Trier[1,2]

[1] Department of Management Information Systems, Paderborn University, Paderborn, Germany
{elnaz.meydani,trier}@uni-paderborn.de,
cduesing@mail.uni-paderborn.de
[2] Department of Digitalization, Copenhagen Business School, Frederiksberg, Denmark
mt.digi@cbs.dk

Abstract. Recommender Systems provide users with recommendations for potential items of interest in applications like e-commerce and social media. User information such as past item ratings and personal data can be considered as inputs of these systems. In this study, we aim to utilize a trust-graph-based Neural Network in the recommendation process. The proposed method tries to increase the performance of graph-based RSs by considering the inferred level of trust and its evolution. These recommendations will not only be based on the user information itself but will be fueled by information about associates in the network. To improve the system performance, we develop an attention mechanism to infer a level of trust for each connection in the network. As users are likely to be influenced more by those whom they trust the most, our method might lead to more personalized recommendations, which is likely to increase the user experience and satisfaction.

Keywords: Recommender systems · Trust-aware recommendations · Autoencoders · Attention mechanism

1 Introduction

Information overload is one of the major problems in many online applications such as e-commerce and social networking websites. Recommender Systems (RSs) have become a promising tool to handle this problem by generating individualized recommendations [1]. Collaborative Filtering (CF) is one the most popular algorithms in RSs, which predicts a user's interest in an item through mining the patterns of the existing rating information of other similar users/items [2]. The main idea of CF is to predict future ratings or purchases based upon collected user-item interactions, represented in a user-item interaction matrix. The approach additionally considers the preferences of associated users modeled as a user-user-connection graph. The user-user connection is usually being defined as friendship or followership between two users, both implying some form of trust between them [3]. Following the basic data structure, RSs based

© The Author(s), under exclusive license to Springer Nature Switzerland AG 2021
F. Ahlemann et al. (Eds.): WI 2021, LNISO 47, pp. 72–77, 2021.
https://doi.org/10.1007/978-3-030-86797-3_5

on Graph Neural Networks (GNNs) have been developed which have shown promising results in applications such as e-commerce and social media [4–6].

The theory of social homophily describes that similarity breeds connection. Accordingly, the people's networks of those whom they trust are more homogenous concerning many sociodemographic, behavioral, and interpersonal characteristics, including attitude towards certain commodities [7]. Consequently, from the observation of trust, possible interests can be derived from associated users in a trust graph [7]. Following this idea, some studies have utilized this concept to not only consider the explicit trust observed in a network but also implicit trust and the dynamics of it to recommend a user possible items of interest [1]. The main idea is to employ trust propagation to predict the level of trust in unknown users [8]. These trust metrics, emerging recently as a powerful technique, can then be utilized to personalize the user experience by emphasizing content entered by trusted users and hiding content provided by unreliable ones [8]. In the context of social media, however, this level of trust is rarely expressed directly, and thus has to be inferred from interactions and other side-information for each pair of related users.

In previous researches, both trust-aware and GNN-based RSs were found to perform well [1, 2, 4–6]. In our proposed approach, we aim to jointly utilize the two aforementioned concepts, GNNs, and level of trust, within a novel recommendation model. This GNN-based RS will capture the preferences of each user in a network as well as these users' interrelations to generate item recommendations. In particular, we will train a Deep sociodemographic GNN to not only accomplish such recommendations but also to infer the level of trust for each user to its direct and n-level neighbors. To accomplish the latter, we extend our GNN by an attention mechanism, as it was proposed in [1]. Attention mechanism in GNNs is originally introduced in [6] and allows to learn the contribution of each user to the recommendation for others, whereby this contribution indicates the inferred trust.

The proposed method tries to increase the performance of graph-based RSs by considering the inferred level of trust and its evolution. As users are likely to be influenced by those whom they trust the most, including the level of trust in our method might lead to more accurate recommendations. Thus, the contribution of our work is to generate more personalized recommendations using our model that aggregates the information from the most trusted users in the trust network. This is likely to increase user loyalty, satisfaction, and experience in online applications and respectively increase provider sales.

2   Related Literature

2.1   Trust-based Recommendations

The consideration of trust as side information in RSs, also referred to as Trust-aware RSs (TARS), has been investigated in several studies [1, 9, 10]. Typically, the trust network has been created from real-world observations. The concept of trust could either be revealed explicitly by the users or be inferred implicitly from their friendship or followership relations [2]. Both methods collect information about the direct associates of each user. The resulting network consists of nodes representing users and edges representing the trust between them [1]. In a weighted trust network, these edges are also weighted by the observed level of trust [1]. Within a trust-network, the level of trust between non-direct neighbors can then be inferred concerning the distance between users and the individual level of trust of each relation along the shortest path [10]. Both observed and implied levels of trust are then utilized to weight the effect of each user in a network on the recommendation for a specific user of interest. The more the target user trusts other users in his/her network, the more his/her recommendations are affected by other users' preferences [1]. The TARS approach has been shown to predict more accurate ratings and hence more individualized recommendations than traditional RSs by considering the trust factor [1].

2.2 Attention Mechanism

TARS relies on observations of trust within a network [1, 9, 10]. However, users trust others to varying degrees, even though this might not be included in the information about a network. To address this problem, Graph Attention Networks (GATs) can be used to learn the weights of each connection between users in a network [11]. GATs implement an attention mechanism, which allows learning a weight per edge [11]. These weighted connections characterize how strong the recommendations for a user u_i depends on the information received from the associated user u_j [11]. According to the theory of social homophily [7] and its bonding preference for similar actors, it can be logically derived that a target user is being influenced more by the users, whom they trust the most. Hence, the learned weight for each edge serves as an indicator for the level of trust between the related users [11].

2.3 Graph-Based Autoencoder

The application of autoencoders, an unsupervised deep learning algorithm, in RSs has shown promising results in recent studies [12, 13]. Due to their good performance, they have been jointly applied with GNNs [4]. The framework proposed in [4] is capable of recommending items to a user based on his/her past interactions with items as well as his/her connections to other users within a network [4]. Thus, direct neighbors affect the recommendations more than other users. Van Berg et al. [4] did not consider weak or strong ties between users and assign each user the same relevance for the recommendation. They propose the application of attention mechanisms in future research [4]. While Feng et al. in [14] followed the idea of integrating attention mechanisms into GNNs, the combination of trust-graph-based autoencoders with attention mechanisms to infer a level of trust between each user remains a gap in the existing research. Although the performance of both approaches shows promising results, applying a combination of both methods might outperform their isolated application. Recent research proved that such all-in-one approaches significantly improve the quality of results compared with single applications one after another [4].

3 Methodology

In this study, we adopt the Design Science Research Methodology (DSRM) process model proposed by Peffers et al. (2007) and develop a model to improve the performance of RSs, aiming at generating more personalized recommendations. The DSRM process model consists of six main activities [15]. The first two activities are the identification of a problem and motivation, and the objectives for a solution, which are illustrated in the introduction part of this paper. In this sub-section, we explain the details of the design and development of our proposed model. In the "Experiments" sub-section, we provide details about the experiments and the evaluation of our proposed model. The proposed model can be divided into three main phases: trust-graph creation phase, training phase, and recommendation phase.

3.1   Trust-graph Creation Phase

The Epinions dataset consists of information about the rating users made on items on one hand, and information about which users trust others on the other hand. The trust is a binary value in this dataset and does not include a differentiated level of trust [16]. The trust-graph is created by combining both types of information. The nodes and their relations are taken from the source of user-user trust information. After that, each node obtains features based on their past item ratings. These features are composed of information about each existing item and if/ how a user rated them. Based on this graph, the GNN Autoencoder will be trained in the next step.

3.2   Training Phase

In this phase, we train the GNN autoencoder to combine neighboring information with the observed ratings of each user and to predict ratings for such items, where no direct ratings were observed so far. During the process and due to the nature of GNNs, information about each node will be passed along the connections in the network, which allows learning the recommendations based upon the information of each n-level neighbors in the network, where, n arises from the number of layers in the network and will be selected concerning the best results. The attention mechanism is also included in the architecture of the underlying model and will allow learning a level of trust for each pair of directly associated users. For users who are not directly related, the overall procedure finds an implicit level of trust between them. Figure 1 shows the formerly unweighted trust-network (a), received from the creation phase. With the help of the attention mechanism, these edges could now be weighted (b). The level of trust will be used to weight the influence on the recommendations.

3.3   Recommendation Phase

The trained model outputs the expected ratings each user has for each item, but with a special level of trust learned from the training phase. These predicted ratings will be compared with the truly observed ratings. At each point, where the prediction gives a good rating for an item, for which a user has not rated yet, a recommendation will be accomplished. By doing so, the model is of special interest when users with very few or no ratings at all are considered. Even for such users, a recommendation can be attained.

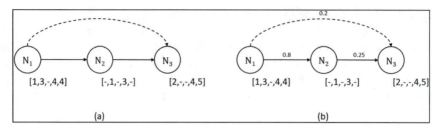

Fig. 1. Trust-network including rating information for each user. (a) is created directly from the data and (b) results after the application of the attention mechanism.

4 Experiments

Within the limited scope of this short paper, we provide a summary of the details of the experiments and evaluation. To measure the performance of our proposed framework, we will conduct experiments on two datasets and compare the results of our model with the graph-based state-of-the-art models. We choose GCMC +SN [4], GraphRec [17], and DANSER [18] models as evaluation baselines in our study. These experiments will be applied to two public known benchmark datasets, namely the Epinions and Ciao datasets[1]. Both datasets consist of user-item rating pairs with rating scores from 1 to 5, as well as the directed trust information between users. Trust is a binary value in both datasets and does not include a differentiated level of trust.

To evaluate the quality of our proposed recommendation algorithm, we adopt two popular metrics, namely, Mean Absolute Error (MAE) and Root Mean Squared Error (RMSE). Following the work of van den Berg et al. (2017), we use these evaluation metrics to evaluate the predictive accuracy of our proposed model and to compare our model with state-of-the-art baseline models. A smaller value of MAE and RMSE means less error score for the predicted item ratings and consequently a better performance of the model. The first results on both datasets show the superior performance of our proposed model. We believe that combining trust information into the recommendation process mitigates the cold-start users/items and data sparsity problem. To investigate the performance of our proposed model for cold-start users, we will test the model in the presence of users with only a few ratings (cold-start users) and monitor the MAE/RSME.

5 Outlook

In this paper, we present a novel approach to improve graph-based recommendations by including information obtained from a user-user trust-network to increase the overall performance and especially the quality of recommendations for users new to the network, which so far remains a challenge even for state-of-the-art RSs. This method is likely to increase the satisfaction of the users and the sales of providers. In the next step, we will continue to increase the performance of our model with special respect to cold-start users and items. Moreover, we will provide insights into how a level of trust can be inferred, how this trust evolves, and how it improves the quality of recommendations. Further evaluation of real-world applications will follow in the future.

---

[1] https://www.cse.msu.edu/~tangjili/datasetcode/truststudy.htm.

References

1. Li, J., Yang, R., Jiang, L.: DTCMF: Dynamic trust-based context-aware matrix factorization for collaborative filtering. In: 2016 IEEE Information Technology, Networking, Electronic and Automation Control Conference, Chongqing, pp. 914–919 (2016)
2. Li, J., Sun, C., Lv, J.: TCMF: trust-based context-aware matrix factorization for collaborative filtering. In: 2014 IEEE 26th International Conference on Tools with Artificial Intelligence, Limassol, pp. 815–821 (2014)
3. Massa, P., Avesani, P.: Trust-aware recommender systems (2007)
4. Berg, R.V.D., Kipf, T.N., Welling, M.: Graph convolutional matrix completion. arXiv preprint arXiv:1706.02263 (2017)
5. Pande, A., Ni, K., Kini, V.: SWAG: Item recommendations using convolutions on weighted graphs. In: 2019 IEEE International Conference on Big Data (Big Data), pp. 2903–2912 (2019)
6. Guo, Z., Wang, H.: A deep graph neural network-based mechanism for social recommendations. IEEE Trans. Industr. Inf. **17**, 2776–2783 (2020)
7. McPherson, M., Smith-Lovin, L., Cook, J.M.: Birds of a feather: homophily in social networks. Ann. Rev. Sociol. **27**, 415–444 (2001)
8. Avesani, P., Massa, P., Tiella, R.: A trust-enhanced recommender system application: moleskiing. In: Proceedings of the 2005 ACM Symposium on Applied Computing, pp. 1589–1593 (2005)
9. Golbeck, J.A.: Computing and applying trust in web-based social networks (2005)
10. Alahmadi, D.H., Zeng, X.-J.: Twitter-based recommender system to address cold-start: A genetic algorithm based trust modelling and probabilistic sentiment analysis. . In: 2015 IEEE 27th International Conference on Tools with Artificial Intelligence (ICTAI), Vietri sul Mare, pp. 1045–1052 (2015)
11. Veličković, P., Cucurull, G., Casanova, A., Romero, A., Lio, P., Bengio, Y.: Graph attention networks. arXiv preprint arXiv:1710.10903 (2017)
12. Li, X., She, J.: Collaborative variational autoencoder for recommender systems. In: Proceedings of the 23rd ACM SIGKDD International Conference on Knowledge Discovery and Data Mining, pp. 305–314 (2017)
13. Liang, D., Krishnan, R.G., Hoffman, M.D., Jebara, T.: Variational autoencoders for collaborative filtering. In: Proceedings of the 2018 World Wide Web Conference, pp. 689–698 (2018)
14. Feng, C., Liu, Z., Lin, S., Quek, T.Q.S.: Attention-based graph convolutional network for recommendation system. In: ICASSP 2019–2019 IEEE International Conference on Acoustics, Speech and Signal Processing (ICASSP), Brighton, pp. 7560–7564 (2019)
15. Peffers, K., Tuunanen, T., Rothenberger, M.A., Chatterjee, S.: A design science research methodology for information systems research. J. Manag. Inf. Syst. **24**, 45–77 (2007)
16. Zhong, H., Zhang, S., Wang, Y., Shu, Y.: Study on directed trust graph based recommendation for e-commerce system. Int. J. Comput. Commun. Control. **9**, 510–523 (2014)
17. Fan, W., et al.: Graph neural networks for social recommendation. In: The World Wide Web Conference, pp. 417–426 (2019)
18. Wu, Q., et al.: Dual graph attention networks for deep latent representation of multifaceted social effects in recommender systems. In: The World Wide Web Conference, pp. 2091–2102 (2019)

A Holistic Framework for AI Systems in Industrial Applications

Can Kaymakci[1,2(✉)], Simon Wenninger[3,4], and Alexander Sauer[1,2]

[1] Fraunhofer Institute for Manufacturing Engineering and Automation IPA, Stuttgart, Germany
{can.kaymakci,alexander.sauer}@ipa.fraunhofer.de
[2] Institute for Energy Efficiency in Production EEP, University of Stuttgart, Stuttgart, Germany
[3] FIM Research Center, University of Applied Sciences Augsburg, Augsburg, Germany
simon.wenninger@fim-rc.de
[4] Project Group Business and Information Systems Engineering of the Fraunhofer FIT,
Augsburg, Germany

Abstract. Although several promising use cases for artificial intelligence (AI) for manufacturing companies have been identified, these are not yet widely used. Existing literature covers a variety of frameworks, methods and processes related to AI systems. However, the application of AI systems in manufacturing companies lacks a uniform understanding of components and functionalities as well as a structured process that supports developers and project managers in planning, implementing, and optimizing AI systems. To close this gap, we develop a generic conceptual model of an AI system for the application in manufacturing systems and a four-phase model to guide developers and project managers through the realization of AI systems.

Keywords: Manufacturing AI system · Intelligent agents · Machine learning

1 Introduction

The digitization and automation of products, plants and manufacturing processes continues to increase and receives new impulses from modern information technology. Companies are constantly forced to adapt to new technologies and remain competitive. Today companies are facing the next big change - artificial intelligence (AI) systems [1]. Due to the relatively new approach of integrating AI into manufacturing systems, by integrating not only preset programs with explicit instructions and programmed control processes, but also knowledge-based on historical data, the acceptance of these systems is not very pronounced. In research AI systems in manufacturing are historically proposed and developed but not yet widely used in practice [2].

Especially in manufacturing, numerous use cases have been identified where AI-controlled applications for pattern recognition, process automation, computer vision, nonlinear control, robotics, data mining or process control systems can be used and existing solutions can be made more efficient and effective or even enable solutions at all [4]. Thus, company goals such as cost reduction or quality improvement can

F. Ahlemann et al. (Eds.): WI 2021, LNISO 47, pp. 78–93, 2021.
https://doi.org/10.1007/978-3-030-86797-3_6

be supported to remain competitive. Nevertheless, compared to big tech companies like Google, Facebook or Microsoft, the manufacturing industry still has problems integrating AI-driven approaches to optimize and automate manufacturing processes [5].

The manufacturing industry is the backbone of today's economy. In order to remain competitive, the manufacturing industry began early to experiment with AI applications (predictive maintenance, quality control and demand planning) [6]. Despite many successful individual AI experiments and use case, implementations in industry, which concentrate on individual details, a holistic concept for the planning, implementation, and optimization of AI systems, is missing.

A conceptual modeling of AI-based information systems enables the use of AI as well as the continuous improvement of the models. Additionally, a conceptual model that supports industrial companies in the introduction and implementation of AI systems to increase the dissemination of the systems, is needed. To close this gap the following two research questions (RQs) are formulated:

Which components are part of an AI system and how can an AI system be defined generically in a conceptual model?

How should a generic process for planning, implementation, and optimization of AI systems be structured?

We address the RQs by defining and describing an AI system with a conceptual model and developing a generic process to plan, implement and optimize an AI system following a design science research approach. With the aim of laying the foundation of a generic approach of modelling AI systems, we contribute by first deriving the necessity of a holistic concept modeling an AI system in the manufacturing industry by identifying the requirements of intelligent systems used in manufacturing. Second, we propose a set of components to model an AI system. The specific attributes and the relationships between the components are developed. Third, we define a process model to plan, implement and optimize the modeled AI system into existing manufacturing and information system environments considering the specific requirements in manufacturing such as maintaining process stability.

This article is structured in eight sections. The second section attempts to define AI systems and the motivation for manufacturing companies of the described concept are elaborated by analyzing existing literature and comparing state-of-the-art processes/concepts. Second, in Sect. 3 we introduce our methodological approach before our conceptual model for an AI system with its components is described (Sect. 4) and a phase model for developing AI systems is introduced in a third step (Sect. 5). In Sect. 6 we demonstrate our designed artifacts with a use case of an anomaly detection in energy consumption for a German metal processing company. We discuss and validate the design artifacts with findings from the use case and expert interviews in Sect. 7 before we conclude in the final Sect. 8.

2   Why the Manufacturing Industry Needs a Holistic Concept

The continuous improvement and optimization of processes is one of the key require-ments of manufacturing systems [7]. Therefore, AI techniques, especially machine learn-ing, are applicable for realizing intelligent systems [2]. The terminology of AI is difficult to define clearly, but its most common interpretation is that of automation of rational behavior [8]. First, AI in manufacturing was used to improve quality, especially in the semiconductor industry [3]. In recent years, with the advent of large amounts of data, intelligent sensors and improved computing power, AI has also been used in other areas such as process control, demand planning or logistics [1]. Nevertheless, the introduc-tion of AI systems still poses major challenges for manufacturing companies, especially data quality, data processing, model selection or cyber security issues [5]. In research and practice many attempts have already been made to develop frameworks and tools to address these challenges. The published approaches, which are not limited to application in manufacturing systems, can be divided into two segments, whereby the distinction is partly fluent. One segment focuses on the generic description of AI systems by means of a conceptual model that encompasses features, functions, or the underlying components of AI systems. The second segment deals with processes for the introduction, develop-ment, or operation of AI systems. The focus is not necessarily on AI systems, but rather on machine learning applications.

The research on conceptual models shows heterogeneous results regarding the def-inition of AI systems, their functionalities and components, and the structure for their description. Nalchigar et al. [9] present a conceptual modeling framework for designing business analytics systems by determining the requirements of the analytical solution. They introduce the layers business, analytics, and data preparation. Another approach to define a holistic industrial AI ecosystem, where different technologies are catego-rized into operation, platform, analytic and data technology, is depicted by Lee et al. [2]. Their industrial AI ecosystem focuses on building and integrating AI systems in existing information systems. Wang et al. [10] create an architecture for self-organized multi-agent systems for smart factories. The specific architecture focuses on the interop-erability between different machines, information systems and other data sources. Van den Heuvel and Tamburri [11] divide an AI system into three different layers - data, intelligence and application. In contrast, Simard et al. [12] present a non-technical app-roach to design AI systems by differentiating between machine learning and machine teaching. Whereas "machine learning" focuses more on implementing the appropriate algorithm and model, "machine teaching" specifies the steps (e.g. labeling, feature engi-neering, schema definition) for teaching the model by using domain knowledge. It can be observed that there is no uniform understanding of the subject of AI systems in liter-ature. Sculley et al. [13] postulate a lack of an abstract description of AI systems, since there is no abstraction to support AI systems compared to the modeling of relational databases. Much more, a generic, understandable, and applicable definition and descrip-tion of AI systems is necessary. The listed approaches and frameworks set different priorities, such as the integration of AI systems into an existing ecosystem of informa-tion systems, without specifying the AI system itself. In addition, the description of the central component of the agent, which we will introduce in Sect. 4, is missing in the specifications. The variety of different frameworks and perceptions of AI systems makes it difficult to deploy AI systems in a targeted and value adding way for companies that have not yet acquired comprehensive knowledge about the application of AI systems in their production systems.

The second of literature segment investigating processes for the introduction, development, or operation of AI systems is even more diverse. Next to the classic data mining approaches like Knowledge Discovery in Databases (KDD) [14], Cross Industry Standard Process for Data Mining (CRISP-DM) [15] or Team Data Science Process (TDSP) [16], which focus on the process of how to gain information or knowledge from large datasets, other workflow and process models related to machine learning have been developed. Transferring the data mining approaches to the operational use of AI systems in industry reveals a weak point. The approaches focus on extracting information from static historical data in order to create a data-driven model and evaluate it without or only partially considering integration and use as an information system that is interoperable with the manufacturing processes themselves. This is particularly important for the practical use of AI systems. In addition, software solutions that support processes such as data understanding or model management are missing [17]. A possible approach to implement AI systems into existing information systems is to extend software engineering and design practices by considering the specifics in machine learning projects [18]. Amershi et al. [19] elaborates the differences between traditional and AI-based software engineering. Kessler et al. [20] introduce a holistic machine learning lifecycle process from business understanding to model optimization and maintenance as well as implications for enterprise data management based on the type of data, the different roles in machine learning groups and the life cycle of machine learning models. Moreb et al. [21] show a framework for the technical implementation on a coding level for machine learning applications in health information system to enhance the systems efficiency. Kriens and Verbelen [22] present current techniques and methods to manage complex AI-based software. They postulate to package AI models to capture all necessary metadata for automating the deployment process. Lwakatare et al. [23] analyzed software-intensive systems with ML components in industrial settings and derived five different evolution stages of AI systems – prototyping, non-critical deployment, critical deployment, cascading (more than one model) deployment and Autonomous Systems in a case study. The comparison of the different approaches and processes shows that, despite their generic character, the processes mostly provide no precise guidelines for actual implementation in practice or only for individual phases in the AI system life cycle. Several challenges have been described in literature supporting this finding. Chen et al. [24] define four specific challenges in building production ready AI systems. First, the multitude of different tools and frameworks available for the development of AI systems makes it almost impossible to know all tools and frameworks. Second, most of the available tools do not have a particular experiment tracking implemented. Third, the reproducibility of AI systems is a major challenge when transferring models into production. Last, deploying models can be challenging with regard to training and inference. Sculley et al. [13] conclude that modeling, learning and predicting with a data-driven model represents only the smallest part in building an AI system. They found that aspects such as configuration, data acquisition or monitoring are more important than the ready-to-use models from research. To avoid pipeline jungles or dead experimental code paths, the entire life cycle of machine learning must be planned [13]. To solve the mentioned challenges further software packages and platforms were developed by Google [25], Uber and Chen et al. [24]. Nevertheless, to date, it is necessary to stack different tools and frameworks together to get an end-to-end solution for an AI system that supports manufacturing processes.

Summarizing, the problem is not the availability and maturity of the technology and AI solutions themselves, but rather that each company has its own individual systems and characteristics as well as no uniform understanding of AI systems. Hence, there is a need for an abstract definition of an AI system within a conceptual model. Missing methods, processes, and frameworks available in the literature guiding engineers, developers, and project managers in manufacturing companies in the planning, implementation, and optimization of AI systems require a generic end-to-end process based on the conceptual model of AI systems. The transfer of classical procedures of systems engineering and software development to AI systems is insufficient and does not cover the specifics of data-driven approaches [18, 19]. For manufacturing companies to withstand increasing cost and efficiency pressure, a uniform procedure for the introduction and operation of AI systems is necessary, which can be individually adapted to the company.

3   Methodology and Study Design

We organized research in this paper by the design science in information systems research framework combining behavioral science and design science paradigms [26]. In terms of Gregor and Hevner [27] we contribute an improvement to existing research and solutions. We argue that even though the application domain of AI in industrial applications is relatively high, the solution maturity is low, as we are among the first to define a generic model for AI systems and develop a structured process for its implementation. In a first step we derived requirements from literature conducting a semi-structured literature search in the databases Google Scholar, ScienceDirect, Scopus, Semantic Scholar, and AIS eLibrary with the keywords "AI in manufacturing", "AI system", "software engineering" as well as expert interviews (employees in manufacturing companies, AI research experts), whose results we presented in Sect. 2. The acceptance criteria extracted from expert interviews are completeness of the artifacts, their easy understanding and traceability. After several iterations of designing our artifacts we demonstrated our AI system and applied our generic process with a use case of AI-based anomaly detection in energy consumption (see Sect. 6) and evaluated the final artifacts again with expert interviews (Sect. 7). We communicate our results with this paper enabling practitioners to integrate AI in manufacturing systems and industrial applications.

4   Developing an AI system for Industrial Process Optimization – A Generic System Concept

4.1   AI System

To build an AI system aligned with existing manufacturing processes and information systems a conceptual model of the AI system is necessary. The conceptual model is the interface to the actual requirements of an AI system and can be seen as an abstract, formal description of the AI system [28]. The theoretical foundations on conceptual modeling of information systems are based on the framework presented by Wand et al. [28]. A conceptual model of an AI system structures its underlying components and systems with the purpose of enabling a fast scalability [29]. The conceptual modeling of a system, also called ontological modeling, is an integral part of the implementation-independent conception phase in database design and is regarded as an orientation here [30]. The basic goal of the presented AI system is the beneficial and value-adding transformation (data processing) of incoming data from data sources to outgoing data in the form of actions of an agent. Due to the modular structure of the AI system the conceptual model covers central components and related functionalities. First, physical objects such as sensors or information systems like ERP systems are data sources that can push and pull data to and from other data sources. Components with a data input, data processing and data output functionality are called data processing unit (DPU). Two specific DPUs need to be considered in depth – the data-driven model and the agent.

An AI system consists of at least DPUs, a data-driven model and an agent, which takes predictions of data-driven models as an input and processes it to an action for the subsequent systems or objects. The components of AI systems and their interaction are visualized in Fig. 1. Related to the concept of Russell et al. [8], agents provide a specific benefit manifested as action for the manufacturing system and the associated subsystems. In addition, agents can occur in a wide variety of forms to support the manufacturing system. An agent could be a human in the loop, which interprets the outcome of a model and triggers an action.

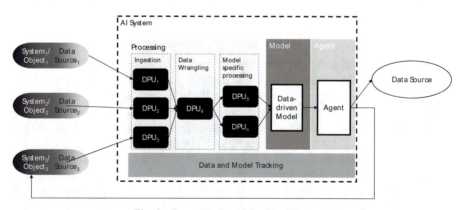

Fig. 1. Conceptual model of an AI system

4.2 Data Source

A data source can be a system or an object that sends one or more variables to another system or object at a specified time interval. It is important to mention that data sources not only have to be backed by a physical object but could also be a relational database or a file server – things that can be encapsulated from the real world. A data source could also receive data. A good example is a programmable logic controller (PLC) that receives data from sensors and sends the data to subsequent systems like an ERP system or an energy management system. The metadata of each attribute is stored within the data source (data type, format, etc.). For the planning and design of an AI system, necessary data sources inside and outside of the manufacturing systems must be identified. Domain expertise and experiences from other systems enable identifying relevant data sources from the environment that can influence the result of the AI system [15, 31]. For the individual and exemplary process of predicting machine failure with an AI system, possible data sources such as power consumption, pressure, temperature or speed must be identified. This allows modelling real phenomena such as machine failure or power consumption [32].

4.3 Data Processing Unit

A data processing unit (DPU) is defined as a base functional module unit within an AI system that consists of a data input, data transformation and data output module. The transformation module processes the input by explicit and rule-based instructions or specific mathematical functions to a fixed data output. The transformation of a data input into a data output is carried out using various tools and methods. The number of DPUs can be varied as required and adapted to the individual case. Modeling and implementing DPUs can be used for data preprocessing and feature engineering steps [14]. One specific task of a DPU could be the deletion of duplicates, the reconstruction of missing values, scaling input parameters, or the standardization of values. Note, that data-driven models and agents are DPUs with a specific structure and functionality described in the next sections.

Data-Driven Model
The data-driven model is a DPU with specific characteristics considering the transformation of the data input into an output. The modelling of the relationship between data input and the desired output is done dynamically by optimizing the parameters of a previously defined model with basic assumptions about its form. The challenge here is to choose the right model depending on the requirements of the AI system and to optimize the parameters of the model. In practice a lot of data-driven models are related to machine learning algorithms such as decision trees or neural networks. The optimization of the parameters is also often referred to as "inductive learning as a process of finding a hypothesis that agrees with the observed examples" [8]. The parameters are optimized by training the model with the data input. Some data-driven models additionally use the model output as a label for the optimization of the parameters (e.g. supervised learning). Especially, when traditional theory-driven approaches for modeling real phenomena are too complex, data-driven approaches are particularly suitable. Data-driven approaches do not follow the exact and simplified modelling of reality by known and established theories, but consider the input of data sources as "ground truth" [33].

AI Service/Agent
An agent is defined as a DPU that can consume the output of the data-driven model(s) and transforms or processes the output for further applications. Other approaches such

as reinforcement learning agents are also capable of action that do not rely on models [8]. The basic goal of an agent developed for industrial applications is to improve a manufacturing process. Three different cases are to be considered. First, an already existing automated process can be improved with the help of an agent (e.g. temperature regulation through reinforcement learning). Second, a manual process can be enhanced (e.g. recommendation system for energy managers). Third, it is possible to fully automate a manual process (e.g. automation of energy procurement). An agent can also describe the interface to other systems or subsystems. Specifically, an agent could be used by other systems such as the Manufacturing Execution System (MES) or a control system. Especially in control systems of industrial energy supply systems agents can be used to optimize the overall performance of a manufacturing system [34]. The integration of the AI system, or information systems in general, with other information systems is one of the big challenges in developing applications in the manufacturing industry. Therefore, easy to use interfaces must be planned and implemented for the interoperability between those systems [35].

Next to the superordinate cases, agents fulfill different functions, which are manifold described in literature. Hofmann et al. [36] provide an overview and define seven general variants of agents which are relevant for the AI system – Perceiving, Feature extraction and identification, Reasoning, Prediction, Decision, Action and Generation. In line with the problem to be solved by the AI system, the listed functionalities can be used to design the agent for each use case.

5 Phase Model for Developing AI Systems

5.1 Developing the Phase Model

After having defined an AI system contributing to understanding its characteristics, we propose a four-phase model for planning, building, and maintaining an AI system– planning, experimentation, implementation, and optimization during operation (see Fig. 2). We derived our phase model from existing frameworks in literature (see Sect. 2) and from the experience gained in current research projects in setting up several AI systems for industrial applications. In a further step, we validated our work with expert interviews in software engineering and machine learning, which led to minor improvements on the way to the current version. The goal is to present the model as understandable as possible and yet generic. In addition, more detailed frameworks can be integrated into our model in individual phases, which allows us to customize the application of our models as desired. Nevertheless, two major points must be considered, which are especially important when building AI systems in a complex information system landscape. The planning phase summarizes all the necessary planning for the AI system, since a corresponding effort must be made to determine the direction for successful further steps. Second, regarding AI systems (especially in manufacturing), it should be noted that a distinction must be made between an experimentation phase and the deployment in production systems.

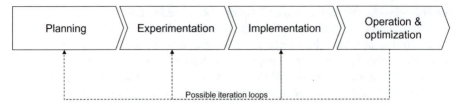

Fig. 2. Phase model for building and operating AI systems

5.2 Planning – Defining the Right Problem to Solve

The main goal of the planning phase of an AI system is to define the specific problem that should be solved and correspondingly the benefit of the AI system. Therefore, the PEAS framework from Russell et al. [8] is used as a foundation, consisting of four dimensions – performance measure, environment, actuators, and sensors. We generalize the framework for our definition of AI systems by using the four dimensions – performance, environment, measures, and data (PEMD). The reason for the change of the terms actuator and sensor to generic measures and data can be explained by the definition of the different data sources in Sect. 4.2, as an AI system does not necessarily have to use physical actuators or sensors as interacting objects but can also be based on information systems or databases.

The **performance** of an AI system is not defined by the evaluation metric of a model (e.g. F1-score in classification or mean squared error in regression) but by the specific performance indicator of the process or problem defined above. Therefore, we differentiate between the model metric for the data-driven model and the system metric for the evaluation or performance metric of the AI system. Whereas the model metrics such as for classification or regression models are well defined, the system metrics are often mentioned but not specified and measured. Furthermore, the relationship of the model metrics and the system metrics are often unclear. The dimension "performance" of the PEMD framework defines the model metrics as well as the system metrics. A typical model metric in binary classification is called recall, which indicates the probability that a positive object is correctly classified as positive. A system metric can be derived from the defined requirements of the AI system. The system metrics are specific business goals such as minimizing costs in manufacturing or increase product quality. By disaggregating the business goal into specific targets, the required models and agents can be derived. The system metric in industrial applications can vary depending on the use case. A typical system metric could be to reduce the energy costs of a manufacturing process. One of the possibilities is to detect load peaks of the process with a classification model and react by smoothing the electrical load using different measures which must be defined in the PEMD dimension "measures". Another well-known system metric in manufacturing goal could be to reduce the number of rejected goods. The goal of the AI system is to maximize or minimize the system metric depending on the problem it solves.

Additionally, the **environment** of the problem must be determined. The environment can be defined as information systems, processes and physical objects that interact with the AI system. A deep understanding of the environment and its processes is also regarded as domain expertise or knowledge in the field of data science. Especially in industrial applications, a multitude of information systems, high degrees of automation and complex dependencies possess challenges that must also be considered when planning AI systems. For further information on (AI-independent) process and system analysis we refer to [37].

The dimension **measures** determines the different actions that one or more agents of the AI system can take to achieve the defined goals and to solve the overall problem. Possible actions must be identified. The agents in industrial applications can take the general measures described in Sect. 4.3. Measures for an industrial application could be generating reports with detected anomalies (generation), regulating variables like the engine speed (action) or giving decision support during production planning (decision). It is important to identify these measures without considering the manifestation of the agents, which can be determined afterwards. The performance of the measures is loosely coupled to the overall performance metric. Therefore, the system metric defined in the dimension "performance" can be combined with the different actions defined in the measure dimension. The measure "turn off machine A" is connected to the system metric "minimizing energy consumption of machine A".

The last dimension **data** defines the sources of information and data that captures the defined environment. It is necessary to determine all possible sources of data like information systems, sensors and actuators as well as external data like weather, customer, or market data. These data sources are described in a data source definition that gives an overview about all the data available, the type of data and how to get access to the data. After the definition of the data sources it is mandatory to model the different data flow processes and the relationships between the data sources. At the end of the planning phase and after determining the performance, environment, measures, and the data a first draft of the AI system can be developed considering our conceptual model for AI systems depicted in Sect. 4.

5.3 Experimentation – Tracking Experiments for the Best Model

The goal of the experimentation phase is to find the best possible data-driven models (Sect. 4.3) in an iterative process based on the previously defined and available performance measure and data in the PEMD framework (Sect. 5.2). Therefore, parts of the classic CRISP-DM [15] or other approaches can be used [17]. Existing frameworks do not mention an end-to-end experiment tracking and logging. Tools such as MLFlow [24] track specific model parameters but not the whole process from data source to agent. Most of the frameworks and tools for model tracking start their logging when compiling or fitting the model to a specific dataset [24, 25]. Nevertheless, the process of data ingestion, preprocessing and feature engineering and selection from data source to evaluating the model performance has to be tracked and optimized. Afterwards a deep analysis of the process or pipelines is possible where e.g. different feature sets can be compared and analyzed. Does the integration of weather data increase the model performance metric? Is there a difference in performance between scaling to unit variance (standard scaler) and scaling from zero to one (min-max scaler)? To generalize the approaches in model and data tracking we define an **experiment** as a process with different data processing steps such as data ingestion, data preprocessing, modeling, and evaluation. The granularity of an experiment can vary from simple changes during data preprocessing to more complex hyperparameter tuning. The experiment can be seen as a controlled setup with controllable parameters such as the model architecture but also the used preprocessing steps. For an effective design of experiments we refer to [38, 39]. The parameters of the whole AI system from the data sources used to the evaluation metrics, are referred to as **experiment metadata**.

In our AI system, an experimental database tracks all metadata during an experiment. A categorization of the metadata that depends on the AI system must be implemented. Experiments should be tracked in a log file or other available approaches to compare different settings. The comparison of experiments and its metadata is the foundation of further optimizing the AI system. Therefore, the PEMD framework for the specific use case can be adjusted when new hypothesis of other influential factors as features are derived. After more research about the overall performance a possible influential factor can be identified (e.g. sensors for measuring the temperature of a process). The new influential factor must be included into the PEMD framework by extending the data dimension. In the initial experimentation phase, after tuning the controllable parameters such as the preprocessing steps and the model architecture the best pipeline depending on the overall performance is chosen. Additionally, during active operation of the AI system the experimentation phase can always be triggered when new experiments are necessary (e.g. new data, modeling technique, processing steps). This also includes the planning phase by extending the specific PEMD framework of the use case.

5.4   Implementation – Software Engineering for AI Systems

After experimenting and identifying a suitable model with satisfactory evaluation metrics, the next phase is to implement the trained model into the AI system that was conceptualized in the planning phase. Therefore, it is necessary to choose the right methods and frameworks to build the system on.

As described in Sculley et al. [13] and Lwakatare et al. [23] the software engineering of AI systems has different challenges compared to traditional software engineering. Especially the written software code for data-driven model consists of few lines of code and is just a minor part of the whole software engineering process. The rest of the system consists of configuration, automation, data collection, data verification, testing and troubleshooting, resource management, model analysis, process and metadata management, deployment infrastructure, and monitoring [13]. One of the biggest efforts especially in manufacturing is the integration of different data sources into the AI system. Depending on the structure and the access of the data source, application programming interfaces to the defined data sources must be implemented. An information system with a REST API is easier to implement than an old industrial oven without any PLC or smart device that can publish data. The conceptualized and optimized DPUs, derived from the planning and experimentation phase, are used in the implementation phase. Furthermore, it is necessary to implement the right interfaces when agents interact with other information systems or objects such as the energy management system or actuators. The interaction of agents and data-driven models requires inference modules. Three different types of inference modules are possible - as micro-services with a REST API to provide online inference, as a model embedded in an edge or mobile device, or as part of a batch inference system.

After implementing and testing the model, the integration with the previous data processing units, model outputs can be evaluated and compared to the experimentation phase. For this, the data flow from the data source is used. If the agent is interacting with other information systems like the energy management system or a MES the engineering of an interface between the agent and the information system is required.

5.5 Operation and Optimization – There is no Closing Time for Optimization

The main goal of the optimization phase is to reassess whether the implemented AI system supports to reach the overall performance goal of solving the specified problem in the planning phase. Therefore, it is necessary to design and plan an AI system management and monitoring functionality for the AI system. To continuously improve the AI system the optimization phase is highly connected to the other phases. The main components to be considered are the monitoring and management of all parameters and metrics defined as experiment metadata in the experimentation phase and the evaluation of the overall defined performance measure from the PEMD framework.

Additionally, the defined processes in the optimization phase should trigger events that start a new iterative cycle of manual or automated experiments. Thus, the processes and the pipeline of the AI system must be monitored and evaluated. Like in the other sectors, we make a distinction between the monitoring and diagnostics of the performance measurement (e.g. energy costs) defined in the PEMD framework and the evaluation metrics (e.g. forecast evaluation metrics) of the implemented models. Furthermore, the inference metrics must be monitored as well. When the time for predicting a value and taking an action is longer than expected an event can be triggered to analyze the problem in the experimentation phase. A solution with visualization methods and automated alerts can help to identify performance issues.

6 An Anomaly Detection Use Case in Energy Consumption

For demonstration purpose we applied our definition of an AI system and our developed process in a real-world use case. We developed an AI system to detect anomalies in the electricity energy consumption of a German metal processing company on an aggregated (electricity grid connection) and appliance (laser punching machine) level. As manufacturing companies are facing the challenge of simultaneously producing at low cost, complying with environmental regulations, and reducing CO_2 emissions while aiming for a cleaner production, energy consumption must be reduced, and energy efficiency enhanced [40]. In this context, the detection of anomalies in energy consumption is a promising option because anomalies leading to higher energy consumption than necessary, e.g. in poorly maintained, outdated or incorrectly controlled systems, can be detected and countermeasures taken. Our AI system features two smart electricity meters (aggregated and appliance level) integrated via a cloud interface, several DPUs for pre-processing and a long-short term memory based autoencoder (LSTM-AE) to detect anomalies in the time series of energy consumption, which feed an alert system and a visualization dashboard. Using the LSTM-AE offers the advantage of not requiring labelled data and can therefore be easily integrated into the surrounding information systems. The AI system's conceptual model is displayed in Fig. 3. The system was gradually developed, implemented, and operated according to the process introduced in Sect. 5.

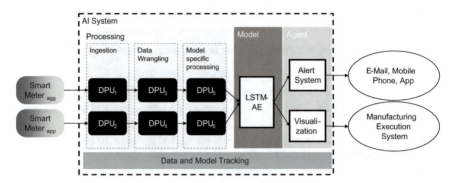

Fig. 3. Proposed AI system for anomaly detection

7 Discussion

Our presented use case allows us to validate and discuss the developed artifacts with findings from the conducted expert interviews. Since it is suitable here, we combine the discussion and validation with limitations and prospects for further research. With our use case we show that it is possible to build an AI system in practice supported by our artifacts. We realize that our current process does not cover economic aspects and that the success and quality level that can be achieved with the AI system is still to some extent uncertain during the planning phase. Therefore, further aspects from a project management and decision-making perspective could be added to our four-stage process in the planning phase. Within our conducted interviews we found further aspects to be addressed specifically for the manufacturing industry. First, the latency of data streams is very critical (e.g. milliseconds for machine control) and thus must be considered when designing an AI system. Learning on historical data and fixed datasets as typically done in CRISP-DM or KDD might here not be suitable, as the design of a system which uses AI must be set in its dynamic environment. The same holds true for approaches in literature that suggest software or software frameworks for machine learning as the superordinate context is often still missing/unclear. Second, safety and reliability of AI systems is very important in manufacturing and must be considered in the planning phase. The modular structure supports this by making e.g. threat modelling easily applicable. Third, interoperability and different levels of automation with different interfaces require generic modeling of systems (= systems engineering) without going into technical details. This supports the statements of all experts with a manufacturing background that one cannot assume that the manufacturing industry has software and machine learning experts, which in turn reinforces our generic and interdisciplinary approach. Fourth, even if everyone talks about industry 4.0 and digital transformation, it actually looks less widespread in reality especially in small and medium-sized companies. Hence, one could even think about of integrating our artifacts in a holistic industry 4.0 roadmap or a digital transformation strategy. Last, some experts mentioned the integrative character of the PEMD framework within the planning phase as well as the integration of agents in the IS ecosystem positively, as e.g. "forecasting of consumption or events seems interesting, but how can I use it in further applications". Summarizing, the acceptance criteria completeness, understandability, and traceability introduced in Sect. 3 could be fulfilled as far as possible, with prospects for further research derived from minor limitations.

8 Conclusion

In our study, we faced the research questions which components are part of an AI system and how a process for planning, implementation, and optimization should be structured. We developed a generic conceptual model of an AI system for use in manufacturing systems and a four-phase model to guide developers and project managers in its realization following a design science research approach. With both research artifacts, we close the knowledge gap of a uniform understanding of components and functionalities of an AI system as well as a structured process for their planning, implementation, and optimization.

Specifically, with our conceptual model for AI systems we depict the central components, structure them, and reveal their relationships. Based on the conceptual model the four-phase model for developing and operating AI systems covers the stages planning, experimentation, implementation, and operation with the possibility to run through iteration loops. Within the planning phase, we provide a structured procedure with our PEMD framework with which the dimensions performance, environment, measures, and data are determined. In the experimentation phase, existing methods such as CRISP-DM can be applied. The implementation phase focuses on the software realization before the operation & optimization covers the processes of the AI system's optimization in operation.

Our developed artifacts have several implications and benefits. The conceptual model as well as the phase model are designed non-technical, which means they are easy to understand and provide a common discussion basis and tool for developers, engineers, data scientists, and managers. This makes the introduction of AI systems easier in practice because there is a clear understanding and a structured procedure for all stakeholders involved. In addition, our phase model is independent of existing frameworks and acts as a meta-model that allows the integration of existing models and frameworks on a more detailed level. Furthermore, our conceptual and phase model is technology-independent and thus enables to draw on the full potential and at the same time, it prevents bias due to possible technological limitations.

References

1. Leo Kumar, S.P.: State of the art-intense review on artificial intelligence systems application in process planning and manufacturing. Eng. Appl. Artif. Intell. **65**, 294–329 (2017)
2. Lee, J., Davari, H., Singh, J., Pandhare, V.: Industrial artificial intelligence for industry 4.0-based manufacturing systems. Manuf. Lett. **18**, 20–23 (2018)

3. Monostori, L., Markus, A., van Brussel, H., Westkämpfer, E.: Machine learning approaches to manufacturing. CIRP Ann. **45**, 675–712 (1996)
4. Patel, A.R., Ramaiya, K.K., Bhatia, C.V., Shah, H.N., Bhavsar, S.N.: Artificial intelligence: prospect in mechanical engineering field—a review. In: Kotecha, K., Piuri, V., Shah, H.N., Patel, R. (eds.) Data Science and Intelligent Applications, vol. 52, pp. 267–282. Springer, Singapore (2021). https://doi.org/10.1007/978-981-15-4474-3_31
5. Wuest, T., Weimer, D., Irgens, C., Thoben, K.-D.: Machine learning in manufacturing: advantages, challenges, and applications. Prod. Manuf. Res. **4**, 23–45 (2016)
6. Capgemini: Scaling AI in manufacturing operations: A Practitioners' Perspective (2019)
7. Mehrabi, M., Ulsoy, A., Koren, Y.: Reconfigurable manufacturing systems: key to future manufacturing. J. Intell. Manuf. **11**, 403–419 (2000). https://doi.org/10.1023/A:1008930403506
8. Russell, S.J., Norvig, P., Davis, E., Edwards, D.: Artificial intelligence. A Modern Approach. Pearson, Boston, Columbus, Indianapolis, New York, San Francisco, Upper Saddle River, Amsterdam, Cape Town, Dubai, London, Madrid, Milan, Munich, Paris, Montreal, Toronto, Delhi, Mexico City, Sao Paulo, Sydney, Hong Kong, Seoul, Singapore, Taipei, Tokyo (2016)
9. Nalchigar, S., Yu, E.: Conceptual modeling for business analytics: a framework and potential benefits. In: 2017 IEEE 19th Conference on Business Informatics (CBI), Thessaloniki, pp. 369–378 (2017)
10. Wang, S., Wan, J., Zhang, D., Li, D., Zhang, C.: Towards smart factory for industry 4.0: a self-organized multi-agent system with big data based feedback and coordination. Comput. Netw. **101**, 158–168 (2016)
11. van den Heuvel, W.-J., Tamburri, D.A.: Model-driven ml-ops for intelligent enterprise applications: vision, approaches and challenges. In: Shishkov, B. (ed.) BMSD 2020. LNBIP, vol. 391, pp. 169–181. Springer, Cham (2020). https://doi.org/10.1007/978-3-030-52306-0_11
12. Simard, P.Y., et al.: Machine teaching a new paradigm for building machine learning systems (2017)
13. Sculley, D., et al.: Hidden technical debt in machine learning systems. Advances in Neural Information Processing Systems (2015)
14. Usama, F., David, H., Stolorz, E.P.: KDD for Science Data Analysis: Issues and examples (1996)
15. Wirth, R., Hipp, J.: CRISP-DM: Towards a standard process model for data mining (2000)
16. Microsoft: Team data science process documentation. Learn how to use the Team Data Science Process, an Agile, Iterative Data Science Methodology for Predictive Analytics Solutions and Intelligent Applications. https://docs.microsoft.com/en-us/azure/machine-learning/team-data-science-process/
17. Kessler, R.: Towards a cross-company data and model platform for SMEs. In: Abramowicz, W., Corchuelo, R. (eds.) BIS 2019. LNBIP, vol. 373, pp. 661–671. Springer, Cham (2019). https://doi.org/10.1007/978-3-030-36691-9_55
18. Colomo-Palacios, R.: Towards a Software engineering framework for the design, construction and deployment of machine learning-based solutions in digitalization processes. In: Visvizi, A., Lytras, M.D. (eds.) RIIFORUM 2019. SPC, pp. 343–349. Springer, Cham (2019). https://doi.org/10.1007/978-3-030-30809-4_31
19. Amershi, S., et al.: Software engineering for machine learning: a case study. In: IEEE/ACM 41st International Conference on Software Engineering: Software Engineering in Practice, Montreal, pp. 291–300 (2019)
20. Kessler, R., Gómez, J.M.: Implikationen von machine learning auf das datenmanagement in unternehmen . HMD Praxis der Wirtschaftsinformatik **57**(1), 89–105 (2020). https://doi.org/10.1365/s40702-020-00585-z

21. Moreb, M., Mohammed, T.A., Bayat, O.: A novel software engineering approach toward using machine learning for improving the efficiency of health systems. IEEE Access **8**, 23169–23178 (2020)
22. Kriens, P., Verbelen, T.: Software engineering practices for machine learning (2019)
23. Lwakatare, L.E., Raj, A., Bosch, J., Olsson, H.H., Crnkovic, I.: A taxonomy of software engineering challenges for machine learning systems: an empirical investigation. In: Kruchten, P., Fraser, S., Coallier, F. (eds.) XP 2019. LNBIP, vol. 355, pp. 227–243. Springer, Cham (2019). https://doi.org/10.1007/978-3-030-19034-7_14
24. Chen, A., et al.: Developments in MLflow. Proceedings of the Fourth International Workshop on Data Management for End-to-End Machine Learning, 1–4 (2020)
25. Baylor, D., et al.: TFX - A TensorFlow-Based Production-Scale Machine Learning Platform, pp. 1387–1395 (2017)
26. Hevner, M.: Park, Ram: design science in information systems research. MIS Q. **28**, 75 (2004)
27. Gregor, S., Hevner, A.R.: Positioning and presenting design science research for maximum impact. MIS Q. **37**, 337–355 (2013)
28. Wand, Y., Monarchi, D.E., Parsons, J., Woo, C.C.: Theoretical foundations for conceptual modelling in information systems development. Decis. Support Syst. **15**, 285–304 (1995)
29. Brodie, M.L. (ed.): On conceptual modelling. Perspectives from Artificial Intelligence, Databases, and Programming Languages, Springer, Berlin (1986)
30. Rishe, N.: Database design. In: The Semantic Modeling Approach. . McGraw-Hill, New York (1992)
31. Felderer, M., Reussner, R., Rumpe, B.: Software engineering und software-engineering-forschung im zeitalter der digitalisierung. Informatik Spektrum **44**(2), 82–94 (2020). https://doi.org/10.1007/s00287-020-01322-y
32. Selcuk, S.: Predictive maintenance, its implementation and latest trends. Proc. Inst. Mech. Eng. Part B: J. Eng. Manuf. **231**, 1670–1679 (2017)
33. Maass, W., Parsons, J., Purao, S., Storey, V.C., Woo, C.: Data-driven meets theory-driven research in the era of big data: opportunities and challenges for information systems research. JAIS **19**(12), 1253–1273 (2018)
34. Kohne, T., Ranzau, H., Panten, N., Weigold, M.: Comparative study of algorithms for optimized control of industrial energy supply systems. Energy. Inform. **3**(1), 1–19 (2020). https://doi.org/10.1186/s42162-020-00115-7
35. Khan, A., Turowski, K.: A survey of current challenges in manufacturing industry and preparation for industry 4.0. Proc. First Int. Sci. Conf. Intell. Inf. Technol. Ind. **450**, 15–26 (2016). https://doi.org/10.1007/978-3-319-33609-1_2
36. Hofmann, P., Jöhnk, J., Protschky, D., Urbach, N.: Developing purposeful ai use cases - a structured method and its application in project management. In: Entwicklungen, Chancen und Herausforderungen der Digitalisierung. Band 1.Proceedings der 15. Internationalen Tagung Wirtschaftsinformatik 2020, GITO Verlag, pp. 33–49 (2020)
37. Krallmann, H.: Systemanalyse im unternehmen. In: Prozessorientierte Methoden der Wirtschaftsinformatik. München, Oldenbourg (2007)
38. Stanley, J.C.: The influence of fisher's "the design of experiments" on educational research thirty years later. Am. Educ. Res. J. **3**, 223–229 (1966)
39. Box, J.F.: R.A. Fisher and the design of experiments, 1922–1926. Am. Stat. 34, 17 (1980)
40. Bauer, D., et al.: Wie IT die energieflexibilitätsvermarktung von industrieunternehmen ermöglicht und die energiewende unterstützt. HMD **58**, 102–115 (2020). https://doi.org/10.1365/s40702-020-00679-8

Managing Bias in Machine Learning Projects

Tobias Fahse$^{(\boxtimes)}$, Viktoria Huber, and Benjamin van Giffen

Institute of Information Management, University of St. Gallen, St. Gallen, Switzerland
{tobias.fahse,benjamin.vangiffen}@unisg.ch,
viktoria.huber@student.unisg.ch

Abstract. This paper introduces a framework for managing bias in machine learning (ML) projects. When ML-capabilities are used for decision making, they frequently affect the lives of many people. However, bias can lead to low model performance and misguided business decisions, resulting in fatal financial, social, and reputational impacts. This framework provides an overview of potential biases and corresponding mitigation methods for each phase of the well-established process model CRISP-DM. Eight distinct types of biases and 25 mitigation methods were identified through a literature review and allocated to six phases of the reference model in a synthesized way. Furthermore, some biases are mitigated in different phases as they occur. Our framework helps to create clarity in these multiple relationships, thus assisting project managers in avoiding biased ML-outcomes.

Keywords: Bias · Machine learning · Project management · Risk management · Process model

1 Introduction

Progress in artificial intelligent (AI) technologies such as machine learning (ML) lead to a wide implementation of intelligent systems in companies and institutions. The ability to learn and act autonomously makes AI different from other technologies and allows for automated decisions and solutions [1]. ML, as a field of AI, refers to algorithms that learn patterns from data without being explicitly programmed [2]. ML-applications support or take over human tasks and decisions in many industries, including issuing of credit loans, determination of insurance rates or provision of health care [3]. Simultaneously, the potential of AI is widely recognized, but there remains a significant uncertainty for organizations in how to manage negative consequences and challenges resulting from AI [4]. Due to the increasing complexity of AI, their usage can lead to negative consequences such as wrong decisions, unfairness, and discrimination [5, 6]. If firms cannot understand the underlying mechanisms of their ML-models, organizations face a loss of trust in their technologies [7] leading to questioning of their accountability and reliability and, in the long term, impact investments into AI in organizations [5, 8]. Many of these obstacles can arise from bias incorporated in the ML developing process [9].

Today, IS research provides only little theory and guidance to systematically identify and mitigate different forms of bias that can occur in ML-projects. There is a need for awareness about possible biases in the ML-project lifecycle and respective mitigation

F. Ahlemann et al. (Eds.): WI 2021, LNISO 47, pp. 94–109, 2021.
https://doi.org/10.1007/978-3-030-86797-3_7

methods to tackle negative consequences [10]. A systematic approach for addressing potential biases is yet missing [11]. Therefore, the objective of this research is to systematically review and integrate available knowledge to improve the management of bias in ML-projects. To frame our research, we pose the following question:

RQ: What types of bias emerge in machine learning projects and how can they be managed?

We perform a systematic literature review to identify different types of biases and respective mitigation methods. We then integrate our findings into CRISP-DM, an established ML-project management framework. CRISP-DM is the most widely adopted process model [12, 13] and provides a practice-oriented and structured approach, including consecutive activities for developing ML-applications that are transferable to different industries [14].

Our research contributes to the emerging body of literature that studies the implementation of ML in organizations and its intended and unintended consequences. First, this paper enhances clarity concerning existing biases and mitigation methods. Hence, a shared terminology can be achieved, which supports further development of solutions. Second, the holistic view of ML-model development and operation improves the understanding of inherent connections between ML-project and bias. Furthermore, temporal dependencies between bias occurrence and mitigation can be detected. Thus, interdependencies in ML-applications that are embedded in broader organizational information systems can be recognized. This makes the management of bias in ML-projects an important aspect of IS development that differs from the development of deterministic software systems.

Our framework serves practitioners as a holistic framework which can be applied to the specific ML-projects at hand.

2 Theoretical Foundation

The adoption of ML-technologies across organizations is growing rapidly and firms are increasingly recognizing the practical opportunities arising from their ability to perform human-like tasks such as learning autonomously, making decisions, or gaining valuable analytical insights from large datasets [1, 4]. In this context, bias describes an unintended or potentially harmful property of data [15] that results in a systematic deviation of algorithmic results [16]. In a broader sense, bias can be defined as unwanted effects or results which are evoked through a series of subjective choices and practices that the ML developing process involves [15].

ML-algorithms differ substantially from deterministic, rule-based algorithms that have been used in the past to perform decision support in organizational context. ML-algorithms, such as Neural Networks, follow a probabilistic approach in which decisions are not made by following programmed rules but by learning patterns from historical data and applying these to new input data. The decision support from ML-algorithms is provided in the form of probabilities, leading to different levels of uncertainty and therefore increased susceptibility to systematic biases. As the learned patterns are non-transparent to the users of the algorithms, existing bias is difficult to identify or mitigate and therefore requires different approaches than deterministic algorithms [17].

A series of potentially subjective choices and actions must be made in the process of an ML-project, any of which can introduce bias and lead to unwanted effects. If datasets incorporate bias, ML-applications will reflect those biases. Even if input data is perfectly unbiased, the decision on how to build the model can introduce bias. Particularly from technical considerations, design decisions must be made, such as which fairness definition or forms of measurement and performance metrics to use. Even if assuming the resulting ML-application is free from bias introduced through data or design decisions, an inappropriate context of use may nevertheless lead to bias [16, 18, 19].

To address the problem of bias, prior work has used fairness metrics as quantification of unwanted bias. This raises concerns about how social goals are abstracted so that they can be used in a prediction task [20]. Such metrics make the implicit assumption that an underlying mathematical concept of fairness can be formulated and operationalized to create a bias-free system [21, 22]. However, there are at least 21 different definitions of fairness [23], and different definitions lead to entirely different results, which makes it impossible to satisfy all fairness definitions simultaneously [24]. Corbett-Davies and Goel [25] and Mitchell et al. [20] demonstrate how popular classes of fairness definitions can, perversely, have a discriminant effect on minorities and also majorities. To prevent this, technical approaches should be complemented with non-technical mitigation approaches that consider more than merely good performance results.

Prior work has emphasized the importance of interpretable outcomes to increase fairness in ML-applications. By increasing the interpretability of outcomes, harmful patterns that have been learned by the ML-algorithm can be revealed and consequently be tackled [7].

IS research is starting to address the negative consequences resulting from bias but the literature about the origins of biases and possible mitigation methods is yet scattered and a systematic approach for addressing potential biases missing [11]. Few existing articles provide a framework with incorporated biases and mitigation methods where the respective terminologies differ substantially and the incorporation is not made in well-established ML-frameworks [15, 16, 26]. To address this, we choose CRISP-DM as an underlying framework for this work as it is the most widely adopted process model [12, 13]. It provides a practice-oriented and structured approach, including consecutive activities for developing ML-applications that are transferable to different industries.

The initial phase of CRISP-DM, Business Understanding (BU), focuses on the understanding of the business objective and translation into data mining goals in order to define the design plan and necessary resources. The Data Understanding (DU) phase then collects and explores initial data to gain insights into data quality and possible concerns. The final dataset is then created from the raw dataset through various activities in the Data Preparation (DP) phase, such as the selection of records and features or transformation and cleaning of data for the modeling tools. Several modeling techniques are then selected in the Modeling (MO) phase and applied to the prepared dataset. The model's performance is evaluated in the Evaluation (EV) phase and put into the context of the business objectives. The Deployment (DE) phase then describes the process of implementing the model in the context of the end-user [14].

Overall, a systematic approach for managing potential biases with a shared terminology and clarity about their occurrence in ML-project lifecycles is yet missing. The challenge is to understand what biases potentially arise in which phase and when to apply which prevention or mitigation method [27]. This underlines the need for guidance to identify sources of harm throughout the full ML-project lifecycle.

3 Methodology

3.1 Research Design

The present paper aims to examine how project managers can systematically identify and mitigate bias in ML-projects. To this end, we perform a systematic literature review to understand existing knowledge about bias through a conceptual lens (CRISP-DM) proposed in former research [28, 29]. This type of literature review is problem-centered and aims to group distinctive problem sources as well as different solution approaches using well-known concepts [29, 30]. First, different types of biases are identified, their terminologies understood and consolidated into distinct categories. Second, possible mitigation methods that address these biases are evaluated. Finally, the findings are incorporated into the CRISP-DM framework regarding their occurrence and application in different project steps.

3.2 Data Collection and Analysis

We determined a threefold data collection strategy. First, a keyword search was conducted considering only leading journals in the field of Information Systems (IS). It focused on 39 journals ranked A+, A, or B based on JourQual3 ranking that are represented in the databases EBSCOhost, AIS Electronic Library, ACM Digital Library, and ScienceDirect. We defined relevant key terms by conceptualizing the topic based on an initial search in IS literature and seminal publications on bias in ML. This resulted in the following search strings: AB ("machine bias" OR "data bias" OR "algorithmic bias" OR "model bias" OR "biased data" OR "biased machine*" OR "biased algorithm*" OR "biased model" OR "bias" or "prejudice" OR "discrimination" OR "stereotypes" OR "historical bias" OR "representation bias" OR "selection bias" OR "measurement bias" OR "aggregation bias" OR "deployment bias" AND TX ("Artificial Intelligence" OR "AI" OR "Algorithm*" OR "Machine Learning")); TX ("machine bias" OR "data bias" OR "algorithmic bias" OR "model bias") AND TX ("artificial intelligence" OR "AI" OR "machine learning" OR "deep learning"). These search strings revealed 57 hits in total, including the initial search. We then conducted a practical screening with inclusion and exclusion criteria. We only considered articles that (i) are peer-reviewed and/or conference proceedings, (ii) define at least one relevant bias (iii) explain at least one relevant identification or mitigation method (iv) address the bias challenge in AI-, or ML-context. After applying these criteria, 22 relevant hits remained. As a third step we performed forward and backward search on the relevant hits using Web of Science [31,

32]. This step added 31 articles based on the same inclusion/exclusion criteria. In a third step, relevant literature was exchanged with senior scholars in the research team [33]. In total, 55 articles were included in the literature review and subsequently examined full text.

In the data analysis phase, types of biases and mitigation methods were subsequently extracted from the articles. Because different synonyms exist in the literature for the same type of bias, biases were then descriptively synthesized based on their mechanism [34]. This allowed us to code the biases in eight distinct categories. Based on an in-depth understanding of the CRISP-DM project steps, the distinct biases were assigned to the phases by matching the mechanism that leads to a specific bias to the tasks of the phases of CRISP-DM. If a different process model was used in the underlying paper, we matched the phases with CRISP DM. We then identified 25 methods and allocated them to the respective bias they address regarding the methods' mechanisms. Finally, the methods were incorporated into the CRISP-DM model steps according to their detailed specifications of where the methods can be applied in the project lifecycle. The allocation was independently conducted by two researchers to enhance inter-coder reliability [35].

4   Results

4.1   Emergence of Bias in Machine Learning Projects

Bias can occur multiple times and in any of the six phases of a ML-project lifecycle. The eight identified biases are located in the CRISP-DM model based on their origin (see Fig. 1) and explained and illustrated in the following.

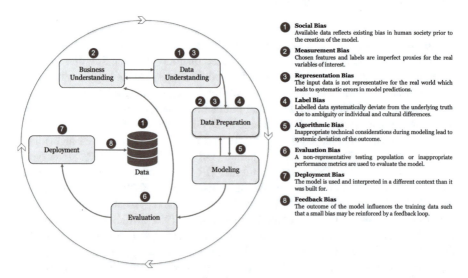

Fig. 1. Emergence of bias in CRISP-DM process model (Chapman et al. 2000)

Social bias occurs when available data mirrors existing biases in society at large. When data embodies social biases that exist independently and prior to the development of an ML-model, the model will most likely lead to unwanted outcomes. Even if the data is perfectly measured and sampled, a normative concern with the current state of the world may exist, that should not be reinforced by the ML-model [9, 19, 33, 36].

Illustration: In 2018, statistical evaluations revealed that only 5% of the Fortune 500 companies' CEOs were women [37]. This unequal distribution was consequently reflected in Google's image search of CEOs that showed only a small fraction of women. Google has recently adapted the search results on images of CEOs showing a higher proportion of women in order not to reinforce gender inequality [15].

Measurement bias can be introduced by humans in the BU-phase through subjective choices about model design. When defining the target variable and necessary features for the data mining problem, they may choose imperfect proxies for the true underlying value or include protected attributes. Protected attributes refer to attributes such as race, gender, ethnicity, etc. that partition a population into different groups that should be treated equally. Using protected attributes as proxies for other features that truly carry the signal of interest may result in a discriminant or inaccurate classifier. But even if the protected attribute is excluded, the discriminant effect can still exist due to the redlining effect. The redlining effect states that protected attributes can correlate with non-protected attributes [9, 15, 25, 38]. Measurement bias can also occur in the DP-phase when features and outcome variables are created. Often, features have to be constructed, derived, or transformed where they may omit important factors or introduce additional noise. When features are inaccurate or if the decision is reduced to only a small number of inappropriate features, the prediction accuracy may vary across groups [9, 38].

Illustration: In a crime prediction application, the feature "number of arrests" is used to predict future criminal activity. Assuming African American and Caucasian defendants commit the same number of drug sales, they have a similar true risk. But arrest rates are possibly recorded differently across ethnic groups, leading to differential predictive power of the application. In minority neighborhoods with heavier policing, African American defendants are likely to have more drug arrests [39]. Despite the similar true risk, the ML-application would consequently rate the African American a higher risk than the Caucasian [40].

Representation bias arises during collection and sampling of data. It emerges if the probability distribution of the development population differs from the true underlying distribution. The algorithm subsequently fails to make good predictions for this group of feature values. The over- or underrepresentation can have several reasons, including difficult or expensive availability of required data. Subsequently, the model will result in less robust outcomes for different subpopulations [9, 15, 41]. Representation bias can also occur when the training data is no longer representative of the data found present when the model is deployed. It arises when the world as it is at the time the application is used is inconsistent with the world as it was when the training data was collected [36].

Illustration: Data can be traumatized by one-time phenomena. An algorithm built for credit card applications uses historical data about the chance of default. In case of an unsuspected event during the collection of data, such as a natural catastrophe in a certain area, people might not be able to pay back their debts. Therefore, applicants from this area will most likely be classified as potential defaults. Thus, the one-time phenomenon is imprinted into the ML-application [36].

Label bias arises when training data is assigned to class labels in the *DP-phase*. Data scientists often face the difficulty of deciding which available label best applies to the present data. Due to ambiguity, cultural or individual differences, labels might systematically deviate. Existing class labels may also fail to precisely capture meaningful differences between classes [9, 36].

Illustration: Assuming a certain number of pictures are to be labeled as "wedding". A person that is educated in the western culture, will likely only label pictures with brides in white dresses and grooms in dark suits as "wedding". An Indian wedding with its colorful dresses and special decorations might then not be labeled as a wedding [36].

Algorithmic bias is introduced during the *MO-phase* and results from inappropriate technical considerations. It can emerge when formulating the optimization problem, in which developers make data and parameters amenable to computers [18, 21, 42]. Resulting ML-models may fail to treat groups fairly under given conditions. The probability of misclassification, i.e., false-positive and false-negative rates, should be equal among groups [19, 27, 38, 41].

Illustration: In COMPAS, a predictive policing application to assess the "risk of crime recidivism", minorities exhibited a higher false-positive rate than majority groups [40, 43].

Evaluation bias can occur, if the population in the benchmark set is not representative of the use population. An algorithmic model is trained and optimized on its training data but evaluated on a test-or benchmark data set in the *EV-phase*.

ML-models are often tested on the same benchmark to allow for an objective comparison. If the benchmark itself is not representative, models could be preferred that perform only well on a subset of the population [15, 42].

Illustration: Choosing the wrong benchmark set can lead to overlooking a potential bias. For example, if a facial recognition algorithm is trained on a dataset with underrepresented dark-skinned females and is tested on a similarly unbalanced benchmark, the bias will remain unrecognized [15].

Deployment bias arises when the system is used or interpreted in inappropriate ways, even if none of the before-mentioned biases are present. This can occur when the ML-application is built and evaluated assuming it operates fully autonomous, but in reality, it works in a complex socio-technical environment and is followed by human decisions. The assumed use population may differ in a significant dimension from the actual use population. They may have a different knowledge base or values and interpret the algorithmic output according to their internalized biases [15, 27, 43].

Illustration: Risk assessment applications are models that aim to predict the likelihood of someone committing a future crime. However, in practice, these models are often seen to be used in different contexts, such as determining the length of defendants sentences [44].

Feedback Bias can arise after the *DE-phase* and after project deployment. It emerges when the output of the ML-application influences features that are used as new inputs and algorithms are refined over time (e.g., through re-training). If the outcome of the ML-application has an influence on the training data, an initially small bias is potentially reinforced through a feedback loop [9, 27, 45].

Illustration: Once a certain content got a good ranking by a rating algorithm based on the number of times it has been clicked, it will affect the position and the promotion of this content, thus leading to even more clicks. A reinforcing feedback loop is created and can lead to decreased user satisfaction as not the best content is promoted to the web user [16, 36].

4.2   Managing Bias in Machine Learning Projects

This section outlines potential mitigation methods for addressing the aforementioned biases and indicates their application within the CRISP-DM project phases. Figure 2 illustrates that a single bias can be mitigated by several methods, and one method can mitigate multiple biases. The methods presented either support project teams in identifying biases or mitigate their unwanted effects. A method that is applied in one phase can address biases that occur in the respective phase or possibly also in later stages of the project. In order to optimally avoid negative consequences resulting from bias, a sociotechnical approach is fostered by including technical and non-technical methods.

CRISP-DM Phase / Bias	Business Understanding	Data Understanding	Data Preparation	Modeling	Evaluation	Deployment
Social Bias			Rapid Prototyping Reweighing Data Massaging Disparate Impact Remover Learning Fair Representation Optimized Pre-Processing	Prejudice Remover Adversarial Debiasing Equalized Odds Multiple Models Latent Variable Model Model Interpretability		
Measurement Bias	Diversity in Teams Exchange with Domain Experts	Proxy Estimation	Rapid Prototyping			
Representation Bias	Diversity in Teams	Data Plotting Exchange with Domain Experts	Reweighing Data Augmentation	Model Interpretability		
Label Bias		Exchange with Domain Experts	Data Massaging			
Algorithmic Bias			Rapid Prototyping	Exchange with Domain Experts Resampling Model Interpretability Multitask Learning		
Evaluation Bias				Resampling	Representative Benchmark Subgroup Validity Data Augmentation	
Deployment Bias	Diversity in Teams Consequences in Context		Rapid Prototyping			Monitoring Plan Human Supervision
Feedback Bias						Human Supervision Randomness

Fig. 2. Bias prevention and mitigation methods in ML-project phases

In the *BU-phase*, the emergence of three biases can be prevented by understanding the business objectives and undertaking actions to ensure a precise translation into data mining problems. Three bias mitigation approaches are relevant in the *BU-phase*.

It is advisable to start addressing bias with the awareness of the project team about different bias types and understand their occurrences. Acknowledging that data does not necessarily represent the world perfectly is helpful to reveal social bias prior to any development [19, 45, 46]. First, **setting up diverse teams** helps to mitigate measurement bias that would typically occur in the *BU-phase*, and to prevent representation and deployment bias from occurring in the *DP- and DE-phase* of the project. Organizations that embrace diverse teams are better capable of identifying potential harms by introducing different perspectives in the development process. This enables the team to better define the data mining problem with more appropriate target variables and features, specify representative populations, and anticipate different use contexts [46, 47]. Second, **exchanging with domain experts** of the specific application context addresses emerging measurement bias and prevents possible representation bias in the *DP-phase*. The interaction with domain experts helps the project team to design the model with appropriate and measurable target variables and features as well as to consider all possible affected populations [36, 38]. Third, it is necessary to discuss technical and social consequences of the use of the application in the respective real-world **context** in order to prevent bias in the deployment stage. A project team should envision the application embedded in a social system and especially consider the prevailing moral values [19, 45]. If possible, multiple contexts of use can be designed. Otherwise, constraints on other user contexts can be articulated in this stage [25, 48].

To identify and prevent possible bias in the *DU-phase*, a good prior understanding of data and its underlying relationship is advisable and can be fostered by the following three methods.

First, a statistical **estimation of appropriate proxy variables** can mitigate the occurrence of measurement bias in the *DP-phase*. Depending on the design specification, it is necessary to choose proxies for variables of interest in case they are not directly observable. Examining the underlying correlations of the proxies and the true variables of interest supports feature selection [25, 38]. Second, **data plotting** can reveal possible spikes (i.e., one-time phenomena) that can be carefully removed in order to prevent representation bias [36]. Third, **exchanging with domain experts** can be effective in the DU phase to ensure a thorough understanding of the features and data in question. Domain experts might better determine affected populations in the application context and can recommend features that should be included for model training to mitigate representation and measurement bias. Also, data scientists often face data labeling challenges in the following *DP-phase*. Gaining insights from experts can help to reduce ambiguity in this decision and consequently prevent label bias [9, 36, 38].

In the *DP-phase*, five mitigation methods can eliminate underlying biases or mitigate discrimination by modifying data prior to modeling activities.

First, **data massaging** can mitigate social bias by strategically relabeling data points near the classification margin according to a ranking of the class probabilities. By relabeling individuals from an unprivileged group to favorable outcomes and simultaneously individuals from privileged groups to unfavorable outcomes, social bias can be reduced while maintaining the overall class distribution. With the class probability ranking, individuals closest to the classification margin can be identified for relabeling to minimally affect the model's accuracy [49, 50]. Second, with **reweighing** it is possible to address representation bias and social bias already present in data. Unrepresentative datasets are balanced out by upweighing underrepresented subgroups with different weights for each combination of group and label. With this approach, discrimination can be significantly reduced while maintaining overall positive class probability [49–53]. Third, **targeted data augmentation** reduces representation bias occurring in the *DP-phase*. It improves the sampling function by populating parts of the underrepresented group in the dataset [51]. Fourth, **rapid prototyping** is an effective approach for identifying different types of unintended bias. By creating a prototype and testing it in the field, practitioners can uncover overlooked populations and prevent representation bias. Furthermore, possible discriminative effects resulting from social bias can be revealed. Also, chosen features and target variables can be tested regarding their suitability to predict the outcome of interest and consequently address measurement bias [19].

Fifth, preprocessing algorithms that transform data can be applied to mitigate social bias or discriminative effects in data. **Disparate impact remover** edits features and labels in the data by learning a probabilistic transformation and applying rank ordering within groups. This ensures that information of the non-protected attributes are preserved and the class belonging can still be correctly predicted [18]. **Learning fair representation** formulates an optimization problem of finding an intermediate representation of the data that encodes it well but simultaneously removes information about membership of a protected group. The new representation space captures true underlying features that differ across groups and can then be used to learn a new classifier in the *MO-phase* that does not use group belonging information [22]. **Optimized preprocessing** formulates a (quasi-) convex problem for the transformation and edits features and labels while complying with fairness constraints [54].

In the *MO-phase*, six model-based methods were identified which conduct modifications of learning algorithms to mitigate bias. Two additional approaches can be applied after modeling that treats the learned model as a black box. These two methods do not modify the training data or the algorithm.

First, **prejudice remover** is an approach to introduce regularization terms or constraints that mitigate social bias during modeling. It considers differences in how the learning algorithm classifies protected non-protected groups and then penalizes the total loss of the loss function based on the amount of the difference [55, 56]. Second, **adversarial debiasing** learns a classifier which maximizes accuracy while simultaneously reduces the adversary's ability to identify the protected attribute(s). The outcome is unable to carry any group discrimination information that the adversary can use, which helps to mitigate social bias during classifier training [57]. Third, **multiple models** is a method used for Naive Bayes Classifiers. Two separate models are learned, one for the protected group and one for the non-protected group. This way, the protected attribute, as well its proxies, no longer influence the outcomes of the separate models. After combining both models, probabilities are modified so that the number of positive labels is kept as high as in the original data set [58]. Fourth, a **latent variable model** discovers the actual class labels that a data set should contain if it was discrimination-free. The parameters of the model are then set in a way such that the likelihood of the data set is maximized [50]. Fifth, the design of **interpretable models** fosters transparency and trust in algorithmic models and aids identification of biases [25, 45, 59]. Sixth, **resampling** multiple training and test set splits is an important part of building a robust classifier and consequently mitigate algorithmic bias. It prevents evaluation bias in the *EV-phase* by improving diversity in the test set [18, 41, 60].

There are two post-processing methods that are applied after the algorithmic training. First, **equalized odds** mitigates social bias by accessing only aggregated data. It can solve a linear problem that finds probabilities with which to change and equalize differences in output labels [25, 61]. Second, **multitask learning** is an efficient decoupling technique that can be added on top of black-box models to learn different classifiers for different groups, thereby mitigating algorithmic bias. It parametrizes different groups differently and learns simpler, multiple functions to account for group differences [42, 62].

In the *EV-phase*, possible evaluation bias can be addressed by two approaches. First, the **representativeness of a benchmark dataset** should be verified regarding its balanced composition of all subgroups present in the model [63]. Second, the **subgroup validity** approach assures to compare performance metrics across groups instead of accepting an aggregated metric, revealing substantial performance gaps between different subgroups. Data augmentation can balance data of underrepresented subgroups [15, 20, 48, 51].

In order to prevent deployment bias and feedback bias in the *DE-phase*, three approaches can be considered. First, a **monitoring plan** can be introduced that accounts for changes in the algorithm when the context evolves [19, 25]. Second, **human supervision** in ML-application lifecycles mitigates possible occurrence of deployment bias and prevents feedback bias. Algorithmic recommendations cannot blindly be accepted because they cannot be expected to be bias-free. Including humans in the application loop to analyze and question the outcomes can enhance objectivity [38]. Third, **randomness** can be introduced. If the outcome of an ML-application has an impact on data generation or sampling distribution, randomness can prevent feedback bias [36].

5   Discussion

The present paper addresses the emerging interest of IS research in challenges resulting from AI implementation in organizations and sheds light on the possible negative consequences of biases in ML-projects. We examined how organizations can identify and mitigate biases. Based on the widely adopted CRISP-DM, we demonstrated a systematic process to guide practitioners when identifying biases in ML-projects and provide a common ground for further theory development. We also presented a brief compilation of methods to consider what suits the specific application and the company.

This paper contributes to theory and novel management challenges in ML-projects twofold: First, the paper summarizes the current state of knowledge about bias in ML-applications in a synthesized way. Unique mitigation methods are allocated both to the bias(es) they address and the project phase they should be applied. The outline supports future researchers to clearly state the addressed problems with shared terminologies helps to solve problems in the analysis and design of ML-applications by highlighting temporal dependencies between bias occurrence and mitigation. Second, failing to recognize interdependencies in ML-models that are embedded (e.g., as modules) in broader organizational information systems can have a significant, detrimental impact on the acceptance and use of such systems as well. In this sense, the management of bias in ML-projects can become a critical aspect in IS development processes and differs fundamentally from, for example, software development.

Our research also has practical implications that could help project teams to address bias in ML-projects. First, it serves as a communication instrument for ML-project teams.

It appears most fruitful to create a shared understanding across industries and to equip teams with methods that are applicable across domains. Second, besides enhancing understanding of the variety of bias types, our work also provides a comprehensive perspective on when bias can occur and how it could be addressed. This allows a better planning and assessment of risks for ML-project managers. Lastly, with our mapping of several applicable methods to particular biases, mitigation methods can be selected. A bias mitigation method should stem from application-specific discussions about what it means to be fair in the particular application context, which determines the individual mix of technical and non-technical methods.

Future research could address the limitation of our work: First, future empirical research could study the practices of how managers and their teams deal with bias in ML-projects. Such research could further substantiate and extend the work presented here. For instance, the interdependencies between different biases are not investigated in this paper. The occurrence of a certain bias may affect the probability of a different bias to occur. Additionally, a certain mitigation method may impact other mitigation methods or biases it is not designed to address. That is, executing a mitigation method to address a certain bias could have an impact on the effectiveness of other mitigation methods or on the probability of other biases to occur. Second, while many of the articles included in this literature review stem from computer science outlets, our research could be extended by further scrutinizing this body of knowledge. Finally, existing frameworks, including the one presented here, still do not capture the full scope of fairness in all situations. Existing frameworks may not deliver clear solutions to ethical challenges in the business and data science community.

Managing Bias in ML-projects is closely related to Explainable Artificial Intelligence (XAI). That is, XAI greatly supports the detection of a ML-model's biases by disclosing the inherent mechanisms that lead to a certain outcome [7, 64]. In this paper, XAI is included as a mitigation method ("interpretable models"). However, XAI is not sufficient to eliminate the risk of bias: Even if the outcomes are interpretable and explainable, some biases can still be introduced through activities in e.g. the DE-phase.

The consolidation of IS research with social sciences and other fields such as law and ethics could provide more guidance on what it means to be fair. How can differences in moral values be handled? How to draw the line between an actual bias and a rationally based differentiation that is justifiable? Algorithms cannot judge or determine what fairness means. While we take serious attention to bias in system development, it should also be recognized that there are limits to what can be accomplished. Some concerns arising from biases go beyond designing and programming algorithms to larger societal problems. IS research could address this issue by encouraging the discussion about the articulation of normative goals that can be computationally resolved in business projects and ensure fair decision making in society.

6 Conclusion

ML-applications can incorporate inadequate properties that lead to both technically incorrect and socially unacceptable results. Besides performance criteria such as reliability, efficiency, and accuracy, freedom from bias is an integral part of the professional (risk) management of AI-systems. Therefore, we have proposed a framework based on the CRISP-DM process model that supports the identification of possible biases and methods for taking countermeasures in the management of ML-projects.

We encourage future research to address some of the limitations of our work. It could be insightful to illustrate the managing of biases and the application of mitigation methods to specific ML-projects with real data. By doing so, the contextual conditions under which each of the identified biases can occur are better captured. Because there is no one-size-fits-all solution to the diverse implementation of ML-applications, technical and social aspects of ML should be combined to bring context-awareness to research and practice.

This paper provides a possible approach by suggesting a framework to which a large part of IS research, project managers, and developers can relate. It fosters the understanding of the occurrence of different types of biases and their possible interactions, which have been so far scattered in the literature and named with different terminologies. Furthermore, we clearly address each type of bias with possible mitigation methods. We demonstrate the necessity to incorporate social and technical aspects in bias mitigation methods that can be tailored to the individual application.

References

1. von Krogh, G.: Artificial Intelligence in organizations: new opportunities for phenomenon-based theorizing. AMD. **4**, 404–409 (2018)
2. Samuel, A.L.: Some studies in machine learning using the game of checkers. IBM J. Res. Dev. **3**, 210–229 (1959)
3. Sauter, V.L.: Decision Support Systems for Business Intelligence. Wiley, Hoboken (2011)
4. Berente, N., Gu, B., Santhanam, R., Recker, J.: Call for papers MISQ special issue on managing AI. MISQ (2019)
5. Mikalef, P., Popovic, A., Eriksson Lundström, J., Conboy, K.: Special issue call for papers: dark side of analytics and AI. Eur. J. Inf. Syst. (2020)
6. O'Neil, C.: Weapons of Math Destruction: How Big Data Increases Inequality and Threatens Democracy. Allen Lane, London (2016)
7. Guidotti, R., Monreale, A., Ruggieri, S., Turini, F., Giannotti, F., Pedreschi, D.: A survey of methods for explaining black box models. ACM Comput. Surv. **51**, 1–42 (2018)
8. Benbya, H., Pachidi, S., Davenport, T., Jarvenpaa, S.: Call for papers: artificial intelligence in organizations: opportunities for management and implications for IS research. J. Assoc. Inf. Syst. (JAIS) MISQ Exec. (MISQE) (2019)
9. Barocas, S., Selbst, A.D.: Big data's disparate impact. Calif. Law Rev. **104**, 671–732 (2016)
10. Bailey, D., Faraj, S., Hinds, P., von Krogh, G., Leonardi, P., Hall, P.: Call for papers special issue of organization science: emerging technologies and organizing. Organ. Sci. (2019)
11. Moreira Nascimento, A., Cortez da Cunha, M.A.V., de Souza Meirelles, F., Scornavacca, E., de Melo, V.V.: A literature analysis of research on artificial intelligence in management information system (MIS). In: AMCIS Proceedings, pp. 1–10 (2018)
12. Mariscal, G., Marbán, Ó., Fernández, C.: A survey of data mining and knowledge discovery process models and methodologies. Knowl. Eng. Rev. **25**, 137–166 (2010)
13. Martínez-Plumed, F., et al.: CRISP-DM twenty years later: from data mining processes to data science trajectories. IEEE Trans. Knowl. Data Eng., 1–1 (2019)
14. Chapman, P., et al.: CRISP-DM 1.0: step-by-step data mining guide. SPSS inc. **9**, 13 (2000)

15. Suresh, H., Guttag, J.V.: A framework for understanding unintended consequences of machine learning. http://arxiv.org/abs/1901.10002 (2019)
16. Baeza-Yates, R.: Bias on the web. Commun. ACM. **61**, 54–61 (2018)
17. Feuerriegel, S., Dolata, M., Schwabe, G.: Fair AI: challenges and opportunities. Bus. Inf. Syst. Eng. **62**, 379–384 (2020)
18. Friedler, S.A., Choudhary, S., Scheidegger, C., Hamilton, E.P., Venkatasubramanian, S., Roth, D.: A comparative study of fairness-enhancing interventions in machine learning. In: Proceedings of the 2019 Conference on Fairness, Accountability, and Transparency, pp. 329–338. ACM, New York (2019)
19. Friedman, B., Nissenbaum, H.: Bias in computer systems. ACM Trans. Inf. Syst. **14**, 330–347 (1996)
20. Mitchell, S., Potash, E., Barocas, S., D'Amour, A., Lum, K.: Prediction-based decisions and fairness: a catalogue of choices, assumptions, and definitions. http://arxiv.org/abs/1811.07867 (2018)
21. Dwork, C., Hardt, M., Pitassi, T., Reingold, O., Zemel, R.: Fairness through awareness. In: Proceedings of the 3rd Innovations in Theoretical Computer Science Conference, pp. 214–226. Association for Computing Machinery, New York (2011)
22. Zemel, R., Wu, Y., Swersky, K., Pitassi, T., Dwork, C.: Learning fair representations. In: International Conference on Machine Learning, Atlanta, GA, USA , pp. 325–333. JMLR (2013)
23. Narayanan, A.: Translation tutorial: 21 fairness definitions and their politics. In: Proceedings of the Conference on Fairness Accountability Transparency, New York, USA, p. 1 (2018)
24. Green, B., Hu, L.: The myth in the methodology: towards a recontextualization of fairness in machine learning. In: Proceedings of the Machine Learning: the Debates Workshop, Stockholm, Sweden (2018)
25. Corbett-Davies, S., Goel, S.: The measure and mismeasure of fairness: a critical review of fair machine learning. http://arxiv.org/abs/1808.00023 (2018)
26. Silva, S., Kenney, M.: Algorithms, platforms, and ethnic bias. Commun. ACM. **62**, 37–39 (2019)
27. Bellamy, R.K.E., et al.: AI fairness 360: an extensible toolkit for detecting, understanding, and mitigating unwanted algorithmic bias. IBM J. Res. Dev. **63** (2018)
28. vom Brocke, J., Simons, A., Riemer, K., Niehaves, B., Plattfaut, R., Cleven, A.: Standing on the shoulders of giants: challenges and recommendations of literature search in information systems research. Commun. Assoc. Inf. Syst. **37**, 205–224 (2015)
29. Rowe, F.: What literature review is not: diversity, boundaries and recommendations. Eur. J. Inf. Syst. **23**, 241–255 (2014)
30. Schryen, G.: Revisiting IS business value research: what we already know, what we still need to know, and how we can get there. Eur. J. Inf. Syst. **22**, 139–169 (2013)
31. Levy, Y., Ellis, T.J.: A systems approach to conduct an effective literature review in support of information systems research. Informing Sci. J. **9**, 181–211 (2006)
32. Webster, J., Watson, R.T.: Analyzing the past to prepare for the future: writing a literature review. MISQ **26**, xiii–xxiii (2002)
33. Randolph, J.: A guide to writing the dissertation literature review. Pract. Assess. Res. Evaluation **14**, 13 (2009)
34. Fink, A.: Conducting Research Literature Reviews: From the Internet to Paper. SAGE Publications (2019)
35. Viera, A.J., Garrett, J.M.: Understanding interobserver agreement: the kappa statistic. Fam. Med. **37**, 360–363 (2005)
36. Baer, T.: Understand, Manage, and Prevent Algorithmic Bias. A Guide for Business Users and Data Scientists. Apress, Berkeley (2019)

37. Zarya, V.: The share of female CEOs in the fortune 500 dropped by 25% in 2018. Fortune.com (2018)
38. d'Alessandro, B., O'Neil, C., LaGatta, T.: Conscientious classification: a data scientist's guide to discrimination-aware classification. Big Data. **5**, 120–134 (2017)
39. Lum, K., Isaac, W.: To predict and serve? Significance **13**, 14–19 (2016)
40. Angwin, J., Larson, J., Mattu, S., Kirchner, L.: Machine Bias. https://www.propublica.org/art icle/machine-bias-risk-assessments-in-criminal-sentencing
41. Lan, J., Hu, M.Y., Patuwo, E., Zhang, G.P.: An investigation of neural network classifiers with unequal misclassification costs and group sizes. Decis. Support Syst. **48**, 582–591 (2010)
42. Suresh, H., Gong, J.J., Guttag, J.V.: Learning tasks for multitask learning. In: Proceedings of the 24th ACM SIGKDD International Conference on Knowledge Discovery & Data Mining, New York, USA, pp. 802–810. ACM (2018)
43. Chouldechova, A.: Fair prediction with disparate impact: a study of bias in recidivism prediction instruments. Big Data **5**, 153–163 (2017)
44. Collins, E.: Punishing risk. Georgetown Law J. **107**, 57 (2018)
45. Martin, K.: Designing ethical algorithms. MIS Q. Exec. **18**, 129–142 (2019)
46. Jones, M.: What we talk about when we talk about (big) data. J. Strateg. Inf. Syst. **28**, 3–16 (2019)
47. Barocas, S., Boyd, D.: Engaging the ethics of data science in practice. Commun. ACM. **60**, 23–25 (2017)
48. Buolamwini, J., Gebru, T.: Gender shades: intersectional accuracy disparities in commercial gender classification. In: Proceedings of the 1st Conference on Fairness, Accountability and Transparency, New York, USA, pp. 77–91. PMLR (2018)
49. Kamiran, F., Calders, T.: Data preprocessing techniques for classification without discrimination. Knowl. Inf. Syst. **33**, 1–33 (2012)
50. Kamiran, F., Calders, T.: Classifying without discriminating. In: 2nd International Conference on Computer, Control and Communication, pp. 1–6. IEEE (2009)
51. Chen, I.Y., Johansson, F.D., Sontag, D.: Why is my classifier discriminatory? In: Advances in Neural Information Processing Systems 31 (NIPS 2018), pp. 3539–3550 (2018)
52. Hajian, S., Domingo-Ferrer, J.: A methodology for direct and indirect discrimination prevention in data mining. IEEE Trans. Knowl. Data Eng. **25**, 1445–1459 (2013)
53. Kamiran, F., Žliobaite, I., Calders, T.: Quantifying explainable discrimination and removing illegal discrimination in automated decision making. Knowl. Inf. Syst. **35**, 613–644 (2013)
54. Calmon, F., Wei, D., Vinzamuri, B., Natesan Ramamurthy, K., Varshney, K.R.: Optimized pre-processing for discrimination prevention. In: Advances in Neural Information Processing Systems 30, pp. 3992–4001. Curran Associates, Inc. (2017)
55. Kamishima, T., Akaho, S., Asoh, H., Sakuma, J.: Fairness-aware classifier with prejudice remover regularizer. In: Flach, P.A., De Bie, T., Cristianini, N. (eds.) ECML PKDD 2012. LNCS (LNAI), vol. 7524, pp. 35–50. Springer, Heidelberg (2012). https://doi.org/10.1007/978-3-642-33486-3_3
56. Zafar, M.B., Valera, I., Rodriguez, M.G., Gummadi, K.P.: Fairness constraints: mechanisms for fair classification. In: Proceedings of the 20th International Conference on Artificial Intelligence and Statistics (AISTATS), Fort Lauderdale, Florida, USA. PMLR (2015)
57. Zhang, B.H., Lemoine, B., Mitchell, M.: Mitigating unwanted biases with adversarial learning. In: Proceedings of the 2018 AAAI/ACM Conference on AI, Ethics, and Society, New York, USA, pp. 335–340. ACM (2018)
58. Calders, T., Verwer, S.: Three naive Bayes approaches for discrimination-free classification. Data Min. Knowl. Discov. **21**, 277–292 (2010)
59. Binder, A., Bach, S., Montavon, G., Müller, K.R., Samek, W.: Layer-wise relevance propagation for deep neural network architectures. In: Kim, K., Joukov, N. (eds.) Information Science

and Applications (ICISA) 2016. LNEE, vol. 376, pp. 913–922. Springer, Singapore (2016). https://doi.org/10.1007/978-981-10-0557-2_87

60. Berardi, V.L., Patuwo, B.E., Hu, M.Y.: A principled approach for building and evaluating neural network classification models. Decis. Support Syst. **38**, 233–246 (2004)

61. Hardt, M., Price, E., Srebro, N.: Equality of opportunity in supervised learning. In: Advances in Neural Information Processing Systems, pp. 3315–3323. Neural Information Processing Systems (NIPS) (2016)

62. Dwork, C., Immorlica, N., Kalai, A.T., Leiserson, M.: Decoupled classifiers for fair and efficient machine learning. http://arxiv.org/abs/1707.06613 (2017)

63. Ryu, H.J., Adam, H., Mitchell, M.: InclusiveFaceNet: improving face attribute detection with race and gender diversity. http://arxiv.org/abs/1712.00193 (2017)

64. Samek, W., Wiegand, T., Müller, K.-R.: Explainable artificial intelligence: understanding, visualizing and interpreting deep learning models. http://arxiv.org/abs/1708.08296 (2017)

Design, Management and Impact of AI-Based Systems

Introduction to the WI2021 Track: Design, Management and Impact of AI-Based systems

Cristina Mihale-Wilson[1], Stefan Morana[2], Alexander Benlian[3],
and Oliver Hinz[1]

[1] Goethe University, Information Systems and Information Management,
Frankfurt am Main, Germany
{mihale-wilson, ohinz}@wiwi.uni-frankfurt.de
[2] Saarland University, Digital Transformation and Information Systems,
Saarbrücken. Germany
stefan.morana@uni-saarland.de
[3] Darmstadt University of Technology, Information Systems and E-Services,
Darmstadt, Germany
benlian@ise.tu-darmstadt.de

1 Track Description

Advances in artificial intelligence (AI), the increased availability of computing power combined with vast amounts of data enable the design and deployment of AI-based systems that offer large benefits in private and business-related contexts. At home, AI-based systems appear in the form of Conversational Agents (CAs) like Amazon's Alexa, Apple's Siri, or Microsoft's Cortana. Some of us might already be asking Alexa for the daily weather forecast, the daily news run-down, or to play music. However, beyond these examples, AI-based systems open up new opportunities for the entire economy as a whole, and especially for those companies that manage to leverage AI's economic potential for themselves. In stark contrast to the multitude of opportunities that AI in general and AI-based systems in particular offer to individuals, companies, or society, several risks and dangers limit the adoption and use of AI-based systems. This track focuses on the impact, optimal design, and management of AI-based systems on an individual, organizational, and societal level.

2 Research Articles

Overall, this track's contributions can be classified in two groups: One group of contributions investigates the adoption and use of AI and AI-based assistants, or Conversational Agents, – as one prominent embodiment of AI-based systems – in the private context. The second group of contributions focuses on AI and AI-based systems for the organizational context.

2.1   AI and AI-Based Systems in the Private Context

Despite the convenience benefits that AI-based systems can afford, their mass-adoption and use in the private context is still limited. While it might be normal for some of us to interact with an AI-based system daily, others still have serious reservations regarding such systems. Aiming to understand the drivers of adoption of CA in the private setting, **Lara Riefle, and Carina Benz** conduct a systematic literature review and identify five determinants that future AI-based systems acceptance research should investigate in more detail: personality, risk aversion, cognitive style, self-efficacy, and desire for control. In a similar vein, to improve the mass adoption of AI-based systems, **Fabian Reinkemeier, Philipp Spreer, and Waldemar Toporowski** present a short paper on a study that tests whether social stimuli and the associated perception of humanity and social presence of AI-based systems. The authors find that providing CAs with many stimuli increases user satisfaction. Nevertheless, users trust less in the integrity of a CA that offers more social stimuli.

2.2   AI and AI-Based Systems in the Organizational Context

Besides the value of AI in the private context, AI can also render competitive advantages in various organizations. **Christian Anschütz, Jan Ibisch, Katharina Ebner, and Stefan Smonik**, for instance, show best practices for AI in modeling traffic volumes and traffic forecasts, while **Raphael Meyer von Wolff, Sebastian Hobert, and Matthias Schumann** focus on AI supporting employees at the workplace.

Despite the advantages that AI and AI-based systems can bring to organizations, AI's adoption and use are still in infancy. One challenge is the implementation process of AI in organizations. Motivated by the high failure rate of projects that implement **Christian Engel, Philipp Ebel, and Benjamin van Giffen** investigate how the unique characteristics of AI (i.e., their context-sensitivity, their black-box character) impose new challenges for project management, and how these challenges are addressed in organizational (socio-technical) contexts. With their study, the researchers help practitioners benchmark their practices and increase their future AI implementations' success rates. Related, **Alexander Stohr and Jamie O'Rourke** present the usefulness of a cognitive functions perspective when implementing AI in organizations and, in particular, into the Predictive Maintenance application context.

Other essential challenges of implementing AI into organizations are the availability of labeled data and AI's black-box character. To improve the labeling of training data, **Julian Schuir, René Brinkhege, Eduard Anton, Thuy Duong Oesterreich, Pascal Meier, and Frank Teuteberg** develop and evaluate a prototype that can help crowdsourcing communities to render labeling tasks more efficient. On a similar note, **Roland Graef** presents and evaluates a new text classification approach that combines recent text representations and automated labeling approaches to label texts more time- and cost-efficiently. Concurrently, **Jessica Ochmann, Sandra Zilker, and Sven Laumer** investigate the black-box problem of AI-based recommendations, while **Kilian Kluge, Regina Eckhardt** exploit Explainable AI methods for the design of user-focused anti-phishing measures.

User-Specific Determinants of Conversational Agent Usage: A Review and Potential for Future Research

Lara Riefle[(✉)] and Carina Benz

Karlsruhe Institute of Technology, Karlsruhe, Germany
{lara.riefle,carina.benz}@kit.edu

Abstract. Conversational agents (CAs) have become integral parts of providers' service offerings, yet their potential is not fully exploited as users' acceptance and usage of CAs are often limited. Whereas previous research is rather technology-oriented, our study takes a user-centric perspective on the phenomenon. We conduct a systematic literature review to summarize the determinants of individuals' acceptance, adoption, and usage of CAs that have been examined in extant research, followed by an interview study to identify potential for further research. In particular, five concepts are proposed for further research: personality, risk aversion, cognitive style, self-efficacy, and desire for control. Empirical studies are encouraged to assess the impact of these user-specific concepts on individuals' decision to use CAs to eventually inform the design of CAs that facilitate users' acceptance, adoption, and use. This paper intends to contribute to the body of knowledge about the determinants of CA usage.

Keywords: Conversational agent use · User behavior · Individual differences · User dispositions · Literature review

1 Introduction

Conversational agents (e.g., customer support chatbots) have become integral parts of providers' service offerings, yet their acceptance and usage are often limited. Providers (e.g., firms), for example, offer conversational agents (CAs) to people in customer service to answer individuals' questions about a firm's offerings [1, 2]. They promise time savings and efficiency gains. Similarly, Apple offers the intelligent agent Siri on its smartphones to assist users with a variety of topics such as meeting scheduling, weather updates, or navigation [2, 3]. Nevertheless, practice reports that after an initial hype, CA usage significantly drops. Users do not continue to use them regularly and often only resort to their assistance for menial tasks such as searching the FAQ or setting a cooking timer [4]. Some people even ignore them completely. Thus, the enormous potential of CAs is not fully exploited and providers withdraw them from their service offerings again [5]. This problem of poor user acceptance and inconsistent usage is also investigated in the literature, with researchers exploring the underlying causes in their search for remedies [3]. Information Systems (IS) literature provides two models that are regularly applied in studies on user behavior: the Technology Acceptance Model (TAM) [6] and the Unified Theory of Acceptance and Use of Technology (UTAUT) [7]. For decades, users' acceptance and usage of technology has been studied based on these two models and recently CAs have become a central research topic. Taking a predominantly technology-focused perspective, researchers have examined how CAs are perceived [e.g., 8], how different design features affect users [e.g., 9], or how the usage experience can be improved [e.g., 10]. Still, existing literature cannot fully explain why people do not accept and use chatbots or intelligent agents. A more user-centric perspective on individuals' acceptance, adoption, and usage of CAs is necessary to understand what drives people to use them. Thus, we intend to answer the following research questions:

What is the current state of research on the determinants of individuals' acceptance, adoption, and usage of CAs? Which concepts should be covered by future research?

To address these questions, we apply a mixed-method approach comprising a systematic literature review (SLR) to provide an overview of the body of knowledge, and an additional interview study to identify overlooked concepts. Thereby we arrive at a research agenda on facilitating individual acceptance and usage of CAs. The literature-based framework compiles the major determinants and corresponding concepts that influence individuals in their decision to use CAs. Five additional concepts emphasizing user-specific factors are identified by means of the interviews. The findings indicate that we need to better understand the users themselves – their individual differences and dispositions – to ultimately be able to advance the acceptance and use of CAs. Overall, this study aims to contribute to the body of knowledge about the determinants of the usage of CAs in particular and AI-based systems in general. The proposed conceptual framework might serve as a basis for both IS researchers and practitioners to successfully design and implement CAs.

The remainder of this paper is structured as follows: First, we provide a brief summary of the background on CAs and research on usage, adoption, and acceptance theories. Second, the research methodology is outlined. Next, we present an integrated framework that aggregates existing research findings on the usage, adoption, and acceptance of CAs. Finally, we derive directions for further research and discuss theoretical and practical implications.

2   Theoretical Background

2.1   Conversational Agents

Conversational agents are defined as software-based systems that interact with the user in natural language [1, 11]. These conversational user interfaces can refer to text-based CAs, such as chatbots, or speech-based CAs, e.g., intelligent agents such as Apple's Siri. Typically CAs are applied in messaging applications, on websites, or, in the case of intelligent agents, embedded in devices, to assist users in various use cases [2, 11]. On e-commerce sites, for example, CAs offer users maximum availability. They can provide fast answers to their questions, or represent a convenient way for users to complete tasks such as ordering food [12]. Smalltalk-oriented CAs can even fulfill users' social needs [12]. Thus, CAs may offer a number of advantages in users' everyday lives. All this is enabled by artificial intelligence (AI), more precisely by machine learning and natural language processing [13].

The use of AI makes CAs and other AI-based systems special [14]. Two crucial aspects distinguish them from other information systems: their degree of interactivity and intelligence [14]. These characteristics allow AI-based systems to interact with users in a human-like way and take over tasks from them. Interactions can even take forms that are so similar to interpersonal communication that emotional bonds between the user and CAs might develop [15]. Researchers have shown that users often perceive AI-based systems as social and autonomous actors [16]. Hence, the anthropomorphism questions basic assumptions of information systems as mere machines or tools [17]. Users' perceptions, attitudes, and beliefs about AI-based systems, particularly CAs, may be fundamentally affected [13, 17].

2.2 Acceptance, Adoption, and Usage Theories in IS

Research on acceptance, adoption, and usage of information systems is of central interest in the IS research stream on user behavior. Although the three terms are often used synonymously, they shall be distinguished in this paper: *Acceptance* is described as a state or an individuals' attitude that marks the start of the *adoption* process; which may eventually end with the *usage* (one-time or continued) [18]. Different models have been introduced over the years to explain users' usage intentions and behavior on the individual level. The most commonly applied theories in IS are the Technology Acceptance Model (TAM) [6] and the Unified Theory of Acceptance and Use of Technology (UTAUT) [7]. Central concepts in these theories are the perceived usefulness and the perceived ease of use, i.e., the user's perceptions of a systems' performance and effort of using it [7, 19, 20]. Incorporated in TAM and UTAUT are the socio-psychological Theory of Planned Behavior (TPB) [21] and the Theory of Reasoned Action (TRA) [22]. These add social and cognitive concepts to the models as further influencing factors of users' behavior [20]. Over the years, TAM and UTAUT have been extended to increase their explanatory power [20]. Still, the underlying assumption of these models is that users' intention to use is a good predictor of actual usage of the system under investigation [20].

Another less frequently used theory to explain user behavior is the IS Continuance Model [23]. In contrast to TAM and UTAUT, the IS Continuance Model is concerned with the post-adoption stage of information systems. The model focuses on users' continued IS use linking satisfaction and perceived usefulness (from TAM) to the individual's intention to continue using a system [23]. Thus, the model draws on consumer behavior research by building on expectation-confirmation theory and including cognitive beliefs and affect to model users' behavior.

The strengths of the theories and models above to explain IS usage lies in a few well-studied determinants: users' perceptions, attitudes, expected outcomes, and their (social) environment. As has been suggested by Schuetz and Venkatesh [17], current advancements of AI-based systems such as CAs make them considerably different from previous information systems. This raises the question in how far user behavior with regard to CAs can be explained drawing on established models and where further research may be needed.

3   Methodology

In order to (1) identify determinants of acceptance, adoption, and usage of chatbots in extant research and (2) derive directions for future research, a mixed-method approach is applied. We conduct a systematic literature review (SLR) according to the guidelines suggested by vom Brocke et al. [24] and Webster and Watson [25] and synthesize the identified determinants of CA acceptance and usage in an integrated framework. This framework is then complemented by a subsequent interview study to identify potential for future research. We conduct 81 structured interviews and analyze them using qualitative content analysis according to Mayring [26]. To facilitate reproducibility and ensure transparency, we adhere to established research methods. The methodological steps taken are outlined below.

Systematic Literature Review (Step 1). To provide an overview of the body of knowledge on why people accept, adopt, and use CAs, we conduct an SLR. The scope of the SLR can be defined by its process, sources, coverage, and techniques [24]: In a sequential search process, four databases (i.e., sources) covering IS research and literature from related fields such as HCI are searched. Representative coverage of literature on the acceptance and usage of CAs is pursued by applying a keyword search, backward search, and forward search (i.e., techniques).

In detail, our *search strategy* involves searching in databases that cover IS research (i.e., AISeL), the related field of HCI research (i.e., ACM Digital Library), as well as interdisciplinary databases (i.e., Scopus, Web of Science) to account for the broad application of CAs across domains. The search string ([""(conversational OR intelligent OR virtual OR cognitive OR smart OR digital OR AI) AND (assistant* OR agent* OR system* OR application*)"] OR chatbot*) AND ["use" OR "usage" OR "adoption" OR "acceptance"] includes related terms for CAs and yields a total of 953 hits (30.06.2020). 122 relevant articles (without duplicates) remain after screening title and abstract and applying the inclusion criteria as outlined in Table 1. 69 respectively six additional articles are added by backward and forward search. To also cover more recent research, next to journal articles also conference publications are included during the selection process. In addition, articles only marginally concerned with CA usage are excluded to ensure only relevant articles that promote further insights are considered. Table 1 provides a more detailed overview of the distribution of articles.

A total of 197 articles are considered in the *literature analysis and synthesis* process. Since our main interest lies in the concepts that have been investigated to understand individual user behavior, we first sort out 155 articles with a strong technology-focus. As suggested by Webster and Watson [25], a concept-matrix to structure the subsequent analysis is created. We scrutinize the full text of 42 articles and extract the concepts that determine individuals' acceptance, adoption, and usage of CAs. Each concept is assigned once per article, yet one article can cover several concepts. This process allows us to build a framework of concepts that have been studied in extant research.

Table 1. Results of the literature search process

Databases	Hits	Relevant	Inclusion criteria
AISeL	38	17	• Peer-reviewed publications in English
ACM	108	22	
Scopus	712	101	• Empirical data is collected
Web of Science	95	25	• Focus on acceptance, adoption, or usage of CAs
Total	953	**122** w/o duplicates	
+ **69** Backward search	+ **6** Forward search		= **197** articles

Interview Study (Step 2). The framework derived from the SLR is complemented with further concepts by an interview study. While the SLR provides an overview of existing knowledge on CA acceptance, adoption, and use, the interview study reveals promising concepts for future research. We interview 81 purposefully sampled interviewees (university students at the age of 21–28, 57% male) about their usage of CAs and the underlying drivers. The structured interviews cover their general attitude towards using CAs, their actual use of CAs, the conditions under which they use CAs, and the influencing factors on their decision to use CAs. 44% of interviewees are regular CA users, 32% occasional users, and 24% non-users, which allows us to investigate a broad spectrum of users.

Qualitative content analysis is performed in an iterative process following the approach by Mayring [26]. Central statements in the interview data are paraphrased, reduced, and aggregated using the software MAXQDA. The initial deductive category assignment aims at verifying the previously identified concepts determining individuals' acceptance, adoption, and usage. Aiming at identifying promising concepts for future research, we next concentrate on those statements that could not be matched with a concept of the literature-based framework but still are relevant to the research questions. During the subsequent inductive category assignment, the statements are coded according to the two-cycle recommendations of Saldaña [27]. In the first cycle, descriptive coding is applied to summarize the main topic of each statement, which is then followed by pattern coding in the second cycle to aggregate the descriptive first-cycle codes to a higher level of abstraction for further in-depth analysis. In this final analysis step, five additional concepts are identified in the interviews that represent concepts in IS and psychology that promise further insights into user behavior with regard to CAs. These five concepts further enrich the framework derived in the SLR and facilitate a more comprehensive view of the determinants of individuals' acceptance, adoption, and usage of CAs.

4 Results

4.1 Determinants and Concepts Investigated in Extant Literature

Existing literature on CA acceptance, adoption, and usage can be classified along three research foci (see Fig. 1): (1) Almost half (48%) of the 197 analyzed articles *evaluate a specific CA artifact*, (2) about one third (31%) compare the *effect of different techno-logical CA features* on users, and (3) only 21% put the user in the center of attention investigating the *determinants of their acceptance and usage* of CAs.

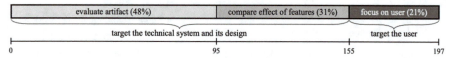

Fig. 1. Focus of existing literature on CA acceptance, adoption, and usage

A total of 79% of analyzed articles, i.e., with research foci (1) and (2), target the technical system and its design. They seek to advance the knowledge of how design features influence the user to finally improve the CAs as such. The evaluation of a specific artifact with users is the main purpose of 95 articles. Typically, CA artifacts are developed, e.g., using a Design Science Research approach [28], and then evaluated by asking users for their acceptance of the artifact and their usage intention. Most often (83%), the articles do not draw on specific concepts from theory for the evaluation [29]. However, in case they do, TAM or UTAUT concepts such as perceived usefulness or ease of use are applied [30]. Overall, very specific CAs built for limited use cases are investigated. Thus, these articles can only marginally contribute to answering the stated research question posed regarding the determinants of individuals' acceptance, adoption, and usage of CAs.

The main purpose of another 60 articles is to compare the effect of different techno-logical CA features on users. For example, they investigate how language style influences information disclosure [e.g., 31] or how CA appearance affects continued human-agent interaction [e.g., 32]. Central topics of interest are social cues, next to error handling mechanisms [e.g., 33], or response characteristics [e.g., 2]. Often, the papers develop design recommendations to improve users' experience during CA usage. The contributions made enhance our understanding of the actual usage phase. However, further literature must be considered to also understand users' decision to accept and use CAs in the first place.

Lastly, 42 articles take a closer look at the users themselves focusing, for example, on their perceptions, attitudes, and experiences. These articles contribute to exploring the usage phase, but also provide further insights into the preceding acceptance and adoption of CA, which is why we examine them in detail. To extract the determinants of individual user behavior the articles are analyzed in a concept-centric approach. The resulting framework is summarized in Table 2 (numbers indicate the number of articles that investigated the concept).

The emphasis on concepts from TAM and UTAUT can clearly be recognized. *Per-ceived usefulness* and *perceived ease of use* from TAM, which are closely related to *per-formance expectancy* and *effort expectancy* from UTAUT, are among the most researched concepts [e.g., 40, 41]. The *perception of risk* (e.g., user's perceived security and data privacy risk) is less commonly investigated [e.g., 42, 43]. The relevance of these estab-lished concepts is further underlined in the interview statements: Interviewee #66, for example, states "I use chatbots in order to save time and get my tasks done more easily".

Table 2. The main determinants of an individual's CA usage investigated in extant research

Concept	Definition	Perception	Attitude	Experience	Motivation	External Factor	Individual Factor
Perceived Usefulness	"the degree to which an individual believes that using a particular system would enhance his or her performance" [6, p. 112]	13					
Performance Expectancy	"the degree to which an individual believes that using the system will help him or her attain gains in performance" [7, p. 447]	7					
Perceived Ease of Use	"the degree to which an individual believes that using a particular system would be free of physical or mental effort" [6, p. 112]	15					
Effort Expectancy	"the degree of ease associated with the use of the system" [7, p. 450]	8					
Perceived Risk	"extent of customers' perception of uncertainty" [34, p. 4297]	9					
Attitude toward CA Usage	"the user's positive or negative feelings (evaluative affect) about performing a specific behavior" [35, p. 247]		10				
Trust	"the extent to which one is willing to ascribe good intentions to and have confidence in the words and actions of other people" [36, p. 39]		11				
Prior Experience with the System	The background and knowledge the individual has with using a particular system [7]			6			
Prior Experience with the Task	The background and knowledge the individual has with completing a particular task [7]			5			
Hedonic Motivation	"pleasure derived from using a technology" [37, p. 161]				6		
Utilitarian Motivation	Behavior driven from functional, goal-oriented motives [38]				1		
Social Motivation	Behavior driven from social and relational motives [12]				1		
Social Influence	"the extent to which consumers perceive that important others (e.g., family and friends) believe they should use a particular technology" [37, p. 159]					5	
Innovativeness	"the degree to which an individual or other unit of adoption is relatively earlier in adopting new ideas than the other members of his social system" [39, p. 22]						3
Demographics	Factors such as age, gender, ethnicity						5

This indicates perceived usefulness or performance expectancy, respectively. Perceived ease of use and effort expectancy are pointed out in statements such as "[the CA is] able to help me quickly and in an uncomplicated manner" (I36) and "chatbots are easy to use" (I6). Statements by I32, I67, I72, I80, and others further support these determinants; i.e., users need to perceive a CA as performance-enhancing and easy to use in order to actually use them. Likewise, the perceived risk associated with CAs is reflected in statements such as "[I am] not quite sure that conversational agents provide a proper data security" (I42) or "I find many conversational agents too intrusive" (I3). Together, these perceptions of users are often studied and seem to be an important determinant of CA acceptance, adoption, and usage.

A user's *attitude toward CA usage* is also well-researched in existing literature [e.g., 41, 44]. TAM also includes the concept of attitude toward usage, which originates from TRA and TPB. This affective response – positive or negative – can also be seen in users' statements: "I love using conversational agents" (I78) or "I am still skeptical of the skills of these machines" (I79). In addition, *trust* toward the CA is investigated by, for example, Kasilingam [42], Laumer et al. [43], or Prakash and Das [45]. Some interviewees expressed a lack of trust as I35's statements documents "I do not really trust the chatbot that it can find the best fitting solution for me. So, I would need to check the result anyway". The interviews show another interesting aspect. Attitudes are formed or reinforced, though not necessarily, based on prior experience (e.g., I79: "This experience verified my skeptical attitude against conversational agents"). In terms of prior experience, a distinction can be made between *prior experience with the system* [e.g., 46], i.e., CAs, and *prior experience with the task* [e.g., 43]. I3's statement "I feel that in 90% of the cases I am not well advised by chatbots and contact the hotline or the support directly" suggests that the concept of prior system experience influences the decision to use a CA.

Hedonic, utilitarian, and *social motivation* are further concepts that are considered by researchers investigating the acceptance, adoption, and usage of CAs [e.g., 12, 40, 45]. While extensions of UTAUT include hedonic motivation as a concept, motivations are originally rooted in social psychology research. Uses and Gratifications Theory [47] assumes that individuals have a clear intent when using a system, i.e., their behavior is goal-driven. In the interviews, these different goals or motivations become apparent: hedonic – e.g., "sometimes I talk to it just for fun" (I47), utilitarian – e.g., "I use them because of higher flexibility" (I67), and social – e.g., "when I am bored, [the CA] is just like a friend to accompany you" (I61). Next to these intrinsic motivations, external factors such as *social influence* can affect an individual in his or her usage decision [34, 40, 43, 45]. For example, I20 states that he has been influenced by his friends to test a certain CA.

As a last determinant, individual factors of the user are investigated in extant research. *Demographic factors* such as age, gender, and ethnicity, and the individual's *innovativeness* are explored as concepts by Kasilingam [42], Nadarzynski et al. [48], or Melián-González et al. [40]. Individual factors, especially innovativeness, are confirmed by statements such as "I was curious to test it" (I20) or "I am trying to familiarize myself with the novel technological tool" (I66).

The outlined determinants and concepts (see Table 2) are the main determinants of users' acceptance, adoption, and usage of CAs that have been regarded in extant literature. The results show that research to date especially contributed to expanding our knowledge about users' perceptions and attitudes towards CAs and the influence of prior experience and friends and family's opinion. Only initial attempts have been made to gain a deeper understanding of individual user-specific factors determining CA acceptance and usage. Yet, our interviews with potential and actual CA users suggest that there are further relevant concepts that might enable us to facilitate CA acceptance and usage.

4.2 Potential for Future Research Based on Concepts Emerging from the Interviews

We have set out to investigate what research has done to understand individuals' acceptance, adoption, and usage of CAs (RQ1). The SLR shows that the majority of existing research is concerned with the technology itself by evaluating a specific artifact with users or comparing the effect of different design features on users. Only little research focuses on the users themselves. These articles on user behavior have examined a multitude of concepts: users' perceptions of the system; their attitudes towards using CAs; users' prior experience; their hedonic, utilitarian, and social motivations; social influence; and individual factors such as innovativeness or demographics. In addition, this study aimed at identifying potential for future research (RQ2). To this end, we conducted interviews and derived five concepts (see Table 3) that offer potential for further research. Our results suggest that user-specific concepts, i.e., individual factors, need to be studied to understand why people accept, adopt, and use CAs.

Personality. Interviewee #66 made the statement "I like to use cutting-edge technologies as I'm a computer geek" (I66), expressing that he seeks new experiences and is generally open to try out novel technologies. I59 stated "I don't like the feeling of talking to a machine [...] I personally would like to hear or feel how the other side reacts to my concern", which indicates that she values personal contact and empathetic conversation in case of a problem. Despite the differences, both statements can be attributed to the concept of *personality,* which is generally described by five traits: openness, agreeableness, neuroticism, conscientiousness, and extraversion known as the Big Five personality traits [54]. Each of these traits is differently pronounced in each individual, which leads to distinct cognitions, emotions, and behavior. In the case of I66, the trait openness ("geek", open to try out) seems to be strong, whereas the wish for establishing relationships and interpersonal interactions in the latter statement by I59 is typical for individuals with a high degree of agreeableness.

Risk aversion. I42 notes that it is "not quite clear in which cases [CAs] can help you and in which they are not that useful", which is why he avoids using them to prevent wasting his time. Similarly, due to uncertainties regarding the "proper data security" of CAs, I7 tries "to either avoid them or at least [does] not provide too much details" about herself. These statements show that both interviewees limit their CA usage due to uncertainties about CAs' usefulness and data security, which points to the concept of *risk aversion.* In

Table 3. Preliminary research agenda on user-specific factors influencing individuals' acceptance, adoption, and usage of CAs

Concept	Definition	Exemplary research questions
Personality	The individually different combination of cognitions, emotions and behavior patterns that evolve from biological and environmental influences [49]	• How can an individual's cognitive style, risk aversion etc. be assessed and inferred from user interactions?
Risk aversion	"An individual's degree of negative attitude toward risk arising from outcome uncertainty" [50, p. 533]	• How do different levels of self-efficacy, desire for control etc. affect the acceptance, adoption, and usage of CAs? • How does current acceptance, adoption, and usage of CAs differ between individuals
Cognitive style	The set of cognitive processes that influence how an individual perceives and forms judgments [51]	with different personality traits, risk aversion, cognitive style etc.? • How should users with certain personality
Self-efficacy	An individual's belief in his/her own skills and abilities [52]	traits be addressed to foster CA usage? • How can we leverage knowledge on individual user characteristics to design CAs
Desire for control	The intensity of an individual's innate psychological need for control [53]	in a way to facilitate their usage?

this context, risk aversion is not only understood in the narrower economic sense, i.e., in terms of calculable financial losses but rather encompasses the general level of risk (arising from outcome uncertainty) that an individual is willing to incur [50]. Different degrees of individual risk aversion lead to different risk-reducing behavior [55]: While I42's risk aversion is so pronounced that he avoids CAs completely, I7's risk aversion is expressed in cautious usage, and I8's risk aversion is so weak that she does "not mind to interact with [CAs]" (I7).

Cognitive Style. Statements such as "for me it is sometimes hard to explain my case by written language" (I63) relate to the fact that individuals are known to prefer different ways of communication and information input (e.g., written, verbal, visual, haptic). Furthermore, I2 states that she "did not consciously make use of [the chatbot]", she just used it when it was presented to her. This shows that her way of processing information is intuitive rather than analytical. Analytical information processing implies decomposing information into its components; as is the case for I16 and I34 who separate the information of becoming aware of the chatbot popping-up, from the information about other alternatives on the website to achieve their goal (e.g., finding product details) and consequently only use the CA after weighing up the alternatives. Both the preference for a particular information representation and the way of processing the presented information are aggregated in the theoretical concept of *cognitive style* [51]. Research investigates a multitude of cognitive styles, i.e., sets of cognitive processes that influence how an individual perceives and forms judgment. Yet, especially the verbal-oriented cognitive style – as indicated in I63's preference for spoken language – and the field-independent cognitive style – observable in I16 and I34's analytic information processing – stood out in the interviews as influencing CA usage [51].

Self-Efficacy. I35's statement "As I assess myself, I am an independent person, preferring doing things by myself" reveals that she thinks she has the necessary skills and abilities to complete the task on her own without CA assistance. Then again, I7 states to resort to the help of CAs to solve problems as this option is "faster than [she] would find an appropriate solution on [her] own" (I7). This varying belief of individuals in their own abilities and skills is reflected in the concept of *self-efficacy* [52, 56]. In our interviews, we observed that depending on the level of self-efficacy, individuals were more or less inclined to use CAs. Individuals (e.g., I35) with a high level of self-efficacy refrained from CA assistance, whereas individuals such as I7 with a lower self-efficacy assessed her abilities in such a way that it seemed better for her to ask the CA for support.

Desire for Control. I62 mentions to enjoy using the chatbot of a retailer as a "shopping assistant to help [her] choose the right style" as it guides her through the shopping process by "prompt[ing] the user to answer some basic questions" (I62). It is in I62's interest that the CA takes the lead during the conversation and decides on how to proceed. Other interviewees, on the contrary, are annoyed by the fact that often the CA controls the interaction, for example, when the customer service chatbot "decides whether to forward the inquiry to a human service employee" (I8). This obviously different innate need for control of the two interviewees is described by the concept of *desire for control* [53]. While some individuals want to have more control over the CA's actions (e.g., I8), others are willing to cede control to the CA and let it decide how to proceed in the conversation (e.g., I62).

Overall, current research on CA acceptance, adoption, and usage has a strong tendency towards technology and design-oriented issues. Thereby, a user's individual characteristics are often only marginally considered which does not correspond to their significance for acceptance, adoption, and usage. It must be considered how users' dispositions influence their perceptions and attitudes. For instance, an individual's unmet desire for control may result in a lack of trust in the system; or a high level of individual risk aversion could increase the amount of perceived risk of CAs, finally leading to the decision to not use the system. Hence, this study aims to reemphasize the value of individual factors for CA acceptance, adoption, and usage. We encourage future research to (re)focus on the user of CAs – their characteristics and dispositions – as determinants for system usage. Only with a sound understanding of the users and their individual differences, CA usage can be reliably predicted and enhanced. For example, only when CA designers are aware of differences in personality and cognitive styles, and their implications for adoption and usage, they can adapt CA design towards individual preferences. Once designers know that the intended system users are characterized by a high degree of self-efficacy influencing their behavior, they can ensure that they design the system in such a way that it does not undermine their competence.

To arrive there, empirical research will be an important means to further explore the user-specific concepts identified in this study, to measure their influence, and examine possible interdependencies. Research questions guiding these endeavors are provided in Table 3: To build a basis for a more nuanced perspective on CA acceptance, adoption, and usage, it is necessary to identify different user profiles in terms of personality traits, cognitive style, risk aversion, self-efficacy, and desire for control. Building on these insights future research should then test and quantify the influence of the identified concepts on individuals' acceptance, adoption, and usage of CAs. Only then will it be possible to design systems that are tailored to the users and ultimately target their enhanced acceptance, adoption, and usage of CAs.

5   Limitations

This study aimed to provide a basis for understanding users' acceptance, adoption, and usage of CAs. This aim has been pursued through a rigorous SLR and a subsequent interview study. We nevertheless acknowledge a few limitations of our study that provide avenues for future research. Although the scope of the SLR is not fully comprehensive, a database-oriented search including journal articles and conference publications was chosen. This way, more recent research could be considered, which is particularly important as the research field of human interaction with CAs is still young and emerging. Regarding the interview study, a drawback is that only a certain group of people, i.e., university students between 21–28, have been interviewed. However, by restricting the interview sample to digital natives familiar with the concept of CAs it was ensured that only relevant data was collected to complement the study. Finally, the overall research focused on the context of CAs as only one type of AI-based systems, which is why it may be an interesting research avenue for future studies to extend the results to other types of AI-based systems (e.g., wearables).

6   Conclusion

In this paper, we investigated the main determinants of individuals' acceptance, adoption, and usage of CAs. Our goal was to better understand what could cause current CA usage to fall short of expectations and, therefore, not fully exploit the potential of these AI-based systems. We took a literature-based approach enriched by empirical insights from interviews. The systematic literature review (SLR) containing 197 articles shows that the strength of existing literature lies in explaining users' perceptions and attitudes. Building on 81 interviews, we derived five additional concepts comprising users' individual factors, i.e., their dispositions and individual differences. On that foundation potential for future research was outlined. We propose that, to enable successful CAs and their continued use, research and practice need to better understand the individual user – their cognitive style, risk aversion, desire for control, etc.. It is important to build a deeper knowledge of users' personality, individual differences, and dispositions. Only then can we facilitate users' acceptance, adoption, and continued usage of CAs and other AI-based systems.

The contribution of this paper is twofold: from a theoretical point of view, we provide a systematic review of existing research on users' acceptance, adoption, and usage of CAs. The integrated framework of concepts may serve as an orientation for researchers in the field of user behavior. In addition, we present five concepts (see Table 3) pertaining to user-specific individual factors that emerged from our study as offering potential for future research. The importance of users' individual characteristics is highlighted, and a research agenda is proposed. From a practical point of view, a better understanding of the user and awareness of individual differences and dispositions will help to figure out how to facilitate the successful acceptance, adoption, and usage of CAs. Hence, a potential starting point toward the individualized design of CAs is presented. All in all, the emerging user-specific factors may serve as a valuable foundation to investigate individual acceptance, adoption, and usage of CAs in more detail.

Acknowledgements. The authors acknowledge the financial support by the Federal Ministry for Economic Affairs and Energy of Germany in the project Service-Meister (project number 01MK20008).

References

1. McTear, M., Callejas, Z., Griol, D.: The Conversational Interface: Talking to Smart Devices. Springer, Heidelberg (2016). https://doi.org/10.1007/978-3-319-32967-3
2. Gnewuch, U., Morana, S., Adam, M., Maedche, A.: Faster is not always better: understanding the effect of dynamic response delays in human-chatbot interaction. In: Twenty-Seventh European Conference on Information Systems (ECIS), Portsmouth, pp. 1–17 (2018)
3. Grudin, J., Jacques, R.: Chatbots, humbots, and the quest for artificial general intelligence. In: Conference on Human Factors in Computing Systems (CHI), Glasgow, pp. 1–11 (2019)
4. Liao, Q.V., et al.: All work and no play? Conversations with a question-and-answer chatbot in the wild. In: Conference on Human Factors in Computing Systems (CHI), Montreal, pp. 1–13 (2018)
5. Ben Mimoun, M.S., Poncin, I., Garnier, M.: Case study-embodied virtual agents: an analysis on reasons for failure. J. Retail. Consum. Serv. **19**, 605–612 (2012)
6. Davis, F.D.: Perceived usefulness, perceived ease of use, and user acceptance of information technology. MIS Q. **13**, 319–339 (1989)
7. Venkatesh, V., Morris, M.G., Davis, G.B., Davis, F.D.: User acceptance of information technology: toward a unified view. MIS Q. **27**, 425–478 (2003)
8. Lee, S., Lee, N., Sah, Y.J.: Perceiving a mind in a chatbot: effect of mind perception and social cues on co-presence, closeness, and intention to use. Int. J. Hum. Comput. Interact. **36**, 930–940 (2020)
9. Go, E., Sundar, S.S.: Humanizing chatbots: the effects of visual, identity and conversational cues on humanness perceptions. Comput. Human Behav. **97**, 304–316 (2019)
10. Biduski, D., Bellei, E.A., Rodriguez, J.P.M., Zaina, L.A.M., De Marchi, A.C.B.: Assessing long-term user experience on a mobile health application through an in-app embedded conversation-based questionnaire. Comput. Human Behav. **104**, 106169 (2020)
11. Følstad, A., Brandtzaeg, P.B.: Chatbots and the new world of HCI. Interactions **24**, 38–42 (2017)
12. Brandtzaeg, P.B., Følstad, A.: Why people use chatbots. In: 4th International Conference of Internet Science (INSCI), Thessaloniki, pp. 377–392 (2017)
13. Maedche, A., et al: AI-based digital assistants. Opportunities, threats, and research perspectives. Bus. Inf. Syst. Eng. **61**, 535–544 (2019)
14. Maedche, A., Morana, S., Schacht, S., Werth, D., Krumeich, J.: Advanced user assistance systems. Bus. Inf. Syst. Eng. **58**, 367–370 (2016)
15. Pfeuffer, N., Benlian, A., Gimpel, H., Hinz, O.: Anthropomorphic information systems. Bus. Inf. Syst. Eng. **61**(4), 523–533 (2019). https://doi.org/10.1007/s12599-019-00599-y
16. Pakkala, D., Spohrer, J.: Digital service: technological agency in service systems. In: 52nd Hawaii International Conference on System Sciences (HICSS), Grand Wailea, Maui, pp. 1886–1895 (2019)

17. Schuetz, S., Venkatesh, V.: The rise of human machines: how cognitive computing systems challenge assumptions of user-system interaction. J. Assoc. Inf. Syst. **21**, 1–42 (2020)
18. Karahanna, E., Straub, D.W., Chervany, N.L.: Information technology adoption across time: a cross-sectional comparison of pre-adoption and post-adoption beliefs. MIS Q. **23**, 183–213 (1999)
19. Davis, F.D., Bagozzi, R.P., Warshaw, P.R.: User acceptance of computer technology: a comparison of two theoretical models. Manag. Sci. **35**, 982–1003 (1989)
20. Constantiou, I.D., Lehrer, C., Hess, T.: Changing information retrieval behaviours: an empirical investigation of users' cognitive processes in the choice of location-based services. Eur. J. Inf. Syst. **23**, 513–528 (2014)
21. Ajzen, I.: The theory of planned behavior. Organ. Behav. Hum. Decis. Process. **50**, 179–211 (1991)
22. Fishbein, M., Ajzen, I.: Belief, Attitude, Intention, and Behavior: An Introduction to Theory and Research. Addison-Wesley, Reading (1975)
23. Bhattacherjee, A.: Understanding information systems continuance: an expectation-confirmation model. MIS Q. **25**, 351–370 (2001)
24. vom Brocke, J., Simons, A., Riemer, K., Niehaves, B., Plattfaut, R., Cleven, A.: Standing on the shoulders of giants: challenges and recommendations of literature search in information systems research. Commun. Assoc. Inf. Syst. **37**, 205–224 (2015)
25. Webster, J., Watson, R.T.: Analyzing the past to prepare for the future: writing a literature review. MIS Q. **26**, xiii–xxiii (2002)
26. Mayring, P.: Qualitative content analysis: theoretical background and procedures. In: Bikner-Ahsbahs, A., Knipping, C., Presmeg, N. (eds.) Approaches to Qualitative Research in Mathematics Education: Examples of Methodology and Methods, pp. 365–380 (2015)
27. Saldaña, J.: The Coding Manual for Qualitative Researchers. SAGE, London (2009)
28. Hevner, A.R., March, S.T., Park, J., Ram, S.: Design science in information systems research. MIS Q. **28**, 75–105 (2004)
29. Rodriguez, J., Piccoli, G., Bartosiak, M.: Nudging the classroom: designing a socio-technical artifact to reduce academic procrastination. In: 52nd Hawaii International Conference on System Sciences (HICSS), Grand Wailea, Maui, pp. 4405–4414 (2019)
30. Hobert, S.: Say hello to 'coding tutor'! Design and evaluation of a chatbot-based learning system supporting students to learn to program. In: Fortieth International Conference on Information Systems (ICIS), Munich, pp. 1–17 (2019)
31. Gnewuch, U., Meng, Y., Maedche, A.: The effect of perceived similarity in dominance on customer self-disclosure to chatbots in conversational commerce. In: Twenty-Eighth European Conference on Information Systems (ECIS), Marrakesh, pp. 1–16 (2020)
32. Liao, Y., He, J.: Racial mirroring effects on human-agent interaction in psychotherapeutic conversations. In: 25th International Conference on Intelligent User Interfaces, Cagliari, pp. 430–442 (2020)
33. Sheehan, B., Jin, H.S., Gottlieb, U.: Customer service chatbots: anthropomorphism and adoption. J. Bus. Res. **115**, 14–24 (2020)
34. Patil, K., Kulkarni, M.S.: Artificial intelligence in financial services: customer chatbot advisor adoption. Int. J. Innov. Technol. Explor. Eng. **9**, 4296–4303 (2019)
35. Malhotra, Y., Galletta, D.F., Kirsch, L.J.: How endogenous motivations influence user intentions: beyond the dichotomy of extrinsic and intrinsic user motivations. J. Manag. Inf. Syst. **25**, 267–300 (2008)
36. Cook, J., Wall, T.: New work attitude measures of trust, organizational commitment and personal need non-fulfilment. J. Occup. Organ. Psychol. **53**, 39–52 (1980)
37. Venkatesh, V., Thong, J.Y.L., Xu, X.: Consumer acceptance and use of information technology: extending the unified theory of acceptance and use of technology. MIS Q. **36**, 157–178 (2012)

38. Childers, T.L., Carr, C.L., Peck, J., Carson, S.: Hedonic and utilitarian motivations for online retail shopping behavior. J. Retail. **77**, 511–535 (2001)
39. Rogers, E.M.: Diffusion of Innovations. Free Press, New York, London, Toronto, Sydney, Singapore (2003)
40. Melián-González, S., Gutiérrez-Taño, D., Bulchand-Gidumal, J.: Predicting the intentions to use chatbots for travel and tourism. Curr. Issues Tour. **0**, 1–19 (2019)
41. Richad, R., Vivensius, V., Sfenrianto, S., Kaburuan, E.R.: Analysis of factors influencing millennial's technology acceptance of chatbot in the banking industry in Indonesia. Int. J. Manag. **10**, 107–118 (2019)
42. Kasilingam, D.L.: Understanding the attitude and intention to use smartphone chatbots for shopping. Technol. Soc. **62**, 101280 (2020)
43. Laumer, S., Maier, C., Gubler, T.F.: Chatbot acceptance in healthcare: explaining user adoption of conversational agents for disease diagnosis. In: Twenty-Seventh European Conference on Information Systems (ECIS), Stockholm-Uppsala, pp. 1–18 (2019)
44. Araújo, T., Casais, B.: Customer acceptance of shopping-assistant chatbots. In: Rocha, Á., Reis, J.L., Peter, M.K., Bogdanović, Z. (eds.) Marketing and Smart Technologies. SIST, vol. 167, pp. 278–287. Springer, Singapore (2020). https://doi.org/10.1007/978-981-15-1564-4_26
45. Prakash, A.V., Das, S.: Intelligent conversational agents in mental healthcare services: a thematic analysis of user perceptions. Pacific Asia J. Assoc. Inf. Syst. **12**, 1–34 (2020)
46. Nadarzynski, T., Miles, O., Cowie, A., Ridge, D.: Acceptability of artificial intelligence (AI)-led chatbot services in healthcare: a mixed-methods study. Digit. Heal. **5**, 1–12 (2019)
47. Rubin, A.M.: Uses and gratifications. In: The SAGE Handbook of Media Processes and Effects, pp. 147–159 (2009)
48. Nadarzynski, T., Bayley, J., Llewellyn, C., Kidsley, S., Graham, C.A.: Acceptability of artificial intelligence (AI)-enabled chatbots, video consultations and live webchats as online platforms for sexual health advice. BMJ Sex. Reprod. Heal., 1–18 (2020)
49. Corr, P.J., Matthews, G.: The Cambridge Handbook of Personality Psychology. Cambridge University Press, Cambridge, New York, Melbourne, Madrid, Cape Town, Singapore, São Paulo, Delhi, Dubai, Tokyo (2009)
50. Mandrik, C.A., Bao, Y.: Exploring the concept and measurement of general risk aversion. Adv. Consum. Res. **32**, 531–539 (2005)
51. Benbasat, I., Taylor, R.N.: The Impact of cognitive styles on information system design. MIS Q. **2**, 43 (1978)
52. Wood, R., Bandura, A.: Social cognitive theory of organizational management. Acad. Manag. Rev. **14**, 361–384 (1989)
53. Bakke, S., Henry, R.: Unraveling the mystery of new technology use: an investigation into the interplay of desire for control, computer self-efficacy, and personal innovativeness. AIS Trans. Human-Comput. Interact. **7**, 270–293 (2015)
54. McCrae, R.R., Costa, P.T.: A five-factor theory of personality. In: Handbook of Personality: Theory and Research, Guilford, New York, pp. 139–153 (1999)
55. Oreg, S., Bayazit, M.: Prone to bias: development of a bias taxonomy from an individual differences perspective. Rev. Gen. Psychol. **13**, 175–193 (2009)
56. Chen, G., Gully, S.M., Eden, D.: Validation of a new general self-efficacy scale. Organ. Res. Methods. **4**, 62–83 (2001)

Voice Assistants in Voice Commerce: The Impact of Social Cues on Trust and Satisfaction

Fabian Reinkemeier[1]($\boxtimes$), Philipp Spreer[2], and Waldemar Toporowski[1]

[1] Chair of Marketing and Retail Management, University of Goettingen, Göttingen, Germany
`fabian.reinkemeier@wiwi.uni-goettingen.de,`
`wtoporo@uni-goettingen.de`
[2] elaboratum GmbH, Hamburg, Germany
`philipp.spreer@elaboratum.de`

Abstract. Voice assistants (VAs) such as Google Assistant and Amazon Alexa are spreading rapidly. They offer users the opportunity to order products online in a spoken dialogue (voice commerce). However, the widespread use of voice commerce is hindered by a lack of satisfaction and trust among VA users. This study investigates whether social cues and the accompanying perception of the VA's humanness and social presence can overcome existing obstacles in voice commerce. The empirical comparison ($N = 323$) of two VAs (low vs. high level of social cues) shows that providing VAs with more cues increases user satisfaction. Nevertheless, the analysis does not reveal entirely positive effects on perceived trust and its dimensions of benevolence, competence, and integrity. Surprisingly, users had less trust in the integrity of a VA with more social cues. For a differentiated view, a more in-depth analysis of the individual cues and their interactions is required.

Keywords: Voice assistants · Voice commerce · Social cues · Trust · Conversational agents

1 Introduction

Recent advancements in artificial intelligence are driving the rapid adoption of voice assistants (VAs). For example, 34.4% of U.S. adults have access to VAs via smart speakers, such as Amazon Echo or Google Home [1]. Companies have the opportunity to use voice commerce to establish an additional e-commerce channel through which their customers can interact with and purchase from the company using spoken language. Despite the manifold advantages of voice commerce, VA users seldom capitalize on this opportunity. Their trust in VAs in terms of successfully carrying out transactions is low and they consider VAs to lack competence and benevolence. Moreover, the interaction experience is perceived to be insufficiently satisfying [2, 3]. As a result, only 14.3% of VA users regularly use them to make purchases [1].

F. Ahlemann et al. (Eds.): WI 2021, LNISO 47, pp. 130–135, 2021.
https://doi.org/10.1007/978-3-030-86797-3_9

Trust and satisfaction are key determinants in traditional sales as well as in e-commerce for the success of product recommendations, providing pleasant shopping experiences, and building positive customer relationships [4, 5]. In a technology-based environment, trust and satisfaction are more difficult to achieve because humanness and social presence are attenuated [6]. According to the "computers are social actors" paradigm [7, 8], the use of social cues can lead VAs to come across as more humanlike and socially present interlocutors [8, 9]. This could in turn increase trust and satisfaction [6, 9]. With this in mind, this study addresses the following research question: *Does the use of social cues in VAs have an impact on user satisfaction and trust in voice commerce, and if so, to what extent?*

To answer this question, we conducted an extensive laboratory experiment with 323 participants who made a simulated purchase in real time using one of two differently designed VAs.

2 Theoretical Foundation and Hypotheses

2.1 Design of VAs with Social Cues

Companies can customize their VAs using social cues as design elements so that the dialog emulates human behavior [10]. For VAs without a visual user interface (e.g., smart speakers such as Amazon's Echo Dot), social cues can be classified into three categories: verbal (e.g., lexical diversity), auditory (e.g., vocal segregates such as "uh-huh"), and invisible (e.g., response time) [10]. Findings from research in other contexts [7, 11, 12] provide evidence that using such social cues triggers an increased perception of the machine having humanlike characteristics and social presence (defined as the perception of interacting with another human being; [13]) and may elicit social responses in users.

2.2 Perceptions of Satisfaction and Trust in Voice Commerce

When customers go to brick-and-mortar stores, trust and satisfaction can be generated based on social elements of face-to-face interactions [14, 15]. In voice commerce, social cues in a VA could take over this task, providing a more natural buying experience [14]. As design elements inspired by human interactions address fundamental social needs of individuals [16, 17], we postulate a first hypothesis (H_1): *The use of social cues has a positive effect on satisfaction with the VA.* According to research from other contexts (websites [13]; recommendation agents [6, 18]), creating a stronger social component in the interaction through the use of social cues could also positively influence perceived trust. Trust is a complex construct that should be captured multidimensionally [19, 20]: A VA's benevolence describes it acting in the user's best interest (Does the VA care about the user?), competence reflects its skills (Is the VA competent in what it does?), and integrity reflects its honesty (Does the VA mean what it says?) [20]. Consequently, we propose a second hypothesis (H_2): *The use of social cues has a positive effect on users' trust in the VA in terms of its benevolence (H_{2a}), competence (H_{2b}), and integrity (H_{2c}).*

3 Empirical Study

3.1 Data Collection

To test the hypotheses, we conducted a laboratory experiment with a between-subjects design in two groups. In the control group, participants interacted with a VA that exhibited only few social cues. In the experimental group, the VA provided various auditory (e.g., speech rate), invisible (e.g., response time), and verbal (e.g., praise) social cues. The VAs developed were based on Amazon Alexa and operationalized on Amazon Echo Dots; all references to Amazon or Alexa were eliminated to avoid any associations with the Amazon brand. Participants were randomly assigned to one of the two groups and asked to order a given book using spoken language via the respective VA. The purchase process included eight interaction points where participants had to make decisions on their own (including selecting a payment method). Afterward, participants completed a questionnaire on tablet PCs. The sample consisted of 323 participants (experimental group: $n = 168$, 50.0% female, $M_{age} = 24.72$ years; control group: $n = 155$, 50.3% female, $M_{age} = 24.64$ years).

3.2 Data Analysis and Results

We coded the independent variable as a binary variable (0 for a low level of social cues in the VA, 1 for a high level). Participants rated six items of perceived humanness [21] and five items of social presence [13]. The manipulation check shows that humanness and social presence of the VA were perceived to be significantly higher ($p < .001$) in the experimental group (confirming the findings from Sect. 2.1 for VAs). Trust in benevolence and competence were measured using three items each, while trust in integrity [18, 20] and satisfaction [22] were each measured with two items. All constructs show satisfactory results in terms of Cronbach's alpha and composite reliability (both criteria > .7; [23]) and average variance extracted (>.5; [24]). Furthermore, they meet the Fornell–Larcker criterion [25].

After the satisfactory testing of the quality criteria, we tested the hypotheses using t tests. The results (see Table 1) show a differentiated picture enabling us to confirm that the use of many social cues in a VA exerts positive effects on satisfaction (H$_1$) as well as trust in its benevolence (H$_{2a}$). However, contrary to the assumption of H$_{2b}$, this does not apply for trust in the VA's competence. H$_{2c}$ must also be rejected: Participants in the experimental group trusted significantly less in the VA's integrity than participants in the control group did.

Table 1. Descriptive statistics and *t*-test results

	Mean		*t* value $(df = 321)$	*p* value	Result
	Control	Treatment			
Satisfaction	4.145	4.640	− 3.092	.002	H$_1$ ✔
Trust: benevolence	4.417	5.242	− 5.692	.001	H$_{2a}$ ✔
Trust: competence	5.602	5.538	.457	.648	H$_{2b}$ ✖
Trust: integrity	5.213	4.583	4.015	.001	H$_{2c}$ ✖

Note. Standard deviations range from 1.239 to 1.494; standard errors range from 0.096 to 1.115; homogeneity of variance is available for all dependent variables (Levene's tests: $p > .05$). The results are not due to significant differences in the groups in terms of age, gender, or experience with VAs (for all variables: $p \geq .816$)

4   Discussion and Outlook

Our empirical comparison shows that the use of social cues and the resulting increased perception of the VA's humanness and social presence have a positive effect on satisfaction but influence the three components of trust in different directions, contrary to results from other research areas [6]. In terms of ability, namely trust in competence [19], our findings reveal no significant difference between VA variants. In terms of morality, however, users trust more humanlike VAs to act in their best interests in the purchase process (benevolence) but perceive the VA to be less honest (integrity). This loss of integrity might result from users perceiving a particular cue or cue combination as intentional manipulation [19] or from the blurring boundary between human and machine being perceived as suspicious and leading to distrust [26]. For companies that want to employ VAs, this results in a clear recommendation to precisely evaluate the effects of social cues as design elements of VAs and to use them in a differentiated manner rather than to pursue the general goal of increased humanness.

We are currently addressing this need for concretization in follow-up studies investigating the effects of individual social cues in isolation as well as specific cue combinations. The results should provide information about which types of social cues cause negative effects (e.g., on perceived integrity) or have the strongest positive effect in voice commerce and which factors are responsible for our initial results.

References

1. Voicebot: Smart Speaker Consumer Adoption Report, April 2020. https://research.voicebot.ai/download-smart-speaker-consumer-adoption-2020-executive-summary. Accessed 24 Aug 2020
2. Rzepka, C., Berger, B., Hess, T.: Why another customer channel? Consumers' perceived benefits and costs of voice commerce. In: Proceedings of the 53rd Hawaii International Conference on System Sciences (HICSS), pp. 4079–4088 (2020)

3. Tuzovic, S., Paluch, S.: Conversational commerce – a new era for service business development? In: Bruhn, M., Hadwich, K. (eds.) Service Business Development, pp. 81–100. Springer, Wiesbaden (2018). https://doi.org/10.1007/978-3-658-22426-4_4
4. Kim, D.J., Ferrin, D.L., Rao, H.R.: Trust and satisfaction, two stepping stones for successful e-commerce relationships. Longitud. Explor. Inf. Syst. Res. **20**, 237–257 (2009)
5. Xiao, B., Benbasat, I.: E-commerce product recommendation agents. Use, characteristics, and impact. MIS Q. **31**, 137 (2007)
6. Hess, T.J., Fuller, M., Campbell, D.E.: Designing interfaces with social presence: using vividness and extraversion to create social recommendation agents. J. Assoc. Inf. Syst. **10**, 889–919 (2009)
7. Nass, C., Moon, Y.: Machines and mindlessness: social reponses to computers. J. Soc. Issues **56**, 81–103 (2000)
8. Nass, C., Steuer, J., Tauber, E.R.: Computers are social actors. In: Proceedings of the ACM CHI Conference on Human Factors in Computing Systems, pp. 72–78 (1994)
9. Diederich, S., Janssen-Müller, M., Brendel, A.B., Morana, S.: Emulating empathetic behavior in online service encounters with sentiment-adaptive responses: insights from an experiment with a conversational agent. In: Proceedings of the 40th International Conference of Information Systems (ICIS), pp. 1–17 (2019)
10. Feine, J., Gnewuch, U., Morana, S., Maedche, A.: A taxonomy of social cues for conversational agents. Int. J. Hum Comput Stud. **132**, 138–161 (2019)
11. Diederich, S., Brendel, A.B., Kolbe, L.M.: Designing anthropomorphic enterprise conversational agents. Bus. Inf. Syst. Eng. **62**(3), 193–209 (2020). https://doi.org/10.1007/s12599-020-00639-y
12. Reeves, B., Nass, C.I.: The Media Equation. How People Treat Computers, Television, and New Media Like Real People and Places. CSLI Publications, Stanford (1996)
13. Gefen, D., Straub, D.: Managing user trust in B2C e-services. e-Service J. **2**, 7–24 (2003)
14. Bickmore, T.W., Picard, R.W.: Establishing and maintaining long-term human-computer relationships. ACM Trans. Comput. Hum. Interact. **12**, 293–327 (2005)
15. Crosby, L.A., Evans, K.R., Cowles, D.: Relationship quality in services selling. an interpersonal influence perspective. J. Mark. **54**, 68–81 (1990)
16. Benlian, A., Klumpe, J., Hinz, O.: Mitigating the intrusive effects of smart home assistants by using anthropomorphic design features: a multi-method investigation. Inf. Syst. J., 1–43 (2019)
17. Nass, C., Gong, L.: Speech interfaces from an evolutionary perspective. Commun. ACM **43**, 36–43 (2000)
18. Qiu, L., Benbasat, I.: Evaluating anthropomorphic product recommendation agents. a social relationship perspective to designing information systems. J. Manag. Inf. Syst. **25**, 145–181 (2009)
19. Xu, J., Cenfetelli, R.T., Aquino, K.: Do different kinds of trust matter? An examination of the three trusting beliefs on satisfaction and purchase behavior in the buyer–seller context. J. Strateg. Inf. Syst. **25**, 15–31 (2016)
20. McKnight, D.H., Choudhury, V., Kacmar, C.: Developing and validating trust measures for e-commerce. Integr. Typology Inf. Syst. Res. **13**, 334–359 (2002)
21. Holtgraves, T., Han, T.-L.: A procedure for studying online conversational processing using a chat bot. Behav. Res. Methods **39**, 156–163 (2007)
22. Han, S., Yang, H.: Understanding adoption of intelligent personal assistants. Ind. Manag. Data Syst. **118**, 618–636 (2018)
23. Nunnally, J.C., Bernstein, I.H.: The assessment of reliability. Psychom. Theory **3**, 248–292 (1994)

24. Bagozzi, R.P., Yi, Y.: On the evaluation of structural equation models. J. Acad. Mark. Sci. **16**, 74–94 (1988)
25. Fornell, C., Larcker, D.F.: Evaluating structural equation models with unobservable variables and measurement error. J. Mark. Res. **18**, 39–50 (1981)
26. Mori, M., MacDorman, K.F., Kageki, N.: The uncanny valley [from the field]. IEEE Robot. Autom. Mag. **19**, 98–100 (2012)

Design of Artificial Neural Networks for Traffic Forecasting in the Context of Smart Mobility Solutions

Christian Anschütz[✉], Jan Ibisch, Katharina Ebner, and Stefan Smolnik

University of Hagen, Chair of Business Information Systems, Hagen, Germany
christian.anschuetz@fernuni-hagen.de

Abstract. In this paper, artificial neural networks (ANNs) are developed to predict traffic volumes using traffic sensor data from the city of Darmstadt as a basis for future smart mobility solutions. After processing the acquired sensor data, information about the current traffic situation can be derived and events such as rush hour, weekends or holidays can be identified. Based on current research findings in the field of traffic forecasting using neural networks, our work shows the first best practices for modeling the traffic volume and an associated traffic forecast. A Long Short-Term Memory (LSTM) network is shown to be superior to a Deep Neural Network (DNN) in terms of prediction quality and prediction horizon. Furthermore, it is discussed whether the enrichment of the training data with additional time and weather data enables an increase of the forecast accuracy. In the sense of a design-theoretical approach, design requirements and design principles for the development of an ANN in a traffic-specific context are derived.

Keywords: Artificial neural networks · Long Short-Term Memory · Deep neural network · Traffic forecasting · Smart mobility

1 Introduction

The population in urban regions in Germany will continue to increase in the coming years [1]. Particularly large cities such as Berlin or Munich will experience strong population growth in the coming years due to the education and jobs available there [1]. This will be accompanied by an increasing burden on the road network due to congestion, traffic noise and emissions [2]. Concepts to meet the challenges in the field of traffic are summarized under the term Smart Mobility (SM) [3]. SM generally refers to an "intelligent, predictive and sustainable control of urban traffic with the help of modern information technologies and pursues the goal of reducing emissions, noise and stress for commuters and residents" [4]. Cities such as Duisburg, Essen, Munich, Bad Hersfeld or Darmstadt already use traffic telematics for traffic management in order to monitor and guide traffic via stationary traffic sensors and, for example, to provide commuters with traffic information. Traffic telematics can support SM solutions by providing data for traffic forecasts, enabling commuters and traffic authorities to react to traffic congestion

© The Author(s), under exclusive license to Springer Nature Switzerland AG 2021
F. Ahlemann et al. (Eds.): WI 2021, LNISO 47, pp. 136–149, 2021.
https://doi.org/10.1007/978-3-030-86797-3_10

in advance [5]. Traffic forecasting as part of an SM solution can help to distribute traffic evenly across different routes, time periods, and transportation modes [6, 7]. Potential congestion can also be preemptively counteracted, resulting in a reduction of environmental impacts (e.g., CO_2 emissions) [6, 8].

For the success of SM solutions, it is crucial that they not only show the acute traffic situation, but also provide a forecast that the user can follow [9]. In the context of a research project, we intend to develop a dynamic traffic forecast that can contribute to the achievement of an optimized traffic flow (e.g., the avoidance of traffic jams or an optimized traffic light switching). For this purpose, artificial neural networks (ANNs) for traffic forecasting are developed in this paper using traffic data from the city of Darmstadt [10]. ANN are suitable for handling non-linear problems and can therefore be used for forecasting in the traffic domain, which is characterized by fluctuations [11]. The development is done with historical sensor data and subsequent evaluation with test data [10]. The added value of the ANNs will be determined by comparison with other forecasting models [12]. Therefore, in the course of developing the ANNs, the following research questions arise:

1. *What design requirements and principles can be used to design ANNs for forecasting traffic in the context of SM solutions?*
2. *Which forecasting model is most appropriate for traffic forecasting?*

To answer these research questions, we first derive four relevant design requirements from the literature in this paper. Furthermore, taking into account the relevant literature on (Smart) Mobility and ANNs as well as building on the concrete development of an ANN, we derive seven design principles. Furthermore, we analyze which prediction model most accurately incorporates past sensor observations into the prediction and how the prediction accuracy develops with increasing prediction horizon. Furthermore, we will examine whether the forecast accuracy can be improved if the existing traffic data are enriched with additional time or weather characteristics. With our research, we can contribute to the development, design and implementation of ANNs, especially in urban and traffic-related contexts. Furthermore, we demonstrate the practical use of ANNs in a concrete application field (traffic), whereby we are convinced that the findings on the processing and use of sensor data in the context of ANNs are relevant for very many application fields, e.g. in the environment of smart cities or smart factories.

2   Related Literature

Two aspects are relevant for the scientific discourse in this paper: SM and the machine learning methodology of an ANN. First, the current state of research of these two aspects is reviewed and relevant research gaps and challenges are identified.

2.1   Smart Mobility

SM is defined in the scientific literature as "*intelligent, predictive and sustainable control of urban traffic with the help of modern information technologies and pursues the*

goal of reducing emissions, noise and stress for commuters and residents" [4] and is
*"applicable and usable for everyone regardless of location and region, regardless of
usage time and duration, regardless of individual abilities and budget"* [13]. The definition can be extended, especially for the inner-city context, to include "proactive and
sustainable management of urban traffic by engaging commuters" to achieve optimal
traffic flow in cities [9]. To enable "smart" mobility with SM solutions, existing solutions are optimized by using information and communication technologies [2, 13, 14].
An example of such technology is traffic telematics [15] with the ability to collect, process, and analyze traffic data via sensors [16]. Among other things, this can be used to
make traffic flows in cities more efficient [17], increase traffic safety [18], and reduce
traffic-related environmental pollution [19]. Some practical implementations in Germany can be found e.g. in Duisburg (public transport priority switching), Essen (digital
traffic signs), Bad Hersfeld (sensor-controlled parking monitoring), Munich (intelligent
mobility stations) or Darmstadt (optimization of traffic control) [16].

In the literature, further practical application scenarios are discussed to enrich traffic telematics systems with data and to optimize traffic [20–22]. One currently much-
discussed approach is traffic optimization by means of a neural network that is supplied
with data from traffic telematics (e.g., stationary sensors) and other data sources (e.g.,
mobile sensors) [6, 23]. The data can be used to make accurate traffic forecasts for urban
traffic [16, 24]. A traffic forecast model obtained from this data enables predictive traffic management, can be considered as a partial aspect of an SM solution, and can thus
contribute to achieving an optimal traffic flow [5, 6].

2.2 Traffic Forecasting Using Artificial Neural Networks

In recent years, judging from the increasing number of publications on the topic of traffic
flow prediction using ANNs, there has been a dynamic development in this field, made
possible by the availability of extensive training data and the development of powerful
hardware and algorithms [25]. The traffic flow prediction problem is, at its core, a time
series prediction problem in which the traffic at a future time is to be estimated using data
collected at monitoring stations in the past [24]. The traffic flow is influenced by time
(time of the day, day of the week, vacations, public holidays, events [26, 27]), weather
(rainfall, temperature [24, 28]), and partially random traffic obstructions (accidents,
closures, road works [29]). Parametric models from statistics and analytical approaches
have not been able to provide convincing predictions so far due to the stochastic and
non-linear characteristics of traffic flow [24, 27, 30]. ANNs, on the other hand, show to
be promising tools as they are able to integrate a variety of different data sources [27,
28], preserve states [24], achieve high prediction accuracy, as well as show robustness
to noisy data [30]. A more in-depth introduction to ANNs is provided by [25, 31], and
[32].

A drawback of using feedforward networks (networks with an input layer, one or
more hidden layers, and an output layer) for the prognosis of time series or other sequential data is their lack of memorability [31]. Each input flows forward to the output layer
independently of the previous input, and no state is passed on [25, 31]. However, this
approach is not suitable especially for the complex patterns in the traffic context, since
it is not sufficient to just pass the knowledge from layer to layer, but the multi-layered

dependencies have to be taken into account [7, 33]. To address this issue, the Recurrent Neural Networks (RNNs) class was created by extending ANNs with feedback loops [25]. As they iterate through the input sequences, they store a state composed of the data processed so far [34]. This can be likened to a feedback loop by which the current output of the neuron ("computational unit") is linked to the input of the next sequence. A disadvantage of this simple setup is that it is not able to learn long-term dependencies between sequences [34]. However, in the context of traffic flow prediction, delay effects often occur, i.e., there may be a longer period of time between the origin of the event and the perception of the consequences [24, 28]. To address these shortcomings, Hochreiter and Schmidhuber [34] developed Long Short-Term Memory (LSTM) networks. Unlike RNNs, these have internal gates that control the flow of information [25]. A key element of the LSTM cell is its cell state, which can be passed across multiple sequences without fading [34]. Therefore, LSTM architectures are particularly suited for time-series prediction [35] but are more computationally intensive as a result.

2.3 Requirements Analysis

In the later deployment phase, the ANN to be developed for traffic forecasting is to provide traffic forecasts and forward them to an SM solution (e.g., a smartphone app) so that the user can make an individual decision regarding his departure time, route, and/or means of transport [6, 10]. From this aspect and from the current state of research in the fields of SM and ANNs [16, 23, 28], different requirements (Design Requirement, DR) arise in the sense of a design-theoretical approach for the development of an ANN for traffic forecasting, as shown in Table 1 below [36].

Table 1. Requirements for the development of an ANN for traffic forecasting

Requirement		Description	References
DR1	Usefulness	The ANN should forecast traffic for a specific route and a suitable travel time window	[6, 7, 37]
DR2	Memorability	The ANN must be able to recognize complex traffic patterns and dependencies of the past in order to derive regularities for future forecasts	[3, 5, 8, 21, 27, 38]
DR3	Prediction quality	The ANN must predict the expected traffic with sufficient prediction quality (accuracy of at least 85%)	[11, 28, 39, 40]
DR4	Usability	The data transmitted by the ANN must be available in a form that can be interpreted by the user	[6, 29, 41]

3 Development and Training of an ANN for Traffic Forecasting

The Cross-Industry Standard Process for Data Mining (CRISP-DM) was used as a procedure for the development of the neural network [10]. This forms a standard procedure for
the creation of ANNs and is divided into the phases of business understanding (includes
the most important requirements from the areas of SM as well as ANNs and is presented
in Sect. 2.3), data understanding, data preparation, modeling, evaluation and deployment
of the application and therefore also forms the basis for our contribution [42, 43].

In the phase of data understanding and data preparation, we dealt in particular
with issues concerning the prediction quality (DR3), which depends significantly on
the database. The basis for our development of the ANN for traffic forecasting is the
traffic data of the city of Darmstadt, which consists of data from over 2,300 different
sensors of various types. This includes induction loop sensors, which are distributed
over numerous intersections and traffic lights in the city and which were also analyzed
as part of the data understanding. These sensors detect a vehicle or metal passing over
them through an electromagnetic coil under the road surface. The number of vehicles per
minute Z and the percent sensor occupancy per minute B are measured. The speed of the
object is not determined. For the neural network training data, only every fifth minute
was downloaded automatically using a script due to the large amount of data. Thus, each
hour consists of a total of twelve measurement points. A period of 23 weeks from the
year 2019 was used as a section of the data, since the fewest complete failures of the
sensor network were present here. Since at the beginning neither the occupancy rate B
nor the number Z alone could be used to make a reliable statement about the utilization
of the traffic network, the number and the occupancy rate were put in relation to each
other. This ratio can be interpreted as the dwell time D of a vehicle on the induction
sensor of the intersection or traffic light. The calculation is shown in formulas (1) and
(2) below:

$$D[sec] = (B \times 0.6)/c, Z > 0 \tag{1}$$

$$D[sec] = B \times 0.6, Z = 0 \tag{2}$$

Figure 1 shows an example of the average dwell time of a vehicle at a sensor. The
inner-city rush hour traffic from Monday to Friday can be clearly identified by the early
morning and evening peaks. Except for the earlier home rush hour traffic on Fridays,
a recurring pattern of traffic congestion can be identified for the weekdays [26]. On
Saturdays and Sundays, rush hour traffic is absent, and the traffic load remains below the
weekday average even at midday. Sufficient coverage of such recurrent patterns in the
data is important for the training (and subsequent prediction performance) of the ANN,
so that the resulting neuronal connections map these central patterns with appropriate
strength.

A frequent error type of the data from Darmstadt during the data preparation were
missing values or several days with sensor values of permanently 0 or 100 for the sensor
occupancy (in % of one minute). For correction, the data of a sensor were completely
discarded after calculation of the dwell time (in seconds based on sensor occupancy and
count value) as soon as more than 90% of all time points had the value 0 s or 20% of all

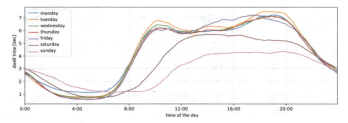

Fig. 1. Average dwell time of a vehicle per day of the week and time of day over the entire data

time points had the value 60 s for the dwell time. Individual missing data points in the time axis were linearly interpolated because a missing reading would be interpreted by an ANN as the absence of a vehicle (Fig. 2).

The sensor data were smoothed using median filtering to avoid jumps through the traffic light phases [27]. The entire process within the data processing serves to ensure sufficient prediction quality. The data used for training should be available with as few gaps as possible, should be interrupted as little as possible by disturbances, and should represent the expected patterns in traffic development (e.g. daily traffic peaks).

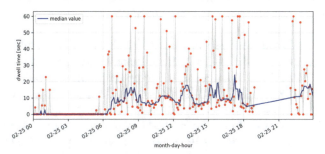

Fig. 2. The dwell time (blue) at sensor A008/D44 after median filtering and interpolation of the measured values (red)

Based on this, we have derived the following design principles (DP), which address DR3 in particular:

DP1: Individual missing sensor data points should be replaced using a workflow (e.g., interpolation). If missing sensor data points cannot be replaced, they must be removed from the datasets.
DP2: Some sensor data (e.g., at the transition of traffic light phases) should be smoothed to allow for meaningful prediction.
DP3: The data used for training must be available for a sufficiently long period of time to recurrently represent the expected patterns in traffic development.

For each data point, the day of the week was derived from the timestamp and coded as a categorical date [16]. Besides, the cyclic feature time of day was encoded by a sine as well as cosine column. Based on the finding of various researchers [8, 24, 27] that the integration of weather data has a positive effect on the forecast accuracies of ANNs, the mean daily temperature as well as minimum and maximum daily temperature and rainfall amount were integrated into the training data, such as those provided by Wetterkontor.

The total data used has a temporal extent T of 32,000 lines. This corresponds to about 111 days. Of this, 80% was used for training and 10% each was used for a validation and test data set. Each column represents a sensor or an additional feature such as day of the week or rainfall. The number of sensor columns used is 531. The number of additional time and weather columns is 13. The value range of the entries is scaled between [0; 1]. In order to arrive at useful forecasts in terms of DR1, forecast models were developed for the time periods of 15, 30 and 60 min. On the one hand, these forecasts can serve the road users to reach their destination stress-free and fast, and on the other hand, they can provide important insights for future traffic planning in cities. As an input pattern for the forecast, the ANN has 36 rows (three hours) of a section of the training matrix randomly selected in the training. For the paper, a subset of ten sensors was used as the output to be predicted. This leads us to the following design principles (cf. DR1 and DR3):

DP4: The traffic data used for training should be enriched with other data that have an influence on the system to be forecast (for traffic, e.g., weather, vacations).
DP5: The targeted forecast horizon must be far enough to allow actors in the system being forecast to react meaningfully to the forecast.

Two basic models are used as a basis for comparison of ANN results: (1) the "Historical Average" (HD) model [44], where the average dwell time at the same time of day and on the same day of the week is looked up for the value to be forecast (Fig. 1); (2) the "Naive Random Walk" (NRW) [45] is used. Here, the traffic flow in the future is predicted using the current value. In the context of modeling, the first ANN has a flattening layer, which transforms the 36×544 matrix to a vector with 19,584 entries. The hidden layers are 600, 300, and 100 neurons in three layers with the rectified linear unit (ReLU) activation function [46]. The output layer has ten neurons with ReLU activation function. Due to the multiple hidden layers, we refer to the model as Deep Neural Network (DNN) in the evaluation. To address the memory (DR2), the second developed ANN has LSTM cells, hereafter referred to as LSTM. The LSTM layer consists of 600 cells and output layer contains ten neurons with ReLU activation function. For both ANNs, experiments with additional layers did not lead to increasing prediction quality on the validation data, but in some cases even to overfitting [31]. In order to evaluate the prediction quality of the prediction models, we consider the Mean Absolute Error (MAE) [33] and the Root Mean Squared Error (RMSE) [7]. In addition, we derive the following design principle with respect to DR2 from the above:

DP6: The ANN design must take into account longer-term dependencies between two relevant measurement points in the system to be forecast (e.g., delay effects in traffic).
The complete project files are available online on the GitHub[1] platform.

---

[1] Available at https://github.com/jaib0001/TrafficFlowPrediction.

4   Results

After training the DNN, the error measures of the validation data for the different architectures and prediction horizons are compared and evaluated in Fig. 3. The NRW is able to outperform the other models only for a prediction horizon of 15 min. As expected, the error values of the NRW increase sharply with larger prediction horizon. The historical average shows itself to be a robust base model, which can only be consistently undercut by the LSTM network in the error measure, regardless of the forecast horizon. The DNN succeeds in achieving constant error values for all prediction horizons. It is on the level of the historical average. For the forecast horizons of 30 and 60 min, the LSTM network shows a significantly lower error measure than all other models. For the LSTM network, a comparatively higher and constant forecast accuracy over wide forecast horizons can be observed for the data.

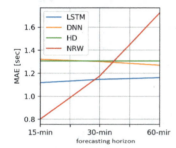

Intervall		HD	NRW	DNN	LSTM
15-Minute	MAE	1,307	0,802	1,301	1,118
	RMSE	-	-	7,623	6,723
30-Minute	MAE	1,307	1,175	1,320	1,147
	RMSE	-	-	7,273	7,160
60-Minute	MAE	1,307	1,723	1,358	1,162
	RMSE	-	-	8,940	7,193

Fig. 3. A comparison of the MAE for all models and forecast horizons

For further illustration, Fig. 4 shows a comparison of the forecast between the LSTM network and the DNN for a forecast horizon of 60 min. For this purpose, a forecast of the dwell time at sensor A008_10 was made for each time of day. The occurring deviations between all ten sensors and the real values were calculated using the MAE.

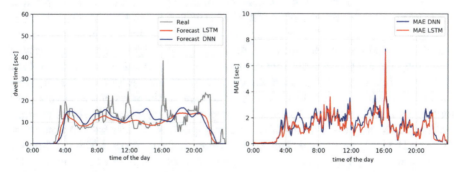

Fig. 4. Forecast and MAE of the LSTM and the DNN for sensor A008_10 on 06/17/2019

A comparison of the two figures shows that the LSTM network depicts the morning rush hour better than the DNN in the forecast. In the selected example, a strong peak in the dwell time at the intersection becomes visible around 16:00. Both networks do not succeed in forecasting this peak, which is noticeable in a strongly deflecting error curve. These random peaks due to unforeseen events (accidents, events, severe weather) are also described by Polson et al. [27] and cannot be predicted by the models. In the following, the influence of the additional time and weather characteristics on the forecast accuracy of the DNN and LSTM networks is investigated (Table 2). For this purpose, the networks were trained under different configurations and the error measures of the validation data were compared.

Table 2. Influence of additional features with a forecast horizon of 60 min

		With add. features	Without add. features	Time-features only	Weather-features only
LSTM	MAE	1,162	1,155	1,164	1,173
	RMSE	7,193	7,171	7,543	7,267
DNN	MAE	1,358	1,226	1,226	1,314
	RMSE	8,941	7,599	7,676	7,442

The results for configurations with and without additional data are indifferent. For the LSTM network, no significant change in the error measure can be seen when the additional features are omitted. The DNN even shows a partial improvement of the error measures under omission of the time and weather features.

5   Discussion

As part of the development of an ANN for traffic forecasting, it was possible to create a forecasting model using proven architectures and procedures from the field of traffic forecasting by means of the traffic sensor data of the city of Darmstadt. The ANN data can be used to provide the user of an SM solution with situation-related and individually tailored traffic forecasts. The modeling was preceded by extensive preparation of the sensor data. The LSTM network was able to achieve the highest forecast accuracy of all developed models. Since the influences of the individual features between DNN and LSTM network are mostly comparable, the forecast advantages of the LSTM network cannot be explained by this alone. An examination of the time axis of the network input for the two models using the "permutation importance" approach [47] shows in Fig. 5 that the LSTM network also considers sensor acquisitions further back in time in the forecast. The DNN, on the other hand, focuses more on the recent past. This confirms the thesis expressed by Polson et al. [27] that an LSTM network is able to incorporate the longer-term temporal dependencies of traffic flow into the forecast. Their observation that more recent observations have a stronger influence than older ones can be confirmed for both architectures [27].

Fig. 5. Comparison of the influence of individual time points in the network input. The lower the index T, the older the sensor acquisition

The analysis of the influence of additional features by means of "permutation importance" showed that especially the time of day coded as sine and cosine columns is significant for the neural network. In addition, the information about the day of the week Friday seems to offer a clear added value (Fig. 6). A comparison with Fig. 1 shows an almost identical course of the dwell time for Friday compared to the other weekdays. Towards the afternoon, however, this is disturbed by the earlier home transport. It can be speculated that this feature is so important for the ANN because it is the only one that provides a clue to distinguish the otherwise uniform weekdays. This allows the network to avoid a strong misprediction for Friday afternoon. The weekdays Saturday and Sunday provide added value, since their patterns are fundamentally very different from the other weekdays. The error measures of the neural networks were hardly affected by omitting the additional time and weather features (Fig. 6) during training.

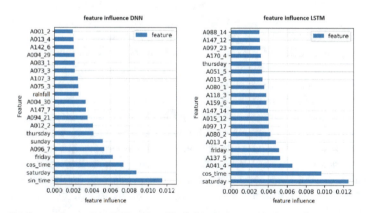

Fig. 6. Comparison of the influence of individual characteristics in the network input

However, an analysis was able to show that the time and weather characteristics, if included in the training of the network, strongly influence the forecast. This seems contradictory at first. However, the hardly measurable effect of omitting these features can be explained by substitution effects. If the network is trained without the additional features, it uses alternative features (i.e., sensors) with similar explanatory power instead. Thus, there are no measurable differences in prediction accuracy. Our analyses revealed that the fewer sensor locations included, the more the two ANNs rely on the additional features. This means that for the comparatively extensive sensor data from Darmstadt, additional enrichment is not necessary. For only a few sensor locations, such as in some of the papers studied (e.g., [23] or [27]), the inclusion of additional features achieves an improvement in forecast accuracy. From the extensive dataset of the city of Darmstadt, only selected data was used for training in a first step. Thus, the data still contains potential for increasing the forecast accuracy and generalization capability of the models by training with data over several months and years. The architectures and their hyperparameters were determined on the basis of the literature studied (e.g. [44–46]). However, the traffic forecasts of the ANN are not easily usable for a subsequent SM solution. For this purpose, the data must be appropriately processed after being provided by the ANN and made available via interface for an SM solution (cf. DR4), which leads us to the following design principle:

DP7: The traffic forecasts have to be processed for subsequent applications.

The explained findings based on the DRs and DPs are to be subjected to further investigations and should finally be transferred into a comprehensive design theory including associated design features [6, 36].

6   Summary and Outlook

In this paper, ANNs were tested for their suitability to develop a forecasting model for traffic congestion based on data from the city of Darmstadt. From the sensor data processed for this purpose, information about the current traffic situation could be derived and events such as rush hour or public holidays could be identified. By analyzing the current state of research, it was possible to identify methods that were applied to the problem. After evaluation of the models, the LSTM network was shown to be superior to the DNN and the basic models in predicting the traffic situation to be expected in the near future. Further analysis showed that the LSTM network also takes into account sensor measurements made in the past, which explains the advantage over the DNN. As expected, all models showed a decreasing forecast accuracy with increasing forecast horizon. Contrary to expectations, a comparison of the error measures for enriching the traffic data with additional time or weather characteristics did not yield any further improvements in forecast accuracy. In the context of further research, however, the evaluation of additional architectures and hyperparameters for the traffic context is a possibility. The optimization of the models as well as their final integration into a comprehensive SM solution also yield concrete opportunities for further research.

References

1. Deschermeier, P.: Die Großstädte im Wachstumsmodus. Stochastische Bevölkerungsprognosen für Berlin, München und Frankfurt am Main bis 2035. IW (2016)
2. Benevolo, C., Dameri, R.P., D'Auria, B.: Smart mobility in smart city. In: Torre, T., Braccini, A.M., Spinelli, R. (eds.) Empowering Organizations. LNISO, vol. 11, pp. 13–28. Springer, Cham (2016). https://doi.org/10.1007/978-3-319-23784-8_2

3. Schmidt, W., Borgert, S., Fleischmann, A., Heuser, L., Müller, C., Schweizer, I.: Smart Traffic Flow. HMD **52**, 585–596 (2015)
4. Wolter, S.: Smart Mobility- Intelligente Vernetzung der Verkehrsangebote in Großstädten. In: Proff H., Schönharting J., Schramm D., Ziegler J. (eds.) Zukünftige Entwicklungen in der Mobilität, pp. 527–548. Gabler Verlag (2012). https://doi.org/10.1007/978-3-8349-7117-3_42
5. Mohammed, O., Kianfar, J.: A machine learning approach to short-term traffic flow prediction: a case study of interstate 64 in Missouri. In: 2018 IEEE International Smart Cities Conference (ISC2), pp. 1–7. IEEE (2018)
6. Ebner, K., Anschütz, C., Smolnik, S.: STREAM – Ein Smart-Mobility-System zur langfristigen Einbindung von Pendlern. In: Proff (Hg.) 2020 – Neue Dimensionen in der Mobilität, pp.. 545–558 (2020)
7. Lv, Y., Duan, Y., Kang, W., Li, Z., Wang, F.-Y.: Traffic flow prediction with big data: a deep learning approach. IEEE Trans. Intell. Transport. Syst., 865–873 (2014)
8. Zhang, D., Kabuka, M.R.: Combining weather condition data to predict traffic flow: a GRU based deep learning approach. In: 2017 IEEE 15th International Conference on Dependable, Autonomic and Secure Computing, 15th International Conference on Pervasive Intelligence and Computing, 3rd International Conference on Big Data Intelligence and Computing and Cyber Science and Technology Congress(DASC/PiCom/DataCom/CyberSciTech), pp. 1216–1219. IEEE (2017)
9. Ebner, K., Mattes, P., Smolnik, S.: Are you responsible for traffic congestion? A systematic review of the socio-technical perspective of smart mobility services. In: Proceedings of the 52nd Hawaii International Conference on System Sciences. Hawaii International Conference on System Sciences (2019)
10. Wirth, R., Hipp, J.: CRISP-DM: towards a standard process model for data mining (2000)
11. Bogenberger, K., Belzner, H., Kates, R.: Ein hybrides Modell basierend auf einem Neuronalen Netz und einem ARIMA-Zeitreihenmodell zur Prognose lokaler Verkehrskenngroessen. In: Ágnes, V.T. (ed.) Egy megkésett vallomás. Z-Press [Miskolc] (2009)
12. Altendeitering, M., Pflügler, C., Schreieck, M., Fröhlich ,S., Wiesche, M., Krcmar, H.: Prognose von Parkplatzdaten. In: Wiesche, M., Sauer, P., Krimmling, J., Krcmar, H. (eds.) Management digitaler Plattformen. Informationsmanagement und digitale Transformation, pp. 193–206. Springer, Wiesbaden (2018). https://doi.org/10.1007/978-3-658-21214-8_13
13. Anschütz, C., Ebner, K., Smolnik, S.: Spielerisch zum Ziel: Initiale Designprinzipien für die nachhaltige Gestaltung von Smart-Mobility-Apps auf Basis einer Marktanalyse. In: WI2020 Zentrale Tracks, pp. 538–553. GITO Verlag (2010)
14. Kagermann, H.: Die Mobilitätswende: Die Zukunft der Mobilität ist elektrisch, vernetzt und automatisiert. In: Hildebrandt, A., Landhäußer, W. (eds.) CSR und Digitalisierung. Management-Reihe Corporate Social Responsibility, pp. 357–371. Springer, Heidelberg (2017). https://doi.org/10.1007/978-3-662-53202-7_27
15. Tcheumadjeu, L.C.T., Suske, D., Sohr, A., Bei, X.: Traffic information systems for smart mobility as part of smart cities. In: International Symposium on Smart Mobility for Smarter Cities (SmartCity 2016) (2016)
16. Jiber, M., Lamouik, I., Ali, Y., Sabri, M.A.: Traffic flow prediction using neural network. In: 2018 International Conference on Intelligent Systems and Computer Vision (ISCV), pp. 1–4. IEEE (2018)
17. Rathore, M.M., Son, H., Ahmad, A., Paul, A.: Real-time video processing for traffic control in smart city using Hadoop ecosystem with GPUs. Soft. Comput. **22**(5), 1533–1544 (2017). https://doi.org/10.1007/s00500-017-2942-7
18. Astarita, V., Festa, D.C., Giofrè, V.P.: Mobile systems applied to traffic management and safety: a state of the art. Procedia Comput. Sci. **134**, 407–414 (2018)

19. Meroux, D., Telenko, C., Jiang, Z., Fu, Y.: Towards design of sustainable smart mobility services through a cloud platform. In: SAE Technical Paper Series. SAE International400 Commonwealth Drive, Warrendale, PA, United States (2020)
20. Chao, Q., et al.: A survey on visual traffic simulation: models, evaluations, and applications in autonomous driving. Comput. Graph. Forum **39**, 287–308 (2020)
21. Wilkie, D., Sewall, J., Lin, M.C.: Transforming GIS data into functional road models for large-scale traffic simulation. IEEE Trans. Visual Comput. Graph. **18**, 890–901 (2012)
22. Ameli, M., Lebacque, J.-P., Leclercq, L.: Improving traffic network performance with road banning strategy: a simulation approach comparing user equilibrium and system optimum. Simul. Model. Pract. Theory **99**, 101995 (2020)
23. Bojarski, M., Yeres, P., Choromanska, A., Choromanski, K., Firner, B., Jackel, L., Muller, U.: Explaining how a deep neural network trained with end-to-end learning steers a car (2017)
24. Jia, Y., Wu, J., Xu, M.: Traffic flow prediction with rainfall impact using a deep learning method. J. Adv. Transp. **2017** (2017)
25. Goodfellow, I., Bengio, Y., Courville, A.: Deep Learning. MIT Press, Cambridge (2016)
26. Schneider, W., Toplak, W.: Verkehrsprognosen mit Visuellem Data Mining und Künstlicher Intelligenz. Elektrotech. Inftech. **125**, 232–237 (2008)
27. Polson, N., Sokolov, V.: Deep learning for short-term traffic flow prediction. Transp. Res. Part C Emerg. Technol. **79**, 1–17 (2017)
28. Essien, A., Petrounias, I., Sampaio, P., Sampaio, S.: Improving urban traffic speed prediction using data source fusion and deep learning. In: 2019 IEEE International Conference on Big Data and Smart Computing (BigComp), pp. 1–8. IEEE (2019)
29. Guo, J., Wang, Z., Chen, H.: On-line multi-step prediction of short term traffic flow based on GRU neural network. In: Proceedings of the 2nd International Conference on Intelligent Information Processing – IIP 2017, pp. 1–6. ACM Press, New York (2017)
30. Liu, Y., Zheng, H., Feng, X., Chen, Z.: Short-term traffic flow prediction with Conv-LSTM. In: 2017 9th International Conference on Wireless Communications and Signal Processing (WCSP), pp. 1–6. IEEE (2017)
31. Chollet, F.: Deep Learning with PYTHON. Manning, Shelter Island (2018)
32. Duda, R.O., Hart, P.E., Stork, D.G.: Pattern Classification. Wiley-Interscience, Hoboken (2012)
33. Wang, W., Bai, Y., Yu, C., Gu, Y., Feng, P., Wang, X., Wang, R.: A network traffic flow prediction with deep learning approach for large-scale metropolitan area network. In: NOMS 2018 - 2018 IEEE/IFIP Symposium, pp. 1–9. IEEE (2018)
34. Hochreiter, S., Schmidhuber, J.: Long short-term memory. Neural Comput. **9**, 1735–1780 (1997)
35. Graves, A., Liwicki, M., Fernández, S., Bertolami, R., Bunke, H., Schmidhuber, J.: A novel connectionist system for unconstrained handwriting recognition. IEEE Trans. Pattern Anal. Mach. Intell. **31**, 855–868 (2009). Seiten
36. Jones, D., Gregor, S.: The anatomy of a design theory. JAIS **8**, 312–335 (2007)
37. Pessa, E.: Neural network models. In: Management Association, I.R. (ed.) Nature-Inspired Computing. Concepts, Methodologies Tools, and Applications, pp. 368–395 (2017)
38. Fajtl, J., Argyriou, V., Monekosso, D., Remagnino, P.: AMNet: memorability estimation with attention (2018)
39. Schimbinschi, F., Nguyen, X.V., Bailey, J., Leckie, C., Vu, H., Kotagiri, R.: Traffic forecasting in complex urban networks: leveraging big data and machine learning. In: 2015 IEEE International Conference on Big Data (Big Data), pp. 1019–1024. IEEE (2015)
40. Biancofiore, F., et al.: Recursive neural network model for analysis and forecast of PM10 and PM2.5. Atmos. Pollut. Res. **8**, 652–659 (2017)
41. Kim, Y., Soo Choi, E., Seo, J., Choi, W.-S., Lee, J., Lee, K.: A novel approach to predicting human ingress motion using an artificial neural network. J. Biomech. **84**, 27–35 (2019)

42. Marban, O., Mariscal, G., Segovia, J.: A data mining & knowledge discovery process model. 1. In: Data Mining and Knowledge Discovery in Real Life Applications. IntechOpen, Rijeka (2009)
43. Nodeh, M.J., Calp, M.H., Şahin, İ: Analyzing and processing of supplier database based on the cross-industry standard process for data mining (CRISP-DM) algorithm. In: Hemanth, D.J., Kose, U. (eds.) ICAIAME 2019. LNDECT, vol. 43, pp. 544–558. Springer, Cham (2020). https://doi.org/10.1007/978-3-030-36178-5_44
44. Oh, S.-d., Kim, Y.-j., Hong, J.-s.: Urban traffic flow prediction system using a multifactor pattern recognition model. IEEE Intell. Transp. Syst. (IEEE Trans. Intell. Transp. Syst.) **16**, 2744–2755 (2015). Seiten
45. Kang, D., Lv, Y., Chen, Y.-y.: Short-term traffic flow prediction with LSTM recurrent neural network. In: 2017 IEEE 20th International Conference on Intelligent Transportation Systems (ITSC), pp. 1–6. IEEE (2017)
46. Zhang, Y.-D., Pan, C., Chen, X., Wang, F.: Abnormal breast identification by nine-layer convolutional neural network with parametric rectified linear unit and rank-based stochastic pooling. J. Comput. Sci. **27**, 57–68 (2018)
47. Ramachandran, R.: Using neural networks to predict icephobic performance (2020)

Sorry, I Can't Understand You! – Influencing Factors and Challenges of Chatbots at Digital Workplaces

Raphael Meyer von Wolff[(✉)], Sebastian Hobert, and Matthias Schumann

University of Goettingen, Goettingen, Germany
{r.meyervonwolff,shobert,mschuma1}@uni-goettingen.de

Abstract. Chatbot research is currently on its rise since many researchers focus on this topic from different perspectives. Thereby, the focus mostly lies on application areas that originate from business contexts. However, application areas and potential outcomes are already subject to research. The business perspective on influencing factors for an application of chatbots at workplaces or their corresponding challenges is underrepresented as less to none research exists. Therefore, we targeting this research gap by an empirical cross-section interview study with 29 domain experts for the application of chatbots at the digital workplace. We categorize the findings with an extension of the TOE-Framework and show that in the core categories of technological, organizational, individual, and environmental 11 sub-influencing factors exist. Furthermore, we also identify 36 challenges, which are relevant in the particular influencing factors.

Keywords: Chatbot · Digital workplace · Influencing factor · Challenge

1 Introduction

Currently, a new research trend emerged: the application of chatbots, which are artificial intelligence and natural language-based human-computer interfaces, to support workers and employees in their daily work [1, 2]. This trend is driven by the current progressing digitalization of society in general and the redesign of the workplace to a digitalized future workplace in specific. Established formerly paper-based working practices vanish, and more and more innovative and digital technologies are used for current daily work tasks. Therefore, almost all working tasks of employees are affected by integrating new technologies [3–6]. As a negative consequence, through the increasing use of information systems and corresponding information sources, the acquisition of information and execution of tasks is becoming obstructed. Regardless of the spread of new and smart systems, the rising information and application overload leads to an increase in the time for searching, editing, using, and sharing of information. Instead of improving work and supporting the employees, this may affect the workers' productivity negatively [6–9]. Therefore, prior research suggests providing user-centric information systems, like chatbots, to assist employees in their daily work by automating tasks or filtering and delivering only the necessary information [1, 10]. Especially for customer service, sales, or financial advisory, these systems are already being used to provide ease of use, faster, and high-quality services [11]. Particularly, the human-like design should contribute to a positive perception and service experience and yet offers the feeling of personal contact [12].

However, the current research mostly focuses on this topic through design research studies where artifacts are published, or their impact, on mostly single application areas, is evaluated [13]. Nonetheless, first empirical studies exist in the chatbots research domain, e.g., on trust, gender, or usability aspects. Overall, however, there is still a lot of research potential, which is due in particular to the novelty/innovativeness. In particular, the business- or management-perspective has received little or no attention so far. Especially, factors influencing or preventing adoption decisions need to be considered, as otherwise, chatbots will not be applied in business contexts, and positive results of the design studies cannot be achieved. Furthermore, the challenges of the technology should be taken into account, as these lead to efforts, which must be made during introduction and operation. Therefore, only if both influencing factors and challenges are known, they can be tackled appropriately by researchers or practice to enable and support the adoption of chatbots at digital workplaces [14]. However, to the best of our knowledge, this is so far only addressed to some extent by [15] for the insurance sector, and, therefore, a research gap for applications at the digital workplace.

Thus, as the initial adoption of chatbots is first of all a corporate decision instead of being based on individual intentions, we examine the issue at the business level [16]. Hereto, we survey the hindering or supporting factors of a chatbot application at the workplace and their underlying challenges. For this, we conducted an empirical cross-section interview study with domain experts, and use an extension of the well-established TOE-framework [14] for the categorization. In doing so, we want to assign influencing factors and challenges to the categories and assess their influences. For this research, we have oriented ourselves on the open research questions on adoption issues in [13], which are answered in the following:

RQ1: *Which factors influence the adoption of chatbots at digital workplaces?*
RQ2: *What challenges arise when applying chatbots at digital workplaces?*

Hereto, the remainder of this paper is structured as follows. First, we point out related research and briefly describe the theoretical framework. Second, we present our research design and corresponding findings. Afterward, we analyze our findings and discuss them. We finish the paper with the limitations and a brief conclusion.

2   Related Research

2.1   Chatbots at Digital Workplaces

Chatbots are a special kind of information system that uses artificial intelligence and machine learning technologies to provide a natural language human-computer interface. Often the terms, conversational agent, or personal assistant are used synonymously [2, 17]. Users can communicate by writing or speaking with a chatbot to carry out (work) tasks or acquire information. The input is processed by natural language processing and further processed. Hereto, the chatbot is integrated with the enterprise systems or databases to provide the functionalities and information [18, 19].

Hereby, chatbots are used in different domains, like customer support or for digital workplace tasks. However, the latter is used often nowadays but not defined commonly. Besides, the by now widely established term of knowledge work is often equated with this concept [6]. Based on corresponding research, we found that the characteristics of the digital workplace are tasks on information, e.g., searching, transforming, or communicating, with a high focus on information systems. Besides, the digital workplace is often location-independent and mobile. Therefore, a digital workplace is not limited to a physical place. Instead, it is a (virtual) confluence of work tasks, processes, applications systems, or technologies, and people [5, 6, 20]. Thus, in this research, we aim at these information-intensive or knowledge work tasks instead of production-processes [21].

Since the last years, different research for the application of chatbots in the different domains was published. For example, mostly prototypes, e.g., for information acquisition [7] or customer service [22] were published. Furthermore, some researchers address more general or meta-level research on chatbots. To mention some, e.g., [23] address the conversation between humans and chatbots and derive a taxonomy of social cues, which a chatbot should encompass. Also, researchers focus on user aspects in the context of chatbots. For example, [24] survey the user experience and motivation when using chatbots and show a general acceptance for chatbots. However, they highlight the importance of handling inquiries efficiently and adequately. A slightly different approach was presented by [25] who examined factors that influence the authenticity of chatbots and, thus, influence the desired outcome like service use and quality or word of mouth. Furthermore, already some overviewing articles for application areas, technological aspects, and so on, were found in the scientific knowledge base, e.g., [2] or [26]. However, despite the different approaches analyzing single aspects, an organizational-level or rather a company-level survey of criteria influencing an application positively or disturbing is only barely studied [13]. Prior to this study, this was only carried out for the insurance sector to survey supporting or hindering adoption factors of chatbots [15]. Thus, a research gap is existent, which should be addressed in order to allow comprehensive research on countermeasures, or on how to successfully introduce chatbots in workplaces.

2.2 Theoretical Background

In today's research, different methodologies are used for the assessment of hindering or supporting factors for the application of technologies in companies. Especially the technology-organization-environment (TOE) framework by [14] has often been used to identify factors affecting adoption decisions [27]. Hereby, *technology* describes internal or external technologies relevant to the company as well as the existent IT-infrastructure [14]. The *organizational* factors, on the contrary, describe organizational measures like decision making structures, size, working cultures, or readiness for IT adoptions [28]. Lastly, the *environmental* domain is the arena in which a company conducts its business like suppliers, competitors, or the government [14]. This framework was applied for example by [29] for assessing influencing or hindering factors of e-businesses at the firm level. Based on a survey, the authors categorized the findings along the TOE-dimensions and calculated the corresponding influence of the dimension. Especially [28] or [30] are to be highlighted, where the TOE-Framework is extended by an *individual* (I) domain. This extension covers factors of future users or decision-makers for the adoption. Thus, these influences based on the employees or rather a user are explicitly shown in order to be addressed.

In the following, we use this extended TOIE-Framework to categorize the findings. In doing so, we want to identify and assess the supporting or hindering factors of chatbot applications at digital workplaces on an business-level [16].

3   Research Design

To identify influencing factors on the adoption of chatbots at digital workplaces (*RQ1*) and underlying challenges (*RQ2*), we conducted a qualitative empirical interview study based on [31] and [32] and followed a three-step research process:

First, we selected potential interview partners. Hereto, we considered managers as domain experts who deal with the future workplace design taking into account the use of natural-language assistance systems like chatbots. To enrich the quality of the findings, the corresponding companies should at least plan to use chatbots or develop them on their own, e.g., software firms. Besides, the experts should already have at least a few years of working practice. To ensure heterogeneity and to achieve a comprehensive cross-section for the research area, we did not limit the industry sector or the company size. By doing so, we want to attain generalizable results, which can be easily reused in further research. Based on the criteria and personal contacts or internet searches, we contacted 68 experts via e-mail of whom 29 experts participated in 27 interview cases (see Table 1).

Table 1. Description of the experts who participated in the study

Case	Expert	Industry	Case	Expert	Industry
01	01	ICT	15	16	ICT
02	02	ICT	16	17	Other manufacturing
03	03	Automotive Engineering	17	18	Other services
04	04	Automotive Engineering	18	19	Finance & Insurance
05	05	ICT	19	20	Other services
06	06	Other services	20	21	ICT
07	07	Finance & Insurance	21	22	ICT
08	08	ICT	22	23	ICT
09	09	Finance & Insurance	23	24	ICT
10	10	Finance & Insurance	24	25 & 26	ICT
11	11	ICT	25	27	Other services
12	12	ICT	26	28	ICT
13	13 & 14	Pharmaceuticals	27	29	Finance & Insurance
14	15	Raw Materials			

Second, we conducted the interviews face-to-face or via conference systems during a four-month period. We used a semi-structured interview guideline as a basis to be able to leave enough room for own ideas or experts' opinions. According to the theoretical saturation [33], we stopped the process as we could not reveal new insights. The interviews were recorded and transcribed if our privacy policy was accepted.

Third, we coded and analyzed our 27 interview cases using a structured content analysis approach. Hereto, the coding was done by two researchers independently using continuous analysis of the transcripts followed by a discussion and an assignment of the codes to the core topics (*RQ1* and *RQ2*) [34]. Lastly, we used the TOIE-framework for categorization and assigned the identified factors and challenges. As the interviews were conducted in German, we translated the final coding into English while preserving the meaning.

4 Findings

Based on the described research design, we coded 597 quotes and statements for the core categories in the 27 interview case transcripts. According to the Technology-Organizational-Individual-Environment Framework of [28] and [30], we classified the influencing factors or challenges as technological, organizational, individual, and environmental. Based on the 27 cases, we identified 11 influencing factors along with corresponding 36 challenges for the adoption and operation of chatbots at digital workplaces (see Fig. 1), which we describe afterward. In the following, the numbers are related to the interview cases instead of the experts. An overview of the influencing factors and the challenges, along with exemplary quotes from the interviews, is available in an online appendix at http://bit.ly/CBInfC.

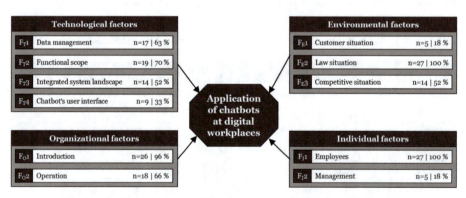

Fig. 1. Identified chatbots' influencing factors (n's based on the 27 cases)

4.1 Technological Factors

We identified four technological influencing factors and corresponding challenges (see Table 2). These represent characteristics of the technology or the enterprise system landscape, which have to be considered for the adoption of chatbots.

The first influencing factor for a chatbot application is the existing **data management** [F_T1] in businesses. In particular, the participants specified that a structured knowledge and data infrastructure that can be accessed via interfaces, which are designed for natural language, is necessary so that the chatbot can use them to generate statements. However, besides these interfaces, especially the creation of the knowledge base is associated with challenges, as existing information is in an inappropriate form or even non-existing [$C_T1.1$]. Additionally, as the chatbot grows over time, further challenges arise for the continuous training and maintenance of the underlying data. Particularly in the customer support area, another challenge arises. As noted by the experts, problems exist when the chatbot statements are not coherent with the statements of real employees, e.g., when the datasets are not up to date or otherwise adulterated [$C_T1.2$]. As users only write or speak with the chatbot, they trust that the chatbot will provide correct information and may not be able to identify incorrect information. This can also refer to organizational issues and factors. Otherwise, acceptance problems or legal effects could be the consequence.

In addition to the data management, the chatbot's **functional scope** [F_T2] is also an influencing factor, which was named by most of the experts. Typically, chatbots answer questions or carry out work tasks [35]. Hereto, they must understand the natural language inputs, provide the requested functions, and execute actions correctly. Thereby, a challenge exists since currently, all conversation paths must be defined in advance [$C_T2.1$]. Despite the claim of artificial intelligence, the functionality is only as extensive as it was implemented before. Thereby, chatbots often fail with the mapping of dynamic, volatile processes [$C_T2.2$]. As a solution to be capable of this kind of conversation, usually, the perpetuation of context is recommended. However, preserving the context over several dialog changes is a challenge for current implementations [$C_T2.3$]. A further challenge arises along with the functional scope: the understanding of expressions or, rather, the localization effort [$C_T2.4$]. As mentioned by the participants, particularly in large companies, many different nationalities, languages, or even just dialects must be taken into account when designing or implementing a chatbot for the employee or customer support. Currently, a chatbot still has to be trained for every single language individually. The corresponding language understanding problems also include, e.g., synonyms or colloquial language, as well as emotions or other forms of rhetoric, e.g., irony, sarcasm.

Furthermore, we identified an **integrated system landscape** [F_T3] as necessary for a chatbot operation. In order to deliver answers or perform tasks, chatbots must access existing databases and systems. Also, chatbots must be integrated with the available information systems so that not only another system is provided. As mentioned by our experts, both of these are current challenges during implementation. First, many of the available databases or information systems have no appropriate natural language-capable interfaces to integrate the existing, often hierarchical grown, landscape with the new technology. Therefore, application programming interfaces have to be developed and also maintained during the operation of chatbots [$C_T3.1$], which becomes more critical the deeper a chatbot is to be integrated into the landscape. Second, chatbots must be integrated into the user interfaces of available information systems, i.e. that users can access the chatbot from the existing information system. Especially for already existing communication tools, this integration must be pursued. As mentioned by some participants, they assess it as critical that a chatbot can be used through these systems [C_T3.2].

A last technological factor is the **chatbots' user interface** [F_T4] or respectively, their setup tools. Chatbots have to be developed, trained, and regularly improved via tools and systems dependent on the used technology or manufacturer. As quoted by the experts, these are challenges in chatbot realizations [C_T4.1]. Current interfaces or tools for chatbots' management are mostly accessible only to technically skilled employees – easy to use administration interfaces for non-technical employees are missing. Therefore, employees who have the best knowledge of the specific application area, e.g., support staff who has daily conversations with customers, cannot directly contribute to the necessary information, questions, or answers. Sometimes, the essential interfaces or tools are absent completely, so all of the content have to be programmed manually. Furthermore, the user interface of chatbots states a second challenge. Based on the one-dimensional characteristics of a chat dialog, it is hard to map complex processes with multidimensional paths or returns. Instead, the content that can be displayed mostly comprises (short) texts, pictures, or videos as well as some control elements [C_T4.2].

Table 2. Technological challenges (n's based on the 27 cases)

		Technological Challenges	n
F_T1	C_T1.1	Provision and maintenance of the required (knowledge) database	16
	C_T1.2	The coherence of the statements of a chatbot and real (service) employee	1
F_T2	C_T2.1	All (conversation-)paths must be defined in advance	4
	C_T2.2	Mapping of dynamic, volatile processes or conversations	8
	C_T2.3	Preserving the conversation context in the conversation process	5
	C_T2.4	Problems with language understanding and effort for language localization	11
F_T3	C_T3.1	Data and process integration with existing information systems and/or databases	12
	C_T3.2	Integration into user interfaces of existing information systems and/or interfaces	5
F_T4	C_T4.1	Inappropriate tools for creating and maintaining chatbots	2
	C_T4.2	Restrictions and limitations within the user interface	9

4.2 Organizational Factors

Our study revealed two organizational influencing factors. These represent aspects and decisions that have to be made or considered prior to the acquisition of chatbots, as well as issues to consider during a productive operation in digital workplace scenarios (see Table 3).

The first influencing factor of the organizational dimension is the successful **introduction** [F_O1]. At the time of the survey, some of the companies have not implemented a strategy or agenda taking into account the application of chatbots (in the workplace) [C_O1.1]. Instead, investments are made in other technologies. Therefore, the chatbot projects are often driven by single responsible persons or departments, which makes coordination among the different projects difficult and partly leads to redundant developments. Additionally, even if the potential of chatbots is often proclaimed, a missing added-value is reported [$C_O1.2$], which also affects user acceptance as in the individual factors. Therefore, value-adding use cases must be identified beforehand [$C_O1.3$]. There is a variety of possible use cases, but not in every case, a chatbot is the best fit. Instead, classical user interfaces are sometimes a better choice. Thus, as a first step in chatbot projects, suitable use cases must be selected, e.g., as pointed out in [35] and following differentiated and defined to address beneficial tasks. Critical is that present processes often cannot be mapped one-to-one by chatbots [$C_O1.4$]. Instead, the current processes must be redefined and adjusted to the natural language user interface and the conversational operation. In addition, the scalability of chatbots is a crucial factor, which includes an easy transfer of established instantiations to new use cases as well as finding use cases where high volumes of questions are existent for the automated answering [$C_O1.5$]. Otherwise, a chatbot only causes costs instead of cost savings. Additionally, a chatbot must be customized and personalized to the application area, as well as to the individual company. Therefore, this is often a time-consuming and cost-intensive process [$C_O1.6$]. Due to this resulting expense and technological requirements, it is often not feasible for small companies. Extending this, all content the chatbot provides is mainly based on the departments' knowledge, e.g., customer support. Therefore, the department's employees, e.g., first-level support staff, are required for creating the knowledge base of the chatbot [$C_O1.7$]. However, these employees should be relieved, or rather the chatbot should take over some of their tasks. Thus, this could lead to some resistance, as employees are afraid of becoming replaceable if they contribute their knowledge completely. Lastly, it is also necessary to integrate the works council in the projects. As mentioned, obstacles can occur thereby since personal data is recorded or can be linked by the system [$C_O1.8$]. Especially the free text input is prone to entering personal or not anonymous data by mistake. Concerning this, the workers' council should be involved from the start, and agreements should be signed.

Table 3. Organizational challenges (n's based on the 27 cases)

		Organizational Challenges	*n*
F_O1	$C_O1.1$	Lack of an agenda for chatbots	5
	$C_O1.2$	Missing of an added-value	17
	$C_O1.3$	Definition and design of use cases	16
	$C_O1.4$	Existing (business processes) processes cannot be mapped by chatbots	2
	$C_O1.5$	Scalability of chatbots	6
	$C_O1.6$	Creating chatbots is time-consuming and cost-intensive	14
	$C_O1.7$	Generation of content for chatbots from the different departments	3
	$C_O1.8$	Obstacles by the works council	10
F_O2	$C_O2.1$	Extensive maintenance and continuous training of chatbots in the company	18
	$C_O2.2$	Missing responsibilities for chatbots	4
	$C_O2.3$	Risk of know-how loss in the company	1

As a second influencing factor, the participants noted the continuous **operation** [F_O2] of a chatbot. Hereto, our participants mentioned a high effort for continuous maintenance and training [$C_O2.1$]. This is necessary to adjust the system and to take previously unaddressed or misunderstood questions into account as shown in the technological factors. Otherwise, user acceptance or usage suffers from it. However, automated training is also critical in this context, as there is sometimes the problem that incorrect contexts or answers are learned. Therefore, additional monitoring has to be introduced. A further challenge arises with responsibilities for the training and maintenance, which are often missing in the companies [$C_O2.2$]. The necessary steps after implementing a chatbot are not allocated probably. Sometimes these steps are outsourced, which, however, can result in dependencies or data privacy/security problems as described in the environmental factors. Lastly, as noted by one participant, the danger of knowledge loss is existent [$C_O2.3$]. If all tasks are operated only by a chatbot, no employee has the knowledge to take them over.

4.3 Individual Factors

In addition, we identified two individual influencing factors and their challenges (see Table 4). These address the future users of chatbots in a respective company, e.g., the employees, as well as the management staff who is responsible for the provision of resources.

One of the most noted influencing factors for a successful chatbot application are the **employees** [F_I1]. As pointed out by our participants, employees often have exaggerated expectations of chatbot capabilities. Mainly due to current advertisements, they assume that all possible questions could be answered [$C_I1.1$]. Despite these high expectations, we found evidence for acceptance problems for this new kind of information system [$C_I1.2$]. On the one hand, especially long-term employees do not see the benefit of an application change, because they have to adapt to new ways of working and forget the familiar. On the other hand, driven by the intended automation and relief, employees perceive chatbots as a threat to their employment [$C_I1.3$]. For all of these three challenges, it is advisable to establish change or rather expectation management. As a result of this, the added value can be demonstrated, and fears can be overcome, e.g., new duties instead of job losses. Furthermore, besides the acceptance, currently, the users lack of experience with chatbots or rather the technology behind. During acquisition, necessary components, as well as the operating principles, are unknown [$C_I1.4$]. During operation, this results in users not knowing how to work with the systems, since they only know the interaction through classic UI's. The situation is intensified by the fact that users have to adapt to the syntax and the dialog structure [$C_I1.5$]. The latter leads to a more difficult and unnecessarily longer execution time, which also harms acceptance. Some participants also mentioned emerging irritations, when chatbots are not recognizable as a chatbot [$C_I1.6$]. The last critical point is that acceptance is negatively affected when chatbots do not provide help after a certain time [$C_I1.7$]. In these cases, the inquiring person should be forwarded to a real employee.

A further individual influencing factor is the **management** [F_I2] of the respective company. Some of the participating experts criticized that the management has a sternly or inadequate assessment of the required effort [$C_I2.1$]. Instead, the assumption dominates that a chatbot can be provided without much effort. So they do not see what additional work needs to be done, e.g., an adaption of existing processes, integration into the landscape, continuous training, or necessary change management in the company. Besides, management support starts to fade after the initial investment [$C_I2.2$].

Instead, the management is often only interested in results, which leads to no further resources being provided.

Table 4. Individual challenges (n's based on the 27 cases)

		Individual Challenges	n
F_I1	$C_I1.1$	Overestimation and high expectations of employees	15
	$C_I1.2$	Acceptance problems of users for chatbots	20
	$C_I1.3$	Fear of job loss	10
	$C_I1.4$	Lack of experience with chatbots or the technology behind	8
	$C_I1.5$	Adapt to the syntax and the dialog structure	7
	$C_I1.6$	Irritation when not recognizing chatbots immediately	5
	$C_I1.7$	Dissatisfaction due to lack of assistance	9
F_I2	$C_I2.1$	Misjudgment of the effort of chatbot projects	3
	$C_I2.2$	Loss of management support during the project	3

4.4 Environmental Factors

Lastly, we identified three environmental influencing factors and their challenges (see Table 5) for the application of chatbots at workplaces. These concerns both, customers as well as legal or competitive situations with which the company is confronted.

Our participants mentioned the **customer situation** [F_E1] of the respective company to be considered as necessary. The application of chatbots, especially in customer-oriented operations, can influence the external perception of the company. If, for example, a service chatbot breaks down and no employees are available, customer inquiries cannot be answered. Besides, the risk evolves that customers fell low esteemed by the impersonal contact over a chatbot. Both factors result in the challenge of customer loss [$C_E1.1$] as well as impersonal communication [$C_E1.2$]. Especially the external application of chatbots is critical since customers would more likely change the company as opposed to employees who would only complain internally.

In addition to the customer situation, the current **law situation** was pointed out in all interviews. Besides the protection of personal data [$C_E2.1$], the data must also be stored securely [$C_E2.2$]. This especially concerns a chatbot application in Europe, as the general data protection regulation must be considered. For proper operation, it is necessary to clarify data processing and storing as well as establish policies. A further solution is the anonymization of inputs. However, technology measures often fail to identify information worth protecting or are complex to implement. Despite all the measures, risks remain. Especially the free text input is prone to entering personal or not anonymous data by mistake, e.g., accidentally free text inputs of private or company-related information. Therefore, a current strategy is the in-house operation of chatbots. Although the data remains in the company, the question arises if a technological lead can be kept or the higher costs justify this.

The last identified influencing factor states the **competitive situation** [F_E3] of the respective company. Most experts pointed out an innovation pressure for chatbots caused by the current hype about artificial intelligence technologies in general and of first-level support chatbots in specific [$C_E3.1$]. Often, chatbot projects are just wanted or implemented without a suitable use case. Instead, the focus lies only on keeping up with competitors. In addition, dependencies with chatbot providers arise [$C_E3.2$]. Companies struggle with the selection of an appropriate provider. Besides choosing an interface that is used by the users, companies must select a corresponding long-term provider. Critical here is that the selection is difficult to undo since current chatbot instantiations cannot be easily transferred to another provider or a different chatbot platform. Especially, since it is unclear which suppliers will be active in the long-term.

Table 5. Environmental challenges (n's based on the 27 cases)

		Environmental Challenges	n
F_E1	$C_E1.1$	Loss of customers	3
	$C_E1.2$	Impersonal customer contact	3
F_E2	$C_E2.1$	Ensuring data protection (concerning GDPR)	27
	$C_E2.2$	Ensuring data security	12
F_E3	$C_E3.1$	Innovation pressure to use chatbots	12
	$C_E3.2$	Dependencies on the provider of chatbot technology	5

5   Analysis and Discussion

Our findings imply that there exist many influencing factors and challenges, corresponding to the TOIE-Framework by [28] when applying chatbots at digital workplace settings. This also underlines the capability of the TOIE-framework for identifying influencing factors and challenges on a business level. Furthermore, although the primary goal was a qualitative study to identify factors and challenges that influence adoption, we have extended the results quantitatively based on the 27 interview cases to assess their influences. This helps in identifying critical factors, which should be addressed as well as in prioritizing countermeasures. Hereto, we summed up the unique number of cases in which they were mentioned.

Overall, we identified 11 influencing factors (see Table 6). Mostly, in all cases ($n = 27$) the *employees* [F_I1] and the *law situation* [F_E2] were noted followed by 26 cases who stated the *introduction* [F_O1] as critical for a successful chatbot application. The *management* [F_I2] and the *customer situation* [F_E1] cause less impact, as mentioned by only 5 experts. The technological influencing factors are mentioned moderately by 9 to 19 experts. In addition, we surveyed challenges, which are existent in each influencing factor, and identified 36 of them. Hereby, mostly the challenge of *ensuring data protection* [$C_E2.1$], especially under consideration of GDPR, was named in all of the cases. The subsequently named challenges are *acceptance problems* [$C_I1.2$] ($n = 20$), *extensive maintenance and continuous training of chatbots* [$C_O2.1$] ($n = 18$), and a *missing benefit* [$C_O1.2$] ($n = 17$). The first technological challenge, the p*rovision and maintenance of the required (knowledge) database* [$C_T1.1$], is named in the fifth place by 16 experts. The least named challenges are *inappropriate tools for creating and maintaining chatbots* [$C_T4.1$] and *existing (business) processes that are not aligned to chatbots* [$C_O1.4$] in two cases, as well as *the coherence of the statements of a chatbot and real employees* [$C_T1.2$] and *risks of know-how loss* [$C_O2.3$] in one case. Thus, two technological challenges are among these, which support the hypothesis that technical aspects are not the problem when applying or operating chatbots in businesses. Furthermore, mostly technological influencing factors are named (see Table 6). This indicates that currently, technical aspects are present, or the focus lies on them. In the case of the mean of mentions, however, the organizational influencing factors are mentioned much more frequently (*mean* = 22). Whereas, the technological factors are the least named (*mean* = 14,75). This distribution is also recognizable for the challenges: Besides the organizational challenges, which are 11 in total, 10 technological challenges where identified. However, on average, our experts mostly stated environmental challenges (*mean* = 10,33) followed by individual challenges (*mean* = 8,89). Therefore, we conclude that: (1) In the case of influencing factors, mostly the organizational factors must be taken into account when applying chatbots in workplaces settings. (2) In the case of challenges, mostly environmental challenges must be considered and addressed to enable a purposeful application of chatbots. (3) In summary, although chatbots are a technology, there are rather organizational, external, or individual aspects, which should be considered

Table 6. Distributions of influencing factors and challenges

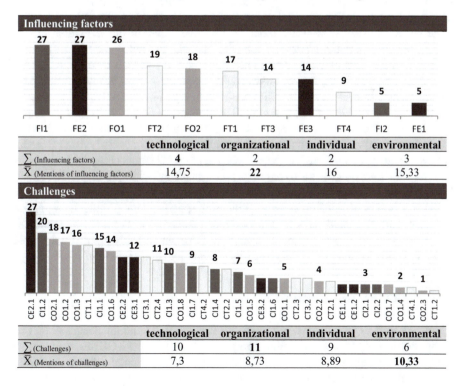

foremost. Nonetheless, as we value the influence based on the number of mentions, this does not necessarily mean that the others are not critical. Instead, they also have the potential to be a showstopper and must be taken into account likewise.

Thus, the results of the study affirmed our initial assumption that the research community should switch from chatbot design research to rather an organizational or management view. As shown, technical aspects are mentioned less. On the contrary, organizational and individual issues have the highest influence on adoption decisions, as well as environmental or individual challenges. Nonetheless, as the design research perspective is often pursued and the identified factors influence individual design decisions, our results should be included in future design research studies for chatbots in business applications. In doing so, possible challenges can be addressed and the corresponding effects can be reduced early in the design stage or in design studies. Additionally, it is also noticeable that many classic IT influencing factors or challenges also apply in particular for chatbot applications at digital workplaces, e.g., data protection, user acceptance, or maintenance and support of the systems.

Furthermore, we could find some clues that related research can be verified by our findings. At first, our study verifies the high influence of the user on introduction and operation. Secondly, we could derive high expectations of the users, which were hinted in [36] or [37]. Additionally, [38] show that environmental and individual factors have a high relevance on adoption decisions, which we were also able to show. Thus, we could contribute that users and usability factors have a high influence on the adoption of chatbots in workplace settings. Although chatbots are technically easy to set up, the major effort concerns the design of social and human aspects to enable an intuitive and natural usage behavior. Also, from a theoretical perspective, many of our individual factors, e.g., *overestimation and high expectation* [$C_I 1.1$], or *lack of experience* [$C_I 1.4$], can be mapped to the core constructs of technology acceptance and their theories, e.g., TAM or UTAUT [39, 40]. Thus, future studies could pursue these approaches in detail. Also, general aspects of system quality were mentioned, e.g., the *syntax* [$C_I 1.5$] or *security* [$C_E 2.1, C_E 2.2.$], which is consistent with IS success research and underlines the importance of these characteristics during chatbot application [41]. In comparison to previous results focusing the environmental issues, we also show that especially data protection and data security are challenging factors when applying chatbots at digital workplaces, e.g., [42]. As this category is also our most noted challenge factor, future studies should focus more on these issues. Especially in comparison to the study of [15], we enrich the knowledge base with specific and comprehensive specifications of influencing factors and their respective challenges for the workplace domain. Furthermore, we could verify the artificial intelligence research agenda of [43], who already pointed out people, (inter-)organizational and societal issues, as relevant for future research.

6   Conclusion and Limitations

In this research paper, we survey influencing factors (*RQ1*) and challenges (*RQ2*) for the application of chatbots at digital workplaces. Based on the TOIE-Framework, we identified technical, organizational, individual, and environmental influencing factors and challenges. As our results indicate, the participants note mostly the organizational influencing factors as opposed to the challenges, where mostly the external ones were mentioned. Comprehensively, we show that despite chatbots are a (new) technology, mostly the non-technical aspects should be taken into account.

However, as with every qualitative study, there exist some limitations, which have to be outlined. *First*, the findings and results are significantly dependent on the interviewee selection and their willingness to participate and provide insights into their experiences. We minimized this influence by: (1) Including a suitably large set of participants with knowledge for the application of chatbots at digital workplaces. (2) Taking into account a cross-section of the industry to achieve generalizable results and to weaken the impact of individual areas. However, our sample consists predominantly of German participants. *Second*, the primary goal was a qualitative study. Nonetheless, we also did some quantitative evaluations based on our interviews. As these sums are only based on our sample, the findings are not representative. Hence, the distribution can be seen as a first indicator of a weighting of factors and challenges when applying chatbots at digital workplaces. *Third*, different researchers might interpret the findings differently. Hereto, we analyzed the interviews by two researchers independently followed by a discussion between them where the findings were merged.

Despite these limitations, our results seem to be comprehensive and generalizable. Thus, with our findings, we contribute to both, research and practice. For the scientific community, firstly, we close the existent research gap for influencing factors and challenges surrounding the chatbot application at digital workplaces. Secondly, we confirm the previous results in this research topic and extend them through our comprehensive survey. Furthermore, we show that especially organizational or management, as well as environmental topics, should be followed in future research. These topics have been given less consideration to date, and our assessment confirms the importance of the factors. For the practice community, we point out comprehensively influencing factors and challenges. Companies can use them for a successful chatbot application. Second, with our influencing factors, decision-makers can prioritize their tasks and address them based on our descriptions and the weighting. Nonetheless, the results still have the potential to be verified on a larger scale, e.g. internationally or in other industries.

References

1. Følstad, A., Brandtzæg, P.B.: Chatbots and the new world of HCI. Interactions **24**, 38–42 (2017)
2. Maedche, A., et al.: AI-based digital assistants. opportunities, threats, and research perspektives. Bus. Inf. Syst. Eng. **61**, 535–544 (2019)
3. Byström, K., Ruthven, I., Heinström, J.: Work and information: which workplace models still work in modern digital workplaces? In: CoLIS Paper 1651. Information Research 22 (2017)
4. Köffer, S.: Designing the digital workplace of the future - what scholars recommend to practitioners. In: Proceedings of the 36th International Conference on Information Systems, pp. 1–21 (2015)
5. Lestarini, D., Raflesia, S.P., Surendro, K.: A conceptual framework of engaged digital workplace diffusion. In: 9th International Conference on Telecommunication Systems Services and Applications, pp. 1–5 (2015)
6. White, M.: Digital workplaces: Vision and reality. Bus. Inf. Rev. **29**, 205–214 (2012)

7. Carayannopoulos, S.: Using chatbots to aid transition. Int. J. Inf. Learn. Technol. **35**, 118–129 (2018)
8. Lebeuf, C., Storey, M.-A., Zagalsky, A.: How software developers mitigate collaboration friction with chatbots. In: Talking with Conversational Agents in Collaborative Action Workshop at the 20th ACM conference on Computer-Supported Cooperative Work and Social Computing, pp. 1–6 (2017)
9. Russell, D.M.: Ubiquitous search for smart workspaces. Univ. Access. Inf. Soc. **11**, 337–344 (2012)
10. Richter, A., Heinrich, P., Stocker, A., Schwabe, G.: Digital work design. Bus. Inf. Syst. Eng. **60**(3), 259–264 (2018). https://doi.org/10.1007/s12599-018-0534-4
11. Gnewuch, U., Morana, S., Maedche, A.: Towards designing cooperative and social conversational agents for customer service. In: Proceedings of the 38th International Conference on Information Systems, pp. 1–13 (2017)
12. Diederich, S., Janßen-Müller, M., Brendel, A.B., Morana, S.: Emulating empathetic behavior in online service encounters with sentiment-adaptive responses: insights from an experiment with a conversational agent. In: Proceedings of the 40th International Conference on Information Systems, pp. 1–17 (2019)
13. Meyer von Wolff, R., Hobert, S., Schumann, M.: How may i help you? - state of the art and open research questions for chatbots at the digital workplace. In: Proceedings of the 52nd Hawaii International Conference on System Science, pp. 95–104 (2019)
14. DePietro, R., Wiarda, E., Fleischer, M.: The context for change: organization, technology and environment. In: Tornatzky, L.G., Fleischer, M. (eds.) The Process of Technological Innovation, pp. 151–175. Lexington, Toronto (1990)
15. Rodríguez Cardona, D., Werth, O., Schönborn, S., Breitner, M.H.: A mixed methods analysis of the adoption and diffusion of chatbot technology in the german insurance sector. In: Proceedings of the 25th Americas Conference on Information Systems, pp. 1–10 (2019)
16. Egbert, D., Paluch, S.: If the app fits - business mobile application assimilation and value creation in SMEs. In: Proceedings of the 40th International Conference on Information Systems, pp. 1–9 (2019)
17. Bittner, E., Shoury, O.: Designing automated facilitation for design thinking: a chatbot for supporting teams in the empathy map method. In: Proceedings of the 52nd Hawaii International Conference on System Science (2019)
18. Berg, M.M.: Modelling of Natural Dialogues in the Context of Speech-Based Information and Control Systems. AKA; IOS Press, Berlin, Amsterdam (2014)
19. Mallios, S., Bourbakis, N.: A survey on human machine dialogue systems. In: 7th International Conference on Information, Intelligence, Systems & Applications, pp. 1–7 (2016)
20. Dery, K., Sebastian, I.M., van der Meulen, R.: The digital workplace is key to digital innovation. MIS Q. **16**, 135–152 (2017)
21. Rüegg-Stürm, J.: The New St. Gallen Management Model. Palgrave Macmillan, London (2005)
22. Chakrabarti, C., Luger, G.F.: Artificial conversations for customer service chatter bots. Architecture, algorithms, and evaluation metrics. Expert Syst. Appl. **42**, 6878–6897 (2015)
23. Feine, J., Gnewuch, U., Morana, S., Maedche, A.: A taxonomy of social cues for conversational agents. Int. J. Hum. Comput. Stud., 138–161 (2019)
24. Følstad, A., Skjuve, M.: Chatbots for customer service. In: Proceedings of the 1st International Conference on Conversational User Interfaces, pp. 1–9 (2019)
25. Wuenderlich, N.V., Paluch, S.: A nice and friendly chat with a bot: user perceptions of AI-based service agents. In: Proceedings of the 38th International Conference on Information Systems, pp. 1–11 (2017)
26. Seeber, I., et al.: Machines as teammates: a collaboration research agenda. In: Proceedings of the 52nd Hawaii International Conference on System Science (2019)

27. Oliveira, T., Martins, M.F.: Literature review of information technology adoption models at firm level. Electron. J. Inf. Syst. Eval. **14**, 110–121 (2011)
28. Rosli, K., Yeow, P., Siew, E.-G.: Factors influencing audit technology acceptance by audit firms: a new I-TOE adoption framework. J. Account. Audit. Res. Pract. **2012**, 1–11 (2012)
29. Zhu, K., Kraemer, K., Xu, S.: Electronic business adoption by European firms: a cross-country assessment of the facilitators and inhibitors. Eur. J. Inf. Syst. **12**, 251–268 (2003)
30. Awa, H.O., Ukoha, O., Igwe, S.R.: Revisiting technology-organization-environment (T-O-E) theory for enriched applicability. Bottom Line **30**, 2–22 (2017)
31. Myers, M.D.: Qualitative Research in Business & Management. London (2013)
32. Döring, N., Bortz, J.: Forschungsmethoden und Evaluation in den Sozial- und Humanwissenschaften. Springer, Heidelberg (2016). https://doi.org/10.1007/978-3-642-41089-5
33. Glaser, B.G., Strauss, A.L.: The Discovery of Grounded Theory - Strategies for Qualitative Research. Aldine, New Brunswick (2006)
34. Mayring, P.: Qualitative Content Analysis. Theoretical Foundation, Basic Procedures and Software Solution. Klagenfurt (2014)
35. Meyer von Wolff, R., Hobert, S., Masuch, K., Schumann, M.: Chatbots at digital workplaces – a grounded-theory approach for surveying application areas and objectives. Pac. Asia J. Assoc. Inf. Syst. **12**, 63–101 (2020)
36. Kraus, D., Reibenspiess, V., Eckhardt, A.: How voice can change customer satisfaction: a comparative analysis between e-commerce and voice commerce. In: Proceedings of the 14th International Conference on Wirtschaftsinformatik, pp. 1868–1879 (2019)
37. Rzepka, C.: Examining the use of voice assistants: a value-focused thinking approach. In: Proceedings of the 25th Americas Conference on Information Systems, pp. 1–10 (2019)
38. Laumer, S., Maier, C., Gubler, F.: Chatbot acceptance in healthcare: explaining user adoption of conversational agents for disease diagnosis. In: Proceedings of the 27th European Conference on Information Systems, pp. 1–18 (2019)
39. Venkatesh, V., Thong, J.Y.L., Xu, X.: Unified theory of acceptance and use of technology: a synthesis and the road ahead. J. Assoc. Inf. Syst., 17 (2016)
40. Davis, F.D.: User acceptance of information technology: system characteristics, user perceptions and behavioral impacts. Int. J. Man Mach. Stud. **38**, 475–487 (1993)
41. DeLone, W.H., McLean, E.R.: The DeLone and McLean model of information systems success: a ten-year update. J. Manag. Inf. Syst. **19**, 9–30 (2003)
42. Pumplun, L., Tauchert, C., Heidt, M.: A new organizational chassis for artificial intelligence - exploring organizational readiness factors. In: Proceedings of the 27th European Conference on Information Systems, pp. 1–15 (2019)
43. Bawack, R.E., Wamba, S.F., Carillo, K.D.A.: Artificial intelligence in practice: implications for information systems research. In: Proceedings of the 25th Americas Conference on Information Systems, pp. 1–10 (2019)

Empirically Exploring the Cause-Effect Relationships of AI Characteristics, Project Management Challenges, and Organizational Change

Christian Engel[✉], Philipp Ebel, and Benjamin van Giffen

Institute of Information Management, University of St. Gallen, St. Gallen, Switzerland
{christian.engel,philipp.ebel,benjamin.vangiffen}@unisg.ch

Abstract. Artificial Intelligence (AI) provides organizations with vast opportunities of deploying AI for competitive advantage such as improving processes, and creating new or enriched products and services. However, the failure rate of projects on implementing AI in organizations is still high, and prevents organizations from fully seizing the potential that AI exhibits. To contribute to closing this gap, we seize the unique opportunity to gain insights from five organizational cases. In particular, we empirically investigate how the unique characteristics of AI – i.e. experimental character, context sensitivity, black box character, and learning requirements – induce challenges into project management, and how these challenges are addressed in organizational (socio-technical) contexts. This shall provide researchers with an empirical and conceptual foundation for investigating the cause-effect relationships between the characteristics of AI, project management, and organizational change. Practitioners can benchmark their own practices against the insights to increase the success rates of future AI implementations.

Keywords: Artificial Intelligence · Project management · Case study · Socio-technical system

1 Introduction

Nowadays, Artificial Intelligence (AI) is a pervasive organizational and economic phenomenon [1]. These developments result from the persistent technological innovations in the areas of algorithmic capability, computing power, and data storage [2, 3]. Thus, AI systems are increasingly applied in various usage contexts to both improve processes, and to enhance or create new products and services [4]. This potential has also been widely recognized in corporate practice. A recent survey among 3000 CIOs shows that the number of companies that has experimented with AI solutions has increased by 270% over the last four years [5]. However, it is estimated that throughout 2022, 85% of AI projects will fail to meet the intended targets and deliver erroneous outcomes [5], which shows a gap between understanding and successfully implementing AI solutions to leverage the potential that AI exhibits.

© The Author(s), under exclusive license to Springer Nature Switzerland AG 2021
F. Ahlemann et al. (Eds.): WI 2021, LNISO 47, pp. 166–181, 2021.
https://doi.org/10.1007/978-3-030-86797-3_12

In this paper, we focus on AI implementation projects as our unit of analysis, i.e. projects that develop and embed AI solutions in organizational (socio-technical) contexts. Particularly, we aim at contributing to paving the way for enriching knowledge on AI project management by seizing the unique opportunity to gain insights from multiple empirical cases. Thus, we pose the following research question:

How do AI projects induce socio-technical challenges into organizations and how can they be addressed by project management?

As research on AI project management practices is still nascent, this implies the need for empirical studies in the field of AI project management as the deduction of concepts from existing conceptualizations and theories is very limited, and (AI) projects are highly context-sensitive. Thus, over the duration of nine months, we engaged in five in-depth case studies with large corporations, which can be viewed as leading in their industries, in order to gain insights into the distinguishable challenges that implementing AI solutions induces into organizations and what the observed resolution approaches of the project management were to manage these challenges.

With this research, we aim to make contributions to both practice and research. First, this study aims at providing practitioners with unique empirical insights gained in real-world organizational settings, which shall create awareness for AI-specific challenges that lie ahead for organizations planning to implement AI solutions, and to present them with resolution approaches observable in corporate practice. Second, we aim to empirically enrich the scientific body of knowledge in the field of project management from a socio-technical perspective. This shall help researchers to better understand the interrelations between AI implementation projects as a focal unit of analysis and the components of socio-technical systems, i.e. the respective organizational context. Third, we aim to contribute to a conceptually sound and empirically rich research foundation on the cause-effect relationships between the characteristics of AI, the induced project management challenges, and the required changes in socio-technical systems. Overall, this shall help to make our unit of analysis, i.e. AI projects in specific, and AI as our phenomenon of interest in general more explainable and predictable.

2   Conceptual Background

We refer to a phenomenon-oriented definition of AI that characterizes it as machines performing the cognitive functions typically associated with human cognition, such as perceiving, interacting, reasoning, and learning [6]. We are aware that the term AI often raises wrong expectations regarding what machines are actually capable of doing, which still leads to hype-induced disappointments in many AI endeavors.

Thus, we narrow down the terminological scope of this paper seizing the common differentiations between "weak AI" that only pretends to think and "strong AI" that refers to a mind exhibiting mental states [7], as well as on a domain-oriented level to the categorization of narrow AI and Artificial General Intelligence (AGI) [8]. While narrow AI refers to an AI that is equally as good or better than a human in a specific domain of tasks, an AGI is posed to be equally as good or better than a human in any domain of tasks [8]. Consequently, when referring to AI in this paper, we mean weak and narrow

AI rather than strong and general AI because the former has already proven its feasibility in the real world, and the latter is still more in the focus of philosophical debates and far away from being technically realized soon [9].

Against this backdrop, AI takes over certain degrees of cognition, which shall provide two types of AI outputs – decisions or solutions [2]. This is facilitated by advancements in computing power, algorithmic capabilities, and data storage [2, 3]. AI systems need to process large amounts of data and even Big Data in short time periods as they are approaching to match the intellectual performance of the human brain [10]. Thus, AI systems often require high levels of computing power. Second, advanced algorithms are used to replicate human cognition by learning from data and adapting to different contextual situations [11]. Thus, productive AI systems incorporate a learning capability to conduct decision making and problem solving [3]. Finally, the advancements in storing the data required for training, testing, commercializing, and maintaining AI solutions, facilitates the creation of a machine memory [12], which is regarded as the basis of intelligent systems [13].

Besides the technological facilitators, the following set of characteristics has been attributed to AI by research: *experimental character (1), context sensitivity (2), black box character (3), and learning requirements (4) of AI*. This set of characteristics is not claimed to be exhaustive but shall cover a representative share of the unique characteristics of AI, which we briefly summarize here:

(1) *Experimental character* refers to AI outcomes being non-deterministic but rather probabilistic [14].
(2) *Context sensitivity* refers to AI solutions being only as good as the data their context provides to reflect and predict the latter [15].
(3) *Black box character* refers to AI systems, especially in the field of deep learning, facing challenges in delivering explanations to humans on what happens between data input and AI output [16].
(4) *Learning requirements* refer to AI solutions constituting entities that just like humans need to learn and develop experience to eventually improve their performance over time [3].

This set of characteristics reflects that technological advancements on the one hand are necessary facilitators of AI solutions but lead to challenges that are induced into organizations intending to implement AI systems that have not existed before this digital era. For instance, the processes of generating AI models differ from programming traditional software applications. Software applications are based on code that runs predictably and deterministically on a computer, while AI models learn from processing data using machine learning [17]. We refer to the following notion of Machine Learning that grasps its underlying mechanism: "A computer program is said to learn from experience E, with respect to some class of task T and performance measure P, if its performance at tasks in T, as measured by P, improves with experience E" [18, p. 2]. Generating machine learning models requires training [19], which refers to the process of extracting knowledge stored in the data by applying machine learning algorithms. This difference between programming software and training AI models has far reaching implications regarding the activities and practices in each type of project.

In this paper, we intend to empirically explore the cause-effect relationships of the set of AI characteristics described above, and how these induce project management challenges against the backdrop of the organizational context. Thus, we view project management challenges and the required organizational IS design and change through the lens of socio-technical systems (STS) theory that takes into account the interrelations of technology, task, structure, and actors [20, 21].

3 Method

We opt for a qualitative, inductive reasoning from multiple cases [1, 22, 23] to identify socio-technical challenges induced by AI technology. The case study method is appropriate for this type of research because the management of AI projects represents a context-sensitive phenomenon on which only little theory is available that acknowledges the technology-specific challenges. Here we describe the phases of *case selection (1), data collection (2), and data analysis (3)* of our research design.

For *case selection (1)*, It was our particular goal to retrieve a discrete set of cases, i.e. AI projects that exhibit potential variation among another – be it variation in project goals or organizational contexts in distinct industries. Therefore, we chose five projects for case analysis, which stem from three distinct industries and exhibit three distinct project goals (see also Table 1). We purposefully selected the combination of project goal and industry in the cases to achieve a high level of variation in the ways that lead to project success according to Mill's method of agreement [24]. This is based on inducing insights from variation in independent case variables with the dependent case variable – i.e., "successfully implemented AI project" – being the same among the cases. To maintain comparability between the cases, we selected the organizational case environment of the particular tasks to be large corporations that already had to have deployed AI systems. Furthermore, we purposefully selected organizations that are leading in their particular industry to base the collection of observed resolution approaches on a revelatory foundation [23].

The process of *data collection (2)* took nine months, in which we investigated the five cases in relation to their particular organizational environment. We were offered with the unique opportunity of conducting case interviews on different hierarchical levels of the organizations. This helped us to develop a more comprehensive understanding of the different perspectives on AI projects in different socio-technical contexts. We approached the interviewees with semi-structured interviews conducted by three researchers from our research team. In doing so, we predefined an interview guideline that assured natural flow of conversations with the interviewees and allowed for variation in topics. Furthermore, this enabled us to adapt to the different levels of hierarchy, professional backgrounds and new themes that eventually may emerge in the interviews [23]. For each project, we additionally gathered case documents that were identified to be directly or indirectly related to the AI project (see also Table 1).

The *data analysis (3)* was carried out on the foundation of the interview transcripts and case documents. Respectively, three researchers extracted data from the material and conducted open, axial, and selective coding iterations [25]. After an open coding iteration of the documents, the coders assigned relationships among the open codes (axial coding)

Table 1. Case information

Project/(Industry)	AI project goal	Interviewees (duration of interviews)	Case data
Alpha (Telco)	Classification and Routing of Incoming Client Emails	Head of Capability Management (30 min), Project Owner from Business (60 min), Project Manager (60 min)	**Interviews:** Transcripts **Internal files:** Project document-ations and presentations **Public Sources:** News articles, company and project websites, and business reports
Beta (Banking)	Translation of Financial Documents from Italian and French to German	Chief Information Officer (40 min), Project Manager (120 min)	
Gamma (Manu-facturing)	Price Setting for Individualized Technical Offerings	Chief Information Officer (30 min), Project Manager (80 min)	
Delta (Banking)	Classification, Routing and Resolution of Internal Incident Tickets	Head of Data and Analytics (40 min), Head of Platform Strategy (35 min), Project Manager (120 min)	
Epsilon (Manu-facturing)	AI-based classification, routing and resolution of internal incident tickets	Vice President IT Innovation (50 min), Project Manager (50 min)	

in a second iteration. Subsequently, we purposefully defined the core variables for selective coding to be "challenges of AI projects" and "resolution approaches", which affect the dependent case variable "successfully implemented AI project". Three coders conducted the selective coding iteration against the backdrop of the conceptual background established for this research. After each coding iteration, the particular coding results were validated in research discussions among the three researchers [25]. This helped to identify a set of specific AI-induced project management challenges and to relate them to the particular socio-technical components of the organizational environments of the projects. Because the selected combinations of the goals and organizational contexts of the AI projects lead to a decent level of variation in the analyzed cases, the AI project management challenges can be induced on a broad conceptual basis [23].

4   Results

Figure 1 provides an overview of the identified set of specific challenges of planning, developing, and embedding AI solutions in organizations, and emphasizes the AI-specific root-causes of each of these challenges along with the observed socio-technical changes that could be observed in the cases. The AI-specific root-causes refer to the distinguishable characteristics of AI that were established in the conceptual background of this work, i.e., experimental character, the context sensitivity, the black box character, and the learning requirements of AI. Overall, this shall provide a first empirical basis for investigating the cause-effect relationships of AI characteristics, project management and organizational change.

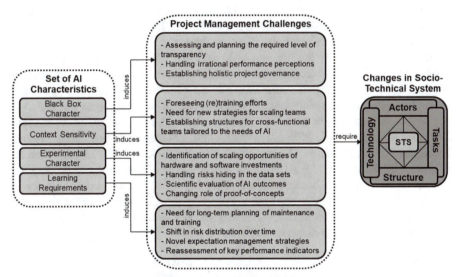

Fig. 1. Proposed cause-effect-relationships of AI characteristics, project management challenges, and changes in the socio-technical system (STS)

4.1   Black Box Character: Induced Challenges and Changes in STS

First, the black box character of AI challenges project management to assess the required level of transparency of certain use cases, which requires change in the STS component of *technology*: The black box character that AI models often exhibit have led to the rise of the research on "explainable AI" that investigates the tradeoff between performance and transparency of models [26]. For project management, this means that project managers need to be aware that some use cases impose restrictions due to inherent transparency requirements rooted in the required auditability of processes. Furthermore, project management needs to control for transparency and hold developers accountable when introducing AI systems – for instance, by implementing rationalization into the system, i.e. the AI verbalizes its functioning [27].

"We use the AI itself to communicate more to the end user. For instance, in this project it is messaged at the beginning of the conversation [...]: 'Hey, now I currently I cannot handle orders but I can do this and that.'" – Project manager (Epsilon)

For example, in the case of the AI-based incident management system in the manufacturing context (project Epsilon). The system uses a chatbot as an interface that, after running testing iterations with users, had to be adapted to verbalize its actions and describe what it is capable of doing and what not. Project managers should foresee situations in which the black box characteristics of AI need to be mitigated, e.g. by further disclosing which sources are used, and what reasoning leads to AI decisions.

Second, the black box characteristics of AI can lead to an irrational performance perception, which requires change in the STS component of *actors*: As AI systems are non-linear systems [17], AI outcomes do not follow tree-like "if-then" structures, which causes dissonance between human decision heuristics and the respective AI output. This challenge is multiplied by the inherent bounded rationality of humans [28]. I.e., even though, AI may lead to objectively better results measured in numbers, people might still not be able to perceive this success due to the black box character of AI, as cases where AI makes mistakes might be easy cases for people observing these mistakes, and vice versa. For instance, in project Epsilon we observed an AI solution that correctly performed a certain task in 80% of the cases while a human actor correctly performed the task in 70% of the cases. However, actors looking into the 20% of cases that are incorrectly performed by the AI systems, might perceive these cases to be easy and obvious cases to handle. In the analyzed case, this led to people questioning the AI project outcomes as it is not transparent to them why the AI models are not able to cope with these "easy" and obvious cases. This can lead to a twist in actors' perception, even though the AI performs better than the human actors.

"You really need to make people understand what AI is, what is within this black box, so that they see for themselves that it is not purely one to one rules that are applied but it is much more." – Project manager (Epsilon)

To cope with the bounded rationality of humans, throughout the cases, the interviewees emphasized the necessity to constantly make people understand what AI is in general, and what hides within AI as a black box to make them understand that AI moves beyond pure one to one rules. For instance, in project Epsilon, collecting and communicating reference cases was observed to be a means of mitigating this challenge: These reference cases should be of high impact to show what the potential behind AI is. In that, it is important to constantly create awareness through various communication channels (face-to-face, and indirect), to repeat the message but also to showcase what is improving in the systems. Another concrete measure observed in the cases is to early integrate the end users of the systems in ideation and development phases. For instance, design thinking workshops were conducted before the actual kickoff of project Epsilon to prototype ideas and to early reach out to the end users.

Finally, the black box characteristics of AI make holistic project governance inevitable, which requires change in the STS component of *structure*: Due to the black box characteristics of AI – these vary in their intensity among the distinct algorithms – it is hard to trace back a certain model output to certain input variables, which imposes the necessity on project management to establish particular governance mechanisms. Project management needs to consider ethical and cultural aspects of governing AI projects. Against the backdrop of recent scandals about racist, gender-discriminating AI solutions that made international news [29], these AI-specific governance mechanisms become of utmost importance for preventing AI projects from causing large-scale harm to the organization and its environment. Especially, when outsourcing AI development, these governance mechanisms lead to project management challenges as not everything is observable between a principal and an agent [30].

"Our company has a general contract with Microsoft and an agreement where most of these governance topics are covered." - Project manager (Epsilon)

In the case of AI-based incident management (project Epsilon) in the manufacturing industry, we could observe that these challenges were largely approached by establishing general contracts with suppliers on data safety and ethical governance, which lowered both transaction costs and project risks.

4.2   Context Sensitivity: Induced Challenges and Changes in STS

The context sensitivity of AI requires to foresee (re)training efforts, which requires change in the STS component of *technology*: Since the performance of AI systems is dependent on the context, it is necessary to account for a change in the environment by early planning the retraining of AI models [31]. For instance, in the case of determining the price level of complex technical offerings (project Gamma), changes in price driving parameters such as prices of natural resources, or changes in laws affecting legal requirements of offerings, e.g. regarding safety, impact whether an AI model is performant over time or not. Also, in project Delta, the models have to be up to date to work in the long run, i.e., taking into account changes in types of incoming incidents.

"[It] depends on what is the quantity of tickets that we get. That is where we need to sit down and discuss in terms of how we do that retraining of the model and the redeployment of the model itself." – Project manager (Delta)

Thus, the project managers early conducted assessments of environmental changes to adequately plan data cleaning and relabeling as part of their sprints based on the timeliness requirements of the data, i.e. planning the intervals of how often the models need to be retrained, making sure that enough of the right data in the right quality and accessibility is available at these points in time [32].

Furthermore, the context sensitivity of AI requires new strategies for scaling respective teams, which requires change in the STS component of *actors*: For scaling AI solutions across a company, distributed computing of the entire model [33], alignment of the distinct data sets as well as redundancies of data sets for individual computing are required [34]. In that, project managers face the challenge to plan and prepare managerial decision making on which parts of the core AI team, i.e., data scientists, data engineers, subject matter experts, product owners need to be scaled.

"[…] The data engineering team can scale because they are the ones who manage it across different servers, or put it into the cloud but from a […] modelling perspective I do not see a need to scale as we want to scale the usage." – Project manager (Delta)

From a data science and model creation perspective, the interviewed project managers did not face a necessity to increase the team size as the machine learning models did not vary heavily. The contrary was the case from a data engineering perspective as there is the challenge to handle the effort for gathering, cleaning, structuring, and storing the data from multiple silos within the organization as the data requirements across the organization can vary. Scaling this designated group of the core team needs to be planned in advance, efforts need to be estimated, and team integration of this particular group has to be managed [35].

Finally, the context sensitivity of AI requires to establish structures for cross-functional teams, which requires change in the STS component of *structure*: Successful AI solutions require both domain expertise, and data science and engineering expertise. This means that business and IT departments need to establish structures to be able to closely collaborate in cross-functional teams as each AI problem is different depending on the organizational context [36]. In that, project managers face the challenge to establish these project structures and harmonize them with organizational structures to reach a close collaboration between business and IT departments to account for the context sensitivity of AI.

"The [external] team consists of computer experts, data experts and business experts. [Internally], there was a data expert, a salesman from the field […], and I was there as a link." – Project manager (Gamma)

We observed in the cases that within the organizations semi-open project onboarding events are conducted with self-selection mechanisms. Furthermore, it became evident during the cases that the context sensitivity of AI requires to establish clear product ownership in the respective business departments that are trying to solve a business problem, as otherwise a continued use of the AI system beyond the project is unlikely.

4.3 Experimental Character: Induced Challenges and Changes in STS

In this vein, we could induce from the cases that the experimental character of AI implies the need to proactively search for scaling opportunities if significant hardware and software investments are necessary, which requires change in the STS component of *technology*: As of now, organizations have started investing in AI technologies but are vigilant and attentive regarding these investment decisions, due to the perceived newness of AI [37]. This is reflected in the size of lighthouse projects being small- and medium-sized in order to serve as a seed of AI that is planted into the organization. For instance, in the case of machine translation (project Beta), a flexible cloud solution could not be seized at the moment, due to the sensitivity of data related to the financial documents that should be translated. Thus, an on-premise server had to be sourced.

"The GPU server was expensive, but we would have found a use for it somewhere else in the company. The business case for the internal GPU server works and thus speaks positively for the GPU server internally." – Project manager (Beta)

In project Beta, project management faced the need to start with a small but measurably successful use case before moving towards scaling the project scope. To justify investments in a GPU server, project management proactively searched for scaling opportunities to other use cases before respective investment decision rounds were triggered with line managers. As a consequence, investments in a GPU server were made in the course of the project with respect to extending it to further use cases, as the AI system for machine translation only uses a small share of the computing capacity of the GPU server.

Moreover, the experimental character of AI leads to a high level of project risks hiding in in the data, which requires change in the STS component of *task*: In the cases, we could find empirical evidence for a large portion of project risk hiding in the data sets that are required for training and testing of models. For instance, while training their AI-based customer incident management system (project Alpha), the project manager of the telecommunication provider observed that, when labelling more data and feeding more data into the AI model, the model's performance became worse, which led to a fair share of initial confusion. However, it could be identified that this was rooted in flawed data sets, which were caused by mistakes committed by the subject matter experts when labelling the data. In a similar vein, the project manager of project Delta summarized the role of data in the respective AI project on incident management.

"[...] I have always been aware of [...] the risk of having the data quality and interpretation of the data, and subject matter knowledge." – Project manager (Delta)

Thus, project management introduced data quality assurance mechanisms into the AI projects and the organization, such as peer data reviews, data stage-gates, and automated data screenings [38].

Furthermore, the experimental character of AI requires a scientific evaluation of results, which requires change in the STS component of *task*: As AI systems operate probabilistically, this requires to evaluate the final AI solution or to test minimum viable products (MVPs) in a scientific manner that is reproducible, rigorous, and robust [39]. For instance, in the case of translating financial documents (project Beta), the bank set the goal to deliver results with higher translation quality than a global market leader of AI-based translation solutions in at least 60% of the cases.

"The team of four translators then spent a maximum of four hours assessing the equivalence of the [benchmark tool] outputs and the in-house tool outputs, from which the quality score was calculated." – Project manager (Beta)

Several individual sentences in the source language with the respective translation from the newly developed AI-based machine translation were compiled for the translators in one document. The translators then had time to comment on the output, e.g. on the style used, spelling, language usage, etc. This was done with 400 test translations. These were generated from the benchmark tool of the global market leader and the developed tool. There were four translators per language, two from the bank's team and two external translators whom the supplier of the AI solution could select. This four-person team of translators then evaluated the equivalence of the benchmark tool outputs and the in-house tool outputs, and a quality indicator was calculated. Test dummies were also built in to test the attention of the translators.

Finally, the experimental character of AI initiatives changes the role of proof-of-concepts (PoCs), which requires change in the STS component of *structure*: Throughout the cases we could observe that the role of proof-of-concepts (PoCs) changes and thus risk is increasingly transferred from the supplier to the buyer. This is especially the case when the AI solution is sourced from outside of the company and project management is more concerned with embedding the AI solution in the socio-technical context. This imposes structure-related challenges on project management as this shift in risk needs to be mitigated to be bearable by the accountable stakeholders. For example, in the case of machine translation of financial documents (project Beta), a PoC was not possible because two neural networks had to be extensively trained.

> *"We made a bonus-malus clause as the classic POC that you always strive for when creating MVPs is often not possible. You have to do it just right, because you can't train a [neural] net with a few data points." –* Chief Information Officer (Beta)

For this reason, in project Beta, a bonus-malus clause tailored to the expected AI performance was negotiated in the supplier contracts in line with value-based pricing. Translating and mediating between sales and purchasing department, external developers, internal solution integrators, and C-level management was part of the project management effort in establishing this bonus-malus clause.

4.4 Learning Requirements: Induced Challenges and Changes in STS

First, the learning requirements of AI induce the need for long-term planning of maintenance, which requires change in the STS component of *technology*: Like an employee, AI systems face the need to learn, and in specific case to even conduct life-long learning. This is due to data value being time-dependent [40] and requires project managers to move beyond the set time frame of a project when conducting planning, and to apply a long-term view on how AI systems need to be maintained to account for long-term changes such as changing user perceptions, values, and culture. In the case of translating financial documents (project Beta), project managers faced the inherent risk that the financial jargon evolves over time [41], which needs to be taken into account when intending to deliver a performant system that is built for the long-run.

> *"It is not like we develop a model today and then it runs for the next ten years. We have to retrain it like a human being. We learn every day, so it also needs to learn on a daily basis. That is the pipeline that we plan to build when we actually go in 'production'." –* Project manager (Delta)

Interviewed project managers emphasized the need to become aware that a model that is developed today does not run successfully in the long-run without retraining it just like a human being needs to regularly be trained to stay up-to-date. Thus, in planning the project, project managers went beyond the time frame of the actual implementation of the AI system to establish a continuous retraining and testing pipeline. E.g. in project Delta, project managers planned to source customer incident data directly via APIs to feed the AI models, even long after the actual project transferred to a productive state. The AI models are then to be continuously evaluated with the new data sets, and then eventually have to be adapted, extended, and improved.

Second, the learning requirements of AI lead to a shift in risk distribution over time, which requires change in the STS component of *task*: The learning requirements of AI lead to the required data volume, quality, and effort of model tuning needed for PoCs being significantly substantial in AI projects. Especially, the data cleaning steps are very time consuming if the initial quality of the data sets is low. In the analyzed cases, we could observe that due to a proliferation of open source AI models, model creation did not induce as much project effort as the data preparation steps. This implies that once feasibility is proven in a PoC, a major share of the project is already finished, which leads to a shift in risk distribution over the time period of AI projects, which needs to be mitigated by project management. To cope with this challenge, throughout the observed cases, project management approached the PoCs in a hypotheses-driven manner for certain building block of the solution by creating a first version of the solution (minimum viable product) and testing it with a small number of end users.

"We gradually processed more and more incoming emails fully automatically until 100% of the requests were processed automatically." – Project manager (Alpha)

After rolling it out in a pilot over the business units, we could observe that throughhut the cases user feedback was gathered, then it was rolled out again to a constantly increasing number of users in a productive environment.

Furthermore, the learning requirements of AI imposes new challenges on stakeholder communication and expectation management, which requires change in the STS component of *actors*: This actor-related challenge is multiplied by the AI hype that is prevalent nowadays [42] and thus imposes challenges on managing expectations towards AI projects. AI solutions constitute learning systems that improve their performance over certain time spans, and as stated earlier in some use cases even require life-long learning. Thus, project management faces the challenge of communicating this to all relevant stakeholders in order to establish understanding of and patience towards expected AI outcomes. In the case of AI-based classification, routing and resolution of internal incidents tickets (project Epsilon), project management thus developed a story around the project to transport the message that their AI system learns and evolves. However, the project management was faced with users expecting that everything works perfectly right after the implementation of the AI solution. This imposed significant communication efforts in terms of providing information on future advancements, in order to manage the expectations of the users.

"AI has to be trained. AI should be regarded as an intern, otherwise users will perceive it as not useful. One team cancelled an AI solution after two weeks because the AI was not able to resolve 100% of the issues." – Project manager (Epsilon)

In project Epsilon, besides announcements that were made to people via email, the AI itself was used to communicate to the end users what it is capable of doing now and what it will be capable of doing after a sufficient learning period and the metaphor of "AI as an intern" was established.

Finally, the learning requirements of AI demand a reassessment of key performance indicators, which requires change in the STS component of *structure*: During the case analysis, it became evident that traditional IT solution performance measurements such as up-time, number of capacity-relate incidents etc. as provided for instance by COBIT (Control Objectives of Information and related Technology) and ITIL (IT Infrastructure Library) need to be tracked for guaranteeing the general stability of the AI solution. However, this is more or less regarded as a hygiene factor but does not establish respective measurement structures for keeping track of the performance of the AI system from a value-oriented perspective [43]. For instance, in the case of AI-based classification, routing and resolution of internal incidents tickets (project Epsilon), the project management faced the challenge to rethink their KPIs, finally moving to a more human-oriented performance assessment that was then applied to the machine.

"What is different in AI projects is that you rather look at KPIs that are relevant for people performance than IT solution performance." – Project manager (Gamma)

To account for the differences that are induced by the learning requirements of AI, project management (project Epsilon) established a KPI system to assess the performance of the AI system based on KPIs that had been originally used to assess the performance of humans rather than IT solution performance. In this specific case, the project manager of project Epsilon had a set of performance KPIs for their human service desk agents in place such as time to provide the solution, first time resolution, and percentage of incorrectly assigned incidents. These were then deployed to assess the performance of the AI system, and combined with the traditional IT performance measures. This shows, how the learning requirements of AI led to a structure-related change in the components of a socio-technical system through inducing respective challenges on implementing AI projects in an organizational environment.

5   Discussion and Contribution to Research and Practice

This research is motivated by the goal to contribute to answering the question of how AI projects induce distinguishable socio-technical challenges into organizations, and how these challenges can be handled, specifically by project management.

We note here that in no way the empirically induced set of AI-specific socio-technical challenges and resolutions can hold to be exhaustive. This is rooted in the nature of empirical work within nascent fields of research. Thus, we acknowledge the extendibility of our results and look forward to future research building up on and extending our empirical findings.

To facilitate this process, the presented insights shall pave the way towards a deeper understanding of implementing AI in organizational settings, and of the specific project management practices required to overcome the obstacles that are induced by the specific characteristics of AI, which lead to a gap between understanding and leveraging the potential of AI in organizations. We purposefully position this paper as a means to provide insights to practitioners and to trigger future research in this nascent field, which shall provide a conceptually valuable and empirically grounded starting point for investigating the following links:

First, in this paper we establish a link between the unique characteristics of AI – i.e. experimental character [14], context sensitivity [15], black box character [16], and learning requirements of AI [3] – and the particular challenges that could be observed in our five cases. This shall provide researchers with the means to build up on these links in order to investigate how the characteristics of AI pose root-causes of required organizational change, and to provide answers from IS research for managing the latter.

Second, we purposefully chose organizations that are leading in their particular industry to base the collection of observed resolution approaches on a revelatory foundation [23]. In that, the presented resolutions shall provide a first – of course neither generalizable nor exhaustive – set of pathways forward. We also acknowledge that the presented resolutions may not be optimal, but however serve the purpose of industry leading organizations in the respective project settings. Through this second link of observed challenges and resolution strategies, which have proven to be successful, practitioners from the realm of project management can seize these aggregated insights to guide future AI implementation endeavors, or benchmark their own existing approaches. On the other hand, researchers can contribute to finding new ways of optimizing the problem-solution links by either enhancing the approaches presented in this paper, establishing new connections between problem and solution space, or extending either of it.

Third, through linking the challenges and resolutions to the dimension of socio-technical systems theory, we intend to embed AI project management practices into a larger organizational context [20, 21], which shall pinpoint the implications that studying project management as a unit of analysis has in the context of AI. For research, this shall make the phenomenon of AI in general, and AI project management in particular more graspable, in a manner of showcasing cause-effect-relationships that need to be taken into account when trying to comprehensively address AI implementation from a project management perspective. The proposed set of cause-effect relationships thus shall serve as an empirical foundation for a vivid scientific discourse and exchange to advance this nascent field. Furthermore, it shall serve as a potential starting point for developing or adapting (new) constructs, models, methods, and ultimately theory in the realm of managing AI projects and the respective organizational change. For practitioners, the proposed cause-effect relationships provide an overview of how AI makes new decisions, solutions, and actions in project management necessary, and how these can affect the distinct socio-technical areas within their organization. Thus, the findings of this study shall support practitioners in assessing the potential consequences of the decisions they make when implementing AI in their organization. This can lower the still high failure rates of these projects [5].

References

1. Bamberger, P.A.: AMD—clarifying what we are about and where we are going. Acad. Manag. Discov. **4**, 1–10 (2018)
2. von Krogh, G.: Artificial intelligence in organizations: new opportunities for phenomenon-based theorizing. ACM Discov. **4**, 404–409 (2018)
3. Jordan, M.I., Mitchell, T.M.: Machine learning: trends, perspectives, and prospects. Science (80-.) **349**, 255–260 (2015)
4. Davenport, T.H.: From analytics to artificial intelligence. J. Bus. Anal. **1**, 73–80 (2018)
5. Rowsell-Jones, A., Howard, C.: CIO survey: CIOs have awoken to the importance of AI (2019)
6. Rai, A., Constantinides, P., Sarker, S.: Editor's comments: next-generation digital platforms: toward human-AI hybrids. Manag. Inf. Syst. Q. **43**, iii–ix (2019)
7. Searle, J.R.: Minds, brains, and programs. Behav. Brain Sci. **3**, 417–457 (1980)
8. Gubrud, M.A.: Nanotechnology and international security. In: Fifth Foresight Conference on Molecular Nanotechnology (1997)
9. Kumar, K., Thakur, G.S.M.: Advanced applications of neural networks and artificial intelligence: a review. Int. J. Inf. Technol. Comput. Sci. **4**, 57–68 (2012). https://doi.org/10.5815/ijitcs.2012.06.08
10. Moravec, H.: When will computer hardware match the human brain? J. Evol. Technol. **1**, 1–12 (1998)
11. Noor, A.K.: Potential of cognitive computing and cognitive systems. Open Eng. **5**, 75–88 (2015)
12. O'Leary, D.E.: Artificial intelligence and big data. IEEE Intell. Syst. **28**, 96–99 (2013)
13. Stanfill, C., Waltz, D.L.: Toward memory-based reasoning. Commun. ACM. **29**, 1213–1228 (1986)
14. Amigoni, F., Schiaffonati, V.: Ethics for robots as experimental technologies: pairing anticipation with exploration to evaluate the social impact of robotics. IEEE Robot. Autom. Mag. **25**, 30–36 (2018)
15. Lieberman, H., Selker, T.: Out of context: computer systems that adapt to, and learn from, context. IBM Syst. J. **39**, 617–632 (2000)
16. Castelvecchi, D.: Can we open the black box of AI? Nature **538**, 20–23 (2016)
17. Wilamowski, B.M., Irwin, J.D.: Intelligent Systems. CRC Press, Boca Raton (2018)
18. Mitchell, T.M.: Machine Learning. McGraw-Hill, New York (1997)
19. LeCun, Y., Bengio, Y., Hinton, G.: Deep learning. Nature **521**, 436–444 (2015)
20. Bostrom, R.P., Heinen, J.S.: MIS problems and failures: a socio-technical perspective, Part I: the causes. MIS Q. **1**, 17–32 (1977)
21. Lyytinen, K., Newman, M.: Explaining information systems change: a punctuated socio-technical change model. Eur. J. Inf. Syst. **17**, 589–613 (2008)
22. Eisenhardt, K.M.: Building theories from case study research. Acad. Manag. Rev. **14**, 532–550 (1989)
23. Yin, R.K.: Case Study Research: Design and Methods. Sage Publications (2013)
24. Savolainen, J.: The rationality of drawing big conclusions based on small samples: in defense of Mill's methods. Soc. Forces **72**, 1217–1224 (1994)
25. Forman, J., Damschroder, L.: Qualitative content analysis. In: Jacoby, L., Siminoff, L.A. (eds.) Empirical Methods for Bioethics: A Primer (Advances in Bioethics, Volume 11), pp. 39–62. Emerald (2007)
26. Theodorou, A., Wortham, R.H., Bryson, J.J.: Why is my robot behaving like that? Designing transparency for real time inspection of autonomous robots. AISB **2016**, 63–66 (2016)

27. Wortham, R.H., Theodorou, A., Bryson, J.J.: What does the robot think? Transparency as a fundamental design requirement for intelligent systems. In: IJCAI-2016 Ethics for Artificial Intelligence Workshop (2016)
28. Bettis, R.A., Hu, S.: Bounded rationality, heuristics, computational complexity, and artificial intelligence. In: Behavioral Strategy in Perspective, pp. 139–150. Emerald Publishing Limited (2018)
29. Zou, J., Schiebinger, L.: AI can be sexist and racist—it's time to make it fair (2018)
30. Akerlof, G.A.: The market for "lemons": quality uncertainty and the market mechanism. Q. J. Econ. **84**, 488–500 (1978)
31. Brézillon, P.: Context in artificial intelligence: II. key elements of contexts. Comput. Artif. Intell. **18**, 425–446 (1999)
32. Wang, R.Y., Strong, D.M.: Beyond accuracy: what data quality means to data consumers. J. Manag. Inf. Syst. **12**, 5–33 (1996)
33. Konar, A.: Artificial Intelligence and Soft Computing: Behavioral and Cognitive Modeling of the Human Brain. CRC Press, Boca Raton (2018)
34. Lawrence, N.D.: Data science and digital systems: the 3Ds of machine learning systems design. arXiv Prepr. arXiv1903.11241 (2019)
35. Huebner, A., le Cessie, S., Schmidt, C.O., Vach, W.: A contemporary conceptual framework for initial data analysis. Obs Stud. **4**, 171–192 (2018)
36. Sandkuhl, K.: Putting AI into context-method support for the introduction of artificial intelligence into organizations. In: 2019 IEEE 21st Conference on Business Informatics (CBI), pp. 157–164 (2019)
37. Brynjolfsson, E., Rock, D., Syverson, C.: Artificial intelligence and the modern productivity paradox: a clash of expectations and statistics (2017)
38. Gao, J., Xie, C., Tao, C.: Big data validation and quality assurance--issues, challenges, and needs. In: 2016 IEEE Symposium on Service-Oriented System Engineering (SOSE), pp. 433–441 (2016)
39. Park, S.H., Han, K.: Methodologic guide for evaluating clinical performance and effect of artificial intelligence technology for medical diagnosis and prediction. Radiology **286**, 800–809 (2018)
40. Heinrich, B., Klier, M.: Assessing data currency—a probabilistic approach. J. Inf. Sci. **37**, 86–100 (2011)
41. Christiansen, M.H., Kirby, S.: Language evolution: consensus and controversies. Trends Cogn. Sci. **7**, 300–307 (2003)
42. Hopgood, A.A.: Artificial intelligence: hype or reality? Computer (Long. Beach. Calif.) **36**, 24–28 (2003)
43. Barrett, D.G.T., Hill, F., Santoro, A., Morcos, A.S., Lillicrap, T.: Measuring abstract reasoning in neural networks. In: International Conference on Machine Learning, pp. 4477–4486 (2018)

Through the Cognitive Functions Lens - A Socio-technical Analysis of Predictive Maintenance

Alexander Stohr[1,2(✉)] and Jamie O'Rourke[3]

[1] Project Group Business and Information Systems Engineering of the Fraunhofer FIT, Augsburg, Germany
[2] FIM Research Center, University of Bayreuth, Bayreuth, Germany
alexander.stohr@fim-rc.de
[3] University of Augsburg, Augsburg, Germany

Abstract. The effective use of artificial intelligence promises significant business value. Effective use, however, requires a thorough exploration of its strengths and weaknesses from different perspectives. Information systems research is particularly invested in the management and use of artificial intelligence in organizations. It has proposed the use of cognitive functions to guide this exploration. In this paper, we evaluate the usefulness of such a cognitive functions lens for a relatively mature application of artificial intelligence, predictive maintenance. Our evaluation is informed by the insights we collected from an embedded single-case study. We find that a cognitive functions lens can indeed be a useful tool to explore artificial intelligence. In particular, it can aid the allocation of tasks between human agents and artificial intelligence-based systems and the design of human-AI hybrids. It is particularly helpful for those who investigate the management of artificial intelligence.

Keywords: Artificial intelligence · Predictive maintenance · Cognitive functions · Embedded single-case study

1 Introduction

The transformative prospect of artificial intelligence (AI) inspires researchers and practitioners in many fields (e.g., transportation, health care, and education) and focus areas (e.g., deep learning, robotics, and collaborative systems) [1]. Since AI reaches many areas of life and might affect a substantial part of our society in the future, the expectations for guidance are substantial. The information systems (IS) community seeks to contribute to this research mainly through the exploration of the socio-technical effects and management of AI, drawing on the community's substantial body of theories and knowledge about the use of conventional IT [2]. Its efforts are directed especially at future workplaces in which human agents and AI-based systems work together [e.g., 3, 4]. In these workplaces, AI-based systems may substitute (*task substitution*) or improve

F. Ahlemann et al. (Eds.): WI 2021, LNISO 47, pp. 182–197, 2021.
https://doi.org/10.1007/978-3-030-86797-3_13

human labor within specific tasks (*task augmentation*), but may as well complement human labor in joint human-AI-teams (*task assemblage*) [5–7].

So far, however, IS research on AI has struggled to find a definition of AI that serves its particular perspectives and needs. While this lack has likely benefitted initial explorations [1], it has also led to a substantial variety in conceptions of AI and a certain vagueness in discussions. To address this issue, Rai et al. [7] propose the use of cognitive functions commonly associated with the human brain, such as reasoning, learning, decision-making, or problem-solving, to describe and characterize AI-based systems. Such a cognitive functions lens could particularly benefit the study of AI-based systems that are designed to perform specific, pre-defined tasks. Exemplary of such task-specific AI-based systems are those for predictive maintenance (PdM) [8].

PdM aims at predicting future maintenance needs by continuously analyzing a machine's operating conditions and predicting when to initiate preventive maintenance activities [9, 10]. PdM offers several benefits and provides organizations with novel opportunities to build knowledge about their products. The implementation of PdM systems, however, requires new maintenance strategies and a new allocation of tasks between the PdM system and human maintenance workers. As such, PdM presents an interesting and relevant case for the application and study of the usefulness of the cognitive functions lens. In this paper, we thus explore the following research question using PdM as our contextual domain:

RQ: How do cognitive functions affect the distribution of tasks in the context of AI-based PdM systems?

To address this question, we conduct an embedded single-case study on a project in which multiple manufacturing organizations and researchers collaboratively developed PdM strategies and implemented prototypes to evaluate their applicability. Based on our case study, we illustrate how the cognitive functions lens can help to better frame human-AI collaboration. In particular, we propose a distinction between cognitive functions that can be performed superbly by a particular AI-based system (core cognitive functions), functions that can be performed either by the system or a human agent (shared cognitive functions), and functions that, so far, human agents excel in. Such a distinction is useful because it allows us to understand Rai et al.'s [7] classification of substitution, augmentation, and assemblage as the result of allocating tasks between human agents and PdM systems based on the (type of) cognitive functions needed to perform the task.

From a theoretical perspective, we contribute to IS research by illustrating how a cognitive functions lens can be a useful tool to explore AI. The cognitive functions lens allows researchers to better understand and frame human-AI collaboration. This is particularly helpful for those who investigate the management and use of information technology. That is, the cognitive functions lens provides researchers with a tool to study the managerial and organizational implications of the implementation of AI-based systems. Moreover, our study has several practical implications. A cognitive functions lens can aid practitioners in better understanding a system's functionalities and support organizations in deciding whether a system fits their needs, which human and organizational capabilities they need, and how to adapt surrounding processes.

2   Theoretical Background

2.1   Artificial Intelligence

Interest in Artificial intelligence (AI) has been growing over the past few years, not only in practice but also in IS research. AI, however, is not a nascent field. Its roots reach back to the 1950s when researchers began to explore the possibilities to compute and simulate intelligence [11]. The first IS publications on AI date back to 1984 [12]. While the 1990s saw various studies on aspects surrounding AI, interest subsided again in the 2000s. However, in the wake of significant technological advancements in hardware (e.g. processing and storage capabilities) as well as the availability of data and data analysis techniques, such as deep learning, AI has begun to regain its earlier foothold in the IS community [1, 12].

This renewed interest has also given birth to various new research streams, many of which revolve around the exploration of AI's impact on corporate strategy, business processes, as well as the future of work [5]. The essential question that underpins these streams is one of the interactions between human agents and AI-based system, that is, whether AI-based systems will change, replace, or enhance human labor [3, 6, 7]. IS research has begun to explore this question from a task-based perspective and identified three archetypical interactions: *task substitution, task augmentation, and task assemblage.* Task substitution refers to the substitution of human labor through an AI agent. Task augmentation describes contexts in which a human or an AI agent performs support functions that allow the supported to perform a task more effectively or efficiently [7]. For instance, AI-based systems can improve human decision-making through highly accurate predictions and decision proposals [13], or human agents can improve an AI-based system's decision-making by factoring in judgment or moral values [14]. Task assemblage refers to contexts where AI and human agents jointly perform a task [7].

The renewed interest in AI has also created new challenges, such as the establishment of a conception of AI that serves the particular perspectives and needs of the IS community. Whereas IS research has been effective in guiding practitioners in understanding and managing traditional information technology [2, 15], the ability of AI-based systems to perform cognitive functions may require a re-examination of various IS concepts [7]. Cognitive functions refer to the various mental processes of the human brain. They are particularly useful to explore task-specific applications of AI because they enable a discussion of the type of intelligence required for the task [16]. Exemplary of such task-specific applications is predictive maintenance (PdM) [8].

2.2   Predictive Maintenance

Traditionally, organizations minimize machine faults through regular maintenance cycles and preemptive activities based on the experience of seasoned maintenance workers. Once a fault has occurred, they respond based on reactive maintenance strategies [10].

PdM presents a fundamental shift from these premises. Technically speaking, PdM is a maintenance management method that is based on a machine's conditions instead of general statistics on a machine's lifetime [9]. It relies on the continuous monitoring of mechanical conditions and system efficiency in order to predict the occurrence of faults and defects and, by extension, allows the prevention of machine failure. PdM systems commonly use techniques such as tribology, oil analysis, vibration analysis, thermography, or process parameter monitoring to collect various data points [9, 17, 18] that are then fed into models that extract meaningful knowledge from the data [19]. PdM enables companies to forecast a machine's future condition and, thus, enhances human decision-making [20].

PdM can have a range of positive effects, such as increased process availability, reduced maintenance costs, increased quality, productivity, safety, and profitability [21]. Successful implementation of PdM, however, requires the addressing of various challenges [22]. For instance, manufacturers need to be able to collect and process data in real-time, provide a data supply chain for simple data transmission among different business units, build knowledge on PdM intelligence and strategy, and enable machines to collaborate with and better assist humans [23].

2.3 Cognitive Functions

Many unresolved issues in the context of AI result from a limited understanding of natural intelligence [24]. One way of examining natural intelligence is by looking at the finite set of cognitive functions of the human brain. These cognitive functions represent all life functions and mental processes that human brains may perform, ranging from very basic and subconscious functions, such as memory or perception, to highly specific and conscious functions, such as recognition or problem-solving [25]. The concept of cognitive functions is based on the idea that "thinking can best be understood in terms of representational structures in the mind and computational procedures that operate on those structures" [26]. Cognitive functions are being explored in many fields, such as psychology, cognitive science, neuro-philosophy, or cognitive informatics [16].

For the design and exploration of AI cognitive informatics, in particular, provides a useful starting point. The discipline focuses on the discovery of information-processing mechanisms as well as cognitive functions of the brain and their application in what we would refer to as AI-based systems [27]. However, not all of the cognitive functions of the human brain are yet transferable to an AI-based system because they are based on the brain's structure with its inherited and acquired life functions and different kinds of memories [16]. But, many applications of AI do not need to draw from the full set of cognitive functions of the human brain because they are not necessary for the task at hand [16]. Russell and Norvig [28], for instance, make only use of a few cognitive functions in describing different types of (rational) AI agents.

Overall, cognitive functions can help researchers to better grasp the gestalt of intelligence and, thus, enrich research in many different AI disciplines [16]. For instance, we follow Rai et al. [7] that cognitive functions are a useful conception of AI that serves the particular perspectives and needs of the IS community in exploring task-specific AI-based systems, such as PdM. In a simplisitc manner, the cognitive functions lens allows us to parse PdM systems into their individual functions and, thus, to describe more precisely what it is that makes such systems AI-based. Moreover, it can help us to better understand the socio-technical aspects and requirements of the adoption of AI-based systems as demanded by Sarker et al. [2]. That is, a cognitive functions lens allows for considering human, social and organisational factors, as well as technical factors, in analyzing and designing PdM systems [29].

3   Research Method

3.1   Case Setting

To address our research goal of understanding how a cognitive function lens can help to conceptualize AI-based PdM systems, we conducted an embedded single-case study guided by the recommendations of Yin [30]. Specifically, we examine an applied research project in which organizations and applied researchers from different backgrounds collaborated to work on PdM strategies and their prototypical implementation in the respective organizations. Embedded single-case studies allow for the analysis of a single-case (the project) while simultaneously considering the specifics of multiple "embedded" units of analysis (participating organizations). According to Yin [30], a single-case is justifiable if it is either critical, unusual, common, revelatory, or longitudinal. Although PdM as a research topic has already gained traction back in the late 1990s, many organizations are still struggling with the implementation of PdM systems [31]. Therefore, we selected a case that reflects common circumstances and conditions faced by many manufacturers.

The applied research project began in early 2018 and concluded just over a year later. The project was publicly funded and saw four non-competing German medium-sized enterprises from the mechanical engineering sector collaborate with two German research organizations to develop intelligent analytics solutions, increase production transparency, and create data-based services and business models. We, as the authors of this paper, were not actively participating in the project. We chose the project because it provided in-depth insights into the PdM implementation process from many different perspectives.

3.2   Data Collection and Analysis

We decided to conduct semi-structured interviews as our primary method of data collection to elicit stories from the participating organizations [32]. Our interviews lasted between 30 and 60 min, were audio-recorded, and fully transcribed afterward. The interviews aimed, inter alia, at eliciting individual viewpoints on either the cognitive functions that experts had already identified in PdM applications or those that they were hoping to make use of for their organization. In several cases, we approached the interviewee again after the interview in order to clarify questions.

We conducted interviews with relevant representatives from all of the involved organizations to take advantage of this unique project setting. We based our selection of interviewees on two aspects. First, we selected only those closely involved in the project and thus able to provide deep insights. Second, we made sure to involve different roles in the interview process, such as managers and engineers, to obtain multiple perspectives. Table 1 provides an anonymized overview of the interviewees.

At the beginning of the interviews, the interviewer introduced himself and the research project followed by an introduction of the interviewee including their background, current organizational position and their experiences within the respective organization. In the further course of the interview, we particularly asked questions related to the cognitive functions of PdM. For instance, we asked the interviewees how they intended to or already used PdM and about the (type of) tasks performed by the PdM system. Moreover, we asked them how their maintenance workers collaborated with the PdM system and how PdM would change their organization's maintenance processes and business models. Lastly, we were also interested in how the organization would need to adapt to implement PdM systems.

Table 1. List of organizations and interviewees

#	Interviewee's Role	Organization	# Employees
1	Data analytics researcher	Research Organization 1	>100
2	Data analytics researcher		
3	Digital business model researcher		
4	IoT researcher		
5	Data analytics researcher	Research Organization 2	<10
6	Data scientist	PdM Implementing Organization 1	>5000
7	Pre-sales management		
8	IT-specialist	PdM Implementing Organization 2	>1000
9	Manager		
10	Engineer	PdM Implementing Organization 3	>1000
11	Engineer		
12	IT-specialist		
13	Manager		
14	Manager	PdM Implementing Organization 4	>1000

To triangulate our results [33], we directly observed workshops that were held as part of the project and analyzed project documentation that the participants provided us with.

In analyzing the collected data, we followed a two-stage process of inductive and deductive coding of data [34]. First, researchers scrutinized and coded the data independently of each other. Subsequently, we discussed our interpretations and constructed categories and subcategories, grouped codes and looked for relationships and patterns. During data analysis, we assigned the codes to higher-level concepts which were either based on our theoretical lens (deductive coding) or emerged during data collection (inductive coding).

4   Findings

We began our analysis of the cognitive functions of PdM by inferring from essential work by Rai et al. [7], Russell and Norvig [28], and Wang et al. [16] eight hypothetical cognitive functions of PdM (creation, decision-making, learning, planning, perceiving.

problem-solving, reasoning, recognition). Out of these, we find five to be relevant in our case study: Decision-making, learning, perceiving, reasoning, and planning.

Moreover, we find that these functions group into two categories depending on their specific manifestation in a PdM system: Core cognitive functions (CCFs) and symbiotic cognitive functions (SCFs) (see Fig. 1). We denote as CCFs those cognitive functions in which a particular AI-based system outperforms human agents. Tasks that require only the CCFs of an AI-based system present substantial opportunity for task substitution. SCFs are those cognitive functions that an AI-based system can provide yet in which it does not necessarily excel human agents. Tasks that require the SCFs of AI-based systems are candidates for task augmentation and task assemblage.

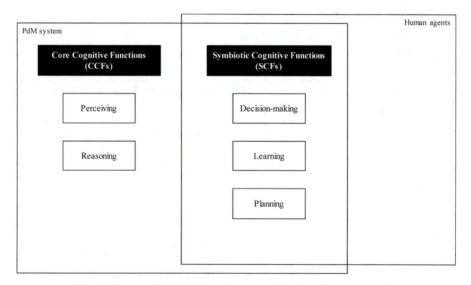

Fig. 1. Human-AI hybrids based on a cognitive functions perspective

4.1   Core Cognitive Functions

As described above, CCFs are those cognitive functions in which AI-based systems significantly outperform human agents either because the human brain cannot perform these functions to the desired extent or because the AI-based system is better at performing the function. In our PdM case, we identified two such CCFs: perceiving and reasoning. The workshop participants and interviewees were either hoping or expecting to make use of these two CCFs to replace human agents when implementing a PdM system in their organization.

Core Cognitive Function of PdM 1: Perceiving. Perceiving refers to an agent's ability to gather information about its environment through means such as sensors and cameras [28]. Sensors involved in PdM range from pressure sensors to thermocouples or resistance temperature detectors, which all measure different types of input data [35]. Popular techniques to analyze this input data are, for example, tribology, oil analysis, vibration analysis, or thermography [9, 17, 18]. We categorize "lower-level" cognitive functions such as audition or tactility that also refer to the processing of such sensory responses under the "higher-level" cognitive function of *perceiving* to better account for different types of PdM systems. One of the major advantages of a PdM system's capability to perceive its environment concerns the analyzability of previously unavailable data sources, such as radio, infrared, GPS, or other wireless signals [28].

"Well, they [the systems] can already pick up sensor signals today, they can also store these sensor signals for a limited period of time and transmit the data." (I_{14})

While one researcher reported about maintenance workers who could detect upcoming faults merely by putting their hands on a machine, such workers are the exception, and PdM systems were broadly expected to outperform human agents in perceiving. This is especially the case if a PdM system can perceive a machine's (or any other product's) direct environment that is not directly accessible for human agents. For instance, some of the organizations need to globally maintain products at isolated customer sites, where accessibility is significantly impeded. Moreover, PdM systems are better at continuously perceiving machine conditions as required to predict imminent failures or other maintenance needs.

Core Cognitive Function of PdM 2: Reasoning. Reasoning refers to the inference of causal conclusions from known pairs of cause and effect [16]. Reasoning can assume different forms. For instance, associational reasoning refers to the use of heuristics to associate data with related solutions [36], deductive reasoning refers to the inference of causalities from the general to the particular, and inductive reasoning is exactly the contrary [37]. Case-based reasoning is a method commonly used for computational reasoning. It simulates human reasoning by searching for similar situations that have occurred in the past (cases) and applying insights from these situations to the current one [38]. Systems capable of reasoning are expected to perform tasks for which they have not been explicitly programmed solely based on raw data whilst reacting rapidly to a continuously and unpredictably changing environment [37, 39].

In PdM systems, reasoning is an important function for analyzing historical data to detect previously unexplored causalities on critical pieces of information, such as system faults or plant diseases [40]. Extracting new information on potential or upcoming machine faults is what most of the interviewees expected or hoped to achieve by using a PdM system. Many interviewees emphasized the ability of PdM systems to discover fault patterns through the collection and analysis of process or fault data.

"I envisioned that we make progress with the analysis part in a way that our manual effort is reduced and that we are relieved of some tasks. For example, I thought that maybe the alarms can be prefiltered, or that different data types can

be combined, such as vibration level, torque, rotation speed, etc. Currently, we have to do a lot of manual work." (I_{10})

All interviewees agreed that making sense of the collected machine data is one of the key challenges for their respective organizations. Human agents, however, do not possess the necessary capabilities to properly analyze these large amounts of data.

"At this point, we entered the project because we had masses of cluttered data that were stored online and to some extent offline. What can we do with it? We have many colleagues who are capable of analyzing data but not those masses. That can't be done by a human." (I_{12})

An intelligent system's capability to discover causality in large amounts of data is one of its biggest strengths where it clearly outperforms human agents in related tasks. Consequently, PdM systems should *substitute* human agents in these kinds of activities.

4.2 Symbiotic Cognitive Functions

SCFs are those cognitive functions that AI-based systems can perform, in which, however, they are not necessarily better than human agents. Tasks that require the SCFs of an AI-based system present opportunities for task assemblage and task augmentation. We found references to SCFs in various statements related to improving existing tasks that the respective organizations were struggling with. Consequently, we do not regard SCFs as a requirement for every PdM system but rather as components whose integration into PdM systems depends on the context.

Symbiotic Cognitive Function of PdM 1: Decision-making. Decision-making is the process of choosing an alternative under a set of options based on one's preferences, for example, in form of utility. Assuming certainty of outcomes, the preferred decision is the one that maximizes the utility [28]. As the world is usually uncertain, different decision approaches exist. Sometimes, people make decisions based on their "gut-feeling" or by applying judgment. However, many organizations have shifted toward data-driven decisions where human agents make decisions based on data analyses.

AI-based PdM systems can support such an approach by recommending certain actions but leaving the final decision to a human agent and his/her judgment [41]. However, they can also completely take over decision-making from human agents. In our case study, most PdM systems are either supposed to or already make maintenance recommendations, yet leave the decision on whether any actions are necessary to the human system users.

"We do now employ a ticket system. That is, we do not need to individually check the data for irregularities, but rather receive a ticket when the system creates an alarm. However, we manually decide on actions." (I_{10})

Many of the involved organizations employed such a ticket-based system, with some systems creating their alert directly for the technician and others for a centralized maintenance unit that decides about required actions. In other words, human agents make the final decision. Despite the possibility, the organizations involved in the project do not (yet) intend to leave the maintenance decision to the PdM system entirely. However, they share the belief that the insights provided by the systems enable them to make better and more accurate maintenance decisions. In summary, the PdM systems *augment* the decision-making of most of the organizations involved in our case study.

Even if decision-making on maintenance needs was delegated to the PdM systems, human agents still would need to decide upon the appropriate algorithm for the PdM systems to be able to excert decision-making abilities. This yields an entirely new form of the decision-making paradox described by Triantaphyllou and Mann [42].

Symbiotic Cognitive Function of PdM 2: Learning. In reference to Schunk [43], learning can refer to a lasting change in behavior or in the capacity to behave as a result of practice or other experiences. The result of learning is improved performance on future tasks compared to the status before the learning process [28]. While shortcomings in data processing capabilities limited machine learning techniques for a long time, these techniques are well established today. Machine learning can generally assume different forms, such as supervised or unsupervised learning [44]. For instance, a system can learn by identifying certain regularities or patterns in (large) data sets, something humans are often not capable of.

Our interviews revealed that PdM systems give organizations the opportunity to learn more about their products, their behavior in an environment outside the organizations' premises, and the actual usage patterns of their customers. A fundamental difference between the cognitive functions of learning and reasoning is that organizations do not intend to leave learning to the systems solely but rather plan to expand their product and customer knowledge by applying PdM. Therefore, PdM systems can enable human agents to perform their tasks better.

> "Additionally, we can benefit from knowing how our products are operated. We usually don't receive field data. This is of course very interesting." (I_{10})

However, human learning processes can also benefit the PdM systems by, for instance, updating the system's knowledge base with new information. Consequently, sharing learning capabilities enables *task augmentation* of the human-AI hybrid in both directions.

Symbiotic Cognitive Function of PdM 3: Planning. Simply put, planning is the creation of an action plan with a given set of information to fulfill a certain goal. The action plan is usually limited by constraints, such as the availability of involved actors [16, 28]. Goals related to maintenance planning are maximizing maintenance resource use and maximizing capacity use of the plant or machine. Especially in the context of large organizations with different customers, maintenance workers and machines, the planning as well as scheduling of maintenance processes can be very challenging and need to be addressed carefully [9]. However, in reactive maintenance settings, organizations do not anticipate and, thus, cannot plan their response to faults and maintenance needs. PdM provides organizations and customers with increased flexibility and corresponding efficiency.

"For me, it [predictive maintenance] has only positive aspects. On the one hand, it increases plannability for the customer because he is notified about maintenance needs in advance. On the other hand, we can eliminate quality problems because we can use the analyses to detect regularities in the process of breakdowns." (I_8)

Moreover, the interviewees pointed out several benefits of this enhanced plannability, such as a reduction of waiting times for spare parts, a reduction of downtimes during business hours and an increase of acceptance on behalf of the customer. Some organizations even intend to take a step further by leaving the planning and scheduling of maintenance activities to the PdM system.

"In markets like Germany, where we can reach our facilities within 30 minutes and have a lot of technicians, we probably would not really need this kind of plannability. However, there are certain markets where it will provide huge benefits." (I_9)

However, automatic and intelligent planning requires decision-making to be left to the system as well. In summary, the allocation of roles can assume different forms depending on the system's design when it comes to planning activities. Task allocation can range from *task augmentation* where the PdM systems support planning activities of the human agents by, for instance, providing flexibility, to *task substitution*, where the system develops a schedule for the maintenance worker.

5 Discussion

Our paper illustrates how a cognitive functions lens can help to better understand and frame human-AI hybrids. Based on an embedded single-case study, we identify both CCFs and SCFs of PdM systems and demonstrate how this differentiation can help to determine the allocation of tasks between human agents and AI-based systems. That is, depending on the (type of) cognitive function needed for a specific task, AI-based systems could, consistent with Rai et al. [7], either replace human agents in performing this task, they could augment each other, or even collaborate on performing the same task. Consequently, we believe that the cognitive function lens is an interesting tool that allows IS researchers to explore the socio-technical effects and management of AI.

Our research contributes to both theory and practice. While research in the field of AI covers many different topics, such as the influence of AI on the workplace of the future [e.g., 4] or specific AI applications such as robotics [e.g., 5], the IS community is mainly interested in the exploration of the socio-technical effects and management of AI [2, 7]. However, so far only very few studies investigate AI-based systems from a managerial perspective. Tarafdar et al. [45], for instance, outline how companies can create value by using AI. The authors focus on the introduction of high-level organizational capabilities, such as data science competence, but lack precise recommendations on a procedural level. Our study contributes to IS research in the field of AI by illustrating how researchers can use cognitive functions as a tool to help conceptualize human-AI hybrids. That is, the cognitive functions lens supports researchers in studying the managerial and organizational implications of the implementation of AI-based systems.

Hence, the lens is particularly helpful for those who investigate the management and use of AI in organizations.

Our study makes some practical contributions as well. The implementation of AI-based systems surely is one of the future (if not today's) key challenges for the manufacturing sector [22, 46]. However, many practitioners and decision-makers lack a deep understanding of AI [47]. Therefore, they will likely struggle to identify the appropriate functionalities of individual systems that fit their organization's needs. Instead, many organizations take competitive actions based on external pressure that questions the organization's AI competency [48]. As a result, many AI-related actions are poorly aligned with the organization's needs and competencies. Here, cognitive functions are a helpful tool that decision-makers can easily understand regardless of their background. Decomposing an AI-based system into its cognitive functions can facilitate the communication of features and requirements between system engineers and business decision-makers. Moreover, practitioners often struggle with creating the appropriate conditions in their organizations to successfully implement AI-based systems [47]. Although AI-related issues can affect the entire organization on a strategic level, problems often arise at a much smaller scale, such as an adequate adaptation of specific processes or appropriate team designs [8]. Organizational decision-makers need to address these challenges by, for instance, creating an appropriate fit between users, systems, and tasks [49]. The cognitive functions lens can aid practitioners in creating this fit. By analyzing a particular AI-based system's CCFs as well as SCFs, practitioners can better design human-AI hybrids and identify associated requirements on process adaptations. In summary, the cognitive functions lens can assist practitioners in getting even more out of their AI endeavors.

PdM systems possess certain capabilities (or cognitive functions) in which they excel, but so do human agents. Tasks addressed by the CCFs of an AI-based system are usually those tasks for which the system substitutes human agents. Consequently, organizations can redirect their human capacities to other tasks improving their resource efficiency. SCFs, on the other hand, support task augmentation and task assemblage. To benefit from these tasks, organizations should adapt their processes, teams, and cultures in a way that supports human-AI collaboration. For instance, organizations should make sure that at least one team member is capable of training the AI-based system with input from the rest of the team, such as contextualized knowledge or error corrections [50]. In particular, skilled workers who, as mentioned in the previous section, can assess a machine's status based on the noise or vibration could be moved along the line to be part of the team that trains the algorithms. Lastly, organizations might develop entirely new tasks where human agents and AI systems perform tasks as an integrated unit.

In line with existing literature, we find that organizations still rely on human capabilities, such as judgment and explanations to make sense of certain irregularities and machine disruptions as well as human creativity [7, 16, 50]. Possessing certain cognitive functions, such as perceiving and reasoning, PdM systems can provide insights on opportunities for the improvement or development of products and services. However, organizations (still) need human input to develop these products or services. In summary, we regard cognitive functions as an interesting concept to better understand human-AI hybrids. In this way, cognitive functions are a valuable tool to further analyze how the implementation of AI-based systems affects the management of organizations. In line with Raisch and Krakowski [51], we further emphasize the inclusiveness of automation and augmentation when using AI-based systems.

6   Limitations and Further Research

Our paper is but a first step toward making effective use of the cognitive functions lens. As such, it has limitations and offers various opportunities for further research. While we consider a single-case study design to be appropriate for our research objective, single-case studies commonly face criticism concerning their generalizability [52]. While we believe that the embedded setting of the project with multiple participating organizations mediates such concerns to some degree, our research would benefit from further validation. Second, we drew our findings from a specific setting, that of a publicly funded, applied research project with medium-sized enterprises from the mechanical engineering sector. While this particular setting provided us with rich, in-depth insights into PdM implementations, future research should investigate the cognitive functions lens also for other applications of AI, different project settings and different types of companies. Third, our case study focuses on organizations that have merely started implementing PdM. Consequently, we cannot – nor do we intend to – provide a conclusive list of cognitive functions of PdM systems or of design options for human-AI hybrids. Rather, we identify cognitive functions as an interesting lens for researchers interested in the intersection of human agents and AI-based systems in organizations. Future research could further benefit from integrating ideas from collective intelligence literature into the design of human-AI hybrids. While Human-Computer Interaction literature, which we do not cover in this paper, provides several studies on the interaction between human agents and AI-based systems on an individual level [49], we argue that the cognitive functions lens will be particularly useful at the organizational level. Moreover, researchers and practitioners could draw from a better understanding of human-AI hybrids to improve the design of AI-based systems in the future.

In conclusion, we believe that our research, despite its limitations, is an initial step toward exploring the management and use of AI-based systems within organizations. We hope it provides fellow IS researchers with a foundation for continued work in this important domain.

Acknowledgements. This paper builds on the preliminary work of the unpublished master's thesis of Jamie O'Rourke (O'Rourke, J.: Cognitive Functions of Predictive Maintenance (Unpublished master's thesis). University of Augsburg, Augsburg, DE (2019)).

References

1. Stone, P., et al.: Artificial Intelligence and Life in 2030. One Hundred Year Study on Artificial Intelligence: Report of the 2015-2016 Study Panel, Stanford, CA, US (2016)
2. Sarker, S., Chatterjee, S., Xiao, X., Elbanna, A.R.: The sociotechnical axis of cohesion for the is discipline: Its historical legacy and its continued relevance. MISQ **43**(3), 695–719 (2019). https://doi.org/10.25300/MISQ/2019/13747

3. Acemoglu, D., Restrepo, P.: Artificial Intelligence, Automation and Work. Working Paper, National Bureau of Economic Research (2018)
4. Davenport, T.H.: The AI Advantage. How to Put the Artificial Intelligence Revolution to Work. MIT Press, Cambridge, MA, US (2018)
5. Aleksander, I.: Partners of humans: A realistic assessment of the role of robots in the foreseeable future. J. Inf. Technol. **32**(1), 1–9 (2017). https://doi.org/10.1057%2Fs41265-016-0032-4
6. Autor, D.H.: Why are there still so many jobs? The history and future of workplace automation. J. Econ. Perspect. **29**(3), 3–30 (2015). https://doi.org/10.1257/jep.29.3.3
7. Rai, A., Constantinides, P., Sarker, S.: Next-generation digital platforms: Toward human–ai hybrids. MISQ **43**(1), iii–ix (2019)
8. vom Brocke, J., Maaß, W., Buxmann, P., Maedche, A., Leimeister, J.M., Pecht, G.: Future work and enterprise systems. Bus. Inf. Syst. Eng. **60**(4), 357–366 (2018). https://doi.org/10.1007/s12599-018-0544-2
9. Mobley, R.K.: An Introduction to Predictive Maintenance. Butterworth-Heinemann, Amsterdam, NL (2002)
10. Swanson, L.: Linking maintenance strategies to performance. Int. J. Prod. Econ. **70**(3), 237–244 (2001). https://doi.org/10.1016/S0925-5273(00)00067-0
11. Simon, H.A.: Artificial intelligence: An empirical science. Artif. Intell. **77**(1), 95–127 (1995). https://doi.org/10.1016/0004-3702(95)00039-H
12. Nascimento, A.M., da Cunha, M.A.V.C., de Souza Meirelles, F., Scornavacca Jr., E., de Melo, V.V.: A literature analysis of research on artificial intelligence in management information system (MIS). In: Proceedings of the 24th Americas Conference on Information Systems (2018)
13. Agrawal, A., Gans, J., Goldfarb, A.: Prediction Machines. The Simple Economics of Artificial Intelligence. Harvard Business Review Press, Boston, MA, US (2018)
14. Daugherty, P.R., Wilson, H.J., Chowdhury, R.: Using artificial intelligence to promote diversity. MIT Sloan Manag. Rev. **60**(2), 1 (2018)
15. Lee, A.: Inaugural editor's comments. MISQ **23**(1), v–xi (1999)
16. Wang, Y., Wang, Y., Patel, S., Patel, D.: A layered reference model of the brain (LRMB). IEEE Trans. Syst., Man, Cybern. C **36**(2), 124–133 (2006). https://doi.org/10.1109/TSMCC.2006.871126
17. Carnero, M.C.: Selection of diagnostic techniques and instrumentation in a predictive maintenance program: A case study. Decis. Sup. Syst. **38**(4), 539–555 (2005). https://doi.org/10.1016/j.dss.2003.09.003
18. Edwards, D.J., Holt, G.D., Harris, F.C.: Predictive maintenance techniques and their relevance to construction plant. J. Qual. Maint. Eng. **4**, 25–37 (1998). https://doi.org/10.1108/13552519810369057
19. Lu, S.C.-Y.: Machine learning approaches to knowledge synthesis and integration tasks for advanced engineering automation. Comput. Ind. **15**(1–2), 105–120 (1990). https://doi.org/10.1016/0166-3615(90)90088-7
20. Lee, W.J., Wu, H., Yun, H., Kim, H., Jun, M.B.G., Sutherland, J.W.: Predictive maintenance of machine tool systems using artificial intelligence techniques applied to machine condition data. Procedia CIRP **80**, 506–511 (2019). https://doi.org/10.1016/j.procir.2018.12.019
21. Zarte, M., Wunder, U., Pechmann, A.: Concept and first case study for a generic predictive maintenance simulation in AnyLogic™. In: Proceedings of the 43rd Annual Conference of the IEEE Industrial Electronics Society, pp. 3372–3377. IEEE, Piscataway (2017). https://doi.org/10.1109/IECON.2017.8216571
22. Wuest, T., Weimer, D., Irgens, C., Thoben, K.-D.: Machine learning in manufacturing: Advantages, challenges, and applications. Prod. Manuf. Res. **4**(1), 23–45 (2016). https://doi.org/10.1080/21693277.2016.1192517

23. Roy, R., Stark, R., Tracht, K., Takata, S., Mori, M.: Continuous maintenance and the future – Foundations and technological challenges. CIRP Ann. Manuf. Technol. **65**(2), 667–688 (2016). https://doi.org/10.1016/j.cirp.2016.06.006
24. Wang, Y., Wang, Y.: Cognitive informatics models of the brain. IEEE Trans. Syst., Man, Cybern. C **36**(2), 203–207 (2006). https://doi.org/10.1109/TSMCC.2006.871151
25. Hwang, K., Chen, M.: Big-Data Analytics for Cloud, IoT and Cognitive Computing. John Wiley & Sons, Newark, NJ, US (2017)
26. Thagard, P.: Mind: Introduction to Cognitive Science. MIT Press, Cambridge (2005)
27. Wang, Y.: The theoretical framework of cognitive informatics. Int. J. Cogn. Informat. Nat. Intell. **1**(1), 1–27 (2007). https://doi.org/10.4018/jcini.2007010101
28. Russell, S.J., Norvig, P.: Artificial Intelligence: A Modern Approach. Pearson Education Limited, Harlow, UK (2016)
29. Baxter, G., Sommerville, I.: Socio-technical systems: From design methods to systems engineering. Interact. Comput. **23**(1), 4–17 (2011). https://doi.org/10.1016/j.intcom.2010.07.003
30. Yin, R.K.: Case study research. design and methods. SAGE, Thousand Oaks, CA, US (2014)
31. Hermes, J.: Lack of expertise makes predictive maintenance a challenge for manufacturers despite promise of IIoT, https://www.environmentalleader.com/2019/03/179592/
32. Myers, M.D., Newman, M.: The qualitative interview in IS research: Examining the craft. Inf. Organ. **17**(1), 2–26 (2007). https://doi.org/10.1016/j.infoandorg.2006.11.001
33. Creswell, J.W., Poth, C.N.: Qualitative Inquiry and Research Design. Choosing Among Five Approaches. SAGE, Thousand Oaks, CA, US (2018)
34. Miles, M.B., Huberman, A.M., Saldaña, J.: Qualitative Data Analysis: A Methods Sourcebook. SAGE, Thousand Oaks, CA, US (2014)
35. Hashemian, H.M., Bean, W.C.: State-of-the-art predictive maintenance techniques. IEEE Trans. Instrum. Meas. **60**(1), 3480–3492 (2011). https://doi.org/10.1109/TIM.2010.2047662
36. Koton, P.A.: A method for improving the efficiency of model-based reasoning systems. Appl. Artif. Intell. **3**(2–3), 357–366 (1989). https://doi.org/10.1080/08839518908949931
37. Watson, I.: A case-based reasoning application for engineering sales support using introspective reasoning. In: Proceedings of the 17th National Conference on Artificial Intelligence and 12th Conference on Innovative Applications of Artificial Intelligence. Austin, TX, US (2000)
38. Leake, D.B.: Case-Based Reasoning: Experiences. Lessons & Future Directions. AAAI Press, MIT Press, Cambridge, MA, US (1996)
39. Georgeff, M.P., Ingrand, F.: Decision-making in an embedded reasoning system. In: Proceedings of the 11th International Joint Conference on Artificial Intelligence. Detroit, MI, US (1989)
40. Tocatlidou, A., Passam, H.C., Sideridis, A.B., Yialouris, C.P.: Reasoning under uncertainty for plant disease diagnosis. Expert. Syst. **19**(1), 46–52 (2002). https://doi.org/10.1111/1468-0394.00188
41. Colson, E.: What AI-Driven Decision Making Looks Like. Harvard Business Review (2019)
42. Triantaphyllou, E., Mann, S.H.: An examination of the effectiveness of multi-dimensional decision-making methods: A decision-making paradox. Decis. Support Syst. **5**(3), 303–312 (1989). https://doi.org/10.1016/0167-9236(89)90037-7
43. Schunk, D.H.: Learning Theories: An Educational Perspective. Pearson, Boston, MA, US (2012)
44. LeCun, Y., Bengio, Y., Hinton, G.: Deep learning. Nature **521**, 436–444 (2015). https://doi.org/10.1038/nature14539
45. Tarafdar, M., Beath, C.M., Ross, J.W.: Using AI to enhance business operations. MIT Sloan Manag. Rev. **60**(4), 37–44 (2019)

46. Thomas, A.J., Byard, P., Evans, R.: Identifying the UK's manufacturing challenges as a benchmark for future growth. J. Manuf. Technol. Manage. **23**(2), 142–156 (2012). https://doi.org/10.1108/17410381211202160

47. Ransbotham, S., Kiron, D., Gerbert, P., Reeves, M.: Reshaping business with artificial intelligence: Closing the gap between ambition and action. MIT Sloan Manag. Rev. **59**(1), 1–17 (2017)

48. Schwartz, J., Hagel, J., Wooll, M., Monahan, K.: Reframing the future of work. MIT Sloan Manag. Rev. **60**(3), 1–6 (2019)

49. Rzepka, C., Berger, B.: User Interaction with AI-enabled Systems: A Systematic Review of IS Research. In: Proceedings of the 39th International Conference on Information Systems (2018)

50. Daugherty, P.R., Wilson, H.J.: Human + Machine Reimagining Work in the Age of AI. Harvard Business Review Press, Boston, MA, US (2018)

51. Raisch, S., Krakowski, S.: Artificial intelligence and management: The automation-augmentation paradox. AMR. **46**(1), 192–210 (2020). https://doi.org/10.5465/amr.2018.0072

52. Walsham, G.: Doing interpretive research. Eur. J. Inf. Syst. **15**, 320–330 (2006). https://doi.org/10.1057/palgrave.ejis.3000589

Augmenting Humans in the Loop: Towards an Augmented Reality Object Labeling Application for Crowdsourcing Communities

Julian Schuir[1]([✉]), René Brinkhege[1], Eduard Anton[1], Thuy Duong Oesterreich[1], Pascal Meier[2], and Frank Teuteberg[1]

[1] Accounting and Information Systems, University of Osnabrück, Osnabrück, Germany
{julian.schuir,rbrinkhege,eduard.anton,thuyduong.oesterreich,
frank.teuteberg}@uni-osnabrueck.de
[2] Smart Enterprise Engineering, German Research Center for Artificial Intelligence,
Osnabrück, Germany
pascal.meier@dfki.de

Abstract. Convolutional neural networks (CNNs) offer great potential for business applications because they enable real-time object recognition. However, their training requires structured data. Crowdsourcing constitutes a popular approach to obtain large databases of manually-labeled images. Yet, the process of labeling objects is a time-consuming and cost-intensive task. In this context, augmented reality provides promising solutions by allowing an end-to-end process of capturing objects, directly labeling them and immediately embedding the data in training processes. Consequently, this paper deals with the development of an object labeling application for crowdsourcing communities following the design science research paradigm. Based on seven issues and twelve corresponding meta-requirements, we developed an AR-based prototype and evaluated it in two evaluation cycles. The evaluation results reveal that the prototype facilitates the process of object detection, labeling and training of CNNs even for inexperienced participants. Thus, our prototype can help crowdsourcing communities to render labeling tasks more efficient.

Keywords: Crowdsourcing · Labeling · Object recognition · Augmented reality

1 Introduction

Data constitute the gasoline fueling artificial intelligence (AI) abilities [1, 2]. With cloud computing, the internet of things (IoT) and social media, data are increasingly abundant and accessible [3]. Yet, the availability of high-quality and structured training data is essential to leverage data for several supervised AI classifiers [4]. Given that up to 80% of corporate data are stored in an unstructured form [5], labeling data can be a costly and time-consuming endeavor [6]. As labeling is still mainly conducted by humans [7], many organizations rely on crowdsourcing platforms to render their labeling tasks more efficient [3]. Therefore, labeling represents a human-in-the-loop approach, in which human skills are needed to gather training data for machine learning [8, 9].

© The Author(s), under exclusive license to Springer Nature Switzerland AG 2021
F. Ahlemann et al. (Eds.): WI 2021, LNISO 47, pp. 198–215, 2021.
https://doi.org/10.1007/978-3-030-86797-3_14

Crowdsourcing platforms such as Amazon's MTurk enable organizations to outsource labeling as so-called "Human Intelligence Tasks" [10]. In this respect, the data type determines the complexity of the labeling job [6]. While high-level classification tasks (e.g. "cat" vs. "no cat" [11]) for images constitute straightforward and speedy annotation jobs, the complexity and duration increase with the requirements for visual perception within a video or image [12]. Consequently, labeling an object within an image is a challenging task that requires the capturing of additional position information within the observed frame [13]. In such cases, even in outsourcing scenarios the efficiency benefits are rather marginal [11]. Given these challenges, there is currently a lack of available solutions for labeling training data for use cases that enable efficient AI-based object recognition [14–16].

To remedy this shortcoming, researchers are increasingly focusing on providing tools that allow direct recognition and labeling of objects within a real-time environment leveraging augmented reality (AR) and convolutional neural networks (CNNs) [17]. AR involves the display of additional information in the user's field of vision and thus enables labeling tasks while capturing images [17, 18]. CNNs, meanwhile, are particularly performant for processing video or image data related to object recognition by utilizing three types of layers: the convolution layer, which generates the activation map enabling the identification of specific properties and defined spatial positions in a frame; the pooling layer, which reduces the dimensionality of the data; and the fully connected layer, which is responsible for linking the neurons from the previous layers [19]. Thus, the synergy of these technologies enables an end-to-end process of capturing objects, direct labeling and immediate embedding of captured information in CNNs' training process [17]. Despite existing solutions for easing the labeling process of objects in images, to the best of our knowledge, there is no solution that is widely scalable to serve the crowdsourcing community. Previous solutions require either stationary hardware [12] or high processing power [17]. Considering this research gap, we derive the following research question (RQ):

RQ: How can the process of capturing and labeling objects be designed and implemented as an AR application for the crowdsourcing community?

Therefore, the aim of this paper is to develop a mobile AR prototype for capturing, labeling and detecting objects based on training CNNs. Our solution is aimed at the crowdsourcing community as it provides the opportunity to capture labeled objects rather than to recruit thousands of workers to manually identify and label objects in images after they are captured.

In accordance with Gregor and Hevner [20], we organize our study as follows: Sect. 2 summarizes related work. Section 3 describes the incremental steps of the artifact development in line with the design science research (DSR) paradigm. This is followed by an explication of the artifact in Sect. 4 and a description of the evaluation in Sect. 5. Subsequently, we discuss our findings in Sect. 6. Finally, the paper concludes by summarizing the main findings.

2   Related Work

With advances in the fields of computer vision and neuroinformatics, artificial neural networks (ANNs) are expected to be increasingly used in business operations [21].

Thereby, CNNs constitute the most commonly used type of ANN architectures applied for image classification [19]. A very promising application area for CNNs is real-time object detection [22]. While the training for this application constitutes a time-consuming task, the subsequent object detection enabled by the trained model is carried out within milliseconds [23]. In view of these capabilities, CNNs are frequently associated with various application scenarios of the IoT age [24]. For example, robots can immediately detect quality deviations in production by using CNNs [25].

However, a basic prerequisite for the effective recognition is the availability of labeled and structured data as well as pre-trained CNNs [4, 10]. To meet this need, several crowd-sourcing tools have already been designed to label data for CNN training. For instance, Lionbridge.ai employs thousands of crowdworkers to label and annotate images, videos and audio recordings [26]. Moreover, various solutions for structuring image data in the fields of medicine, traffic and machinery have been developed in research [16]. However, these solutions require pre-defined sets of images that first must be provided to enable crowdworkers to perform the labeling [6, 10].

The use of AR applications for training neural networks in terms of gathering labeled training data and object detection has been a rarity so far, although AR user interfaces offer unique potential by guiding the user through visual and auditory stimuli [18, 27]. Combined with AR, CNNs have so far mainly been used for the recognition of markers (e.g. barcodes) that facilitate the recognition process [28, 29]. For instance, Dash et al. [30] developed an AR learning environment that identifies markers in the user's field of view, computes the geometric data and seamlessly displays the 3D content in the video stream. To date, however, multiple CNN architectures, like AlexNet and GoogLeNet, have been deployed to allow object recognition without markers [31, 32].

To the best of our knowledge, only one study has combined object labeling, real-time object detection and AR: Hoppenstedt et al. [17] implemented a prototype for labeling objects for the Microsoft HoloLens. The application allows to use voice commands for storing the metadata (e.g. label). Data input generated from the AR labeling is stored in a folding neural network. This network is then trained to classify the images along with the corresponding objects. However, the results of their evaluation indicate that the architecture is more suitable for small classification problems. Furthermore, the application does not provide feedback to the user, which could cause problems for novices. Finally, the use of AR headsets is still not prevalent.

In conclusion, companies, crowdsourcing communities and previous solutions suffer from several shortcomings, which we categorize as belonging to seven central issues (I): The shortage of structured data (I1) leads to high efforts for labeling images (I2), which in turn are often outsourced to crowdworkers. However, crowdworkers often lack the necessary domain knowledge (I3) [5, 16]. Even though a number of solutions have already been developed, they lack scalability (I4) [17]. Moreover, the missing domain knowledge of crowdworkers leads to poor data quality of labeled images and objects (I5), resulting in low accuracy of CNNs (I7) [16]. However, recent technological developments relating to mobile devices have created significant potential for the combination of data collection and labeling [33]. Furthermore, advancements in the field of CNNs are creating opportunities to accelerate training processes (I6) while achieving a comparatively high level of accuracy [16, 17, 34]. In spite of these potentials, research has so far failed to identify a solution that combines the advantages of CNNs, mobile devices and scalable architectures.

3   Research Approach

Given the problem statement outlined in the previous section, we initiated the artifact development and followed the DSR methodology proposed by Peffers et al. [35]. Figure 1 illustrates the research approach in six main stages.

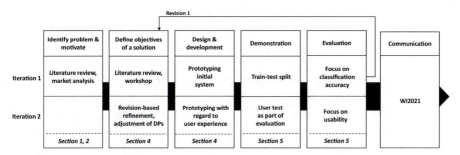

Fig. 1. Design science research approach based on Peffers et al. [35]

First, we examined the current state of practice and research by means of a market analysis and a literature review [36]. The former was conducted in the Apple App Store and the Google Play Store using search terms such as *object labeling* and *augmented reality labeling* [37, 38]. To identify relevant literature, we queried the scientific databases ScienceDirect, IEEE Explore, SpringerLink, ResearchGate and Google Scholar by applying the search string (*artificial neural networks OR connectionist models OR parallel distributed processing models OR convolutional neural networks) AND (augmented reality OR mixed reality) AND (label* OR training)*. This query yielded 43 research papers and two applications of particular importance for our project. To improve objectivity and validity, the screening process was conducted independently by two different researchers in line with the interrater agreement [39].

Second, we used a concept matrix according to Webster and Watson [40] for structuring the literature analysis. Thereby, we identified and categorized issues for the training of neural networks by means of a mobile application in the context of crowdsourcing. To subsequently deduce the meta-requirements (MRs) and design principles (DPs), we conducted a workshop with four researchers from the field of information systems (IS) and applied the anatomy proposed by Gregor et al. [41].

Third, we continued with the development of our artifact. Overall, we carried out two development cycles, each ending with an evaluation step to provide enhancements for the subsequent cycle. We employed two formative and naturalistic ex-post evaluations to examine the artifact's problem-solving ability in a real-world setting [42]. After the first design phase, we conducted a train-test split with 15 objects to validate the functionality of our artifact [43]. The second evaluation involved an experimental study and focused on the user experience. For this step, we applied the User Experience Questionnaire (UEQ) [44]. The two evaluation cycles are presented in Sect. 5.

4   Artifact Description

To address the observed real-world problem under consideration, we start by specifying the MRs, which describe the goals of our solution. These serve as a starting point for the derivation of DPs, which in turn guide the implementation of our artifact [20].

4.1 Meta-requirements and Design Principles

Applying the research approach outlined in Sect. 3, we identified 12 MRs concerning *data labeling*, *system infrastructure* and *model development* (cf. Table 1).

Table 1. Meta-requirements

ID	Meta-requirements
Data labeling	
MR1	**Identification of unknown objects.** The system must help crowdworkers to identify previously unlabeled objects [45, 46]
MR2	**Highlighting the position of objects.** The application needs to enable crowdworkers to highlight the position of objects in the video stream in order to allow labelling [47]
MR3	**Recording multiple labeled data.** The system needs to be capable of recording multiple labeled training data within a short time [17]
MR4	**Intuitiveness.** Users without background knowledge need to be able to carry out the labeling process. Hence, the application needs to be intuitive to use [48]
System infrastructure	
MR5	**Scalability.** Given the need to train several models simultaneously, it is important to be able to train them in a parallel manner and thus enable scalable training [49, 50]
MR6	**Ubiquity of interaction device.** To enable crowdworkers to perform their tasks independent of location, a mobile device is required which functions as the user interface [51]
MR7	**Automation.** As outlined in Sect. 1, the training process requires an understanding of neural networks and does not constitute a trivial task [52]. Therefore, the training process is supposed to be automated to relieve the crowdworkers
Model development	
MR8	**Processing of labeled training data.** To enable training, processing of camera data is required. Simultaneously, the recorded camera image needs to be visible to the user to be able to adjust the orientation of the camera [53]
MR9	**Diversified image data for an object.** To ensure the accuracy of the CNN, heterogeneous data need to be collected by recording the object from different perspectives [45]
MR10	**Time efficiency of training.** The training process needs to achieve useful results within the shortest possible time [34]
MR11	**Classification accuracy.** The CNN is intended to provide as few false positives as possible [54]
MR12	**Recognition and validation of previously trained objects.** To avoid redundant recordings by the user and verify the success of the trainings process, the application needs to notify the user of objects that have been recognized and highlight them [17]

Based on these MRs, we derived three initial DPs that guided us through the design process. In formulating each DP, we followed the anatomy proposed by Gregor et al. [41] to incorporate important elements like *aim, context* and *mechanism* (Table 2).

Table 2. Design principles

ID	Design Principle Specification
Data labeling	
DP1	To allow crowdworkers to identify unlabeled objects in the environment and label them, provide a mobile application with capabilities for detecting and highlighting the objects to be labeled, because this intuitiveness facilitates the capture of objects for users without background knowledge in the domains of labeling and CNN
System infrastructure	
DP2	To enable multiple crowdworkers to capture and label datasets, independently from their location, provide a mobile app that sends the captured data to a central server. This server, in turn, needs to be capable of automatically and simultaneously conducting the trainings process, because the centralization of training tasks enables the use of available resources as effectively as possible and crowdworkers lack the required background knowledge [55]
Model development	
DP3	To allow the system to train CNN algorithms with labeled input in a time-efficient and accurate manner, provide the CNN with heterogeneous, sufficient data and validate them against previously trained objects, because the storage capacity of mobile phones is limited, while neural networks require sufficient training data to maintain high accuracy

Figure 1 visualizes the interrelation between the Is, MRs and DPs. Thus, for example, we address the issue of missing structured image data (I1) by enabling to identify objects that so far have not been labeled (MR1) [14, 15], thereby allowing users without background knowledge to identify and capture them in a structured manner (DP1) (Fig. 2).

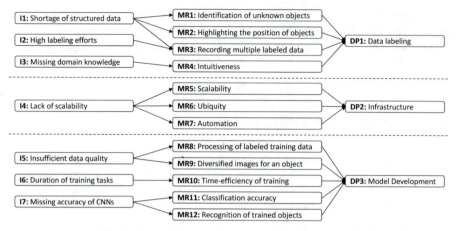

Fig. 2. Issues, meta-requirements and design principles

To sum up, we identified seven Is that were translated into 12 MRs. Based on these, we derived three central DPs concerning *data labeling* (DP1), *infrastructure* (DP2) and *model development* (DP3).

4.2   Application

The design principles DP1, DP2 and DP3 governed the development of the application in the realms of data labeling, infrastructure and model development. The resulting system architecture is depicted in Fig. 3.

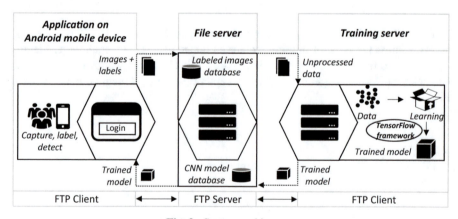

Fig. 3. System architecture

To instantiate DP1, we developed an *application (app)* for mobile Android devices serving as the data collection component of the overall system to capture, label and detect objects within images. Since mobile devices usually do not have sufficient computing power for processing neural networks, we relied on the MobileNetV2 architecture integrated in Google's TensorFlow with regard to DP2 [56]. This resource-efficient architecture enables us to run CNNs on mobile devices [57] by incorporating the high-performance Single Shot MultiBox Detector (SSD), which handles the task of object detection, recognizing the object position in the image and its classification [58].

Once the user has completed the data collection process, the app transfers the information via file transfer protocol (FTP) to the data storage component and stores the data in a specific directory on a Linux server. Simultaneously, the *training server* monitors whether there are unprocessed data records on the *file server*. An implemented script downloads the identified unprocessed records and starts the training of a CNN model for a particular object class to incorporate DP3. Upon completion of the training, the resulting model is transferred back to the file server via FTP.

We developed an app for mobile Android devices on the client side in light of the operating system's corresponding smartphone market share [59]. The integrated camera enables users to capture and store images and the respective required spatial object information. When the user opens the app, the camera is activated, and the user is prompted to actively define a screen area by means of a bounding box in which the observed object is located in case the app does not recognize the object. The app automatically scans the object to check if it can be detected and recognized by previous capturing, labeling and training activities. If the object (e.g. the box of salt) can be detected, a rectangle appears around the object that is augmented on the camera screen with the presumed label and the accuracy in percent (cf. Figure 4, picture on the right). Otherwise, the user creates a new entry by clicking the button "create new object" and assigns a corresponding label (this would be necessary for the stapler in the right picture of Fig. 4).

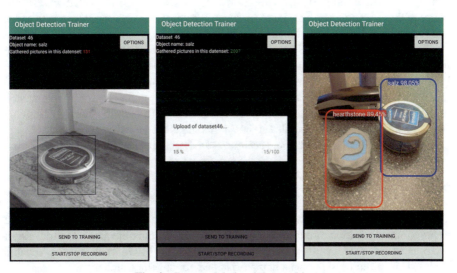

Fig. 4. Capture, label and detect object

Once the object area is marked and the label set (e.g. the box of salt, cf. Figure 4, picture on the left), the image capturing can be initialized. We enabled this procedure by deploying the CSR-DCF tracking method (CSRT) [60]. The first image is used as reference for the marked object area. The follow-up recordings are always validated by the CRST method by determining where the marked area is located on a new image. The CRST method corrects the marker and uses the corresponding input for the object detection. The image capturing is processed in black and white. The user receives meta-information at the top edge of the screen about the current capture and label process by the display of the selected label and the number of already captured images. The number is colored in green as a feedback function when the number of images reaches > 2000 and in red when it is lower than this threshold (cf. Figure 4, picture on the left). The green color indicates that the amount of collected data is sufficient for a CNN training and that the user can proceed with the training process. The threshold for the image count was set at 2,000 because the first beta tests indicated satisfying results with this amount of data. The captured images are temporarily stored locally on the mobile device. To save the label and the information (width, height, xmin, ymin, xmax, ymax), the app also stores a CSV file for each image within the image folder. The coordinates of the object on the image are indicated by *xmin* and *ymin* for the lower left corner and *xmax* and *ymax* for the upper right corner of the bounding box; *width* and *height* refer to the overall image size. By clicking the button "send to training," the captured data is converted into a ZIP archive and transferred to the file server (cf. Figure 3, picture in the middle). After a record has been successfully sent to the file server, the associated data are deleted from the mobile device to free up local storage space. We further implemented several app functions to manage the end-to-end process (e.g. for monitoring the training status of a particular object class).

For the data processing component, we first installed the Python environment Anaconda 3.5 on the training server. This allows us to create independent Python environments without causing conflicts between them. We utilized several open source libraries and frameworks for building the training environment.

The training process starts by unpacking the downloaded ZIP archive and moving the images and labels to the designated locations in the environment. Subsequently, a script is executed that starts the training process. The training process ends when a predefined number of steps has been reached. Upon completion of the training, an implemented function converts the model into a format compatible with mobile devices (tflite) and sends the model via FTP to the file server. At this stage, the model can be used for object detection by displaying the label and accuracy of a detected object within the application.

5   Evaluation

The prototype results from two build-evaluate cycles that enabled us to validate and improve our application through constant feedback. Given our objective was to develop a socio-technical artifact with user-oriented design risks, the FEDS framework by Venable et al. [61] inspired us to pursue a human-risk and effectiveness strategy.

The first evaluation cycle involved an assessment of the classification accuracy within a train-test split, whereas in the second evaluation cycle, we conducted an experiment with real end users to assess usability. Accordingly, in cycle 2, the application was first given to the volunteers to perform three tasks with the artifact: First, the environment had to be scanned for an unknown object. Second, the object had to be captured and labeled. Third, the captured object from the previous step needed to be validated using the application.

5.1 Cycle 1: Classification Accuracy

The first evaluation cycle involved examining the classification accuracy of the machine learning component by means of a train-test split [43]. To this end, 15 individual objects were captured and labeled using the mobile application. Each dataset comprised 2,000 images, with 80% of randomly selected images being used in training. To determine the accuracy, we subsequently analyzed these images by using the trained models and documenting the number of errors. We distinguished between two types of errors: undetected objects (1) and false positives (2). The former refer to errors that occur in cases where the object is in the camera image but is not recognized (type 1 errors), whereas the latter occur once the system indicates having recognized an object even though it is not in the camera frame (type 2 errors). We chose 50% as the baseline for a correctly detected object. Thus, an object is considered as detected if the model estimates the likelihood of being the targeted object to be 50% or higher. Figure 5 summarizes the frequency of the errors that occured during classification.

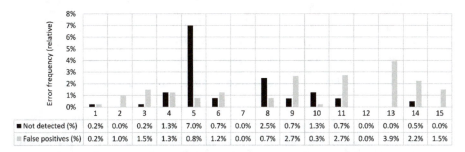

Fig. 5. Error occurrence within classification per object

The average percentage of images with type 1 errors was 1.01%, whereas the corresponding average percentage for type 2 errors amounted to 1.34%. Hence, the share of incorrectly analyzed images can be considered low [17]. As shown in Fig. 5, only the data set for object 5 constitutes an explicit outlier with a share of 7% for the type 1 errors, and we thus examined it in greater depth. Upon inspecting the dataset, we noticed that a number of images were taken by mistake. As the training process cannot independently separate such defective images from high-quality images, those images were also used for training the CNN.

In summary, the CNNs can detect objects at a low error rate. Upon completion of the train-split evaluation, we tested all models with regard to their operability on a mobile device for ensuring the functionality of the object detection functions before proceeding with the experimental evaluation in cycle 2.

5.2   Cycle 2: Usability

To assess the usability of our artifact and derive future research avenues, we adopted the User Experience Questionnaire (UEQ) developed by Laugwitz et al. [44] and supplemented it with an open question section. The participants received 26 word couples (e.g., unpleasant vs. pleasant, inefficient vs. efficient) and applied a 7-point Likert scale to rate the interaction with the technology in a range from -3 to $+3$. Apart from the UEQ questions, 15 participants were asked to submit feedback on the overall quality of the system and potential areas for improvement. Most of them were male (80%) while all of them were between 17 and 50 years old (with an average age of 32.4). One out of three (33.3%) were familiar with the concept of neural networks, and the remaining two thirds had no domain knowledge (66.7%). Nevertheless, all participants succeeded in completing the tasks, with an average duration of 30.42 min. Upon completion, the participants were asked to rate the interaction with the mobile application using the UEQ. Figure 6 illustrates the results of the UEQ survey in accordance with Laugwitz et al. [44].

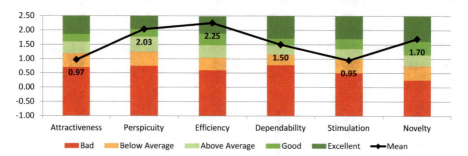

Fig. 6. User Experience Questionnaire results

Overall, the average rating of all 26 items was positive by exceeding the critical mark of 0.8 (mean: 1.5). As proposed by Laugwitz et al. [44], the pre-defined items were aggregated into the six categories of *attractiveness, perspicuity, efficiency, dependability, stimulation* and *novelty*. These six categories achieved a mean value between 0.95 and 2.25 and in all cases a standard deviation below 1 for all six categories, which confirms a homogeneous positive impression of the system. We obtained the highest score for *efficiency* (2.25), a finding that reveals that users can accomplish labeling tasks within a short time. Furthermore, with high means in the categories of *perspicuity* (2.03) and *novelty* (1.70), the interaction with the prototype was on average perceived as "understandable" (2.10), "easy to learn" (2.30) and "clear" (1.80) while being regarded as a rather "creative" (1.40) and "innovative" (2.00) solution. The lowest values were given in the categories *stimulation* (0.95) and *attractiveness* (0.97), resulting from the negative ratings of the requested word couples "attractive" vs. "unattractive" (0.10) and "motivating" vs. "demotivating" (0.10).

Apart from small visual adjustments to the user interface design (e.g., integration of icons and a more user-friendly arrangement of buttons), the participants proposed to integrate a tutorial to guide users through the initial labeling process and thus avoid preventable errors. Another suggested major improvement concerned the highlighting of objects; according to the volunteers, the rectangular shape of the bounding box limits the quality and flexibility of the capturing process. An integration of a customizable shape to adjust the object position within the camera frame would be an enhancement to capture the object from different distances (e.g. by scaling). Moreover, the shape itself needs an indication by means of a striking color (e.g. green instead of black) to increase its visibility during the capturing process (e.g. within dark environments). Further improvement suggestions relate to the image capturing process: first, the user should be instructed on how to change the camera angle to improve the quality of the training data by providing different visual contexts for more heterogeneous images. This instruction can be achieved by displaying arrows that indicate the direction to rotate the camera. To adjust for poor-quality inputs, a function for deleting the last 50 images during the process must be provided.

We used the provided feedback from the second evaluation cycle for further improvement of the artifact. For example, we revised the arrangement of the user interface to provide the user with a more intuitive interaction. In addition, we improved the performance of the application by intensively modifying the source code.

6 Discussion, Limitations and Future Research

The process of labeling objects is a time-consuming and cost-intensive task [12] that is still mainly conducted by humans [7]. Many organizations rely on crowdsourcing platforms to outsource their labeling tasks [3]. As an alternative to manual labeling methods, tools are needed for the direct detection and labeling of objects within a real-environment. Responding to this need, we developed a mobile AR-based prototype for the object recognition, labeling and training of CNNs in three steps. First, we identified and derived the main issues, MRs and DPs based on a thorough literature review and a workshop. Interestingly, most MRs are concerned with model development (MR8-MR12), which underlines the major role of data processing and object recognition within the entire process. Second, we developed a mobile AR-based prototype that consists of three subsystems. Third, the prototype was evaluated in two iterations through an accuracy assessment and a UEQ-based survey conducted among 15 participants. The evaluation results reveal that the artifact facilitates the described process of object detection, labeling and training of CNNs even for inexperienced participants with no prior knowledge in this field. Against this background, we conclude that AR-based labeling constitutes a promising alternative or complement to the manual labeling of pre-defined data sets.

Given these findings, our research is of interest for practitioners for several reasons. First, crowdsourcing platforms and crowdworkers can be informed through our findings about the capabilities of AR-based systems for enhancing object labeling processes. In a similar manner, the proposed system architecture consisting of three interacting subsystems (cf. Section 4.2) is expected to be a more practical alternative compared to conventional system architectures with respect to system resources, system performance and scalability. Thus, we provide a scalable approach to the manual labeling methods of images (of videos) in the crowdsourcing context. For crowdworkers responsible for the tasks, the system can help to avoid cognitive overload and mental stress by facilitating the labeling process. Moreover, for developers, the proposed MRs and DPs can serve as a starting point when attempting to develop similar prototypes for object detection, labeling and training of neural networks. In addition, the mobile-based AR prototype and the corresponding infrastructure can be valuable for companies that are planning to implement AI-based image recognition systems as it facilitates the data entry step required for CNN training. By implementing the system, companies can thus collect structured data and train neural networks in a facilitated manner, thereby enabling real-time object recognition. One promising application area is the domain of logistics, where high-level object recognition can be employed for quality control of picking processes [62].

Apart from the practical relevance, the scientific contributions of this paper are manifold. First, the DPs contribute to the IS discipline by providing high-level guidance for researchers and developers in designing similar prototypes for object detection, labeling and training [35]. In doing so, our study aligns with prior IS research efforts on the interplay between humans and AI-based machines in the context of human-in-the-loop approaches (cf. [4, 9]). We encourage researchers from the IS discipline to critically examine our DPs with regards to modifications and extensions. Second, our findings expand the growing research stream on crowdsourcing human intelligence tasks by providing a mobile AR-based prototype as a substitute for the manual labeling of images [10]. However, the results of the second evaluation round based on the survey of 15 participants indicate major areas for improvement. For example, we found that the factors of attractiveness and stimulation displayed the lowest ratings in the UEQ survey, the latter being a consequence of the workers' lower cognitive loads due to the increase in repetitive tasks. Hence, the design of the user interface is subject to further improvements, along with considerations for how to redesign the user interface such that a well-balanced task-technology fit can be achieved. Therefore, researchers must find a trade-off between an attractive and stimulating design and a level of complexity for workers that is suited to their cognitive abilities [63]. For instance, recent research revealed that the integration of gamification elements represents a suitable instrument to enhance the user experience in terms of enjoyment with regard to labeling tasks [64].

Despite the promising results, our solution is subject to several limitations that highlight worthwhile avenues for future research. First, the MRs and DPs are based on a limited literature sample. Since we searched for literature in a limited number of databases by applying a limited set of search phrases, studies may have been overlooked that could be relevant for our research. Furthermore, the MRs and DPs are mainly literature-based. A possible extension of the requirements engineering step is to triangulate and complement the requirements with insights from experts to form a more practice-oriented view. Another limitation relates to the evaluation conducted to test the practicability and functionality of the prototype. Although we have evaluated the developed artifact, it has not been implemented and tested in a real business setting to date. A deployment of the prototype in a real case study, for example in cooperation with a crowdsourcing provider, constitutes the next step to further examine the impact of such a system on the contractors' and customers' work processes and organization as well as the associated social and economic implications. An important aspect to be considered is the impact of the system's use on the crowdworkers' skills requirements and cognitive performance, since AI-based systems facilitate the entire process of detecting and labeling objects and thereby render the workflows monotonous. Thus, the use of AI-based systems does not necessarily only lead to positive effects such as increased efficiency, but may also have negative consequences for humans in the loop (i.e. crowdworkers). At the same time, the human as an integral part of our socio-technical system constitutes an inherent source of vulnerability since capturing faulty data sets may lead to a decrease in the accuracy of the trained models, as shown in the first evaluation. Since our solution does not yet integrate any quality control mechanisms, the fully automated training could thus result in incorrectly trained models, thereby eliminating the advantage in terms of efficiency compared to existing solutions like Liongbridge.ai [26]. Future research could focus on answering the question of how these negative consequences can be avoided. Finally, our implementation does only concern Android devices. Thus, the use of other mobile devices (i.e. iOS) or devices such as AR glasses is not within the scope of this research and should be considered as a worthwhile avenue for future research. Likewise, conversational agents could be integrated into the system to facilitate the data entry step, especially when using AR glasses to enable hands-free working.

7   Conclusion

This paper presents a mobile AR-based prototype for capturing, labeling and detecting objects based on training CNNs following the design science research paradigm. Based on seven issues, we derived initial meta-requirements and design considerations from the scientific literature, that were translated into three design principles. We subsequently instantiated these design principles to develop a mobile AR-based prototype that consists of three subsystems. We evaluated and re-designed the artifact in two iterations though a train-test split and a usability assessment with 15 test users. The findings of the evaluations reveal that the proposed mobile-based AR prototype enables novices to detect objects and label them. A central server allows CNNs to be trained using the labeled data, generating models with a high degree of classification accuracy. Against this background, our research provides researchers and practitioners with a mobile application as a scalable alternative to the manual labeling methods of images in the context of crowdsourced labeling. The derived design principles serve as a higher-level guidance for system designers and IS researchers in the realm of AI-based assistance systems with regards to object labeling and recognition. Future studies should investigate the influence of AR-based labeling on crowdworkers' skill requirements and the integration of control mechanisms to ensure data quality.

Acknowledgements. The authors would like to thank the reviewers for their positive and constructive feedback. This contribution was prepared within the research training group "va-eva: Vertrauen und Akzeptanz in erweiterten und virtuellen Arbeitswelten" at the University of Osnabrück.

212 J. Schuir et al.

References

1. He, J., Baxter, S.L., Xu, J., Xu, J., Zhou, X., Zhang, K.: The practical implementation of artificial intelligence technologies in medicine. Nat. Med. **25**, 30–36 (2019)
2. Sun, T.Q., Medaglia, R.: Mapping the challenges of Artificial Intelligence in the public sector: evidence from public healthcare. Gov. Inf. Q. **36**, 368–383 (2019)
3. Gu, Y., Leroy, G.: Mechanisms for automatic training data labeling for machine learning. In: 40th ICIS 2019. München, Germany (2019)
4. Maedche, A., et al.: AI-based digital assistants. Bus. Inf. Syst. Eng. **61**(4), 535–544 (2019). https://doi.org/10.1007/s12599-019-00600-8
5. Accenture: Natural Language Processing Applications in Business. (2019)
6. Haq, R.: Enterprise Artificial Intelligence Transformation. John Wiley & Sons Inc, Hoboken, New Jersey (2020)
7. Sun, Y., Lank, E., Terry, M.: Label-and-learn: visualizing the likelihood of machine learning classifier's success during data labeling. In: Proceedings of the 22nd International Conference on IUI, USA, pp. 523–534 (2017)
8. Anton, E., Behne, A., Teuteberg, F.: The Humans behind Artificial Intelligence-an operationalisation of AI Competencies. In: 28th ECIS 2020. Marrakech, Morocco (2020)
9. Traumer, F., Oeste-Reiß, S., Leimeister, J.M.: Towards a future reallocation of work between humans and machines – taxonomy of tasks and interaction types in the context of machine learning. In: 38th ICIS 2017. Seoul, Korea (2017)
10. Kauker, F., Hau, K., Iannello, J.: An exploration of crowdwork, machine learning and experts for extracting information from data. In: Yamamoto, S., Mori, H. (eds.) HIMI 2018. LNCS, vol. 10904, pp. 643–657. Springer, Cham (2018). https://doi.org/10.1007/978-3-319-92043-6_51
11. Chang, J.C., Amershi, S., Kamar, E.: Revolt: collaborative crowdsourcing for labeling machine learning datasets. In: Proceedings of the 2017 CHI Conference on Human Factors in Computing Systems. pp. 2334–2346. ACM, New York, USA (2017)
12. Ramirez, P.Z., Paternesi, C., De Gregorio, D., Di Stefano, L.: Shooting labels: 3D semantic labeling by virtual reality. arXiv preprint arXiv:1910.05021. (2019)
13. Girshick, R., Donahue, J., Darrell, T., Malik, J.: Rich feature hierarchies for accurate object detection and semantic segmentation. In: Proceedings of the IEEE Computer Society Conference on Computer Vision and Pattern Recognition 2014. USA (2014)
14. Gao, P., Sun, X., Wang, W.: Moving object detection based on Kirsch operator combined with optical flow. In: IASP 10 - 2010 International Conference on Image Analysis and Signal Processing. USA (2010)
15. Rangel, J.C., Martínez-Gómez, J., Romero-González, C., García-Varea, I., Cazorla, M.: Semi-supervised 3D object recognition through CNN labeling. Appl. Soft Comput. **65**, 603–613 (2018)
16. Zhang, J., Wu, X., Sheng, V.S.: Learning from crowdsourced labeled data: a survey. Artif. Intell. Rev. **46**(4), 543–576 (2016). https://doi.org/10.1007/s10462-016-9491-9
17. Hoppenstedt, B., Kammerer, K., Reichert, M., Spiliopoulou, M., Pryss, R.: Convolutional Neural Networks for Image Recognition in Mixed Reality Using Voice Command Labeling. In: De Paolis, L.T., Bourdot, P. (eds.) AVR 2019. LNCS, vol. 11614, pp. 63–70. Springer, Cham (2019). https://doi.org/10.1007/978-3-030-25999-0_6
18. Milgram, P., Kishino, F.: A taxonomy of mixed reality visual displays. IEICE Trans. Inf. Syst. **77**, 1321–1329 (1994)
19. O'Shea, K., Nash, R.: An introduction to convolutional neural networks. arXiv Prepr. https://arxiv.org/abs/1511.08458. (2015)

20. Gregor, S., Hevner, A.R.: Positioning and presenting design science research for maximum impact. MIS Q. Manag. Inf. Syst. **37**, 337–355 (2013)
21. Wäldchen, J., Mäder, P.: Plant species identification using computer vision techniques: a systematic literature review. Arch. Comput. Method Eng. **25**(2), 507–543 (2017). https://doi.org/10.1007/s11831-016-9206-z
22. Ren, S., He, K., Girshick, R., Sun, J.: Faster R-CNN: towards real-time object detection with region proposal networks. IEEE Trans. Pattern Anal. Mach. Intell. **39**, 1137–1149 (2017)
23. Pezeshk, A., Hamidian, S., Petrick, N., Sahiner, B.: 3D convolutional neural networks for automatic detection of pulmonary nodules in chest CT. IEEE J. Biomed. Heal. Informatics. **23**, 2080–2090 (2018)
24. Jain, S.K., Rajankar, S.O.: Real-time object detection and recognition using internet of things paradigm. Int. J. Image, Graph. Signal Process. **1**, 18–26 (2017)
25. Quack, T., Bay, H., Van Gool, L.: Object recognition for the internet of things. In: Floerke-meier, C., Langheinrich, M., Fleisch, E., Mattern, F., Sarma, S.E. (eds.) IOT 2008. LNCS, vol. 4952, pp. 230–246. Springer, Heidelberg (2008). https://doi.org/10.1007/978-3-540-78731-0_15
26. Lionbridge Technologies: Lionbridge, https://lionbridge.ai/ (Accessed 14 Dec 2020)
27. Chen, C.H., Wu, C.L., Lo, C.C., Hwang, F.J.: An augmented reality question answering system based on ensemble neural networks. IEEE Access. **5**, 17425–17435 (2017)
28. Billinghurst, M., Clark, A., Lee, G.: A survey of augmented reality. Found. Trends Hum.-Comput. Interact. **8**, 73–272 (2014)
29. Neges, M., Koch, C., König, M., Abramovici, M.: Combining visual natural markers and IMU for improved AR based indoor navigation. Adv. Eng. Informatics. **31**, 18–31 (2017)
30. Dash, A.K., Behera, S.K., Dogra, D.P., Roy, P.P.: Designing of marker-based augmented reality learning environment for kids using convolutional neural network architecture. Displays **55**, 46–54 (2018)
31. Krizhevsky, A., Sutskever, I., Hinton, G.E.: ImageNet classification with deep convolutional neural networks. Commun. ACM. **60**, 84–90 (2017)
32. Szegedy, C., et al.: Going deeper with convolutions. In: Proceedings of the IEEE Computer Society Conference on Computer Vision and Pattern Recognition, pp. 1–9. USA (2015)
33. Vakharia, D., Lease, M.: Beyond mechanical turk: an analysis of paid crowd work platforms university of Texas at Austin. In: Proceedings of the I Conference 2015. pp. 1–17. USA (2015)
34. Holzinger, A., et al.: Interactive machine learning: experimental evidence for the human in the algorithmic loop: a case study on ant colony optimization. Appl. Intell. **49**, 2401–2414 (2019)
35. Peffers, K., Tuunanen, T., Rothenberger, M.A., Chatterjee, S.: A design science research methodology for information systems research. J. Manag. Inf. Syst. **24**, 45–77 (2007)
36. vom Brocke, J., Simons, A., Niehaves, B., Riemer, K., Plattfaut, R., Cleven, A.: Reconstructing the giant: On the importance of rigour in documenting the literature search process. 17th ECIS 2009. Verona, Italy (2009)
37. Google: Google Play Store, https://play.google.com/ Accessed 14 Dec 2020
38. Apple: Apple App Store, https://www.apple.com/ios/app-store/ Accessed 14 Dec 2020
39. LeBreton, J.M., Senter, J.L.: Answers to 20 questions about interrater reliability and interrater agreement. Organ. Res. Methods. **11**, 815–852 (2008)
40. Webster, J., Watson, R.T.: Analyzing the Past to Prepare for the Future: Writing a Literature Review. MIS Q. Manag. Inf. Syst. **26**, xiii–xxiii (2002)
41. Gregor, S., Kruse, L.C., Seidel, S.: The anatomy of a design principle. J. Assoc. Inf. Syst. **21**, 1622–1652 (2020)

42. Venable, J., Pries-Heje, J., Baskerville, R.: A comprehensive framework for evaluation in design science research. In: Peffers, K., Rothenberger, M., Kuechler, B. (eds.) DESRIST 2012. LNCS, vol. 7286, pp. 423–438. Springer, Heidelberg (2012). https://doi.org/10.1007/978-3-642-29863-9_31
43. Bronshtein, A.: Train/test split and cross validation in python. Underst. Mach. Learn. (2017)
44. Laugwitz, B., Held, T., Schrepp, M.: Construction and evaluation of a user experience questionnaire. In: Holzinger, A. (ed.) USAB 2008. LNCS, vol. 5298, pp. 63–76. Springer, Heidelberg (2008). https://doi.org/10.1007/978-3-540-89350-9_6
45. Kent, D., Behrooz, M., Chernova, S.: Crowdsourcing the construction of a 3D object recognition database for robotic grasping. In: Proceedings - IEEE International Conference on Robotics and Automation, pp. 3347–3352. IEEE (2014)
46. Valdenegro-Toro, M.: End-to-end object detection and recognition in forward-looking sonar images with convolutional neural networks. In: Proceedings of the IEEE/OES Auton. Underwater Vehicles (AUV), pp. 144–150. Tokyo, Japan (2016)
47. Li, C., Parikh, D., Chen, T.: Extracting adaptive contextual cues from unlabeled regions. In: Proceedings of the ICCV 2011. Barcelona, Spain (2011)
48. Chatzimilioudis, G., Konstantinidis, A., Laoudias, C., Zeinalipour-Yazti, D.: Crowdsourcing with smartphones. IEEE Internet Comput. **16**, 36–44 (2012)
49. Lee, S., et al.: Improving scalability of parallel CNN training by adjusting mini-batch size at run-time. In: 2019 IEEE International Conference on Big Data 2019. pp. 830–839, IEEE (2019)
50. Radovic, M., Adarkwa, O., Wang, Q.: Object recognition in aerial images using convolutional neural networks. J. Imaging. **3**, 1–9 (2017)
51. Goncalves, J., Hosio, S., Rogstadius, J., Karapanos, E., Kostakos, V.: Motivating participation and improving quality of contribution in ubiquitous crowdsourcing. Comput. networks. **90**, 34–48 (2015)
52. Cui, Y., Zhou, F., Lin, Y., Belongie, S.: Fine-grained categorization and dataset bootstrapping using deep metric learning with humans in the loop. In: Proc. of the IEEE conf. on Computer Vision and Pattern Recognition, pp. 1153–1162, IEEE (2016)
53. Kawano, Y., Yanai, K.: FoodCam-256: A large-scale real-time mobile food recognition system employing high-dimensional features and compression of classifier weights. In: MM 2014 - Proc. of the 2014 ACM Conference on Multimedia. pp. 761–762, ACM (2014)
54. Navalpakkam, V., Itti, L.: Sharing resources: buy attention, get object recognition. Int. Work. Atten. Perform. Comput. Vis. WAPCV, pp. 73–79 (2003)
55. Briese, C., Schlüter, M., Lehr, J., Maurer, K., Krüger, J.: Towards deep learning in industrial applications taking advantage of service-oriented architectures. Procedia Manuf. **43**, 503–510 (2020)
56. Abandi, M., Agarwal, A., Barham, P., Al., E.: TensorFlow: large-scale machine learning on heterogeneous distributed systems. ArXiv preprint arXiv:1603.04467. (2015)
57. Sandler, M., Howard, A.: MobileNetV2: The next generation of on-device computer vision networks. https://ai.googleblog.com/2018/04/mobilenetv2-next-generation-of-on.html (Accessed 16 Dec 2020)
58. Liu, W., et al.: SSD: single shot multibox detector. In: Leibe, B., Matas, J., Sebe, N., Welling, M. (eds.) ECCV 2016. LNCS, vol. 9905, pp. 21–37. Springer, Cham (2016). https://doi.org/10.1007/978-3-319-46448-0_2
59. Statista: Mobile operating systems' market share worldwide from January 2012 to December 2019. (2020)
60. OpenCV: OpenCV: cv: TrackerCSRT Class Reference. (2000)
61. Venable, J., Pries-Heje, J., Baskerville, R.: FEDS: a framework for evaluation in design science research. Eur. J. Inf. Syst. **25**, 77–89 (2016)

62. Stoltz, M.H., Giannikas, V., McFarlane, D., Strachan, J., Um, J., Srinivasan, R.: Augmented reality in warehouse operations: opportunities and barriers. IFAC-PapersOnLine **50**, 12979–12984 (2017)
63. Goodhue, D.L., Thompson, R.L.: Task-technology fit and individual performance. MIS Q. Manag. Inf. Syst. **19**, 213–236 (1995)
64. Spatharioti, S.E., et al.: Tile-o-Scope AR: an augmented reality tabletop image labeling game toolkit. In: FDG 2020 Proc. pp. 1–4. USA (2020)

Leveraging Text Classification by Co-training with Bidirectional Language Models – A Novel Hybrid Approach and Its Application for a German Bank

Roland Graef[✉]

Institute of Business Analytics, University of Ulm, Ulm, Germany
roland.graef@uni-ulm.de

Abstract. Labeling training data constitutes the largest bottleneck for machine learning projects. In particular, text classification via machine learning is widely applied and investigated. Hence, companies have to label a decent amount of texts manually in order to build appropriate text classifiers. Obviously, labeling texts manually is associated with time and expenses. Against this background, research started to develop approaches exploiting the knowledge contained in unlabeled texts by learning sophisticated text representations or labeling some of the texts in an automated manner. However, there is still a lack of integrated approaches, considering both types of approaches to further reduce time and expenses for labeling texts. To address this problem, we propose a new hybrid text classification approach combining recent text representations and automated labeling approaches in an integrated perspective. We demonstrate and evaluate our approach using the case of a German bank where the approach could be applied successfully.

Keywords: Machine learning · Text classification · Co-training · Bidirectional Long Short-Term Memory Networks

1 Introduction

Machine learning is becoming a main driver for automating processes and developing new business models as well as products [1]. As a consequence, companies worldwide and of all sizes are increasingly investing in machine learning [2]. For instance, machine learning is also becoming more and more established amongst German companies as a recent study by the International Data Group [1] shows. In this regard, the share of German companies dealing with the application of machine learning has risen by 20% up to 73% compared to the year 2019. Since machine learning can particularly be used to find sophisticated patterns in texts, it excels at the task of text classification [3–10]. Indeed, organizations use machine learning for text classification within diverse value creating tasks. PayPal, for instance, as an operator of a worldwide online payment system successfully employs the machine learning platform RapidMiner for a real-time text classification of customers' feedback messages in terms of sentiment. Thereby, PayPal

F. Ahlemann et al. (Eds.): WI 2021, LNISO 47, pp. 216–231, 2021.
https://doi.org/10.1007/978-3-030-86797-3_15

aims to enable an instant reaction to displeased customers for preventing churn [11]. In order to develop a machine learning application for text classification a decent amount of training data in terms of labeled texts is required. In practice, organizations prefer, or may even be forced, to collect training data by labeling their internal texts so that machine learning approaches can learn the specific context. In particular, if a company has a domain-specific language or specific classes are required, it is necessary to label internal texts. For example, companies in specific domain areas (e.g. insurance) developing a text classification approach for an inbound routing of incoming customer mails, need to use their customers' texts and label them by hand with respect to their predefined desired domain-specific classes. Actually, labeling training data increasingly represents the largest bottleneck for machine learning projects [12]. A recent study found that 25% of time for machine learning projects is allocated to data labeling [13]. Consequently, labeling large amounts of texts as training data for building an adequate text classification approach via machine learning represents a time consuming and expensive task [3–6, 12, 13]. These expenses are even further increased if domain experts are required to label texts.

To address this challenge and tap the potential of text classification, research has started to develop approaches exploiting unlabeled texts in order to enhance text classifiers trained only on a small set of labeled texts [3–8, 14–19]. On the one hand, authors focus on a sophisticated semantic text representation by training deep learning models on a large amount of unlabeled texts [7, 8, 14–18, 20]. By this means, downstream text classifiers based on machine learning are supported in learning to adequately distinguish classes. On the other hand, literature provides approaches to increase the amount of labeled data based on automated labeling procedures [3–6, 19]. However, there is still a lack of integrated approaches considering both. Therefore, in the problem context of reducing time and expenses associated with manually labeling texts for text classification approaches based on machine learning, merging these two research streams seems very promising to cope with our problem. To address this research gap, we propose a new hybrid text classification approach leveraging the capabilities of text classifiers based on recent text representations as well as automated labeling approaches by exploiting unlabeled data in an integrated approach. Thereby, we aim at reducing time and effort for labeling texts as well as enhancing text classification accuracy when the number of labeled texts is limited.

Following a design-oriented approach (cf., e.g. Peffers et al. [21]), the remainder of this paper is structured as follows: In the next section, we provide an overview of the related work and the research gap. In Sect. 3, we propose a hybrid text classification approach combining recent text representation and automated labeling approaches. In Sect. 4, we demonstrate and evaluate our approach based on the case of a German direct banking institution. Finally, we conclude with a summary of the findings, a discussion of limitations and an outlook on future research.

2 Related Work and Research Gap

Text classification via machine learning approaches is widely applied and investigated by recent research [3–10]. Since labeling a large amount of texts as training data for machine learning is a time consuming and expensive task, particularly if domain experts are required [3–6, 12], literature started to develop approaches which require a rather small amount of manually labeled texts and therefore exploit unlabeled texts. A recent survey examines a wide range of these so-called semi-supervised approaches while presenting a respective taxonomy [22]. In case of text data, however, research particularly focuses on producing a sophisticated semantic representation of text [7, 8, 14–18, 20] or develops approaches to label data in an automated manner [3–6, 19]. To cope with our problem of further reducing time and expenses required for labeling texts, both research streams seem promising.

Recent surveys already review the great evolvement of semantic representations of text in order to solve diverse downstream tasks of Natural Language Processing as, for example, text classification [9, 10]. In this regard, research aims at deriving so-called embeddings, representing the semantics of texts within dense vectors. In this context, embeddings are usually gained by training Neural Networks on large text corpora so that the Neural Networks learn to decode the semantic meaning of words based on the context [7, 8, 14–18, 20]. Although embeddings can be trained simultaneously when training Neural Networks for text classification (e.g. by using an embedding layer [23]), such an approach does not profit from unlabeled texts [10]. As a consequence, research started to develop Neural Network approaches, which can be trained on unlabeled texts. Subsequent to training, these Neural Networks can be applied to produce embeddings as an input for downstream text classifiers.

Embeddings can be particularly divided into single global [14, 15, 20] and context-dependent representations of words [7, 8, 18, 24, 25]. Research focusing on embeddings started with the development of single global representations of words and gained high popularity with approaches as, for instance, Word2Vec [14] or GloVe [15]. As both of these famous examples are limited to the vocabulary they have been trained on, more general approaches have been investigated. For example, the widely used single global embeddings from Kim et al. [20] overcome the issue of building embeddings for unknown words by processing words character by character. However, due to their global representation of context, single global embeddings fail at accurately representing polysemous words (e.g. the word "apple" may refer either to the fruit or the company) [9, 10]. Consequently, research addressed this challenge by building context-dependent representations using single global embeddings as a basis [7, 8]. To do so, authors started to exploit the capabilities of bidirectional Long Short-Term Memory Networks (biLSTMs) [7, 8, 18, 24, 25]. BiLSTMs constitute a specific type of Recurrent Neural Networks, which are designed to process sequential data from both sides while learning long term dependencies as, for instance, contextual information contained in natural language [18, 26]. In terms of text, mostly words of a sentence are passed step-by-step to the biLSTMs as sequential data. For training biLSTMs with unlabeled data usually the same texts in two different languages [8, 17] or words from the surrounding context [7, 18] are used as labels. As a result, a biLSTM can be used to produce the context-dependent embedding of a word given its preceding and following words in a sentence [7, 9]. One of the first authors approaching context-dependent word embeddings with biLSTMs are Kawakami and Dyer [17], who trained their biLSTM by using cross-lingual supervision. More precisely, their approach predicts a target word from a different language based on a sentence from the source language. By this means, the representation of polysemous words is context-dependent as these words are usually not polysemous in the target language (e.g. translating the word of the fruit "apple" to the German word "Apfel" avoids any confusion with the company when context-dependent embeddings are learnt). Further authors using training data from different languages, developed the well-known context-dependent word embeddings CoVe on the basis of English-to-German translation [8]. On this account, they exploited an encoder and decoder architecture, trained with GloVe [15] as input vectors for the source language. Subsequent to training, the encoder, consisting of two layers of biLSTMs, is used to produce the CoVe embeddings. Others obtained their context-dependent embeddings by training their biLSTM models to predict a target word based on the preceding and following sequences of words in sentences [7, 18]. Melamud et al. [18], for instance, further developed the idea of Word2Vec [14] by additionally creating context vectors to single global word embeddings with their Context2Vec approach. Thereby, they demonstrated that their context vectors outperform averaged Word2Vec embeddings to represent the context of sentences in different Natural Language Processing tasks. Meanwhile, the probably most popular context-dependent embeddings based on biLSTMs are those of the ELMo approach [7]. The concept behind ELMo is to train L layers of biLSTMs for predicting a target word based on its surrounding context words while also using single global embeddings as input. In contrast to other approaches, ELMo not only uses the top layer biLSTM to produce the context-dependent embeddings but rather collapses the output of all layers based on a task specific weighting to gain the ELMo embeddings. By this means, the single global embedding and multiple context-dependent embeddings are combined and offset with each other.

Other researchers exploit unlabeled text data by developing approaches to automatically label data, which subsequently can be used as training data [3–6]. To do so, these authors rely on the famous co-training approach [19]. The idea behind co-training is to train two classifiers on the same training data, but provide each with a different view (e.g. set of features) of the data. Subsequently, each classifier can be applied to classify some of the unlabeled data, which can in turn be used to train the respective other classifier. This procedure can be repeated until a stopping condition is met (e.g. if all unlabeled data has been labeled or a given number of iterations is reached). Authors benefitting from co-training within their text classification approaches either use different representations of text as views [5, 6], adjust the co-training approach [3, 27] or even do both [4]. For instance, Kim et al. [6], employed three different representations of text as views and trained a classifier for each view within their co-training approach. More precisely, their respective views of text representations constitute the statistical term weighting representation tf-idf, the generative topic model Latent Dirichlet Allocation as well as the Doc2Vec approach, which is an evolution of the Word2Vec approach for whole documents. Others as, for example, Katz et al. [3], overthought the co-training approach by saving and using all classifiers within each iteration of the co-training process to classify texts. As a result, the most recent classifiers are used as an ensemble to classify the test data.

To sum up, both, context-dependent embeddings based on biLSTMs as well as co-training seem very promising means to reduce time and expenses associated with manually labeling texts as training data by exploiting the knowledge contained in unlabeled texts. However, first promising approaches dealing with both types of knowledge expansion through unlabeled texts do not fully exploit the capabilities of individual context-dependent embeddings based on biLSTMs [4, 28] or require additional human knowledge for modeling [5]. Chen et al. [4], employ co-training by using a single global embedding in terms of Word2Vec as one view of the text and context-dependent embeddings in terms of ELMo as the other view. Therefore, one of their classifiers is only provided with single global embeddings of text and cannot resolve context-dependent relationships as, for instance, polysemous words. Lim et al. [28], employ co-training from a broader view by combining multiple context-dependent embeddings from different biLSTMs. Thus, they only add up information contained in multiple embeddings using them as different views in co-training but do not take advantage of the information offered by already one context-dependent embedding based on biLSTMs. Actually, a more in-depth combination of context-dependent embeddings based on biLSTMs and co-training could be integrated into their approach to reach further improvement. Karisani et al. [5] who rely on context-dependent embeddings based on the very recent bidirectional transformer architecture [9], require further human knowledge to model different concepts of texts, which are subsequently used as different views in co-training. Hence, time and expenses for manual tasks are not necessarily reduced. Indeed, further exploiting the information contained in embeddings based on the transformer architecture via co-training is hardly possible without human modeling of features. Although the transformer architecture is entitled bidirectional, it is rather alldirectional in the sense that it processes sentences from both directions at the same time instead of once in each direction [16]. Hence, context-dependent embeddings based on the transformer architecture do not provide two different views of the same text, which is the prerequisite for designing co-training approaches.

To the best of our knowledge, so far none of the studies in text classification has considered embeddings based on biLSTMs in conjunction with co-training while at the same time taking an integrated perspective by not only using embeddings as different views in co-training but rather combining research streams by merging co-training into context-dependent embeddings based on biLSTMs. To address this gap, we follow a design oriented approach (cf., e.g. Peffers et al. [21]) and aim at developing, a novel hybrid text classification approach, combining embeddings based on biLSTMs with co-training in a well-founded way.

3   Hybrid Approach for Leveraging Text Classification by Co-training with Bidirectional Language Models

3.1   Basic Idea and Overview of the Hybrid Approach

The aim of this paper is to develop a text classification approach, which reduces the amount of labeled texts required to train sound machine learning classifiers and consequently reduces time and expenses to label texts by hand. To reach this goal our approach exploits unlabeled data, on the one hand, for generating context-dependent embeddings based on biLSTMs for a sophisticated text representation. On the other hand, we enable an automated labeling of texts to expand training data by relying on the well-known co-training approach. By these means, our approach is well-suited to leverage the capabilities of text classification approaches when only a small amount of labeled data is available. Hence, accuracy of text classification can be improved while simultaneously reducing time and expenses for labeling texts by hand. Our approach comprises two phases (cf. Figure 1).

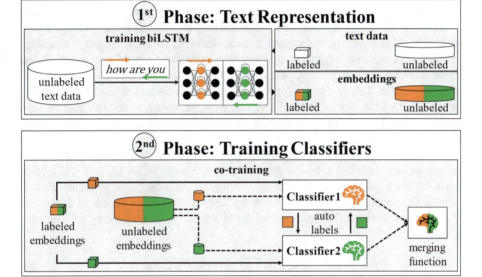

Fig. 1. Hybrid text classification approach

In the first phase, the semantic information contained in text is decoded into machine readable form. To do so, we rely on biLSTMs while suggesting approaches from language modeling for training biLSTMs on a large corpus of unlabeled texts. Afterwards, the trained biLSTMs can be used to represent text data in terms of context-dependent embeddings. Since biLSTMs decode text once in reading direction and once in the opposite direction, they provide context-dependent embeddings with two different views by design thereby drawing on the past and future context of the text, respectively. The second phase of our approach builds upon the context-dependent embeddings of the first phase. As context-dependent embeddings based on biLSTMs provide two different views on the text by design, we make use of these views by designing a co-training approach. Accordingly, two classifiers are trained, each on a different view, to label text data for the respective other classifier in an automated manner. We refer to these labels as auto labels. Obviously, a larger training set enhances the text classification capabilities of the classifiers. At last, we propose a merging function to combine the results of the trained classifiers for deployment. In the following subsections, we present our hybrid approach for reducing time and expenses associated with manual text labeling in detail.

3.2   Text Representation: Context-Dependent Embeddings Based on BiLSTMs

The aim of the first phase is to reach a context-dependent representation of text based on unlabeled text data to make the information contained in natural language accessible for classifiers. Additionally, the desired representation shall offer two different views on the text so that the following phase can profit of these views in terms of co-training. Since context-dependent embeddings based on biLSTMs are the most recent and popular text representations offering two different views by design [9], we rely on approaches based on biLSTMs. On this account, research in context-dependent embeddings heavily relies on the concept of language modeling while reaching convincing results [4, 7, 9, 10, 18, 24, 25, 28]. Consequently, we propose to train biLSTMs based on language modeling. Note that although we suggest to use language modeling to build context-dependent embeddings, our approach is not limited to text representations based on language modeling approaches. Indeed, our approach can exploit each context-dependent embedding based on biLSTMs. For instance, CoVe embeddings, using an encoder and decoder architecture on the basis of English-to-German translation [8], are also very well-suited for usage in our approach.

Language modeling can be described as estimating a probability distribution over a sequence of words based on the preceding or following words [7, 9, 10, 25]. More precisely, for a given sequence of n words $(w_1, \ldots, w_n)$ language modeling aims to estimate the probability of that sequence by factorizing it either based on the past or future context. In case of the past context, the factorization is described by the following equation:

$$p(w_1, \ldots, w_n) = \prod_{i=1}^{n} p(w_i | w_1, \ldots, w_{i-1}) \tag{1}$$

To estimate the conditional probability $p(w_i | w_1, \ldots, w_{i-1})$ unidirectional Long Short-Term Memory Networks (LSTMs) are trained to predict the word w_i given its past context words $(w_1, \ldots, w_{i-1})$. By this means, unlabeled text data can be exploited for training. As a by-product, LSTMs learn to represent internally the context of the target word w_i, which can be extracted as the context-dependent embedding. In order to do so, LSTMs keep an internal memory, combining knowledge of previously processed words with the words they are currently processing. Since the internal memory is capable of storing information over an extraordinary long period, even long-term dependencies among words are established. In the same vein, language modeling can be approached by relying on the future context of words, as shown in the following equation:

$$p(w_1, \ldots, w_n) = \prod_{i=1}^{n} p(w_i | w_{i+1}, \ldots, w_{ns}) \tag{2}$$

Similarly, unidirectional LSTMs are trained to predict the word w_i, but this time based on the future context comprising the words $(w_{i+1}, \ldots, w_n)$. Employing both, LSTMs based on the past context as well as LSTMs based on the future context of words, results in biLSTMs. In this regard, embeddings from the past and future context are concatenated, resulting in the context-dependent embeddings based on biLSTM. Further on, popular research [7, 8, 25] suggests to represent the past $(w_1, \ldots, w_{i-1})$ and future $(w_{i+1}, \ldots, w_n)$ context words by means of single global embeddings (e.g. GloVe [15]) as input for the biLSTMs to improve learning the context-dependent representation. A further enhancement is proposed by the most recent ELMo approach [7] by training L layers of biLSTMs, each further processing the output of the preceding layer. On this basis, each biLSTM layer outputs a context-dependent embedding. Finally, the ELMo embedding is determined by offsetting all context-dependent embeddings as well as the single global embedding, serving as input, with each other based on a task specific weighting. In fact, training biLSTMs to reach context-dependent embeddings requires a large amount of unlabeled text data and computational resources. The ELMo approach, for example, was trained on the basis of the one billion word benchmark [7]. Hence, it is common practice, to make use of a pretrained biLSTM approach to generate context-dependent embeddings. Subsequently, the trained biLSTM can be used to generate context-dependent embeddings representing the unlabeled as well as labeled text data necessary for training text classifiers in the following phase. If the amount of unlabeled text data is large enough, both phases of our approach can rely on the same unlabeled texts.

To sum up, state of the art approaches train biLSTMs on an huge amount of unlabeled text data via language modeling. By this means, biLSTMs learn to provide a text representation in terms of context-dependent embeddings based on two views. On this basis, both labeled and unlabeled text data are represented by means of context-dependent embeddings. The better the text representation, the easier it is for the following phase to identify patterns for assigning the right class to a text. Thus, the text representation based on biLSTMs not only enables a more accurate text classification in the following phase but also offers a past and a future context view of the text, which allows to further enhance the text classifiers based on the unlabeled data through co-training.

3.3 Training Classifiers: Expanding Classifiers' Capabilities by Co-training

The aim of the second phase is to enhance the accuracy of machine learning classifiers for text classification by providing them with additional training data based on unlabeled data. To reach this goal, unlabeled texts are labeled in an automated manner. One of the most famous approaches exploiting the knowledge in unlabeled data by automated labeling is co-training [19]. Indeed, co-training approaches are applied with convincing results for text classification [3–6, 27]. Further on, co-training-based approaches are designed to take advantage of two different views or representations of data as given by the context-dependent embeddings from the first phase. Consequently, we rely on a co-training-based approach to leverage text classifiers' capabilities based on auto labeled texts and hence, reduce time and effort for labeling.

Transferring the original co-training approach to the task of text classification it can be described as the process of training two classifiers and successively retrain both after providing each classifier with text labeled by the respective other classifier [19]. In detail, co-training requires two different views of text in order to train each classifier based on the set of labeled texts L but each based on a different view of the texts. Subsequently, both classifiers are employed to classify or rather auto label a subset of unlabeled texts U' randomly chosen of the set of unlabeled texts U. The X^c most confidently auto labeled texts for each class are then added to the set of labeled texts L. In the case of machine learning classifiers, this confidence is determined by the probabilities assigned by the classifiers regarding the auto labeled texts. One iteration of co-training is closed by retraining the classifiers on the expanded set of labeled texts L. Accordingly, the next iteration starts by drawing a new subset U' of the unlabeled texts U. This procedure is repeated until all texts of the set of unlabeled data U have been labeled or a predefined number of iterations k is reached. The concept behind co-training, which enhances both classifiers with each iteration, is based on the two different views used to train the classifiers. Since one classifier provides the other with labels it is most certain, these auto labels show a high probability of being correct while they may provide a higher degree of difficulty of classification for the classifier operating with the other view. By this means, both classifiers are provided with different auto labeled texts they are not necessarily certain how to classify by themselves and hence, can be improved by training on them without the need of labeling texts by hand.

In our case, the context-dependent embeddings from the first phase of our approach provide two different views by design. One view is represented by the part of the embeddings based on the past context words $(w_1, \ldots, w_{i-1})$ whereas the other view is based on the future context words $(w_{i+1}, \ldots, w_n)$. Consequently, we design our second phase, by splitting up the context-dependent embeddings so that co-training can be approached by training one classifier based on each part of the context-dependent embeddings. Further on, we decided to not limit the design of this phase to a specific co-training approach. Indeed, there exist several recent extensions of co-training, which might enhance the classical co-training approach depending on the text classification task and the dataset [3, 4]. For instance, Chen et al. [4] refined the selection of the auto labels, which are added to the set of labeled texts L in each iteration. By employing their "double-check" strategy they only select those auto labels for training which are assigned by both classifiers to the same class and additionally provide a given similarity to manually labeled texts of the same class. Others, as Katz et al. [3], develop co-training further by saving in each iteration the respective classifiers and thereby train an ensemble of classifiers. Of course, implementing the mentioned approach requires greater memory capacities. Going a step further, also a combination of compatible co-training approaches, as those of Chen et al. [4] and Katz et al. [3], represents a conceivable realization of this phase.

In order to combine the classifiers after co-training for deployment in text classification tasks, we propose a merging function $m(p_1^c, \ldots, p_n^c)$. By this means, the probabilities p_i^c assigned from each classifier i that a given text corresponds to class c can be offset to a unified class probability. For example, in accordance with the original co-training approach, the average of the probabilities p_i^c can be used to specify the function $m(p_1^c, \ldots, p_n^c)$ [19].

To sum up, the second phase generates auto labels to expand the training data for text classifiers by relying on co-training. To do so, the texts represented by the context-dependent embeddings from the first phase are split into two views necessary for co-training based on the past and future context contributing to the embedding. As a result, co-training can be approached by training one classifier per view and using each for generating auto labels for the respective other classifier. Subsequently, the classifiers can be retrained based on the labeled and auto labeled texts. This procedure is repeated multiple times to stepwise increase the labeled data and hence, improve the classifiers' capabilities. Thus, the time and expenses to label texts by hand can be reduced. Finally, the trained classifiers can be employed for text classification tasks while their outputs are combined by a merging function $m(p_1^c, \ldots, p_n^c)$.

4 Demonstration and Evaluation

4.1 Case Setting and Dataset

In order to demonstrate the practical applicability and evaluate the effectiveness of our approach, we used the case of a German direct banking institution. The institution is specialized in the field of community banking and maintains an online social network where customers are encouraged to discuss issues regarding financial services and products. For instance, users have the opportunity to discuss the conditions to obtain a loan from the bank or exchange experiences about saving and investment. In order to monitor the mood within public forums and be able to intervene when users continue to negatively impact the atmosphere, an adequate text classification approach is needed. In this case, texts shall be classified regarding their sentiment resulting in the classification task of sentiment analysis. In particular, the money forum, where concrete financial investment opportunities are shared or new financial products and services are proposed, reaches a high popularity amongst users of the banking institution. As a consequence, a domain-specific language is used within the money forum so that texts from the forum have to be labeled to be able to train a well-adapted classifier. For these reasons, the money forum provides an appropriate setting to apply our novel hybrid approach in order to reduce time and expenses associated with manually labeling texts for text classification approaches based on machine learning. Therefore, the banking institution provided us with a unique dataset comprising 308,087 texts written between the 1st September 2009 and 11th November 2016 in German language. The dataset contains on average approximately 31 words per text.

4.2 Demonstration of Our Approach for the German Bank

In the following, as an essential part of the Design Science research process (cf., e.g. Peffers et al., [21]), we demonstrate the applicability of our approach. To do so, a small amount of labeled texts is required. Hence, 3,000 randomly selected texts of our dataset have been labeled into the classes positive, negative and, as recommended by Go et al. [29], neutral. As a result, we obtained 612 (20.40%) texts labeled positive, 661 (22.03%) texts labeled negative and 1,727 texts (57.57%) belonging to the neutral class. We use 80% of these labeled texts as training data within our approach and keep the remaining 20% as test set for evaluation purposes in Subsect. 4.3 while retaining the class distribution for each set.

Following the first phase of our approach, we used the recent and well-known ELMo approach to reach context-dependent embeddings trained via language modeling [7]. In this regard, we used the pre-trained *ELMoForManyLangs* python implementation from Che et al. [30] providing an ELMo model for the German language. By this means, we were able to represent both labeled and unlabeled texts as context-dependent embeddings. In detail, the used ELMo implementation provides the average of three different embeddings extracted from different consecutive layers of the ELMo model (cf. Figure 2).

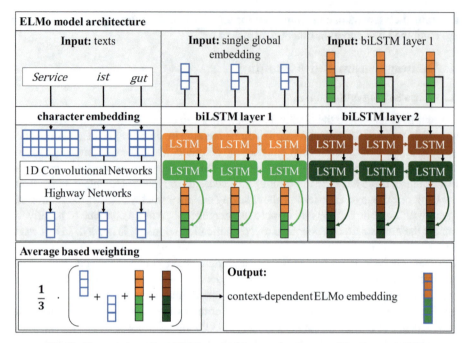

Fig. 2. Context-dependent ELMo embeddings as implemented by Che et al. [30]

On the one hand, a single global embedding arising from the output of a so-called character level Convolutional Neural Network in terms of a vector with 512 units. This type of embedding is gained by processing each word character by character, thereby representing each character as an embedding vector and further processing all character embeddings from each word with, at first, 1D-Convolutional Networks and subsequently with Highway Networks to reach a single global embedding for each word. For further details of this architecture, we refer to Kim et al. [20]. On the other hand, two context-dependent representations are gained from two consecutive biLSTM layers, each producing a vector with 1,024 units per word based on 512 units from the past context and 512 units from the future context, respectively. The average of the three embeddings is computed by first, building a new vector with 1,024 units using the 512 units of the single global embedding twice (once for the past and once for the future context) and second, computing the average of the three vectors unit-wise. As a result, each word of labeled and unlabeled texts is represented by an ELMo vector comprising 1,024 units of averaged embeddings.

For the second phase of our approach, an implementation of a co-training approach is required to label texts in an automated manner. In this regard, we rely on the original co-training approach [19] so that implementations of enhanced co-training approaches could even further improve the results. To do so, we used two Multi-Layer Perceptrons (MLPs) with the same architecture trained by the Keras module within the Tensorflow 2.0 library [23]. We provide each MLP with a different view on the texts by splitting the context-dependent ELMo embeddings from the first phase based on the past and future context units. By this means one MLP is trained by using the first 512 units of each ELMo embedding while the other is trained based on the last 512 units per word. To find a sound architecture and configuration for our MLPs as well as for the parameters of our co-training implementation, we had limited access to an NVIDIA Tesla P100 GPU via the Google Cloud Platform[1]. As a result, the architecture of each MLP comprises an input, three dense and an output layer. The input layer receives the concatenated embeddings from the first 50 words of each text. Since MLPs require inputs of the same size and the average text contains around 31 words, we found that a padding to 50 words is a sound configuration to avoid large sparse vectors for shorter texts while at the same time being able to adequately process longer texts. The dense layers contain from bottom to top 128, 64 and 32 neurons all using ReLU as activation function. The output layer consists of three neurons, each for one class, activated by the softmax function. We chose only 10% of the training data as validation data to still have enough labeled texts for actual training. On this basis, we trained our MLPs for 50 epochs with a batch size of 64 using early stopping if the loss on the validation data does not decrease within three epochs. As usual for classification tasks, we used the categorical cross entropy as loss function and employed the adam optimizer. To parameterize our co-training implementation, we found that a subset of $U' = 1,000$ randomly selected unlabeled texts per iteration constitutes a sensible choice. Further, we generate our auto labels within $k = 40$ iterations of our co-training, while expanding the set of labeled texts L in each iteration by the respective most confidently labeled 11 negative, 27 neutral and 10 positive texts. By this means, we retain the class distribution similar to Blum and Mitchell [19]. In line with research, we specify our merging function $m(p_1^c, p_2^c)$ as the average of the probabilities p_i^c per class c assigned by the MLPs [3, 19]. By this means, each classifier contributes to the same extent to the final classification result.

Summing up, to train two MLPs by exploiting unlabeled texts, we relied on pre-trained context-dependent embeddings from the ELMo approach and implemented the original co-training approach to generate auto labels. Hence, institutions can be provided with a sound text classification while the time and expenses associated with manual labeling of texts can be reduced.

4.3 Evaluation

In order to evaluate our approach, we compared its performance on the test set against that of well-established competing artifacts for text classification [7, 23, 31]. To ensure comparability, all considered approaches are based on the same MLP architecture introduced within the demonstration of our approach in Sect. 4.2 while varying the input layer based on the competing text representation. In this regard, we chose three approaches as baselines for comparison. First, the most widely used statistical term weighting representation tf-idf [31]. Thereby, each word is weighted based on the frequency of its occurrence in the respective text as well as in the whole dataset. More precisely, each word occurrence in the respective text to be classified increases its tf-idf weighting and hence, increases influence on the classification output. In turn, the weighting for frequently occurring words in the whole dataset decreases. This is due to the idea that

---

[1] https://cloud.google.com/.

a frequently occurring word does not add specific value to the text to be classified. The representation of text by the tf-idf weighting can be improved by an adequate pre-processing. Thus, we applied pre-processing insofar as words had been cleared from stop words, transformed to lower case and reduced to their word stems. Second, a single global embedding representation learned via using an embedding layer as input layer [23]. By this means, single global embeddings are gained simultaneously when training the MLP. Third, the context-dependent embeddings from the ELMo approach using the pre-trained German embeddings from the *ELMoForManyLangs* implementation [30]. Further on, we report the results of our hybrid approach for multiple numbers of co-training iterations k. Please note that a comparison to a competing co-training approach using two different text representations (e.g. ELMo and CoVe) as views is not fair, since further information would be added. Actually, such a broader co-training approach could be improved by using our hybrid approach in each view leading to a recursive co-training approach.

To assess text classification performances, we calculated the well-known metrics *accuracy* as well as the F_1-*Score* for each class. Since our test set is rather small and text classification performance of MLPs can vary based on the randomly chosen initial weights, we repeated the training of the classifiers for 40 times and thereby determined the macro-average for our evaluation metrics. Additionally, we report a 99%-confidence interval for the macro-averages, relying on the t-distribution, which is often applied for building confidence intervals for a mean based on a small sample size. On this basis, we were able to rigorously evaluate text classification approaches in our setting (cf. Table 1).

Table 1. Evaluation of our approach in comparison with competing artifacts

Competing artifacts /Metrics in percent	Accuracy	F_1-Score (positive)	F_1-Score (neutral)	F_1-Score (negative)
Tf-idf	56.38 ± 0.96	22.82 ± 5.75	71.30 ± 0.92	26.4 ± 3.84
Global embedding	57.75 ± 0.27	0.45 ± 1.11	73.09 ± 0.18	9.17 ± 5.01
ELMo	61.13 ± 0.70	29.05 ± 4.72	75.49 ± 0.59	35.07 ± 4.49
Hybrid approach ($k = 0$)	61.30 ± 0.58	21.02 ± 4.69	75.57 ± 0.50	33.35 ± 3.03
Hybrid approach ($k = 10$)	62.50 ± 0.60	31.12 ± 3.80	76.50 ± 0.51	36.50 ± 3.41
Hybrid approach ($k = 20$)	63.05 ± 0.44	33.25 ± 2.60	76.80 ± 0.46	38.42 ± 2.61
Hybrid approach ($k = 40$)	**63.18 ± 0.52**	**34.16 ± 3.57**	**76.82 ± 0.46**	**39.04 ± 2.18**

Accordingly, our hybrid approach started with an accuracy of 61.30% (±0.58%) without any auto labels from co-training ($k = 0$) and gradually increased with co-training iterations. In contrast , the ELMo approach reached an accuracy of 61.13% (±0.70%). In this regard, it was to be expected that the ELMo approach does only marginally differ from the initial state of our approach for $k = 0$ as both receive the same information and differ only in the processing. While the ELMo approach receives the full context-dependent embeddings and processes them by one MLP classifier, our approach for $k = 0$ receives the splitted ELMo embeddings, processes them by two MLP classifiers and outputs the merged results. However, already $k = 10$ iterations of co-training within our approach are enough to outperform the competing approaches for all of the evaluation metrics. Additionally, further iterations further improve results for each metric. Moreover, after $k = 10$ iterations even the confidence intervals for the accuracy of our approach do not touch those of the competing approaches. With 57.75% ($\pm 0.27\%$) the directly trained single global embeddings had the second lowest value for accuracy. However, as can be seen from the F_1-Scores, this approach assigned most of the texts to the neutral class. Although the tf-idf baseline performed worst in terms of accuracy, it was able to distinguish the three classes to some extent as reflected by the F_1-Scores for each class. Indeed, our results are in line with literature as accuracy for sentiment analysis for short messages is often below 60% for the multiclass case including a neutral class [32].

To gain more detailed insights with respect to reducing manual labeling of texts when applying our approach, we evaluated our approach using only 2,000 instead of 2,400 labeled texts for training our MLP classifiers. On this basis, our approach started with an initial accuracy of 60.13% ($\pm 0.63\%$) for $k = 0$ iterations while also obtaining F_1-Scores below the ELMo approach. Surprisingly, we reached similar results for $k = 10$ as those in Table 1 when all labeled texts have been used for training. For $k = 40$ iterations of our approach with reduced labeled texts we obtained an accuracy of 62.70% ($\pm 0.63\%$) and F_1-Scores for the positive, neutral and negative class of 32.24% ($\pm 2.58\%$), 76.23% ($\pm 0.43\%$) and 40.38% ($\pm 2.40\%$). Hence, our approach is even able to outperform the competing artifacts when trained with less labeled texts.

5 Conclusion, Limitations and Future Research

Machine learning is nowadays becoming more and more established in companies while offering great potential for the task of text classification as sophisticated patterns have to be identified. However, training sound text classification approaches via machine learning requires a decent amount of manually labeled texts. Since labeling texts requires time and is associated with expenses, research provides promising approaches to exploit the knowledge in unlabeled texts by learning sophisticated semantic representations [7, 8, 14–18, 20] or by labeling texts in an automated manner through co-training [3–6, 19]. Nevertheless, until now literature does not provide sufficient approaches combining these two research streams. Hence, we contribute to research and practice by proposing a novel hybrid text classification approach combining text representations based on biLSTMs with co-training approaches in an integrated perspective to reduce time and expenses associated with labeling texts. Our approach takes benefit of the past and future context representations obtained from biLSTMs by integrating them as different views into co-training. We demonstrated and evaluated our approach using the case of a German bank. The results of the evaluation reveal that our hybrid approach provides greater text classification capabilities compared to other state-of-the-art approaches even if trained with less labeled texts.

Nevertheless, our work also has some limitations which may constitute the starting point for future research. In this paper we focused on embeddings based on biLSTMs from an in-depth perspective. Future research could further exploit unlabeled texts by adding different single global embeddings (e.g. Word2Vec and GloVe) to the respective views in our approach or even design recursive co-training approaches by integrating our approach as one view in a broader co-training approach. Furthermore, we only considered one dataset, for which we applied and evaluated our approach. As in our case the dataset was skewed towards the neutral class, it would be interesting to investigate the performance of our approach on datasets with different class distributions (e.g. equally sized classes) as well as with further variations regarding the amount of labeled texts. Summing up, we believe that our hybrid approach is an important step towards combining embeddings based on biLSTMs with co-training. Going a step further, the question arises how to ensure that co-training approaches do not learn undesired patterns when trained on auto labeled texts. As promising starting point, it seems reasonable to make use of explainable artificial intelligence approaches to retrace results and guarantee plausibility [33]. With this in mind, we hope to stimulate future research to push this exiting research field forward.

References

1. International Data Group Research Services: Studie Machine Learning 2020 (2020)
2. Algorithmia: 2020 state of enterprise machine learning (2020)
3. Katz, G., Caragea, C., Shabtai, A.: Vertical ensemble co-training for text classification. ACM Trans. Intell. Syst. Technol. **9**, 1–23 (2017)
4. Chen, J., et al.: Co-training semi-supervised deep learning for sentiment classification of MOOC forum posts. Symmetry **12**, 8 (2019)
5. Karisani, P., Ho, J., Agichtein, E.: Domain-guided task decomposition with self-training for detecting personal events in social media. In: Web Conference, pp. 2411–2420 (2020)
6. Kim, D., Seo, D., Cho, S., Kang, P.: Multi-co-training for document classification using various document representations: TF-IDF, LDA, and Doc2Vec. Inf. Sci. **477**, 15–29 (2019)
7. Peters, M., et al.: Deep contextualized word representations. In: NAACL, pp. 2227–2237. ACL (2018)
8. McCann, B., Bradbury, J., Xiong, C., Socher, R.: Learned in translation: contextualized word vectors. In: NIPS, pp. 6294–6305 (2017)
9. Liu, Q., Kusner, M.J., Blunsom, P.: A survey on contextual embeddings. ArXiv (2020)
10. Qiu, X., Sun, T., Xu, Y., Shao, Y., Dai, N., Huang, X.: Pre-trained models for natural language processing: a survey. ArXiv (2020)
11. Bitkom: Big Data und Geschäftsmodell-Innovation in der Praxis: 40+ Beispiele (2015)
12. Ratner, A., Bach, S.H., Ehrenberg, H., Fries, J., Wu, S. and Ré, C.: Snorkel: rapid training data creation with weak supervision. In: International Conference on VLDB, vol. 11, pp. 269–282 (2017)
13. Cognilytica Research: Data Engineering, Preparation, and Labeling for AI 2020. Getting Data ready for Use in AI and Machine Learning Projects (2020)
14. Mikolov, T., Chen, K., Corrado, G., Dean, J.: Efficient estimation of word representations in vector space. ArXiv (2013)

15. Pennington, J., Socher, R., Manning, C.D.: Glove: global vectors for word representation. In: Conference on EMNLP, pp. 1532–1543 (2014)
16. Devlin, J., Chang, M.-W., Lee, K., Toutanova, K.: BERT: pre-training of deep bidirectional transformers for language understanding. In: NAACL, pp. 4171–4186. ACL (2019)
17. Kawakami, K., Dyer, C.: Learning to represent words in context with multilingual supervision. In: Workshop ICLR (2016)
18. Melamud, O., Goldberger, J., Dagan, I.: context2vec: learning generic context embedding with bidirectional LSTM. In: 20th SIGNLL CoNLL, pp. 51–61 (2016)
19. Blum, A., Mitchell, T.: Combining labeled and unlabeled data with co-training. In: 11th COLT, pp. 92–100 (1998)
20. Kim, Y., Jernite, Y., Sontag, D., Rush, A.M.: Character-aware neural language models. ArXiv (2015)
21. Peffers, K., Tuunanen, T., Rothenberger, M.A., Chatterjee, S.: A design science research methodology for information systems research. JMIS **24**(3), 45–77 (2007)
22. van Engelen, J.E., Hoos, H.H.: A survey on semi-supervised learning. Mach. Learn. **109**(2), 373–440 (2019). https://doi.org/10.1007/s10994-019-05855-6
23. Abadi, M., et al.: Tensorflow: A system for large-scale machine learning. In: 12th USENIX OSDI, pp. 265–283 (2016)
24. Howard, J., Ruder, S.: Universal language model fine-tuning for text classification. ArXiv (2018)
25. Peters, M.E., Ammar, W., Bhagavatula, C., Power, R.: Semi-supervised sequence tagging with bidirectional language models. ArXiv (2017)
26. Graves, A., Schmidhuber, J.: Framewise phoneme classification with bidirectional LSTM and other neural network architectures. Neural Netw. **18**, 602–610 (2005)
27. Wu, J., Li, L., Wang, W.Y.: Reinforced co-training. ArXiv (2018)
28. Lim, K., Lee, J.Y., Carbonell, J., Poibeau, T.: Semi-supervised learning on meta structure: multi-task tagging and parsing in low-resource scenarios. In: AAAI Conference (2020)
29. Go, A., Bhayani, R., Huang, L.: Twitter sentiment classification using distant supervision. In: CS224N project report, Stanford 1 (2009)
30. Che, W., Liu, Y., Wang, Y., Zheng, B., Liu, T.: Towards better UD parsing: deep contextualized word embeddings, ensemble, and treebank concatenation. In: CoNLL 2018, pp. 55–64 (2018)
31. Salton, G., Buckley, C.: Term-weighting approaches in automatic text retrieval. Inf. Process. Manage. **24**, 513–523 (1988)
32. Socher, R., et al.: Recursive deep models for semantic compositionality over a sentiment treebank. In: Conference on EMNLP, pp. 1631–1642 (2013)
33. Holzinger, A., Kieseberg, P., Weippl, E., Tjoa, A.M.: Current advances, trends and challenges of machine learning and knowledge extraction: from machine learning to explainable AI. In: International CD-MAKE, pp. 1–8 (2018)

The Evaluation of the Black Box Problem for AI-Based Recommendations: An Interview-Based Study

Jessica Ochmann[1]([✉]), Sandra Zilker[2], and Sven Laumer[1]

[1] Schöller Endowed Professorship for Information Systems (Digitalization in Business and Society), Friedrich-Alexander-University Erlangen-Nuremberg, Nuremberg, Germany
{jessica.ochmann,sven.laumer}@fau.de
[2] Chair of Digital Industrial Service Systems, Friedrich-Alexander-University Erlangen-Nuremberg, Nuremberg, Germany
sandra.zilker@fau.de

Abstract. Organizations are increasingly adopting artificial intelligence (AI) for business processes. AI-based recommendations aim at supporting users in decision-making, e.g., by pre-filtering options. However, users can often hardly understand how these recommendations are developed. This issue is called "black box problem". In the context of Human Resources Management, this leads to new questions regarding the acceptance of AI-based recommendations in the recruiting process. Therefore, we develop a model based on the theory of planned behavior explaining the relation between the user's perception of the black box problem and the attitude toward AI-based recommendations distinguishing between a mandatory and voluntary use context. We conducted 21 interviews with experts from recruiting and AI. Our results show that the perception of the black box problem conceptualized by the awareness and the evaluated relevance relates to the user's attitude toward AI-based recommendations. Further, we show that the use context has a moderating effect on that relation.

Keywords: Black box · AI-based recommendations · Human resources management

1 Introduction

The increasing demand for information technologies within the organizational context changes the way companies handle their business-related processes. Organizations have early recognized that the implementation of new technologies is beneficial for the company's success. Therefore, companies are ambitious to expand the use of information systems further in order to design their processes more efficiently [1]. In this regard, artificial intelligence (AI) is increasingly addressed [2]. One possible application of AI are recommender systems. In general, recommender systems are software tools and techniques, providing suggestions for items that are of use to a user [3]. In the private context, AI-based recommendations are well-known. For example, if a person wants to watch a movie on Netflix, the platform suggests possible movies based on the user's preferences, which is determined by personal data, like previously watched movies or shows. In comparison, AI-based recommendations are also becoming more and more present in the business context in general and in the human resources management (HRM) in particular [4]. Focusing on HRM, AI-based recommendations offer new possibilities to realize various advantages from the organization's perspective [4]. Primarily the automated recruiting of candidates gains importance as organizations expect various benefits such as faster application handling and relief of recruiters [5]. In this regard, organizations make considerable efforts to push the application of AI-based recommendations in their recruiting process [5, 6]. One of the general advantages of these recommendations is that the information overload for the user is minimized. For example, by pre-filtering possible candidates with the use of AI, recruiters are provided with a pre-select list of job seekers that fit the vacancy. Therefore, information overload is prevented, and the recruiter's decision is supported. However, the application of AI-based systems in organizations also encourages controversial discussions as the prediction quality of the underlying technology of Machine Learning (ML) has continuously advanced by simultaneously increasing the complexity of the learning process. As a result, it is nearly impossible for humans to understand what the system is doing [7]. This so-called "black box problem" leads to challenges for organizations. For example, organizations have to develop a basic understanding of AI-based systems and clarify both potentials of this technology such as the production of accurate results and risks such as regulatory requirements [2]. In this regard, also the acceptance of AI-based technologies must be addressed as individuals might behave hesitantly when they are uncertain about the basis of decision-making and have difficulties to appraise the consequences [8].

Regarding AI-based recommendations in HR, the system undertakes the role of the recruiter. In this particular case, it is a debatable point whether the recruiter follows an AI-based recommendation on their own responsibility when neither the basis of decision-making (e.g., why a system makes a certain recommendation) nor the consequences of a certain decision (e.g., what happens if the system fails) are clear. Moreover, the extent to which the recruiter is willing to accept the competence-shift from the human to the system is questionable [9, 10]. Given these challenges and considering that "people factors" like user acceptance gain in importance for the successful adoption of AI-based recommendations [5], it is crucial to discuss the purport of black boxes for individuals in an organizational context. Prior research on the black box problem focuses primarily on the technical perspective and aims to identify methods that uncover how systems recognize patterns and make predictions [7, 11, 12]. However, the existing research lacks in covering the individual point of view in an organizational context. Nonetheless, it is essential to understand the consequences of non-interpretable AI-based recommendations for individuals. Against this backdrop, it has to be clarified how users (e.g., recruiters) of AI-based recommendation systems evaluate the consequences of missing transparency-provided that these users are aware of the black box accompanied by the application of AI-based systems. Based on this research gap, we intend to answer the following research question (RQ):

"RQ: How does the perception of the black box problem influence an individual's attitude toward AI-based recommendations?"

As the field of HRM is highly underrepresented in current research in regards to the black box problem of AI and it is of high relevance for individuals, we focus on this specific domain. To frame our research, we focus on the theoretical lens of attitude-based technology acceptance [13]. We also consider the use context of the AI-based recommendation following the approach presented by Krönung et al. [14]. In addition, we explain the terms AI-based recommendations and black box problem. From a methodology perspective, we conducted 21 explorative interviews. Based on the results extracted from these interviews, we discuss the relation between the perception of the black box problem and the user's attitude toward AI-based recommendations and we show that the use context moderates this relation. Finally, the paper consolidates the findings, shows limitations, and discusses research as well as practical implications.

2 Related Work

In this section, we will summarize related work on attitude-based technology acceptance research and the black box problem of AI-based recommendations to highlight the specific research gap that our approach is intended to fill.

2.1 Attitude-Based Technology Acceptance Research

To examine a user's attitude toward AI-based recommendations in general and gain a basic understanding of the behavioral implications regarding the attitude toward the black box problem in particular, we build on attitude-based technology acceptance research. This research stream is based on the theory of planned behavior (TPB) that links users' behavioral beliefs to the attitude toward an object. In this context, attitude is defined as an individual's evaluation (i.e., positive or negative) of a certain object [15]. More precisely, TPB postulates that behavior is influenced by attitude, and attitude is influenced by beliefs [13]. As we strive to analyze how beliefs regarding the black box problem shape the attitude toward AI-based recommendations, TPB seems to be the most appropriate starting point to develop comprehensible models. In the context of our research, beliefs are defined as the perception of the black box problem. Complementary, we consider the attitude toward an object with the object being specified as AI-based recommendations. Besides, we consider the use context where a particular belief emerges as different perspectives might result in divergent attitudes. Behavioral theory suggests that the use context influences the attitude of users and thereby affecting their acceptance [16]. In other words, the actions users take when using an information system depend on the attitude they have in a particular situation and that the attitude formation process varies in different contexts. Therefore, we adopted an approach proposed by Krönung et al. [14]. The authors show that the use context influences the attitude formation process in the respective context of using information systems. The use context can either be mandatory or voluntary. A mandatory use context is characterized by the obligatory use of information systems. For example, an organization requires its employees to use a certain technology and deny them to handle business-related tasks without the applied technology. In comparison, in a voluntary use context, the organization offers information systems as a supportive tool. However, the use is not required to fulfill the business-related task, and employees can decide themselves if they want to apply a certain system. In sum, this paper considers the perception of the black box problem as a belief that shapes the attitude toward an object, which are in our approach AI-based recommendations. In addition, we investigate the use context, thereby distinguishing between a voluntary and a mandatory technology use as an individual's attitude toward AI-based recommendations might differ in relation to the use context.

2.2 Recommender Systems in Human Resources Management

Recommender systems describe information systems that process user data to provide personalized recommendations for products or services that match user preferences [3]. By sorting and filtering alternatives, recommender systems aim to reduce possible information overload for users and support them in making reasonable decisions. In the last decade, recommender systems have been increasingly implemented in a variety of application domains with a strong focus on e-commerce and media in the consumer context [17] to reduce a consumer's effort to find relevant products or services. In contrast, in an HR context, two types of recommender systems are discussed depending on their aim to support either the organization or the job seeker. The first ones are job recommender systems that support job seekers in their job search by matching vacancies with their job preferences. The second group is CV recommender systems that are implemented by organizations and support recruiters by pre-selecting suitable candidates for a certain vacancy.

For realizing a data-driven recommender system, there are different kinds of approaches like collaborative or content-based filtering [18]. Besides these more traditional statistical metrics, the methods behind those approaches are nowadays increasingly based on AI models that lead to more user-centric AI-based recommendations [19].

Given the ubiquity of recommender systems, scholarly research put much effort to investigate factors that influence the acceptance of both the recommender systems and the underlying recommendations in a business-to-consumer context. Prior research shows, for example, that personalization and familiarity positively influence the acceptance of recommender systems [18], while system biases might decrease the adoption of such systems [20]. However, it remains unclear under which circumstances these results can be adapted to a business-related context, which is characterized by higher stakes of the decisions. While the consequences of a failed product recommendation are comparability low, a wrong business decision might lead to more serious economic consequences. In an HR context, for example, the recruitment of an unskilled employee due to an insufficient recommendation might damage the company's reputation if this new employee is not able to perform adequately. Besides, the application of such recommender systems in HR can be either mandatory or voluntary, depending on the organization's strategy [14]. A review of the literature shows that academic research evaluates automation in HRM predominantly positive [21–23]. However, little is known about its consequences for organizational users in general and recruiters in particularly [24]. Accordingly, the understanding of how organizations can proactively influence the attitude toward these AI-based recommendations remains limited.

Therefore, it is essential to look at recommendations in the business context in general and in the HR context in particular as individuals might show different acceptance behaviors toward the use of recommender systems in organizations.

2.3 Black Box Problem

Recent AI-based systems based on deep learning achieve higher predictive quality while at the same time gaining in complexity. Therefore, individuals find it increasingly difficult to understand the underlying reasoning for a certain recommendation. This phenomenon is subsumed under the term "black box problem". Black boxes miss providing further information about how predictions are generated [25] as they cover multiple levels of abstraction that are barely interpretable [26]. Prior research has highlighted that uncertainty about the reliability of AI predictions might hurt trust in AI-based systems and reduce acceptance of an AI-based recommendation [12]. Hence, transparency and explainability of data-based decisions are crucial for most business processes (e.g., recruiting of candidates) and medical (e.g., interpretation of radiographic images) or safety-critical (e.g., autonomous driving) as well as commercial (e.g., lending decisions) applications [7, 11, 12]. Individuals want to understand the reasons for a certain recommendation to appraise the consequences and especially when they are responsible for a certain task to verify a decision. In comparison, black boxes might be acceptable in most business-to-consumer contexts as referred services (e.g., translation services, consumer entertainment, e-commerce) are merely uncritical, and the consequences of failed AI-based recommendations are unspectacular and manageable [12]. Thus, transparency requirements for AI-based systems might be higher for Business-to-Business than for Business-to-Consumer contexts [25].

To address this issue, regulatory authorities and other initiatives have lately focused on the transparency of algorithms and started to promote the concept of explainable AI (XAI). According to Zanni-Merk [27], the overall goal of XAI is to build an explainable model. This is, understandable by humans, yet providing justification for predictions or decisions. Previous research focuses on the black box problem from a technical perspective (e.g., underlying explanatory structures of an algorithm) [7, 11, 12, 26, 28], in the medical domain [29–32], or in the financial sector [25, 33, 34]. However, the impact of the black box problem in an organizational context in general and in HRM in particular is mostly unaddressed. Especially in HRM, it is crucial to understand how the output of an AI-based system is generated. First, the consequences of failed recommendations might be business-critical (e.g., algorithms with discriminatory tendencies, which harms a company's reputation). Second, from an organization's perspective, the individual's attitude toward an AI-based recommendation must be investigated to encourage the usage of such systems. We aim to address this research gap by conducting an exploratory interview analysis to unveil the user's perception of the black box problem to gain insights regarding the attitude toward AI-based recommendations.

3 Research Method

The overall aim of this paper is to explain attitude-based technology acceptance of AI-based recommendations against the backdrop of the black box problem. To reveal the user's attitude toward AI-based recommendations in HR, we applied a two-stage approach. First, we conducted interviews to get further insights regarding the black box problem as a determinant for the user's attitude toward AI-based recommendations. Second, we examined the influence of the use context on the relation between the perception of the black box problem and the attitude toward AI-based recommendations. As already mentioned before, our research focuses on applications in the business context, more specifically on the application in HRM. Furthermore, we distinguish between a mandatory and a voluntary use context.

3.1 Study Design

Overall, 21 semi-structured interviews with experts from various fields (HRM, AI and ML, law, data protection) were conducted to gain a broad understanding of fundamental beliefs and concerns regarding the acceptance of AI-based recommendations in HRM [35]. All interviewed experts (I1–I21) have experience with recruiting of candidates and can assess the black box problem as they deal with the potentials of innovative AI-technologies in their daily work. Our interviewees provide both a perspective from an organizational and from an individual point of view as the experts indicate that the black box problem affects the organization in general and the user of AI-based systems in particular. The identification of potential experts took place by screening their business-related networking sites in order to assess their involvement in the topic. In sum, 56 potential participants were contacted via E-Mail or the professional network platform LinkedIn. Twenty-eight contacted persons did not respond, and seven persons stated they could not take part due to time issues or because they are not highly involved in recruiting processes. In the end, we interviewed 21experts exclusively in person or by phone. Table 1 illustrates the demographic characteristics.

Table 1. Overview on the study design

Characteristics	Attribute	Share
Gender	Male	12 (56,1%)
	Female	9 (42,9%)
Age	24–29	7 (33,3%)
	30–39	2 (9,5%)
	40–49	4 (19,1%)
	50–59	4 (19,1%)
	> 59	4 (19,1%)
Background	Recruiting	9 (42,9%)
	AI and ML	7 (33,3%)
	Law/ Data Protection	5 (23,8%)

We conducted an interview guideline considering questions regarding the *awareness and relevance* of the black box problem, the evaluation of lack in transparency and explainability of AI-based recommendations (i.e., *positive vs. negative*), as well as the importance of an application's use context (i.e., *mandatory vs. voluntary*). The interview guideline follows a semi-structured format. This approach gives respondents sufficient freedom to describe their overall attitude toward AI-based recommendations. Moreover, it allows for consistency across the interviews and enables the interviewer to explain specific and new insights [36, 37]. To reduce possible response bias and encounter social desirability, the authors assured them to treat all answers anonymous and strictly confidential.

3.2 Interview-Based Research

The transcription in preparation for the data analysis was accomplished after each interview using MAXQDA. This approach ensured that no thematic aspect is missing in the analysis. The systematic analysis and categorization of the insights from the interviews followed the method of qualitative content analysis [38]. In order to generate insights regarding the perception of the black box problem from the user's perspective in an organizational context, we followed an exploratory, inductive approach to code the interviews [38, 39]. Coding the interviews inductively allows the consideration of alternative solutions as we searched for statements that reflect alternative adoption behaviors as well as determinants for the attitude toward AI-based recommendations, thereby avoiding a bias toward the black box problem [35, 40].

4   Results

Based on the interviews, we could derive two propositions, P1 and P2. A synthesis of determinants for the attitude toward AI-based recommendations results in the research model shown in Fig. 1.

In our analysis, we identified the black box problem (i.e., awareness and relevance) as a determinant to explain the user's attitude toward AI-based recommendations (P1). Additionally, we found evidence that the use context (i.e., voluntary vs. mandatory) moderates the relation between the black box problem and user's attitude toward AI-based recommendations (P2). In the following subchapters, we will describe the resulting implications in more detail.

4.1   Black Box and Attitude Toward AI-Based Recommendations

To explain the user's attitude toward AI-based recommendations, we examine the black box problem from an individual's perspective in an organizational HRM context. Thereby, we identified users' awareness regarding the lack of transparency and explainability of AI-based recommendations. Based on our analysis, we highlight users' evaluation of the black box problem by scrutinizing the relevance of a black box when users rely on AI-based recommendations. In general, the interviews show that users are aware of the black box problem of AI-based recommendations and assess this issue as highly relevant for HR. Black boxes seem to be the major challenge when an organization considers the application of AI-based recommendations in HR-related processes, as the following statements show:

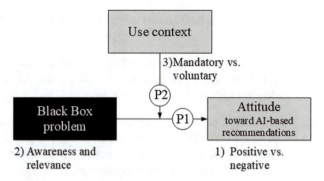

Fig. 1. Relation between black box problem and attitude toward AI-based recommendations.

"At the moment, black boxes are the greatest challenge for AI systems, because we do not know how they come to their decisions." (I1)

"[…] there is no transparency, the accountability is lost, and these systems are not traceable." (I13)

More precisely, respondents criticize the incomprehensibility of AI-based recommendations resulting from obscure data processing. They are not able to interpret the recommendation's underlying reasoning and would prefer a higher level of transparency:

"The problem when applying AI-based recommendations is that data is inserted and then an answer emerges. It is unclear, however, how this answer has been produced. […]. It is incomprehensible." (I14)

HR-related processes are linked to a certain degree to responsibility regarding the consequences of a decision. Therefore, users find it difficult to trust non-transparent recommendations and to assume responsibility for the consequences, as the following interviewee stated:

"I imagine working together with an AI to be complicated, as I would need to raise a lot of trust, if not understanding its inner workings […] because I like to understand causes and procedures." (I21)

To increase the attitude toward AI-based recommendation in HR, organizations have to clarify the level of responsibility for the users with regard to the acceptance of AI-based recommendations.

Especially in an organizational HRM context, users want AI-based systems to provide additional information regarding the underlying processes. Respondents see it critical when AI-based systems miss to exemplify how recommendations are generated and believe that AI-based recommendations should offer some detailed explanation for the suggested solution:

"The user of AI systems should not only be told: 'This is the result now and you trust it.' Rather, requests should be allowed. For example: 'When was a candidate filtered out?' And then the user himself also thinks about what the reasons are.

However, explainable artificial intelligence is still very much in development."
(I3)

Regarding "soft skills" (e.g., empathy and intuition), humans are currently superior to systems [9]. Anyhow, respondents see potentials in the application of AI-based systems, in particular when it comes to processing a huge data amount:

"In feeling, in intuition, in perception – generally in all 'human competencies', AI systems are inferior to humans. An AI system has no chance in this respect. On the other hand, where man has no chance is when it comes to the evaluation of very many numbers. If thousands of people apply for a job in a large corporation, then people have no chance to match their skills as quickly as AI." (I2)

AI-based recommendations might also be an appropriate instrument to prevent discriminatory tendencies in HRM as unbiased, and correctly programmed algorithms are directly linked to consistent and impartial decisions [41].

"When it comes to recruiting, AI has the biggest potential here. It will help human beings to overcome their conclusive biases when making a decision. But again, AI or any intelligent system is only as good as the data you are feeding it with." (I7)

However, there are also more critical voices regarding the underlying algorithms of AI-based recommendations programmed by humans as the black box contains-strictly speaking also the opinion of the programmer and represents his beliefs:

"An algorithm is not objective. An algorithm does not have a moral. The machine does what humans tell it to do. In the end, in particular, it depends on humans becoming aware when making the decision to use an algorithm or AI system that ultimately, it is error-prone and, furthermore, where the boundaries and possibilities of the system lie." (I6)

In summary, the interviews show that users are aware of the black box problem in an organizational context and evaluate it as a relevant issue that influences their attitude toward AI-based recommendations. Particularly in HRM, where personal data is processed, transparent decisions are inevitable. For example, insufficient explanations in the process of applicant selection can harm an organization's reputation due to discrimination accusations and even induce legal consequences [10]. Therefore, it is important that users of AI-based recommendations are aware of the consequences resulting from a lack of transparency and explainability.

Hence, we argue that there is a relation between the black box problem and the user's attitude toward AI-based recommendations. This applies when the user is aware of the lack of transparency and explainability. Simultaneously, the user has to evaluate the relevancy of the given challenge as crucial. Provided that both aspects are given, the user's attitude toward AI-based recommendations is more negatively connoted. Therefore, we conclude that the perception of the black box problem, conceptualized by awareness and relevance, influence the attitude toward AI-based recommendations, such that we assume:

P1: The higher (lower) a user's perception of the black box problem in terms of awareness and relevance, the lower (higher) is the user's attitude toward AI-based recommendations.

4.2 The Influence of the Use Context

In our interview-based study, we examined the influence of the use context on the relation between the black box problem and the user's attitude toward AI-based recommendations. Organizations might pursue the mandatory use of AI-based systems to realize advantages from the organization's perspective (e.g., increase labor productivity). In a mandatory use context, the organization constrains its employees to use a specific AI-based system. Users have no other choice and must accept the recommendation created by the AI. For example, an organization implements a mandatory CV parser. Users have to accept the recommendations from the CV parser instead of screening CVs independently – even if they are not able to understand a certain recommendation and are eventually responsible for the consequences.

In contrast, organizations can implement AI-based systems as a supportive tool that can be used voluntarily by employees to support them in their daily work routine.

In our interviews, we found evidence that users' attitude toward AI-based recommendations depends on the level of voluntariness provided by an organizational AI-based system. In general, the interviews indicate that users hesitate to trust a mandatory tool to make business-critical decisions. Respondents evaluate it critically if AI-based systems force users to select a certain option without giving them any guidance regarding the consequences, even when the objective of an AI-based recommendation is relieving the user (e.g., recruiter), illustrated by the following statement:

"But I don't think the AI should decide whether I want to hire someone or not, it should just simplify what the HR person does for them." (I12)

More precisely, the interviews show that users want to make the final decision (e.g., selection of candidates in the recruiting process) and are critical of AI-based systems that act autonomously:

"That [who is responsible for AI-based decisions] is already a discussion. But AI should not be the ultimate decision-maker. The decision maker is the one who uses this tool." (I1)

Furthermore, respondents stated that users might feel uncomfortable to follow such a non-transparent recommendation when they are personally responsible for the decision. Moreover, interviewees find it difficult to verify a decision they are not able to interpret. Especially when they cope with reconstructing the reasoning of an AI-based recommendation:

"The users receive some recommendations that should lead to a decision respectively contribute to a decision making the process. But in the end, the human decision maker, e.g., the recruiter, is held responsible for the decision." (I1)

In comparison, a voluntary use context allows the user to consider AI-based systems as a supportive tool. The recommendations provided are a kind of guidance for the user. For example, recruiters receive AI-based recommendations for a job platform regarding appropriate candidates. The recruiter can accept these recommendations and contact the proposed candidates or ignore them. In this particular case, AI-based systems support the user in self-assessment:

> "So, if the recommendation of the AI is not understandable, then I feel uncomfortable with it. If this is something where you would have come to the same conclusion or you can check the recommendation (e.g., by running an assessment center independently of the AI recommendation), then perhaps AI will help you to rethink your assessments." (I3)

Simultaneously, in a voluntary use context, the user receives enough freedom to make their own decisions. In this case, the black box problem is less critical. AI-based recommendations are merely options and support the user in the daily work – but the final decision resides with the user:

> "So I'm always a friend of any kind of support, but the last decision must be made by the human being." (I9)

In summary, the interviews indicate that the relation between the black box problem and user's attitude is moderated by the use context. A mandatory use context strengthens the negative relation between the perception of the black box problem and the attitude toward an AI-based recommendation, whereas a voluntary use context weakens this effect. Especially when users are responsible for a decision, they want to understand the underlying reasoning of a recommendation and evaluate the use of mandatory AI-based systems more negatively. In contrast, AI-based recommendations are evaluated positively when they are considered as a supportive tool, and the user maintains the decisional power. Therefore, we propose:

> P2: The use context moderates the relation between the black box problem and user's attitude toward AI-based recommendations such that the relation is stronger (weaker) in a mandatory (voluntary) use context.

5 Discussion

We propose that the attitude toward AI-based recommendations is based on the perception of the black box problem in terms of awareness and relevance and that the influence of this perception depends on the context of AI-based recommendations, whereas we assume that the effect is stronger in mandatory use contexts. This proposed theoretical model has implications for theory and practice, as we will discuss in the following. Prior studies have generated insights by outlining the technical perspective of the black box problem, thereby focusing on methods to increase explainability of the underlying algorithms [7, 11, 12, 28]. Further, approaches that deal with the black box problem consider in particular the medical domain [29–32] as well as the financial sector [25, 33, 34] with a strong focus on the technical perspective, thereby unveiling *how* an algorithm works to derive recommendations.

The issue of *why* perceptions on the black box problem influence an individual's attitude toward AI-based recommendations in HR is largely unaddressed, especially in regard to the use context (i.e., mandatory vs. voluntary). Therefore, our theoretical model contributes to the outlined XAI discussion in the literature by providing an individual focused perspective that explains how AI users evaluate the black box problem in HR and if the black box problem shapes their attitude toward AI-based recommendations. This perspective enriches the rather technical perspective in the literature as it highlights the need for a comprehensive model to explain the relation of the black box problem of AI-based recommendations and the role of the use context. Our proposed model addresses this challenge by providing valuable insights regarding the black box perceptions on the attitude toward AI-based recommendations. The overall results show that the attitude toward AI-based recommendations is more negative when user awareness and user evaluation as determinants of the black box problem are high. Furthermore, we contribute by considering the organizational use context as a moderator on the relation between AI-based recommendations and the perception of the black box problem. We show that a mandatory use context, which is characterized by the obligated use of AI-based systems, strengthens the relation between the black box problem and user's attitude toward AI-based recommendations. In contrast, users evaluate the voluntary use of AI-based systems as beneficial because the given recommendations are experienced as suggestions and support them in their business-related tasks.

Regarding research dealing with AI-based systems in HRM, we followed the call for an examination of attitude-based technology acceptance research [42]. So far, much research has focused on the application of AI to enhance the strategic role of HR [43]. AI-based systems are implemented to increase value creation for the company and therefore realize economic advantages. Furthermore, research has focused on using AI to improve employees' performance from an organizational point of view [44]. In this context, research has tackled the challenges of discrimination and unfairness and discussed AI as an appropriate instrument to prevent both discriminatory tendencies and unfairness [41]. Besides these research efforts linking AI and HRM and to focus on general challenges such as discrimination, less is known about how HR employees value the use of AI in their job. Hence, this paper contributes to this stream of research by focusing on the user's attitude toward such AI-based systems in HR. Our study contributes to this discussion in the literature as it shows that HR employees are aware of the black box problem. They evaluate the lack of transparency and explainability as critical, especially when they are responsible for a decision, which they are not able to verify (mandatory use context). However, HR employees see potential in AI-based systems as recommendations can support them in non-critical business-related decision making (voluntary use context). Our findings also give practical implications. When implementing AI-based systems, companies should be aware of the fact that user acceptance depends on the transparency and understandability of such systems. In addition, AI-based recommendations are not suitable for every business-related task. When users are of high responsibility for the possible consequences, they wanted to be more involved in the decision-making process and hesitate to trust AI-based recommendations unconditionally.

Besides these contributions, the presented paper underlies several limitations. First, the generalizability of the findings is restricted as only 21 German experts with experience in recruiting or AI affinity were interviewed. As the majority of respondents deal with innovative technologies and AI in their daily business, the sample might be biased in regard to awareness of the black box problem. Based on our findings, we aim at expanding future research in regard to the implementation of XAI in HRM. In this context, it is not only important to understand the perception of the black box problem within an organization, but also to focus on the black box problem for AI-based recommendations that are provided to external individuals, such as in an HR context potential employees. Therefore, future research should expand our study to black box problems of AI-based recommendations offered for candidates. This might enable to study additional use contexts that are relevant in the general AI-based recommendation context. In addition, the identified effects can be further validated by using a quantitative study that enables tests of additional context factors such as user personality or experience with AI. These factors have not been tested in the development of the proposed model so far, but they are expected to better explain which users in which contexts especially perceive the black box problem such that it influences their attitude toward AI-based recommendations.

6   Conclusion

This paper contributes to both academia and practice. We provide insights into the application of XAI in HRM. We highlight the importance of perception of the black box problem conceptualized by the awareness and the relevance in regard to AI-based recommendation systems. Adding to the existing technical-oriented literature on the black box problem, this work recognizes the individual perspective and examines an attitude-based view on this strategically relevant topic. According to use of these findings in practice, we highlight the need for awareness regarding the trade-off between realization of an organization's efficiency and the user's responsibility for their decisions.

Acknowledgements. This project is funded by the Adecco Stiftung "New Ways for Work and Social Life".

References

1. Melville, N., Kraemer, K., Gurbaxani, V.: Information technology and organizational performance: an integrative model of IT business value. MIS Q. **28**, 283–322 (2004)
2. Ransbotham, S., Kiron, D., Gerbert, P., Reeves, M.: Reshaping business with artificial intelligence: closing the gap between ambition and action. MIT Sloan Manag. Rev. **59**, 1–17 (2017)
3. Recommender Systems Handbook: Springer. US, Boston, MA (2011)
4. Eckhardt, A., Laumer, S., Maier, C., Weitzel, T.: The transformation of people, processes, and IT in e-recruiting. Empl. Relat. **36**, 415–431 (2014)
5. van Esch, P., Black, J.S., Ferolie, J.: Marketing AI recruitment: the next phase in job application and selection. Comput. Hum. Behav. **90**, 215–222 (2019)

6. Strohmeier, S., Piazza, F.: Artificial intelligence techniques in human resource management—a conceptual exploration. In: Kahraman, C., Çevik Onar, S. (eds.) Intelligent Techniques in Engineering Management. ISRL, vol. 87, pp. 149–172. Springer, Cham (2015). https://doi.org/10.1007/978-3-319-17906-3_7
7. Castelvecchi, D.: Can we open the black box of AI? Nature **538**, 20–23 (2016)
8. Nugent, C., Cunningham, P.: A case-based explanation system for black-box systems. Artif. Intell. Rev. **24**, 163–178 (2005)
9. Jarrahi, M.H.: Artificial intelligence and the future of work: human-AI symbiosis in organizational decision making. Bus. Horiz. **61**, 577–586 (2018)
10. Orwat, C.: Diskriminierungsrisiken durch verwendung von algorithmen. In: Eine Studie erstellt mit einer Zuwendung der Antidiskriminierungsstelle des Bundes. Nomos; Antidiskriminierungsstelle des Bundes, Baden-Baden (2019)
11. Ghahramani, Z.: Probabilistic machine learning and artificial intelligence. Nature **521**, 452–459 (2015)
12. Explainable, A.I.: Interpreting. Explaining and Visualizing Deep Learning. Springer International Publishing, Cham (2019)
13. Ajzen, I.: The theory of planned behavior. Organ. Behav. Hum. Decis. Process. **50**, 179–211 (1991)
14. Kroenung, J., Eckhardt, A.: The attitude cube: a three-dimensional model of situational factors in IS adoption and their impact on the attitude–behavior relationship. Inf. Manag. **52**, 611–627 (2015)
15. Ajzen, I., Fishbein, M.: Attitude-behavior relations: a theoretical analysis and review of empirical research. Psychol. Bull. **84**, 888–918 (1977)
16. Mallat, N., Rossi, M., Tuunainen, V.K., Öörni, A.: The impact of use context on mobile services acceptance: the case of mobile ticketing. Inf Manag. **46**, 190–195 (2009)
17. Lu, J., Wu, D., Mao, M., Wang, W., Zhang, G.: Recommender system application developments: a survey. Decis. Support Syst. **74**, 12–32 (2015)
18. Komiak, B.: The effects of personalization and familiarity on trust and adoption of recommendation agents. MIS Q. **30**, 941 (2006)
19. Dietvorst, B.J., Simmons, J.P., Massey, C.: Overcoming algorithm aversion: people will use imperfect algorithms if they can (even slightly) modify them. Manage. Sci. **64**, 1155–1170 (2018)
20. Adomavicius, G., Bockstedt, J.C., Curley, S.P., Zhang, J.: Do recommender systems manipulate consumer preferences? a study of anchoring effects. Inf. Syst. Res. **24**, 956–975 (2013)
21. Bondarouk, T.V., Ruël, H.J.M.: Electronic Human Resource Management: challenges in the digital era. Int. J. Hum. Resour. Manag. **20**, 505–514 (2009)
22. Bondarouk, T., Harms, R., Lepak, D.: Does e-HRM lead to better HRM service? Int. J. Hum. Resour. Manage. **28**, 1332–1362 (2017)
23. Ruta, C.D.: HR portal alignment for the creation and development of intellectual capital. Int. J. Hum. Resour. Manage. **20**, 562–577 (2009)
24. Wirtky, T., Laumer, S., Eckhardt, A., Weitzel, T.: On the untapped value of e-HRM – a literature review. Commun. Assoc. Inf. Syst. **38**, 20–83 (2016)
25. Samek, W., Müller, K.-R.: Towards explainable artificial intelligence. In: Samek, W., Montavon, G., Vedaldi, A., Hansen, L.K., Müller, K.-R. (eds.) Explainable AI: Interpreting, Explaining and Visualizing Deep Learning. LNCS (LNAI), vol. 11700, pp. 5–22. Springer, Cham (2019). https://doi.org/10.1007/978-3-030-28954-6_1
26. LeCun, Y., Bengio, Y., Hinton, G.: Deep learning. Nature **521**, 436–444 (2015)
27. Zanni-Merk, C.: On the need of an explainable artificial Intelligence. In: Borzemski, L., Świątek, J., Wilimowska, Z. (eds.) ISAT 2019. AISC, vol. 1050, pp. 3–3. Springer, Cham (2020). https://doi.org/10.1007/978-3-030-30440-9_1

28. Zhu, J., Liapis, A., Risi, S., Bidarra, R., Youngblood, M.: Explainable AI for designers: a human-centered perspective on mixed-initiative co-creation. In: Proceedings of the 2018 IEEE Conference on Computational Intelligence and Games (CIG'18) (2018)
29. Holzinger, A., Biemann, C., Pattichis, C.S., Kell, D.B.: What do we need to build explainable AI systems for the medical domain? CoRR abs/1712.09923 (2017)
30. Holzinger, A., Langs, G., Denk, H., Zatloukal, K., Müller, H.: Causability and explainability of artificial intelligence in medicine. WIREs Data Mining Knowl. Discov. **9**, e1312 (2019)
31. Lamy, J.-B., Sekar, B., Guezennec, G., Bouaud, J., Séroussi, B.: Explainable artificial intelligence for breast cancer: a visual case-based reasoning approach. Artif. Intell. Med. **94**, 42–53 (2019)
32. Meldo, A.A., Utkin, L.V.: A new approach to differential lung diagnosis with CT scans based on the Siamese neural network. J. Phys.: Conf. Ser. **1236**, 12058 (2019)
33. Weller, A.: Transparency: motivations and challenges. In: Samek, W., Montavon, G., Vedaldi, A., Hansen, L.K., Müller, K.-R. (eds.) Explainable AI: Interpreting, Explaining and Visualizing Deep Learning. LNCS (LNAI), vol. 11700, pp. 23–40. Springer, Cham (2019). https://doi.org/10.1007/978-3-030-28954-6_2
34. Wang, D., Yang, Q., Abdul, A., Lim, B.Y.: Designing theory-driven user-centric explainable AI. In: Proceedings of the 2019 CHI Conference on Human Factors in Computing Systems - CHI '19, pp. 1–15. ACM Press, New York, New York, USA (2019)
35. Gioia, D.A., Corley, K.G., Hamilton, A.L.: Seeking qualitative rigor in inductive research. Organ. Res. Methods **16**, 15–31 (2013)
36. Myers, M.D.: Qualitative Research in Business & Management. Sage, Los Angeles (2010)
37. Bryman, A.: Social Research Methods. Oxford University Press, Oxford (2016)
38. Mayring, P.: Qualitative content analysis: theoretical foundation, basic procedures and software solution. Klagenfurt (2014)
39. Schreier, M.: Qualitative Content Analysis in Practice. Sage, Los Angeles, London, New Delhi, Singapore, Washington DC (2012)
40. Yin, R.K.: Case Study Research and Applications. Design and Methods. Sage, Los Angeles, London, New Dehli, Singapore, Washington DC, Melbourne (2018)
41. Xu, P., Barbosa, D.: Matching résumés to job descriptions with stacked models. In: Bagheri, E., Cheung, J.C.K. (eds.) Canadian AI 2018. LNCS (LNAI), vol. 10832, pp. 304–309. Springer, Cham (2018). https://doi.org/10.1007/978-3-319-89656-4_31
42. Burton-Jones, A., Stein, M., Mishra, A.: IS Use. MIS Q. Res. Curations (2017)
43. Marler, J.H., Parry, E.: Human resource management, strategic involvement and e-HRM technology. Int. J. Hum. Resour. Manage. **27**, 2233–2253 (2016)
44. Tursunbayeva, A., Di Lauro, S., Pagliari, C.: People analytics—A scoping review of conceptual boundaries and value propositions. Int. J. Inf. Manage. **43**, 224–247 (2018)

Explaining the Suspicion: Design of an XAI-Based User-Focused Anti-Phishing Measure

Kilian Kluge[✉] and Regina Eckhardt

Institute of Business Analytics, University of Ulm, Ulm, Germany
{kilian.kluge,regina.eckhardt}@uni-ulm.de

Abstract. Phishing attacks are the primary cause of data and security breaches in businesses, public institutions, and private life. Due to inherent limitations and users' high susceptibility to increasingly sophisticated phishing attempts, existing anti-phishing measures cannot realize their full potential. Against this background, we utilize methods from the emerging research field of Explainable Artificial Intelligence (XAI) for the design of a user-focused anti-phishing measure. By leveraging the power of state-of-the-art phishing detectors, our approach uncovers the words and phrases in an e-mail most relevant for identifying phishing attempts. We empirically show that our approach reliably extracts segments of text considered relevant for the discrimination between genuine and phishing e-mails. Our work opens up novel prospects for phishing prevention and demonstrates the tremendous potential of XAI methods beyond applications in AI.

Keywords: Phishing prevention · Explainable artificial intelligence · Interpretable machine learning · User-centric XAI

1 Introduction

During the first weeks of the COVID-19 pandemic, a large number of US citizens received an e-mail ostensibly from their employers' payroll department. The e-mail informed them that the federal government was considering a financial relief package, entitling them to a $1000 check. In order to benefit from this measure, they would need to verify "their email account for new payroll directory" by following a "Secure Link" included in the e-mail [1]. These e-mails are exemplary for a phishing attack: To gain sensitive information for malicious purposes, the sender imitates a trustworthy source and promises a personal benefit to deceive the user [2, 3].

Phishing attacks are the primary way in which identity theft and security breaches occur in businesses, public institutions, and private life [4–6]. Virtually all users of electronic communication are frequently subject to phishing attempts [6–8]. In light of this perpetually growing threat, IT security researchers and practitioners have developed a large variety of anti-phishing measures. Commonly, these are divided into three categories: Blocking malicious e-mails before they reach users, warning users, and training users not to fall for phishing [2, 4, 6, 8]. All of these measures are applied in practice with

F. Ahlemann et al. (Eds.): WI 2021, LNISO 47, pp. 247–261, 2021.
https://doi.org/10.1007/978-3-030-86797-3_17

some success. Ultimately, however, due to inherent limitations, neither is effective in preventing phishing attempts from succeeding. While state-of-the-art phishing detectors that aim to identify and filter out phishing attempts are robust and versatile, they suffer from their limited accuracy [2, 8, 9]. In order to avoid a high number of false positives i.e., mistakenly blocking genuine e-mails the detectors are generally tuned for maximum precision [6]. Consequently, many e-mails that a detector identified as suspicious of constituting a phishing attack reach the user [2, 8, 9]. Therefore, user behavior is of paramount importance in phishing prevention.

While the response rate to phishing e-mails varies widely between users and particular variants of phishing attacks, on average, 10 to 20% of users that receive a phishing e-mail act on it [5, 10, 11]. Anti-phishing training aims to reduce this rate by educating users on how to identify phishing attempts [2, 8]. However, while users successfully learn to spot telltale signs of phishing, they nevertheless fall for it in everyday situations, which is overwhelmingly attributed to a lack of awareness when performing routine tasks in a familiar and trusted environment [10–16]. Existing anti-phishing measures that aim to raise the users' attention, such as warning messages, are often ignored, as they are perceived as too generic [4, 6–8]. In summary, on the one hand, the need to avoid false positives prevents phishing detectors from realizing their full potential [6]. On the other hand, users do not benefit from the knowledge gained in anti-phishing training and remain susceptible to phishing because, in everyday life, they lack the required attention [11, 12].

Against this background, approaches from the emerging field of Explainable Artificial Intelligence (XAI) [17, 18] harbor to date untapped potential for the design of more effective user-focused anti-phishing measures [9]. In particular, XAI methods designed to explain the classification of text documents by black-box models [19, 20] could convey to the user which elements in an e-mail most strongly influenced a phishing detector in identifying it as suspicious. These explanations, which could be provided for all e-mails that a detector had to let pass to avoid false positives, constitute highly specific warnings that are expected to effectively raise the users' attention [3, 9, 11, 14]. Pursuing this basic idea, we design a novel approach that identifies phishing cues in suspicious e-mails by generating explanations for the output of a phishing detector. Thereby, we not only pave the way for more effective user-focused anti-phishing measures but provide a glimpse of the potential applications of XAI in the realm of IT security and beyond.

Following the Design Science methodology [21], the remainder of the paper is structured as follows: In Sect. 2, we survey research from the fields of phishing prevention as well as XAI and conclude with the research gap. Subsequently, in Sect. 3, we describe the design of a novel XAI approach to extract cues and phrases from e-mails that contribute to their assessment by a black-box phishing detector. In Sect. 4, we demonstrate and evaluate the applicability of the approach using a real-world dataset. Subsequently, in Sect. 5, we summarize our findings and conclude our paper with a discussion of the limitations of our research and an outlook on future work.

2   Related Work and Research Gap

To lay the foundation for the design of our novel approach, in the following, we first summarize research on phishing attacks and the cues based on which both automatic detectors and users can distinguish phishing attempts from legitimate communication. Then, we provide a brief overview of existing anti-phishing measures and their respective strengths and drawbacks. Last, we introduce the research field of Explainable Artificial Intelligence (XAI) and survey XAI methods for explaining document classification.

2.1 Phishing Attacks and Phishing Cues

Phishing is a social engineering attack that aims to exploit specific weaknesses of users [4, 5, 7]. The attacker imitates a trustworthy source to gain sensitive information for malicious purposes [2, 4, 5]. A phishing attack typically consists of three phases [5, 6]: Circumventing IT security measures (e.g., a phishing detector) to deliver an electronic communication (e.g., an e-mail) to a user, convincing the user to engage in the intended activity (e.g., click on a link to a counterfeit website and enter their credit card details), and finally gaining from the attack (e.g., receive a payment). Most phishing attacks are carried out via e-mail and traditionally target a broad audience, e.g., all users of a popular online platform [5–7]. The e-mails include a link to a forged website, where users are asked to enter their login credentials, on which the attackers then capitalize. Increasingly, personalized attacks target employees of specific company departments or public offices using elaborately crafted e-mails that imitate communication by superiors or co-workers [5–7, 10]. Often, the goal is to initiate large payments or gain access to confidential information [5, 8, 10].

Researchers have identified cues that are helpful to distinguish between genuine and phishing e-mails through user studies [10, 13, 14, 22] and analyzing e-mails [3, 14, 23].

Among the main discriminatory elements are the sender's address and other technical information in the e-mails' header, the links included in the e-mail, and words and phrases in the e-mails' text [3, 10, 14]. In contrast, the graphical design of an e-mail, visual elements, and the presence of legal information (e.g., a disclaimer) are of little informative value [3, 14].

Textual information is arguably the most relevant for users when distinguishing between genuine and phishing e-mails. On the one hand, increasingly sophisticated imitation of the style and design of e-mails renders these features unsuitable as discriminators [11, 14]. On the other hand, textual cues such as urgency require complex judgment and background knowledge [10, 23]. Thus, in contrast to technical cues (e.g., URL spoofing), they often cannot be unambiguously detected by automated filters [5–7]. Indeed, anti-phishing training places emphasis on textual cues and caution users' against just considering the superficial properties of an e-mail [3, 11]. Table 1 summarizes typical categories of textual phishing cues.

2.2 Technical and User-Focused Anti-Phishing Measures

Measures for phishing prevention are commonly divided into technical and user-focused anti-phishing measures. While the former aim to block malicious e-mails before they reach users, the latter intend to prevent users from falling for phishing attempts [2, 4, 6].

Technical anti-phishing measures detect phishing e-mails by searching for common characteristics [6, 7]. Typical approaches include rule-based filters and machine-learning-based detectors [6]. Filters are based on manually assembled blacklists [2, 25]

Table 1. Typical categories of textual cues in phishing e-mails [2, 3, 10, 11, 14, 22, 23]

Category	Example from the IWSPA v2.0 dataset [24]
Urgency	You have 72 h to verify the information, …
(Appeal to) authority	A message from the CEO …
Importance	We have reason to believe that your account was accessed by a third party
Positive consequence (reward)	In return we will deposit $70 to your account …
Negative consequence (loss)	If you do not verify yourself, your account will be suspended
References to security and safety	Security is one of our top goals at our company …
Spelling mistakes and grammatical errors	You were qualified to participate in $50.00 reward surwey
Lack of personalization	Dear Valued Customer, …

and are thus inherently constrained to already known cues and patterns [5–7]. In contrast, machine-learning-based detectors learn to detect phishing e-mails from training on examples [6]. While earlier approaches relied on predefined features [7], modern deep learning methods autonomously identify intricate patterns in raw data and have demonstrated excellent performance in phishing detection [8, 26]. However, phishing detectors have to be configured such that no genuine e-mail is mistakenly classified as a phishing attempt and thus discarded [6, 9]. Indeed, it is the "concern over liability for false positives [that] is the major barrier to deploying more aggressive heuristics" [6, p. 79], which in turn limits the effectiveness of phishing detectors.

Depending on the type of attack and target audience [cf. 5], studies found that between 5% and close to 50% of users that receive a phishing e-mail fall for the attempt [5, 10, 11]. Against this background, user-focused anti-phishing measures aim to reduce users' susceptibility to phishing attacks. They comprise anti-phishing training as well as preventive mechanisms and warning facilities [2, 6]. Trainings aim to raise users' awareness of the threat and educate them on how to identify phishing attempts. They are administered in the form of resources for self-study (e.g., texts [8], videos [27], or games [28, 29]), classroom-style training, and interventional training [2, 8, 10, 11]. In the course of the latter, imitated phishing e-mails are sent to users. When they fall for the simulated attack (e.g., by clicking on an included link), they are immediately presented with self-study material [2, 6, 10]. However, anti-phishing training is not sufficient to prevent users from falling for phishing attacks [2, 12]. While trainings have been shown to increase users' ability to identify phishing attempts when tasked to do so [2, 6], trained users nevertheless fall for phishing in everyday situations [8].

Researchers have theorized and demonstrated that the cause for users' high susceptibility to phishing is their lack of attention when performing routine tasks in a familiar and trusted environment [8, 12, 16, 30]. It is further amplified by users' tendency to underestimate their vulnerability to phishing attacks [10, 28, 31]. Thus, preventive mechanisms such as regular reminders [10], warning messages [4, 10], or tooltips that help users to evaluate URLs [32] are employed to motivate users to stay alert and scrutinize all communication for phishing cues [6, 10, 32]. However, users often overlook or outright ignore these warnings when they are passive indicators or not perceived as specific and relevant to their current situation [2, 4, 7, 8, 10].

2.3 Explainable Artificial Intelligence and Generation of Explanations for Document Classification

Since at least the rise of deep learning, AI systems have become ubiquitous. Thus, an increasing number of people are faced with the consequences of decisions and recommendations generated by effectively black-box systems [17, 33]. Against this background, the research field of Explainable Artificial Intelligence (XAI) focuses on automatically generating explanations for AI decisions [17, 18, 33, 34].

XAI methods can be distinguished by their aim and their dependency on a particular kind of machine learning model [18, 34]. In the context of explanations for AI systems for text and document classification (such as phishing detectors), both researchers and practitioners have taken a particular interest in outcome explanations [20, 35]. This kind of explanation is not concerned with revealing the inner workings of the AI system but aims to provide a human-understandable reasoning for one specific decision [34, 36].

One avenue to explain an AI system's decisions in this manner is through local feature importance [18, 34]. The underlying idea is to assign a weight to each of the input's features that reflects how strongly it contributes positively or negatively to the AI system's decision. The SHAP family constitutes a popular example of such methods [37]. Some of its variants are model-agnostic, i.e., do not require access to the AI system's internals and are thus applicable to any kind of AI system [36, 37]. A study by Weerts et al. [38] suggests that SHAP explanations succeed in drawing user's attention to particularly influential features that they would otherwise have overlooked. However, explanations based on local feature importance do not necessarily transfer to other decisions by the same AI system [19, 34].

This limitation is addressed by several more robust XAI methods, which can be divided into search-based approaches and document classifiers with integrated explanation capabilities. Martens and Provost [20] define "explanations" as minimal sets of words that, if removed from the particular document under investigation, change the classifier's prediction. To find explanations, they utilize a best-first heuristic search with search tree pruning. In the case of a non-linear classifier, two post-processing optimizations aim to ensure that the found set is indeed minimal [20]. Fernandez et al. [39] generalize this approach to replacing words instead of removing them and introduce a variable cost for replacement, allowing for more fine-grained control of the explanations' properties. Similar to these "explanations," the "anchors" introduced by Ribeiro et al. [19] are sets of words. However, instead of constituting a minimal set of words required for the classification, "anchors" aim to be representative of the AI system. They are defined as a set of words that, if present, is sufficient to guarantee the classification independent of changes to the remainder of the document. "Anchors" are built up word by word through local beam search [19].

Instead of generating explanations post-hoc [34], Lei et al. [35] train two joint machine-learning models to find explanations for the classification of texts. While an "encoder" model classifies a text, a "generator" model extracts the corresponding "rationales," which are short phrases that, individually, are classified similarly as the full text. An objective function ensures both correct classification and the "rationales'" characteristics, namely conciseness and coherence [35, 40]. With their τ-SS3 classifier, Burdisso et al. [41] again pursue a different approach. τ-SS3 is inherently interpretable, i.e., the AI system itself transparently reveals which word sequences in a text stream contributed most to its output.

2.4 Research Gap

Phishing is a pervasive threat for businesses, public institutions, and private individuals alike. Technical anti-phishing measures filter out malicious e-mails with increasing effectiveness. However, due to their limited accuracy, phishing e-mails nevertheless reach the inboxes of users, which consequently have a decisive role to play [2, 6, 7, 9]. Despite efforts to educate users, they frequently fall for phishing attempts, in particular for those that are sophisticated imitations of genuine e-mails [8, 10]. It is, however, generally not a lack of knowledge or awareness of the grave consequences but a lack of attention in everyday situations that makes users vulnerable [10, 12, 16]. Existing preventive mechanisms such as warning messages often remain without effect, as users perceive them as too unspecific and disregard them [4, 7, 8, 10].

In light of the power of modern phishing detectors, methods from the field of XAI appear as a promising foundation for the design of more specific, and thus, more effective user-focused anti-phishing measures [9]. Following this idea, based on outcome explanation methods for document classification [19, 20, 35], we design a novel approach that uncovers words and phrases in e-mails that are telltale signs of phishing. Our work paves the way for user-focused anti-phishing measures that effectively raise users' attention and guide their assessment of suspicious communication [11, 15, 30, 31]. It further serves as an example of the potential of XAI methods to address problems of high practical relevance beyond the field of artificial intelligence.

3   A Novel XAI Approach to Uncover Phishing Cues in E-Mails

We design a novel XAI approach to draw the user's attention to the telltale signs of phishing in a suspicious e-mail. The underlying basic idea is to generate explanations for a phishing detector's assessment of an e-mail that serve as highly specific warnings.

The starting point for our approach is a phishing detector. In the following, we describe it as a model m that takes an e-mail x as its input and outputs a score $s \in [0, 1]$ and treat it as a black box otherwise. All incoming e-mails for which $m(x) = s > t_{phish}$ are considered phishing e-mails and are filtered out before they reach a user's inbox. Since the detection threshold t_{phish} has to be set such that no genuine e-mails are discarded [cf. 6], many e-mails to which the detector assigns a high score – and thus, a high likelihood of being a phishing attempt – nevertheless reach the user [6, 8, 9].

Three design decisions characterize our approach. First, to be widely applicable and to not adversely interfere with the phishing detector's performance, we design the approach to be model-agnostic [19, 39]. Second, we focus exclusively on textual cues, as these are most relevant to distinguish phishing from genuine e-mails and easiest to assess for laypeople [3, 11, 14, 23]. Third, to assist the users' assessment, we strive to highlight precisely the telltale signs of phishing (cf. Table 1 and Fig. 1). For this, we identify the words and phrases in an e-mail that significantly contribute to the phishing detectors score. In the following, we describe the design of our approach in detail and elaborate on the design decisions.

3.1 Designing Explanations as Text Highlights

The goal of our approach is to assist users in reliably identifying phishing e-mails. Thus, the explanations produced by our approach should match how people evaluate e-mails [11, 33, 42, 43]. Phishing research suggests that textual cues are most relevant to distinguish between genuine and phishing e-mails (cf. Section 2.1). On the one hand, textual cues are easiest to comprehend and evaluate for laypeople [3, 14]. On the other hand, they are the only cues present in types of phishing e-mails that do not rely on technical manipulation [6, 10, 11].

Against this background, we design our approach to produce explanations in the shape of text highlights (cf. Fig. 1). Specifically, we highlight short sequences of text [35, 41], which offers three advantages. First, people are familiar with this concept from everyday life [cf. 42]. Second, the interpretation of the explanations does not require technical knowledge about their production [19, 44]. Further, the focus on textual cues avoids the adverse effects of cognitive biases associated with quantitative indicators such as confidence scores [33]. Third, the interpretation of text highlights demands substantial cognitive effort and thus encourages thorough evaluation [42], which is favorable for users' ability to accurately identify phishing attempts [11, 15, 31].

To formalize the notion of text highlights, we represent an e-mail as a sequence of words $x = [x_0, x_1, \ldots, x_N]$ [35, 45]. A text highlight explanation can then be represented by a binary vector a of the same length as x, where $a_i = 1$ indicates that the word x_i is highlighted and $a_i = 0$ indicates that it is not.

3.2 Characteristics of Suitable Explanations

The basic idea of our approach is to convey to the user which words and phrases in an e-mail influenced a phishing detector's classification of the e-mail as suspicious. In the realm of XAI, the task of explaining a model's output by uncovering which parts of the input contributed to its assessment has attracted considerable research attention (cf. Section 2.3). In the following, we draw from this prior work to derive and define the characteristics of explanations required in our application context.

As worked out in the previous section, our explanations take the shape of text highlights. To ensure that the highlighted phrases indeed represent phishing cues, we demand that the phishing detector classifies them as suspicious themselves. In that regard, the explanations generated by our approach are similar to the "rationales" proposed by Lei et al. [35]. Taking into account that this assessment might be coincidental, we require the phrases themselves to be sufficient for the classification of the entire e-mail. More specifically, similar to the anchors defined by Ribeiro et al. [19], replacing the remainder of the e-mail with different words should have a negligible influence on the phishing detector's assessment [cf. 39].

We capture these characteristics in the concept of a document anchor. For its formal definition, we resort to the perturbation set D_x introduced by Ribeiro et al. [19]. For a given e-mail x, this set contains all possible variants z that can be generated by replacing words in x with either blanks or similar words [19, 39]. A particular sequence of highlighted words in an e-mail is a document anchor if it is present in most $z \in D_x$ that are classified similarly as the original e-mail, but not present in the $z \in D_x$ for which this is not the case. More formally, a text highlight described by a binary vector a is a document anchor for x if for any $z \in D_x$

$$|z \odot a| = |a| \Rightarrow m(z) \geq m(x) - \tau, \tag{1}$$

where τ is an application-specific constant.

In general, many document anchors exist for any given e-mail x. However, not all of them constitute a good explanation [19, 42]. On the one hand, an anchor that covers the entire document ($a_i = 1 \forall i$) always fulfills the definition, but conveys no information to the user that is particularly helpful in distinguishing between phishing and genuine e-mails. On the other hand, while a few specific words might be sufficient to guarantee the correct classification, the user perceives text in phrases [41]. Thus, while prior work strives to find a minimal number of words in an explanation [19, 20, 39], the shortest possible explanation is not necessarily the best in the eyes of the user [40, 42]. Based on these considerations, we require that the document anchors chosen as explanations both contain an appropriate number of words and consist of at most a few connected phrases. We encode these characteristics in an objective function that takes on a minimum value for an optimal anchor:

$$\mathcal{O}(a) = (|a| - l)^2 + \beta \cdot \sum_i |a_i - a_{i-1}| \tag{2}$$

The first term measures how far the number of highlighted words contained in the document anchor described by a deviates from the desired target l. The second term measures the coherence, i.e., the number of connected sequences of words [35]. The coefficient β weights the two terms and allows for fine-tuning of the explanations' characteristics.

3.3   Model-Agnostic Generation Of Explanations For Suspicious E-Mails

Up to this point, we have defined the shape of the explanations and developed the concept of document anchors to capture their desired characteristics. What remains in the design of our approach is to devise a method that, for a given e-mail x, generates a document anchor a that minimizes the objective function $\mathcal{O}(a)$ [cf. 19].

As our approach is based on an existing phishing detector, the search for a suitable anchor cannot make any assumptions regarding the model's inner workings. Therefore, we design our approach to be model-agnostic. This not only allows it to be used with any kind of phishing detector [18, 36]. It further ensures that the phishing detector's functionality and performance are not affected in any way [19, 40]. Conversely, the phishing detector's properties do not impose restrictions on the design of the method for the generation of explanations [34, 36].

Incorporating these benefits, we follow the general idea of search-based approaches [cf. 45]. The basic concept is to find and construct an anchor for an e-mail x by probing the detector with perturbed versions of that e-mail [19, 20, 39]. Addressing the requirement that our approach should generate explanations that consist of phrases, we construct an anchor a by combining individual phrases p $(a = \sum p)$.

In our approach, we generate perturbed versions $z \in D_x$ by replacing words in the e-mail [19, 39]. In line with the definition of a document anchor, we iteratively search for phrases p that are present in those versions z that the detector identifies as suspicious, but absent from versions of the e-mail that the detector considers genuine. To this end, we utilize local beam search [19, 45], which we initialize with N seed phrases. Each iteration of the search consists of three steps. First, we generate N_{child} child phrases from each of the N phrases by growing, shrinking, or shifting the highlighted sequences of words. Second, we use the KL-LUCB algorithm [46] to determine the N best phrases among the $N \cdot N_{child}$ children [19]. For this, we estimate the expectation value for a $z \in D_x$ that contains the phrase p to be classified as suspicious by the model [19]:

$$\mathbb{E}(p) = \mathbb{E}_{|z \odot p| = |p|}[m(z) \geq m(x) - \tau] \tag{3}$$

We repeatedly refine these estimates until the lower bound on the expectation value of the Nth-best phrase surpasses the upper bound on the next-best phrase's expectation value by at least Δ_{min}. The N best phrases then form the set of N phrases for the next iteration. To boost convergence, we keep a set of the N_{elite} best phrases that we add to the child phrases in every round of the search [45]. In the third and final step of each iteration, we merge the current set of N phrases to an anchor candidate. If the objective function's value for this candidate falls below a previously specified threshold or the number of iterations surpasses a given maximum, the search terminates. Both the threshold and the maximum number of iterations, as well as the beam search parameters N, N_{child}, and N_{elite} influence the efficiency of the search and the consistency of the document anchors' characteristics [19, 45].

4 Demonstration and Evaluation

In the following, as an essential part of the Design Science research process [21], we demonstrate and evaluate the efficacy of our approach. For this, we instantiate it using a real-world dataset and conduct a series of summative evaluations adhering to the Framework for Evaluation in Design Science Research (FEDS) [47].

4.1 Dataset and Phishing Detector

The instantiation and subsequent evaluation of our approach requires a phishing detector and a set of both phishing and genuine e-mails. We use the English-language IWSPA-AP v2.0 dataset [24, 26] that was compiled to enable the comparison of machine-learning-based phishing detectors. It consists of 452 phishing and 3505 legitimate e-mails. We randomly select 80% of each kind for the training set and leave the remaining e-mails as the test set.

Using the training set, we instantiate a bidirectional LSTM (long short-term memory) recurrent neural network as the phishing detector, which is a standard model for text classification [45]. In line with real-world requirements [6], we aim to set the threshold above which we discard an e-mail as phishing t_{phish} such that the false positive rate is minimal. To avoid fatigue due to frequent unsubstantiated warnings, the threshold t_{susp} above which an e-mail is considered suspicious should be set such that the probability that these e-mails are indeed phishing attempts is reasonably high [6, 10]. We find that for the given detector and dataset, $t_{phish} = 0.98$ and $t_{susp} = 0.20$ achieve these goals, resulting in a false positive rate of 0.43% and the classification of 16 genuine and 11 phishing e-mails as suspicious. Just 2.2% of phishing e-mails reach the user without explanations.

4.2 Instantiation

Our approach generates text highlight explanations by performing a local beam search guided by an objective function and repeated estimation of the expectation value $\mathbb{E}(p)$ (Eq. 3). Accordingly, in the following, we parametrize the required components.

To generate the samples $z \in D_x$ needed to estimate $\mathbb{E}(p)$, we randomly replace words in the e-mail x with blanks. Since evaluating $\mathbb{E}(p)$ for a given phrase p requires a z for which $|z \odot p| = |z|$ (cf. Eq. 3), we can optimize the search's efficiency by maximizing the likelihood that this condition is fulfilled. As p generally consists of connected sequences of words, we do not randomly replace words but generate $z \in D_x$ that each contain a single sequence of varying length. To obtain an unbiased estimate of $\mathbb{E}(p)$, the unconditional probability $P(m(z) \geq m(x) - \tau)$ should be close to 0.5. We find that for the given phishing detector, $\tau = 0.15m(x)$ is a suitable choice. We generate at most 1024 samples $z \in D_x$ to limit the load on the phishing detector.

To instantiate the search component, we first parametrize the local beam search. We use a beamwidth of $N = 10$ and maintain an elite set of size $N_{elite} = 4$. We initialize the search with randomly placed phrases of three words. In each round, we generate $N_{child} = 2$ new phrases from each of the N current best phrases by appending one word or shifting them in either direction. Finally, we parametrize the objective function (Eq. 2) with a target length of $l = 10$ and $\beta = 4$, which we find to strike a suitable balance between highlighting relevant phishing cues and comprehensibility. We stop when $\mathcal{O}(a) \leq 16.0$ or five iterations have passed. Figure 1 displays an example of an explanation generated by our approach.

4.3 Evaluation

As suggested by FEDS, we explicate the goals and evaluation strategy before designing particular evaluation episodes [47]. The goal of the evaluation is to investigate whether our approach succeeds in generating explanations for suspected phishing attempts that help users distinguish between genuine and phishing e-mails. Owing to our research's

| ... login to your account and give us the necessary information. Complete the necessary verification tasks within 5 days, or your account might get temporarily suspended. Proceed with the link below. | For more information on protecting yourself from fraud, please review our Security Tips. Protect Your Password: You should never give your PayPal password to anyone, including PayPal employees. |

Fig. 1. Example of text highlights generated by our approach for a phishing e-mail that seeks to persuade users to provide their PayPal login credentials by invoking a sense of urgency, suggesting impending negative consequences, and alluding to standard security practices.

exploratory nature, the main risks in the design of our approach are technically-oriented. Thus, FEDS' "Technical Risk & Efficacy" strategy, which prescribes a series of increasingly summative and naturalistic evaluations, is an appropriate choice [47].

For the individual evaluation episodes, we utilize the established concept of functionally-grounded evaluation of explainable systems defined by Doshi-Velez and Kim [48] and assess explanations using three proxy measures. Each proxy measure operationalizes a particular goal of our design.

First, the highlighted segments of text should be classified similarly to the entire e-mail, i.e., as suspicious. Thus, we take the score that the phishing detector attributes to the text highlights as the corresponding proxy measure (*Score*).

Second, the explanations should be comprehensible for laypeople. For this, an explanation should consist of connected phrases rather than individual words scattered across the e-mail. Therefore, we take the number of highlighted sequences as the corresponding proxy measure (*Comprehensibility*).

Finally, to draw the users' attention to those elements in a suspicious e-mail relevant to assessing the threat, the highlighted parts of the text should represent phishing cues. To evaluate this, we let two researchers code the words in each of the suspicious e-mails according to the categories in Table 1 and measure the text highlights' overlap with the humans' assessment. To account for the vastly different amount of phishing cues in the e-mails (ranging from 0% to 50% of words), we divide this value by the ratio of cues expected to be found when randomly selecting words to be highlighted (*Relevance*).

To benchmark the values obtained for the proxies, we utilize two competing approaches: As the baseline, we create explanations by randomly highlighting $l = 10$ words in an e-mail (Random). Further, to assess the effect of the information our approach obtains from the phishing detector, we perform the local beam search with a fixed $\mathbb{E}(p) = 1$ (Search-only). To obtain statistically sound conclusions, we apply each approach fifty times for each of the 27 suspicious e-mails, assess the resulting explanations, and aggregate the results (Fig. 2).

We find that our approach outperforms the competing approaches for all three proxy measures. First, the *Score* of the text highlights generated by our approach is significantly higher and exhibits a smaller variance (1st/2nd/3rd quartile .70/.92/.98) compared to Random (.12/.43/.84) and Search-only (.05/.29/.89). Second, our approach selects only 2.1 ± 1.0 phrases in an e-mail to be highlighted, rendering its explanations comprehensible. Third, despite selecting the fewest phrases, the words highlighted by our approach exhibit higher *Relevance* for distinguishing between phishing and genuine e-mails (.99/1.6/2.3) than the text highlights generated by Search-only (.44/.98/1.5),

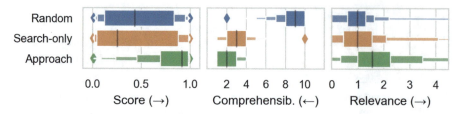

Fig. 2. Aggregated evaluation results. The arrows indicate the direction of better values.

whose *Relevance* is similar to that of the Random baseline (.60/.98/1.3). The difference in *Relevance* is significant (Mann-Whitney $U = 1.20 \cdot 10^6$, $n_1 = n_2 = 1350$, $p < 10^{-3}$ one-sided, effect size 0.66), which validates that through $\mathbb{E}(p)$ our approach indeed extracts the required information on phishing cues from the detector.

In summary, our approach successfully generates explanations in the shape of text highlights that are well suited to draw the users' attention to phishing cues in an e-mail.

5   Conclusion, Limitations, and Outlook on Further Research

Phishing is a threat to businesses, public institutions, and private individuals alike. Current anti-phishing measures ultimately fail at effectively preventing users from falling for phishing attacks. Against this background, XAI methods offer a promising path towards more effective user-focused anti-phishing measures that leverage the power of state-of-the-art phishing detectors. Pursuing this idea, we designed a novel XAI approach that identifies telltale signs of phishing in suspicious e-mails. Building on research in phishing susceptibility and anti-phishing training, we designed its explanations to raise users' attention and assist their assessment of the potential threat. We demonstrated our approach utilizing a real-world dataset and a deep learning phishing detector. Rigorous functionally-grounded evaluation indicates that our approach succeeds in producing explanations that are both relevant and comprehensible. In addition to the design of a novel XAI approach, our research contributes to theory and practice in two ways. On the one hand, it validates the feasibility of utilizing XAI methods for the design of user-focused anti-phishing measures. On the other hand, it serves as an example of how XAI methods can be applied to address problems of high practical relevance beyond the field of AI.

Although our work constitutes a substantial step, it is subject to several limitations that call for further research. First, by design, our approach can only uncover cues and phrases that the phishing detector identifies as suspicious. While our demonstration suggests that the detectors' assessment matches that of users, this might not be the case for any phishing detector, restricting the applicability of our approach. Second, although we utilized a real-world dataset, a real phishing detector, and included human labelers, our evaluation is nevertheless artificial. With the technical design risks out of the way, an evaluation based on established concepts for the evaluation of user-focused anti-phishing measures is an essential next step. Third, while the design of the explanations was informed by research in phishing susceptibility, our approach in itself does not constitute a full user-focused anti-phishing measure. Further development towards its real-world application will, amongst others, require extensive user interface design. These limitations notwithstanding, our approach provides a first glimpse of the exciting potential of XAI methods for applications in IT security and beyond.

Acknowlededgments. We kindly thank Rakesh M. Verma (University of Houston) for providing us the dataset.

References

1. O'Donnell, L.: Coronavirus 'Financial Relief' Phishing Attacks Spike, (2020) https://threat post.com/coronavirus-financial-relief-phishing-spike/154358/. Accessed 28 Aug 2020
2. Kumaraguru, P., Sheng, S., Acquisti, A., Cranor, L.F., Hong, J.: Teaching johnny not to fall for phish. ACM Trans. Internet Technol. **10**, 1–31 (2010)
3. Parsons, K., Butavicius, M., Pattinson, M., McCormac, A., Calic, D., Jerram, C.: Do users focus on the correct cues to differentiate between phishing and genuine emails? In: 26th Australasían Conference on Information Systems, Adelaide, Australia (2016)
4. Gupta, B.B., Arachchilage, N.A.G., Psannis, K.E.: Defending against phishing attacks: taxonomy of methods, current issues and future directions. Telecommun. Syst. **67**(2), 247–267 (2017). https://doi.org/10.1007/s11235-017-0334-z
5. Pienta, D., Thatcher, J., Johnston, A.: A taxonomy of phishing: attack types spanning economic, temporal, breadth, and target boundaries. In: Proceedings of the 13th Pre-ICIS Workshop on Information Security and Privacy, AIS, San Francisco, CA, USA (2018)
6. Hong, J.: The state of phishing attacks. Commun. ACM **55**, 74–81 (2012)
7. Khonji, M., Iraqi, Y., Jones, A.: Phishing detection: a literature survey. IEEE Commun. Surv. Tutorials **15**, 2091–2121 (2013)
8. Nguyen, C.: Learning not to take the bait: an examination of training methods and overlerarning on phishing susceptibility. PhD thesis. University of Oklahoma, Norman, OK, USA (2018)
9. Albakry, S., Vaniea, K.: Automatic phishing detection versus user training, Is there a middle ground using XAI? In: CEUR Workshop Proceedings, vol. 2151 (2018)
10. Williams, E.J., Hinds, J., Joinson, A.N.: Exploring susceptibility to phishing in the workplace. Int. J. Hum. Comput. Stud. **120**, 1–13 (2018)
11. Harrison, B., Svetieva, E., Vishwanath, A.: Individual processing of phishing emails: how attention and elaboration protect against phishing. Online Inf. Rev. **40**, 265–281 (2016)
12. Dennis, A.R., Minas, R.K.: Security on autopilot: why current security theories hijack our thinking and lead us astray. Database Adv. Inf. Syst. **49**, 15–38 (2018)
13. Parsons, K., McCormac, A., Pattinson, M., Butavicius, M., Jerram, C.: Phishing for the truth: a scenario-based experiment of users' behavioural response to emails. In: Janczewski, L.J., Wolfe, H.B., Shenoi, S. (eds.) SEC 2013. IAICT, vol. 405, pp. 366–378. Springer, Heidelberg (2013). https://doi.org/10.1007/978-3-642-39218-4_27
14. Blythe, M., Petrie, H., Clark, J.A.: F for fake: four studies on how we fall for phish. In: CHI 2011, pp. 3469–3478, ACM, Vancouver, BC, Canada (2011)
15. Vishwanath, A., Herath, T., Chen, R., Wang, J., Rao, H.R.: Why do people get phished? Testing individual differences in phishing vulnerability within an integrated, information processing model. Decis. Support Syst. **51**, 576–586 (2011)
16. Vishwanath, A., Harrison, B., Ng, Y.J.: Suspicion, cognition, and automaticity model of phishing susceptibility. Communic. Res. **45**, 1146–1166 (2018)

17. Gunning, D.: Explainable Artificial Intelligence (XAI), 2017, https://www.darpa.mil/pro gram/explainable-artificial-intelligence (Accessed 20 Aug 2020)
18. Guidotti, R., Monreale, A., Ruggieri, S., Turini, F., Giannotti, F., Pedreschi, D.: A survey of methods for explaining black box models. ACM Comput. Surv. **51**, 1–42 (2019)
19. Ribeiro, M.T., Singh, S., Guestrin, C.: Anchors: high-precision model-agnostic explanations. In: Thirty-Second AAAI Conference on Artificial Intelligence, pp. 1527–1535, AAAI, New Orleans, LA, USA (2018)
20. Martens, D., Provost, F.: Explaining data-driven document classifications. MIS Q. **38**, 73–99 (2014)
21. Hevner, A.R., March, S.T., Park, J., Ram, S.: Design science in information systems research. MIS Q. **28**, 75–105 (2004)
22. Jakobsson, M.: The human factor in phishing. In: Priv. Secur. Consum. Inf. (2007)
23. Kim, D., Hyun Kim, J.: Understanding persuasive elements in phishing e-mails. Online Inf. Rev. **37**, 835–850 (2013)
24. Zeng, V., et al.: Diverse datasets and a customizable benchmarking framework for phishing. In: IWSPA '20, pp. 35–41, ACM, New Orleans, LA, USA (2020)
25. Sheng, S., Wardman, B., Warner, G., Cranor, L.F., Hong, J., Zhang, C.: An empirical analysis of phishing blacklists. In: Sixth Conference on Email Anti-Spam, Mountain View, CA, USA (2009)
26. Verma, R.M., Zeng, V., Faridi, H.: Data quality for security challenges: case studies of phishing, malware and intrusion detection datasets. In: CCS '19, pp. 2605–2607, ACM, London, UK (2019)
27. Karumbaiah, S., Wright, R.T., Durcikova, A., Jensen, M.L.: Phishing training: a preliminary look at the effects of different types of training. In: Proceedings of the 11th Pre-ICIS Workshop on Information Security and Privacy, AIS, Dublin, Ireland (2016)
28. Sheng, S., et al.: Anti-phishing phil: the design and evaluation of a game that teaches people not to fall for phish. In: SOUPS 2007, pp. 88–99, Pittsburgh, PA, USA (2007)
29. Canova, G., Volkamer, M., Bergmann, C., Borza, R.: NoPhish: an anti-phishing education app. In: Mauw, S., Jensen, C.D. (eds.) STM 2014. LNCS, vol. 8743, pp. 188–192. Springer, Cham (2014). https://doi.org/10.1007/978-3-319-11851-2_14
30. Moody, G.D., Galletta, D.F., Dunn, B.K.: Which phish get caught? An exploratory study of individuals' susceptibility to phishing. Eur. J. Inf. Syst. **26**, 564–584 (2017)
31. Wang, J., Li, Y., Rao, H.R.: Overconfidence in phishing email detection. J. Assoc. Inf. Syst. **17**, 759–783 (2016)
32. Volkamer, M., Renaud, K., Reinheimer, B.: TORPEDO: tooltip-powered phishing email detection. In: Hoepman, J.-H., Katzenbeisser, S. (eds.) SEC 2016. IAICT, vol. 471, pp. 161–175. Springer, Cham (2016). https://doi.org/10.1007/978-3-319-33630-5_12
33. Wang, D., Yang, Q., Abdul, A., Lim, B.Y.: Designing theory-driven user-centric explainable AI. In: CHI 2019, ACM, Glasgow, UK (2019)
34. Lipton, Z.C.: The mythos of model interpretability. Queue **16**, 1–27 (2018)
35. Lei, T., Barzilay, R., Jaakkola, T.: Rationalizing neural predictions. In: EMNLP 2016, pp. 107–117, ACL, Stroudsburg, PA, USA (2016)
36. Ribeiro, M.T., Singh, S., Guestrin, C.: "Why Should I Trust You?": Explaining the predictions of any classifier. In: KDD 2016, pp. 1135–1144, ACM, San Francisco, CA (2016)
37. Lundberg, S., Lee, S.-I.: A unified approach to interpreting model predictions. In: NIPS 2017, pp. 4765–4774, Curran Associates, Long Beach, CA, USA (2017)
38. Weerts, H.J.P., van Ipenburg, W., Pechenizkiy, M.: A human-grounded evaluation of SHAP for alert processing. In: Proceedings of the KDD Workshop on Explainable AI, Anchorage, AK (2019)
39. Fernandez, C., Provost, F., Han, X.: Counterfactual explanations for data-driven decisions. In: ICIS 2019, AIS, Munich, Germany (2019)

40. Förster, M., Klier, M., Kluge, K., Sigler, I.: Evaluating explainable artificial intelligence – what users really appreciate. In: ECIS 2020, AIS (2020)
41. Burdisso, S.G., Errecalde, M., Montes-y-Gómez, M.: t-SS3: a text classifier with dynamic n-grams for early risk detection over text streams. arXiv:1911.06147 (2019)
42. Gedikli, F., Jannach, D., Ge, M.: How should I explain? A comparison of different explanation types for recommender systems. Int. J. Hum. Comput. Stud. **72**, 367–382 (2014)
43. Ribera, M., Lapedriza, A.: Can we do better explanations? A proposal of user-centered explainable AI. In: Joint Proceedings of the ACM IUI 2019 Workshop, ACM, Los Angeles, CA (2019)
44. Bhatt, U., et al.: Explainable machine learning in deployment. In: FAT*20, pp. 648–657, ACM, Barcelona, Spain (2020)
45. Verheij, B., Wiering, M. (eds.): BNAIC 2017. CCIS, vol. 823. Springer, Cham (2018). https://doi.org/10.1007/978-3-319-76892-2
46. Kaufmann, E., Kalyanakrishnan, S.: Information complexity in bandit subset selection. J. Mach. Learn. Res. **30**, 228–251 (2013)
47. Venable, J., Pries-Heje, J., Baskerville, R.: FEDS: a framework for evaluation in design science research. Eur. J. Inf. Syst. **25**, 77–89 (2016)
48. Doshi-Velez, F., Kim, B.: Considerations for evaluation and generalization in interpretable machine learning. In: Escalante, H.J., et al. (eds.) Explainable and Interpretable Models in Computer Vision and Machine Learning. TSSCML, pp. 3–17. Springer, Cham (2018). https://doi.org/10.1007/978-3-319-98131-4_1

Human Computer Interaction

Introduction to the WI2021 Track: Human Computer Interaction

Alexander Maedche[1], Mario Nadj[1], and Fenne große Deters[2,3]

[1] Karlsruhe Institute of Technology, Karlsruhe, Germany
[2] Weizenbaum Institute, Berlin, Germany
[3] University of Potsdam, Potsdam, Germany

1 Track Description

Human Computer Interaction (HCI) is an interdisciplinary research field that focuses on the design and evaluation of information and communication technologies concentrating on the interaction with humans with the aim of improving usability, productivity, quality of life, and the well-being of users. With the rapidly developing capabilities of interactive technologies, sensor technology, intelligent real-time data processing and the almost universal presence of IT in all areas of life, new challenges and opportunities for Information Systems research in the context of HCI are arising. The track "Human Computer Interaction" focuses on research that helps to understand and shape the interaction of users with digital artifacts. Submissions of any methodological orientation were invited, which make theoretically and practically relevant contributions to a better understanding and design of the HCI of information systems. Accepted papers in this track provide insights into the development of and human interactions with conversational agents and smart personal assistants, introduce new aspects of web interface designs, and discuss design elements potentially reducing toxic behavior in online multiplayer video games.

2 Research Articles

2.1 ArgueBot: A Conversational Agent for Adaptive Argumentation Feedback (Thiemo Wambsganss, Sebastian Guggisberg, and Matthias Soellner)

The paper presents the development of a conversational agent which uses machine learning approaches to identify different parts of an argument. An exemplary use case in the context of education illustrates potential benefits of new artefacts built in the context of human computer interaction.

2.2   Do you Feel a Connection? How Human-like Design of Conversational Agents Influences Donation Behavior (Johannes Bührke, Alfred Benedikt Brendel, Sascha Lichtenberg, Stephan Diederich, and Stefan Morana)

The effects of social cues on perceived humanness and social presence of a conversational agent representing a charitable organization are assessed with an online experiment. The paper contributes to our understanding on how these design elements might influence the outcomes of interactions with conversational agents.

2.3   'Let us work Together' – Insights from an Experiment with Conversational Agents on the Relation of Anthropomorphic Design, Dialog Support, and Performance (Sascha Lichtenberg, Johannes Bührke, Alfred Benedikt Brendel, Simon Trang, Stephan Diederich, and Stefan Morana)

The paper explores the role of anthropomorphic and persuasive elements in the design of conversational agents and their effect on individuals' willingness to keep working on tasks. The presented results have implications for conversational agents and persuasive system design.

2.4   Persuasive Design for Smart Personal Assistants - A Theory-Motivated State-of-the-Art Analysis (Dennis Benner, Sofia Schöbel, and Andreas Janson)

With a systematic literature analysis this paper provides an overview of the status quo of design of persuasive smart personal assistants and how persuasive design features like gamification and nudging are currently incorporated. Important research gaps are identified and the paper might stimulate research in this emerging area.

2.5   Buy Online, Trust Local – The Use of Regional Imagery on Web Interfaces and its Effect on User Behavior (Tobias Menzel and Timm Teubner)

The short paper introduces the construct of regional presence on web interfaces to the IS literature by presenting the results of a qualitative content analyses. Avenues for future research assessing the effects of regional presence on trust and purchase intentions of customers are outlined.

2.6   Curing Toxicity - A Multi-Method Approach (Bastian Kordyaka and Björn Kruse)

This short paper focuses on antecedents of the online disinhibition effect and resulting aggressive behaviors in online multiplayer video games. Apart from an introduction into the topic the paper proposes a survey study with video game players and a workshop with subject experts.

ArgueBot: A Conversational Agent for Adaptive Argumentation Feedback

Thiemo Wambsganss[1(✉)], Sebastian Guggisberg[1], and Matthias Söllner[2]

[1] Institute of Information Management, University of St.Gallen (HSG), St.Gallen, Switzerland
thiemo.wambsganss@unisg.ch,
sebastian.guggisberg@student.unisg.ch
[2] Information Systems and Systems Engineering, University of Kassel, Kassel, Germany
soellner@uni-kassel.de

Abstract. By combining recent advances in Natural Language Processing and Conversational Agent (CAs), we suggest a new form of human-computer interaction for individuals to receive formative feedback on their argumentation to help them to foster their logical reasoning skills. Hence, we introduce Argue-Bot, a conversational agent, that provides adaptive feedback on students' logical argumentation. We, therefore, 1) leveraged a corpus of argumentative student-written peer-reviews in German, 2) trained, tuned, and benchmarked a model that identifies claims, premises and non-argumentative sections of a given text, and 3) built a conversational feedback tool. We evaluated ArgueBot in a proof-of-concept evaluation with students. The evaluation results regarding technology acceptance, the performance of our trained model, and the qualitative feedback indicate the potential of leveraging recent advances in Natural Language Processing for new human-computer interaction use cases for scalable educational feedback.

Keywords: Argumentation learning · Argumentation mining · Pedagogical conversational agents

1 Introduction

In today's world most information is readily available and the importance of the ability to reproduce information is decreasing. This results in a shift of job profiles towards interdisciplinary, ambiguous and creative tasks [1]. Thus, educational institutions are asked to evolve in their curricula when it comes to the compositions of skills and knowledge conveyed [2]. Especially teaching higher order thinking skills to students, such as critical thinking, collaboration or problem-solving, have become more important [3]. This has already been recognized by the Organization for Economic Co-operation and Development (OECD), which included these skills as a major element of their Learning Framework 2030 [4]. One subclass represents the skill of arguing in a structured, reflective and well-formed way [5]. Argumentation is not only an essential part of our daily communication and thinking but also contributes significantly to the competencies of communication, collaboration and problem-solving [6]. Starting with studies from

Aristoteles, the ability to form convincing arguments is recognized as the foundation for persuading an audience of novel ideas and plays a major role in strategic decision-making and analyzing different standpoints especially in regard to managing digitally enabled organizations. To develop skills such as argumentation, it is of great importance for the individual to receive continuous feedback throughout their learning journey, also called formative feedback [7, 8] However, universities, face the challenge of providing individual learning conditions, since every student would need a personal tutor to have an optimal learning environment to learn how to argue [9]. However, this is naturally hindered due to traditional large-scale lectures or due to the growing field of distance learning scenarios such as massive open online courses (MOOCs) [10].

A possible solution avenue lies in leveraging Natural Language Processing (NLP) and Machine Learning (ML) to provide students with adaptive and ongoing feedback, e.g., on texts and instant messages by a Conversational Agent (CA) [11] and thus provide them access to formative argumentation feedback. CAs are software programs that communicate with users through natural language interaction interfaces [12, 13]. The successful application of CAs to meet individual needs of learners and to increase their learning outcomes has been demonstrated for learning various skills such as problem-solving skills [14], programming skills [15], mathematical skills [16] as well as for learning factual knowledge [17], and also offers potential for training argumentation skills. A possible solution to provide adaptive support of argumentation could be the utilization by argumentation mining, a proven approach to identify and classify argumentation in texts. The potential of argumentation mining has been investigated in different research domains, such as automated skill learning support for students [18–20], accessing argumentation flows in legal texts [21], better understanding of customer opinions in user-generated comments [22], or fact-checking and de-opinionizing of news [23]. Hence, we suggest that the advantages of argumentation mining could be leveraged to design a new form of human-computer interaction for individual to receive scalable formative argumentation feedback [24]. In fact, Lippi and Torroni (2016) [25] and Chernodub et al. (2019) [26] designed static argumentation web interfaces that can be used to automatically identify and classify argumentation components from English input texts. However, these tools fall short to provide an educational embedding, a user-friendly form of human-computer interaction, e.g., through a conversational interface, and lack application for German content, since they were trained on English corpora. Therefore, we aim to close this gap by designing a CA that can be used by individual learners to receive formative argumentation feedback, e.g., while writing an argumentative text. Overall, we aim to contribute to research and practice by answering the following research question:

RQ:*How do students perceive a conversational agent which provides adaptive argumentation feedback on a given text based on Argumentation Mining?*

To tackle the research question, we develop a CA in *Slack*[1] (Slack bot) called *Argue-Bot* (short for *Argumentation Bot*), which provides students feedback on the logical argumentation of given texts on the baseline of existing theory (cognitive dissonance based on [27]). We believe cognitive dissonance theory could explain why formative

---

[1] https://slack.com/.

feedback on an individual's argumentation will motivate the individual to learn how to argue. With adaptive formative feedback, we implicate a CA which provides individual and real-time feedback to individuals on a given text.

We follow the Cross Industry Standard Process for Data Mining (CRISP-DM) Model [28] to build a novel model that identifies argumentation flaws in texts. For training our argumentative feedback model, we leverage the German business model feedback corpus of [29]. We develop a novel modelling approach to identify argumentative structures and build a CA in Slack, which provides individuals with formative argumentation feedback based on given textual messages. To answer our research question, we evaluate ArgueBot in a first proof-of-concept evaluation, where we ask students to write an argumentative text and use our CA to receive feedback on the argumentation structure. The measured technology acceptance, the positive qualitative feedback and the strong performance of our model compared to state-of the art approaches suggest using new forms of conversational human-computer interaction based on NLP to provide students with argumentation support in different scenarios.

The remainder of the paper is structured as follows: First, we provide the necessary conceptual background on argumentation learning, argumentation mining and CAs based on a systematic literature review [1]. Next, we present our CRISP-DM methodology in section three and explain the implementation and evaluation of our model and *ArgueBot* in section four. Finally, we present and evaluate our results, followed by a discussion about the limitations and contributions of our study.

2 Conceptual and Theoretical Background

2.1 Adaptive Argumentation Learning

As Kuhn (1992) [6] states, the skill to argue is of great significance not only for professional purposes like communication, collaboration and for solving difficult problems but also for most of our daily life: *"It is in argument that we are likely to find the most significant way in which higher order thinking and reasoning figure in the lives of most people. Thinking as argument is implicated in all of the beliefs people hold, the judgments they make, and the conclusions they come to; it arises every time a significant decision must be made. Hence, argumentative thinking lies at the heart of what we should be concerned about in examining how, and how well, people think"* ([6], pp. 156–157). However, teaching argumentation is limited. [30] identified three major causes for that: *"teachers lack the pedagogical skills to foster argumentation in the classroom, so there exists a lack of opportunities to practice argumentation; external pressures to cover material leaving no time for skill development; and deficient prior knowledge on the part of learners"*. Therefore, many authors have claimed that fostering argumentation skills should be assigned a more central role in our educational system [31, 32]. Adaptive support approaches for argumentation learning (e.g., 15, 30–32) describe a rather new field of argumentation learning supported by IT-based systems. The aim is to provide pedagogical feedback on a learner's action and solutions, hints and recommendations to encourage and guide future activities in the writing processes or automated evaluation to indicate whether an argument is syntactically and semantically correct. However, the combination of NLP, ML and pedagogically evaluated formative feedback in a student's learner journey is merely investigated due to high complexity. As Scheuer (2015) identifies, *"rigorous empirical research with respect to adaptation strategies is almost absent; a broad and solid theoretical underpinning, or theory of adaptation for collaborative and argumentative learning is still lacking"* [36]. Therefore, we aim to address this research gap and design an easy-to-use argumentation learning tool based on a conversational human-computer interaction design. Thus, we built on the application of recent developments in NLP and ML, in which argumentation mining has been a proven approach to identify and analyze argumentative structures of a given text in real time [19, 29, 37, 38].

2.2 Argumentation Mining

The foundation of argumentation mining is argumentation theory. Argumentation theory is about analyzing the structure and the connection between arguments. One of the most prominent argumentation models is the Toulmin model [39]. Toulmin's model asserts that a "good" argument involves a logical structure built on ground, claim and warrant, whereas the grounds are the evidence used to prove a claim. Walton et al. (2008) [40] developed the so-called "argumentation schemes" that use the Toulmin's type of reasoning. It is commonly considered that *"Claim"*, *"Premise"*, and *"Warrant"* are the main components of every argument, and the rest are supporting sub-argument parts that may or may not exist in an argument. Argumentation mining itself aims to identify these components of an argumentation model with NLP and ML. It falls under the category of computational argumentation, which encompasses a variety of tasks. These tasks include identifying the argumentation style [41], in which arguments are classified as "factual" or "emotional" in order to understand the characteristics better, identifying the reasoning behind the stance of the author by creating a classifier using the stance classification [42], identifying arguments to be used as summarization pointers [43] or ranking arguments according to how convincing they are using a joint model with one deep learning module in it [44]. Following [45], the most related subtasks of argumentation mining can be summed up as:

- **Argument Identification,** which is concerned with identifying the argumentative parts in raw text and setting up its boundaries versus a non-argumentative text.
- **Argument component classification,** which is the subtask of finding out what the primary purpose is to classify the components of the argument structure. Classifying an argumentative text into claims or premises is one popular way of tackling the target of this subtask.
- **Argumentative discourse analysis,** during this subtask, the researcher tries to identify the discourse relations between the various components existing in the argument. A typical example of this subtask is the identification of whether a support or an attack relationship exists between the claim and the premise.

In our study we are focusing on the challenges of argument identification and argument component classification since these are usually the first two steps of an argumentation mining architecture and, thus, the foundation of every argumentation mining application. The potential of argumentation mining has been investigated in different research domains. However, it has merely been leveraged to build a conversational learning tool to provide individuals with formative and adaptive argumentation feedback on a commonly available communication platform such as Slack [20, 37].

2.3 Adaptive Argumentation Feedback Tools and Conversational Agents

Although argumentation mining is a growing field of research and many studies have been conducted, only very few practical tools exist that provide individuals – non-programmers – with access to this technology. In a systematic literature review, we found only two tools available that provide individuals with access to argumentation mining. Lippi and Torroni (2016) [25] developed the first online argumentation mining tool that was made available for a broad audience. Their tool, MARGOT, is available as a web application and processes a text that is input in the corresponding editor field. After processing and analyzing the text, the results are displayed on the user interface. Claims are displayed in bold font, whereas premises are displayed in italic style [25]. The second and most recent tool that provides individuals with access to argumentation mining was published by [26]. Similar to MARGOT, in their system called TARGER a user can analyze the argumentative structure of an input text. The results are then presented below the input, whereas claims are highlighted in red and premises are marked in green. However, both approaches are only available in English, not designed from an educational perspective and thus not necessarily easy-to-use and easy-to-access for students in their learning journey, since a user would always have to open the website, select a certain model and then copy his or her text into the input field. Therefore, we suggest building a novel conversational interface for leveraging argumentation mining for argumentation feedback for students.

CAs are software programs that are designed to communicate with users through natural language interaction interfaces [12, 13]. In today's world, conversational agents, such as Amazon's Alexa, Google's Assistant or Apple's Siri, are ubiquitous, with their popularity steadily growing over the past few years [46, 47]. They are implemented in various areas, such as customer service [11], collaboration [48], counselling [49] or education (e.g., [50, 51]). Hobert and Wolff (2019) [52] define CAs used in education as a special form of learning application that interacts with learners individually. We believe that a CA can offer new forms of providing argumentative feedback to students through a conversation interface. Therefore, we aim to tackle the challenge of adaptive argumentation support to individuals by building a novel model based on argumentation mining and prototype a conversational interface on an open platform such as Slack.

2.4 Cognitive Dissonance Theory

We built our research project on cognitive dissonance theory. We believe that this theory might supports our underlying hypothesis that individual and personal feedback on a individuals' argumentation motivates the individual to improve her skill level. Cognitive dissonance refers to the unsatisfying feeling that occurs when there is a conflict between one's existing knowledge and contradicting presented information [27]. This uncomfortable internal state results in a high motivation to solve this inconsistency. According to Festinger's theory, an individual experiencing this dissonance has three possible ways to resolve it: change the behavior, change the belief or rationalize the behavior. Especially for students in a learning process, dissonance is a highly motivating factor to gain and acquire knowledge to actively resolve the dissonance [53]. It can be an initial trigger for a student's learning process and thus the construing of new knowledge structures [54]. However, the right portion of cognitive dissonance is very important for the motivation to solve it. According to Festinger, individuals might not be motivated enough to resolve it if the dissonance is too obvious, whereas a high level of dissonance might lead to frustration. Therefore, we believe that the right level of feedback on a student's skill through a conversational interface on an open communication platform, could lead to cognitive dissonance and thus to motivation to change the behavior, belief or knowledge to learn how to argue [55].

3   Research Methodology

To answer our research question, we develop an artifact following the Cross Industry Standard Process for Data Mining (CRISP-DM) Model, which is illustrated in Fig. 1 [28]. The model describes a standardized approach for Data Mining problems from a practical point of view, followed by the data understanding, the data preparation, and the data modelling.

Our approach is divided into five iterative stages. In the first stage, we analyzed the current state of argumentation learning and argumentation mining achievements in literature based on a systematic literature review [1]. Second, we investigated different corpora and their results at the current state in argument classification across multiple domains. We built on the corpus of [29] since it fulfills our requirements of a large data set, a rigorous annotation study and has been successfully used to provide students adaptive argumentation feedback [19]. Third and fourth, we built a model using NLP and Deep Learning (DL) algorithms to classify a text piece as a claim, premise or non-argumentative following the model of [37, 39, 56]. We iteratively evaluated the performance of our model and revised it based on various performance metrics such as the f1-score. In a fifth step, the model is deployed as the back-end algorithm of our conversational agent *ArgueBot* using the Slack communication platform. We chose Slack since it is a team communication platform widely used with a strong user growth [57]. Moreover, Slack offers an easy-to-use API for building CAs. We believe that a Slack bot might lower the barrier for students to use such a feedback tool in their daily learning journey. Finally, to we evaluate *ArgueBot* in a proof-of-concept evaluation, following the evaluation patterns of artefacts of Sonnenberg and vom Brocke (2012).

Our approach is developed using the programming language Python 3.7 for Machine Learning (ML) applications, since it is widely known, easy to use and supports major libraries for NLP and ML tasks. For Deep Learning, *TensorFlow* and its integrated *Keras* [59] are called. Additionally, the framework FARM by *deepset*[2] was used.

---

[2] https://github.com/deepset-ai/FARM.

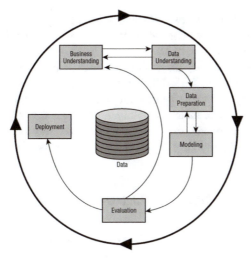

Fig. 1. Cross industry standard process for data mining (CRISP-DM) [28]

4 Implementation and Evaluation of ArgueBot

To answer our research question, we aim to build a CA that provides adaptive feedback
on the argumentation structure of a given text input by identifying claims, premises and
non-argumentative sections. In order to accomplish this, we propose to train a model
on a transfer learning approach based on Deep Bidirectional Transformers for Language Understanding (BERT) as seen in [60]. The first phase of CRISP-DM, business
understanding, is explained in the introduction and the theoretical background of this
work.

4.1 Data Understanding and Data Preparation

For training our argumentative feedback model, we leverage the German business model
feedback corpus of [29] since it provides a) a large data base of 1000 argumentation annotated student texts in German language, is b) annotated based on the argumentation theory
of Toulmin [39] and c) provides a rigorous annotation study with a moderate agreement.
We split the corpus' texts into tokens and assigned the corresponding label. In our case,
the label includes two parts. The first part represents the *IOB-encoding* following [61].
The *IOB-encoding* indicates whether a token is the beginning of an argument component
("B" = *beginning*), is covered by an argument component ("I" = *inside*) or not included
in any argument component ("O" = *outside*). Additionally, we include the specific argument type in the label, which results in labels such as "*B-Premise*" (standing for a token
being the beginning of a premise) or "*I-Claim*" (standing for a token being inside a
claim). Since several authors reached satisfying results with bidirectional Long-Short-
Term-Memory-Conditional-Random-Fields classifiers (BiLSTM-CRF), we started with
such a modelling architecture [26, 62]. To prepare the data accordingly, the tokens are
replaced by their index in the corresponding word embeddings vocabulary (GloVe) [63].

However, since we did not receive sufficient accuracy in the further refinement of our model, the architecture was switched to the Bidirectional Encoder Representations from Transformers (BERT) proposed by Devlin et al. (2018) [60] in a second modelling cycle (see Sect. 4.2). Therefore, the tokens are further split into word pieces to fulfill the preparation requirements for BERT. This also requires providing additional labels for the word piece endings. Finally, the data are transformed to *PyTorch Tensors*[3], which represent multi-dimensional matrices containing a single data type, in order to match the model's input requirements for the used framework. The special preprocessing for BERT was conducted by utilizing the tokenizer and processor provided by the FARM framework from *deepset*.

4.2   Iterative Modelling: Identifying Claims and Premises

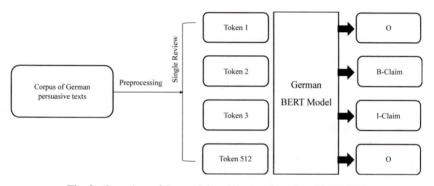

Fig. 2. Overview of the model architecture based on BERT [60]

The goal of our model is to provide accurate predictions to identify and classify argument components that can be used for an automated argument feedback system. We split the data into 70% training, 20% validation and 10% test data. We iteratively developed our model in two cycles. In the first cycle, the current state-of-the-art model, a bidirectional LSTM-CRF classifier with *GloVe* embeddings input, was created following the approach for persuasive essays of [62]. However, since we only reached an unsatisfying f1-score of 57%, we decided to follow a more novel transfer learning approach in the second modelling interaction. In fact, we decided to change the architecture of our model to the Bidirectional Encoder Representations from Transformers (BERT) proposed by Devlin et al. (2018) [60]. BERT has been successfully used to model argumentations across different domains [38]. A German BERT model is available through the framework FARM. For the proposed architecture, the inputs and outputs are adapted to the sequence classification task of argument component identification and classification. The last hidden layer is a Recurrent Neural Network with 512 nodes that takes the BERT output and learns to feed into a *sigmoid layer* that classifies each token according to the predicted label. Figure 2 illustrates the basic architecture of our model following BERT.

---

[3] https://pytorch.org/docs/stable/tensors.html.

The proposed model was finetuned in several iterations and the best performing set of hyperparameters included a *learning rate of 5e^{-5}*, a *warmup* and *embedding dropout probability* of *0.1* and *0.15* respectively. As presented in Table 1, BERT clearly outperforms other state-of-the-art model architectures for argumentation mining for persuasive essays (e.g., [62]). Whereas the bidirectional LSTM-CRF classifier achieved a macro f1-score of 0.57, the German BERT model performed about 28% better, reaching a macro f1-score of 0.73 on the token classification task on the German student written business model review corpus.

Table 1. Overview of overall performance of the BiLSTM-CRF and BERT

Model	Precision	Recall	F1-Score
BiLSTM-CRF	0.60	0.55	0.57
BERT	0.74	0.72	0.73

After a set of iterative refinements, we achieved satisfying results for the classification of argumentative components of the texts using the BERT model of *deepset*. The results are stated in Table 2 for the different labels.

Table 2. Overview of results of BERT for the classification of argumentative components

Label	Precision	Recall	F1-Score
B-Claim	0.66	0.74	0.69
I-Claim	0.72	0.62	0.66
B-Premise	0.66	0.75	0.70
I-Premise	0.75	0.68	0.72
O	0.91	0.82	0.86

4.3 Deployment: Building ArgueBot - a CA for Adaptive Argumentation Feedback

In order to contribute to our research question, the next step incorporated to deploy our trained model in a conversational interface so that students can receive formative feedback on their argumentation structure, e.g., when writing an argumentative essay. Therefore, the trained model was exported and implemented in the back-end of our CA *ArgueBot* which identifies and classifies argument components and provides feedback on the argumentative structure. We chose Slack as a platform for *ArgueBot* since it is a team communication platform widely used by many large organizations. We believe that a CA in Slack (Slack bot) might lower the barrier for using such a feedback system in daily learning activities. A screenshot of our final CA in Slack is illustrated in Fig. 3.

The functionality and usability are kept rather simple so that students can access our CA without any pre-knowledge or onboarding. The user can enter a message and send it to *ArgueBot*, e.g., an argumentative essay or an important email (see Fig. 3). This message is then sent to our trained model. Claims, premises and non-argumentative tokens are being classified and sent back to the frontend. Following [25], claims are then displayed in bold font, whereas premises are displayed in italic style (see Fig. 3). Besides, *ArgueBot* is providing a short summarizing feedback based on the number of premises and claims in the message (see Fig. 3). For example, if the message contains less than two premises or contains more claims than premises, the user receives a corresponding feedback indicating that the argumentation is not sufficient. We believe that this individual and personal feedback on an individual's argumentation motivates the individual to improve her skill level.

Mobile version of our CA   *Desktop version of our CA*

Fig. 3. Screenshots of our CA *ArgueBot* providing argumentative feedback to a student

4.4   Proof-of-Concept Evaluation of ArgueBot

In order to answer our research question and evaluate the feasibility of *ArgueBot* we performed a proof-of-concept evaluation following the evaluation patterns of technical artifacts of [58]. Hence, our aim was to investigate *how do students perceive a conversational agent which provides adaptive argumentation feedback on given texts*. Therefore, we performed a qualitative and a quantitative evaluation. We designed a laboratory experiment, where we asked students to write an argumentative text message, e.g., a statement about a business model. The participants were told that the test message should contain at least three sentences (around 50 words). We asked the participants to use *ArgueBot* to receive feedback on the argumentation structure of their text and revise it accordingly, if wished. After that the participants were asked to conduct a post-survey. We captured the *perceived usefulness, intention to use* and *ease of use* following the technology acceptance model of [64, 65]. Exemplary items for the three constructs are: "*Imagine the feedback tool would be available in your daily working life, I am encouraged to use it. "*, *"I would find the feedback tool useful for receiving feedback on my argumentation. "*, *"Using the feedback tool would allow me to write more argumentative messages."* or *"The feedback tool is easy to use."* All these items were measured with a 7-point Likert scale (1: strongly disagree to 7: strongly agree, with 4 being a neutral statement). In addition, we collected demographic information, such as age, gender and occupation. Finally, the participants were asked to provide qualitative feedback regarding the strengths, weaknesses and suggestions for useful additional features.

In total, ten users participated in our experiment; eight male and two females, who were between the ages of 22 and 25. Four participants were software development trainees working in a software company, six participants were business students on master level. The quantitative evaluation of the results showed that the CA is considered to be *easy to use* with an overall score of 6.33. The *intention to use* and the *perceived usefulness* were rated similar positively, with total scores of 5.5 and 5.63 respectively. A positive technology acceptance is especially important for learning tools to ensure students are perceiving the usage of the tool as helpful, useful and easy to interact. This will foster motivation and engagement to use the learning application. The perceived usefulness and intention to use provides promising results to use this tool as a feedback application in different learning settings.

Moreover, we performed a qualitative evaluation by asking the participants to provide a more detailed feedback on what they particularly liked or disliked about the tool. We clustered the answers to form a more concise feedback. Based on that, it seems that the short adaptive feedback on the argumentation structure is highly appreciated. The participants mentioned several things about the conversational interaction, such as about the format of the feedback (*"The formatting of the feedback is very clear"*), the reaction time of the CA (*"The fast reaction of the system (feedback time) is pleasant"*), the differentiation of claims and premises (*"I like the division of my statement into Claim and Premise"*) or the overall feedback system (*"The tool really helps to build up a meaningful argumentation structure, it recognized my rather bad argumentation immediately"*). However, three of ten participants mentioned that the tool did not find the right argument components. Further, one participant also criticized the speed and the representation of the feedback, since the analysis takes too long and especially the premises (italic) are not clearly highlighted. Besides, several suggestions have been made for further development of such a feedback system, such as clear suggestions to improve the argumentation, spelling checks, scoring or a more detailed description of claims and premises.

5   Discussion and Conclusion

In our paper, we aimed to investigate if a conversational agent based on a novel modelling approach might provide a new form of human-computer interaction for formative argumentation skill feedback. To answer our research question, we develop a new argumentation classification pipeline based on the current state of transfer learning to build a CA that provides students with formative feedback on their argumentation, e.g., when writing an argumentative essay. We built on an existing corpus of argumentation annotated student texts in German to develop a novel modelling approach to identify argumentative structures and build a CA in Slack, which can be used by students in their daily learning activities to receive adaptive and ongoing feedback independent of an instructor, time and location. To evaluate how *do students perceive a conversational agent which provides adaptive argumentation feedback on given text*, we performed a first proof-of-concept evaluation, where we asked participants students to write an argumentative text and to use our CA for receiving adaptive feedback. Our results indicate that students would intent to use a conversational argumentation feedback tool. Moreover, the measured perceived usefulness and perceived ease of use provides evidence that this new form of human-computer interaction might help to leverage recent advantages in NLP to provide students with writing support through a conversational interface. In order to successfully use a learning tool in a real-world scenario, positive technology acceptance is very important to ensure students perceive the usage of the tool as helpful, useful and easy to interact with. This will foster motivation and engagement to use the learning application.

We build our research on cognitive dissonance theory [27]. We argue that a learning tool for argumentation skills (and possibly also meta cognition skills) like our CA increases the motivation of students to learn how to apply the certain skills, for example, learn how to argue, and thus improve the learning outcome. For example, our *ArgueBot* which provides instant and individual feedback should increase the individual's motivation to resolve dissonance and therefore construct new knowledge. This goes along with other studies on adaptive argumentation support in the literature of HCI research (e.g., [19, 55]).

Thereby, our study contributes to two different research areas in information systems: first, we contribute to new forms of human-computer interaction in adaptive education, suggesting a use case to employ a conversatioanl interaction with potential benefits for educational institutions and organizations to foster adaptive and on-going skill feedback. We show how an exemplary case, based on a CA and a novel NLP model, can be leveraged to provide individual support and feedback to enable students to receive feedback on a certain skill. Second, we contribute to the field of digital learning innovations, by embedding a recent technology from NLP and ML to help students to learn how to argue independent of a human, time and location.

Nevertheless, our study faces some limitations. First, our evaluation displays a proof-of-concept evaluation about the technology acceptance of our CA. We did not evaluate the influence of argumentation feedback through a CA on the actual argumentation skills. However, we believe cognitive dissonance theory might explain how adaptive feedback leads to the motivation to learn. Moreover, our evaluation is based on a rather small sample size. More participants in an evaluation are needed to strengthen the findings. Therefore, we call for future research to further investigate the potential of new conversation-based forms of human-computer interaction for adaptive skill learning. Empirical studies are needed to investigate the effects of new interactive learning tools on students' skill level. Moreover, we did not investigate and evaluate specific design cues of a CA for adaptive argumentation feedback, since we wanted to provide a proof-of-concept study rather than a design science research approach. A more user-centered design approach, however, would be necessary to further investigate design parameters and design principles for adaptive conversation-based learning tools.

All in all, we contribute to a new, unified approach for adaptive argumentative support of students by showing an exemplary use case for argumentation skill learning. Researcher can build on this to investigate new HCI use cases for other skills in which adaptive feedback might be necessary for formative learning in large-scale or distance learning scenarios. With further advances of NLP and ML, we hope our work will attract researchers to design more intelligent tutoring systems for other learning scenarios or metacognition skills and thus contribute to the OECD Learning framework 2030 towards a metacognition-skill-based education.

References

1. vom Brocke, J., Simons, A., Riemer, K., Niehaves, B., Plattfaut, R., Cleven, A.: Standing on the shoulders of giants: challenges and recommendations of literature search in information systems research. Commun. Assoc. Inf. Syst. **37**, 205–224 (2015). https://doi.org/10.17705/1cais.03709
2. Topi, H.: Using competencies for specifying outcome expectations for degree programs in computing: lessons learned from other disciplines. In: 2018 SIGED International Conference on Information Systems Education and Research (2018)
3. Fadel, C., Bialik, M., Trilling, B.: Four-dimensional education: the competencies learners need to succeed (2015)
4. OECD: The Future of Education and Skills - Education 2030 (2018)
5. Toulmin, S.E.: The uses of argument: Updated edition. (2003). https://doi.org/10.1017/CBO9780511840005
6. Kuhn, D.: Thinking as argument. Harv. Educ. Rev. **62**, 155–179 (1992). https://doi.org/10.17763/haer.62.2.9r424r0113t670l1
7. Black, P., Wiliam, D.: Developing the theory of formative assessment. Educ. Assess. Eval. Acc. **21**, 5–31 (2009). https://doi.org/10.1007/s11092-008-9068-5
8. Hattie, J., Timperley, H.: The power of feedback. Rev. Educ. Res. **77**, 81–112 (2007). https://doi.org/10.3102/003465430298487
9. Vygotsky, L.S.: Mind in Society: The Development of Higher Psychological Processes. Harvard University Press, Cambridge (1980)
10. Seaman, J.E., Allen, I.E., Seaman, J.: Higher Education Reports - Babson Survey Research Group (2018)
11. Zierau, N., Wambsganss, T., Janson, A., Schöbel, S., Leimeister, J.M.: The anatomy of user experience with conversational agents : a taxonomy and propositions of service clues. Icis **2020**, 1–17 (2020)
12. Shawar, B.A., Atwell, E.S.: Using corpora in machine-learning chatbot systems. Int. J. Corpus Linguist. **10**, 489–516 (2005). https://doi.org/10.1075/ijcl.10.4.06sha
13. Rubin, V.L., Chen, Y., Thorimbert, L.M.: Artificially intelligent conversational agents in libraries. Libr. Hi Tech. **28**, 496–522 (2010). https://doi.org/10.1108/07378831011096196
14. Winkler, R., Büchi, C., Söllner, M.: Improving problem-solving skills with smart personal assistants: insights from a quasi field experiment. In: Fortieth Internatioanl Conference on Information System, pp. 1–17 (2019)
15. Hobert, S.: Say hello to coding tutor! design and evaluation of a chatbot-based learning system supporting students to learn to program. In: 40th International Conference Information System ICIS 2019, pp. 1–17 (2019)

16. Cai, W., et al.: MathBot: A Personalized Conversational Agent for Learning Math. (2019)
17. Ruan, S., et al.: QuizBot: a dialogue-based adaptive learning system system for factual knowledge, pp. 1–13 (2019). https://doi.org/10.1145/3290605.3300587
18. Stab, C., Gurevych, I.: Identifying argumentative discourse structures in persuasive essays. In: Conference on Empirical Methods in Natural Language Processing (EMNLP 2014), Association for Computational Linguistics, p.(to appear), pp. 46–56 (2014).
19. Wambsganss, T., Niklaus, C., Cetto, M., Söllner, M., Leimeister, J.M., Handschuh, S.: AL : an adaptive learning support system for argumentation skills. In: ACM CHI Conference on Human Factors in Computing Systems, pp. 1–14 (2020)
20. Wambsganss, T., Söllner, M., Leimeister, J.M.: Design and evaluation of an adaptive dialog-based tutoring system for argumentation skills. In: International Conference on Information Systems (ICIS). Hyderabad, India (2020)
21. Moens, M., Boiy, E., Reed, C.: Automatic detection of arguments in legal texts. Proceedings of the 11th International Conference on Artificial Intelligence and Law. ACM. (2007)
22. Boltuži, F., Šnajder, J.: Back up your stance : recognizing arguments in online discussions. In: Proceedings of the First Workshop on Argumentation Mining, pp. 1–43 (2014)
23. Dusmanu, M., Cabrio, E., Villata, S.: Argument mining on twitter: arguments, facts and sources. In: Proceedings of the 2017 Conference on Empirical Methods in Natural Language Processing, pp. 2317–2322 (2018)
24. Lawrence, J., Reed, C.: Argument mining: a survey. Comput. Linguist. **45**, 765–818 (2019). https://doi.org/10.1162/COLIa00364
25. Lippi, M., Torroni, P.: MARGOT: a web server for argumentation mining. Expert Syst. Appl. **65**, 292–303 (2016). https://doi.org/10.1016/j.eswa.2016.08.050
26. Chernodub, A., et al.: TARGER: neural argument mining at your fingertips, pp. 195–200 (2019). https://doi.org/10.18653/v1/p19-3031
27. Festinger, L.: Cognitive dissonance. Sci. Am. **207**, 93–106 (1962). https://doi.org/10.1038/scientificamerican1062-93
28. Chapman, P., et al.: Step-by-step data mining guide. SPSS inc. **78**, 1–78 (2000)
29. Wambsganss, T., Niklaus, C., Söllner, M., Handschuh, S., Leimeister, J.M.: A corpus for argumentative writing support in German. In: 28th International Conference on Computational Linguistics (Coling) (2020)
30. Jonassen, D.H., Kim, B.: Arguing to learn and learning to argue: design justifications and guidelines. Educ. Technol. Res. Dev. **58**, 439–457 (2010). https://doi.org/10.1007/s11423-009-9143-8
31. Driver, R., Newton, P., Osborne, J.: Establishing the norms of scientific argumentation in classrooms. Sci. Educ. **84**, 287–312 (2000). https://doi.org/10.1002/(SICI)1098-237X(200005)84:3%3c287::AID-SCE1%3e3.0.CO;2-A
32. Kuhn, D.: Education for Thinking. Harvard University Press (2005)
33. Pinkwart, N., Ashley, K., Lynch, C., Aleven, V.: Evaluating an intelligent tutoring system for making legal arguments with hypotheticals. Int. J. Artif. Intell. Educ. **19**(4), 401-424 (2009).
34. Huang, C.J., Chang, S.C., Chen, H.M., Tseng, J.H., Chien, S.Y.: A group intelligence-based asynchronous argumentation learning-assistance platform. Interact. Learn. Environ. **24**, 1408–1427 (2016). https://doi.org/10.1080/10494820.2015.1016533
35. Stab, C., Gurevych, I.: Recognizing insufficiently supported arguments in argumentative essays. In: Proceedings of the 15th Conference of the European Chapter of the Association for Computational Linguistics: Volume 1, Long Papers (2017)
36. Scheuer, O.: Towards adaptive argumentation learning systems (2015)
37. Lippi, M., Torroni, P.: Argumentation mining: state of the art and emerging trends. IJCAI International Conference Artifical Intelligence, pp. 4207–4211 (2015). https://doi.org/10.1145/2850417

38. Wambsganss, T., Molyndris, N., Söllner, M.: Unlocking transfer learning in argumentation mining: a domain-independent modelling approach. In: 15th International Conference on Wirtschaftsinformatik, Potsdam, Germany (2020). https://doi.org/10.30844/wi_2020_c9-wambsganss

39. Toulmin, S.E.: Introduction to Reasoning (1984).

40. Walton, D., Reed, C., Macagno, F.: Argumentation Schemes. Cambridge University Press, Cambridge (2008). https://doi.org/10.1017/CBO9780511802034

41. Oraby, S., Reed, L., Compton, R.: And That's A Fact: Distinguishing Factual and Emotional Argumentation in Online Dialogue. arXiv Prepr. (2000)

42. Hasan, K.S., Ng, V.: Why are you taking this stance ? identifying and classifying reasons in ideological debates. In: Proceedings of the 2014 Conference on Empirical Methods in Natural Language Processing (EMNLP), pp. 751–762 (2014)

43. Chowanda, A.D., Sanyoto, A.R., Suhartono, D., Setiadi, C.J.: Automatic debate text summarization in online debate forum. Procedia Comput. Sci. **116**, 11–19 (2017). https://doi.org/10.1016/j.procs.2017.10.003

44. Habernal, I., Gurevych, I.: Which argument is more convincing ? Analyzing and predicting convincingness of Web arguments using bidirectional LSTM. In: Proceedings of 54th Annual Meeting Association Computational Linguistics (Volume 1 Long Pap), pp. 1589–1599 (2016)

45. Lippi, M., Torroni, P.: Argumentation mining : state of the art and emerging trends. ACM Trans. Internet Technol. **16**(2), 1-25 (2016)

46. Krassmann, A.L., Paz, F.J., Silveira, C., Tarouco, L.M.R., Bercht, M.: Conversational agents in distance education: comparing mood states with students' perception. Creat. Educ. **09**, 1726–1742 (2018). https://doi.org/10.4236/ce.2018.911126

47. eMarketer: Alexa , Say What?! Voice-Enabled Speaker Usage to Grow Nearly 130% This Year. (2017)

48. Elshan, E., Ebel, P.: Let's team up: designing conversational agents as teammates. International Conference on Information Systems (ICIS) (2020)

49. Cameron, G., et al.: Towards a chatbot for digital counselling. In: HCI 2017 Digit. Make Believe - Proceedings 31st International BCS Humans Computer Interactation Conference HCI 2017. 1–7 July (2017). https://doi.org/10.14236/ewic/HCI2017.24

50. Wambsganss, T., Winkler, R., Schmid, P., Söllner, M.: Unleashing the potential of conversational agents for course evaluations: empirical insights from a comparison with web surveys. In: Twenty-Eighth European Conference on Information Systems (ECIS2020). pp. 1–18, Marrakesh, Morocco (2020)

51. Wambsganss, T., Winkler, R., Söllner, M., Leimeister, J.M.: A conversational agent to improve response quality in course evaluations. In: ACM CHI Conference on Human Factors in Computing Systems (2020)

52. Hobert, S., Wolff, R.M. Von: say hello to your new automated tutor – a structured literature review on pedagogical conversational agents. In: 14th International Conference Wirtschaftsinformatik, Siegen, Germany (2019)

53. Elliot, A.J., Devine, P.G.: On the motivational nature of cognitive dissonance: dissonance as psychological discomfort. J. Pers. Soc. Psychol. **67**, 382–394 (1994). https://doi.org/10.1037/0022-3514.67.3.382

54. Piaget, J., Brown, T., Thampy, K.J.: The equilibration of cognitive structures: the central problem of intellectual development. Am. J. Educ. **94**, 574–577 (1986). https://doi.org/10.1086/443876

55. Wambsganss, T., Rietsche, R.: Towards designing an adaptive argumentation learning tool. In: 40th International Conference on Information Systems. ICIS 2019, pp. 1–9. Munich, Germany (2020)

56. Fromm, H., Wambsganss, T., Söllner, M.: Towards a taxonomy of text mining features. In: European Conference of Information Systems (ECIS), pp. 1–12 (2019)

57. Statista: Slack - total and paying user count. https://www.statista.com/statistics/652779/wor ldwide-slack-users-total-vs-paid/. Accessed 24 Nov 2019
58. Sonnenberg, C., vom Brocke, J.: Evaluation patterns for design science research artefacts. In: Helfert, M., Donnellan, B. (eds.) EDSS 2011. CCIS, vol. 286, pp. 71–83. Springer, Heidelberg (2012). https://doi.org/10.1007/978-3-642-33681-2_7
59. Chollet, F.: Keras Documentation, (2015).
60. Devlin, J., Chang, M.-W., Lee, K., Toutanova, K.: BERT: Pre-training of Deep Bidirectional Transformers for Language Understanding (2018)
61. Ramshaw, L.A., Marcus, M.P.: Text Chunking using Transformation-Based Learning. (1995)
62. Eger, S., Daxenberger, J., Gurevych, I.: Neural end-to-end learning for computational argumentation mining. In: Proceedings of the 55th Annual Meeting of the Association for Computational Linguistics (Volume 1: Long Papers), pp. 11–22. Association for Computational Linguistics, Stroudsburg, PA, USA (2017). https://doi.org/10.18653/v1/P17-1002
63. Pennington, J., Socher, R., Manning, C.D.: GloVe: global vectors for word representation. In: EMNLP 2014 - 2014 Conference on Empirical Methods in Natural Language Processing, Proceedings of the Conference, pp. 1532–1543. Association for Computational Linguistics. (ACL) (2014). https://doi.org/10.3115/v1/d14-1162
64. Venkatesh, V., Bala, H.: Technology acceptance model 3 and a research agenda on interventions. Decis. Sci. **39**, 273–315 (2008). https://doi.org/10.1111/j.1540-5915.2008.001 92.x
65. Venkatesh, V., Morris, M.G., Davis, G.B., Davis, F.D.: User acceptance of information technology: toward a unified view. MIS Q. **27**, 425–478 (2003)

Do You Feel a Connection? How the Human-Like Design of Conversational Agents Influences Donation Behaviour

Johannes Bührke[1]($\boxtimes$), Alfred Benedikt Brendel[2], Sascha Lichtenberg[1], Stephan Diederich[1], and Stefan Morana[3]

[1] Chair of Information Management, University of Goettingen, Göttingen, Germany
{johannes.buehrke,stephan.diederich}@stud-goettingen.de,
sascha.lichtenberg@uni-goettingen.de
[2] Chair of Business Informatics, Esp. Intelligent Systems and Services, Technische Universität Dresden, Dresden, Germany
alfred_benedikt.brendel@tu-dresden.de
[3] Junior Professorship of Digital Transformation and Information Systems, Saarland University, Saarbrücken, Germany
stefan.morana@uni-saarland.de

Abstract. Conversational agents (CAs) are rapidly changing the way humans and computers interact. Through developments in natural language processing, CAs are increasingly capable of conducting human-like conversations with users. Furthermore, human-like features (e.g., having a name or an avatar) lead to positive user reactions as if they were interacting with a real human conversational partner.

CAs promise to replace or supplement traditional interactions between humans (e.g., counseling, interviews). One field of CA-human interaction that is not yet fully understood in developing human-like CAs is donating to a good cause. Notably, many charities rely on approaching people on the streets to raise funds.

Against this background, the questions arise: How should a CA for raising funds for non-profit organizations be designed and how does human-like design of a CA influence the user's donation behavior. To explore these two questions, we conducted a 2×2 experiment with 134 participants.

Keywords: Conversational agents · Human-like design · Social cues · Donation behavior · Charity

1 Introduction

Since the 1960s, the development of CAs (e.g., chatbots) has been continuously improved in technological aspects to enhance the way users interact with the information and communication interface [1]. Over the past years, the focus on human-like communication, enabled by real-time natural language processing, has increased rapidly [2]. Specifically, in the context where traditional interfaces could not successfully replace or supplement

F. Ahlemann et al. (Eds.): WI 2021, LNISO 47, pp. 283–298, 2021.
https://doi.org/10.1007/978-3-030-86797-3_19

human-to-human interactions (for instance, many aspects of customer service), CAs offer a new and potentially more efficient way to satisfy user demands and requests [3]. For example, Google's CA "Duplex" offers users a natural conversation atmosphere through voice support for service encounters (e.g., scheduling appointments) [4].

While improving CAs technology, such as natural language processing and machine learning continuously [5], understanding and enhancing the user experience remains a complex area [6]. For instance, the effective design and handling of open conversations remain open [7]. In this context, previous research has identified that designing CAs with social cues (e.g., having a name, avatar, greeting users) can change the users perception [8, 9], leading to social responses (e.g., reacting to the CAs similar to a human) [10, 11]. These responses can be positive (e.g., increasing enjoyment [12]) or negative (leading to a feeling of eeriness and uncanniness), depending on various factors, including the context and user expectations [13, 14]. Hence, an emerging body of research has been broadened to understand the interrelation of CA design and the various factors influencing perception and user reaction [8, 15].

One context of traditional human-to-human interaction is raising funds for charity. Many charities have volunteers engaging individuals on the streets, asking for donations [16]. Personal dispositions, such as altruism, empathy, and enjoyment, are important factors in a person's decision to donate [17, 18]. Furthermore, a personal aspect of having a human ask for donations increases the success rate significantly compared to flyers or letters [19]. For humans, persuasion is the bread and butter of daily interaction, and humans are arguably considered the strongest persuaders [20].

However, due to the constantly improving CA technology and human-computer interaction, in this context, CAs could potentially provide a new and additional way to ask for donations while maintaining the human-like feeling during the interaction. To the best of our knowledge, there is currently no evidence on how such a CA needs to be designed. Against this background, this study investigates the effects of a human-like CA design on the user's donation behavior to a charity organization with the following research question:

RQ: *How does the human-like design of a CA influence the user's donation behavior to a charitable organization?*

We address this research question using an online experiment in a user self-information context. Our paper is structured as follows: First, we continue by providing a theoretical research background for our study. In the next step, using CA design theories and the underlying research in donation behavior, we develop our hypotheses to analyze the effects of human-like CA design on the actual donation behavior. We then present our research design, followed by analyzing our results regarding perceived humanness, perceived social presence, and the individual donation behavior. Finally, we discuss theoretical and practical implications for the design of CAs, outline the limitations of our study, and state future research opportunities.

2 Theoretical Research Background

The interaction between CAs and users is driven by natural language speaking software, supporting the CAs capabilities [21]. In contrast to an impersonal graphical user interface, the information exchange in the human-CA interaction is followed by the principle of human-to-human interaction [1, 2]. At present, CAs have become a widespread and commonly known software artifact to society's everyday life [2], communicating via spoken language like virtual personal assistants [22] or written text defined as chatbots or dialogue systems [23]. CAs can be physically embodied (e.g., Robot "Pepper") [24], interactive digital embodied (e.g., Microsoft dynamic Avatar) [25], or static digital embodied (e.g., chatbot) [26]. The application context can serve general-purposes or be used in specific areas [21], such as in private life and the professional business context. Examples of the use of CAs in different areas include customer service [8, 24, 27], human resources [28], learning context [29], or data analysis [30]. Our study focuses on text-based CAs in the context of a charity customer self-service information.

In the 1960s, Weizenbaum [31] was the first to program a text-based CA in the form of a chatbot called ELIZA, which compared users' statements with certain patterns and responded to them according to technical rules. Since then, human-computer interaction has emergently improved and is still enhancing to achieve more convenient interfaces suited to the customers' demand [32]. Today, CAs offer convenient access to information and manage customer requests [27] using machine learning to improve their natural language speaking capabilities continuously [21]. At the same time, interest in CA research is steadily increasing [33], as is the number of emerging corporate CAs [34] and solutions for designing chatbot applications [35]. Companies from different industries introduced text-based CAs to automate tasks and support customers with information 24/7 the week. CAs provide a high efficiency [36] and reduced labor effort for the operator [5]. Due to technical improvement, CAs might overcome the basic human performance quality of today [5].

2.1 Design of Conversational Agents

Despite the recent adoption of CAs in our personal and business interactions, social cues affect user perception and behaviors are still inconsistent [22]. The successful design remains a major challenge to satisfy high user expectations, for example, through problems in adaptive interaction behavior [37]. Failures are caused by technical aspects, for example, natural language and architecture issues. Also, processing problems (e.g., limited vocabulary) and errors associated with the CA-human relation take a substantial part of user dissatisfaction [38]. Although present studies mostly focus on technical aspects, there is a knowledge gap about the CA-human interaction existing [6, 23]. Due to the limited capabilities of CAs, errors occur that are negatively affecting the perception of users also lead to a negative attitude towards the long-term use of CAs [38]. The design and development of these capabilities remain a complex area to be explored and improved by theoretical and practical research to provide an optimal user experience. In their contribution to the International Journal of Human Computer Studies in 2019, Feine et al. [9] provide a systematic overview of relevant categories of social cues that can contribute to CAs design. The social cues identified can be categorized along four dimensions, verbal (e.g., praise, excuse) [26], visual (e.g., gender, avatar) [39], auditory (e.g., the gender of voice) [40], and invisible (e.g., response time) [11].

2.2 Social Response Theory and Social Presence in the Context of CA

CAs implemented with social cues [26] transfer behavioral and social signals while interacting within a user interface [41]. The interaction begins to feel more human-like, similar to a natural communication between two people [15, 42]. This paradigm is reported by the research of Nass et al. [41], who identified that human-like CA characteristics trigger social responses by users, better known as the Computers Are Social Actors (CASA) paradigm. The paradigm states that humans tend to mindlessly respond socially to anything that displays human-like characteristics (e.g., technology, animals) [15, 41]. Consequently, the paradigm is used to understand user behavior and perception of CA-human interaction better [8].

Another theoretical concept that is considered in the context of CAs is social presence. Social presence can be described as the sense or a feeling of a human contact embodied in a system [43]. Therefore, in our study, social presence describes how a CA is perceived as real to a certain extent.

Despite the absence of a real human interlocutor in user interaction with a CA, studies have shown that social presence can be increased by adding social cues [44]. One way to do this is by adding personal greetings [45] or human images [46]. Nevertheless, how the user perceives a CA is not only dependent on the variation of social cues [22], as the user perception can also be influenced by factors such as gender [21] and appearance [47].

Considering these two perspectives, social response and social presence, Seeger et al. [26] provide a design framework that characterizes three different dimensions of social cues to elicit positive user perception. The proposed design framework consists of human identity (e.g., such as name, gender avatar) [48], non-verbal cues (e.g., dynamic delayed responses) [11], and verbal cues (e.g., express emotions) [49]. Besides stimulating social presence positively, social cues are attested to positively contribute to traits such as perceived humanness [8], trust [50], and empathy [51].

2.3 Donating to Charity

There are various forms of donations, ranging from voluntary work, blood donations to monetary donations [18]. According to research by Hoolwerf and Schuyt [52], more than 87.5 billion euro were donated in Europe in 2013. In addition, more than 418 billion dollars were given to charity in the US [53]. Both studies indicate that donations and charity make up a large part of the international economy, which has grown steadily in recent years [52, 53]. However, the underlying reasons why someone would donate, and the amount donated depends on various factors.

In this relation, research has identified factors including personal dispositions (e.g., altruism, empathy, enjoyment) [17, 18], the demographics of a person (e.g., age, income, children) [54], the image of an organization [17], and the perceived relationship with the charity [55]. The donors' perception in the donation interaction process also plays an important role for or against a donation [55]. In particular, prior work has shown that human-like design (e.g., using social cues) can influence people's judgments and behaviors [56, 57].

In this context, Zhou et al. [55] investigated that enhancing money with social cues in an interaction (e.g., asking for a "one Hamilton" instead of $10) had a positive effect on donation behavior. The focus on social cues displayed by a human-like CA during a user interaction could also play a valuable role in the individual's donation behavior since CAs' social cues can induce the users' perception positively (e.g., trust, satisfaction) [8, 11]. Since many different studies have been conducted to understand the individuals' tendency for or against a donation [17, 18, 54], up until now, a knowledge gap exists where donation behavior is affected by the user interaction with a human-like CA. Our study investigates the context of CA-human interaction, especially with the background of social cues (e.g., human-like design) to fill this gap.

3 Research Model and Hypothesis

To better understand the interaction between the human-like design of a CA and the individual's donation behavior, we conducted a two-conditions online CA experiment, with two differently designed instances from the same chatbot (see Fig. 1).

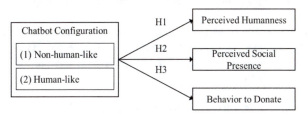

Fig. 1. Research model

Consistent with the research of Seeger et al. [26] (CA design framework) and Feine et al. [9] (social cue taxonomy), we define our CA design based on their findings to social cues in CA-human interaction. The experiment context provided the user with a self-information service encounter providing real information about a charitable organization. After interacting with the CA service encounter, the user was kindly given the opportunity to donate to charity.

3.1 Perceived Humanness

According to the social response theory [15], the human-like design offers the potential to contribute to the humanness of CAs. We base our CA design on various social cue elements; for example, we equipped the human-like CA with a Name and 2D avatar, implemented self-reference (e.g., using 'I' and 'me'), and applied dynamic response times [8, 9, 26]. Based on the social response theory [15, 58], we expect various social cues to increase human-like perception. Therefore, we postulate the following hypothesis:

H1: The human-like design of a CA leads to a positive effect on the perceived humanness.

3.2 Perceived Social Presence

Social presence describes the feeling of human contact in a mediated interaction [43] and the degree to which a conversation partner is perceived as a real person [44]. In the present research, the increased perceptions of social presence can be explained by social signals, and social presence could be created without actual human contact [43] (e.g., image). In correlation to human-like design elements, one can assume that social cues provide the user with a sense of human contact. Therefore, we postulate the following hypothesis:

H2: The human-like design of a CA leads to a positive effect on the perceived social presence.

3.3 Donation Behavior

Previous research has identified that a CA's human-like design does not only have a positive influence on user perception (e.g., trust, empathy), but also on perceiving a CA more human-like and socially present (e.g., human contact, personalness, warmth, sensitivity) [8]. As identified by Zhou et al. [55], social cues can be positively associated with the users' perception in a donation context and elicit an individual's donation behavior.

This phenomenon could help us to better understand if the human-like design of a chatbot, using social cues, can also affect the donation behavior. By applying existing knowledge of social cues in the donation context to the CA-human interaction, we postulate the following hypothesis:

H3: The human-like design of a CA leads to a positive effect on donation behavior.

4   Research Design

To test our hypotheses, we conducted an online experiment with a between-subjects design based on Boudreau, Gefen, and Straub [59] to avoid carryover effects. To analyze the context of donation behavior, we developed an intuitive chatbot-based self-information service encounter interface. The experiment took place in April 2020 for three weeks.

On average, the participation time per experiment took around five minutes. The study had an initial sample size of n = 149. After filtering out 15 invalid surveys, 134 data sets were analyzed. The study's participants' ages ranged from 17 to 58 years (M = 24.8 years, SD = 5,76), with a rate of 49% female and 50% male. 1% of the participants made no statement regarding their gender. The participants were recruited through personal networks and social media.

4.1 Data Collection Procedure and Sample

Before starting the experiment, participants received a briefing document explaining the CA interaction structure and context. Subsequently, the tasks related to the service meeting were explained and illustrated. Each participant received similar information to ensure that the participants had the same level of knowledge [60]. Then, comprehensive questions about the experimental context had to be answered to confirm the user's understanding. After the successful completion of the questions, a link to the experiment was provided. The provided link randomly assigned the participants to one of the two possible chatbot instances to guarantee a non-biased and random assignment. After completing the experimental service encounter interaction, the participants were requested to participate in our survey.

In order to interact with the user in a way that resembles a real human-to-human dialogue in a donation context, the experimental user task consisted in gaining information about different areas of the fields of activity of a non-profit organization first. Only after the users had gathered knowledge about the organization and its activities, the chatbot made a request for a user's donation. Additionally, to provide the user with a true relation to this experiment, we have decided to refer to a real-world charity. The charity organization was selected randomly from several charity organizations (e.g., German Red Cross, Caritas International, United Nations International Children's Emergency Fund (UNICEF)). Based on a lottery, the UNICEF organization was selected and then integrated into the CA test scenario with real information. The experimental service encounter included six steps:

(1) Welcome and introduction of the chatbot instance, stating UNICEFs corporate reason (e.g., objective United Nations Children's Fund that is active worldwide).
(2) The chatbot offered six different categories (e.g., targets, emergency assistance, child protection) to receive information for (participants had to gather information from at least three of them).
(3) After stating the possibility of receiving information from at least three different categories, the participants were asked whether they would like to continue (i.e., gathering information for the remaining categories) or to end the interaction.
(4) Each participant was offered to participate in a raffle for an online shopping voucher worth €5 (6 vouchers were raffled).
(5) The chatbot then offered the participant the opportunity to donate the value of the voucher to UNICEF.
(6) The chatbot instances were confirming the completion of the experiment with a link to the quantitative survey.

4.2 Control and Treatment Configurations

For our experiment, we implemented two CA instances of the same chatbot: one chatbot instance was designed with social cues (see Fig. 3), and the other instance had little to no social cues (see Fig. 2). Both CA were implemented into a straightforward web interface to provide direct access. The interface allowed for participation via computers and smartphones. Moreover, the CA instances were trained to understand typing errors and variations of different wordings of the same statement.

Conducting the human-like chatbot instance, we considered three types of social cue dimensions (e.g., using human identity, verbal cues, and non-verbal cues) [9, 26] in order to establish positive effects on perceived humanness, social presence, and donation behavior. Our charity-based chatbot represented a female customer service agent named Lena, situated with a comic avatar within the chatbot interface in perspective to the dimension of human identity.

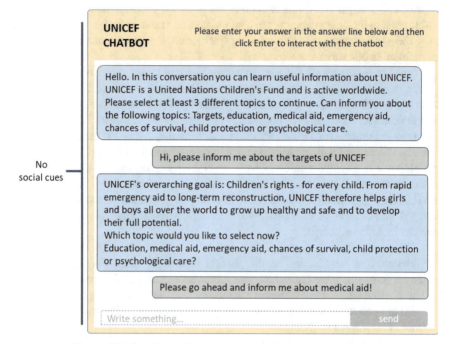

Fig. 2. Web interface with control treatment (translated to English)

In addition, Lena's verbal cues were implemented by self-references such as, "I am very pleased about your interest in UNICEF" and emotional expressions like "great, I'm glad to hear that." Furthermore, to use non-verbal cues with chatbots, we equipped the human-like instance with emojis and dynamic response delays (using a visual indicator that the chatbot is writing).

4.3 Measures

After the participants completed the chatbot interaction, an online survey was conducted regarding the CA's perceived humanness and perceived social presence. We adapted measurement instruments previously established and applied in CA research [43, 61]. We measured perceived humanness on a 9-point semantic Likert-scale, while for perceived social presence, we conducted a 7-point Likert scale.

However, for measuring the donation behavior [55], we used a single-scale item to conduct a manipulation check based on a nominal scale. To verify the factor loadings to each construct and its items, we conducted a confirmatory factor analysis (CFA). In this regard, only elements with a factor loading higher than the threshold value of .60 have been considered [62]. All constructs were further evaluated and supported by Cronbach's

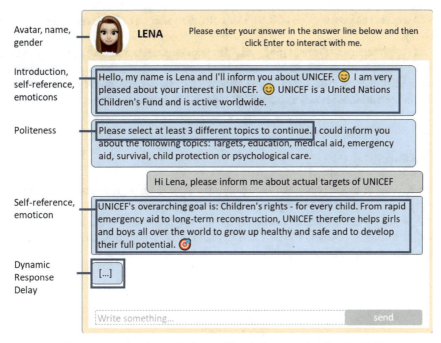

Fig. 3. Web interface with human-like design (translated to English)

Alpha (α) and the composite reliability (CR). Referring to Urbach and Ahlemann [63], both values require a minimum level larger than 0.80, and the average variance extracted

Table 1. Items, measures, factor loadings, and sources

Constructs and Items	Loadings	Source
Perceived humanness	.810	[61]
(α = .861, CR = .894, AVE = .587) [metric scale]	.769	
extremely inhuman-like – extremely human-like	.688	
extremely unskilled – extremely skilled	.717	
extremely unthoughtful – extremely thoughtful	.705	
extremely impolite – extremely polite	.889	
extremely unresponsive – extremely responsive		
extremely unengaging – extremely engaging		
Perceived social presence	.924	[43]
(α = 928, CR = .944, AVE = .771) [metric scale]	.790	
I felt a sense of human contact with the system	.864	
I felt a sense of personalness with the system	.911	
I felt a sense of sociability with the system	.899	
I felt a sense of human warmth with the system		
I felt sense of human sensitivity with the system		
Donation Behavior	1.000	[55]
(α = 1.00, CR = 1.00, AVE = 1.00) [nominal scale]		
Would you like to donate the money to charity?		

α = Cronbach's Alpha, CR = Composite Reliability, AVE = Average Variance Extracted.

(AVE) requires at least a value of 0.50. Our constructs met all of these requirements (see Table 1).

As suggested by DiStefano [64], weighted sum scores were then calculated to create a metric variable for perceived humanness and perceived social presence. Table 1 summarizes the three constructs, including Cronbach's alpha (α), composite reliability (CR), and average variance (AVE) extracted, as well as the items, measured factor loadings, and sources.

5 Results

After collecting the survey data, we analyzed the data through descriptive statistics. We applied a t-test for measuring our metric variables (perceived humanness, perceived social presence) and a Fisher's exact test for the single nominal scale item of donation behavior to obtain answers to our three hypotheses. Furthermore, we carried out our analyzes by using SPSS version 26.

Table 2. Descriptive statistics and t-test results

		Condition		t-value	p-value
		Control (n=58) [non-human-like]	Treatment (n=76) [human-like]		
Perceived Humanness	Mean	4.50	5.51	*(df132)* *3.61*	0.000
	SD	1.45	1.51		
	SE	0.19	0.17		
Perceived Social Presence	Mean	1,90	2.70	*(df129)* *3.11*	0.002
	SD	1.26	1.43		
	SE	0.16	0.16		

SD = Standard deviation, SE = Standard error

The homogeneity of variance was successfully proven to the construct of perceived humanness by conducting a Levene-test [65] (F(132) = 0.989, p = 0.000). For perceived social response, we utilized the Welch-test because the homogeneity of variance was not successfully proven [66] (F(132) = 0.989, p = 0.033). Afterward, we tested for a significance between the non-human-like control group and the human-like treatment group. For both hypotheses (H1 + H2), we found significance (see Table 2).

Our data indicate that social cues to influence perceived humanness (H1) can be supported. Second, regarding perceived social presence (H2), our analysis reveals that there is a significance considering the control and treatment conditions too. Hence, we can attest that our CA treatments have been developed accordingly to influence perceived humanness and perceived social presence significantly, as illustrated in Table 4. In order to find evidence for our third hypothesis concerning the construct of behavior donation, Fisher's exact test [67] was conducted to examine the control and treatment groups.

Table 3. 2 × 2 Table – Human-like treatment x Donation behavior

		Donation behavior		Overall
		No	Yes	sum
Human-like	Yes	23	53	76
treatment	No	15	43	58
Overall sum		38	96	134

Table 3 illustrates the human-like treatment of a CA in correlation with the construct of donation behavior. Since the p-value of Fisher's exact test is higher than 0.05 (0.669), we do not have sufficient evidence for a significant association between human-like treatment and the participants' donation behavior. Hence, we cannot support H3 (see Table 4).

Table 4. Results for hypothesis

Hypothesis	Result
H1: The Human-like design of a CA leads to a positive effect on the perceived humanness	Supported
H2: The Human-like design of a CA leads to a positive effect on the perceived social presence	Supported
H3: The Human-like design of a CA leads to a positive effect on donation behavior	Not Supported

6 Discussion

Our study aimed to examine the effect of human-like CA design on the individual's donation behavior. Thereby, perceived humanness, perceived social presence, and the individual's donation behavior was analyzed. We show that the participants perceived the different CA treatments regarding perceived humanness and perceived social presence as hypothesized across our two experimental treatments. Our results provided no support for our hypothesis regarding human-like CA design on donation behavior. Consequently, participants who had experienced a human-like chatbot instance did not decide to donate more often than participants who interacted with the less human-like chatbot. In contrast to the findings of Zhou et al. [55], who examined a strong correlation of donation behavior by donating money with social cues, we were unable to find similar results for the context of CAs. This outcome is consistent with research on CAs in other contexts, such as the perception of human-like typing errors [68] and self-introduction of CA

[69]. Understanding the interaction between humans and CA in the right way remains complex.

Even though this study did not find any significance for the donation behavior through human-like design, it can be reported that a remarkable 70% of the participants chose to donate. The share of online donations has rapidly increased over the past years (60% since 2012), with a value of $31 billion in 2017 [19], rendering CAs as a valuable opportunity to expand the success in online donations further. Therefore, our study is a good starting point for future research to conduct a more in-depth investigation of CAs effective design for gathering donations. For instance, adding persuasive messages [70, 71] to the interaction could increase an individual's donation behavior. We propose that future research explore the benefits of CA human-like design [e.g., 5, 15] in the area of donation further, for example, through a cooperative study with a real organization that has implemented CA already.

Since we consider our experimental conduction as a constraint, our study is not free of further limitations. Even if illustrating that our control and treatment group are designed in the right way (e.g., non-human like and human-like), the design of human-computer interaction remains a complicated task. Thus, the results of our study may depend on the social cues designed [26]. Therefore, a further variation of different social cues that customer interaction is confronted with might cause a different contribution to donation behavior. Furthermore, research into human-to-human interaction (e.g. persuasion strategies of volunteers on the street) is essential to improve the future design of CAs and to better understand the influence of human-like CAs on donation behavior for the future.

7 Conclusion

Our research contributes to human-computer interaction by providing knowledge to CA design effects in a donation context. Our study has shown that the human-like design of a CA, using social cues, does not necessarily lead to an increase in donations. While our results show a positive significance on social cues to perceived humanness and social presence, the results do not suggest a significant effect of human-like CAs design on a user's donation behavior. Overall, our study provides future research with a base to improve the design of CAs for gathering donations, directing research to extend beyond inducing the perception of humanness and social presence.

Acknowledgements. We would like to thank Ho Ching Florence Tran for her support during this research project.

References

1. Berg, M.M.: Modelling of Natural Dialogues in the Context of Speech-based Information and Control Systems. Kiel, Germany (2014)
2. McTear, M., Callejas, Z., Griol, D.: Conversational interfaces: past and present. In: The Conversational Interface, pp. 51–72. Springer, Cham (2016). https://doi.org/10.1007/978-3-319-32967-3_4

3. Maedche, A., et al.: AI-based digital assistants. Bus. Inf. Syst. Eng. **61**(4), 535–544 (2019). https://doi.org/10.1007/s12599-019-00600-8
4. Leviathan, Y., Matias, Y.: Google Duplex: an AI system for accomplishing real-world tasks over the phone, https://bit.ly/38csuBn. Accessed 10 Aug 2020
5. Larivière, B., et al.: Service encounter 2.0: an investigation into the roles of technology, employees and customers. J. Bus. Res. **79**, 238–246 (2017)
6. Grudin, J., Jacques, R.: Chatbots, humbots, and the quest for artificial general intelligence. In: Conference on Human Factors in Computing Systems - Proceedings (2019). https://doi.org/10.1145/3290605.3300439
7. Luger, E., Sellen, A.: Like having a really bad pa: the gulf between user expectation and experience of conversational agents. In: Conference Human Factors Computer System – Proceedings, pp. 5286–5297 (2016). https://doi.org/10.1145/2858036.2858288.
8. Araujo, T.: Living up to the chatbot hype: the influence of anthropomorphic design cues and communicative agency framing on conversational agent and company perceptions. Comput. Hum. Behav. **85**, 183–189 (2018)
9. Feine, J., Gnewuch, U., Morana, S., Maedche, A.: A taxonomy of social cues for conversational agents. Int. J. Hum. Comput. Stud. Stud. **132**, 138–161 (2019). https://doi.org/10.1016/j.ijhcs.2019.07.009
10. Von Der Pütten, A.M., Krämer, N.C., Gratch, J., Kang, S.H.: It doesn't matter what you are! Explaining social effects of agents and avatars. Comput. Hum. Behav. **26**, 1641–1650 (2010)
11. Gnewuch, U., Morana, S., Adam, M.T.P., Maedche, A.: Faster is not always better: understanding the effect of dynamic response delays in human-chatbot interaction. In: Proceedings of the European Conference on Information Systems (ECIS). S, pp. 1–17. Portsmouth, United Kingdom (2018)
12. Diederich, S., Brendel, A.B., Kolbe, L.M.: Designing anthropomorphic enterprise conversational agents. Bus. Inf. Syst. Eng. **62**(3), 193–209 (2020). https://doi.org/10.1007/s12599-020-00639-y
13. Tinwell, A., Sloan, R.J.S.: Children's perception of uncanny human-like virtual characters. Comput. Hum. Behav. **36**, 286–296 (2014)
14. Mori, M., MacDorman, K.F., Kageki, N.: The uncanny valley. IEEE Robot. Autom. Mag. **19**, 98–100 (2012)
15. Nass, C., Moon, Y.: Machines and mindlessness: social responses to computers. J. Soc. Issues **56**, 81–103 (2000)
16. Meijers, M.H.C., Verlegh, P.W.J., Noordewier, M.K., Smit, E.G.: The dark side of donating: how donating may license environmentally unfriendly behavior. Soc. Influ. (2015). https://doi.org/10.1080/15534510.2015.1092468
17. Bennett, R.: Factors underlying the inclination to donate to particular types of charity. Int. J. Nonprofit Volunt. Sect. Mark. (2003). https://doi.org/10.1002/nvsm.198
18. Verhaert, G.A., Van den Poel, D.: Empathy as added value in predicting donation behavior. J. Bus. Res. (2011). https://doi.org/10.1016/j.jbusres.2010.12.024
19. Nonprofits Source: The Ultimate List Of Charitable Giving Statistics For 2018, https://nonprofitssource.com/online-giving-statistics/#:~:text=Overall giving increased 4%25 last, donated money to nonprofit organizations. Accessed 10 Aug 2020
20. IJsselsteijn, W., de Kort, Y., Midden, C., Eggen, B., van den Hoven, E.: Persuasive technology for human well-being: setting the scene. In: IJsselsteijn, W.A., de Kort, Y.A.W., Midden, C., Eggen, B., van den Hoven, E. (eds.) PERSUASIVE 2006. LNCS, vol. 3962, pp. 1–5. Springer, Heidelberg (2006). https://doi.org/10.1007/11755494_1
21. Nunamaker, J.F., Derrick, D.C., Elkins, A.C., Burgoon, J.K., Patton, M.W.: Embodied conversational agent-based kiosk for automated interviewing. J. Manag. Inf. Syst. **28**, 17–48 (2011)

22. Schuetzler, R.M., Grimes, G.M., Giboney, J.S.: An investigation of conversational agent relevance, presence, and engagement. In: Proceedings of the Americas Conference on Information Systems (AMCIS). S. 1–10. New Orleans, USA (2018)

23. Følstad, A., Brandtzæg, P.B.: Chatbots and the new world of HCI. Interactions **24**, 38–42 (2017)

24. Stock, R.M., Merkle, M.: Customer responses to robotic innovative behavior cues during the service encounter. In: Proceedings of the International Conference on Information Systems (ICIS). S, pp. 1–17. San Francisco, USA (2018)

25. Groom, V., Nass, C., Chen, T., Nielsen, A., Scarborough, J.K., Robles, E.: Evaluating the effects of behavioral realism in embodied agents. Int. J. Hum. Comput. Stud. **67**, 842–849 (2009)

26. Seeger, A.-M., Pfeiffer, J., Heinzl, A.: Designing anthropomorphic conversational agents: development and empirical evaluation of a design framework. In: Proceedings of the International Conference on Information Systems (ICIS). S, pp. 1–17. San Francisco, USA (2018)

27. Gnewuch, U., Morana, S., Maedche, A.: Towards designing cooperative and social conversational agents for customer service. In: Proceedings of the International Conference on Information Systems (ICIS), pp. 1–13. Seoul, Korea (2017)

28. Liao, Q.V., et al.: All work and no play? conversations with a question-and-answer chatbot in the wild. In: Proceedings of the ACM CHI Conference on Human Factors in Computing Systems, pp. 1–13. Montréal, Canada (2018)

29. Fridin, M., Belokopytov, M.: Acceptance of socially assistive humanoid robot by preschool and elementary school teachers. Comput. Hum. Behav. (2014). https://doi.org/10.1016/j.chb.2013.12.016

30. Fast, E., Chen, B., Mendelsohn, J., Bassen, J., Bernstein, M.: Iris: a conversational agent for complex tasks. In: Proceedings of the ACM CHI Conference on Human Factors in Computing Systems, pp. 1–12. Denver, USA (2017)

31. Weizenbaum, J.: ELIZA—a computer program for the study of natural language communication between man and machine. Commun. ACM. **9**, 36–45 (1966)

32. Ben Mimoun, M.S., Poncin, I., Garnier, M.: Case study-embodied virtual agents: an analysis on reasons for failure. J. Retail. Consum. Serv. **19**, 605–612 (2012). https://doi.org/10.1016/j.jretconser.2012.07.006

33. Diederich, S., Brendel, A.B., Kolbe, L.M.: On Conversational agents in information systems research: analyzing the past to guide future work. In: Proceedings of the International Conference on Wirtschaftsinformatik, pp. 1550–1564 (2019)

34. Kraus, R.: Facebook is really proud of its 300,000 business bots, despite claiming it will put 'people first. https://bit.ly/2TUGM19. Accessed 07 Aug 2020

35. Diederich, S., Brendel, A.B., Kolbe, L.M.: Towards a taxonomy of platforms for conversational agent design. In: Proceedings of the International Conference on Wirtschaftsinformatik (2019)

36. Wünderlich, N.V., Paluch, S.: A nice and friendly chat with a bot: user perceptions of AI-based service agents. In: Proceedings of the International Conference on Information Systems (ICIS), pp. 1–11. Seoul, Korea (2017).

37. Morana, S., Friemel, C., Gnewuch, U., Maedche, A., Pfeiffer, J.: Interaktion mit smarten Systemen – Aktueller Stand und zukünftige Entwicklungen im Bereich der Nutzerassistenz. Wirtschaftsinformatik Manag. **5**, 42–51 (2017)

38. Brandtzæg, P.B., Følstad, A.: Chatbots: changing user needs and motivations. Interactions **25**, 38–43 (2018)

39. Leathers, D.G., Eaves, M.: Successful Nonverbal Communication: Principles and Applications. Routledge (2015)

40. Nass, C., Moon, Y., Green, N.: Are machines gender neutral? gender-stereotypic responses to computers with voices. J. Appl. Soc. Psychol. (1997). https://doi.org/10.1111/j.1559-1816.1997.tb00275.x
41. Nass, C., Steuer, J., Tauber, E.R.: Computers are social actors. In: Proceedings of the ACM CHI Conference on Human Factors in Computing Systems, p. 204. Boston, USA (1994)
42. Feine, J., Morana, S., Gnewuch, U.: Measung service encounter satisfaction with customer service chatbots using sentiment analysis. In: Proceedings of the International Conference on Wirtschaftsinformatik, pp. 0–11 (2019)
43. Gefen, D., Straub, D.: Gender differences in the perception and use of e-mail: an extension to the technology acceptance model. Manage. Inf. Syst. Q. **21**, 389–400 (1997)
44. Gunawardena, C.: Social presence theory and implications of interaction and collaborative learning in computer conferencing. Int. J. Educ. Telecommun. (1995). https://doi.org/10.1111/j.1541-0420.2011.01694.x
45. Gefen, D., Straub, D.: Managing User Trust in B2C e-Services. e-Service J. **2**, 7–24 (2003)
46. Cyr, D., Head, M., Larios, H., Pan, B.: Exploring human images in website design: a multi-method approach. Manag. Inf. Syst. Q. **33**, 539 (2009)
47. Baylor, A.L.: Promoting motivation with virtual agents and avatars: Role of visual presence and appearance. Philos. Trans. R. Soc. Bio. Sci. **364**(1535), 3559-3565 (2009)
48. Cowell, A.J., Stanney, K.M.: Manipulation of non-verbal interaction style and demo-graphic embodiment to increase anthropomorphic computer character credibility. Int. J. Hum. Comput. Stud. **62**, 281–306 (2005)
49. Wang, N., Johnson, W.L., Mayer, R.E., Rizzo, P., Shaw, E., Collins, H.: The politeness effect: pedagogical agents and learning outcomes. Int. J. Hum. Comput. Stud. **66**, 98–112 (2008)
50. Seeger, A.-M., Pfeiffer, J., Heinzl, A.: When do we need a human? anthropomorphic design and trustworthiness of conversational agents. In: Special Interest Group on Human-Computer Interaction, pp. 1–6 (2017)
51. Diederich, S., Janßen-Müller, M., Brendel, A.B., Morana, S.: Emulating empathetic behavior in online service encounters with sentiment-adaptive responses: insights from an experiment with a conversational agent. In: Proceedings of the International Conference on Information Systems (ICIS), pp. 0–17. Munich, Germany (2019)
52. Hoolwerf, B., Schuyt, T.: Giving in Europe - The current state of research on household dona-tions, corporations, foundations and charity lotteries to charitable organisations in Europe. Eur. Res. Netw. Philanthr. **280** (2013)
53. Giving USA: Giving USA 2019: The Annual Report on Philanthropy for the Year 2018, https://bit.ly/3p127Ej. Accessed 30 July 2020
54. Sargeant, A.: Charitable giving: towards a model of donor behaviour. J. Mark. Manag. (1999). https://doi.org/10.1362/026725799784870351
55. Zhou, X., Kim, S., Wang, L.: Money helps when money feels: money anthropomorphism increases charitable giving. J. Consum. Res. **45**, 953–972 (2018). https://doi.org/10.1093/jcr/ucy012
56. Aggarwal, P., McGill, A.L.: Is that car smiling at me? schema congruity as a basis for evaluating anthropomorphized products. J. Consum. Res. **34**, 468–479 (2007)
57. Chandler, J., Schwarz, N.: Use does not wear ragged the fabric of friendship: thinking of objects as alive makes people less willing to replace them. J. Consum. Psychol. **20**, 138–145 (2010)
58. Reeves, B., Nass, C.: The Media Equation: How People Treat Computers. The Center for the Study of Language and Information Publications, Television and New Media Like Real People and Places (1996)
59. Boudreau, M.C., Gefen, D., Straub, D.W.: Validation in information systems research: a state-of-the-art assessment. MIS Q. Manag. Inf. Syst. **25**, 1–16 (2001)

60. Dennis, A.R., Valacich, J.S.: Conducting experimental research in information systems. Commun. Assoc. Inf. Syst. **7**, 1–41 (2001)
61. Holtgraves, T.M., Ross, S.J., Weywadt, C.R., Han, T.L.: Perceiving artificial social agents. Comput. Hum. Behav. **23**, 2163–2174 (2007)
62. Gefen, D., Straub, D.: A practical guide to factorial validity using PLS-graph: tutorial and annotated example. Commun. Assoc. Inf. Syst. **16**, 91–109 (2005). https://doi.org/10.17705/1cais.01605
63. Urbach, N., Ahlemann, F.: Structural equation modeling in information systems research using partial least squares. J. Inf. Technol. Theory Appl. **11**, 5–40 (2010)
64. DiStefano, C., Zhu, M., Mîndrilă, D.: Understanding and using factor scores: considerations for the applied researcher. Pract. Assessment, Res. Eval. **14**(1), 20 (2009)
65. Kubinger, K.D., Rasch, D., Moder, K.: To the legend of the pre-requisites of t-tests for non-dependent samples. Psychol. Rundschau. **60**, 26–27 (2009)
66. Ruxton, G.D.: The unequal variance t-test is an underused alternative to student's t-test and the mann-whitney U test. Behav. Ecol. **17**, 688–690 (2006)
67. Yates, F.: Tests of significance for 2×2 contingency tables. J. R. Stat. Soc. Ser. A. **147**, 426–449 (1984)
68. Westerman, D., Cross, A.C., Lindmark, P.G.: I Believe in a thing called bot: perceptions of the humanness of chatbots. Commun. Stud. **70**, 295–312 (2019). https://doi.org/10.1080/10510974.2018.1557233
69. Hendriks, F., Ou, C.X.J., Khodabandeh Amiri, A., Bockting, S.: The power of computer-mediated communication theories in explaining the effect of chatbot introduction on user experience. In: Proceedings of 53rd Hawaii International Conference System Science (2020). https://doi.org/10.24251/hicss.2020.034
70. Diederich, S., Lichtenberg, S., Brendel, A.B., Trang, S.: Promoting sustainable mobility beliefs with persuasive and anthropomorphic design: insights from an experiment with a conversational agent. In: Proceedings of the International Conference on Information Systems (ICIS), pp. 0–17. Munich, Germany (2019)
71. Lehto, T., Oinas-Kukkonen, H., Drozd, F.: Factors affecting perceived persuasiveness of a behavior change support system. In: International Conference on Information Systems, ICIS 2012 (2012)

'Let Us Work Together'– Insights from an Experiment with Conversational Agents on the Relation of Anthropomorphic Design, Dialog Support, and Performance

Sascha Lichtenberg[1(✉)], Johannes Bührke[1], Alfred Benedikt Brendel[2], Simon Trang[1], Stephan Diederich[1], and Stefan Morana[3]

[1] Chair of Information Management, Georg-August-Universität Göttingen, Goettingen, Germany
{Sascha.Lichtenberg,Strang}@uni-goettingen.de,
{johannes.buehrke,stephan.diederich}@stud.uni-goettingen.de
[2] Chair of Business Informatics, Esp. Intelligent Systems and Services, Technische Universität Dresden, Dresden, Germany
Alfred_Benedikt.Brendel@tu-dresden.de
[3] Chair of Digital Transformation and Information System, Universität Des Saarlandes, Saarbrücken, Germany
stefan.morana@uni-saarland.de

Abstract. In the human interaction with CAs, research has shown that elements of persuasive system design, such as praise, are perceived differently when compared to traditional graphical interfaces.

In this experimental study, we will extend our knowledge regarding the relation of persuasiveness (namely dialog support), anthropomorphically designed CAs, and task performance. Within a three-conditions-between-subjects design, two instances of the CA are applied within an online experiment with 120 participants. Our results show that anthropomorphically designed CAs increase perceived dialog support and performance but adding persuasive design elements can be counterproductive. Thus, the results are embedded in the discourse of CA design for task support.

Keywords: Conversational agents · Persuasive system design · Task performance · Dialog support · Chatbot · Human computer interaction

1 Introduction

Information Systems (IS) can be designed to attain various goals. Following Benbasat [1], one of the goals is to increase the effectiveness and efficiency of users in the completion of a task, such as finding and purchasing a product online. However, IS also exhibits substantial potential to influence individual beliefs and behavior [2], for instance, regarding environmental sustainability [3] or health [4]. Studies in the context of persuasive

© The Author(s), under exclusive license to Springer Nature Switzerland AG 2021
F. Ahlemann et al. (Eds.): WI 2021, LNISO 47, pp. 299–315, 2021.
https://doi.org/10.1007/978-3-030-86797-3_20

systems and their design have received increasing attention recently, which is reflected in calls for more research [5].

While the vast majority of studies in the area of persuasive system design focuses on software with graphical user interfaces [6], we follow the notion that conversational agents (CAs) offer the opportunity to design even more persuasive IS. CAs, defined as software with which users interact through natural language (i.e. written or spoken word) [7], have been shown to trigger mindless social responses (i.e. users treat computers like it is a human being [8]) as formulated in the paradigm of computers-are-social-actors (CASA) [8, 9]. Due to the social nature of human interaction with CAs, we argue that elements of persuasive system design, such as praise or social roles [10], can be leveraged to influence individual behavior.

Initial work in the area of persuasive and anthropomorphic CAs underlines this potential. For example, Diederich, Lichtenberg, et al. [11] investigated how persuasive messages of a CA can influence an individual's environmental sustainability beliefs, finding that a anthropomorphic design of a CA increase the perceived persuasiveness. Similarly, Gnewuch et al. [12] argue that CAs can be a useful means to enable more sustainable energy consumption behavior of consumers, due to their feedback provided for the user. However, we still lack an understanding of whether persuasive CAs can extend beyond the scope of emotion and cognition, influencing actual user behavior (e.g., task performance).

In this experimental study, we address this research gap regarding the relation of persuasive, anthropomorphic CAs, and actual behavior in the form of performance. The performance of an individual can be measured by the number of completed tasks (e.g., in the context of gamification, by completed rounds [13], or the number of steps per day [14]). We conducted an experiment with three different treatment groups (no CA, anthropomorphic CA and anthropomorphic CA extended with persuasive features) in a task completion setting. Specifically, participants had to complete a certain number of tasks, with the option to voluntarily complete more of them. Against this background, this study aims to answer the following research question:

RQ: How can persuasive and anthropomorphic design of conversational agents positively influence performance?

2   Research Background

The following section contains the relevant background information for understanding this work: (1) persuasive system design and performance and (2) anthropomorphic conversational agents and social response theory.

2.1   Persuasive System Design and Performance

The observation that technology can influence human cognition, emotion, and behavior has been made around two decades ago. On this basis, the paradigm of CASA [9, 11, 16] has been formulated. The paradigm of CASA posits that individuals mindlessly apply social rules and expectations to computers once they receive cues associated with human traits or behavior [17]. Against this background, research in the domain of persuasive design investigates the social responses people show to computers [9, 10]. Research in this context entails the development and application of design elements intended to shape user perception and promote desired behavior. An example of this is the display of anthropomorphic communication features, such as humor, empathy, and praise, to trigger social dynamics, such as competition or cooperation [10].

These persuasive design elements can be distinguished into five types of social cues Fogg [2]: physical (e.g., touch, facial expressions, movement), psychological (e.g., empathy, humor), language (e.g., written or spoken language, turn-taking in a conversation), social dynamics (e.g., praise, judgment), and social roles (e.g., guide, partner). In sum, designers are provided with a wide selection of design elements and cues that can be used to persuade individuals in a variety of application domains, such as environmental sustainability, work, or education [18]. Regarding the effects of these social cues, four different categories can be distinguished [10]: (1) primary task support (e.g., individual tailoring of information), (2) dialog support (e.g., providing praise), (3) credibility support (e.g., displaying trustworthiness), and (4) social support (e.g., referring to social facilitation).

In the domain of work and performance, persuasive design offers the opportunity to incline individuals to perform their primary task [10]. In the context of performance, for instance, this can mean enabling an individual to measure their primary task progress via self-monitoring [6] (e.g., displaying heart rate while exercising to ensure progress and commitment [19]). Similar examples can be found in the context of the academic performance of students [20], promoting physical activity at the workplace [4] and provoke "work-like" performance in experimental contexts [21, 22]. Dialog support has shown that users are encouraged to use the enhanced IS and consecutively motivated to perform their primary task [23]. One example is praise in the form of images, symbols, or words [6] to support a person in achieving his or her goals (e.g., increase the number of steps per day [14]).

2.2 Anthropomorphic Conversational Agents and Social Response Theory

Through technological progress regarding natural language processing and machine learning, CA-related technology has become widely available [24]. Consequently, CAs are currently attracting strong interest from research and practice [7, 24, 25]. Users can interact with CAs using written (e.g., chatbots) or spoken language (e.g., personal assistants like Siri or Microsoft Cortana). Furthermore, CAs can be disembodied, have a virtual embodiment [26], or a physical embodiment, e.g. service robots [27]. Through various means, CAs can display human characteristics, such as having a human name and participating in a dialogue with turn-taking [28]. These anthropomorphic characteristics trigger mindless social responses by users [28, 29], as postulated in the social response theory [17, 30].

The intensity of these social responses varies according to the degree of perceived anthropomorphism (i.e., human-likeness) of a CA [31]. Current studies on CA design found that a higher degree of anthropomorphism can lead to various positive effects, such as an increase in service satisfaction [32], trustworthiness [33], and persuasiveness [11]. In order to better understand the relation of anthropomorphic CA design,

perceived anthropomorphism, and related benefits, CAs are studied in various application areas, such as customer service (e.g., marketing and sales [34]), and healthcare
[35]). Synthesizing current research on anthropomorphic CA design, Seeger et al. [15]
developed a conceptual framework that comprises three dimensions: (1) human identity, (2) verbal cues, and (3) non-verbal cues. The dimension of *human identity* includes
cues regarding the representation of the agent, for example, having an avatar [31]. The
second dimension of *verbal cues* comprises the language used by a CA, for instance,
using self-references ("I think that…" [36]), expressing artificial thoughts and emotions
("In my experience…" [37]), or variability in syntax and word choice [15]. The third
dimension of *non-verbal cues* includes conveying information on attitudes or emotional
state [38], such as indicating thinking through dynamic response times depending on
message length and complexity [32] or using emoticons to express emotions [39].

3   Research Model and Hypotheses

Our research will contribute to a better understanding of the relation between CA design,
its perception, and user performance. Our research model is depicted in Fig. 1. Specifically, we hypothesize that CAs equipped with social cues as part of an anthropomorphic
design [15] persuade users to complete a higher number of tasks when combined with
persuasive design elements, such as dialog support [40].

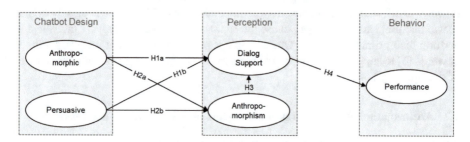

Fig. 1. Research model

Based on the paradigm of CASA [17, 30], technology influences individual beliefs
and behavior [2]. CAs equipped with anthropomorphic characteristics, such as a human
name and participating in a dialogue with turn-taking [28], trigger social responses by
users [28, 29]. The human appearance leads individuals to perceive the CA as more
persuasive, giving it the potential to influence the beliefs and behavior of individuals.
Specifically, CAs provide users with the option to interact with the system via written
dialog, providing dialog support [23]. Thus, we formulate the following hypothesis:

*H1a: An anthropomorphically designed chatbot yields a higher level of perceived
dialog support than no chatbot.*

In the context of this study, we focus on CAs that are praising the user for their
performance and award points for certain achievements, thereby providing dialog support

[23]. Kamali et al. [41] were able to show that praise was expected (i.e., for specific behavior) when elderly people interact with a CA. Similarly, receiving points for certain behavior increases participation [42]. Therefore, we formulate our next hypothesis as follows:

H1b: A persuasively and anthropomorphically designed chatbot yields a higher level of perceived dialog support than an anthropomorphically designed chatbot.

Furthermore, CAs offer various possibilities for anthropomorphic design. An agent equipped with a name, gender, and avatar [31], displaying emotions through verbal cues [8], and applying nonverbal cues, such as dynamic response delays to indicate thinking or typing [32], can contribute to the perception of the agent as more anthropomorphic, even when users are aware of the artificial nature of it. Thus, we propose the following hypothesis:

H2a: An anthropomorphically designed chatbot yields a higher level of perceived anthropomorphism than no chatbot.

Furthermore, CAs additionally displaying persuasive cues, such as praising their user, add further to the anthropomorphic perception [10]. For instance, the study of Xu and Lombard [43] have shown that even a small cue (e.g., the name of the CA) can change the perception of the CA. Therefore, we hypothesize that such cues contribute to users anthropomorphizing the agent:

H2b: A persuasively and anthropomorphically designed chatbot yields a higher level of perceived anthropomorphism than an anthropomorphically designed chatbot.

Recent studies, which explore the interaction of anthropomorphic design of CAs and their persuasiveness, suggest that perceived anthropomorphism can increase the persuasiveness of the agent. For instance, Harjunen et al. [44] found that virtual offers are more likely to be accepted when the agent shows typical human behavior, such as smiling or touching (with a haptic glove). Similarly, Adler et al. [45] showed that a CA displaying positive emotions leads to a higher degree of perceived persuasiveness compared to a CA without emotionally loaded language. Against this background, we hypothesize:

H3: Perceived anthropomorphism positively impacts perceived dialog support.

Following Lehto et al. [23], persuasive design elements have the potential to reinforce, change, or shape the behavior of individuals by increasing the overall persuasiveness of information systems. Superficially, dialog support has shown to encourage users to perform their primary task, such as increasing the amount of physical exercise [14]. Thus, we propose the following hypothesis:

H4: Perceived dialog support positively impacts performance.

4   Research Design

To test our hypotheses, we conducted an online experiment with three-conditions (no design, anthropomorphic design, and persuasive design) in a between-subjects design, avoiding carryover effects [46]. We conducted an a priori power analysis using GPower [47] to estimate the required sample size. We assume a large effect and estimated a minimum amount of 102 participants, given an effect size f = 0.4, alpha = .05 and power (beta) = 0.95). We collected data from the 2nd to the 15th of October 2019 until we had at least forty observations per treatment, resulting in a total of 120 participants. Overall, the sample consisted of 37% of females (5% of the participants preferred not to specify their gender). The age of the participants ranges from 18 to 83 (mean 33), and all participants are currently residing in Germany.

4.1   Data Collection Procedure and Sample

The experiment consisted of four steps: (1) Explanation of the experiment, (2) chat with the chatbot, (3) perform the task, and (4) fill out the questionnaire. In the first step, the participants received a briefing screen, which explained the context [48] and the structure of the experiment (completing five of 15 slider tasks with a subsequent survey) and described the tasks. Every participant received the same explanations to make sure that all participants have the same information [49]. Following the instructions, participants got two attempts to answer three comprehension questions. Those who failed both attempts were excluded from the experiment. This procedure ensures that no participant completed more tasks because the rules related to the number of completed tasks were not understood properly. After this step, all participants were randomly assigned to one of the three treatments and proceeded to step 2. The second step is divided into two sub-steps: (2a) chat with chatbot and (2b) perform the task. In step 2a, the participants had to chat with a chatbot. Via the chatbot, participants were able to start a task and end the experiment (see Control and Treatment Configuration section for details). If the participant was not in a chatbot treatment, the start of a task, and the end of the experiment could be triggered by a button. In step 2b, users had to perform slider tasks [48]. For the slider task, the participants had to set five sliders from 0 to 50 by using the mouse pointer. After completing each task, the participants returned to step 2a. When five tasks were completed, participants had the option to proceed to the questionnaire or complete up to ten more tasks. In step (3), participants had to fill out a questionnaire (see Measures section for details) (Fig. 2).

4.2   Control and Treatment Configurations

Our experiment had three conditions: (1) no chatbot (control treatment), (2) anthropomorphic chatbot, and (3) persuasive chatbot. Every participant was randomly assigned to one experimental condition (between-subjects design). For condition (1), users did not have the option to communicate with a chatbot. For conditions (2) and (3), two chatbots were developed via the natural language processing platform Dialogflow by Google. Both chatbots received the same training phrases (i.e., exemplary statements that users might make during the interaction) to train them to understand a user's intent

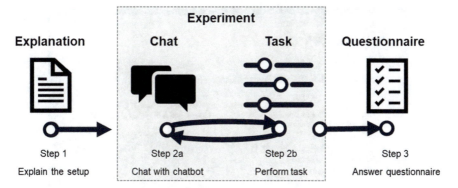

Fig. 2. Procedure of the experiment

and provide the correct reply. The chatbots were able to process different variations of sentences with the same meaning and could extract parameters, such as the intention to proceed to the next task or to exit the experiment and react appropriately. We further implemented a custom-built web interface to provide convenient access to the chatbots, ensure device independence, and minimize distraction (Fig. 3, 4).

Fig. 3. Slider task

Both chatbots were equipped with various cues for anthropomorphic CA design according to the three dimensions (human identity, verbal, non-verbal) as suggested by Seeger et al. [19] to establish a baseline for perceived anthropomorphism. Regarding the human identity, we equipped the chatbot with the name "Laura," a female gender, and a human pictogram representing a female individual. Concerning verbal communication, the CA was designed to use self-references, turn-taking, and a personal introduction ("Hi! I am Laura and I will…"), including a greeting in the form of a welcome message. Regarding the non-verbal anthropomorphic CA design dimension, we implemented blinking dots in combination with dynamic response delays depending on the length of the previous message to simulate thinking and typing of replies by the CAs [32].

Overall, both chatbot instances were identical except for the addition of persuasive messages for condition (3). The chatbot provides dialog support by using praise, suggestions, and rewards [10]. The persuasive chatbot praises users after every task completed ("Wow! You finished your task very quickly."), whereas the anthropomorphic chatbot renounces praise. Furthermore, in case users want to end the experiment and proceed to the questionnaire, the chatbots suggests continuing and completing more tasks ("Maybe

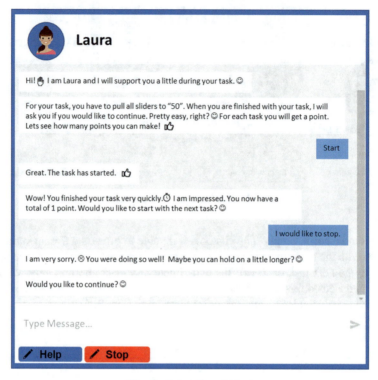

Fig. 4. Persuasive chatbot

you can hold on a little longer? Would you like to continue?"). Lastly, the chatbot introduces a point system, rewarding the user with one point for every completed task ("You
now have a total of X points").

4.3 Measures and Descriptive Statistics

Our research variables included experimentally manipulated variables, questionnaire-
based variables (i.e., dialogue support and control variables), and the task outcome
variable.

First, the effect of the experimentally manipulated variables for the different types
of chatbots. As the three treatments build on one another, we detangled the different
effects and coded variables that capture commonalities and differences between the
treatments. Second, dialog support, anthropomorphism, and control variables in terms
of age, gender, education, and experience with chatbots were captured using a questionnaire. All items were measured on a scale from 1 (strongly disagree) to 7 (strongly
agree). For the design of the survey, only established constructs from previous studies
were considered. Additionally, we included attention checks by asking two questions
that prompt the participant to select a specific number on a scale. If the participant failed
to answer the questions correctly, the data was not considered for the analysis. Perceived
dialog support was measured using a 7-Point Likert scale adapted from [23]. Perceived

Table 1. Questionnaire Items *(Note that the items are translated from German to English.)*

Constructs and Items	FL	REF
Perceived Dialogue Support (α = .911)		
I believe that the tool has supported me with appropriate feedback.	.873	
I believe that the tool has encouraged me to continue working on the task.	.909	[23]
I believe that the tool motivated me to complete the task by praise.	.889	
Perceived Anthropomorphism(α = .934)		
I believe that the tool has a mind.	.759	
~~I believe that the tool has a purpose.~~	~~.305~~	
I believe that the tool has free will.	.909	
I believe that the tool has a consciousness.	.926	[15]
I believe that the tool desires something.	.857	
I believe that the tool has beliefs.	.912	
I believe that the tool has the ability to experience emotions.	.602	
Perceived Persuasiveness (Single Scale)		[23]
I believe that the tool convinced me to perform the task.	-	

FL = factor loadings, REF = reference, α = Cronbach's alpha;

anthropomorphism is based on a 7-Point Likert scale adapted from [15]. Additionally, we measured perceived persuasiveness [23] as a single-scale item to conduct a manipulation check. The items are displayed in Table 1. Third, the outcome variable of the task was measured in terms of the number of completed tasks, where the number of completed tasks equals the times a participant positioned all sliders correctly.

5 Results

In the following two sub-sections, we will present our results regarding the descriptive statistics and structural model.

5.1 Descriptive Statistics

The group averages of the performance show that the anthropomorphic chatbot ($M = 7.375$, $SD = 5.309$) and anthropomorphic chatbot with persuasive elements ($M = 4.3$, $SD = 2.893$) differ from the control group, which yields a lower number of tasks performed ($M = 3.150$, $SD = 3.519$). Similarly, we observed that the perceived dialog support is lower for the control group (M = 2.45, SD = 1.693) when compared to the anthropomorphic chatbot ($M = 5.15$, $SD = 1.743$) and anthropomorphic chatbot with persuasive elements ($M = 2.858$, $SD = 1.571$). As for anthropomorphism, the system is perceived lower in the control group ($M = 2.107$, $SD = 1.318$) when compared to the treatments anthropomorphic chatbot ($M = 3.279$, $SD = 1.734$) and anthropomorphic chatbot with persuasive elements ($M = 2.504$, $SD = 1.045$) (see Table 2).

To test whether our manipulation of the interface designs for the three different treatments was successful, we assessed users' perceived social persuasiveness. A test for variances homogeneity was not significant ($F(2, 117) = 13.467$; $p = .597$). Based on this result, we conducted a one-way ANOVA. The ANOVA was significant with F(2,117) 13.467; p < .001. The result of a Tuskey HSD post hoc comparison revealed following significant differences between for control (M = 2.7; SD = 1.951) – anthropomorphic chatbot (M = 4.88; SD = 1.977) (p < .001), and anthropomorphic chatbot - anthropomorphic chatbot with persuasive elements (M = 3.08; SD = 1.789) (p < .001). We applied PLS (partial least squares) to evaluate the measurement model and estimate the structural model. As our analysis includes dialog support as a latent variable, we applied a structural equation approach. We used partial least squares (PLS) path modeling and employed SmartPLS 3.2.9. In the following paragraph, we first inspect the measurement models and will then estimate and interpret the structural model.

Table 2. Descriptive statistics

Dependent variables	Treatments (N = 40 for all treatments)				
	All		Control	AC	ACwPE
Performance	Mean	4.942	3.150	7.375	4.300
	SD	4.387	3.519	5.309	2.893
Perceived Dialogue Support	Mean	3.486	2.450	5.150	2.858
	SD	2.042	1.693	1.743	1.571
Perceived Anthropomorphism	Mean	2.629	2.107	3.279	2.504
	SD	1.467	1.318	1.734	1.045
Perceived Persuasiveness (Manipulation Check)	Mean	3.55	2.7	4.88	3.08
	SD	1.903	1.951	1.977	1.789

SD = Standard deviation, AC = Anthropomorphic, ACwPE = AC with Persuasive Elements.

5.2   Measurement Model and Structural Model

The measurement model includes manifest variables in terms of the experimentally manipulated variables, the number of completed tasks, and reflective constructs. From the experimental treatments, we derived four variables (see Table 3). The no chatbot variable (control treatment) was not included (reference group).

We then assessed the reflective measurement model of anthropomorphism and dialogue support for individual item reliability, convergent validity, and discriminant validity. The model displays good measurement properties: all factor loadings are meaningful and significant, the composite reliability is above .7, the average variance extracted is above .5, and the Fornell–Larker criterion is satisfied. We then applied a bootstrap resampling procedure (with 4999 samples) to test the relationships. We favor the SEM for our research design with latent variables because it takes into account measurement errors or multidimensional structures of theoretical constructs [50]. The PLS estimator has advantages with respect to restrictive assumptions and is therefore widely used in experimental research [51, 52]. The different experimental conditions (no chatbot, anthropomorphically designed chatbot, persuasively and anthropomorphically designed chatbot) were

Table 3. Inter-Construct correlations, CR, and AVE

(Latent) Variable	CR	AVE	1	2	3	4	5
1. Number of Completed Tasks	–	–	–				
2. Dialogue Support	.95	.86	.43	**.93**			
3. Anthropomorphism	.94	.69	.33	.53	**.83**		
4. Anthropomorphic Chatbot Design	–	–	.17	.14	.08	–	
5. Persuasive Chatbot Design	–	–	– .11	– .25	– .11	.58	–

CR = composite reliability, AVE = average variance extracted

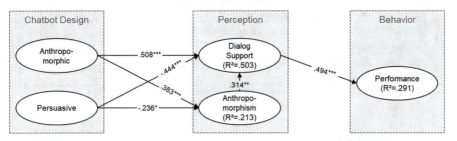

Fig. 5. PLS Structural Model ****p ≤ .001, **p ≤ .01, *p ≤ .05*

dummy coded for our structural model, to compare the manipulations with a baseline condition (no chatbot). The structural model explains variances in Anthropomorphism ($R^2 = .213$, $f^2 = .156$), Dialog Support ($R^2 = .503$, $f^2 = .312$) and Performance (measured as number of completed tasks) ($R^2 = .291$). The results of the PLS estimation are illustrated in Fig. 5.

In summary, we find support for hypotheses H1a, H2a, H3, and H4. We find contradicting results for H1b and H2b, namely the role of the persuasive design (see Table 4). Concerning, our control variables, we find significant effects for prior experience with chatbots on Anthropomorphism ($\beta = -.239$, $p < .05$). Moreover, we find a significant effect on Gender on Number of Completed Tasks ($\beta = -.181$, $p < .05$), with male participants comple-ting fewer tasks.

6 Discussion

Our experiment aimed to explore the relationship between the persuasive and anthropomorphic design of conversational agents and performance. The results have implications for CA and persuasive system design. In this regard, we provide empirical evidence for the relation of anthropomorphism and persuasive design in CAs. We found contradicting evidence for our hypotheses that persuasive cues (explicitly praise, suggestion, and rewards) lead to higher perceived anthropomorphism and dialogue support. These results can be explained from different perspectives.

Table 4. Results for hypotheses

Hypothesis	B	t	
1 a) An anthropomorphically designed chatbot yields a higher level of perceived dialog support than no chatbot.	.51***	6.11	s
b) A persuasively and anthropomorphically designed chatbot yields a higher level of perceived dialog support than an anthropomorphically designed chatbot.	-.44***	5.25	c
2 a) An anthropomorphically designed chatbot yields a higher level of perceived anthropomorphism than no chatbot.	.38***	4.02	s
b) A persuasively and anthropomorphically designed chatbot yields a higher level of perceived anthropomorphism than an anthropomorphically designed chatbot.	-.24*	2.49	c
3 Perceived anthropomorphism positively impacts perceived dialog support.	.31**	3.96	s
4 Perceived dialog support positively impacts the number of completed tasks.	.49***	6.41	s

s = supported, c = contradicted, ns = non-supported, B = path coefficient

6.1 Implications for Research

First, when looking at CA literature, Seeger et al. [15] state that simply applying more social cues and anthropomorphic design elements will not automatically lead to a higher level of perceived anthropomorphism. Selecting and combining them should be done with caution. In this context, Clark et al. [53] see the expectations of a user as decisive. Users are experienced with the interaction with humans and know the mistakes they make in an interaction. However, computers make errors that can rarely be found in humans. Therefore, these errors are unexpected. Regarding our CA design, the anthropomorphic chatbot was well perceived, leading to higher perceived anthropomorphism and dialog support. However, by adding the intended-to-be-persuasive elements to the design, the perception of the chatbot is vastly different from the other one. This observation indicates that users did not expect the added social cues.

Second, it could also be hypothesized that the persuasive chatbot appears to be disingenuous. A slider task does not require specific skills, qualifications, or knowledge [48]. Furthermore, unlike tasks in crowdsourcing, such as labeling pictures, performing a slider task has no trigger for enjoyment (task enjoyment leading to increased performance [54]), has no deeper meaning (perceived meaning is linked with satisfaction and performance [55]), and does not enable a user to contribute to a greater good (like voluntary work where the reward is intrinsic to the act of volunteering [56]). Hence, we would suggest that individuals perceive the high level of praise, combined with suggestions to keep going and receiving arbitrary point rewards, as disingenuous and not fitting the task.

Lastly, the negative perception of the persuasive chatbot might be explained by the cognitive fit theory [57]. The theory proposes that the fit between task and presentation of supporting information shapes the task performance. Our results indicate that an anthropomorphic CA provides a better information presentation in terms of dialog support, fitting the task at hand. This fit leads to higher performance. Thus, through the lens of the cognitive fit theory, the addition of persuasive elements appears to reduce the fit between task and task support.

In summary, our results can be embedded in the current discourse of CA design for task support. However, the significant negative change in the CA's perception by adding persuasive elements was unexpected. Thus, our results highlight a research opportunity to investigate the design of CAs for task support. Specifically, the framing and nature of a task appear to interact with the perception of a CA. CAs should meet expectations, appear genuine, and be adapted to the nature of the task. However, understanding how to design such a CA has yet to be addressed.

6.2 Implications for Practice

For practice, our result indicates that using a CA to frame and support tasks can be beneficial. To be specific, we would relate our results to the context of crowdworking. In crowdworking, crowd workers perform multiple tasks [58], which fits the experimental setup of this study. Our participants were inclined to complete more tasks than necessary. This indicates that adding the option to perform more tasks, accompanied by an anthropomorphic CA, can lead crowd workers to do more tasks. Furthermore, our study provides a blueprint regarding the design of such an anthropomorphic CA. Specifically, we would advise against adding persuasive messages or other design elements to an anthropomorphic CA that is intended to provide dialog support. Therefore, our results can be used to better design chatbots in the context of (crowdworking) tasks.

6.3 Limitations and Future Research

Our study is not free of limitations and offers different opportunities for future research. We conducted the online experiment in a rather controlled setting, with a set of specific tasks that every participant was asked to complete, and a single interaction with the conversational agent. Moreover, we did not compare the provided CA's with a CA without any social cues. Thus, we benefitted from control yet lacked realism in our research design [49]. Similarly, our results are limited by the selection and reimbursement of participants. In a real-world work environment, individuals are under the constant influence of expecting and receiving payment for work. For instance, crowd workers primarily perform tasks to be paid [58]. In our setting, participants did not receive a comparable form of pay. They were allowed to participate in a raffle for 10€ online shopping vouchers. Thus, it is safe to assume that participants were motivated by other factors, such as curiosity or escaping boredom.

7 Conclusion

In this study, we set out to explore the relation of persuasive and anthropomorphic CA design and performance (measured as the number of completed tasks). By means of a three-condition online experiment with two chatbots and 120 participants, we find empirical evidence for the positive influence an anthropomorphic CA has on an individual's perceived dialog support, mediated by the perceived anthropomorphism. However, a CA that displays the same anthropomorphic features and additionally provides persuasive messages, intended to provide further dialog support, is negatively perceived. This observation supports the proposition of Seeger et al. [15] that merely adding social cues and anthropomorphic characteristics to a CA is not always beneficial. In this context, our results indicate that a chatbot that provides dialog support (in our case praise, suggestions, and rewards) for simple tasks appears to be disingenuous. Therefore, our results indicate a potential for future research regarding the interaction of task and persuasive CA design. Our study makes three main contributions: First, we empirically demonstrate how the application of anthropomorphic characteristics and persuasive messages can influence performance. Thereby, we add to the body of knowledge regarding the perception and influence anthropomorphic IS has on users. Second, we present CAs as a new type of persuasive IS that triggers social responses by users and offers new opportunities for interface and task design. Third, we bridge the gap between knowledge on persuasions and anthropomorphism of IS and the design of CA for dialog support.

Acknowledgements. We would like to thank Jonas Gehrke and Jessica Lühnen for their support during this research project.

References

1. Benbasat, I.: HCI research: future challenges and directions. AIS Trans. Hum.-Comput. Interact. **2**(2), 16–21 (2010)
2. Fogg, B.J.: Computers as persuasive social actors. In: Persuasive Technology. Morgan Kaufmann Publishers, San Francisco, USA, pp. 89–120 (2003)
3. Loock, C.-M., Staake, T., Thiesse, F.: Motivating energy-efficient behavior with green is: an investigation of goal setting and the role of defaults. Manag. Inf. Syst. Q. **37**(4), 1313–1332 (2013)
4. Haque, M.S., Isomursu, M., Kangas, M., Jämsä, T.: Measuring the influence of a persuasive application to promote physical activity. CEUR Workshop Proc. **2089**, 43–57 (2018)
5. Slattery, P., Vidgen, R., Finnegan, P.: Persuasion: an analysis and common frame of reference for is research. Commun. Assoc. Inf. Syst. **46**, 30–69 (2020)
6. Oinas-Kukkonen, H., Harjumaa, M.: A systematic framework for designing and evaluating persuasive systems. In: Oinas-Kukkonen, H., Hasle, P., Harjumaa, M., Segerståhl, K., Øhrstrøm, P. (eds.) PERSUASIVE 2008. LNCS, vol. 5033, pp. 164–176. Springer, Heidelberg (2008). https://doi.org/10.1007/978-3-540-68504-3_15
7. McTear, M., Callejas, Z., Griol, D.: The Conversational Interface: Talking to Smart Devices. Springer Publishing Company, Basel, Switzerland (2016)
8. Wang, N., Johnson, W.L., Mayer, R.E., Rizzo, P., Shaw, E., Collins, H.: The politeness effect: Pedagogical agents and learning outcomes. Int. J. Hum. Comput. Stud. **66**(2), 98–112 (2008)
9. Reeves, B., Nass, C.: The Media Equation: How People Treat Computers. The Center for the Study of Language and Information Publications, Television and New Media Like Real People and Places (1996)
10. Oinas-Kukkonen, H., Harjumaa, M.: Persuasive systems design: key issues, process model, and system features. Commun. Assoc. Inf. Syst. **24**(1), 96 (2009)

11. Diederich, S., Lichtenberg, S., Brendel, A.B., Trang, S.: Promoting sustainable mobility beliefs with persuasive and anthropomorphic design: Insights from an experiment with a conversational agent November 2019
12. Gnewuch, U., Morana, S., Heckmann, C., Maedche, A.: Designing conversational agents for energy feedback. In: Chatterjee, S., Dutta, K., Sundarraj, R.P. (eds.) DESRIST 2018. LNCS, vol. 10844, pp. 18–33. Springer, Cham (2018). https://doi.org/10.1007/978-3-319-91800-6_2
13. Koeder, M.J., Tanaka, E., Mitomo, H.: Lootboxes in digital games - a gamble with consumers in need of regulation? An evaluation based on learnings from Japan. In: 22nd Bienn. Conference International Telecommunation Social Beyond boundaries Challenges business, policy Social (2018)
14. Toscos, T., Faber, A., An, S., Gandhi, M.P.: Chick clique: persuasive technology to motivate teenage girls to exercise. In: CHI 2006 Extended Abstracts on Human factors in Computing Systems, pp. 1873–1878 (2006)
15. Seeger, A.M., Pfeiffer, J., Heinzl, A.: Designing anthropomorphic conversational agents: development and empirical evaluation of a design framework. In: ICIS, pp. 1–17 (2018)
16. Nass, C., Steuer, J., Tauber, E.R.: Computers are social actors. In: ACM CHI, p. 204 (1994)
17. Nass, C., Moon, Y.: Machines and mindlessness: social responses to computers. J. Soc. Issues 56(1), 81–103 (2000)
18. Langrial, S., Lehto, T., Oinas-Kukkonen, H., Harjumaa, M., Karppinen, P.: Native mobile applications for personal wellbeing: a persuasive systems design evaluation. In: PACIS, pp. 1–16 (2012)
19. Consolvo, S., Everitt, K., Smith, I., Landay, J.A.: Design requirements for technologies that encourage physical activity. In: Conference on Human Factors in Computing Systems - Proceedings, vol. 1, pp. 457–466 (2006)
20. Filippou, J., Cheong, C., Cheong, F.: Modelling the impact of study behaviours on academic performance to inform the design of a persuasive system. Inf. Manag. 53(7), 892–903 (2016)
21. Lichtenberg, S., Brendel, A.B.: Arrr you a pirate ? towards the gamification element 'Lootbox, AMCIS (Forthcoming) (2020)
22. Lichtenberg, S., Lembcke, T., Brenig, M., Brendel, A.B., Trang, S.: Can Gamification lead to Increase Paid Crowdworkers Output ?. In: 15. Internationale Tagung Wirtschaftsinformatik December 2019 (2020)
23. Lehto, T., Oinas-Kukkonen, H., Drozd, F.: Factors affecting perceived persuasiveness of a behavior change support system. ICIS 3, 1926–1939 (2012)
24. Diederich, S., Brendel, A.B., Kolbe, L.M.: On conversational agents in information systems research: analyzing the past to guide future work. In: Proceedings Internationa Conference Wirtschaftsinformatik, pp. 1550–1564 (2019)
25. Oracle, "Can Virtual Experiences Replace Reality? The future role for humans in delivering customer experience, p. 19 (2016)
26. Wünderlich, N.V., Paluch, S.: A nice and friendly chat with a bot: user perceptions of AI-based service agents. In: ICIS, no. 1, pp. 1–11 (2017)
27. Stock, R.M., Merkle, M.: Can humanoid service robots perform better than service employees? a comparison of innovative behavior cues (2018)
28. Feine, J., Gnewuch, U., Morana, S., Maedche, A.: A taxonomy of social cues for conversational agents. Int. J. Hum. Comput. Stud. 132, 161 (2019)
29. Verhagen, T., van Nes, J., Feldberg, F., van Dolen, W.: Virtual customer service agents: using social presence and personalization to shape online service encounters. J. Comput. Commun. 19(3), 529–545 (2014)
30. Fogg, B.J., Nass, C.: How users reciprocate to computers. In: ACM CHI, p. 331 (1997)
31. Gong, L.: How social is social responses to computers? The function of the degree of anthropomorphism in computer representations. Comput. Hum. Behav. 24(4), 1494–1509 (2008)

32. Gnewuch, U., Morana, S., Adam, M.T.P., Maedche, A.: Faster is not always better: understanding the effect of dynamic response delays in human-chatbot interaction. In: ECIS, pp. 1–17 (2018)
33. Araujo, T.: Living up to the chatbot hype: The influence of anthropomorphic design cues and communicative agency framing on conversational agent and company perceptions. Comput. Hum. Behav. **85**, 183–189 (2018)
34. Hanus, M.D., Fox, J.: Persuasive avatars: The effects of customizing a virtual salespersons appearance on brand liking and purchase intentions. Int. J. Hum. Comput. Stud. **84**, 33–40 (2015)
35. Sebastian, J., Richards, D.: Changing stigmatizing attitudes to mental health via education and contact with embodied conversational agents. Comput. Hum. Behav. **73**, 479–488 (2017)
36. Sah, Y.J., Peng, W.: Effects of visual and linguistic anthropomorphic cues on social perception, self-awareness, and information disclosure in a health website. Comput. Hum. Behav. **45**, 392–401 (2015)
37. Schuetzler, R.M., Giboney, J.S., Grimes, G.M., Nunamaker, J.F.: The influence of conversational agents on socially desirable responding. HICSS **9**, 283–292 (2018)
38. Ekman, P., Friesen, W.V.: The repertoire of nonverbal behavior: categories, origins, usage, and coding. Semiotica **1**(1), 49–98 (1969)
39. Mayer, R.E., Johnson, W.L., Shaw, E., Sandhu, S.: Constructing computer-based tutors that are socially sensitive: politeness in educational software. Int. J. Hum. Comput. Stud. **64**(1), 36–42 (2006)
40. Shevchuk, N., Oinas-Kukkonen, H.: Exploring green information systems and technologies as persuasive systems: a systematic review of applications in published research. In: ICIS, pp. 1–11 (2016)
41. El Kamali, M., Angelini, L., Caon, M., Andreoni, G., Khaled, O.A., Mugellini, E.: Towards the Nestore e-Coach: A tangible and embodied conversational agent for older adults, in UbiComp/ISWC 2018, pp. 1656–1663 (2018)
42. Hamari, J.: Transforming homo economicus into homo ludens: a field experiment on gamification in a utilitarian peer-to-peer trading service. Electron. Commer. Res. Appl. **12**(4), 236–245 (2013)
43. Xu, K., Lombard, M.: Persuasive computing: feeling peer pressure from multiple computer agents. Comput. Hum. Behav. **74**, 152–162 (2017)
44. Harjunen, V.J., Spapé, M., Ahmed, I., Jacucci, G., Ravaja, N.: Persuaded by the machine: the effect of virtual nonverbal cues and individual differences on compliance in economic bargaining. Comput. Hum. Behav. **87**, 384–394 (Oct. 2018)
45. Adler, R.F., Iacobelli, F., Gutstein, Y.: Are you convinced? a wizard of oz study to test emotional vs. rational persuasion strategies in dialogues. Comput. Hum. Behav. **57**, 75–81 (2016)
46. Boudreau, M.C., Gefen, D., Straub, D.W.: Validation in information systems research: a state-of-the-art assessment. MIS Q. Manage. Inf. Syst. **25**(1), 1–16 (2001)
47. Erdfelder, E., FAul, F., Buchner, A., Lang, A.G.: Statistical power analyses using G*Power 3.1: tests for correlation and regression analyses. Behav. Res. Meth. **41**(4), 1149–1160 (2009). https://doi.org/10.3758/BRM.41.4.1149
48. Lezzi, E., Fleming, P., Zizzo, D.J.: Does it matter which effort task you use? a comparison of four effort tasks when agents compete for a prize. SSRN Electron. J. (2015)
49. Dennis, A.R., Valacich, J.S.: Conducting experimental research in information systems. Commun. Assoc. Inf. Syst. **7**(5), 1–41 (2001)
50. Bagozzi, R.P., Yi, Y.: On the use of structural equation models in experimental designs. J. Mark. Res. **26**(3), 271 (1989)

51. Fombelle, P.W., Bone, S.A., Lemon, K.N.: Responding to the 98%: face-enhancing strategies for dealing with rejected customer ideas. J. Acad. Mark. Sci. **44**(6), 685–706 (2015). https://doi.org/10.1007/s11747-015-0469-y
52. Trenz, M., Veit, D., Tan, C.-W.: Disentangling the impact of omnichannel integration on consumer behavior in integrated sales channels. Manag. Inf. Syst. Q. **44**(3) (2020)
53. Clark, L., et al.: What makes a good conversation? Challenges in designing truly conversational agents. In: Conference on Human Factors in Computing Systems - Proceedings, vol. 12 (2019)
54. Puca, R.M., Schmalt, H.D.: Task enjoyment: a mediator between achievement motives and performance. Motiv. Emot. **23**(1), 15–29 (1999)
55. Wrzesniewski, A., Dutton, J.E., Debebe, G.: Interpersonal sensemaking.pdf. Res. Organ. Behav. **25**, 93–135 (2003)
56. Bussell, H., Forbes, D.: Understanding the volunteer market: the what, where, who and why of volunteering. Int. J. Nonprofit Volunt. Sect. Mark. **7**(3), 244–257 (2002)
57. Agarwal, R., Sinha, A.P., Tanniru, M.: Cognitive fit in requirements modeling: a study of object and process methodologies. J. Manag. Inf. Syst. **13**(2), 137–162 (1996)
58. Durward, D., Blohm, I., Leimeister, J.M.: The nature of crowd work and its effects on individuals' work perception. J. Manag. Inf. Syst. **37**(1), 66–95 (2020)

Exploring the State-of-the-Art of Persuasive Design for Smart Personal Assistants

Dennis Benner[1(✉)], Sofia Schöbel[1], and Andreas Janson[2]

[1] University of Kassel, Information Systems, Kassel, Germany
{dennis.benner,sofia.schoebel}@uni-kassel.de
[2] Institute of Information Management, University of St, GallenSt. Gallen, Switzerland
andreas.janson@unisg.ch

Abstract. Driven by technological advances, smart personal assistants (SPA) have gained importance in human–computer interaction. SPA can influence user behavior and persuade users to reach a specific outcome. However, users often lack the motivation to interact with SPA. One way to support this interaction is persuasive system design – considering concepts as gamification and nudging. Although SPA research has increased recently, there is still no shared knowledge about persuasive designs. Therefore, we aim to identify the current state-of-the-art Design for persuasive SPA to understand how interactions and designs can be improved. Thus, we conduct a systematic literature analysis to represent how gamification and digital nudging are used to design SPA and conclude if and how those concepts can support SPA interactions. Consequently, we contribute to theory, providing better understanding about SPA interaction and design to make SPA more engaging and entertaining. Practitioners can use this contribution for persuasive SPA designs.

Keywords: Smart personal assistants · Persuasive Design · Persuasive agents

1 Introduction

With the increasing digitalization and influx of new information technologies, the impact of machines on people's lives is growing [1]. This growing impact extends to human decision-making, influencing human behavior as well as the interaction between humans and computers [2]. One trend that heavily impacts this human–computer interaction (HCI) is smart technical objects (STO). They are context-sensitive technical artifacts that use artificial intelligence (AI) and support (semi-)autonomous behavior to enhance the interaction [3]. STO include smart personal assistants (SPA), which are software programs that use AI and natural language to communicate with humans in a human-like fashion [4, 5]. SPA fulfil tasks, provide assistance or smart services to users that change the user experience as well as personal satisfaction [6–8]. This technology offers various possible applications for research and practice, which have been successfully applied in the past [9, 10]. For example, SPA are used in the context of e-commerce and customer service [7] because they can deliver a human-like experience that is always

F. Ahlemann et al. (Eds.): WI 2021, LNISO 47, pp. 316–332, 2021.
https://doi.org/10.1007/978-3-030-86797-3_21

available [11]. These properties can positively transform the provider–user interaction and user experience permanently [12, 13], which may prove to be a key success factor for companies [14]. Consequently, the interest in SPA is expected to grow, as Gartner predicts that by 2020 up to 25% of all customer service operations will make use of SPA [15]. Therefore, SPA are expected to be the new standard path for users to interact with service providers [16]. Overall, the global market of SPA is expected to grow by 24,3% until 2025. This equals a total market net worth of 1.25 billion US-Dollar [17].

However, SPA do have their share of problems. A recent survey on the interaction of users with an SPA shows that 58% of users could not complete their task (customer support inquiry), 52% did not like the interaction and 73% stated that they did not enjoy SPA in general [18]. Academic studies confirm these issues and highlight that users get demotivated because of bad SPA design, as Pricilla et al. [19] and Adam et al. [7] find in their studies in the field of e-commerce and self-service. These problems will eventually result in unsatisfactory experiences [7], bad performance and ultimately also to the failure of badly designed SPA [20]. Oftentimes, this bad design refers to the general ability to motivate users to engage and interact with the SPA as well as the ability to create joyful and satisfying user experiences. This shortcoming in current SPA design indicates that such designs lack the means for sustainable user motivation and engagement, thus missing to deeply consider the psychological needs of users and reducing effects on desired behavioral changes in users. This in return may lead to users not properly interacting with SPA, aborting their interaction and eventually rejecting SPA in total. Therefore, the need for an engaging and motivating SPA design arises that satisfies the needs of users and thus prevents failures [16, 20].

Current literature regarding SPA design lacks knowledge about design elements and configurations [21], especially in the area of persuading users to motivate and engage them to change their behavior towards a desired goal. To solve this problem, it can be referred to concepts that engage users and guide them during the interaction with an SPA, combining motivating components with components that alter a user's behavior. In doing so, service providers can, for example, make users disclose more non-private information to the SPA with the ultimate goal of improving the interaction (e.g., providing better assistance or recommending better suited products to the customer).

Two related ways to implement such components is to refer to persuasive system designs, which considers gamification [22] and digital nudging [23]. Gamification in its essence is the use of game design elements in a non-game context [24] that can positively impact motivation and engagement as well as change behavior [25, 26]. Digital nudging (or simply "nudging"), on the other hand, simply makes use of small design elements that persuade humans to pursue a specific behavior [23]. This can be illustrated with an example: interacting with an SPA more effectively and thus receiving better service is in the interest of both user and service provider. Consequently, we propose the design idea of "persuasive smart personal assistants" (pSPA). The concept of pSPA relies on persuasive technology and design that motivates users (in a gameful fashion) and persuades (or nudges) them to change their behavior in favor of a desired outcome [27].

Therefore, we aim to combine the two related concepts of gamification and digital nudging in the effort to create a first pSPA concept in order to increase the motivation of users during the interaction with SPA. Thus, we seek to address the research gap on SPA design and answer the following two research questions (RQ):

RQ1: What is the state-of-the-art design for persuasive smart personal assistants?

RQ2: How do current SPA incorporate persuasive design features?

We will answer these two questions by conducting a systematic analysis of current literature [28–31]. Ultimately, our research will contribute to the knowledge base for SPA design by analyzing current SPA designs with persuasive features.

The structure of this research paper is as follows. First, the theoretical background for relevant topics, like SPA and persuasive system design, is explained. Then the research methodology is presented. Next, the results of the literature review are discussed. The paper then closes with a conclusion, implications of the results and the importance for future research as well as a planned research agenda.

2 Theoretical Background

2.1 Smart Personal Assistants and User Interaction

The term "Smart Personal Assistant" (SPA) is an umbrella term for technological artifacts (i.e., computer programs) that use voice, vision and contextual information to interact with humans [32]. The general idea behind SPA is a technology-based approach to fulfill tasks and to provide assistance for humans [3, 5, 33]. Modern SPA additionally make use of AI – including machine learning (ML) and natural language processing (NLP) – to interact with humans [4]. Such SPA are nowadays omnipresent, as in the Facebook messenger app [9].

In the narrow sense modern SPA are often defined as "smart voice assistants" and restricted to examples like Alexa or Siri. However, with this study, we want to analyze the state of the art of how to make user–SPA interactions more engaging to support users in changing their behavior. Consequently, in this research paper we use a broader definition that includes all kinds of assistants that often are used synonymously with "intelligent assistants", "virtual assistants" and "conversational agents". Such a broader definition also includes simple rule-based chatbots that may not be "smart" but may incorporate persuasive design features, which may prove to be useful for our planned contribution. Additionally, human-like artifacts such as robots will be included in this research, since the outcome of SPA and robots (i.e., embodied agents that may appear human-like) is the same [34]. We apply this broader scope to evaluate as many implementations and concepts – like gamification or digital nudging – as possible that may be applicable to our proposed persuasive design concept for smart personal assistants. Hence, the definition of SPA in this paper is any technological artifact that interacts in a human-like fashion with the user to fulfill a task or provide assistance.

Accordingly, SPA and users interact with each other. To better design interactive dialogues between a user and an SPA, they also incorporate techniques that include social norms and emotional aspects of interpersonal communication to address the psychological needs of users [4, 5, 35]. SPA imitate humans and try to address the psychological needs of humans, which are defined as the universal, basic needs inherent in every person.

These needs are a driving factor behind engagement, motivation as well as an efficient and effective user–SPA interaction. If users are not satisfied, they get demotivated or frustrated easily [36].

2.2 Persuasive System Design and Corresponding Concepts

Persuasion can be defined as a form of communication with the intention to influence decisions and behaviors of people so that a desired outcome is achieved [37, 38]. Thus, the aim of persuasive technology and persuasive systems – henceforth Persuasive System Design (PSD) – is to influence users and their behavior to achieve a desirable outcome using persuasive design for information technology and systems [27]. To design persuasive technology or persuasive systems, the most prominent and effective concepts are gamification and digital nudging.

Gamification can be considered a persuasive technology that aims to exert influence over human behavior, which can be more powerful than monetary incentives [25]. A popular and widely accepted definition of gamification with a broad scope is the use of game design elements in a non-game context [24]. In addition to changing user behavior towards a desired outcome, gamification can provide a joyful experience and address hedonic aspects of products (i.e., services employing an SPA), which is significant for the user experience [39, 40].

Digital nudging, on the other hand, does not offer such joyful experiences but rather "nudges" humans towards a desired outcome [41]. Nudging, however, focuses on persuading people to change their behavior towards a desired outcome by using small design elements that influence the choice and behavior of people in a predictable way [23]. The main difference to gamification is that nudging explicitly affects user choice and must not forbid any options or change monetary incentives to achieve the desired behavior. However, both gamification and digital nudging are related and can support users in changing their behavior – or, more precisely, persuade users to reach a specific outcome a desired behavior.

Thus, we aim to highlight what similarities between gamification and digital nudging exist and how they can be applied to persuasive design for SPA. To compare and combine gamification and digital nudging, one must consider the different theoretical backgrounds and psychological needs these two persuasive methods employ. Despite the differences, gamification and nudging can be compared regarding their theoretical background [42]. An overlap regarding the psychological effects can be identified, which are (1) social norms, (2) priming, (3) motivation, (4) choice and (5) representation. Accordingly, gamification and digital nudging try to address the inner human needs of autonomy, relatedness and competence. This way, both gamification and digital nudging address similar basic psychological needs in human beings while also using similar theoretical backgrounds [36].

Apart from the shared goal of addressing psychological needs, gamification and nudging refer to design elements that instantiate the design of a persuasive technology. Gamification makes use of game design elements that address the psychological effects just mentioned. These design elements can be organized in a taxonomy along factors and attributes [43]. In our research we use the established game design element taxonomy introduced by Schöbel et al. [43]. On the one hand, factors represent the overarching category of design elements and the mechanic they use (e.g., progress, rewards and guidance). On the other hand, attributes express the actual implementations that refer to the overarching category (i.e., factors). For example, the attributes of *points* and *badges* refer to the factor *rewards*, while the attributes of *feedback avatars* and *representing avatars* refer to the factor *guidance*.

Similar to gamification, nudging also uses some specific design elements. However, unlike game design elements used in gamification that provide an established taxonomy, the categorization of design elements used for nudging is fairly new. Nevertheless, categorization is possible as Schöbel et al. [44] demonstrate. This taxonomy presents the following categories: default, representation and framing, information, feedback, time delay, social, and progress. The default nudge refers to default settings (e.g., cookie settings of a website). Representation and framing addresses visual factors like colors. Information and feedback nudges focus on providing knowledge, with information nudges being more general and feedback nudges being focused on a specific task or context. The time delay nudge is essentially equal to the time pressure game design element of gamification, limiting the user's time to make decisions. The social nudge refers to the user's social needs (e.g., social comparison), similar to how leaderboards address the need for social comparison in gamification. The progress element is also almost identical between nudging and gamification.

By comparing gamification and nudging design elements, a clear overlap between some elements can be observed. The most obvious overlapping design elements between gamification and nudging are time and progress, which are almost identical. Further, feedback is similarly defined in both gamification and nudging. However, gamification may focus more on visual feedback in this regard, while nudging may focus more on text-based feedback [43, 44]. Nevertheless, at the core both variants are identical in the sense that they keep the user aware about a circumstance or situation during the use of an information system [43, 44]. Apart from this overlap, some elements are unique to gamification and nudging, like gatherable points or badges to gamification and the default element to nudging.

With this background in mind, gamification and nudging can be combined in two ways. On the one hand, due to the existing overlap, the two concepts already support each other. On the other hand, both concepts provide exclusive design elements that can close the gaps between them and thus combine the advantages of mitigating possible disadvantages if applied on their own. For example, badges rely on a visual representation of the reward. This is not possible with voice assistants. Here, information and feedback nudges that mimic the content of the badge may be useful. This also highlights the importance of adjusting persuasive design elements to the properties of SPAs. Hence, gamification and digital nudging can both complement each other in addressing the psychological needs of users and translate them into a viable design for pSPA that are adjusted to the pSPA properties. In other words, persuasive design elements should be used according to the user–SPA interaction in question. Because the goal of this paper is to provide a broad view on options to apply PSD to SPA, restrictions like on digital nudging [23] are dropped. Consequently, we use the following definition for PSD in this research paper: Persuasive system design is the usage of any design element that exerts influence over users to change their behavior in a desirable fashion. To derive our concept of pSPA, we will take a closer look at what previous research studies have done to consider digital nudges and gamification in relation to SPA. Afterwards, we will try to find similarities between both concepts to better understand how we can support users with pSPA.

3 Research Methodology

To answer the research questions, a systematic literature review was conducted. The literature review was conducted according to the suggestions proposed by Cooper [28], Fettke [30] and Vom Brocke et al. [29]. A simplified process of our structured literature review that we adapted from Fettke [30] can be seen in Fig. 1 below.

Fig. 1. Structured literature review process

Starting with the definition of our review, the goal was to explore the current state-of-the-art design options for pSPA. Hence, we focused on the integration of results with a focus on used design elements. The scope of the literature review was explorative so that the spectrum of state-of-the-art designs is as complete as possible. Accordingly, the structure was thematical and methodical (Table 1).

Table 1. Literature review classification

Characteristic	Category		
Goal	Integration	Criticism	Central topics
Scope	Representative	Selective	Explorative
Focus	Outcomes	Designs	Theories
Structure	Historical	Thematical	Methodical

The next step was the preparation of our literature search. Here, we defined necessary keywords and search strings that we used for our database search. Hence, we defined keywords that represent various forms and descriptions of SPA. These keywords included "virtual assistants", "smart assistants" and "conversational agents" as well as "gamification" and "nudging". Additionally, we also included the term "collaboration" as an optional keyword to highlight the collaborating factor in user–SPA interaction. We did this because of the role of SPA in collaborative settings, where users and SPA create value together in smart services [3]. Accordingly, we formulated the following search string (optional search terms are in square brackets) that we adapted to the specifications of every database including the use of wildcards:

```
[collab* AND] (virtual OR smart OR conversational)
AND (agent? OR assistant?) AND (nudg* OR Gamif*)
```

As for the databases, ScienceDirect, AISeL, IEEEXplore, EBSCOhost and ACM were included. Because of the novelty of this specific topic and the desired broad scope for the review, the literature was not subjected to any restrictions like publication date, peer-reviewed literature or ratings, and grey literature was considered as well, since it can provide value and broaden the horizon [45]. Additionally, we conducted a forward and backward as well as open search for further literature. A total of 5017 papers were found during the initial database literature search. Those papers were narrowed down to 691 papers, selected by title and abstract. Of those 691 papers, only 135 were selected for further reading after scanning their content. Those 135 papers were then examined thoroughly, and 23 papers remained and were found as relevant. These findings include forward and backward as well as open search. We based the inclusion or exclusion of studies on the implementation of gamification and nudging as well as the implemented artifact. Concerning the latter, we here referred to the taxonomy of Knote et al. [3]. However, we also included artifacts that do not fit to this taxonomy, based on the findings of Tussyadiah and Miller [34], who state that robotic artifacts are similar to virtual agents, which are defined in the taxonomy, and provide the same outcome. Concerning gamification and nudging, we included studies that apply to the definitions we describe in the theoretical background and excluded those that do not.

Consequently, the results of the gathered literature are then organized in concept matrices according to Webster and Watson to gain a deeper understanding of the composition of current persuasive design elements for SPA [31]. SPA come in different forms and shapes with various features; thus, SPA need to be categorized accordingly. To categorize SPA a simplified taxonomy by Knote et al. [3] is used, where only categories relevant to this topic are included, such as communication and representation. Literature that does not implement SPA but instead theorizes about SPA or implements related artifacts such as robots is listed in the "other" category. Gamification and digital nudging design elements will be categorized according to simplified taxonomies by Schöbel et al. [43, 44]. These taxonomies will be narrowed down to relevant categories and combined considering similarities and differences of design elements of gamification and digital nudging.

4   Results

The 23 analyzed papers show a heterogenous mixture of journal and conference contributions as well as gray literature. Unlike the composition, the publication dates are more homogenous; almost all publications are from the late 2010s with a few exceptions from the 2000s. We examined the 23 resulting papers regarding their implementation of SPA and use of persuasive design elements such as gamification and digital nudging. The detailed results regarding the composition of SPA and similar artifacts can be found in Table 2 (see 4.1). Detailed results regarding the composition of persuasive design elements can be found in Table 3 (see 4.2).

4.1 Status Quo of SPA Design with Persuasive Features

The table below shows the status quo of the design of SPA that include persuasive design features from the literature we included. We used the taxonomy provided by Knote et al. [3] as a blueprint and simplified the taxonomy for our research.

Table 2. Status quo of smart personal assistants with persuasive features

Author (Year)	Communication T	A	V	P	Directionality U	B	Complexity 1	2	Behavior S	D	Representation N	C	O	Other
Backhaus et al. (2018)		X	X			X						X	X	X
Brotman et al. (2015)				X										X
Dokukina/Gumanova (2020)	X													X
Eigenbrod/Janson (2018)														X
Falk et al. (2018)	X					X	X		X	X				
Filimon et al. (2019)		X				X	X		X	X				
Fischbach et al. (2018)		X	X		X		X					X	X	X
Fogli et al. (2016)	X				X		X		X			X		X
Hwang et al. (2019)	X				X		X	X			X			X
Kocielnik et al. (2016)														X
Kuz et al. (2017)	X				X		X		X		X			
Lange et al. (2020)	X				X		X		X		X			X
Lechler et al. (2019)	X				X		X		X		X			
Maedche et al. (2019)														X
Martinez-Miranda et al. (2008)	X		X		X		X		X			X		X
Sheth et al. (2019)	X				X		X		X		X			X
Silva-Coira et al. (2016)	X					X	X		X	X				
Smutny/Schreiberova (2020)	X	X	X			X	X		X			X	X	X
Strohmann et al. (2018)														X
Turk (2017)		X	X			X	X		X			X	X	X
Tussyadiah/Miller (2019)														X
Weisz et al. (2019)	X					X	X	X	X		X			
Xiao et al. (2019)	X					X	X	X	X		X			
Sum (23)	13	5	5	1	8	8	9	6	10	5	9	7	4	16

T = text; A = audio/voice; V = video/visual; P = passive; U = unidirectional; B = bidirectional;
1 = low complexity (rule-based, basic NLP); 2 = high complexity (advanced NLP and ML);
S = static; D = adaptive; N = none; C = virtual character; O = audio/voice only
Other = including non-SPA artifacts such as robots or literature simply theorizing about persuasive design for SPA (e.g., future research directions)

We observed that most implementations in this study are mainly text-based (13 out of 23 studies), with a few exceptions that incorporate audio or voice (5) and visual forms (5) of communication. The interaction directionality (i.e., whether the interaction is one- or two-sided) is split relatively evenly (8 studies each). The complexity of the viewed SPA is also split with a slight tendency towards lesser complexity, with 9 studies choosing less complex and 6 studies opting for a more complex SPA design. This suggests that the current SPA design is built upon less complex methods like simple rule-based SPA or simple natural language applications in contrast to complex and advanced natural language processing and machine learning methods. SPA behavior is also tilted towards less complex static SPA in contrast to adaptive SPA (e.g., SPA that can be personalized), with 10 studies opting for static and only 5 for adaptive. The representation of SPA is mixed. Most text-based SPA do not use any form of representation (9), whereas SPA that use other forms of communication tend to have visual (7) and/or voice (4) representation. Additionally, it is noteworthy that many studies, regardless of whether they implement an actual SPA or not, at least indirectly acknowledge the existence of some persuasive influence in their study.

4.2 Persuasive Design Elements from Literature

A large portion of literature we analyzed does not directly implement an SPA. Instead, many authors rather chose to theorize about persuasive designs for SPA or simply highlighted persuasive effects they observed. Moreover, unlike the overall design of SPA with persuasive features as presented above, the use of design elements referring to digital nudging and gamification is less consistent, as can be seen in Table 2 above.

However, analyzing the designs of the included SPA, we can still identify a certain pattern. There is a clear tendency towards the use of information elements (14) exclusively from nudging and feedback elements (10), which exist in both gamification and nudging. Moreover, 10 studies also combine feedback and information elements (see [34, 46–54]), resulting in what we call an information-feedback pattern. However, looking at other elements from both nudging and gamification on their own, we observe a rather nonuniform distribution of several design elements. Some elements – specifically from nudging – are missing entirely, like the default element to induce a desired behavior. Thus, we could not observe a clear tendency in design elements referring to gamification only, unlike with design elements that refer to digital nudging only (i.e., information elements). Regardless, game design elements are used for SPA to a certain degree. The most prominent observation of a game design element that exclusively refers to gamification is design elements that address the collection (5) mechanic. These include the collection of points or badges. Persuasive design elements that refer to both gamification and digital nudging, like design elements that address social norms and interactions, are being used as well. Studies use social comparison (3), as in rankings, and social collaboration (2), as in teamwork or trading things (e.g., virtual goods).

Additionally, it is noteworthy that some persuasive design elements are not being used at all. We could not observe design elements referring to progress (e.g., progress bars, levels) and default (e.g., default settings).

Table 3. State-of-the-Art Persuasive Design Elements from Literature

Author (Year)	R	I	F	T	L	S	P	C	A	Z
Backhaus et al. (2018)								X		
Brotman et al. (2015)	X		X	X						
Dokukina/Gumanova (2020)	X	X	X					X		
Eigenbrod/Janson (2018)		X			X					
Falk et al. (2018)		X								
Filimon et al. (2019)					X			X		
Fischbach et al. (2018)						X				
Fogli et al. (2016)						X		X		
Hwang et al. (2019)		X	X							
Kocielnik et al. (2016)		X	X							
Kuz et al. (2017)										X
Lange et al. (2020)		X								
Lechler et al. (2019)	X	X	X							
Maedche et al. (2019)										
Martinez-Miranda et al. (2008)								X	X	
Sheth et al. (2019)		X								
Silva-Coira et al. (2016)	X	X	X							
Smutny/Schreiberova (2020)										
Strohmann et al. (2018)		X	X							
Turk (2017)	X	X	X							
Tussyadiah/Miller (2019)		X	X		X					
Weisz et al. (2019)		X	X							
Xiao et al. (2019)		X	X							
Sum (23)	5	14	11	1	3	2	0	5	1	1

R = representation (framing, avatars); I = information (knowledge, hints); F = feedback (response);
T = time (pressure); L = social comparison (leaderboards); S = social collaboration (interaction, exchange); P = progress (levels, bars); C = collection (points, badges); A = aspiration (goals, quests); Z = gameful or playful design only

R = representation (framing, avatars); I = information (knowledge, hints); F = feedback (response);
T = time (pressure); L = social comparison (leaderboards); S = social collaboration (interaction, exchange); P = progress (levels, bars); C = collection (points, badges); A = aspiration (goals, quests);
Z = gameful or playful design only

4.3 Text-Based Information and Feedback Assistants

In the results of our structured literature analysis we found a common design pattern among existing SPA. This pattern defined by its usage of persuasive design elements and general SPA properties. We define this pattern of text-based information and feedback assistants as TIFA, which can be considered a subcategory and/or design pattern of SPA. Artifacts that can be categorized as TIFA also show a tendency to unidirectional communication, static behavior and low complexity. This highlights the role of artifacts that fit the TIFA pattern. This approach to pSPA focuses on simple, unidirectional user–SPA interaction without adaptive behavior or advanced NLP/ML methods, which indicates some sort of "mentor" or "instructor" role of those pSPA. This TIFA pattern diverges from general observed SPA design in two ways. To illustrate how general SPA or pSPA compare to TIFA, we compare the concepts (see Fig. 2; note that scales are relative and not an absolute representation of literature). First, TIFA are less complex regarding technology and implementation than regular SPA or other observed pSPA implementations. Second, TIFA focus entirely on two persuasive design elements – information and feedback. However, this does not imply TIFA cannot be supported by other persuasive design elements.

Fig. 2. Comparison of observed SPA and TIFA pattern

We observed that some TIFA may implement design elements that use collection and social comparison, although these are not the norm for this pSPA pattern. The only true exception to this pattern is "ElliQ" [52], which is an embodied agent (e.g., robotic artifact) that combines information and feedback with focus on audiovisual interaction. This advanced artifact is also able to adapt to user behavior and the emotional state to provide adequate feedback.

5 Discussion and Contributions

5.1 The State of SPA Research and Persuasive Design

The goal of our systematic literature review was to provide an overview of designs with persuasive elements currently used in SPA research. In doing so, we answered two research questions with this study. Firstly, we want to stress that methodological research concerning a persuasive design for SPA is lacking and should be pursued in further research to gain more detailed knowledge. Secondly, we must clarify that some authors do not explicitly call their artifact an SPA or state that they implemented a persuasive design. Instead, some simply call their artifacts "agents" (e.g., [34, 55]) and/or highlight persuasive effects such as behavioral changes trough persuasive design elements (e.g., [34, 49, 55, 56]). Additionally, some other authors do not implement an SPA, persuasive design or other artifact at all. However, they do theorize about persuasive design regarding SPA. Many highlight the positive effects of designing the interaction in an engaging, game-like way, citing possible persuasive design elements derived from gamification such as rewards or reminders (e.g., [46, 50, 57–60]). Many other authors highlight the possible effects and uses of digital nudging for SPA by theorizing about its effects or implementation (e.g., [9, 34, 47–49, 51–54, 61–63]). Simply selecting and combining game design elements (or nudge elements respectively) does not necessarily support the intended behavioral change of users. There is some support in literature that one cannot refer to standardized solutions by simply integrating badges or points [64] to make an SPA interaction more entertaining. Likewise, when designing pSPA it needs to be considered how game design elements and nudge elements need to be designed and adapted to a context an SPA is interacting in. In general, authors that choose to focus on theorizing about the uses of persuasive design or effects on user behavior of SPA always include either gamification or digital nudging, with the latter being the prevalent theme. Authors repeatedly recognize the potential effects on user behavior and acknowledge future research potential regarding the application of gamification and/or digital nudging to SPA (e.g., [9, 64]).

In our study we find several persuasive design elements are being used that refer to the concepts of gamification and digital nudging. Some of them are used less frequently with no recognizable pattern, and others are used rather often with a recognizable pattern, often even combined. The prime example for this is the combination of the design elements of information and feedback [34, 46–54]. As described, many authors use those design elements either on their own or in combination. All studies, except one, that combine these elements use text-based SPA. This marks the greatest commonality that can be observed when analyzing current SPA that implement persuasive design elements. According to our literature analysis, this seems to be the go-to pattern for designing persuasive smart personal assistants. We emphasize on this pattern that we found in literature specifically, because of its prevalent usage over in multiple studies, where no other combination of design elements and SPA properties has shown usage to such an extent. However, this does not imply that there are no other patterns or combinations that may be relevant as well which other studies may find.

In general, many SPA designs incorporate persuasive elements, and authors use a persuasive design for their SPA, although most often only in an implicit way. In other words, many researchers do not explicitly apply persuasive design to their SPA but instead recognize the persuasive character and potential of their implementations retrospectively. This may point towards a lack of awareness about persuasive design and theory. On the other hand, authors are in fact aware of the effects. Considering the shortcomings in current SPA design and research as well as the highlighted potential of pSPA, we want to emphasize the importance of gaining awareness and consequently knowledge about this topic. Nevertheless, first approaches to designing persuasive agents or at least theorizing about persuasive effects of SPA designs that include gamification or digital nudging concepts can be found in the current literature. Another factor we want to highlight is that the majority of studies do not focus on the use of theories, psychological needs and effects or the preferences of the users but rather use ad hoc implementations of persuasive design. Another issue present in current SPA design research is the choice of persuasive design elements. While a common theme for information and feedback design elements can be observed, this cannot be said for other persuasive design elements.

Lastly, we want to state it may be valuable to examine progress, default and status quo design elements more closely to get an understanding why these are not used in the literature and may not work for pSPA design. In this regard, other studies may find different patterns similar to TIFA or entirely new ones in the future as research continues, designs change, and new artifacts are developed.

5.2 Theoretical and Practical Contributions

With our study, we provide implications for research and practice. Our research contributes to theory regarding general SPA interaction and design as well as theory about gamification and digital nudging. As a result of our systematic literature analysis, we identified the state-of-the-art persuasive design of today's SPA that is leaning towards SPA that primarily incorporate digital nudging and, to a certain degree, some game design elements. We introduce the TIFA pattern as a prevalent state-of-the-art theme for the design of current pSPA. We also identified several general shortcomings in current SPA design research and presented possible approaches to address those issues. Therefore, we contribute to theory by highlighting areas for future research about pSPA and about how to make a human–SPA interaction more meaningful. Practical implications can be given to developers of SPA about what to consider to better motivate and support users in an interaction with an SPA. From a practical perspective it is important to consider SPA designs that focus on how to better engage users in a SPA interaction to make it more effective and efficient for both the user and the constructor or a SPA (mainly a company or an institution). As a result, with our work, we provide a novel approach to practitioners about what to care about when constructing pSPA.

6   Conclusion, Limitations and Future Research

The goal of our paper was twofold. First, we wanted to provide an overview of the status quo of SPA design in order to describe a state-of-the-art design for persuasive smart personal assistants (RQ1). Second, we wanted to analyze how current SPA designs incorporate persuasive design features that refer to the concepts of gamification and nudging (RQ2). To address our research questions, we therefore conducted a structured literature review using established literature review methodology.

We presented theoretical studies and practical insights about the potential of SPA in general as well as the emerging opportunities for future research and practical applications of pSPA. In this regard we also presented a prevalent theme or pattern in current

SPA with persuasive features that we define as TIFA. This pattern takes both techni-cal properties of SPA as well as persuasive design features into account that refer to gamification and digital nudging concepts. Additionally, as a result of our structured lit-erature review, we find that today there is virtually no methodical research that directly addresses persuasive design approaches for SPA. However, studies that use gamification and nudging in combination do acknowledge the persuasive character of their artifacts to a certain degree. However, we also have to address our own limitations in this regard. As with all literature-based research, our contribution as well is limited by our decisions to include or exclude certain studies, our definition of keywords and our search pro-cess. Moreover, the TIFA pattern we found in literature may or may not be supported by other, future studies based on the literature they include. As we earlier mentioned, we may have also missed other commonalities or themes in SPA research that refer to persuasive design. Disregarding potential limitations of our research, we in general want to highlight a potential research gap for the persuasive design of SPA that offers direc-tions for future research. Future research should therefore focus on methodical design approaches, such as DSR, towards generalizable pSPA designs. Furthermore, conduct-ing a meta-analysis on the topic of persuasive designs for SPA or pSPA designs may be a worthwhile proposition for future research.

Overall, based on our structured literature analysis we can summarize that explicit persuasive design in SPA research provides promising future research directions since many studies already acknowledge the implicit persuasive character of their SPA. We hope our contribution will encourage researchers to address the limitations and future directions that we presented.

Acknowledgements. The research presented in this paper was funded by European Regional Development Fund (ERDF) in the context of the project KI-based Subscription Business Automa-tion (20007305), Grant No. pending. The project is conducted in cooperation with billwerk GmbH (see https://billwerk.com/forschungsprojekt-kiba/).

References

1. Bitkom e.V.: Die wichtigsten CRM-Trends im Check. https://www.bitkom.org/Themen/Tec hnologien-Software/CRM/CRM-Trends-2017/3-Chatbots.html
2. Skjuve, M., Haugstveit, I.M., Følstad, A., Brandtzaeg, P.B.: Help! Is my chatbot falling into the uncanny valley? an empirical study of user experience in human-chatbot interaction. Hum. Technol. **15**, 30–54 (2019)
3. Knote, R., Janson, A., Söllner, M., Leimeister, J.M.: Value co-creation in smart services: a functional affordances perspective on smart personal assistants. J. Assoc. Inf. Syst. (JAIS) **22**(2), 5 (2020)
4. Guzman, A.: Making AI safe for humans: a conversation with siri. Socialbots and their Friends: Digital Media and the Automation of Sociality, pp. 69–85 (2017)
5. Zhao, S.: Humanoid social robots as a medium of communication. New Media Soc. **8**, 401–419 (2006)
6. Medina-Borja, A.: Editorial column—smart things as service providers: a call for convergence of disciplines to build a research agenda for the service systems of the future. Serv. Sci. **7**, ii–v (2015)

7. Adam, M., Wessel, M., Benlian, A.: AI-based chatbots in customer service and their effects on user compliance. Electron. Mark. **31**(2), 427–445 (2020). https://doi.org/10.1007/s12525-020-00414-7

8. Beverungen, D., Müller, O., Matzner, M., Mendling, J., Vom Brocke, J.: Conceptualizing smart service systems. . Electron Mark. **29**, 7–18 (2019)

9. Maedche, A., et al.: AI-based digital assistants. Bus. Inf. Syst. Eng. **61**(4), 535–544 (2019). https://doi.org/10.1007/s12599-019-00600-8

10. Oracle: Can Virtual Experiences Replace Reality? The future role for humans in delivering customer experience (2019)

11. Meuter, M.L., Bitner, M.J., Ostrom, A.L., Brown, S.W.: Choosing among alternative service delivery modes: an investigation of customer trial of self-service technologies. J. Mark. **69**, 61–83 (2005)

12. Forbes: AI And Chatbots Are Transforming The Customer Experience. https://www.for bes.com/sites/shephyken/2017/07/15/ai-and-chatbots-are-transforming-the-customer-experi ence/

13. Reddy, T.: How chatbots can help reduce customer service costs by 30%. https://www.ibm. com/blogs/watson/2017/10/how-chatbots-reduce-customer-service-costs-by-30-percent/

14. Lemon, K.N., Verhoef, P.C.: Understanding customer experience throughout the customer journey. J. Mark. **80**, 69–96 (2016)

15. Gartner: Gartner Says 25 Percent of Customer Service Operations Will Use Virtual Customer Assistants by 2020. https://www.gartner.com/en/newsroom/press-releases/2018-02-19-gar tner-says-25-percent-of-customer-service-operations-will-use-virtual-customer-assistants-by-2020

16. Følstad, A., Brandtzæg, P.B.: Chatbots and the new world of HCI. Interactions **24**, 38–42 (2017)

17. Business Insider: Chatbot Market Size to Reach $1.25 Billion by 2025 I CAGR: 24.3%: Grand View Research, Inc. I Markets Insider

18. Koelwel, D.: Chatbots im E-Commerce: Entwicklung eilt der Akzeptanz voraus. https://www.estrategy-magazin.de/e-commerce/artikel/chatobots-im-e-commerce-entwicklung-eilt-der-akzeptanz-voraus-001543.html

19. Pricilla, C., Lestari, D.P., Dharma, D.: Designing interaction for chatbot-based conversational commerce with user-centered design. In: 5th International Conference on Advance Informat-ics: Concepts, Theory and Applications. ICAICTA, 14–17 August 2018, Beyond Resort, Krabi, Thailand, pp. 244–249. IEEE, Piscataway, NJ (2018)

20. Brandtzaeg, P.B., Følstad, A.: Chatbots: changing user needs and motivations. interactions **25**, 38–43 (2018)

21. Følstad, A., Brandtzaeg, P.B.: Users' experiences with chatbots: findings from a questionnaire study. Qual. User Exp. **5**(1), 1–14 (2020). https://doi.org/10.1007/s41233-020-00033-2

22. Morana, S., Friemel, C., Gnewuch, U., Maedche, A., Pfeiffer, J.: Interaktion mit smarten Systemen — Aktueller Stand und zukünftige Entwicklungen im Bereich der Nutzerassis-tenz. Wirtschaftsinformatik Manage. **9**(5), 42–51 (2017). https://doi.org/10.1007/s35764-017-0101-7

23. Thaler, R.H., Sunstein, C.R.: Nudge. Improving decisions about health, wealth, and happiness. Yale Univ. Press, New Haven, Conn (2008)

24. Deterding, S., Dixon, D., Khaled, R., Nacke, L.: From game design elements to gameful-ness: defining gamification. In: Proceedings of the 15th International Academic MindTrek Conference Envisioning Future Media Environments, pp. 9–15 (2011)

25. Blohm, I., Leimeister, J.M.: Gamification Bus Inf. Syst. Eng. **5**, 275–278 (2013)

26. Deterding, S.: Situated motivational afforances of game elements: a conceptual model. Computer Human Interfaces (2011)

27. Fogg, B.J.: Computers as persuasive social actors. In: Persuasive Technology, pp. 89–120. Elsevier (2003)
28. Cooper, H.M.: Organizing knowledge syntheses: a taxonomy of literature reviews. Knowl. Soc. **1**, 104–126 (1988)
29. Vom Brocke, J., Riemer, K., Plattfaut, R.: Standing on the shoulders of giants: challenges and recommendations of literature search in information systems research. CAIS 37 (2015)
30. Fettke, P.: State-of-the-Art des State-of-the-Art. Wirtsch. Inf. **48**, 431 (2006)
31. Webster, J., Watson, R.T.: Analyzing the past to prepare for the future: writing a literature review. MIS Q. 13–21 (2002)
32. McTear, M., Callejas, Z., Griol, D.: The conversational interface. Talking to smart devices. Springer, Cham (2016)
33. Hauswald, J., et al.: Designing future warehouse-scale computers for sirius, an end-to-end voice and vision personal assistant. ACM Trans. Comput. Syst. **34**, 1–32 (2016)
34. Tussyadiah, I., Miller, G.: Nudged by a robot: Responses to agency and feedback. Ann. Tour. Res. **78**, 102752 (2019)
35. Skalski, P., Tamborini, R.: The role of social presence in interactive agent-based persuasion. Media Psychol. **10**, 385–413 (2007)
36. Deci, E.L., Ryan, R.M.: The What and why of goal pursuits: human needs and the self-determination of behavior. Psychol. Inq. **11**, 227–268 (2000)
37. Simons, H.W., Morreale, J., Gronbeck, B.E.: Persuasion in society. SAGE, Thousand Oaks, Calif. (2001)
38. Briñol, P., Petty, R.E.: Chapter 2 Persuasion. In: Zanna, M.P. (ed.) Advances in experimental social psychology, 41, pp. 69–118. Academic Press, London, Amsterdam, Oxford, Burlington, MA, San Diego, Calif. (2009)
39. Zhou, H., Fu, X.: Understanding, measuring, and designing user experience: the causal relationship between the aesthetic quality of products and user affect. In: Proceedings of the 12th International Conference on Human-Computer Interaction: Interaction Design and Usability, pp. 340–349. Springer-Verlag, Berlin, Heidelberg (2007). https://doi.org/10.1007/978-3-540-73105-4_38
40. Sharp, H., Preece, J., Rogers, Y.: Interaction design. Beyond human-computer interaction (2019)
41. Acquisti, A., et al.: Nudges for privacy and security. ACM Comput. Surv. **50**, 1–41 (2017)
42. Lieberoth, A., Holm Jensen, N., Bredahl, T.: Selective psychological effects of nudging, gamification and rational information in converting commuters from cars to buses: a controlled field experiment. Transp. Res. Traffic Psychol. Behav. **55**, 246–261 (2018)
43. Schöbel, S., Ernst, S.-J., Söllner, M., Leimeister, J.M.: More than the sum of its parts - towards identifying preferred game design element combinations in learning management systems. short paper. International Conference on Information Systems (2017)
44. Schöbel, S., Barev, T.J., Janson, A., Hupfeld, F., Leimeister, J.M.: Understanding user preferences of digital privacy nudges – a best-worst scaling approach. In: Hawaii International Conference on System Sciences, pp. 3918–3927 (2020)
45. Mahood, Q., van Eerd, D., Irvin, E.: Searching for grey literature for systematic reviews: challenges and benefits. Res. Synth. Meth. **5**, 221–234 (2014)
46. Dokukina, I., Gumanova, J.: The rise of chatbots – new personal assistants in foreign language learning. Procedia Comput. Sci. **169**, 542–546 (2020)
47. Hwang, I., Lee, Y., Yoo, C., Min, C., Yim, D., Kim, J.: Towards interpersonal assistants: next-generation conversational agents. IEEE Pervasive Comput. **18**, 21–31 (2019)
48. Kocielnik, R., Xiao, L., Avrahami, D., Hsieh, G.: Reflection companion: a conversational system for engaging users in reflection on physical activity. Proc. ACM Interact. Mob. Wearable Ubiquitous Technol. **2**, 1–26 (2018)

49. Lechler, R., Stoeckli, E., Rietsche, R., Uebernickel, F.: LOOKING beneath the tip of the iceberg: the two-sided nature of chatbots and their roles for digital feedback exchange. In: European Conference on Information Systems (ECIS) (2019)
50. Silva-Coira, F., Cortinas, A., Pedeira, O.: Intelligent virtual assistant for gamified environments. Pacific Asia Conference on Information Systems (2016)
51. Strohmann, T., Fischer, S., Siemon, D., Brachten, F., Lattemann, C.: Virtual moderation assistance: creating design guidelines for virtual assistants supporting creative workshops. Pacific Asia Conference on Information Systems (2018)
52. Turk, V.: Home robot helps to keep you on your toes. New Sci. **233**, 9 (2017)
53. Weisz, J.D., Jain, M., Joshi, N.N., Johnson, J., Lange, I.: BigBlueBot: teaching strategies for successful human-agent interactions. IUI **19**, 448–459 (2019)
54. Xiao, Z., Zhou, M.X., Fu, W.-T.: Who should be my teammates: using a conversational agent to understand individuals and help teaming. IUI **19**, 437–447 (2019)
55. Brotman, R., Burleson, W., Forlizzi, J., Heywood, W., Lee, J.: Building change: constructive design of smart domestic environments for goal achievement. In: Begole, B., Kim, J., Inkpen, K., Woo, W. (eds.) Proceedings of the 33rd Annual ACM Conference on Human Factors in Computing Systems - CHI 2015, pp. 3083–3092. ACM Press, New York, New York, USA (2015)
56. Falk, J., Poulakos, S., Kapadia, M., Sumner, R.W.: PICA: proactive intelligent conversational agent for interactive narratives. In: Proceedings of the 18th IVA, pp. 141–146 (2018)
57. Filimon, M., Iftene, A., Trandabăţ, D.: Bob - a general culture game with voice interaction. Procedia Computer Science **159**, 323–332 (2019)
58. Fogli, D., Lanzilotti, R., Piccinno, A., Tosi, P.: AmI@Home: a game-based collaborative system for smart home configuration. AVI, pp. 308–309 (2016)
59. Martinez-Miranda, J., Bernhard, J., Payr, S., Petta, P.: The intermediary agent's brain: supporting learning to collaborate at the inter-personal level. In: Proceedings of 7th International Conference on Autonomous Agents and Multiagent Systems, pp. 1277–1280 (2008)
60. Smutny, P., Schreiberova, P.: Chatbots for learning: a review of educational chatbots for the facebook messenger. Comput. Educ. **151**, 103862 (2020)
61. Eigenbrod, L., Janson, A.: How digital nudges influence consumers - experimental investigation in the context of retargeting. In: European Conference on Information Systems (ECIS) (2018)
62. Sheth, A., Yip, H.Y., Shekarpour, S.: Extending patient-chatbot experience with internet-of-things and background knowledge: case studies with healthcare applications. IEEE Intell. Syst. **34**, 24–30 (2019)
63. Lange, P. de, Goschlberger, B., Farrell, T., Neumann, A.T., Klamma, R.: Decentralized learning infrastructures for community knowledge building. IEEE Trans. Learn. Technol. 1 (2020)
64. Liu, D., Santhanam, R., Webster, J.: Toward meaningful engagement: a framework for design and research of gamified information systems. MIS Q. **41**, 1011–1034 (2017)

Buy Online, Trust Local – The Use of Regional Imagery on Web Interfaces and Its Effect on User Behavior

Tobias Menzel[1,2]([envelope]) and Timm Teubner[1,2]

[1] Trust in Digital Services, Technische Universität Berlin, Berlin, Germany
`tobias.menzel@campus.tu-berlin.de, timm.teubner@tu-berlin.de`
[2] Einstein Center Digital Future, Berlin, Germany

Abstract. While regional cues are omnipresent in offline consumer life, the use of regional imagery is a still emerging trend in online retail. Applying a multi-method approach, we investigate the use of regional imagery on web interfaces and its effects on consumer behavior. We find that social, nature, and regional imagery is frequently used on energy provider websites and identify cityscapes and monuments as primary regional motives. Further, we outline an experiment to assess whether regional imagery promotes trust within online retail and how the presence of regionality interacts with the concepts of Social Presence and Nature Presence. Our contribution is twofold: First, we propose the psychological construct of Regional Presence to the IS literature, link it to theory, and describe its application in online retail. Second, we sketch out an experimental design to systematically study the effects of regional imagery on web interfaces.

Keywords: Social presence · Nature presence · Regional presence · Trust · Online retail

1 Introduction

References to people's home region have become a common practice in offline retail – think of ads promoting fruits "from the region". Such references are supposed to indicate quality [1], sustainability [2], local business support [3], and appeal to patriotism [4]. More recently, we observe an expansion of this practice to online retail – in particular in the form of regional imagery (e.g. of an identity-establishing building, landmark, or place). This study aims to increase understanding of a) the use of regional imagery on web interfaces and b) its effects on consumer behavior.

Since there is very little research on this phenomenon in the online retail context, our first research objective is of exploratory nature aiming to systematically capture a new phenomenon in IS research [5]. By means of content analysis of 318 energy provider websites, we set out to better understand the use of regional imagery on existing web interfaces. This qualitative method is well-established [6] and will increase the proposed study's practical applicability down the line [7]. To isolate the behavioral effects of perceived regionality, we focus on the electricity retail market for mainly two reasons:

© The Author(s), under exclusive license to Springer Nature Switzerland AG 2021
F. Ahlemann et al. (Eds.): WI 2021, LNISO 47, pp. 333–339, 2021.
https://doi.org/10.1007/978-3-030-86797-3_22

First, analyzing a homogenous *credence good* eliminates potential confounding effects based on product quality (e.g. freshness of a fruit produced in close geographic proximity may indeed be higher compared to other fruit and consumers can distinguish this product property either at the point of purchase or at least after having consumed the fruit. In contrast, electricity generated in closer proximity is physically identical with that generated further away). Second, it is supplied through networks. This eliminates the transportation cost effect since network fees are charged to consumers regardless of electricity's geographic origin. Hence, any effects can be fully attributed to the very idea of regionality. Our first research question reads:

RQ1:*To what extent do energy providers apply regional imagery on their websites? What types of regional imagery are used?*

The use of imagery to affect consumer behavior is well established in the fields of Marketing and Information Systems (IS; e.g. [8, 9]). Primarily, IS research has focused on social cues to generate consumer trust and trigger purchases. Gefen and Straub [8] have transferred Social Presence (SP) Theory to IS research to explain these effects. More recently, Schmuck et al. [10] have attested similar impact to nature imagery. Expressing the similarities to the SP construct, we use an analogous phrasing for Regional Presence (RP) and explore whether perceived regionality triggers similar effects as SP (i.e. trust, purchase intentions). Further, the interaction of the three concepts is of interest. Accordingly, our second research question asks:

RQ2: *Does Regional Presence promote trust (and ultimately purchase intentions) in online retail? How does it interact with Social and Nature Presence?*

To address these questions, we sketch out the design for an online experiment. Figure 1 provides an example (icons highlight the three concepts).

Fig. 1. Website Example with Regional, Social, and Nature Cues. Source: https://www.stadtw erke-goerlitz.de/privatkunden

2 Theoretical Background

To explain the behavioral effects of social, nature, and regional cues, several theories can be readily applied, including Social Presence Theory [11], the Biophilia Hypothesis

[12], and Consumer Ethnocentrism [13]. Ultimately, all theories build on evolutionarily patterns which we exploit to develop the RP construct.

Social Presence (SP). Social Presence Theory originates in the field of psychology, describing communication media's ability to transmit social cues [11]. Gefen and Straub [8] have transferred this concept to IS research and shown that social imagery on web interfaces generates perceived "personal, sociable, and sensitive human contact" (p. 410) despite the fact that online retail is characterized by a lack of such. The sensation of interpersonal contact decreases consumer anxiety towards online transactions which improves trust in the website and purchase intentions [9]. Ultimately, this is driven by the evolutionary pattern that humans increased chances of survival when interacting with other human beings [14, 15].

Nature Presence (NP). Similar to the above, natural imagery generates a virtual nature experience in the absence of real nature which provokes positive brand attitude and purchase intentions [10]. The Biophelia Hypothesis explains such effects by "the urge to affiliate with nature" (p. 85) [12]. Other evolutionary psychologists invoke restoration of attention [16] and stress reduction [17]. This is ultimately driven by the critical relevance of nature to human survival through provision of water, nutrition, and defense advantages [17].

Regional Presence (RP). In a similar fashion, evolutionary biology lends itself well to rationalize human preferences for regionality as well. For centuries, cohesion and solidarity of social groups like tribes and families have been essential to survival [18] which, today, translates into ethnocentric consumer behavior on a regional or national level [19]. This means is buying from the *in-group* (defined as the set of people with "which an individual identifies", p. 280) is preferred over buying from the *out-group* [13]. Practically speaking, Consumer Ethnocentrism suggests that consumers prefer regional products and services as purchasing otherwise "is wrong because […] it hurts the domestic economy, causes loss of jobs, and is plainly unpatriotic" (p. 280) [13]. We hypothesize that – similar to social and nature cues – the use of regional cues can influence users' psychology, subconsciously promoting trusting beliefs and, in turn, purchase intentions. RP can therefore be defined as the *sensation of regionality in a set-up characterized by geographic independence.*

3   Study 1: Content Analysis of *Stadtwerke* Websites

Methodology. Examining **RQ1**, we shortlisted 318 regional energy providers from an online resource [20], selecting corporations (AG or GmbH) referring to themselves as regional utilities (*"Stadtwerke"*). Next, we devised a web-scraper to take screenshots of all 318 landing webpages. These screenshots were coded for regional, social, and nature cues by two researchers individually. With Cohen's kappa [21] of 0.74 for regional, 0.75 for social, and 0.68 for nature cues, inter-rater reliability indicates substantial agreement [22]. Conflicting cases were resolved by a third researcher. Further, we classified regional imagery with regard to its content (e.g. cityscapes).

Results. As displayed in Fig. 2, the majority of the evaluated energy providers (215 out of 318) employ at least one of the three concepts. Social imagery is the dominant cue (125) but regional (78) and nature (69) imagery are often used as well. The most frequent combination is between regional and nature cues (27) while only three websites combine all three types. Figure 3 provides a breakdown of regional cues: In more than half of all cases (44 out of 78), the images show cityscapes. Other motives are buildings (15), monuments (13), and cultural events (6).

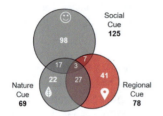

Fig. 2. Coding results   **Fig. 3.** Classification of regional cues

4   Study 2 (in progress): Design of an Online Experiment

Research Model and Hypothesis Development. Addressing **RQ2**, we seek to experimentally evaluate whether RP promotes trust (and purchase intentions) and how it interacts with SP and NP (see Fig. 4). We build on Gefen and Straub [8] and expand their model for RP, NP, and potential interaction effects. The relationship of SP on trust (e.g. [8, 9]) and, in turn, purchase intentions (e.g. [23]) is commonly accepted. Similar results have been found for NP (e.g. [10]). Hence, our hypotheses focus on 1) whether RP similarly promotes trust and 2) the interaction effects of RP, SP, and NP. We control for standard demographic variables, individual trusting disposition [24], environmental concern [25], and attitude towards home region [26].

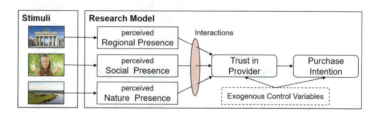

Fig. 4. Research model

Experiment Design. We plan to engage Prolific.ac [27] to recruit a German sample of around 350 participants (ensuring sufficient payment and attention checks). We will apply a full-factorial $2 \times 2 \times 2$ between-subjects design with regional, social, and nature cues as binary treatment variables (either present or not). Participants engage on a mock-up website with randomly assigned stimulus combinations. Social and nature imagery is drawn from provider websites while regional imagery will be participant specific. Therefore, participants will be asked to state their home region and the survey tool will build on this answer to draw stimulus material from a database of ~500 landmark images. We use validated 7-point Likert scales [28, 29]. For Social Presence, we draw on Gefen and Straub [28] and derive the NP and RP instruments from that.

5 Discussion and Concluding Remarks

Findings. Two out of three regional energy providers use regional, social, or nature imagery on their landing webpages. The frequent use of regional imagery (>20%) suggests that providers intentionally employ it to influence consumer behavior. When regional imagery is used, we observe a variety of different motives – with a tendency towards cityscapes (in particular aerial perspectives).

Theoretical Contributions. By addressing the "surprisingly understudied topic of regionality" (p. 44) [30], our (proposed) study promises contributions to IS research in multiple ways. First, while the usage and benefits of SP (and NP) cues are widely accepted in research on human-computer interaction, the proposed study could provide arguments to also include regional cues in future research projects. Second, we introduce a new theoretical concept that is potentially capable of capturing an important aspect of user perceptions when dealing or interacting with online interfaces. Motivated by the rich literature on the SP phenomenon, we propose a tangible measure for perceptions of regionality or one's home region. This alone provides a tool for shedding further light on the concept of (Consumer) Ethnocentrism which hypothesizes favorable consumer attitudes towards products based on their and the products' origin [13]. We extend this view in the sense that origin-match may not always be clear, let alone a dichotomous matter. In order to capture this, the proposed scale of RP allows to assess consumers' perspective. Third, with regard to tangible IS solutions such as load management [31] or peer-to-peer energy markets [32], we offer a new mean to generate trust in the energy provider that goes beyond the trust building letters to consumers proposed by Stenner et al. [31].

Practical Implications. For practitioners, our study yields new insights for the improvement of web interfaces in the energy sector. This sector has been subject to numerous calls for Green IS research to counter climate change [e.g.33–35]. In particular, IS solutions to "support decision making for more sustainable practices" (p.527) are needed [36]. Our findings could inform the design of web interfaces to support consumers in their decision making in favor of more renewable and regional (i.e., decentral) products and hence drive the sector's transition towards the triangular objective of *digitalization, decentralization,* and *decarbonization* [37]. Against this background, the design of websites is particularly relevant for regional energy providers as their websites are one of their major digital sales channels [38]. Also, insights gained in this study can be applied to other interface designs in the energy sector. With the rise of the platform economy in the energy sector, trust-infusing platform interfaces will be critical for the sectors' platformization and sustainabilization [39].

Limitations and Future Work. First, we have focused on imagery in this study. While this may be the most obvious cue type, we plan to expand our study to other elements such as textual keys (e.g. "Your partner from the region"). Second, our work focuses on energy providers as trust target, as suggested by [40]. Future work should also consider additional trust targets (e.g. the website itself). Third, the presented findings could be misused by non-regional providers and lead to a situation in which "consumers may intentionally be deceived" (p. 43) [30]. Further work should analyze this phenomenon of *regional washing* and assess discrepancies between perceived regionality and geographic proximity. Fourth, study 2 is drawing on a variance-based approach. Future work could methodically triangulate and apply additional analytical angles such as qualitative comparative analysis [41].

References

1. Loureiro, M.L., McCluskey, J.J.: Assessing consumer response to protected geographical identification labeling. Agribusiness Int. J. **16**, 309–320 (2000)
2. Darby, K., Batte, M.T., Ernst, S., Roe, B.: Willingness to pay for locally produced foods: a customer intercept study of direct market and grocery store shoppers. In: American Agricultural Economics Association Annual Meeting. AAEA, Long Beach, California (2006)
3. Hu, W., Batte, Ma. t., Woods, T., Ernst, S.: Consumer preferences for local production and other value-added label claims for a processed food product. Euro. Rev. Agri. Econ. **39**, 489–510 (2012)
4. Morse, A., Shive, S.: Patriotism in your portfolio. J. Financ. Mark. **14**, 411–440 (2011)
5. Trauth, E.M.: The choice of qualitative methods in IS research. In: Qualitative Research in IS, pp. 1–19. IGI Global (2001)
6. Rourke, L., Anderson, T.: Validity in quantitative content analysis. Educ. Tech. Res. Dev. **52**, 5–18 (2004)
7. Kruse, J., Lenger, A.: Zur aktuellen Bedeutung von qualitativen Forschungsmethoden in der deutschen Volkswirtschaftslehre – Eine programmatische Exploration. ZQF–Zeitschrift für Qual. Forsch. **14**, 105–138 (2014)
8. Gefen, D., Straub, D.W.: Consumer trust in B2C e-Commerce and the importance of social presence: experiments in e-Products and e-Services. Omega **32**, 407–424 (2004)
9. Hassanein, K., Head, M.: The impact of infusing social presence in the web interface: an investigation across product types. Int. J. Electron. Commer. **10**, 31–55 (2005)
10. Schmuck, D., Matthes, J., Naderer, B., Beaufort, M.: The effects of environmental brand attributes and nature imagery in green advertising. Environ. Commun. **12**, 414–429 (2018)
11. Short, J., Williams, E., Christie, B.: The Social Psychology of Telecommunications. Wiley, London (1976)
12. Wilson, E.O.: Biophilia. Harvard University Press, Cambridge, Massachusetts (1984)
13. Shimp, T.A., Sharma, S.: Consumer ethnocentrism: construction and validation of the CETSCALE. J. Mark. Res. **24**, 280–289 (1987)
14. Riva, G., Mantovani, F., Waterworth, E.L., Waterworth, J.A.: Intention, action, self and other: an evolutionary model of presence. In: Lombard, M., Biocca, F., Freeman, J., IJsselsteijn, W., Schaevitz, R.J. (eds.) Immersed in Media, pp. 73–99. Springer, Cham (2015). https://doi.org/10.1007/978-3-319-10190-3_5
15. Lee, K.M.: Why presence occurs: Evolutionary psychology, media equation, and presence. Pres. Teleoper. Virtual Environ. **13**, 494–505 (2004)

16. Kaplan, R., Kaplan, S.: The Experience of Nature: A Psychological perspective. Cambridge University Press, Cambridge (1989)
17. Ulrich, R.S.: Biophilia, biophobia, and natural landscapes. In: Kellert, S.R., Wilson, E.O. (eds.) The biophilia hypothesis, pp. 73–137. Island Press, Washington, DC (1993)
18. van den Berghe, P.L.: The Ethnic Phenomenon. Praeger, Westport, CT and London (1981)
19. Bizumic, B.: Effects of the dimensions of ethnocentrism on consumer ethnocentrism an examination of multiple mediators. Int. Mark. Rev. **36**, 748–770 (2019)
20. Stadtwerke in Deutschland: Liste der deutschen Stadtwerke, https://stadtwerke-in-deutschla nd.de. Accessed 05 Feb 2020
21. Cohen, J.: A coefficient of agreement for nominal scales. Educ. Psychol. Measure. **20**, 37–46 (1960)
22. Viera, A.J., Garrett, J.M.: Understanding interobserver agreement: the kappa statistic. Fam. Med. **37**, 360–363 (2005)
23. Lim, S.H., Hur, Y., Lee, S., Koh, C.E.: Role of trust in adoption of online auto insurance. J. Comput. Inf. Syst. **50**, 151–159 (2009)
24. Gefen, D.: E-commerce: the role of familiarity and trust. Omega **28**, 725–737 (2000)
25. Schuhwerk, M.E., Lefkoff-Hagius, R.: Green or non-green? does type of appeal matter when advertising a green product? J. Advert. **24**, 45–54 (1995)
26. Lentz, P., Holzmüller, H.H., Schirrmann, E.: City-of-origin effects in the German beer market: transferring an international construct to a local context. Adv. Int. Mark. **17**, 251–274 (2006)
27. Palan, S., Schitter, C.: Prolific.ac — a subject pool for online experiments. J. Behav. Exp. **17**, 22–27 (2018)
28. Gefen, D., Straub, D.: Managing user trust in B2C e-services. e-Serv. J. **2**, 7–24 (2003)
29. Everard, A., Galletta, D.F.: How presentation flaws affect perceived site quality, trust, and intention to purchase from an online store. JMIS. **22**, 56–95 (2005)
30. Herz, M., Diamantopoulos, A.: Deceptive use of the 'regionality' concept in product labelling: an abstract. In: Pantoja, F., Wu, S., Krey, N., (eds.) AMSWMC 2019, pp. 43–44 (2019). https://doi.org/10.1007/978-3-030-42545-6_9
31. Stenner, K., Frederiks, E.R., Hobman, E. v., Cook, S.: Willingness to participate in direct load control: The role of consumer distrust. Appl. Energ. **189**, 76–88 (2017)
32. Ableitner, L., Tiefenbeck, V., Meeuw, A., Wörner, A., Fleisch, E., Wortmann, F.: User behavior in a real-world peer-to-peer electricity market. Appl. Energ. **270**, 115061 (2020)
33. Melville, N.P.: Information System innovation for environmental sustainability. MIS Q. **34**, 1–21 (2010)
34. Watson, R.T., Boudreau, M.-C., Chen, A.J.: Information systems and environmentally sustainable development: energy informatics and new directions for the IS community. MIS Q. **34**, 23–38 (2010)
35. Dedrick, J.: Green IS: Concepts and issues for information systems research. Commun. Assoc. Inf. Syst. **27**, 173–184 (2010)
36. Gholami, R., Watson, R.T., Hasan, H., Molla, A., Bjørn-Andersen, N.: Information systems solutions for environmental sustainability: how can we do more? J. Assoc. Inf. Syst. **17**, 521–536 (2016)
37. di Silvestre, M.L., Favuzza, S., Riva Sanseverino, E., Zizzo, G.: How decarbonization, digitalization and decentralization are changing key power infrastructures. Renew. Sustain. Energ. Rev. **93**, 483–498 (2018)
38. Dringenberg, H.: Interview with Horst Dringenberg (2020)
39. Menzel, T., Teubner, T.: Green Energy Platform Economics - understanding platformization and sustainabilization in the energy sector. Int. J. Energy Sect. Manag. **15**, 456–475 (2021). https://doi.org/10.1108/IJESM-05-2020-0022
40. Söllner, M., Hoffmann, A., Leimeister, J.M.: Why different trust relationships matter for information systems users. EJIS. **25**, 274–287 (2016)
41. Ragin, C.C.: The Comparative Method: Moving Beyond Qualitative and Quantitative Strategies. University of California Press, Oakland, CA (1987)

Curing Toxicity – A Multi-method Approach

Bastian Kordyaka[1]([⊠]) and Björn Kruse[2]

[1] Chair of Information Systems, University of Siegen, Siegen, Germany
bastian.kordyaka@uni-siegen.de
[2] South Westfalia University of Applied Science, Meschede, Germany
kruse.bjoern@fh-swf.de

Abstract. Enabled by technological advancements, a contemporary form of technology use that particularly became popular are online multiplayer video games, which are played with others in real time. Besides various positive impacts on the user experience (e.g., fun, additional social exchange) adverse consequences have occurred as well (e.g., stress, anger). Most recently, a sincere problem gaining increased attention is toxic behavior (i.e., a behavior spreading negative effects and bad mood during play). With our study, we propose a way to handle toxic behavior on a level of video game design by using a multi-method approach. First, we will consult the online disinhibition effect and its antecedents to identify design related relationships. Afterwards, we will conduct a qualitative workshop engaging video game designers and players to reshape in-game experiences by incentivizing players to buffer toxicity.

Keywords: User experience engineering · Toxic behavior · Online disinhibition effect · Multi-method approach

1 Introduction

Accompanied by the widespread digitalization during the last decades, new forms of technology use emerged. One such instance is computer-mediated communication (CMC), which occurs through the use of technological devices supporting the communication of individuals [1]. Besides various beneficial consequences (e.g., effective communication, location independent work) the dissemination of CMC had some adverse impacts on health and well-being of individuals (e.g., stress and strain mediated through technology) [2, 3].

One form of technology use that became particularly popular and is driven by CMC are online multiplayer video games (OMGs). They are collaboratively played in real time over the internet with other players around the world. Collaboratively playing games online is an important leisure activity in times of the world-wide corona pandemic, as it creates opportunities to establish additional forms of social exchange largely missing in real life. In this context, a phenomenon that already has attracted the attention of academia [4–6] and practice [7] is toxic behavior (TB). TB can be understood as a form of aggressive behavior towards members of the own team, which contributes to an increasingly negative affect and bad mood during gameplay [6]. Currently, TB is

F. Ahlemann et al. (Eds.): WI 2021, LNISO 47, pp. 340–346, 2021.
https://doi.org/10.1007/978-3-030-86797-3_23

considered one of the sincerest problems and a main driver of the churn of players in OMGs that largely remains unsolved [8].

With our study, we seek to utilize the (unexploited) potential of video game design to buffer TB. For this, we refer to present findings that showed substantial influences of the online disinhibition effect (ODE) as a predictor of TB [8] and identified antecedent variables of the ODE indicating its potential to be addressed on the level of game design (i.e., dissociative anonymity, invisibility, asynchronicity, solipsistic introjection, dissociative imagination, and minimization of authority) [9]. Specifically, we propose the application of a multi-method approach. First, we want to identify meaningful ODE antecedent variables explaining TB using a quantitative survey. Second, we will use the derived information to qualitatively explore manifestations on the level of video game design elements. By carrying out a workshop with various stakeholders (e.g., game designers, social and computer scientists) to identify mechanisms to buffer TB. Our paper is guided by the subsequent research questions:

RQ1: *What antecedent variables related to the ODE explain TB?*
RQ2: *What design elements hold the potential to reduce the occurrence of TB?*

With our short paper, we seek to make the following contributions. First, it will allow academia to better understand the occurrence of TB and its influences of a new class of potential predictor variables (ODE antecedents), opening up a variety of subsequent research questions regarding new forms of CMC and aggressive behavior online. Second, it provides practical implications for the video game industry to better handle TB. This substantially improves the user experience for their communities and prevent the churn of players significantly lowering profit margins.

2   Related Work

2.1   Video Games as Popular Form of Technology Usage

Enabled through the technological advancements during the last decade, OMGs disrupted the market of video games regarding popularity and revenue, whereby this development is closely linked to the meaningfulness of competitive multiplayer games [10, 11]. OMGs such as League of Legends (LoL) or Fortnite allow thousands of people around the world to interact with each other in real-time and can be considered elementary pillars of the contemporary digital culture. As an example, LoL has more than 115 million active players and made around $1.4 billion revenue in 2018 [15, 16]. For the purpose of our paper, we refer to LoL because of its team-based design and high levels of interactivity between players. As a consequence, toxic behavior can be considered an ordinary form of behavior that occurs in almost every game. This allows us to holistically explore toxicity in one of the most popular multiplayer contexts [17].

2.2   The Adverse Impact of Toxic Behavior

For the purpose of our paper, we understand TB as an aggressive behavior that occurs when a video game player comes across a negative event during a game, that generates anger and frustration, leading to a harmful, contaminated, and disseminated toxic type of communication using pings and text chat primary towards members of the own team [6]. Manifestations of TB are behaviors such as flaming, trolling, or insulting other players. Moreover, TB is a genuine problem in various OMGs because the necessity for players to cooperate and interact with each other in real time to win becomes undermined. As a consequence, TB scares away new players and leads to the churn of existing players. Opposed to related constructs of online aggressive behavior on the internet such as cyberbullying, TB occurs in a rather short period of time (the ordinary game length is around 30 min) and can be understood as state variable that can be executed by a single individual (in the case of cyberbullying more than one perpetrator is necessary). Additionally, TB is an ordinary part of the relevant gaming cultures, which underlines its wide dissemination. Taken together, TB remains a sincere problem for different video game communities. While previous research occasionally dealt with TB and it is still unclear how to holistically buffer toxicity from a theoretical standpoint on a level of game design [8, 18, 19].

2.3   Online Disinhibition Antecedents

Disinhibition can be understood as the perceived lack of restraint an individual feels when communicating online compared to communicating in-person, due to decreased behavioral inhibitions [9]. Usually, the ODE is operationalized with two different dimensions: benign disinhibition (i.e., positive behavior such as helping others, and showing kindness) and toxic disinhibition (i.e., negative behavior such as hostile expressions, and inappropriate behaviors). In previous research, the ODE already illustrated its potential to explain aggressive behavior on the internet [20–23]. Referring to the context of TB, a recent study showed the meaningfulness of toxic disinhibition as a predictor for TB [8]. Additionally, various antecedent variables of the ODE were identified: dissociative anonymity (e.g., perceived anonymity), invisibility (e.g., not being physically visible), asynchronicity (e.g., communication does not happen in real-time), solipsistic introjection (e.g., self-constructed characteristics of others), dissociative imagination (e.g., being in an alternative reality), and minimization of authority (e.g., reduced responsibility). We believe that the antecedent variables are particularly suitable to be addressed on a level of game design influencing both dimensions of disinhibition. To the best of our knowledge no study tried to explore the influences of the ODE variables as predictors of TB, which is a knowledge gap we seek to close with our study.

3   Methodology

3.1   Research Design and Data Analysis

To answer our two research questions, we plan to carry out a multi-method approach using quantitative and qualitative methods respectively, which will give us the opportunity to derive unique and connecting aspects of knowledge. First, we want to better understand influences of the ODE antecedent variables during the occurrence of TB using co-variance-based statistics. Since the main goal of our study is the identification of opportunities to buffer TB on a level of game design and not the development or continuation of existing theories, we decided out of reasons of parsimony to not specify concrete hypotheses for our quantitative analysis because we understand it as an initial and explorative step of our multi-method approach. Second, we want to use the derived information from the quantitative part and conduct a moderated focus group workshop engaging game designers and players to designate design elements to buffer TB. For this, we will define and explain the most important antecedent variables as a framework condition. The workshop will consist of a semi-structured narrative phase with pre-formulated questions and a discussion phase to identify additional design elements following a structured procedure from previous research [24, 25]. Its main goal is to derive design principles based on the relevant predictors of our quantitative study, to buffer TB on a level of game design. Additionally, we plan to develop a heuristic prototype that addresses different usage scenarios (e.g. pre-game/post-game, in-game, and game client) (Research model).

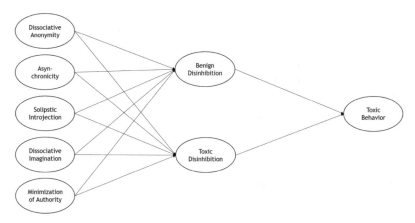

Fig. 1. Research model of the quantitative approach

3.2 Participants and Data Collection

We will collect two different data samples. First, we use an online survey to ask individuals who frequently play LoL about variables related to the ODE as explanations for TB. In order to acquire a significant number of respondents (N > 300), we will use the crowdsourcing marketplace Mechanical Turk. Second, we will recruit a sample (N > 10) consisting of different groups of stakeholders who are familiar with the design of video games (i.e., technology development, game designers, and social and computer sciences) to participate in our workshop. Accordingly, we will derive a convenient sample of respondents from the internal and external networks of our institution, while ensuring a maximum of diversity regarding academic background and demographics.

3.3 Quantitative Measurements

To measure the quantitative constructs in our study, we will use empirically validated scales adssjusted to the context of our study. The majority of scales will use a seven-point Likert scale ranging from 1 ("strongly disagree") to 7 ("strongly agree"). Additionally, we will measure various demographic (e.g., age, sex, education, origin) and control variables (e.g., enjoyment, hours of play, experience of play, game type) to prevent unwanted confounding effects.

Dependent Variable: Toxic behavior will be measured by using five items from (e.g., "If I get mad during a game, I insult others") [4].

Mediating Variables: We plan to use an existing scale to measure ODE: benign disinhibition will be measured with six items (e.g., "I have an image of the other players in my head when I read their messages") and toxic disinhibition with four items (e.g., "There are no rules online therefore you can do whatever you want") [21].

Independent Variables: We will use a scale comprising of thirty-eight items to measure the ODE antecedent variables, which consists of the dimensions dissociative anonymity (e.g., "I can hide my identity"), invisibility (e.g., "My actions are invisible"), asynchronicity (e.g., "I can control the pace of communication"), sollipstic introjection (e.g., "I assign a character to that player I am communicating with."), dissociative imagination (e.g., "My game related life is separated from the offline world") and minimization of authority (e.g., "I can get rid of authority") [26].

4   Conclusion and Outlook

Embedded in the assumptions of the ODE, in this short paper we propose a multi-method approach to identify design elements to buffer TB in OMGs. For this, we outlined our two-step approach and how we plan to identify and use the potential of the ODE variables to buffer toxicity in OMGs. Specifically, we will derive design principles based on the relevant predictors of our quantitative study to buffer TB on a level of game design and develop a heuristic prototype that can be used in subsequent experimental research. Academia can build on the findings, integrate them within existing frameworks, and pursue the derived body of knowledge. Developers and video game designers can utilize the findings to better handle TB and substantially improve the user experience of OMG players resulting in larger player bases and increased revenues eventually.

References

1. McQuail, D.: McQuail's Mass Communication Theory. Sage Publications (2010)
2. Tarafdar, M., Tu, Q., Ragu-Nathan, B.S., Ragu-Nathan, T.S.: The impact of technostress on role stress and productivity. J. Manag. Inf. Syst. **24**, 301–328 (2007)
3. Fuglseth, A.M., Sørebø, Ø.: The effects of technostress within the context of employee use of ICT. Comput. Hum. Behav. **40**, 161–170 (2014)

4. Kordyaka, B., Klesel, M., Jahn, K.: Perpetrators in league of legends: scale development and validation of toxic behavior. In: Proceedings of the 52nd Hawaii International Conference on System Sciences, pp. 1–10 (2019)
5. Blackburn, J., Kwak, H.: STFU NOOB!: predicting crowdsourced decisions on toxic behavior in online games. ACM Press, pp. 877–888 (2014)
6. Neto, J.A.M., Yokoyama, K.M., Becker, K.: Studying toxic behavior influence and player chat in an online video game. In: Proceedings of the International Conference on Web Intelligence, pp. 26–33 (2017)
7. Fair Play Alliance. http://www.fairplayalliance.org/. Accessed 26 Apr 2020
8. Kordyaka, B., Jahn, K., Niehaves, B.: Towards a unified theory of toxic behavior. Internet Res. **30**, 1081–1102 (2020)
9. Suler, J.: The online disinhibition effect. Cyberpsychol. Behav. **7**, 321–326 (2004)
10. Martinello, League of Legends generated $1.5 billion revenue in 2019. https://dotesp orts.com/league-of-legends/news/league-of-legends-generated-1-5-billion-revenue-in-2019. Accessed 08 Apr 2020
11. Goslin, A.: Fortnite has 78.3 million monthly players, according to Epic, https://www.polygon.com/fortnite/2018/9/20/17884036/how-many-fortnite-monthly-players-2018. Accessed 07 Apr 2020
12. Kordyaka, B., Hribersek, S.: Crafting identity in league of legends – purchases as a tool to achieve desired impressions. In: Proceedings of the 52nd Hawaii International Conference on System Sciences (HICSS-52), Maui, Hawaii, pp. 1506–1515 (2019)
13. Wohn, D.Y., Freeman, G., McLaughlin, C.: Explaining viewers' emotional, instrumental, and financial support provision for live streamers. In: Proceedings of the 2018 CHI Conference on Human Factors in Computing Systems, pp. 1–13 (2018)
14. Cai, J., Wohn, D.Y., Mittal, A., Sureshbabu, D.: Utilitarian and hedonic motivations for live streaming shopping. In: Proceedings of the 2018 ACM International Conference on Interactive Experiences for TV and Online Video, pp. 81–88 (2018)
15. Riot: League of legends is the world leader in PC gaming revenue since the start of 2017. https://www.akshonesports.com/article/2017/08/league-legends-world-leader-pc-gaming-revenue-since-start-2017. Accessed 14 Feb 2018
16. Tassi, P.: Riot games reveals "League of Legends" has 100 million monthly players. https://www.forbes.com/sites/insertcoin/2016/09/13/riot-games-reveals-league-of-legends-has-100-million-monthly-players/. Accessed 14 Sept 2017
17. Adinolf, S., Turkay, S.: Toxic behaviors in Esports games: player perceptions and coping strategies. In: Proceedings of the 2018 Annual Symposium on Computer-Human Interaction in Play Companion Extended Abstracts –CHI PLAY 2018, Extended Abstracts, pp. 365–372 (2018)
18. Shores, K.B., He, Y., Swanenburg, K.L., Kraut, R., Riedl, J.: The identification of deviance and its impact on retention in a multiplayer game. ACM Press, pp. 1356–1365 (2014)
19. Kwak, H., Blackburn, J., Han, S.: Exploring cyberbullying and other toxic behavior in team competition online games. ACM Press, pp. 3739–3748 (2015)
20. Barlett, C.P., Gentile, D.A., Chew, C.: Predicting cyberbullying from anonymity. Psychol. Popular Media Cult. **5**, 171 (2016)
21. Udris, R.: Cyberbullying among high school students in Japan: development and validation of the online disinhibition scale. Comput. Hum. Behav. **41**, 253–261 (2014)
22. Lowry, P.B., Moody, G.D., Chatterjee, S.: Using IT design to prevent cyberbullying. J. Manag. Inf. Syst. **34**, 863–901 (2017)
23. Runions, K.C., Bak, M.: Online moral disengagement, cyberbullying, and cyber-aggression. Cyberpsychol. Behav. Soc. Netw. **18**, 400–405 (2015)

24. Mueller, M., Heger, O., Kordyaka, B., Kampling, H., Niehaves, B.: Beyond intuition: towards a framework for empirical-based design theory building in design science research. In: Proceedings of the 52nd Hawaii International Conference on System Sciences, pp. 5715–5724 (2019)
25. Stahl, B.C., Tremblay, M.C., LeRouge, C.M.: Focus groups and critical social IS research: how the choice of method can promote emancipation of respondents and researchers. Eur. J. Inf. Syst. **20**, 378–394 (2011)
26. Cheung, C.M.K., Wong, R.Y.M., Chan, T.K.H.: Online disinhibition: conceptualization, measurement, and relation to aggressive behaviors. In: Proceedings of International Conference on Information Systems, pp. 1–10 (2016)

Information Security, Privacy and Blockchain

Introduction to the WI2021 Track: Information Security, Privacy, and Blockchain

Ali Sunyaev[1], and Jens Grossklags[2]

[1] Karlsruhe Institute of Technology, Institute of Applied Informatics and Formal
Description Methods, Karlsruhe, Germany
sunyaev@kit.edu
[2] Technical University of Munich, Department of Informatics, Munich, Germany
jens.grossklags@in.tum.de

1 Track Description

With the increasingly ubiquitous use of IT systems in most areas of our lives—spanning from government, to banking, health, and retail management—problems associated with information privacy and information security are becoming a focal issue for various stakeholders around the globe. Moreover, the emergence and proliferation of novel internet-based technologies and applications as well as mobile IT further increase the importance of information privacy and information security. This results in intense public discussions at all levels. For example, the Cambridge Analytica scandal [1] showcased the extent and dangers of user data collection and caused major concerns worldwide. Further examples of ongoing debates are related to the blockchain and cryptocurrency ecosystems, genetic privacy, or the usage of a multitude of tracking and tracing technologies, for example, in the context of Covid-19.

2 Research Articles

The track received twenty submissions addressing information security and information privacy challenges in various contexts including blockchain and cryptocurrencies. After a rigorous review process, we selected five full papers, and one short paper for presentation at the conference. We would like to express our sincere gratitude to all the authors, the reviewers, and our Associate Editors.

2.1 Blockchain and Data Protection: An Evaluation of the Challenges and Solutions mentioned by German Stakeholders

Distributed ledger technology (DLT) is an emerging technology that promises to reshape how information is processed in online environments [2]. The paper "Blockchain and Data Protection: An Evaluation of the Challenges and Solutions mentioned by German Stakeholders" written by Frank Ebbers and Murat Karaboga explores challenges and presents possible solutions for DLT-based applications regarding current legislation, compliance and administrative actions on data protection.

2.2   CyberSecurity Challenges for Software Developer Awareness Training in Industrial Environments

Secure code development is not only a policy issue but also a practical challenge for developers [3]. Tiago Espinha Gasiba, Ulrike Lechner, and Maria Pinto-Albuquerque present a serious game for software developers. The idea of the game is to raise awareness among software developers with regard to secure code development. The paper is entitled "CyberSecurity Challenges for Software Developer Awareness Training in Industrial Environments".

2.3   On the Relationship between IT Privacy and Security Behavior: A Survey among German Private Users

Information privacy and information security have an intricate relationship [4], which also impacts the interplay of privacy and security preferences and behaviors [5]. The goal of the paper "On the Relationship between IT Privacy and Security Behavior: A Survey among German Private Users" by Tom Biselli and Christian Reuter is to conceptualize the relationship between security, privacy, and corresponding behaviors. The results of the paper are a further step towards empowering users in facing security and privacy challenges in the use of digital services.

2.4   The Hidden Value of Patterns – Using Design Patterns to Whitebox Technology Development in Legal Assessments

How to incorporate legal requirements (e.g., data protection principles) into design is a long-standing challenge [6]. The paper "The Hidden Value of Patterns – Using Design Patterns to Whitebox Technology Development in Legal Assessments" by Ernestine Dickhaut, Andreas Janson, and Jan Marco Leimeister presents interdisciplinary design patterns for the representation of technical systems in order to support legal professionals during legal proceedings on the legal compliance of digital technology with data protection legal requirements.

2.5   Understanding Privacy Disclosure in the Online Market for Lemons: Insights and Requirements for Platform Providers

To go beyond the current provision of ineffective privacy notices [7], platform providers need to better understand their customers. Andreas Engelmann and Gerhard Schwabe wrote a paper entitled "Understanding Privacy Disclosure in the Online Market for Lemons: Insights and Requirements for Platform Providers". The paper studies user's sensitivity to personal data disclosure on peer-to-peer used car markets and their willingness to trade disclosure of personal data for money.

2.6   Towards GDPR Enforcing Blockchain Systems

Smart contracts are a promising feature of blockchain systems; however, their use in practice is still challenging [8]. The short paper "Towards GDPR Enforcing Blockchain Systems" by Hauke Precht and Jorge Marx Gómez discusses a conceptual proposal to use smart contracts in order to enable GDPR-compliant data processing control.

3   Associate Editors for our Track

We are grateful for the contributions of the seventeen Associate Editors, who were part of the review process and selected suitable external reviewers for each submission:

- Annika Baumann, Weizenbaum Institute
- Zinaida Benenson, University of Erlangen–Nuremberg
- Tobias Dehling, Karlsruhe Institute of Technology
- Christian Djeffal, Technical University of Munich
- Tatiana Ermakova, Fraunhofer FOKUS
- Torsten Eymann, University of Bayreuth
- Daniel Fischer, TU Ilmenau
- Michael Friedewald, Fraunhofer ISI
- Steffi Haag, University of Erlangen–Nuremberg
- Paula Helm, University of Hagen
- Dominik Herrmann, University of Bamberg
- Thomas Hupperich, University of Münster
- Timo Jakobi, University of Siegen
- Mathias Klier, University of Ulm
- Peter Niemeyer, Leuphana University of Lüneburg
- Simon Trang, University of Göttingen
- Liudmila Zavolokina, University of Zurich

References

1. Hu, M.: Cambridge Analytica's black box. Big Data and Society. 7, 1–6 (2020). https://doi.org/10.1177/2053951720938091
2. Kannengießer, N., Lins, S., Dehling, T., Sunyaev, A.: Trade-offs between distributed ledger technology characteristics. ACM Computing Surveys. 53, 42:1-42:37 (2020). https://doi.org/10.1145/3379463
3. Bednar, K., Spiekermann, S., Langheinrich, M.: Engineering privacy by design: Are engineers ready to live up to the challenge? The Information Society. 35, 122–142 (2019). https://doi.org/10.1080/01972243.2019.1583296
4. Toch, E., Bettini, C., Shmueli, E., Radaelli, L., Lanzi, A., Riboni, D., Lepri, B.: The privacy implications of cyber security systems: A technological survey. ACM Computing Surveys. 51, 36:1–36:27 (2018). https://doi.org/10.1145/3172869
5. Grossklags, J., Barradale, N.J.: Social status and the demand for security and privacy. In: De Cristofaro, E. and Murdoch, S.J. (eds.) Privacy Enhancing Technologies. pp. 83–101. Springer International Publishing, Cham (2014)
6. Mulligan, D.K., King, J.: Bridging the gap between privacy and design. Journal of Constitutional Law. 14, 989–1034 (2012)
7. Sunyaev, A., Dehling, T., Taylor, P.L., Mandl, K.D.: Availability and quality of mobile health app privacy policies. Journal of the American Medical Informatics Association. 22, e28–e33 (2015). https://doi.org/10.1136/amiajnl-2013-002605
8. Drummer, D., Neumann, D.: Is code law? Current legal and technical adoption issues and remedies for blockchain-enabled smart contracts. Journal of Information Technology. 35, 337–360 (2020). https://doi.org/10.1177/0268396220924669

Blockchain and Data Protection: An Evaluation of the Challenges and Solutions Mentioned by German Stakeholders

Frank Ebbers[(✉)] and Murat Karaboga

Fraunhofer Institute for Systems and Innovation Research ISI, Breslauer Str. 48,
76139 Karlsruhe, Germany
{frank.ebbers,murat.karaboga}@isi.fraunhofer.de

Abstract. This paper analyzes data protection challenges and possible solutions associated with the usage of the blockchain (BC) technology from the perspective of 94 German companies and organizations. This paper clusters 537 data protection-relevant statements into three subject areas: (1) relevance of data protection in BC, (2) articulated challenges and (3) proposed solutions. Each group is then collated with insights from computer science. The results show that a majority of the respondents do see data protection issues with using BC, which mainly relate to data erasure and identifying the data controller. However, the majority also consider these problems to be solvable utilizing already available technologies, e.g. off-chain storage, encryption, pseudonymization or usage of private BCs. Comparing these proposals with the findings in computer science literature shows that especially off-chain storage, encryption and redactable blockchains can be regarded as adequate solutions.

Keywords: Blockchain · Data protection · Protection of personal data · Privacy · Content analysis

1 Introduction

Distributed ledger technologies (DLT) use decentralized data storage on the computers of many users. One variant is the blockchain (BC) technology, which has become one of the top five strategic decisions for many companies worldwide [1]. Since BC has gradually been approaching commercialization [2], the discussion concerning an appropriate regulatory framework has also recently gained momentum worldwide. The data protection requirements of the General Data Protection Regulation (GDPR) are the most important regulatory challenge in the European Union (EU). Among the various data protection (DP) challenges, the following two are the most serious for BC applications: the difficulty of identifying the data controller, and the DP implications of the immutability of the data stored in a blockchain [3].

Companies expect disruptive changes and economic gains if BCs are operated in compliance with data protection [e.g. 4]. Therefore, an intensive debate is ongoing in academia, industry and regulatory authorities on the compatibility of BC applications

© The Author(s), under exclusive license to Springer Nature Switzerland AG 2021
F. Ahlemann et al. (Eds.): WI 2021, LNISO 47, pp. 353–369, 2021.
https://doi.org/10.1007/978-3-030-86797-3_24

with the data protection framework [5–7]. Although this debate is intensive, it lacks empirical evidence of how stakeholders actually assess the DP challenges. Research in this area generally focuses on two strands. First, there are studies which only ask companies whether they perceive regulations such as DP as an obstacle. Second, there is intensive research, particularly from a legal and technical perspective, into solutions to DP challenges (see Sect. 2.2).

Several research gaps can be identified here. The analyses of DP challenges usually remain on an abstract level (in the sense of: is regulation/data protection considered an obstacle to the use of blockchains in your company?). Quantitative analyses are missing of the concrete data protection-related challenges that companies face. In addition, surveys among companies generally do not enquire whether they consider solutions to the challenges possible.

Thus, our study aims to find out whether and how companies and organizations are trying to overcome these challenges. Since there is a lack of quantitative analyses of the possible solutions being discussed, computer science research also lacks analyses of the usefulness of such proposed solutions. Against this background, we ask the following research questions:

- RQ1: What challenges and possible solutions do stakeholders see with regard to data protection and blockchain issues?
- RQ2: How are the proposed solutions to be evaluated from a technical point of view?

We answer these questions in two steps. To answer RQ1, we rely on a text-based qualitative content analysis of the statements of 130 actors who participated in the 2019 blockchain consultation of the German government. To answer RQ2, we assess the challenges articulated and the proposed solutions based on state of the art technical BC research in computer science literature.

Our study has implications for academia, practitioners and policy makers by providing qualitative insights into how companies and organizations evaluate the DP challenges and solutions concerning BC technology.

2 State of Research

2.1 Background of Blockchain Technology

DLT are a type of database with globally decentralized data storage across multiple computers, so-called nodes [8]. Each node has a partial or full copy of the ledger and can interchange data formally as a peer-to-peer network without a central authority [9]. Blockchain is a DLT, but consolidates new data into blocks, which are chained to the preceding one by means of cryptographic hash functions [10]. This results in an append-only structure, where prior blocks cannot be deleted or edited without changing all the subsequent blocks. If something tries to change a block, the corresponding hash value changes, resulting in a breakage of the chain [8]. As every node has a copy of the ledger, tampering with a single node cannot manipulate the blockchain. This should ensure full transparency and traceability. This consensus mechanism is, however, only possible for financial data, as the nodes check whether the total amount, e.g. of Bitcoins, is still valid after a transaction. This is to ensure that no one can transfer coins they do not own. In public BCs, nodes are unknown and there is no administrator. In contrast, permissioned/private or consortium BCs have one or a group of known nodes with special rights able to grant access to new users (such as nodes, miners or programmers) and thus control the BC.

The concept emerged during the global financial crisis in 2008, when an author with the pseudonym Satoshi Nakamoto introduced the crypto currency Bitcoin to provide non-manipulable financial transactions on the internet by avoiding intermediaries, e.g. financial institutions [9, 10]. The term "blockchain" only appeared 2013, but the under-lying technology of storing chained hash values of documents already existed in 1991 [9].

2.2 Data Protection in Blockchain Technologies

The EU considers data protection a fundamental right (see Art. 8 of the Charter of Fundamental Rights of the EU) and strives for economic growth (see Recitals 2 and 7 GDPR). Consequently, the GDPR aims to guarantee a high and harmonized level of data protection for the personal data of EU citizens on the one hand, and to strengthen the digital single market by removing obstacles that impede the free movement of personal data on the other (see Recitals 9 and 10 GDPR.). The GDPR represents a comprehensive and complex set of rules with which these goals are to be achieved. A wide range of provisions must be complied with in order to ensure that personal data is processed in accordance with data protection regulations. These include the material and territorial scope, the definition of personal data, the rules on the lawfulness of processing, the rights of the data subject, and the obligations of the data controller. The GDPR has two requirements that stand out in particular for blockchain applications.

First, Art. 4 (7) GDPR is based on the assumption that one or more relatively clearly identifiable data controllers are responsible for the processing operation, and against whom the data subject can assert his or her DP rights. However, the technical mode of operation of public blockchain technology does not provide for clear responsibility. Instead, it explicitly relies on the decentralization of responsibility. Due to their influence on determining the means and purposes of BC data processing, nodes and users can be considered controllers (but not only these depending on the BC). Since both nodes and users are controllers, the provisions of Art. 26 GDPR on joint controllers must be fulfilled. In the case of traditional data processing, the joint responsibility of the data controllers has to be regulated in an agreement. However, as there is insufficient knowledge of all controllers in public BCs, a contractual sharing of joint responsibility is not possible [3]. The European Data Protection Board (EDPB) has finally clarified in its most recent Guidelines (see recital 167) that, in such cases, each individual controller must comply with the obligations of the GDPR [11]. In a public blockchain, data is passed on to an unmanageable group of people and the granting of data subject rights is extremely difficult. Therefore, nodes and users will generally not be able to meet their obligations [3, 7]. The Schrems II ruling has further complicated the issue. The ruling clarified that (joint) data controllers must also ensure compliance with the GDPR in the case of transfers of personal data to countries outside the EU that do not have an adequate level of data protection [12]. Since, in a public blockchain, every person from any part of the world can become a node or a user, fulfilling this requirement is also difficult.

Second, the GDPR grants the data subjects the right to rectify and erase their data. However, the distinctive feature of BC technology is the immutability of the stored data, in order to achieve maximum transparency and data integrity [3]. As this brief discussion has made clear, there are still challenges with regard to the privacy-compliant operation of a public BC, which make it necessary to adapt BC architecture to the legal requirements.

Nonetheless, many companies expect disruptive changes due to BC technology. Thus, awareness of the challenges posed by DP law has led to an intensive debate. A number of recent surveys have been carried out to identify the concerns of the business community. A PricewaterhouseCoopers survey [13] of 600 corporate executives from 15 countries found that 27% considered regulatory uncertainty the biggest barrier to the use of BCs. A Bitkom survey [14] of 1,004 companies revealed that 66% regarded DP requirements as a challenge. According to Deloitte's survey [1], 32% of 1,488 companies surveyed named regulatory issues as hindering BC adoption. This study is the only one that asked companies whether and to what extent they saw possibilities to overcome the DP challenges. Indeed, 83% of respondents indicated that they were very or somewhat confident that they would be able to meet the regulatory requirements [1]. Such surveys mainly focus on finding out whether companies see DP as a challenge, but they do not ask what exactly they regard as challenges or how they will try to overcome them.

Until a few years ago, IS literature considered DP to be guaranteed, e.g. due to the anonymity of the nodes [15]. Today, a growing number of papers, mainly in the fields of computer science [10, 16] and law [3], acknowledge DP challenges, and search for possible solutions. Some of these deal with the challenges in great depth. To the authors' best knowledge, there is no literature on the possible solutions discussed in the business world and no literature comparing stakeholder views.

The German government published its BC strategy in September 2019 [17]. It laid down the framework conditions for the further development of the technology and announced several dozen measures in five fields of action. The subsequent reactions ranged from clear support [18] to skeptical relief [19] and fundamental criticism [20]. In particular, the lack of uniform goals and a binding timetable was criticized.

With regard to DP issues in connection with BC applications, the German government stated that it saw no need to amend the GDPR. Instead, the uncertainties of developers and users with regard to data protection law were to be addressed using existing technical solutions (including hash values, pseudonymization, ZKP) and holding a "round table" on the topic of blockchain and data protection [17].

3 Methodology

We conducted a text-based, qualitative content analysis (CA) following [21], because "it is a research technique for making replicable and valid inferences from texts" [21].

Unitizing: As the basis for our analysis, we used the document provided by [22], containing all the officially published answers given in the consultation process for the blockchain strategy of the German government. In total, there were 6,261 answers from 130 respondents, which we transferred into a machine-readable format.

Sampling: From this corpus of data, we identified data protection-relevant answers and questions by applying a keyword search to the statements. Since the blockchain consultation was conducted in German, we decided to use the terms shown in Table 1 (case insensitive, incl. substrings). These are terms found in the German and English version of the GDPR as well as synonyms in the relevant data protection literature. In Table 1, we also provide the percentage of mentions of each keyword within questions (Q) and given answers (A). We ended up with 537 relevant questions and answers in total, which we refer to as statements from now on (8.6%).

Table 1. Keywords and percentage of mentions in all statements (Q = question, A = answer)

Keyword	% in Q	% in A		Keyword	% in Q	% in A
Datenschutz	14.90%	35.94%		private Daten	0.00%	0.74%
Privatsphäre	21.23%	5.40%		DS-GVO	0.00%	0.19%
personenbezogen	29.24%	18.06%		Privatheit	0.00%	0.13%
DSGVO	3.91%	22.53%		private data	0.00%	0.03%
privacy	0.00%	5.96%		personal data	0.00%	0.00%
GDPR	0.00%	3.72%		Data protection	0.00%	0.00%
persönliche Daten	0.00%	1.68%				

Coding: Two persons coded the statements. Both were familiar with the subject of data protection; the principal coder (C1) had additional technical expertise in BC technology. C1 processed all 537 statements and defined the final category set. The second coder (C2) processed a representative sample of 50 statements from more than ten percent of the respondents, as suggested by [23].

C1 applied iterative inductive-deductive coding. Based on our research question, we predefined three subject areas, i.e. "problem relevance", "articulated challenges" and "proposed solutions". In total, 57 codes were identified for each subject area. Additionally, C1 always noted the usage domain in which the question was situated.

After this initial coding, C2 relied on the codes by C1 and processed the coding of the representative sample to ensure reproducibility [21]. Our analysis showed a moderate strength of agreement, manifesting in a Cohen's Kappa of 0.53 for intercoder reliability.

Reducing: We applied hybrid card sorting in order to reduce the number of codes and created clusters based on insights from literature. For example, [16] and [24] considered pruning, Merkle trees, and chameleon hash functions as erasure methods, as all aim at (physically) deleting data. This process resulted in a reduction from 57 to 31 categories (Table 2). Finally, we consulted an expert panel of n = 8 to check the codes were collectively exhaustive and mutually exclusive, as suggested by [21].

Table 2. Quantitative representation of codes and categories for each subject area

Group of themes	No. of code categories	No. of codes
Problem description	4	5
Articulated challenges	15	19
Proposed solutions	8	26
General remarks	4	7
Total	31	57

Inferring: In order to "bridge [...] the gap between descriptive accounts of texts and what they mean, refer to, entail, provoke, or cause" [21], we compared the respondents' statements with findings from the literature. This yields important insights, as most respondents are generalists rather than BC experts.

Narrating: We present the procedures and results, theoretical and practical contributions, and upcoming questions of the content analysis in the next chapters.

4   Results

In this section, we provide a descriptive overview of all DP-related statements of the respondents. First, we show how relevant DP issues are for the respondents. Second, we present the specific challenges stated and, finally, we give an overview of the proposed solutions to these challenges. In total, there were 130 companies and organizations, of which 94 (72%) provided DP-relevant answers. Their 537 statements form the basis for this analysis. The respondents are active in different industries, with a majority in the IT sector (38%), followed by research institutions (18%) and Fintech (13%). Although our focus is on companies, the analysis involves different types of stakeholders. Based on our analysis, we cannot identify structural differences in the answers between the different sectors, as there were not enough data available. The available data indicate that the automotive, financial and energy sectors are particularly skeptical about the compatibility of data protection and blockchain. In contrast, the healthcare and IT sectors are particularly optimistic.[1]

4.1   Problem Relevance

The first subject area represents how relevant companies and organizations assess DP in the field of blockchain. The relevance is shown in eight coding categories (Fig. 1). These results are independent of specific usage domains, but an analysis of the provided application domains shows similar results.

---

[1] Compare the *online appendix* for a table in which the assessment of how serious the problems are and whether there are possible solutions was divided by sector.

Out of the total of 94 respondents, a majority (81%) agree that DP is a challenge in BC applications, whereas only 21 respondents (22%) see no DP challenges, at least in some usage domains[2]. 19 respondents (20%) consider DP issues to be so serious that they expect a showstopper effect for companies. This means that they see no possible solution to DP issues of BC, either now or in the future. Very few respondents believe these challenges will discourage companies from adopting blockchain applications. A majority of 66 respondents are confident that solutions to DP issues are possible. About one third (29%) of respondents even argue that BC can enhance DP. For example, they mention "self-sovereign identity" (7%), which helps users to track and configure how their data must be processed [25].

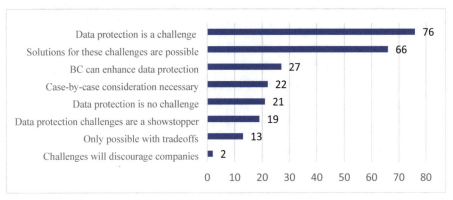

Fig. 1. Relevance of data protection issues in blockchain applications in absolute numbers, n = 94 (own analysis, multiple responses possible)

4.2 Articulated Challenges

Guaranteeing the data subject's rights is seen by 53 respondents as the biggest challenge. In Fig. 2, we refer to these rights with the heading "grouped". Of these, 50 respondents (94%) consider deletion to be the main problem, 38 (72%) say rectification and six (11%) see the right of data portability as challenging. 12 respondents (23%) mention guaranteeing these rights in general as problematic. The second most mentioned challenge by 43 respondents (46%) is that all personal data in the BC is visible to everyone. The third most frequently mentioned problem was the (non-)identifiability of the data controller (31 times, 33%). 15 respondents (16%) criticized the current encryption technologies for personal data, fearing they could be cracked in the near future. 14 actors (15%) doubted the effectiveness of pseudonymization and regard de-pseudonymization as a problem. Seven (7%) criticized the security of storage, which is particularly important in the case of possible off-chain storage or storage of the keys required for encryption. Four respondents (4%) expressed concerns about the integrity or quality of the input

---

[2] As the respondents see no challenges in some specific usage domains, the total number of mentions is 97 (103%), instead of max. 94.

data and stated that it is difficult to verify the correctness of data relating to objects in the physical world. Finally, three respondents (3%) criticized the high computing power requirements of zero-knowledge proofs (ZKP) and the effectiveness of anonymizing personal data.

In addition, seven respondents (7%) drew attention to the legal problems arising from the transfer and data storage outside the EU. In the same context, seven respondents (7%) criticized the unclear legal situation, both with regard to divergent legal frameworks worldwide, which made the use of a global BC more difficult, and with regard to the - from their perspective - unclear legal situation in the EU.

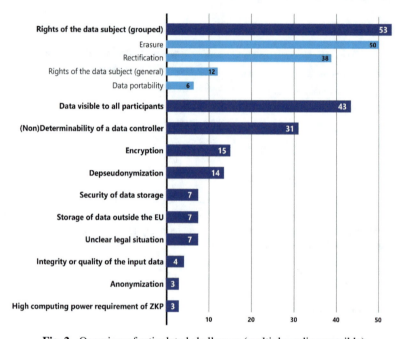

Fig. 2. Overview of articulated challenges (multiple coding possible)

4.3 Proposed Solutions

A majority of the respondents believe that solutions to DP issues in blockchain technology are generally possible. In the following section, we briefly present the proposed solutions that were mentioned by the respondents.

Figure 3 shows that the majority of respondents (62 or 66%) believed that a solution to the DP challenges was already possible using existing technology. This included off-chain storage in the first place (43 or 46%), closely followed by encryption technologies (37 and 39%). 18 actors (19%) considered pseudonymization to be a useful approach. The use of zero-knowledge proofs (ZKP) represented a possible solution for 13 actors (14%). Twelve actors (13%) thought that there are possibilities for deleting data. The use of existing anonymization methods was mentioned by eleven actors (12%).

The second most frequently mentioned proposal (38 actors/40%) was to simply refrain from storing personal data in a BC. 31 stakeholders (33%) were in favor of restricting access by using a private BC. 29 actors (31%) mentioned legal adjustments. Of those, 27 (29%) mention the concretization and amendment of the GDPR, four (4%) the creation of legal bases that apply worldwide (4 or 14%), and two (2%) cooperation with other countries.

29 respondents (31%) expressed the opinion that further technical developments and standards were necessary to operate BCs in conformity with data protection laws. With the help of organizational security measures, such as user roles or data aggregation, a solution to DP problems could be found, according to 17 actors (18%). This included user roles and rights (9 or 10%), assigning different protection levels to different types of data (8 or 9%), and the exclusive storage of data aggregates (3 or 3%).

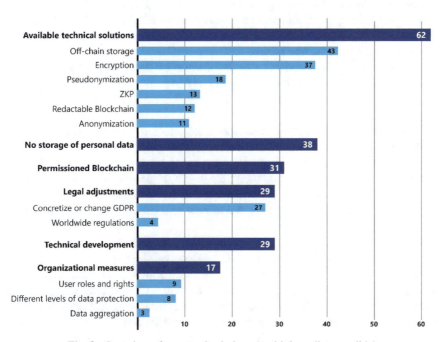

Fig. 3. Overview of proposed solutions (multiple coding possible)

5 Discussion

In this section, we compare the articulated challenges and proposed solutions with the state of research. The results show that the majority of respondents (81%) consider data protection a challenge in BC. However, many of the respondents in the BC consultation consider the challenges to be manageable. Our results also show that many respondents promote BC technology, whereas others are rather critical or cannot make a generally valid statement. Further, our results suggest that many companies and organizations are not very familiar with "the BC issue" or have no desire to delve deeper into it. This can be seen, for example, in the fact that almost a third of the respondents urged to concretize or amend the GDPR and called on public authorities to offer guidelines. Whereas publishing guidelines is certainly a realistic option for action (as the recent EDPB guidelines on accountability have shown), amendments of the GDPR are most unlikely at this point in time [26]. In the following subsections, we discuss the statements articulated by the respondents.

5.1 General Statements

Several respondents raise questions concerning information security goals, i.e. confidentiality, integrity and availability, which we want to discuss briefly. While immutability and distributed storage fulfill integrity and availability requirements; the blockchain "is not specifically designed to support or maintain data confidentiality" [27]. Although the company Achelos suggests using *encryption* to tackle these problems, encryption cannot prevent internal errors, such as misuse.

Additionally, a few respondents note that the inserted data is not verified. Thus, data quality control is an issue. The literature agrees on that point, as the BC technology "does not guarantee or improve data quality" [28]. Neither the respondents nor the literature suggest possible solutions.

Almost one third of the respondents articulate the need for technical developments and standards to operate BCs in a DP-compliant manner. According to the company DB Systel, there are currently only "trade-offs between security, data protection, efficiency, flexibility, platform complexity and user-friendliness for developers" (own translation). The literature acknowledges that the prerequisites for successful research have been created and it is likely that a large number of new applications will emerge in the near future [29].

Finally, for about one fifth of the respondents, technical solutions do not seem to be sufficient at this point of time. Instead, they suggest three types of *organizational measures*: (1) introduction of user roles and rights, (2) allocation of different protection levels to different types of data, e.g. medical data, and (3) exclusive storage of data aggregates. The literature also discusses such measures for BC applications, e.g. [30] find that "organizational measures need to be taken to fulfill the boundary conditions, before blockchain can be used successfully". Generally, private BCs can comply with these three types of measures, as a central authority can be defined. For (1), a predefined data controller could allow new users and assign rights and roles, which could be themselves stored in the BC using smart contracts [7]. For (2), it is technically possible to assign data categories that define conditions of use and specify a group of privileged recipients [3]. [31] describe a method for service providers to carry out data processing directly in the user's network without accessing raw data. This can ensure that users can only access certain data. At present, there does not seem to be a sufficient solution for the (3) measure. Researchers agree that performing privacy-preserving data aggregation is challenging due to advancements in data processing using big data and artificial intelligence [32].

5.2   Rights of the Data Subject: Erasure, Rectification and Data Portability

Problem Description: By far the most frequently mentioned problem relates to guaranteeing the rights of data subjects to the erasure or rectification of their data. This is hardly possible, because of the immutable nature of BCs. Several researchers agree that these are the most pressing points when considering DP in BC applications [24]. Another problem mentioned by the respondents is data portability. This calls for data being stored in structured, commonly used and machine-readable formats. However, there is no standard exchange format in the blockchain [33].

Suggested Solutions and Evaluation: Most respondents suggest *off-chain storage*. In this case, only a reference hash value of the original file will be stored in the BC. As hash values are collision-free, changes to the original file can be detected and thus transparency achieved, while being able to continue the blockchain [34]. Contrary to the original BC idea, the operator must be trusted, since there are ways to change stored data afterwards. Such methods are often referred to as *redactable blockchains* [24]. One prominent example mentioned by the respondents are *chameleon hash functions*, which have collision-free algorithms that enable a group of controllers to delete data while leaving a "scar" [35]. However, deletion is only possible in permissioned BC architectures, because data controllers need to coincide and deletion is an exception [24]. Another drawback is the possible identification of a hash value in a small search space [36]. For example, a modern graphic card can calculate the double-sha256 hashes of all human names (7.6 bn) in under 4 s [37]. Thus, there is the need to add random data, a so-called "secret". To identify users as data holders, this secret must be transmitted. However, attacks could compromise the transition and intercept the secret.

To overcome this problem, some respondents suggest *Merkle trees,* which are used, e.g. in the Bitcoin blockchain, to reclaim disk space [9]. These combine hashes of different data fields, such as the hash of the name and the hash of the birthdate and create a new hash. This results in a tree-like structure. Only the uppermost hash (analogous to the tree trunk) is saved in the BC [38], so that no single person can identify the original hash. Especially in the Bitcoin BC, Merkle trees are used to verify data blocks to ensure that no miner transmits a manipulated financial transaction.

Zero knowledge proofs (ZKP) represent another solution, which dispenses with the release of the "secret". They do not use a person's real data, but rather a proof that the datum exists or is correct [39]. In such a way, one could easily check whether a person is older than 18, without revealing the actual birthdate. However, there are two disadvantages. First, the literature suggests that an attacker could try out all possible input values until the proof is verified [40]. Second, the respondents note that ZKP require considerable computing power. Whereas the transactions are stored on-chain, the computation and storage are performed off-chain.

Other respondents mentioned *tombstones* and *data revocation keys* as deletion methods. However, both these methods only mark data as invalid and do not physically delete it, as required by Art. 17 GDPR. Here, at first glance, *forking* seems a solution. It presents an irreversible separation from a BC. However, if data changes and deletions have to occur frequently, the chain needs to be split very often. This contradicts the basic BC idea, since short chains may counteract transparency [41]. The so-called *pruning* is a deletion method already used in the Bitcoin blockchain. Pruning removes old and thus no longer needed parts of the chain while maintaining the integrity of the whole chain using Merkle trees [9]. However, this can only delete transaction values that have been "consumed" (i.e. spent Bitcoin). No other data could be pruned [6].

Concerning the right of data portability, it is unlikely that a standard file format will evolve in the near future, as lock-in effects are economically advantageous to companies. The current diversity of the blockchain market underlines this problem [2]. The question also arises as to who should guarantee the rights of those affected (see the following subsection).

5.3 Identification of the Data Controller

Problem Description: To protect the rights of a data subject, the GDPR provides for a (joint) data controller who, for example, acts as an addressee for data subjects to assert their rights, or who fulfills the transparency requirements of the Articles 13 and 14. One third of all respondents were of the opinion that the difficulty in identifying the data controller (see also Sect. 2.2) makes it considerably harder to comply with the legal requirements.

Suggested Solutions and Evaluation: Respondents suggest using a permissioned *private or consortium blockchain,* as the participants are known there. Researchers, such as [3], agree with this, even though this contradicts the basic BC idea of transparency and distributed responsibility. Nevertheless, in light of recent developments in case law and EDPB recommendations, we concur with this assessment. In view of the vast number and geographical location of different nodes and users, we do not expect that it will be possible to fulfill the data protection requirements regarding the obligations of data controllers in a public BC. Alternatively, the problem of responsibility could be solved by limiting the personal nature of data to a manageable group of actors (see the following subsection on encryption) [3, 7].

5.4 Encryption

Problem Description: In connection with the above-mentioned problems of identifying the data controller and guaranteeing the rights of those affected by data processing, an important strand of the debate is devoted to solutions using *encryption.*

Suggested Solutions and Evaluation: Many respondents point out that the DP challenges related to erasure could be solved by *encryption.* The respondents' assumptions sound simple: data would only be considered personal for those actors who have the access key. In this regard, eco - the Association of the Internet Industry demands that the verified destruction of a decryption key should be considered sufficient for anonymization.

The French Data Protection Authority CNIL agrees with this opinion. However, [3] points out the need for further regulatory advice on this issue, as under the current conditions, even nodes that do not actually have significant control over the encrypted data could still be considered responsible.

From a technical point of view, encryption is not identical to physical erasure - it only makes data inaccessible. In this respect, both respondents and researchers fear that current encryption methods could be cracked in the future and data made accessible [7]. However, (a)synchronous encryption algorithms such as AES or RSA are commonly used to encrypt bulk data [42] and cracking these is very unlikely in practice, as AES-256 and RSA-2048 are considered secure for the next decades [43]. However, BC creates an immutable technology architecture, which relies on cryptographic procedures. In case of an error in a procedure, the entire chain would be affected forever. Thus, as long as no further regulatory guidance is provided, only erasure methods as discussed in Sect. 5.2 could help to overcome the problems.

5.5 Storage Outside the European Union

Problem Description: The GDPR requires that if any personal data is transferred outside the EU, it must meet the requirements of Articles 44–49 GDPR. As a public BC is distributed among many (unidentifiable) users, personal data could be stored outside of the EU, which causes compliance difficulty.

Suggested Solutions and Evaluation: The respondents referred to the use of a *private or consortium blockchain*. Indeed, this would solve some challenges, as only EU citizens could be allowed to join. However, it would thwart the BC's goal of maximizing transparency. While relying on a public chain, *geo-blocking* could be a solution, but is not in accordance with European law [44]. Furthermore, VPN software can easily circumvent geo-blocking.[3] Apart from the possibilities mentioned above, the transfer of data outside the EU is currently an ongoing problem (not only) in the BC context.

5.6 Data Readability and Writability for BC Participants

Problem Description: Another important challenge articulated by the respondents is that all blockchain users can read and write all data, even personal data, as there is no possibility of verification for non-transactional data. Here a dilemma arises: while the visibility of all data ought to support transparency, readability and writability also raises significant DP concerns, because any user can add personal data to the BC. This poses a challenge even if limiting responsibility to the owner of the private keys would enable DP-compliant operation of a BC. Indeed, other users could enter unencrypted personal data into BC at any time and thus invalidate its data protection compliance.

Suggested Solutions and Evaluation: Most respondents suggest using *access-restricted (private) blockchains* to let only registered users participate. Although this could relieve several DP challenges, it runs counter to the BC intention of ensuring

---

[3] *Please note that this assessment was made before July 16, 2020, when the European Court of Justice ruled that the EU-US Privacy Shield is invalid.*

full transparency. Other respondents suggest a rather pragmatic approach: simply *no Storage of Personal Data*. However, technical or organizational measures cannot fully achieve this. Firstly, data that are not personal today, could become so in future [45]. Secondly, content filters could be easily circumvented by experienced users, and excluding these users is also very difficult [46]. Respondents also discuss *pseudonymization* as an effective method to veil personal references. However, it has become relatively easy to re-assign data. For example, [47] de-pseudonymized up to 60% of the IP addresses used to execute Bitcoin transactions. The literature does not provide effective solutions to render de-pseudonymization impossible, as even TOR network users can be identified by their Bitcoin transactions [48]. Another possible solution is a Bitcoin mixer, which combines several transactions into a large bitcoin pool and then distributes the coins to the receivers [49]. However, the service provider still knows the user's bitcoin address and could de-anonymize data. Furthermore, the mixing service could be a honeypot set up by governments to identify users. For the same reason, *anonymization* cannot be guaranteed for all BC applications. Even Monero, which claims to be an anonymous cryptocurrency, is prone to de-anonymization errors [50].

6   Conclusions and Outlook

The data protection-related challenges of BC technology are taking center stage for many companies in different industry sectors. Despite a broad debate, little was known about the concrete challenges facing companies and how they intend to overcome them.

Our results augment the existing literature in several regards. First, our study contributes to undermining the view that DP regulations are an insurmountable hurdle to the use of BCs. The number of actors perceiving a challenge (81%) and believing it can be overcome (70%) is very similar. Second, our analysis provides insights into which challenges the stakeholders regard as particularly important. Immutability is the biggest challenge for most respondents. Whereas many answers relate to public BCs and guaranteeing data subjects' rights, some respondents even promote BC as improving DP, e.g. via self-sovereign identities. Third, our results also show that the majority consider the problems solvable with already available technologies, in particular off-chain storage, encryption, pseudonymization and ZKPs. However, a comparison with state-of-the-art scientific literature reveals that only off-chain storage and encryption are advisable. Finally, a considerable number of actors also demanded the use of a private BC, promotion of further technical developments, and concretization or modification of the GDPR. These results show that stakeholders are aware that there is no silver bullet to overcome DP-related challenges. Instead, solutions depend strongly on the specific implementation and use case. Ultimately, our results show that most challenges arise in the field of public BCs. Thus, academia should focus on solutions here (e.g. chameleon hash functions). Furthermore, computer science research could benefit from empirical insights into how BC stakeholders perceive the challenges and solutions, and how these coincide with research. Practitioners can benefit from the evaluation of solutions to installing a BC architecture that best addresses DP demands. Additionally, our results offer important insights for policy makers, as they can see what specific challenges companies face and which research to support.

Although we rely on a large sample of 94 stakeholders, it is not representative for all industry sectors, since the sample contains only actors who took part in the consultation. The quantity and quality of coders is another common criticism of content analysis. However, our reliability measure shows moderate strength.

Future research could make a quantitative analysis of how often the proposed solutions are mentioned by stakeholders across all industry sectors. This would also pave the way for sector-specific analyses to find out whether, for example, certain sectors see greater challenges, or whether economic actors and researchers hold different views.

Funding and Acknowledgement. This research has been funded by the German Federal Ministry of Education and Research (BMBF) within the Project "Forum Privatheit und selbstbestimmtes Leben in der Digitalen Welt". We would like to thank our colleagues from the "Forum Privatheit" as well as Dirk Achenbach and Jochen Rill from FZI Research Center for Information Technology, for detailed and helpful feedback during the development of this paper.

References

1. Deloitte: Deloitte's 2020 Global Blockchain Survey (2020)
2. Grover, P., Kar, A.K., Janssen, M.: Diffusion of blockchain technology. JEIM **32**, 735–757 (2019)
3. Finck, M.: Blockchain and the General data protection regulation. Can distributed ledgers be squared with European data protection law? European Parliament, Brussels (2019)
4. Holotiuk, F., Pisani, F., Moormann, J.: The impact of blockchain technology on business models in the payments industry. In: Proceedings of Wirtschaftsinformatik (2017)
5. European Commission: European countries join Blockchain Partnership (2018). https://ec. europa.eu/digital-single-market/en/news/european-countries-join-blockchain-partnership
6. Farshid, S., Reitz, A., Roßbach, P.: Design of a forgetting blockchain: a possible way to accomplish GDPR compatibility. In: HICSS-52 (2019)
7. Fridgen, G., Guggenberger, N., Hoeren, T., Prinz, W., Urbach, N.: Chancen und Herausforderungen von DLT (Blockchain) in Mobilität und Logistik, Berlin (2019)
8. Nofer, M., Gomber, P., Hinz, O., Schiereck, D.: Blockchain. Bus. Inf. Syst. Eng. **59**, 183–187 (2017)
9. Nakamoto, S.: Bitcoin: a peer-to-peer electronic cash system (2008)
10. Hughes, L., Dwivedi, Y.K., Misra, S.K., Rana, N.P., Raghavan, V., Akella, V.: Blockchain research, practice and policy: applications, benefits, limitations, emerging research themes and research agenda. IJIM **49**, 114–129 (2019)
11. EDPB: Guidelines 07/2020 on the concepts of controller and processor in the GDPR (2020)
12. CJEU: Data Protection Commissioner v Facebook Ireland Limited and Maximillian Schrems: Case C 311/18 (2020)
13. PwC: Global Blockchain Survey 2018 (2018)
14. Gentemann, L.: Blockchain in Deutschland – Einsatz, Potenziale, Herausforderungen. Studienbericht 2019. Berlin (2019)
15. Yli-Huumo, J., Ko, D., Choi, S., Park, S., Smolander, K.: Where is current research on blockchain technology?-A systematic review. PloS One **11**, e0163477 (2016)
16. Florian, M., Henningsen, S., Beaucamp, S., Scheuermann, B.: Erasing data from blockchain nodes. In: 2019 IEEE European Symposium on Security and Privacy Workshops (EuroS&PW), pp. 367–376. IEEE (2019)

17. Press and Information Office of the Federal Government: Blockchain Strategy of the Federal Government (2019)
18. Sausen, T.: BVDW lobt Blockchain-Strategie der Bundesregierung (2019). https://www.bvdw.org/der-bvdw/news/detail/artikel/bvdw-lobt-blockchain-strategie-der-bundesregierung/
19. Brandenburg, M.: Die Blockchain-Strategie der Bundesregierung – ein überfälliges Positionspapier (2019). https://www.btc-echo.de/die-blockchain-strategie-der-bundesregierung-ein-ueberfaelliges-positionspapier/
20. Streim, A., Hansen, P.: Bitkom: Blockchain-Strategie gibt Aufbruchsignal (2019). https://www.bitkom.org/Presse/Presseinformation/Bitkom-Blockchain-Strategie-gibt-Aufbruchsignal
21. Krippendorff, K.: Content Analysis. An Introduction to Its Methodology. Sage Publication, Thousand Oaks (2004)
22. BMWi, BMF: Online-Konsultation zur Erarbeitung der Blockchain-Strategie der Bundesregierung (2019). https://www.bmwi.de/Redaktion/DE/Downloads/-Stellungnahmen/Stellungnahmen-Blockchain/stellungnahmen.pdf
23. Lombard, M., Snyder-Duch, J., Bracken, C.C.: Content analysis in mass communication: assessment and reporting of intercoder reliability. Hum. Commun. Res. **28**, 587–604 (2002)
24. Ateniese, G., Magri, B., Venturi, D., Andrade, E.: Redactable blockchain – or – rewriting history in bitcoin and friends. In: IEEE European Symposium on Security and Privacy (EuroS&P), Piscataway, NJ, pp. 111–126. IEEE (2017)
25. Schwerin, S.: Blockchain and privacy protection in the case of the European general data protection regulation (GDPR): a Delphi study. JBBA **1**, 1–77 (2018)
26. EC: Data Protection as a Pillar of Citizens' Empowerment and the EU's Approach to the Digital Transition. Communication from the Commission to the European Parliament and the Council (2020)
27. Warkentin, M., Orgeron, C.: Using the security triad to assess blockchain technology in public sector applications. IJIM **52**, 102090 (2020)
28. Piscini, E., Dalton, D., Kehoe, L.: Blockchain & Cyber Security (2017)
29. Belchior, R., Vasconcelos, A., Guerreiro, S., Correia, M.: A survey on blockchain interoperability: past, present, and future trends (2020)
30. Behnke, K., Janssen, M.F.W.H.A.: Boundary conditions for traceability in food supply chains using blockchain technology. IJIM **52**, 101969 (2020)
31. Zyskind, G., Nathan, O., Pentland, A.S.: Decentralizing privacy: using blockchain to protect personal data. In: 2015 IEEE Security and Privacy Workshops (SPW), Piscataway, NJ, pp. 180–184. IEEE (2015)
32. Memon, I.: An analysis of privacy preserving data aggregation protocols for WSNs. In: Park, J.J., Zomaya, A., Yeo, S.-S., Sahni, S. (eds.) NPC 2012. LNCS, vol. 7513, pp. 119–128. Springer, Heidelberg (2012). https://doi.org/10.1007/978-3-642-35606-3_14
33. Jaikaran, C.: Blockchain: Background and Policy Issues (2018)
34. BSI: Blockchain sicher gestalten. Konzepte, Anforderungen, Bewertungen (2019)
35. Lumb, R., Treat, D., Jelf, O.: Editing the uneditable Blockchain. Why distributed ledger technology must adapt to an imperfect world (2016)
36. Kohn, W., Tamm, U.: Mathematik für Wirtschaftsinformatiker: Grundlagen und Anwendungen. Springer, Heidelberg (2019). https://doi.org/10.1007/978-3-662-59468-1
37. Bitcoin Wiki: Non-specialized hardware comparison (2020). https://en.bitcoin.it/wiki/Non-specialized_hardware_comparison
38. Fill, H.-G., Haerer, F.: Knowledge blockchains: applying blockchain technologies to enterprise modeling. In: HICSS-51 2018 (2018)

39. Fatz, F., Hake, P., Fettke, P.: Confidentiality-preserving validation of tax documents on the blockchain. In: Gronau, N., Heine, M., Poustcchi, K., Krasnova, H. (eds.) WI2020 Zentrale Tracks, pp. 1262–1277. GITO (2020)

40. Yung, M.: Zero-knowledge proofs of computational power. In: Quisquater, J.-J., Vandewalle, J. (eds.) EUROCRYPT 1989. LNCS, vol. 434, pp. 196–207. Springer, Heidelberg (1990). https://doi.org/10.1007/3-540-46885-4_22

41. Avital, M., Beck, R., King, J.L., Rossi, M., Teigland, R.: Jumping on the blockchain Bandwagon: lessons of the past and outlook to the future. In: Proceedings of the 37th ICIS (2016)

42. Thambiraja, E., Ramesh, G., Umarani, R.: A survey on various most common encryption techniques. Int. J. Adv. Res. Comput. Sci. Softw. Eng. (IJARCSSE) **2**, 226–233 (2012)

43. Bernstein, D.J., Lange, T.: Post-quantum cryptography. Nature **549**, 188–194 (2017)

44. European Parliament: Distributed ledger technologies and blockchains: building trust with disintermediation (2018). http://www.europarl.europa.eu/doceo/document/TA-8-2018-0373_EN.html

45. Tönnissen, S., Teuteberg, F.: DSGVO und die Blockchain. Datenschutz und Datensicherheit **44**, 322–327 (2020)

46. Matzutt, R., Henze, M., Ziegeldorf, J.H., Hiller, J., Wehrle, K.: Thwarting Unwanted Blockchain Content Insertion. In: Chandra, A. (ed.) 2018 IEEE IC2E, Piscataway, NJ, pp. 364–370. IEEE (2018)

47. Biryukov, A., Tikhomirov, S.: Deanonymization and linkability of cryptocurrency transactions based on network analysis. In: Proceedings of the 4th IEEE EuroS&P, pp. 172–184. IEEE (2019)

48. Jawaheri, H.A., Sabah, M.A., Boshmaf, Y., Erbad, A.: Deanonymizing Tor hidden service users through Bitcoin transactions analysis. Comput. Secur. **89**, 101684 (2020)

49. Ciaian, P., Rajcaniova, M., Kancs, d.'A.: The digital agenda of virtual currencies: can BitCoin become a global currency? Inf. Syst. E-Bus Manag. **14**, 883–919 (2016)

50. Möser, M., et al.: An empirical analysis of traceability in the Monero blockchain. In: Proceedings of PoPETs (2018)

CyberSecurity Challenges for Software Developer Awareness Training in Industrial Environments

Tiago Gasiba[1,2]([✉]), Ulrike Lechner[2], and Maria Pinto-Albuquerque[3]

[1] Siemens AG, Munich, Germany
tiago.gasiba@siemens.com
[2] Universität der Bundeswehr München, Munich, Germany
{tiago.gasiba,ulrike.lechner}@unibw.de
[3] Instituto Universitário de Lisboa (ISCTE-IUL), ISTAR, Lisbon, Portugal
maria.albuquerque@iscte-iul.pt

Abstract. Awareness of cybersecurity topics facilitates software developers to produce secure code. This awareness is especially important in industrial environments for the products and services in critical infrastructures. In this work, we address how to raise awareness of software developers on the topic of secure coding. We propose the "CyberSecurity Challenges", a serious game designed to be used in an industrial environment and address software developers' needs. Our work distills the experience gained in conducting these CyberSecurity Challenges in an industrial setting. The main contributions are the design of the CyberSecurity Challenges events, the analysis of the perceived benefits, and practical advice for practitioners who wish to design or refine these games.

Keywords: Cybersecurity · Serious games · Awareness · Industry · Capture-the-flag · Education

1 Introduction

Over the last years, the number of industrial security-related incidents, e.g., reported by the ICS-CERT [8], has been steadily increasing. When malicious parties exploit security vulnerabilities present in products and services, the outcome of its exploitation has serious negative consequences for society, the customers, and the company that produced the software. Think, e.g., of critical infrastructures as the grid, transportation, or production lines: a security vulnerability in the code may cause interruptions in service quality or cause safety issues for society or individual customers when critical machinery fails. Several efforts can be made to increase the level of security in critical infrastructures. These efforts include, among others: analysis of threat and risks, implementing a secure software development lifecycle process, deployment of static application security testing tools, code reviews, and training. This paper addresses the software vulnerabilities through awareness training of software developers in the industry, based on a serious game: the CyberSecurity Challenges (CSC). Serious Games are

F. Ahlemann et al. (Eds.): WI 2021, LNISO 47, pp. 370–387, 2021.
https://doi.org/10.1007/978-3-030-86797-3_25

games that are *designed for a primary purpose other than pure entertainment* [9]. The serious game "CyberSecurity Challenges" (CSC) aims at raising awareness of secure coding topics among industrial software engineers. In this game, software developers are trained to spot security vulnerabilities in software and write secure code. i.e., code that is free from known vulnerabilities and adheres to secure coding policies. Previous work introduced the CyberSecurity Challenges from a theoretical point-of-view [11, 16] and focused on particular aspects [15]. The current work extends previous publications by a presentation of a unified view on the design process, tailoring to the industry's needs and the perceived usefulness of the CSC events. Our results are based on data from several CSC events held in the industry from 2017 to 2020. As such, the main contributions of this work are:

- **CSC Artifact**: consolidated view of the design and deployment of CSCs, based on results from thirteen events held in an industrial context, and
- **CSC Evaluation:** analysis of results from industry events covering the following aspects: adequacy of CSC as a means to raise secure coding awareness, impact of CSC on software developers, and success factors for CSC events.

This paper aims to guide practitioners who wish to develop or refine a software developer awareness training in an industrial context, provide a solid reference to the research community who wishes to address serious games for the industry, and close the existing literature gap. This work is organized as follows. In the following section, we give a summary of the game idea and logic of CSC games. Section 3 presents related work. In Sect. 4, the research method and research questions are introduced. The unified view of the CSC artifact is presented in Sect. 5. Section 6 presents a summary of the survey results, together with critical discussions. Finally, Sect. 7 concludes the paper with an outlook of next steps.

2 Cybersecurity Challenges at a Glance

The CyberSecurity Challenges (CSCs) are a serious game, designed to raise awareness for cybersecurity topics among industrial software engineers. A CSC game consists of several challenges designed to raise awareness on secure coding guidelines and secure coding on software developers. These challenges are oriented towards improving the defensive skills of the participants. Defensive challenges are challenges that help the players write code that has no (known) vulnerabilities and adheres to secure coding guidelines.

The Capture-the-Flag genre was the original inspiration for the game. Capture the-Flag (CTFs) are associated with offensive skills, e.g., system penetration, and reverse engineering, and they can often last hours or even days [23]. Unlike CTF games, which teach the participants to attack and break into systems, CSC focus on improving skills to write and develop secure code. These games thus have no intention to cause any harm or inspire unlawful actions – they are about "defensive" skills. The challenges are composed of C, C++, Java, and Web exercises. The focus on these programming languages and genre inspiration is rooted in internal demand for training and internal decisions taken in the company where CSC is developed. Thus, the games are designed to match software developers' interests and organizations' needs for developer training. This interest can be motivated by several factors, e.g., the need to show due diligence and certification purposes.

The CSC event is delivered as a single event (Standalone type) or after a workshop on secure coding (Workshop type). In both cases, the duration of the event is designed to fit a single working day. During the game, the participants solve secure coding challenges related to secure coding guidelines, either individually or as part of a team. Although the challenges can include an offensive part (e.g., on how malicious parties exploit systems), the main focus and emphasis of the challenges is on developing secure software, i.e., on the defensive perspective. For each solved challenge, points are awarded, and the winner of the game is the one with the highest number of points. Participants to the event can have either a background in a single programming language or be mixed, e.g., both C and Web developers.

3   Related Work

Although several methods exist to deal with software vulnerabilities, e.g., requirements engineering and code reviews, we focus on awareness training for software developers. Several previous studies indicate that software developers lack secure programming awareness and skills [2, 26, 31]. In 2020, Bruce Schneier, a well-known security researcher, and evangelist stated that "more than 50% of software developers cannot spot security vulnerabilities in software" [29]. His comment adds to a discussion on secure coding skills: In 2011, Xie et al. [32] did an interview study with 15 senior professional software developers in the industry with an average of 12 years of experience. Their study has shown a disconnect between "software developers' understanding of security concepts and their attitudes in their jobs". Awareness training on information security is addressed in McIlwraith [22], which looks at employee behavior and provides a systematic methodology and a baseline on implementing awareness training. In their work, Stewart et al. [30] argue that communicators, e.g., trainers, must understand the audiences' constraints and supporting beliefs to provide an effective awareness program.

There is a stream of literature on compliance with security policies, which deals with employees in general and not with software developers specifically. This stream of literature explores many reasons why people do not comply with IT-security policies. The unified framework by Moody et al. [24] summarizes the academic discussion on compliance with IT-security policies. Empirical findings include that neither deterrence nor punishment such as e.g., public blame, works to increase compliance. However, increasing IT-security awareness increases the level of compliance [30]. In their seminal review article, Hänsch et al. [20] define IT-security awareness in the three dimensions: *Perception*, *Protection*, and *Behavior*. The concept of IT-security awareness is typically used in IT security management contexts, and we use this concept to evaluate our work. While these findings are for the compliance of employees with IT-security policies and awareness of IT security, little empirical research is done on IT-security awareness in software development and what makes software developers comply with security policies in software development.

Graziotin et al. [19] show that *happy developers are better coders*, i.e., produce higher quality code and software. Their work suggests that by keeping developers happy, we can expect that the code they write has a better quality and, by implication, be more secure. Davis et al. [7] show that cybersecurity games have the potential to increase the overall happiness of software developers. Their conclusions support our approach to use a serious game approach to train software developers in secure coding. Awareness games are a well-established instrument in information security and are discussed in defacto standards as the BSI Grundschutz-Katalog [5] (M 3.47, Planspiele) as one means to raise awareness and increase the level of security. Frey et al. [10] show both the potential impact of playing cybersecurity games on the participants and show the importance of playing games as a means of cybersecurity awareness. They conclude that cybersecurity games can be a useful means to build a common understanding of security issues. Rieb et al. [27] provide a review of serious games in cybersecurity and conclude that there are many approaches. However, only a few have an evaluation of their usefulness and are available beyond the immediate context of a consulting or cyber-security company. The games listed mainly address information security rather than secure coding. Documented and evaluated games are [4] and [27].

Capture-the-flag is one particular genre of serious games in the domain of Cyber-security [7]. Game participants win flags when they manage to solve a task. Forensics, cryptography, and penetration testing are skills necessary for solving tasks and capturing flags. They are considered fun, but there are hardly any empirical results on these games' effects on participants' skill levels. The present work uses serious games to achieve the goal of *raising secure coding awareness of software developers in the industry*. Previous work on selected design aspects and a smaller empirical basis on the CSC includes [11–18].

4 Method

The design science paradigm, according to Hevner [21], Baskerville and Heje [3] guides our research in the industry. Design and evaluation of designs in iterative approaches are an integral part of design research: this article presents our design after 13 CSC events and the evaluation of the design. The events took place from 2017 to 2020, with more than 200 game participants.

Table 1 summarizes the CSC events. CSC games were designed n three design cycles: 1) Initial Design (events 1–5), 2) Refinement (events 6–9) and 3) Sifu/Online (events 10–13).

The CSC events participants were all software developers specializing in web technologies and the C/C++ programming language. The events took place mostly in Germany but also in China and Turkey. The players' age ranged from 25 to 60, the background industry of the participants was critical infrastructures, in particular, industry automation (50.85%), energy (37.29%), and healthcare (11.86%), the overall number of years of work experience was as follows: one year (13.7%), two years (11.0%), three years (19.2%), four years (6.8%) and five or more years (49.3%). Regarding the average number of security training over the previous five years, the results are as follows: Germany –3.57, China 2.10, and Turkey 1.50.

Table 1. Overview of cybersecurity challenges events

No.	Date	Type	Focus	Where	NP	Data collection
1	Nov. 2017	Standalone	Mixed	Germany	11	SSI
2	May. 2018	Standalone	Web	Germany	12	SSI
3	Jul. 2018	Standalone	Web	Germany	6	SSI
4	Jul. 2018	Standalone	Mixed	Germany	30	SSI
5	Sep. 2018	Standalone	Web	Germany	16	SSI
6	Aug. 2019	Workshop	C/C++	China	14	Survey
7	Aug. 2019	Workshop	Web	China	15	Survey
8	Sep. 2019	Workshop	Web	Germany	7	Survey
9	Oct. 2019	Workshop	C/C++	Turkey	23	Survey
10	Jun. 2020	Standalone	C/C++	Online	15	Survey*
11	Jul. 2020	Standalone	C/C++	Online	21	Survey*
12	Jul. 2020	Standalone	C/C++	Online	20	Survey*
13	Jul. 2020	Standalone	C/C++	Online	15	Survey*

NP: No. of players, **SSI**: semi-structured interview, (*) for survey description see [15]

According to the first and second design cycles, the evaluation of these CSC events is structured according to the following research questions. For analysis of the survey results concerning the Sifu platform, we refer the reader to [15].

– **RQ1**: To what extent are CSC adequate to raise awareness about secure coding?
– **RQ2**: What is the impact that CSC workshops have on the participants?
– **RQ3:** Which factors are considered essential for a successful CSC event?

To address these research questions, the authors have conducted semi structured interviews (SSI) [1] and developed a small survey. The semi-structured interview questions were asked to the participants, one after another in a round-the-table. The participants' answers were recorded on paper. The semi-structured interviews were performed during the first design cycle and were part of the feedback round after the CSC event. They were based on the following questions: a) "what went well, and you would you like to keep" and b) "what did not go well and would you like to change". These questions gave a good insight and allowed us to improve later versions of the game. They were also fundamental for requirements elicitation (see [11]).

The survey was administered to the CSC participants, in the refinement cycle, after completion of the event. The survey consisted of an online survey. Participation in the SSI and the survey was opt-in. Furthermore, all participants consented to participate in research, and the collected data was anonymized. We have used a more formal survey methodology to evaluate the game's usefulness concerning the level of awareness and the skills in secure coding. Table 2 shows the questions that were asked in the survey and the related research questions. The survey used a five-point Likert scale of agreement with the following mapping: strongly disagree (1), disagree (2), neutral (3), agree (4), and strongly agree (5). RQ1 addresses the aspect of the usefulness of the CSC artifact, and the corresponding survey questions are based and adapted from the three dimensions of awareness, as defined by Hänsch et al. [20]: Perception (PE – knowing existing software vulnerabilities), Protection (PR – knowing how to write secure software) and

Behavior (BE – actual behavior of software developer) (cf. Sec. Related Work). The questions for RQ2 focus on clarity of the description of the challenges, the coaches' role during the game, and the general motivation of training secure coding. These questions address the design of CSC games and events. RQ3 questions address the challenges and their relation to software developers' everyday work practices in the industry. The survey questions for RQ2 and RQ3 are based on the authors' experience in industrial software engineering, feedback from CSC evaluations of events 1 to 5, and various discussions with colleagues. All the collected data were processed using the statistics package RStudio 1.2.5019. Availability of the gathered data is provided in the same authors' included references and on a forthcoming publication.

Table 2. Survey 1: questions

RQ	CT	QID	Question
			By participating in this awareness training _____
	PE	Q1.1	I learned new techniques and principles of secure software development
		Q2.1	I understand the possible consequences of a security breach
		Q3.1	I feel that I am prepared to handle secure coding related issues at work
		Q4.1	I understand the need to have secure development life-cycle activities
RQ1	BE	Q5.1	I feel more prepared to work with static code analysis tools (e.g. SAST)
		Q6.1	I know how to use the information about secure coding guidelines
		Q7.1	Focusing on the challenges improves my practical secure coding skills
		Q8.1	I have learned about new issues that I would like to check in my own code
	PR	Q9.1	I know where I can find more information about secure coding guidelines
		Q10.1	I understand the importance of secure coding guidelines
		Q11.1	The learning goals of the challenges were clearly explained
RQ2	–	Q12.1	CSC games help me to understand the need to develop secure software
		Q13.1	The help from the coaches was adequate
		Q14.1	I want to learn about new tools, even if I do not use them at work
		Q15.1	I prefer to solve challenges sequentially rather, even if it takes too much time
		Q16.1	Working in teams is better than working individually on the challenges
RQ3	–	Q17.1	I like the fact that different kinds of challenges are presented
		Q18.1	I prefer challenges that address the same problem from different point-of-views
		Q19.1	I prefer challenges that are related with my work environment
		Q20.1	I prefer challenges that are based on real-life examples
		Q21.1	I prefer challenges that can be systematically solved with some tool

RQ: Research Question, **CT**: Construct , **QID**: Question Identifier, **PE**: Perception,
BE: Behavior, **PR**: Protection

5   Design of the CyberSecurity Challenges

In this section, we present the design of the CyberSecurity Challenges for industrial software developers. The sub-sections provide a detailed overview of the architecture, the schedule, and the design of challenges. The results presented in this section distill the experience obtained through the three design cycles of the CSC games, i.e., of the thirteen CSC events.

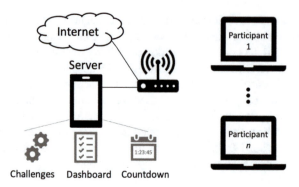

Fig. 1. Architecture of CyberSecurity Challenges infrastructure

5.1 Architecture

Figure 1 shows the architecture of the CSC infrastructure. Each participant, either individually or after forming a team, accesses the challenges through a computer. A server hosts the applications that run the game logic, a "countdown" clock, and a dashboard that records individual players and teams' progress. The dashboard uses the open-source CTFd [6] project. A description of the challenges will be given in the following.

5.2 CSC Time Schedule

Table 3 shows a typical time-plan for the one-day CSC event consisting of seven blocks: 1) welcome, 2) team building, 3) introduction, 4) main event, 5) winner announcement, 6) feedback and 7) walk-through. The last block, the walk-through, was not initially planned and is the direct result of players feedback—the participants preferred to dedicate one hour of the main event to provide final explanations and closure on selected exercises. The authors decided to place the feedback and survey before the walk-through to increase the chance of collecting feedback from the participants.

Table 3. Agenda for a one-day cybersecurity challenges game event

Duration	What	Description
10 min	Welcome	Welcome to participants and accessing CSC infrastructure
20 min	Team building	Participants select partners and build teams that will play against each other
30 min	Introduction	Challenge types are presented. One challenge in each category is solved in order to show the participants how the game works
320 min	Main event	Game is open and teams are free to play the game. They are responsible for defining their own strategy for time-out (e.g. for lunch break).
10 min	Winner	Game is closed and teams can no longer submit points to the dashboard. Winning team is announced. A brief review of the game-play is done together with the participants.
30 min	Feedback	Participants are asked to fill out a survey about the game. Additionally, discussions with players is held in short non-systematic interviews. Main points of discussions is recorded for later analysis.
60 min	Walk-through	Participants are shown solution to the exercises they considered most difficult. These exercises are solved together in interaction with all the participants. Discussion on how to solve the challenge is highly encouraged.

The duration of similar training events ranges from several days [23] (less common) to a single day [28] (more common). Note that the first CTF is done in academia, while a commercial provider does the latter. Additionally, a difference to typical Capture-the-Flag events are the two agenda items *Introduction* and *Walk-through*.

5.3 Defensive Challenges

The primary focus of the CSC game's challenges are Web and C/C++. In contrast to C/C++, for the web challenges, it was decided not to focus on a single programming language or framework since many of these programming languages and frameworks are in everyday use in the company where the CSC game was developed. In this case, we chose a generic approach based on the Open Web Application Security Project – OWASP [25]. The challenges' design took two approaches: 1) based on open-source components and 2) design of own challenges. The first approach was used in the Refinement design cycle, while the second approach in the Sifu/Online design cycle. A common approach to the design of the challenges is given in [16]. Each challenge is presented to the participants according to the following phases: *Phase 1* - introduction, *Phase 2* - challenge, and *Phase 3* - conclusion. The types of challenges are: Single Choice Questions (SCQ), Multiple-Choice Questions (MCQ), Text-Entry Questions (TEQ), Associate-Left-Right (ALR), Code-Snippet Challenge (CsC), and Code-Entry Challenge (CEC). Second, Phase 1 presents an introduction to the challenge and sets up the scenario; the main part of the challenge is phase 2; phase 3 concludes the challenge by adding additional text related to secure coding guidelines or additional questions related to phase 2.

Challenges using Open-Source Components. Challenges on secure coding for software developers can be implemented by using and adapting existing open-source components. Since most of the available projects focus on the offensive perspective, the following adaptations are suggested: 1) include an incomplete description on how to solve the challenge, and 2) provide follow-up questions related to secure coding guidelines. Figure 2, 3 and 4 shows an example of a challenge for Web developers using OWASP JuiceShop. This challenge's learning goal is to understand what SQL injections are and how to identify an SQL injection quickly. Phase 1 sets the stage for the challenge (Fig. 2). In Phase 2, the player is assisted with how to find the vulnerability, through the textual description, as in Fig. 3, or also directed by the game coaches. The last phase consists of an additional question related to the exercise, as shown in Fig. 4, which directs the player to secure coding guidelines. Table 4 shows the open-source projects and components in which have been used to design CSC challenges for Web and for C/C++, along with the expected effort required to modify them. Note that the design of these challenges is based on open-source components that include an offensive perspective. Therefore, after the components' adaptation, these types of challenges are described as being *defensive/offensive*.

Defensive Challenges using Sifu Platform. The Sifu platform hosts code projects containing vulnerabilities in a web application. The reason to choose a web interface is to avoid that the players need to install any software on their machine, which might be difficult in an industrial setting. The players' task is to fix the project's source code to

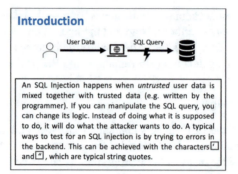

Fig. 2. Web challenge: phase 1

Fig. 3. Web challenge: phase 2

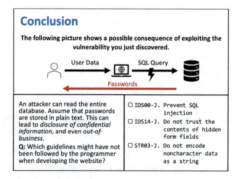

Fig. 4. Web challenge: phase 3

bring it to an acceptable solution (therefore focusing on the defensive perspective). An acceptable solution is a solution where the source code is compliant to secure coding guidelines and does not have known vulnerabilities. The Sifu platform contains two main components: 1) challenge assessment and 2) an automatic coach. The challenge assessment component analyses the proposed solution submitted by a player and determines if it is acceptable. Analysis is based on several tools, e.g., compiler output, static code

Fig. 5. Sifu platform

Table 4. Open-source tools used for cybersecurity challenges

Type	Project	Effort	Description
Web/Java	Juice Shop	Minimal	Insecure web application for training purposes from the OWASP project.
Web/Java	Java SEI-CERT	Medium	Secure coding guidelines dedicated to Java from Carnegie Mellon University
Web	Vulnerable API	Medium	REST API containing several vulnerabilities
C/C++	MBE	Small	Vulnerable code from RPISEC course at Rensselaer Polytechnic Institute
C/C++	C/C++ SEI-CERT	Medium	Secure coding guidelines dedicated to C/C++ from Carnegie Mellon University
C/C++	Vulnerable code snippets	High	Vulnerable C/C++ code from NIST (Juliet Set)

analysis, and dynamic code analysis. The automatic coach component is implemented through an artificial intelligence technique that provides hints to the participant when the solution is not acceptable, with the intent to guide the participant to an acceptable solution. Figure 5 shows the Sifu platform. Note that only phase 2 is shown in the figure. The player can browse the different files of the project. All the hints issued by the automatic coach are available on the right-hand side. If the player experiences errors when using the platform, these can be reported for later analysis and improvement. The Sifu platform's main advantage is that the participants do not need to install any software in their machine - a browser with internet or intranet access is sufficient. However, since untrusted and potentially malicious code will be executed in the platform during the analysis stage, several security mechanisms need to be implemented to guarantee that the players cannot hack it. These challenges were developed in the Sifu/Online design cycle, and further and detailed information on the implementation is available in [15]. For more information about the Sifu platform we also refer the reader to [14]. The Sifu platform is available for download as an open-source platform under the MIT license in [18].

6   Results

This section presents a quantitative analysis of the CSC artifact based on the semi-structured interviews and online survey collected during the design cycles Initial Design and Refinement.

6.1   Initial Design Cycle—CSC 1 to 5

As discussed in Sect. 4, in this design cycle, the participants were asked to provide feedback on what should be kept and what should be changed in the CSC event. The participants were encouraged to discuss openly what they felt was important. These discussions were used to inform the design of future CSC events. In this cycle, requirements were collected on traits that serious games for software developers in the industry should have. A summary of the findings is as follows: 1) *challenges should focus on the defensive perspective*, 2) *challenges should reflect real-world examples*, 3) *challenges should be aligned with the work environment*, 4) *careful planning in terms of duration should be performed*, and 5) *participants should be able to solve challenges without knowledge of extra tools*. A more in-depth analysis of the feedback and resulting requirements is available in [11].

6.2   Artifact Refinement Cycle—CSC 6 to 9

Figure 6 shows the overall results of the answers to the survey. The research questions are used to group the results. We observe an overall agreement on all the survey questions. In particular, considering negative answers ($-$), neutral answers (N) and positive answers ($+$), this table shows the following overall results for each research question: $RQ1^- = 7.89\%$, $RQ1^N = 16.13\%$, $RQ1^+ = 75.99\%$, $RQ2^- = 4.82\%$, $RQ2^N = 12.05\%$, $RQ2^+ = 83.13\%$, $RQ3^- = 4.19\%$, $RQ3^N = 12.56\%$, and $RQ3^+ = 83.26\%$.

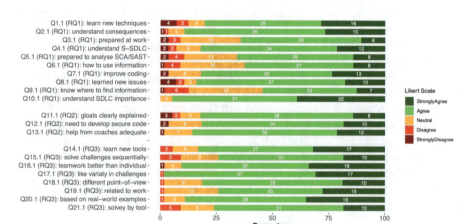

Fig. 6. Evaluation of usefulness of CSC events 6–9

These results give a good indication that CSC games are suitable as a means to train software developers in secure coding guidelines, as the factors on awareness (RQ1) and impact on participants (RQ2) have high levels of agreement (i.e., higher than 75%. However, we observe the difficulty in making every participant happy, in particular, due to the residual values on negative and neutral answers. Further analysis is required to understand this. Based on our experience, we believe that this fact might be correlated with the participants' previous experience.

Table 5 shows a ranking of the different survey questions, grouped by research question. The ranking is performed by sorting the questions based on the average agreement value. In terms of adequacy (RQ1), and impact on the participants (RQ2), the two highest-ranking answers are: to understand the importance of SDLC (Q10) and understand consequences of a breach (Q2) for RQ1, and help from coaches (Q13), and understand the need to develop secure software (Q12) respectively. The lowest-ranked factors for RQ1 are "find more information" (Q9) and "prepared to handle secure coding issues at work" (Q3). Although the rank is low, the average agreement is positive. The surprising result obtained for Q3 is likely related to the large number of neutral answers. Further investigations are required to determine the root cause of this observation.

Table 5. Analysis of Research Questions for Survey on CSC Events 6–9

	Rank	1	2	3	4	5	6	7	8	9	10
RQ1	W.Avg.	4.34	4.11	3.98	3.93	3.89	3.84	3.66	3.66	3.63	3.53
	QID	Q10.1	Q2.1	Q7.1	Q4.1	Q1.1	Q8.1	Q5.1	Q6.1	Q3.1	Q9.1
RQ2	W.Avg.	4.04	3.93	3.82	-	-	-	-	-	-	-
	QID	Q13.1	Q12.1	Q11.1	-	-	-	-	-	-	-
RQ3	W.Avg.	4.27	4.22	4.21	4.09	4.00	4.00	3.85	3.83	-	-
	QID	Q17.1	Q20.1	Q16.1	Q14.1	Q18.1	Q19.1	Q21.1	Q15.1	-	-

The collected results for RQ3 serve to inform practitioners who wish to design such games for an industrial context. It provides a ranked list of factors that participants consider having a positive impact on CSC games. The three top factors that contribute to the success of a CSC game that should be considered by practitioners who wish refine the CSC game are the following: different kinds of challenges (Q17), based on real-life examples (Q20), and participants should work in teams rather and individually (Q16).

In terms of awareness, taking into consideration negative answers ($-$), neutral answers (N), and positive answers (+), the perception (PE), behavior (BE), and protection (PR) show the following results: $PE^- = 8.04\%$, $PE^N = 7.14\%$, $PE^+ = 84.82\%$, $BE^- = 7.89\%$, $BE^N = 20.79\%$, $BE^+ = 71.33\%$, $PR^- = 7.78\%$, $PR^N = 14.37\%$, $PR^+ = 77.84\%$. These results show similar values for the negative answers (around 8%), which might be related to the players' background. The highest result is related to perception, which also has the least number of neutral answers. While we observe strong agreement on the behavior and protection constructs (more than 70%), there are still many neutral answers. We believe that the large number of neutral answers is also related to player background and the fact that the challenge type is not purely defensive, i.e., it is defensive/offensive, as discussed in Sect. 5. The reasoning for this is based on the better results obtained in the study of the Sifu platform (see [15]).

6.3   Sifu/Online Cycle—CSC 10 to 13

In this design cycle, the CSC challenges were further developed as the Sifu platform [15]. The participants were asked to evaluate the platform through 5point Likert scale questions. Survey questions were based on the Awareness [20], and Happiness [19] dimensions. The following is a summary of the results, in terms of the three awareness dimensions: perception (PE), behavior (BE), and protection (PR); and in terms of happiness (HP). $PE^- = 2.22\%$, $PE^N = 8.89\%$, $PE^+ = 88.89\%$, $BE^- = 0.0\%$, $BE^N = 8.06\%$, $BE^+ = 91.94\%$, $PR^- = 6.67\%$, $PR^N = 11.11\%$, $PR^+ = 82.22\%$, $HP^- = 8.22\%$, $HP^N = 10.27\%$, $HP^+ = 81.51\%$. The negative results $(-)$ correspond to strongly disagree and disagree, neutral (N) to neutral answers, and positive results (+) correspond to agree and strongly agree. A more in-depth analysis of these results, along with the Sifu platform's design, and the survey questions, can be found in [14]. The collected answers again indicate an agreement with the awareness theory, in the following sequence: behavior, perception, and finally, protection. Also, the participants report having fun and being happy while playing challenges in the Sifu platform.

The Hellinger distance is used to measure the distance between two probability mass functions (PMF). The distance between the PMF of the three awareness constructs was computed to compare the results obtained in the second (refinement) and third cycle (Sifu/Online). The obtained results are as follows (from higher distance value to smaller distance value): behavior $(d = 0.25)$, perception $(d = 0.10)$, and protection $(d = 0.04)$. These results show that using the Sifu platform results in the most significant improvement in agreement on the behavior construct. Although both cycles indicate positive results, the participants have a more substantial agreement that solving the Sifu platform's challenges helps in actual behavior (i.e., using defensive challenges), than using defensive/offensive challenges. In terms of protection, the distance between the PMF is low (0.04), indicating that the agreement level is similar for the protection construct for both the defensive/offensive and the defensive challenges. These results were as expected since the improvements to the challenges and the corresponding design cycles performed in the Sifu platform increase the adequacy to improve software developer awareness in terms of behavior.

6.4   Discussions

In this work, we have presented and evaluated an awareness training program for software developers in the industry, which was designed through three design cycles [21]. The types of CSC challenges for each design cycle were as follows: offensive, defensive/offensive, and defensive. The initial design cycle was mostly used for requirements elicitation to further develop and refine the CyberSecurity Challenges for software developers in the industry. In the second design cycle, defensive/offensive challenges were introduced. These challenges adapt existing open-source projects to adopt a defensive perspective. Finally, in the third design cycle, defensive challenges are introduced using the Sifu platform. Our experience has shown that software developers highly appreciate playing CSC games based on direct feedback from participants. It was also observed that playing CSC games can be done as either a standalone event or after a secure coding training. Furthermore, the participants have claimed that the challenges have helped solidify, understand, and practice secure coding in real scenarios, the concepts discussed during training. While the challenges, as described for the second and third design cycle, seem to address software developers and management's needs adequately, the third design cycle was shown to result in a higher agreement in terms of the behavior (BE) awareness construct.

Participants report on the happiness and fun in participating in these events. However, a long-term study on the impact of CSC events on software quality is not possible. The reason for this is related to the large number of factors that hinder this study, which include, among others: job rotation, changing and evolving IT security technologies, discovery of new attack vectors, and evolving programming languages and programming language standards. Therefore, we need to suffice with the fact that these events are both welcome by software developers and, with the fact that CSC has had continuous management approval throughout the years, and also the fact that it has been introduced in the standard teaching curriculum in the company where it was developed.

While previous work such as McIlwraith [22] provides a generic approach for awareness training, we show a method that explicitly addresses software developers in the industry and is based on a serious game inspired by the Capture-the-Flag format. Nevertheless, some of the traits introduced by McIlwraith are also common with our artifact, e.g., the usage of web-based media and web-based text. While the CSC artifact was designed for Web and C/C++ challenges, we think our approach can be generalized to other programming languages. Other possible usages of our artifact include a refresher on previously acquired knowledge, a self-evaluation tool for individuals, and a recruiting tool used by human resources. However, further work might be required either for non-industrial environments or participants with different backgrounds, e.g., management or human resources.

6.5 Threats to Validity

There are threats to the validity of or findings - threats as they are typical or inherent to design research. Both the evaluation of the game in a survey and in the mixed workshop might lead to socially desired bias. Moreover, participants might evaluate the game positively in order to be able to get the awareness training done as it is a task that is mandated to them by management. The authors cannot control the types of workshops and the participants; however, we think that the conclusions are valid as they contributed to improving the serious game over time.

The authors claim that the game has a positive impact on IT security awareness. The path from awareness training to secure products and services is long and potentially tedious, and other kind of research would be needed to evaluate whether such a game has an impact on the quality of code. Due to the large number of factors that affect code quality, this is, in practice, not possible. Nevertheless, awareness is a well-established endpoint in IT security research.

As in any design research, we cannot argue that our solution is the best, and we need to suffice with the argument that our artifact and outcome of research is useful, both in terms of developers' happiness and management approval. There are several external variables that we cannot control in an industrial setting that can limit our evaluations' validity. Although we have explicitly mentioned to the participants that the survey questions refer to the CSC event, we cannot exclude questions' misinterpretation due to the participants' different cultural and language backgrounds.

Also, we cannot exclude a bias for socially desired answers and positive bias with the game setting. However, for the validity of our findings, we refer to the fact that all game participants were industrial software engineers, and participation in the survey was not mandatory. Our results demonstrate that these are a viable method for awareness training on secure coding in the industry in terms of the CSC game's usefulness. We base this observation on the fact that it is approved by management, has high internal demand, and is liked and enjoyed by most participants.

7   Conclusions and Further Work

In this work, we provide an overview of the design and implementation of CyberSecurity Challenges - a serious game to raise awareness on secure coding for software developers in the industry. The CyberSecurity Challenges have been developed following a design science research design structured in three design cycles: Initial Design, Refinement, and Sifu/Online. The design cycles extended from 2017 until 2020 and consisted of thirteen events where more than 200 software developers participated. Our contribution addresses practitioners who wish to develop or refine a software developer awareness training for the industry and the research community by understanding the usage of serious games targeting software developers in the industry.

This paper consists of two main parts: 1) an overview of the design of the CyberSecurity Challenges and 2) an evaluation of the CyberSecurity Challenge game and events, including the usefulness of CyberSecurity Challenges. In the first part, we presented a consolidated view of CyberSecurity Challenges. This consolidated view is the result of all the lessons learned throughout the three design cycles. We provide an analysis and report of the main results that practitioners can use to design a similar awareness training program. We also discuss the differences and similarities to other existing awareness training programs. In the second part, we analyze results from semi-structured interviews from the first design cycle and a survey collected during the second design cycle. Overall, software developers enjoy playing CyberSecurity challenges, either as a standalone event or together with a training workshop on secure programming. Furthermore, we present results on the impact that the game has on the participants and discuss essential factors for successful awareness training. Our positive results, continuous management endorsement, and the fact that these games have been introduced as a standard part of the company's teaching curricula validate our design approach. Additionally, our results show that CyberSecurity challenges are a viable approach for awareness training on secure coding.

As further steps, the authors would like to design a systematic approach to identify topics for challenges and assessing these challenges for relevance. Towards this, more empirical analyses are required. Thus, parallel and next steps include an empirical study on the awareness of various secure coding topics to tailor the challenges to different software developer groups' needs. Also, as the COVID-19 crises limits travel and physical presence, we will continue to enhance the online version of the game. We also plan to enrich the scope of defensive challenges.

Acknowledgements. The authors would like to thank the participants of the CyberSecurity Challenges for their time and their valuable answers and comments. Also, the authors would also like to thank Kristian Beckers and Thomas Diefenbach for their helpful, insightful, and constructive comments and discussions.

This work is financed by national funds through FCT - Fundação para a Ciência e Tecnologia, I.P., under the projects FCT UIDB/04466/2020 and UIDP/04466/2020. Furthermore, the third author thanks the Instituto Universitário de Lisboa and ISTAR, for their support.

References

1. Adams, W.: Conducting semi-structured interviews. In: Newcomer, K., Hatry, H., Wholey, J. (eds.) Handbook of Practical Program Evaluation, chap. 19, pp. 492–505. Wiley Online Library (2017)
2. Assal, H., Chiasson, S.: 'Think secure from the beginning' a survey with software developers. In: Proceedings of the 2019 CHI Conference on Human Factors in Computing Systems, pp. 1–13. CHI'19, Association for Computing Machinery, New York, NY, USA (2019)
3. Baskerville, R., Pries-Heje, J.: Explanatory design theory. Bus. Inf. Syst. Eng. **2**(5), 271–282 (2010)
4. Beckers, K., Pape, S.: A serious game for eliciting social engineering security requirements. In: 2016 IEEE 24th International Requirements Engineering Conference (RE). IEEE (2016)
5. Bundesamt für Sicherheit in der Informationstechnik: BSI IT-Grundschutz-Katalog, 2016, 15. ed. (2016). https://tinyurl.com/zkbmfb6
6. Chung, K.: CTFd: The Easiest Capture The Flag Framework. https://ctfd.io/
7. Davis, A., Leek, T., Zhivich, M., Gwinnup, K., Leonard, W.: The fun and future of CTF. 2014 USENIX Summit on Gaming, Games, and Gamification in Security Education (3GSE 14), pp. 1–9 (2014). https://tinyurl.com/y97enbtr
8. Department of Homeland Security: Industrial Control Systems - Computer Emergency Response Team. https://us-cert.cisa.gov/ics. Accessed on 26 Aug 2020
9. Dörner, R., Göbel, S., Effelsberg, W., Wiemeyer, J. (eds.): Serious Games. Springer, Cham (2016). https://doi.org/10.1007/978-3-319-40612-1
10. Frey, S., Rashid, A., Anthonysamy, P., Pinto-Albuquerque, M., Naqvi, S.A.: The good, the bad and the ugly: a study of security decisions in a cyber-physical systems game. IEEE Trans. Software Eng. **45**(5), 521–536 (2019)
11. Gasiba, T., Beckers, K., Suppan, S., Rezabek, F.: On the requirements for serious games geared towards software developers in the industry. In: Damian, D.E., Perini, A., Lee, S. (eds.) Conference on Requirements Engineering Conference, pp. 286–296. IEEE, Jeju, South Korea (2019). https://doi.org/10.1109/re.2019.00038

12. Gasiba, T., Lechner, U., Cuellar, J., Zouitni, A.: Ranking secure coding guidelines for software developer awareness training in the industry. In: Queirós, R., Portela, F., Pinto, M., Simões, A. (eds.) First International Computer Programming Education Conference (ICPEC 2020). OpenAccess Series in Informatics (OASIcs), vol. 81, p. 11:1–11:11. Schloss Dagstuhl–Leibniz-Zentrum für Informatik, Dagstuhl, Germany (2020)
13. Gasiba, T., Lechner, U., Pinto-Albuquerque, M.: Awareness of secure coding guidelines in the industry - a first data analysis. In: The 19th IEEE International Conference on Trust, Security and Privacy in Computing and Communications. IEEE, Online (2020)
14. Gasiba, T., Lechner, U., Pinto-Albuquerque, M.: Sifu - A cybersecurity awareness platform with challenge assessment and intelligent coach. In: Special Issue on Cyber-Physical System Security of the Cybersecurity Journal. SpringerOpen (2020)
15. Gasiba, T., Lechner, U., Pinto-Albuquerque, M., Porwal, A.: Cybersecurity awareness platform with virtual coach and automated challenge assessment. In: Katsikas, S., et al. (eds.) CyberICPS/SECPRE/ADIoT -2020. LNCS, vol. 12501, pp. 67–83. Springer, Cham (2020). https://doi.org/10.1007/978-3-030-64330-0_5
16. Gasiba, T., Lechner, U., Pinto-Albuquerque, M., Zouitni, A.: Design of secure coding challenges for cybersecurity education in the industry. In: Shepperd, M., Brito e Abreu, F., Rodrigues da Silva, A., Pérez-Castillo, R. (eds.) QUATIC 2020. CCIS, vol. 1266, pp. 223–237. Springer, Cham (2020). https://doi.org/10.1007/978-3-030-58793-2_18
17. Gasiba, T., Lechner, U., Rezabek, F., Pinto-Albuquerque, M.: Cybersecurity games for secure programming education in the industry: gameplay analysis. In: Queirós, R., Portela, F., Pinto, M., Simões, A. (eds.) First International Computer Programming Education Conference (ICPEC 2020). OpenAccess Series in Informatics (OASIcs), vol. 81, p. 10:1–10:11. Schloss Dagstuhl–Leibniz-Zentrum für Informatik, Dagstuhl, Germany (2020)
18. Gasiba, T.: Sifu Platform (2020). https://github.com/saucec0de/sifu
19. Graziotin, D., Fagerholm, F., Wang, X., Abrahamsson, P.: What happens when software developers are (un)happy. J. Syst. Softw. **140**, 32–47 (2018)
20. Hänsch, N., Benenson, Z.: Specifying IT security awareness. In: 25th International Workshop on Database and Expert Systems Applications, Munich, Germany, pp. 326–330. IEEE, Munich, Germany (2014). https://doi.org/10.1109/DEXA.2014.71
21. Hevner, A.R., March, S.T., Park, J., Ram, S.: Design science in information systems research. MIS Q. **28**(1), 75 (2004)
22. McIlwraith, A.: Information Security and Employee Behavior: How to Reduce Risk Through Employee Education. Gower Publishing, Ltd, Training and Awareness (2006)
23. Mirkovic, J., Peterson, P.A.: Class Capture-the-Flag exercises. In: 2014 {USENIX} Summit on Gaming, Games, and Gamification in Security Education (3GSE 14) (2014)
24. Moody, G.D., Siponen, M., Pahnila, S.: Toward a unified model of information security policy compliance. MIS Q. **42**(1), 1–50 (2018)
25. OWASP Foundation: Open Web Application Security Project. https://owasp.org/
26. Patel, S.: 2019 Global Developer Report: DevSecOps finds security roadblocks divide teams (2020). https://about.gitlab.com/blog/2019/07/15/globaldeveloper-report/. (Online; posted on July 15, 2019]
27. Rieb, A.: IT-Security Awareness mit Operation Digitales Chamäleon. Ph.D. thesis, Universität der Bundeswehr München, Neubiberg (2018)
28. SANS Institute: SEC642: Advanced Web App Penetration Testing, Ethical Hacking, and Exploitation Techniques. https://tinyurl.com/yytoawyn, online, Visited Nov 2020
29. Schneier, B.: Software Developers and Security. Online (2020). https://www.schneier.com/blog/archives/2019/07/softwaredevelo.html

30. Stewart, G., Lacey, D.: Death by a thousand facts: criticizing the technocratic approach to information security awareness. Inf. Manag. Comput. Secur. **20**(1), 29–38 (2012)
31. Tahaei, M., Vaniea, K.: A survey on developer-centered security. In: 2019 IEEE European Symposium on Security and Privacy Workshops (EuroS&PW), pp. 129–138. IEEE (2019)
32. Xie, J., Lipford, H.R., Chu, B.: Why do programmers make security errors? 2011 IEEE Symposium on Visual Languages and Human-Centric Computing (VL/HCC) pp. 161–164 (2011). https://doi.org/10.1109/VLHCC.2011.6070393

On the Relationship Between IT Privacy and Security Behavior: A Survey Among German Private Users

Tom Biselli[✉] and Christian Reuter

Science and Technology for Peace and Security (PEASEC), Technical University of Darmstadt, Darmstadt, Germany
{biselli,reuter}@peasec.tu-darmstadt.de

Abstract. The relevance of adequate privacy and security behavior in the digital realm is higher than ever. However, the exact relationship between privacy and security behavior is rarely discussed in the literature. This study investigates this relationship and the role of socio-demographic factors (gender, age, education, political ideology) in such behavior. Results of a survey among German private users ($N = 1,219$) show that privacy and security behavior are only weakly correlated and not similarly influenced by socio-demographic factors. While security behavior significantly differs between age and education groups (younger and less educated show less security behavior), no such differences exist for privacy behavior. Additionally, political ideology has no influence on privacy and security behavior. Thus, this study sheds light on the concepts of privacy, security and corresponding behavior and emphasizes the need for a fine-grained differentiation if either privacy or security behavior is to be improved.

Keywords: Security · Privacy · Behavior · Relationship

1 Introduction

The advancing digitalization leads to the ever-increasing pervasion of the internet into the daily lives of individuals. In this context, individuals increasingly share sensitive data and use software to facilitate their everyday life. This has implications both with regard to privacy and security in the realm of information technology[1]. The Deutsche Telekom (Europe's largest telecommunications company) hereby reported 46 million attacks on their honeypots in 2019 [1], an increase of 12 million attacks compared to 2018. In addition, the Federal Criminal Police Office (Bundeskriminalamt) reported around 87,000 incidents of cybercrime with a particularly growing focus on mobile malware and an associated financial loss of around 60 million euros [2].

Apart from such illegal activities that reveal the need for enhanced security, the advancing digitalization also fuels an increased interest of private companies and state institutions to increasingly collect private data about individuals. Companies are mainly

---

[1] In this paper, privacy and security thus always refer to IT privacy and IT security.

F. Ahlemann et al. (Eds.): WI 2021, LNISO 47, pp. 388–404, 2021.
https://doi.org/10.1007/978-3-030-86797-3_26

interested in better understanding their customers in order to offer individualized products and enable personalized advertising. State actors, on the other hand, are expanding their surveillance activities in cyberspace to prevent or solve crimes, in the context of which the interests of individuals who value their privacy are potentially affected. Negative consequences of increased collection of private data could be observed in the case of Cambridge Analytica, where data was analyzed and misused for political purposes and thus used in a completely different context than originally intended by the user [3].

In this digital environment, individuals should therefore have an interest in maintaining their privacy and security through appropriate protective behavior. In line with this, a representative study by the German Federal Office for Information Security (Bundesamt für Sicherheit in der Informationstechnik, BSI) in 2017 showed that 97% of German internet users consider security to be very important [4]. However, only a third of those surveyed specifically inform themselves about security. Further studies have confirmed that there is a growing security awareness among private individuals, especially with regard to the widespread use of smartphones [5, 6]. Similarly, users usually highly value their privacy but often do not act accordingly, a phenomenon also known as the *privacy paradox* [7, 8]. Thus, there is a general concern to support users in both their privacy and security needs. Privacy and security behavior have a common basis, as they both deal with threats in a digital world. By avoiding public WIFI-spots, for example, one can avoid both security risks and unwanted access to private data. However, the one does not necessarily go hand in hand with the other. Performing regular updates of the operating system of one's computer might be an effective security behavior, but does not prevent the provider from collecting private data. Therefore, the exact relationship between privacy and security remains of high importance. If both privacy and security behavior is to be effectively enhanced, it must be understood how both are related, whether they are conceptually similar or different and whether different factors similarly influence privacy and security behavior. Only on the basis of a better understanding of this can it be ensured that appropriate interventions and software are developed which support users in their need for both privacy and security.

To address this issue, an online study representative for the German population (with regard to age, gender, state, income and education) with 1,219 participants was conducted. In the following sections related work is presented (Sect. 2), followed by the hypotheses (Sect. 3) and the methods applied (Sect. 4). After the illustration of the results (Sect. 5) the findings are discussed in a broader context (Sect. 6) and conclusions are drawn (Sect. 7).

2   Related Work

Theoretical Conceptualizations. The causes of existing insufficiencies and possibilities for improving both privacy and security behavior are being studied intensively. IT security in general refers to the protection of computer systems from theft and damage of hardware, software and information as well as the disruption of services they are supposed to provide [9]. A good conceptualization of this protection is provided by the so called CIA triad: secure IT systems should therefore maintain confidentiality, integrity and availability [10]. Confidentiality hereby refers to the prevention of unauthorized viewing, integrity to the unauthorized modification and availability to the preservation of access [10]. Based on these definitions, security does not necessarily cover the privacy domain, but may incorporate it to some extent. There is a particular overlap in the factor confidentiality, since unauthorized viewing is associated with both unauthorized access as a security breach and with the possible exposure of sensitive information about individuals as a privacy breach. Integrity and availability, on the other hand, tend to describe factors that can be distinguished from privacy more easily.

Privacy in general refers to the prevention of exposure of sensitive information about (groups of) individuals. This includes, among other things, the nondisclosure of behavior, communications and descriptive personal data [11]. The general understanding of the term "privacy" today is still quite close to Westin's widely known definition in 1967, which described privacy as "the claim of individuals, groups, or institutions to determine for themselves when, how, and to what extent information about them is communicated to others" [12]. However, preserving privacy in the rapidly changing digital environment is much more difficult today, which may be one reason why there is still no general agreement on the exact scope of the term privacy. Since the focus in this study is on the exposure of sensitive information in the realm of information technology, we refer to privacy in the IT context throughout this manuscript.

Based on these conceptualizations, privacy and security can both be seen as essential protections which are related to a certain degree - especially in the factor confidentiality, which describes the unauthorized viewing of data and is relevant for both privacy and security. Nevertheless, they can also vary widely in which specific elements they protect. While security refers to protection in a more general way, privacy refers specifically to the protection of personal, informational data.

Previously, the technology threat avoidance theory (TTAT) has been introduced as a possible framework to better understand personal motivations when facing IT threats [13, 14]. The TTAT hereby tries to conceptualize the cognitive processes taking place when individuals appraise threat and seek solutions with the goal to avoid technology-related threats. Although the TTAT does not explicitly distinguish between privacy and security, both represent essential areas in which IT-threats can be avoided. TTAT posits that, when confronted with IT threats, the two processes *threat appraisal* and *coping appraisal* take place and determine the answer to the threat [14]. While both privacy and security have their common ground in representing IT-related threats, they could also differ in those processes. For example, security threats such as ransomware often have immediate negative effects for users while privacy threats often have negative consequences only at a later stage and also on a societal rather than individual level (as in the Cambridge Analytica case). Thus, depending on whether the threat is a security or privacy threat, the threat appraisal could differ and result in different behavior. Taken together, the TTAT provides a framework on the basis of which it can be expected that privacy and security behavior are related to a certain extent, but nevertheless differ in specific aspects of the corresponding behavior.

Empirical Conceptualizations. In order to find relevant literature, we used several databases (IEEE Xplore, Web of Science, ACM Digital Library), looking for the combination of the search terms privacy, security and relationship. After initially including several studies containing both privacy and security even without a specific conceptualization of their relationship in order to illustrate the problem, we proceeded to only include studies making some kind of statement about the presumed relationship. This approach revealed that despite the reported differences on a theoretical level, privacy and security (and corresponding behavior) are often used together without a finer distinction. They are hereby treated as quite identical with the (mostly implicit) assumption, that they describe a common construct. In this context one study, for example, argues for the importance of usable privacy and security and how social processes play a major role in a number of privacy and security related behaviors [15]. However, instead of explicitly conceptualizing the relationship between security and privacy, both terms are mainly used in combination. Similar cases with a lack of disentangling privacy from security behavior can be seen throughout the literature [16–18]. Only few studies explicitly justify the approach to treat both privacy and security as closely related. For example, in one instance it is explicitly argued that they are indeed closely related and might be best conceptualized as two dimensions of a single construct [19].

Apart from studies that cover privacy and security as closely related or without an explicit conceptualization, some voices argue for a finer distinction between privacy and security, and define these concepts more explicitly in distinction to each other [20–23]. Bansal, for example, distinguishes privacy and security via developing a scale with dimensions which are unique to security concerns and show no overlap to privacy concerns, such as data integrity, authentication and improper access during transmission [24]. Pavlou also explicitly distinguishes information privacy concerns and information security concerns as distinct antecedents of purchasing behavior in an online environment representing uncertainty factors [25]. Finally, Oetzel and Krumay distinguish privacy and security conceptually and based on a content analysis of company websites, even though they acknowledge that some relationship exists between the concepts to a certain degree [26]. One group of studies explicitly examines the relationship between privacy and security attitudes and find that they are not equally influenced by individual characteristics, with the correlation between privacy and security attitudes being only weak [27, 28].

Finally, some studies rather use a hierarchical approach to conceptualize privacy and security, although sometimes only implicitly. In one study, influencing factors on privacy and security behavior are discussed without a clear distinction between the two concepts [17]. Implicitly, however, privacy is treated as a subcategory of security concerned with the protection of access to personal data. The subsumption of privacy into the security domain is confirmed by further studies which define information privacy as a part of the broader construct web security [29] and generally as being part of a security framework [30]. The other direction of a hierarchical relationship has also been suggested, e.g. in the sense that the problem area of improper access to data as a security concern can also be considered as a part of the superordinate category privacy [31]. An overview of the most commonly proposed relationships is provided in Fig. 1.

Influencing Factors on Privacy and Security Behavior. In order to better conceptualize the relationship between privacy and security behavior, it is also promising to examine it from different points of view and analyze how factors such as age, gender, education and political ideology influence the corresponding behavior. Age and gender, for example, have previously been associated with differences in security behavior. Here, it has mainly been shown that women show less security knowledge, experience and behavior than men [32, 33]. With regard to age, especially younger people below 25 years have been associated with weaker security behavior [34, 35]. As for education, it has previously been shown that those with higher levels of education tend to be more concerned about privacy [36] and show more security awareness [37]. Political ideology has so far mainly been reported as relevant to privacy attitudes and behavior [7, 38, 39]. There is a consensus in this respect that people who see themselves as rather left-wing are more critical of the (predominantly state-organized) data collection on individuals. If the concepts of privacy and security were indeed as closely related as they are often discussed, the moderating factors described should be applicable to each other's behavior. Thus, political ideology should have an influence on security behavior, age and gender should have an influence on privacy behavior and education levels should have similar effects on both privacy and security behavior.

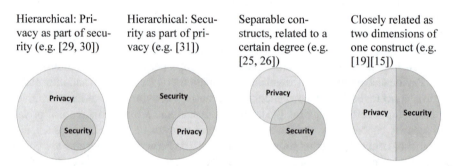

Fig. 1. Conceptualizations of the relationship between privacy and security proposed in the literature (inspired by [20])

Importantly, privacy and security attitudes and behavior can potentially differ between cultures [40, 41]. Thus, we focus on a sample from Germany providing an opportunity for cross-country comparability in future studies. Private users are thereby of special interest since everyday behavior in the digital realm can have negative consequence for everyone, such as the already described security incidents (e.g. mobile malware) and privacy breaches (e.g. Cambridge Analytica).

Research Gap. Generally, there is no consensus with regard to the relationship between privacy and security and plenty of studies using both terms actually do not conceptualize their relationship at all, but use both in parallel and assume some kind of implicit, close relationship. Importantly, the vast majority of studies trying to conceptualize some kind of relationship focus either on theoretical considerations or on corresponding privacy/security attitudes as opposed to behavior. Thus, there exists a gap with regard to illuminating the relationship between privacy and security behavior. If the ultimate goal is to increase privacy and security behavior, which is a desirable objective as previously outlined, further empirical data on the relationship between them is needed. Especially the question, to what extent privacy behavior goes hand in hand with security behavior, and thus whether both could eventually be improved by similar interventions and technical implementations has been neglected so far. Accordingly, this study aims to answer the following research question: *"Are privacy and security behavior closely related and similarly influenced by demographic factors and political ideology?".*

3 Hypotheses

In order to fill the described research gap, this study investigates the relationship between privacy and security behavior of private users in Germany, taking into account demographic factors such as gender, age, education and political ideology. *Private users* are hereby defined as individuals who use information and communication technology, such as computers and the internet for their personal use. Based on the literature review, we do not expect privacy and security behavior to be not related at all and that they would constitute completely separable domains. Instead, we aim at illuminating the relationship between the two by assessing the correlation and influencing factors on corresponding behavior at different levels. Due to the literature describing privacy and security (sometimes implicitly) predominantly as closely related, a correlation and a similar influence of demographic factors and political ideology on both privacy and security behavior is expected. However, no assumptions are made about the expected strength of the correlation, as there is preliminary evidence to suggest that privacy and security may be conceptually more different than often treated in the literature. As demographic factors have previously been shown to influence especially security behavior, these factors should influence privacy behavior in a similar way, if both were conceptually closely related. Similarly, political ideology, which has previously been shown to influence privacy behavior, should also influence security behavior if both were closely related. If there were no similar influence of these factors on the corresponding behavior, this would indicate that the two concepts of privacy and security behavior need to be distinguished more thoroughly. Based on the previously reviewed literature, the following hypotheses are therefore postulated:

- **H1: Privacy behavior and security behavior correlate positively**
- **H2: Demographic factors such as gender, age, and education have a similar influence on both privacy and security behavior**
- **H3: Political ideology has a similar influence on both privacy and security behaviour.**

4 Method

4.1 Study Design and Participants

To assess privacy and security behavior and their relationship, a representative online survey with German citizens was conducted in May 2019, using LimeSurvey and the panel provider GapFish (Berlin)[2]. GapFish is certified according to the ISO norm 26362 ensuring the quality of access-panels in market, opinion and social research [42]. The sample (N = 1,219) was matched to the distribution of age, gender, income, region and education according to the general German population [43, 44] during the data collection by the panel provider using corresponding quotas. The sample covers an age-range from 14 to 87 years, of which 52% are women and 48% are men.

The survey included four questions related to security behavior and eight questions related to privacy behavior. The overall survey further included questions on security and privacy knowledge, media use in crisis situations and data misuse which, however, are not part of this study. As the privacy and security behavior questions were posed prior to the other questions, a possible bias through the other questions can be ruled out. Answers to the items were given on a 5-point rating scale by Rohrmann, ranging from *1 – I disagree* to *5 – I strongly agree* [45]. To get more reliable answers, the option *no answer* was provided for all questions and all questions were posed in German.

The items were developed based on the recommendations of the German Federal Office for Information Security (BSI) on how to secure one's computer, smartphone and online generated data [46, 47]. Some survey instruments already exist with regard to privacy and security. However, we found none to be suitable for our specific case, in which we wanted to analyze German private users with regard to their everyday behavior. The Human Aspects of Information Security Questionnaire (HAISQ), for example, aims at evaluating information security threats caused by employees within organizations rather than assessing private users in their everyday life [48] and the Internet Users Information Privacy Concerns (IUIPC) scale focuses on attitudes rather than actual behavior [49]. For the item development we therefore focused on (1) behavioral actions rather than intentions, (2) private users in their everyday-life as opposed to specific (e.g. work-related) contexts and (3) suitable contexts for German private users. The latter was the main motivation to use recommendations of a German institution such as the BSI. The recommendations do not explicitly distinguish between privacy and security behavior but rather touch on both topics. For the purpose of this study, however, the resulting items have been treated as items separately for privacy and security, based on face validity. Since the recommendations do not explicitly distinguish between privacy and security behavior and we wanted to include all recommendations to cover enough topics, an uneven number of items for assessing privacy and security behavior resulted. With regard to their security behavior, the participants had to answer questions such as whether they would install software updates immediately, or use antivirus software. With regard to their privacy behavior, the participants had to answer questions such as whether they inform themselves about the privacy policy of apps before installing them, or avoid online services that require a name or e-mail address (an overview of all items used in the analysis can be found in Figs. 2 and 3).

---

[2] Some of the subsequently analyzed data with regard to security behavior (but not privacy behavior) overlaps with a data analysis of a different published manuscript of our group. However, the focus here is explicitly on the relationship between privacy and security behavior, which was not examined at all in the other study. There, the focus was on the extent to which knowledge about security-relevant issues can predict appropriate security behavior [33].

Because the aim of this study was to evaluate the relationship between privacy and security behavior of the German population with regard to demographics like age and gender, education but also political ideology, corresponding questions were also included in the survey. For the latter, two items were included which asked for the personal opinion regarding the responsibility for data protection on the internet (*state* vs. *company*) since different political ideologies can be expected to yield different answers here (e.g. more left-wing socialist types might expect greater state interference than more right-wing liberal types [50]). In these, participants were asked, whether they think that the state is responsible for data protection on the internet (item 1) and whether they think, that the companies collecting the data are responsible for data protection on the internet (item 2). The items were developed based on theoretical considerations and answers were given on the same 5-point Rohrmann-scale as the other items. Another item asked directly about the political orientation on a left to right spectrum (*left-wing, fairly left-wing, center, fairly right-wing, right-wing*).

4.2 Analysis

The analysis was conducted using the software tools Microsoft Excel and RStudio Version 4.0.2. Answers with the rating *no response* were excluded as missing values from the subsequent analysis. An initial descriptive analysis for the items for both the privacy behavior scale and security behavior scale was conducted. The reliability of the corresponding scales was investigated based on the internal consistency (Cronbach's Alpha). In order to find group differences, participants were grouped into roughly equal age categories (15–29, 30–44, 45–59, >60). Education levels were grouped into three categories: *low* (no degree and German Hauptschul-degree), *medium* (German Realschul-degree) and *high* (Highschool & University degree). The individual level of privacy and security behavior was determined by calculating the mean across all items of the corresponding scale. The factor *attribution of responsibility for data protection on the internet* was calculated based on the two items with regard to state- or company-responsibility. If a participant reported a higher responsibility for the state than the company, he was grouped in the factor level state and vice versa.

Differences in privacy and security behavior depending on the group factors *gender*, *age* and *education* were analyzed using a multivariate analysis of variance (MANOVA). A separate MANOVA was carried out for the factors *political orientation* and *attribution of responsibility for data protection on the internet* (together representing political ideology) as they can be assigned to a different theoretical framework than the former factors. Since the assumption of multivariate normality and homogeneity of covariance matrices could not be confirmed for the available data, a parametric bootstrap resampling approach with 10,000 iterations was used to calculate the test statistics. This method was implemented using the MANOVA function from the R package "MANOVA.RM" [51].

Subsequent univariate analyses were conducted using factorial analyses of variance (ANOVA) when corresponding assumptions such as normal distribution and homogeneity of variances were fulfilled and robust factorial ANOVAs with trimmed means (trimming level = 0.2) if they were violated [52, 53]. The robust approach also uses bootstrapping to obtain an empirically derived critical p-value. In this context, no degrees of freedom are reported since an adjusted critical value instead of a critical value based on a known sampling distribution is used. The reported test statistic Q refers to the robust ANOVA test statistic for trimmed means. Subsequent robust post-hoc tests (test statistic: ψ) for disentangling observed main effects are also based on percentile bootstraps for the p values [53]. Because all tests were performed with the same sample, the 5% - alpha level was corrected with the Bonferroni-Holm method [54].

5   Results

5.1   Descriptive Analysis

To evaluate the reliability of the constructed privacy behavior and security behavior scales, the internal consistency of Cronbach's Alpha was analyzed. After two items for the privacy behavior scale and one item for the security behavior scale were rejected and not used for further analyses (due to a low correlation of the item with the overall scale) they showed moderate values of $\alpha_{\text{privacy-behavior}} = .72$ and $\alpha_{\text{security-behavior}} = .65$. The internal consistency is usually considered acceptable from around $\alpha = .70$ [55]. A possible underestimation of α due to few and heterogenous items is a known phenomenon, which can be neglected to a certain degree, since the analysis does not focus on individual scores but on aggregated group scores, which are not strongly affected by measurement errors due to a lower reliability [55].

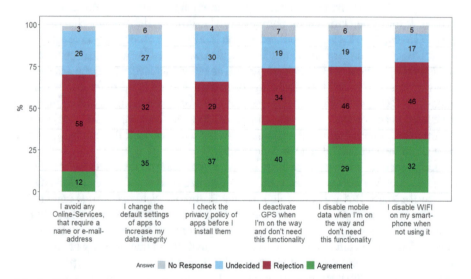

Fig. 2. Percentage frequencies for the questions of the *privacy behavior* category, N = 1,219.

A descriptive analysis of the responses gave a nuanced picture of the participants' self-reported privacy behavior. As shown in Fig. 2 ("Rejection" combines *"I strongly disagree"* and *"I hardly agree"* answers while "Agreement" combines *"I fairly agree"* and *"I strongly agree"* answers), agreement and rejection with regard to privacy-related items are mostly balanced with the exception of one item (*"I avoid Online-Services, that require a name/email-address"*) where only 12% of participants agree and 58% disagree. Moreover, a fairly high percentage of participants were undecided about their privacy behavior, with response rates ranging from 17% to 30%.

A descriptive analysis of the responses with regard to security revealed that the majority of participants indicated a rather high level of self-reported security behavior. Figure 3 shows the percentage frequencies for the corresponding *security behavior* items. It becomes apparent that agreement to all security-related items exceeds rejection (70% vs. 18%, 51% vs. 25%, 58% vs. 18%) and also undecided or no response answers (which are all below 20%).

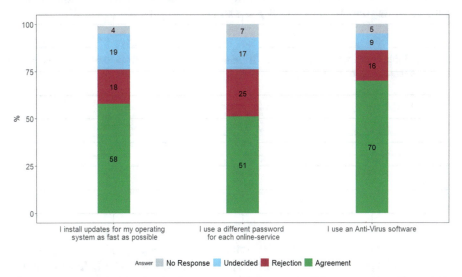

Fig. 3. Percentage frequencies for the questions of the *security behavior* category, N = 1.219.

5.2 Hypothesis Testing

H1: Privacy Behavior and Security Behavior Correlate. To test H1, a Spearman's rank correlation was calculated with the mean values of privacy and security behavior across the corresponding items. The correlation was weakly positive, $r = .18, p < .001$. The overall privacy behavior ($M = 2.81, SD = 0.86$) thereby was considerably lower than the overall security behavior ($M = 3.76, SD = 1.07$) across all participants.

H2: Demographic Factors such as Gender, Age, and Education have a Similar Influence on Both Privacy and Security Behavior. One main goal of the analysis was to assess, whether privacy and security behavior can be considered as conceptually closely related. If that were the case, gender, age and education should have a similar influence on both privacy and security behavior. The corresponding robust MANOVA revealed that while gender did not influence privacy and security behavior at all (Wald-type statistic: $W(df=2) = 0.85, p = 0.99$) both age ($W(6) = 32.11, p < .001$) and education ($W(4) =$

21.61, $p = .003$) influenced privacy and security behavior. To disentangle these effects, univariate ANOVAs were conducted separately for privacy behavior and security behavior. This revealed that age ($F(1,995) = 0.07, p = .79$) and education ($F(1,995) = 2.01, p = .78$) did not influence privacy behavior. In contrast, security behavior was significantly influenced by both age ($Q = 44.94, p = .01$) and education ($Q = 12.88, p = .02$). Subsequent robust post-hoc comparisons showed that young people below the age of 30 reported significantly less security behavior than those in the age groups 30–44 ($\psi = -0.69, p < .001$) and 45–59 ($\psi = -0.81, p = .001$). Furthermore, older people in the age group over 60 reported significantly higher security behavior than those in the age group 30–44 ($\psi = -1.08, p < .001$), but significantly lower security behavior that those in the age group 45–59 ($\psi = -1.20, p < .001$) (see Table 1).

Table 1. Table for trimmed mean values (trimming level = 0.2) and standard deviations of the *security behavior* score per age category

Age (in years)	Security behavior score	
	Mean value (M)	Standard deviation (SD)
<30	3.43	1.03
30–44	3.75	1.04
45–59	3.93	1.08
>=60	3.84	1.07

With regard to the level of education, robust post-hoc comparisons revealed that those with a low education reported significantly lower security behavior both compared to those with medium education ($\psi = -0.94, p = < .001$) and high education ($\psi = 1.30, p = < .001$) (see Table 2).

Taken together, the results show that contrary to expectations, privacy and security behavior are not similarly influenced by the categories of gender, age and education. While different groups with regard to age and education report significantly diverging security behavior, no such differences are seen for privacy behavior. Thus, the hypothesis could not be confirmed based on the current data.

Table 2. Table for trimmed mean values (trimming level = 0.2) and standard deviations of the *security behavior* score per education category

Education	Security behavior score	
	Mean value (M)	Standard deviation (SD)
Low	3.63	1.14
Medium	3.84	0.98
High	3.90	1.03

H3: Political Ideology has a Similar Influence on both Privacy and Security Behavior. Besides the described demographic factors such as gender, age and education, it was hypothesized that political ideology might have an influence on privacy and security behavior. Again, if privacy and security can be considered as conceptually closely related, political ideology should have a similar influence on privacy and security behavior. The corresponding MANOVA included the factors "attribution of responsibility for data protection on the internet" (*state* vs. *company*) and political orientation (*left, rather left, center, rather right, right*). The results showed that neither the data protection attribution ($W(8) = 17.51$, $p = .18$) nor political orientation ($W(4) = 5.56$, $p = .94$) were significantly associated with privacy and/or security behavior.

6 Discussion

Summary of Results. The main goal of this study was to quantify the relationship between privacy and security behavior and assess, whether they can be regarded as closely related. We tried to illuminate this relationship from different points of view by examining whether the corresponding behaviors correlate and whether they are similarly influenced by factors such as demographics and political ideology. Only then it would be valid not to disentangle them and explicitly explain their relationship when researching these concepts, as is often the case. However, the present results show that privacy and security behavior are actually only weakly correlated. Furthermore, influencing factors on privacy and security behavior are not consistent. While young people (<30) and those with low education (no degree and German Hauptschul-degree) reported significantly less security behavior than older and more educated people, no such differences could be found for privacy behavior. Political ideology had no influence, neither on privacy nor on security behavior.

Relationship Between Privacy and Security Behavior. Based on these results, the notion, that privacy and security are closely linked and those who behave securely necessarily also behave privately must be questioned. This finding stands in contrast to some research, which does not explicitly distinguish between privacy but uses both in parallel [16–18]. Thus, the danger exists that findings which implicitly rather target security improvements might be falsely attributed to privacy improvements when they are only suitable to improve security – and vice versa. This could be relevant, for example, for both the education of children and adults with regard to improving privacy and security behavior and for software developers who need to be aware in which relation they view privacy and security and to what extend one and the other shall be protected.

Especially with regard to the examination of privacy and security behavior as opposed to corresponding attitudes, the findings of this study add to the existing literature. They are hereby in line with findings, that attitudes towards privacy and security also are not similarly influenced by personality characteristics and the correlation between privacy and security attitudes is only weak [27, 28]. Existing evidence, according to which individuals differ in their privacy needs based on their political ideology [38, 39] could not be shown in corresponding behavior. One reason for this could be the fact, that we assessed political orientation on a 5-point scale. Even though it can be argued that too many points can also confuse respondents, there is evidence that a 10-point and 11-point left-to-right scale can lead to a higher validity [56]. Thus, we might have been able to detect corresponding effects if we had used a more fine-grained scale.

In general, up until today there is no consensus on the exact relationship between privacy and security. Sometimes implicitly, sometimes explicitly hierarchical relationships are proposed (privacy as part of security [29, 30, 57], security as part of privacy [31]) both are described as rather separable constructs [25, 26] or as related dimensions of one underlying construct [15, 19]. Since we found at least some correlation between both privacy and security but couldn't identify the common drivers to be demographic factors or political ideology the question then arises where the common ground between privacy and security could lie. As previously outlined, the TTAT might provide a suitable framework for conceptualizing both the similarities and differences between privacy and security. The TTAT makes assumptions about cognitive processes such as threat appraisal and coping appraisal, which determine subsequent behavior in the face of IT-related threats [14]. Threat appraisal hereby includes the *perceived susceptibility* and *perceived severity*, i.e. gravity of consequences associated with an IT threat. While TTAT does not explicitly distinguish between privacy and security related IT threats, the dimension of perceived severity of the corresponding IT threat (security or privacy related) could be one, where privacy and security behavior are differentially influenced. Specifically, only if an individual considers the unregulated collection of personal data as having grave consequences, would he engage in behavior that prevents this, and thus show high privacy behavior. However, since the consequences of a security threat such as a computer virus are usually more immediate, an individual could show high security behavior and at the same time underestimate the consequences of not protecting his privacy, and thus show low privacy behavior. Consequently, there might be a common factor such as avoidance of technology related threats in general, as posited by the TTAT, which explains that privacy and security behavior are correlated, albeit weakly. However, in certain aspects of this common factor, such as the exact threat appraisal via assessing the perceived severity of the IT threat, depending on the core beliefs of an individual, differences in privacy and security behavior might arise. This would explain that factors such as age and education have a differential influence on privacy and security behavior. Given the weak correlation and inconsistent role of demographic factors and political ideology for privacy and security behavior, it is not obvious whether our results rather suggest that privacy and security overlap as distinct concepts, or whether they can rather be seen as two dimensions of a common construct. However, combined with the considerations presented in the light of the TTAT, we suggest that corresponding privacy and security behavior might be best conceptualized as two dimensions of a common construct which, based on TTAT, possibly represents some form of technical threat avoidance.

Limitations. Some limitations of this study need to be considered, before drawing too broad conclusions. First, *(1)* the results are based on the participants' self-reported privacy and security behavior which is not necessarily identical with their actual behavior. The discrepancy between intentions and actual behavior has been reported before [7, 58] and represents a general limitation of the survey methodology. Furthermore, *(2)* the used items can only be seen as an approximation to the surveyed constructs because no previously validated questionnaire was used. This caveat regarding the validity of the scales was confirmed by a rather low internal consistency, especially with regard to security behavior. The exact wording of items could be refined, e.g. disabling WIFI on one's smartphone could be more relevant in public than at home. In addition, *(3)* relatively few items were used to assess complex privacy and security behavior with many potential influencing factors [59, 60], a problem exacerbated by the elimination of two items due to their low correlation with the corresponding behavior scale. Consequently, the items and should be reviewed and revised. However, since the items were based on recommendations of the German Federal Office for Information Security, they are still considered sufficiently suitable for an approximation to the described topic.

7   Conclusion

In view of ever-increasing threats to privacy and security, methods to improve both privacy and security behavior are being studied intensively. However, an explicit conceptualization of the relationship between privacy and security is often missing, although both terms are usually used in combination. In general, there is no consensus on how best to describe the relationship and the extent to which one goes hand in hand with the other. Based on the results of this study, we found that privacy and security behavior of German private users actually correlate only weakly and is differentially influenced by demographic factors such as age and education. Thus, even though privacy and security are often treated as closely related concepts, it is not necessarily possible to improve security behavior and rely on automatically improving privacy behavior (and vice versa). Instead, a fine-grained differentiation is necessary if privacy or security behavior in particular is to be improved. The results of this study shed light on the relationship in that there might exist a common driver which influences both privacy and security behavior to a certain degree, but which we could not show to be related to demographics and political ideology. Future studies should take a step back from the circumscribed concepts privacy and security and explicitly try to uncover common drivers of those behaviors. Also, the findings of this study should be validated, taking into account the described limitations. Only through such studies and a better understanding of the concepts and the relationship between privacy and security behavior can they be effectively improved and private users empowered to meet the challenges in the digital realm.

Acknowledgements. This research work has been funded by the German Federal Ministry of Education and Research and the Hessian Ministry of Higher Education, Research, Science and the Arts within their joint support of the National Research Center for Applied Cybersecurity ATHENE and by the Deutsche Forschungsgemeinschaft (DFG) – SFB 1119 (CROSSING) – 236615297 as well as GRK 2050 (Privacy & Trust) – 251805230.

References

1. Knirsch, R.: Telekom legt aktuelle Zahlen zur Cybersicherheit vor [Telekom presents current numbers on cyber security] | Deutsche Telekom. https://www.telekom.com/de/medien/medieninformationen/detail/telekom-legt-aktuelle-zahlen-zur-cybersicherheit-vor-573046. Accessed 31 July 2020
2. Bundeskriminalamt: Cybercrime Bundeslagebild [Federal situation picture] (2018)
3. Isaak, J., Hanna, M.J.: User data privacy: Facebook, cambridge analytica, and privacy protection. Computer **51**, 56–59 (2018)
4. Deutsches Bundesamt für Sicherheit in der Informationstechnik (BSI): Die Lage der IT-Sicherheit in Deutschland [The state of IT security in Germany] 2018. 100 (2018)
5. Reuter, C., Häusser, K., Bien, M., Herbert, F.: Between effort and security: user assessment of the adequacy of security mechanisms for app categories. In: Proceedings of Mensch und Computer, pp. 287–297 (2019)
6. Ben-Asher, N., Kirschnick, N., Sieger, H., Meyer, J., Ben-Oved, A., Möller, S.: On the need for different security methods on mobile phones. In: Mobile HCI - 13th International Conf. on Human-Computer Interaction with Mob. Devices and Services, pp. 465–473 (2011)
7. Acquisti, A., Grossklags, J.: Privacy attitudes and privacy behavior. In: Camp, L.J., Lewis, S. (eds.) Economics of Information Security, vol. 12, pp. 165–178. Springer, Heidelberg (2006). https://doi.org/10.1007/1-4020-8090-5_13
8. Alashoor, T., Baskerville, R.: The privacy paradox: the role of cognitive absorption in the social networking activity. In: International Conference on Information Systems: Exploring the Information Frontier. ICIS (2015)
9. Mihajlov, M., Josimovski, S., Jerman-Blazič, B.: A conceptual framework for evaluating usable security in authentication mechanisms - usability perspectives. In: 5th International Conference on Network and System Security, NSS 2011, pp. 332–336 (2011)
10. Pfleeger, C.P.: Security in Computing. Pearson Education, Delhi (2009)
11. Pfleeger, S.L., Pfleeger, C.P.: Harmonizing privacy with security principles and practices. IBM J. Res. Dev. **53**, 1–12 (2009)
12. Westin, A.F.: Privacy and Freedom. Atheneum, New York (1967)
13. Chen, H., Li, W.: Mobile device users' privacy security assurance behavior: a technology threat avoidance perspective. Inf. Comput. Secur. **25**, 330–344 (2017)
14. Liang, H., Xue, Y.: Avoidance of information technology threats: a theoretical perspective. MIS Q. **33**, 71–90 (2009)
15. Das, S., Kim, T.H., Dabbish, L.A., Hong, J.I.: The effect of social influence on security sensitivity. In: SOUPS: Symposium on Usable Privacy and Security, pp. 143–157 (2014)
16. Halevi, T., Lewis, J., Memon, N.: A pilot study of cyber security and privacy related behavior and personality traits. In: WWW Companion - Proceedings of the 22nd International Conference on World Wide Web, pp. 737–744 (2013)
17. Kang, R., Dabbish, L., Fruchter, N., Kiesler, S.: "My data just goes everywhere:" user mental models of the internet and implications for privacy and security. In: SOUPS - Proceedings of the 11th Symposium on Usable Privacy and Security, pp. 39–52 (2015)
18. Redmiles, E.M., Kross, S., Mazurek, M.L.: How well do my results generalize? Comparing security and privacy survey results from mturk, web, and telephone samples. In: IEEE Symposium on Security and Privacy, pp. 1326–1343. Institute of Electrical and Electronics Engineers Inc. (2019)
19. Flavián, C., Guinalíu, M.: Consumer trust, perceived security and privacy policy: three basic elements of loyalty to a web site. Ind. Manag. Data Syst. **106**, 601–620 (2006)
20. Hurlburt, G.F., Miller, K.W., Voas, J.M., Day, J.M.: Privacy and/or security: take your pick. IT Prof. **11**, 52–55 (2009)

21. Ermakova, T., Fabian, B., Kornacka, M., Thiebes, S., Sunyaev, A.: Security and privacy requirements for cloud computing in healthcare. ACM Trans. Manag. Inf. Syst. **11**, 1–29 (2020)

22. Buck, C., Kessler, T., Eymann, T.: Nutzerverhalten als Teil der IT-Security – ein IS- Lit-eraturüberblick [User behavior as part of IT security - an IS literature overview]. In: Wirtschaftsinformatik (WI) Proceedings, pp. 1115–1130 (2015)

23. Maass, M., Walter, N., Herrmann, D., Hollick, M.: On the difficulties of incentivizing online privacy through transparency: a qualitative survey of the German health insurance market. In: Wirtschaftsinformatik (WI) Proceedings (2019)

24. Bansal, G.: Security concerns in the nomological network of trust and Big 5: first order vs. second order. In: International Conference on Information Systems, pp. 2117–2132. ICIS (2011)

25. Pavlou, P.A.: State of the information privacy literature: where are we now and where should we go? MIS Q. **35**, 977–988 (2011)

26. Oetzel, M.C., Krumay, B.: Differentiating privacy and security: a content analysis of B2C websites. In: 17th Americas Conference on Information Systems, AMCIS, pp. 1891–1900 (2011)

27. Egelman, S., Peer, E.: Predicting privacy and security attitudes. ACM SIGCAS Comput. Soc. **45**, 22–28 (2015)

28. Egelman, S., Peer, E.: Scaling the security wall : developing a security behavior intentions scale (SeBIS). In: Conference on Human Factors in Computing Systems – Proceedings, pp. 2873–2882 (2015)

29. Kim, M.S., Ahn, J.H.: Comparison of trust sources of an online market-maker in the e-marketplace: Buyer's and seller's perspectives. J. Comput. Inf. Syst. **47**, 84–94 (2006)

30. Clarke, R.: Privacy impact assessment: its origins and development. Comput. Law Secur. Rev. **25**, 123–135 (2009)

31. Smith, H.J., Milberg, S.J., Burke, S.J.: Information privacy: measuring individuals' concerns about organizational practices. MIS Q. Manag. Inf. Syst. **20**, 167–195 (1996)

32. McGill, T., Thompson, N.: Gender differences in information security perceptions and behaviour. In: ACIS - 29th Australasian Conference on Information Systems, pp. 1–11 (2018)

33. Herbert, F., Schmidbauer-Wolf, G.M., Reuter, C.: Differences in IT security behavior and knowledge of private users in Germany. In: WI2020 Community Tracks, pp. 168–184 (2020)

34. Jagatic, T.N., Johnson, N.A., Jakobsson, M., Menczer, F.: Social phishing. Commun. ACM. **50**, 94–100 (2007)

35. Sheng, S., Holbrook, M., Kumaraguru, P., Cranor, L.F., Downs, J.: Who falls for phish? A demographic analysis of phishing susceptibility and effectiveness of interventions. In: Conference on Human Factors in Computing Systems, pp. 373–382 (2010)

36. O'Neil, D.: Analysis of internet users' level of online privacy concerns. Soc. Sci. Comput. Rev. **19**, 17–31 (2001)

37. Öğütçü, G., Testik, Ö.M., Chouseinoglou, O.: Analysis of personal information security behavior and awareness. Comput. Secur. **56**, 83–93 (2016)

38. Rykkja, L.H., Lægreid, P., Fimreite, A.L.: Attitudes towards anti-terror measures: the role of trust, political orientation and civil liberties support. Crit. Stud. Terror. **4**, 219–237 (2011)

39. Bergström, A.: Online privacy concerns: a broad approach to understanding the concerns of different groups for different uses. Comput. Human Behav. **53**, 419–426 (2015)

40. Li, Y., Kobsa, A., Knijnenburg, B.P., Carolyn Nguyen, M.-H.: Cross-cultural privacy prediction. In: Proceedings on Privacy Enhancing Technologies, pp. 113–132 (2017)

41. Reuter, C., Ludwig, T., Kaufhold, M.-A., Spielhofer, T.: Emergency services' attitudes towards social media: a quantitative and qualitative survey across Europe. J. Hum. Comput. Stud. **95**, 96–111 (2016)

42. ISO 26362:2009: Access panels in market, opinion and social research - vocabulary and service requirements. https://www.iso.org/standard/43521.html. Accessed 09 Nov 2020

43. Destatis: Bildungsstand: Allgemeine Schulausbildung [Educational level: General school education] - Statistisches Bundesamt. https://www.destatis.de/DE/Themen/Gesellschaft-Umwelt/Bildung-Forschung-Kultur/Bildungsstand/Tabellen/bildungsabschluss-privathaush-allgemeine-schulausbildung-insgesamt.html. Accessed 10 July 2020

44. Statistisches Bundesamt: Datenreport 2016. Ein Sozialbericht für die Bundesrepublik Deutschland [Data Report 2016: A Social Report for the Federal Republic of Germany] | WZB. https://www.wzb.eu/de/publikationen/datenreport/datenreport-2016. Accessed 10 July 2020

45. Rohrmann, B.: Empirische Studien zur Entwicklung von Antwortskalen für die sozialwissenschaftliche Forschung [Empirical studies on the development of response scales for social science research]. Zeitschrift für Sozialpsychologie. **9**, 222–245 (1978)

46. Bundesamt für Sicherheit in der Informationstechnik: Zehn Maßnahmen zur Absicherung gegen Angriffe aus dem Internet [Ten measures to safeguard against attacks from the Internet]. https://www.bsi-fuer-buerger.de/BSIFB/DE/Service/Checklisten/Massnahmen_gegen_Internetangriffe.html. Accessed 30 July 2020

47. Bundesamt für Sicherheit in der Informationstechnik (BSI): Sichere private Nutzung des Internets [Safe private use of the Internet] (2013)

48. Parsons, K., Calic, D., Pattinson, M., Butavicius, M., McCormac, A., Zwaans, T.: The human aspects of information security questionnaire (HAIS-Q): two further validation studies. Comput. Secur. **66**, 40–51 (2017)

49. Malhotra, N.K., Kim, S.S., Agarwal, J.: Internet users' information privacy concerns (IUIPC): the construct, the scale, and a causal model. Inf. Syst. Res. **15**, 336–355 (2004)

50. Fuchs, D., Klingemann, H.: Das Links-Rechts-Schema als politischer Code: ein interkultureller Vergleich auf inhaltsanalytischer Grundlage [The Left-Right Scheme as Political Code: An Intercultural Comparison Based on Content Analysis]. Campus Verl, Frankfurt am Main (1989)

51. Friedrich, S., Konietschke, F., Pauly, M.: Resampling-based analysis of multivariate data and repeated measures designs with the R package MANOVA RM. R J. **11**, 380–400 (2019)

52. Field, A.P., Wilcox, R.R.: Robust statistical methods: a primer for clinical psychology and experimental psychopathology researchers. Behav. Res. Ther. **98**, 19–38 (2017)

53. Mair, P., Wilcox, R.: Robust statistical methods in R using the WRS2 package. Behav. Res. Methods **52**(2), 464–488 (2019). https://doi.org/10.3758/s13428-019-01246-w

54. Victor, A., Elsässer, A., Hommel, G., Blettner, M.: Judging a Plethora of p-values: how to contend with the problem of multiple testing. Dtsch. Ärzteblatt Int. **107**, 50–56 (2010)

55. Moosbrugger, H., Kelava, A.: Testtheorie und Fragebogenkonstruktion [Test Theory and Questionnaire Construction]. Springer, Heidelberg (2012). https://doi.org/10.1007/978-3-642-20072-4

56. Kroh, M.: Measuring left-right political orientation: the choice of response format. Public Opin. Q. **71**, 204–220 (2007)

57. Bubaš, G., Orehovački, T., Konecki, M.: Factors and predictors of online security and privacy behavior. J. Inf. Organ. Sci. **32**, 79–98 (2008)

58. Kokolakis, S.: Privacy attitudes and privacy behaviour: a review of current research on the privacy paradox phenomenon. Comput. Secur. **64**, 122–134 (2017)

59. Furnell, S., Rajendran, A.: Understanding the influences on information security behaviour. Comput. Fraud Secur. **2012**, 12–15 (2012)

60. Leach, J.: Improving user security behaviour. Comput. Secur. **22**, 685–692 (2003)

The Hidden Value of Patterns – Using Design Patterns to Whitebox Technology Development in Legal Assessments

Ernestine Dickhaut[1]([⊠]), Andreas Janson[2], and Jan Marco Leimeister[1,2]

[1] Information Systems, University of Kassel, Kassel, Germany
{ernestine.dickhaut,leimeister}@uni-kassel.de
[2] Information Systems, University of St. Gallen, St. Gallen, Switzerland
{andreas.janson,janmarco.leimeister}@unisg.ch

Abstract. Higher legal standards with regards to data protection of individuals such as the European General Data Protection Regulation (GDPR) increase the pressure on developing lawful technologies. The development requires feedback from stakeholders such as legal experts that lack technical knowledge but are required to understand IT artifacts. As a solution, patterns can support interdisciplinary system development. We demonstrate how design patterns can support legal experts in arguing about technologies in court by introducing a law simulation study which is a well-known evaluation method in law. Our results show that patterns support legal experts in their argumentation about technologies in court. We provide theoretical contributions concerning cognitive fit theory about how patterns act as a bridge between the internal and external representation of problems and improve problem-solving performance related to the legal assessment of technology. In addition, we provide practical guidance for codifying and communicating design knowledge through patterns.

Keywords: Design pattern · Law simulation study · Cognitive fit theory

1 Introduction

Socio-technical system development has become increasingly important, since not only the technical system is considered in isolation, but also the user and their environment [1, 2]. When building information systems (IS), more and more disciplines like psychology, marketing, economics, law, and sociology are considered. Thus, not only software developers play a decisive role in the design and implementation but also lawyers and legal experts who deal with issues of legal aspects in information systems.

Two factors are crucial in the development and assessment of lawful technologies, the development, and the legal assessment. On the one side, higher legal standards with regards to the data protection of individuals such as the European general data protection regulation (GDPR) are increasing the pressure on developers of IT artifacts [3]. In practice, it is often the case that the measures necessary to launch a system on the market are only considered at the end of the development process [4]. Usually, it

© The Author(s), under exclusive license to Springer Nature Switzerland AG 2021
F. Ahlemann et al. (Eds.): WI 2021, LNISO 47, pp. 405–421, 2021.
https://doi.org/10.1007/978-3-030-86797-3_27

happens with the least possible amount of attention so that the system just about meets the minimum requirements of the legal system. For example, due to the COVID-19 situation, video conference systems such as ZOOM have become increasingly important. However, especially ZOOM was subject to major violations of the GDPR in the huge European market that ultimately led to extensive ad-hoc changes in the system functionalities as well as heavily revised privacy statements [5]. These technologies have to comply with legal requirements to avoid penalties. This could be prevented by paying sufficient attention to legal requirements in advance and in a systematic manner. Concerning the legal assessment related to the tradeoff between the quality of an IT artifact and its lawfulness, there is indeed a "legal limbo" [6]. Through questions of interpretation and the complex nature of legal aspects, there is also room for specific design decisions of IT artifacts that could be more or less compatible to legal regulations. To support the lawful system development a way must be found that support developers in understanding and implement legal requirements by capturing legal design knowledge and makes it accessible and applicable to developers [7].

On the other side, if there is a violation of the law, the IT artifact will be subject to court cases, and the lawfulness of the systems must be negotiated. Here, lawyers often lack technical knowledge and do not have the knowledge to investigate the background of the technology. In the legal assessment, lawyers use the information they get from their clients by using documents like contracts, reports, or documentation [8]. There is, to the best of our knowledge, no approach that supports lawyers in understanding complex socio-technical systems.

In the development of systems, (design) patterns are proven support for the development [9]. Patterns describe frequently occurring problems and outline the core of possible solutions [10]. In the form known so far, patterns usually support (only) developers in the implementation of technical problems by presenting possible solutions.

By providing patterns with legal and technical knowledge, i.e., patterns that make legal knowledge accessible for software engineers, the added value of patterns not only supports developers but also supports legal experts in understanding complex socio-technical systems, e.g., to argue about technical facts in court cases but also a priori when assessing newly developed IT artifacts. The goal of our paper is to present an approach in which patterns also provide an added value for legal experts in their work dealing with IT systems and it is based on the following research question (RQ):

RQ: How can design patterns support legal experts in the assessment of complex socio-technical systems in court?

To answer our research question, we use a pattern catalog that considers legal and user experience requirements. With the help of the pattern catalog, a SPA [11] for the teaching context is developed. To investigate the use of the pattern catalog by giving legal experts an understanding of the development, we use the catalog as support for lawyers in court. For this purpose, we use a law simulation study, which is a well-known evaluation method among law researchers for capturing the lawfulness of IT artifacts [12]. When considering a design science research (DSR) perspective on evaluation, we, therefore, maximize the summative and naturalistic evaluation perspective through the simulation study [12]. Thus, we contribute to theory by extending cognitive fit theory to improve a missed cognitive fit [13] between internal and external representation by using interdisciplinary patterns as a bridge to improve the understanding of the negotiated technology. In addition, we contribute to practice by deriving insights how far patterns support negotiation in a court case and whitebox the development of complex IT artifact, by making the procedure and the details of the development accessible to external parties.

2 Related Work and Theoretical Background

2.1 Application of Design Patterns

In system development, design patterns document known and proven solutions to recurring problems [14]. In the literature, patterns contain templates to describe information in tabular form and represent established instruments to make complex knowledge accessible and applicable [15]. Thus, the use of patterns has become established in various disciplines. In Human-Computer Interaction (HCI), patterns have already been proven in many studies to teach design principles and design concepts [4, 16, 17]. Originally design patterns were used by Christopher Alexander in the area of architecture [9]. In system development, patterns were established first through the Gang of Four (GoF) [14]. In addition to the previously used application areas, patterns can be used to enable a broad understanding of periphery disciplines [18]. There are already approaches that map legal knowledge into patterns [10, 19, 20]. With increasing time and success, the scope of the application of design patterns has been expanded and new advantages were discovered (see Table 1).

Table 1. Application scenarios of design patterns

Application context	Source
Communication of complex concepts between designers	[21]
Record and encourage the reuse of "best practices"	[21]
Recurring design in building architecture	[9]
Record and reuse existing design knowledge	[14]
Teaching HCI design	[10, 17, 18]
Best practice of programming languages such as "Smalltalk"	[22]
Improving design skills	[23]
Develop lawful technologies	[10, 19, 20]

Design patterns are an approach to codify design knowledge. Design knowledge is a special form of knowledge, namely, knowledge to design a system including methods and constructs [24]. As soon as design knowledge is codified for a group that differs in its expertise, further challenges arise. These challenges arise especially in interdisciplinary teams when considering socio-technical system development, which also encompasses engineering aspects that relate to legal aspects that we focus on in this paper. In this context, the codification of design knowledge is gaining importance, because members of an interdisciplinary team come from different disciplines that solve the same problem from different perspectives, with their own method and individual language, which harms knowledge sharing [25–27]. It should be guaranteed that the design knowledge is formulated in a clear, unambiguous, accessible language, and is free from inconsistencies and contradictions [28].

2.2 Cognitive Fit Theory and Knowledge Transfer

Cognitive fit theory was developed to understand how the fit between a task to be solved and the mental representation influences the skill to solve a problem [29]. A human characteristic is the abstract mental representation of situations and characteristics. Accordingly, the performance in solving a problem depends on the representation of the problem and the task. If there is a mismatch between both, the performance of problem solving a specific task will suffer [30]. Cognitive fit theory suggests that when both the problem representation and the problem to resolve correspond, a cognitive fit will occur. The cognitive fit produces a consistent mental representation for problem solving, and subsequently leads to faster and a more accurate performance in decision-making [31]. In recent decades, cognitive fit theory has been used to explain a wide range of problem-solving phenomena [13, 30, 32, 33].

The knowledge level is important and has an influence on the problem-solving performance. In interdisciplinary system development the level of knowledge and the transfer of knowledge gain in importance. In literature, differences regarding the level of knowledge due to different knowledge backgrounds exist such as levels of experience, and various disciplines are regarded as so-called knowledge boundaries, which must be resolved in the interaction of interdisciplinary teams [34]. Many studies have investigated how knowledge can be shared in interdisciplinary teams [34–38]. In the development of socio-technical systems, where many different disciplines come together, interdisciplinary cooperation is indispensable. Translations and interpretations between developers and other disciplines are still necessary [39]. By reusing and recombining knowledge, effectiveness, and efficiency can also be achieved, knowledge transfer of solutions to new use cases must be enabled [40]. Thus, we consider cognitive fit theory as a prime candidate for better understanding the value of patterns in complex socio-technical systems and scaffolding the subsequent theory development accordingly.

3   Methodology: Law Simulation Study and Content Analysis

The law simulation study is an established method among legal experts to evaluate technology in a practical manner in regard to their lawfulness [41]. A key characteristic is that it allows creating realistic conditions while damage is prevented. Therefore, it is desirable to provoke critical situations [12]. With the help of the simulation study, we are able to make statements about our goal to what extent the patterns make system development understandable for legal experts, besides contributing to a lawful system design. With the help of the simulation study, we are able to address legal requirements and assess the realization through the system before the system is launched to the market [42]. There-fore, we have the possibility to evaluate systems in an early state of implementation such as by evaluating prototypes. To our knowledge, it is currently the only known evaluation method that makes it possible to negotiate the lawfulness of technologies before they are launched to the market. The simulation study enables developers to receive legal feedback early (e.g. on prototypes). In addition, compared to legal opinion gathered a priori, the simulation study as an evaluation method reveals a richer picture related to the lawfulness of an IT artifact because it involves multiple rounds of negotiation between the stakeholders.

Simulation studies in general can be divided into two parts, starting with a user evaluation, and followed by a simulated court case. With the help of the design patterns, we have developed a smart personal assistant (SPA) which is used as a support in exam preparation as part of a course. The first part of the study evaluates the use with users, while the second part examines the lawfulness of the SPA in simulated court cases.

3.1 Pattern Development and Pilot Study

In the following, we want to provide a brief insight into the development of the pattern catalog as well as into the execution of a pilot study, in which developers evaluated the patterns regarding aspects such as the understanding, application, and usefulness.

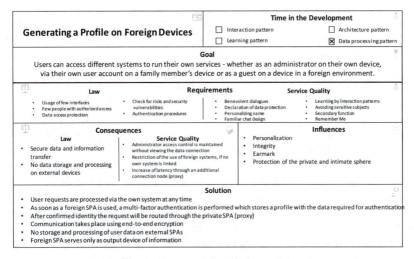

Fig. 1. One exemplary design pattern

The development of the patterns was carried out in an iterative process consisting of several iterations to evaluate the patterns at an early stage and incorporate feedback. In a first step, a research team consisting of legal experts and computer scientists conduct literature reviews to investigate recurring issues that occur in the development of lawful SPAs. In addition to the theoretical insights, they conduct a workshop with developers (N = 6). Based on the insights acquired through literature they prepare an overview of issues to match them with practical problems in the development. This procedure makes it possible to compare the results of the literature review with practice.

Based on the list of issues, the research team worked on proven solutions in the literature. In a second workshop with the practitioners, they extend the proposed solutions resulting in an overview of eleven issues and corresponding solutions at the end. The codification of the design knowledge into the patterns (see Fig. 1) was carried out by an author of the paper. Based on a literature review on the codification of design knowledge and theories, such as cognitive load theory, the results were codified in patterns [43].

To make sure that the pattern developers support developers in developing lawful technologies, we have conducted a pilot study. In a 2×2 fully randomized field study we used manipulation to investigate how the support of patterns in the development of prototypes affects the assessment of legal experts. The results show that the group that was supported by pattern led to significantly better ratings of lawfulness [43].

For the user evaluation, we have used an IT artifact, which we developed in another study using interdisciplinary patterns [43]. The IT artifact is a voice-based conversational agent for exam preparation in university courses.

3.2   First Part – User Evaluation

The primary goal of the first part of the law simulation study is the use of the SPA by real users, similar to a usability evaluation [12]. This procedure enables the generation of legal violations by using the system in practice, as they might occur in reality. Therefore, violations of law are simulated for the later court case. Particular attention is paid to the fact that the violations have only been simulated and do not occur during the first part by using technology to avoid real damage. Nevertheless, the simulation of the violations is carried out as close to reality as possible to get a real situation.

In the user evaluation, we let students in a basic course for economics and business administration use the conversational assistant for half an hour a day for one week to revise the course material before the upcoming final assessment. Therefore, we prepared the teaching material to include it in the SPA. The teaching material is prepared as a flashcards quiz to make it as comprehensible and supportive as possible. The subjects use the SPA within the given time period and then give feedback on the use in questionnaires. This enables us to draw two conclusions. First, we can early evaluate the usability and user experience and improve it before launching on the market. On the other hand, a trial of the technology in case of an emergency is conducted, which helps us to improve the technology before market entry. During the user evaluation, legal experts observed the use and created four cases that could lead to court action. These cases are now used in the second part of the simulation study as a basis for the court cases.

3.3   Second Part – Court Cases

Based on the user evaluation, we have simulated four court cases. The simulation study was carried out before German courts according to German and European law. Overall, six legal experts participated in our law simulation study. Among them were two judges and four lawyers who conducted the four court cases. All participants have completed the second state examination in law and already have several years of professional experience as a lawyer or judge. One participant was female, the other five males. The oral hearings lasted 45 and 60 min. All participating lawyers received the patterns used in the development and a note that they were implemented in the development. The judges in the court cases, on the other hand, only received the evidence and material that was contributed to the court by the lawyers (as it would be in reality).

Two cases were heard before the civil court and two before the administrative court. To get a general impression of the support of our patterns, we conducted the civil cases in written form and the two administrative law processes in oral form. Each of the four trials involved a judge, a lawyer from the defendant's side, a lawyer from the plaintiff, the plaintiff, and the defendant. As plaintiffs, we recruited voluntary participants of the first part of the simulation study to present the process as realistically as possible. In all four cases, the defendant's side was represented by the university, which used the IT artifact in the lecture course.

In preparation for the oral hearings written preliminary proceedings took place. In a seven-page written pleading, the plaintiff's lawyer set out the facts of the case and the reasons for the action and called on the defendant to refrain from using the IT artifact in university teaching. The reason for one of the four actions was the collection of personal data beyond the purpose of processing, as well as information about the duration and purpose of data storage. In a five-page statement of defense, the defendant's lawyer commented on the action. In the statement of defense, the lawyer refers to the patterns that were used in the development process of the IT artifact.

The judge invites to an oral hearing to dispute the action. To be able to answer questions regarding the development of the IT artifact an expert who was involved in the development of the SPA. The expert leaves the courtroom before the start of the hearing and only joined to answer questions about the development. According to the administrative court rules, the oral proceedings began (after the case was called,) with the presentation of the essential content of the files. The judge first presented the facts of the case and discussed the reasons for the action. After the plaintiff's lawyer confirmed the facts of the case and set out the grounds of the action in more detail, the two lawyers and the judge examined the facts. Both parties now had the opportunity to present their side and the judge could get an impression of the situation. The negotiations end with the pronouncement of a judgment.

In addition to the four court cases and the written correspondence, we interviewed the judges and lawyers to gain insights into the support for our pattern catalog. The interview took place at once after the end of the simulation study with all participants. The interview allowed the participants to exchange views on the use of the patterns as well as to extract and discuss critical aspects necessary for the revision of the patterns. The advantage of conducting a group interview is that the participants can address aspects of the others. These insights allow us to draw a few conclusions about the added value of the patterns for the legal experts.

3.4 Qualitative Content Analysis

Through the simulation study, we received documents (see Fig. 2) from four court cases, which we examined in a structuring qualitative content analysis according to Mayring [44]. With the results of our analysis, we want to gain insights into how legal experts experienced working with interdisciplinary patterns to better understand how complex socio-technical systems can be designed. For this purpose, we have inductively formed categories based on our insights and the documents of the simulation study.

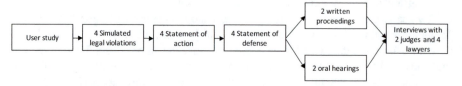

Fig. 2. Use of the design patterns in court cases

As a result, the two categories *technical understanding* and *supporting argumentation* emerged. Based on the categories, we have categorized our qualitative data. The data includes 1) two transcripts of the oral proceedings 2) the related correspondence between the lawyers and the judge before both oral proceedings 3) the documents of both written proceedings, and 4) the interviews of the lawyers and judges after the hearings. In the first step, paraphrasing, we cut out all the text components that are not content bearing. We have generalized the resulting statements and thus combined redundant statements into one common statement. In a second reduction, we summarized similar statements and combined them into general statements.

4   Findings and Theoretical Propositions

Regarding the intention of a qualitative content analysis, we screened our documents, and inductively formed two core categories in which the patterns were used, namely: *understanding technical mechanisms*, and *supporting argumentation*. Using the insights, we want to get detailed conclusions about how legal experts use the patterns in court. The first category *technical understanding* shows that legal experts support using patterns to get a better understanding of the technology to be negotiated (see Table 2). In court, the lawyers and judges argue about an action of a technology to clarify the state of affairs. Each of the two lawyers pursues its own search for a solution to the problem. The plaintiff's lawyer argues against the use of the technology, while the defense lawyer argues why the technology did not lead to any violations of the law. The judge uses both arguments and tries to understand the technology to come to a judgment. For all parties, this means that the problem representation is formed from the action, the understanding of the technology, and the previous knowledge of the problem domain. To solve the problem the lawyer uses his mental representation about the problem domain together with the external representation about the technology. According to cognitive fit theory, a cognitive fit appears if each information matches.

Through further information and explanations in the pattern that goes beyond the technical solution, the contents of the pattern can be applied to the practical case (all following quotes are translated to English):

> "[…] to meet the secondary burden of explanation, I have described the application and used the pattern." lawyer 1 (L1).

The patterns are used to refer to the development in the argumentation and to be empowered to describe actual facts from the technology. The clear and uniform presentation of the patterns means that the necessary information can be found directly. Formulations that require no technical background make the patterns used stand out from technical documentation. These are difficult to understand and therefore offer little basis for developing a technical understanding:

"The technical information in the pattern is easy to understand, even for laymen with no technical background." lawyer 4 (L4).

Table 2. Use of the patterns in court cases

Category	Reduction from the content analysis	Participant
Technical understanding	Information goes beyond technical solution	L1, L3, L5
	Applicable in court	L1, L3, L5
	Reference to the development in the argumentation	L2
	Supporting secondary burden of proof	L3, L5
	Support the understanding of the technology	L1, L2
	Clear, uniform presentation	L1, L4, J2
	No need for technical background	L4
Supporting argumentation	Linking law and technology	L1, L3, J2
	Support to find arguments	J1, L4
	Offer helpful information	L2, L3
	Negotiation on technical basis	L1
	Clarity leads to fast overview	L1
	Negotiations of fines	L3

Nevertheless, the possibility remains to use documentation as an addition to the patterns to get a more detailed insight into the development of the system. Through additional information, such as user stories and examples, the content of the patterns is not misunderstood and does not lead to false statements in court. The links to other additional patterns and additional information in the patterns are specially mentioned. With the help of links to other patterns and influencing factors, the contents can be applied to practice and be understood as a whole. Hence, we propose that further information in design patterns support the understanding of the technology.

Proposition 1 (P1): Design patterns act as a bridge between internal representation and external representation and contribute to a better problem representation, which can be used for the problem-solving task.

The second category *supporting argumentation* summarizes statements about the support in the formation of arguments and the justification based on the knowledge gained from the patterns in the court case. By linking law and technical requirements, the patterns show the conflict between user experience and law and that an attempt was made to meet the needs of both. In this way, a link to legal implementations in the technology can be drawn from the patterns in the case of technical points of attack.

"The patterns are, in the end, aid for finding the argumentation." lawyer 3 (L3)
"They offer information to write a statement of defense." lawyer 2 (L2).

Especially in situations where background knowledge and understanding are missing, it is difficult to find convincing arguments. This is where patterns come in and provide the basis for the formation of arguments about the development that are nevertheless understandable. Because the other side's lawyer also understands the technical arguments, negotiations can be continued on a technical basis.

"The fact alone, that the pattern has been taken into account in the development shows the importance of protection of personal data in the development."

The use of the pattern already shows that the will was generally there to develop a lawful system. This could be used to the advantage of the defendant's technology, especially at the beginning of the trial. When it comes to negotiating fines, it is often a question of whether the person in charge has even thought about it:

"Here you can explain the first step, which means that the fines will be reduced. The more concretely one can then explain this, the better the argumentation." judge 1 (J1).

Proposition 2 (P2): Design patterns contribute to a comprehensive mental representation of the problem domain, thus expanding the space of possible solutions.

The interdisciplinary pattern catalog supports the formation of arguments during the trial but does not serve as independent evidence. The confirmation that the pattern has been implemented in the system completely without deviations is missing. With little time in the negotiation to react to arguments from the other side, the patterns must quickly provide exactly the information that is needed at that moment. Due to the clarity and the fact that all patterns correspond to the same structure, you can quickly get the used information and build arguments. The link between law and technology leads to an understanding of how the system functions technically, and provide an understanding of which legal requirements have been observed, and use it for argumentation:

"[...] you can see that the instructions were followed to implement legal requirements and argue with it." lawyer 1 (L1).

Proposition 3 (P3): Design patterns enable to through clear presentation of solutions to achieve a fit between problem representation and problem-solving task that, ultimately, leads to a better mental representation of a possible task solution.

Besides insights into the usefulness and comprehensibility of the patterns, we have also gained insights into the situations in which the lawyers used the patterns in the negotiation. At the oral hearing, arguments were presented on the basis of five patterns.

In the second oral hearing, five patterns were used throughout the court proceedings for the argumentation. In both written procedures' patterns were also used to illustrate the development of the lawful IT artifact. Six patterns were used in the third process. While in the fourth process, six patterns were used to generate arguments. To show the use of the patterns, we use an extract from an oral hearing to show which arguments were used in the respective legal dispute (see Table 3).

Table 3. Pattern as support for evidence

Phase	Issue	Evidence
Action	Data storage	Data protection policy
Defense	Data minimization principle Art. 5 sect. 1 lit. c. GDPR	Statement of expert
		Pattern "Data protection-friendly user profile"
		Pattern Differentiated purposes of use"
		Pattern "Non-linkability"
		Pattern "Prevention of personal data"
		Pattern "Deleting routines"
		Pattern "Transparent data processing procedures"
		Pattern "Setting options by the user"
		Pattern "No complete user profile"
		Pattern "Learning through relevance assessments"
		Pattern "Learning through interaction patterns"
In court	Data storage	Pattern "Deleting routines"
		Statement of the expert
	Cancellation right	Pattern "Data protection friendly user profile"
		Statement of the expert
		Data protection policy
	Storage purpose	Pattern "Differentiated purposes of use"
		Pattern "Prevention of personal data"
		Pattern "Setting options by the user"
		Pattern "No complete user profile"

The court case consists of a written preliminary hearing, in which the claim and defense are exchanged, and the oral hearing occurs. The key reason for the action is data minimization which supposedly has not been complied with. In his statement of defense, the lawyer refers to ten patterns:

> *"The design pattern 'privacy-friendly user profile' proposes that only data that are necessary to [...] should be stored. It is also recommended to give the user the possibility to decide which data may be processed." lawyer 1 (L1).*

The reference to the design pattern enables the lawyer to shift the discussion from a legal argumentation level to a technical level. While the hearing has previously focused on the data minimization principle art. 5 sect. 1 lit. c. GDPR, the lawyer was able to show with the help of the design pattern that data minimization was generally taken into account and he has the possibility to show how this was implemented in the technology.

Proposition 4 (P4): Design patterns contribute to the extension of existing domain knowledge and for the acquisition of new knowledge.

To support his argument, he mentions further patterns in his argumentation. Due to the change from the negotiation of purely legal aspects to the technical implementation of the legal requirements, the judge sees no need to discuss general questions about the extent to which data minimization was implemented. All further questions afterward relate to the question of whether the patterns mentioned were actually implemented in the technology in this way. The lawyer can confirm this with the following statement:

> *"These proposed solutions from the pattern "Data Protection Friendly User Profile" were fully considered and implemented when programming [...]." lawyer 1 (L1).*

In the end, the judge invites the expert who should confirm that the mentioned patterns have really been implemented. All further questions refer to the actual implementation of the pattern in the technology.

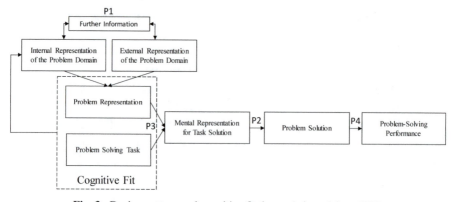

Fig. 3. Design pattern and cognitive fit theory (adapted from [13])

Based on the findings we consider a cognitive fit between the understanding of a technology to be negotiated (mental representation) by legal experts and the clarification of the facts (problem-solving task) to be a decisive factor for a negotiation on the lawfulness of a technology in court (P3). The mental representation consists of the internal representation of the problem domain, i.e., the existing knowledge about the technology to be negotiated, and the external representation of the problem, the technology itself. As in practice legal experts often lack the necessary domain knowledge on complex socio-technical systems hence the internal presentation of technical domain knowledge that can be accessed is limited. In our case, the external presentation of the technology consists of technical documentation and programming code which is difficult to understand for legal experts and difficult to use for negotiation. Therefore, we see the extension of a bridge between the internal and external representation in the extended cognitive fit model of [33] as a crucial factor in building the cognitive fit and thus improving problem-solving performance. We see an opportunity (see Fig. 3) in which the cognitive fit can be produced with the help of further information (in our case the use of interdisciplinary patterns).

A crucial point that must be taken into account is that the person is aware of a mismatch and lack of cognitive fit and realizes this amongst other things in the fact that he cannot solve the task this way. They then look for information that help them to solve the task (P1). The information acts between the internal and external representation (P2) of the problem and bridges the mismatch of understanding, leading to a mental representation that leads to a problem solution. At any time, when new information is added to the internal representation, the mental representation is compared with the task to be solved and it is decided whether a) further information is needed or b) the problem can be solved by the circumstances of the mental representation. Our simulation study shows the benefit in legal patterns that act as a bridge between the internal and external representation by codifying and accessing design knowledge from different domains in a layman's language to improve the negotiation in court (P4).

5   Discussion

5.1   Theoretical and Practical Implications

Our findings show that the use of interdisciplinary design patterns in the context of court cases increase the understanding of technical mechanisms. A connection between legal requirements and influences on the technical solution is mapped, which offers links between law and development.

Hong et al. [30] argues that the same type of representing the solving task and the mental representation is crucial for the cognitive fit. According to [30] we assume that a bridge between the internal and external representation can support the cognitive fit because both representations should be on the same professional level of the domain knowledge. By formulating the interdisciplinary patterns in a layman's language, they help the legal experts to understand, (build a mental representation of the technology [29]) and support the possibility to negotiate the technology. For example, technical documentation of the code is usually poorly understood by lawyers and cannot be used to understand the problem domain, which would lead to no cognitive fit [31].

From a design science theoretical perspective, patterns provide a means to the end for accumulating design knowledge of IT artifacts in a way that is comprehensible enough to not only build IT artifacts but also communicate IT artifact design effectively across disciplines [14]. Accordingly, patterns are a carrier of design knowledge, which serves as a mediator between developers and legal experts by acting as a bridge between the external representation (technology itself) and the internal representation (legal experts' knowledge of the technological domain). Thus, on the one hand, design patterns provide guidance on the code and technical implementation [9]. On the other hand, lawyers and judges are trained in technical understanding in order to negotiate the state of affairs in court.

Our findings indicate the added value of patterns in two cases, the development and the legal assessment. In both cases the patterns act as support. In the development the patterns support the legal understanding of the developer and provide proven solutions for recurring legal problems.

5.2 Limitation and Future Research

Our study is limited by a few factors that provide directions for future research. First, by having evaluated the use of the patterns in a natural scenario, the results can only be generalized to a limited extent. The methodology of the simulation study has the limitation that a technology is evaluated extensively, but with a small sample size. At the evaluation in court, seven legal professionals were asked and observed, which does not offer a strong evidence base. Nevertheless, we have provided a first insight into possible scenarios of patterns in the work of legal experts. We see a need for further research, which, among other things, will examine the usefulness of a larger sample.

Second, the fact that our infringements are based on the user evaluation of the simulation study means that they are invented. Thus, it cannot be guaranteed that exactly these cases would happen in reality. In preparing the legal infringements, we have used years of practical experience of lawyers who have extracted simulated legal infringements to the best of their knowledge. Nevertheless, there is a bias that must be taken into account in any case.

Third, the legal validity of the patterns as evidence could lead to the fact that now everyone designs interdisciplinary patterns and refers to them in case of an action. The problem of developing lawful technologies is the interpretation of the law. Law is technology-neutral which leaves room for interpretation. The lawfulness of a technology has to be reconsidered in each individual case. Therefore, patterns act as a support to provide information and solutions but are no guarantee to develop lawful technologies. To close the gap between the development and the legal assessment we include a field in which the implementation can be confirmed. To prevent a large number of legal patterns from being created that claim to help design legal technologies, we see the need for certification of the patterns. Further work could, therefore, deal with a certification of legal patterns. In particular, the content should be checked for its correctness to support developing lawful technologies. Additionally, the interpretability of the patterns should not leave too much room for negotiation so that the patterns cannot be interpreted the wrong way. Further work in this area could, for example, be oriented towards certification types for medical technology and use their experience. This is the only way to guarantee that the expansion of patterns, as we know it from system development, can be extended to other disciplines, such as law, and bring high-quality added value.

Fourth, the method of simulation study we use is, in its current form, linked to the European legal system. In comparison to other legal systems, European law and especially the GDPR represent strict legal requirements. In particular, the protection of personal data is in focus and is strictly protected. Nevertheless, we see the necessity to use the interdisciplinary pattern catalog in other legal systems as well and to focus on its utility.

6 Conclusion

We present an approach in which interdisciplinary patterns provide an added value for legal experts in understanding complex socio-technical systems. The law simulation study enables us to gain practical insights into the work with the patterns. We use the interdisciplinary pattern catalog to support lawyers in their argumentation and evidence during court cases. So, we have the opportunity to study the process of using the pattern in a unique scenario. We investigate the use of the pattern catalog in a natural setting that would not be possible in a laboratory study. In addition, to gain insights into the support of the pattern to make the development of the IT artifact transparent for legal experts, the simulation study enables a statement about the lawfulness of the developed technology.

The socio-technical system development would benefit from the approach of combining a two-sided added value from patterns, especially with regard to higher legal standards for data protection of individuals such as the GDPR. So far, the process of how systems were developed and what thoughts developers had in mind for lawyers has remained a black box, which makes it difficult to argue in court. This issue is especially prevalent when considering new AI-based technologies due to their complexity and blackbox character [45]. Technical documentation and further technical explanations would mostly be difficult to understand for laymen and, therefore, not sufficient for the formation of argumentations. In the development of socio-technical systems, various stakeholders are becoming increasingly relevant, which is why it is important to codify the meaning of design knowledge. Since, in practice, there is often a lack of exchange between the individual disciplines in the development of socio-technical systems, we see the use of interdisciplinary patterns to create knowledge bridges as useful.

Acknowledgements. Our thanks go to all participating lawyers and judges without whose support the study would not have been possible. This paper presents research that was conducted in context of the project AnEkA (project number: 348084924), funded by the German Research Foundation (DFG).

References

1. Hoffmann, A., Söllner, M., Fehr, A., Hoffmann, H., Leimeister, J.M.: Towards an Approach for Developing socio-technical Ubiquitous Computing Applications (2011)

2. Sarker, S., Chatterjee, S., Xiao, X., Elbanna, A.: The Sociotechnical axis of cohesion for the is discipline: its historical legacy and its continued relevance. MISQ **43**, 695–720 (2019)
3. Kühling, J., Martini, M.: Die Datenschutz-Grundverordnung: Revolution oder Evolution im europäischen und deutschen Datenschutzrecht (2016)
4. Compagna, L., Khoury, P.E., Massacci, F., Thomas, R., Zannone, N.: How to capture, model, and verify the knowledge of legal, security, and privacy experts. In: International Conference on Artificial Intelligence and Law, pp. 149–153 (2007)
5. Security Week: www.securityweek.com/zooms-security-and-privacy-woes-violated-gdpr-expert-says. Accessed 25 June 2020
6. Scott, J.: In legal limbo: post-legislative guidance as a challenge for European administrative law. Common Mark. Law Rev. **48**(2) (2011)
7. Morse, W.C., Nielsen-Pincus, M., Force, J.E., Wulfhorst, J.D.: Bridges and barriers to developing and conducting interdisciplinary graduate-student team research. Ecol. Soc. **12**(2), 8 (2007)
8. Morcón, C.R., García, J.P., Pizarro, J.A.S.: Knowledge management in a law firm. J. Knowl. Manag. (2000)
9. Alexander, C.: A Pattern Language: Towns, Buildings, Construction. Oxford University Press, Oxford (1977)
10. Compagna, L., El Khoury, P., Krausová, A., Massacci, F., Zannone, N.: How to integrate legal requirements into a requirements engineering methodology for the development of security and privacy patterns. Artif. Intell. Law **17**, 1–30 (2009). https://doi.org/10.1007/s10506-008-9067-3
11. Knote, R., Janson, A., Söllner, M., Leimeister, J.M.: Value co-creation in smart services: a functional affordances perspective on smart personal assistants. JAIS **22**, 5 (2020)
12. Pordesch, V., Roßnagel, A., Schneider, M.: Simulation study mobile and secure communication in healthcare. DuD 76–80 (1999)
13. Shaft, T.M., Vessey, I.: The role of cognitive fit in the relationship between software comprehension and modification. Manag. Inf. Syst. Q. **30**, 29–55 (2006)
14. Gamma, E., Helm, R., Johnson, R., Vlissides, J.: Design Patterns: Elements of Reusable Object Oriented Software. Addison-Wesley Professional, Boston (1994)
15. Alexander, C.: The Timeless Way of Building. Oxford University Press, New York (1979)
16. Borchers, J.: Teaching HCI design patterns: experience from two university courses. CHI (2002)
17. Koukouletsos, K., Khazaei, B., Dearden, A., Ozcan, M.: Teaching usability principles with patterns and guidelines. In: Kotzé, P., Wong, W., Jorge, J., Dix, A., Silva, P.A. (eds.) Creativity and HCI: From Experience to Design in Education, vol. 289, pp. 159–174. Springer, Cham (2009). https://doi.org/10.1007/978-0-387-89022-7_11
18. Wania, C.: Exploring design patterns as evaluation tools in human computer interaction education. In: MWAIS (2019)
19. Hoffmann, A., Schulz, T., Zirfas, J., Hoffmann, H., Roßnagel, A., Leimeister, J.M.: Legal compatibility as a characteristic of sociotechnical systems. Bus. Inf. Syst. Eng. **57**(2), 103–113 (2015). https://doi.org/10.1007/s12599-015-0373-5
20. Yskout, K., Scandariato, R., Joosen, W.: Do security patterns really help designers? In: International Conference on Software Engineering, pp. 292–302 (2015)
21. Beck, K., et al.: Industrial experience with design patterns. In: Proceedings of IEEE 18th International Conference on Software Engineering, pp. 103–114 (1996)
22. Roberts, D., Brant, J., Johnson, R.: A refactoring tool for smalltalk. Theory Pract. Object Syst. **3**, 253–263 (1997)
23. Prechelt, L., Unger-Lamprecht, B., Philippsen, M., Tichy, W.F.: Two controlled experiments assessing the usefulness of design pattern documentation in program maintenance. IEEE Trans. Softw. Eng. **28**, 595–606 (2002)

24. Gregor, S., Hevner, A.R.: Positioning and presenting design science research for maximum impact. MIS Q. **37**, 337–355 (2013)
25. Chandra Kruse, L., Seidel, S., Purao, S.: Making use of design principles. In: Parsons, J., Tuunanen, T., Venable, J., Donnellan, B., Helfert, M., Kenneally, J. (eds.) Tackling Society's Grand Challenges with Design Science, vol. 9661, pp. 37–51. Springer, Cham (2015). https://doi.org/10.1007/978-3-319-39294-3_3
26. Chandra Kruse, L., Seidel, S.: Tensions in design principle formulation. In: DESRIST, pp. 180–188 (2017)
27. Phuwanartnurak, A.J.: Interdisciplinary collaboration through wikis in software development. IEEE, Piscataway (2009)
28. Lukyanenko, R., Jeffrey, P.: Design theory indeterminacy: what is it, how can it be reduced, and why did the polar bear drown? JAIS **21**, 1–59 (2020)
29. Vessey, I., Galletta, D.: Cognitive fit: an empirical study of information acquisition. Inf. Syst. Res. **2**, 63–84 (1991)
30. Hong, W., Tam, J.Y., Tam, K.Y.: The effects of information format and shopping task on consumers' online shopping behavior: a cognitive fit perspective. JMIS **21**, 149–184 (2004)
31. Agarwal, R., Sinha, A.P., Tanniru, M.: Cognitive fit in requirements modeling: a study of object and process methodologies. J. Manag. Inf. Syst. **13**, 137–162 (1996)
32. Claes, J., Vanderfeesten, I., Gailly, F., Grefen, P., Poels, G.: The Structured Process Modeling Theory (SPMT) a cognitive view on why and how modelers benefit from structuring the process of process modeling. Inf. Syst. Front. **17**(6), 1401–1425 (2015). https://doi.org/10.1007/s10796-015-9585-y
33. Khatri, V., Vessey, I., Ramesh, V., Clay, P., Park, S.-J.: Understanding conceptual schemas: exploring the role of application and is domain knowledge. Inf. Syst. Res. **17**, 81–99 (2006)
34. Kotlarsky, J., van den Hooff, B., Huysman, M.: Bridging knowledge boundaries in cross-functional groups: the role of a transactive memory system. ICIS (2009)
35. Bittner, E.A.C., Leimeister, J.M.: Creating shared understanding in heterogeneous work groups: why it matters and how to achieve it. J. Manag. Inf. Syst. **31**, 111–144 (2014)
36. Carlile, P.R.: Transferring, translating, and transforming: an integrative framework for managing knowledge across boundaries. Organ. Sci. **15**, 555–568 (2004)
37. Linden, T., Cybulski, J.: Refining the process of sharing problem-solving experience across domain: a hermeneutic study. In: AMCIS (2006)
38. Winkler, M., Huber, T., Dibbern, J.: The software prototype as digital boundary object: a revelatory longitudinal innovation case (2014)
39. Pawlowski, R.: Bridging user organizations: knowledge brokering and the work of information technology professionals. MIS Q. **28**, 645 (2004)
40. vom Brocke, J., Winter, R., Hevner, A., Maedche, A.: Accumulation and evolution of design knowledge in design science research–a journey through time and space. JAIS (2019)
41. Roßnagel, A., Schuldt, M.: The Simulation Study as a Method of Evaluating Socially Acceptable Technology Design, pp. 108–116 (2013)
42. Otto, P.N., Anton, A.I.: Addressing legal requirements in requirements engineering. In: 15th IEEE International Requirements Engineering Conference, pp. 5–14 (2007)
43. Dickhaut, E., Janson, A., Leimeister, J.M.: Codifying interdisciplinary design knowledge through patterns – the case of smart personal assistants. In: Hofmann, S., Müller, O., Rossi, M. (eds.) Designing for Digital Transformation. Co-Creating Services with Citizens and Industry. LNCS, vol. 12388, pp. 114–125. Springer, Cham (2020). https://doi.org/10.1007/978-3-030-64823-7_12
44. Mayring, P.: Qualitative content analysis: theoretical foundation, basic procedures and software solution (2014)
45. Rahwan, I., et al.: Machine behaviour. Nature **568**, 477–486 (2019)

Understanding Privacy Disclosure in the Online Market for Lemons: Insights and Requirements for Platform Providers

Andreas Engelmann[✉] and Gerhard Schwabe

Department of Informatics, University of Zurich, Zurich, Switzerland
{engelmann,schwabe}@ifi.uzh.ch

Abstract. Future used car markets may use personal data to reduce information asymmetries between car sellers and buyers, e. g. on past driving behavior. Reducing information asymmetries is attractive for used car platforms as they can move from pure information provision to orchestrating transactions. However, car sellers and buyers have to agree to sharing personal data. What kind of data is interesting for them? Under what circumstances are they willing to share this data? What should a platform do to support data sharing? We explore those research questions as part of the Cardossier project by conducting experiments with the Car-Market Game, simulating a future car market. The results indicate that there is no market for pure personal data (e. g. photographs of sellers), but there is a market for car usage data. From future used car platforms the participants expect disclosure control and disclosure transparency in an environment free of interpersonal trust.

Keywords: Privacy preferences · Personal data disclosure · Trust · Used car platforms

1 Introduction

The used car market is characterized by information asymmetries: The seller of a car knows more about the quality of a car than a potential buyer. As already noted by Akerlof [1], markets with such information asymmetries are prone to fail as 'lemons' (= bad cars) drive out 'peaches' (= good cars) until the market collapses. It is thus in the primary interest of used car platforms, such as Autoscout24, to decrease information asymmetries. If potential buyers could gain sufficient information about the quality of a used car, they would not need leave the platform to physically inspect many cars or turn to professional used car dealers because of their reputation and guarantees. This would increase traffic on the platform and ultimately the revenue of the platform.

Systems like Cardossier promise to increase market transparency: They collect all important events in the lifecycle of a car, e. g. registrations, accidents, repairs, and driving behavior. So, used car platforms are interested to integrate them into their offering. However, the history of a car can contain sensitive data about the car's drivers and owners. European data protection laws require the consent of the car sellers for the

F. Ahlemann et al. (Eds.): WI 2021, LNISO 47, pp. 422–439, 2021.
https://doi.org/10.1007/978-3-030-86797-3_28

release of such sensitive data. So, the question arises: What can a platform do to acquire this consent from car sellers?

As a first step, the platform needs to understand what sensitive information car buyers are interested in when looking for a used car. Interesting sensitive information may not be limited to information about the car's history. Car buyers may also want to establish interpersonal trust in the car seller in order to accept any remaining information asymmetries; and car sellers may want to establish trust in the car buyer to make sure that they receive the payment for the car and that the car is not misused while they are still legally responsible for it. Such interpersonal trust building could be mediated [2] by platforms by providing certified information about the seller or the buyer. So, we ask very generally:

RQ1: What sensitive data are sellers and buyers interested in and willing to share?

Only if information consumers (= classically: the buyers) are 'sufficiently' interested in getting access and information providers (= classically: the sellers) are 'sufficiently' willing to provide data, there is a chance that they can share data on the platform. Economically, 'sufficient' means that the information consumers need to value information at least as high as the information providers value the compromised privacy. If this is the case, a platform can facilitate the exchange of data, e. g. by asking the information consumer to remunerate the information provider. In a first exploratory study, we will address research question 1. The answer provides the platform insights, *what* data should be provided.

However, willingness to share is not free of context. Car sellers may want to release sensitive data only to selected buyers and only once the negotiation has progressed to a certain stage. So, the question *how* data sharing should be orchestrated remains. We will address this question in a second exploratory study, asking:

RQ2: What preferences and expectations do individuals have when disclosing their personal information in the used car market?

The answer to this question will provide used car platforms with requirements for building systems that facilitate data exchange and ultimately reduce information asymmetries in the market for lemons.

The subsequent section will first introduce related work on emerging changes in the used car market and the role of platforms as a mediator and as a car data market. As the envisioned markets do not yet exist, behavioral data on privacy preferences and privacy disclosure behavior is still lacking. We therefore inform our research from the closest existing domain: eCommerce. We ask how privacy is conceptualized there, what people expect, and how data disclosure is managed.

After the related work, we introduce the chosen research methodology, the research setting, and the data collection. As we strive to improve the market position of the used car platform, we selected a design research approach. The research is situated as a part of the Cardossier project. Data is collected from experiments with Car-Market Game. Car-Market Game is a game that simulates a future used car platform.

The subsequent results section offers the data collected in two experiments. Data from the first experiment indicates that there is no market for purely personal data (e. g. a photograph of the other party), but there is a market for car usage data. Data collected in the second round of experiments validates the insights from the first experiments.

In addition, results indicate that participants expect disclosure control and disclosure transparency in an environment free of interpersonal trust.

The subsequent discussion section analyzes what the insights mean for used car platforms, translates those insights into requirements for platform owners, and present novel insights concerning privacy in eCommerce. Conclusions and limitations close the paper.

2   Background and Related Work

2.1   Emerging Changes in the used Car Market

Cars become increasingly software-intensive [3] and car manufacturers strive to develop platforms [4] to generate value from the data gathered during car usage. EU initiatives limit their power, forcing car manufacturers to provide open interfaces for third parties to make use of the data. Other actors in the car ecosystem, such as garages, insurances, mobility service providers, and registration authorities, wake up and see the opportunities in generating value from their 'data treasures'. They team up in Blockchain consortia [5] to jointly generate value in a distributed setting [6]. One value proposition is a jointly generated Cardossier that reduces the information asymmetries in the used car market. While such a Cardossier may be a double-edged sword for garages and established used car dealers [7], used car platforms will be net-benefactors. Until now, their activities have been limited to the information search phase [8] of a used car sale. The actual deal is closed outside the platform with a used car dealer or a private person. A trustworthy and complete Cardossier turns a used car into a commodity and it may be traded without inspection just like a new car. This allows used car platforms to expand their offering up to the actual transaction phase, i. e. deals can be negotiated and closed over the platform. The platform can then offer new services such as payments, certified data or trust mediation.

Prior research indicates that there indeed is a market for trusted car data [9] and that a complete Cardossier has a value in the order of 100 Euros. This research assumes that this data is available in the market place and stakeholders are willing to share it. Researchers have addressed multiple issues here such as the architecture of such a system [5], assuring data quality [10], the inclusion of the public sector [11], and the building of an appropriate governance [12]. It is also clear that car usage data can be sensitive and is protected by GDPR [13]. Therefore, its use on platforms needs the car owner's consent. However, it remains unclear whether the sellers are actually willing to share sensitive data and where the buyers see value.

There are three types of data that is potentially relevant for used car sales:

1. The static core data of a car, such as its brand, age, color, or weight. This data is readily available as soon as the car has been produced and it is captured in public platforms for little charge. Most countries agree that this data is not sensitive.

2. The car usage data covering what has been done with the car and what has happened to it, e. g. repair data, accident data, registration data, or driving behavior data (who?, where?, when?, how careful? etc.). In Europe, this data is regarded as sensitive data under GDPR.
3. The personal data of the sellers (or buyers), i. e. their names, addresses, picture, job, credit history etc. This data is also sensitive.

Static core data is or will soon be readily available in many countries and is not sensitive. Therefore, it is not relevant for this study. The other two types of data are relevant. If car usage data is relevant and the platform can persuade the stakeholders to release it, the platform can not only expand its reach on the value chain, but also establish itself as an actor in car data trade [9]. If personal data of the sellers or buyers is important, a used car platform can establish itself as a mediator of interpersonal trust [2]. Research on this issue should take into account what we already know about privacy in the eCommerce sector.

2.2 Privacy in eCommerce: Privacy Behavior and Privacy Negotiations

Privacy can be defined as a dynamic process of social boundary management by which individuals grant or deny access to other individuals or one's group [14]. *Privacy boundaries* are often negotiated between the involved parties and readjusted over time. However, if they are not clearly defined or the parties differ in their privacy rules, conflicts arise. These conflicts can affect the willingness to disclose information and hinder the relationship between the parties, or worse, lead to reluctance [15].

In the eCommerce context, *online privacy* can be referred to as the process of controlling access to the self while using Internet services. A distinction is made between the *desired level of online privacy* (the extent of control users want) and the *achieved level of online privacy* (factual privacy that users acknowledge having and executing) [14]. Bringing their achieved online privacy in line with their desired level is a continuous process of optimizing privacy and self-disclosure. Thereby, individuals follow the *privacy calculus* that posits: Online self-disclosures are based on a cost-benefit tradeoff [16] that is influenced by the lack of control resulting from the risk of fraudulent actions and mistrust towards the information recipient (in eCommerce mostly a company) [17]. The literature, however, stresses that emotional, situational, affect-based and contextual factors also influence this calculation [18], especially in online contexts [19]. The actual *online privacy behavior* furthermore depends on the user's attitude towards privacy. The user's attitude is influenced by past experiences with privacy breaches and by their skills in using the Internet (literacy) [20].

Privacy behavior and privacy calculus manifest themselves in user preferences on withholding and revealing personal information. These preferences can be administered by privacy management. An appropriate privacy management does not only allow users to control data access, but also offers *traceability* of data use by the platform, data providers, and data consumers [21]. Previous research covered traceability of personal data in social networking sites [22], on mobile phones [23], and towards third parties in business relations [21]. However, there is currently no insight into a peer-to-peer used car market.

The used car market resembles more peer-to-peer markets like eBay than business-to-consumer markets like the core of Amazon. In these consumer-to-consumer markets, the quality of products is frequently uncertain, and prices are frequently agreed upon in auctions or negotiations. The used car business distinguishes itself from even those consumer-to-consumer platforms, as it deals with a highly valuable product with a history that is potentially sensitive. Hence, it is unclear whether the disclosure control and trust building strategies suggested by literature (e. g. [17, 24]) can be applied in this context.

3   Research Design and Methodology

This research was conducted as part of an Action Design Research [25] project striving to develop the Cardossier. The research reported here strives to uncover requirements for enhancing the trade of sensitive data in used car markets. Requirements are a typical outcome of design research [26, 27]. The requirements were elicited in two exploratory studies. In each of them, users were exposed to the Car-Market Game, an experimental platform that simulates a future used car market. This Car-Market Game provided features for searching for cars, buying and selling data from the Cardossier, negotiating with potential sellers, and settling a transaction. After playing the Car-Market Game, the participants were asked to state their privacy expectations and to evaluate existing privacy features. The first study explored the interest in sensitive data and the willingness to share personal information to find an answer to our RQ1. The second study investigated the car sale negotiation process for an in-depth understanding of the privacy disclosure behavior and inherent preferences of the participants to derive requirements as an answer to our RQ2. For data collection we used a mixed-method approach, including quantitative and qualitative methods [28]. The next sections will briefly introduce the Cardossier project and the methods for data collection before it will go into details on the experimental design.

3.1   The Cardossier Project[1]

The "Cardossier Project" aims to develop an electronic record for the used car trade in Switzerland based on a consortium distributed ledger. The initial consortium of companies and organizations consisted of an insurance company, a car dealer and importer, a car sharing company, a road traffic authority, a software company, and two universities. The main objective of this project is the reduction of information asymmetries by providing a car's history that decreases uncertainty and increases trust between the parties involved. It aims to digitalize and improve the processes, minimize redundancies, and establish a trusted *digital ecosystem* for car-related data management between all the players participating in the life cycle of a car. The different stakeholders contribute car-specific data, utilization-related personal data and personal data to the Cardossier. A more detailed explanation can be found in [10, 29].

---

[1] https://www.cardossier.ch (Last accessed: 11/30/2020).

3.2 Data Collection

We conducted two experimental games with the Car-Market Game in 2018 and 2019. After each game, we applied surveys to gather information on privacy preferences and expectations [30]. The survey applied open questions, closed questions, and Likert scales. The questionnaire in the first survey consisted of the following sections that are of relevance for this study:

- Demographic data of the test persons
- Assessment of relevance of personal information
- Willingness to buy/trade personal information
- Importance to control the disclosure of personal information

The questionnaire in the second survey consisted of the following sections that are of relevance for this study:

- Demographic data of the test persons
- Willingness to disclose data
- Importance of control
- Importance of traceability
- Evaluation of design elements

The survey after the second experiment was augmented with semi-structured interviews [31] with a subset of the participants. Each interview addressed the following topics: general questions about the interviewee, attitude to data markets and attitude to disclosure of data. These interviews were recorded and transcribed in a verbatim manner [30]. Based on this, two researchers deductively and inductively processed the core themes to understand the relations between them (axial coding). This process generated insight concerned with, e.g. interest in data, willingness to buy/sell, disclosure behavior and negotiation behavior as presented below [32].

3.3 Experimental Design

The Car-Market Game can be configured to simulate a traditional or future used car platform (i. e. AutoScout24.ch). Buyers find information on cars posted by the seller and then can negotiate directly within the platform about the sales price using a chat dialog. In each experiment, the participants had to sell (role of seller) respectively buy (role of buyer) a car. The goal was to maximize the relative revenue[2] when buying or selling a car.

In the first experiment (E1), 50 bachelor students participated. The students volunteered for the experiment but received incentives (shopping vouchers). Table 1 shows their demographic data. To communicate the intentions of the Cardossier project in a clear and readily understandable manner before the experiment, a moderator held a presentation using a screencast that showed the features of the game. Each participant was

---

[2] Computed from the final sales/purchase price and the actual value of the car.

428 A. Engelmann and G. Schwabe

randomly assigned either the role of a buyer or the role of a seller. Sellers were provided with cars and information on cars from an existing collaborating used car platform. Buyers were provided with a budget for buying the car. The experiment consisted of two game rounds in which different versions of the game were played. After each round, the test persons had to fill out a questionnaire about their willingness to trade or their interest in the data items.[3] In the first round, the participants played a classical scenario (*classical round*), similar to existing conventional online used car platforms. In the second game round, car buyers and sellers could buy verified car lifecycle information from the Cardossier (*round with Cardossier*).

After analyzing the results of the first experiment, we changed and extended the game application according to our findings and feedback.

In the second experiment (E2), 48 university students participated voluntarily (see Table 1 for their characteristics). All took part in the subsequent survey and five volunteers were interviewed directly after the experiment. The main objective of the experiment was to investigate the test persons' privacy disclosure behavior while negotiating about used cars. Therefore, the subjects played only the game version with the Cardossier.

Table 1. Demographic data of test persons

Character		E1 (n = 48/50) (See footnote 3) Frequency (%)		E2 (n = 48) Frequency (%)	
Gender	Male	38	(79.2%)	37	(77.1%)
	Female	10	(20.8%)	11	(22.9%)
Age	20–30	44	(91.7%)	47	(97.9%)
	31–40	3	(6.2%)	1	(2.1%)
	41 and above	1	(2,1%)	–	(–)
No. of used cars bought so far	0	35	(72.9%)	34	(70.8%)
	1	10	(20.8%)	9	(18.8%)
	2 and more	3	(6.3%)	5	(10.4%)
Already bought a car via an online platform?	Yes	13	(27.1%)	7	(14.6%)
	No	35	(72.9%)	41	(85.4%)

4   Results

We structure our findings according to our two exploratory studies and the research questions raised in the introductory section.

---

[3] Note: 2 persons failed to complete the survey after the first round.

4.1   First Study: Exploring Interest in Data and Willingness to Share

In the first study, we addressed the first research question (RQ1): What sensitive data are sellers and buyers interested in and willing to share?

After playing the conventional game (classical round without the Cardossier), the subjects were asked to evaluate the potential relevance of sensitive data (Table 2). The vast majority of the buyers and sellers selected the history of accidents as relevant. Half the buyers and the vast majority of the sellers also regarded driving behavior as relevant. So, all in all, utilization related personal data clearly appears to be relevant. The picture is less clear on personal data. While a little more than half the participants regarded name, address, and date of birth as relevant, only a minority regarded bank data and information on the driving experience (as indicated by how long the person has had a driver's license) as relevant.

Table 2. Assessment of the relevance of personal information by item type

Personal data	Car Buyers (n = 24)[4] Frequency (%)	Car Sellers (n = 24)[5] Frequency (%)
Name, date of birth, address	13 (54.2%)	12 (50.0%)
Bank/payment data	9 (37.5%)	8 (33.3%)
Driving experience	4 (16.7%)	12 (50.0%)
Utilization-related personal data		
History of accidents	21 (87.5%)	20 (83.3%)
Driving behavior (frequent/infrequent)	12 (50.0%)	20 (83.3%)

In the second game round of the first experiment, the participants were exposed to the Cardossier. Therefore, we could ask more specifically for their willingness to buy or offer the data items after this game. The picture is similar to results after the first round (Table 3): The majority of the sellers would be willing to sell the history of accidents and the past driving behavior. A majority of the car buyers would also be willing to buy a history of accidents. However, only 40% would buy data on driving behavior. Their willingness to buy personal data is even lower: It ranges between 20% and 32% while less than half of the sellers would be willing to sell this data.

We conclude from this experiment that it is dubious whether market participants are really interested in personal data and willing to share it for money. The picture is more positive for data on car usage: Here, participants appear to be interested and willing to trade for money.

---

[4] Question: "What personal information about the seller would influence your buying decision?"
[5] Question: "What personal information about yourself would you provide to a potential buyer in order to obtain a higher price, if necessary?"

Table 3. Assessment of the willingness to buy/offer personal information by item type

Personal data	Car Buyers (n = 25)[6] Frequency (%)	Car Sellers (n = 25)[7] Frequency (%)
Name, date of birth, address	8 (32%)	11 (44%)
Bank/payment data	6 (24%)	8 (32%)
Driving experience	5 (20%)	10 (40%)
Utilization-related personal data		
History of accidents	20 (80%)	19 (76%)
Driving behavior (frequent/infrequent)	10 (40%)	14 (56%)

4.2 Designing for Privacy in the Car-Market Game

Beyond those key insights on willingness to share, interviews and questionnaires from the first experiment offered additional insight for the designing for privacy in the Car-Market Game. Participants voiced a clear preference for controlling the disclosure of sensitive data. In the questionnaire, the participants rated its importance with 5.48 on a Likert scale from 1 = 'Not at all important' to 7 = 'Extremely important'. The analysis of the interviews led to the identification of three important topics: The global disclosure of information to all participants of the platform, the disclosure of information to a specific partner during the course of the negotiation and the transparency of the public profile.

We therefore implemented the following design elements:

- *Global Disclosure Control* (global, see Fig. 2, on the left,): Buyers and sellers can define, if and for which price they disclose data to all users of the platform.
- *Individual Disclosure Control*: Sellers can define, which car usage data they disclose to their current negotiation partner for free (Fig. 3).
- *Privacy Preview* (see Fig. 2, on the right): Buyers and sellers can see what their public profile looks like.

We furthermore added a personal photograph of the seller or buyer (see Fig. 2, on the upper left) to the prior personal information as an element that could enhance interpersonal trust.

In the actual game, all users would sign in and set their global privacy settings (Fig. 2). The sellers would then finish their car profile (e. g. adding sales price) and wait for interested buyers to start a negotiation. The buyers select cars from the marketplace (Fig. 1) and start a negotiation (Fig. 3). During the negotiation, sellers can release sensitive data for free.

---

[6] Question: "What personal information about the seller would you pay for to support your purchase decision?"

[7] Question: "What personal information about yourself would you provide in the Cardossier in order to achieve a higher return (higher sales price/revenue for your provided data)?"

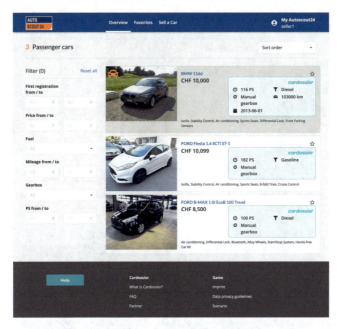

Fig. 1. Searching for cars in the marketplace

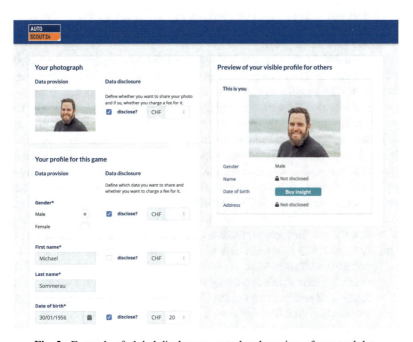

Fig. 2. Example of global disclosure control and preview of personal data

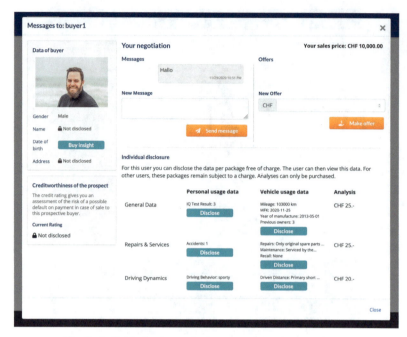

Fig. 3. Individual privacy disclosure and chat for negotiation

4.3 Second Exploratory Study: Identifying Preferences and Expectations

The second study had two goals:

First, we wanted to validate the insights from the first study: Is personal data of car buyers and sellers really not relevant in the course of a car sale? And is car usage data really relevant? To get more insights we made the privacy choices more personal for the test participants: We added real pictures of them to their player profile to make the personal data more realistic. And we personalized their car data through in-game tests: an IQ test was used to calculate the accident history for the sellers' cars (the more fault points, the more accidents) and an online driving test was used to derive the driving behavior data of their cars[8]. We also made the privacy choices more economically sound: Both buyers and sellers were not only asked about their willingness to sell or buy personal data, but could also set a price for their personal data in their global settings and offer it there. Since the participants were exposed to privacy management features in the game, we could not only ask for their preferences but also study their behavior. The results should finally answer RQ 1 on *what* data should be provided by a platform.

The second goal addresses RQ2: *How* should this data be provided, and privacy be managed? Assuming that at least some sensitive data is relevant, we wanted to understand, how buyers and sellers accepted the disclosure control design elements and what further preferences they had for disclosure control.

---

[8] To comply with ethical guidelines, the players could opt out of using their real data; genuine data use was incentivized by a flat payment of 20 Swiss francs and 72% of the participant opted for it.

a) **Results for RQ1: What sensitive data are sellers and buyers interested in and willing to share?**
In the questionnaire the participants voiced only limited willingness to disclose personal data (Table 4). The ratings show that the willingness to disclose data toward an individual counterpart has a moderate agreement, for personal data as well as car usage data. The disclosure free of charge has the lowest approval, and the general disclosure of car usage data is also rated slightly positive.

Table 4. Willingness to disclose. (Average rating on a scale from 1 = 'I do not agree at all' to 7 = 'I totally agree'; n = 48).

	Willingness to disclose globally	*Willingness to disclose for free*	*Willingness to disclose to an individual Counterpart*
Personal data	3.8	3.0	4.1
Utilization-related personal data	4.3	3.6	4.4

Consequently, only gender data was released for free by the majority (Table 5). For the other data items the information providers either asked for a fee (27%–54%) or did not disclose them at all (20–35%).

Table 5. Global disclosure of data (n = 48)

Personal data	*Not disclosed* Frequency (%)	*For free* Frequency (%)	*For a fee* Frequency (%)
Photo	17 (35.4%)	11 (22.9%)	20 (41.7%)
Gender	3 (6.2%)	32 (66.7%)	13 (27.1%)
Name	10 (20.8%)	15 (31.3%)	23 (47.9%)
Date of birth	11 (22.9%)	11 (22.9%)	26 (54.2%)
Address	17 (35.4%)	5 (10.4%)	26 (54.2%)
Utilization-related personal data (sellers only; n = 24)			
Accident history	7 (29.2%)	2 (8.3%)	15 (62.5%)
Driving behaviour	9 (37.5%)	6 (25.0%)	9 (37.5%)

How does this offer impact the actual market transactions on sensitive data? (Table 6). Nearly no transactions on personal data occurred. So, the valuation of the seller was consistently higher than the valuation of the buyers. Therefore, we conclude: There is no market for personal data in the used car market.

Table 6. Purchases from game data of E2 (n = 48)

Personal data	Number of purchases	Average amount of purchases	Expected average price[9]
Photo	1	CHF 50.00	CHF 117.09
Gender	0	–	CHF 32.62
Name	0	–	CHF 70.19
Date of birth	0	–	CHF 76.16
Address	0	–	CHF 56.50
Utilization-related personal data			
Accident history	14	CHF 119.29	CHF 93.93
Driving behaviour	1	CHF 15.00	CHF 70.00

The picture is different for car usage data. Although only a minority offered this data for free, quite a few transactions happened (see Table 6). So, there is a market for car usage data what is slightly confirmed with the results of our survey: On a scale from 1 = 'I do not agree at all' to 7 = 'I totally agree' the respondents rated the statement of being willing to buy utilization-related personal data with 4.2. The interviews supported this observation without providing further insights.

b) **Results for RQ2: What preferences and expectations do individuals have when disclosing their personal information in the used car market?**
   All three new design elements were evaluated positively.

Global Disclosure: All participants actually used global disclosure in their general offering to the marketplace. In the questionnaire the global disclosure mechanism (Fig. 4) was rated transparent[10] with a 4.9 on a Likert scale from (1 = 'I do not agree at all' to 7 = 'I totally agree'). So, we conclude that the participants of the used car market expect a global disclosure control (= preference P1).

Individual Disclosure: Willingness to provide data to individuals was rated highest in the questionnaire (Table 4) and 15 participants actually used individual disclosure control in their negotiations. Thus, we conclude that the participants of the used car market expect a context-dependent individual disclosure control (= Preference *P2*).

Privacy Preview: During the game all participants used the preview function (located on the same page in the right; see Fig. 2). After the game we asked the test persons if the preview function made the disclosure settings transparent[11] and got an agreement with a mean of 5.0. For this reason, we formulate as third preference (*P3*): Car buyers and sellers want to have a preview of the disclosure outcome.

---

[9] Values higher or equal to CHF 1000 were regarded as outliers and left out
[10] Question: "I can track to whom I share my data and when".
[11] Question: "The preview function made the release settings easy to understand".

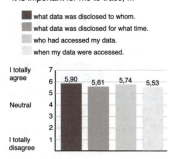

"It is important for me to trace, ..."

Fig. 4. Importance of traceability regarding time and accessing actor

Tracebility: We furthermore asked the participants of the second experiment whether tracing is important to them, i. e. to see to whom and for how long data was disclosed and who has accessed it, at what time. We got a clear agreement in all cases (Fig. 4), although a traceability support was currently not yet implemented in the game. Thus, based on these answers, we state our fourth preference (*P4*): Data providers prefer traceability of data access and accessing actor.

In the discussion section, we will develop the insight and preferences towards requirements that online used car platforms should address.

5 Discussion

The study results offer several insights for used car platform providers. *What sensitive data are sellers and buyers interested in and willing to share?* The results indicate that buyers and sellers do not have significant interest in each other's personal data. Thus, it is not promising for the platform providers to design their system as a mediator for interpersonal trust [2]. Rather, they should opt for a platform that is free of this kind of trust [33], via which car buyers and sellers negotiate to release information about their primary object of interest: the car and its history. In principle, a market exists for car usage data; and buyers and sellers are willing to engage in transactions of data. Thus, a Cardossier does not only promise to enhance traffic on a car platform, but platform providers may also extend their business model to providing certified car data [34]. This has further implications for used car ecosystems such as the Cardossier ecosystem. They should focus their efforts on collecting data on car usage and shy away from collecting data on the car owners. This is good news as personal data is even more difficult to handle and the collection of such data is even more difficult to justify than car usage data.

What preferences and expectations do individuals have when disclosing their personal information on the used car market? Buyers and sellers prefer global disclosure control (P1), individual disclosure control (P2), a preview of the disclosure outcome (P3), and to trace data access and the accessing actor (P4). This leads to the three generic requirements of 'Selective Disclosure Control', 'Disclosure Information Transparency' and 'Disclosure Process Transparency' (Table 7).

Selective Disclosure Control: We define selective disclosure control as the possibility to disclose data continuously or for a single instance according to the preferences and the situation of the data subject. Selective disclosure control enables car sellers to keep control over their data depending on their own perception of sensitivity (cf. [35, 36]). Our results indicate that selective disclosure control in the used car market can be globally, i. e. context-independent (*P1*) or individually, i. e. context-dependent (*P2*).

Table 7. Summary of requirements derived from preferences

Preference	Generic Requirements
P1: Individuals expect global disclosure control	Selective Disclosure Control
P2: Individuals expect context-dependent individual disclosure control	
P3: Individuals expect to have a preview of the disclosure outcome	Disclosure Information Transparency
P4: Individuals expect to trace data access and the accessing actor	Disclosure Process Transparency

Disclosure Information Transparency: The ability to transmit how disclosure information is presented can be conceptualized as an instance of information transparency ([37], p. 4). Disclosure information transparency can thus been defined as the degree of the data subject being enabled to monitor and comprehend the information used as the basis of personal data disclosure and to assess their quality and suitability. Disclosure information transparency enables data subjects to effectively prevent undesired consequences and produce a desired profile toward others [36].

Disclosure Process Transparency: The ability to trace information use can be conceptualized as an instance of process transparency ([38], p. 280). Disclosure process transparency can thus be defined as the degree of the data subject being able to follow and comprehend the performed activities with their personal data. In the context of a used car market, buyers and sellers can not only use disclosure process transparency to protect their privacy but also as a strategic instrument in their negotiation. For example, if a seller knows that a buyer has accessed a critical information item (e. g. on an accident), the seller may negotiate differently than if the buyer has not accessed the information item.

The need for selective disclosure control, disclosure information transparency, and disclosure process transparency reveals that the general privacy calculus known from eCommerce is incomplete: In the used car market, online self-disclosure is not only based on a cost-benefit tradeoff [16] on the personal impact and risks of data release, but also on the cost-benefit analysis of releasing data as a tactical instrument during negotiations in an environment free of interpersonal trust. Car sellers may hide (or highly price) sensitive car data of lemons or may signal high quality by making it available for free.

6   Conclusions, Limitations and Future Research

Used car platforms were the primary addressees of this paper and, indeed, they have a lot to gain if they manage to include car usage data into their platform. They can take a larger share of the used car market and establish themselves as data traders. The insights, requirements, and design elements proposed in this paper should be more comprehensively implemented and evaluated to understand how exactly car sellers and buyers can be enabled to efficiently and effectively manage car usage data and how this relates to the value proposition of a future used car platform. Results indicate that platforms should provide selective disclosure control, disclosure information transparency and disclosure process transparency. While it is quite obvious, how global disclosure control should be implemented, individual disclosure control is more challenging: What exactly defines the individual context? How can disclosure control be embedded in the communication and negotiation process? Future research in this direction can not only guide platform providers in building better used car platforms but also lead to a better understanding what the privacy calculus in such settings is.

Future research should also validate the presented results in other contexts as the current results come with limitations. The Car-Market Game and the contained design elements were tested and evaluated with students as test persons. This test group was quite homogenous and the average age was about 25, which is younger than the average used car buyer. In this group, only about half of the participants had have experience with buying used cars. And the experiment was situated in a safe environment; car sellers and buyers may value personal data and interpersonal trust-building higher, if their opponents are potentially threatening.

Other stakeholders will have to react to the threat of being disintermediated. Used car dealers may not only use the remaining information asymmetries as a basis for their business but also apply car usage data to improve their advice giving and to provide new products [7]. Also, car manufacturers, car importers, and garages may re-evaluate the value of their data treasure and use it to create platforms that compete established used car platforms. They can make different, potentially more attractive, offers for car usage data than car platforms, for example free or discounted services. But all need to understand the needs of car owners, requiring control and transparency. Future research will need to understand how those other stakeholders can take them into account.

References

1. Akerlof, G.A.: The market for "lemons": quality uncertainty and the market mechanism. In: Uncertainty in Economics, pp. 235–251. Academic Press (1978)
2. Söllner, M., Hoffmann, A., Hoffmann, H., Wacker, A., Leimeister, J.M.: Understanding the formation of trust in IT artifacts. In: ICIS (2012)
3. Massaro, E., et al.: The car as an ambient sensing platform. Proc. IEEE. **105**, 3–7 (2017)
4. Lovas, R., Marosi, A.C., Emödi, M.: PaaS-oriented IoT platform with connected cars use cases. In: International Conference on Sensor Networks and Signal Processing, SNSP (2018)
5. Zavolokina, L., Ziolkowski, R., Bauer, I.: Management, governance and value creation in a blockchain consortium. MIS Q. Exec. (2020)
6. Notheisen, B., Cholewa, J.B., Shanmugam, A.P.: Trading real-world assets on blockchain. Bus. Inf. Syst. Eng. **59**(6), 425–440 (2017). https://doi.org/10.1007/s12599-017-0499-8
7. Baumann, J., Zavolokina, L., Schwabe, G.: Dealers of peaches and lemons: how can used car dealers use trusted car data to improve their value proposition? In: Hawaii International Conference on System Sciences, HICSS (2021)
8. Luo, C., Sia, C.-L., Shi, Y., Chen, H.: Managing uncertainty - an exploratory study of information seeking strategies of online consumers. In: ICIS (2009)
9. Bauer, I., Zavolokina, L., Schwabe, G.: Is there a market for trusted car data? Electron. Mark. **30**(2), 211–225 (2019). https://doi.org/10.1007/s12525-019-00368-5

10. Zavolokina, L., Spychiger, F., Tessone, C.J., Schwabe, G.: Incentivizing data quality in blockchains for inter-organizational networks-learning from the digital car dossier. In: International Conference on Information Systems (2018)
11. Schwabe, G.: The role of public agencies in blockchain consortia - learning from the Cardossier. Inf. Polity **24**, 437–451 (2019)
12. Ziolkowski, R., Miscione, G., Schwabe, G.: Decision problems in blockchain governance: old wine in new bottles or walking in someone else's shoes? J. Manag. Inf. Syst. **37**, 316–348 (2020)
13. Jakobi, T., Stevens, G., Seufert, A.-M.: Privacy-By-Design für das Connected Car - Architekturen aus Verbrauchersicht. Datenschutz und Datensicherheit. **42**, 704–707 (2018). https://doi.org/10.1007/s11623-018-1029-7
14. Trepte, S., et al.: Do people know about privacy and data protection strategies? Towards the "Online Privacy Literacy Scale" (OPLIS). In: Gutwirth, S., Leenes, R., de Hert, P. (eds.) Reforming European Data Protection Law. LGTS, vol. 20, pp. 333–365. Springer, Dordrecht (2015). https://doi.org/10.1007/978-94-017-9385-8_14
15. Petronio, S.: Boundaries of Privacy. SUNY Press, New York (2012)
16. Dienlin, T., Metzger, M.J.: An extended privacy calculus model for SNSs: analyzing self-disclosure and self-withdrawal in a representative U.S. sample. J. Comput.-Mediat. Commun. **21**, 368–383 (2016)
17. Olivero, N., Lunt, P.: Privacy versus willingness to disclose in e-commerce exchanges: the effect of risk awareness on the relative role of trust and control. J. Econ. Psychol. **25**, 243–262 (2004)
18. Kehr, F., Wentzel, D., Mayer, P.: Rethinking the privacy calculus - on the role of dispositional factors and affect. In: ICIS (2013)
19. Li, H., Sarathy, R., Xu, H.: The role of affect and cognition on online consumers' decision to disclose personal information to unfamiliar online vendors. Decis. Support Syst. **51**, 434–445 (2011)
20. Büchi, M., Just, N., Latzer, M.: Caring is not enough: the importance of Internet skills for online privacy protection. Inf. Commun. Soc. **20**, 1261–1278 (2016)
21. Wohlgemuth, S., Echizen, I., Sonehara, N.: On privacy-compliant disclosure of personal data to third parties using digital watermarking. J. Inf. Hiding Multimedia Sig. Process. **2**, 270–281 (2011)
22. Lalas, E., Papathanasiou, A., Lambrinoudakis, C.: Privacy and traceability in social networking sites. In: Panhellenic Conference on Informatics, pp. 127–132 (2012)
23. Mun, M., et al.: Personal data vaults: a locus of control for personal data streams. In: Proceedings of the 6th International Conference, November 2010
24. McKnight, D.H., Choudhury, V., Kacmar, C.: Developing and validating trust measures for e-commerce - an integrative typology. Inf. Syst. Res. **13**, 334–359 (2002)
25. Sein, M.K., Henfridsson, O., Purao, S., Rossi, M., Lindgren, R.: Action design research. MIS Q. **35**, 37–56 (2011)
26. Peffers, K., Tuunanen, T., Rothenberger, M.A., Chatterjee, S.: A design science research methodology for information systems research. J. Manag. Inf. Syst. **24**, 45–77 (2007)
27. Hevner, A.R., March, S.T., Park, J., Ram, S.: Design science in information systems research. MIS Q. **28**, 75–105 (2004)
28. Dubé, L., Paré, G.: Rigor in information systems positivist case research: current practices, trends, and recommendations. MIS Q. **27**, 597–635 (2003)
29. Bauer, I., Zavolokina, L., Leisibach, F., Schwabe, G.: Exploring blockchain value creation - the case of the car ecosystem. In: Hawaii International Conference on System Sciences (2019)
30. Myers, M.D., Newman, M.: The qualitative interview in IS research - examining the craft. Inf. Organ. **17**, 2–26 (2007)

31. Flick, U., von Kardoff, E., Steinke, I.: A Companion to Qualitative Research. SAGE, Thousand Oaks (2004)
32. Saldana, J.: The Coding Manual for Qualitative Researchers. SAGE, Thousand Oaks (2015)
33. Hawlitschek, F., Notheisen, B., Teubner, T.: The limits of trust-free systems: a literature review on blockchain technology and trust in the sharing economy. Electron. Commer. Res. Appl. **29**, 50–63 (2018)
34. Stahl, K., Strausz, R.: Certification and market transparency. Rev. Econ. Stud. **84**, 1842–1868 (2017)
35. Yoon, C., Rolland, E.: Knowledge-sharing in virtual communities: familiarity, anonymity and self-determination theory. Behav. Inf. Technol. **31**, 1133–1143 (2012)
36. Menard, P., Bott, G.J., Crossler, R.E.: User motivations in protecting information security: protection motivation theory versus self-determination theory. J. Manag. Inf. Syst. **34**, 1203–1230 (2018)
37. Nussbaumer, P., Matter, I., Schwabe, G.: Enforced vs. casual transparency - findings from IT-supported financial advisory encounters. ACM Trans. Manag. Inf. Syst. (TMIS) **3**, 1–19 (2012)
38. Nussbaumer, P., Matter, I.: What you see is what you (can) get? designing for process transparency in financial advisory encounters. In: Campos, P., Graham, N., Jorge, J., Nunes, N., Palanque, P., Winckler, M. (eds.) Human-Computer Interaction. LNCS, vol. 6946, pp. 277–294. Springer, Heidelberg (2011). https://doi.org/10.1007/978-3-642-23774-4_24

Towards GDPR Enforcing Blockchain Systems

Hauke Precht[(⊠)] and Jorge Marx Gómez

Business Information Systems/VLBA, Carl Von Ossietzky
University of Oldenburg, Oldenburg, Germany
{hauke.precht,jorge.marx.gomez}@uol.com

Abstract. This paper gives an overview of current research areas considering GDPR and blockchain. It is shown that GDPR is often seen as a problem, limiting blockchain use cases. However, approaches towards more data protection for the data subjects based on blockchain technology emerge. In this paper, we evaluate a first step towards a GDPR enforcing blockchain by using a combination of smart contracts within Hyperledger Fabric, evaluating if a *joint controllership agreement* is in place. Such agreement is required for joint controller to process personal data. Based on this rather simple use case evaluation, it is discussed that a combination of the different research areas around GDPR and blockchain should be further evaluated and combined, aiming to GDPR enforcing blockchain systems.

Keywords: Blockchain · GDPR · Joint controllership agreement

1 Introduction – GDPR and Blockchain

As blockchain gains more and more popularity and new application domains are included, the legal issues of blockchain are analyzed more often. Even though a variety of blockchains exist, they are typically classified in public, private, permissioned and permissionless blockchains [1]. Independent of this classification, they all build around the feature of the immutability of data. This is due to the fact, that the actual data structure "blockchain" is built as an ordered list of blocks, which contain transactions, chained via the hash representation of the previous block [1]. By combining this specific data structure with computational constraint and incentivizing block creation, a tamper-resistant and revisioning resistant decentralized system is built [1], which is also often referred to as blockchain. As the most used blockchain systems, Bitcoin, Ethereum and Hyperledger Fabric [2] all share the same described approach, they are all subject to the immutability feature. For the rest of the paper, when we speak about blockchains in general, we especially mean those blockchain systems which follow the described immutability feature by using a similar data structure. This immutability of data is of especially high interest in legal analysis as this can lead to violations of the General Data Protection Regulation (GDPR) rules when personal data is processed (e.g., the right of erasure cannot be fulfilled).

The most used approach to avoid possible violations is to store no personal data on the blockchain as done for example in [3]. However, in open systems like Bitcoin

F. Ahlemann et al. (Eds.): WI 2021, LNISO 47, pp. 440–446, 2021.
https://doi.org/10.1007/978-3-030-86797-3_29

or Ethereum it is up to the user what they store, so violations are still possible. To avoid on-chain storage but still maintaining decentralized storage, approaches around the InterPlanetary File System (IPFS), which is a distributed file system on a peer-to-peer basis [4], emerged. Note, that even though decentralized off-chain storage could be used to store private data, it still falls under the GDPR, meaning a decentralized deletion of data must be possible. Note, that the idea to store private data in an encrypted way, especially on public blockchain with accessibility and readability for everyone is not considered to be GDPR compliant, as pointed out by Fridgen et. al. in their report for the German Federal Ministry of Transport and Digital Infrastructure [5, p. 137]. The authors argue, that as the encrypted data is stored *ad infinitum* on a public blockchain, the used encryption algorithm can be broken in the future leading to a state where the data can be considered publicly available, then violating the GDPR rules [5, p. 137]. But in the past few years, approaches were evaluated towards redactable blockchains, which aim to enable the modification of already accepted blocks [6–10]. This way, a possible modification or even erasure of data in a blockchain should be made possible to comply with the GDPR. But there also exist approaches, in which blockchain is considered as an enabler towards data sovereignty of the data subject. For example, blockchain technology is used to empower the data subject to manage its personal data via a blockchain-based personal data management platform [11, 12].

However, the GDPR does not only state the rights of data subjects, which can be challenging to fulfill in blockchain systems but also guidelines, targeting companies that process personal data. For example, in case personal data is processed by multiple controllers, Art. 26 GDPR must be considered [13], requiring a *joint controllership agreement (JCA)* between these controllers. In such a JCA, the controllers must define the internal relationship, stating whom of them are responsible to fulfill the different duties based on the GDPR. For example, it must be stated which controller(s) must fulfil the data subjects right of access as stated in Art. 15 GDPR. Considering blockchains in general, independent of access scope, i.e. private or public, all participants who operate a node take part in data processing and in case of processing personal data, GDPR must be considered [14]. Due to the high number of participants and anonymity in public blockchains, however, it is difficult to identify the actual controllers within such public blockchain networks. But in private blockchains, with limited and known participants, the controllers can be identified as well as the joint controllership [14] meaning a JCA can and must be implemented. Therefore, we will focus in the following of this paper on private and permissioned blockchain systems. In case no JCA is agreed on, every controller must provide the ability to fulfil possible requests from the data subjects as well as general duties based on the GDPR. Ignoring these duties and not creating a JCA high fines must be paid. Nevertheless, often there is no explicit JCA defined [15], but data is still processed in the blockchain system by smart contracts. In this paper, the authors evaluate a proposal consisting of a combination of smart contracts, enforcing a JCA to be in place before any data processing can be executed, therefore preventing legal uncertainty. Moreover, it is discussed to evaluate possibilities to include such feature, and GDPR enforcing features in general, directly in (private and permissioned) blockchain systems. This could lead to further legal certainty and supporting the privacy by design approach as stated in Art. 25 GDPR. The paper is structured as follows: First, an overview of related work is given. Next, a prototypical implementation for a JCA smart contract combination within a private blockchain (Hyperledger Fabric) is given. This paper concludes with a short discussion towards GDPR enforcing blockchain systems.

2 Related Work

To ensure GDPR compliant implementation, different approaches can be identified. Wirth and Kolain presented in their paper a privacy by blockchain design, taking a step towards incorporating the privacy by design approach mentioned in GDPR, stating an interdisciplinary approach [16]. That an interdisciplinary approach is required to ensure legally compliant code, especially for smart contracts and blockchain systems, is also explained by Precht and Saive, who evaluate the integration of legal specialists into the scrum process [17]. The term smart contract was already coined by Szabos in 1979 [18]. In conjunction with blockchain, a new hype around smart contracts started. In general, a smart contract contains contractual rules as software code which is stored and executed on a blockchain [19]. To the best of the authors' knowledge, only two approaches explicitly dealing with the digitization of a JCA or related contract called data processing contract (DPC) with smart contracts. In [20] the authors propose a new specification of an intelligible contract, as a "gap between traditional contracts and digital contracts towards the goal of making them intelligible and legal valid."[20]. They implemented a data processing agreement based on their newly created approach leading to a complex system [20]. In [13] the authors propose a different approach towards a digitized JCA. They evaluate, from a legal and technical perspective, the possibility to store the JCA on a private blockchain while also creating a smart contract around it, allowing parties to initiate, accept or to propose changes to a JCA. As the handling of the JCA is done on-chain as well, the whole development and creation phase of the JCA is transparent to all parties at every given time. Therefore, it can be said that this focus is towards the handling and tracking of the JCA process itself as an asset on the blockchain between parties, while [20] focuses on the way of translating legal contracts to machine-readable contracts while also making the newly created machine-readable contract automatically executable. As we aim to further incorporate the existing of a JCA into other smart contacts as a basis to decide if the processing of data is legal, we will focus in the following on the approach proposed by [13].

3 Using the JCA-SC to Ensure Legal Compliance for Data Processing in Smart Contracts

As mentioned, we use the proposed approach in [13] and analyze the possibility and the sufficiency of using the JCA smart contract (JCA-SC) as a base contract to other contracts. The goal is to build a legally compliant system, which refuses data processing in a private permissioned blockchain system if no active and valid JCA is in place. The initial implementation of the JCA-SC is used from [13] which was built for the Hyperledger Fabric platform. Thus, we also used the Hyperledger Fabric platform for our prototype. Hyperledger Fabric itself is a permissioned blockchain for enterprises [21] and

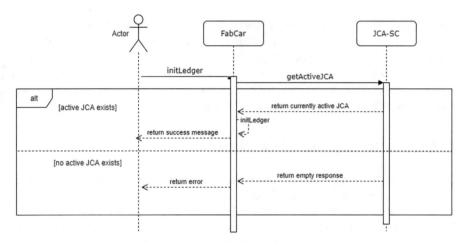

Fig. 1. Sequence diagram combining FabCar contract and the JCA

is one of the most used blockchain systems [2]. Within Hyperledger Fabric, two different kinds of nodes exist: Peer nodes, which hold onto the ledgers and smart contracts [22] and ordering nodes who order transaction and group them into new blocks [23] which are then distributed. Further, Hyperledger Fabric introduced the channel concept, which allows us to create "subnets" which can only be accessed by a selected and configured set of network members [24]. Note, that each channel has its own, independent blockchain, meaning that, as a single peer can be part of multiple channels, a single peer also holds onto multiple blockchains.

To evaluate our proposed smart contract combination from a technical point of view, we make use of the existing Hyperledger Fabric smart contract example *fabcar*, representing a car selling contract. We modified the fabcar smart contract in a way, that, before any processing of data takes place, the JCA-SC is called to verify the existing of a JCA. In Fig. 1 the sequence diagram shows how the actor interacts with the fabcar contract and how the fabcar contract itself interacts with our JCA-SC. The actor first needs to initialize the fabcar contract in which a default set of cars is stored on the ledger. Before data is processed, i.e. written to the ledger, the JCA-SC is called, checking if an active and valid JCA is in place. The returned result by the JCA-SC is then checked by the calling fabcar smart contract. If the returned result is positive, i.e. the JCA-SC confirmed an existing and accepted JCA, the init function of the fabcar smart contract will continue the data processing by initializing the ledger and will return a success message to the actor. In case the returned result is negative, i.e. the JCA-SC states that no JCA exists or that the JCA is not yet accepted by the required parties, the init method of the fabcar smart contract will abort and an error message is returned to the actor. By aborting the init method, any data processing is stopped as no legal certainty exist, based on the JCA-SC evaluation.

We found that the integration, i.e. the calling of the JCA-SC from the existing fabcar contract to be considered simple. This is due to the fact, that the Hyperledger Fabric system explicitly encourages developers to integrate and connect different smart contracts, providing the necessary functions and features. However, a major drawback is the mentioned integration which must be done manually by the developer. This means, that at every method of the fabcar contract, which processes data, a call to the JCA-SC must be implemented. Therefore, possible repetitive development and code duplicities are to be expected. Note that the sequence diagram only shows the sequence for the ledger initialization but is similar for other methods within the fabcar contract. Abstraction and reusing code will help to reduce the possible code duplicities.

4   On GDPR Enforcing Blockchains

The simple example above shows the general feasibility of combining a GDPR related smart contract, in this case, the JCA-SC, and contracts dealing with actual business logic. Manual integration can be considered error-prone like any other manual process. Therefore, it is next to discuss, if the integration of such features directly into the core functionality of a given blockchain, e.g. Hyperledger Fabric, is possible. Considering Hyperledger Fabric, such integration could take place in the Contract Interface in which several utility features are already implemented to ease the development of smart contracts so that the developer can focus on the actual business logic. Further, it must be evaluated if a general concept of such integration can be identified and then be applied to other blockchain systems as well. This exposes further possible new research directions, by shifting the focus of GDPR and blockchain from a perspective of problems (e.g. erasure of personal data in blockchains) towards the perspective of possibilities to further enforce GDPR and legal regulations in general. This could lead to legally compliant and compliance enforcing blockchain systems. Another use case for such smart contracts could be the digitization of *Standard Contractual Clauses* which gaining attention after the judgment of the Court of Justice of the European Union invalidates the EU-US Data Protection Shield [25]. In general, a combination of existing work towards GDPR enforcing blockchain-based approaches must be evaluated. The mentioned personal data management platform, for example, could be connected to the emerging research field of redactable blockchains [6–10]. It could be analyzed if a revoke of consent from the data subject via a respective system could trigger a block change if personal data is affected. Further, it can be evaluated if the JCA-SC can be enhanced in a way that it can automatically verify specific terms defined within the JCA. The work by [20] could serve as a starting point for such research. The proposed approach and ideas presented in this paper should serve as a starting point, aiming to design compliant and GDPR enforcing blockchain systems.

References

1. Xu, X., et al.: A taxonomy of blockchain-based systems for architecture design. In: ICSA 2017: 2017 IEEE International Conference on Software Architecture: Proceedings: 3–7 April 2017, Gothenburg, Sweden, Gothenburg, Sweden, pp. 243–252 (2017). Accessed 7 Mar 2019
2. Hileman, G., Rauchs, M.: Global blockchain benchmarking study. Cambridge Centre for Alternative Finance (2017). https://www.ey.com/Publication/vwLUAssets/ey-global-blockchain-benchmarking-study-2017/$File/ey-global-blockchain-benchmarking-study-2017.pdf. Accessed 22 Aug 2019

3. Fridgen, G., Guggenmoos, F., Lockl, J., Rieger, A., Schweizer, A., Urbach, N.: Developing an Evaluation Framework for Blockchain in the Public Sector: The Example of the German Asylum Process (2018). Accessed 15 Mar 2019
4. Benet, J.: IPFS - Content Addressed, Versioned, P2P File System: (DRAFT 3). https://github.com/ipfs/papers/raw/master/ipfs-cap2pfs/ipfs-p2p-file-system.pdf. Accessed 11 Apr 2019sss
5. Fridgen, G., Guggenberger, N., Hoeren, T., Prinz, W., Urbach, N.: Chancen und Herausforderungen von DLT (Blockchain) in Mobilität und Logistik (2019). https://www.bmvi.de/SharedDocs/DE/Artikel/DG/blockchain-grundgutachten.html. Accessed 18 Nov 2020
6. Ateniese, G., Magri, B., Venturi, D., Andrade, E.: Redactable blockchain – or – rewriting history in bitcoin and friends. In: 2017 IEEE European Symposium on Security and Privacy (EuroS&P), Paris, April 2017, pp. 111–126 (2017)
7. Farshid, S., Reitz, A., Roßbach, P.: Design of a forgetting blockchain: a possible way to accomplish GDPR compatibility. In: Proceedings of the 52nd Hawaii International Conference on System Sciences (2019)
8. Florian, M., Henningsen, S., Beaucamp, S., Scheuermann, B.: Erasing data from blockchain nodes. In: 2019 IEEE European Symposium on Security and Privacy Workshops (EuroS & PW), Stockholm, Sweden, June 2019, pp. 367–376 (2019)
9. Marsalek, A., Zefferer, T.: A correctable public blockchain. In: 2019 18th IEEE International Conference on Trust, Security and Privacy in Computing and Communications/13th IEEE International Conference on Big Data Science and Engineering (TrustCom/BigDataSE), Rotorua, New Zealand, August 2019, pp. 554–561 (2019)
10. Precht, H., Marx Gómez, J.: Redactable blockchain – leveraging chameleon hash functions for a GDPR compliant blockchain. In: Konferenzband zum Scientific Track der Blockchain Autumn School 2020, Mittweida, pp. 66–70 (2020)
11. Truong, N.B., Sun, K., Lee, G.M., Guo, Y.: GDPR-compliant personal data management: a blockchain-based solution. IEEE Trans. Inform. Forensic Secur. **15**, 1746–1761 (2020). https://doi.org/10.1109/TIFS.2019.2948287
12. Vargas, J.C.: Blockchain-based consent manager for GDPR compliance. In: Open Identity Summit 2019, pp. 165–170 (2019)
13. Janicki, T., Precht, H.: Smart-contract-basierter joint controllership agreements in privaten blockchains. In: Den Wandel begleiten - IT-rechtliche Herausforderungen der Digitalisierung (2020)
14. Janicki, T., Saive, D.: Privacy by Design in Blockchain-Netzwerken: Verantwortlichkeit und datenschutzkonforme Ausgestaltung von Blockchains, ZD 2022, Zeitschrift für Datenschutz, pp. 251–256 (2019)
15. Gierschmann, S.: Gemeinsame Verantwortlichkeit in der Praxis – Systematische Vorgehensweise zur Bewertung und Festlegung, ZD 2022 Zeitschrift für Datenschutz, pp. 69–73 (2020)
16. Wirth, C., Kolain, M.: Privacy by BlockChain Design: A BlockChain-enabled GDPR-Compliant Approach for Handling Personal Data (2018)
17. Precht, H., Saive, D.: Compliant Programming - Juristen in der agilen Softwareentwicklung. In: Tagungsband Herbstakademie 2019, pp. 581–595 (2019). https://beck-online.beck.de/?vpath=bibdata/zeits/DSRITB/2019/cont/DSRITB.2019.595.1.htm
18. Szabo, N.: Smart Contracts: Building Blocks for Digital Markets. http://www.fon.hum.uva.nl/rob/Courses/InformationInSpeech/CDROM/Literature/LOTwinterschool2006/szabo.best.vwh.net/smart_contracts_2.html. Accessed 12 May 2020
19. Mattila, J.: The Blockchain Phenomenon: The Disruptive Potential of Distributed Consensus Architectures. ETLA Working Papers, no. 38 (2016). http://pub.etla.fi/ETLA-Working-Papers-38.pdf
20. Cervone, L., Palmirani, M., Vitali, F.: The intelligible contract. In: Proceedings of the 53rd Hawaii International Conference on System Sciences (2020)

21. Hyperledger Fabric: Hyperledger Fabric: Open, Proven, Enterprise-grade DLT (2020). https://www.hyperledger.org/wp-content/uploads/2020/03/hyperledger_fabric_whitepaper. pdf. Accessed 13 May 2020
22. Hyperledger Fabric, Peers. https://hyperledger-fabric.readthedocs.io/en/release-2.0/peers/ peers.html. Accessed 13 May 2020
23. Hyperledger Fabric, Orderer. https://hyperledger-fabric.readthedocs.io/en/release-2.0/ord erer/ordering_service.html. Accessed 13 May 2020
24. Hyperledger Fabric, Channels. https://hyperledger-fabric.readthedocs.io/en/latest/channels. html. Accessed 13 May 2020
25. Court of Justice of the European Union, The Court of Justice invalidates Decision 2016/1250 on the adequacy of the protection provided by the EU-US Data Protection Shield. Luxembourg (2020). https://curia.europa.eu/jcms/upload/docs/application/pdf/2020-07/cp2000 91en.pdf. Accessed 26 Nov 2020

Social Media and Digital Work

Introduction to the WI2021 Track: Social Media and Digital Work

Hanna Krasnova[1], Matthias Trier[2], Christian Meske[3], and Milad Mirbabaie[4]

[1] University of Potsdam, Faculty of Economics and Social Sciences,
Potsdam, Germany
krasnova@uni-potsdam.de
[2] Paderborn University, Faculty of Business Administration and Economics,
Paderborn, Germany
matthias.trier@upb.de
[3] Freie Universität Berlin, School of Business and Economics, Berlin, Germany
christian.meske@fu-berlin.de
[4] University of Bremen, Faculty of Business Studies and Economics,
Bremen, Germany
milad.mirbabaie@uni-bremen.de

1 Track Description

Social media have become part of the digital work and digital life of millions of users. These platforms rely on individual members for content creation and their success hinges on active user involvement and participation. Related platforms allow anyone to virtually share information and knowledge within a virtual team or even a global audience. Despite the ubiquitous nature of social media use, we still need to better understand the role and long-term consequences of this phenomenon for digital transformation on individual, organizational and societal levels.

On the one hand, proponents argue that social media promote creation of social capital, result in increased interconnectedness, or facilitate social support and collective action. On the other hand, opponents express strong concerns over the dangers of social media. The sheer quantity and the sensitivity of the information users disclose, gives rise to strong privacy concerns. Furthermore, the impact of social media on users' mental health has been questioned, with empirical evidence hinting at such undesirable developments as addiction, depression, mood disorders. In companies the multivocality, afforded by social media, can yield tensions for organizational coherence. Finally, the phenomenon of fake news and hate speech has recently emerged as a dangerous development, posing significant challenges for platform providers and users.

This track consists of publications examining the role social media is playing in transforming the networked society and businesses at large. We focus on research that reaches out beyond IS theories, which is grounded in multiple reference disciplines and applies new intriguing perspectives to document and understand the transformatory impact of social media and social media-related smartphone use.

2   Research Articles

2.1   Don't Want It Anymore? Resilience as a Shield Against Social Media-Induced Overloads (Bermes, Alena; Gromek, Clara-Lea)

This paper highlights the overlooked concept of resilience in the IS realm, raises awareness on resilience's function as a shield against the adverse effects of social media, and provides a comprehensive outlook for future research.

2.2   Problems and Solutions in Digital Work – Exploring Measures for Team Identification in Virtual Teams (von Thülen, Geeske; Hartl, Eva)

This study addresses the question of how companies can support team identification in virtual teams. Combining a literature review with multiple case studies. The authors derive an overview of solutions to foster team identification and link these to problems in virtual team identification. The authors derive propositions for future research based on identified research gaps and inconsistencies.

2.3   A No-Code Platform for Tie Prediction Analysis in Social Media Networks (Schötteler, Sebastian; Laumer, Sven; Schuhbauer, Heidi; Scheidthauer, Niklas; Seeberger, Philipp; Miethsam, Benedikt)

Conventional methods for tie prediction analysis in social media networks are often code-intensive and encompass complex steps. To tackle this, authors used design science research to develop a no-code tie prediction analysis platform. The evaluation indicates that the platform significantly reduces tie prediction analysis complexity and, depending on the network size, also total prediction time.

2.4   Crowd Analysts vs. Institutional Analysts – A Comparative Study on Content and Opinion (Bankamp, Steffen; Neuss, Nicole; Muntermann, Jan)

In this study, the authors examine the informational value of crowd analyst reports regarding their timeliness in publishing and their originality as for content and opinion. The findings suggest that crowd analysts strongly rely on previously published institutional reports.

2.5   Design Principles for Digital Upskilling in Organizations (Cordes, Ann-Kristin; Weber, Julia)

The research goal of this paper is to provide an action-oriented guideline in form of design principles supporting organizations to handle digital upskilling. To achieve this goal a hermeneutic literature review and semi- structured expert interviews as well as a focus group discussion have been performed in order to deduce design principles.

Don't Want It Anymore? Resilience as a Shield Against Social Media-Induced Overloads

Alena Bermes[(⊠)] and Clara-Lea Gromek

Chair of Marketing, Heinrich Heine University Düsseldorf, Düsseldorf, Germany
{alena.bermes,clara-lea.gromek}@uni-duesseldorf.de

Abstract. Social media have become part of millions of users' everyday life, leading to the proliferation of the daily stressors associated with them, particularly social media-induced overloads. Therefore, understanding the individual characteristics that enable users to resist such stress factors and ultimately buffer negative follow-up effects, such as exhaustion and discontinuance behavior, is important for researchers and practitioners. Grounded in psychological resilience theory, we examine if a user's resilience (one's ability to bounce back) has the power to mitigate the effects of this critical chain of influence by inhibiting the stressors. Structural equation modelling on survey data from 194 social network users confirms that resilience decreases perceived information and social overload. We also find that self-efficacy is a protective factor leading to resilience. Therein, this short paper raises awareness on resilience's function as a shield against the adverse effects of social media and provides a comprehensive outlook for future research.

Keywords: SNS resilience · Protective (resilience) factors · Social media-induced overloads · Technostress

1 Introduction

The concept of *resilience* is omnipresent. While it holds different meanings depending on the context [1], researchers and practitioners, regardless of the discipline, agree that it serves as shield for individuals, groups, and society [2]. Grounded in psychological research, specifically, resilience refers to an individual's ability to bounce back in the face of adversity and stress [3]. Since a high number of individuals are affected by technology-induced stress every day [4, 5] and since technostress is reported to be a major concern due to lowered end-user productivity [6], satisfaction [7], and well-being [8], Klesel et al. [9] introduced the concept of resilience to Information Systems (IS) research, conceptualizing it as one's ability to counteract technology-related stressors. Therein, the theoretical relevance of the concept of resilience for IS research has been acknowledged, but crucial questions remain to be addressed. The mitigating effect of resilience on specific technology-related stressors has not yet been proven empirically, and the question remains as to how resilience in the IS domain can be developed.

© The Author(s), under exclusive license to Springer Nature Switzerland AG 2021
F. Ahlemann et al. (Eds.): WI 2021, LNISO 47, pp. 451–458, 2021.
https://doi.org/10.1007/978-3-030-86797-3_30

We seek to address this gap by examining resilience in the face of social media-induced stressors, particularly social overload (SO) and information overload (IO). The context is relevant and timely since the widespread use of social network sites (SNS), having become one of the most popular Internet services globally [10], is known to induce perpetual obsessions and create pressure for users to keep up to date and react to each other's postings [11]. Moreover, both types of overloads are particularly prevalent in the time of COVID-19 [12], therefore augmenting the call to understand how they may be mitigated [11]. Importantly, earlier research demonstrates that overloads on SNS do not only place the business models of SNS providers at risk (by leading users to discontinue their social network use) [13], but also significantly decrease users' well-being [14]. Hence, in this short paper, we specifically shed light on the concept of *SNS resilience* by addressing the following research questions:

RQ1. Does SNS resilience have the power to inhibit social media-induced overloads?

RQ2. If so, how can SNS resilience among social media users be build?

2   Conceptual Development

2.1   Resilience as a Means to Combat Stressors

The concept of resilience is derived from the Latin word 'resilire', meaning to jump back or rebound [3]. It is best exemplified by the metaphor of metals bending (not breaking) when stressed [15] and marks an aspect of focus for different communities of practice (for selected reviews see [16] for psychological resilience and [2] for social (ecological) resilience). This work builds on previous psychological resilience research that mostly explores the concept at the individual level [17]. At the individual level, resilience not only describes one's ability to withstand stress, but also emerge from that situation better equipped for future adversities [16]. The scant work done in the area of IS and user behavior is striking, as psychologists have long demonstrated that resilient individuals are able to endure adversities (e.g., trauma) better than non- or less resilient individuals [1]. Moreover, IS-adjacent scholars (i.e., in management and marketing) have started to demonstrate that resilience can serve as a shield in work-related [17] or consumption-related stress processes [18], for example, in terms of job (dis)satisfaction [19], turnover intentions [20], or consumer experiences of austerity [21].

Despite the construct of resilience having been conceptualized in a number of ways, most modern scholars agree that resilience is not a trait that one must be born with to have; rather, it can partly be learned [22]. Moreover, the notion of 'adversity' is inherent in most definitions [16] and today it is of no question that adversity is associated with not only major disasters (e.g., death of a spouse), but also modest disruptions embedded in everyday lives [23]. In our study, acceding to the request that resilience researchers outline their notion of adversity [24], we specifically examine users' *SNS resilience* as the ability to bounce back in the face of social media-induced stressors. By adhering to the understanding of resilience as a capacity [17], we acknowledge that individuals can be trained to become resilient [25], which makes the construct particularly valuable.

Overload perceptions – the individual's evaluation that the number of demands from the environment exceeds one's ability to deal with [13] – represent common social-media induced stressors that are present in social media. Particularly *IO* and *SO* are known to be major technology-induced stressors that users experience on a daily basis. While the former refers to information volumes exceeding a user's processing capacity in a certain unit of time [13], the latter concerns an overwhelming number of requests from online contacts that demand a user's attention [26]. As such, both constitute an imbalance between a user's perceived demands and coping abilities, leading to strain and, ultimately, negative outcomes [4].

Drawing on psychological resilience theory [27] we assume that users' resilience has the power to mitigate such overload perception, because it entails the ability to bounce back. As such, users with high resilience should appraise stressors as less harmful and experience them less strongly, because they intrinsically possess the ability to resist stress factors and perceive them as less troublesome [16]. Prior empirical research also suggests that resilience inhibits stressors similar in nature to IO and SO. For example, Richards et al. [28] revealed that resilience decreases overloads in the context of work stress, i.e., role overloads. Accordingly, we posit that SNS resilience decreases perceived IO (H1) and SO (H2).

2.2 Protective Factors Leading to Resilience

Resources within individuals and their environment, referred to as protective or resilience factors, promote an individual's ability to have resilience [27]. As such, external or internal protective factors are an integral part of resilience theory. Psychological research shows that protective factors often function in cumulative ways [29] and exist across three levels: individual, social, and community/society [1]. Social support and self-efficacy are particularly well-documented factors for resilience within an individual and their immediate social environment [30, 31].

While psychological resilience research describes *social support* as support received by an individual through social ties to others [32], social support in the digital era has specifically been defined as the extent to which SNS users are taken care of by their online friends [33]. Such support from one's immediate environment should operate as a protective factor leading to resilience, because it reinforces the user's ability to positively adapt by providing a generally positive, caring context [34]. To be precise, already, the very earliest resilience studies have found that children who were born into adverse conditions (e.g., into families troubled by chronic discord) profited from the external support of surrogate parents or the community (e.g., caring neighbors) and could develop into resilient individuals later, although their origin would have suggested otherwise [35]. Hence, drawing on psychological resilience theory and prior empirical findings, we hypothesize that social support increases SNS resilience (H3).

Self-efficacy in relation to SNS usage (i.e., SNS self-efficacy) might best be described as an individual's efficacy in addressing specific SNS-related stressors. This definition is derived from Marakas et al.'s [36] broader concept of computer self-efficacy. According to psychological resilience research, self-efficacy should lead to resilience because it improves the user's adaptational system [22] and increases their motivation and perseverance [37]. In particular, there is vast empirical evidence showing that self-efficacy is one of the most important resilience (protective) factors [38] and increases one's resilience in contexts such as academia [37], entrepreneurship [39], or military combat [31]. Based on psychological resilience theory and previous empirical research, we therefore hypothesize that (SNS) self-efficacy increases SNS resilience (H4).

3 Empirical Study

To examine our hypotheses, we conducted an online survey via a consumer panel in Germany in July 2020. A total of 232 participants completed the survey. We only considered datasets from participants currently using SNS and showing careful response patterns [40], resulting in 194 valid responses (female $= 70.1\%$, $M_{age} = 29.66$, $SD_{age} = 10.85$). All respondents used more than one SNS and the majority of the respondents (87.6%) reported that SNS were an integral part of their daily lives.

For measurement purposes, we used well-established and reliable multi-item scales from prior academic literature, ranging from "strongly disagree" (1) to "strongly agree" (7). SNS resilience was adapted from Smith et al. [3] and Klesel et al. [9]. We included the specific context into the scale as per Klesel et al. [9], asking the respondents to imagine situations where SNS use caused stress, followed by the items of the renowned Brief Resilience Scale [3, 41], e.g., "… I tend to bounce back quickly". IO and SO were assessed based on Zhang et al. [42] and Maier et al. [26]. Items included "I find that I am overwhelmed by the amount of information I have to process on a daily basis on SNS" (IO) and "I pay too much attention to posts of my friends on SNS" (SO). Social support was measured as per Lo [33] (e.g., "I get a lot of social support from my friends on SNS") and SNS self-efficacy was adapted from Marakas et al. [36] by replacing references to the computer with SNS (e.g., "I have the ability to describe how SNS work"). Where available, validated German translations were used (e.g., [43]).

To analyze the data, we employed the partial least squares (PLS) method. Specifically, SmartPLS3 [44] was used following the two-stage approach [45] to estimate both the measurement model and structural model. First, to validate the measurement model, we assessed the reliability, convergent validity, and discriminant validity of the constructs. Cronbach's alpha values ranging from 0.80 to 0.94 [46], composite reliabilities ranging from 0.87 to 0.96 [47], average variances extracted (AVE) ranging from 0.63 to 0.81 [48], and standardized factor loadings ranging from 0.70 to 0.93 [49] exceeded the recommended thresholds, signifying sufficient reliability and convergent validity. The square root of the AVE for each construct exceeded the interconstruct correlations, indicating discriminant validity [48]. Furthermore, we evaluated the common method bias (CMB) by employing the marker variable approach [50] with the theoretically unrelated marker variable 'attitude toward the color blue'. The results showed that CMB was not a concern. Second, we estimated the PLS results of the structural model. The results revealed that resilience decreased both IO ($\beta = -0.522$, $t = 10.413$, $p < 0.001$) and SO ($\beta = -0.377$, $t = 5.550$, $p < 0.001$), supporting H1 and H2. Moreover, self-efficacy was found to increase SNS resilience ($\beta = 0.312$, $t = 5.391$, $p < 0.001$), confirming H4. However, social support was found to decrease SNS resilience ($\beta = -0.261$, $t = 4.484$, $p < 0.001$), rejecting H3 and the notion that social support is a protective factor for SNS resilience. The model explained 15.2% of the variance of SNS resilience and 27.3% and 14.2% of the variances of IO and SO.

4 Discussion and Outlook

This study was a first step taken to examine whether SNS resilience inhibits stressors and to determine how it can be built. With our efforts, we heed the call to explore mitigating mechanisms within the SNS-induced stress process [11] and to establish the construct of resilience in the IS realm [9]. Grounded in psychological resilience theory, our study confirms the mitigating power of SNS resilience against IO and SO. This initial proof of resilience's function as a shield may explain why some users can handle technostress better than others. Future research could also examine resilience against other 'dark sides' of SNS, e.g., addictive use [51], or other IS-related adversities [52].

For the question of which factors lead to SNS resilience, our study shows mixed results. While self-efficacy increases SNS resilience, social support decreases it. The latter is striking as psychological theory clearly proposes that external support leads to resilience [31]. Yet, selected research also shows that the required type of support may change over time as a function of personal development and environmental interaction [53]. Moreover, studies on SNS discontinuance show that social support on SNS can transform into social overload due to reciprocal dynamics [54]. This may explain social support's inhibiting effect as it may be perceived as a burden in itself. Future studies should investigate which theoretically founded factors truly enhance SNS resilience.

Our results highlight that SNS resilience is a noteworthy concept that researchers and practitioners alike should consider, as it can mitigate the stressors leading to strain and negative outcomes [13]. SNS providers can profit from our findings by integrating SNS resilience into their customer relationship management process [55]. For example, by segmenting users based on their level of resilience, providers can address each segment specifically. Moreover, intervention strategies to foster resilience are highly recommended. These programs often rely on strengthening the protective factors [25]. To this end, computerized trainings [56] or mobile games [57] may be valuable tools.

As any, our study has limitations, each equally leaving room for future research. First, as this is a cross-sectional study, we will continue with a longitudinal design to examine potential changes in SNS resilience over time [34] and understand resilience's exact role as an inhibitor in the causal stress process related to SNS usage. Second, this study was based on a gender imbalanced sample. Future studies will be more weighted and also perform group analyses for gender and age (both known to affect technostress perception [13, 58]). Third, in subsequent studies, we will also examine the context dependence of resilience [22] and test our conceptual model within the different SNS, given that different types of networks may fulfill different purposes for the user [26].

References

1. Windle, G.: What is resilience? A review and concept analysis. Rev. Clin. Gerontol. **21**, 152–169 (2011)
2. Keck, M., Sakdapolrak, P.: What is social resilience? lessons learned and ways forward. Erdkunde **67**, 5–19 (2013)
3. Smith, B.W., Dalen, J., Wiggins, K., Tooley, E., Christopher, P., Bernard, P.: The brief resilience scale: assessing the ability to bounce back. Int. J. Behav. Med. **15**, 194–200 (2008)

4. Ayyagari, R., Grover, V., Purvis, R.: Technostress: technological antecedents and implications. MIS Q. **35**, 831–858 (2011)
5. Maier, C., Laumer, S., Weinert, C., Weitzel, T.: The effects of technostress and switching stress on discontinued use of social networking services: a study of Facebook use. Inf. Syst. J. **25**, 275–308 (2015)
6. Tarafdar, M., Tu, Q., Ragu-Nathan, B.S., Ragu-Nathan, T.S.: The impact of technostress on role stress and productivity. J. Manag. Inf. Syst. **24**, 301–328 (2007)
7. Tarafdar, M., Tu, Q., Ragu-Nathan, T.S.: Impact of technostress on end-user satisfaction and performance. J. Manag. Inf. Syst. **27**, 303–334 (2011)
8. Tarafdar, M., D'Arcy, J., Turel, O., Gupta, A.: The dark side of information technology. MIT Sloan Manag. Rev. **56**, 60–70 (2015)
9. Klesel, M., Narjes, N., Niehaves, B.: Conceptualizing IT resilience: an explorative approach. In: Multikonferenz Wirtschaftsinformatik, pp. 1008–1019 (2018)
10. Global Web Index. http://www.globalwebindex.com/reports/social. Accessed 23 Nov 2020
11. Lee, A.R., Son, S.-M., Kim, K.K.: Information and communication technology overload and social networking service fatigue: a stress perspective. Comput. Hum. Behav. **55**, 51–61 (2016)
12. Bermes, A.: Stop it! Consumer resilience as a buffer against daily stressors accompanying COVID-19. In: Proceedings of the 23rd International Conference on Multidisciplinary Studies: "Resilience for Survival", Cambridge, UK (2020)
13. Zhang, S., Zhao, L., Lu, Y., Yang, J.: Do you get tired of socializing? An empirical explanation of discontinuous usage behaviour in social network services. Inf. Manag. **53**, 904–914 (2016)
14. Lee, S.B., Lee, S.C., Suh, Y.H.: Technostress from mobile communication and its impact on quality of life and productivity. Total Qual. Manag. Bus. Excell. **27**, 775–790 (2016)
15. Lazarus, R.S.: From psychological stress to emotions: a history of changing outlooks. Ann. Rev. Psychol. **44**, 1–21 (1993)
16. Fletcher, D., Sarkar, M.: Psychological resilience: a review and critique of definitions, concepts, and theory. Eur. Psychol. **18**, 12–23 (2013)
17. Kossek, E.E., Perrigino, M.B.: Resilience: a review using a grounded integrated occupational approach. Acad. Manag. Ann. **10**, 729–797 (2016)
18. Bhattacharyya, A., Belk, R.W.: Consumer resilience and subservience in technology consumption by the poor. Consum. Mark. Cult. **22**, 489–507 (2019)
19. Youssef, C.M., Luthans, F.: Positive organizational behavior in the workplace: the impact of hope, optimism, and resilience. J. Manag. **33**, 774–800 (2007)
20. Bande, B., Fernández-Ferrín, P., Varela, J.A., Jaramillo, F.: Emotions and salesperson propensity to leave: the effects of emotional intelligence and resilience. Ind. Mark. Manag. **44**, 142–153 (2015)
21. Szmigin, I.T., O'Loughlin, D.M., McEachern, M.G., Karantinou, K., Barbosa, B., Lamprinakos, G., Fernández-Moya, E.M.: Keep calm and carry on: European consumers and the development of persistent resilience in the face of austerity. Eur. J. Mark. **54**, 1883–1907 (2020)
22. Masten, A.S.: Ordinary magic: resilience processes in development. Am. Psychol. **56**, 227–238 (2001)
23. Davis, M.C., Linda, L., Lemery-Chalfant, K.: Resilience in common life: introduction to the special issue. J. Pers. **77**, 1637–1644 (2009)
24. Luthar, S.S., Cicchetti, D., Becker, B.: The construct of resilience: a critical evaluation and guidelines for future work. Child Dev. **71**, 543–562 (2000)
25. Macedo, T., Wilheim, L., Gonçalves, R., Coutinho, E.S.F., Vilete, L., Figueira, I., Ventura, P.: Building resilience for future adversity: a systematic review of interventions in non-clinical samples of adults. BMC Psychiatry **14**, 227 (2014)

26. Maier, C., Laumer, S., Eckhardt, A., Weitzel, T.: Giving too much social support: social overload on social networking sites. Eur. J. Inf. Syst. **24**, 447–464 (2015)

27. Richardson, G.E.: The metatheory of resilience and resiliency. J. Clin. Psychol. **58**, 307–321 (2002)

28. Richards, K.A.R., Levesque-Bristol, C., Templin, T.J., Graber, K.C.: The impact of resilience on role stressors and burnout in elementary and secondary teachers. Soc. Psychol. Educ. **19**(3), 511–536 (2016). https://doi.org/10.1007/s11218-016-9346-x

29. Vanhove, A.J., Herian, M.N., Perez, A.L.U., Harms, P.D., Lester, P.B.: Can resilience be developed at work? A meta-analytic review of resilience-building programme effectiveness. J. Occup. Organ. Psychol. **89**, 278–307 (2016)

30. Lee, J.H., Nam, S.K., Kim, A.R., Kim, B., Lee, M.Y., Lee, S.M.: Resilience: a meta-analytic approach. J. Couns. Dev. **91**, 269–279 (2013)

31. Southwick, S.M., Charney, D.S.: The science of resilience: implications for the prevention and treatment of depression. Science **338**, 79–82 (2012)

32. Ozbay, F., Johnson, D.C., Dimoulas, E., Morgan, C.A., III., Charney, D., Southwick, S.M.: Social support and resilience to stress: from neurobiology to clinical practice. Psychiatry (Edgmont) **4**, 35–40 (2007)

33. Lo, J.: Exploring the buffer effect of receiving social support on lonely and emotionally unstable social networking users. Comput. Hum. Behav. **90**, 103–116 (2019)

34. Rutter, M.D.: Psychosocial resilience and protective mechanisms. Am. J. Orthopsychiatry **57**, 316–331 (1987)

35. Werner, E.: Resilience and recovery: findings from the Kauai longitudinal study. Res. Policy Pract. Child. Ment. Health **19**, 11–14 (2005)

36. Marakas, G.M., Johnson, R.D., Clay, P.F.: The evolving nature of the computer self-efficacy construct: an empirical investigation of measurement construction, validity, reliability and stability over time. J. Assoc. Inf. Syst. **8**, 16–46 (2007)

37. Cassidy, S.: Resilience building in students: the role of academic self-efficacy. Front. Psychol. **6**, 1781 (2015)

38. Masten, A.S., Cutuli, J.J., Herbers, J.E., Reed, M.-G.J.: Resilience in development. In: Lopez, S.J., Snyder, C.R. (eds.) Oxford Handbook of Positive Psychology, pp. 117–131. Oxford University Press, Oxford (2009)

39. Bullough, A., Renko, M.: Entrepreneurial resilience during challenging times. Bus. Horiz. **56**, 343–350 (2013)

40. Meade, A.W., Craig, S.B.: Identifying careless responses in survey data. Psychol. Methods **17**, 437–455 (2012)

41. Windle, G., Bennett, K.M., Noyes, J.: A methodological review of resilience measurement scales. Health Qual. Life Outcomes **9**, 8 (2011)

42. Zhang, S., Zhao, L., Lu, Y., Yang, J.: Get tired of socializing as social animal? An empirical explanation on discontinuous usage behavior in social network services. In: Proceedings of the 19th Pacific Asia Conference on Information Systems. Singapore (2015)

43. Chmitorz, A., Wenzel, M., Stieglitz, R.-D., Kunzler, A., Bagusat, C., Helmreich, I., Gerlicher, A., Kampa, M., Kubiak, T., Kalisch, R., Lieb, K., Tüscher, O.: Population-based validation of a German version of the Brief Resilience Scale. PLoS ONE **13**, e0192761 (2018)

44. Ringle, C.M., Wende, S., Becker, J.-M.: SmartPLS 3. SmartPLS GmbH, Boenningstedt (2013)

45. Hair, J.F., Black, W.C., Babin, B.J., Anderson, R.E.: Multivariate Data Analysis: A Global Perspective. Prentice-Hall, Englewood Cliffs (2010)

46. Nunally, J.C., Bernstein, I.H.: Psychometric Theory. McGraw Hill, New York (1978)

47. Bagozzi, R.P., Yi, Y.: On the evaluation of structural equation models. J. Acad. Mark. Sci. **16**, 74–94 (1998)

48. Fornell, C., Larcker, D.F.: Evaluating structural equation models with unobservable variables and measurement error. J. Mark. Res. **18**, 39–50 (1981)

49. Barclay, D., Higgins, C., Thompson, R.: The partial least squares (PLS) approach to causal modeling: personal computer use as an illustration. Technol. Stud. **2**, 285–309 (1995)
50. Lindell, M.K., Whitney, D.J.: Accounting for common method variance in cross-sectional research designs. J. Appl. Psychol. **86**, 114–121 (2001)
51. Tarafdar, M., Maier, C., Laumer, S., Weitzel, T.: Explaining the link between technostress and technology addiction for social networking sites: a study of distraction as a coping behavior. Inf. Syst. J. **30**, 96–124 (2019)
52. Maier, C., Laumer, S., Eckhardt, A.: Information technology as daily stressor: pinning down the causes of burnout. J. Bus. Econ. **85**(4), 349–387 (2014). https://doi.org/10.1007/s11573-014-0759-8
53. Southwick, S.M., Bonanno, G.A., Masten, A.S., Panter-Brick, C., Yehuda, R.: Resilience definitions, theory, and challenges: interdisciplinary perspectives. Eur. J. Psychotraumatol. **5**, 25338 (2014)
54. Sun, Y., Wenping, Z., Wang, N., Shen, X.-L.: Dual Processes, buffering/coping effects, and reciprocal dynamics: the social demands–resources model of SNS discontinuance. In: Proceedings of the 40th International Conference on Information Systems, Munich (2019)
55. Reinartz, W., Krafft, M., Hoyer, W.D.: The customer relationship management process: its measurement and impact on performance. J. Mark. Res. **41**, 293–305 (2004)
56. Sanchez-Lopez, A., De Raedt, R., van Put, J., Koster, E.H.: A novel process-based approach to improve resilience: effects of computerized mouse-based (gaze) contingent attention training (MCAT) on reappraisal and rumination. Behav. Res. Ther. **118**, 110–120 (2019)
57. Aboody, D., Siev, J., Doron, G.: Building resilience to body image triggers using brief cognitive training on a mobile application: a randomized controlled trial. Behav. Res. Ther. **134**, 103723 (2020)
58. Tarafdar, M., Tu, Q., Ragu-Nathan, T.S., Ragu-Nathan, B.S.: Crossing to the dark side: examining antecedents and consequences of technostress. Commun. ACM **54**, 113–120 (2011)

Challenges in Digital Work – Exploring Solutions to Improve Team Identification in Virtual Teams

Geeske von Thülen$^{(\boxtimes)}$ and Eva Hartl

LMU Munich, Munich, Germany
`hartl@bwl.lmu.de`

Abstract. The emergence of digital work leads to an increasing number of teams that collaborate virtually. The physical absence of team members and other problems that occur due to the virtual context hinder the formation of team identification, which however is essential for employee's work motivation and team effectiveness. Our study addresses the question of how companies can improve team identification in virtual teams. Combining a literature review with interviews with five case teams, we derive an overview of solutions to improve team identification and link these to problems in virtual team identification. Our results provide guidance to practitioners and we further derive propositions for future research based on identified research gaps and inconsistencies.

Keywords: Virtual teams · Team identification · Digital work · Remote work · Enterprise social media

1 Introduction

The rapid development of new digital technologies is characterizing our current business era. New technological opportunities combined with social and economic trends, like globalization or vertically-aligned corporate structures, are triggers for the emergence of digital work, in which ever more teams are locally distributed and have to collaborate virtually [1]. Virtual teams (VT) are characterized by not being located in the same physical space and using computer-mediated communications. Thus, they do have only little physical contact [2].

Researchers argue that physical absence of team members can reduce team identification (TI) [3] and that the establishment of TI with computer-mediated communication is difficult [4] as well as time- and effort-intense [5]. TI however is an important contributor to the success of teams as it describes the degree to which members align their personal interest to the team's and thereby determines their work engagement [6]. TI can thus increase team performance, bonding, and satisfactions and reduce team conflicts [7]. Missing TI negatively impacts team performance [8], team consensus [9] and individual interaction [10]. Thus, TI is a crucial prerequisite for team success. With COVID-19 having led to a sudden increase of virtual collaboration and with an expected increase in VT also in future, firms urgently need to find solutions for how to achieve and uphold TI in a virtual context.

Motivated by recent relevance of the topic and urgent need of practitioners, this study therefore addresses the question: what are solutions to improve TI in VT? This paper thereby intends to improve three issues with existing literature: 1) presented solutions are scattered throughout literature and an overview is missing, what issues yet need solving, 2) recent research criticizes that literature is lacking behind practice and suggests that existing findings in literature need to be extended by recent developments in practice, and 3) some solutions in literature hold paradoxes which require solving. We combine an extensive literature review with interview research to provide an extensive overview of solutions to improve TI in VT and give insights into their practical application. Based on the TI process, we first outline problems in team identification that occur due to the virtual context of teams. The results of our study then provide an overview of solutions to improve TI in VT and how they solve problems in virtual team identification. Our results provide practitioners with guidance and allow us to identify promising areas for future research.

2 Theoretical Background

2.1 Team Identification

Based on Tajfel's (1978) concept of social identity, team identification (TI) can be defined as the sharing of common goals with the team and feeling of psychological belongingness to and connection with the team's kismet. TI stems from the basic human tendency to classify oneself and others into social categories. Social identity theory and social categorization theory propose that individuals ascribe certain categorical characteristics of a group to themselves and thereby start to identify with that group and to integrate the specific categories into their self-concept [11, 12]. With many citations and a high level quality rank, the paper of Fiol and O'Connor (2005) is the very central paper in the TI discipline. Since there are barely any concrete TI processes present in existing literature, we combine their model of the TI process with insights from Thatcher and Zhu (2006) and Lembke and Wilson (1998) [8], to give a holistic five-phase model beyond the state of the identification decision that guides our research (see Fig. 1).

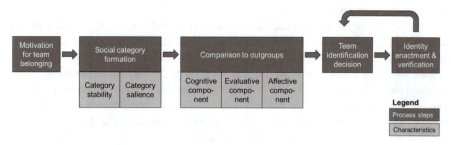

Fig. 1. Depiction of team identification process.

First, the *motivation* of the individuals to belong to a team (in-group) is an essential prerequisite for TI. In VT, this motivation stems predominantly from the desire to reduce existing subjective uncertainties, such as on relationships with others [13, 14]. Given their motivation, individuals *form social categories* based on the team's characteristics that are meaningful to the individual [15] and make the team stand out from other teams (out-groups) [16]. Social category formation is influenced by the team's category stability, i.e. how consistent the team characteristics are perceived to be, and category salience, i.e. the degree of perceived importance of the team as an identification target. Subsequent to category formation, the *team's characteristics are compared* to the individuals' self-concept and relevant out-groups based on cognitive, evaluative, and affective components [17, 18]. Thereby, a strong congruence between the individual's self-concept and the group's characteristics [12], a high valuation of the group membership [18], and an emotional attachment to the group [19] as well as perceived benefits of the team membership are desirable [20, 21]. In the resulting *team identification* itself, individuals adopt the team's characteristics to their self-concept [22]. However, in order for sustained TI, individuals need to enact the team identity by behaving accordingly to the team's characteristics and receive confirmation on the identity by others (verification), which reduces the risk of team members to lose identification with the team or start seeking other identifications.

2.2 Virtual Teams

VT are characterized by being distinct to traditional work teams in that they are (at least partly) geographically or organizationally separated and thus have a significant lower or even absent physical contact [13]. Based on the degree of geographical and organizational separation of the team, VT are distinguished into purely virtual and hybrid VT. This paper adopts the notion of VT as pure virtual, if all team members are geographically distributed from each other and do not have physical contact on a regular basis. We use the term hybrid VT, when there is some physical contact [13] and/or when some, but not all, team members are located at the same site (onsite) whereas other members are geographically dispersed [23].

With VT becoming ever more important in practice due to technological developments, also research in this field has significantly increased since 2000 [24]. VT have been studied on individual, group and organizational level [24]. Thematically, VT research has investigated factors impacting VT work, such as leadership, team compositions and communication technologies [e.g. 25], VT processes and activities, such as knowledge management [e.g. 26] or identity [e.g. 3], as well as from VT resulting output factors, such as performance indicators, like team efficiency [e.g. 27] and team satisfaction [e.g. 1] [for a literature overview cf. 24, 28]. This growing body of research suggests that the particularities of VT lead to multiple problems along the TI process. The subsequent overview of problems for TI in virtual work was compiled based on our literature review (see Sect. 3 for methodological details). From this literature review, we identified a list of problems that we set in relation to the TI process dependent on where in the process the problem was found to hinder TI. We further grouped the problems into 4 themes based on common causes: physical absence of team members, computer-mediated communication, team diversity, and volatile organizational environments.

One central characteristic of VT is the **physical absence of team members** which hinders TI in multiple ways. The absence of team members leads to a low external visibility of the team as an entity, thus reduces the desirability of the team as an identification target and reduces *identification effort*. Physical absence evokes social distance which further reduces the motivation to establish a positive team orientation which can result in *reduced openness in communication* and can negatively impact group process contentment [29]. Since physical distance leads to a *decreased interaction* between team members [3] it also negatively impacts identity enactment and verification and thus decreases the chance for mutual team member identity verification [5]. Also, the *presence of external groups* might negatively impact TI. Members of VT are often physically surrounded by different groups of other people. The higher visibility and identification salience of external groups thus threatens the identification with the specific VT [3]. While in pure VT all members work remotely from each other, in hybrid VT some members do work also physically together – a circumstance that might lead to *subgroup identification in hybrid teams*. The geographical closeness to some team members [30] as well as the higher frequency of interaction and physical meetings between collocated team members compared to the intensity of interaction with the physical distant members lead to the fact that the collocated employees tend to forget about the remote ones [29]. The higher level of interaction also reveals more identity cues of the team members and thereby fosters the visibility of similarities within this perceived in-group [13]. Additionally, literature suggests that there is a level of mistrust coming from people working onsite towards the work efficiency of remotely working employees, which negatively impacts the building of overall TI [3, 29].

With only little or no physical contact, VT have to rely on **computer-mediated communication**. Lean communication technology, such as E-Mail, is characterized by not having many features to transfer communication cues, such as gestures and mimes. This leads to *ineffective communication* [3] and might trigger *intra-team conflicts* due to misunderstandings [31]. Communication via lean technologies also reduces the speed of communication, thereby the number of interactions and leads to an overall reduced visibility of team members – ultimately resulting in *reduced team identity salience* [4]. Paradoxically, also rich media, such as video conferencing, which allows for the transfer of communication and identity cues holds threats to identity salience and stability. When starting to use rich communication media, transmitted identity cues can lead to the disconfirmation of previous assumptions on identity and result into category instability [13].

VT are often geographically dispersed in different countries, leading to a higher probability and degree of **team diversity** (e.g. in terms of culture) compared to traditional teams, which leads to an overall lower identity salience [13, 32, 33]. Further, diversity of team members can *reduce their mutual socio-emotional* understanding. Literature proposes that reduced socio-emotional understanding has a negative impact on team category salience, which in turn will decrease identification [4].

Further, VT are often set up in **volatile organizational environments** and with team members expecting the team constellation to change soon, thus reducing the *motivation of the team members to identify* [5]. Such changes in work context constantly challenge

TI by continuously triggering identity reflection which influences the motivation as well as the verification stage of TI [3].

This long list of problems emerging along the TI process due to the specifics of virtual teams stresses the importance to find solutions to improve TI in virtual team contexts. Our research thus aims to provide an overview of known and available solutions to improve TI in virtual teams and point out potential areas for future research.

3 Methodology

In order to derive an overview of solutions to TI problems in virtual teams, we conducted an extensive literature review in combination with interviews with five case teams. As outlined in the introduction, this paper aims to address three issues with existing literature that guided our methodological approach. First, solutions to improve TI in VT are scattered presented in existing literature and an overview is missing on what problems in virtual TI are already addressed and what problems yet need solving. As a first step, we thus decided to conduct a literature review to get an overview of known solutions. Second, we decided to complement the literature review with empirical data, because a) we wanted to illustrate research results with concrete examples from practice, and b) there is recent criticism of research lacking behind solutions applied in practice [34], thus suggesting that the findings of our literature review need to be extended by recent developments in practice. Third, existing literature holds some paradoxes in suggested solutions (e.g. anonymity vs. sharing personal information) that require a critical review of their application and success in practice. This issue is addressed by our discussion of solutions presented in literature and their application in practice. Both, the literature review and interviews were conducted in 2019.

Data Collection for Literature Review: Conducting our literature review, we followed the approach of Webster and Watson [35]. We applied the following search string: "(virtual OR hybrid OR remote) AND team* AND (identity OR identification)" to search for relevant papers in the databases Google Scholar, EBSCO and AISeL. The three databases were chosen due to their holistic compilation of recent research within the IS and other relevant disciplines. Additionally, we conducted forward and backward search from the central and high quality ranked seminal paper for TI by Fiol and O'Connor (2005) [13]. In total, 330 papers were screened by their title and abstract for their relevance on TI in VT. The screening process was stopped thereafter because the proportion of relevant papers decreased significantly and after reviewing, we expected no further insights. To ensure scientific rigor, only peer-reviewed articles were considered and we strived for a minimum C-ranking (VHB-Jourqual 3). Further, papers were excluded when their focus was not on identification and when there were no results when searching for the keyword "identi*" within the full text. Resulting from this, 95 papers were selected for further reading. Beyond this, papers, that did not deal with virtual or organizational contexts and papers, that did not focus on TI but solely on organizational- or self-identification, were not further included as these are different levels of identification [36]. This process resulted in 58 papers that were included in the literature review. The selected papers were published between 1984 and 2018 with ca. 73% dating back to 2010 or earlier. Further, 46% of the papers have a relation to IS discipline and almost 40% bear upon the Organization (ORG) and Human Resources (PERS) discipline. This shows that in fact, IS makes a significant contribution to research on the topic of TI in VT. Gilson, Maynard, Jones Young, Vartiainen and Hakonen [34] criticize that current literature is outdated. We therefore decided to complement our literature review with recent empirical data from case team interviews.

Data Collection for Complementary Conducted Interviews: We collected data from five virtual teams from different companies with the aim to extend identified solutions from our literature review and to illustrate the practical application of solutions with concrete examples. The five case teams were purposefully selected, following the criterion sampling logic [37], under following criteria: 1) the team had already started to collaborate virtually; 2) the physical contact with the remote team members is less than 50% of working time [based on 38] and 3) the team consists of at least four team members [based on 39–41]. In addition, we aimed to increase the variety between case teams and deliberately considered structural differences (team- and organizational size, -structure and geographical dispersion) in our case team selection. The case teams were identified from the researchers private and professional network and conducting online research. For each case team, three team members including one member in a leading function were interviewed. The interviews followed a semi-structured interview guideline that followed the steps of the TI process. We asked open questions with the aim to identify problems to TI as well as applied solutions to improve TI in the respective TI process steps. As recommended for qualitative interviews [42], the guideline for team members was pilot-tested with one test interview partner, who is not part of the actual data collection sample. Further, the interview questions were continuously improved for the upcoming interviews during the constant review of conducted interviews. The interviews lasted on average one hour and were transcribed verbatim.

Data Analysis: Our data analysis followed a combined inductive and deductive coding approach. That is, initially one researcher performed inductive coding of the gathered data, i.e. sections of the papers included in our literature review referring to problems and solutions for TI in VTs were coded thematically and code descriptions for determining the coding rules were created. Subsequently, the codes were refined and grouped into categories by two researchers. In line with Mayring [43], the codes as well as their description have been dynamically adapted and checked back during the coding process, grouping or breaking down codes into categories where appropriate. Conflicts in coding were resolved via discussing the respective coding rules and relating them back to existing concepts in literature. The interview data was coded as described for the literature review and finally the derived codes and categories were deductively matched to the codes from the literature overview. Our data analysis was guided by the TI process in that we related identified problems and solutions to the respective stages in which they were found to occur.

Table 1. Overview of investigated case teams.

Company # of employees	Industry and activities	Distribution of team members
Team A ~ 3,000	International B2C fashion retailer with main focus on e-commerce	2 collocated in Germany, 4 collocated in Bulgaria
Team B ~ 10	National online job platform for apprenticeships and integrated degree positions in Germany	2 permanently remote, others collocated in HQ
Team C ~ 10	B2B SaaS provider for automatically market and company researches	1 located in Mexico, others collocated in Germany
Team D ~ 115,000	Two merging companies in the B2B and B2C energy producing, supplying as well as infrastructure and grid operating industry in Germany	5 members overall, all work from different offices 2 work in the same city
Team E ~ 50	B2B content marketing service and SEO solutions provider	Fully virtual, all 50 members work permanently remote

4   Results

While we also identified general solutions to foster TI, e.g. longstanding collaboration and/or company affiliation, shared goal commitment, success and interpersonal sympathy, we in the following address solutions that were found to be specifically relevant within a virtual context or that specifically address problems stemming from virtuality. For increased readability, the identified solutions are presented along three categories: team actions, tools and digital leadership. These categories were derived by grouped solutions according to common characteristic and first and foremost follow the aim to structure our results for easier readability, thus don't raise claims on singularity or prominence.

Team actions describe organizational or structural solutions that teams can actively conduct to address problems in virtual TI. One action VT can perform to increase the interaction among all team members is to *foster work interdependencies* [41]. An increased amount of interactions between team members can solve many problems stemming from physical absence: frequent interaction can increase socio-emotional understanding amongst team members, gives opportunity to identify team characteristics and thereby fosters team identity salience. This solution therefore helps to improve TI by essentially supporting the social category formation and identity verification steps of the TI process. When enforced for all team members, increased amount of interactions can resolve unequal contact and thus the potential for subgroup identification in hybrid teams [32]. Team D for example is working in different tandem constellations with each team member at a different point in time. Further, actively initiating *frequent communication* can help to reduce a feeling of separateness that is caused by physical absence. Frequent communication increases personal interaction and thus counteracts the problem of missing possibilities for spontaneous and unplanned meetings in virtual collaboration

[38]. Therefore, team B established regular update calls as well as the possibility to contact each other for spontaneous communication throughout the working day. Some of their calls even last for hours, which again improves TI by supporting the social category formation and verification steps. In addition, *conversations on non-work-related topics* were also mentioned as essential for building TI in VT [38]. Non-work-related communication helps to get to know the team members better on a more personal level. Proactive communication and active questioning of latest happenings before or at the end of a call, as performed in team D, give the team members the necessary scope to implement this action. Further, sharing non-work-related pictures in group chats and using informal language further promote communication on non-work-related topics, as performed by team A.

Next, interactions can be further increased via *physical meetings and (virtual) team events*. Physical meetings, especially at the beginning of the collaboration, can foster a mutual understanding for individual behaviors and communication characteristics and thus reduce future misunderstandings [5]. However, they require travel time, which might lower the intrinsic motivation to participate. In order to decrease this burden, offering team events on a voluntary basis to decrease the feeling of obligation but convey the idea of an invitation is proposed by team B. Team C even proposes to conduct content-driven team events virtually.

Further actions reduce the risk of miscommunication by addressing the lack of relevant communication cues. Technological media limit the transfer of communication cues that are relevant to grasp the meaning of words. Giving each other regular *acknowledgement and feedback* [5] in a kind way generates more clarity and, as the interview results show, helps to establish a *common understanding on terminologies*. Beyond, establishing an *open team culture* provides the team members with psychological safety that makes them more comfortable to address their concerns openly [44]. Team E for example established an error tolerance as part of their feedback- and open team culture by inviting the team members to openly share their challenges within the team to give and receive support. Beyond, team D points out the importance to get mutual cultural understanding if the team is international.

Additional actions to improve TI in VT stated in literature include first, the *transfer of employees* between different collocated sub-groups in order to build up communication networks [32]. If within a team, sub-groups have established that hinder the overall TI, literature suggests to even restructure the team by relocating employees of sub-groups to the location of other team members [23]. Next, being *permanently available* for collaboration and communication is found to be helpful for TI as well [45]. However, this can increase the team members' perceived stress level and thus have negative consequences on their TI [46]. In order to foster mutual understanding by proactively sharing contextual information, i.e. information, that is not available to all team members due to geographic distance, such as environmental events, it is proposed to *train* the team members on their awareness on the importance of this issue [32]. Beyond this, enabling the members to communicate and vote in certain aspects *anonymously* leads to a more open communication [2]. Another aspect that is promoted in literature is the fact that teams should *differentiate* themselves from outgroups and outline their benefits compared to other teams. This is especially relevant for the phases of category formation and comparison [5].

Tools are technical solutions that can be implemented to support TI in VT. First, *information archives, issue tracking technologies* and *chat programs* can positively contribute to TI, as the interview results show. Internationally distributed teams may face the challenge of being located across different time zones and thus having differences in working hours. This makes it challenging for them to organize meetings and conversations as well as to perform knowledge management as the interviewees in team C stated. Team A, for example, uses group chats that allow for a team-wide transparent communication and switched its chat program to a tool that enables the functionality of accessing the chat history. Issue tracking technology generates awareness on the fact that all team members together contribute to achieve the team goal and thus helps to create membership awareness as team B states in the interviews. This makes the team aspect even more visible to the members and thus increases team salience. Team B tracks the progress of the individual tasks in a central program where they also store all relevant related information to these tasks. Further, in team E chat channels are dedicated to specific non-work-related topics to facilitate communications on those. Further, the interview results show that the integration of technological features into communication media that *show the respective times of availability* of each team member is a helpful tool, especially for internationally distributed teams. Team E integrated a time zone tracking feature into their communication tool which increased the awareness, enhances mutual understanding for possibly delayed replies, and facilitates the coordination of finding an appointment date.

Apart from this, some *advanced technological communication tools* allow for the transfer of more communication cues. While in audio conferences, gestures and mimes can only be transferred by acoustic signals, video conferences provide additional visual components, which make gestures and facial expressions directly visible [47]. In both however, there is a strong dependence on connectivity and equipment quality which is nowadays still an issue. Team D sometimes made use of telepresence technology. However, this technology is rarely applied due to limited facility availability. Moreover, *virtual reality (VR) features* [48], such as avatars [49], can support communication beyond words.

In addition, the interviewees state that *real-time document sharing functions* can help to reduce misunderstandings by allowing for simultaneous access to documents. In the interviews it was stated that without physical meetings in which team members can look at the same device, discussing and editing documents is prone to miscommunication without real-time sharing functionalities. Team B highlights the importance of this feature in remote work. Additionally, literature proposes the integration of *automatic team update notifications* that inform all team members on the latest happenings within the team [45]. However, none of the teams interviewed is currently using such a feature.

Enterprise social networks, i.e. web-based platforms that allow workers to communicate via messages, identify relevant coworkers, and share information via posts and files [50], offer an integration of all technological functions that were mentioned in this paragraph. Therefore, they play a key role in TI building in VT. *Enterprise social network profiles* that offer a platform for sharing personal information as well as a newsfeed for the remote locations to stay informed about critical happenings can be supportive to foster non-work-related communication. According to the interview outcomes, detecting common fields of personal interests can help to overcome the issue of missing gambits when not being located at the same place. Team C has integrated personal profiles in their intranet, allowing each team member to share all kinds of personal information in different formats (video, pictures, text etc.).

Digital leadership describes all actions that can be especially performed by the team leader. As the interview results show, leaders can *act as a role model* by expressing their identification with the team towards the members and thereby positively influence the team members to act the same way. Team B's team leader initiated the sharing of non-work-related information to inspire the team members to do the same. As proposed in literature, an aptitude-based team *member selection* when setting-up the team is a fundament to ensure that the team members are capable to work in virtual settings. Optimally, the team leader should be experienced in leading in virtual settings [51].

Next, individual inclusion of all team members into communication is an essential activity [52]. By *communicating thoughtfully* with regard to honesty and friendliness in wording [53] and parallelly *minimizing non-transferrable communication cues*, as shown in the interviews, the leader can make sure to involve all team members equally. Especially in giving feedback, thoughtful and honest communication is very important according to team E. With regards to onboarding, ensuring an *introduction of new team members* to the team is of high relevance as the interviews show. In this way, the basis for future interaction is laid. Team A shows that actively introducing new members to the team positively contributes to TI. Further, the interview results show that demanding and *fostering active participation* from all team members increases the interaction within the team and thereby improves TI. When the team leader in team A demanded active participation, the perceived TI within the team was stronger compared to times, when participation was not actively forced.

Finally, as stated in the interviews, *measuring TI* ensures to stay informed about the current TI situation. Having information on the current TI within the team helps to take additional solutions in time, if necessary. In team E, for example, TI is tracked regularly by small weekly surveys which ask the team members to reflect on the previous week, plan the next week and share their feelings. Additionally, more encompassing quarterly surveys are conducted, to explicitly ask for feedback and improvement potential as well as the team member's wellbeing.

In the theoretical background section, we outlined problems in TI due to the virtual context of teams in detail along the TI process. In the subsequent Table 2, we now link all identified solutions to improve TI in VT to the respective problems these solutions solve. The thereby derived matrix provides a comprehensive overview of problems and solutions in virtual TI and gives insight into the distribution of findings from literature and our conducted interviews.

Table 2. Matrix linking solutions to problems in virtual team identification.

Problems category	Problems	Foster work interdependence	Physical meetings	Acknowledgement & feedback	Common terminologies	Frequent communication	Non-work-related communication	Open team culture	Employee transfer	Permanent availability	Communication training	Anonymous communication	Differentiation	Information archive	Issue tracking	Chat programs	Advanced techn. communication	Real-time document sharing	Enterprise social media profiles	Availability times visibility	Team update notifications	VR features	Role model	Thoughtful communication	Minimize non-transferrable cues	Introduction of new members	Fostering active participation	Measuring TI	Member selection
		Team Actions												**Tools**									**Digital Leadership**						
Changes in work context	Reduced identification efforts	Ø				Ø																	X	X			X		O
Diversity within VT	Reduced socio-emotional understanding		Ø				Ø	Ø			Ø								X	X			X	Ø		X			
Computer-mediated communication	Reduced team identity salience	Ø	Ø	Ø		Ø	Ø		Ø		Ø		O	X	X	X	O		X	X	O	O	X	Ø		X			
	Intragroup conflict			Ø	X			Ø							X			X			O								
	Ineffective communication			Ø	X									X			O	X						Ø	X				
	Subgroup identification in hybrid teams	Ø	Ø						Ø			Ø										O							
Physical absence of team members	Non-open communication		Ø	Ø		Ø	Ø	Ø			Ø			X					X				X	Ø					
	Reduced interaction	Ø				Ø	Ø		Ø	Ø		Ø				X			X				X			X			
	No self-enhancement		Ø	Ø																							X		O
	Identification with external group	Ø	Ø										O										X						

Legend: „O" Solutions only in literature review; „X" Solutions only from interviews; „Ø" Solutions from literature review and interviews

5 Discussion

Comparison of Solutions from Literature and Their Application in Our Empirical Interview Research: Comparing the identified solutions to improve TI in VT from literature and the insights gained from the conducted interviews with our case teams (see Table 2 for an overview), some consensus as well as new insights can be derived. First, we found *congruence in literature and practice* on the effectiveness of several solutions to improve TI in VT, namely: foster work interdependencies, encourage acknowledgement and feedback, introduce audio & video-conferencing, implement communities for mutual learning, e.g. working-tandems for knowledge-exchange, as well as real-time document sharing.

We further found some solutions that were *proposed in literature but not applied in practice*. While literature suggests to differentiate the team from others to decrease the risk of outgroup identification [53], we found no such application in practice but rather solutions to increase ingroup awareness, such as team-building events. One potential reason for this could be that ingroup activities might be seen as socially more accepted than differentiation. Another reason might be that our interview partners did not perceive the presence of outgroups as threat for TI. Another proposition by literature for hybrid VT is to transfer employees between sites to trigger exchange between locational subgroups. In order to foster the sharing of contextual information, literature proposes to train the team members. In practice, sharing of contextual information is performed in dedicated time frames in regular meetings.

Further, our interview data reveals several *solutions to improve TI that have yet not been mentioned in literature*. The interview results point out the relevance for real-time document sharing and the possibilities to enable simultaneous accesses to one document for several team members. Especially the topic of digital leadership as support for TI in VT thus seems a promising field for future research. Interestingly, a lot of our studied case teams still relied on eventually bringing team members physically together, e.g. via onboarding events. We therefore call for future research to further investigate this issue in order to derive a better understanding of which elements of TI can and which cannot be virtually substituted. Further, for some of the problems to TI in VT, we identified *only a small number of potential solutions* and therefore call for future research on how these problems might be solved. Especially for the problem of reduced identity efforts in VT, all our identified solutions stem from our interviews revealing a lack of knowledge in the existing body of literature. In terms of onboarding new employees in VT, it would be helpful to find out more about solutions that help the new employees to identify with the team in a situation where the values for collaboration are usually already set.

Applied Solutions Might Trigger New Problems: The insights from the conducted interviews with our case teams reveal an issue that is yet unaddressed in literature: that the applied solutions potentially lead to further problems. Three problems triggered by solutions to improve TI seem to be especially challenging because there are no immediate solutions available. As outlined, the implementation of IT can solve many issues in virtual TI, however this can trigger new problems in form of connection quality, technological incompatibility, and (technological) facility availability. The effectivity of audio-, video- and telepresence conferences is highly dependent on good internet connectivity quality. While this factor is internally influenceable by investments in IT quality, the issue is however also dependent on external factors, such as the maximum available internet speed, which seems to be still a big issue nowadays. Moreover, technological incompatibility is an issue that cross-company teams might face when there is no common base of technological tools and if the different internal rules of the companies hamper tool integration. Third, offering facilities, both technological, such as equipment for telepresence, as well as spatial, like quiet office spaces, comes along with high investment costs. In addition, the individual working conditions for employees who work from home can be very different and make it especially hard to provide them with access to such facilities. In summary, applied solutions to TI in VT might evoke new problems and although existing solutions can help to overcome some of the issues, not all problems can be fixed the short-term nor are they all fully influenceable internally. We therefore call for future research to explicitly consider these (often technology-related) issues when identifying or proposing solutions for virtual TI. Future research should set a strong focus on providing insight into what requirements technological tools have to meet in order to be used in VT.

Discussion Opportunities for TI Due to Virtuality: Contrary to what was expected when researching problems and solutions for TI issues in VT, the interview results provide plentiful insights on opportunities for TI that occur due to the virtual context. First, being physically distant from superiors creates a feeling of freedom in action, fosters creativity and the implementation of own ideas. This increases the degree of personal contribution to the team success. Second, communicating over distance decreases the inhibition level of posing questions and representing a specific point of view in discussions. Even though this fact is not explicitly stated as an opportunity in literature, there are proposals on anonymity features that could make this opportunity possible [2]. However, communication over distance can also have downsides to TI, as it is more difficult to casually address more critical issues in an informal atmosphere. Finally, using video conferences in the home office allows much more private insights into the private circumstances of the team members than conversations onsite would allow for. Thus, team members have the chance to get to know each other on an even more private level.

6   Contribution

In conclusion, our study combines an extensive literature review with interviews conducted with five case teams to identify solutions to improve TI in VT and give insights into their practical application. Based on the TI process, we first identified problems to TI stemming from a virtual context and then linked these problems to potential solutions identified in our research. Overall, our research provides an overview of known solutions to problems in virtual TI that allows us to identify promising areas for future research.

With increasing digitalization and ever more teams working together, our work contributes to research on digital work. First, our study extends the understanding of the TI process by explicitly considering also the phase of identification enactment and verification which is critical for long-term TI preservation. Second, we compile a list of problems to TI in VT and link them to their occurrence in the TI process. Third, we provide a comprehensive overview of known solutions to problems in virtual TI and exemplify their application in practice. Our results go beyond a mere literature review and also integrate insights from interview data collected at five case teams, our study reveals new solutions and opportunities that enrich the scope of available solution solutions as they have not been found in literature before. These insights can give hands-on guidance for practitioners in how existing issues with TI in VT can be solved. Based on our results, we further outline promising areas for future research due to non-attended problems and emerging issues that teams might be confronted with when deciding to apply these solutions.

We further acknowledge some limitations to our study. First, due to the enormous amount of search results we limited our screening efforts to 330 papers as basis for our literature review as no further insights thereafter were expected. Future research could however extend our literature review by including more papers, e.g. also from the discipline of psychology. Second, we extended our literature review with insights from five case teams. Due to the limitations given by the empirical interview research design, the insights on the application of solutions to improve TI in VT are therefore not generalizable. Future research could extend our findings with insights from more cases via e.g. a quantitative assessment. However, we believe that our qualitative approach allowed us to gain insights into the practical application of solutions stated in literature and identify new solutions of how to improve TI in VT.

References

1. Lurey, J.S., Raisinghani, M.S.: An empirical study of best practices in virtual teams. Inf. Manag. **38**, 523–544 (2001)
2. O'Leary, M.B., Cummings, J.N.: The spatial, temporal, and configurational characteristics of geographic dispersion in teams. MIS Q. **31**(3), 433–452 (2007)
3. Thatcher, S.M., Zhu, X.: Changing identities in a changing workplace: identification, identity enactment, self-verification, and telecommuting. Acad. Manag. Rev. **31**, 1076–1088 (2006)
4. Shapiro, D.L., Furst, S.A., Spreitzer, G.M., Von Glinow, M.A.: Transnational teams in the electronic age: are team identity and high performance at risk? J. Organ. Behav. **23**, 455–467 (2002)
5. Sivunen, A.: Strengthening identification with the team in virtual teams: the leaders' perspective. Group Decis. Negot. **15**, 345–366 (2006)
6. Han, G., Harms, P.D.: Team identification, trust and conflict: a mediation model. Int. J. Confl. Manag. **21**, 20–43 (2010)
7. Kramer, R.M.: Intergroup relations and organizational dilemmas: the role of categorization processes. In: Cummings, L.L., Staw, B.M. (eds.) Research in Organizational Behavior, vol. 13, pp. 191–228. JAI, Greenwich CT (1991)
8. Lembke, S., Wilson, M.G.: Putting the "team" into teamwork: alternative theoretical contributions for contemporary management practice. Hum. Relat. **51**, 927–944 (1998)
9. Moore, D.A., Kurtzberg, T.R., Thompson, L.L., Morris, M.W.: Long and short routes to success in electronically mediated negotiations: group affiliations and good vibrations. Organ. Behav. Hum. Decis. Process. **77**, 22–43 (1999)
10. Eckel, C.C., Grossman, P.J.: Managing diversity by creating team identity. J. Econ. Behav. Organ. **58**, 371–392 (2005)

11. Turner, J.C.: Towards a cognitive redefinition of the social group. In: Tajfel, H. (ed.) Social Identity and Intergroup Relations, pp. 15–40. Cambridge University Press, Cambridge (1982)
12. Dutton, J.E., Dukerich, J.M., Harquail, C.V.: Organizational images and member identification. Adm. Sci. Q. **39**, 239–263 (1994)
13. Fiol, C.M., O'Connor, E.J.: Identification in face-to-face, hybrid, and pure virtual teams: untangling the contradictions. Organ. Sci. **16**, 19–32 (2005)
14. Hogg, M.A.: Subjective uncertainty reduction through self-categorization: a motivational theory of social identity processes. Eur. Rev. Soc. Psychol. **11**, 223–255 (2000)
15. Tajfel, H.: Social identity and intergroup behaviour. Soc. Sci. Inf. **13**, 65–93 (1974)
16. Turner, J.C., Oakes, P.J., Haslam, S.A., McGarty, C.: Self and collective: cognition and social context. Pers. Soc. Psychol. Bull. **20**, 454–463 (1994)
17. Tajfel, H., Turner, J.C.: An integrative theory of intergroup conflict. In: Austin, W.G., Worchel, S. (eds.) The Social Psychology of Intergroup Relations, pp. 56–65. Brooks Cole, Monterey (1979)
18. Tajfel, H.: Social psychology of intergroup relations. Annu. Rev. Psychol. **33**, 1–39 (1982)
19. Allen, N.J., Meyer, J.P.: The measurement and antecedents of affective, continuance and normative commitment to the organization. J. Occup. Psychol. **63**, 1–18 (1990)
20. Tajfel, H.: Social categorization, social identity and social comparison. In: Tajfel, H. (ed.) Differentiation Between Social Groups: Studies in the Social Psychology of Intergroup Relations, pp. 61–76. Avademic Press, London (1978)
21. Lembke, S., Wilson, M.: The psychology of teamthink: a journey towards highly productive teamwork. In: The 1996 International Conference on Work Teams, Proceedings. The University of North Texas (1996)
22. Reicher, S.D., Spears, R., Postmes, T.: A social identity model of deindividuation phenomena. Eur. Rev. Soc. Psychol. **6**, 161–198 (1995)
23. Webster, J., Wong, W.: Comparing traditional and virtual group forms: identity, communication and trust in naturally occurring project teams. Int. J. Hum. Res. Manag. **19**, 41–62 (2008)
24. Kirkman, B.L., Gibson, C.B., Kim, K.: Across Borders and Technologies: Advancements in Virtual Teams Research, vol. 2. The Oxford Handbook of Organizational Psychology (2012)
25. Kahai, S.S., Cooper, R.B.: Exploring the core concepts of media richness theory: the impact of cue multiplicity and feedback immediacy on decision quality. J. Manag. Inf. Syst. **20**, 263–299 (2003)
26. Rafaeli, S., Ravid, G.: Information sharing as enabler for the virtual team: an experimental approach to assessing the role of electronic mail in disintermediation. Inf. Syst. J. **13**, 191–206 (2003)
27. May, A., Carter, C.: A case study of virtual team working in the european automotive industry. Int. J. Ind. Ergon. **27**, 171–186 (2001)
28. Raghuram, S., Hill, N.S., Gibbs, J.L., Maruping, L.M.: Virtual work: bridging research clusters. Acad. Manag. Ann. **13**, 308–341 (2019)
29. Andres, H.P.: The impact of communication medium on virtual team group process. Inf. Res. Manag. J. (IRMJ) **19**, 1–17 (2006)
30. Panteli, N., Davison, R.M.: The role of subgroups in the communication patterns of global virtual teams. IEEE Trans. Prof. Commun. **48**, 191–200 (2005)
31. Bhappu, A.D., Crews, J.M.: The effects of communication media & conflict on team identification in diverse teams. In: Proceedings of the 38th Annual Hawaii International Conference on System Sciences. IEEE, NW Washington, DC (2005)
32. Cramton, C.D., Hinds, P.J.: Subgroup dynamics in internationally distributed teams: ethnocentrism or cross-national learning? Res. Organ. Behav. **26**, 231–263 (2005)
33. Workman, M.: The effects from technology-mediated interaction and openness in virtual team performance measures. Behav. Inf. Technol. **26**, 355–365 (2007)

34. Gilson, L.L., Maynard, M.T., Jones Young, N.C., Vartiainen, M., Hakonen, M.: Virtual teams research: 10 years, 10 themes, and 10 opportunities. J. Manag. **41**, 1313–1337 (2015)
35. Webster, J., Watson, R.T.: Analyzing the past to prepare for the future: writing a literature review. MIS Q. **26**(2), xiii–xxiii (2002)
36. Miscenko, D., Day, D.V.: Identity and identification at work. Organ. Psychol. Rev. **6**, 215–247 (2016)
37. Patton, M.Q.: Qualitative Research and Evaluation Methods. Sage Publications, Thousand Oaks (2002)
38. Dubé, L., Robey, D.: Surviving the paradoxes of virtual teamwork. Inf. Syst. J. **19**, 3–30 (2008)
39. Cramton, C.D.: The mutual knowledge problem and its consequences for dispersed collaboration. Organ. Sci. **12**, 346–371 (2001)
40. Millward, L.J., Haslam, S.A., Postmes, T.: Putting employees in their place: the impact of hot desking on organizational and team identification. Organ. Sci. **18**, 547–559 (2007)
41. O'Leary, M.B., Mortensen, M.: Go (Con) figure: subgroups, imbalance, and isolates in geographically dispersed teams. Organ. Sci. **21**, 115–131 (2010)
42. Hennink, M., Hutter, I., Bailey, A.: Qualitative Research Methods. SAGE Publications Limited, London (2020)
43. Mayring, P.: Qualitative Inhaltsanalyse. Grundlagen und Techniken. 12., überarbeitete Auflage. Beltz. Weinheim (2015)
44. Brandon, D.P., Pratt, M.G.: Managing the formation of virtual team categories and prototypes by managing information: a SIT/SCT perspective. Acad. Manag. Proc. **1999**, D1–D6 (1999)
45. Wu, Y., Cui, T., Deng, Y.: How does mobile computing develop transactive memory in virtual team? A social identification view. In: Thirty Seventh International Conference on Information Systems, Dublin (2016)
46. Fonner, K.L., Roloff, M.E.: Testing the connectivity paradox: linking teleworkers' communication media use to social presence, stress from interruptions, and organizational identification. Commun. Monogr. **79**, 205–231 (2012)
47. Pauleen, D.J., Yoong, P.: Facilitating virtual team relationships via internet and conventional communication channels. Int. Res. Electron. Netw. Appl. Policy **11**, 190–202 (2001)
48. Guegan, J., Segonds, F., Barré, J., Maranzana, N., Mantelet, F., Buisine, S.: Social identity cues to improve creativity and identification in face-to-face and virtual groups. Comput. Hum. Behav. **77**, 140–147 (2017)
49. Ellis, J.B., Luther, K., Bessiere, K., Kellogg, W.A.: Games for virtual team building. In: Proceedings of the 7th ACM Conference on Designing Interactive Systems, pp. 295–304. Cape Town South Africa (2008)
50. Leonardi, P.M., Huysman, M., Steinfield, C.: Enterprise social media: definition, history, and prospects for the study of social technologies in organizations. J. Comput.-Mediat. Commun. **19**, 1–19 (2013)
51. Rezgui, Y.: Exploring virtual team-working effectiveness in the construction sector. Interact. Comput. **19**, 96–112 (2007)
52. Scott, M.E.: "Communicate through the roof": a case study analysis of the communicative rules and resources of an effective global virtual team. Commun. Q. **61**, 301–318 (2013)
53. Hallier, J., Baralou, E.: Other voices, other rooms: differentiating social identity development in organisational and Pro-Am virtual teams. N. Technol. Work. Employ. **25**, 154–166 (2010)

A No-Code Platform for Tie Prediction Analysis in Social Media Networks

Sebastian Schötteler[1,2(✉)], Sven Laumer[2], Heidi Schuhbauer[1], Niklas Scheidthauer[1], Philipp Seeberger[1], and Benedikt Miethsam[1]

[1] Faculty of Computer Science, Nuremberg Institute of Technology, Nuremberg, Germany
{sebastian.schoetteler,heidi.schuhbauer,scheidthauerni63750,
seebergerph64032,miethsambe65044}@th-nuernberg.de
[2] Schöller Endowed Chair for Information Systems (Digitalization in Business and Society),
FAU Erlangen-Nuremberg, Nuremberg, Germany
sven.laumer@fau.de

Abstract. Conventional methods for tie prediction analysis in social media networks are often code-intensive and encompass complex steps. Against this backdrop, we used design science research to develop a no-code tie prediction analysis platform. Our evaluation indicates that the platform significantly reduces tie prediction analysis complexity and, depending on the network size, also total prediction time. Moreover, it maintains a prediction accuracy similar to that of conventional, code-intensive methods. Thus, our artifact substantially facilitates tie prediction analysis for social media network researchers and practitioners.

Keywords: Social media networks · Tie formation concepts · Tie prediction algorithms · Tie prediction analysis platform · Social media analytics

1 Introduction

Humans, as social beings, naturally strive for social embeddedness [1]. Thus, social networks, such as friendship and communication networks, have been commonplace since the emergence of mankind [1]. What is new, however, is the proliferation of public and enterprise social media, such as Twitter and Yammer, and their novel potentials to achieve social embeddedness [2]. Nowadays, social networks based on social media (more briefly "social media networks") have become ubiquitous [3].

Social media networks are a subset of social networks and have their own distinct characteristics [2]. They confront researchers and managers with novel questions and challenges. In this context, a fundamental challenge is the social media tie prediction problem, which is concerned with inferring future or missing ties among actors – such as friends, employees, or students – from given social media network snapshots [4–6]. Addressing this problem provides major benefits, as would an eventual solution to it.

For instance, one application domain that benefits from research on social media tie prediction is the development of contact recommender systems for employees [6, 7]. Such systems can guide community emergence [8, 9] and prevent information overload

F. Ahlemann et al. (Eds.): WI 2021, LNISO 47, pp. 475–491, 2021.
https://doi.org/10.1007/978-3-030-86797-3_32

[10]. Another domain is the detection of anomalies, such as crucial missing ties [7, 11], which can indicate conflicts that harm communication and knowledge transfer or collaboration [12, 13]. Further domains are the detection of influential communities [6, 7, 9] and the modeling of network evolution processes [6, 7, 14].

Driven by the tie prediction problem relevance induced by the various application domains, several studies have contributed to its solution [5–7, 9, 15, 16]. However, a review of these studies indicates that social media tie prediction research is complex and prone to errors, and it often relies on code-intensive methods [16–21]. This situation is particularly caused by the large number of prediction approaches [4, 5, 22] as well as the interdependencies [23] and large sizes [9] of network data samples.

Against this backdrop, our goal is to develop a no-code analysis platform – that is, a platform that enables analysis without programing – to facilitate common tie prediction analysis tasks in social media networks. This would support researchers (and perhaps practitioners) in the generation of new insights into the tie prediction problem. More specifically, our platform should facilitate three common tasks. First, it should simplify comparing the accuracy of various fundamental tie prediction approaches (Sect. 2) with reference to a given social media network [5–7, 9, 16, 21, 24]. Second, it should facilitate evaluating the accuracy of specific fundamental tie prediction approaches across various (types of) social media networks [15, 21, 24]. Lastly, it should simplify combining different tie prediction approaches into strong overarching predictors [5, 9, 15, 18, 19]. Thus, the following research question is addressed [25]:

> *How can we implement a no-code platform for tie prediction analysis in social media networks that facilitates the three aforementioned common tie prediction tasks?*

To answer the research question, we followed the methodology by Peffers et al. [26], best practices from Gregor and Hevner [25], and guidelines from Hevner et al. [27]. First, we defined the problem, motivations for solving it, and objectives of a suitable solution. Then we designed and developed the platform, alias "artifact", based on the problem statement and solution objectives. Finally, we demonstrated and evaluated the platform and communicated the findings.

In line with Gregor and Hevner [25], the paper is structured as follows. The next section provides a concise literature review on tie prediction analysis in social media networks. It moreover provides a literature review on tie formation concepts and tie prediction algorithms in social media networks and on further tie prediction artifacts relevant for the development of our platform. This is followed by a detailed description of the applied methodology, after which the developed no-code analysis platform is demonstrated. The next section describes our evaluation of the platform, followed by a discussion of the main findings. The last section concludes and summarizes the paper.

2 Related Work

In line with recommendations by Gregor and Hevner [25], we built our literature review on descriptive (Ω) and prescriptive (Λ) knowledge. Descriptive knowledge is the "what" knowledge that sharpens the understanding of the problem, including its context and relevance, and how our proposed artifact may solve this problem [25]. Prescriptive knowledge is the "how" knowledge of relevant developed artifacts, such as concepts, algorithms, metrics, architectures, and system instantiations, which contribute to the development of our intended artifact [25]. Against this backdrop, this section contains four subsections. The first subsection contains a description of the relevant descriptive knowledge (Ω). The second subsection addresses fundamental tie formation concepts [23] in social media networks (Λ_1), meaning concepts that explain common drivers of tie formation in social media networks, which in turn can be used to predict ties. The third subsection deals with fundamental tie prediction algorithms [4] in social media networks (Λ_2), meaning algorithms that were explicitly developed for tie prediction purposes and which have been applied to social media networks. The fourth subsection describes further relevant artifacts for the development of our artifact (Λ_3).

To derive the aforementioned descriptive (Ω) and the prescriptive knowledge (Λ), we conducted a systematic literature search. More specifically, we used the search string "TITLE-ABS-KEY(("link" OR "tie") AND ("prediction" OR "formation") AND ("social media" OR "social network"))" to query the basket of journals and conferences named by [28] with the help of the Scopus database. We then studied the identified literature sources relevant to our topic, including their references and citations, to collect descriptive (Ω) and prescriptive knowledge (Λ) and further relevant sources. The findings derived from these literature sources constituted the knowledge base for the development of our platform (Sect. 4).

2.1 Tie Prediction Analysis in Social Media Networks (Ω)

Building on the definition provided by Wasserman and Faust [1], a social network, and thus also a social media network [2], consists of a finite set of actors (e.g., friends, employees, or students) and the ties (e.g., friendship, collaboration, or communication ties) defined on them. A fundamental challenge in such social media networks is the social media tie prediction problem, which is concerned with inferring future or missing ties among actors [4–6]. Several studies have contributed to its solution, leading to benefits for theory (e.g., novel insights into social media network evolution) and practice (e.g., techniques to enhance contact recommender systems) [5–7, 9, 15, 16]. However, social media tie prediction research is complex and prone to errors, and often relies on code-intensive methods, which may mitigate scientific progress [16–21].

To solve this problem, our goal is to develop a no-code platform with the objective to facilitate common tie prediction analysis tasks in social media networks by reducing complexity (e.g., coding complexity) while at the same time achieving a tie prediction velocity and accuracy comparable to those of conventional analysis methods [16–21]. More specifically, our platform should facilitate three common tasks derived from our literature review. First, the platform should simplify comparing the accuracy of various fundamental tie prediction approaches with reference to a given social media network [5–7, 9, 16, 21, 24]. Second, it should facilitate evaluating the accuracy of specific fundamental tie prediction approaches across various (types of) social media networks [15, 21, 24]. Third, it should simplify combining different tie prediction approaches into strong overarching predictors [5, 9, 15, 18, 19]. This would support researchers (and perhaps practitioners) in the generation of new insights into the social media tie prediction problem. We could not identify any no-code platform for tie prediction analysis in social media networks in the existing literature, which facilitates these tasks.

2.2 Tie Formation Concepts in Social Media Networks (Λ_1)

Homophily: This concept implies that actors tend to form ties with other similar actors [29]. Homophily is often described with the idiom "birds of a feather flock together" [29]. Several types of homophilous tendencies can be observed in various types of social media networks [15, 30], indicating that this concept is relevant in such networks. For instance, past research has determined that tie formation in social media networks is driven by homophily in status [31], gender [32], function [30], topic [15], location [30], and hierarchy [32].

Dyadic Social Balance: This concept was first described by Heider [33] and explains (inter alia) tie reciprocation tendencies between two actors who are embedded in a dyad. Heider argued that unreciprocated ties in a dyad may lead to cognitive dissonance or social imbalance, which in turn may lead to uncertainty and instability [34]. Thus, actors embedded in such dyads naturally strive for reciprocity to establish cognitive consistence or social balance [33]. Research has shown that reciprocity drives tie formation in various types of social media networks [5, 30, 35, 36], suggesting that dyadic social balance is a relevant concept in social media networks.

Triadic Social Balance: The aforementioned social balance concept can be extended to the triadic level. Heider argues that, analogously to the dyadic level, actors embedded in triads tend to strive for cognitive consistence, which in turn influences triadic formation tendencies [33]. For instance, to avoid cognitive dissonance in a triad, a focal actor's alters (i.e., actors connected with him) may form a common tie, thus leading to a transitive triadic closure [37]. Colloquially, this social balance tendency is often expressed as "a friend of my friend should be my friend" [23]. Studies have determined that transitive triadic closure drives tie formation in various types of social media networks [8, 30, 38], indicating that triadic social balance is a relevant concept in social media networks. It seems to be slightly more relevant in public than in enterprise social media networks [14].

Rich-get-Richer: The rich-get-richer concept implies that the tendency of an actor to form a tie with a potential alter is proportional to the alter's tie "richness" (i.e., number of his pre-existing ties). Hence, rich actors become even more central over time [39]. This concept is also often referred to as cumulative advantage [39] or preferential attachment [14]. Ultimately, it may lead to scale-free networks that follow a power-law distribution [40]. Research has shown that tie formation in social media networks may often – yet not always [30] – be explained by this concept [14, 39, 41, 42].

In summary, tie formation in social media networks can be conceptualized using the homophily, dyadic social balance, triadic social balance, and the rich-get-richer concepts. As shown in past studies, the accuracy of tie prediction artifacts in social media networks can be enhanced when these formational concepts are considered [5, 8, 15]. Therefore, our intended artifact considers these concepts. The above list may not be exhaustive;

for example, structural hole closing and transaction memory may also be relevant [23]. However, based on our systematic literature search, we are confident that the list reflects the most fundamental concepts [23] for developing our artifact.

2.3 Tie Prediction Algorithms for Social Media Networks (Λ_2)

Common Neighbors: This is a fundamental algorithm for predicting ties in various types of social networks [5, 9, 16, 22]. It is described in Eq. (1):

$$Common\ neighbors\ (x, y) = |\Gamma(x) \cap \Gamma(y)| \tag{1}$$

The rationale behind this algorithm is that the more structurally similar two focal actors (x and y) are, as expressed by the number of their common neighbors (i.e., $|\Gamma(x) \cap \Gamma(y)|$, where $\Gamma(x)$ is the neighborhood of x, or in other words, his alters), the greater the odds of the actors establishing a common tie. Several social media network studies have applied the common neighbors algorithm for tie prediction purposes. Depending on the underlying social media network, the algorithm has achieved low [5, 9], medium [6, 7, 16, 21], or high [15, 21, 24] prediction accuracy.

Jaccard Coefficient: This is another fundamental algorithm for predicting ties in various social network types [5, 9, 16, 22, 43]. It can be defined as shown in (2).

$$Jaccard\ coefficient(x, y) = \frac{|\Gamma(x) \cap \Gamma(y)|}{|\Gamma(x) \cup \Gamma(y)|} \tag{2}$$

It operates similarly to the common neighbors algorithm, but additionally divides the number of common neighbors across two focal actors by the number of actors that are neighbors of at least one of the focal actors (i.e., $|\Gamma(x) \cup \Gamma(y)|$). This enables addressing structural dissimilarities between the two focal actors more precisely, resulting in a more accurate representation of structural similarity. Several studies have applied this algorithm to predict ties in social media networks and have demonstrated low [9, 24], medium [5, 15, 16, 21], or high [6, 21, 24] prediction accuracy.

Adamic-Adar Index: This algorithm was originally used to predict ties between personal homepage networks [44]. Over time, it has evolved into a fundamental tie prediction algorithm that is applicable in various social network types [5, 9, 16, 22]. The algorithm is described in Eq. (3).

$$Adamic - Adar\ index\ (x, y) = s \sum_{z \in \Gamma(x \cap \Gamma(y))} \frac{1}{\log(|\Gamma(z)|)} \tag{3}$$

As in the common neighbors algorithm, the Adamic-Adar index algorithm counts the number of common neighbors between two focal actors. However, unlike the common neighbors algorithm, it assigns less connected common neighbors a greater weight (note that $\log(|\Gamma(z)|)$ resembles the logarithmic degree centrality of a common neighbor $z \notin \Gamma(x) \cap \Gamma(y)$). The reasoning for the weighting approach is that two focal actors with ties to common neighbors having low connectivity are relatively likely to share unique characteristics, which in turn can increase the chance of a common tie emerging [44].

This algorithm has been used in various studies to predict ties in social media networks. Depending on the underlying social media network, the accuracy of prediction was low [5], medium [16, 21], or high [6, 21, 24].

Preferential Attachment: This is another fundamental tie prediction algorithm used in various social network types [5, 9, 16, 22]. It can be described as in (4).

$$\text{Preferential attachment } (x, y) = |\Gamma(x)| \cdot |\Gamma(y)| \qquad (4)$$

Building on the rich-get-richer concept (Sect. 2.2), research has shown that the probability of a tie occurring between two focal actors is correlated with the product of their degree centrality (i.e., $|\Gamma(x)| \cdot |\Gamma(y)|$) [4]. The preferential attachment algorithm has been used to predict ties in various types of social media networks, and has achieved low [6, 9, 16], medium [5, 21], or high [21] prediction accuracy.

The aforementioned list is not exhaustive. Nevertheless, after reviewing the various literature sources derived from our systematic literature search, we are confident that the list encompasses the most fundamental tie prediction algorithms [22] that should be considered in our artifact.

2.4 Further Relevant Tie Prediction Artifacts (Λ_3)

The literature review indicated that researchers often combine different tie prediction concepts and algorithms with the help of classification machine learning algorithms, such as the decision tree [5, 9, 15, 18, 19], random forest [18, 19], k-nearest-neighbors [18, 19], and logistic regression algorithm [5], to achieve a higher prediction accuracy.

Moreover, studies often rely on the AUC (area under curve) metric to evaluate their achieved prediction accuracy, expressed by a value between 0 (lowest accuracy) and 1 (highest accuracy) [9, 11, 16, 22]. These artifacts were also considered for our platform.

Lastly, we could not identify any no-code platform for tie prediction analysis in social media networks in the existing literature, which addressed the aforementioned descriptive (Ω) and prescriptive knowledge (Λ). This lack was underpinned by the fact that, as far as evident, the aforementioned social media tie prediction studies derived from our systematic literature search have all relied on more complex methods (e.g., code-intensive methods [16–21]). The most similar derived artifact is the tie prediction architecture by Schall [24]. However, it lacks relevant complexity reduction features, such as an analysis preparation component, which allows translating the complete architecture into an integrated no-code platform. Nonetheless, it supplied a sound basis for our artifact and was therefore incorporated.

3 Methodology

The goal of this research was to develop a no-code platform to facilitate tie prediction analysis in social media networks (Sect. 1). This objective is congruent with design science research, which aims to create and evaluate artifacts, such as constructs, models, methods, and – as in this paper – system instantiations, to solve relevant problems [27].

Activity 1: Define Problem and Motivate	Activity 2: Define Solution and Objective	Activity 3: Design and Development	Activity 4: Artifact Demonstration	Activity 5: Artifact Evaluation	Activity 6: Artifact Communication
"Complexity of tie predictions in social media networks"	"A no-code platform to facilitate tie predictions"	"Creation of the no-code tie prediction platform"	"Application of the platform on one social media network"	"Comparison against a code-intensive method"	"Publication of the research in a professional IS outlet"
Sections Mapping: 2.1	**Sections Mapping:** 2.1	**Sections Mapping:** 2.2, 2.3, 2.4 & 4.1	**Sections Mapping:** 4.2	**Sections Mapping:** 5	**Sections Mapping:** 1 to 7

Fig. 1. Design science research approach (adapted from [26])

Thus, we adopted the design science research guidelines, best practices, and methodology proposed by Hevner et al. [27], Gregor and Hevner [25], and Peffers et al. [26], respectively. Figure 1 illustrates the applied design science research approach.

In the first activity, we collected descriptive knowledge (Ω) [25] to specify the research problem, namely the high complexity of conventional tie prediction analysis methods in social media networks; we also used this knowledge to motivate why solving this problem would be valuable (Sect. 2.1) [26]. Next, we further used this knowledge [25] to infer a solution to the problem and the main objective of that solution. The solution was a platform with the objective to facilitate tie prediction analysis via a no-code paradigm (Sect. 2.1) [26]. In the third activity, we collected prescriptive knowledge (Λ) [25] (Sects. 2.2 to 2.4) and used it to translate the solution into an artifact, namely the proposed platform. This activity involved defining the artifact's requirements and architecture as well as actually creating the artifact (Sect. 4.1) [26]. Next, we demonstrated how the artifact could be used to solve the specified research problem. We did so by conducting an experimental [27] tie prediction analysis in an empirically derived social media network (Sect. 4.2) [26]. In the fifth activity, we evaluated the artifact's complexity, velocity, and accuracy (as three common performance metrics [27] also relevant for our artifact (Sect. 2.1)) compared with a conventional, code-intensive method [17]. We used two social media networks for this task and repeatedly returned to activity 3 until the evaluation results were satisfactory (Sect. 5) [26], thus incorporating the iterative build-and-evaluate paradigm of design science research [27]. The last activity was communicating the research findings to diffuse the created body of knowledge and the artifact. The communication process explains the specified problem and its relevance, and indicates how – and how well – the artifact solves the problem [26]. This paper represents the fulfilment of this step. Moreover, we published the created artifact into a public software repository to make it publicly available for use and refinement[1].

Following the logic of Merwe et al. [45], we mapped each activity to the corresponding sections proposed in the design science research publication schema by Gregor and Hevner [25]. This paper's structure has thus been defined, and more detailed insights regarding each activity appears in the relevant sections (Fig. 1).

---

[1] Public repository link: https://github.com/social-media-analytics-research/tie-prediction-tool.

4 Artifact

This section has two subsections. The first describes the development procedure of the artifact, starting from a requirements definition and progressing to the architectural conception and ending with the actual artifact creation [26]. The second subsection demonstrates the developed artifact [26], namely our no-code platform to facilitate social media tie prediction analysis by reducing complexity (e.g., coding complexity).

4.1 Development

Requirements: Based on the research question (Sect. 1) and the review of the relevant descriptive (Ω) and prescriptive (Λ) knowledge (Sect. 2), we defined ten requirements for our artifact. These are as follows: First, the artifact should enable the use of (1) the derived tie formation concepts (Sect. 2.2) and (2) prediction algorithms (Sect. 2.3) as tie prediction approaches. Moreover, it should enable (3) comparison of various approaches with reference to a given social media network and (4) evaluation of a specific approach across several social media networks (Sect. 2.1). In addition, the artifact should enable (5) combining different approaches into a strong predictor (Sect. 2.1) via the determined (6) machine learning algorithms (decision tree, random forest, k-nearest-neighbors, and logistic regression algorithm) (Sect. 2.4). Lastly, the artifact should meet all the above requirements while also (7) following a no-code paradigm, thus rendering programing obsolete (Sect. 2.1). This no-code paradigm should (8) substantially reduce analysis complexity compared to conventional tie prediction analyses, while achieving a tie prediction (9) velocity and (10) accuracy comparable to those of conventional analyses (Sect. 2.1).

Architecture: To conceptualize the architecture of our artifact, we relied on the literature review findings and adapted the modular tie prediction architecture proposed by Schall [24] (Sect. 2.4). Our artifact architecture is presented in Fig. 2.

The data layer contains an import library that enables migrating social media networks into the network database, which is also situated in this layer. The stored networks can then be loaded from the tie predictor in the prediction layer.

The tie predictor is the main component of the prediction layer. In the first step, the tie predictor loads a network N selected from the database and extracts from it a random tie subset of specified size, while maintaining the same actor set as in N, resulting in a test network N_{TE}. This process is then repeated using the network N_{TE} to derive a training network N_{TR} [24], such that $N_{TR} \subseteq N_{TE} \subseteq N$ [6, 16, 46, 47]. Subsequently, the tie predictor uses one of the prediction approaches stored in the concepts (Sect. 2.2) or algorithms library (Sect. 2.3) to calculate the associated prediction scores for each pair of network actors (x,y) in N_{TR} and N_{TE}. This step can be augmented by combining different tie prediction approaches into a strong predictor via the implemented machine learning algorithms. To meet the defined requirements, we decided to implement the machine learning algorithms derived from the literature review, namely decision tree, random forest, k-nearest-neighbors, and logistic regression algorithms (Sect. 2.4). After calculating these prediction scores, the tie predictor uses the scores derived for the

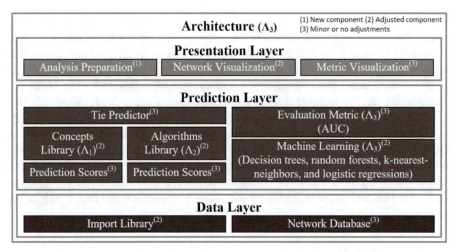

Fig. 2. Artifact architecture (adapted from [24])

network N_{TR} together with N_{TR} itself to train its prediction accuracy. Lastly, the tie predictor evaluates its accuracy via the prediction scores derived for the network N_{TE}, N_{TE} itself, and the implemented evaluation metric. For this, we relied on the AUC metric determined in the literature review, which quantifies the achieved prediction accuracy as a value between 0 (lowest accuracy) and 1 (highest accuracy) (Sect. 2.4).

The presentation layer contains an analysis preparation component. It is used to prepare the tie prediction analysis by selecting the network N from the database, the sample sizes of the networks N_{TR} and N_{TE}, the tie prediction approach(es), and further tie prediction parameters, if available (Fig. 3). This component is further used to start the core prediction process. After that process is complete, the network visualization component can be used to derive the (correctly and incorrectly) predicted ties in the network N_{TE} (Fig. 4). Moreover, the metric visualization component can be used to determine the AUC metric values for the networks N_{TR} and N_{TE}, including an associated AUC graph that visualizes the achieved accuracy (Fig. 4).

We made various adaptations to the baseline architecture to reduce complexity and to implement our findings from the literature review. First and potentially most importantly, we added an analysis preparation component to unify all necessary preparation steps into an integrated no-code dashboard. Next, we adjusted the network visualization component to enable displaying the predicted ties. Furthermore, we adjusted the concept, algorithm, and machine learning components as per our literature review findings. Lastly, we extended the import library so that standard network data formats such as GEFX, GML, GraphML, and CSV [20] could be imported easily. The residual components underwent only minor or no adjustments.

Creation: In the data layer, we used PostgreSQL for the network database [48] and Python [49] together with NetworkX [20] to develop the import library. In the prediction layer, we used Python and NetworkX [20] for the tie predictor, the concepts, and algorithms library, and for each prediction score and the AUC evaluation metric component. Next, we used the Scikit-learn [50] Python package for the machine learning component. We opted for Scikit-learn because it is a well-established package both in academia and practice [50] and covers the common machine learning algorithms used for social media tie prediction identified by our literature review (Sect. 2.4). Moreover, it is simpler to configure compared to alternatives, such as PyTorch or TensorFlow [50], thus facilitating a further development of our platform by other users, if required. Although the two aforementioned packages contain more advanced machine learning techniques, future implementations of our platform can efficiently overcome this limitation with the help of specialized Scikit-learn wrappers, such as Skorch (a wrapper that augments Scikit-learn by PyTorch machine learning techniques) [51]. In the presentation layer, we used D3.js [52] and AngularJS [53] for the analysis preparation and each visualization component.

4.2 Demonstration

For the artifact demonstration, we empirically collected an enterprise social media network, N^D, from a geographically dispersed organization. The network contained 17 employees, and displayed 160 present and 112 absent directed collaboration ties [9]. Moreover, N^D contained employee attributes such as business function and location, which enabled homophily-based tie prediction analysis. We used the common neighbors algorithm and the homophily concept as prediction approaches. The artifact enables assigning global relevance weights to the various homophily attributes of the embedded

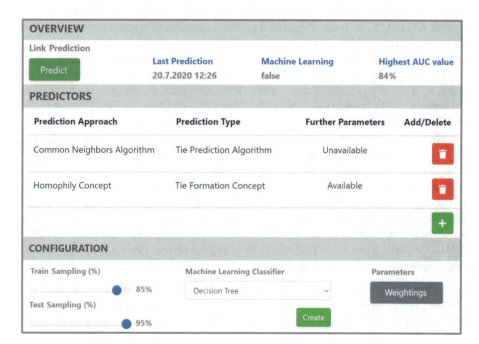

Fig. 3. Analysis preparation dashboard: aggregated representation

employees. As N^D was geographically dispersed, we decided to focus solely on locational homophily. The analysis preparation is illustrated in Fig. 3. The predicted ties and achieved accuracies (i.e., AUC values) are presented in Fig. 4.

We used the preparation dashboard to configure our prediction approach. First, we imported, named, and described our network sample N^D. Next, we adjusted the prediction settings by selecting the prediction approaches, homophily weightings (via the button "Weightings"), and a network split of $N_{TR}^D = 85\%$ and $N_{TE}^D = 95\%$. Then, we started the actual prediction process (via the button "Predict"). Figure 3 illustrates the analysis preparation dashboard after completion of the tie prediction process.

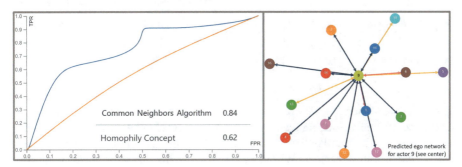

Fig. 4. Metric (left) and network visualization dashboard (right): aggregated representation

The metric visualization dashboard (left panel) presents the achieved N_{TE}^D AUC values for the chosen prediction approaches; these were 0.84 for the common neighbors algorithm and 0.62 for the locational homophily concept. Both approaches achieved a higher-than-random (i.e., > 0,5) accuracy. However, as reflected by the higher AUC value, the first approach achieved more accurate predictions. The dashboard augmented the values with an AUC graph. Lastly, the network visualization dashboard (right panel) allowed for selecting an actor's (e.g., actor 9's) egocentric network to examine his correctly (orange) and incorrectly (red) predicted ties. Blue ties were already present in N_{TR}^D. Both prediction approaches considered N^D to be undirected.

5   Evaluation

To evaluate our artifact ("ART"), we compared its performance against an alternative tie prediction method ("ALT"). For this, we built upon the alternative method from Bojanowski and Chroł [17]. For this, we used RStudio [54], a statistical programming tool often used for tie prediction analysis [17], augmented by preprocessing, tie prediction, and machine learning features. The methods were compared by assessing four performance metrics, collected along two prediction approaches and networks. The result was four evaluation cases with four value comparisons in each case (Table 1).

As mentioned earlier, we compared the methods by measuring and juxtaposing their achieved prediction performances in two different prediction approaches. For the first approach ("Approach 1"), we used the Adamic-Adar index algorithm. For the second

Table 1. Evaluation results

Approach 1: *Adamic-Adar index algorithm*				$N_{TR}^{E(n)} = 80\% \Big\vert N_{TR}^{E(n)} = 95\%$			
Approach 2: *Logistic regression machine learning combining the Jaccard coefficient and preferential attachment algorithms*							
Network	*UCI network* (N^{E1})			*Twitter network* (N^{E2})			
Approach	Approach 1		Approach 2		Approach 1		Approach 2
Method	ART	ALT	ART	ALT	ART	ALT	ART	ALT
Complexity (min:sec)	<u>03:10</u>	12:45	<u>03:31</u>	07:30	<u>00:27</u>	14:25	<u>00:44</u>	09:35
Velocity (min:sec)	03:46	<u>00:11</u>	05:56	<u>00:27</u>	00:13	<u>00:06</u>	00:24	<u>00:10</u>
Total time (min:sec)	<u>06:56</u>	12:56	09:27	<u>07:57</u>	<u>00:40</u>	14:31	<u>01:08</u>	09:45
Accuracy (AUC)	<u>0.80</u>	0.77	<u>0.91</u>	<u>0.91</u>	<u>0.84</u>	0.83	<u>0.81</u>	0.80

approach ("Approach 2"), we used logistic regression machine learning to combine the Jaccard coefficient and the preferential attachment algorithm into a strong predictor.

Each approach was applied to two networks. The first network ("UCI network (N^{E1})") comprised 1899 students from a Facebook-like internal social media platform at the University of California, Irvine (UCI). It encompassed 20,296 present and 3,584,006 absent directed communication ties [55]. The second network ("Twitter network (N^{E2})") was derived from Twitter via Gephi [56] and encompassed 745 Twitter users as well as 1204 present and 553,076 absent directed communication ties.

We defined four metrics to quantify the achieved performance of each method in each approach-network combination or evaluation case. Complexity represented the effort, in minutes, to prepare the analysis. Velocity displayed the minutes of the actual prediction calculation process. Total time indicated the cumulated complexity and velocity time. Accuracy represented the achieved AUC value. Each performance metric was recorded for each method in each evaluation case by a researcher with basic experience in both methods.

Better performance metric values in each evaluation case are underlined twice. The artifact achieved better (lower) complexity scores than the alternative method. However, the alternative method achieved better (lower) velocity scores, particularly in the second approach ("Approach 2"). Nevertheless, the artifact achieved better (lower) total prediction time scores in three of the four evaluation cases. Lastly, the methods achieved similar accuracy scores, indicating that the prediction approaches have been correctly implemented into the artifact; small variances may be attributed to the randomness factor in the tie extraction step (Sect. 4.1). These results are discussed in Sect. 6.

6   Discussion

The goal was to reduce tie prediction complexity while maintaining a velocity and accuracy similar to those attained by conventional methods. For this purpose, we developed a no-code tie prediction platform. Our evaluation results indicate that our artifact significantly reduces tie prediction complexity while maintaining similar accuracy. However, the alternative method (the chosen conventional method) achieved better velocity scores, particularly in the machine learning approach. However, for the chosen social media networks, the artifact's lower total prediction time largely overcompensated for its slower velocity. However, it is to be expected that this compensation effect diminishes proportionally to the network size. Nevertheless, various studies (e.g., [21, 57]) have used sizes for which our artifact may perform similarly, or better than, the alternative method regarding the total time. Thus, while future studies should enhance our artifact's prediction velocity, it is already suitable for tie prediction analysis – even for larger networks, if velocity is not the main priority.

Due to the iterative nature of the design science research methodology, the evaluation step was repeated several times. Here, we determined two further differences between the methods. First, the artifact displayed a substantially lower learning curve. While the researcher required several hours to perform a first tie prediction analysis in the alternative, he only required a few minutes in the artifact. Second, the artifact's no-code paradigm guarded the researcher against common pitfalls and errors that occurred in the alternative, such as mistakes in the network splitting process. Thus, the artifact promotes valid and correct prediction procedures. On the other hand, the no-code paradigm may sometimes restrict researchers. For instance, although the artifact allows random undersampling, augmenting it through additional sampling techniques could improve its accuracy [58]. Another useful addition would be to enable time-variant tie prediction analysis [6]. In general, future studies could augment the artifact by various additional features, thus aligning its flexibility with that of conventional methods.

Congruent with our evaluation results, we conclude that our developed artifact answers the research question proposed in Sect. 1. Furthermore, the artifact meets the requirements in Sect. 4.1, apart from (9), which is only partially met due to the velocity concerns. Thus, with reference to the tie prediction problem stated in the introduction, our artifact reduces tie prediction complexity and facilitates the generation of novel insights. For instance, researchers could use the artifact to more easily explore formation mechanisms through which communities in social media networks evolve [6, 7, 9, 14], and could use the findings in order to develop guidelines to foster fruitful community evolution. Moreover, practitioners could use the artifact to more easily infer tie formation antecedents in order to develop their own recommender systems [7, 46].

7   Conclusion

Readers should consider the artifact's limitations, namely the improvable velocity score and the room for further tie prediction features. As an outlook, two optimization measures could mitigate these limitations. Firstly, to substantially enhance platform velocity, realizing artifact compatibility with alternative Python compilers, such as the PyPy just-in-time compiler, seems promising [59]. Secondly, to enable even more sophisticated tie prediction analyses, exploiting the features of the Scikit-learn package more strongly or even implementing a wrapper that augments this package, such as Skorch (Sect. 4.1), should prove valuable [51]. Another limitation is that the artifact was created upon literature mainly derived from the social media network domain. Although probable, it is not clear whether the artifact is directly applicable to other social network types. Lastly, future studies may strengthen the platform evaluation using additional prediction approaches, social media networks, metrics, or users [27].

Despite its limitations, our artifact extends the current body of knowledge by three novel contributions. First, conventional methods for tie prediction analysis in social media networks often rely on code-intensive approaches that encompass a set of complex steps [16–21]. In this context, our artifact provides the advantage of a no-code paradigm to reduce this complexity and to facilitate tie prediction analyses while maintaining an accuracy and, depending on the network sample size, total prediction time similar to that of conventional methods. Second, another advantage of the no-code paradigm is that it reduces the risk of mistakes and leads to a low learning curve, thus allowing to achieve valid results rapidly. Lastly, the artifact contains tailored features, such as an overview of the predicted ties and homophily type-based prediction analysis calibrations, enabling uncomplex but fine-grained analyses.

From a theoretical perspective, we contribute to research by augmenting Schall's tie prediction architecture [24] with an analysis preparation component. Our evaluation results imply that this architectural extension has various positive outcomes for resultant system instantiations (e.g., reduction of complexity, lower learning curves, and less user mistakes).

References

1. Wasserman, S., Faust, K.: Social Network Analysis – Methods and Applications Cambridge. University Press, Cambridge (1994)
2. Labianca, G., Kane, G, Alavi, M., Borgatti, S.: What's different about social media networks? Framework and Research Agenda. MISQ 38, 274–304 (2013)
3. Meske, C., Junglas, I., Schneider, J., Jaakonmaeki, R.: How social is your social network? Toward a measurement model. In: Proceedings of the Fortieth International Conference on Information Systems (ICIS '19), pp. 1–9. Association for Information Systems, Munich, Germany (2019)
4. Liben-Nowell, D., Kleinberg, J.: The link prediction problem for social networks. In: Proceedings of the Twelfth International Conference on Information and Knowledge Management (CIKM '03), pp. 556–559. Association for Computing Machinery, New York, USA (2004)
5. Cheng, J., Romero, D., Meeder, B., Kleinberg, J.: Predicting reciprocity in social networks. In: Proceedings of the 2011 IEEE Third International Conference on Privacy, Security, Risk and Trust (PASSAT '11) and 2011 IEEE Third International Conference on Social Computing (SocialCom '11), pp. 49–56. IEEE Computer Society, Boston, USA (2011)
6. Yin, D., Hong, L., Davison, B.: Structural link analysis and prediction in microblogs. In: Proceedings of the 20th ACM International Conference on Information and Knowledge Management (CIKM '11), pp. 1–6. Association for Computing Machinery, Glasgow, UK (2011)
7. Tsugawa, S., Kito, K.: Retweets as a predictor of relationships among users on social media. PLoS ONE 12, 1–19 (2017)
8. Brzozowski, M., Romero, D.: Who should I follow? Recommending people in directed social networks. In: Proceedings of the Fifth International Conference on Weblogs and Social Media (ICWSM '11), pp. 458–461. Association for the Advancement of Artificial Intelligence, Barcelona, Spain (2011)

9. Valverde-Rebaza, J., de Andrade Lopes, A.: Exploiting behaviors of communities of twitter users for link prediction. Soc. Netw. Anal. Min. **3** 1063–1074 (2013)
10. Chen, X., Wei, S.: Enterprise social media use and overload: a curvilinear relationship. J. Inf. Technol. **34**, 22–38 (2019)
11. Luo, P., Li,Y., Wu, C., Chen, K.: Detecting the missing links in social networks based on utility analysis. J. Comput. Sci. **16**, 51–58 (2016)
12. Oostervink, N., Agterberg, M., Huysman, M.: Knowledge sharing on enterprise social media: practices to cope with institutional complexity: knowledge sharing on enterprise social media. J. Comput.-Mediat. Comm. **21**, 156–176 (2016)
13. Azaizah, N., Reychav, I., Raban, D., Simon, T., McHaney, R.: Impact of ESN implementation on communication and knowledge-sharing in a multi-national organization. Int. J. Inf. Manage. **43**, 284–294 (2018)
14. Wiesneth, K.: Evolution, structure and users' attachment behavior in enterprise social networks. In: Proceedings of the 49th Hawaii International Conference on System Sciences (HICSS '16), pp. 2038–2047. IEEE Computer Society, Koloa (2016)
15. Aiello, L., Barrat, A., Schifanella, R., Cattuto, C., Markines, B., Menczer, F.: Friendship prediction and homophily in social media. ACM Trans. Web. **6**, 1–33 (2012)
16. Martinčić-Ipšić, S., Močibob, E., Perc, M.: Link prediction on twitter. PLOS ONE **12**, 1–21 (2017)
17. Bojanowski, M., Chroł, B.: Proximity-Based Methods for Link Prediction in Graphs with R Package 'linkprediction'. Kozminski University, Warsaw (2019)
18. Fire, M., Katz, G., Rokach, L., Elovici, Y.: Links reconstruction attack. In: Altshuler, Y., Elovici, Y., Cremers, A., Aharony, N., Pentland, A. (eds.) Security and Privacy in Social Networks. pp. 181–196. Springer, New York (2013). https://doi.org/10.1007/978-1-4614-4139-7_9
19. Fire, M., Tenenboim, L., Lesser, O., Puzis, R., Rokach, L., Elovici, Y.: Link prediction in social networks using computationally efficient topological features. In: Proceedings of the 2011 IEEE Third International Conference on Privacy, Security, Risk and Trust (PASSAT '11) and 2011 IEEE Third International Conference on Social Computing (SocialCom '11), pp. 73–80. IEEE Computer Society, Boston (2011)
20. Hagberg, A., Schult, D., Swart, P.: NetworkX: Network Analysis in Python. https://networkx.github.io/documentation/latest/. Accessed 12 Jul 2020
21. Gao, F., Musial, K., Cooper, C., Tsoka, S.: Link prediction methods and their accuracy for different social networks and network metrics. Sci. Program. **2015**, 1–13 (2015)
22. Zhou, T., Lü, L., Zhang, Y-C.: Predicting missing links via local information. Eur. Phys. J. B. **71**, 623–630 (2009)
23. Contractor, N., Wasserman, S., Faust, K.: Testing multi-theoretical multilevel hypotheses about organizational networks: an analytic framework and empirical example. Acad. Manag. Rev. **31**, 681–703 (2006)
24. Schall, D.: Link prediction in directed social networks. Soc. Netw. Anal. Min. **4**, 157 (2014)
25. Gregor, S., Hevner, A.: Positioning and presenting design science research for maximum impact. MISQ **37**, 337–356 (2013)
26. Peffers, K., Tuunanen, T., Rothenberger, M., Chatterjee, S.: A design science research methodology for information systems research. JMIS **24**, 45–77 (2007)
27. Hevner, A., March, S., Park, J., Ram, S.: Design science in information systems research. MISQ **28**, 75–105 (2004)
28. Wang, P., Xu, B., Wu, Y., Zhou, X.: Link prediction in social networks: the state-of-the-art. Sci. China Inf. Sci. **58**, 1–38 (2015)
29. McPherson, M., Smith-Lovin, L., Cook, J.: Birds of a feather: homophily in social networks. Annu. Rev. Sociol. **27**, 415–444 (2001)

30. Kim, Y., Kane, G.: Online tie formation in enterprise social media. APJIS **29**, 382–406 (2019)
31. Šćepanović, S., Mishkovski, I., Gonçalves, B., Nguyen, T., Hui, P.: Semantic homophily in online communication: evidence from twitter. OSNEM **2**, 1–18 (2017)
32. Di Tommaso, G., Gatti, M., Iannotta, M., Mehra, A., Stilo, G., Velardi, P.: Gender, rank, and social networks on an enterprise social media platform. Soc. Netw. **62**, 58–67 (2020)
33. Heider, F.: Attitudes and cognitive organization. J. Psychol. **21**, 107–112 (1946)
34. Festinger, L., Hutte, H.A.: An experimental investigation of the effect of unstable interpersonal relations in a group. J. Abnorm. Psychol. **49**, 513–522 (1954)
35. Rode, H.: Analyzing motivational determinants of knowledge-sharing in enterprise social media platforms. Acad. Manag. Proc. **2015** 6 (2015)
36. Quercia, D., Capra, L., Crowcroft, J.: The social world of twitter: topics, geography, and emotions. In: Proceedings of the International Conference on Weblogs and Social Media (ICWSM '12), pp. 298–305. Association for the Advancement of Artificial Intelligence, Dublin (2012)
37. Granovetter, M.: The strength of weak ties. Am. J. Sociol. **78**, 1360–1380 (1973)
38. Sadri, A.M., Hasan, S., Ukkusuri, S., Lopez, J.: Analysis of social interaction network properties and growth on twitter. Soc. Netw. Anal. Min. **8**, 2–13 (2018)
39. Su, J., Sharma, A., Goel, S.: The effect of recommendations on network structure. In: Proceedings of the 25th International Conference on World Wide Web (WWW '16), pp. 1157–1167. Association for Computing Machinery, Montréal (2016)
40. Johnson, S., Faraj, S., Kudaravalli, S.: Emergence of power laws in online communities: the role of social mechanisms and preferential attachment. MISQ **38**, 795–808 (2014)
41. Kumar, A., Kushwah, S., Manjhvar, A.: A review on link prediction in social network. Int. J. Grid Distrib. Comput. **9**, 43–50 (2016)
42. Overbey, L., Greco, B., Paribello, C., Jackson, T.: Structure and prominence in twitter networks centered on contentious politics. Soc. Netw. Anal. Min. **3**, 1351–1378 (2013)
43. Jaccard, P.: Distribution de la Flore Alpine dans le Bassin des Dranses et dans quelques régions voisines. Bull. Soc. Vaud. Sci. Nat. **37**, 241–272 (1901)
44. Adamic, L., Adar, E.: Friends and neighbors on the web. Soc. Netw. **25**, 211–230 (2003)
45. Van der Merwe, A., Gerber, A., Smuts, H.: Mapping a design science research cycle to the postgraduate research report. In: Liebenberg, J., Gruner, S. (eds.) ICT Education, Communications in Computer and Information Science, vol. 730, pp. 293–308. Springer, Cham (2017). https://doi.org/10.1007/978-3-319-69670-6_21
46. Yin, Z., Gupta, M., Weninger, T., Han, J.: A unified framework for link recommendation using random walks. In: Proceedings of the 2010 International Conference on Advances in Social Networks Analysis and Mining (ASONAM '10), pp. 152–159. IEEE Computer Society, Odense (2010)
47. Clauset, A., Moore, C., Newman, M.: Hierarchical structure and the prediction of missing links in networks. Nature **453**, 98–101 (2008)
48. Ahmed, I., Fayyaz, A., Shahzad, A.: PostgreSQL Developer's Guide. Packt Publishing Ltd, Birmingham (2015)
49. Langtangen, H.: Python Scripting for Computational Science. Springer, Heidelberg (2009)
50. Hackeling, G.: Mastering Machine Learning with Scikit-learn. Packt Publishing Ltd, Birmingham (2017)
51. Tietz, M., Nouri, D., Bossan, B.: Skorch 0.9.0 Documentation: A scikit-learn Compatible Neural Network Library That Wraps PyTorch. https://skorch.readthedocs.io/en/stable/. Accessed 7 Nov 2020
52. Bostock, M., Ogievetsky, V., Heer, J.: D3 Data-driven documents. IEEE Trans. Visual. Comput. Graph. **17**, 2301–2309 (2011)
53. Körner, C.: Data Visualization with D3 and AngularJS. Packt Publishing Ltd, Birmingham (2015)

54. Gandrud, C.: Reproducible Research with R and R Studio. CRC Press, Boca Raton (2018)
55. Panzarasa, P., Opsahl, T., Carley, K.: Patterns and dynamics of users' behavior and interaction: network analysis of an online community. J. Am. Soc. Inf. Sci. **60**, 911–932 (2009)
56. Hammer, L.: Guide: Analyzing Twitter Networks with Gephi 0.9.1. https://lucahammer.com/2016/09/06/guide-analyzing-twitter-networks-with-gephi-0-9-1/. Accessed 18 Jul 2020
57. Divakaran, A., Mohan, A.: Temporal link prediction: a survey. N. Gener. Comput. **38**(1), 213–258 (2019). https://doi.org/10.1007/s00354-019-00065-z
58. Blagus, R., Lusa, L.: Smote for high-dimensional class-imbalanced data. BMC Bioinform. **14**, 106 (2013)
59. Bolz, C., Cuni, A., Fijalkowski, M., Rigo, A.: Tracing the meta-level: pypy's tracing jit compiler. In: Proceedings of the 4th Workshop on the Implementation, Compilation, Optimization of Object-Oriented Languages and Programming Systems (ICOOOLPS '09), pp. 18–25. Association for Computing Machinery, New York (2009)

Crowd Analysts vs. Institutional Analysts – A Comparative Study on Content and Opinion

Steffen Bankamp[(✉)], Nicole Neuss, and Jan Muntermann

Chair of Electronic Finance and Digital Markets, University of Goettingen, Goettingen, Germany
{steffen.bankamp,nicole.neuss}@uni-goettingen.de,
muntermann@wiwi.uni-goettingen.de

Abstract. The ongoing digital transformation shapes the world of information discovery and dissemination for investment decisions. Social investment platforms offer the possibility for non-professionals to publish financial analyst reports on company development and earnings forecast and give investment recommendations similar to those provided by traditional sell-side analysts. This phenomenon of "crowd analyst reports" has been found to provide an adequate alternative for non-professional investors. In this study, we examine the informational value of these crowd analyst reports regarding their timeliness in publishing and their originality as for content and opinion. Our findings suggest that crowd analysts strongly rely on previously published institutional reports. Therefore, crowd analysts do not pose a threat to institutional analysts at this time, however, they provide a more accessible information basis and improve decision-making for individual investors.

Keywords: Social investment platforms · Social media · Crowd analysts · Financial analysts · Natural language processing

1 Introduction

In this paper, we examine the information dissemination role of financial analyst reports made available by non-professional "crowd" analysts on social investment platforms compared to institutional reports, issued by professional sell-side financial analysts. The number of crowd analyst reports has increased in recent years and research has only just started to investigate these information intermediaries [1–3]. We investigate how content and expressed opinion of crowd and institutional analyst reports are related to each other. We also investigate to what extent and how fast both report types incorporate up-to-date information.

The emergence of crowd analysts is a relatively new phenomenon, creating "additional content that adds to or otherwise affects the information content of firm disclosures […] as a result of changes in technology and the media" [4]. Their analyses are made available to other market participants via social investment platforms. These platforms allow crowd analysts to publish their reports, analyses, interpretations, or recommendations. In contrast to institutional analyst reports, the information published on these platforms is also available to non-professional investors who cannot afford institutional reports, as subscriptions often cost several thousand dollars per user [5–7].

We therefore ask the following overall research question: What is the role of crowd analysts within the market of financial information intermediaries? Previous studies have come to different conclusions on this question. While Drake et al. [8] see crowd analysts as a threat to the business of institutional analysts, Kommel et al. [9] cannot confirm this. In contrast to these prior studies, our study examines both kinds of reports (institutional and crowd) on a textual level. This will allow us to gain a deeper insight into the kind of content these two report types bring to the market. This sheds light on the informational contribution crowd reports can provide for investors. With this study, we also contribute to the literature of the changing environment of financial analysts in general, as crowd analysts emerge as a new phenomenon in the age of social media and platform services.

We analyze 7,836 company-related analyst reports from a social investment platform of all companies listed in the Dow Jones Industrial Average (DJIA) between 2015 and 2019. These reports are compared to 24,606 institutional reports for the same companies and time period. Further, we use 730 conference call (CC) transcripts of these companies to identify important news keywords discussed in the CCs and examine whether institutional and crowd analysts took up these keywords. For examining similarities between the institutional and crowd analyst reports, we use TF-IDF-based cosine similarity [10]. Our empirical results show that crowd analysts provide similar information as institutional analysts, however, with a time lag of a few days.

This paper is structured as follows: Firstly, we provide a theoretical background on traditional financial analysts and crowd analysts. Based on this, we develop research questions and hypotheses and explain the methodological background. This is followed by a description of the dataset and its pre-processing. A detailed description of our analysis and our empirical results are presented afterward. Within the discussion section, we provide further interpretations of our results. The paper closes with a conclusion and an outline of possible directions for future research.

2 Theoretical Background

2.1 Institutional Analysts

According to New Institutional Economics, the existence of financial analysts is justified by the demand of information intermediaries reducing information asymmetries between market participants, precisely between managers possessing insider information and investors without access to this information [11, 12]. The role of traditional financial analysts has been examined in depth by existing literature. In their role as information intermediaries, they create information by discovery and interpretation. They reduce the asymmetry by disseminating information, thus making it available to (potential) investors and reducing information asymmetry [13–15]. This role is particularly relevant at times when companies publish financial earnings and it reduces the time to information incorporation at the financial markets, which in turn improves market efficiency [13, 14, 16]. Sell-side institutional analysts are often employed in brokerage firms, research institutes, or investment banks. Brokerage firms and research institutes are usually commissioned to produce analyst reports [17].

Institutional analyst reports are characterized by analyzing information on the financial and earnings position of companies and macro- and microeconomic factors and pass on information interpretations in order to facilitate better decisions [18]. Assumingly, financial analysts have privileged access to non-public company information, why their information is considered particularly relevant [14]. A traditional analyst report contains an earnings forecast, a stock price target, and a recommendation about buying, holding or selling the financial instrument, as well as arguments to support the recommendation [18]. A substantial share of all analyst reports is published in direct conjunction or shortly after a firm's CC, often adopting and disseminating the CCs' content and providing a related interpretation [19]. CCs are quarterly meetings of the firm's management and analysts to discuss the firm's development and answer questions of analysts.

2.2 Crowd Analysts

Similar to institutional analyst reports, crowd analyst reports usually provide investors with an earnings forecast and a recommendation about the company's stock, fulfilling an information dissemination role [3]. The main difference to traditional analyst reports lies in the audience, that are, mainly private investors. Most of the analysts providing reports on investment platforms are non-professionals. The author collective of social investment platforms also contains investment professionals and experienced individuals from the financial sector conducting the research in their free time [20].

In recent years, the literature has started to investigate the phenomenon of crowd analysts. Chen et al. [1] find that non-institutional crowd analyst reports can be used to predict stock price developments and earnings surprises. Similar results can be found for the crowd's earnings forecasts, even stronger when the contributing crowd is larger [2]. The existence of crowd reports also helps investors to mitigate a negative bias in institutional reports, improving the prediction of earnings surprises [21]. A recent study supports the growing relevance of crowd analysts, finding that bearish recommendations provide more accurate stock price prediction than recommendations in traditional analyst reports [3]. Campbell et al. [22] find that stock markets react with a price increase to articles with a positive tone, indicating their credibility. Farrell et al. [6] focus on the benefit for individual investors, that are provided with more and accessible information through the social investment platform, decreasing the information advantage compared to professionals, while liquidity on financial markets increases. This aspect can be supported by easier readability of crowd reports that at the same time provide a higher information density, potentially leading to lower costs of information processing [23]. Another strand of literature has examined the relationship between crowd analysts and institutional analysts. Crowd analysts and their confirmed effect on the accessibility of information to non-institutional investors have the potential of disciplining traditional analysts by lowering the incentive to publish pessimistic and too conservative short-term earnings forecasts [24]. The authors find the forecasts being more optimistic yet accurate. They also find crowd earnings forecast to be published much later than earnings forecast from their institutional peers. Drake et al. [8] investigate crowd analyst reports and their findings suggest a competitive threat through pre-empting traditional analysts' reports.

2.3 Research Question and Hypothesis Development

In the previous literature on crowd analysts, the main focus is dedicated to the evaluation of crowd analyst reports' accuracy and performance [1, 3]. Comparative studies that consider institutional and crowd analyst reports are rare and provide mixed evidence [8, 9]. These studies essentially compare the sentiment of crowd analyst reports with price forecasts from analyst databases (e.g., I/B/E/S). However, these studies cannot determine what information is provided by these groups of analysts and to what extent interdependencies exist between these groups in content and expressed opinion. Comparing crowd analysts and institutional analyst on a textual level has not been extensively covered in research. To close this gap, we compare the text contents provided by them. This is crucial for a better understanding of the role of crowd analysts in relation to their professional peers. Because after all, it is the text that analysts use to communicate their findings to the capital market.

To answer our overall research question, we split it into two sub-questions. As analysts function as information intermediaries and information discovery is one of their primary roles [19], the timely supply of relevant information to investors has to be fulfilled. This leads to RQ1.

RQ1: How does the capability of timely information discovery, creation and dissemination distinguish between institutional and crowd analysts?

Besides reporting in a timely manner, reporting new information is another element of the information discovery role, leading to RQ2:

RQ2: To what extent do institutional and crowd analysts provide related content and similar opinions?

Aspects such as a possible closer relationship to firm management and greater resources regarding financials and information processing possibilities establish a privileged access on the side of institutional analysts [19, 25, 26]. We assume that institutional analysts can analyze and publish new information faster than crowd analysts and therefore, contribute more to the reduction of information asymmetry. These advantages would justify the existence of institutional analysts in the context of New Institutional Economics [12], even though low-priced or free alternatives are made available by crowd analysts. We assume the topicality of institutional analyst reports to be higher and formulate the following hypothesis addressing RQ1.

H1: Institutional analysts provide more topical information to investors compared to crowd analysts.

Regarding RQ2 we assume a high degree of similarity in content and opinion between reports of crowd and institutional analysts. However, we assume that crowd reports are more related to preceding institutional reports than institutional reports to preceding crowd reports. As crowd analysts have fewer resources for information retrieval and information processing compared to their professional peers mostly employed by international brokerage companies, they have a strong incentive to rely stronger on the research conducted by institutional analysts and, therefore, disregard their own content and opinions.

H2.1: The originality of crowd reports content is lower than that of institutional reports.

H2.2: The originality of crowd reports opinion is lower than that of institutional reports.

3   Research Methodology

To compare the similarity of the reports' content, we use cosine similarity as a widely used approach in accounting and finance contexts to analyze documents of financial communication, e.g., analyst reports [27], financial product descriptions [28] or annual reports [29]. We apply this measure on a TF-IDF (term frequency – inverse document frequency) document representation [30]. The cosine similarity (1) is calculated between the word vectors A and B for each document pair. The cosine similarity is a measure for the angle between the vectors A and B [31]. The score can take a value between 0 and 1, while a high similarity score indicates a higher similarity between the two documents. The cosine similarity is especially useful for the comparison of sparse vectors (vectors containing many zero values) because it is robust against the extension of vectors by more zero values [31]. Since vectors of a term-document-matrix are typically very sparse, the cosine similarity is suitable for our application. The combination of cosine similarity and TF-IDF has proven to be a good measure for detecting documents containing new information in the area of novelty detection [32]. Since we are confronted with a very similar problem, we apply this measure.

$$Cosine\ Similarity(A, B) = \frac{Cross\ product(A, B)}{\sqrt{Cross\ Product(A) * Cross\ Product(B)}} \qquad (1)$$

To evaluate the opinion addressed within the reports, we use sentiment. In the context of finance and accounting research, measuring the sentiment provides insights on how the author of a document perceives corporate information such as financial news [33], annual reports [34], or analyst reports [35]. We use a dictionary-based approach, assigning each word within a document a positive, negative, or neutral connotation [36]. We apply the Loughran/McDonald positive and negative word lists developed for finance-related documents [37]. The sentiment score of a document can take a value between -1 and 1.

$$Sentiment\ Score = \frac{n\ positive - n\ negative}{n\ positive + n\ negative} \qquad (2)$$

4   Dataset and Descriptive Statistics

Our dataset is compiled from three sources. Institutional analyst reports as well as CC transcripts are obtained from Refinitiv Thomson ONE and the crowd analyst reports are from an online platform providing crowd equity research. The observation period of four years ranges from 07-01-2015 to 06-30-2019. To ensure that the observed companies are sufficiently covered by both professional and crowd analysts, we have selected the 31 companies that have been a constituent of the DJIA during our observation period as a sample. Our sample consists of 24,606 institutional and 7,836 crowd analyst reports written in the English language. Only reports are selected that cover one individual company exclusively. We consider the transcripts of 482 CCs that took place during the observation period. In addition, 248 CC transcripts taking place before the start of our investigation period have been indirectly included in our analysis as reference transcripts (further outlines on this in the analysis section).

To prepare the documents for further analysis, we apply standard pre-processing methods. We follow Huang et al. [19] and remove any boilerplate, disclaimer, tables and graphs from the analyst reports. From conference call transcripts we separately extract metadata (e.g., who is speaking) and content-related data (transcript of the spoken word). As the conference call transcripts have a clearly defined structure, i.e., the metadata and the actual content is consistently separated by the same text pattern, the separation between meta- and content-related data is done by applying a simple rule-based string processing. For all document types, we drop punctuation, figures, and non-ASCII characters and transform the text to lower case. Utilizing *gensim* phrase detection allows us to concatenate common multi-word expressions (e.g. cash flow $\geq$ cashflow). The text is tokenized to unigrams and then stemmed utilizing the Porter stemmer [38]. We further drop the respective company name and security ticker as well as stopwords (e.g. "and", "the"), and words with one or two letters, as these words will most likely not add actual content.

To get a better understanding of analysts' information, we analyze their research output. In Fig. 1, research output is plotted against the time relative to the companies' CC. The left plot is showing the number of reports, whereas the right plot is showing their length. Huang et al. [19] highlight the importance of CCs for institutional analysts. They found that most reports are published on the (following) day of the companies' CC. Our data confirm this observation. For crowd analysts, we see a similar pattern. However, the timeframe of increased publication activity is considerably broader. As the research output of institutional analysts drops to the normal level only four days after the CC, we observe increased publication activity until ten days after the CC for crowd analysts. Furthermore, the crowd analysts are less focused on the CC, as they publish relatively more reports between CCs than professional analysts.

The evidence from report length (after described removal of boilerplate and disclaimer) shows the inverted case. Reports published close to the CC are considerably shorter than reports published between conference calls. This effect is stronger for institutional reports, which are longer in general. This finding is less surprising, as analysts, that want to publish their reports on the day of the CC, are faced with notable time constraints.

5 Analysis

5.1 Information Topicality

To answer RQ1, we first have to identify analyst specific news. One approach would be to use public news streams and filter for news related to the corresponding company. This would give us a comprehensive collection of news, but it would not tell us whether a certain news item is important for shareholders, and thus for analysts. We would also

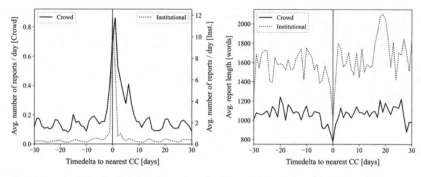

Fig. 1. Publication pattern and report length around CCs

oversee news, which might have an impact on the company but where the company name is not mentioned in the news article (e.g., macroeconomic or political events).

To overcome this issue, we chose an indirect approach to extract relevant news. We compare the corpus of CCs and extract words that have been discussed substantially within a CC (mentioned five times or more) but were not mentioned within the last eight CCs (two years). The CCs are usually held in the context of quarterly financial reports [39]. These words could either describe news that emerged between the current and the last CC or new information that is just released by the management. The last eight CCs are chosen to get a reference corpus that is comprehensive enough to filter words usually discussed within a CC. For this reason, we also use the transcripts of CCs conducted prior to the observation period's beginning. As the timeframe of the reference corpus ranges over two years, seasonal influences are prevented. The threshold of five mentions for the extracted keyword was determined after a manual review of the keyword lists. A low threshold results, especially in the extraction of misspelled words, whereas a higher threshold leads to important news being overlooked. A threshold of five balanced out these effects quite well. We also ran the analysis with different thresholds and the results remained robust.

To get a better understanding of the nature of the extracted keywords, we provide an example. From Apple's CC on the 1st of August 2017 the keyword "ARKit" was extracted, which referred to a platform for developing augmented reality applications previously announced by Apple during their 2017 developer conference on the 5th of June 2017. During the CC the ARKit was mentioned within the presentation and discussion section.

We only consider CCs happening from 12-31-2015 onwards (N = 421) to ensure that enough reports being observed before the respective CC. However, our results remain stable when considering all CCs. For 264 (62,71%) of the remaining CCs we could identify at least one keyword. We assigned analyst reports to these CCs that cover the same company and have been published within a timeframe of 360 days around the CC. A single report might be assigned to multiple CCs. For each assignment, we check whether the report contains at least one extracted keyword. If so, we labeled the specific CC/report combination as news adapted.

In Fig. 2, the proportion of report/CC combinations with existing news adoption is plotted against the time difference of CC and report. For clarity, the plotted data is aggregated on a weekly interval. The solid vertical line indicates the CC the keyword was extracted from. Just after the previous CC (dashed-dotted vertical line) the adoption of these words into the reports increases, as the news start to become public.

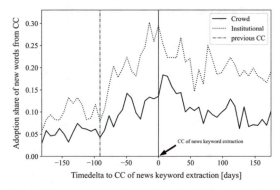

Fig. 2. News adoption of crowd and institutional analysts

This is identical to the presented example, as Apple's ARKit was announced before the CC where it was discussed. The spread in news adoption between institutional and crowd analysts widens, as the institutional analysts are more likely to cover the news.

For the reports published during the day of the CC (solid vertical line) and the following six days, we see that news adoption for institutional reports peaked (29.47%). During this time period of highest analyst output, only 13.55% of the published crowd analyst reports covered the extracted news keywords. χ^2 test proves this difference to be highly significant ($p < 0.001$). Crowd reports only reach their maximum news adoption in the second week after the CC (18.47%).

The results clearly show that institutional analysts can filter relevant news even before the CC from the continuous news stream to a greater extent than crowd analysts. This allows them to awaken investors' awareness regarding these topics, whereas crowd analysts take considerably longer and only reach their maximum news adaptation more than one week after the topic has already been discussed in the CC. However, the news adoption is by then still significantly lower than for institutional analysts before. This result corroborates H1 and further shows that institutional analysts satisfy their task of information discovery [19] better than crowd analysts.

5.2 Information and Opinion Originality

To evaluate the extent, crowd analysts provide similar information and opinion as institutional analysts and vice versa (RQ2), we compare each report with all reports of the opposing group published within a tight timeframe. To implement this approach, we build report pairs consisting of one institutional and one crowd analyst report as shown in Fig. 3. Thereby, only pairs are formed that were published within the *PairingInterval*.

The length of the *PairingInterval* has to be specified. The cosine similarity (1) between the TF-IDF vectors of paired reports is calculated. For the similarity analysis, we reduce our feature set by excluding words occurring in more than 90% or less than 0.02% of all corpus documents. These cutoffs are useful to extract only words with high information content [40]. The upper cutoff of 90% is applied to exclude very frequent words that do not add information to the text but are not already filtered out as stopwords. The lower cutoff of 0.02% (equivalent to six reports) filters especially wrong spelled words.

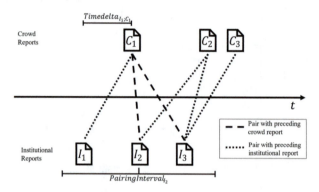

Fig. 3. Building of report pairs

The sample of report pairs is divided into pairs with preceding institutional and preceding crowd reports. Within each subsample, we group the pairs by their time difference (number of days between publication of paired reports). For each group, the mean cosine similarity was calculated and plotted in Fig. 4. The error bars indicate the 95% confidence interval of means. The highest similarity can be observed for same-day report pairs, which is not surprising. For this kind of report pairs, we cannot determine whether the institutional or the crowd report is proceeding. When looking at pairs with a time difference of one day or more, we observe an interesting pattern. For pairs with preceding crowd report (dashed line) we observe a steep decline in similarity just from the time difference of one day. However, if the institutional report was published first, the similarity remains relatively high up to a time difference of five days. For report pairs with larger time differences, the similarities of both groups are aligned again, and the effect is strongly reduced. This indicates that crowd reports tend to refer more to institutional reports than vice versa.

In order to deepen this analysis, we look at all report pairs together, which have a time difference between one and ten days (*PairingIntervall*: $[-10; -1 \& +1; +10]$). Report pairs published on the same day cannot be considered, as it is not possible to determine which report was published first. As already discussed and derived from Fig. 4, it is inappropriate to include report pairs with very long time differences as the effect is mainly observed between report pairs with a few days time difference. When combining all these report pairs as mentioned above, we get 71,011 report pairs with preceding institutional and 54,807 pairs with preceding crowd report. The mean cosine similarity across pairs with preceding institutional (crowd) report is 0.1684 (0.1585). The delta of 0.0099 is highly significant ($p < 0.001$). This gives evidence for H2.1 being

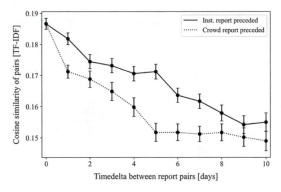

Fig. 4. Originality of content

institutional analyst reports more original in content than their non-professional peers. To provide an intuition for the absolute level of cosine similarity of 0.1684 and 0.1585 respectively, we compare it to the average similarity of report pairs within each report type (crowd and institutional). For crowd (institutional) reports the cosine similarity amounts to 0.2301 (0.2206). We already discussed the importance of the CC. To refine our analysis, we divide our sample into pairs published close to the CC (CC-timeframe: ranges ten days prior to ten days past the CC) and pairs published outside of this interval (Non-CC-timeframe). Pairs extending over both timeframes are excluded. Within the CC-timeframe, we observe an overall higher similarity (Table 1). This is not surprising, as the CC expose both groups to similar information.[1] The delta between the groups (inst. preceding / crowd preceding) is however 96% larger during Non-CC-timeframes. This indicates that crowd analysts make relatively greater use of information from their institutional peers in times of low information density.

In addition to the comparison of content, we also compare the authors' opinions expressed within the document. Based on the finance-related sentiment dictionary of Loughran and McDonald [37], we count the number of positive and negative words within each document and calculate the documents' sentiment polarity by applying (1). On average, we observe a more positive sentiment of institutional reports (mean polarity: +0.017) compared to crowd reports (mean polarity: −0.060). This finding is in line with the comprehensive literature on institutional analyst optimism [41].

We use the same matching applied for content comparison. To evaluate whether both analyst groups have a similar opinion regarding a specific company during a specific point in time, we calculate the Pearson correlation between the sentiment polarities of matched reports. We find a highly significant positive correlation between the sentiment polarity of crowd and institutional reports for all subsections (Table 2). Since we are interested in whether the institutional analysts or crowd analysts are opinion leaders, we

---

[1] The strong influence of the conference call on the content of the reports is also evident when calculating the average similarity between the reports and the conference call transcript for this period. Pairings between conference calls and crowd reports show a similarity of 0.2706 whereas the pairings between conference calls and institutional reports show similarities of 0.2912. These values are higher than the similarity between crowd and institutional reports.

Table 1. Cosine similarity between different group report pairs

Sample	Group	Cosine similarity	N
Overall	Inst. preceding	0.1684	71,011
	Crowd preceding	0.1585	54,807
	Delta	*0.0099****	
CC-timeframe	Inst. preceding	0.1711	44,615
	Crowd preceding	0.1643	30,493
	Delta	*0.0068****	
Non-CC-timeframe	Inst. preceding	0.1651	22,555
	Crowd preceding	0.1518	19,813
	Delta	*0.0133****	

***p < 0.001

examine the correlation coefficients' delta. Overall, pairs with preceding institutional reports have a significantly higher correlation, indicating institutional analysts to be opinion leaders. We apply Fisher-z transformation to evaluate the significance of the difference in correlation coefficients.

Conversely to the adaptation of content, we recognize that crowd analysts might be especially influenced by the opinion of institutional analysts during the CC timeframe. During this timeframe, the correlation coefficient is 57.1% higher for pairs with a preceding institutional report (0.1904) compared to pairs with a preceding crowd report (0.1212). Outside of the CC timeframe, we observe only a small, insignificant delta in favor of the professional analysts. To make sure that the result from CC-timeframe is not purely driven by the sentiment conveyed within the CC, we controlled for the CC's sentiment polarity by applying partial correlation [42].[2] Our results remain robust and the delta of the correlation coefficients during the CC time span remains significantly positive. Moreover, the adaptation of the opinion from the CC is significantly higher for institutional analysts ($r = 0.2374$) than for crowd analysts ($r = 0.0635$). These values are not based on the report-to-report pairing used above but by mapping the reports from within the CC-timeframe against the corresponding CC. If only reports published after the CC are considered, the correlation for crowd reports increased slightly but the correlation of institutional reports is remaining the same.

Our results suggest that the opinion of institutional analysts might influence crowd analysts during times of high information density. Thus, we can confirm H2.2 for the timeframe of the CC. During times of low information density, they rather form their own opinion. This is in line with the Social Impact Theory proposed by Latané [43],

---

[2] The correlation of the sentiment scores of the paired institutional and crowd reports is calculated after the influence of the sentiment from the conference call is eliminated from both variables. The partial correlation can be implemented by regressing the sentiment scores first from the crowd and second from the institutional reports against the conference call sentiment and then calculating the correlation between the residuals of these two regressions.

Table 2. Correlation of sentiment polarity between different group report pairs

Sample	Group	Correlation (Pearson)	Partial correlation†	N
Overall	Inst. preceding	0.1646***		71,011
	Crowd preceding	0.1087***		54,807
	Delta	*0.0559****		
CC-timeframe	Inst. preceding	0.1904***	0.1680***	44,615
	Crowd preceding	0.1212***	0.1220***	30,493
	Delta	*0.0692****	*0.0460****	
Non-CC-timeframe	Inst. preceding	0.1065***		22,555
	Crowd preceding	0.0924***		19,813
	Delta	*0.0141*		

***$p < 0.001$ † Partial correlation controls for the sentiment of the CC.

which states that the crowd size is positively related to crowd influence. The evidence of low adoption of CC sentiment by crowd analysts compared to institutional analysts can be attributed to the fact that the extraction of information from an analyst report appears to be much easier than the information processing of a CC transcript.

6 Discussion

Our results clearly show that institutional analysts are still intermediaries ensuring the timely publishing of new information. These findings are in line with Jame et al. [24], finding a delay of crowdsourced earnings forecasts. Crowd reports lack significantly in the timely provision of relevant news. This indicates the high relevance of institutional analysts for information dissemination, reduction of information asymmetry, and ensuring efficiency on capital markets. Not only do the results show a timelier adoption of news from the CC, but also the capability to identify relevant information before a CC. For crowd analysts the adoption of news is significantly lower, relevant information is reported later after it was already confirmed within the CC. Therefore, institutional analysts fulfill the function of information discovery [19] better than crowd analysts. To answer our first research question, it is apparent that crowd analysts take more time than institutional analysts to fulfill the information dissemination function. A reason can be the lack of resources, such as time and accessibility, or delayed quality control mechanisms of the platforms in opposition to institutional providers that aim to publish their services as soon as possible, while institutional analysts receive privileged access to information. A potential disrupting influence towards the financial analyst business cannot be confirmed in the question of timeliness.

Addressing the second research question on originality of content, cosine similarity results suggest that crowd reports provide similar information as preceding institutional reports significantly more than institutional reports to preceding crowd reports within a short timeframe of ten days. The ratio converges for longer timeframes. Referring to the analysis on timeliness of the reports, the results hint to crowd analyst reports not only being delayed in adopting and disseminating information but also relying on institutional analyst reports as an information basis. The division into two timeframes shows that this effect is lower during times of the CC and higher between CCs. In times of low information density when the firms provide no information, crowd analysts rely more on institutional analysts than in high information density times. Lower information availability outside of CC timeframes leads to higher costs of information procurement, incentivizing crowd analysts with fewer resources to rely on content previously created by institutional analysts.

Examining the opinion through sentiment polarities, we find that both crowd and institutional analysts adopt the sentiment of the CC to a large extent. This effect is stronger for institutional analysts. A reason may lie in the possibility of institutional analysts attending the CCs and contribute to shaping the opinion [44]. Not only in content but also in opinion, we observe crowd analysts adopting the interpretational tone of institutional analysts. This result is strong for the high information density timeframe. Interestingly, this observation cannot be made in times of low information density, indicating the creation of original opinions by crowd analysts. Another reason can also be attributed to the fact that information extraction from analyst reports appears to be easier than from CC transcripts. Our findings clearly show that institutional investors are still leading in content and opinion compared to crowd analysts, even though lower-priced or free alternatives are available to investors. This justifies the existence of institutional analysts in the context of New Institutional Economics [12].

Our study is subject to some limitations. To ensure appropriate coverage among crowd analysts and institutional analysts on the sample companies, we are restricted to an equity index with a rather small number of companies. We use a TD-IDF document representation to apply cosine similarity analysis on analyst reports. Other document representation, especially topic models, might enhance interpretability and add further assumptions and complexity to the analysis. Alternatively, mean word embeddings (e.g., word2vec or GloVe) or document embeddings (e.g., doc2vec) could be used as text representation. As a robustness check, we performed our analyses using meaned word embeddings based on pre-trained GloVe embeddings [45]. Thereby each document is represented by a 300-dimensional vector. The basic structure of the results remains stable.[3] The advantage of word embeddings is that the semantic similarity of different words is considered. In the area of novelty detection, however, the loss of word specificity in word embeddings based measures leads to underperformance compared to TF-IDF-based similarity measures on novelty detection tasks [46]. Numerous alternatives to the cosine similarity are available, but this measure's effectiveness has been demonstrated in practical applications despite its limited theoretical foundation. Moreover, it is less sensitive to document length than, for example, the Manhattan distance [32]. For this reason, we consider it appropriate to calculate the similarity of documents based on TF-IDF in combination with cosine similarity.

For the sentiment analysis, we decided to use a dictionary approach designed for financial contexts, widely used in analyst report research. It has no need for labeling

---

[3] The results of the sensitivity check are not included into this document but are available upon request.

that could be affected by the subjective opinions of the person conducting the labeling. However, for text mining in analyst reports, other approaches such as a naïve Bayes approach have been assessed as more accurate [35]. Furthermore, we cannot rule out the possibility that professional analysts are also enrolled on the equity research online platform and we, therefore, allocate institutional analysts' ability to a certain extent to the abilities of crowd analysts.

7   Conclusion

In this paper, we examine the information dissemination role of financial analyst reports made available by non-professional "crowd" analysts on social investment platforms compared to institutional reports issued by traditional financial analysts. In recent years, the number of institutional analysts is decreasing [47], whereas platform business models and social media are constantly growing. Non-institutional analyst reports are available for a wider range of market participants, especially individual investors, and therefore allowing a better basis for decision-making in financial markets. We examine institutional and crowd reports from 2015 to 2019 concerning their capability of disseminating new information derived from CCs and their similarity to each other. We find that institutional analysts are faster in disseminating news and relevant information. Leading in topicality, institutional analysts mainly use CCs for their analysis, while crowd analysts tend to rely on institutional analyst reports as an information source. This effect is more pronounced in times of a low information density between CCs. We also find that crowd analysts are influenced by the opinion expressed in institutional analyst reports during the time of the CC. In times of low information density, they disseminate a more individual opinion.

Our study provides evidence on the role of crowd analysts. First of all, findings on a more topical news adoption from institutional analysts (RQ1) indicate possible incentives for crowd analysts to follow the content and opinion of institutional analysts rather than conducting their own research. This presumption is precisely confirmed when looking at the relation of content and opinion (RQ2) between crowd and institutional analysts. Since the observed delay is only a few days, this does not mean that crowd reports are worthless. Rather, it shows that the vehicle of crowd reports can provide information to investors that is otherwise only available to institutional investors with high research budgets. The delay might be less serious for investors with long-term investment horizons. For investors with high investment volumes and short-term investment horizons, it seems reasonable to continue relying on expensive institutional reports despite the low-cost alternative of crowd reports.

Our research contributes to the literature on the role of crowd analysts and the value they can provide to market participants through social investment platforms in contrast to institutional analysts. We also provide a deeper understanding of crowd analysts' role within the capital market for individual investors, institutional analysts, researchers and regulators. Social investment platforms can use these results to derive measures on how to improve their information creation processes and objectives on how to become more independent from institutional business research. Crowd analysts should be encouraged to search for private information to create additional value for market participants. We also provide an approach on how to extract relevant keywords from documents such as

CCs without requiring a topic modeling approach. The results indicate that even though crowd analysts currently do not pose a threat to the market position of traditional analysts, there is some potential to grow in relevance, especially for less sophisticated and non-institutional investors. Through better accessibility and easier information processing of crowd reports for market participants, crowd analysts might shape the market of business research in the future.

References

1. Chen, H., De, P., Hu, Y.J., Hwang, B.-H.: Wisdom of crowds: the value of stock opinions transmitted through social media. Rev. Financ. Stud. **27**(5), 1367–1403 (2014)
2. Jame, R., Johnston, R., Markov, S., Wolfe, M.C.: The value of crowdsourced earnings forecasts. J. Account. Res. **54**(4), 1077–1110 (2016)
3. Jin, Y., Ye, Q., Gao, C., Xia, H.: The value of amateur analysts' recommendations extracted from online investment communities. In: PACIS 2019 Proceedings (2019)
4. Miller, G.S., Skinner, D.J.: The evolving disclosure landscape: how changes in technology, the media, and capital markets are affecting disclosure. J. Account. Res. **53**(2), 221–239 (2019)
5. Brush, S., Spezzati, S.: How do you put a price on investment research? https://www.bloomberg.com/professional/blog/put-price-investment-research-2/. Accessed 27 Nov 2020
6. Farrell, M., Green, T.C., Jame, R., Markov, S.: The Democratization of investment research: implications for retail investor profitability and firm liquidity (2018). SSRN 3222841
7. Gomez, E., Heflin, F., Moon, J., Warren, J.: Crowdsourced financial analysis and information asymmetry at earnings announcements. In: Georgia Tech Scheller College of Business Research Paper (2018)
8. Drake, M.S., Moon, J., Twedt, B.J., Warren, J.: Are social media analysts disrupting the information content of sell-side analysts' reports? (2019). SSRN 3456801
9. Kommel, K.A., Sillasoo, M., Lublóy, Á.: Could crowdsourced financial analysis replace the equity research by investment banks? Financ. Res. Lett. **29**, 280–284 (2019)
10. Tata, S., Patel, J.M.: Estimating the selectivity of TF-IDF based cosine similarity predicates. SIGMOD Rec. **36**(2), 7–12 (2007)
11. Frankel, R., Li, X.: Characteristics of a firm's information environment and the information asymmetry between insiders and outsiders. J. Account. Econ. **37**, 229–259 (2004)
12. Rischkowsky, F., Döring, T.: Consumer policy in a market economy: considerations from the perspective of the economics of information, the new institutional economics as well as behavioral economics. J. Consum. Policy **31**, 285–313 (2008)
13. Chen, X., Cheng, Q., Lo, K.: On the relationship between analyst reports and corporate disclosures: exploring the roles of information discovery and interpretation. J. Account. Econ. **49**(3), 206–226 (2010)
14. Frankel, R., Kothari, S.P., Weber, J.P.: Determinants of the informativeness of analyst research. J. Account. Econ. **41**(1–2), 29–54 (2006)
15. Lawrence, A.: Individual investors and financial disclosure. J. Account. Econ. **56**(1), 130–147 (2013)
16. Elgers, P.T., Lo, M.H., Pfeiffer, R.J.J.: Delayed security price adjustments to financial analysts' forecasts of annual earnings. Account. Rev. **76**(4), 613–632 (2001)
17. Brown, L.D., Call, A.C., Clement, M.B., Sharp, N.Y.: Inside the "black box" of sell-side financial analysts. J. Account. Res. **53**(1), 1–47 (2015)
18. Asquith, P., Mikhail, M.B., Au, A.S.: Information content of equity analyst reports. J. Financ. Econ. **75**(2), 245–282 (2005)

19. Huang, A.H., Lehavy, R., Zang, A.Y., Zheng, R.: Analyst information discovery and interpretation roles: a topic modeling approach. Manag. Sci. **64**(6), 2833–2855 (2018)
20. Chen, H., Hu, Y.J., Huang, S.: Monetary incentive and stock opinions on social media. J. Manag. Inf. Syst. **36**(2), 391–417 (2019)
21. Schafhäutle, S., Veenman, D.: Crowdsourced earnings expectations and the salience of sell-side forecast bias (2019). SSRN 3444144
22. Campbell, J.L., DeAngelis, M., Moon, J.R.J.: Skin in the game: personal stock holdings and investor's response to stock analysis on social media. Rev. Acc. Stud. **24**(3), 732–779 (2019)
23. Palmer, M., Bankamp, S., Muntermann, J.: Institutional versus crowdsourced analyst reports: who puts it in a nutshell? In: PACIS 2020 Proceedings (2020)
24. Jame, R., Markov, S., Wolfe, M.: Does crowdsourced research discipline sell-side analysts? (2019). SSRN 2915817
25. Clement, M.B.: Analyst forecast accuracy: do ability, resources, and portfolio complexity matter? J. Account. Econ. **27**(3), 285–303 (1999)
26. Clifton Green, T., Jame, R., Markov, S., Subasi, M.: Access to management and the informativeness of analyst research. J. Financ. Econ. **114**, 239–255 (2014)
27. Eickhoff, M., Muntermann, J.: They talk but what do they listen to? Analyzing financial analysts' information processing using latent Dirichlet allocation. In: PACIS 2016 Proceedings (2016)
28. Hoberg, G., Phillips, G.: Text-based network industries and endogenous product differentiation. J. Polit. Econ. **124**(5), 1423–1465 (2016)
29. Lang, M., Stice-Lawrence, L.: Textual analysis and international financial reporting: large sample evidence. J. Account. Econ. **60**(2–3), 110–135 (2015)
30. Salton, G., Buckley, C.: Term-weighting approaches in automatic text retrieval. Inf. Process. Manag. **24**(5), 513–523 (1988)
31. Han, J., Kamber, M., Pei, J.: Getting to know your data. In: Han, J., Kamber, M., Pei, J. (eds.) Data Mining, 3rd edn., pp. 39–82. Morgan Kaufmann, Boston (2012)
32. Zhang, Y., Callan, J., Minka, T.: Novelty and redundancy detection in adaptive filtering. In: Proceedings of the 25th Annual International ACM SIGIR Conference on Research and Development in Information Retrieval, pp. 81–88. Association for Computing Machinery (2002)
33. Liebmann, M., Hagenau, M., Neumann, D.: Information processing in electronic markets measuring subjective interpretation using sentiment analysis. In: ICIS 2012 Proceedings (2012)
34. Huang, X., Teoh, S.H., Zhang, Y.: Tone management. Account. Rev. **89**(3), 1083–1113 (2014)
35. Huang, A.H., Zang, A.Y., Zheng, R.: Evidence on the information content of text in analyst reports. Account. Rev. **89**(6), 2151–2180 (2014)
36. Loughran, T., McDonald, B.: The use of word lists in textual analysis. J. Behav. Financ. **16**(1), 1–11 (2015)
37. Loughran, T., McDonald, B.: When is a liability not a liability? Textual analysis, dictionaries, and 10-Ks. J. Financ. **66**(1), 35–65 (2011)
38. Porter, M.F.: An algorithm for suffix stripping. Program **14**(3), 130–137 (1980)
39. McKay Price, S., Doran, J.S., Peterson, D.R., Bliss, B.A.: Earnings conference calls and stock returns: the incremental informativeness of textual tone. J. Bank. Finance **36**(4), 992–1011 (2012)
40. Patwardhan, S., Pedersen, T.: Using WordNet-based context vectors to estimate the semantic relatedness of concepts. In: Proceedings of the Workshop on Making Sense of Sense: Bringing Psycholinguistics and Computational Linguistics Together (2006)
41. Brown, L.D.: Earnings forecasting research: its implications for capital markets research. Int. J. Forecast. **9**(3), 295–320 (1993)

42. Johnson, R.A., Wichern, D.W.: Applied Multivariate Statistical Analysis. Prentice Hall, Upper Saddle River (2002)
43. Latané, B.: The psychology of social impact. Am. Psychol. **36**(4), 343–356 (1981)
44. Cornaggia, J., Cornaggia, K.J., Xia, H.: Revolving doors on wall street. J. Financ. Econ. **120**(2), 400–419 (2016)
45. Pennington, J., Socher, R., Manning, C.D.: GloVe: global vectors for word representation. In: Proceedings of the 2014 Conference on Empirical Methods in Natural Language Processing (EMNLP), pp. 1532–1543 (2014)
46. Wang, F., Ross, R.J., Kelleher, J.D.: Exploring online novelty detection using first story detection models. In: Yin, H., Camacho, D., Novais, P., Tallón-Ballesteros, A.J. (eds.) IDEAL 2018. LNCS, vol. 11314, pp. 107–116. Springer, Cham (2018). https://doi.org/10.1007/978-3-030-03493-1_12
47. Lee, J.: Analyst jobs vanish as a perfect storm crashes into research. https://www.bloomb erg.com/news/articles/2019-12-19/analyst-jobs-vanish-as-a-perfect-storm-hits-wall-street-research. Accessed 27 Nov 2020

Design Principles for Digital Upskilling in Organizations

Ann-Kristin Cordes[(⊠)] and Julia Weber

University of Münster, ERCIS, Münster, Germany
cordes@ercis.uni-muenster.de, j_webe35@wwu.de

Abstract. The workforce of an organization plays a critical role for the success (or failure) of digital innovation; they need to have specific skills, which are required for creating the needed digital change. Therefore, organizations need to continuously upskill their workforce. Different ways to prepare and upskill the workforce for the digital future exist. However, a structured approach to guide organizations on how to retrain and upskill their workforce is lacking. In the light of this context, the research goal is to provide an action-oriented guideline in form of design principles supporting organizations to handle digital upskilling. To achieve this goal a hermeneutic literature review and semi-structured expert interviews as well as a focus group discussion have been performed to deduce design principles. Based on an applicability check proposed by Rosemann and Vessey [1] the usefulness and applicability of the resulting 15 design principles in organizations are validated.

Keywords: Digital upskilling · Applicability check · Design principles · Digital intelligence

1 Call for Digital Upskilling in Organizations

Digitalization accelerates the spread and use of digital technologies like cloud services, big data, internet of things, artificial intelligence, and smart workspaces. Widespread adoption has a significant impact on how organizations stay competitive in today's globalized economy. It requires organizations to adapt their established business models and operations to keep pace with the ever-changing environment.

One crucial aspect of such a change is that digital systems and human systems co-evolve and continuously transform each other. Companies like Facebook, Uber, Airbnb, and Alibaba were built to operate in a digital economy from the very beginning and can, therefore, be considered as pioneers in utilizing digital technologies to generate the highest possible business value [2]. On the other hand, companies that are not structured around a digital economy at their core need to go through a process of digital transformation in order to stay competitive, including their cyber and human systems [2]. For instance, companies like Henkel, L'Oréal, Voith, PriceWaterhouse Coopers (PwC), and Amazon run upskilling programs to equip their workforce with the new skills and mindset to tackle organizational digital transformation, making sure that both their technology as well as their human resources are endowed with what they need to thrive [3–5]. This

© The Author(s), under exclusive license to Springer Nature Switzerland AG 2021
F. Ahlemann et al. (Eds.): WI 2021, LNISO 47, pp. 509–525, 2021.
https://doi.org/10.1007/978-3-030-86797-3_34

pattern shows that there is a global call for digital upskilling initiatives, although many organizations report that they lack the digital talent, i.e. "someone who is proficient in at least one of the 24 hard digital skills and in at least four of the eight soft digital skills" [6, p. 1], to run these initiatives successfully [6].

To successfully realize digital upskilling, organizations need to continuously upskill their workforce [7]. Putting the focus onto the workforce reveals widely discussed challenges like the increasing talent gap especially for digital skills [6]. There are different ways to prepare the workforce for the digital future: "retrain, redeploy, hire, contract, and release" [7, p. 50]. The latter four, redeploy, hire, contract, and release seem to be less appropriate because of the existing talent gap [3, 6, 7], budget restrictions [8], and the effort to integrate them in the organizational routines. That is why retraining is becoming more and more a reasonable approach for digital upskilling. However, a structured approach to guide organizations on how to retrain their workforce is lacking.

In the light of this context, the research goal is to provide an action-oriented guideline in form of design principles supporting organizations to handle digital upskilling of their workforce. No specific target workers are addressed in this article since the target workers depends on the focus of the intended digital upskilling initiative of the respective organization. It could be the whole workforce or only a specific department. The development of the design principles is based on the conceptual framework for developing organizational digital intelligence proposed by Cordes and Rosemann [9] as that framework is formulated on a high level of abstraction and a guideline for organizations on how to apply that framework is missing. Therefore, the main theoretical contribution is the instantiation of Cordes and Rosemann's [9] organizational digital intelligence framework by giving recommendations in form of design principles for applying the framework. By extending the framework, it demonstrates the applicability of it in the organizational context. Hence, it contributes to the context-extension [10]. The managerial contribution of this article is to provide a tangible artifact that guides organizations dealing with digital upskilling, aimed at facilitating digital upskilling. To achieve this goal a hermeneutic literature review and semi-structured expert interviews have been performed in order to deduce design principles. Based on an applicability check in form of a conducted focus group discussion proposed by Rosemann and Vessey [1], the usefulness and applicability of the design principles in organizations are validated.

In the remainder of this paper, the research background is introduced followed by the research method. Next, the design principles are presented and discussed. The paper concludes with potential limitations, and highlights future research opportunities.

2 Theoretical Background

2.1 Organizational Digital Upskilling

Digital upskilling refers to equipping the existing workforce with the right digital skills that enable them to participate in organizational digital transformation by providing learning and development offers that add value to the whole organization. It is one way of creating the workforce of the future [11]. It is a means to give "people the opportunity to gain the knowledge, tools, and abilities they need to use and understand advanced and ever-changing technologies in the workplace and their daily lives" [11, p. 2]. The aim is to teach them how to acquire the mindset and the behavior to confidently succeed in a digitally-enabled surrounding [11].

Digital upskilling can be done in three ways, that can also be applied in conjunction: (1) raising the workforce's capacity of skills, by teaching them new or different skills, (2) increasing the level of the workforce's existing skills, and (3) hiring entry-level employees to develop their skill set according to the organization's needs [7].

Organizations are already offering learning and development measures, including upskilling programs to equip their employees with the necessary skills. However, a survey about the investigation of a digital talent gap in companies of 753 surveyed employees working in the USA, Western Europe, or India reports not being satisfied with the upskilling programs offered by their organizations [6]. Moreover, 48% of the interviewed employees feel that they are not given enough time to attend upskilling opportunities. This leads to the observation that senior management and human resources departments need to ensure that the initiatives provided to the organization are perceived as both more attractive and more effective by the workforce, and that front-line managers actively encourage their employees to participate. In addition, employees should be given sufficient time to upskill [6].

Continuously informing the workforce about new ideas and plans for the organizational future helps to keep employees motivated to strive for the organization's goals. Staying connected and investing into the development of current employees promises more commitment and acceptance from their side and facilitates the management of the changing circumstances to be beneficial for the organization [8].

In conclusion, digital upskilling is crucial for organizations dealing with digital transformation [3]. Due to the widening talent gap [6] and budget limitations [8], digital upskilling is a reasonable alternative [7] for organizations to remain competitive in an increasingly digitally enabled business environment [2].

2.2 Organizational Digital Intelligence Framework

Cordes and Rosemann [9] introduce a conceptual framework entitled 'organizational digital intelligence framework', which addresses the organizational digital transformation from a dynamic-capabilities-perspective with a focus on the human resources of an organization. They define organizational digital intelligence "as [...] the capability of an organization to assess, understand, evaluate, implement and appropriately use digital technologies" [9, p. 4].

The framework has two layers, as displayed in Fig. 1: the phase layer and the activity layer. The first layer consists of three phases that structure the process of developing digital intelligence in organizations. The phases are (1) digital ambition, (2) digital skills, and (3) digital literacy. The second layer contains more specific organizational activities, each related to one of the three phases [9].

The first phase of the digital intelligence framework, (1) digital ambition, aims at fostering a drive for continuous exploration of an organization's environment for technology-related opportunities to improve their business and build competitive advantage [9]. The activity, (1.1) scanning, refers to the effort of becoming aware of ideas for technology-driven change by searching external sources of information [9, 12]. The second activity, (1.2) shaping, relates to building on the results from the (1.1) scanning activity to develop and communicate a clear digital strategy along with the specification of required skill needs [9].

The second phase, (2) digital skills, intends to specify how an organization can develop the previously identified skills that are required to pursue the digital strategy and to provide an environment that enables the organization's workforce to acquire these skills successfully. The activity, (2.1) selecting, invokes the compiling of the desired skill portfolio. This means that an organization needs to identify the skills its workforce requires and to put it together in a selection of skills, that is a skill portfolio. These skills could already be available internally or could be taught through training offerings. The (2.2) structuring activity includes creating a learning infrastructure that enables the workforce to acquire the previously defined desired skillset. A well-thought-through learning environment and approach will help the workforce to create the motivation and the ability to acquire the required skills [9].

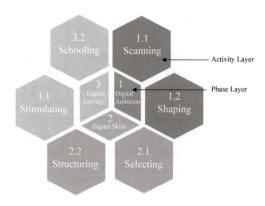

Fig. 1. Organizational digital intelligence framework: phases and activities [9]

The final phase of the organizational digital intelligence framework called (3) digital literacy, reflects a state of continuous alignment between the digital strategy and existing organizational operations. The phase includes the motivation and preparation of the workforce to pursue the organization's digital strategy and execute the needed change. (3.1) Stimulating includes inspiring and encouraging the employees to integrate the organization's digital strategy into their daily operations, making them develop their own ambition to strive for a digitally enhanced future, aligned with their organization's digital ambition. (3.2) Schooling is the second activity and comprises the actual teaching and acquisition of knowledge, and the learning process of the organization. During this activity, the workforce acquires the identified skills [9].

3   Research Approach

The article's goal is to define a guideline that helps organizations with designing digital upskilling initiatives. This guideline is presented in form of design principles (DP).

Design principles are a method used in design science research "to specify design knowledge in an accessible form" [13, p. 1622] and popular due to their compactness and instructing action-oriented character [14] and therefore suitable for the research goal, because the developed guideline should comprise key aspects of a complex project described as compact as possible and prompting for specific actions. Gregor and Hevner [15] consider design principles as an artifact, originated from nascent design theory, that is more abstract allowing a condensed description of what to do.

In order to develop a preliminary set of design principles, different research methods are combined. First, a hermeneutic literature review proposed by Boell and Cecez-Kecmanovic [16] and semi-structured expert interviews have been conducted. Moreover, the initial version of the design principles has been validated by conducting an applicability check in form of a focus group discussion [1].

In the context of this article, proceeding through the first circle of a hermeneutic literature review following Boell and Cecez-Kecmanovic [16] allowed an initial understanding of what is meant by digital upskilling in organizations, who is currently dealing with the topic in practice, and which organizations have already triggered such initiatives. The second circle was executed to identify major theoretical concepts that address digital upskilling in a narrow or broad sense and decide on methods for data collection, enabling the inclusion of practice-oriented information.

Qualitative data is gathered using semi-structured interviews, which allow a more detailed investigation around a set of fixed research topics. The interviews are used to investigate what recommendations can be given for organization when planning digital upskilling initiatives. To ensure a systematic and consistent procedure, an interview guide has been developed and used. It includes an introduction to the purpose of the interview and research, a set of central topics ((1) requirement definition, (2) initiative execution, (3) communication and change management, and (4) quality of initiative results) including predefined questions, anticipated probes and prompts, as well as closing comments. The interview questions were phrased based on previous knowledge, such as the central research goal, the findings of the literature review and the organizational digital intelligence framework [9, 17]. As interview partners, experts from the industry were chosen to improve the research relevance for practice. Each interviewee has a different organizational function and thereby introduces insights from different perspectives [17]. Each interview lasts 45–60 min to cover the topics defined in the interview guide in a satisfying depth [18]. The interviews are recorded and transcribed for a re-assessment at a later point in time. The content has been analyzed and embedded into the argumentation of each design principle [19]. Table 1 presents an overview of the three experts involved.

All experts interviewed are involved with the digital upskilling initiative at a German DAX30 company that operates globally in the business-to-business market as well as the business-to-consumer market. The organization is structured as a matrix organization with business units that each focus on one core business field of the organization and supporting corporate functions such as human resources, digital, finance, and IT. Interviewee 1 has been working for the selected organization for eleven years, with eight years of experience as head of the area learning and development. Interviewee 2 has been working at the same organization for 21 years, heading the collaboration topic for six years. The collaboration topic is part of the digital workplace team that is responsible for providing the tools and processes for the workforce to work digitally and initiate upskilling initiatives to enable the people to work within the provided workplace. Interviewee 3 works for the same organization as a business consultant on the topic of change management related to the introduction and use of IT-related solutions. This person can draw from experiences with upskilling programs at other organizations, mainly German DAX companies. These experts were selected due to the diversity of areas and functions within the organization that they represent. It allows a thorough investigation from different and potentially opposing perspectives.

Table 1. Overview of the Interviewees

Role of interviewee	Data collection method	Reference
Interviewee 1: Head of learning and development (Human resources department; HR)	Semi-structured interview	Interview #1
	Focus group	Focus group
Interviewee 2: Head of collaboration (Information technology department; IT)	Semi-structured interview	Interview #2
	Focus group	Focus group
Interviewee 3: Change management expert (Business consultant with psychology background)	Semi-structured interview	Interview #3
	Focus group	Focus group

The results of the literature review together with three semi-structured expert interviews provided the basis for developing a preliminary set of design principles for digital upskilling. This work was done in a deductive approach [20] based on theories and ideas from literature and statements from the experts.

The preliminary set of design principles was then tested in one focus group discussion, according to the applicability check approach by Rosemann and Vessey [1]. As recommended by the authors [1], a focus group discussion can be conducted as an applicability check. During the focus group discussion, the role of the researcher is to act as a facilitator, encouraging the focus group members to exchange ideas with one another. This research approach enables the researcher to get insights into people's experiences, opinions, ways of thinking, and social interactions. It also allows the focus group members to highlight aspects important to them [21, 22].

One of the objectives of the focus group discussion is to examine any major discrepancies in the results. For each potential discrepancy, questions were prepared upfront and outlined in a dedicated guideline. Possible comments and questions are anticipated upfront and incorporated in the focus group guideline as well. Three focus group participants and two researchers took part in the discussion. The participants were selected because they have experience with a digital upskilling initiative recently launched in their organization; each of them brings in a different perspective, as they work in different departments and roles (see Table 1). The focus group discussion was limited to 60 min and took place at their organization's site. Prior to the focus group discussion, the set of

14 design principles for digital upskilling has been shared with the focus group for evaluation, so that the focus group discussion could focus on significant discrepancies only. A question guideline has been created and served as an orientation for the person conducting the check. It included a rough outline of what is to be covered during the discussion. However, it leaves enough room for the participants to freely exchange their opinions and add further comments if needed. For the analysis of the content, the core statements of the focus group discussion were noted and incorporated in the argumentation for each design principle.

4 Design Principles for Digital Upskilling

In the following it is elaborated how each of the design principles (DP) is built based on the supporting literature and how they are informed by statements from the expert interviews, as well as statements from the focus group discussion. Each design principle is formulated in a format that allows a focus on action and gives the desired outcome as proposed by Chandra et al. [14]. Table 2 gives an overview of the design principles.

Table 2. Design principles for digital upskilling in organizations

Topic	Design principle
Principle of board sponsorship	**DP1:** Define one board member, who is empowered by the complete board, to drive the initiative and to articulate the digital ambition
Principle of dedicated budget	**DP2:** Provide budget, especially human resources dedicated to digital upskilling exclusively, to ensure capacities and commitment for executing the initiative
Principle of digital upskilling team	**DP3:** Form a digital upskilling team with diverse skills, topic and change management experience, and access to an organization-wide network to steer digital upskilling
Principle of vision and strategy	**DP4:** Define a digital upskilling strategy that is closely linked to the organization's digital strategy, to realize defined objectives and to achieve the organizational digital vision
Principle of stakeholders	**DP5:** Identify and involve stakeholders in the preparation phase who can potentially impede or promote organizational change to reduce misunderstandings and obstacles
Principle of planning and timing	**DP6:** Define a detailed planning, with milestones and timings, which allows for iterations of stages and activities, to prepare and execute the initiative within time and budget

(continued)

Table 2. (*continued*)

Topic	Design principle
Principle of workforce involvement in requirement definition	**DP7:** Consult market trends, scientific research, consultancies, upskilling experts, topic experts, and especially job-family representatives to define digital skill requirements and levels that reflect job-family-specific needs
Principle of digital skill level review	**DP8:** Analyze the digital skill set and level of each employee, from different perspectives, to get insights on the organizational status and the magnitude of upskilling
Principle of digital skill fit	**DP9:** Provide customized digital upskilling recommendations to each employee, according to skill level and job family, to offer personalized learning and development where required
Principle of learning system	**DP10:** Provide a learning system, with a comfortable atmosphere, a convenient toolbox, and suitable training content, to allow effective learning during work time
Principle of role models	**DP11:** Engage workforce representatives, who are well-recognized amongst their colleagues and can motivate them to participate, to act as role models, to establish a link to the workforce, and to reduce their concerns
Principle of benefit communication	**DP12:** Publicize successful change and personal benefits, things the workforce can relate to, to create interest and ambition in the workforce to improve their digital skills
Principle of communication and collaboration	**DP13:** Utilize diverse communication channels, for a regular exchange of information and knowledge with the workforce, to manage expectations proactively, and to foster organization-wide collaboration and organizational learning
Principle of monitoring	**DP14:** Define evaluation criteria, success factors and mechanisms, that can reflect the skills set and level of the workforce, to monitor the progress of the initiative and to ensure sustainable digital upskilling
Principle of interorganizational alliances	**DP15:** Form or enter interorganizational alliances, with other organizations who also work on digital upskilling, to exchange best practices and lessons learned

DP 1 – Principle of Board Sponsorship: *Define one board member, who is empowered by the complete board, to drive the initiative and to articulate the digital ambition.*
Within the organizational digital intelligence framework by Cordes and Rosemann [9] the responsibility for scanning the environment and articulating the organization's digital ambition is assigned to the top-level management of an organization [9, 23, 24]. Vahs [25] also sees the need for top-level management to be committed to the change, for it to be successful. An analysis of the expert interviews shows that it is prudent to have a board member sponsoring the initiative, for example, the head of human resources or the head of information technology (Interview #2). It requires someone, like the chief executives, who invites the workforce to participate in the initiative. It is important that the workforce does not feel forced to participate but rather participates voluntarily (Interview #2).

Further research shows that having the whole board support the organizational changes such as digital upskilling, can empower the coordination between the different areas in an organization [26]. This is also confirmed by expert interviews and the focus group discussion. The HR expert states that in addition to one board member who owns the initiative, the whole board should push the initiative and empower that person to drive the initiative (Interview #1). The focus group agrees that all board members need to generally support the digital upskilling initiative to leverage its full potential.

DP 2 – Principle of Dedicated Budget: *Provide budget, especially human resources dedicated to digital upskilling exclusively to ensure capacities and commitment for executing the initiative.*
The principle of dedicated budget fits in the order after (1.2) shaping, because it assumes that a board member sponsors the initiative (see DP1).

Burnes [26] argues in his model for managing organizational change that it is prudent to dedicate specific resources to change projects. To fulfill that need, budget is to be dedicated specifically to change management. Additionally, the analysis of the expert interviews shows that there is a need for drawing attention to the importance of dedicating budget to digital upskilling. All interviewed experts (#1 - #3) report that they are often restricted in terms of time and resources that relate to budget. Besides, like Burnes [26], the experts point out that the workforce cannot cope with the change during their regular work time, while still delivering the same performance (Interview #2, #3). Thus, capacities and commitment for digital upskilling need to be ensured.

DP 3 – Principle of Digital Upskilling Team: *Form a digital upskilling team with diverse skills, topic and change management experience, and access to an organization-wide network to steer digital upskilling.*
According to the experts, it is *"definitely important"* (Focus Group) to have a team in place that manages digital upskilling. Burnes [26] also describes the need for creating a team that manages the change. In addition, as elaborated before, people cannot permanently deal with change on top of their normal job (Interview #2, #3), which is why resources should be allocated to managing digital upskilling. The team responsible for managing the digital upskilling in the organization should be diverse in terms of competences, background, and organizational function (Focus Group). The team should be populated with representatives of the different employee groups who are affected by

the initiative, as well as topic experts from the different organizational areas (Interview #1, #2), a change expert, and a sponsor from the management board [26].

DP 4 – Principle of Vision and Strategy: *Define a digital upskilling strategy that is closely linked to the organization's digital strategy, to realize defined objectives and to achieve the organizational digital vision.*

Digital upskilling is a form of change, because it requires a transformation of the workforce [11]. Thus, it requires a strategy for its execution. Therefore, a clear strategy, concrete actions and a plan to execute them have to be defined to execute a digital upskilling initiative [9]. Each action can then be assigned to human resources who will be responsible for completing the action [26]. Vahs [25] remarks that it is crucial to communicate a clear vision for successful change. It is essential to set clear objectives, i.e., clearly defining what the outcome of the initiative should be (Interview #3). The focus group recommends that the digital upskilling team has to clearly define what should be accomplished by running the initiative (Interview #2, Focus Group) as clear objectives will provide a guidance [26].

DP 5 – Principle of Stakeholders: *Identify and involve stakeholders in the preparation phase who can potentially impede or promote organizational change to reduce misunderstandings and obstacles.*

Burnes [26] postulates that it is important to identify key people and groups within the organization who can promote or impede changes [9]. Johnson et al. [27] refer to those people as stakeholders, providing the following definition: "Stakeholders are those individuals or groups who depend on an organization to fulfill their own goals and on whom, in turn, the organization depends" (Focus Group). Further, it is important to identify the people in the organization who have an influence on the collective opinion of the people who surround them. It is crucial to involve these people and to make sure they understand the reasons and urgency for the planned change. If they favor the change, it is likely that the people on whom they have an influence also tend to favor the change. If they do not favor the change, the opposite can happen [26]. The expert interviews reveal that it is judicious to consider the following type of people as stakeholders for digital upskilling in order to reduce misunderstandings and obstacles: (1) the workforce as a whole, especially those who are affected by the digital upskilling, (2) the area representatives who are involved in the requirement definition, (3) the sponsor of the initiative, and (4) the board of directors (Interview #1; Interview #2).

DP 6 – Principle of Planning and Timing: *Define a detailed planning, with milestones and timings, which allows for iterations of stages and activities, to prepare and execute the initiative within time and budget.*

This design principle has the goal to raise the awareness of how important it is to have a planning that considers the defined objectives of the initiative and formulates a procedure that shows how to achieve the objectives [26, 28, 29]. The interviewed change expert also highlights the importance of defining a clear planning with milestones, timings, and allocation of the responsibility for meeting them to the digital upskilling team (Focus Group). It was said that it is difficult to define realistic timings for most of the activities, especially iterative ones (where the number of required iterations may not be known). But the publication of the trainings, timings, or rather deadlines can be a means to convey the urgency of the participation in the initiative to the workforce (Focus Group). Vahs [25] also states that a lack of understanding the urgency of the change is factor for failure of organizational transformation.

DP 7 – Principle of Workforce Involvement in Requirement Definition: *Consult market trends, scientific research, consultancies, upskilling experts, topic experts, and especially job-family representatives to define digital skill requirements and levels that reflect job-family-specific needs.*

Aguninis [30] argues from a performance management perspective that people who are involved in the creation of something are more willing to "support what they help create" [30, p. 172]. Wilson [31] states that organizational change could fail if the people affected by the change are not involved. Giving responsibility to the people will most likely make them more likely to support the change [26]. According to the interviewed experts, it seems most effective to visit team meetings, to talk to people personally, to accompany them during their daily work and – most importantly – to "listen to the organization" (Interview #2), granting the word-of-mouth high importance (Interview #1). But also the topic experts from areas like finance or marketing should provide their input, to make sure the skill requirements reflect job-families' specifics (Interview #2, #3). A job-family is a cluster of jobs with the same or very similar qualification profiles like salespersons. The digital intelligence framework by Cordes and Rosemann [9] addresses the need for defining a skills portfolio to deal with digital transformation in organizations in the form of establishing digital intelligence. The activity that comprises the skill portfolio definition is called (2.1) Selecting.

DP 8 – Principle of Digital Skill Level Review: *Analyze the digital skill set and level of each employee, from different perspectives, to get insights on the organizational status and the magnitude of upskilling.*

The knowledge about the current skill set and level of the workforce, enables the management to decide what other measures are necessary to digitally upskill the workforce. According to McKinsey Global Institute, there are five actions to equip the workforce with the digital skills that will be needed to handle digital transformation successfully: "retrain, redeploy, hire, contract, and release" [7, p. 50]. The key challenge for surveying the digital skill set and level of the employees is that it varies day-to-day (Focus Group). Ideally, an information technology system would analyze the skill sets and levels of the individual employees, providing customized development measures to each employee, but that is currently not yet possible (Focus Group).

DP 9 – Principle of Digital Skill Fit: *Provide customized digital upskilling recommendations to each employee, according to skill level and job-family, to offer personalized learning and development where required.*

The provision of customized upskilling measures makes it more likely that the affected people are more willing to make use of the offers and pursue the continuous improvement [26] of their digital skills. It is important to make sure the workforce effectively benefits from the digital upskilling initiative (Interview #1–#3). It seems reasonable to train job-family-specific skills, such as digitalizing content in the marketing area, or utilizing sales-specific applications in the sales area (Interview #2).

DP 10 – Principle of Learning System: *Provide a learning system, with a comfortable atmosphere, a convenient toolbox, and suitable training content, to allow effective learning during work time.*

External providers can provide training material for the basic functionalities of employed tools. When it comes to organization-specific content, area representatives may have to contribute (Interview #1). The HR department is responsible for preparing organization-specific learning and development offers (Interview #2). The training material for digital upskilling is often a combination of content provided by digital solution providers (e. g., Microsoft), organization-specific material provided by the HR department, and job-family-specific content provided by the job-family-representatives and topic experts (Interview #2). In addition, the workplace should be designed to inspire the employees to acquire new ways of working [11]. Furthermore, Cordes and Rosemann [9] emphasize to design a motivating learning environment for successful digital upskilling in the activity (2.2) structuring.

DP 11 – Principle of Role Models: *Engage workforce representatives, who are well-recognized amongst their colleagues and can motivate them to participate, to act as role models, to establish a link to the workforce, and to reduce their concerns.*

The principle of role models is intended to express the importance of supporters in the organization who are enthusiastic about digitally upskilling themselves and who delightedly motivate their colleagues also to upskill themselves. The term role models, "a person looked to by others as an example to be imitated," [32] was chosen because it is a commonly known and understood term and because it summarizes all other potential terms mentioned by the interviewed experts that express the same idea, such as key users (Interview #2), ambassadors (Interview #3) or gurus (Interview #1), freeing them from company-specifics or relying on area-specific knowledge. Key users, for instance, is a term that is often used amongst the employees of the information technology department (Interview #2). Cordes and Rosemann [9] point out the need for motivating the workforce to take part in digital upskilling, expressed in form of the first activity of the (3) digital literacy phase in their framework: (3.1) stimulating. The design principle of *role models* refers to those people in the organization who embody a role model function, inspiring others, independent of their formal role [26] and are willing to push change on top of their normal duties.

DP 12 – Principle of Benefit Communication: *Publicize successful change and personal benefits, things the workforce can relate to, to create interest and ambition in the workforce to improve their digital skills.*

Cordes and Rosemann [9] draw the attention to the need for motivating the workforce to upskill themselves, conveyed in the (3.1) stimulating activity of the (3) digital literacy phase of their framework. (3.1) Stimulating aims to raise the workforce's ambition to become digitally upskilled [9]. In addition to engaging role models for motivating the workforce's participation, communicating the benefits that the initiative brings to the employee's daily work and their personal life is an option [26]. Even though it is important to make the workforce aware of the benefits they receive from digital upskilling, it is a challenge to do so on an individual basis (Focus Group). Moreover, it can be supportive if the trained workforce sees that the offered solution works properly and can effectively improve their daily work (Interview #3).

DP 13 – Principle of Communication and Collaboration: *Utilize diverse communication channels, for a regular exchange of information and knowledge with the workforce, to manage expectations proactively, and to foster organization-wide collaboration and organizational learning.*

Communication is key for an organization going through a process of change [26]; communication should be bi-directional between the people affected by the change and the people managing the change [25]. It is important to provide and use channels for regular two-way communication encouraging employees to talk about and understand their ideas and concerns. The interviewed experts recommend making use of diverse communication channels, "to meet the people where they are" (Focus Group). This allows the change management team to better understand what drives the workforce and what fosters their willingness to learn. Keeping up the communication to the people affected by the digital upskilling initiative is advisable [31]. The focus should be on presenting features that are beneficial for them (Interview #2), connecting use cases to the different job-families to which they apply (Interview #3).

DP 14 – Principle of Monitoring: *Define evaluation criteria, success factors and mechanisms, that can reflect the skills set and level of the workforce, to monitor the progress of the initiative and to ensure sustainable digital upskilling.*

Change is an ongoing process that needs continuous management [26]. To assure that the defined digital upskilling objectives are achieved, it is required to monitor the progress of ongoing activities [26] and the skill level of the employees by collecting feedback [26]. Experience shows that training evaluation surveys are "happy sheets" asking questions like "did you like the training?" and "was the trainer nice?". Instead, a personal conversation may reveal more constructive feedback that can show whether people have actually understood the training and can apply their newly acquired skills (Interview #3). Therefore, for monitoring the progress of the organization, it is essential to maintain contact with the people by talking to the teams, joining their team meetings, and providing interactive question and answer sessions, because the progress of digital upskilling cannot be measured by only regarding hard facts, like number of emails sent (Interview #3). Therefore, it is crucial to "listen to the organization" (Interview #2). since (3.2) schooling focuses on the organizational learning process [9] that should be monitored regularly, to ensure the sustainability of digital upskilling.

DP 15 – Principle of Interorganizational Alliances: *Form or enter interorganizational alliances, with other organizations who also work on digital upskilling, to exchange best practices and lessons learned.*

The focus group discussion has crystalized the demand for interorganizational cooperation in regards to digital upskilling in organizations. In addition, one of the experts articulated strong interest in the results of further research regarding digital upskilling that is aimed at surveying other organizations about their approaches to digital upskilling, in addition to: "I sense that all the companies are at the same point. And all are struggling with the same things. So, if these people would exchange on the lessons learned, that would help. Because everyone is doing the same mistakes in this" (Focus Group). Furthermore, surveys published by consultancies prove that there are many organizations nowadays dealing with digital upskilling [33]. Therefore, it seems to be a strong demand for a knowledge exchange with other organizations, to learn from their mistakes and to generate best practices. However, even though the experts seem to be aware of other companies dealing with digital upskilling, their organization is not part of an interorganizational alliance on digital upskilling (Focus Group).

5 Discussion

5.1 Final Set of Design Principles

The previous section presented the final set of design principles. One challenge was to find the right amount of design principles and the appropriate level of detail each of the design principles expresses. The aim was to avoid overwhelming the audience with too many or too detailed design principles while ensuring to cover the most important aspects at a level of detail that is useful for people applying the guideline to practice. The set of principles was established through an iterative approach of adapting the content and formulation throughout the research.

The design principles that were developed are intended to be generic enough to serve different types of organizations while being detailed enough for practitioners to get an adequate overview of concrete actions required for a successful digital upskilling in their organization. However, smaller organizations who operate regionally or locally, or organizations that do not have a central human resources department and information technology department that have a corporate reach, may need a slightly modified set of design principles. For instance, organizations without a management board but a single director, would need to interpret the principle of board sponsorship as the principle of organizational head sponsorship. A reoccurring statement in literature and the conversations with experts also confirms that there is no one-size-fits-all-approach for digital upskilling in organizations. Therefore, the set of design principles developed in this article may need minor modifications for each specific use case.

The conducted research and the results of the focus group discussion emphasized that it is required to distill meaningful design principles, comprising all key aspects, in a single sentence. Still, the provision of further explanation seems recommendable, since the focus group discussion revealed that people might interpret individual terms differently, that simply cannot be avoided completely just in the phrasing of one sentence.

The design principles of role models and benefit communication could be combined because both are related to motivating the workforce to participate in the initiative. However, both aspects are important for themselves and were mentioned by the experts explicitly (Focus Group; Interview #1–#3). Therefore, they are listed as separate design principles to give each of them sufficient attention, especially in the first reading of the presented set of design principles.

The measures of motivating the workforce to participate in digital upskilling, focus on non-monetary incentives, such as higher reputation as a result of successful upskilling, gamification of the upskilling results, and clearly visualizing the added convenience for their daily work. The reported expert experience suggest that non-monetary incentives are more effective than monetary incentives. The decision on which kind of incentive to employ depends on the organizational setup, the culture, and the desired outcome of the planned initiative. Therefore, monetary incentives should also be considered as a reasonable means to get people engaged with digital upskilling.

5.2 Modifications of Design Principles After the Focus Group Discussion

As an outcome of the focus group discussion, minor changes in the wording of the following design principles for digital upskilling were made and one additional design principle was formulated.

The principle of benefit communication originally stated 'Publicize personal benefits and success to create intrinsic motivation [...]', but the first part was rephrased because the focus group agreed that it is difficult for the digital upskilling to generate 'intrinsic motivation' in the workforce for participating in the initiative. The change management expert argued that it is something very personal and hard to influence, and the other focus group members agreed (Focus Group). Therefore, 'intrinsic motivation' was rephrased to 'interest and ambition' that all discussants agreed on (Focus Group).

The design principle of workforce involvement in requirement definition does not further specify an additional boundary condition, because it does not seem to be adding value to the message of the design principle but rather prolongs it unnecessarily. Therefore, no explicit boundary condition was phrased because the principle was understood and perceived as important and applicable by the participants of the focus group discussion (Focus Group).

The principle of communication and collaboration was also rephrased. The focus group pointed out that the original wording excludes, for example, emails, from the scope of the design principles by referring to communication platforms. Since emails are a crucial part of the communication, the participants suggested the term communication channels instead of platforms. In addition, the focus group highlighted the importance of utilizing existing communication channels, to "meet the people where they are", that can be diverse and should be used regularly (Focus Group).

Even though the focus group confirmed that the developed set of design principles does not lack any key aspects and that it can serve as an adequate starting point for other organizations dealing with digital upskilling, the principle of interorganizational alliances was added to further enhance the final set of design principles. While the principle of stakeholders and the principle of workforce involvement in requirement definition, both addressing the cross-functional cooperation, were pointed out as vital design principle one additional design principle was deduced from the discussions. Especially the following statements led to the decision to enhance the set of design principles by adding a principle of interorganizational alliances: "I sense that all the companies are at the same point. And all are struggling with the same things. So, if these people would exchange on the lessons learned, that would help. Because everyone is doing the same mistakes in this" (Focus Group).

6 Conclusion

The aim of this article was to develop a set of design principles for digital upskilling that enhances the organizational digital intelligence framework [9] by providing guidance on how to apply the framework. The developed set of 15 design principles is supposed to be phrased generically enough to be applied in different kinds of organizations as well as sufficiently detailed to enable practitioners to get an adequate impression of what aspects to consider when designing digital upskilling initiatives in their organization. The guideline shall help employees who are in charge of designing and executing a digital upskilling initiative with an organization-wide reach.

As with every research, this paper is subject to limitations and leaves room for further research work. Future research could focus on developing a set of methods, along with decision criteria regarding the method selection, for each of the design principles. Each of the presented principles would benefit from a collection of methods developed to provide guidance on possible approaches to conform with the principle. Moreover, the perspectives of other organizational areas than those departments represented by the interviewed experts could be examined how they perceive digital upskilling. The clear demand for personalized upskilling recommendations suggests that further research could focus on developing a system or technology that can analyze the employees' skills set and levels and make recommendations based on that analysis.

Concluding, digital upskilling initiatives are a suitable approach for upskilling the workforce of organizations, enabling them to thrive in an increasingly digital future. The herein presented design principles provide an adequate guideline for designing and executing digital upskilling in organizations.

References

1. Rosemann, V.: Toward improving the relevance of information systems research to practice: the role of applicability checks. MIS Q. **32**, 1 (2008)
2. Gimpel, H., Röglinger, M.: Digital transformation: changes and chances - insights based on an empirical study, Augsburg, Bayreuth (2015)
3. Moritz, B.E., et al.: Navigating the rising tide of uncertainty (2020)
4. Stubbings, C.: The case for change: new world. New skills. https://www.strategy-business.com/blog/The-case-for-change-New-world-new-skills?gko=1482a
5. Wittenhagen, J.: Wir stehen am Beginn einer Lernreise. Digital Upskilling bei Henkel. Lebensmittel Zeitung (2019)
6. Buvat, J., Crummenerl, C., Slatter, M., Puttur, R.K., Pasquet, L., van As, J.: The digital talent gap. Are companies doing enough? (2017)
7. Bughin, J., Hazan, E., Lund, S., Dahlström, P., Wiesinger, A., Subramaniam, A.: Skill shift. Automation and the future of the workforce (2018)
8. Heath, B., Christidis, A.: Invest in people to best manage through disruption. Employee development may be a complex, long-term priority, but it's more effective than short-term responses to disruption. MIT Sloan Manag. Rev. (2020)
9. Cordes, A.-K., Rosemann, M.: Developing organizational digital intelligence: a conceptual framework. In: 28th European Conference on Information Systems 2020 (2020)
10. Berthon, P., Pitt, L., Ewing, M., Christopher, L.: Potential research space in MIS. A framework for envisioning and evaluating research replication, extension, and generation. Inf. Syst. Res. **13**, 416–427 (2002)
11. Stubbings, C., Sethi, B., Brown, J.: Talent trends 2019. Upskilling for a digital world (2019)
12. Albright, K.S.: Environmental scanning: radar for success. Inf. Manag. J. **38**, 38–44 (2004)
13. Gregor, S., Chandra Kruse, L., Seidel, S.: The anatomy of a design principle. J. Assoc. Inf. Syst. **21**, 1622–1652 (2020)

14. Chandra, L., Seidel, S., Gregor, S.: Prescriptive knowledge in IS research: conceptualizing design principles in terms of materiality, action, and boundary conditions. In: 2015 48th Hawaii International Conference on System Sciences, pp. 4039–4048. IEEE (2015)
15. Gregor, S., Hevner, A.R.: Positioning and presenting design science research for maximum impact. MIS Q. **37**, 337–355 (2013)
16. Boell, S.K., Cecez-Kecmanovic, D.: A hermeneutic approach for conducting literature reviews and literature searches. CAIS **34** (2014)
17. Wilson, C.: Semi-structured interviews. In: Interview Techniques for UX Practitioners, pp. 23–41. Elsevier (2014)
18. Robson, C., McCartan, K.: Real World Research. A Resource for Users of Social Research Methods in Applied Settings. Wiley, Chichester (2016)
19. Gläser, J., Laudel, G.: Experteninterviews und qualitative Inhaltsanalyse als Instrumente rekonstruierender Untersuchungen. VS Verlag, Wiesbaden (2010)
20. Saunders, M., Lewis, P., Thornhill, A.: Critically reviewing the literature. Chapter 3. In: Saunders, M., Lewis, P., Thornhill, A. (eds.) Research Methods for Business Students, pp. 58–105. Pearson Education, Harlow (2009)
21. Kitzinger, J.: Qualitative research. Introducing focus groups. BMJ (Clin. Res. Ed.) **311**, 299–302 (1995)
22. Nyumba, T.O., Wilson, K., Derrick, C.J., Mukherjee, N.: The use of focus group discussion methodology: insights from two decades of application in conservation. Methods Ecol. Evol. **9**, 20–32 (2018)
23. Teece, D.J., Pisano, G., Shuen, A.: Dyn. Capabil. Strateg. Manag. **18**, 509–533 (1997)
24. Teece, D.J.: Dynamic capabilities as (workable) management systems theory. J. Manag. Organ. **24**, 359–368 (2018)
25. Vahs, D.: Organisation. Ein Lehr- und Managementbuch. Schäffer-Poeschel, Stuttgart (2012)
26. Burnes, B.: Managing Change. Pearson Educación, Harlow (2004)
27. Johnson, G., Scholes, K., Whittington, R.: Exploring Corporate Strategy. Prentice Hall, Harlow (2009)
28. Kotter, J.P.: Leading change: why transformation efforts fail. Harvard Bus. Rev. 57–67 (1995)
29. PMI: A Guide to the Project Management Body of Knowledge (PMBOK Guide). PMI, Newtown Square (2008)
30. Aguinis, H.: Performance Management. Pearson, Boston (2013)
31. Wilson, J.P.: Human Resource Development. Learning & Training for Individuals & Organizations. Kogan Page, London (2005)
32. LEXICO: Role Model—Meaning of Role Model by Lexico. https://www.lexico.com/definition/role_model
33. Sethi, B., Stubbings, C.: Upskill my workforce for the digital world. https://www.pwc.com/gx/en/services/people-organisation/upskill-my-workforce-for-the-digital-world.html

Student Track

Introduction to the WI2021 Track: Student Track

Martin Matzner[1] and Thomas Grisold[2]

[1] Friedrich-Alexander-Universität Erlangen-Nürnberg, School of Business, Economics and Society, Nuremberg, Germany
martin.matzner@fau.de
[2] University of Liechtenstein, Institute of Information Systems, Vaduz, Principality of Liechtenstein
thomas.grisold@uni.li

1 Track Description

The student track has been an important part of the WI and MKWI conferences since 2016. Initiated by Jan vom Brocke from the University of Liechtenstein, the idea has been to promote and support aspiring IS students to gain first experiences in a scientific environment. Over the years, several IS students have used this experience as a springboard into the academic world and enrolled in PhD programs. Looking at this year's promising contributions, we hope that this trend will continue.

This year's student track, to be held at the WI2021 in Duisburg-Essen, attracted an exceptionally large number of interesting contributions. In total, 29 student papers were submitted to the track. We had submissions from various universities in Germany, Austria and Switzerland, including the *University of Heilbronn, University of Muenster, Friedrich-Alexander-University Erlangen-Nuremberg, University of Applied Sciences Aachen, University of Siegen, University of Innsbruck, Karlsruhe Institute of Technology, Technical University of Munich, Martin Luther University Halle-Wittenberg, Leuphana University Lüneburg, University of St. Gallen, University of Hildesheim, Chemnitz University of Technology, Technical University of Dortmund, OTH – Technical University of Applied Sciences Regensburg* and the *University of Stuttgart.*

As every year, renown professors from various German-speaking universities formed the program committee. They peer-reviewed the research works of students and provided constructive suggestions on how to improve their works. Students have been using these reviews to improve their works to subsequently virtually present them in front of a top-class academic audience.

The quality of the papers were impressive. Several reviewers highlighted the high relevance of the individual topics, the rigorous application of various qualitative and quantitative methodologies we well as the thorough presentation of the results.

Based on the review results, we selected 16 papers for a full presentation and 13 paper for poster presentations. As every year, the AIS chapter Liechtenstein will award the best student paper with 500 Euros.

2   Research Articles

The papers submitted and published in the Student Track span a diverse field of research topics. A first major cluster of works investigates organizational challenges relating to digital transformation. Rebecca Lueg and Paul Drews investigate how software development teams select roles. Daniel Heinz, Fabian Hunke and Gregor Felix Breitschopf aim at bridging between topics and concepts in the areas of innovation management and organizational resilience. Sandy Schmidt, Marius Voß, Hendrik Wache, Sarah Hönigsberg and Barabara Dinter explore how value co-creation in SME networks can be improved by using digital technology. Céline Madeleine Aldenhoven, Dominik Korbinian Brosch, Barbara Prommegger and Helmut Krcmar compare the skill sets requested for agile positions in the US and in Germany.

Three publications focus on digital services and digital (industrial) platforms. Jan Abendroth, Lara Riefle and Carina Benz created a taxonomy of B2B co-creation platforms. Christoff Schaub, Matthias Hille, Johannes Schulze and Freimut Bodendorf describe their implementation of a decision support system that assists business developers in creating smart services in the construction industry. Corinna Zarnescu and Sebastian Dunzer present their ontology for platform ecosystems.

Three of the accepted articles relate to the topic areas smart city and society. Michael René Schulte, Lukas-Walter Thiée, Jonas Scharfenberger and Burkhardt Funk suggest an approach for tracking parking lot availability using object recognition and neural networks. Coralie Werkmeister, Thorsten Schoormann and Ralf Knackstedt examine the extent to which carpooling can be nudged using the prototype of a mobility application. Anna Katharina Frische, Julia Felicitas Kirchner, Caroline Pawlowski, Sebastian Halsbenning and Jörg Becker derive design principles for public warning systems in view of federal structures.

Two papers explore the topic of data management and governance. Giulio Behringer and Marcel Hizli conduct a systematic literature review to define the term "data governance" more precisely and to identify interdependencies between different areas of governance. Cornelia Zeiler and Rhena Krause shed light on the role of master data management for succeeding with IoT applications.

Two articles are dedicated to Business Process Management (BPM). Frederik Wolf, Jens Brunk and Jörg Becker update and extend an existing framework for Predictive BPM by including the process context as an additional dimension. Karolin Bosch, Linda Mosenthin and Christian Schieder describe the current state of digitalization in dental practices in Germany based on expert interviews and survey data.

Finally, Raphael Weidhaas, Stephan Schlögl, Veikko Halttunen and Theresa Spieß present findings on how consumer choose media on video-on-demand platforms. Maximilian Schulte and Mathias Eggert collected data from different freely available sources like Twitter and used the information to predict the hourly bitcoin prices.

Conceptualizing Role Development in Agile Transformations: Deriving Design Goals and Principles for Agile Roles

Rebecca Lueg$^{(\boxtimes)}$ and Paul Drews

Institute of Information Systems, Leuphana University Lüneburg, Lüneburg, Germany
paul.drews@leuphana.de

Abstract. Design knowledge on agile role development is still nascent. Following the call for a theoretical and empirical investigation into the formation of roles in agile transformations, we elicited three design goals, six design principles and defined the pathway to achieving these goals. Our concept provides new insights into the dynamic and cohesive character of agile roles and adds role development as a key activity to the core of agile transformation. The results are based on a qualitative research methodology and design science research. We contribute to theory by providing a grounded approach for the situational development of dynamic agile roles based on design goals and principles, while practice can profit from the approach as our concept provides greater flexibility than the strict role definitions of agile frameworks.

Keywords: Agile roles · Agile transformation · Design goals and principles

1 Introduction

With the emergence of agile software development methods since the late 1990s [1–4], especially software dominated companies have an increasing interest in applying agile methodologies and agile frameworks. Scaling agile methods beyond the team level and conducting an agile transformation of entire departments or organization wide became a protruding and contemporary phenomenon [5–7]. Scaled agile frameworks like SAFe [8], Less [9], or DAD [10] provide guidance for conducting an agile transformation and maintaining an agile way of working, including suggestions and rules on how to apply certain agile methods, define artifacts, and describe roles and role structures. The understanding of agility as the ability to create change rapidly, embrace change reactively and proactively, and learn from change [11] is mostly applied to agile methods and processes. The development and evaluation of roles in agile settings remains a blackbox. We argue that agility also impacts the design of roles and calls for a concept that supports the contextualized development of roles.

Although nascent research and theoretical fundamentals exist, the development of roles in agile transformation processes is mostly neglected [12, 13]. Previous research outlines the precise role definitions in practical frameworks like SAFe [8] and Scrum

© The Author(s), under exclusive license to Springer Nature Switzerland AG 2021
F. Ahlemann et al. (Eds.): WI 2021, LNISO 47, pp. 531–547, 2021.
https://doi.org/10.1007/978-3-030-86797-3_35

[14]. However, the role transition in transformation processes are still unclear [15]. For instance, Moe et al. [13] postulate a lack of research regarding the process of forming teams and defining roles in agile settings. Initial research, however, provides implications of role development in agile and software development settings, giving insights into influencing factors like the system perspective [9, 16], and the product or artifact-orientation [17]. Jovanović et al. [12], emphasize the difficulties of role transitioning in agile transformations, specifically the different character of agile roles and the challenges of agile role development and transition. Besides the Information Systems perspective, organization theory and sociological concepts provide also approaches to the structuring of work (e.g. [18, 19]), and a starting point for the terminology of roles and their dynamic evolvement [20]. However, these concepts are predominantly suited for stable and predictable environments and traditional coordination practices. Finally, scaled agile frameworks, like SAFe [8], LeSS [9], and DAD [10], address the need for renewed roles and the formulation of roles as flexible blueprints, as a one-fits-all solution, but neglect the provision of guidance for role development and customization.

As no studies or frameworks explicitly guide the development of roles in agile transformations in conjunction with the underlying principles, we propose to link agile values to the development of the respective roles and thus lay the foundation for a critical reflection of roles and possible strategies for role development and refinement. Therefore, this study is guided by the following two research questions: (RQ1) *Which design goals and principles should be considered for developing roles in agile transformations?* and (RQ2) *How can a concept to develop agile roles look like?*

As a contribution, we identify design goals and principles for role development in agile transformations, along with a design concept and a theoretical instantiation. This research follows the design-oriented approach [21] and manifest on the empirical data collection and interpretative qualitative data analysis with the theoretical investigations of literature reviews, concepts, approaches, frameworks, and case studies.

Our presentation of research is structured as follows: First, we provide the theoretical background and the state-of-the-art research on agile transformations and agile roles, along with the investigation of sociological and organizational concepts. Afterwards, we introduce the chosen research methodology, followed by the presentation of the results. Subsequently, we conclude with theoretical and practical implications and an outlook on further research.

2   Theoretical Background

In order to continuously and proactively create change, and institutionalize the ability for learning and continuous improvement [11], organizations are scaling up their use of agile methodologies. Agile transformations change processes, collaboration procedures, roles, and mindset beyond the team level [5–7]. Research on agile transformation is gaining increasing momentum highlighting the challenging character of the adoption of agile methods and the thrive for more agility as the organization grows, and the dependencies and complexity between projects and teams increase [22].

The research area of roles in agile transformations is diversified and fragmented. Studies in the area of IS focus, for instance, on the importance of having defined roles and their effect on involvement, commitment, and personal responsibility, as well as on the need for ongoing refinement of role definitions [23]. Other studies outline the precise and diverse role definitions in practical frameworks like SAFe and Scrum [15] or focus on specific roles like the architect [24]. Although defining the nature of roles as self-organizing and enabling has become a hallmark of agile methods, less attention is paid to the development of agile roles. A first attempt to identify and develop adequate job descriptions and roles in modern software development teams was proposed by Downey [17] with the artifact-centric skill framework. The study depicts the software development process as mostly comparable between different companies and suitable for creating more adequate role descriptions based on the associated artifacts within a development process.

The theoretical investigation of the role concept in agile transformations extends the research towards interdisciplinary research grounds. The sociological role theory [20] investigates the organization of social behavior and define roles as a group of behaviors and attitudes that are considered to belong together. Role theory assumes that instead of mechanically playing the role, individuals shape and define the roles on their own, in order to interact in a meaningful way with other relevant roles [25]. The development of roles is ascribed to differentiation practices to sort and separate actions. In organizations, roles often face a discrepancy between role definition and role behavior.

In contrast, organization theory addresses roles from the starting point of building organizational structures. As the terminology of positions [18] or jobs [19] is more common, jobs represent the essential building block in organizations and are composed of stable bundles of tasks executed by individuals under administrative titles [26]. The development of organizational structures is part of the intertwined approach of organizational differentiation and integration [27]. Organizational differentiation addresses the question of the most favorable division and allocation of tasks [18], whereas organizational integration focuses on the coordination of tasks. Organization and management theory are criticized for being prescriptive and postulating to place well-understood tasks into stable jobs and therefore being mechanistic and narrow [26, 27]. More recent studies propose the concept of job assembling instead of job design, following the activities of organizing work that impact the allocation of tasks [26]. As today's work differs from the traditional model and is confronted with increasing dynamic environments, like ambiguous, team-oriented, abstract, and changeable work activities [28], studies emphasize the increasing need for taking a system perspective in order to structure tasks [16, 27], along with cross-functionalism and abstract role design [28]. Furthermore, job crafting [29], as physical and cognitive changes made by job holders, and the emergence of teams and group-based forms of working have gained increasing interest by scholars [30, 31].

The literature review of different research disciplines along with the multitude of roles named in scaled agile frameworks, and case studies (e.g. [32–34]), indicate the inadequacy of a one-fits-all approach for agile roles in software development settings. Studies show that role definitions used in the industry vary significantly from those role definitions defined in the frameworks and literature [15]. Role tailoring and role customization processes are needed to find the appropriate roles for the relevant project activities and goals. Additionally, the variety of required roles differs with the size of the organization and results in the merging of roles in smaller organizations or the implementation of additional roles in larger ones [15]. Organizational conditions in terms of problem areas and capabilities determine the resulting role definitions and structures, leading from well-defined and detailed role descriptions to abstract understandings of role responsibilities.

As studies named team set-up and role formation as one essential prerequisite for the success of agile transition and adoption [7, 35], a concept for agile role development and a clear definition of the role terminology is needed to support the individual adoption of frameworks and expand the possibilities of role assessment. Furthermore, we follow the research calls for strategies for organizational role structuring [12, 15], the exploration of the development of agile teams [13], and more practical guidance in agile transformations [36–38].

3   Research Method

To investigate and develop a concept suitable for identifying agile roles in agile transformations, the research process follows the implications of design science research (DSR) [39, 40]. The DSR methodology postulates a problem-solving paradigm and seeks to create new and innovative artifacts intended to solve an identified organizational problem. This study aims to design an abstract artifact without physical existence, but communication in the form of a concept [41]. The iterative design and development of artifacts facilitate continuous reflection and refinement of the incremental results [21] (see Fig. 1).

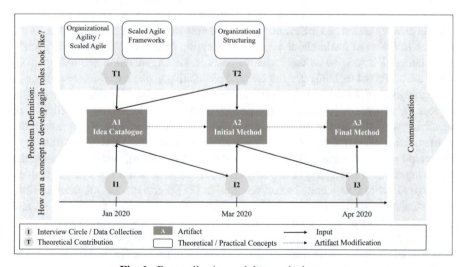

Fig. 1. Data collection and data analysis process

We base our research on primary and secondary data from multi-case organizational settings. Explorative in-depth interviews were conducted with eleven international experts in the field of agile transformation and scaled agile. The iterative conduction of the interviews led to the division of three interview cycles. The interviews were conducted in December 2019, January 2020, and March/April 2020. After each circle, the data was analyzed and processed. The last interview circle served as a feedback loop, where the designed concept was presented in its entirety. Finally, the company SoftwareCorp was accompanied in the exemplary theoretical application of the artifact, which enriches the collection of data for the final reflection and the rigor of the results. The primary data was collected with international experts from Germany, Netherlands, India, the United States of America, Ireland, Belgium, and Switzerland.

We collected secondary data to enable triangulation of the results, where possible. The secondary data is based on case studies and experience reports on agile transformation and scaling agile. The material was identified in the systematic process of in-depth literature research in academic databases AIS electronic library, EBSCOHost, IEEE explore, and Google Scholar. For the conducted searches, the following search terms were used: scaled, scaling agile, large-scale agile, large-scale scrum, scaling scrum, and agile transformation. The selected articles were analyzed for their richness of information to specific roles, role definitions, and role structures. The objectivity criteria excluded all cases which were not independent from the publisher of a specific scaling agile framework. Ultimately, six cases [32–34, 42–44] were identified, which provided enough information to investigate and analyze role definitions and structures. Additionally, sources in the form of three scaled agile frameworks, SAFe [8], LeSS [9], and DAD [10] were also included for best practices in agile roles and role structures.

The data analysis followed the inductive grounded theory approach [45]. The generated data was transcribed and along with the case studies transmitted into the analysis tool MAXQDA. In alignment with the grounded theory approach, the three coding stages, open coding, axial coding, and selective coding were applied (see Appendix for detailed information). Following, design goals and principles were derived from the coding and backed up with theoretical evidence. For the concept building, the core codes were put into relation which derived in a four-phased concept to develop roles in agile transformations. Finally, a summative evaluation approach, with a five-point Likert-scale questionnaire, was applied to receive comprehensive feedback. Furthermore, the evaluations validate the initial results, evaluate the utility, and the level of completeness and applicability [21]. The instantiation at our participating organization, SoftwareCorp, serves as a "proof-of-concept" for the value of the artifact [41] and assessed the originality and benefit.

4   Results

In the following, we present the (1) design goals (DG), as a requirement for the definition of agile roles and the design principles (DP), as the underlying logic of sufficient agile roles. The resulting (2) concept as a designed artifact is derived from the design goals and principles. Finally, (3) an exemplary theoretical instantiation of the artifact for the development of agile role definitions and structures is presented to establish its utility.

4.1 Design Goals and Principles for Agile Roles

Design Goals as Requirement for Agile Roles. Design goals (causa finalis) serve as meta-requirements to specify the type of artifact to which the theory applies and reflect the boarders of applicability [46]. We identified three generalizable design goals.

Agility requires organizations to have a customer-centric capacity for fast value creation [35, 47]. Generating customer value corresponds with a strong product focus [48], leading to a rethinking of structures and processes, as well as new ways of working [8]. Agile role definitions and structures demand a corresponding role designing logic, from creating output in different independent silos and strictly task-oriented role definitions towards outcome focus in terms of activities that generate customer value [17]. Hence, the first design goal requires a **customer value-based role development process (DG1)**.

Since the environment and the customer's needs can change continuously, agile roles should incorporate the ability to adapt to change. Allowing freedom of movement in role definitions and structure serves to facilitate the responsiveness of the organization and its ability to adapt [28]. Therefore, the second design goal calls for **flexible and adaptable role definitions and structures (DG2)**. Flexible and adaptable roles are therefore a prerequisite for agility, as, for instance, one expert noted that *"a specific job description is [...] not good for an agile transformation, so it doesn't help it is contradicting, even."* *(TPDT07)*.

Finally, **relentless improvement of role definitions and structures (DG3)** serves as the underlying premise, as agility unfolds its potential in turbulent ever-changing environments [49, 50]. SAFe named relentless improvement as one of the critical pillars to unlock agility [8]; also, LeSS suggests continuous improvement by experimenting and providing the organization capability for teams to improve and adapt [9]. Incorporating the premise of relentless improvement emphasizes the dynamic character of agile roles and postulates a non-mechanical approach to ensure sustainable evolvement of agile roles in disruptive environments [37]. One expert (TPAM08) emphasized the importance of relentless improvement, as inevitable impediments necessarily lead to deviation from the role definitions.

Design Principles as Abstract Blueprints for Agile Roles. Design Principles (causa formalis) describe the principles of form and function [46] for developing roles in agile transformations. We identified six principles that serve as an abstract blueprint of the requirements for achieving adequate agile roles.

In order to foster customer value creation (DG1), **DP1** implies **value stream-driven role definitions and structures.** Value streams represent the series of steps needed to create customer value and follow a chronological flow of activities [8, 48]. The underlying goal is to break down barriers between silos and departments to increase efficiency and minimize delays through dependencies and waste [48]. Also, in terms of role development, value streams facilitate the identification of specific roles, teams, and actions needed to process the value stream and deliver solutions, by fostering customer-centricity, and delivering value in the shortest lead time (DG3).

Agile settings face an increasing need for balancing the relentless focus on delivering customer value (DG1) with technical excellence. As noted by one expert, there is: *"the natural friction process between the developer who wants to build [the product] technically perfect, but never finishes, and the Product Owner, who wants to build the perfect product and has this delivery pressure."* *(TPTL06, translated)* that needs to be managed. **Responsibility differentiated role definitions and structures** as **DP2** manage the frictions within a team by splitting the areas of focus. The division of responsibility suggests no form of hierarchy [9]. Instead, it facilitates the most efficient localization and processing of knowledge and activities to achieve a common goal. Concerning the definition of agile roles, DP2 facilitates the design of dynamic role descriptions, as the differentiation of responsibility defines the scope of action for each area within one team.

DP3 targets **autonomous decision-making through aligned cross-functional teams in agile role structures**. *"Team autonomy is a fundamental design principle, [...] because we believe that it is beneficial to working in a faster and more efficient manner, when decisions are being made as far down the line as possible, so, directly in the teams."* *(TPTL06, translated).* Autonomous and flexible teams enable fast value creation (DG1,2) and minimize delay and waste, as a viable decision can be made independently [51]. Diverse and inclusive teams increase the likelihood of being able to act autonomously [13]. An implicit implementation of the premise of autonomy and cross-functionalism in role definitions and structures, support the embedding of an agile mindset into the foundations of the organizational structures of roles.

For relentless improvement (DG3) of the role definitions and structure with continuously changing conditions, **DP4** proposes **role definition and structure review cycles** as necessary routines in the development of agile roles. The routine in the form of regular reviews represents a valuable source of flexibility and change [52] (DG2). One expert proposed three factors in order to review the role structure: *"Are we solving the problem we want so solve, is somebody behaving in the expected behavior and [...] what is the perspective of the person himself."* *(TPDT07).* Continuous reflection encourages learning and improvement [8] and does not only promote a central review process of roles, but also recommend role inhabitants to review and redefine themselves as a form of 'role' crafting [29] and how they perceive other roles.

The execution of role review cycles is facilitated by **DP5**, which proposes **focusing on simplicity in role definitions and structures**. Simplicity, "the art of maximizing the amount of work not done" [4], postulates the prevention of unnecessary complexity. The application of this DP to agile roles prevent the paths to structural inertia (DG2,3). The implementation of simplicity is manifold. Simplicity can occur in terms of lightweight processes, in forms of knowledge acquisition, or manifest in personal communication between the team and the customer [53].

DP6 advises the development of role definitions and structures to **extend towards (product) abstraction level integration**. Organizations need to handle a lot of information and knowledge about the product in terms of requirements, on varying levels of abstraction and detail [54]. Agile roles need to tackle these abstraction levels from high-level conception to detailed operationalization and the subsequent responsibilities. Therefore, role definitions can be abstracted as the product requirements are assigned; for instance, to the product level, feature level, function level, and component level [54]. It simultaneously promotes a flexible approach, as the levels can change with the customer's requirements (DG2).

As a result of the defined design goals and principles, we define agile roles as a set of responsibilities and expectations of a person or group of people in a social system.

Agile roles possess the ability to create themselves, to optimize themselves, and to adapt dynamically and autonomously to constantly changing influences. Agile roles are characterized by an embedded agile mindset as well as by the goal of relentless improvement and self-reflection for the most efficient creation of value.

4.2 A Concept for Developing Agile Roles in Agile Transformations

The following concept represents the systematic application of the aforementioned design goals and principles. The concept, as an abstract artifact, shows how organizations can follow the systematic procedure of identifying and designing agile roles. The concept consists of four repetitive phases, which guide organizations through the individual development of roles in the agile transformation (see Fig. 2).

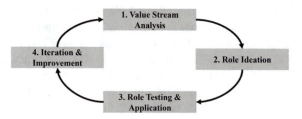

Fig. 2. A concept for developing agile roles

1. Value Stream Analysis. The identification of product value streams serves as the starting point for role development and depict the design room for role creation (DP1). Product value streams represent the activity flow and the core processes from a customer perspective, which are necessary for the creation of customer value. Identifying product value streams represents an essential step in rethinking and redefining the role structures, as this demands the construction of cross-functional and silo independent value flows. A high-level description of the activities reduces complexity (DP5) and fosters flexibility (DG2).

2. Role Ideation. Role ideation manifests in the orchestration of the activities to dimensions of responsibility (DP2), derived from a value and product-oriented perspective. The concept distinguished between the (1) product, (2) technology, and (3) flow responsibility dimension. Each dimension consists of a factual and integration area, which, in combination, represent the building blocks for agile roles in each responsibility dimension. The factual areas cover the main areas of content responsibility in the dimensions and serve as a minimum standard, whereas integration areas represent necessary integrative aspects. These are essential to align and coordinate all responsibility dimensions.

The Product Responsibility Dimension. The responsibility of the product dimension lies in the ability to represent the customer and adequately serve as their proxy. The factual coverage of the product dimension contains at least: product vision and roadmap, product requirements definition, product requirements prioritization, and product demonstration.

The Technology Responsibility Dimension. The technology dimension takes over the responsibility for delivering working and tested product steps that fit customer needs and generate customer value. The coverage of the technology dimension consists at least of: technical vision and roadmap, technical requirements definition, technical requirements prioritization, and technical development and operations.

The Flow Responsibility Dimension. The flow responsibility dimension acts as an enabler for the other dimensions, fostering an efficient way of working towards fast delivery and a customer value-based role development process. The flow responsibility dimension covers: agile coaching, process management, risk management, release or delivery management, and resource management.

The ideation of roles leads to generic role definitions. Figure 3 gives an example of three product-related roles. The gray marked bars above each factual area indicate the extent to which, for instance, Role III covers the factual area 'Product Requirements definition'. As some requirement definitions are predefined on the overall product level and apply to more than one activity, Role I on the product level covers the remaining responsibilities in this factual area on the higher abstraction level. The dashed areas show that the granularity of the responsibilities regarding requirement definitions vary depending on which team Role III is cooperating with.

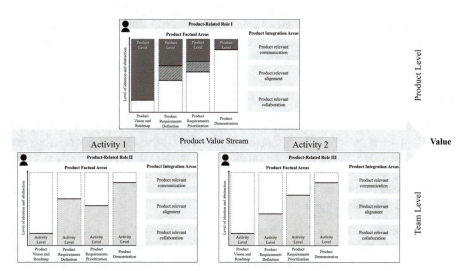

Fig. 3. Example of designed product-related roles

The design for technology- and flow-related roles follows the same systematic. The simplicity of these role definitions (DP5) balances structure with flexibility, as these definitions offer mandatory orientation and guidance while having room for adaptability (DG2). Furthermore, the orientation of agile roles towards different responsibilities and factual areas circumvents the definition of specifying and detailing tasks. The uniform role design approach alleviated the comparability of roles on different levels. It also enables the systematic and logic-guided assessment of possible consequences of role adjustments and changes.

3. Role Testing and Application. The concept suggests validating the resilience and feasibility of the agile roles with a systematic testing phase (DP4). The ideation of the agile roles is tested against three possible challenges. First, people-related challenges, like change resistance or lack of acceptance as, for instance, *"most people are used to more traditional job descriptions."* *(TPPM02)*. Second, operational challenges, like existing HR instruments, as one expert notes that: *"All the instruments don't fit there."* *(TPPL09, translated)*, or staffing. Finally, managerial or organizational challenges, like impact and scope of the transformation, or the re-orchestration of decision-making, as noted by one expert: *"making decisions is something you have to adjust to."* *(TPAM08, translated)*. Testing is a prerequisite for continuous improvement and constant adaptation to changing conditions and emphasizes the utopia of one-fits-all solutions, as these are strongly dependent on organizational resources and capabilities.

4. Iteration and Improvement. Finally, the iteration and improvement phase emphasize the ongoing development cycle and activation of the organizational capacity to develop and adapt roles (DG2,3) (DP4). The generalized nature of the design goals and principles allows the application of various role scenarios and coping mechanisms for occurring challenges. The importance of generalizable principles is emphasized by one expert, who emphasized: *"Don't change the principles, [...] only change the structure and the way of working, slightly."* *(TPDT07)*. In conclusion, the design of the responsibility dimensions provides a tool to make adaptations and modifications of role definitions and structures which are visible for the role inhabitants. It also facilitates the measurement and reviewal of improvement efforts.

4.3 Exemplary Instantiation

The theoretical application represents an instantiation of the artifact. SoftwareCorp is a software development consultancy, supporting the client in the development of a software developer platform and agile transformation. The product encompassed seven teams and over 70 team members. The instantiation shows how SoftwareCorp followed the methodological implications of the developed artifact, as well as what the theoretical result looked like (see Fig. 4).

1. Value Stream Analysis. SoftwareCorp focuses on its work on customer-centricity and the development of value for the user (DG1). The user journey designed from SoftwareCorp corresponds with the identification of the product value stream, proposed by the aforementioned method (DP1).

2. Role Ideation. SoftwareCorp introduced the product and team level for the initial creation of roles, to avoid complexity added by hierarchy (DP5). The abstraction levels (DP6) are differentiated into: user story, feature, and goal. This categorization results from the structure of the road map, breaking down goals into realizable features and feasible user stories. SoftwareCorp applied the suggested factual areas and linked the coverage to the abstraction levels. The factual areas cover in their abstractness the real scenario with its activities at SoftwareCorp. The role ideation phase leads to six generic role definitions for SoftwareCorp. Three on the product level and three on the team level, being applicable for multiple teams.

3. Role Testing and Application. SoftwareCorp evaluates and tests the developed role ideation against the real constellation in practice and the challenge areas mentioned by the method above (DG3). For instance, SoftwareCorp outlines that some people are not accustomed to the agile mindset and the way of working and therefore need more guidance in the form of more detailed role definitions. Additionally, also staffing represents a valid challenge as it is hugely influenced by the available budget and the most suitable staffing constellation. Finally, also resource utilization influences the designed role structure. The chosen constellation is the result of adequately covering the factual areas based on the skills, capabilities, and experiences of the corresponding resources. The implementation of these constellations leads to the open time capacities of certain roles and the coverage of more than one responsibility dimension by one role.

4. Iteration and Improvement. SoftwareCorp outlines that based on experiences, a dynamic role construct is more than necessary as, in reality, roles adapt continuously due to changes in required skills, expertise, or product context. Conscious role reviews increase the observations of role efficacy and adequacy (DP4), whilst still maintaining the focus on learning and improvement above control (DG3). Continuous role review demands generic role definitions that rest on responsibilities and goals instead of tasks.

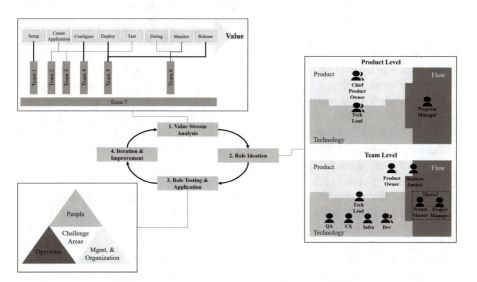

Fig. 4. Agile role development at SoftwareCorp

5 Discussion

Theoretical Implications. Our research provides several theoretical implications. First, the study extends the theoretical investigation of roles in agile transformations and follows the call for a theoretical analysis of agile role development [12, 15, 24]. This study goes beyond the current research by looking behind the fixed roles offered by frameworks and linking the agile values and principles to the agile role development process. The concept reflects the system perspective [9, 10], by incorporating the identification of value streams, customer-centricity, and changing external and internal influences in the development system of agile roles. Furthermore, this study addresses the proactive side of agile roles and the pursuit of relentless improvement, instead of designing roles in a traditionally reactive nature [18]. The proposition of generic agile role definitions serves as an individual blueprint for roles in an organization but are subject to the principles of relentless improvement and flexibility.

Second, the study addresses the inconsistency of the term 'role' and suggests a convergence of research disciplines to provide a holistic picture of the role phenomena. In theory, different research streams use either the term role [20] or the term jobs [18], whereas some scaled agile frameworks clearly distinguish between the two [9, 10]. Both terms have their advantages in either describing the tasks and the resulting organizational structure or the interactions between individuals that lead to structure and organization. Our data analysis suggests that the design of agile roles could not solely be explained by organizational approaches of traditional differentiation and integration [18], as these approaches are dominantly task-oriented. Moreover, classic integration mechanisms require some form of chain-of-command or treat the chain of command as the mechanism for integration [27]. Newer approaches, such as job design [26] or job crafting [51], also focus on the allocation of tasks, either as a process conducted by managers or other internal authorities, or as the power of job inhabitants to redefine the jobs themselves. The design of agile roles demands a broader orientation anchor than tasks. The derived method phases for role definitions and structures in agile transformations incorporates the idea of job design/assembling [26] as an interrelated process between problem-areas and institutional demands. As a consequence of interaction dynamics, our concept also incorporates the advantages of job crafting through self-reflection and refinement. Therefore, our study follows the idea of defining roles with responsibilities and expectations, rather than tasks and acknowledges the dynamics of interaction as a role structuring premise [20].

Third, the study contributes to the scientific research base in the form of design goals and principles and reflect abstract theoretically and empirically-validated guidelines for the development of agile role definitions and structures. As noted by Gregor and Jones [46], meta requirements aim to develop a design theory suitable for a class of artifacts, typified by these requirements. Therefore, the boundaries of applicability are defined. The design goals apply to the design of agile role definitions and structures and not to a single role structure in one specific organization. This component allows the comparison of new theories with similar goals and scopes [46]. Therefore, the study postulates that agile role definitions and requirements can be abstracted to design goals and principles and sheds light on the object of a role as a dynamic, flexible construct which enables value creation in an agile manner. Following this, the derived concept suggests a novel design of agile role development by applying the design goals and principles and thus postulating a modified approach for the structuring of work.

Practical Implications. Our study positions agile role definitions and structures within the context of agile transformations and reflects the matter-of-course implementation of predefined roles from frameworks. Surprisingly, research and practitioners still tend to focus on the optimization of processes and the implementation of new agile practices with the one-fits-all role structure. The investigation of transformation challenges and empirical case studies, however, suggest that many problems have their roots in people-related issues; including, unclear or overlapping roles (e.g. [34, 55]). We recommend practitioners treating agile roles as mutable and thus provide a tool for testing and improving roles in a systematic but flexible manner. Our concept suggests an all-participatory approach, combining the ideas of external 'role' design [18] and 'role' crafting [29] from the role inhabitants themselves. Therefore, the concept, along with the design goals and principles, provides a comprehensible design routine and distributes the wealth of information into managerial steps, enabling a focus on the incremental flow of improvement and optimization.

6 Concluding Remarks and Further Research

Our research contributes to theory and practice by developing three design goals, six design principles, and a concept that can serve as an underlying guideline for organizations to build adequate and flexible roles in agile transformations. The study explicitly links the understanding of agility with the concept of roles and deepens the understanding of the underlying strategies of agile role development and refinement.

The study is not without limitations. First, the data collection in software and IT dominated organizations limit the generalizability and application of the results in non-IT industries and departments. Second, the concept is imprecise in the explicit illustration of strategic imperatives, as the research has a dominant focus on the operational level. Furthermore, the DSR method is not non-judgmental, as the design of the artifact can be subjected by the desire to yield a specific benefit and reach a particular objective [40]. Finally, the qualitative analysis of the interviews is also naturally affected by the researcher's biases and assumptions [45], despite the strict adherence to the grounded theory methodology.

To better understand the implications of this research and the results, further research should address the applicability of the method and the design goals and principles in cross-sector investigations. Quantitative studies could measure the importance and prioritization in practical applications and determining the causes and effects between the design goals and principles and the corresponding role definitions and structures. Additionally, qualitative case studies could provide a broader picture of agile roles concerning industry and context factors. As the study could not rely on a grounded definition or conceptualization of agile roles; we recommend further field spanning and integration of the whole research field (Table 1).

Appendix

Table 1. Coding example

Selective coding	Axial coding	Open coding	Exemplary data
Role development challenges	People challenges	Change resistance and uncertainty	*"People say [...] this is not my job description from my employment contract that's why I won't do it." (TPAM08, translated)*
		People's abilities and capabilities	*"Minimal training in agile [...]and all of a sudden you need to act differently and the people in your team need to act differently and become self-steering and you need to become a servant leader while you are actually a command-and-control type that's a double difficulty." (TPOE03)*
	Operational challenges	Staffing and resources	*"It can be difficult depending on what resources (people) are available." (TPAD04)*
		Finances	*"The number of team members is strictly shaped by the budget." (TPPM11)*
	Man. and org. challenges	Decision-making	*"Here again one would have to look at how certain decisions have to be made (e.g.) with the management." (TPAM08, translated)*

References

1. Beck, K.: Extreme Programming Explained Embrace Change. Addison-Wesley, Boston (1999)
2. Schwaber, K., Beedle, M.: Agile Software Development with SCRUM. Prentice Hall, Upper Saddle River (2002)
3. Stapleton, J.: DSDM: Dynamic Systems Development Method. Addision-Wesley, Harlow (1997)
4. Manifesto for Agile Software Development. https://agilemanifesto.org/. Accessed 20 Nov 2020

5. Laanti, M.: Agile transformation model for large software development organizations. In: Tonelli, R. (ed.) Proceedings of the XP2017 Scientific Workshops on – XP '17, pp. 1–5. ACM Press, New York (2017)

6. Denning, S.: The ten stages of the agile transformation journey. Strateg. Leadersh. **47**, 3–10 (2018)

7. Gandomani, T.J., Nafchi, M.Z.: The essential prerequisites of agile transition and adoption: a grounded theory approach. J. Internet Comput. Serv. **17**, 173–184 (2016)

8. Leffingwell, D.: SAFe Reference Guide. Scaled Agile Framework for Lean Software and Systems Engineering: SAFe 4.5. Scaled Agile Inc., Pearson Addison-Wesley, Boulder (2018)

9. Larman, C., Vodde, B.: Large-Scale Scrum More with Less. Addison-Wesley, Boston (2017)

10. Ambler, S.W., Lines, M.: Disciplined Agile Delivery. A Practitioner's Guide to Agile Software Delivery in the Enterprise. IBM Press, New Jersey (2012)

11. Conboy, K.: Agility from first principles. Reconstructing the concept of agility in information systems development. Inf. Syst. Res. **20**, 329–354 (2009)

12. Jovanović, M., Mas, A., Mesquida, A., Lalić, B.: Transition of organizational roles in agile transformation process. A grounded theory approach. J. Syst. Softw. **133**, 174–194 (2017)

13. Moe, N.B., Stray, V., Hoda, R.: Trends and updated research agenda for autonomous agile teams. In: Hoda, R., van der Aalst, W., Mylopoulos, J., Rosemann, M., Shaw, M.J., Szyperski, C. (eds.) A Summary of the Second International Workshop at XP2019. Agile Processes in Software Engineering and Extreme Programming – Workshops. XP 2019 Workshops, Montreal, QC, Canada, pp. 13–19 (2019)

14. Schwaber, K., Sutherland, J.: The Scrum Guide. The Definitive Guide to Scrum: The Rules of the Game. https://www.scrumguides.org/scrum-guide.html#events. Accessed 04 Oct 2020

15. Yilmaz, M., O'Connor, R., Clarke, P.: Software development roles. a multi-project empirical investigation. ACM SIGSOFT Softw. Eng. **40**, 1–5 (2015)

16. Burlton, R.T.: Business Process Management. Profiting from Process. Sams, Indianapolis (2001)

17. Downey, J.: An artifact-centric method for creating software job descriptions. In: Lending, D., Vician, C., Riemenschneider, C., Armstrong, D.J. (eds.) Proceedings of the 2008 ACM SIGMIS CPR Conference on Computer Personnel Doctoral Consortium and Research - SIGMIS-CPR '08, pp. 12–21. ACM Press, New York (2008)

18. Schreyögg, G., Geiger, D.: Organisation. Grundlagen moderner Organisationsgestaltung: mit Fallstudien. Springer, Wiesbaden (2016). https://doi.org/10.1007/978-3-8349-4485-6

19. Cohen, L.E., Burton, M.D., Lounsbury, M.: Introduction: Bringing jobs back in. Toward a new multi-level approach to the study of work and organizations. In: Cohen, L.E., Burton, M.D., Lounsbury, M. (eds.) The Structuring of Work in Organizations, pp. 1–22. Emerald Group Publishing Limited, Bingley (2016)

20. Turner, R.H.: Role theory. In: Turner, J.H. (ed.) Handbook of Sociological Theory, pp. 233–254. Springer, Riverside (2006). https://doi.org/10.1007/0-387-36274-6_12

21. Hevner, A.R., March, S.T., Park, J., Ram, S.: Design science in information systems research. MIS Q. **28**, 75–105 (2004)

22. Dybå, T., Dingsøyr, T.: Empirical studies of agile software development. A systematic review. Inf. Softw. Technol. **50**, 833–859 (2008)

23. Dubinsky, Y., Hazzan, O.: Roles in agile software development teams. In: Eckstein, J., Baumeister, H. (eds.) XP 2004. LNCS, vol. 3092, pp. 157–165. Springer, Heidelberg (2004). https://doi.org/10.1007/978-3-540-24853-8_18

24. Uludag, O., Kleehaus, M., Xu, X., Matthes, F.: Investigating the role of architects in scaling agile frameworks. In: 2017 IEEE 21st International Enterprise Distributed Object Computing Conference (EDOC), pp. 123–132. IEEE (2017)

25. Mead, G.H.: Mind, Self, and Society. From a Standpoint of a Social Behaviorist. University of Chicago Press, Chicago (1934)

26. Cohen, L.E.: Assembling jobs: a model of how tasks are bundled into and across jobs. Organ. Sci. **24**, 432–454 (2013)
27. Lawrence, P.R., Lorsch, J.W.: Organization and Environment Managing Differentiation and Integration. Harvard University Press, Cambridge (1967)
28. Cohen, S.G., Mankin, D.: The changing nature of work: managing the impact of information technology. In: Mohrman, S.A., Galbraith, J.R., Lawler, E.E. (eds.) Tomorrow's Organization. Crafting Winning Capabilities in a Dynamic World, pp. 154–178. Jossey-Bass Publ, San Francisco (1998)
29. Wrzesniewski, A., Dutton, J.E.: Crafting a job: revisioning employees as active crafters of their work. Acad. Manag. Rev. **26**, 179–201 (2001)
30. Gully, S.M., Incalcaterra, K.A., Joshi, A., Beauien, J.M.: A meta-analysis of team-efficacy, potency, and performance: interdependence and level of analysis as moderators of observed relationships. J. Appl. Psychol. **87**, 819–832 (2002)
31. Kozlowski, S.J.W., Bell, B.S.: Work groups and teams in organizations. In: Weiner, I.B. (ed.) Handbook of Psychology, vol. 42, pp. 333–375. Wiley, Hoboken (2013)
32. Kalenda, M., Hyna, P., Rossi, B.: Scaling agile in large organizations: practices, challenges, and success factors. J. Softw. Evol. Process **30**, 1–24 (2018)
33. Paasivaara, M.: Adopting SAFe to scale agile in a globally distributed organization. In: 2017 IEEE 12th International Conference on Global Software Engineering (ICGSE), pp. 36–40 (2017)
34. Paasivaara, M., Behm, B., Lassenius, C., Hallikainen, M.: Large-scale agile transformation at Ericsson. A case study. Empir. Softw. Eng. **23**, 2550–2596 (2018)
35. Misra, S.C., Kumar, V., Kumar, U.: Identifying some important success factors in adopting agile software development practices. J. Syst. Softw. **82**, 1869–1890 (2009)
36. Fuchs, C., Hess, T.: Becoming agile in the digital transformation: the process of a large-scale agile transformation. In: Thirty Ninth International Conference on Information Systems, San Francisco, pp. 1–17 (2018)
37. Gerster, D., Dremel, C., Kelker, P.: "Agile meets non-agile": implications of adopting agile practices at enterprises. In: Twenty-Fourth Americas Conference on Information Systems, New Orleans, pp. 1–10 (2018)
38. Kiely, G., Kiely, J., Nolan, C.: Scaling agile methods to process improvement projects: a global virtual team case study. In: Twenty-Third Americas Conference on Information Systems, Boston, pp. 1–9 (2017)
39. Meth, H., Mueller, B., Maedche, A.: Designing a requirement mining system. J. Assoc. Inf. Syst. **66**, 799–837 (2015)
40. Peffers, K., Tuunanen, T., Rothenberger, M.A., Chatterjee, S.: A design science research methodology for information systems research. J. Manag. Inf. Syst. **24**, 45–77 (2007)
41. Gregor, S., Hevner, A.R.: Positioning and presenting design science research for maximum impact. MIS Q. **37**, 337–355 (2013)
42. Kim, S., Lee, H., Kwon, Y., Yu, M., Jo, H.: Our journey to becoming agile. experiences with agile transformation in Samsung electronics. In: Asia-Pacific Software Engineering Conference, vol. 23, pp. 377–380 (2016)
43. Paasivaara, M., Lassenius, C.: Scaling scrum in a large globally distributed organization: a case study. In: IEEE 11th International Conference on Global Software Engineering, pp. 74–83 (2016)
44. Gat, I.: How BMC is scaling agile development. In: Proceedings of AGILE 2006 Conference (2006)
45. Corbin, J.M., Strauss, A.L.: Basics of Qualitative Research. Techniques and Procedures for Developing Grounded Theory. SAGE, Los Angeles (2015)
46. Gregor, S., Jones, D.: The anatomy of a design theory. J. Assoc. Inf. Syst. **8**, 312–335 (2007)

47. Gunasekaran, A.: Agile manufacturing. A framework for research and development. Int. J. Prod. Econ. **62**, 87–105 (1999)
48. Womack, J.P., Jones, D.T.: Lean thinking—banish waste and create wealth in your corporation (1996)
49. Sambamurthy, V., Bharadwaj, A., Grover, V.: Shaping agility through digital options: reconceptualizing the role of information technology in contemporary firms. MIS Q. **2**, 237–263 (2003)
50. Overby, E., Bharadwaj, A., Sambamurthy, V.: Enterprise agility and the enabling role of information technology. Eur. J. Inf. Syst. **15**, 120–131 (2006)
51. Hur, W., Shin, Y., Rhee, S., Kim, H.: Organizational virtuousness perceptions and task crafting. Career Dev. Int. **22**, 436–459 (2017)
52. Feldman, M.S., Pentland, B.T.: Reconceptualizing organizational routines as a source of flexibility and change. Adm. Sci. Q. **48**, 94–118 (2003)
53. Santos, W.B., Cunha, J.A.O.G., Moura, H., Margaria, T.: Towards a theory of simplicity in agile software development: a qualitative study. In: Felderer, M., Holmström Olsson, H., Skavhaug, A. (eds.) 43rd Euromicro Conference on Software Engineering and Advanced Applications. SEAA 2017: Proceedings, 30 August–1 September 2017, Vienna, Austria, pp. 40–43. IEEE, Piscataway (2017)
54. Gorschek, T., Wohlin, C.: Requirements abstraction model. Requir. Eng. **11**, 79–101 (2005)
55. Dikert, K., Paasivaara, M., Lassenius, C.: Challenges and success factors for large-scale agile transformations. A systematic literature review. J. Syst. Softw. **119**, 87–108 (2016)

Organizing for Digital Innovation and Transformation: Bridging Between Organizational Resilience and Innovation Management

Daniel Heinz[1]([✉]), Fabian Hunke[1], and Gregor Felix Breitschopf[2]

[1] Institute of Information Systems and Marketing, Karlsruhe Institute of Technology (KIT), Karlsruhe, Germany
daniel.heinz@student.kit.edu, fabian.hunke@kit.edu
[2] Department of Accounting, The London School of Economics and Political Science (LSE), London, UK
g.breitschopf@lse.ac.uk

Abstract. Increased digitalization offers today's organizations novel opportunities to enhance value propositions for customers, but also poses significant challenges for traditional businesses. To navigate through the difficult process of digital transformation in this turbulent environment, organizations need to integrate successful innovation management practices and build organizational resilience.

In this paper, we propose a conceptual framework that bridges between these two constructs: We describe innovation management as the continuous activity of anticipating and responding to ongoing trends in an organization's environment through innovation, whereas we understand organizational resilience as the capability to adapt or transform an organization's business. By analyzing two illustrative cases, we find indications that a successful digital transformation is not possible without one or the other. Furthermore, we contribute key factors for building organizational resilience and showcase two examples of how to leverage organizational resilience by transforming business models through digital innovation and, thus, avoiding the innovator's dilemma.

Keywords: Organizational resilience · Digital transformation · Innovation management · Digital innovation · Digitalization

1 Introduction

The unprecedented success of modern tech-companies, e.g., Amazon, Netflix, or Uber, illustrates the impact of the ongoing wave of digitalization [1]. Novel business potentials challenge traditional companies to reinvent themselves by transforming their business models and internal processes to remain competitive in the digital age [2, 3]. The ability to detect relevant technological advances and to anticipate their business applicability has become a strategic necessity across industries [2, 4]. The continuous process of digital transformation requires companies to successfully integrate digital innovation management practices into their workflow [5]. The need for digital innovation challenges extant innovation management theory [6, 7] and requires research priority to lead the transition process from innovation management towards *digital innovation management* [5].

To contribute, we suggest organizational resilience as a mean to exploit digital innovation opportunities and organize for these temporal windows of opportunities to successfully navigate through the challenging digital age [5]. Organizational resilience describes an organization's ability to remain successful by undergoing adaptive or transformative processes when facing challenges and adversity. Furthermore, being resilient not only implies reacting to external forces, but rather creating the conditions to anticipate unknown but high-risking threats and, thus, allows them to stay in control and act flexibly and adaptively. In contrast, we see (digital) innovation management as a set of ongoing practices and processes to anticipate and respond to ongoing trends in an organization's environment through (digital) innovation.

This study addresses this potential linkage by asking the following research question: *"How are the research streams of organizational resilience and digital innovation management interrelated, which related insights from organizational theory enhance knowledge in IS research about digital innovation and transformation, and what are fruitful areas of future research to strengthen the linkage between both concepts?"*.

As a first step to address this broad research question, we analyze two illustrative success stories of digital innovation and transformation [8] – 1) Apple's innovation of the iPod and iPhone enabled through digital technology, and 2) Netflix's transformative and adaptive capabilities by reinventing itself as a leading streaming provider for video content. We retrieve success factors for building organizational resilience and, thereby, identify organizational resilience as a critical enabler for companies to strive and grow their business by digitally transforming existing business models. Subsequently, we put our findings in the context of digital transformation by outlining how state-of-the-art innovation management research should adapt ideas of organizational resilience theory as part of a transition towards *digital* innovation management. We contribute by bridging between the concepts of organizational resilience originated in organizational theory and digital transformation and (digital) innovation management in IS research and provide possibilities for future research endeavors. Practitioners might also benefit as we showcase two examples of how to leverage organizational resilience by transforming business models through digital innovation [9] and, thus, avoiding the innovator's dilemma [10].

In the following chapter, we compile foundational and related work on organizational resilience as well as digital innovation management and digital transformation. In Sect. 3, we define organizational resilience with a conceptual framework and derive nine potential success factors from related literature. Additionally, we present a systematic procedure for the conducted cross-case study. We examine the two cases of Apple and Netflix as success stories of a resilient adaptation to technological change in Sect. 4 and discuss our findings across both cases. In Sect. 5, we put our results into the context of digital transformation and innovation management, summarize our findings, address the limitations of our study, and point out possibilities for future work.

2 Foundations and Related Work

2.1 Organizational Resilience Research

The term "resilience" was shaped by two scientific currents in the 1970s and early 1980s: The ecologist Holling [11] introduced the concept of resilience to describe the survivability of an ecological system; the psychologist Werner [12] examined factors of resilience that helped children and adolescents to successfully deal with biological and psychosocial risk factors. With their pioneering work, the authors established two competing approaches to study resilience, namely systemic resilience and personal resilience.

In economic sciences, the work of Staw et al. [13] and Meyer [14] on organizational responses to external threats was pioneering. In the 1980s, measures to increase internal reliability and security moved into scientific focus, with resilience being examined as part of the strategy of high-reliability-organizations [15]. Linnenluecke [9] divides the subject of contemporary organizational resilience research into three main topics: The management of employee strengths [16–18], resilient supply chain design [19, 20], and the *adaptability of business models*. In the following, we mainly focus on literature related to the latter topic since the adaptability of business models is the most relevant in the context of our study. This type of resilience, often coined as organizational resilience [21, 22], combines aspects of both systemic and personal resilience research.

Sutcliffe and Vogus [21] examine organizational resilience as a means of creating conditions for successfully using internal and external resources to deal with threats. They investigate possible conditions at several levels of the organization (individual, team, organizational). In Sect. 3, factors of organizational resilience are presented in more detail. Hamel and Välikangas [23] emphasize the innovative capacity of companies as a decisive criterion for measuring organizational resilience. They see it as a serious challenge for established companies to create a suitable corporate culture and hierarchical structures to anticipate future disruptions and remain adaptable by developing novel business models or products.

Endres et al. [24], on the other hand, tie in with past research (e.g. [15]) by describing a significantly increased vulnerability of modern companies in times of digitalization and related paradigms such as the Internet of Things and Industry 4.0. The authors, therefore, recommend establishing resilience management practices as an evolution of risk management on best-practice learnings from high-reliability-organizations. Particularly, this includes the establishment of a positive error culture to identify weaknesses and, thus, initiate learning processes, and a shift of operational decision-power away from non-specialized management towards the employees with the most specific expertise.

Palzkill and Schneidewind [25] transfer existing systemic resilience research to management theory by introducing the concept of Business Model Resilience. They use dimensions of resilience, which were previously introduced by Walker et al. [26] to describe socio-ecological systems and, hence, obtain appropriate management strategies. In doing so, they differ between the relevance of risks due to vulnerability (precariousness and latitude) and the (non-)transformability of an organization (resistance and panarchy). Based on this, the authors point out that the resilience of a system is always directly related to the resilience of its super- and sub-systems [25, 26]. Thus, organizational change requires not only the company's resilience capabilities as a closed system but also the adaptability of its employees or departments (sub-system) as well as its environment, e.g. a local community or business partners (super-system). As an illustrative example, the authors discuss the finite nature of fossil resources as a threat to the automotive industry. In this context, the business model of offering shared electric vehicles might be an alternative strategy to create value while mostly maintaining its initial value proposition. In the establishment of this adaptational or transformational process, the business model resilience of the organization, and especially the internal and external transformability (resistance and panarchy), play a major role in the successful establishment of this business model innovation [25].

2.2 Digital Innovation Management and Digital Transformation

The wave of digitalization has an impact on many different levels and, thus, exerts holistic pressure on companies and their business models [1]. Changing conditions that confront companies include shifting customer expectations and work processes, new sales channels and markets, social media, real-time information and availability, and a range of new possibilities through the analysis of existing data [2, 27]. Throughout our study, we refer to different related concepts in this context, namely digitalization, digital transformation, digital innovation, and digital innovation management. In Table 1, we provide a brief definition of our understanding of the respective concepts and link to related work in IS research.

Table 1. Key concepts in the context of digital innovation management.

Concept	Summary and related work
Digitalization	The sociotechnical phenomena and processes of adopting and using digital technologies in broader individual, organizational, and societal contexts [1, 28]
Digital transformation	The process that aims to improve an entity by triggering significant changes to its properties through combinations of information, computing, communication, and connectivity technologies [29, 30]
Digital innovation	The creation of (and consequent change in) market offerings, business processes, or models that result from the use of digital technology [5, 7], which can include activities of initiating, developing, implementing, and exploiting [31]
Digital innovation management	The practices, processes, and principles that ensure the effective orchestration of digital innovation [5]

Digital technological advancement is an essential foundation of digital business models and forces companies to react to the emerging digital environment [3, 4, 32]. Studies such as the Cisco Visual Networking Index [33], according to which the number of Internet-enabled mobile devices will exceed the world population by a factor of 1.5 by 2022, illustrate the rapid progress of digital change. This upheaval can be both an opportunity and a risk for companies. On the one hand, new potential sources of revenue arise for companies due to changes within their business models, such as the introduction of new sales channels or access to new markets [34–36]. Further potential lies in the collection and analysis of data, which can be used to either make internal value chains more efficient, wrap new functions around existing value propositions, or even innovate completely novel business models [37–39]. Besides that, data and analytics can increase the probability of success of marketing measures through targeted customer targeting [40, 41].

At the same time, however, this change also involves a major risk for companies. If a competitor earlier identifies and exploits a window of opportunity for digital innovation, the disruptive characteristics of digital technologies might severely threaten the market position of traditional players [42, 43]. Hereby, established companies often face the innovator's dilemma [10] of having to choose between maintaining still successful business models and uncertain innovations at the expense of current profits. This dilemma might lead companies to (fatal) decisions against innovation for fear of cannibalizing their own business and risking their position as a market leader. Companies that meet the challenges of the digital world with an open mind will therefore benefit - companies that insist on existing structures will lose out [23].

Even though digitalization nowadays affects any industry, the degree of digitalization is not equally advanced across all industries. This difference can be illustrated, for example, by the digitalization index for German SMEs [44], indicating that digitalization is already more advanced in some industries, while other industries could face even more disruptive upheavals. This is the starting point of this work, using the entertainment industry as an example to show how building organizational resilience might enable a company to successfully manage the complex requirements of digitalization. The insights gained from this analysis can serve as a recommendation for future actions so that, especially in less digitized industries, companies can successfully master the transition to the digital age thanks to preventive measures.

3 Research Methodology

3.1 Conceptualizing Organizational Resilience

In this subsection, we present a framework that depicts how organizational resilience impacts the long-term success of a firm. This framework specifies our understanding of organizational resilience and serves as a foundation for our cross-case study. Afterward, we derive potential success factors for building organizational resilience from existing literature. Ultimately, these foundational steps allow us to systematically examine how firms can strive through digital innovation and transformation.

As a systematic literature review of Linnenluecke [9] shows, related literature about resilience in the organizational context does not apply the phenomenon of resilience as a clear distinct concept. For example, resilience is used as a target variable, as a set of measures to respond to internal disruptions, or as a positive outcome of recovery efforts after a disaster. In this paper, we refer to *organizational resilience* as a set of moderating positive systemic and personal factors that are present in an organization already before an immediate threat becomes visible, and which enable an organization facing threats or other adversarial circumstances to successfully deal with them.

Similar to biological or socio-ecological systems in other application fields, organizations cannot strive in adverse conditions only by having resilient characteristics [45]. A system or organization must use its resilient capabilities to trigger transformative or adaptive processes to drive change within the organization itself, for its employees and its stakeholders. While for only temporarily threatening events such as accidents or supply chain difficulties, the return to the initial state might be desirable in the long run, the context of digital innovation requires a permanent transformation of the organization to remain successful [46]. In Fig. 1, we propose a conceptual framework depicting how organizational resilience consisting of systemic and personal factors has a positive effect on an organization's long-term business success by triggering transformative or adaptive processes when facing adversarial circumstances.

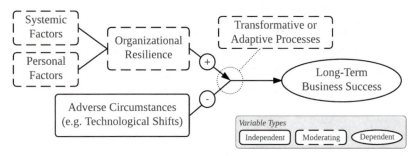

Fig. 1. Conceptual framework on the moderating effect of organizational resilience [22].

Several studies grasp the concept of organizational resilience by describing different factors of it. These factors can be classified by the associated level of hierarchy (individual, team, organization, ecosystem), by the respective nature (personal or systemic), or other unifying attributes. For example, a widely recognized work [9] on resilience in organizations of Sutcliffe and Vogus [21] examines factors of organizational resilience at three levels of hierarchy and further divides these factors into two categories: 1) resources that enable the development and maintenance of competencies, and 2) motivation systems and processes that promote effectiveness and growth. Accompanied by a call for more sustainable leadership, Avery and Bergsteiner [47] analyze 23 leadership style elements and identify 3 key performance drivers to build resilience and, thus, enable a long-term successful business performance: strategic and systematic innovation, employee retention, and quality.

In addition to existing scientific literature, we looked into the standard ISO 22316, published in 2017 [48], which describes 9 different factors as principles and attributes of organizational resilience. We found that there is a broad agreement between the wide range of proposed factors of resilience attributes in related literature [15, 21, 22, 25, 47] and the ISO standard. Moreover, recent studies begin to adopt the ISO standard's factors as a basis for qualitative empirical studies on organizational resilience (e.g. [49]). Hence, we decided to take the distinct set of nine factors as a starting point for our research and triangulated them by gradually adjusting them following the discussed literature and categorizing them into five systemic (S1–S5), and four personal (P1–P4) factors of organizational resilience. The final set of factors of organizational resilience, which guided our case study analysis, are represented in Table 2.

Table 2. Systemic (S1–S5) and personal (P1–P4) factors of organizational resilience [48].

ID	Organizational resilience factor
S1	Mutual learning by **sharing information and knowledge**
S2	**Availability of resources** to enable rapid adaptation to changing circumstances
S3	Development and **coordination of business units** geared to strategic goals
S4	Support of a **continuous improvement process** to constantly evaluate results and identify opportunities
S5	Ability to **anticipate change** and manage necessary adjustments
P1	**Shared vision**, goals, and values; clarity about the purpose of the organization
P2	**Understanding and influencing** the internal and external **context**
P3	Effective and **encouraging leadership** by leaders, e.g. to accept uncertainty and failure
P4	**Positive culture** towards values, attitudes, and behaviors **that promote resilience**

3.2 Case Study Approach

In this paper, we use a case study-based approach to link the concept of organizational resilience to present research questions in the field of IS, especially in the context of digital innovation management and digital transformation. In doing so, our procedure corresponds to the guidelines developed by Glaser and Strauss [50] and Eisenhardt [8].

Conducting a case study is a common approach in organizational resilience research [9, 22], since the organizational effects of resilience can hardly be simulated or reconstructed, and collecting representative data is difficult due to accessibility, timeliness, and confidentiality. As Eisenhardt [8] explains, case studies are particularly suitable in novel research areas such as organizational resilience research. Since real events serve as the basis for theory formation, the author believes that the insights gained from the cases are often universally valid and transferable to other applications.

1) Selection of Cases. To select highly-promising cases, Eisenhardt [8] recommends a theoretical sampling approach. In doing so, extreme situations or polar opposable cases are selected that reflect or extend the examined theory by showing a high variation concerning the examined concept. However, regarding concepts not examined in the study, the cases should be mostly similar to keep the influence of confounding factors low. Therefore, we focused on the entertainment industry, which was affected by disruptive technological change early-on throughout digitalization. Throughout the selection of cases, we looked out for scientific studies that already linked the concept of organizational resilience with the success of particular companies through digital innovation (cf. [51,

52]) and focused on well-known cases in IS research. With the cases of Apple and Netflix, we selected historical digital upheavals (MP3, DVD, broadband internet access) in the entertainment industry and compared the success factors of both firms with the decline of their competitors Sony Walkman and Blockbuster Video.

2) Data Collection and Evaluation. It is difficult to collect internal data on resilience in companies (e.g. through questionnaires) due to the high strategic importance and confidentiality of such data. Therefore, we examined the selected cases using existing scientific literature, complemented by journalistic articles and public reports of the firms. The scientific literature was collected through keyword searches in the databases Scopus and Google Scholar as well as forward and backward searches of the included papers [53]. To decide on the relevance of articles, we looked out for technological triggers and factors for success or failure associated with a firm's organizational resilience. Regarding non-academic material, we discussed the quality and added value of the resources among the authors and only included high-quality articles, which added valuable insights to the scientific literature. The final set of the included material is listed in Table 3. By applying the principle of dual control among the authors throughout the data collection and evaluation phase, we obtained complementary insights and ensured the reliability of our results [8].

Table 3. Scientific and non-scientific material included in the case study.

Case	Scientific literature	Additional material
Apple	[43, 51, 54–56]	[57, 58]
Netflix	[52, 59–63]	[64–68]

3) Within-Case Analysis and Cross-case Pattern Search. We analyzed both cases in the authors' team by comparing the successful firm with its unsuccessful competitor regarding our proposed framework on organizational resilience. Subsequently, we looked for cross-case patterns, i.e. effective resilience attributes, to distinguish generalizable factors from case-specific characteristics to contribute to the knowledge of organizational resilience in the context of digital innovation management [9].

4) Formation of Hypotheses and Transferability of the Results. Based on the cross-case and case-specific patterns identified throughout our case study, we discussed the relevance and benefits of bridging between existing research on organizational resilience and digital innovation management and digital transformation. By linking these different research strings, we encourage future theory-building to better understand the specifics of *digital* innovation management [5].

5) Enfolding Literature and Outlook. In the final step, we tied together our findings with extant literature by analyzing related IS literature for similar findings as well as research in conflict with our results [8]. To deepen the understanding of the linkage between organizational resilience theory and IS concepts, we developed questions for subsequent research endeavors.

4   Case Study Results

In this chapter, we present the results of our cross-case study. For each case, we briefly summarize its outline in a case vignette by describing the initial market situation, relevant technological shifts, and how the market developed throughout the case. Afterward, we focus on the firms' organizational resilience and discuss how it enabled successful digital innovation through adaptational and transformational processes.

4.1   Organizational Resilience Paved the Way for Apple iPod's Success

Table 4. Case vignette of Apple iPod's success story.

Case vignette: organizational Resilience paved the way for Apple iPod's success
Initial Situation: Sony introduced its Walkman in 1979, which set new standards for portable music devices and revolutionized the music market [57]. Throughout the 1980s, Sony's Walkman became a status symbol and emblem of youth culture [54]. Apple, however, was struggling to compete in its core business of personal computing after Steve Jobs was driven from the company in 1985. Ultimately, in 1997, Steve Jobs returned to Apple and continued leading the company as CEO
Technological Shift: The progressive spread of PCs, the breakthrough of the Internet, and the invention of digital music file compression (MP3) in the early-mid 1990s made the use of digital storage media conceivable for portable music players [55]
Market Development: While the first respectably successful portable MP3 players appeared in 1998, the most successful one came to market in 2001 with the Apple iPod. The iPod was the first device to fully meet the expectations of customers: A large increase in storage capacity (>80 h playtime) allowed the iPod to unfold the most valuable advantage over physical media and to provide its user a previously unknown level of convenience, accompanied by a simple and plain design and a couple of novel other features [55]
With the introduction of iTunes and the integrated iTunes store in 2003, Apple enhanced its value proposition by offering its customers a service to digitally manage and purchase their favorite music. This marked the final breakthrough of the iPod and digital music services in general [58] and resulted in a dominant market share of up to 48% for the Apple iPod among MP3 players, accompanied by a rapid decline for portable CD players such as the Sony Walkman [55]
Despite its huge success, Apple remained one of the top innovative companies with products such as the iPod Shuffle and iPod touch. Finally, in 2007, Apple introduced the iPhone - an innovation that, again, changed the whole industry by leveraging mobile data connectivity but also cannibalized most of Apple's iPod sales. With the introduction of the App Store in 2008, the iPad in 2010, and the Apple Watch in 2014, Apple continued to increase its portfolio by innovative market-leading products and services

The continuous reinvention of a company through pioneering innovations is considered as a distinguishing feature of resilient companies; especially in today's fast-moving digital world, where business models' life cycles rapidly decline [23]. A closer look at the success story of the Apple iPod, which is described in Table 4, indicates that Apple's business success cannot be explained solely with a one-time successful product innovation. Instead, its ongoing innovation capability indicates that Apple's *organizational resilience* was a critical success factor throughout the past 20 years [51]. Without this capability, Apple probably would not have been able to identify three highly profitable windows of opportunities (iPod, iPhone, and iPad) in one decade and to provide the necessary resources to make its production a core part of their business. Moreover, with the iTunes Store and the App Store, Apple innovated a new type of digital marketplace and created a whole ecosystem around their physical products [43].

In their study on resilience, Teixeira and Werther [51] classify Apple as an anticipatory company and, thus, distinguish it from reactive and proactive companies. This means that Apple has internal resources and processes (S2) at its disposal to continuously develop industry-changing innovations based on the anticipation of changing conditions (S5). The authors differentiate between Apple's future-oriented opportunity-seeking orientation (S4) and Sony's problem-solving orientation at the time of the introduction of the iPod. According to Teixeira and Werther [51], further enablers were the interaction of leadership and followers (P3), an open corporate culture (P4), strategic planning (S3), and innovation as the "way of life" (P1).

In the case of Apple, two particular aspects should be mentioned: First, the leadership approach and corporate culture that Steve Jobs re-established after returning to Apple as CEO in 1997. Jobs placed great emphasis on simplicity and focus, quality and perfectionism as well as unconventional ideas and approaches. He applied these personal qualities to the entire way the company operates, creating the right environment for Apple's innovative product development [56]. Secondly, Apple showed a keen sense of the right timing of strategic decisions. For example, the iPod was not introduced until the necessary boundary conditions (P2), i.e. a whole mp3 player ecosystem, were in place [58].

These success factors enabled Apple to leverage different technological changes brought by digitalization as highly profitable opportunities for digital innovation. For this reason, Apple can be seen as one of the most resilient companies in the last 20 years and as an archetype for organizational resilience. In comparison, Sony was more reluctant to adapt to technological changes, such as MP3 files in our case study of the Sony Walkman. Other related cases, such as the decline of Sony Ericson Walkman phones and Sony's missed change towards LCD-powered televisions support this interpretation. However, at the same time, Sony also innovated revolutionary digital products such as the PlayStation, and earlier the Sony Walkman. For this reason, we cannot extrapolate from our results to the company Sony as a whole. Nevertheless, the case of Sony Walkman illustrates the effects of hesitant reactions to technological changes in the business environment.

4.2 Netflix's David vs. Goliath Story of Constant Innovation

The case of Netflix's success story, summarized in Table 5, shows how Netflix repeatedly managed to anticipate environmental changes through innovation over the past 20 years [59]. Similar to Apple, Netflix's success today is not built on a single successful product innovation but rather on several internal capabilities, which allow Netflix to continuously reinvent itself. Thanks to these resilient characteristics, the company has been able to set

Table 5. Case vignette of Netflix's success story.

Case vignette: Netflix's David vs. Goliath story of constant innovation
Initial Situation: The mass production of video equipment in the early 1980s opened up a large market for video stores, such as the US rental chains Blockbuster Video or Movie Gallery, that rented VHS cassettes for a minor fee
Technological Shift: DVDs as a lower-weighted storage technology, the rapid evolution of e-commerce in the early 2000s, and later, the wide-spread access to broadband infrastructure put high pressure on brick-and-mortar stores in the video-on-demand business [60]
Market Development: Founded in 1997 as an online DVD rental service, Netflix relied exclusively on DVDs from the very beginning and offered a novel business model by solely accepting orders online and sending the requested movies per mail. This innovation was only possible due to the lower weight of the DVD compared to the VHS technology and became even more radical with Netflix's introduction of a flat-rate subscription model in 1999 [59]. Thanks to its trailblazing business model, Netflix's market share in the growing online video-rental segment was approx. 85% in the early-mid 2000s, even though established firms such as Blockbuster reluctantly developed a similar online mail order service [59]
With the expansion of faster broadband connections and the development of more efficient data transmission algorithms, Netflix saw the opportunity and necessity to transform its business model as a home theater service provider. In 2007, they began to make movies and TV series accessible through ad-free online streaming and expanded this service all around the globe in the early 2010s. By gaining a first-mover advantage for the second time, Netflix increased its number of subscribers from 22 million in 2011 to nearly 150 million in 2019 [65] and had an annual profit of $1.2 billion in 2018 [66]. Due to shared subscriptions, the amount of actual users of Netflix's offerings even exceeds the number of subscribers and represented approximately 37% of all global Internet users in 2019 [65]
Another remarkable business decision of Netflix was to create and stream their own productions, beginning with House of Cards in 2011, which is considered a key success factor in a nowadays highly-competitive segment [59]. By leveraging data-driven insights in customer needs as a competitive advantage [64], Netflix not only sets new standards in the video-on-demand business but also initiates changes in the entire movie and television industry [61, 67]

itself apart from other video-on-demand providers such as Blockbuster Video, but also established film studios like Disney.

Poupakis [64] describes the reluctance of film studios to enter the market of streaming with Christensen's [10] *innovator's dilemma,* since the film studios might fear cannibalizing their pay-tv and box office business and, thus, put their high-profit business models at risk. However, especially in the face of disruptive technological changes such as digitalization, this can become a rapidly growing threat to established companies due to new competitors [42]. Due to the importance of network effects and the collection of vast amounts of user data, digital disruptions such as streaming platforms are more likely to be accompanied by "winner-takes-it-all" markets than traditional businesses [43]. However, if a company has sufficient organizational resilience, it can successfully deal with this threat through adaptive or transformative processes. In Netflix's case, the transformation of the company from an online DVD rental service to a streaming provider, but also the adaptation by adding in-house productions, are illustrative examples. Both times, the company managed to anticipate the change and transformed the threat into an opportunity for even greater success (S5). Despite extensive changes in its business model, Netflix retained its original mission, i.e. affordably providing its customers with their favorite movies and series with a high level of convenience, complemented with a mature recommendation system [62].

A key reason for Netflix's success lies in its innovative corporate culture and informal human resources practices. Netflix's human resources approach closely overlaps with our proposed factors of organizational resilience: Netflix emphasizes acting in the interest of the company (P1), sharing knowledge (S1), delegating responsibility (S3, P4), openly addressing mistakes (P3), and mutual understanding of the context (P2) [63, 68]. Ideas such as the Netflix Prize - an open innovation challenge to improve Netflix' recommendation system with a $1 million reward - are another indicator for Netflix's innovative mindset to identify opportunities for improvement (S4) and ensuring the availability of resources for a rapid innovation (S2) [62].

4.3   Cross-case Patterns

Comparing the cases of Apple and Netflix, we found that both companies repeatedly developed groundbreaking innovations that became an integral part of today's entertainment industry. In contrast, other major players (Sony, Blockbuster, eventually Disney) have shied away from these necessary adoptions of their business model for too long. As described in the previous subsection, this hesitation can be attributed to the innovator's dilemma [10, 64]. Apple and Netflix, on the other hand, seem to have recognized the right time to gradually replace their market-leading and highly profitable products such as the iPod and DVD distribution with more advanced innovations such as the smartphone and online streaming.

Hamel and Välikangas [23] and Teixeira and Werther [51] describe this *ability to continually reinvent oneself through innovation* as a core characteristic of organizational resilience in today's highly volatile business environment. This ability reflects, in particular, the following factors of organizational resilience (cf. Table 2): Availability of resources (S2), Coordination of business units (S3), Continuous improvement process (S4), Ability to anticipate change (S5), and Understanding and influencing the context (P2).

In addition to the ability to respond to a changing context through innovation, both share a distinctive *corporate culture that strengthens trust in employees and facilitates the necessary processes of change*. Both companies, similarly, select only excellent applicants but then transfer great freedom to them [56, 63]. The managers in both companies establish a corporate culture that reflects the following factors of organizational resilience (cf. Table 2): Sharing information and knowledge (S1), Shared vision (P1), Understanding and influencing the context (P2), Encouraging leadership (P3), and Positive culture that promotes resilience (P4).

As a major difference between the analyzed cases of Apple's iPod and Netflix, we identified the timing of market entry. While Apple released its products with a certain delay compared to other MP3 players and early smartphones, Netflix used the first-mover advantage for both online DVD distribution and its streaming service. However, both cases indicate a deep understanding of the context and conditions of the respective markets. Therefore, Apple and Netflix both were able to identify just the right temporal window of opportunity for digital innovation, which we identify as a critical success factor for their digital transformation.

5 Discussion and Conclusion

Meanwhile, digitalization is affecting almost all established industries and business models with disruptive forces. As a result, innovation cycles are becoming increasingly shorter, and companies hesitating to change eventually get overwhelmed by the rapid change of digital disruptions [42]. Prominent examples give evidence for the widespread upheavals brought about by digitalization: Kodak's decline in the photo business, Uber's success vis-à-vis the established cab industry, and the success stories of Airbnb, Spotify, and Zalando. Netflix's founder Reed Hastings emphasizes in an interview that a successful way of working in creative companies like Netflix or Apple is fundamentally different from conventional industrial companies. While the latter primarily aim to reduce variance and thus errors, creative companies are successful by increasing variance and thus innovation [63]. This conflict poses severe and unsolved challenges for traditional companies aiming to digitally transform their organizations.

In this paper, we contribute to an understanding of digital innovation management by linking the concepts of organizational resilience and digital innovation and transformation. With a cross-case study of Apple and Netflix, we examine the decisive role of organizational resilience for successful digital innovation and transformation and show that digital transformation through innovation is a necessity to strive in the digital age. Thereby, our study reveals the following implications: First, we find systemic and personal resilience factors of organizational resilience, which help companies to prepare for temporal "distensions" facilitated by digital technologies providing opportunities for digital innovation. Aligned with innovation management, which is constantly looking out for these opportunities, this empowers companies to rapidly transform their business with digital innovation when the right moment has come. Second, we bridge between organizational theory and traditional innovation management as part of a transition towards *digital* innovation management by introducing a conceptual framework, which depicts the moderating effect of organizational resilience in the face of adverse circumstances such as technological disruptions. Finally, practitioners might use our case study as guidance as we showcase two examples of how to leverage organizational resilience by digitally transforming one's business [9] and, thus, avoiding the innovator's dilemma [10].

Our research certainly comes with some *limitations*. First, throughout our cross-case study, we mainly focused on two cases in a similar industry and business environment. Therefore, our results can only indicate the potential of organizational resilience for IS theory building in the context of digital innovation management and digital transformation. Second, due to the nature of the examined concept, it was difficult to collect sufficient internal data, which is why we also considered external data and journalistic material. Finally, we based our findings only on relevant literature and the insights from our case study, whereas they still lack a rigorous evaluation in practice.

However, these limitations at the same time leave the potential for *future research*. First, subsequent research might use our results for an in-depth qualitative or quantitative empirical study on the current digital readiness in less digitized industries such as construction and agriculture, e.g. by using questionnaires as in the work of Heller et al. [49]. Second, our work could serve as a basis for future endeavors aiming to derive targeted measures for companies to build organizational resilience and, thus, create preventive conditions to successfully deal with digital disruptions [42]. Finally, future work might apply our conceptualization as part of a case study in other industries, such as the financial or energy sector, to review and expand our findings, and thus, contribute to understanding the impact of organizational resilience for IS research.

References

1. Legner, C., et al.: Digitalization: opportunity and challenge for the business and information systems engineering community. Bus. Inf. Syst. Eng. **59**(4), 301–308 (2017). https://doi.org/10.1007/s12599-017-0484-2
2. Rachinger, M., Rauter, R., Müller, C., Vorraber, W., Schirgi, E.: Digitalization and its Influence on business model innovation. J. Manuf. Technol. Manag. **30**, 1143–1160 (2019). https://doi.org/10.1108/JMTM-01-2018-0020
3. Wiesböck, F., Hess, T.: Digital innovations. Electron. Mark. **30**(1), 75–86 (2019). https://doi.org/10.1007/s12525-019-00364-9
4. Abolhassan, F.: Was treibt die Digitalisierung? Warum an der Cloud kein Weg vorbeiführt (2016)
5. Nambisan, S., Lyytinen, K., Majchrzak, A., Song, M.: Digital innovation management: reinventing innovation management research in a digital world. MIS Q. Manag. Inf. Syst. **41**, 223–238 (2017). https://doi.org/10.25300/MISQ/2017/41:1.03
6. Henfridsson, O., Mathiassen, L., Svahn, F., Henfridsson, O.: Managing technological change in the digital age: the role of architectural frames (2014). https://doi.org/10.1057/jit.2013.30
7. Yoo, Y., Henfridsson, O., Lyytinen, K.: Research commentary-the new organizing logic of digital innovation: an agenda for information systems research. Inf. Syst. Res. **21**, 724–735 (2010). https://doi.org/10.1287/isre.1100.0322
8. Eisenhardt, K.M.: Building theories from case study research. Acad. Manag. Rev. **14**, 532–550 (1989). https://doi.org/10.2307/258557
9. Linnenluecke, M.K.: Resilience in business and management research: a review of influential publications and a research agenda. Int. J. Manag. Rev. **19**, 4–30 (2017). https://doi.org/10.1111/ijmr.12076
10. Christensen, C.: The innovator's dilemma: when new technologies cause great firms to fail (2013)
11. Holling, C.S.: Resilience and stability of ecological systems. Annu. Rev. Ecol. Syst. **4**, 1–23 (1973). https://doi.org/10.1146/annurev.es.04.110173.000245
12. Werner, E.E.: Vulnerable but Invincible. A longitudinal study of resilient children and youth. Acta Paediatr. Int. J. Paediatr. Suppl. **86**, 103–105 (1982). https://doi.org/10.1111/j.1651-2227.1997.tb18356.x
13. Staw, B., Sandelands, L.E., Dutton, J.E.: Threat rigidity effects in organizational behavior: a multilevel analysis. JSTOR (1981). https://doi.org/10.2307/2392337
14. Meyer, A.D.: Adapting to environmental jolts. Adm. Sci. Q. 515–537 (1982). https://doi.org/10.2307/2392528
15. Weick, K., Sutcliffe, K., Obstfeld, D.: Organizing for high reliability: processes of collective mindfulness. Res. Organ. Behav. **21**, 81–123 (1999)

16. Luthans, F.: The need for and meaning of positive organizational behavior. J. Organ. Behav. **23**, 695–706 (2002). https://doi.org/10.1002/job.165
17. Luthans, F., Vogelgesang, G.R., Lester, P.B.: Developing the psychological capital of resiliency. Hum. Resour. Dev. Rev. **5**, 25–44 (2006). https://doi.org/10.1177/1534484305285335
18. Shin, J., Taylor, S., Seo, M.-G.: Resources for change: the relationships of organizational inducements and psychological resilience to employees' attitudes and behaviors toward organizational change. Acad. Manag. J. **55**, 727–748 (2012). https://doi.org/10.5465/amj.2010.0325
19. Sheffi, Y., Rice, J.B.: A supply chain view of the resilient enterprise. MIT Sloan Manag. Rev. **47** (2005)
20. Sáenz, M.J., Revilla, E.: Creating more resilient supply chains. MIT Sloan Manag. Rev. **55**, 22–24 (2014)
21. Sutcliffe, K.M., Vogus, T.J.: Organizing for resilience. Posit. Organ. Scholarsh. Found. New Discip. 94–110 (2003)
22. Di Bella, J.: Unternehmerische Resilienz (2014)
23. Hamel, G., Valikangas, L.: The quest for resilience. Harv. Bus. Rev. **81**, 52–63 (2003)
24. Endres, H., Weber, K., Helm, R.: Resilienz-management in Zeiten von Industrie 4.0. IM+io Das Mag. für Innov. Organ. und Manag. (2015)
25. Palzkill, A.: Managementperspektiven für die Zivilgesellschaft des 21. Jahrhunderts. Manag. für die Ziv. des 21. Jahrhunderts, pp. 27–43 (2014). https://doi.org/10.1007/978-3-658-02523-6
26. Walker, B., Holling, C.S., Carpenter, S.R., Kinzig, A.: Resilience, adaptability and transformability in social-ecological systems. Ecol. Soc. **9** (2004). https://doi.org/10.5751/ES-00650-090205
27. Ostrom, A.L., Parasuraman, A., Bowen, D.E., Patrício, L., Voss, C.A.: Service research priorities in a rapidly changing context. J. Serv. Res. **18**, 127–159 (2015). https://doi.org/10.1177/1094670515576315
28. Brennen, J.S., Kreiss, D.: Digitalization. Int. Encycl. Commun. Theory Philos. 1–11 (2016). https://doi.org/10.4324/9780203736319-36
29. Vial, G.: Understanding digital transformation: a review and a research agenda. J. Strateg. Inf. Syst. **28**, 118–144 (2019). https://doi.org/10.1016/j.jsis.2019.01.003
30. Hinings, B., Gegenhuber, T., Greenwood, R.: Digital innovation and transformation: an institutional perspective. Inf. Organ. **28**, 52–61 (2018). https://doi.org/10.1016/j.infoandorg.2018.02.004
31. Kohli, R., Melville, N.P.: Digital innovation: a review and synthesis. Inf. Syst. J. **29**, 200–223 (2019). https://doi.org/10.1111/isj.12193
32. Hunke, F., Seebacher, S., Schuritz, R., Illi, A.: Towards a process model for data-driven business model innovation. In: 2017 IEEE 19th Conference on Business Informatics, vol. 1, pp. 150–157 (2017). https://doi.org/10.1109/CBI.2017.43
33. Barnett, T.J., Sumits, A., Jain, S., Andra, U.: Cisco visual networking index (VNI) update global mobile data traffic forecast (2015)
34. Davenport, T.H., Harris, J.G.: Competing on Analytics: The New Science of Winning. Harvard Business Review Press, Boston (2017)
35. Porter, M.E., Heppelmann, J.E.: How smart, connected products are transforming competition (2014)
36. Hunke, F., et al.: Geschäftsmodelle 4.0. In: Stich, V., Schumann, J.H., Beverungen, D., Gudergan, G., Jussen, P. (eds.) Digitale Dienstleistungsinnovationen, pp. 167–183. Springer, Heidelberg (2019). https://doi.org/10.1007/978-3-662-59517-6_9

37. Hartmann, P.M., Zaki, M., Feldmann, N., Neely, A.: Capturing value from big data – a taxonomy of data-driven business models used by start-up firms. Int. J. Oper. Prod. Manag. **36**, 1382–1406 (2016). https://doi.org/10.1108/IJOPM-02-2014-0098
38. Schüritz, R., Seebacher, S., Satzger, G., Schwarz, L.: Datatization as the next frontier of servitization: understanding the challenges for transforming organizations. In: ICIS 2017 Proceeding, pp. 1098–1118 (2017)
39. Hunke, F., Seebacher, S., Schüritz, R., Satzger, G.: Pathways from data to value: identifying strategic archetypes of analytics-based services. In: Proceeedings of 15th International Conference on Wirtschaftsinformatik (2020). https://doi.org/10.30844/wi_2020_j7-hunke
40. Kim, Y.S., Street, W.N.: An intelligent system for customer targeting: a data mining approach. Decis. Support Syst. **37**, 215–228 (2004). https://doi.org/10.1016/S0167-9236(03)00008-3
41. Habryn, F., Kunze von Bischhoffshausen, J., Satzger, G.: A business intelligence solution for assessing customer interaction, cross-selling, and customization in a customer intimacy context. In: ECIS 2012 Proceedings (2012)
42. Skog, D.A., Wimelius, H., Sandberg, J.: Digital disruption. Bus. Inf. Syst. Eng. **60**(5), 431–437 (2018). https://doi.org/10.1007/s12599-018-0550-4
43. Gawer, A., Cusumano, M.A.: Industry platforms and ecosystem innovation. J. Prod. Innov. Manag. **31**, 417–433 (2014). https://doi.org/10.1111/jpim.12105
44. Deutsche Telekom AG: Digitalisierungsindex Mittelstand 2019/ 2020: Der Digitale Status Quo im Deutschen Handel, pp. 1–12 (2019)
45. Folke, C.: Resilience: the emergence of a perspective for social-ecological systems analyses. Glob. Environ. Chang. **16**, 253–267 (2006). https://doi.org/10.1016/j.gloenvcha.2006.04.002
46. Dahles, H., Susilowati, T.P.: Business resilience in times of growth and crisis. Ann. Tour. Res. **51**, 34–50 (2015). https://doi.org/10.1016/j.annals.2015.01.002
47. Avery, G.C., Bergsteiner, H.: Sustainable leadership practices for enhancing business resilience and performance. Strateg. Leadersh. **39**, 5–15 (2011). https://doi.org/10.1108/108 78571111128766
48. ISO: ISO 22316:2017 - Security and Resilience - Organizational Resilience - Principles and Attributes. https://www.iso.org/standard/50053.html. Accessed 15 Oct 2020
49. Heller, J., Huemer, B., Preissegger, I., Drath, K., Zehetner, F., Amann, E.G.: Messung organisationaler Resilienz: Zentrale Elemente, Schutz - und Risikofaktoren. In: Heller, J. (ed.) Resilienz für die VUCA-Welt, pp. 133–139. Springer, Wiesbaden (2019). https://doi.org/10. 1007/978-3-658-21044-1_9
50. Glaser, B., Strauss, A.: Discovery of Grounded Theory: Strategies for Qualitative Research. Routledge, Milton Park (2017)
51. Teixeira, E.d.O., Werther, W.B.: Resilience: continuous renewal of competitive advantages. Bus. Horiz. **56**, 333–342 (2013). https://doi.org/10.1016/j.bushor.2013.01.009
52. Meniuc, C.: Adaptive cycle of resilience: Netflix case study. (V)ODC Course 2013/2014 (2013)
53. Webster, J., Watson, R.T.: Analyzing the past to prepare for the future: writing a literature review. MIS Q. **26**, xiii–xxiii (2002). https://doi.org/10.2307/4132319
54. Hosokawa, S., Ollrogge, B.: Der Walkman-Effekt. Merve, Berlin (1987)
55. Bull, M.: Investigating the culture of mobile listening: from walkman to iPod. In: O'Hara, K., Brown, B. (eds.) Consuming Music Together. Computer Supported Cooperative Work, vol. 35, pp. 131–149. Springer, Dordrecht (2006). https://doi.org/10.1007/1-4020-4097-0_7
56. Isaacson, W.: The real leadership lessons of steve jobs. Harv. Bus. Rev. 93–102 (2012)
57. Pothitos, B.A.: The history of portable music. Mob. Ind. Rev. 1–9 (2011)
58. Adner, R.: From Walkman to iPod: what music tech teaches us about innovation. Atl. 1–6 (2012)

59. Voigt, K.-I., Buliga, O., Michl, K.: Entertainment on demand: the case of Netflix. In: Voigt, K.-I., Buliga, O., Michl, K. (eds.) Business Model Pioneers, pp. 127–141. Springer, Cham (2017). https://doi.org/10.1007/978-3-319-38845-8_11

60. Sim, G.: Individual disruptors and economic gamechangers: Netflix, new media, and neoliberalism. In: Netflix Effect: Technology and Entertainment 21st Century, pp. 185–201 (2016)

61. Burroughs, B.: House of Netflix: streaming media and digital lore. Pop. Commun. **17**, 1–17 (2019). https://doi.org/10.1080/15405702.2017.1343948

62. Rayna, T., Striukova, L.: 360° business model innovation: toward an integrated view of business model innovation. Res. Technol. Manag. **59**, 21–28 (2016). https://doi.org/10.1080/08956308.2016.1161401

63. McCord, P.: How Netflix reinvented HR. Harv. Bus. Rev. 1–14 (2014)

64. Poupakis, S.: The reason Hollywood giants waited so long to challenge Netflix. Quartz, 12 Nov 2019

65. Watson, A.: Netflix - statistics & facts. Statista. 1–6 (2020)

66. Watson, A.: Netflix: net income 2000–2018. Statista. **2018**, 2019–2021 (2020)

67. Barnes, B.: The streaming era has finally arrived. Everything is about to change. N. Y. Times, 1–5 (2019)

68. Hastings, R.: Netflix culture: freedom & responsibility. Netflix Jobs, 16 (2009)

Replicating a Digital Transformation Case

Sandy Schmidt[(✉)], Marius Voß, Hendrik Wache, Sarah Hönigsberg,
and Barbara Dinter

Chemnitz University of Technology, Business Information Systems – Business Process and
Information Management, Chemnitz, Germany
{marius.voss,hendrik.wache,sarah.hoenigsberg,
barbara.dinter}@wirtschaft.tu-chemnitz.de

Abstract. This study is a methodological replication of the PROFUND method
for the implementation of digital transformation projects in small and medium-
sized enterprises (SMEs). In the original study, a method for improving the Value
Co-Creation (VCC) of an SME network was applied in the digital transformation
of a network of textile manufacturers to validate four existing propositions for
improving the VCC. This study replicates (1) the procedure in the case study, (2)
the guidelines for improving the VCC, and (3) the evaluation of the results via the
DART model and transfers them to a network in the metal industry. The method
was transferable and the propositions could be reconfirmed. The results of this
study confirm the results of the original study and thus validate the procedural
structure used there.

Keywords: Value Co-Creation · Digital transformation · Replication

1 Introduction

Companies are currently facing special challenges which are being increased by the
digitalization in the society. Small and medium-sized enterprises (SMEs) are particularly affected by this and often face higher hurdles when trying to take part in digital
transformation projects in order to keep pace with the digitalization of society [1, 2].
Particular challenges of SMEs include limited resources (e.g. funds but also staff) [3,
4], strong networking with other partner companies (with many dependencies to consider) [5, 6] and lack of digitalization skills (e.g. as the owner often holds almost all
management functions at once) [1, 7]. The digital transformation can be described as:
"a process that aims to improve an entity by triggering significant changes to its properties through combinations of information, computing, communication, and connectivity
technologies" [8]. Especially in large companies, DT is a strategically driven issue, with
digital business strategies and new roles such as chief digital officers [9–12]. In contrast, "[c]ompared with large firms which have greater resources, SMEs are sometimes
struggling with survivals rather than peacefully planning long-term strategies" [13].

The value network of SMEs is becoming increasingly complex as companies specialize in their skills in order to compete globally [2, 3]. This fragmentation and close

© The Author(s), under exclusive license to Springer Nature Switzerland AG 2021
F. Ahlemann et al. (Eds.): WI 2021, LNISO 47, pp. 565–581, 2021.
https://doi.org/10.1007/978-3-030-86797-3_37

interlocking of companies makes transformation processes for SMEs very negotiation-intensive [5], as digital solutions inevitably have to be designed across several actors [14]. However, digitalization in the value network offers the opportunity to minimize the differences between customers and partners by closely interconnecting them and promotes value co-creation (VCC) [12, 15, 16].

The research topic of DT from SMEs has gained importance in recent years, but is still scarcely considered [1, 3, 4], even though over 99% of European companies are considered SMEs [17]. Furthermore, studies show that digitalization continues to grow significantly in importance for SMEs [18]. However, previous research results are often insufficient for SMEs. For example, a twenty-man company, given the limited resources available, will not be able to afford a chief digital officer, an innovation lab, and often not even an IT department or a strategy development project spanning several years. Furthermore, DT initiatives are often described as strategically planned projects, but in the SME context it is clear that these projects should be planned considering the VCC at a network level [19]. There are still few empirical results available on the topic of DT of VCCs in SME networks. In recent years, there have been repeated calls for empirical studies to investigate the joint value creation and also its digitalization (e.g. via digital platforms) in network settings (several companies working together in a real setting) [20–22]. These studies, especially as long-term studies, offer a deep insight into the interdependencies in the network, but due to their high complexity they are preferably carried out as single embedded case studies [23], which makes these studies vulnerable with regard to their generalizability.

For this reason, this paper examines an SME network and its possibilities for the DT of their VCC, which is designed as a replication of an already published study. Both studies focus on the question of how the network VCC can be improved through the use of digital technologies. Replication research is gaining significance in IS research, because by replicating (i.e. repeating in a modified form) studies, our discipline can increase the rigor of research and thus strive for a higher degree of maturity [24]. In the present paper, therefore, a replication approach is pursued, based on a case study in the textile industry, in order to verify the transferability of the obtained insights to another SME value network in the metal industry. This involves a methodical replication of a case study of [19, 25–27], which applies the same method as the original study in a different context. A positive result, which confirms the findings of the original study, allows the generalization of the original contribution to the new context; if the previous results cannot be replicated, this does not mean that the previous results are 'wrong', but that they cannot be transferred to the new context, which offers further opportunities for further research [24]. The remainder of the paper briefly describes the replicated case after the foundations and research approach, before discussing the case comparison. The paper ends in a conclusion.

2   Foundations of Digital Transformation and Value Co-Creation

Digital transformation is a technology-induced change and comprises a goal-oriented transformation in the areas of organization, processes and technologies, which is nec-essary for the success of companies in the digital age [28]. It significantly changes the company's relationships with its key stakeholders such as customers, suppliers or employees [14, 29]. As part of the digital transformation, information technology and information systems are positioned more visibly in the economy and society [28]. This means that digital technologies are used to have a positive influence on the business [10] and in the process the company is changed from the processes to the organizational structure to the business model. As a demarcation to the IT-enabled transformation, at the end of the digital transformation there is a newly created business identity [30] which can be achieved through innovations in the business model [31]. The focus is not on the effects in the individual company but on the radiation into the value network [8]. Automation plays a central role as an important mechanism of digitalization. Advantages that arise can be seen in increases in turnover or productivity, innovations in value creation and new forms of interaction with customers [10]. In addition to efficiency-enhancing measures such as process digitalization and automation, joint value creation with customers and partners plays a key role in the digital transformation of companies [12, 14, 29]. Furthermore, practical studies show the importance of this topic [18], with 69 percent of the companies surveyed stating that customer communication is the decisive success factor for digitalization.

In the digital era, cooperation includes activities at the relational level to contribute and maintain resources, and actions at the network level to improve resource integration [22]. Companies should initiate an open communication process with their stakeholders and strive for new ways of value creation [15]. For many years now, traditional value creation concepts and conservative patterns of interaction (e.g. mass producing goods or rendering standardized service) have been considered to cause little customer satisfaction and companies are encouraged to strive for co-creation and personalized interaction [32]. Prahalad and Ramaswamy [32] identify Dialogue, Access, Risk-Benefits and Transparency, or DART for short, as the basis for VCC interaction. These four prerequisites for interaction are also referred to below as characteristics or building blocks of the VCC. VCC can be seen as a collaborative and dyadic process [33]. It is about jointly identifying and solving problems and not about transferring activities to the customer, as in self-service, or simply satisfying the customer [32, 33]. There is a shift from value-in-exchange to value-in-use and the cognition the beneficiary (e.g. customer) is always involved in the process of value creation [21]. Apart from the dyadic perspective, the VCC can appear as a network phenomenon [22]. Considering the distributed character of the VCC in this case the definition of VCC as the processes and activities of resource integration that involves different actors in the service ecosystem (networked actors) is more appropriate [21].

3 Research Approach

3.1 Case Setting

The industries in Germany that are still least digitalized include not only healthcare and vehicle construction, but also other manufacturing industries [18]. Therefore, the choice of a network from the area of 'manufacturing of metal products' in this case study as a representative of the manufacturing industry is a good example of an area with a high pressure to digitalize. The replicated case is hereafter referred to as the metal case.

Three companies, whose value creation is carried out in a shared value creation network, were investigated for over four months and represent the unit of analysis in the metal case (conducted in a master thesis). The company C1 has a total of ten employees, eight of whom work in production. Company C2 is the smallest company with a total of 3.5 employees. Company C3 can be classified as a small enterprise, with a total of 20 employees. All three companies follow the engineer-to-order approach in their production. The individual products are individually tailored to customer needs and are produced in small quantities [34]. The network relationship is structured as follows: C3 is the supplier of metal parts for both network partners. C2 additionally purchases external edge smoothing services for parts of C1, which it has had lasered by C3. C3 purchases bending services from C1 within the scope of a cooperation if it cannot produce the parts itself. Due to this type of production, the setting under consideration represents a process industry, since not discrete units but rather work steps are offered. The network works exclusively in the B2B context. In comparison to this, four textile companies with 12–235 employees over a period of more than three years were considered in the original case, hereinafter referred to as the textile case. Similar to the metal case, the companies act as service providers to each other, from knitters and weavers to finishers and coaters. The technical textile industry is also a process industry. The companies follow an engineer-to-order approach for technical textiles as well. This network also works exclusively in the B2B context.

While the sampling in the textile case is a theoretical sampling along the textile value chain, the metal case is a convenience sample to map a small portfolio section of the focal company where one of the authors is employed [35]. It will be checked whether the results can be transferred to another industry, from textile to metal, with the same setting in terms of engineer-to-order, B2B, SME, and process industry.

3.2 Procedure for the Replication Study

According to Niederman and March [36], "[c]ase studies present a rich and open set of possibilities for replication" and "subsequent case studies can act as a kind of natural replication of the original." In this paper we perform a methodological replication [24] by reusing a procedural structure from a prior case study in a different context. This is intended to validate and generalize the previously obtained findings by confirming them in a different context. Another type of replication is exact replication, where, in addition to the research methodology, the context should also be replicated exactly [24]. In our case this would mean to replicate the case study again in the textile industry with the same contextual parameters. However, this does not correspond with the goal of using the procedural structure of the prior case study for validation and generalization in another context (e.g. the metal industry) and is therefore unsuitable for our purposes. The third type of replication is the contextual replication, which deliberately uses a different methodological approach (for example a quantitative survey) to answer the same research question [24]. Since we believe that our due to the procedural structure we want to validate in a network context, that a single embedded case study is the best methodological approach to verify the findings of the original study.

Three aspects of the original study are applied to the new context: (1) the process in the case study, (2) propositions for improving VCC, and (3) evaluation of the results using the DART model. In the textile case, a method for the DT of VCCs in SME networks was derived based on observations of the network over several years. This method specifies (1) the process of the case study. The aim is to check to what extent the method is transferable to another case. It was considered that only suitable sections of the method should be used and that the companies should make their own adaptations and justify them for themselves. The steps are identical, but the instruments such as questionnaires, interviews, etc. were freely chosen within the method in both cases. The sequence and structure of the method steps in this paper are therefore also reflected in the subsections of Sect. 4 the Metal Case.

The process in the case study (1) is structured as follows: In the first step, the common goals and the vision of the network are defined or formulated in interviews and surveys. Subsequently, the VCC process in the network is recorded. The modeling of the VCC process in both cases takes place with the help of the Business Process Model and Notation (BPMN). In both cases, the stages of digitalization were determined by online questionnaires, which were sent out in advance of the interviews. Afterwards the current and desired degree of digitalization was determined in both cases with regard to the modeled process and the resulting phases. Subsequently, recommendations for digitalization were developed with all partners in the network. In the penultimate step of the case study, the actual and desired degree of digitalization was compared in tabular form. In a final online questionnaire and interviews, possible measures were presented and then prioritized. In the last step of the case study, the actual implementation of digitalization measures takes place at the company level. The method used for this phase is primarily prototyping, which is intended to define the requirements of the user and provide him with a preliminary system for test purposes. In the metal case a combination of real life and simulated situation was used, where the simulation prototype with a low design is implemented in real circumstances by a lower manufacturing effort. In the textile case, the IT solutions such as a joined IT platform [27], were fully implemented and transitioned to real operations.

(2) Four propositions to facilitate the network VCC (P1-4) were derived from previous literature, and used as kernel theory for the IT platform development in the textile case [25]. To facilitate the network VCC, (P1) the internal processes should be modular and have defined interfaces, so that the individual process steps of different network actors can be combined at will. To facilitate the network VCC, (P2) all actors involved in the VCC process of the network should be treated as equal participants. To facilitate the network VCC, (P3) efficient and standardized communication for the transfer of information and knowledge should be established between the actors of the network. To facilitate the network VCC, (P4) there should be a cross-organizational IT support for the modular VCC processes in the network, allowing efficient standardized communication between the equal actors of the network. Previous work [25] showed that the propositions were supported by the empirical data collected in the textile case study. The propositions were confirmed according to the case study methodology [37] by analytical generalization based on empirical findings as opposed to the inference-based statistical generalization used in the survey methodology. In the metal case these four propositions were examined again and, in addition, their transferability to a different industrial context was evaluated.

(3) Evaluation of the results via the DART model: In both cases, the DART model of Prahalad and Ramaswamy [32] was used to validate that the DT of the VCC also has a positive effect on the VCC as anticipated. The DART model with its components can be used to check whether a successful VCC has been established, as it describes four basic prerequisites that must be present between co-creating actors. Dialogue refers to the equal two-way interaction between actors, which is supported by Access (to important information), and Transparency (information symmetry between actors). Risk-Benefits additionally addresses the empowerment of actors to assess the risks of interactions in the VCC [32]. The application of the DART model therefore represents the same validation tool for both cases.

3.3   Data Collection and Analysis for the Metal Case

For the realization of the presented single embedded case study, (online as well as physical) questionnaires, interviews and observation techniques were used to collect the data, thus enabling triangulation [37]. To this end, data collected using the various techniques were analyzed as part of a data triangulation to determine which findings could be supported by multiple sources of evidence or data collection techniques [37]. In addition to the questionnaires, a short interview was conducted with each of the owners. In particular, the use of open-ended questions was intended to extend the answers given so far to achieve more comprehensive results. In the course of semi-structured interviews, questions were asked about the companies' goals and vision, the answers to the online questionnaire, and the degree of digitization in the individual phases of the value creation process.

In addition to documentaries and interviews, observations were made in the metal case. One author is an employee in one of the companies of the network, so that the work process could be recorded through participant observation. Furthermore, the methodology of direct observation was applied, which can be divided into formal (observation of meetings) and informal (during field research) data collection measures [37]. In particular, formal and informal observations were made by inspecting the general premises and shop floors of the companies.

For the data analysis the questionnaires were evaluated. After the evaluation of the first online questionnaire, the companies were sent a document by e-mail in the lead-up to the interviews for a final decision on specific topics. The interview could only take place once all three companies had reached agreement. The interviews were evaluated using the qualitative content analysis according to Mayring [38]. For this purpose, the structuring content analysis using the MAXQDA tool was selected. The main categories in the coding were deductively defined by the textile case, but subcategories were freely coded. In the textile case, data from 2017–2020 were collected via interviews, questionnaires, workshops, observations, and document analysis and also evaluated with MAXQDA in a rather abductive procedure [cf. 39].

4   The Metal Case

4.1   Goals, Vision and Process

The goals and visions of the three companies were surveyed with the help of interviews. The clearest and most concise goal to be pursued by the DT initiative was to increase the degree of digitalization and thus optimize processes. In addition, goals were also named which would provide an insight into the work of the other companies and create suggestions for their own work, as well as reveal opportunities to work *"hand in hand"* or to stimulate cooperation. The vision is defined as the development or introduction of an information system or program that is installed across partners and customers. Each actor can place requests according to his orders and share them with several other actors as well as gain insight into the status of the completion. The goals and visions are formulated considering the value creation process in the network. The development of the comprehensive VCC process in the network was carried out in interviews with the companies, where the companies agreed on the structuring of the process and worked out which interfaces they use between the actors. The inclusion of the already modular value creation process in the observed network and, above all, the definition of the interfaces facilitates joint value creation from the point of view of the companies, since the individual process steps can be combined with the help of defined interfaces between the actors in the network. On this basis the value creation process was divided into the following phases: (1) customer needs, (2) feasibility analysis, (3) network construction and calculation, (4) production and (5) logistics and project end. The interfaces are mostly not fully digital and also not standardized; they range from technical drawings to job tickets to completion notifications. The process was recorded in a detailed BPMN, which was used as a common basis for discussion in the DT initiative. Especially in the production phase it could be observed that the bidirectional exchange with customers and partners only takes place in case of problems. This is completely different in other phases, such as 'customer needs' or 'logistics & project end', where regular exchange takes place. In the 'feasibility analysis' phase, access to information could be optimized, since relevant information is currently either stored in the head of employees or noted on slips of paper and scattered on computers. Here, the transparency of feasible services to customers and partners could also be improved. In summary, it can be said that companies want to adapt these aspects internally in order to achieve an increase in VCC. The goal in the metal case is to use digitalization as the basis for tight integration in the network, which makes the boundaries between customers and providers dissolve. Due to the lack of hierarchies in the VCC process, all participants are thus on an equal level. In practice, the implementation of this in the metal case was initially rather difficult. Even internally, not all employees are equal, especially in terms of access to information and knowledge, which is also due to the different work areas and departments. Although the companies see the advantage of a higher production capacity utilization here, they always regard the competition as a danger: *"[...] if the customer knows everything, exactly how everything is done, then he can also use this knowledge to apply it against the competition again. So, there you have to be careful that this is not counterproductive, the whole story."* In the course of the case, however, the idea of an equal exchange platform developed more and more: *"Well, the optimum would be if there was a program where all companies had access, both supplier and customer* [...]*."* However, the most important criterion here is controlling the visibility of sensitive information, which shows that trust is a key element for the network VCC in our network. Nevertheless, the dominant impression from the inter-company information exchange in the interviews is that *"paper chaos"*, *"knowledge in the head"* and *"isolated small databases where we have already entered a little bit of information"* are predominant. The cross-organizational IT support in the metal case is intended to provide access to resources and focus on continuous information supply and easy knowledge exchange.

4.2 Digitalization Level, Potentials and Recommendations

With help of process modeling, the actual degree of digitalization per company for the individual phases of the VCC process in the network was recorded during the interviews. This was considered for customer communication, partner communication and internal communication. In line with the textile case [19, 25–27], the degree of digitalization in the metal case is also differentiated into five levels in order to ensure comparability. In stage one, "Volatile", information is passed on verbally on an ad hoc basis and is not always documented; communication is error-prone and time-consuming. This stage includes personal conversation, a telephone call or communication via handwritten notes. In stage two "Persistent-Simple" communication takes place via e.g. e-mail, in which the content is stored but not in a structured way. Digitalization in the third stage, "Persistent-Structured", can be described as more efficient, in which templates, such as Word/Excel templates, are already used to structure and, if necessary, standardize the content. If documents are stored and shared in a common repository, as is possible with Dropbox or Google Drive, for example, the fourth stage of digitalization is "Persistent-Structured-Shared". The most efficient and optimized communication takes place in the last stage, the "Persistent-Structured-Shared-Controlled" stage. Here, information systems are used to support the process flow, whereby the structured data is forwarded to the right actor in the process.

In customer communications, the highest level of digitalization was achieved in the "network design & calculation" phase. The decisive factor here is that digital templates are used to send offers or order confirmations by e-mail. The lowest level of digitalization in all companies is found in the "production" phase. The reason for this is that, especially in the case of problems in production, communication is done by telephone. The same low level of digitalization across all companies in the "logistics and project end" phase is due to customer queries about the delivery status by e-mail or telephone. Partner communication is by far the least digitalized, followed by customer communication. A somewhat more positive picture emerges in the case of companies' internal communication, which is somewhat more digitalized and standardized, see Fig. 1.

The internal communication and thus used systems differ more between companies than with the other two communication types. C3 is the most digitalized, which is mainly due to the existing PPS/ERP system, which is used in almost all phases. In the system *"all the articles* [...] *are recorded, are given a unique ID in the system. In there* [...] *then also the cost centers* [...] *for processing are titled, yes, and in there all further links are made with our CAD program...".* C1 and C2 do not have such a system, only individual databases or Excel lists, calculation programs and digital

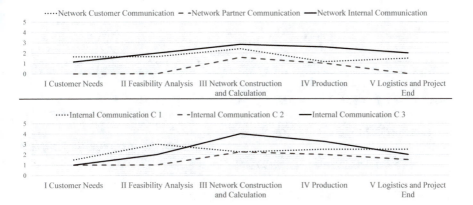

Fig. 1. Level of digitalization in the metal case

templates. The companies have been able to identify that this lack of comprehensive IT support hinders the efficient flow of information and knowledge and that there is a need for action here. Overall, the companies have a low level of digitalization. From the Sects. 4.1 and 4.2 some recommendations and potentials can be derived for the enterprises with the help of the propositions as assistance. A recommendation is based in particular on the consideration that the (P1) VCC process can be broken down into individual steps and that it is important to draw clear boundaries between the actors and to define responsibilities and rights. Furthermore, (P2) equality among the actors represents a facilitation in the process, which in turn would lead to an increase in the VCC. These two points are present, but should be strengthened. In connection with (P3) efficient information and knowledge flow and (P4) comprehensive IT support, a centralized knowledge base, where information is stored and made accessible, would be an important component. IT can take on the role of an initiator, supporter or enabler. The result could be a shared IT platform, which would facilitate the VCC process. It is important to create a comprehensive IT support and not to establish an unmanageable system landscape in the company. Based on these findings, the companies in the metal case then derived individual digitalization measures to achieve improved IT support.

4.3 Prioritization and Implementation

A target digitalization level was determined and concrete digitalization proposals were recorded. From the interviews and the questionnaires, all comments on digitalization measures were collected. The differences between the actual and target level of digitalization give rise to additional considerations. From the digitalization suggestions that were made, such as an internal messenger, digitalization measures along the VCC process could be worked out together with the actual and the target level of digitalization: *"Well, internal communication, there it would be again with the internal messenger, that you could now communicate order-accompanying special features internally or if the customer actually calls, what does it look like? That you could also prioritize this internally, for example, again".*

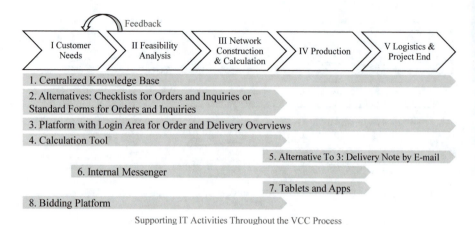

Fig. 2. Digitalization initiatives in the metal case

After the development of nine measures, these were evaluated by means of an online survey and presented to the companies with examples. The actual suitability for implementation in the company was specifically asked, but always with regard to the individual communication types. They were able to choose between "suitable", "not suitable" or "not specified". Figure 2 shows the respective measures, evaluated by the companies according to their importance. Seven of the nine measures are applied in the first three phases, with measure three and five representing alternatives to each other. The online survey also revealed the ranking of the measures. With the ranked measures and the digitalization potential that arises per phase of the VCC process, the companies in the metal case have developed an implementation plan for joint IT support. Due to the shorter runtime of the metal case, not all measures were started in the implementation phase and none were completely finished. Started were the installation of an internal messenger, negotiations with suppliers regarding the calculation tool and the implementation of the login area for orders and delivery overviews as well as the implementation of a centralized knowledge base in the network.

5   Discussion

The metal case study was conducted as a methodological replication of the textile case study [19, 25–27]. Both studies focus on the question of how the network VCC can be improved through the use of digital technologies. By replicating the textile case in the new context of the metal industry, it was possible to show that the results were independent of the industry, i.e. a transfer from the technical textile industry to the metal processing industry was possible. Some context variables were deliberately retained, firstly that it is a process industry, so no discrete goods are produced, that an engineer-to-order approach is followed, so new developments are carried out according to customer orders, and both cases are SME networks serving a B2B market. These contextual variables lead to the fact that the studied networks rely on strong information and knowledge exchange in their shared value creation in order to satisfy customer needs, since there is a low degree of product standardization. Even though both are SME networks, there is a range in company sizes; while the first network with one company with over 200 employees and several 10–30 employee companies represents small to medium sized companies, the second network with the largest companies with 20 employees and the smallest company with 3.5 employees represents small companies and micro companies. Both networks feature partners with over 100 years of history, but also younger companies with less than 30 years of operating history. Thus, both networks include companies that went through far-reaching disruptions during wartime and in the history of Eastern Germany, but also companies that were founded in the reunified Germany leading to different company traditions.

The original study developed a method to support the introduction of new digital technologies and evaluated four propositions that had a positive impact on the VCC in the network. The method was transferable and the proposition could be supported again. By validating the results, the research question can be answered in such a way that the VCC in these SME networks can be improved by cross-partner planning and steering the technology introduction on the network level (method) considering the four propositions.

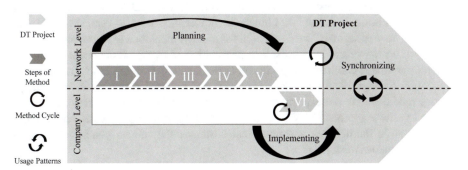

Fig. 3. Depiction of the method

Although the main points of the study were confirmed, there are some deviations of the results which are shown in the following tables. The method was developed in the textile case. The steps and their sequence were defined as well as a hierarchical break-down of the digitalization initiatives (total DT project, method cycles, and individual IT implementations). Additionally, usage patterns were found: IT planning at network level, implementation in the own company, and synchronization of the network VCC (see Fig. 3). In the metal case, the method was transferred. The steps could be retained, but the sequence was varied e.g. by switching planning steps (in Fig. 3 I-V) or by jumping back in the step sequence. The hierarchical breakdown was seen as an important aid to structuring the DT project. The usage pattern was again observed in this way, but one company from the company level was the active leader on the network level. The implication is that the original method could be adapted with some changes, as a kind of evolution. On the one hand, the sequence of steps was made more flexible and new role constellations were considered in the use of the method.

Table 1. Comparison - (P1) internal modular VC processes with clear interfaces

Textile	It could be observed, that the companies in the textile case are aware of the necessity of process modularity and practice it to configure their VCC. In fact, their value creation is even dependent on frequent recombination and therefore a wide variety of modularization concepts have become established in the network. However, the standardization using interfaces is lacking, which occasionally results in coordination problems and higher complexity due to frequent iterations in the process
Metal	It could be observed that modularity in the value creation process is recognizable and modules could be clearly identified by the companies when modelling the process. In contrast, the interfaces were only considered in the course of the case study and newly defined. Transfers between process sections were previously unstructured and ad-hoc. The step of interface definition was identified as an important step forward in the cooperation between the companies

This means that in both cases the internal modularity of the value creation process for cross-network configuration of the VCCs can already be observed (cf. Table 1). In both cases the interfaces are insufficient, one time too little standardized and digitalized and another time almost undefined. In both cases, however, it has also been shown that the companies have recognized great potential for improvement through the standardization and digitalization of the interfaces. The proposition (P1), which demands modularity and interfaces was confirmed, it partly supports the VCC building block transparency. Innovation through recombination of internal and external resources in the form of service modules with defined interfaces in a service system is also discussed in other studies as a new approach to VCC [40]. The modularization of services enables their mobilization in the network and thus creates transparency about which resources are available in the network [41].

Table 2. Comparison - (P2) equalization of the actors in the network

Textile	In the beginning, the concern about the oversharing of sensitive information dominated, which was drastically reduced in the course of the case study. The lack of awareness for the necessary digitalization of inter-actor communication became a hindering factor for the VCC. Despite the partnership philosophy in the direct network environment, co-production plays an important role and companies tend to fall into conservative stakeholder classifications
Metal	On the one hand, a cooperative behavior in the direct interaction between the examined companies is to be seen in the close co-production and by the willingness of the larger company to assume the economic responsibility for digitalization measures in the network. On the other hand, the companies have struggled with the general idea of equal partners, as they often appear as competitors and thus the concern of losing their competitive advantage arises

The claim of the second proposition was supported by the observations in the face-to-face interaction of actors in both cases, but not when considering digital communication or documentation, where legacy processes are in place (cf. Table 2). In addition, it was observed in both cases that at the beginning the standardized sharing of internal information was perceived as a danger of over sharing sensitive information. In the long-lasting case, this phase was almost completely overcome after two years by exploring technical possibilities and intensive cooperation in the companies' digitalization project. In the shorter case, where only four months were spent working on a joint digitalization project, this learning process could only begin. The building block dialogue is supported above all by the second proposition, where equal partners act together as problem solvers [32, 33]. Although the partnership approach between the companies has a positive effect on their VCC and this is also said by the companies themselves, the cases, which were considered in varying lengths of time, made it clear that the SMEs first have to learn certain skills for the successful use of new digital technologies in a prosperous VCC [42]. This supports the fact that SMEs in networks have to build up relational skills such as human or cultural relational capabilities [5]. This learning process then takes place again in the context of digital technologies, for example with platform capabilities, where relational capabilities have to be learned in a new environment [1, 7].

Table 3. Comparison - (P3) efficient and standardized communication between actors

Textile	The previous predominant logic in the textile network has led to companies only optimizing their own information flows and thus neglecting the integration of other actors. A lot of critical information only exists in the minds of individual employees such as the information "which actor can perform which service". In addition, the answer to the question "Which process step adds which functions to the textile" is only known by each supplier in his field of expertise
Metal	On the one hand, the degree of digitalization in the metal case differs greatly between the large and the small companies in the network, on the other hand communication between the partners usually takes place at a very low digitalization level (telephone)

The third proposition could not be confirmed due to an absence of an efficient information flow in the two cases (cf. Table 3). However, the companies in both cases stated that insufficient information flow poses their collective biggest challenge and thus indirectly support the proposition and they identify knowledge bases and mutual access to them as prerequisites for their network VCC. Therefore, the focus was placed on various digitalization initiatives to improve the communication between the partners as well as to the customers. Both networks initially experienced problems with the efficient information and knowledge flow from the third proposition. This information asymmetry negatively influences both the building block transparency and the risk assessment of the VCCs [32]. However, due to the longer case study duration in the textile case, the VCC could be improved by increasing the digitalization of information and knowledge flows through the introduction and use of a shared IT platform [26]. In the metal case, concrete measures to improve these flows, such as the introduction of a messenger, are being implemented. It has been shown that efficient sharing of information and knowledge is a key element of the VCC and by disclosing critical information not only transparency is increased, but if, for example, feasibility can be assessed at an early stage, the risk of losses for the actors involved is also reduced [33].

A cross-organizational IT support could not be observed in both cases (cf. Table 4). Therefore, the fourth proposition could not be confirmed by an existing IT solution, instead, the companies described a joint IT solution along the VCC process as their envisioned approach to facilitate the VCC. Access as the last building block of the VCC was also not supported at the beginning of the two case studies, but could be realized in the textile case through the successful implementation of a shared IT platform for partners and customers with a common knowledge base. Meanwhile, in the metal case, an orchestration of several small IT solutions and joining an existing bidder platform as cross-organizational IT support was initiated to improve the VCC.

Table 4. Comparison - (P4) cross-organizational IT support for VCC

Textile	The companies in the textile case are facing varying challenges with different grades of digitalization and standardization in their internal processes. The internal IT infrastructure of the companies already forms an important basis for cross-company IT support, but obstacles in the IT of individual companies can also transfer to the network
Metal	Internal IT is not yet strongly developed in the metal case. The low level of digitalization is particularly noticeable in small companies, which means that the larger company has been designated by the companies as host for the IT solutions in the network

IT infrastructures form the basis for the digital value creation strategies in which a large number of actors are connected [43]. In the two cases under consideration, two contrasting strategies for the realization of cross-organizational IT support can be recognized. In the textile case an IT platform was newly developed, which is then jointly owned and operated, corresponding to a digital manifestation of a strategic alliance as it can also be found in the newspaper industry [44]. In contrast to this, in the metal case, the aim was to use digital solutions available on the market and to join an existing marketplace platform operated by an intermediary, as often the case with SMEs due to limited resources [1].

Subsequent to this promising replication study in another industry, initial steps were taken to conduct a more extensive replication with more variation in context variables. To this end a case comparison of the textile case and a case in the Australian construction industry was conducted. It became apparent that there was a significant overlap of findings even though the Australian case was a B2B retailer network and the company in question, with over 300 employees, is no longer considered an SME. These insights were used as an impetus to aim for yet another replication study as further research, where again in Germany an SME retailer network in the textile industry was chosen, where the collaboration is accompanied by a clothing manufacturer and its retail stores with a digitalization project. This changes many of the context variables, it is no longer engineer-to-order, it is not a process industry, and the retailers are already operating in a B2C market.

6   Conclusion

In our replication study we were able to confirm the findings of the original study. The implications for research are that the developed method and propositions were validated beyond the previous context. Furthermore, the studies address calls for research in the context of the VCC in networks [21]. As an implication for practice, the method for digital transformation and propositions for the improvement of VCC can be used by SME's across industries. As a limitation, we have merely carried out a methodological replication and additionally transferred it to a very similar context. Therefore, as future research we are working on a replication in a network of SME's in the retail sector.

Acknowledgements. The research described in this paper was supported by a grant from the German Ministry for Research and Education (BMBF), project name: PROFUND grant number: 03ZZ0618C.

References

1. Li, L., Su, F., Zhang, W., Mao, J.Y.: Digital transformation by SME entrepreneurs: a capability perspective. Inf. Syst. J. **28**, 1129–1157 (2018)
2. Mahmood, K., Lanz, M., Toivonen, V., Otto, T.: A performance evaluation concept for production systems in an SME network. Procedia CIRP **72**, 603–608 (2018)
3. Goerzig, D., Bauernhansl, T.: Enterprise architectures for the digital transformation in small and medium-sized enterprises. Procedia CIRP **67**, 540–545 (2018)
4. Barann, B., Hermann, A., Cordes, A.-K., Chasin, F., Becker, J.: Supporting digital transformation in small and medium-sized enterprises: a procedure model involving publicly funded support units. In: 52nd Hawaii International Conference on System Sciences, Maui, pp. 4977–4986 (2019)
5. Ngugi, I.K., Johnsen, R.E., Erdélyi, P.: Relational capabilities for value co-creation and innovation in SMEs. J. Small Bus. Enterp. Dev. **17**, 260–278 (2010)
6. Stojanova, T., Suzic, N., Orcik, A.: Implementation of mass customization tools in small and medium enterprises. Int. J. Ind. Eng. Manag. **3**, 253–260 (2012)
7. Cenamor, J., Parida, V., Wincent, J.: How entrepreneurial SMEs compete through digital platforms: the roles of digital platform capability, network capability, and ambidexterity. J. Bus. Res. **100**, 196–206 (2019)
8. Vial, G.: Understanding digital transformation: a review and a research agenda. J. Strateg. Inf. Syst. **28**, 118–144 (2019)
9. Kane, G.C., Palmer, D., Phillips, A.N., Kiron, D., Buckley, N.: Strategy, not technology, drives digital transformation. https://sloanreview.mit.edu/projects/strategy-drives-digital-transform ation/. Accessed 01 May 2019
10. Matt, C., Hess, T., Benlian, A.: Digital transformation strategies. Bus. Inf. Syst. Eng. **57**(5), 339–343 (2015). https://doi.org/10.1007/s12599-015-0401-5
11. Singh, A., Hess, T.: How chief digital officers promote the digital transformation of their companies. MIS Q. Exec. **16**, 1–17 (2017)

12. Bharadwaj, A., El Sawy, O.A., Pavlou, P.A., Venkatraman, N.: Digital business strategy: toward a next generation of insights. MIS Q. **37**, 471–482 (2013)
13. Wang, Y.C.W., Chang, C.-W., Heng, M.: The levels of information technology adoption, business network, and a strategic position model for evaluating supply chain integration. J. Electron. Commer. Res. **5**, 85–98 (2004)
14. Rogers, D.L.: The Digital Transformation Playbook: Rethink Your Business for the Digital Age. Columbia University Press, New York (2016)
15. Pagani, M.: Digital business strategy and value creation: framing the dynamic cycle of control points. MIS Q. **37**, 617–632 (2013)
16. Breidbach, C.F., Maglio, P.P.: Technology-enabled value co-creation: an empirical analysis of actors, resources, and practices. Ind. Mark. Manag. **56**, 73–85 (2016)
17. Muller, P., et al.: Annual Report on European SMEs 2018/2019 Research & Development and Innovation by SMEs, Brussels (2019)
18. Bundesministerium für Wirtschaft und Energie (BMWi): Monitoring-Report Wirtschaft Digital 2018, München (2018)
19. Hönigsberg, S., Dinter, B.: Toward a method to foster the digital transformation in SME networks. In: 40th International Conference on Information Systems, Munich, pp. 1–8 (2019)
20. De Reuver, M., Sørensen, C., Basole, R.C.: The digital platform: a research agenda. J. Inf. Technol. **33**, 124–135 (2018)
21. Lusch, R.F., Nambisan, S.: Service innovation: a service-dominant logic perspective. MIS Q. **39**, 155–175 (2015)
22. Jaakkola, E., Hakanen, T.: Value co-creation in solution networks. Ind. Mark. Manag. **42**, 47–58 (2013)
23. Halinen, A., Törnroos, J.-A.: Using case methods in the study of contemporary business networks. J. Bus. Res. **58**, 1285–1297 (2005)
24. Dennis, A., Valacich, J.: A replication manifesto. AIS Trans. Replication Res. **1**, 1–4 (2014)
25. Hönigsberg, S., Dinter, B.: Network value co-creation goes digital – a case study. In: 25th Americas Conference on Information Systems, Cancun, pp. 1–10 (2019)
26. Hönigsberg, S., Dinter, B., Wache, H.: The impact of digital technology on network value co-creation. In: 53rd Hawaii International Conference on System Sciences, Maui, pp. 5233–5242 (2020)
27. Hönigsberg, S.: A platform for value co-creation in SME networks. In: 15th International Conference on Design Science Research in Information Systems and Technology, Kristiansand (2020)
28. Legner, C., et al.: Digitalization: opportunity and challenge for the business and information systems engineering community. Bus. Inf. Syst. Eng. **59**(4), 301–308 (2017). https://doi.org/10.1007/s12599-017-0484-2
29. Gimpel, H., Hosseini, S., Huber, R.X.R., Probst, L., Röglinger, M., Faisst, U.: Structuring digital transformation: a framework of action fields and its application at ZEISS. J. Inf. Technol. Theory Appl. **19**, 31–54 (2018)
30. Wessel, L., Baiyere, A., Ologeanu-Taddei, R., Cha, J., Blegind-Jensen, T.: Unpacking the difference between digital transformation and IT-enabled organizational transformation. J. Assoc. Inf. Syst. (2020, forthcoming)
31. Teece, D.J.: Business models and dynamic capabilities. Long Range Plann. **51**, 40–49 (2018)
32. Prahalad, C.K., Ramaswamy, V.: Co-creation experiences: the next practice in value creation. J. Interact. Mark. **18**, 5–14 (2004)
33. Aarikka-Stenroos, L., Jaakkola, E.: Value co-creation in knowledge intensive business services: a dyadic perspective on the joint problem solving process. Ind. Mark. Manag. **41**, 15–26 (2012)
34. Hicks, C., McGovern, T., Earl, C.F.: Supply chain management: a strategic issue in engineer to order manufacturing. Int. J. Prod. Econ. **65**, 179–190 (2000)

35. Glaser, B.G., Strauss, A.L.: The Discovery of Grounded Theory Strategies for Qualitative Research. AldineTransaction, New Brunswick (1967)
36. Niederman, F., March, S.: Reflections on replications. AIS Trans. Replication Res. **1**, 1–16 (2015)
37. Yin, R.K.: Case Study Research and Applications: Design and Methods. SAGE Publications Inc., Los Angeles (2018)
38. Mayring, P.: Qualitative content analysis. In: Flick, U., von Kardoff, E., Steinke, I. (eds.) A Companion to Qualitative Research, pp. 266–270. SAGE Publications Inc., London (2004)
39. Baiyere, A., Salmela, H., Tapanainen, T.: Digital transformation and the new logics of business process management. Eur. J. Inf. Syst. 1–22 (2020)
40. Beverungen, D., Lüttenberg, H., Wolf, V.: Recombinant service systems engineering. Bus. Inf. Syst. Eng. **60**(5), 377–391 (2018). https://doi.org/10.1007/s12599-018-0526-4
41. Blaschke, M., Riss, U., Haki, K., Aier, S.: Design principles for digital value co-creation networks: a service-dominant logic perspective. Electron. Mark. **29**(3), 443–472 (2019). https://doi.org/10.1007/s12525-019-00356-9
42. Eze, S.C., Chinedu-Eze, V.C.: Examining information and communication technology (ICT) adoption in SMEs - a dynamic capabilities approach. J. Enterp. Inf. Manag. **31**, 338–356 (2018)
43. Tan, B., Pan, S.L., Lu, X., Huang, L.: The role of is capabilities in the development of multi-sided platforms: the digital ecosystem strategy of alibaba.com. J. Assoc. Inf. Syst. **16**, 248–280 (2015)
44. Kazan, E., Ghanbari, H., Tuunanen, T., Li, M., Tumbas, S.: Strategic design towards platform collaboration in the newspaper industry: a design science research study. In: 53rd Hawaii International Conference on System Sciences, Maui, pp. 5086–5095 (2020)

Differences in Skill Requirements for Agile Workers in the German and the US IT Industries

Céline Madeleine Aldenhoven(✉), Dominik Korbinian Brosch, Barbara Prommegger, and Helmut Krcmar

Chair for Information Systems and Business Process Management, Technical University of Munich, Munich, Germany
{celine.aldenhoven,dominik.brosch,barbara.prommegger, helmut.krcmar}@tum.de

Abstract. The IT industry is getting more and more agile. Therefore, it is important to know about the required skills for agile workers in this industry. In this study, we analyzed 1000 job advertisements from online job portals to determine the differences in skill requirements for agile workers in the IT industry in Germany versus the U.S. We found that searches for non-technical skills are greater in the U.S. than in Germany. Test and Requirements Management are the most important management concept searches in both countries. JavaScript is searched more often in the U.S. This study contributes to a better understanding of the required skills of agile workers in Germany and the U.S.

Keywords: Skills · Agile · IT workforce · Programming languages · Non-technical skills

1 Introduction

Over the last several years, digital globalization has grown exponentially, fueled by highly skilled IT professionals working behind the scenes. As a result of this ongoing transformation, skilled workers are in high demand, leading to more openings in the IT industry [29]. But how are software projects efficiently organized? According to a survey among IT professionals in the U.S. [12], most software projects are already done with an agile or leaning toward the agile approach. The survey revealed that in 2004, only 4% of the surveyed companies used agile methodologies. By 2014, all the firms had adopted them. One significant benefit of the agile approach mentioned by the respondents was, "agile enhances collaboration between teams that usually do not work together". Therefore, collaboration skills are an essential component of the non-technical skills requested by recruiters. This is also reflected in the first principle of the Agile Manifesto [25]: "Individuals and interactions over processes and tools".

This is why we proposed the question, what skills are recruiters actually looking for today as they recruit personnel for an agile environment. As technology changes and agile working methodologies evolve, the required skills for a successful career in the IT industry evolve with the market. The shift to agile methodologies specifically requires more team interaction [25]. Therefore, soft skills for agile workers become increasingly important [23]. Several studies have been conducted on the skills and requirements needed to serve the rapidly expanding IT market, particularly from its new hires [4, 10, 21]. Those studies exposed two important gaps: 1) between the skills recruiters searched for versus the skills required by future employers [10] and 2) between the skills employers need and the skills learned in academia [4, 21]. Unfortunately, most of these studies were conducted in the U.S. with U.S. datasets. There is a lack of surveys in this area with European datasets. Due to the change to agile methodologies, we expect that the required skills of the IT workforce have also changed. Therefore, a review of sought-after technical and non-technical skills of agile workers is necessary.

The study aims to identify the required skills for workers in agile positions in the U.S. and in Germany (Ger) and uncover the differences in required skills in these two countries. Our paper also elaborates on the reasons behind these differences.

2 Theoretical Background

To learn more about previous research conducted in related fields, we reviewed the literature on the topics of agile skills, IT industry skills, skills, agile, and skill recruitment. A surprising number of papers were primarily focused on the technical skills required in the IT industry, whereas others studied required non-technical skills [10, 15]. Most of the papers evaluating job advertisements also categorized the skills. During our research, we also found substantial evidence on the impact of non-technical skills on the performance of IT teams [3, 5, 7, 19, 23], underlining the importance of these skills. Furthermore, some papers studied the change in required skills over time and made predictions for future job requirements [9, 11].

2.1 Changing Requirements Have Led to Changing Job Advertisements

Over the years, the information systems researchers reviewed technical and non-technical requirements in job advertisements. Technical skills were always important and evolved as the technology required but not so much quantitatively. Litecky et al. [17] stated it best in an analysis of job advertisements from the 1990s and 2000s, *"Although application and web development skills are still in demand, the programming languages and tools used for development have changed.".* This notion is apparent in work by Todd et al. [20]. Non-technical requirements were usually less prevalent in job advertisements, although Gallivan et al. and Lee et al. [10, 16] showed the increased need for them. Work by Gallivan et.al. [10] revealed the need for more non-technical skills even as the rate of communication and interpersonal skills was declining. The results indicated a recruitment gap between the required skills in job listings and the actual skills required by employers. The discrepancy was noted by Wade et al. [24].

As of the mid-2000s, non-technical skills gained prominence in job advertisements. In 2007, Kennan et al. [15] looked at the required skills in job listings for information systems graduates in Australia and learned that *"Personal Characteristics and Communications Skills [...] were mentioned in close to 75% of ads."* and *"Computer Languages occurred in more than 50% of the ads.".* This finding was also reflected by Florea et al.

[8], who analyzed the skills required for software testers. The study showed that non-technical skills, including communication, are very important for testers. They saw an increase in the *"requirements regarding being a team-player, flat-learner, independent-working and having openness and adaptability skills."*. Furthermore, they found minimal difference in a comparison of skills required for testing in an agile environments and positions where agile knowledge was not explicitly stated.

2.2 Skills of the Agile Workforce

Working agile changed the requirements for workers on agile teams. Workers are required to communicate more and to know about the whole value chain of development [30]. Therefore, the skill profile of agile workers must be much more differentiated than the one of non-agile workers.

Further investigation of non-technical skills in IT and information systems jobs revealed papers highlighting the importance of non-technical skills for successful IT projects. Csapo et al. [5] showed that *"employees spend more than 75% of their time communicating in interpersonal situations, as well as on a variety of other levels within the organization and externally."*. This finding reinforces the importance of non-technical skills, especially communication skills. Venkatesh et al. [23] provided another view on the agile work environment and showed that organizational skills are critical in reducing stress and enabling success in IT teams. Emotional intelligence supports the same goals [19]. The importance of non-technical skills is also apparent in employer surveys [13, 14]. Interestingly, this is more important for software and IT service providers than for non-IT companies, as they search more for non-technical skills [11].

3   Research Method

Given the lack of literature analyzing the differing requirements in IT skills between the U.S. and Germany, especially in the agile context, we chose to take an explorative approach to find unexpected results. To that end, we performed a qualitative analysis of two different job sites and collected 1000 job advertisements using the keyword "agile". We followed the guidelines of the skill paper by Gallivan et al. [10] and others [4, 6, 18], for the data collection process via Monster.com. Our U.S. data were sourced from monster.com following previous research in the field [4, 6, 18]. Monster.com was used because of its popularity and continuity of information [10]. For German job postings, we used stepstone.de, a popular job advertisement platform in the country [32]. We designed our workflow to be as generic and reproducible as possible to facilitate further work in the field.

Our workflow was divided into three stages, as illustrated in Fig. 1. First, we extracted the data from job sites and pushed them into a database. Next, we developed a tool for manually extracting skills from full-text job descriptions and categorized them using a general skill layout to simplify the evaluation process. Finally, we developed a tool to generate real-time tables from the categorized skills layout and other data, such as the title/role of the job or the location of the job.

Fig. 1. Data collection process

3.1 Data Crawling and Collection

Initially, we explored the structure of both sites to develop a structure for our database. We collected a unique identifier for each job, the job title, company name, job description, job location country, and data source, in our case stepstone.de or monster.com. Where available, we extracted the industry name, job location city, posting date, job category, and other metadata seen in our publicly available code[1].

With our initial database configuration complete, we developed the corresponding crawler for both monster.com and stepstone.de. For each crawler, we queried one job offer at a time with a slight delay in between to ensure that no relevant extra load was put on the servers. After letting our crawlers run, we noticed that many job advertisements on monster.com were posted in the "Staffing/Employment Agencies" industry. These advertisements were very generic and allowed little conclusion about the required skills and responsibilities of the role. Therefore, we decided to filter them out and focus only on companies directly searching for employees. To limit our dataset to job ads requiring "agile" knowledge, we filtered the job description with the word "agile".

3.2 Skill Extraction and Classification

Our team of two people reviewed 50 job postings each to get a sense of the different skill requirements and to make categorization notes. In a later meeting, we created a coding scheme on the basis of experience, technical, and non-technical skills. In the experience category, we stated the required minimum for an educational degree and years of work experience. We categorized technical skills into multiple categories on the basis of our knowledge of previously analyzed datasets. Programming Languages and Frameworks, Management Concepts, Non-Technical Skills, Certificates, Degree, Testing Knowledge, Deployment Knowledge, and Job Title were the final categories in our tables.

We include three of the above categories in this paper, as they reveal the most interesting results: 1) Non-technical skills, as seen in Table 4 2) Programming Languages and Frameworks (defined as Programming languages to implement algorithms such as JavaScript, Java, or PHP, as well as scripting and markup languages such as HTML/CSS and XML, we categorized Frameworks under their main written language), and 3) Management Concepts (covering software development processes such as Scrum

---

[1] https://bitbucket.org/agiletum/monster-crawler/,   https://bitbucket.org/agiletum/stepstone-crawler/, https://bitbucket.org/agiletum/monster-server/.

and IT project management concepts and methodologies such as Continuous Integration, Microservices, or DevOps).

To further categorize non-technical skills, we adapted the coding scheme created by Ahmed [28] and extended it with six more categories as seen in Table 4 of the appendix. Exact pattern matches and other details of our workflow are available in our source code[1] and in Table 4.

4   Results

We analyzed 500 datasets from the U.S. and Germany, respectively, for a total of 1000 job advertisements. The following results are based on the categories of "non-technical skills", "management concepts", and "programming languages and frameworks". In our dataset, U.S. job listings mentioned 24.7 skills in average, while German ones mentioned 13.3 in those categories.

First, we provide insights into the most frequently mentioned non-technical skills for agile workers. Table 1 provides an overview of in-demand non-technical skills. We found that non-technical skills, such as communication skills, problem solving skills, and leadership skills were mentioned more often in the U.S. than in Germany. U.S. job advertisements searched 37.5% more often for communication skills (U.S.: 59.4%, Ger: 43.2%), two times more often for analytical and problem-solving skills (U.S.: 78.0%, Ger: 38.6%) and over two times more often for leadership skills (U.S.: 84.0%,

Table 1. Non-technical skills of agile workers in the U.S. and in Germany

Skill	The U.S. (total)	The U.S. (%)	Germany (total)	Germany (%)
Work in teams	451	90.2	355	71.0
Leadership skills	420	84.0	200	40.0
Organizational skills	394	78.8	196	39.2
Analytical and problem-solving skills	390	78.0	193	38.6
Being innovative	350	70.0	197	39.4
Being motivated	323	64.6	136	27.2
Communication skills	297	59.4	216	43.2
Work with clients	288	57.6	143	28.6
Interpersonal skills	194	38.8	85	17.0
Fast learner	176	35.2	33	6.6
Presentation skills	115	23.0	29	5.8
Ability to work independently	87	17.4	102	20.4
Open and adaptable to change	50	10.0	43	8.6
Travelling	39	7.8	71	14.2
Languages	16	3.2	323	64.6
Other	9	1.8	61	12.2
Total	498/500	99.6	489/500	97.8

Ger: 40.0%). Organizational skills were mentioned twice as often in the U.S. than in Germany (U.S.: 78.8%, Ger: 39.2%). The skills more often searched for in Germany than in the US were language skills and the ability to work independently.

Next, we provide insights into the most requested knowledge concerning management concepts for agile workers. Table 2 provides an overview of the results mentioning management concepts. In Germany, the most important skills are Scrum, Test Management, and Requirements Management. In the U.S., our findings were similar, except that Scrum was replaced by IT Project Management. Continuous Integration/Deployment (CI/CD) knowledge is almost three times more often requested in the U.S. than in Germany (U.S.: 30.4%, Ger: 10.2%). A similar trend is visible for Test-Driven Development (TDD), which is more than two times more popular in the U.S. (U.S.: 10.2%, Ger: 4.8%). Test management is 72.8% more in demand in the U.S. (U.S.: 58.4%, Ger: 33.8%). Finally, project management skills are 2.8 times more prevalent in U.S. job advertisements (U.S.: 64.2%, Ger: 22.6%).

Table 2. Management concepts of agile workers in the US and in Germany

Skill	The U.S (total)	The U.S. (%)	Germany (total)	Germany (%)
IT project management	321	64.2	113	22.6
Requirement management	310	62.0	126	25.2
Test management (automation, continuous)	292	58.4	169	33.8
Scrum	194	38.8	187	37.4
CI/CD	152	30.4	51	10.2
Coding practices	96	19.2	46	9.2
Risk management	95	19.0	14	2.8
DevOps	76	15.2	61	12.2
TDD	51	10.2	24	4.8
Design patterns	46	9.2	14	2.8
User stories	44	8.8	17	3.4
Microservices	37	7.4	18	3.6
Scaled agile	37	7.4	18	3.6
Kanban	34	6.8	60	12.0
Industry knowledge (business & markets)	30	6.0	14	2.8
Other	175	35.0	120	24.0
Total	491/500	98.2	500/500	100.0

Finally, we provide insights into the most requested programming languages and frameworks of agile workers in our dataset. Table 3 provides an overview of the results. JavaScript was more popular in the U.S. than in Germany. While 28.2% of all U.S. agile job advertisements in IT mentioned JavaScript knowledge, only 17.6% of German job advertisements in our dataset searched for this language. According to our collected data, JavaScript dominates the U.S. IT industry in terms of programming languages. Furthermore, HTML/CSS knowledge is more than 2.8 times more requested in the U.S. than in Germany (U.S.: 22.2%, Ger: 7.8%). Of the top five programming languages in the U.S. and Germany, all executable programming languages have support for object-oriented development; 49% of German job advertisements and 26% of U.S. job ads did not mention any specific programming language.

Table 3. Programming languages and frameworks of agile workers in the US and in Germany

Skill	The U.S. (total)	The U.S. (%)	Germany (total)	Germany (%)
JavaScript (including frameworks)	140	28.0	88	17.6
SQL	140	28.0	75	15.0
Java (including frameworks)	128	25.6	106	21.2
HTML/CSS	111	22.2	39	7.8
Python	76	15.2	45	9.0
C#	74	14.8	51	10.2
C++	47	9.4	35	7.0
Scala	38	7.6	6	1.2
NoSQL	23	4.6	18	3.6
XML	15	3.0	1	0.2
Bash/Shell/PowerShell	11	2.2	5	1.0
PHP	10	2.0	13	2.6
C	4	0.8	9	1.8
ERP/CMS	4	0.8	8	1.6
Other	77	15.4	54	10.8
Total	370/500	74.0	255/500	51.0

5   Discussion

The following section reveals our results, including theoretical and practical implications, and points to possibilities for future research.

5.1   Geographical Differences in Non-technical Skills for Agile Workers

Our results show that communication, problem-solving, and leadership skills are mentioned more in the U.S. than in Germany. Almost all U.S. job advertisements search for these skills versus three-quarters of the job ads in Germany. This finding draws a different picture than the one provided by Gallivan et al. [10]. They stated that he *"found ongoing evidence of a recruitment gap where, despite many firms' stated emphasis on well-rounded individuals with business knowledge and strong 'soft skills,' the job advertising aspect of the recruiting process continues to focus on 'hard skills'."* [10, p. 1]. Our findings, 16 years later, show an improvement in this regard, closing the recruitment gap (where soft skills are needed but not listed in job advertisements), identified by Gallivan et al. [10], at least for agile job postings in the IT industry.

Language skills are the most important non-technical skill for agile workers in Germany. More than three-fifth of the job offers explicitly require knowledge of a language, mostly German or English. Therefore, the question is whether the same soft skills recruitment gap that Gallivan et al. identified [10] can be identified in Germany several years later. The answer would require further research as to the skills that German firms really want from their agile workers. Assuming the recruitment gap by Gallivan et al. [10] exists in Germany 16 years later, it would be an interesting topic to research to learn whether recruitment trends from the U.S. are swapping over to Germany in a timely manner.

According to our results, U.S job listings mentioned almost twice as many skills than German ones on average. Therefore, the result that non-technical skills are more important in the U.S. could also be the case because U.S. job listings had included more skills in general. Our findings state that U.S. firms ask for more skills in general, which may indicate that U.S. job listings are structured differently than German ones. This could be a result of cultural differences of the recruitment process. For future research it is interesting to see if all the skills mentioned in U.S. job listings really have to be fulfilled from the new hire.

Our results support Venkatesh et al. [23] who highlighted the agile workers' need for organizational skills. The authors stated, although the use of the agile methods may improve clear role perceptions and work exhaustion of developers, organizational skills are needed to effectively collaborate. Thus, the high value of non-technical skills in U.S. job listings for the IT industry is a very good step toward hiring effective agile teams. German employers should place more emphasis on non-technical skills in the recruitment process of agile workers, or they risk falling behind [23].

5.2 Agile Workers in the US Need to Have a Broader Knowledge of the Whole Workflow than in Germany

Our results show that CI/CD knowledge, TDD and test management skills, and requirement management are more important for agile workers in the U.S. than in Germany. This indicates that in the U.S., agile team members must know the whole workflow, from requirements engineering through test management and deployment, whereas in Germany, the workflow is distributed into multiple roles.

The findings also suggest that agile job descriptions follow the Agile Manifesto [25] more closely. The goal "Working software over comprehensive documentation" is reflected in the adoption of Test-Driven Development, meaning that the functions of the software are defined by tests rather than extensive documentation and specification. This aligns with the need for test management and requirements management, as good requirement management is needed for planning and writing tests. The need for CI and CD skills is reflected in the usable product increment, a very important part of the Scrum process [26]. It is surprising to see that CI/CD is much less important for German agile workers.

5.3   High US Demand for Web Technologies and JavaScript for Agile Workers

Surprisingly, there is a big difference between programming languages used in the agile working IT industry in Germany and the U.S., as shown in Table 3. Although JavaScript, including frameworks such as JQuery, React, Vue, and Angular, is the most searched for programming language in the U.S., with less than one-third of ads mentioning it, only about one-fifth of German job ads request JavaScript knowledge. When comparing this to programming languages currently used by developers worldwide, on the basis of the 2020 StackOverflow Developer Survey [27], we notice that our results for the U.S. are quite similar to those of the survey, and they both show the lead of JavaScript. Additionally, HTML/CSS, C#, and Python are all more popular in the U.S. than in Germany. Java is the most required language in Germany in agile jobs, with more than one-fifth of the advertisements requiring it, according to our results.

Comparing our results with data collected by Gallivan et al. [10], the change is clearly visible. In 2001, C was the most popular programming language. Today, it is not even in the top ten. Similarly, COBOL has completely vanished from our results. By contrast, although object-oriented programming languages were required in less than nine percent of job advertisements in 2001, currently, all the top five programming languages except HTML/CSS, which is not an executable programming language, allow object-oriented programming. Compared with the results by Gallivan et al. [10], we see a similar pattern in Germany as in the U.S., with a clear focus on object-oriented languages. C is still more popular in Germany than in the U.S. Generally, it seems as though newer frameworks, such as Node.js and Angular, or generally newer programming concepts, are more widespread in the agile IT industry in the U.S. than in Germany. This might be an indication that German companies adopt new technologies slower than U.S. companies. However, this requires further study.

The radical change in the last two decades serves as an example of the need to learn and adopt new technologies in the IT industry. Programming languages required today will not be the same ones required 20 years from now, although current graduates entering the job market will then still be in the middle of their careers.

5.4   Implications for Theory and Practice

With our paper, we contribute to two fields of research. First, we contribute to skills literature [1, 2, 4, 7, 8]. Our results provide a better understanding of the current skill requirements in Germany and the U.S. Second, we contribute to agile literature [3, 23, 26, 30]. We show differences in agile working between the two countries.

With our updated dataset and the focus on agile skills, we have looked at the recruitment gap from previous researchers [10, 24] and compared it to our findings. We found the recruitment gap to be larger in Germany than in the U.S. This study contributes to recruitment gap research both in the U.S. and in Europe. Furthermore, we show that universities should focus even more on building soft skills to make their students more competitive in the job market. This assertion supports previous research in the field from other countries.

Apart from that, our paper has direct practical relevance for companies, students, and young professionals. For German companies, it might serve as a reminder to promote critical non-technical skills in job advertisements, as these are the skills used in everyday business. Communication skills, problem solving skills, and leadership skills are underrepresented in the German job market. The differences we illuminated regarding the adoption of new technologies might encourage employers to actively search for employees with knowledge in recently introduced technologies. Finally, this paper serves as a useful summary for students and young professionals on the non-technical skills required for agile jobs in Germany and the U.S.

5.5 Limitations

Our research was conducted with certain limitations. First, the term "agile" limited our search to jobs containing this particular tag. This leaves room for fitting job advertisements on our topic that we do not analyze. There may exist some job advertisements mentioning Scrum or Kanban for instance, but not the word "agile". Those job advertisements do not contribute to our findings in any way. Second, with our decision to choose the monster.com and stepstone.de platforms, we cannot be sure that we captured a representative dataset for all agile jobs in Germany and the U.S. However, we do not suspect any bias regarding specific skills in stepstone.de and monster.com. Third, there could also be cultural differences in the recruitment process. This might influence the way recruiters formulate their job advertisements, which is not a factor analyzed in our data. Hence, the conclusion that US workers need more soft skills might be a derivative from a cultural difference. Ahmed et al. concluded that *"cultural difference does not have a major impact on the choice of soft skills requirements in hiring new employee in the case of the software development profession."* [31, p. 1]. Therefore, it could also be the case that the soft skills requirements are the same for the U.S. and Germany, but U.S. firms explicitly state them in their job listings, while German ones do not. This is not analyzed in our paper.

5.6 Further Research

With our system for evaluating job listings, it is now possible to expand the analyzed categories to include more subdomains, such as operating systems, deployment methods, and testing methods, to allow further research in the field of IT job requirements. Additionally, more work is required to further evaluate if and how many trends in technology are adopted first in the U.S. and then in Germany, which might provide interesting insights into the future development of the German IT skills market.

592   C. M. Aldenhoven et al.

Although many of the well-known tech companies, such as Apple or Google, are from the U.S., more research is needed to see how the required skills in job listings are reflected in the success of agile teams. It would also be very interesting to review how the performance of agile teams compares to non-agile teams and how this is reflected in job advertisements.

Furthermore, as previously mentioned in our limitations, it would be interesting to review the influence of cultural differences in job advertisements and how the content of the job listings reflect the actual needs of employers.

6 Conclusion

As the digitalization expands globally, more jobs are being created in the IT industry. To fill those jobs with highly qualified workers, it is essential to know what skills are needed by the companies operating in the IT industry. With the increasing adoption of agile practices in IT, the required skills for agile workers are of critical importance.

This paper aims to fill a research gap, as most of the studies about required skills have been made using U.S. rather than European datasets. By investigating current job listings in the U.S. and Germany, we provide a better understanding of the required skills for workers in agile positions.

There were three key findings in our results. First, we learned that non-technical skills, including communication, problem solving, and leadership skills, are more important in the U.S. than in Germany. Second, we found that Test Driven Development (TDD) and Continuous Integration/Deployment (CI/CD) skills are required more often in the U.S. than in Germany. Third, we saw that JavaScript is more popular in the U.S. than in Germany, as are general modern web development languages such as HTML and CSS.

With our findings, we contribute to a better understanding of the required skills of agile workers in the U.S. and Germany. There are many other directions to investigate using the foundation of our data. These include assessing new job advertisements with our tools, studying U.S. trends as they move to Germany, and venturing further into the details of the data that we already collected.

Appendix

Table 4. Soft skill categorization by [28] and coding scheme for the skills of agile workers Germany and the US

Soft skill	Definition according to Ahmed (2012)
Communication skills	The ability to convey information so that it's well received and understood
Interpersonal skills	The ability to deal with other people through social communication and interactions under favorable and inauspicious conditions
Analytical and problem-solving skills	The ability to understand, articulate, and solve complex problems and make sensible decisions based on available information
Team player	Someone who can work effectively in a team environment and contribute toward the desired goal
Organizational skills	The ability to efficiently manage various tasks and to remain on schedule without wasting resources
Fast learner	The ability to learn new concepts, methodologies, and technologies in a comparatively short timeframe
Ability to work independently	Can carry out task with minimal supervision
Innovative	The ability to come up with new and creative solutions
Open and adaptable to change	The ability to accept and adapt to changes when carrying out a task without showing resistance
Additional soft skill	**Definition based on analyzed job offers**
Work with clients	The ability to work directly with clients
Traveling	The ability to travel for a certain part of the work time
Languages	The ability to speak a certain language
Motivated	Being motivated, a self-starter or similar
Leadership skills	The ability to lead a team and motivate others
Presentation skills	The ability to present in front of an audience

References

1. Aasheim, C.L., Williams, S., Butler, E.S.: Knowledge and skill requirements for IT graduates. J. Comput. Inf. Syst. **49**(3), 48–53 (2009)
2. Alghamlas, M., Alabduljabbar, R.: Predicting the suitability of IT students' skills for the recruitment in saudi labor market. Paper presented at the 2019 2nd International Conference on Computer Applications and Information Security (ICCAIS) (2019)
3. Barke, H., Prechelt, L.: Role clarity deficiencies can wreck agile teams. PeerJ. Comput. Sci. **5**, e241 (2019)
4. Capiluppi, A., Baravalle, A.: Matching demand and offer in on-line provision: a longitudinal study of monster.com. Paper presented at the 2010 12th IEEE International Symposium on Web Systems Evolution (WSE) (2010)

5. Csapo, N., Featheringham, R.D.: Communication skills used by information systems graduates. Issues Inf. Syst. VI **1**, 311–317 (2005)
6. Debortoli, S., Müller, O., vom Brocke, J.: Comparing business intelligence and big data skills. Bus. Inf. Syst. Eng. **6**(5), 289–300 (2014)
7. Debrah, Y.A., Reid, E.F.: Internet professionals: job skills for an on-line age. Int. J. Hum. Resour. Manag. **9**(5), 910–933 (1998)
8. Florea, R., Stray, V.: Software tester, we want to hire you! An analysis of the demand for soft skills. Paper presented at the International Conference on Agile Software Development (2018)
9. Gallagher, K.P., et al.: A typology of requisite skills for information technology professionals. Paper presented at the 2011 44th Hawaii International Conference on System Sciences (2011)
10. Gallivan, M.J., Truex, D.P., III., Kvasny, L.: Changing patterns in IT skill sets 1988–2003: a content analysis of classified advertising. ACM SIGMIS Database DATABASE Adv. Inf. Syst. **35**(3), 64–87 (2004)
11. Goles, T., Hawk, S., Kaiser, K.M.: Information technology workforce skills: the software and IT services provider perspective. Inf. Syst. Front. **10**(2), 179–194 (2008)
12. Hewlett Packard Enterprise LP: Agile is the new normal. https://softwaretestinggenius.com/docs/4aa5-7619.pdf. Accessed 21 Oct 2020
13. Janicki, T.N., Lenox, T., Logan, R., Woratschek, C.R.: Information systems/technology employer needs survey: analysis by curriculum topic. Inf. Syst. Educ. J. **6**(18), 3–16 (2008)
14. Keil, M., Lee, H.K., Deng, T.: Understanding the most critical skills for managing IT projects: a Delphi study of IT project managers. Inf. Manag. **50**(7), 398–414 (2013)
15. Kennan, M.A., Willard, P., Cecez-Kecmanovic, D., Wilson, C.S.: IS early career job advertisements: a content analysis. In: PACIS 2007 Proceedings, vol. 51, (2007)
16. Lee, D.M., Trauth, E.M., Farwell, D.: Critical skills and knowledge requirements of IS professionals: a joint academic/industry investigation. MIS Q. 313–340 (1995)
17. Litecky, C., Prabhakar, B., Arnett, K.: The IT/IS job market: a longitudinal perspective. Paper presented at the Proceedings of the 2006 ACM SIGMIS CPR Conference on Computer Personnel Research: Forty Four Years of Computer Personnel Research: Achievements, Challenges and the Future (2006)
18. Park, S.-K., Jun, H.-J., Kim, T.-S.: Using online job postings to analyze differences in skill requirements of information security consultants: South Korea versus United States. Paper presented at the PACIS (2015)
19. Rezvani, A., Khosravi, P.: Emotional intelligence: the key to mitigating stress and fostering trust among software developers working on information system projects. Int. J. Inf. Manag. **48**, 139–150 (2019)
20. Todd, P.A., McKeen, J.D., Gallupe, R.B.: The evolution of IS job skills: a content analysis of IS job advertisements from 1970 to 1990. MIS Q. 1–27 (1995)
21. Trauth, E.M., Farwell, D.W., Lee, D.: The IS expectation gap: industry expectations versus academic preparation. MIS Q. 293–307 (1993)
22. Valentin, E., Carvalho, J.R.H., Barreto, R.: Rapid improvement of students' soft-skills based on an agile-process approach. Paper presented at the 2015 IEEE Frontiers in Education Conference (FIE) (2015)
23. Venkatesh, V., Thong, J.Y., Chan, F.K., Hoehle, H., Spohrer, K.: How agile software development methods reduce work exhaustion: insights on role perceptions and organizational skills. Inf. Syst. J. (2020)
24. Wade, M.R., Parent, M.: Relationships between job skills and performance: a study of webmasters. J. Manag. Inf. Syst. **18**(3), 71–96 (2002)
25. Beck, K., et al.: Manifesto for agile software development. Agile Manifesto. http://agilemanifesto.org. Accessed 2 Sept 2020

26. Scrum Guide: Scrum Guides. https://www.scrumguides.org/scrum-guide.html. Accessed 2 Sept 2020
27. Stackoverflow: Stackoverflow Developer Survey 2020. https://insights.stackoverflow.com/survey/2020#technology-programming-scripting-and-markup-languages-professional-dev elopers. Accessed 2 Sept 2020
28. Ahmed, F., Capretz, L.F., Campbell, P.: Evaluating the demand for soft skills in software development. Paper published by the IEEE Computer Society (2012)
29. U.S. Bureau of Labor Statistics: Which industries need workers? Exploring differences in labor market activity. https://www.bls.gov/opub/mlr/2016/article/which-industries-need-wor kers-exploring-differences-in-labor-market-activity.htm. Accessed 18 Oct 2020
30. Agile Connection: Practice soft skills through collaboration to become truly agile. https://www.agileconnection.com/article/practice-soft-skills-through-collaboration-become-truly-agile. Accessed 18 Oct 2020
31. Ahmed, F., Capretz, L.F., Bouktif, S., Campbell, P.: Soft skills requirements in software development jobs: a cross-cultural empirical study. J. Syst. Inf. Technol. (2012)
32. Institute for Competitive Recruiting: Deutschlands Beste Jobportale 2020. http://deutschla ndsbestejobportale.de/index.html. Accessed 25 Dec 2020

Opening the Black Box of Digital B2B Co-creation Platforms: A Taxonomy

Jan Abendroth[(✉)], Lara Riefle, and Carina Benz

Karlsruhe Institute of Technology, Karlsruhe, Germany
jan.abendroth@student.kit.edu, {lara.riefle,carina.benz}@kit.edu

Abstract. Digital B2B platforms are becoming increasingly important for value co-creation in today's business networks, leading to the emergence of a diverse landscape of platforms and intensifying research efforts. Yet, practitioners and researchers alike lack a means to structure existing knowledge and distinguish between different B2B platforms. In this paper, we apply Nickerson et al.'s method for taxonomy development to derive a taxonomy of B2B co-creation platforms drawing on 36 research articles and 63 real-world platform cases. We find 17 dimensions that describe B2B co-creation platforms in terms of their platform architecture, their actor ecosystem, and their value creation process. Thereby, we contribute to research and practice: First, we provide a holistic perspective on B2B co-creation platforms by aggregating existing knowledge and identifying the fundamental properties relevant for their distinction. Second, we provide a decision aid for practitioners to evaluate which platform to join or how to design B2B co-creation platforms.

Keywords: Digital B2B platforms · Platform taxonomy · Co-creation

1 Introduction

Digital platforms—as a business and organizational model—are one of the key drivers of digital transformation [1, 2]. In the B2C sector, digital platforms, like Google, Facebook, or Airbnb, often have an almost monopolistic status and continue to maintain their position [3]. In contrast, the landscape of digital platforms in the B2B sector is more scattered: Aiming to tap their potential to foster collaboration and co-creation of value [1], we observe intensified efforts to establish and operate own digital platforms (e.g., GE Predix [4], thyssenkrupp toii [5]). Accordingly, companies aiming to join other parties' platform ecosystem, are challenged with reviewing and comparing an ever increasing number of digital platforms with different application-, industry- and technology-foci [6].

Hence, practitioners and researcher alike would benefit from a comprehensive view on B2B platforms and their respective characteristics. While prior research has already made attempts to aggregate and structure knowledge on B2B platforms, they are either limited to a specific perspective (e.g., technical platform architecture [7], platform complementors [8]) or type of platform (e.g. IIoT platforms [9]). Therefore, this paper aims

© The Author(s), under exclusive license to Springer Nature Switzerland AG 2021
F. Ahlemann et al. (Eds.): WI 2021, LNISO 47, pp. 596–611, 2021.
https://doi.org/10.1007/978-3-030-86797-3_39

to lay the foundation for holistically classifying digital B2B co-creation platforms by consolidating existing knowledge in the form of a taxonomy. Taxonomies have proven to be a valuable tool to understand, analyze, and structure the knowledge within emerging research fields [10]. Hence, the following research question can be formulated: *What are the conceptually grounded and empirically validated characteristics that describe B2B co-creation platforms?*

The taxonomy development follows the process of Nickerson et al. [10]. Building on a data corpus of 63 real-world platform cases and 38 academic articles identified by a structured literature review [11], we iteratively develop our taxonomy. We determine 17 key dimensions (e.g., core value proposition, platform openness, and complementor types) that systematically characterize B2B co-creation platforms. The final taxonomy is evaluated regarding its usefulness and general applicability.

Our taxonomy contributes to theory and practice: On the one hand, it provides a comprehensive reference work that takes a holistic view on B2B co-creation platforms instead of focusing on selected aspects. Therefore, is represents a tool for researchers to systematically compare platforms, position their research, and identify research directions. On the other hand, it enables practitioners to compare and benchmark different platforms, and to identify options for platform design.

This paper is structured as follows. Section 2 provides an overview of extant literature on B2B platforms and existing attempts to structure this knowledge. Section 3 describes the methodological approach to develop the taxonomy, which is presented, applied and evaluated in Sect. 4. Finally, Sect. 5 concludes the paper with a discussion of the taxonomy's implications and future research opportunities.

2 Background

Originally defined as "layered modular technology architectures in business networks" [12, p. 186], digital platforms represent socio-technical systems that enable and coordinate the interaction of actors and resources in an ecosystem facilitating value co-creation and innovation [1, 7, 13]. By providing a stable core, whose functionality can be extended with modular services [14, 15], digital platforms are an essential means for facilitating collaboration between firms, innovation, and, thus, value co-creation in today's service ecosystems [2, 14, 16]. Especially, in the realm of business-to-business interactions, digital platforms become increasingly popular, leading to the development of a diverse platform landscape [1]. For example, we find data platforms such as *AVIATION DataHub* that bring together data from the aviation industry and facilitate data exchange [17]; industrial internet of things (IIoT) platforms such as *Cumulocity IoT* that integrate physical devices of manufacturers and allow third parties to provide additional resources or develop complementary applications [18]; supply chain management platforms such as *RailSupply* that foster the communication and collaboration of firms across the supply chain; or cloud platforms such as *Azure IoT* that offer flexible and scalable IT resources as a service. Further, there are retail platforms such as *WUCATO* that provide marketplaces for products and services bringing together the supply and demand side. Yet, in our paper, we focus on digital platforms that enable value co-creation of different actors directly on the platform. Thus, we refer to *B2B co-creation platforms* as *modular structures that enable the interaction of actors and resources to facilitate value co-creation*

[13, 19]. These digital platforms are particularly important for businesses in today's competitive environment as they facilitate effective and efficient information exchange, integrate resources across firm boundaries, thereby facilitating joint innovation and value co-creation, enabling new business models and, thus, ultimately promoting long-term market success. These benefits encourage companies to join B2B platforms or even develop their own ones. However, as the range of available digital platforms is diverse and often difficult to assess, the need for a means to structure and analyze them arises.

The literature offers several approaches for structuring and classifying digital B2B platforms and their surrounding ecosystems: Guggenberger et al. [20] provide a typology of generic ecosystem configurations aggregating different ecosystem conceptualizations in IS research. Yet platforms as the core of ecosystems are not considered in depth. Furthermore, they solely take a literature-based approach and do not include practice-oriented findings. Engert et al. [8] focus on the aspect of platform complementors and develop a taxonomy for complementor assessment by conducting a multiple-case study on the partner programs of 14 B2B software platforms. Even though they propose criteria and metrics for assessing platform complementors, they neither consider the platforms' architecture nor the value creation processes. Blaschke et al. [7] take a technical view on platforms' architecture developing a taxonomy to distinguish digital platforms based on their underlying technical configuration of components. For example, they provide insights into platform access options (e.g., open standards, devices) and technical core artefacts of software and hardware, however the network of actors and their relations, as well as complementor roles are not in the scope of their taxonomy. While Blaschke et al. [7] focus on technical aspects, Hodapp et al. [9] limit their study to a business view investigating IoT platforms' business models. The authors analyze 195 IoT platforms to characterize their business model and derive IoT business model archetypes. Similarly, Täuscher and Laudien [21] examine the business model characteristics of platforms with a focus on marketplaces in the areas of C2C, B2C, and B2B. However, both articles focus a specific platform type (i.e., IoT platforms or marketplaces) and do not consider further value co-creation activities or facilitating platform characteristics. Summing up, all these approaches to structure and analyze digital B2B platforms are limited either on certain aspects of the platform or on specific platform types, which further emphasizes the need for a comprehensive characterization that reflects the diverse nature of B2B co-creation platforms.

3 Methodology

We aim to identify characteristics of digital co-creation platforms in the B2B field, which serve as basis for the discrimination of platform types and provide assistance for their design. For that purpose, we develop a taxonomy following Nickerson et al. [10]. A taxonomy is a set of dimensions used to classify objects of interest [10]. Mutually exclusive and collectively exhaustive characteristics construct each dimension, i.e., in each dimension, each object must exhibit precisely one characteristic [10].

The taxonomy development method is an iterative method. It starts with the def-inition of the meta-characteristics and ending conditions. The meta-characteristic is an initial comprehensive characteristic, which will serve as the basis for the choice of characteristics in the taxonomy [10]. Ending conditions define the state in which the taxonomy development process is terminated. Nickerson et al.'s process [10] includes seven steps that are iteratively repeated until the ending conditions are met. For each iteration, either a conceptual-to-empirical or empirical-to-conceptual approach must be selected. Conceptual-to-empirical is a deductive approach in which the taxonomy's dimensions are conceptualized first, and then the dimensions' characteristics are identified. The empirical-to-conceptual approach in turn, examines real-life objects and identifies their common characteristics that are grouped into dimensions.

3.1 Input Data for Taxonomy Development

As a basis for the development of the taxonomy an extensive data corpus is compiled with both scientific literature and real-world platform cases from practice. For the conceptual-to-empirical approach, we rely on dimensions that have previously been identified in the literature. We therefore conduct a systematic literature review following Webster and Watson [11]. The search string *[(platform AND ecosystem) OR ((platform OR ecosystem) AND (digital OR B2B OR industry OR IoT OR business))]* is applied to the title of articles in four databases: AISeL, Scopus, EBSCOhost, and Web of Science. The AISeL database provides a distinct information systems perspective, while the others provide a more general and interdisciplinary view on research on B2B platforms.

The search yields 3948 unique search results, which are screened for relevance by screening their title, abstract, and full text. The literature screening and reduction follows a three-step process: First, we consider the title and reduce the literature base to 395 articles. Only articles that deal with the research objectives in a non-trivial and non-marginal way are included in the literature base. Articles that do not exhibit a relevant domain focus or context (i.e., IS, business, or B2B focus) are excluded. Thus, articles from the domains of medicine, biology, media, or physics, articles with a clear B2C focus, and articles with a purely technical focus (e.g., middleware) are excluded. Second, we screen the abstracts to exclude articles that only marginally cover value co-creation platforms, leaving 82 articles. For example, we exclude articles examining pure marketplaces or platforms that are used as passive information repositories. Third, by screening the full text we arrive at 29 articles that can provide meaningful insights (i.e., dimensions, platform characteristics) for the taxonomy development. Finally, after the screening process and a backward and forward search 38 relevant articles remain, which build a sound basis for the conceptual-to-empirical taxonomy development approach.

Following the empirical-to-conceptual approach, we draw on real-world platform cases. A total of 63 real-world platforms are identified by (1) screening the publications identified for cases mentioned and (2) by referring to reports from German public research institutes and industry associations [6, 22–25]. Following, we collect publicly available information on the 63 platforms. Information sources include primary sources (e.g., the platforms' websites or press releases), and secondary sources (e.g., analyst reports, YouTube videos, tech blog entries) [26]. We analyze the collected data applying qualitative content analysis [27], which is supported by the software MAXQDA. This systematic approach allows to identify characteristics of B2B co-creation platforms that serve as input for the taxonomy development process.

3.2 Taxonomy Development

The taxonomy development process starts with definition of the meta-characteristics and ending conditions. The meta-characteristic is formulated as "describing the platform structure and value co-creation process", hence it adapts to the taxonomy purpose of distinguishing platform instances. Second, we define the ending conditions that terminate the taxonomy development: both the eight objective and five subjective ending conditions from Nickerson et al. [10] are adopted. Third, we start the iterative part of the development process with the first iteration choosing the conceptual-to-empirical approach to build on the foundation of existing research. The final taxonomy of B2B co-creation platforms is developed throughout eight iterations: Iterations one and six follow the conceptual approach, whereas iterations two to five, seven and eight follow the empirical approach. In each iteration we revise the initial dimensions and characteristics of the B2B co-creation platform taxonomy by repeatedly examining sets of platform objects (empirical-to-conceptual approach) or refining dimensions and characteristics based on scientific literature (conceptual-to-empirical approach).

Figure 1 visualizes the taxonomy development process and presents an overview of the iterations and modifications to the taxonomy. In particular, iteration one establishes the initial taxonomy with 23 dimensions, which is refined in iterations two to five by adding and revising characteristics and dimensions based on real-world platform cases. This process leads to 24 preliminary dimensions, as the dimension *revenue stream* is split up into *revenue stream from complementors* and *revenue stream from users* to better reflect relevant differences in real-world platforms. Iteration six pursues the goal to consolidate previously identified dimensions to improve the taxonomy's conciseness. Therefore, the preliminary 24 dimensions are consolidated to 17 dimensions based on scientific literature. Iteration seven leads to no further changes and after the eighth iteration, all objective and subjective ending conditions are met. Thus, the taxonomy development process ends. The final taxonomy comprises 17 dimensions with the corresponding characteristics that comprehensively classify B2B co-creation platforms. Since the taxonomy's purpose is to provide a valuable tool to researchers and practitioners to distinguish and eventually design B2B platforms, we subsequently evaluate the taxonomy regarding its usefulness and ease of use [10] and demonstrate its applicability.

4   Results

In this section, we first present the developed B2B co-creation platform taxonomy. We find that B2B co-creation platforms can be distinguished according to their value creation process, their platform architecture, and their actor ecosystem, which we structure in 17 dimensions. Furthermore, we present the evaluation results that confirm the usefulness of our taxonomy. Lastly, we demonstrate the taxonomy's applicability by classifying all 63 platform instances, two of which are illustrated, and outline initial insights on the landscape of B2B co-creation platforms.

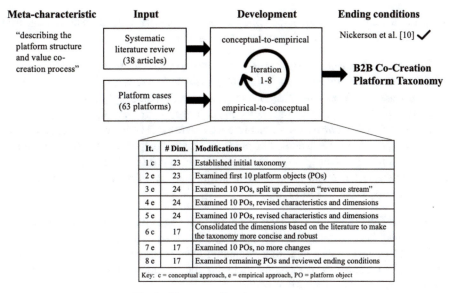

Fig. 1. Taxonomy development process

4.1 B2B Co-creation Platform Taxonomy

Drawing on existing literature and 63 real-world platform cases, we find that B2B co-creation platforms can fundamentally be classified by their value creation, their architecture, and their actor ecosystem. These three essential distinguishing properties are specified in 17 dimensions that constitute the taxonomy and provide a first answer to the posted research question. Figure visualizes the taxonomy as a morphological box as it grants intuitive insight into the structure [28].

Value Creation. The dimensions summarized as value creation address the unique value that is offered by the platform and describe how this value is created. Therefore, the taxonomy includes the core value proposition offered to platform participants, the medium of exchange, the revenue streams from complementors and users, as well as the options provided to users to extend the platform according to their own needs.

Core Value Proposition (What are the core capabilities offered by the platform?): Our study unveils that platforms offer six core capabilities: Whereas some platforms only offer basic *device connectivity and management services* (e.g., Telekom Cloud of Things, Cisco Jasper Control Center), others additionally offer *advanced analytics* capabilities (e.g., Flutura Cerebra) or *orchestrate a network*, i.e., optimize the collaboration and exchange between the platform members, often in a supply-chain context (e.g., VW Discovery). On *exchange* platforms, physical or virtual goods and services are traded (e.g., Telekom Data Intelligence Hub) and platforms with a *Cloud PaaS* capability offer a collection of fully managed tools to connect assets, manage and analyze data, and support the development of new solutions (e.g., Azure IoT, AWS IoT Core). The characteristics *IIoT enablement* refers to platforms that offer connectivity capabilities, data analytics, tools for developers, and applications and services in the domain of industrial applications (e.g., Siemens MindSphere, ADAMOS).

Options for Extensibility (How does the platform enable the user to extend the platform?): This dimension can be split into five characteristics. While some platforms do *not allow users to extend the platform* (e.g., SupplyOn Railsupply), the majority provides this option through additional code. In particular, platforms either provide a highly abstracted *low code environment* (e.g., Flutura Cerebra), or, in other cases, more programming *code-based* effort in a dedicated programming language (e.g., Exosite Murano) is required. Similarly, in an *open-source* approach, the platform can be extended through open-source interfaces and programming languages (e.g., Kaa IoT) or even *multiple* options are offered (e.g., GE Predix).

Medium of Exchange (What is the primarily exchanged on the platform?): Platforms create value by exchanging various items [29]. These can be pieces of *information* (e.g., in the case of SAP AIN), *data* (e.g., Telekom Data Intelligence Hub), *services* (e.g., Homag tapio), or also *multiple* items, including the simultaneous exchange of capacity and services (e.g., Siemens MindSphere).

Revenue Stream from Users (How does the platform owner capture value from the platform users?): Our study finds seven characteristics that describe the revenue stream from platform users [30]. While some platforms offer their services *free* of charge (e.g., Lufthansa Technik Aviation Data Hub), most platforms apply one or *multiple* (e.g., SAP Cloud Platform) of the following revenue models. *Freemium* models offer platform users basic functionalities for free and charge for additional services (e.g., Siemens Healthineers teamplay). In the case of a *transaction-based* revenue model (e.g., HPE Universal IoT Platform) the user is charged for different kinds of transactions (e.g., per connected device, per API call, or generated traffic [31]) while in the commonly used *subscription-based* model (e.g., ABB Ability) users pay a fixed subscription fee. A *hybrid* model combines the subscription- and transaction-based revenue model, i.e., the platform charges a recurring fixed fee plus transaction-dependent costs (e.g., Bosch IoT Suite). A few platforms also offer a *license* model (e.g., BEDM Industrie 4.0 Framework).

Revenue Stream from Complementors (How does the platform owner capture value from the platform complementors?): The platform owner also generates revenue through the complementors either by a *transaction-based* revenue model (e.g., Cogobuy) where the complementor is charged per transaction (e.g., per connected device, per API call, or generated traffic [31]), or a *subscription-based* model (e.g., DKE Agrirouter), or *licensing* (e.g., Exosite Murano). In addition, some platforms do *not charge* their complementors (e.g., Telekom Data Intelligence Hub).

Platform Architecture. The dimensions summarized as platform architecture describe the fundamental organizational layout of the platform, including its components and governing principles. On the one hand, the taxonomy specifies how the platform is integrated in businesses' IT systems and what type of support is offered to participants and on the other hand, it looks into different aspects of openness, i.e., platform openness, decisional openness, and complementor openness.

	Dimension	Characteristics					
Value creation	Core value proposition	Device management	Analytics	Network orchestration	Exchange	Cloud PaaS	IIoT enablement
	Options for extensibility	None	Low code	Code-based	Open source		Multiple
	Medium of exchange	Information		Data	Services		Multiple
	Revenue stream from users	None	Freemium	Transaction-based	Subscription-based	Hybrid	License	Multiple
	Revenue stream from complementors	None		Transaction-based	Subscription-based		License
Platform architecture	Platform integration	Stand-alone		Vertical	Horizontal		End-to-end
	Platform openness	Fully proprietary	Hardware proprietary	Software proprietary	Open source	
	Decisional openness	Lead organization-governed			Participant-governed		
	Complementor openness	Open	Conditions for access	Selected partners	Closed	
	Type of support	Non-personal technical support		Personal technical support		Personal technical and business support	
Actor ecosystem	Industry focus	Single vertical industry			Multiple vertical industries		
	Origin of platform	Company internal		External customers in own domain		External customers in new domain	
	Geographic distribution	National		Regional		International	
	Platform owner	SME		Large enterprise	Joint venture		Open source
	Platform owner background	IT and software systems	Automation, control and equipment systems	Telco and carrier systems	Automotive	Aviation and aerospace	Emergent innovator	Mixed
	Complementor types	None	Technology partner	Resource integrator	Technology & integration	Technology & resource	All types
	Participation incentives	None		Non-monetary		Monetary and non-monetary	

Fig. 2. B2B co-creation platform taxonomy

Platform Integration (How is the platform integrated into the business' IT system?): Regarding a platforms integration into the business' IT system, we find four characteristics [32]: The *vertical* integration means that various IT systems are integrated at different hierarchical levels (sensor-to-ERP) (e.g., HPE Universal IoT Platform, Cisco Jasper Control Center) while *horizontal* integration refers to the integration of various IT systems used in different stages of the value chain (e.g., Crowdfox). *End-to-end* integration combines both horizontal and vertical integration (e.g., Software AG Cumulocity IoT), in contrast to a *stand-alone* solution that is not integrated into the business's IT system (e.g., Telekom Data Intelligence Hub).

Platform Openness (How open is the platform towards external modifications to the platform's underlying code?): For the platform's openness, which is defined as "the extent to which platform boundary resources support complements" [1, p. 127]), scholars distinguish between four characteristics [33]. First, *fully proprietary* means that external developers have no access to modifying the platform's underlying code or exchange data with the platform on open source-based interfaces. Second, when the *hardware is proprietary*, only specific devices can be integrated into the platform, for example, only specific devices can transfer data to the platform (e.g., Schaeffler Smart Ecosystem). Third, *software proprietary* means that the platform can be run on any device, but the platform code is not openly accessible (e.g., PTC Thingworx). Fourth, in an *open-source* approach the platform can run on any third-party device and the platform code is open to external modifications (e.g., ADAMOS).

Decisional Openness (Who holds the decision-making authority?): We find two typical governance models [34]: In a *lead organization-governed* platform all key decisions are made by a single participating member, usually the platform owner, which leads to a highly centralized and asymmetrical power distribution [35] (e.g., Siemens MindSphere, Telekom Data Intelligence Hub). In multi-firm strategic alliances or partnerships (e.g., ADAMOS, DKE Agrirouter) [35] often the platform members themselves govern the platform, which is called a *participant-governed platform*.

Complementor Openness (How open is the platform for complementors?): Four different complementor openness characteristics can be distinguished [13]: The two edge cases are a fully *closed* platform that does not allow complementors to join at all (e.g., ZF Openmatics) and an *open* platform where any complementor is free to join (e.g., DeviceHive IoT). Apart from these, a platform owner can dictate *specific conditions for complementors* to join and offer their services on the platform (e.g., Ayla Agile IoT Platform) or the owner may invite *selected partners* to join (e.g., Flutura Cerebra).

Type of Support (What type of support does the platform offer for participants?): The level of support ranges from *non-personal technical support* providing documentation and online forums (e.g., Flutura Cerebra), to additional *personal technical support* teams (e.g., Lufthansa Technik Aviatar), to full *personal technical and business support* including business consulting services related to the platform (e.g., DeviceHive IoT).

Actor Ecosystem. The dimensions summarized as actor ecosystem describe platform participants and their roles. In particular, it provides an overview of the platform's origin and geographic as well as industry focus, the platform owner and its background, and the complementors including the incentives to join.

Industry Focus (What is the target market of the platform?): Either a platform focuses on a *single vertical industry*, e.g., discrete manufacturing, aviation, and healthcare (e.g., Siemens Healthineers Teamplay), or it targets *multiple different verticals* simultaneously (e.g., PTC Thingworx) [33].

Origin of Solution (Why was the platform originally developed?): This dimension describes whether the platform was developed for internal use or external customers. In particular, some platforms (e.g., GE Predix, Thyssenkrupp toii) were initially developed for a *company internal use* and only later offered to external customers. In contrast, others were explicitly developed as a platform for *external customers*, either targeting the company's *primary domain of expertise* (e.g., Siemens MindSphere, Lufthansa Technik Aviation Data Hub) or focusing on a *new domain* (e.g., Software AG Cumulocity IoT).

Geographic Distribution (How is the platform positioned globally?): We find that platforms either focus on a *specific country* (e.g., Hitachi Lumada), *region* such as DACH or SE Asia (e.g., Davra IoT Platform), or they pursue an *international* strategy (e.g., Homag tapio) [36].

Platform Owner (Who holds the ownership rights to the platform?): Scholars distinguish between four owners [30], namely *SME, large enterprise, joint venture*, and *open source*. For our taxonomy we adopt the European Commission's definition of a SME (e.g., Flutura) and large enterprises (e.g., Siemens) [37] and refer to joint ventures when a merger of two or more companies establish a platform (e.g., DKE Agrirouter), or to open source when the platform results from an open-source project (e.g., DeviceHive IoT).

Platform Owner Background (What is the platform owner's main domain of expertise?): Our study reveals five distinct backgrounds, namely *IT and software systems* (e.g., SAP Cloud Platform); *automation, control and equipment systems* (e.g., Bosch IoT Suite); *telco and carrier systems* (e.g., Telekom Data Intelligence Hub); *aviation and aerospace* (e.g., Lufthansa Technik Aviatar); *automotive* (e.g., ZF Openmatics); and *emergent innovator* (e.g., QiO Foresight) meaning that the owner is a new market entrant. Lastly, in *joint ventures* (e.g., ADAMOS), *mixed* backgrounds can also occur.

Complementor Types (Which types of complementors are active on the platform?): Three different types of complementors can be part of a platform and appear *alone* or *together* in different permutations. *Technology partners* include software and hardware developers as well as cloud infrastructure providers. *Integration support* refers to system integrators that support the platform's technical implementation, and consulting firms that offer business consulting and transformation services in connection with the platform. The third type of complementors are *resource integrators*, i.e., firms that provide tangible and intangible types of resources, such as data, physical products, manufacturing capacity, or financing. These three complementor types can appear in five different permutations or not at all, as is the case when the platform owner provides all these services.

Participation Incentives (How does the platform owner incentivize complementor participation?): Some platforms offer *no explicit incentives* to complementors to join the platform (e.g., Lufthansa Technik Aviatar), while others offer *non-monetary* incentives such as sales and technical training, application developer tools or technical support (e.g., QiO Foresight) or a combination of these *non-monetary incentives with monetary incentives* such as discounts or access to business developer funds (e.g.; Siemens MindSphere) [38].

4.2 Taxonomy Evaluation and Demonstration of Application

The taxonomy is evaluated with regard to its usability and applicability. To assess its usability, eight experts—four selected for their theoretical knowledge and four chosen for their practical experience with B2B platforms—are asked to classify two real-world platforms using the taxonomy. We chose Siemens MindSphere and Telekom Data Intelligence Hub as cases for the evaluation, as they differ greatly and provide extensive publicly available information. Subsequent to the classification, the experts are asked to evaluate the taxonomy's perceived usefulness and ease of use with survey items adapted from Davis [39]. The evaluation results indicate that our taxonomy of B2B co-creation platforms is useful (mean = 6.3, SD = 0.4, scale from 1 = extremely unlikely to 7 = extremely likely) and easy to use (mean = 6.0, SD = 0.5, scale from 1 = extremely unlikely to 7 = extremely likely). Furthermore, it fulfilled the experts' expectations (mean = 6.4, SD = 0.5, scale from 1 = extremely unlikely to 7 = extremely likely) and is extensive (mean = 6.1, SD = 0.3, scale from 1 = extremely unlikely to 7 = extremely likely). Moreover, the high classification agreement (Siemens case: 69.9%, Telekom case: 70.1%) among the experts illustrates the taxonomy's ability to classify B2B platforms consistently. As a consequence of the evaluation, the description of the dimension *platform integration* was revised to enhance its clarity. To demonstrate the taxonomy's practical applicability and capability to characterize B2B co-creation platforms, we classified all 63 platform objects of our data corpus. Figure 3 shows the frequency of each characteristics' occurrence across all platforms and visualized exemplary platforms: Siemens MindSphere and Telekom Data Intelligence Hub.

Siemens MindSphere is an IIoT enablement platform that operates internationally in multiple vertical industries. It offers ample ways for customers to create value by providing, among other things, end-to-end integration, a low code environment and the possibility to integrate open-source software. Open application programming interfaces enable customers to connect their machines and equipment to the platform to exchange data and value-adding services. The ecosystem consists of Siemens, a large enterprise that owns and governs the platform, customers from Siemens' domain of expertise (i.e., automation, control, and equipment systems) and technology partners as well as complementors offering integration support. Complementors are offered monetary and non-monetary incentives to join, yet they must meet certain conditions and pay a subscription fee. In contrast, the core value proposition of Telekom's international platform

Data Intelligence Hub is the exchange of data. Telekom, with a background in telco and carrier systems, retains sole decision control on the platform, which is used by a wide range of customers that mainly are from outside Telekom's core domain of expertise. Users can extend the stand-alone platform by using open-source interfaces, whereas external developers are not allowed to extend the underlying code. While all types of complementors can freely join without any payment, Telekom does not offer explicit participation incentives.

Dimension		Characteristics					
Value creation	Core value proposition	Device mgmt. 15.9%	Analytics 12.7%	Network orch. 6.3%	Exchange 14.3%	Cloud PaaS 19.0%	IIoT enable. 31.7%
	Options for extensibility	None 15.9%	Low code 7.9%	Code-based 19.0%	Open source 7.9%		Multiple 22.2%
	Medium of exchange	Information 31.7%		Data 22.2%	Services 19.0%		Multiple 27.0%
	Revenue stream from users	None 11.1%	Freemium 6.3%	Transaction 9.5%	Subscription 25.4%	Hybrid 4.8%	License 3.2%	Multiple 17.5%
	Revenue stream from complementors	None 14.3%		Transaction-based 1.6%	Subscription-based 12.7%		License 3.2%
Platform architecture	Platform integration	Stand-alone 14.3%		Vertical 25.4%	Horizontal 12.7%		End-to-end 41.3%
	Platform openness	Fully proprietary 22.2%	Hardware proprietary 3.2%	Software proprietary 15.9%		Open source 44.4%	
	Decisional openness	Lead organization-governed 88.9%			Participant-governed 11.1%		
	Complementor openness	Open 27.0%	Conditions for access 33.3%		Selected partners 15.9%		Closed 1.6%
	Type of support	Non-personal tech. support 17.5%		Personal technical support 31.7%		Pers. tech. & business supp. 34.9%	
Actor ecosystem	Industry focus	Single vertical industry 28.6%			Multiple vertical industries 69.8%		
	Origin of platform	Company internal 7.9%		Ext. customer in own domain 50.8%		Ext. customer in new domain 38.1%	
	Geographic distribution	National 1.6%		Regional 4.8%		International 87.3%	
	Platform owner	SME 28.6%	L. enterprise 61.9%		Joint venture 4.8%		Open source 4.8%
	Platform owner background	IT and software systems 36.5%	Aut., cntrl and equip. systems 23.8%	Telco and carrier systems 3.2%	Automotive 3.2%	Aviation and aerospace 6.3%	Emergent innovator 23.8%	Mixed 1.6%
	Complementor types	None 1.6%	Technology partner 25.4%	Resource integrator 9.5%	Technology & integration 25.4%	Technology & resource 11.1%	All types 20.6%
	Participation incentives	None 36.5%		Non-monetary 20.6%		Monetary and non-monetary 11.1%	
Key: ▲ Siemens MindSphere ● Telekom Data Intelligence Hub							

Fig. 3. Application demonstration of proposed taxonomy[1]

When comparing the taxonomy characteristics' occurrences across all 63 platforms, it stands out that the core value propositions *Cloud PaaS* and *IIoT enablement* are the most

---

[1] The missing percent to 100 are platforms for that not enough data was available to classify.

common in the data set. To support the value creation process, the majority of platforms (57%) offer at least one option for extensibility, while 22.2% even offer multiple. The revenue models vary widely, with a tendency towards *subscription-based revenues* from users as well as complementors. Regarding the platform architecture, a high divergence can be observed. However, an *end-to-end platform integration* (41.3%) and an *open-source* approach (44.4%) to platform openness are predominant. Most platforms *limit complementor access* (50.8%), while providing extensive support to their users. Looking at the actor ecosystem, additional insights can be derived: *Large enterprises* (61.9%) stand out as platform owners, while *joint ventures* (4.8%) or *open-source projects* (4.8%) only rarely occur. Although the two dominant platform owner backgrounds are *IT and software systems* (36.5%) and *automation, control and, equipment systems* (23.8%), almost a quarter of platforms is owned by *emergent innovators* (23.8%). The majority of platforms (88.9%) were *initially developed for external customers*, primarily in the *platform owner's main domain of expertise* (50.8%). Furthermore, 69.8% of platforms target *multiple vertical industries*, most often on an *international level* (87.3%). 27% of platforms are *entirely open* to complementors with *technology partners* (25.4%) being the prevalent complementor type, either on their own or in *combination with other partners.*

5   Discussion and Conclusion

This study aimed at identifying the conceptually grounded and empirically validated characteristics that describe B2B co-creation platforms. Therefore, we propose a taxonomy of B2B co-creation platforms highlighting their distinguishing features and building blocks. Thereby the paper provides a comprehensive view on this emerging research field, and a useful tool to classify B2B platforms. Drawing on 38 articles identified by a structured literature review [11] and 63 real-world platform cases, we ensure scientific and practical grounding.

Following the approach of Nickerson et al. [10], 17 dimensions describing and distinguishing B2B co-creation platforms form our final taxonomy. These dimensions describe a platform's value creation process, the platform architecture, and the actor ecosystem. Usefulness and ease of use is demonstrated by an expert evaluation. Furthermore, the taxonomy's applicability is shown and initial insights on the landscape of B2B co-creation platforms are presented.

Hence, our taxonomy of B2B co-creation platforms entails important implications for research and practice. The scientific contribution stems from a comprehensive analysis and structuring of knowledge within the emerging research field of B2B platforms. By aggregating the existing knowledge, we provide a sound foundation for future work. Furthermore, our taxonomy is one of the first to take a holistic perspective, rather than focusing on single platform types or specific platform aspects. It thereby contributes to a clear differentiation of the various B2B co-creation platforms and identifies fundamental characteristics to distinguish them.

Practitioners may benefit from the taxonomy's ability to facilitate decision-making and design: Being able to distinguish B2B co-creation platforms along 17 dimensions, allows decision-makers to structure their assessments and informs decision-making in terms of platform selection and joining. Furthermore, platform owners and designers are put in the position to emphasize their competitive advantage and discover potential for improvement by systematically comparing their own platform to competitor solutions.

Although the taxonomy is developed applying a theoretically founded and empirically validated approach, our study is not free of limitations. Even Nickerson et al. [10] acknowledge that a taxonomy can never be optimal, it still provides an effective means to analyze and structure knowledge on a topic. First, Nickerson et al.'s [10] method for taxonomy development only provides basic guidelines and heuristics for a taxonomy development process. Hence, the results are not free of ambiguity. Second, we explicitly excluded pure marketplaces for the taxonomy development, as our goal was to specifically investigate platforms that enable the interaction and collaboration of actors. Therefore, the taxonomy may be extended to additionally incorporate the distinguishing aspects of this type of B2B platforms. Third, we rely on a set of 63 real-world platforms and corresponding publicly available information to develop the taxonomy. As the market of B2B platforms is rapidly developing, there might be more platforms and information that has not yet been considered in our study. By including a greater number of platform cases, the taxonomy development process might further be improved. Forth, we are aware that the evaluation results are limited in their generalizability. Applicability was demonstrated by classifying the set of platform cases that were used to develop the taxonomy. Moreover, the limited number of evaluation participants only provides initial indication for the taxonomy's usability.

By providing a concise and robust taxonomy of B2B co-creation platforms we enable a common understanding among researchers and, hence, lay the foundation for future research. Addressing the limitations of this study, future research should collect more platform cases to validate the taxonomy and evaluate it with a larger group of experts with different perspectives (e.g., platform owner, platform participants). More important, our taxonomy provides the basis for a deeper theorizing process. Subsequent research may build on our taxonomy and conduct a cluster analysis to identify archetypes of B2B platforms. Using the taxonomy, typical characteristics of these archetypes could then be described and condensed in profiles. This way, the cluster analysis not only unveils prevalent platform types, but also enables the identification of the properties of successful platforms. Further qualitative and quantitative studies should then deepen the investigation of success factors of B2B platforms. Qualitative studies could examine why certain design choices are made and how different platform designs are perceived by the platform participants. For example, interviews with complementors could bring additional insights on how different platform architectures and governance principles resonate with platform participants. In addition, quantitative studies might be used to examine the effect of different platform configurations on platform success. For example, one could compare how different levels of platform and complementor openness affect platform growth. Longitudinal studies may complement this research by providing insights into the evolution of B2B platforms and their distinct characteristics. Finally, all these research efforts lead to a better understanding of B2B co-creation platforms and facilitate their development and design.

References

1. De Reuver, M., Sørensen, C., Basole, R.C.: The digital platform: a research agenda. J. Inf. Technol. **33**, 124–135 (2018)
2. Hein, A., et al.: Digital platform ecosystems. Electron. Mark. **30**(1), 87–98 (2019). https://doi.org/10.1007/s12525-019-00377-4
3. Schreieck, M., Wiesche, M., Krcmar, H.: Design and governance of platform ecosystems–key concepts and issues for future research. In: 24th European Conference on Information Systems (ECIS), pp. 1–20 (2016)
4. Sebastian, I.M., Ross, J.W., Beath, C., Mocker, M., Moloney, K.G., Fonstad, N.O.: How big old companies navigate digital transformation new. MIS Q. **16**, 197–213 (2017)
5. VDMA EV, McKinsey & Company I: Customer centricity as key for the digital breakthrough. What end-customer industries expect from mechanical engineering companies on platforms and apps (2020)
6. Lichtblau, K.: Institut der deutschen Wirtschaft Köln Consult GmbH: Plattformen - Infrastruktur der Digitalisierung (2019)
7. Blaschke, M., Haki, K., Aier, S., Winter, R.: Taxonomy of digital platforms: a platform architecture perspective. In: 14th International Conference on Wirtschaftsinformatik, pp. 1–15 Siegen (2019)
8. Engert, M., Hein, A., Krcmar, H.: Partner programs and complementor assessment in platform ecosystems: a multiple-case study. In: Americas Conference on Information Systems (AMCIS), pp. 1–10 (2017)
9. Hodapp, D., Remane, G., Hanelt, A., Kolbe, L.M.: Business models for internet of things platforms: empirical development of a taxonomy and archetypes. In: 14th International Conference on Wirtschaftsinformatik, pp. 1783–1797 (2019)
10. Nickerson, R.C., Varshney, U., Muntermann, J.: A method for taxonomy development and its application in information systems. Eur. J. Inf. Syst. **22**, 336–359 (2013)
11. Webster, J., Watson, R.T.: Analyzing the past to prepare for the future : writing a literature review. MIS Q. **26**, xiii–xxiii (2002)
12. Kazan, E., Tan, C.W., Lim, E.T.K., Sørensen, C., Damsgaard, J.: Disentangling digital platform competition: the case of UK mobile payment platforms. J. Manag. Inf. Syst. **35**, 180–219 (2018)
13. Lusch, R.F., Nambisan, S.: Service innovation: A service-dominant logic perspective. MIS Q. Manag. Inf. Syst. **39**, 155–175 (2015)
14. Tiwana, A., Konsynski, B., Bush, A.A.: Platform evolution: coevolution of platform architecture, governance, and environmental dynamics. Inf. Syst. Res. **21**, 675–687 (2010)
15. Baldwin, C.Y., Woodard, C.J.: The architecture of platforms: a unified view. In: Gawer, A. (ed.) Platforms, Markets and Innovation, pp. 19–44 (2009)
16. Gawer, A.: Bridging differing perspectives on technological platforms: toward an integrative framework. Res. Policy. **43**, 1239–1249 (2014)
17. Bundesverband der Deutschen Industrie e.V.: Deutsche digitale B2B-Plattformen (2019)
18. Mineraud, J., Mazhelis, O., Su, X., Tarkoma, S.: A gap analysis of Internet-of-Things platforms. Comput. Commun. **89–90**, 5–16 (2016)
19. Löfberg, N., Åkesson, M.: Creating a service platform – how to co-create value in a remote service context. J. Bus. Ind. Mark. **33**, 768–780 (2018)
20. Guggenberger, T.M., Möller, F., Haarhaus, T., Gür, I., Otto, B.: Ecosystem types in information systems. In: 28th European Conference on Information Systems (ECIS), pp. 1–21 (2020)
21. Täuscher, K., Laudien, S.M.: Understanding platform business models: a mixed methods study of marketplaces. Eur. Manag. J. **36**, 319–329 (2018)
22. Gartner Inc.: Magic Quadrant for Industrial IoT Platforms (2019)

23. Krause, T., Strauß, O., Scheffler, G., Kett, H., Lehmann, K., Renner, T.: IT-Plattformen für das Internet der Dinge (IoT) - Basis intelligenter Produkte und Services. FRAUNHOFER VERLAG, Stuttgart (2017)
24. Rauen, H., Glatz, R., Schnittler, V., Peters, K., Schorak, M.H., Zollenkop, M.: Plattformökonomie im Maschinenbau (2018)
25. Koenen, T., Heckler, S.: Deutsche digitale B2B-Plattformen (2019). https://bdi.eu/artikel/news/deutsche-digitale-b2b-plattformen/. Accessed on 22 Oct 2020 S
26. Yin, R.K.: Case Study Research and Applications. SAGE Publications Ltd, Thousand Oaks (2018)
27. Mayring, P.: Qualitative content analysis: theoretical background and procedures. In: Bikner-Ahsbahs, A., Knipping, C., and Presmeg, N. (eds.) Approaches to Qualitative Research in Mathematics Education: Examples of Methodology and Methods, pp. 365–380 (2015)
28. Ritchey, T.: Problem structuring using computer-aided morphological analysis. J. Oper. Res. Soc. **57**, 792–801 (2006)
29. Zutshi, A., Grilo, A.: The emergence of digital platforms: a conceptual platform architecture and impact on industrial engineering. Comput. Ind. Eng. **136**, 546–555 (2019)
30. Penttinen, E., Halme, M., Lyytinen, K., Myllynen, N.: What influences choice of business-to-business connectivity platforms? Int. J. Electron. Commer. **22**, 479–509 (2018)
31. Hodapp, D., Remane, G., Hanelt, A., Kolbe, L.M.: Business models for internet of things platforms: empirical development of a taxonomy and archetypes. In: 14th International Conference Wirtschaftsinformatik, pp. 1783–1797 (2019)
32. Gerrikagoitia, J.K., Unamuno, G., Urkia, E., Serna, A.: Digital manufacturing platforms in the industry 4.0 from private and public perspectives. Appl. Sci. **9**, 2934–2946 (2019)
33. Gawer, A., Cusumano, M.A.: Industry platforms and ecosystem innovation. J. Prod. Innov. Manag. **31**, 417–433 (2014)
34. Fürstenau, D., Auschra, C., Klein, S., Gersch, M.: A process perspective on platform design and management: evidence from a digital platform in health care. Electron. Mark. **29**, 581–596 (2019)
35. Provan, K.G., Kenis, P.: Modes of network governance: structure, management, and effectiveness. J. Public Adm. Res. Theory. **18**, 229–252 (2008)
36. Arica, E., Oliveira, M.: Requirements for adopting digital B2B platforms for manufacturing capacity finding and sharing. In: IEEE International Conference on Emerging Technologies and Factory Automation (ETFA), pp. 703–709. IEEE (2019)
37. European Commission: User guide to the SME Definition (2015)
38. Daiberl, C.F., Oks, S.J., Roth, A., Möslein, K.M., Alter, S.: Design principles for establishing a multi-sided open innovation platform: lessons learned from an action research study in the medical technology industry. Electron. Mark. **29**, 711–728 (2019)
39. Davis, F.D.: Perceived usefulness, perceived ease of use, and user acceptance of information technology. MIS Q. Manag. Inf. Syst. **13**, 319–339 (1989)

Implementation of a Decision Support System for the Development of Digital Services Within Supplying Companies in the Construction Industry

Christoff Schaub[(✉)], Matthias Hille, Johannes Schulze, and Freimut Bodendorf

Chair of Information Systems for for Services, Processes, and Intelligence,
Friedrich-Alexander-Universität Erlangen-Nürnberg, Nuremberg, Germany
{christoff.schaub,matthias.hille,johannes.schulzev,
freimut.bodendorf}@fau.de

Abstract. In the building supply industry, there is increasing price pressure for semi-finished products. This price pressure is strongly influenced by the commoditisation of the product business. One way to differentiate from competitors in product-heavy industries such as the construction industry is to develop and offer digital services. Digital services can be used to expand existing product solutions and provide them with additional functionality, as well as to develop completely independent solutions. Problematic for existing supplier companies is the strongly product-focused know-how and the low level of competence in the development of digital solutions. This paper presents the conception and development of a decision support system for the technical implementation of modular services. Therefore, a systematic procedure for requirements specification as well as a user-centred description of the essential functional features is explained. Finally, the system is tested within the framework of an evaluation with 16 test persons from product development and business development in practical case studies.

Keywords: Smart services · Digitalisation · Decision support · Digital transformation · Business modelling · Construction industry · Digital services

1 Introduction

Up to now, various supplier industries have relied on the production of semi-finished products and products with comparatively low added value [1]. For many products, technical standardisation is increasing while the number of variants remains high. As a result, the product-side differentiation between individual competitors is shifting towards a price war. Due to a tense price situation, falling margins are increasingly worsening the competitive situation of existing companies [2]. Besides mechanical engineering and manufacturers of finished products, manufacturers of semi-finished products are also under increasing pressure from the market [3]. One strategy to counteract falling margins is to offer complementary smart services (also called digital services). By offering complementary services or stand-alone digital solutions, companies can open up

© The Author(s), under exclusive license to Springer Nature Switzerland AG 2021
F. Ahlemann et al. (Eds.): WI 2021, LNISO 47, pp. 612–626, 2021.
https://doi.org/10.1007/978-3-030-86797-3_40

new business areas and thus ensure their competitiveness [4, 5]. For this paper, smart services are defined as solutions that collect, process and interpret information and are marketed as value-added digital solutions through digital distribution channels [6–8]. This paper focuses on the supply sector of the construction industry. Subcontracting companies in the construction industry often lack experts in the design, evaluation and technical development of software and digital services [9, 10]. The aim is to simplify the development of intelligent service portfolios from a strategic, organisational and technical perspective with a decision support system (DSS). The system intervenes after the idea generation for digital services and leads through a structured process up to the technical conception. The final evaluation gives an outlook on which advantages and influences the system represents in business practice. The testing in practice shows how the development of digital services can be improved in the environment of producing companies.

2 Research Structure and Theoretical Foundations

This student paper starts with the requirements analysis for the implementation of digital services in the construction supply industry. Based on the elicited requirements, the conception and development of a prototype for decision support is presented. This system serves to provide structured process support for the technical design of digital services. The primary objective is to answer the following two research questions:

Q1: What are the requirements for a system to support the technical design of digital services in a structured way?

Q2: How can a DSS for modular service development be implemented in the construction supply industry?

2.1 Development of Digital Services

Classic methods of product development are waterfall models and V-models, which have been extended by iterative and agile approaches for some time [11]. The first two classical approaches are rigid, not very flexible and at the same time offer hardly any possibilities to respond to rapidly changing market and customer needs. Agile and iterative approaches support rapid adaptation to changing market and customer needs [12]. Product development processes often focus on a finished product to be developed. These approaches are usually unsuitable or only partially suitable for digital services, since they do not take into account the service provision and subsequent phases of further development [13]. Based on the DIN phase model for the development of services, an adapted and modern development process can be implemented in connection with the modularisation of services, especially for manufacturing industries [14].

2.2 Modularisation of Digital Services

In contrast to the development of classic, tangible products, the development of digital services is significantly more complex, especially for supplier companies and traditional product developers. One approach to counteracting the increased complexity and thus keeping development time and cost structures under control at the same time is the application of modularity principles [15]. According to [15], the modularisation of services "[...] achieves an increase in standardisation while ensuring the necessary degree of customisation [...]" [15]. [16] describes modularity as the degree to which a system can be separated into its individual parts and recombined. Basically, the goal of modularly structured systems is to master complex but recurring demands on systems. By reusing, standardising and individualising individual technical functions, an overall system can be put together with self-contained building blocks (modules). A modular service architecture increases flexibility while controlling complexity [17].

For the implementation of the later support system, a modular kit with technical building blocks for digital services is used. This modular kit has already been derived from a comprehensive market analysis using the Service Modularity Function [18], Modular Service Architectures [19] and Design Structure Matrix [20] and is not a core component of this paper.

2.3   Decision Support Systems

DSS are applications generally used by middle and senior management in companies. Information from various sources is used to find solutions to problems and support decision-making processes. DSS are primarily used for semi-structured and unstructured decision problems [21].

DSS with a focus on collected and analysed market data can provide valuable information to decision makers in situations with difficult or hard-to-predict alternatives [22].

In this thesis, a data driven DSS for improving and structuring the development process of digital services in supplier companies is designed and prototypically implemented.

3   Requirements Development and Conception

The requirements development and conception as well as the subsequent implementation are based on the GORE model [23]. The GORE model provides a theoretical framework for requirements specification. It covers the following four steps, which are described in detail in the next sections: Goal elaboration, object modelling, responsibility assignment and operationalisation.

3.1   Requirements in Smart Service Development

1.   Step GORE Model - Goal Formulation

According to the GORE model, the elaboration of objectives is divided into several sub-steps. First, basic goals are derived from the literature. Based on this, the questions of why and how are to be answered within the goal formulation. The derivation of the basic goals is done with the help of a review. 24] describes the five necessary phases for conducting the review as follows:

- Problem formulation
- Literature search
- Literature review
- Analysis and interpretation
- Presentation

The problem is already formulated in research question 1. The causes that prevent companies from digitising are examined. This is exemplified by supplier companies in the construction industry within the DACH region. In the literature search phase, "the aim is to research the literature suitable for the research question" [24]. Due to the specificity of the research focus, only a few suitable sources can be found for the given problem. During the literature search, nine suitable articles focusing on the construction industry in the DACH region were identified on the relevant platforms Google Scholar, Business Source Complete and Springer Link.

Subsequently, the identified works are to be systematised and examined with regard to their significance [24]. The literature found that fits thematically into the problem is shown in Table 1. Only literature is listed that deals with obstacles in the implementation of digital services from supplier companies in the construction industry.

In the literature, the authors list various reasons for the problems in the digitalisation of the construction industry, which result from their research. The most frequently mentioned problems are listed below, divided into directly and indirectly solvable problems. Directly solvable problems are part of the development process in the bidding company. Indirectly solvable problems can be solved by developing more tailored services through simplified service development.

Table 1. Identified problems in the digitalisation of the construction supply industry

Year	Source	Title
2017	[25]	Study: Potentials of digitalisation in the construction industry
2018	[26]	Digitalisation in the construction sector
2018	[27]	Business implications of the digital transformation
2018	[28]	Analysis of work processes and determination of qualification needs taking into account digitalisation in Saxon construction companies
2018	[29]	Bits and Bricks: Digitisation of business models in the real estate industry
2018	[30]	Business models and structures must change for the meaningful implementation of digital tools (original source in german, see source column)
2018	[31]	Artificial neural networks in use for serviceability assessment of single-shell mechanised tunnel construction
2019	[32]	Building the Future
2019	[33]	Digitalisation in small businesses: Results from the construction, logistics and outpatient care sectors

Direct problems in the design of digital services

1. Lack of knowledge of companies and employees [25, 30, 33].
2. Qualification and human resources development [27, 33].
3. Lack of operational capacity [30, 33].
4. No employee participation in decisions [27]
5. Too many different individual software solutions [29, 32, 33].
6. Lack of a digitisation strategy [33]
7. Term digitisation not meaningful [33].
8. Work-oriented use of digital technology is not the focus [33].
9. Only little and heterogeneous data on digital services [31, 32].
10. Rejection of technologies [28]

Indirect problems with digital services

1. Planning and organisation not consistent, through many different participants and trades [26, 30, 32, 33].
2. Communication problems and thus information asymmetries [26, 29, 32].
3. Perceived advantages of the previous, analogue solutions [28].
4. Complexity of the construction projects [32]
5. Existing funding opportunities hardly known [33]
6. Directly produced work has so far been little digitised [33].

The results found answer the question of why, which according to the GORE model takes place in the first step (goal formulation). These results are now evaluated on the basis of the problem formulation established at the beginning [24]. The focus is on problems that can be solved through support in the development process or at least result in process improvement within a supplier company.

A DSS to be designed can solve the identified obstacles partly directly and partly indirectly. Directly, a DSS can help companies with the problem of the lack of knowledge of the companies and the employees [34]. The hurdle of lack of expert knowledge and limited experience with the development of digital services can also be lowered by a DSS [21]. The support system to be designed should not take over the development of services, rather it should guide the technical conception.

3.2 Concept as a Decision Support System

After deriving the basic goals and answering the why, the question of how is answered with the conception as DSS. This concludes the first step of goal development.

The system is designed as an automated question catalogue, which assigns the requested information to individual technical modules. Overall, the DSS support service is based on the concept of modularised services. The approach states that the technical implementation of a digital service is carried out by means of modularisation into smaller, easy-to-handle technical building blocks. In practice, the technical design requires a translation service between the requirements of an idea presented by a user to technical modules.

In the DSS, the user is presented with a selection of questions about his or her existing idea. Based on the user's input and on dependencies between individual modules and external factors, necessary technical components are recommended to the user for implementation. Thus, the technical conception of a digital service is simplified and considerably accelerated. After using the system, the result set can be further processed, shared with colleagues and external partners and documented. This enables the company to check one or more existing ideas for technical feasibility, to compare and evaluate them. With the recommendations of the DSS, ideas can be evaluated and further implementation decided on more quickly than was previously possible with the conventional approach. In the next step, after the technical rough conception with appropriately selected modules, the result set is used to move on to a technical discussion on implementation planning with the company's own IT department or external IT companies.

2. Step GORE Model - Object Modelling

After describing the how, the object modelling takes place in the second step of the GORE model. In order to make the object modelling as concrete as possible, the process of the DSS is described with the help of a user journey and the respective roles involved. For this purpose, the concrete process of digital service development starts with business development (BD) from the user's perspective. In this step, ideas for digital services are generated.

In many cases, however, the BD staff lack the expertise to assess what is necessary for a technical implementation of these services [25, 30, 33]. Users of the system, e.g. from the areas of BD, product management or innovation, are provided with an individual, technical conception by the DSS.

The basis of the technical recommendations the user receives is based on an extensive market analysis and subsequent modularisation of existing digital services within the construction industry [35]. Alternatively, it is possible for a company to customise the existing data set. This makes the technical modules, individual questions and the logic in the questionnaire adaptable to company and department-specific requirements.

In both cases, an employee first selects a data set provided by an administrator. Then the user describes his or her existing idea using the intelligent questionnaire. The individual and dynamic adaptation of the questionnaire to the user's concrete situation makes the questionnaire intelligent. While answering, the user can access help on the individual questions and also view market statistics. Based on the user's answers and possible dependencies, further, necessary questions are dynamically reloaded. After answering the questions, the user receives individualised recommendations for the technical implementation of his idea. Finally, the results can be edited, shared and compared.

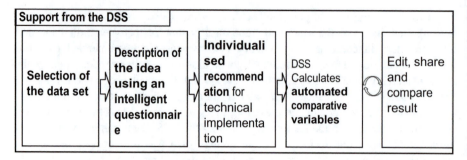

Fig. 1. User journey through the DSS

3. Step GORE Model - Allocation of Responsibility

Step three of the GORE model deals with the allocation of responsibilities, which in this case is described by a role model. In the present DSS, the role model consists of three roles: Developer, Administrator, and User. The developer is responsible for the implementation of the application, as well as for incidental maintenance tasks, for example in the context of occurring errors. The administrator's tasks are to maintain the data records using standardised CSV format. These tables contain the questions and technical modules for the system as well as the logic for dependencies, market statistics and external factors. Subsequently, a corresponding JSON data set is automatically generated from the CSV files for use in the system. The user uses the system in the creation process of a digital service.

First, an initial idea for a smart service is developed and then the system is deployed as described in Sect. 3.2.

4. Step GORE Model - Operationalisation

The fourth step of the GORE model consists of operationalisation, i.e. the identification of functional and non-functional requirements. This step is covered in Sect. 4 together with the actual implementation of the designed DSS.

4   Practical Implementation

4.1   Functional and Non-functional Requirements

Functional and non-functional requirements for the DSS result from the requirements development and conception: A functional requirement for the application is the provision of technical recommendations for an existing service idea. Furthermore, the system should offer the possibility to edit and individually change files through a file management. To simplify collaboration, the sharing of results should also be made possible. Non-functional requirements are intuitive usability and the possibility to access the application from any end device via a browser in order to create permanent and easy access.

4.2   System Architecture

The system architecture describes the structure of a system and is represented by the software architecture and the data model.

Software Architecture

The practical implementation of the DSS is realised with the help of a so-called three-tier architecture pattern, which consists of a frontend, a backend and a database [36]. The architecture of the system, with the associated technology stack, is shown in Fig. 2. The frontend is responsible for the user's interactions with the application. The technologies Angular and HTML 5 are used for this purpose. The user's read requests are processed completely with these two technologies. However, as soon as changes are made to data, the frontend forwards the requests to the backend for processing. The communication between the front-end and back-end runs via an application programming interface (API) that follows the REpresentational State Transfer (REST) paradigm. The REST paradigm was developed to improve standardised communication in web applications and is considered a widely used standard [37].

The task of the backend is to map the application logic and data management of the application, as well as to abstract the access to the data management layer [38]. For these tasks, Java is used in combination with Spring Boot. MongoDB, an object-oriented database, is used for data storage.

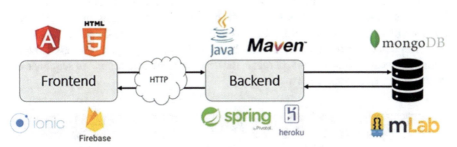

Fig. 2. Architecture of the implemented DSS

Data Model

The data model is realised using a JSON taxonomy, as this can be easily stored and accessed in a MongoDB. It consists of three components: Questions, answers and technical modules. Questions have different attributes such as ID, question title and description. A question has up to n different answers. By selecting one or more answers, n more questions can be added to the question list and m technical modules can be added to the result set. The data model thus allows for dynamic reloading of questions based on answers provided by the user. The result set is displayed to the user after all questions have been answered and forms the first draft of a possible technical implementation through the attributes contained in the individual modules. From the data model described, it can be deduced that the present system is a data-driven DSS. The reason for this is that the recommendations are based on an analysis of pre-modularised digital services and the answers given by the user.

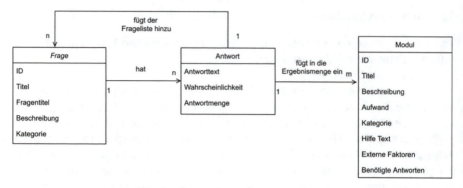

Fig. 3: Data model of the designed DSS

4.3 Implementation

The implementation of the main functionalities is separated into two essential parts. On the one hand, there is the data storage, which takes place in a MongoDB database and is based on the data model. On the other hand, the presentation of the questions/answers and the implementation of the logic. The current JSON file is made available via the backend. With the help of Spring Boot, the JSON files are stored in the JSON Controller class via a repository in the database. A timestamp is saved for each file. When the frontend is called, a request is sent to the backend, which returns the last saved or uploaded file. After the file with questions, answers and all technical modules are sent to the frontend, the questions can be displayed to the user. The questions are displayed according to categories. For this purpose, the categories are run through in sequence and the respective questions are displayed.

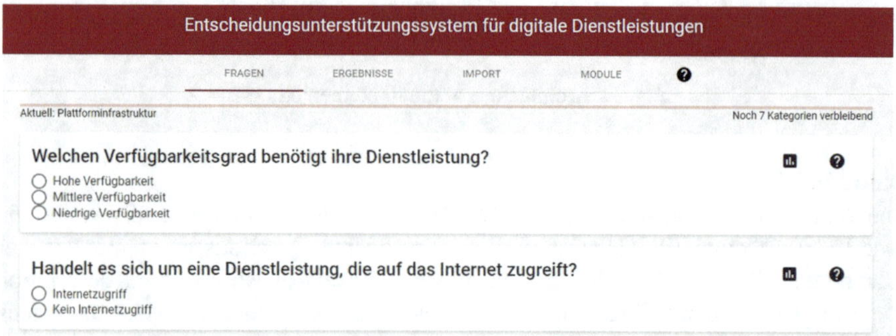

Fig. 4. Example of the questions of a category in the DSS

The user answers the questions displayed to him or her. In the case of a single-choice question, this is done by selecting a radio button (cf. Fig. 4) and in the case of a multiple-choice question by selecting any number of check boxes. By answering the individual questions, a set of answers is added to the temporary result list. The questions are divided into categories and are thus processed in a thematically coherent manner.

After answering the individual question catalogue, the system switches to the results display. The result overview can be seen in Fig. 5. Two processes are distinguished in the results component. If the user does not design a digital service himself, but wants to retrieve a previously saved result, this is possible by entering a result ID. In the case of a generated result, the user can save and share the result at any time or have the result ID displayed. The collected data about the user's answers are evaluated in the frontend to display the necessary technical modules. In the process, all existing technical modules are iteratively checked to determine which modules should be added to the final result list based on the collected answers and dependencies. The results are also displayed to the user via the corresponding Results overview displayed and thus represent the recommendation for a technical implementation of the digital service.

Fig. 5. Overview of results of the DSS

The system is made available to the user as a web application and can be used with all current browsers. The frontend is hosted via Google Firebase[1], the backend application via Heroku[2] and the database as MongoDB[3] by mLab[4].

5 Evaluation

The DSS is evaluated for usability in the following. Usability is defined according to DIN EN ISO 9241-11 by effectiveness, efficiency and user satisfaction [39]. It is a metric that determines the intention to use a system. A high usability predicts a high degree

---

[1] https://firebase.google.com/.
[2] https://www.heroku.com/.
[3] https://www.mongodb.com/de.
[4] https://mlab.com/.

of utilisation. The evaluation thus pursues the purpose of identifying improvements in order to achieve a use of the DSS in practice. The evaluation of the three aspects of usability is carried out in semi-structured interviews with experts from the construction industry in a multiple case study design [40]. The questionnaire design for the usability survey follows [39]. For the selection of questions, the UTAUT model of [41] is used. The questionnaire contains both closed and open questions.

A total of nine questions are defined for effectiveness, based on the aspects of facilitating conditions (FC). For efficiency, eight questions are formed based on the effort expectancy (EE). The last part deals with three questions user satisfaction based on performance expectancy (PE). The evaluation of the closed questions is carried out by means of a five-point Likert scale by the experts interviewed. All respondents have tested the DSS with their own practical examples of smart services to be developed [41, 42].

The target group for the survey is not only the construction supply industry but also leading construction companies and management consultancies with clients in this sector. The respondents are chosen so that they already have project experience in the development of smart services in corresponding companies. In order to minimise company-specific influences and to comply with the multiple case study approach, 16 experts from nine different companies are interviewed. Detailed information on the 16 interviewees is presented in Table 2.

Table 2. Experts interviewed on the effectiveness of the developed DSS

Expert	Position designation	Operational affiliation (years)	Number of employees	Turnover of the company (million €)	Interview duration (min.)
1	New Business Development	[5–10]	[10.000–50.000]	[3.000–6.000]	50
2	Software Architect	[1–5]	[0–2.500]	[0–250]	45
3	Consultant	[1–5]	[2.500–10.000]	[250–1.000]	40
4	Consultant	[1–5]	> 50.000	> 10.000	40
5	Innovation Architect	[1–5]	[10.000–50.000]	[3.000–6.000]	45
6	Senior Innovation Architect	[1–5]	[10.000–50.000]	[3.000–6.000]	60
7	Senior Innovation Architect	[1–5]	[10.000–50.000]	[3.000–6.000]	45
8	Product Manager Digitisation	[1–5]	[10.000–50.000]	[3.000–6.000]	60

(continued)

Table 2. (*continued*)

Ex-pert	Position designation	Operational affiliation (years)	Number of employees	Turnover of the company (million €)	Interview duration (min.)
9	Innovation Architect	[1–5]	[10.000–50.000]	[3.000–6.000]	50
10	Project Manager	[1–5]	]10.000–50.000]	[3.000–6.000]	35
11	Consultant	[1–5]	> 50.000	> 10.000	40
12	Project Manager	>10	[10.000–50.000]	>10.000	55
13	Innovation Coordinator	> 10	[10.000–50.000]	> 10.000	40
14	Project Manager Lean Construction	[1–5]	[10.000–50.000]	[3.000–6.000]	45
15	Lean Manager	[1–5]	[10.000–50.000]	[3.000–6.000]	50
16	Requirement-manager	[1–5]	[0–2.500]	[250–1.000]	55

The average duration per interview is 47 minutes. Prior to this interview, the interviewees have already used the DSS with at least one, usually two to three, examples of their own application. All interviews are transcribed and subsequently coded and summarised. Table 3 summarises the results averaged across the evaluation dimensions, consisting of effectiveness, efficiency, and user satisfaction.

Table 3. Results of the quantitative survey

Assessment dimension	UTAUT-Model	Questions- number	Median	Mean value	Standard deviation
Effectiveness	FC	9	1,44	1,53	0,60
Efficiency	EE	8	1,19	1,40	0,59
User satisfaction	PE	3	1,67	1,79	0,76

The survey of the experts shows that all three dimensions of usability are positively evaluated. According to the model of [41], a high acceptance of the DSS can be predicted based on the overall evaluation.

In a further step, the effect of the DSS is examined qualitatively in the expert interviews [40, 43]. The interviewees state that the impact of the DSS can be measured according to financial, temporal as well as quality-oriented dimensions. These dimensions have an influence on the entire development process of smart services. For example, the DSS has a quality-enhancing effect that is particularly strong at the beginning in the requirements analysis. In the further course of development, the DSS also has a cost- and time-reducing influence, as developments can be parallelised, and modules can be reused.

6 Summary and Limitations

This paper describes a structured methodology developed on the basis of the GORE model for the requirements definition of a support system in the development of digital services. With the processing of problems from practice, correspondingly detailed requirements for process improvements can be derived and presented. The actual development process of digital services in product-focused companies is adapted to the characteristics of digital solutions and improved with the designed DSS.

The concept of the DSS, which was first derived theoretically, is implemented as a prototypical version and presented in detail in chapter 4. It is based on the principle of modularisation of IT systems and supports the user in selecting the necessary modules for the implementation of a specific digital service. The peculiarities and special requirements of the building supply industry are taken into account. Finally, the system is tested in practice with different roles and companies. In the course of the interviews conducted with the experts, practical examples of digital services are simulated. The experts come to the conclusion that the designed and implemented DSS delivers measurable added value in the development of digital services. This means that in the future, business developers in the construction industry will be able to integrate the DSS presented into their development process for smart services.

Through the DSS, smart services can be developed faster, with lower costs and in high quality.

One limitation is the transferability to other sectors and their use cases. Technological innovations that are not yet included in the existing data set must be entered manually. A structured process and easy-to-process data formats for individualising and adapting the data sets are available for this purpose. Future research should accompany the application of the developed system in development projects. Furthermore, it is recommended to investigate how the system can be extended for further phases of the development process.

References

1. Lusch, R.F., Nambisan, S.: Service innovation: a service-dominant logic perspective. MIS Q. **39**, 155–176 (2015)
2. Jacob, F., Ulaga, W.: The transition from product to service in business markets: an agenda for academic inquiry. Ind. Mark. Manage. **37**, 247–253 (2008)
3. Moeller, S.: Characteristics of services - a new approach uncovers their value. J. Serv. Mark. **24**, 359–368 (2010)
4. Gebauer, H., Gustafsson, A., Witell, L.: Competitive advantage through service differentiation by manufacturing companies. J. Bus. Res. **64**, 1270–1280 (2011)

5. Agarwal, N., et al.: User-generated service systems for the digital transformation of organisations. In: Digital Service Innovations, pp. 281–306. Springer, Cham (2019). https://doi.org/10.1007/s10796-021-10112-0
6. Pöppelbuß, J.: Smart service. https://www.enzyklopaedie-der-wirtschaftsinformatik.de/lexikon/informationssysteme/Sektorspezifische-Anwendungssysteme/smart-service
7. Beverungen, D., Breidbach, C.F., Poeppelbuss, J., Tuunainen, V.K.: Smart service systems: an interdisciplinary perspective. Inf. Syst. J. **29**, 1201–1206 (2019)
8. Kagermann, H., et al.: Smart service welt. implementation recommendations for the future project Internet-based services for the economy (final report) (2015)
9. Oesterreich, T.D., Teuteberg, F.: Understanding the implications of digitisation and automation in the context of Industry 4.0: a triangulation approach and elements of a research agenda for the construction industry. Comput. Ind. **83**, 121–139 (2016)
10. Boton, C., Rivest, L., Forgues, D., Jupp, J.: Comparing PLM and BIM from the product structure standpoint. In: Harik, R., Rivest, L., Bernard, A., Eynard, B., Bouras, A. (eds.) PLM 2016. IAICT, vol. 492, pp. 443–453. Springer, Cham (2016). https://doi.org/10.1007/978-3-319-54660-5_40
11. Brehm, L., et al.: Configuration of hybrid project management for the development of technical physical products. processes, technology, applications, systems and management. In: 2017, Proceedings of the 30th AKWI- Conference, pp. 30–39 (2017)
12. Engeln, W.: Methoden der Produktentwicklung. Oldenbourg Industrieverlag (2006)
13. Meyer, K., Klingner, S., Zinke, C. (eds.): Service Engineering. Springer, Wiesbaden (2018). https://doi.org/10.1007/978-3-658-20905-6
14. DIN Deutsches Institut für Normung e.V.: Service engineering. development-accompanying standardisation for services. German Institute for Standardisation, Berlin (1998)
15. Eissens-Van der Laan, M., Broekhuis, M., van Offenbeek, M., Ahaus, K.: Service decomposition: a conceptual analysis of modularizing services. Int. J. Operat. Prod. Manage. (2016)
16. Schilling, M.A.: Toward a general modular systems theory and its application to interfirm product modularity. Acad. Manag. Rev. **25**, 312–334 (2000)
17. Mikkola, J.H.: Management of product architecture modularity for mass customization: modeling and theoretical considerations. IEEE Trans. Eng. Manage. **54**, 57–69 (2007)
18. Voss, C.A., Hsuan, J.: Service architecture and modularity. Decis. Sci. **40**, 541–569 (2009)
19. Böhmann, T., Junginger, M., Krcmar, H.: Modular service architectures: a concept and method for engineering IT services (2003)
20. Browning, T.R.: Applying the design structure matrix to system decomposition and integration problems: a review and new directions. IEEE Trans. Eng. Manage. **48**, 292–306 (2001)
21. Keen, P.G.: Decision support systems: a research perspective. decision support systems: Issues and challenges: Proceedings of an international task force meeting (1980)
22. Islam, O., Alfakeeh, A., Nadeem, F.: A framework for effective big data analytics for decision support systems. Int. J. Comput. Netw. Appl. **4**, 1 (2017)
23. Van Lamsweerde, A.: Goal-oriented requirements enginering: a roundtrip from research to practice [enginering read engineering]. In: Proceedings. 12th IEEE International Requirements Engineering Conference, pp. 4–7 (2004)
24. Fettke, P.: State-of-the-Art des State-of-the-Art. WIRTSCHAFTSINFORMATIK **48**, 257–266 (2006)
25. Goger, G., Piskernik, M. and Urban, H.: Studie: potenziale der digitalisierung im bauwesen, http://www.forschung-bau.at/media/1369/201802_studie-potenziale-der-digitalisierung.pdf (2017)
26. Kocijan, M.: Digitalisation in the construction sector. ifo Schnelldienst **71**, 42–45 (2018)
27. Krause, S., Pellens, B.: Betriebswirtschaftliche Implikationen der digitalen Transformation. Springer Fachmedien Wiesbaden, Wiesbaden (2018)

28. Martin, S., Niethammer, M.: Analyse von Arbeitsprozessen und Bestimmung des Qualifizierungsbedarfs unter der Berücksichtigung der Digitalisierung in sächsischen Bauunternehmen. Final report in the project "Bau's mit BIM", Technische Universtiät Dresden. Dresden (2018)

29. Moring, A., Maiwald, L., Kewitz, T.: Bits and Bricks: Digitalisation of Business Models in the Real Estate Industry. Springer Fachmedien Wiesbaden, Wiesbaden (2018)

30. Rieder, A., Bröckl, A.: Business models and structures must change for the meaningful implementation of digital tools: Anton Rieder, Managing Director of the construction company RIEDERBAU on potentials in digitalisation in the construction industry and the impact of new technologies on the world of work. AMS Info 2018 (2018)

31. Wenighofer, R., Galler, R.: Artificial neural networks in use for serviceability assessment of single-shell mechanised tunnelling. BHM Berg- Huettenmaenn. Monatsh. **163**, 517–523 (2018)

32. Oprach, S., Bolduan, T., Steuer, D., Vössing, M., Haghsheno, S.: Building the future: of the construction industry through artificial intelligence and platform thinking. Digitale Welt, 40–44 (2019)

33. Fikret Öz: Digitalisation in small businesses: Results from Construction, Logistics and Outpatient Care: Forschung Aktuell. Institute for Work and Technology (IAT), Gelsenkirchen, http://hdl.handle.net/10419/193137

34. Sprague Jr, R.H.: A framework for the development of decision support systems. MIS Q. 1–26 (1980)

35. Anonymised for review process. In:

36. Shah, R.C., Roy, S., Jain, S., Brunette, W.: Data mules: Modeling and analysis of a three-tier architecture for sparse sensor networks. Ad Hoc Netw. **1**, 215–233 (2003)

37. Feng, X., Shen, J., Fan, Y.: REST: An alternative to RPC for web services architecture. In: 2009 First International Conference on Future Information Networks, pp. 7–10. IEEE (2009)

38. DATACOM Buchverlag GmbH: Three-Tier-Architektur (2019). https://www.itwissen.info/ Three-Tier-Architektur-three-tier-architecture.html

39. Schneider, W.: Ergonomic design of user interfaces: Commentary on the basic standard DIN EN ISO 9241–110. Beuth Verlag (2008)

40. Yin, R.K.: Case study research and applications. Sage (2018)

41. Venkatesh, V., Morris, M.G., Davis, G.B., Davis, F.D.: User acceptance of information technology: toward a unified view. MIS Q. 425–478 (2003)

42. Esser, E., Hill, P.B., Schnell, R.: Methoden der empirischen Sozialforschung (9th, updated edition). Oldenbourg Wissenschaftsverlag GmbH, Munich (2011)

43. Huberman, A.M., Miles, M., Saldana, J.: Qualitative Data Analysis: A Methods Sourcebook. SAGE Publications, New York (2014)

A Domain Ontology for Platform Ecosystems

Corinna Zarnescu[✉] and Sebastian Dunzer

DISS, Friedrich-Alexander-Universität Erlangen-Nürnberg, Nürnberg, Germany
{corinna.zarnescu,sebastian.dunzer}@fau.de

Abstract. Platforms have disrupted several business sectors and daily life in general. Platforms facilitate collaboration between different partners, which leads to the emergence of an ecosystem. During recent years, both research fields platforms and ecosystems have made significant progress. Since the terminologies originate from different backgrounds and are put into play in various sectors, a certain vagueness surrounds platforms and ecosystems. The present paper, therefore, adds to academia by providing an ontology – an abstraction of a real-world phenomenon – for platform ecosystems. The ontology comprises concepts from the platforms, business ecosystems, and platform ecosystems domains. The evaluation with three real-world platform ecosystems from different industries verifies that the platform-ecosystem-specific requirements were met in the ontology.

Keywords: Platform ecosystem · Domain ontology · Platform · Ecosystem

1 Introduction

Platforms shape nowadays' business environments. The platform Airbnb supplies its users with more accommodations than the five largest hotel brands together. Uber overshadows local taxi companies by having a network of over seven million drivers [1]. Thus, interest in platforms has sharply increased since the 1990s [2]. Platforms like Airbnb and Uber have established a sharing economy, where competition is about attracting platform activity instead of controlling the value chain [3]. As a result, the platform concept gains momentum for both managers and researchers [4].

Status-quo literature defines platforms from two perspectives, the market-oriented and technological perspective. The market-oriented perspective describes platforms as markets that enable transactions between different groups of actors. In contrast, the technological perspective defines platforms as one fixed core with a variable periphery [5]. Often companies and their partners use a platform to build an ecosystem around it [4]. Research has named these ecosystems *platform ecosystems.* These platform ecosystems comprise a platform as the core and actors in the periphery. Subsequently, platform ecosystems enable value creation by coordinating activities among the different actors [1].

Platform ecosystems have become a rather complex phenomenon since they unify multiple perspectives on platforms and ecosystems. The conceptual ambiguity of platform ecosystems aggravates communication about them [3]. Hence, creating a formal

© The Author(s), under exclusive license to Springer Nature Switzerland AG 2021
F. Ahlemann et al. (Eds.): WI 2021, LNISO 47, pp. 627–641, 2021.
https://doi.org/10.1007/978-3-030-86797-3_41

ontology – an abstraction of a real-world phenomenon – might help achieve a structured view of platform ecosystems [2].

This contribution aims to develop a domain ontology for platform ecosystems, to provide a consolidated and formal view on the existing knowledge base. Based on a method adapted from Brusa et al. [6], this paper creates the domain ontology. Ontology users who set up or operate a platform ecosystem can gain an overview of the influences in platform ecosystems. Furthermore, an ontology acts as a communication medium between people with different backgrounds and information systems. An ontology should assist the acquisition, representation, structuring, and organizing libraries of knowledge [7].

After presenting the domain ontology, three online case studies demonstrate how the ontology expresses the real-world platform ecosystems Amazon, an airport, and Airbnb.

This paper is structured as follows. Section 2 outlines the theoretical background of this study and related work. After describing the underlying method in Sect. 3, Sect. 4 presents the resulting domain ontology in an entity-relationship model with Chen notation. In Sect. 5, the ontology is evaluated by mapping the entities from the ontology to three real-world platform ecosystems. Section 6 discusses the results, outlines the contribution, and clarifies limitations to this study. In the end, the paper is shortly summarized, and future research is proposed in Sect. 7.

2   Theoretical Background

2.1   Platforms

Two perspectives dominate the platform literature: the market-oriented perspective and the technological perspective. The market-oriented perspective defines platforms as markets that enable exchange between two or more groups of actors. Therefore, platforms are often referred to as multisided-markets [5]. The central idea of the market-oriented perspective are network effects, which arise between different groups of actors. Research distinguishes two kinds of network effects: direct and indirect network effects. According to De Reuver et al. [3], if the success of the platform depends on the number of users in the same group of actors, network effects are direct. An example of platforms with direct network effects are social media networks. The more people use the platform, the more popular it is, and more new users are attracted to join it [3]. For indirect network effects, however, the success of a platform depends on the number of users in the different groups. An example of platforms with indirect network effects are video game consoles: the more developers are developing compatible games for the console are on the platform, the more people are interested in buying this video game console [3]. Sometimes indirect network effects can also negatively affect the value of a platform. For example, the more advertising partners a search engine has, the lower its value gets for those users who search for independent information [3]. The success of a platform is determined by network effects, which is why platforms must solve the "chicken-and-egg" problem in the initial phase. This problem arises as the platform does not have any users initially and must attract them by itself. For example, Microsoft initially paid developers to develop apps for the Windows Phone platform to get more users onto the platform [2].

From a technological perspective, platforms have a modular structure. They consist of a fixed core and a variable periphery. The core can contain several components that do not change over time. The core generates economies of scale and economies of scope. An increased production volume decreases fixed costs and lowers the cost of developing new products as the core is fixed [5]. The periphery, on the other hand, is variable and can be adjusted, replaced, or even left out as desired. Platforms connect the core and the periphery via interfaces. These allow the platforms to facilitate innovation and co-creation [8]. Depending on how much information interfaces provide to external groups, the more platform users can participate in the innovation process. However, the technological view of platforms is limited since it cannot explain how the entire platform, including its core, is evolving [2].

Despite the similar architecture of platforms, these have different manifestations. Evans and Gawer [9] classify platforms as four types: transaction platforms, innovation platforms, integrated platforms, and investment platforms. Transaction platforms enable exchanging a service, product, or technology between different users, e.g., PayPal, Netflix, and Spotify [9]. When a platform allows other companies to develop complementary technologies, products, or services, it is an innovation platform. Typical innovation platforms are Intel and Microsoft [9]. If a technology, product, or service is a transactional and an innovation platform, it is called an integrated platform; for instance, Google, Facebook, and Apple. Last, investment platforms consist of companies that have developed a platform portfolio strategy, whereby they act as a holding company. For this definition, Softbank 2015 is a corresponding platform [10].

2.2 Platform Ecosystems

The term ecosystem refers to a union of organisms that relate to each other [10]. Business ecosystems are the fixed arrangement of actors around a focal firm, intending to fulfill a focal value proposition [11]. Thus, an ecosystem has a solid structure, which determines the position of an actor.

Actors are independent economic entities that contribute to the fulfillment of the ecosystem's value proposition. Actors do not need a direct connection to the focal firm to be part of the ecosystem, as its value proposition determines its boundaries. Therefore, an actor contributing to the focal value proposition belongs to an ecosystem. On Airbnb, for example, a host uses pictures from a professional photographer to promote her accommodation. Here, the photographer contributes to the value of the ecosystem without any connection to Airbnb.

To fulfil the focal value proposition, actors depend on each other's activities within the ecosystem. Activities are actions carried out by actors to fulfill the focal value proposition [12]. The ecosystem's strategy is based on how a focal firm determines the arrangement of the actors and ensures its role in the competitive ecosystem. The actors pursue different strategies that affect the structure, roles, and risks of the ecosystem. Finally, the focal firm has the task of arranging its partners as envisioned in its strategy. A company in the ecosystem either plays the role of a follower or a leader [11]. While focal firms are the leaders who enforce strategy and governance, followers must accept the provisions of the focal firm. Therefore, internal competition between companies regarding position, role, and activities emerges. In addition to internal competition, an ecosystem also competes with other ecosystems [11].

If an ecosystem revolves around a platform, the result is a platform ecosystem with the platform as the core. An essential aspect for platform ecosystems is that the platform opens up and allows complementors to offer products and services via the platform [2]. Complementors are external companies or groups with no direct relationship to the platform owner, but they contribute to the platform [10]. Boundary resources are tools, regulations, or other resources, which enable co-creation within platform ecosystems [13]. The platform takes care of different activities within the ecosystem: The platform determines roles. The aim for the platform is to control ownership, the number of groups it brings together, power-sharing, and relationships with stakeholders.

Furthermore, the platform regulates pricing and revenue distribution within the ecosystem. It determines the competitive strategy of the platform ecosystem, which can be either collaborative, competitive, or a mixture of both [2].

2.3   Related Work

This paper aims to consolidate the literature on platform ecosystems to resolve conceptual ambiguities. Therefore, other structured views on platform ecosystems are considered as related work for the present paper.

Derave et al. [14] present a domain ontology for digital platforms. In doing so, they analyze the most important features of a digital marketplace and present them in an ontology. They divide the overall ontology into three sub-ontologies. The first sub-ontology shows the service offering. In the second ontology, they depict the negotiation within a marketplace. The last ontology displays marketplace service delivery [14]. These ontologies have a specific view of digital marketplaces as they represent different services. While these sub ontologies show some characteristics of platforms and ecosystems, they mainly concentrate on digital platforms. Thus, the market-oriented and the technological perspectives are missing in this representation. The present paper aims to add to existing ontologies with a high-level conceptual overview representing the essential characteristics of platform ecosystems.

Schreieck et al. [2] give an overview of current research on platform ecosystem. Hence, the authors conduct a literature review to denominate the most relevant concepts of platform ecosystems. The paper contributes to the understanding of platform ecosystems in information systems literature [2]. In addition to their work, the domain ontology provides a formal view on platform ecosystems. According to [15] a definition is formal if it provides a an unambiguous specification that is generally understandable and machine processable. Therefore, an ontology acts as a communication medium and also assists to structuring and organizing libraries of knowledge [7].

3   Method

Ontologies specify the common syntax and definitions of terminology systems [16]. It also defines the relations between terms and is shared by many people in a formal way [17]. An ontology that describes phenomena in a particular domain or discipline is a domain ontology [16]. The paper develops a domain ontology for platform ecosystems partly based on the four step method from Brusa et al. [6].

First, the goal and scope of the ontology need to be identified. The scope defines the concepts of the domain that must be included and the ones that must not [6]. The ontology for platform ecosystems focuses on the structure and the flows of money, goods, and services within a platform ecosystem. As a result, the connections between different platform ecosystems and other third parties were excluded from the ontology.

Second, the target domain is analyzed. This analysis identifies the essential components, relationships, and characteristics of platform ecosystems. Hence, specific requirements for the ontology could be identified. While finding the specific requirements the own expectations towards the ontology should also be taken into account [18]. A literature search was carried out to determine specific requirements for platform ecosystems. Section 2 presents the insights from the review. This procedure sets out the following specific requirements for an ontology for platform ecosystems:

- The platform from the market-oriented and technological point of view
- The integration of actors and activities in a platform ecosystem
- The collaboration between ecosystem and platform
- Value creation within the platform ecosystem

Third, based on the specific requirements, the ontology was designed. Therefore, the requirements were categorized so that different components, types, or relationships can be identified [18]. The requirements above can be divided into the category's *platform*, *ecosystem,* and *value creation*. These categories were designed one after the other and merged at the end to achieve the overall ontology. The ontology was developed as an entity-relationship-model using Chen's notation.

Finally, ontologies should be evaluated, adjusted, and improved based on the results. The evaluation verifies whether all requirements have been implemented. Here, various use cases of the target domain can be used to check the quality of the domain ontology [18]. Platform ecosystems with different features were used for this purpose.

4   A Domain Ontology for Platform Ecosystems

This section presents the domain ontology for platform ecosystems. Figure 1 depicts the resulting ontology. Color-codes were used in the figure to indicate the field of origin for each entity and relationship. All green elements are representing the characteristics of an ecosystem. The blue components originate from platforms, and yellow parts are features of platform ecosystems. Parentheses in the metamodel indicate the sources.

Platform Ecosystem Entities and Relationships. At first, the entities and relationships that represent the characteristics of platform ecosystems are introduced.

A platform ecosystem consists of an ecosystem that revolves around a platform [2]. The relationship *consists_of* illustrates this by connecting the entities *Platform Ecosystem, Platform, and Ecosystem*. Because an ecosystem and platform can belong to multiple platform ecosystems, both are 1-to-N relationships. Also, the entity *Platform*

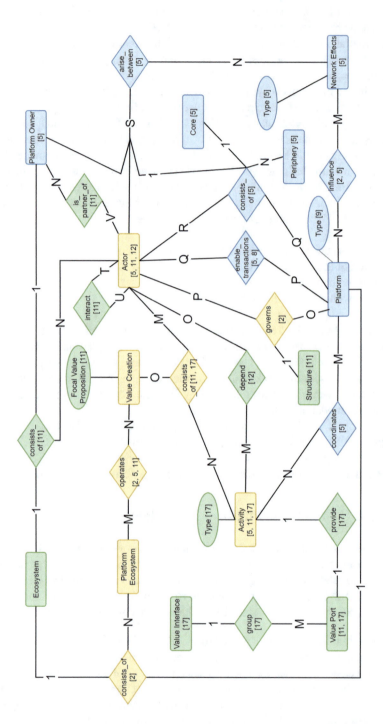

Fig. 1. A domain ontology for platform ecosystems

Ecosystem was added to the *operates* relationship leading to the *Value Creation* entity to show that value creation occurs in a platform ecosystem.

In an ecosystem, a value creation comprises actors, and activities within the relationship *consists_of*. Actors are members of a platform ecosystem who contribute to its value creation by providing different activities [11]. This relationship is an N-to-M relationship, as distinct actors offer different activities to operate other value creations.

A governance mechanism of platform ecosystems is the determination of pricing and revenue distribution by the platform [2]. In a platform ecosystem, the platform further determines the structure. In the ontology, this is visualized by the relationship *governs* between *Platform*, *Actor*, and *Structure*. A platform ecosystem has only one fixed structure. Therefore, one is selected as the cardinality between the platform and structure.

Ecosystem Entities and Relationships. Next, the main characteristics of ecosystems were designed. Adner [11, p. 42] defines ecosystems as follows: "The ecosystem is defined by the alignment structure of the multilateral set of partners that need to interact in order for a focal value proposition to materialize." According to the definition of Adner (2016), an ecosystem has one focal firm.

The focal firm determines the arrangement of the actors and, thereby, the structure of the ecosystem. As a result, the same actors in a different arrangement represent another ecosystem [11]. In a platform ecosystem, the focal firm is always the platform owner. The *Actors* are partners of the *Focal Firm*. In the ontology, this is represented by the relationship *is_partner_of*. Since actors and focal firms can collaborate in more than one ecosystem, the relationship has an N-to-M cardinality. The focal firm and its partners pursue a *Focal Value Proposition* [11]. The ontology, therefore, adds *Focal Value Proposition* as an attribute of the entity *Value Creation*. All components of the ecosystem participate in the relationship *consists_of* between the entities *Ecosystem*, *Actor*, and *Platform Owner*. As a focal firm exists only once in an ecosystem, one is selected as the cardinality between the ecosystem and platform owner.

The recursive relationship *interact* depicts the interaction between *Actors*. As multiple actors can interact with each other, this is an N-to-M relationship.

To realize the focal value proposition, the ecosystem operates value creation, which is shown in the model by the relationship *operates* between the entities *Ecosystem* and *Value* Creation. In [19], the value creation is represented by several so-called value objects that match specific needs or are used to produce other value objects. While a single ecosystem can offer multiple value objects, a value object can also be a part of different ecosystems' value creation. As a consequence, an N-to-M relationship was chosen for the ontology.

Activities need to be carried out to materialize the focal value proposition of an ecosystem [11]. Hence, value objects are activities in the ontology. An activity can be goods, services, or cash-flow. The attribute *Type* of the *Activity* entity in the ontology indicates whether it is a good, service, or money. Activities are carried out or provided by actors [19]. The same actor can perform multiple activities; meanwhile, multiple actors can perform the same activity [11].

To create value, actors depend on each other's activities [12]. Therefore, the N-to-M relationship *depend* is modeled between *Actor* and *Activity*. To enable the exchange of activities in an ecosystem, actors utilize value ports to deploy or request activities. Value ports are summarized by value interfaces [19]. In the ontology, this can be seen in the relationships *are_provided* and *group*. An *Activity* is provided through a *Value Port*, while several value ports are grouped by one *Value Interface*.

Platform Entities and Relationships. Finally, the platform aspects were added to the ontology. Therefore, the attribute *Type* was added to the entity *Platform*. According to [20] there are for types of platforms: transaction platforms, innovation platforms, integrated platforms, and investment platforms.

Further, both platform perspectives – market-oriented and technological – are included in the ontology. In the market-oriented view, platforms are influenced by network effects.

Network effects occur between groups of actors. There are two different types of network effects, direct and indirect network effects [5], which is why the *Network Effects* entity has an attribute named *Type*. In the ontology, the influence is represented by the relationship *influence* between the entities *Platform* and *Network Effects*. Within a platform, there can be several network effects, which is why an N-to-M relationship is chosen. As network effects only arise between actors, the relationship *arise_between* concerns *Network Effects* and *Actors*.

From the technological perspective, a platform consists of a core and a periphery. In the ontology, the relationship *consists_of* between the entities *Platform*, *Core*, and *Periphery* illustrates the technological perspective. There is only one core in a platform, which is why all these relationships are 1-to-N relationships. Other components of a platform that belong to the *consists_of* relationships are actors and the platform owner, which use the platform to create value.

The platform also enables transactions between the actors, which is visualized with the *enable_transactions* relationship. A platform creates value by coordinating the activities of actors. It coordinates activities, which in turn are coordinated by a single platform. This is represented by the 1-to-N relationship *coordinates* [5].

Boundary resources belong to the central concepts of platforms. These can be tools, regulations, or other resources used for co-creation [13]. In the ontology, *Boundary Resources* are defined as another type of activity. Platforms are often supported by complementors who offer products that expand the platform's value [5].

5 Evaluation

Platform ecosystems from different industries were analyzed to evaluate the developed ontology and to verify the implementation of the specific requirements. For this purpose, three online case studies were conducted. The selected platform ecosystems are Airbnb, the Albrecht-Dürer Airport from the tourism and travel industry, and Amazon as an online marketplace. For the evaluation examples from the selected platform ecosystem are mapped for every entity in the ontology. Thereby, the existence of this concepts in the real world is given. The results from the online case studies are summarized in Table 1.

Table 1. Mapping between ontology and real-world platform ecosystems

Entities	Case1: Airbnb	Case 2: Albrecht-Dürer Airport	Case 3: Amazon
Platform	Airbnb	Albrech-Dürer Airport	Amazon
Platform Owner	Airbnb, Inc.	Flughafen Nürnberg GmbH	Amazon.com, Inc.
Actor	Host, Travelers	Passengers, Airlines, Shopkeepers, Advertisement partners, Travel agencies	Customers, Companies, Sellers, Logistics
Focal Value Proposition	Convey accommodations and experiences	Provide pleasant traveling experience	Operate online-marketplace
Activity	24-hour-service, templates	Check-in, salesrooms	Goods, templates
Core Periphery	Website backend Web interface	Airport Facilities Service providers	Website backend Web interface
Network Effects	Indirect, Traveler ⇔ Hosts	Indirect, Airlines ⇔ Passenger ⇔ Shopkeeper	Indirect, Customer ⇔ Seller

5.1 Airbnb

Airbnb is a platform where accommodations and experiences can be booked. In return, the platform offers travelers customer service and travel security [21]. Airbnb does not own any accommodations itself. These are only provided by hosts. Hosts have the option to offer their accommodations on Airbnb and pay a service fee to the platform every time a traveler books their accommodation. Besides, Airbnb offers hosts a 24-h service and pays them the surplus of their accommodation after the traveler has checked-in [22].

First, the components that belong to the main characteristics of platform ecosystems are checked. A platform ecosystem consists of an ecosystem and a platform. The platform, in this case, is Airbnb itself and has the type transaction platform. The ecosystem consists of the platform owner, that is the owner of Airbnb, and the actors. The actors are the travelers and the hosts. They are also partner of the platform owner.

The platform ecosystem operates value creation by offering accommodations to travelers. The focal value proposition in value creation is to provide its customers with affordable accommodations and experiences. Further, value creation consists of activities. Airbnb provides hosts a 24-h-service which is an activity of the type service. A money flow activity, for instance, is Airbnb paying the surplus to the host after the check-in of the customer. Also, boundary resources are used by Airbnb. Boundary resources are, for example, templates they offer so hosts can post their accommodations on the platform. Activities are provided through value ports, which are themselves grouped by value interfaces. These entities cannot be seen in real life as they are used to represent the willingness to provide and to group activities. Actors depend on each other's activities as without the hosts providing their accommodations, the traveler cannot book any.

The platform is the core of the platform ecosystem as it coordinates all activities. It also enables transactions between the actors as the booking process takes place over the platform. The platform consists of a core, and periphery. The platform's core is the backend of the platform since Airbnb is a digital platform. The periphery comprises different user interfaces that travelers or hosts use to interact with the platform.

Last, the platform is influenced by network effects. The network effects arise between the hosts and the customer. The more travelers Airbnb attracts, the more hosts are tempted to post their accommodations on the platform. Thus, the network effects in the case of Airbnb are indirect.

The first real-world case shows that platform ecosystem aspects of Airbnb can be captured within the domain ontology.

5.2 Albrecht-Dürer Airport

Next, the Albrecht-Dürer airport Nürnberg – a physical platform ecosystem – is analyzed. Passengers can book tickets for flights and events at the airport. The airport offers passengers check-in, baggage drop-off, parking, and other services such as flight information or barrier-free travel [23]. Furthermore, the Albrecht-Dürer airport incorporates shopping facilities provided by shopkeepers. They can rent salesrooms for their shops on the platform [24]. The platform offers airlines various services, such as ground handling or the provision of runways, which they can use for a fee [25]. Besides, advertising space is available at the airport, which partners can rent. Travel agencies receive information about the airport and discounted parking via a website [26].

The platform ecosystem consists of a platform and an ecosystem. The platform is the Albrecht-Dürer airport and has the type transaction platform. The ecosystem consists of a platform owner who is the Flughafen Nürnberg GmbH and several actors. These actors are passengers, airlines, shopkeepers, advertisement partners, and travel agencies. They are partners of the platform owner.

A platform ecosystem operates value creation by carrying out flights. The focal value proposition of the value creation is to provide passengers with pleasant traveling experiences. To fulfill the value creation, activities are carried out by the actors. Activities of the type services are, e.g., offering check-in and baggage drop-off. The airlines must pay a fee to use services provided by the airport which is an activity of the type money flow. Boundary resources are, for instance, salesrooms. Selling goods is an activity of the type flow of goods. The actors depend on each other's activities.

The platform is again the core of the ecosystem as it coordinates all activities and enables transactions between the actors. Further, the platform governs the actors and the structure of the platform ecosystem.

The platform consists of a core, periphery, and a platform owner. The core is the building and the central concept of the airport. The periphery are the different services that are provided to and by groups of actors.

Indirect network effects influence the airport. They arise between the airlines and the passengers and between the shopkeepers and passengers.

The Albrecht-Dürer airport is a non-digital platform that interacts with many actors, which is why many activities take place within the platform ecosystem. Nevertheless, this platform could also be represented with the ontology.

5.3 Amazon

The last platform ecosystem to be analyzed is Amazon. Amazon is a marketplace where retailers offer their products. Retailers can publish their products on the platform, and Amazon provides shipping, payment processing, marketing and advertising services [27]. For these services, retailers pay a monthly contribution to Amazon.

The platform is customer-oriented and tries to make the shopping experience as pleasant as possible. On Amazon, customers are offered many services such as Amazon Prime, Prime Now, and especially for businesses, Amazon Business. These services are subscriptions. Amazon Prime offers customers free shipping on some products and many other services, such as streaming series and movies through Prime Video. Prime Now is included in Amazon Prime and offers customers the delivery of products within one or two hours [28].

Amazon partners with logistics companies. For example, the platform provides them with training or accounting services. The logistics partners receive certain tariffs for the delivery of orders [29].

This platform ecosystem consists of an ecosystem and the platform Amazon. The platform is an integrated platform. The ecosystem consists of the platform owner Amazon and the actors. Actors of this ecosystem are customers, companies who place orders via Amazon from sellers, and logistic partners. They are partners of the platform owner.

The platform ecosystem operates value creation by selling goods and services online. The focal value proposition is to provide their customers with a pleasant shopping experience. Activities that are carried out to fulfill the value proposition include providing services like Amazon Prime or Prime Now. Also, activities of the type goods and money flows are carried out. For instance, selling goods is an activity of the type goods, and paying for the goods is of the type money flow. Amazon provides as boundary resources, e.g., trainings for logistic companies. The actors depend on each other's activities.

In this platform ecosystem, the platform is again the core. It coordinates the activities as the buying process is carried out through the platform. Also, the platform enables transactions between the actors and governs them and their structure.

The platform consists of a core, periphery, and a platform owner. The core is again the backend of the platform, and the periphery are the user interfaces the actors use to interact with the platform.

Amazon is an integrated platform that is customer-oriented. Customer orientation can be seen in the fact that many services are offered to consumers. All essential characteristics of the platform ecosystem are documented in the ontology.

6   Discussion

As the three online case studies in the evaluation show, the ontology can capture the essential concepts of those platform ecosystems. Further, the fulfillment of the requirements requires verification.

The first requirement is to represent platforms from both the market-oriented and technological perspectives. The use case of an airport shows this incidence particularly well. On the one hand, network effects from the market-oriented perspective arise between the platform owner and the other actors since the airport itself functions as a marketplace. On the other hand, the mere physical facilities of the airport, i.e., the building, runways, and airplane and car parking lots, function as the technological core of the platform. Additionally, complementors, i.e., airlines, shop owners, and tourism offices, create a pleasant stay at the airport for travelers. Thus, the ontology can express even physical platforms from both the technological and the market-oriented perspective on platforms.

The evaluation presents the integration of actors and activities in a platform ecosystem. The entities Activity and Actors relate to entities that represent characteristics of platforms and ecosystems. Therefore, they are also the entities that show the collaboration between the ecosystem and the platform. Another entity that connects the platform and the ecosystem is the Value Creation as both the ecosystem and the platform operate it.

In conclusion, the ontology met all previously defined requirements. However, since an ontology is a far abstraction of a real-world phenomenon, some information is always be obscured. For instance, when focusing on a digital platform, boundary resources like application programming interface gains importance. The present ontology tries to capture platform ecosystems at their essence, which is neither merely digital nor physical. Thus, the scope of the ontology was set up in a broader sense.

The ontology contributes a clearer understanding of platform ecosystems. According to Schreieck et al. [2] the literature provides different perspectives on platform ecosystems. Nevertheless, platform-based businesses cannot be described by only one of the perspectives. To better understand platform ecosystems, the perspectives must be integrated as they do not exclude each other.

De Reuver et al. [3] describes a conceptual ambiguity in literature as new research challenges arise. These are a result of the exponentially growing platform innovation, the increasing difficulty of platform architectures, and the spread of digital platforms to different industries. In this paper, a domain ontology was established to counteract the conceptual ambiguity.

Despite the best efforts, the present paper underlies some limitations. The paper aims to develop a domain ontology that contains the main concepts of platform ecosystems. The ontology is not based on a structured literature review. However, since this paper relies on the structured overview in Schreieck et al. [2], the ontology should capture common knowledge about platform ecosystems.

Further, the literature about platforms and ecosystems often contains various definitions. Sometimes the definitions differ from each other, which is why those had to be bridged together. Especially, the business ecosystem literature spreads wide regarding its main subjects. The present paper focuses on the core platform ecosystems concepts instead and is thereby not intended to capture the full stream of ecosystems and platforms by themselves. Additionally, the depiction of an ontology is aggravated by the mere number of subjects. Nevertheless, the selection provides a solid foundation for platform ecosystems.

The present paper contributes a platform ecosystems ontology to theory and practice. While researchers may use the ontology to facilitate clear communication about their subject of interest, practitioners aiming to develop a platform ecosystem may find it useful to see the relations and entities in it. Hence, the paper contributes to a unified view of platform ecosystems.

7 Conclusion

This paper develops an ontology, an abstraction of real-world phenomena, to contribute to a unified understanding of platform ecosystems. An ontology serves as a common ground when communicating and analyzing a particular subject of interest. The ontology was developed using the four-step method adapted from Brusa et al. [6]. Platform-ecosystem-specific requirements were derived from the literature. The resulting entity-relation model incorporates concepts from the business ecosystems, platforms, and platform ecosystems domains. The evaluation of the ontology shows that it can map three real-world platform ecosystems from different industries to the modeled elements. Therefore, the ontology has fulfilled the requirements. To this end, the domain ontology can represent the main characteristics of platform ecosystems. It includes all the main concepts of platform ecosystems that also occur in different industries. Further, the ontology can represent non-digital platforms, i.e., an airport.

The ontology provides a high-level view of platform ecosystems, representing their characteristics in an abstract manner. Facets of platform ecosystems, such as activities, relationships, ecosystem strategies, etc., could be encoded into sub ontologies to create an expandable and exhaustive abstraction of platform ecosystems. Furthermore, an interview-based evaluation of platform-ecosystem concepts and thereby, the presented ontology might provide deeper insights into the importance of every single aspect in the literature.

References

1. Hein, A., et al.: Digital platform ecosystems. Electron. Mark. **30**(1), 87–98 (2019). https://doi.org/10.1007/s12525-019-00377-4
2. Schreieck, M., Wiesche, M., Krcmar, H.: Design and governance of platform ecosystems - key concepts and issues for future research. In: 24th European Conference Information System ECIS 2016. (2016). https://doi.org/10.1057/jit.2010.21
3. De Reuver, M., Sørensen, C., Basole, R.C.: The digital platform: a research agenda. J. Inf. Technol. **33**, 124–135 (2018). https://doi.org/10.1057/s41265-016-0033-3
4. Gawer, A., Cusumano, M.A.: Industry platforms and ecosystem innovation. J. Prod. Innov. Manag. **31**, 417–433 (2014). https://doi.org/10.1111/jpim.12105
5. Gawer, A.: Bridging differing perspectives on technological platforms: toward an integrative framework. Res. Policy. **43**, 1239–1249 (2014). https://doi.org/10.1016/j.respol.2014.03.006

6. Brusa, G., Caliusco, M.L., Chiotti, O.: A process for building domain ontology: an experience in a government budgetary ontology. (2006). https://doi.org/10.1109/ICEEI.2011.6021572
7. Uschold, M., King, M., Moralee, S., Zorgios, Y.: The Enterprise Ontology. (1996). https://doi.org/10.1017/s0269888998001088
8. Baldwin, C.Y., Woodard, C.J.: The architecture of platforms: a unified view. Platforms Mark. Innov. 19–44 (2009). https://doi.org/10.4337/9781849803311.00008
9. Evans, P., Gawer, A.: The Rise of the Platform Enterprise: A Global Survey. The Center for Global Enterprise, New York (2016)
10. Bünte, C.: Tschüss, Einzel-App – willkommen, Plattform-Ökosystem: Die Grundlage der digitalen Revolution. In: Die chinesische KI-Revolution, pp. 81–115. Springer, Wiesbaden (2020). https://doi.org/10.1007/978-3-658-29795-4_5
11. Adner, R.: Ecosystem as structure: an actionable construct for strategy. J. Manage. **43**, 39–58 (2016). https://doi.org/10.1177/0149206316678451
12. Jacobides, M.G., Cennamo, C., Gawer, A.: Towards a theory of ecosystems. Strateg. Manag. J. **39**, 2255–2276 (2018). https://doi.org/10.1002/smj.2904
13. Petrik, D., Herzwurm, G.: Complementor satisfaction with boundary resources in IIoT ecosystems. In: Abramowicz, W., Klein, G. (eds.) BIS 2020. LNBIP, vol. 389, pp. 351–366. Springer, Cham (2020). https://doi.org/10.1007/978-3-030-53337-3_26
14. Derave, T., Sales, T.P., Verdonck, M., Gailly, F., Poels, G.: Domain Ontology for Digital Marketplaces. In: Guizzardi, G., Gailly, F., Suzana Pitangueira Maciel, R. (eds.) ER 2019. LNCS, vol. 11787, pp. 191–200. Springer, Cham (2019). https://doi.org/10.1007/978-3-030-34146-6_17
15. Bork, D., Fill, H.-G.: Formal aspects of enterprise modeling methods: a comparison framework. https://doi.org/10.1109/hicss.2014.422
16. Bittner, T.: From top-level to domain ontologies: ecosystem classifications as a case study. In: Winter, S., Duckham, M., Kulik, L., Kuipers, B. (eds.) COSIT 2007. LNCS, vol. 4736, pp. 61–77. Springer, Heidelberg (2007). https://doi.org/10.1007/978-3-540-74788-8_5
17. Hofferer, P.: Achieving business process model interoperability using metamodels and ontologies (2007)
18. Frank, U.: Domain-specific modeling languages: requirements analysis and design guidelines. In: Reinhartz-Berger, I., Sturm, A., Clark, T., Cohen, S., and Bettin, J. (eds.) Domain Engineering: Product Lines, Languages, and Conceptual Models, pp. 1–404 (2013). https://doi.org/10.1007/978-3-642-36654-3
19. Fatemi, H., van Sinderen, M., Wieringa, R.: E3value to BPMN model transformation. In: Camarinha-Matos, L.M., Pereira-Klen, A., Afsarmanesh, H. (eds.) PRO-VE 2011. IAICT, vol. 362, pp. 333–340. Springer, Heidelberg (2011). https://doi.org/10.1007/978-3-642-23330-2_37
20. Gawer, A., Evans, P.C.: The rise of the platform enterprise (2016)
21. Airbnb, I.: So funktioniert Airbnb. https://www.airbnb.de/d/howairbnbworks. Accessed 06 Jul 2020
22. Airbnb, I.: Vermiete dein Zimmer, deine Wohnung oder dein Haus bei Airbnb. https://www.airbnb.de/host/homes?from_footer=1. Accessed 25 Jul 2020
23. Flughafen Nürnberg GmbH: Airport Nürnberg - Entspannt abheben. https://www.airport-nuernberg.de. Accessed 18 Jul 2020
24. Flughafen Nürnberg GmbH: Airport Nürnberg - Das Unternehmen. https://www.airport-nuernberg.de/unternehmen. Accessed 18 Jul 2020
25. Flughafen Nürnberg GmbH: Entgeltordnung
26. Flughafen Nürnberg GmbH: Infos für Reisebüros. https://www.airport-nuernberg.de/infos-fur-reiseburos-d19dc2d6d7e654c2. Accessed 25 Jul 2020

27. Pfister, F.: Marktplatz Amazon - Das Erfolgskonzept im Gespräch. https://www.k5.de/e-commerce-vortraege/marktplatz-amazon-das-erfolgskonzept-im-gespraech/. Accessed 13 Jul 2020
28. Amazon Europe Core S.à r.l.: Amazon Prime Now. https://primenow.amazon.de/onboard?forceOnboard=1&sourceUrl=%2Fhome. Accessed 20 Jul 2020
29. Amazon Europe Core S.à r.l.: Erfolg aus eigenem Antrieb | amazon

Parking Space Management Through Deep Learning – An Approach for Automated, Low-Cost and Scalable Real-Time Detection of Parking Space Occupancy

Michael René Schulte[1](✉), Lukas-Walter Thiée[2], Jonas Scharfenberger[2], and Burkhardt Funk[2]

[1] Leuphana University, Lüneburg, Germany
`michael@web-schulte.de`
[2] Institute of Information Systems, Leuphana University, Lüneburg, Germany
`{lukas-walter.thiee,jonas.scharfenbereger,`
`burkhardt.funk}@leuphana.de`

Abstract. Balancing parking space capacities and distributing capacity information play an important role in modern metropolitan life and urban land use management. They promise not only optimal urban land use and reductions of search time for suitable parking, but also contribute to a lower fuel consumption. Based on a design science research approach we develop a solution to parking space management through deep learning and aspire to design a camera-based, low-cost, scalable, real-time detection of occupied parking spaces. We evaluate the solution by building a prototype to track cars on parking lots that improves prior work by using a TensorFlow deep neural network with YOLOv4 and Deep-SORT. Additionally, we design a web interface to visualize parking capacity and provide further information, such as average parking times. This work contributes to camera-based parking space management on public, open-air parking lots.

Keywords: Design science research · Parking space management · Object detection · Deep learning

1 Introduction

With the increasing population in city centers and the advancement of metropolitan areas, not only the traffic situation is becoming an increasing challenge, but also the search for parking spaces. Every day, millions of people invest time searching for a suitable parking space near their destination. A large-scale study from 2017 by INRIX describes the "impact of parking pain" [1]. Asking 17.868 car drivers in the 30 largest cities in the USA, Great Britain and Germany, Cookson and Pishue [1] study the average search time and economic consequences. The study reveals that German car drivers spend an average of over 41 h over the course of one year looking for parking space. This does not only lead to considerable time losses, but also causes a tremendous waste of fuel.

© The Author(s), under exclusive license to Springer Nature Switzerland AG 2021
F. Ahlemann et al. (Eds.): WI 2021, LNISO 47, pp. 642–655, 2021.
https://doi.org/10.1007/978-3-030-86797-3_42

The study estimated an economic impact of over 40 billion Euros, due to decreased productivity. The picture in the USA is even more alarming, with economic costs of over 72 billion US Dollars [2]. However, Cookson and Pishue conclude that this is "a problem that technology can help fix" [3].

One technological approach to reduce "parking pain" is the implementation of parking space management systems and the distribution of parking capacity information. Conventional parking space management systems, such as barrier and gate systems, are installed to monitor entry and exit of parking lots and provide information of the total capacity, i.e. 40 of 80 parking spaces free. While this number is very intuitive and can be used for traffic routing through parking guidance systems, it does not provide information on individual parking spots, e.g. handicapped parking, and is usually not available online for public use. Other technologies, such as induction [4] or RFID sensors [5] can be installed on individual parking spots. Even though this approach provides accurate data on individual parking spots, it has two major disadvantages. First, it is difficult to install these sensors after construction and second, it is rather expensive in initial investment and in long-term maintenance compared to other approaches and therefore less scalable.

A promising approach, which is cheaper, and still provides detailed parking information is parking space surveillance with camera systems and image recognition. In this case, a single camera can capture and assess the occupancy of a large number of parking spaces. Both a subsequent installation of camera systems and the use of already installed cameras is possible, provided that these are connected to the internet. Whereas prior work [10–14] has been focusing primarily on the optimization of individual aspects of such camera systems, we derive the requirements of a parking lot surveillance system and design a ready-to-use artifact that can potentially help reduce the aforementioned problem. For this purpose, we propose a deep learning solution harnessing state-of-the-art frameworks and off-the-shelf hardware components, to ensure resource efficiency, low cost and scalability. This paper goes beyond the experimental test setup of a proof of concept and presents a fully applicable solution, that was tested under real-world conditions.[1] Additionally, in order to provide parking information online, we draft a web user interface. This work contributes to parking space management, focusing on public, open-air parking lots.

2 Research Method

In this paper we apply a design science research (DSR) approach. DSR is a framework that develops, tests and finally evaluates potential solutions for a specific real-world problem [6, 7]. The goal of DSR is to address a well-defined general problem and to develop and design the optimal solution based on a systematic approach. The definition and evaluation of requirements for this solution play a pivotal role. DSR is therefore often described as an outcome driven research method that focuses not only on explaining a circumstance, but on creating a useful and feasible artifact. As a framework, design science research aims to create a better understanding for the application of such solutions and provide new insights through the documentation of the results. In our case we

---

[1] Real-world test on a webcam in New York: http://96.56.250.139:8200/mjpg/video.mjpg.

consider it very useful to apply DSR for two reasons. First, DSR offers the necessary scientific and practical guidelines for such projects. And second, we want to present an applicable artifact [8]. Here, we follow Österle et al. [8] and go through the steps problem identification (Sect. 3), design requirements (Sect. 4), proposed solution (Sect. 5), and finally evaluation (Sect. 6). Based on the real-world challenges of parking space management mentioned in the introduction, we present related work in the field of parking space surveillance through camera systems and image recognition algorithms. The discussion and categorization of the related work serves the identification of open problems to be solved. We derive our design requirements from related work and real-world challenges and highlight the applicability. We narrow down the possible solutions within our problem identification, and therefore only present one solution to this problem. In order to provide real-time information to end-users, our proposed solution offers a web interface, utilizing state-of-the-art deep learning frameworks. The evaluation of our solution takes place in two ways. First, established machine learning evaluation metrics [9], then qualitative design requirements are discussed in the light of our proposed solution.

3 Related Work

Deep learning object recognition in images is a growing field of research with a broad range of applications [10]. That is why different attempts to integrate deep learning object recognition algorithms in the field of camera-based parking lot surveillance have also been explored. This approach promises various benefits, such as cost reduction and time savings, as well as easy identification and higher security.

Conducting a keyword-based literature search on the AIS eLibrary and Google Scholar, we use the search terms "car object detection", "parking lot detection" and "parking lot deep learning". Since we only want to include most recent deep learning approaches, we limit the search to the past four years (2016–2020). Despite similar objectives, we find very different approaches in the literature. We generally distinguish these approaches into three categories 1) background subtraction, 2) image classification, and 3) object detection. In total, we identify five relevant papers which we describe and analyze with regard to the areas of software and hardware, user interface, and data. We summarize our comparison in a concept matrix (Table 1). The matrix is divided into three areas, namely software and hardware, data, and application. Finally, we derive the gap in research and practice and discuss the relevance of our proposed solution.

Soo [11] identifies regions of interest, i.e. image coordinates indicating potential cars, through background subtraction. Therefore, he uses an image of an empty parking lot and subtracts it from a current image of the same parking lot. By subtracting the numeric values of the pixels, only those places with significant differences remain. This method is computationally efficient, since both images are processed as a matrix and then calculated in a single step. However, this method only finds the pixel difference of two images and cannot distinguish objects per se. Thus, to detect cars, Soo has to apply a supplemental classifier. Combining background subtraction and a classifier, Soo is able to count cars on a given image. Yet, he is not able to assign these cars to parking spaces.

Instead of using background subtraction, Amato et al. [12] and Acharya et al. [13] try to achieve the assignment of cars to parking spots by manually defining image sections each showing exactly one parking spot. They use image classification, applying a customed-trained convolutional neural network (CNN) on these image sections. This serial approach yields an accurate assignment. Nevertheless, manually cropping and individually classifying image parts is slow in terms of process. A significant advantage, however, is that single image classification is less resource-intensive in terms of memory (RAM) and computing intensity, than object localization. For this reason, the possibility arises to run a classifier even on a computationally weak edge device. For instance, Amato et al. [12] employ a Raspberry Pi 2, which offers a cost-effective overall solution and high scalability compared to server-side computation.

Another approach for parking space evaluation is object detection. For object detection, it is not necessary to pre-define regions on the image or cropping the image. Instead, the neural network is trained to detect and mark all cars in the frame with bounding boxes. This enables the detection of cars, regardless of their position on the image. Therefore, Chen et al. [14] and Ordonia [15] use the object detection algorithm "You Only Look Once" (YOLO) [16] for car detection. YOLO is a single shot detector (SSD) which processes the entire image in a single step. Chen et al. [14] evaluate the occupation of the parking lot by comparing detected cars to a predefined map of the parking spots, utilizing an Nvidia Jetson edge device. However, the focus of the work is not on parking space surveillance per se. Instead, the authors use a miniature model of road side parking, to develop a smart street lighting system. Their solution is limited to a small number of parking spots.

Ordonia [15] focuses on the reliability of the car identification task with the detector, for which he compares different versions of YOLO on two public datasets. Ordonia focuses on the accuracy of object detection, only counting the cars present, from which he derives detailed capacity statistics. However, he does not map the detected cars to marked parking spaces. Since there is no information given about the hardware used, we assume that a desktop computer was running the demo system.

The papers discussed above only cover specific aspect of the whole system, such as the most reliable image recognition or optimization of computational resources. The authors do excellent work and reveal insights into new frameworks and system approaches. In the course of our research, however, we aspire to design a complete solution, that closely follows the DSR approach.

This paper extends the presented prior work, in particular the work of Ordonia [15]. Based on his findings, e.g. to analyze an entire image in a single step, we also decide to use object detection. Modern object detectors can run on edge devices and offer the possibility to track single objects, which is not possible with common classifiers. Tracking objects enables us to record more sophisticated data, such as parking duration. As we present the related work as basis for our proposed solution, our design science research is focused on three key issues, that we identify (Table 1). First, previous work does not use most recent versions and frameworks in their deep learning application, second, none of the presented solutions feature an end user interface, and third, the data are rarely visualized and forecasted to that extent, that an interpretable result, in the form of "parking space available or not" is given.

Table 1. Concept matrix of related work

Concept	Sander Soo [11]	Giuseppe Amato et al. [12]	Debaditya Acharya et al. [13]	Lun-Chi Chen et al. [14]	Samuel Ordonia [15]
Software and hardware					
Computer vision algorithm	Background subtraction (MOG) with classifier	Classification	Classification	Object detection	Object detection
Detection framework	Custom trained CNN for classification	Custom trained CNN for classification	Custom trained CNN for classification	SSD (YOLOv3)	SSD (YOLOv3)
Computation platform	Desktop	Edge device (Raspb. Pi)	Desktop	Edge device (Nvidia Jetson TX2)	Desktop
Specific hardware solution	No –proposed webcam	Yes	No	Yes	No
Data					
Research environment	Simulated model	Real world application	Real world application	Simulated model + real photos	Real world application
Process mode	Real-time	Real-time	On test dataset	Real-time	Real-time
Training dataset	Custom	Public (PKLot); custom (CNRPark-EXT)	Custom (transfer learning on PKLot and ImageNet dataset)	CNRPark + EXT	Public (CNR, CPARK)
Application					
End user interface	No	No	No	No	No
Practical application	No – just simulated in a model	No – no end user inter-face and no data workflow	No	No – just simulated in a model and no focus on status interpretation	No – missing Hardware and end user interface

4 Design Requirements

Compared to design principles, which are more high-level and generic, design requirements in information systems (IS) research "are defined as documented physical and functional needs that a particular product or service must fulfil" [17]. The requirements here are of qualitative nature and the proposed solution needs to be evaluated against them later on. To address the challenges of parking space management, namely capacity tracking and forecasting, our proposed solution is designed to be user-centric, i.e. that it provides a software solution and hardware recommendations. The solution must primarily make a statement on a level that an end user understands, i.e. online information of "parking available or occupied" (DR1.1). An end user in our context can either be a parking lot operator (e.g., admin interface) or a driver (e.g., parking guidance). Since the result must be retrievable and easily interpretable for the user, it has to be processed online and it has to have some kind of easy-to-read visualization (DR1.2). The real-time data are supposed to be viewed and filtered via a web interface. The solution sought is primarily intended to provide a digital real-time overview of the parking situation, therefore, it is important that both the camera evaluation and the server updates are performed live (DR1.3). In addition, the system should be able to be operated permanently and long-term (DR3.2). As we aspire a low-cost solution, we aim to use off-the-shelf hardware (DR2.1). Further, no changes should be made to the parking spaces themselves, such as the installation of sensors or other infrastructure, except camera installation, if needed. The preferred use-case works with pre-installed camera systems. Hence, we are able to implement our solution without any interventions (DR2.2). This requirement is directly related to the scalability of the solution. It should be possible to apply the developed solution on new parking spaces without great effort, which could be important for operators of multiple or complex parking facilities (DR3.1). Since the artifact shall be available to public and feature latest frameworks, the solution is supposed to be built upon open-source software (DR3.3). In order to ensure usefulness of the solution, high accuracy is to be achieved, i.e. F_1 score of at least 95% (DR3.4). We summarized the design requirements in Table 2.

We are aware that privacy and data security play an extremely important role in video surveillance of parking lots. A public or commercial use of our solution should therefore consider these aspects. Our proposed solution shall be able to recognize individual vehicles, but no information about driver, passengers or license plate shall be tracked here. As we focus on the technical solution, we will not convert this into a separate design requirement. However, we want to emphasize that, in our approach, we do not need to store video stream or image data permanently.

Table 2. Summary of the design requirements

Number	Description
DR1	**Provide status information of current parking situation**
DR1.1	Provide online interface
DR1.2	Display visual representation
DR1.3	Offer real-time status
DR2	**Ensure low-cost implementation**
DR2.1	Use off-the-shelf hardware
DR2.2	Minimize modification/intervention of main infrastructure, only camera with internet connection, if necessary
DR3	**Provide system package (hardware, software)**
DR3.1	Ensure scalability
DR3.2	Permanent operation
DR3.3	Use open-source software modules
DR3.4	Ensure reliability: F_1 score $> 95\%$

5 Proposed Solution

In order to provide a useful artifact to parking space management on public, open-air parking lots and ultimately to address the introduced problem of "parking pain", we propose a solution, that can display real-time occupancy of monitored parking spaces via a web application. For this purpose, we use camera images that are automatically evaluated with a deep learning model. Utilizing cameras is a suitable approach, since many parking lots have already installed cameras or can mount them with as little interference as possible and at low cost.

Our proposed solution includes two parts. First, we describe our technical approach, which highlights the deep learning algorithm for the automated recording and evaluation of parking spaces. Second, the implemented approach is presented, which includes the hardware system and an end-user interface in the form of a web app for real-time display of free and occupied parking spaces. As we strive for an applicable artifact, the proposed solution must be consistent from input to output. The system we present includes three layers, namely the preprocessing of a camera stream, image interpretation with deep learning and the visual representation in a web app. The layers and the schematic data flow are presented in Fig. 1.

5.1 Deep Learning Approach

In this section we present an object detection based solution for automated assessment of occupied and free parking spaces. The solution covers the object detection algorithm for detecting cars, the algorithm for determining the occupancy of parking spots, and object tracking for determining parking durations of each car.

Ordonia [15] compares the first three versions of YOLO, achieving an accuracy level over 90% with YOLOv3, and confirms YOLO's reliable and relatively resource-friendly approach as a single-shot-detector. The release of YOLOv4 promises even better performance.

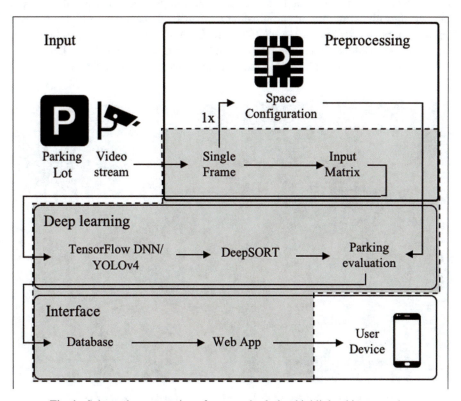

Fig. 1. Schematic presentation of proposed solution highlighted in grey color.

[18] indicates that YOLOv4 is the most accurate open-source, real-time detector, tested on the Microsoft's Common Objects in Context (COCO) dataset.

Therefore, our solution takes up the YOLOv4 algorithm. We use YOLO's Tensor-Flow implementation, since TensorFlow is an essential anchor point in the artificial intelligence industry. Our model is pretrained on an ImageNet dataset [19]. This dataset includes images of people, animals, but also cars, trucks and other vehicles. Thus, this pretrained model serves as a perfect basis, since the deeper layers are already trained to detect vehicles. Fine tuning of the model is performed on a dataset of images taken over a 24-h period at three-minute intervals in the test parking lot. 90% of the annotated data is used for training (395 images) and testing (113 images) and 10% (57 images) for later evaluation of the results. Therefore, we apply transfer learning, which is a technique to transfer and leverage the learning results of a trained neural network to a related task. This method requires comparatively small datasets, which is useful in our case, i.e. training a neural network to recognize parked cars [20].

Instead of just detecting an object on a single image, we can also track this object over several frames. This technique is called object tracking and enables us to identify and track cars over time by assigning a unique ID to each car. This allows our system to collect parking data, such as durations, spots, or daytime. Hence, our solution can automatically produce a variety of statistics and can ultimately be used to predict parking data. Object tracking algorithms are used in combination with object detection algorithms. A recent approach to object tracking is DeepSORT (Simple Online and Realtime Tracking) [21] which uses the Kalman Filter and deep learning. Our approach combines DeepSORT with our previously trained YOLOv4 model in order to track detected cars.

Fig. 2. Frame with YOLOv4 (objects), DeepSORT (IDs) and occupation (green/red color)

Further, after detecting and tracking unique cars, we map their position on the regarding parking lot to evaluate the occupancy (Fig. 2). For every pre-defined parking box, our algorithm compares each detected car object with this spot and considers a parking space to be occupied if a recognized car covers this space to at least 60%. We use the python package Shapely to calculate this intersection. The threshold value needs to be chosen based on the camera angle and the individual parking style of the drivers and might differ from parking lot to parking lot. If the percentage value is too low, the bounding box of a car may also cover parts of a parking spot behind it. Hence, this parking spot would be falsely marked as occupied. Furthermore, it is possible that a car was not parked exactly inside the parking spot and it is falsely interpreted as free.

5.2   Edge Device

Our hardware approach is based on the edge device Nvidia Jetson Xavier NX. We choose the Jetson Xavier NX because of its high performance, resource-efficient operation and small size. With 8 GB RAM, 4 CPU cores and a 32 GB micro SD card, the Xavier NX fulfills all requirements to perform the entire parking lot analysis. At the same time, the system runs at only 10 watts. To access video data, we embed the video stream of the corresponding parking lot. We don't specify the connected camera. Since we use the OpenCV library to convert the video streams into individual frames, our solution can handle a multitude of common video formats, that are supported by OpenCV. We load the latest image into our model. The results are then saved locally and sent to the central server running the web app. Experience shows that the process of entering and exiting the parking lot takes about half a minute, an actual real-time analysis is not necessary. Therefore, we decide to analyze and evaluate the most recent frame of the live video just every 20 s. Despite this huge reduction in data size and transfer, we can still provide almost real-time information within the web app.

5.3 Implemented Solution

The goal of our solution is to provide end users with an intuitive and clear overview of the current parking situation. In our opinion a web application offers the fastest and most flexible approach to this. The software is therefore platform independent and doesn't require installation. Users can access the URL[2] and view the parking lot with an internet-capable device. This is useful, since one-time parking visitors can quickly view the parking situation without any prerequisites. Figure 3 represents the bird's-eye view of the parking lot in a graphical representation and indicates them as free (green) or occupied (red). This is not only very useful for potential parking visitors, but also for parking lot operators. We further provide an admin interface. The admin panel offers a number of additional functionalities, such as a heat map of daily utilization of individual parking boxes, total and average parking times. An occupancy rate graph allows, on the one hand, to compare the daily utilization and on the other hand, it serves as a forecast for the current day. Another graph visualizes the number of unique visitors ().

6   Evaluation and Results

6.1   Evaluation of the Deep Learning Application

In order to provide useful information to visitors and operators, accuracy and reliability of the algorithm are essential, i.e. the accuracy of the object recognition and the correct classification of free and occupied parking spaces.

We follow the approach of splitting our dataset into 70% training, 20% test and 10% evaluation data. Therefore, we evaluate our algorithm on 57 images of the parking lot containing both daytime and nighttime images. In total we evaluate our model on 4845 parking spaces – 3855 free and 990 occupied spaces (Table 3) – on accuracy, precision and recall [9]. Our model achieves an accuracy of 99.48% on our test data, i.e. nearly every classification (free or occupied) is correct. However, since the number of free and occupied spaces is imbalanced the accuracy could be misleading here. Therefore, we also take the precision and recall into account. We calculate a recall of 98.57% and a precision of 99.89%. This leads to an F_1 score of 99.22%, verifying the high reliability of our predictions.

---

[2] Link to the web app: https://sparkle-network.com/app/

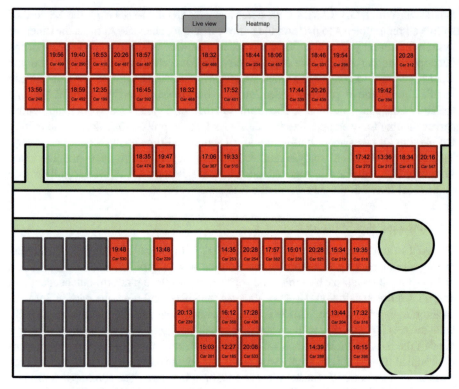

Fig. 3. Live overview of the parking situation in the web interface

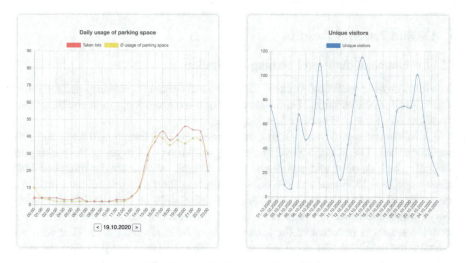

Fig. 4. Visualization of parking data

Table 3. Confusion matrix

	Actual occupied spot	Actual free spot
Predicted occupied spot	966	1
Predicted free spot	24	3854

6.2 Evaluation of the Requirements

We conduct a test of our solution for several weeks and qualitatively compare our result with the design requirements from chapter 4. The main goal of our solution is to provide status information of the current parking situation. We provide a web app, that displays visual information. Therefore, DR1.1 and DR1.2. are fulfilled.

As discussed in Sect. 5.2, the server updates occur in real-time, however, for a better system performance, it has proven to be best to analyze the parking lot only every 20 s, which in a narrow sense does not fulfill DR1.3 (real-time). Nevertheless, due to the fact that drivers need some time to park their car, this did not have any substantial effect on the quality of the results in the test system. Our system still meets the qualitative requirement of a current overview of the parking situation. The proposed solution has been developed with existing standard hardware. The Jetson Xavier NX has been optimized by Nvidia for the operation of neural networks. Thus, DR2.1 regarding off-the-shelf hardware is achieved. Furthermore, the one-time hardware costs for the Jetson computer, a suitable case and a SD card only add up to 530€. The annual operating costs of the Jetson at 10 watts and an electricity price of 0.28€/kWh are estimated to be around 25€. Especially with regard to comparable solutions such as built-in sensors in individual parking boxes, both the initial investment costs and the long-term operating costs are remarkably lower, satisfying DR2.1. Since our system offers the possibility to use already existing cameras, the modification of the parking lot in this scenario is minimal. DR2.2 however, requires no or only little modification of the parking lot. This is the only way to realize a low-cost approach. We consider this objective as achieved with respect to alternative solutions. We highlight that the cameras need internet and power supply to send the analysis data to the server. DR3 refers to a fully functional system. Since our test phase shows that the Jetson is capable of performing the entire computation, the requirements DR3.1, a scalable system, and DR3.2, permanent operation, are also satisfied. Instead of having a bottleneck due to a central server approach, the entire computation is done on the local device. Only the result data are transferred to the server. This reduces the data traffic and allows a resource-saving implementation of further systems on other parking spaces. Additionally, the system is based on an open-source approach. The neural network YOLOv4 for image recognition is publicly available and was trained by us through transfer learning on a custom dataset. Thus, the procedure meets the requirements of DR3.3. In addition to the operation itself, the reliability and accuracy of the system are essential. An evaluation based on test data has resulted in an accuracy of over 99% for the used parking space and thus satisfies the requirement DR3.4.

Summarizing, the previously defined requirements have been taken into account and fulfilled in our system. Nevertheless, the developed solution is limited to some extent, e.g. the camera must be able to cover the whole parking lot. Potentially more than one camera has to be in use. Also, the solution still needs to be evaluated with end users.

7 Conclusion

In this paper we provide a solution for camera-based parking space management with a focus on low-cost public and open-air scenarios. Based on a design science approach, we apply existing deep learning approaches in the field and select hardware to construct a useful and feasible artifact, which is the very core of design science research. Our deep learning approach features TensorFlow, YOLOv4 and DeepSORT and is able to automatically identify free parking spaces at a 99% accuracy level. We use transfer learning to train the model on self-labeled data from a selected public parking lot. Our hardware approach, using an edge device, enables a resource efficient and scalable concept and ensures low costs. Additionally, we design a web application, that can potentially assist drivers as well as parking lot managers to view live information about the parking space.

We evaluate our solution qualitatively against the design requirements, that we derive from prior work and challenges in the field. We can successfully meet the majority of the requirements. Within our deep learning algorithm, we integrate the SSD Detector YOLOv4, which proves to be very reliable regarding object recognition of a large number of small objects. The achieved accuracy refers both to the car detection and to the parking lot evaluation. A major challenge in this evaluation arises with the camera angle, i.e. in an acute angle objects cannot be classified correctly. Another challenge is given by the computation power of the edge devices. We solve this issue by utilizing Nvidia Jetson Xavier NX, which offers sufficient memory (RAM).

A key challenge in the deep learning approach is certainly the generalization of the dataset. In order to avoid retraining the system for each new parking space, the neural network must reliably recognize cars under a wide variety of conditions and camera angles. Future research should therefore try to collect significantly larger and more diverse training datasets, in order to gain better generalization. Since we evaluate the solution only on a single parking environment, we engage other researches to use our approach to test a variety of other parking spaces.[3] The project was primarily driven by the focus on a useful artifact and viable prototype. Our solution was tested in real-world conditions and can be the basis for further development of camera-based parking space management and ultimately help to optimize urban land use and traffic routing.

Future research can also integrate advanced functionalities in the system, such as automatically recognizing parking lot boundary lines, or enhancing the system with a predictive algorithm for future occupancy scenarios. Another feature could be the integration of GPS functions in the web app to enable on-parking navigation. The goal would be to develop a complete program that combines all these individual functionalities and runs as a standalone product. A long-term goal could be the cross-platform integration of this solution with various digital parking management solutions such as sensors in parking garages or roadside scanning from car manufacturers. By pooling different solutions

---

[3] Our code is available on GitHub: https://github.com/derm1ch1/spARkle.

in one platform, individual solutions for specific parking scenarios can be developed and integrated, thus contributing even better to a holistic urban traffic and city planning.

1. References

1. Cookson, G., Pishue, B.: Stress durch Parkplatzsuche in Deutschland. INRIX, Inc. (2017)
2. Cookson, G., Pishue, B.: Impact of parking pain in the U.S. INRIX, Inc. (2017)
3. Cookson, G.: https://inrix.com/blog/2017/07/parkingsurvey/. Accessed 04 Oct 2020
4. Revathi, G., Dhulipala, V.R.: Smart parking systems and sensors: a survey. In: International Conference on Computing, Communication and Applications (2012)
5. Pala, Z., Inanc, N.: Utilizing RFID for smart parking applications, pp. 101–118 (2009)
6. Hevner, A.R., March, S.T., Park, J.: Design science in information systems research, pp. 75–105 (2004)
7. Peffers, K., Tuunanen, T., Rothenberger, M. A., Chatterjee, S.: A design science research methodology for information systems research, pp. 45–78 (2007)
8. Österle, H., Becker, J., Frank, U.H.T., Karagiannis, D., Krcmar, H., Sinz, E.J.: Memorandum on design-oriented information systems research (2011)
9. Hossin, M., M.N, S.: A review on evaluation metrics for data classification evaluations (2015)
10. Dargan, S., Kumar, M., Ayyagari, M.R., Kumar, G.: A survey of deep learning and its applications: a new paradigm to machine learning (2019)
11. Soo, S.: Object detection using Haar-cascade Classifier. U. o. T. Institute of Computer Science (2014)
12. Amato, G., Carraraa, F., Falchia, F., Gennaroa, C., Meghinia, C., Vairoa, C.: Deep learning for decentralized parking lot occupancy detection. ISTI-CNR (2017)
13. Acharya, D., Yan, W., Khoshelham, K.: Real-time image-based parking occupancy detection using deep learning. The University of Melbourne, Infrastructure Engineering (2018)
14. Chen, L.-C., Sheu, R.-K., Peng, W.-Y., Wu, J.-H., Tseng, C.-H.: Video-based parking occupancy detection for smart control system. MDPI (2020)
15. Ordonia, S.: Detecting cars in a parking lot using deep learning. San Jose State University (2019)
16. Redmon, J., Divvala, S., Girshick, R., Farhadi, A.: You only look once: unified, real-time object detection (2016)
17. Koppenhagen, N., Gaß, O., Müller, B.: Design science research in action – anatomy of success critical activities for rigor and relevance. IISM (2012)
18. Bochkovskiy, A., Wang, C.-Y., Liao, H.-Y. M.: YOLOv4: optimal speed and accuracy of object detection (2020)
19. ImageNet. http://image-net.org/. Accessed 04 Oct 2020
20. Pratt, L.U., Mostow, J., Kamm, C.A.: Direct transfer of learned information among neural networks. In: AAAI (1991)
21. Wojke, N., Bewley, A., Paulus, D.: Simple online and realtime tracking with a deep association metric (2017)

Promoting Carpooling Through Nudges: The Case of the University Hildesheim

Coralie Werkmeister[✉], Thorsten Schoormann, and Ralf Knackstedt

Department of Information Systems and Enterprise Modeling (ISUM), Institute for Business Administration and Information Systems, Hildesheim, Germany
{thorsten.schoormann,ralf.knackstedt}@uni-hildesheim.de

Abstract. Mobility is an essential need that requires novel opportunities enabling us to travel more sustainably. In attempting to address this, our university—the University Hildesheim—, located within a city of about 100.000 residents seeks to improve especially the student's and employee's arrival approaches to, for instance, reduce greenhouse emissions caused by traffic, relax the current parking situation, and limit traffic jams. By drawing on a literature review, an analysis of a university-wide mobility survey, and several interviews, this study (1) deduced a set of eight requirements for choosing more environmentally-friendly mobility options and (2) developed a mobile application (app) that promotes carpooling through the help of digital nudges. With this, we hope to contribute to current mobility challenges especially due to increased traffic.

Keywords: Sustainability · Green mobility · Digital nudging · Design science

1 Introduction

Mobility is one of the fundamental needs of our modern world. Through mobility, there is a wide range of possibilities for our society and for companies such as worldwide traveling to meet our family and friends, to arrive at our workplace, as well as to experience other cultures and countries. Due to challenges such as in terms of climate change, it is however a necessary prerequisite to create mobility solutions that are affordable for everyone without accelerating the deterioration of the natural environment. Particularly the pollution caused by car traffic plays a big role in the overall greenhouse emission, which is evident by several facts: In Europe, transportation is the most significant source of CO_2 [1]; in Germany, transportation makes 165 tons of CO_2, representing 20,5% of the overall greenhouse emission [2]; car traffic takes 60,6% of that—so, overall 12,4% of the emission in Germany [3].

In addition to these general facts, it is also a great challenge in local areas. In line with this, at our university—the University Hildesheim, Germany—mobility is one of the most important problems because there are, for example, only very restricted areas for parking lots causing complaints from residents as well as employees who have to handle long times for searching free spaces, high emission values, and an increased volume of traffic causing in traffic jams. Nonetheless, as shown by a recent survey on

© The Author(s), under exclusive license to Springer Nature Switzerland AG 2021
F. Ahlemann et al. (Eds.): WI 2021, LNISO 47, pp. 656–672, 2021.
https://doi.org/10.1007/978-3-030-86797-3_43

mobility conducted by the Green Office Hildesheim [4], the most preferable option to arrive at our university is still by car. In consequence, there is a need for employing novel approaches such as carsharing [5, 6], carpooling, or self-driving services [7] that help to reduce car traffic and thereby lower negative impacts on the environment.

A promising approach to open up the possible solution space of mobility options as well as to foster the selection of options that are more sustainable (e.g., in terms of emissions caused by driving cars individually) is given by nudging. In broad terms, nudging can be used as a tool to increase the transparency of decision situations so that people, hopefully, choose more sustainable mobility options more frequently without intervening in the people's opinion [8]. According to Thaler and Sunstein [9], a nudge "is any factor that significantly alters the behavior of humans" (p. 6). Since information systems (IS) are generally seen as an enable for new mobility services and business models in the context of sustainability [10, 11], this study focuses on 'digital nudging'. When nudging digitally, (technology-driven) user-interface design elements are involved to intervene in choices [12, 13]. Based on that, we seek to improve the current mobility situation at our university by encouraging students and employees to choose a more environmentally-responsible arrival option in particular. Therefore, we raise the following research question: *How can people be fostered to arrive in a more environmentally-friendly way at University Hildesheim?*

In attempting to answer this question, we developed and evaluated a prototypical mobile app that aims at connecting several students and employees to collectively arrive at the university by means of carpooling. Based on a triangulation of literature on nudging and mobility, the analysis of an available university-wide survey [4], and interviews with students and staff from the university, we identified different problems and objectives in terms of how and why people decide on a certain mobility option. By using mechanisms of nudging these objectives were translated into different solution concepts from which the most promising approach has been selected and implemented through a prototype. For evaluation, students and employees were interviewed across several rounds to give detailed feedback on the prototypical app.

2 Research Background: Mobility and Nudging

The term 'mobility' refers to the means of transport, in this paper especially everyday transport as we focus on a specific case in which students and employees should select arrival options more responsibly. Many people rely on mobility, but it comes with financial as well as natural and societal costs such as huge amounts of greenhouse emissions caused by transportation, especially car traffic (e.g., see statistics in [2, 3]). Because of that, there is a need for more sustainable mobility. Whereas sustainability often distinguishes between ecological, economic, and social dimensions, this paper mostly focuses on ecological concerns, which are often called 'green'.

In attempting to face this challenge, research and practice have started to blend both streams of mobility and nudging. Generally, the verb *nudge* can be described as pushing somebody in a direction. In this mean, nudging does not try to intervene in the people's opinion but rather discretely influences them [9]. Referring to this study's context, nudging was used in other studies to influence mobility behavior such as in the online flight booking process [14]. Because many decision situations such as the flight booking process happen nowadays in digital environments, digital nudges can have a larger impact, even in real-world behavior [12]. Moreover, the high volume of information available in digital environments, but also the declining attention spans, makes rational choices harder [15]. Since previous research gives good reasons that nudging effectively motivates users to make more sustainable choices in terms of mobility, this paper especially relies on digital nudges. To operationalize nudging and to make it applicable in prototypes, there are several mechanisms that can be implemented. Table 1 gives more information about the different nudging mechanisms and how they can be used in a digital environment (based on [12, 13, 16–22]).

Table 1. Selected nudge mechanisms and exemplary use case

Nudge mechanism	Description	Example of digital nudge
Default settings	Predefined and suggested options that accelerate the decision process	The (online) cookie-selection of a site is set to "necessary" or "accept all"
Expecting errors	Expects errors from people and being as forgiving as possible when they do	When typing, the software automatically correct minor mistakes
Feedback	The user is shown his/her behavior and the influencing factors that come with it	*Garmin Connect*: Showing the user data about their latest workout
Information	Framing the information about the decision to be made	*Instagram*: Notifying when a live stream of someone they follow is started
Incentive	Encouraging the user by giving them salient incentives	*TK Fit*: Giving the user badges and points that they can redeem
Social norms	Represents the behavior or decision of somebody else, acting as a 'role model'	*WhatsApp*: Showing the user's online status and if they read a message
Structure complex choices	Simplifying or reducing alternatives in each decision situation	*Immowelt*: Implemented filters so that just relevant offers will be shown
Understanding mapping (from choice to welfare)	Giving a clear choice architecture with an overview of the different characteristics of a decision	*Google Maps*: Showing the duration that different means of transportation need

3   Research Design

The research design of this paper draws on two procedure models, namely the *Design Science Research Methodology* (DSRM) with a problem-centered initiation as proposed by Peffers et al. [23] and the *Digital Nudge Design Method* (DNDM) by Mirsch et al. [24] that complements the DSRM through specific activities for designing digital nudges (Fig. 1). Even though we are aware of the availability of other methods for designing nudges that generally have some overlaps and similarities such as designing and testing the nudge (e.g., [25, 26]), we selected the DNDM because it details each of the abstract phases through sub-steps and is evaluated in terms of (practical) interviews that emphasize the applicability. Furthermore, we believe that the DNDM can be easily arranged with the DSRM.

The first phase, **identify problem & motivate,** started with a triangulation of a literature review, the analysis of an available mobility survey [4], and six interviews with the target group (i.e., students and employees of the university). First, the literature review was executed in three different databases: *AISeL, Google Scholar,* and *Web of Science.* Furthermore, articles from the journals *Transportation Part D* and *Part F* were included because we assume that these are helpful for the field of sustainable transportation. In total, 21 articles were examined. With the literature review, several requirements (REQ) could be derived, supporting an effective nudge development. Second, the results from the mobility survey gave more details about the case, the target group as well as the mobility behavior. Third, for structuring the interviews, the model from [27] was used. Six people were interviewed, taking into consideration that there had to be a range of different characters to explore different arrival situations and to possibly identify multiple approaches/situations that can be nudged.

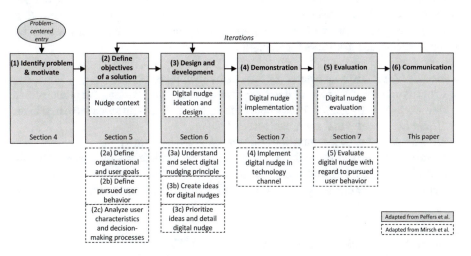

Fig. 1. Overall research process (adapted from Peffers et al. and Mirsch et al.)

In the second phase, the **objectives of the solution** were defined based on the results of the triangulation, the obtained REQs in particular. Therefore, organizational and user goals were specified. This was done by analyzing the fundamental needs and primary goals of the interviewees. Besides, several user characteristics, and decision-making processes in terms of individual mobility options could be disclosed.

In the third phase, **design and development**, different nudging approaches were created within a brainstorming session. Reviewing the examples from the literature, the results from the mobility survey, and analyzing the interviews with the target group, the, in our opinion, most promising approach was selected for further prototype development, namely a mobile app for university-wide carpooling. Different options to address the target group with the approach of carpooling were created (i.e., different combinations of nudge mechanisms and designs), and prototypes were built.

For **demonstration** and **evaluation**, the prototype including its implemented nudges was used to illustrate potential usage scenarios as well as tested in three major evaluation activities: First, the participants were shown the prototype (i.e., mobile app) and should provide critical feedback; Second, after incorporating that feedback, the participants should provide positive feedback to the overall functions and the revised features; Third, the participants tested and rated the prototype's usability.

4   Problem Formulation: The Case of the University Hildesheim

The mobility survey done by the Green Office Hildesheim [4] indicates that 38,9% of the students and employees are unsatisfied and 15,7% very unsatisfied with the mobility situation regarding the arrival at University Hildesheim. They found out that especially the duration, costs, the distance between residence and university, access to supporting offers or platforms, as well as the ownership of, for example, a car or bike, can influence the mobility choice. Even though Hildesheim is a rather small city with about 100.000 residents, general-purpose (e.g., apps such as Google Maps) and city-specific (i.e., offers that especially focus just on this city) in the form of analog and digital offers to arrive at the university are available, for example:

- *Google Maps*[1] gives an overview of routes by foot, bike, and car.
- Citizens can arrive by bike, and in case of any damage or questions can participate in free workshops by *Fazze*[2]. Bulky items can be transported with so-called cargo bikes (*Hilde Lastenrad*[3]) that are useable free of charge.
- *DB Navigator*[4] shows connections that are available by train or bus.
- Electric cars can be used, which are provided by the local electricity provider *EVI*[5]—recently introduced a prototype for electronic car-sharing.
- Various e-scooter can be rented across the city via a mobile app (*TIER*[6])

---

[1] Google Maps: https://www.google.de/maps (Accessed:12.09.2020).

[2] Fazze: https://fazze.asta-hildesheim.de/ (Accessed:12.09.2020).

[3] Hilde Lastenrad: https://hilde-lastenrad.de/ (Accessed:12.09.2020).

[4] DB: https://www.bahn.de/p/view/service/mobile/db-navigator.shtml (Accessed: 12.09.2020).

[5] EVI: https://www.evi-hildesheim.de/ (Accessed: 12.09.2020).

[6] TIER: https://www.tier.app/de/ (Accessed: 20.09.2020).

Generally, students can use public transportation free of charge because of their student tickets. The employees do not have such an opportunity when it comes to public transport. Still, they can take advantage of the job ticket by the state of Lower Saxony to reduce the overall costs. Nevertheless, plenty of the students and employees from the university still rely on cars which reinforced the mentioned challenges.

5 Specification of Solution Objectives

In this section, we derive requirements (REQ) based on the literature on nudging and mobility that acts as the basis for our artifact. Afterward, we refined this set through interviews disclosing reasons why, for instance, students and employees rely on cars.

5.1 Requirements and Objectives Based on Existing Literature

As explained in the Research Design, three academic databases and additional journals for transportation were used to collect important aspects and findings from recent research. Our sample of 21 articles offered more information about how to create a nudge in the context of (sustainable) mobility. Not all these articles focused directly on nudging, but on related and adjacent topics such as decision-making [28], persuasive design [29], or gamification [30]. Also, different niches were explored, from smart charging [28], public transport systems [31, 32], sustainable travel [33], to general pro-environmental behavior [34]. During the analysis, we especially focus on tools that were used: Some of the explorative articles decided to work with apps, notifications, or feedback systems. Others chose to use offline possibilities like more space for pedestrians, cyclists, and busses [35] or test-tickets for trying public transportation services and convince the users of their advantages [36]. After examining the relevant articles, it was possible to develop REQs about how a nudge in terms of fostering mobility should look like. In the following, these REQs are presented in more detail.

The approach of tracking the user's activities and giving them feedback or more information about their behavior is used in more than half of the articles examined [28, 31, 37]. Ortmann et al. [38] summarized different behavioral intervention strategies towards a more efficient transportation system where the evidence for information/education is generally estimated as high. In the case of shifting travel to off-peak periods, it is rated with medium confidence. Bardal et al. [39] explored the "barriers for designing and implementing policies for the transition to more environmentally sustainable urban mobility" (p. 1). The authors identified that amongst other things, the lack of knowledge, evaluation, communication, or tools could be a barrier for the transitions to greener mobility. To face this, it is possible to make use of specific nudge mechanisms that draw on the lack of information, as presented in Sect. 2 (e.g., information, structure complex choices). Therefore, the following REQ is specified as follows: *REQ1—The more information is available for the user about available alternatives, more sustainable ways to arrive at their destination, the more users would make more sustainable decisions in that matter.*

In the article 'goal framing in smart charging' [28], which also adopted the concept of Mirsch et al. [13] to nudge more flexible charging, the researchers allowed the user to set their own goals in terms of environmental, social, and financial aspects. The authors explained that goal-framing for reducing pollution regarding health led to 8–10% more energy conservation and, therefore, better decision-making. In general, six of the articles took fundamental needs or primary goals of the user into consideration while developing the nudge (e.g., [29, 40]). Sandau et al. [31] built an architecture of a demand platform that includes the special demands and local road attributes so that the proposed trip would fit the users' needs and goals. Overall, it can be said that addressing fundamental needs or primary goals of the user could support a nudge. Therefore, the next REQ is specified as follows: *REQ2—The more a nudge would address the fundamental mobility needs/primary mobility goals of a user, the more useful this nudge would be.*

Andersen et al. [32] investigated smart nudging, including sensing, analyzing, and informing and nudging. They listed discouraging and encouraging factors for different transportation types to sense where the users could be hindered from using a specific means of transportation. To analyze the user, they listed main user profile dimensions, such as personal data or goals, and user-related information that could be useful for the nudging, like calendar events or current locations. They claimed that it is crucial to be aware of the user's current situation, their former ones, the plans like calendar events, but also bus and train schedules. Additional predictions about the weather, pollution levels, and schedule deviations were considered significant. With this personalized information, the nudge could have been more effective or, like the authors said: "smarter". Wallann [41] also emphasized that the current, past, and future weather "affect the travel decisions of people living in an area" (p. 14). Furthermore, the road conditions, traffic, parking situation, and health conditions are considered as important information, so that a nudge could also advise about outdoor clothing for specific means of transportation. Accordingly, the next REQ is specified as follows: *REQ3—The more a nudge is personalized to the user, the more useful this nudge would be.*

5.2 Requirements and Objectives Based on Interviews

Based on the initial list of requirements gathered from the literature, we sought to complement this through specific insights, needs, and challenges when choosing a means of transport from real students and employees of the university. These additional insights were intended to increase or decrease the importance of a single requirement in the context of our specific problem situation. To obtain this and understand how potential users make decisions in terms of mobility, six students and employees were interviewed. Each of the interviews was separated into five main blocks: First, general information about the arrival process including morning routines. Second, options that are available to arrive at the university as well as influencing factors and fundamental needs that are essential for choosing a means of transportation (e.g., Do you always use the same means of transportation? Why do you not choose other options?). Third, the general opinion about more environmental options, the awareness of all the possibilities to arrive at the university, and possible reasons to choose an ecological option (e.g., What do you think is the mist environmental option?). Fourth, validation of initial requirements from the literature (e.g., Would a financial incentive convince you to choose another option?), Fifth, personal information including courses details.

In a nutshell, half of the interviewees tried to make more environmental decisions on purpose (see 2, 4, 5) like by avoiding domestic flights. One of them also stated that the factor to behave more sustainable may be a great thing to do, but for most, it is just one factor included in a bigger decision process. The other half of the interviewees choose environmental options without specific purposes (see 1, 3, 6). Next, we summarize the main observations and insights gained from the interviews.

Personal Factors and Needs.   Table 2 summarizes the influencing factors and fundamental needs of the different interviewees when choosing a means of transport. It indicates that every person has different influencing factors and fundamental needs because every arrival situation is unique. The most common needs were cleanness, free space, low volume, and transportation from A to B. Taking a look at the influencing factors, costs, time to work or read, the daily schedule of the person, and the general environmental impact, were most often mentioned. Therefore, a nudge could include an aspect of personalization—supporting the initial REQ3.

Table 2. Summary of influencing factors for mobility choices and needs

ID	Role	Influencing factors	Fundamental needs
1	Student	Comfort, costs, available time to work/read during transport	Cleanness, free space, low background noises
2	Student	Costs, daily schedule, environmental impact, weather	Customer experience, free space, predictability, regularity, reliability, security
3	Student	Convenience, free space	Cleanness, punctuality
4	Employee	Daily schedule, exercise, flexibility, health problems, weather	Free space, low background noise, transport from A to B
5	Employee	Environmental impact, speed, available time to work/read during transport	Comfort, environmental impact, free space, time maximum
6	Employee	Cleanness, costs, daily schedule, available time to work/read during transport, transport luggage or dog(s)	Comfort, regularity, transport from A to B

5.3   Summary of Requirements and Objectives

Table 3 synthesizes both the requirements derived from the literature and the interviews with students and employees. REQ1–3 have not been revised and REQ4–8 have been added during the interviews.

Table 3. Requirements for the artifact to be developed (i.e., university carpooling)

ID	Formulation of the requirement (REQ)
REQ1	Information about the environmental impact of a means of transport affects the user's behavior in terms of their mobility choices
REQ2	The more a nudge would address the user's mobility needs and primary mobility goals, the more useful this nudge would be
REQ3	The more a nudge is personalized to the students or employees of the University Hildesheim, the more useful this nudge would be
REQ4	More information about the means of transportation regarding trustworthiness affects the behavior of the students and employees of the University Hildesheim regarding their mobility choices
REQ5	More information about the means of transportation regarding reliability affects the behavior of the students and employees of the University Hildesheim regarding their mobility choices
REQ6	The possibility to connect with colleagues, fellow students, or professors while arriving from the University Hildesheim affects the behavior of the students and employees regarding their mobility choices
REQ7	Flexibility or keeping up with the daily schedules of a means of transportation affects the behavior of the students and employees of the University Hildesheim regarding their mobility choices
REQ8	The opportunity of working or reading while traveling affects the behavior of the students and employees of the University Hildesheim regarding their mobility choices

6 Design and Development

After examining the REQs, different approaches to nudge the mobility options at University Hildesheim were created during creative brainstorming sessions. The most promising approach, discussed within the author team, was to simplify the building of carpools so that students and employees do not need to drive a car on their own when they, for instance, need to transport larger objects or need to be flexible in time. Carpooling has the potential to reduce the environmental impact, the costs when it comes to arriving at University Hildesheim, and the parking situation (see problem description) as well as allows for making new acquaintances. Moreover, even though there is a great environmental potential of carpooling as a mobility service, there is only limited research in information systems focusing on that topic [7]. As argued before, some people need to arrive by car and with our solution (i.e., carpools), we seek to still allow using cars in those cases where it is important (e.g., transport of bulky objects) but also to provide an approach that might have a lower impact on the environment. Referring to University Hildesheim, a user-organized system for carpool building would be suitable because there is already a huge amount of people arriving by car (as indicated by the mobility survey).

Table 4. Implemented features and applied nudging mechanisms

Feature category	Description of features (F)	Nudging mechanism
Searching and filtering	• *Use filter (F1):* Since people rely on cars because of specific reasons, different filter options such as taking children or the possibility to work during the drive are implemented to fit a carpool	Structure complex choices
Rating	• *Create rating (F2):* All users can rate each other after the carpool regardless of being a provider or consumer	Feedback
	• *View ratings (F3):* To overcome the barrier of trust, users can see the rating of other users to assess if they are trustworthy	Social norms
Motivating through gamification elements	• *Perform quests (F4):* When the user accesses the application for the first time, quests will be available that are easy to complete, for example, booking or providing their first carpool	Incentive
	• *Earn achievements (F5):* Users can receive profile badges to visualize achievements	Feedback, incentive
	• *Compare rankings (F6):* Through leaderboards, users can compare their achievements • *Give incentives (F7):* The app indicates what needs to be done to improve rankings	Feedback, social norms

Being aware that the implementation of a carpooling mobile app could have different focuses such as on building trust between users or on punctuality through tracking cars, this study blends nudging mechanisms with elements proposed by gamification [42] in order to motivate users to participate in carpooling. In Table 4, we describe the main features implemented through our mobile app according to three categories, namely (1) searching and filtering, (2) rating, and (3) motivating through gamification elements.

Figure 2 presents exemplary screens of the prototype, i.e. the mobile app. The language in the prototype is German because it was tested at a German University.

| My Profile: | My Quests: | My Achievements: | Search Options: | Rankings: |
| Feature 3 | Feature 4 | Feature 5 | Feature 1 | Feature 6 |

Fig. 2. Prototype screen examples

7 Demonstration and Evaluation

For evaluation, three people were selected to give feedback to the prototype in three rounds. They all already participated in the previous interviews and therefore have a basic understanding of the facts discussed during the last sections. After each round, the prototype was adjusted according to the feedback given. In the first round, the participants gave critical feedback. Misunderstandings made in the previous interviews about the needs of the interviewed persons were discovered, such as specific search options. In the second round, all participants gave positive feedback highlighting the positive aspects of the prototype. The participants could test the usability with a clickable prototype in the third round. After that, they were asked to rate the prototype by usability-attributes. In the following, (1) feedback, lessons learned, and observations made across all evaluation rounds are provided (2) and the prototype is discussed in terms of how it fulfills the derived REQs.

Features for Searching and Filtering (1). To address the fundamental needs, the users could have the opportunity to differentiate between carpool offers by selecting given attributes as mentioned in the previous section. Through that, the user would have more structured information of a carpool and the possibility to evaluate if it fits their needs. The prototype sets the university as a standard destination or starting point. Search options for travel needs, like the possibility to work or read while traveling, could lead to more frequent use of the carpools provided (REQ3 and REQ8). To simplify the selection of different options, the main options that could change from day to day have to be selected every time, but more general options can be selected over a separate filter that is saved. With these options, the nudging mechanism of structuring complex choices is addressed, and the user will find a suitable carpool faster. Moreover, both users and providers do not have match details. Therefore, the prototypes implement feature for addressing the user's needs and the possibility to search for a carpool that is suitable for the unique personal situation (REQ2 and REQ3). Because a user can select to work or read during the carpool, REQ8 could be addressed. The users could also specify their latest departure and arrival time, which provides a sense of reliability (REQ5). Moreover, through building the carpools a connection to other students and employees is provided (REQ6). In the evaluation, all participants stated that this feature is necessary for a final version and implementation. The option to filter specific search settings on another site was added after it has been noted that is it laborious to select all the different search options every time. Also, search options were added and changed, for example, the possibility to select if the carpool was children friendly and gender selection was added.

Features for Rating (2). Trust is a relevant factor when it comes to carpool building. As already mentioned in the interviews, when no trust or general knowledge of the person is available, driving, or taking them in their carpool becomes insecure. One possibility to overcome the barrier of trust is to let the users rate each other. An example of this is the application Google Play[7], where the users can see the overall rating of an application, the comments of other users to explain their rating, but also the editor's recommendations about what they appreciate in the app. Another example is the application Kleiderkreisel[8], where the users can rate each other after a transaction. In the example of University Hildesheim, a rating of other users, respectively, carpool providers, could increase the trust and, therefore, the use of the application in general (REQ3 and REQ4). We hope to achieve a sense of trust for the users and to provide information about the reliability of the users (REQ5). Participants of the evaluation, particularly for the positive feedback, rated this as an essential feature for the providing of feedback for their behavior.

Features for Motivating through Gamification Elements (3). In broad terms, gamification employs game-mechanisms in a non-game-context to influence the user's behavior positively [43, 44]. Referring to this study, this might be helpful as we seek to motivate carpool building in the sense of playing a game, for example, to get awards when providing the most carpools within a day—also known from other applications (e.g., Pokémon Go[9] or [45]). Adapting this to the example of University Hildesheim, students and employees could also get rewards when, for example, providing or booking a specific number of carpools. In combination with a rating mechanism to support the trust between the users (REQ4), they could even get rewards when reaching a high number of five-star ratings. In the prototype built, typical gamification elements in the form of *quests* (i.e., tasks the user must fulfill to get rewards), *achievements* (i.e., rewards that can be collected such as in the form of points or badges), and *ranking/leaderboards* (i.e., an overview of all users and their progress in terms of achievements) were used (e.g., [44, 46–48]). By using the leaderboard element, for example, the app offers a comparison between the users, so that *Social norms* as a nudging mechanism can be also fostered. This also addresses REQ6 because of the social aspect to connect with other users and compare rankings. Besides, all gamification elements provide a feedback mechanism for the user, which can support the regular use of the application.

Before the first evaluation was performed, the gamification elements were not visible on the starting screen when entering the application. The participants stated that

---

[7] Google Play Store: https://play.google.com/store (Accessed: 20.09.2020).

[8] Kleiderkreisel: https://www.kleiderkreisel.de/app (Accessed: 20.09.2020).

[9] Pokémon Go: https://pokemongolive.com/de/ (Accessed: 20.09.2020).

it could be useful to see the users' progress immediately after entering the application. Therefore, the level-bar was added to the first site and the overview with the quests. By completing quests, the user can collect points that raise their level. Moreover, the overall theme of the gamification-element design was included in the whole prototype. One participant suggested adding little stars at the end of each quest-bar to make the possibility of an achievement more visible. Moreover, the possibility to show other users their favorite achievement was added. In summary, all participants agreed that the gamification elements gave an effective incentive to use the app more often.

Additional Features and Design Decisions. Besides gaining insights regarding features that are already implemented, evaluation participants suggested additional features and comments in terms of the prototype design: First, the selection of nearby bus stops or subway stations as pick up locations to protect the user's privacy, which would also reduce the required information to pick up users, for example. Second, as a payment system, a non-commercial variant such as buying and receiving free kilometers for the carpool would be conceivable—this would also cover the costs of the carpool providers. Third, since all participants like the idea of gamification, they suggested implementing the gamification design throughout the entire application—therefore, gender-specific design of questions, for instance, need to be considered.

8   Discussion and Conclusion

8.1   Summary and Implications

Mobility is an essential prerequisite to support positive aspects such as meeting friends and family, engaging with other cultures, or getting to work. In contrast, mobility can have negative impacts on the natural environment, particularly in terms of greenhouse emissions [2, 3] that need to be taken into account. Therefore, novel approaches such as sharing vehicles need to be promoted. From a more specific view, this study's case of the University Hildesheim faces challenges in terms of restricted parking lots, emissions, and traffic jams in particular. Against this backdrop, the present study raised the research question of *how people can be fostered to arrive in a more environmentally-friendly way at University Hildesheim*. For answering this question, we combined approaches from design science and digital nudging to plan the activities for developing and evaluating a mobile app that makes use of nudge mechanisms.

In doing this, our contribution is threefold: First, we derived a set of eight requirements (REQ1-REQ8) from literature, a university-wide mobility survey, and interviews with students and employees. These requirements served as a foundation for the development of our artifact but also can be picked up in further studies that aim at designing nudges for mobility. Second, we developed and evaluated a prototypical mobile app for carpooling at our university. With this app, we hope to pool different students and employees to collectively arrive at the university and thereby help to reduce the number of required parking lots as well as the general traffic during the university's peak times. Moreover, since there is only limited IS research on carpooling in the context of sustainable mobility [7], we provide an artifact that complements current research streams in this field. Third, we contribute to the research stream of digital nudging [12, 13] by laying a focus on the achievement of more sustainable arrival procedures through carpooling—especially environmentally-friendly arrival. Our nudges complement the repertoire of available nudges for mobility such as [49] who developed a nudge in the form of a reminder card placed on the windshield that visually reminds carsharing users to inspect the car before starting with the trip, [14] who examined different nudges for reducing emissions during flight booking, or [50] who investigated how eco-labels can help to select more sustainable vehicles.

8.2 Limitations and Future Directions

Even though we could obtain some promising results, our study is not free of limitations, which open avenues for future research endeavors. First, since we evaluated the entire prototype, we could hardly provide information on (a) which nudges are most effective and (b) which nudges are leveraged by which gamification-elements. Further research may focus on separating these items and test them individually in experiments. Second, whereas we focus on the implementation of digital nudges, which is in line with the available literature (e.g., half of the articles prefer digital solutions), analog nudges might be helpful too. We believe that digital nudges are more suitable for this study's case because students and employees are used to rely on digital technology and make use of this in their daily life. The potential of digital nudges is further evident by research (e.g., [12, 13]) who emphasized the increasing use of digital devices. Besides these effects, it might however be helpful to explore how analog nudges can be implemented to support the general use of the carpooling app. As an example, some interviewees discussed points such as providing an initial credit of free kilometers when students matriculate at the university. Accordingly, some default options can leverage the actual use and popularity of the app. Third, while related literature often provides approaches that focus on creating awareness for acting environmentally-friendly (e.g., [16, 34, 37]), we especially focus on nudging people for action. The prototype focuses on the users themselves and their needs. Nonetheless, the combination of awareness and action is already emphasized in previous research for which reason future steps could (a) investigate whether the prototype has already an effect on the user's awareness and (b) how the prototype might be complemented to address both. For instance, it could be helpful to provide information about the positive factors such as emissions of carpool building in terms of the environment. Fourth, the prototype does not include financial incentives because of the inconsistencies between the literature and the interviews. The next steps could deal with (a) investigating under which circumstances it makes sense to integrate financial features and (b) how this might look like.

Nonetheless, the preliminary evaluation gives promising indications that the carpooling app will be used by students and employees of the university, which ultimately may contribute to sustainable mobility.

References

1. Grelier, F.: CO$_2$ emissions from cars: the facts. transport & environment, european federation for transport and environment AISB, Brussels, Belgium (2018)

2. Umweltbundesamt: Emission der von der UN-Klimarahmenkonvention abgedeckten Treibhausgase. Umweltbundesamt, Nationale Treibhausgas-Inventare, UBA (2020)
3. BMU (Bundesministerium für Umwelt, Naturschutz und nukleare Sicherheit): Klimaschutz in Zahlen: der Sektor Verkehr (2019). www.bmu.de/publikationen
4. Green Office Hildesheim: Mobilitätsbefragung 2019/2020. Universität Hildesheim (2019)
5. Schoormann, T., Behrens, D., Knackstedt, R.: Carsharing Geschäftsmodelle – Entwicklung eines bausteinbasierten Modellierungsansatzes. In: Thomas, O., Nüttgens, M., Fellmann, M. (eds.) Smart Service Engineering: Konzepte und Anwendungsszenarien für die digitale Transformation. pp. 303–325. Springer Fachmedien, Wiesbaden (2017). https://doi.org/10.1007/978-3-658-16262-7_14
6. Degirmenci, K., Breitner, M.: Carsharing: A literature review and a perspective for information systems research. In: Multikonferenz Wirtschaftsinformatik. Paderborn, Germany (2014)
7. Brendel, A., Mandrella, M.: Information systems in the context of sustainable mobility services: a literature review and directions for future research. In: Americas Conference on Information Systems. San Diego (2016)
8. Lehner, M., Mont, O., Heiskanen, E.: Nudging – a promising tool for sustainable consumption behaviour? J. Clean. Prod. 134, 166–177 (2016)
9. Thaler, R.H., Sunstein, C.R.: Nudge: improving decisions about health, wealth, and happiness. Penguin (2009)
10. Hildebrandt, B., Hanelt, A., Piccinini, E., Kolbe, L., Nierobisch, T.: The value of is in business model innovation for sustainable mobility services - the case of Carsharing. In: Wirtschaftsinformatik. Osnabrück, Germany (2015)
11. Schoormann, T., Behrens, D., Kolek, E., Knackstedt, R.: Sustainability in business models–a literature-review-based design-science-oriented research agenda. In: European Conference on Information Systems. Istanbul, Turkey (2016)
12. Nudging, D.: Weinmann, M., Schneider, C., Brocke, J. v. Bus. Inf. Syst. Eng. 58, 433–436 (2016)
13. Mirsch, T., Lehrer, C., Jung, R.: Digital nudging: altering user behavior in digital environments. In: Wirtschaftsinformatik, pp. 634–648. St Gallen, Switzerland (2017)
14. Székely, N., Weinmann, M., Brocke, J. v.: Nudging people to pay CO_2 offsets - the effect of anchors in flight booking processes. In: European Conference on Information Systems. Istanbul, Turkey (2016)
15. Lembcke, T.-B., Engelbrecht, N., Brendel, A.B., Herrenkind, B., Kolbe, L.M.: Towards a unified understanding of digital nudging by addressing its analog roots. In: Pacific Asian Conference on Information Systems. Xi'an, China (2019)
16. Byerly, H., et al.: Nudging pro-environmental behavior: evidence and opportunities. Front. Ecol. Environ. 16, 159–168 (2018)
17. Löfgren, Å., Nordblom, K.: A theoretical framework explaining the mechanisms of nudging. University of Gothenburg, Department of Economics (2019)
18. Garmin Connect: Garmin Connect. https://connect.garmin.com/. Accessed: 12 Dec 2020
19. Immowelt: Immobilienangebote als mobile Apps. https://aktion.immowelt.ag/de/app/?_ga=2.128939212.1794498132.1599830182–630382709.1597767396 . Accessed 12 Dec 2020
20. Instagram: Instagram. https://www.instagram.com/. Accessed 12 Dec 2020
21. Google Maps: Google Maps, https://www.google.de/maps (Accessed: 12.12.2020)
22. Techniker Krankenkasse: Die TK-App. https://www.tk.de/techniker/leistungen-und-mitgliedschaft/online-services-versicherte/die-tk-app-2027886. Accessed 12 Dec 2020
23. Peffers, K., Tuunanen, T., Rothenberger, M.A., Chatterjee, S.: A design science research methodology for information systems research. J. Manag. Inf. Syst. 24, 45–77 (2007)
24. Mirsch, T., Lehrer, C., Jung, R.: Making digital nudging applicable: the digital nudge design method. In: International Conference on Information Systems. San Francisco (2018)

25. Schneider, C., Weinmann, M., vom Brocke, J.: Digital nudging-guiding choices by using interface design. Commun. ACM **61**, 67–73 (2017)
26. Meske, C., Potthoff, T.: The DINU-Model - a process model for the design of nudges. In: European Conference on Information Systems, pp. 2587–2597. Guimarães, Portugal (2017)
27. Krell, C., Lamnek, S.: Leitfaden (2016). https://www.beltz.de/fileadmin/beltz/downloads/Onl inematerialienPVU/28269_Lamnek/(2)_Qualitatives_Interview/Beispielleitfaden.pdf
28. Huber, J., Jung, D., Schaule, E., Weinhardt, C.: Goal framing in smart charging – increasing BEV Users' charging flexibility with digital nudges. In: European Conference on Information Systems. Stockholm-Uppsala, Sweden (2019)
29. Anagnostopoulou, E., Bothos, E., Magoutas, B., Mentzas, G., Stibe, A.: How to not be annoying: adjusting persuasive interventions intensity when nudging for sustainable travel choices. In: Personalization in Persuasive Technology Workshop, Persuasive Technology, pp. 88–92. Waterloo, Canada (2018)
30. Lieberoth, A., Holm, N., Bredahl, T.: Selective psychological effects of nudging, gamification and rational information in converting commuters from cars to buses: a controlled field experiment. Transp. Res. Part F **55**, 246–261 (2018)
31. Sandau, A., Gómez, J.M., Stamer, D., vom Berg, B.W., Halberstadt, J.: Model of mobility demands for future short distance public transport systems. In: CONF-IRM (2016)
32. Andersen, A., Karlsen, R., Yu, W.: Green Transportation choices with IoT and smart nudging. In: Maheswaran, M., Badidi, E. (eds.) Handbook of Smart Cities, pp. 331–354. Springer, Cham (2018). https://doi.org/10.1007/978-3-319-97271-8_13
33. Andersson, H.: Designing digital nudges for sustainable travel decisions. http://urn.kb.se/res olve?urn=urn:nbn:se:umu:diva-161076 (2019)
34. Henkel, C., Seidler, A.-R., Kranz, J., Fiedler, M.: How to nudge pro-environmental behaviour: an experimental study. In: European Conference on Information Systems. Stockholm-Uppsala, Sweden (2019)
35. Freudendal-Pedersen, M.: Sustainable urban futures from transportation and planning to networked urban mobilities. Transp. Res. Part D Transp. Environ. **82**, 102310 (2020)
36. Thorun, C., et al.: Nudge-Ansätze beim nachhaltigen Konsum: Ermittlung und Entwicklung von Maßnahmen zum, Anstoßen "nachhaltiger Konsummuster (2016)
37. Baird, T.D.: Towards nudging active travel: behavioral interventions using mobile technology. Master Thesis, University of Wisconsin, USA (2014). https://open.library.ubc.ca/cIRcle/col lections/ubctheses/24/items/1.0166848
38. Ortmann, A., Dixit, V.: Nudging towards a more efficient transportation system: A review of non-pricing (behavioural) interventions. Unpublished Manuscript (2017)
39. Bardal, K.G., Gjertsen, A., Reinar, M.B.: Sustainable mobility: policy design and implementation in three norwegian cities. Transp. Res. Part D Transp. Environ. **82**, 102330 (2020)
40. Pihlajamaa, O., Heino, I., Kuisma, S.: Nudging towards sustainable mobility behaviour in nature destinations: Parkkihaukka mobile information service. In: ITS European Congress. Brainport, Netherlands (2019)
41. Riggs, W.: Painting the fence: Social norms as economic incentives to non-automotive travel behavior. Travel Behav. Soc. **7**, 26–33 (2017)
42. Wallann, H.: RoadAhead - Removing uncertainty in travel. creating a data warehouse for green transportation nudging, Master thesis, The Arctic University of Norway, Norway (2019). https://munin.uit.no/handle/10037/15735
43. Blohm, I., Leimeister, J.M.: Gamification: Gestaltung IT-basierter Zusatzdienstleistungen zur Motivationsunterstützung und Verhaltensänderung. Wirtschaftsinf. **55**, 275–278 (2013)
44. Deterding, S., Khaled, R., Nacke, L.E., Dixon, D.: Gamification: toward a definition. In: CHI 2011 Gamification Workshop. Vancouver BC, Canada (2011)

45. Schacht, S., Morana, S., Mädche, A.: The project world - gamification in project knowledge management. In: European Conference on Information Systems. Tel Aviv, Israel (2014)
46. Vinichenko, M.V., Melnichuk, A.V., Kirillov, A.V., Makushkin, S.A., Melnichuk, Y.A.: Modern views on the gamification of business. J. Internet Bank. Commerce (1970)
47. Sailer, M., Hense, J., Mandl, J., Klevers, M.: Psychological perspectives on motivation through gamification. Interact. Des. Architect. J. 28–37 (2014)
48. Wiegand, T., Stieglitz, S.: Serious fun-effects of gamification on knowledge exchange in enterprises. In: GI-Jahrestagung, pp. 321–332 (2014)
49. Swacha, J.: Gamification in knowledge management: motivating for knowledge sharing. Polish J. Manage. Stud **12**(2) (2015)
50. Namazu, M., Zhao, J., Dowlatabadi, H.: Nudging for responsible carsharing: using behavioral economics to change transportation behavior. Transportation **45**(1), 105–119 (2016). https://doi.org/10.1007/s11116-016-9727-1
51. Folkvord, F., Veltri, G.A., Lupiáñez-Villanueva, F., Tornese, P., Codagnone, C., Gaskell, G.: The effects of ecolabels on environmentally-and health-friendly cars: an online survey and two experimental studies. Int. J. Life Cycle Assessment (2019)

Leave No One Behind: Design Principles for Public Warning Systems in Federalism

Anna Katharina Frische$^{(\boxtimes)}$, Julia Felicitas Kirchner, Caroline Pawlowski,
Sebastian Halsbenning, and Jörg Becker

University of Münster, ERCIS, Münster, Germany
{anna.frische,julia.kirchner,
caroline.pawlowski}@uni-muenster.de, {halsbenning,
becker}@ercis.de

Abstract. The effectiveness of public warning systems (PWS) can be challenged by federal structures as the failure of the first nationwide German "Warntag" (Warning Day) showed. By designing PWS to address specific challenges of federal systems, the effectiveness of public warning might be improved. In this paper, we derive design principles for PWS which aim to address these specific challenges. Based on a thorough literature review, challenges regarding responsibility, coordination, and interoperability, as well as functional and technical requirements for PWS in federal systems were identified. By applying a design-oriented research approach, 16 design principles in the categories strategy and governance, standards and templates, and technology are articulated. The research provides guidance for responsible authorities in federal systems for the implementation or evaluation of public warning systems.

Keywords: Public warning system · Public warning · Federalism · Design principles · Design science

1 Introduction

In 2020, public warning received public attention in Germany when the first nationwide "Warntag" (Warning Day) was declared a failure by the Ministry of Interior [1]. One of the reasons was that the warning apps NINA and KATWARN pushed warning messages delayed or not at all, as warning messages were accidentally triggered simultaneously on the federal, state, and local level [2]. As public warning systems (PWS) and administrative and governance structures are directly linked to each other, state structures can challenge the effectiveness of PWS [3]. For example, the German PWS is regarded as highly influenced by the federal character of the civil protection responsibility [3, 4]. Every citizen must be entitled to receive a warning of equal quality if they are potentially affected by an emergency. From a federal perspective, this means an increased need for guidelines to ensure that the same quality of warning is delivered throughout the federal system [5].

F. Ahlemann et al. (Eds.): WI 2021, LNISO 47, pp. 673–686, 2021.
https://doi.org/10.1007/978-3-030-86797-3_44

This paper addresses these challenges of public warning in a federal administrative system by the *development of design principles for public warning systems in federal administrative systems*. The design principles serve the purpose of guiding through the implementation of a new PWS. To meet the research goal appropriately, this paper follows a design-oriented research approach proposed by Österle et al. [6].

The following section of this paper introduces the research background and relevant concepts regarding public warning, including the means of public warning, challenges for public warning in a federal system, and the requirements for public warning. In the next section, the paper's overall research design to achieve the research goal is explained. Afterward, design principles derived from prioritized requirements are presented as the results of the research and applied to the German case. Finally, the results are discussed, including the study's limitations and implications for research and practice.

2   Research Background

2.1   Public Warning

Public warning is "the provision of timely and effective information, through identified institutions, that allows individuals exposed to a hazard to take action to avoid or reduce their risk and prepare for effective response" [7]. To obtain relevant information in risk situations, four types of communication can be classified [8]: (1) from citizen to authorities, (2) among authorities, (3) from authorities to citizens, and (4) among citizens. This paper focuses on the third type of communication, which is achieved by PWS [8], through which authorities provide the citizens with relevant emergency-related information as well as suggested actions to be protected in risk situations [8].

Means of informing, alerting, and warning the population have changed over the years. Regardless, the traditional warning system, the siren, is still in use since it is recognized as a "universal language" for an emergency and therefore makes people aware of an occurring emergency [9, 10]. However, sirens have limited capabilities to provide the population with more information about the emergency and could fail to operate due to their outdoor location [9]. Through the information era, people impose high demands in the information flow about events before acting, as they are used to being consistently provided with sufficient information [3]. Established and new media, like radios, warning-apps, or TV broadcasts, can warn the population and simultaneously advise the necessary action in time [10].

2.2   Public Warning and Federalism

The nature of a public warning system is closely related to the administration and governance structures of the country in which it is applied [3]. A state's complex and often contradictory social and administrative relationships shape and influence its actions and responses to disasters [11]. Therefore, managing risk in multilevel systems is strongly influenced by policy decisions and institutions on multiple administrative levels.

As they differ in administrative and governance structures, each federal administrative system faces its own administrative and governance challenges, influencing the adopted solutions for public warning significantly [3]. In the case of multilevel systems, complexity increases, and challenges regarding responsibility [12, 13], coordination [12, 14, 15] and interoperability [3, 15, 16] occur. In the case of multilevel systems, complexity increases. The literature review revealed responsibility [12, 13], coordination [12, 14, 15], and interoperability [3, 15, 16] as the main challenges of public warning in federal systems.

Responsibility. In a multilevel system, responsibilities are usually delegated among different federal and state departments, and critical conflicts and gaps can occur within these relationships [15]. In multilevel systems, clear responsibilities, especially for warning system implementation, need to be defined [13].

Coordination. In a multilevel system, coordination ensures that all levels of the system work together in a synchronized manner. This is one of the most prevailed challenges of public warning in multilevel systems and inadequate coordination between different levels is a significant barrier for the functioning of warning systems [13].

Interoperability. Another challenge related to public warning in a federal system is interoperability. Barriers to the interoperability of public warning systems are higher when civil protection is decentralized [3]. The literature describes different perspectives and levels of interoperability. In contrast, some authors address interoperability in regards to the need for interoperable communication systems [15], and others stress the importance of interoperability of neighboring countries [9] and Europe-wide interoperability of public warning and alert systems [17].

There are also distinct advantages concerning public warning in federal systems. Federal structures and the resulting necessity to involve multiple actors in public warning processes can lead to a constructive competition of ideas, and productive knowledge exchange among institutions [14]. A positive outcome of complex governance networks is that actors from multiple levels are urged to jointly reach decisions on parallel activities or coordinative measures, which might facilitate common standards in civil protection [14].

3   Research Design

To meet our research goal, we follow the design-oriented research approach by Österle et al. [6]. Design-oriented research explicitly focuses on solving problems by developing IT artifacts in four phases. In the first phase, *Analysis,* the research problem is identified, and the methods to be applied for solving the problem are planned. In the following phase, *Design,* the actual development of the artifact is conducted, which is critically tested in the third phase—the *Evaluation.* Lastly, the results of the research are disseminated during the fourth phase, *Diffusion.*

For the *Analysis,* we made practical and scientific considerations and further investigated the areas of public warning and federalism. As a result of this, we uncovered several competing characteristics of warning systems and federal structures underlining the relevance of our investigations, which finally led to the formulation of our research

676   A. K. Frische et al.

goal. To address this goal, we firstly derived requirements for public warning systems in federal systems by conducting a literature review and an expert interview.

The literature review was conducted according to Webster and Watson [18]. The literature consisted of relevant articles from the databases Web of Science and Scopus between 2010 to 2020. A total number of 21 academic sources were considered relevant to the previously introduced problem. Additionally, a manual search of the titles in all volumes and issues between 2010 and 2020 of the Journal of Contingencies and Crisis Management and the Journal of Emergency Management and Homeland Security was conducted, which resulted in two additional relevant academic sources. Finally, the sources identified in the first two steps were used for backward and forward research, which added another five sources to the literature review.

The literature review resulted in a set of relevant academic sources that covered functional as well as technical requirements for PWS in general [18], as well as specific requirements that address the previously identified challenges of responsibility, coordination, and interoperability of public warning for federal administrative systems. Requirements from all sources were synthesized and evaluated regarding their applicability to the challenges of federalism. Applicable requirements were categorized in line with the following statement by Párraga Niebla [3, p. 231]: "public warning is effective if the following conditions are met: 1) the citizens at risk receive, notice, understand and trust warning messages on time; 2) the citizens at risk are prepared to act, i.e., are sufficiently familiar with warning procedures and trained to act upon". As the latter is not within the scope of PWS, applicable requirements were categorized according to the first part of the statement. The statement was chosen as a framework as the paper ultimately aims to support the effectiveness of public warning, which is what Párraga Niebla [3] refers to.

To ensure the applicability and completeness of the requirements determined in the literature review, we conducted one expert interview with a focus on public warning in federal states. The interviewee is employed in the middle management of an agency for civil protection in a federal administration. The interview lasted 73 min, was recorded, and then transcribed. We analyzed the interview according to the specificities of public warning systems in federal states, corresponding requirements, and our design principles. Together with further insights from documents of other organizations involved in civil protection and hazard management, we obtained our final set of requirements. Based on these requirements, we proceeded with the development of our design principles. Design principles are artifacts that apply to a class of problems and go beyond a classical instantiation [19]. An iterative and incremental approach was chosen to derive the design principles. The authors took turns in developing first drafts and reviewing the other authors' work. In total, three iterations were carried out until the set of principles was finished. The IT artifact was developed argumentatively. Consequently, we created our artifact to offer guidelines for introducing or evaluating PWS in federal systems.

The preliminary *Evaluation* of the design principles was two-fold: First, we conducted a feature comparison [20] against the requirements a PWS in federal systems should meet. Second, we tested their applicability exemplary for the German case.

We already started with the *Diffusion* of our findings with a presentation in front of seven academic professionals and a group of 24 students. We are planning to further disseminate our work on the 16. Internationale Tagung Wirtschaftsinformatik.

4 Requirements

4.1 Literature Review

The literature review revealed applicable requirements in three out of the four conditions necessary to ensure effective public warning as referred to in the statement by Párraga Niebla, [3], in Sect. 2.2, namely "receive", "understand" and "trust". No requirements in the category "notice" were considered relevant to the specific challenges.

Receive. Seven applicable requirements aim to ensure that the population receives warning messages distributed by authorities. The first requirement refers to *using a multi-channel approach in order to reach all people threatened by a hazard in all contexts.* Several sources concluded that a multi-channel approach increases the effectiveness of public warning or is less risky as all channels have limitations [4, 5, 14, 21–23]. Further supporting arguments insist on the need for (ubiquitous) coverage and high penetration of warning technologies [3, 24]. Furthermore, the population needs to be warned in different contexts, which cannot be reached by the same warning channels [3, 5, 8, 9]. Also, people's access to one technology (e.g., their mobile phone or specific applications) cannot be guaranteed [5, 25]. Brynielsson et al. [26] further reason that people's perceptions of source credibility and trust differ, which is another argument for using different channels to make PWS more effective.

Second, authorities should be *able to activate all necessary channels easily and without issues* [4]. Besides, *channels and technologies should be compatible* [16, 27]. In this context, Párraga Niebla et al. [4] refer to the introduction of the Common Alerting Protocol (CAP) as an essential step. Fourth, *warnings should be sent based on citizens' current location (geotargeting)* [3, 5, 8, 9, 14], in order to "avoid excessive panic" [24, p. 154]. Due to this requirement, cell broadcasting might not be an appropriate technology for large countries, as cells tend to cover large areas [5]. The fifth requirement relates to *warning the population in a timely manner*, not only but also by using appropriate technologies [3, 5, 8, 14, 16, 24, 26, 28]. Lastly, the literature stresses the need to *use highly available* [3], *reliable and resilient* [3, 5], *as well as redundant* [16]*technologies to prevent failures.* For federal countries, Aloudat and Michael [5] mention the need to *establish clear protocols for information dissemination to ensure the correctness of the destination* of the message which also relates to the trust in concept of trust later mentioned in this section.

Understand. Three distinct requirements aim to ensure that recipients of warning messages understand them. Firstly, when formulating and sending alerts, authorities should use a targeted approach by considering different needs and capabilities of the population, including for example age groups and people with disabilities [8, 27–29]. This also includes the support of (configuring) different presentation modes or multi-media content [3, 8]. Alerts via text messages might, for example, be very beneficial to deaf and hearing-impaired [5]. Secondly, *alerts should be offered in a language understandable by the population*, which implies the need to provide information in several languages [3, 5, 8]. Lastly, *authorities should provide citizens with all or sufficient relevant information*, including where to find further details [3, 4, 8], *in a specific* [26]*and accurate manner* [5].

Trust. Four applicable requirements were assigned to the category of "trust". Párraga Niebla [3], Preinersdorfer et al. [16], and Green et al. [30] mention the need for PWS to *include security features*. Examples of this can be authentication methods or limiting web-based access to PWS to prevent manipulation and cybersecurity threats. Further, it needs to be ensured that an *"all-clear" message will be sent using the same communication channels* once the threat is over [14]. Concerning the challenges for federal countries, Aloudat and Michael [5] note the necessity to *ensure consistent quality at all locations*, thus also across state borders. Experts interviewed by Aloudat and Michael [5] stated that every citizen is entitled to alerts of the same quality, leading to the need to specify guidelines by a central (national) agency on what that meant. Furthermore, the authors mention the need to *establish clear protocols for information dissemination to ensure the correctness of the content* of the message [5].

Further Requirements. Two federalism-specific requirements do not fall into the previously introduced categories. Firstly, Aloudat and Michael [5] mention the need for a *common approach to public warning* specified by a central (national) agency. Secondly, inadequate coordination is highlighted as the primary barrier for warning systems by three authors [3, 12, 13], which supports the call for *appropriate governance structures* to mitigate this issue. Preinersdorfer et al. [16] hereby highlight that structures need to ensure that alerts can be sent from different administrative levels according to the prevailing disaster management structures.

4.2 Document Analysis and Expert Interview

Following the review of academic literature, further documents, for example, those published by international organizations, were used to validate the list of requirements. Additional sources put a specific emphasis on appropriate governance structures and clear responsibilities as well as standardized procedures and protocols to ensure effective warning of the population [31–33]. In addition, the European Telecommunications Standards Institute (ETSI) defines a list of scenarios in which citizens need to be reached [34]. It widens the definition of citizens at risk, including those "entering the area or in close proximity to the area during the emergency" [34, p. 9], which specifies the first requirement (see Receive) as derived from academic literature. One additional requirement, namely, to ensure appropriate training of warning personnel [32], was added to the list.

Besides, the requirements from the literature were cross-referenced with insight from the expert interview. Insights from the interview confirmed four requirements that had previously been identified by other sources: The need to use a multi-channel approach with technologies that provide attention-calling features, to reach all people at risk in all contexts and locations. As stated by the interviewee: "In our opinion there is not just one warning channel [...] because every warning channel has some advantages and disadvantages. The radio is still the most widespread warning multiplier [...] the disadvantage is that you do not wake up when the radio is switched off - you need something to wake people up with". The interviewee also emphasized the need to provide the population with "all clear" messages that "need to be formulated in such a way that the citizen understands it".

5 Design Principles

Based on the finalized list of requirements, we developed design principles in the areas strategy and governance, standards and templates, and technology. The design principles in the category strategy and governance aim for a common and jointly developed public warning concept, highlighting essential aspects that have to be considered and defined. For example, is it important to define clear responsibilities between federal, state, and local authorities to warn the population on time as well as with the appropriate means of public warning. However, a lower authority should be able to send warning messages to a larger territorial area within the same state if necessary. For this, the authority should receive prior approval from a respectively higher authority. The design principles in the category standards and templates focus on guaranteeing every citizen, no matter in which federal state they are located, the same quality of warning. This can be fulfilled by developing templates and offering training to responsible authorities. The last feature, technology, focuses on the implementation of the previously defined changes as well as the provision of the technologies.

Strategy and Governance. The principles in this category are based on the identified requirement to ensure a common approach as well as on establishing appropriate governance structures, including a description of responsibilities. A joint concept of strategy and governance supports the avoidance of coordination issues during an emergency between different levels of authorities and means of public warning. The following principles are defined:

(1) Federal authorities in coordination with state and local authorities work out and use a common concept to warn the public in case of occurring emergencies.
(2) The concept should consider and define scenarios in which citizens need to be reached (e.g., at home, at work, outside, in transit, etc.) and assign at least one technology to each scenario. At least one technology needs to be used across the entire country, while further technologies can be specified individually by each authority.
(3) The concept should consider and define warning levels as a basis for assigning responsibilities as well as the choice of public warning means. For each warning level, it needs to be specified which scenarios need to be covered when sending a warning message.

(4) The concept should consider and define clear responsibilities based on warning levels and (territorial) administrative responsibilities. In predefined emergencies, authorities should be able to warn the population in proximity to but outside their jurisdiction. In order to reach out to a larger area, the responsible authority[1] should receive prior approval from the respective higher administrative level.

(5) The concept should consider and define whether and when affected[2] authorities are allowed to change or adapt a message passed on from the authority responsible for that disaster.

(6) The concept should consider and define whether responsibilities for warning messages and all-clear signals can change over the course of a disaster.

Standards and Templates. The design principles listed in the category standards and templates address the requirement category "understand", which considers different needs and capabilities of the population when sending alerts (targeted approach). To warn the whole country in case of an emergency, it is of high importance that every person can understand the message (provide information in several languages). The following principles are defined:

(7) Public warning messages should be based on common standards to ensure equal quality and understanding of messages for the entire population and avoid delays despite split responsibilities.

(8) The responsible authorities should jointly agree on standards for each technology/means of warning (e.g. protocols for information dissemination) to ensure equal quality of warning in a timely manner.

(9) The responsible authorities should jointly agree on standards that consider the needs and capabilities of the population to avoid exclusion of parts of the population.

(10) The responsible authorities should jointly agree on standards which define templates for warning messages for each means of warning, to provide the same information to every citizen despite their source of information (e.g., relevant content, specific and accurate phrasing, languages).

(11) The responsible authorities should jointly agree on standards that define training guidelines. They should further ensure joint training and workshops to enable an exchange of experiences among different levels. Thereby, every person in charge is able to use the provided standards and templates in a correct manner.

Technology. The last category, containing five design principles, addresses the formerly defined requirements of the category "receive". It is important that all citizens are able to receive the same warning message using a centrally provided technology, to avoid

---

[1] The responsible authority is understood to be the authority responsible for sending out the initial warning message. The administrative level of the authority might depend on the warning level of the disaster.

[2] The affected authority is understood to be an authority in (close) proximity of the disaster (but outside the jurisdiction/competence area of the responsible agency) which receives the warning message and can send it to its citizens.

mixed information and late responses to the warning message. The following principles are defined:

(12) A (national) authority should provide basic infrastructure and interfaces for the PWS which can be accessed by all authorities involved in public warning. Thereby, it should be assured that this infrastructure is redundant and protected against failures.

(13) Furthermore, country-wide used technologies should be provided centrally (e.g., by a national authority or private provider), which allows states and municipalities to additionally connect further warning technologies. This provides a way to assure highly available, reliable, and resilient technologies are used.

(14) The technology of the PWS needs to ensure that all relevant scenarios according to warning levels are covered (e.g., by choice of at least one technology in that category) when sending a warning message. In each relevant scenario, at least the country-wide used technology needs to be used, in order to ensure that all people are reached in the same scenarios despite their location.

(15) Lastly, the responsibilities and access rights should be represented in the PWS and (16) the PWS should enable to reassign responsibility of a warning message to other levels in case of changing responsibilities (e.g., "all-clear" message from authority closest to disaster). The means used for updates of all-clear messages should not be adaptable over the course of the disaster.

6 Exemplary Case Application: The German Case

In Germany, warning and alerting the population is a task shared between the federal and state administrations. Whereas the federal administration is responsible for civil protection, especially in defense situations, the states are responsible for protecting the population in case of most other disasters [35]. For this purpose, the Federal Office of Civil Protection and Disaster Assistance (BBK) operates the Modular Warning System (MoWaS), which has been used by federal and state authorities since 2013 [36]. It allows the triggering of all connected warning technologies via a central user interface [36].

In order to uncover opportunities to further increase the effectiveness of public warning through MoWaS, the design principles were applied to the German case. Each principle was individually checked against information collected through the expert interview, analysis of available documents, and web research. In case the design principles were not fully adhered to, recommendations based on the design principles were formulated. In case information was limited due to access restrictions, for example, regarding higher warning levels, we focused on the parts of the system we did have information about. The opportunities for improvement were summarized in Table 1.

It should be noted that the further development of MoWaS is and was the central concern of a project carried out jointly by federal and state governments. It aimed to finish by the end of 2020 and was funded through the Internal Security Fund (ISF) [38]. Some of the recommendations, such as connecting the remaining authorities to MoWaS, might therefore already being addressed.

The exemplary application to the German case emphasizes that the proposed design principles can be a valid approach to assess a PWS in a federal administrative system. Despite not being able to evaluate all parts of the system due to restricted access to information, we could still derive recommendations that might be valuable for improving the effectiveness of MoWaS.

Table 1. Opportunities for increasing the effectiveness of MoWaS

#	Opportunity for improvement
1	The involved authorities should agree on a comprehensive warning concept which brings together the information identified in different sources and defines clusters of technologies (scenarios) as well as the respective, country-wide used technology for each scenario. Responsibilities and rights should be clearly defined (including, for example, exceptional situations and the right to warn neighboring municipalities). The guidelines agreed upon by federal and state governments in 2019 [37] provide a starting point to include these design recommendations
2	Templates should be created for each means of public warning considering the needs and capabilities of the population. The templates should include (only) the relevant content and be explicitly phrased and accurately. Templates need to exist in different languages
3	The remaining authorities relevant for public warning from the different administrative levels should be connected to MoWaS
4	It should be ensured that the previously defined country-wide used technologies are provided centrally for all citizens by public or private organizations, as are, for example, NINA or KATWARN
5	Changes based on the previous recommendations should be reflected in MoWaS, for example through authorities' (access) rights and the obligation to choose country-wide used technologies as well as predefined templates for warning messages. Warning updates should only be possible using the same warning technologies

7   Discussion and Conclusion

We have developed a set of design principles in the categories strategy and governance, standards and templates, and technology that aim to guide through the implementation of a new PWS in federal administrative systems. Natural and human-made disasters can affect large areas of an authority's population. Equally, public warning has become more critical as a consequence of increasing and exacerbating numbers of incidents over the past years [28]. Even though technological development and digitalization have led to an improvement in PWS, administrative and governance structures also play an essential role in effective public warning, especially in complex systems as federalism [3, 5, 39].

To achieve the research goal, we conducted a systematic literature review on the requirements for public warning in federal administrative systems according to Webster and Watson [18], which detected three challenges of public warning in federal systems: missing clear responsibilities, lacking coordination, and interoperability. Furthermore, general requirements of a PWS, as well as federalism-specific requirements, have been identified. These requirements addressed the categories receive, notice, understand, trust as well as further requirements outside those categories. Based on the results of the literature review, the design principles were developed.

7.1 Limitation and Further Research

Despite basing the research design on proven research approaches, our work is subject to limitations that emphasize the need for further research. Firstly, the literature review, especially its manual steps, might be subjective to some extent. It could also be difficult to distinguish between generally relevant challenges and requirements as well as those that were only applicable in the case discussed by the authors of the article in question. Further, the literature review revealed only a limited literature basis for requirements regarding administrative structures and especially federalism. This fact was mitigated by consulting further documents in the following steps of the research.

Further research should, thus, aim to extend the literature basis in this field. Due to the increasing importance of public warning, scholars could, for example, compare the effectiveness of different public warning systems considering their academic background. Secondly, even though the basic phases for design-oriented IS research as proposed by Österle et al. [6] were followed to derive the IT artifact, the design principles were not finally evaluated by experts. Future research should aim to increase the involvement of experts in the field of PWS in federalism to verify and test the design principles, for example through focus groups. As a next step, research could test the design principles together with experts to investigate and improve its practical applicability.

Furthermore, part of the information regarding public warning in Germany is classified, which might have influenced the results of the demonstration. We are also not the intended addressees of the artifact. As we used only one case for demonstrating the artifact, we chose a case in which public warning is substantially influenced by the structures of the federal system [3]. This implies that it might indeed be strongly affected by the discovered challenges pose a good example for other cases. Scholars could now investigate the applicability of our design principles in other federal administrative systems, such as Belgium or Australia. Lastly, due to scope, we decided to apply only one iteration of Österle et al.'s [6] method. The decision to leave improvements of the artifact to the following projects, for example, due to the nature of research, is recognized as legitimate [40]. Even though further iterations might improve the artifact, it already provides a starting point for further research. It provides value to both theory and practice. Other researchers can for example use the artifact as groundwork and contribute to improving it with their own knowledge and experiences.

Most importantly, however, it should be kept in mind that, even though the focus of our research was solely on PWS, an effective PWS does not necessarily directly lead to an effective public warning. Citizens need to be appropriately prepared, for example, by being trained to act upon warning messages [3]. Therefore, future research should extend the design principles considering the preparation of citizens.

7.2 Theoretical and Practical Implications

Despite its limitations, we identified key implications for theory and practice which emerge from our research. Firstly, the literature review contributes to the closure of the identified research gap regarding effective PWS and federalism and highlighted the difference in the maturity of the research fields of general public warning (systems) and public warning in federalism. Secondly, the design principles provide a starting point for national governments and practitioners in responsible agencies to work with. They can be used as a basis for discussions with involved parties and draw attention to factors that are important for effective public warning. A validated set of design principles will eventually enable federal governments to review their overall warning systems and discover potentials for improvement. This is especially important considering a European Union directive that commits member states to have mobile number-based PWS (or equivalent regarding its effectiveness) in place by 21 June 2022 [41]. While it influences the choice of warning technologies included in a multi-channel approach for public warning, it also generally implies the necessity for a review of existing PWS and used technologies. Thirdly, not only federal governments can benefit from the results of this paper. As stated by Gregor and Hevner, an "artifact that is presented with a higher level degree of abstraction can be generalized to other situations" [19, p. 352]. The design principles were kept on a reasonably abstract level; thus, any national government can use an adapted version of the model as guidance for a review of its PWS. An essential step of the process was to gather overall requirements for effective PWS, which can be used as a basis to design an improved system. Lastly, irrespective of the administrative level, state or local governments can refer to the design principles to drive bottom-up change, which is especially important as they are close to the citizens and might be the first to sense when changes in an existing system become necessary.

7.3 Conclusion

All in all, the study contributes to filling a research gap, as well as enabling governments to identify federal specific areas of improvement in their existing PWS or guide the introduction of PWS in federal systems. Eventually, this way the use of our design principles can lead to a more effective public warning system. This might in turn positively influence the trust of the public in the warning system as well as the awareness of measures in case of disasters. In the case of Germany, a more effective public warning system might lead to a more positive connotation of the subject and a higher acceptance during the next "Warntag" (Warning Day).

References

1. Bundesministerium des Innern für Bau und Heimat: Probealarm zum "Warntag 2020" fehlgeschlagen. https://www.bmi.bund.de/SharedDocs/pressemitteilungen/DE/2020/09/war ntag-fehlgeschlagen.html
2. Die Zeit: App-Alarm stark verzögert: Der Warntag wird zum Fehlschlag. https://www.zeit. de/news/2020-09/10/erster-bundesweiter-warntag-um-11-uhr-heulen-die-sirenen

3. Párraga Niebla, C.: Communication technologies for public warning. In: Wireless Public Safety Networks 1: Overview and Challenges, pp. 229–260. Elsevier Inc. (2015). https://doi.org/10.1016/B978-1-78548-022-5.50008-X
4. Párraga Niebla, C., Mulero Chaves, J., De Cola, T.: Design aspects in multi-channel public warning systems. In: Wireless Public Safety Networks 2: A Systematic Approach. pp. 227–261. Elsevier Inc. (2016). https://doi.org/10.1016/B978-1-78548-052-2.50008-6
5. Aloudat, A., Michael, K.: Toward the regulation of ubiquitous mobile government: a case study on location-based emergency services in Australia. Electron. Commer. Res. **11**, 31–74 (2011)
6. Österle, H., et al.: Memorandum on design-oriented information systems research. Eur. J. Inf. Syst. **20**, 7–10 (2011)
7. ISDR: Terminology: basic terms of disaster risk reduction. www.unisdr.org/eng/library/lib-terminology-enghome.htm
8. Mulero Chaves, J., De Cola, T.: Public Warning Applications: Requirements and Examples. In: Wireless Public Safety Networks 3: Applications and Uses, pp. 1–18. Elsevier (2017). https://doi.org/10.1016/B978-1-78548-053-9.50001-9
9. Crowe, A.: When status quo becomes obsolete: the changing use of outdoor warning sirens. J. Homel. Secur. Emerg. Manag. **7**, 1–5 (2010)
10. Jagtman, H.M.: Cell broadcast trials in The Netherlands: using mobile phone technology for citizens' alarming. Reliab. Eng. Syst. Saf. **95**, 18–28 (2010)
11. Corfee-Morlot, J., Cochran, I., Hallegatte, S., Teasdale, P.-J.: Multilevel risk governance and urban adaptation policy. Clim. Change. **104**, 169–197 (2011)
12. Wolf, F., Pfohl, T.: Zeitschrift für Vergleichende Politikwissenschaft **8**(1), 259–285 (2014). https://doi.org/10.1007/s12286-014-0189-6
13. Marchezini, V.: "What is a sociologist doing here?" An unconventional people-centered approach to improve warning implementation in the sendai framework for disaster risk reduction. Int. J. Disaster Risk Sci. **11**(2), 218–229 (2020). https://doi.org/10.1007/s13753-020-00262-1
14. Karutz, H., Geier, W., Mitschke, T. (eds.): Bevölkerungsschutz. Springer, Heidelberg (2017). https://doi.org/10.1007/978-3-662-44635-5
15. Reed, K.: Disaster relief. Nova Science Publishers, Hauppauge, NY (2011)
16. Preinerstorfer, A., Egly, M., Gojmerac, I., Hochwarter, C., Schuster, C., Stocker, R.: Requirements for the next generation Public Warning and Alert System for Austria. In: Proceedings of the 14th International Conference on Telecommunications - ConTEL 2017, pp. 115–122. Institute of Electrical and Electronics Engineers Inc., Zagreb, Croatia (2017)
17. Dittmer, C., Lorenz, D.F.: Disaster Situation and Humanitarian Emergency – In-Between Responses to the Refugee Crisis in Germany. Int. Migr. (2019)
18. Webster, J., Watson, R.: Analyzing the past to prepare for the future: writing a literature review. MIS Q. **26**, XIII–XXIII (2002)
19. Gregor, S., Hevner, A.R.: Positioning and presenting design science research for maximum impact. MIS Q. **37**, 337–355 (2013)
20. Siau, K., Rossi, M.: Evaluation techniques for systems analysis and design modelling methods - a review and comparative analysis. Inf. Syst. J. **21**, 249–268 (2011)
21. Alhmoudi, A.A., Aziz, Z.: Integrated framework for early warning system in UAE. Int. J. Disaster Resil. Built Environ. **7**, 361–373 (2016)
22. Nakamura, I., Morioka, C.: Effect of communication regarding dam operation on the evacuation of residents: a case study of the 2018 inundation of the Hijikawa river in Japan. Geosciences. **9**, 444 (2019)
23. Perry, R.W.: Defining Disaster: An Evolving Concept. In: Rodríguez, H., Donner, W., Trainor, J.E. (eds.) Handbook of Disaster Research. HSSR, pp. 3–22. Springer, Cham (2018). https://doi.org/10.1007/978-3-319-63254-4_1

24. Zhang, H., Wang, G., Lu, M., Wang, D., Xu, P.: Emergency warning and bidirectional communication via digital audio broadcast. IEEE Trans. Consum. Electron. **65**, 150–159 (2019)

25. Jasmontaite, L., Dimitrova, D.: Online disaster management: applicability of the european data protection framework and its key principles. J. Contingencies Cris. Manag. **25**, 23–30 (2017)

26. Brynielsson, J., Granåsen, M., Lindquist, S., Narganes Quijano, M., Nilsson, S., Trnka, J.: Informing crisis alerts using social media: best practices and proof of concept. J. Contingencies Cris. Manag. **26**, 28–40 (2018)

27. Malizia, A., Onorati, T., Diaz, P., Aedo, I., Astorga-Paliza, F.: SEMA4A: an ontology for emergency notification systems accessibility. Expert Syst. Appl. **37**, 3380–3391 (2010)

28. Basher, R.: Global early warning systems for natural hazards: systematic and people-centred. Phil. Trans. R. Soc. A. **364**, 2167–2182 (2006)

29. Marchezini, V., Trajber, R., Olivato, D., Muñoz, V.A., de Oliveira Pereira, F., Oliveira Luz, A.E.: Participatory early warning systems: youth, citizen science, and intergenerational dialogues on disaster risk reduction in Brazil. Int. J. Disaster Risk Sci. **8**(4), 390–401 (2017). https://doi.org/10.1007/s13753-017-0150-9

30. Green, A., Dodson, K., Woszczynski, A.B., Easton, P.: Responding to cybersecurity challenges: Securing vulnerable U.S. emergency alert systems. Commun. Assoc. Inf. Syst. **46**, 187–208 (2020).

31. European Emergency Number Association (EENA): Public Warning. V3.0. (2019)

32. UN Inter-Agency Secretariat of the International Strategy for Disaster Reduction: Developing Early Warning Systems: A Checklist, Bonn (2006)

33. United Nations: Sendai Framework for Disaster Risk Reduction 2015–2030. Switzerland, Geneva (2015)

34. European Telecommunications Standards Institute: TS 102 182 - V1.4.1 - Emergency Communications (EMTEL); Requirements for communications from authorities/organizations to individuals, groups or the general public during emergencies. Sophia Antipolis Cedex, France (2010)

35. Bundesamt für Bevölkerungsschutz und Katastrophenhilfe: Wie werde ich gewarnt?. https://www.bbk.bund.de/DE/AufgabenundAusstattung/Krisenmanagement/WarnungderBevoelke rung/Wie_werde_ich_gewarnt/Wie_werde_ich_gewarnt_node.html;jsessionid=272A501B9 976A8A7C2610B5F31553F10.2_cid355#doc12868476bodyText5.

36. Bundesamt für Bevölkerungsschutz und Katastrophenhilfe: Das Modulare Warnsystem des Bundes und der Länder (Zusatzinformation). Bonn

37. Bundesamt für Bevölkerungsschutz und Katastrophenhilfe: Leitlinien für ein Gemeinsames Warnkonzept von Bund und Ländern, Bonn (2019)

38. Bundesamt für Bevölkerungsschutz und Katastrophenhilfe: BBK Bevölkerungsschutz 1 | 2018. (2018)

39. Scholta, H., Niemann, M., Halsbenning, S., Räckers, M., Becker, J.: Fast and federal—policies for next-generation federalism in Germany. In: Proceedings of the 52nd Hawaii International Conference on System Sciences (HICSS), pp. 3273–3282 (2019)

40. Peffers, K., Tuunanen, T., Rothenberger, M.A., Chatterjee, S.: A design science research methodology for information systems research. J. Manag. Inf. Syst. **24**, 45–77 (2008)

41. European Parliament: Directive (EU) 2018/1972 of the European Parliament and of the Council of 11 December 2018 establishing the European Electronic Communications Code (Recast) (Text with EEA relevance) (2018)

Data Governance: State-of-the-Art

Giulio Behringer[(⊠)] and Marcel Hizli

Hochschule Heilbronn, Fachbereich Wirtschaftsinformatik, M. Sc.
Wirtschaftsinformatik – Informationsmanagement und Data Science, Heilbronn, Germany
{gbehring,mhizli}@stud.hs-heilbronn.de

Abstract. To survive in today's economy, it is no longer enough to stick to old habits and corporate structures. In the age of digitalization, it is much more important to recognize innovation and optimization potential in good time and to constantly question them. In the long term, this can only be ensured by establishing suitable data governance in the company. In addition to data governance, IT, information and corporate governance play an important role in installing organizational frame conditions in companies. In relation to the starting position described above, the current state of scientific research on data governance and the mutual dependencies on the adjacent types of governance: corporate, information and IT governance, will be presented by means of a literature search according to Fettke (2006) and Webster and Watson (2002).

Keywords: Governance · Data governance · Corporate governance · IT-governance · Information-governance

1 Introduction

For a better understanding, at the beginning of the scientific work, the problem and question are first discussed before the objective provides information about the added value of the scientific contribution.

1.1 Problem Definition

In the age of digitalization Data is heralded as "the new oil", but organizations are still struggling to generate value for their business [1]. Many organizations are interested in new opportunities in the context of managing big data. However, they are often inhibited by seemingly tedious data issues [2]. Issues of quality, availability, or accuracy complicate data efforts. However, solving these in isolation is only a short-term solution [3]. Extracting value from data requires an organization-wide approach and as such cannot be solved by IT alone. Here, data governance has been identified by both practitioners and academics as a promising approach to solving these organizational data problems [4, 5]. In this regard, a precise delimitation and the interdependencies of adjacent governance domains offer optimization potential in order to make a significant contribution to value creation in companies [6, 7].

F. Ahlemann et al. (Eds.): WI 2021, LNISO 47, pp. 687–699, 2021.
https://doi.org/10.1007/978-3-030-86797-3_45

1.2 Research Question

In the age of digital transformation, every company will ask itself what measures need to be taken to ensure optimal use of data and information. Consequently, an organization must establish data governance to ensure that data is handled in accordance with the rules. The various areas of corporate, information, IT and data governance must be examined more closely in order to establish a suitable regulatory framework for companies. Derived from this, the following research question crystallizes: What is the current state of science regarding data governance? In this respect, the research question can be differentiated into further sub-questions: What is data governance and which mutual relationships exist with regard to corporate, information and IT governance? What challenges and goals are associated with data governance?

1.3 Objectives

The goal of this scientific contribution is to gain insight into data governance, as well as corporate, information, and IT governance. With the help of a systematic, scientific literature search, the current state of knowledge of research in the field of data governance and related governance types is mapped. Based on the literature found, the initial focus is on the characterization, challenges and goals of data governance, as well as a comparative view of regulatory frameworks for corporate, information, IT and data governance. As a result of the findings of this paper, further areas of research will be identified.

1.4 Structure

This scientific paper is divided into a total of five chapters. In the introduction, an overview of the scientific contribution is first given. Thereby, the problem and the research question are explained first, in order to formulate a suitable objective thereupon. In order to make the current starting point understandable, the second chapter explains the basics and the most important terms, which form the basis for the scientific paper. In the following Sect. 3, the methodology for the literature analysis is presented and the procedure how the used literature was filtered out of the listed databases and conferences is explained in more detail. The penultimate of the five chapters presents the results of the paper based on the literature described in Sect. 3 and refers to the research question posed at the beginning. In the final Sect. 5, the summary of the results, as well as a critical appraisal takes place. This should once again clarify the findings and provide an outlook for further research.

2 Fundamentals and Terms

In the following section, the relevant basics and terms are explained in more detail. For an optimal starting point, the topic of data governance is first explained. Following this, the most important, related types of governance: corporate, IT and information governance are described in more detail in order to create a common basis for answering the research question. For a collective understanding of the different governance types, the term "governance" is defined in advance according to [8]: Governance "refers to the responsible, sustainable organization and control of activities aimed at long-term value creation, and thus to the entire system of internal and external performance, control and monitoring mechanisms."

2.1 Data Governance

Data governance is a discipline of data management for managing data and information assets in an organization. This is done through formal oversight of the people, processes, technologies, and lines of business that affect data and information outcomes in order to improve business performance. Through standards and policies, data governance ensures that the quality, as well as the protection and security, of data is maintained that the legal framework is complied [4]. According to [9], data governance can be described as an organizational approach to data management that formalizes a set of policies and procedures to cover the entire lifecycle of data. The focus of data governance is on policies and guidelines for the proper handling and maintenance of data. In this regard, data governance is strongly aligned with the business objectives of the organization [10]. In doing so, data governance helps organizations adopt a set of rules and regulations for managing data to meet the standards or requirements of the organization [11].

2.2 Corporate Governance

Corporate governance represents an institutional regulatory framework for organizations. Concrete specifications and guidelines can be derived from this, which in turn can be adapted to all areas of the organization [10]. An important component of corporate governance touches on essential areas of corporate management in terms of customers, processes, guidelines, laws and institutions. In addition, the interaction and cooperation with various stakeholders, such as directors, managers, shareholders, employees, suppliers, customers, etc., plays an important role in achieving corporate goals. Corporate governance is implemented using various models within the company. Ideally, corporate governance should enable productive and efficient operation while preventing corruption and abuse of power [12].

2.3 IT- Governance

[13] describe IT-Governance as a framework that supports organizations in decision making, assessment, and implementation in the context of IT. IT-Governance is a type of institution that lists various management principles in order to comply with the policies on the part of business and IT. The definition of [12] focuses on processes and structures and states as follows: "IT-Governance is the process and structure that ensure that organizations use their IT investments appropriately to ensure that the resulting activities -whether programs, projects, or operations that fund them- are executed properly and achieve the desired results." The focus is on the governance and organizational structures, as well as processes, that ensure IT maintains and extends the organization's strategy and goals [14].

2.4 Information Governance

Information governance describes the way in which data and information are managed in an organization, including all business processes [15]. [16] define information governance as a contemporary approach to manage the use of information better and to protect and maximize its value inside and outside organizations. In accordance with [16], information governance encompasses an environment of capabilities, rules, and decisions for assessing, creating, collecting, analyzing, distributing, storing, using, and controlling information [16, 17]. In this context, information governance is not a one-time process, but a continuous process. On the one hand, information governance defines the decision-making rights and at the same time provides a framework for accountability in order to promote desirable behaviour regarding the assessment, creation, storage, use, and archiving and deletion of information and data. This includes processes and roles, as well as standards and metrics to ensure optimal use of information in organizations [18].

3   Methodology for Literature Analyses

In this section, the methodology for the literature analysis is presented in detail. The procedure with which the literature analysis was carried out is explained in more detail. Thereupon the used literature databases and conferences are described in detail, as well as the used search queries and search terms. For better traceability of the literature analysis, the search filters used, as well as the limitation of the time frame for the literature search and finally the characterization of the literature analysis are given.

3.1 Procedure

For a first insight into the topic of data governance, as well as the already mentioned adjacent topics, a literature analysis of the German and English-language literature is carried out. With the help of a structured literature analysis according to [19], the aim is to show as much relevant literature as possible. The subsequent forward and backward search according to [20] serves to verify the completeness of the literature in relation to the research question.

3.2 Literature Sources

A more detailed overview of the source finding and evaluation process is shown in the table below.

The relevant literature was obtained using the following literature databases: AIS Electronic Library (AISel), Association for Computing Machinery Digital Library (ACM), Institute of Electrical and Electronics Engineers (IEEE), Emerald Insights, and Springer Link. Furthermore, the Americas Conference on Information Systems (AMCIS) and the European Conference on Information Systems (ECIS) were reviewed for potential literature.

In order to proceed as efficiently as possible with the literature search, it is suitable to use special search terms and search queries for the respective databases. To get a first

Table 1. Evaluation of the literature research

Quelle	Term 1	Term 2	Term 3	Term 4
AISel	275	67	41	29
ACM	263	22	14	7
Emerald	170	26	23	28
IEEE	114	5	6	3
SL	77	80	76	66
AMCIS	51	13	8	5
ECIS	39	10	4	2
Query results	**989**	**223**	**172**	**140**
Duplicate	723	150	121	113
Sighting the Abstracts	117	44	37	23
Scientific qualification	46	31	24	19
relevance of content	6	7	2	3
Backward and forward research		30		
Total contributions		**48**		

overview of the topic of data governance, the search term: (search term 1: "data governance") was used. Based on this, the adjacent governance types: Corporate, Information and IT Governance were examined in more detail to identify hidden potential for Data Governance implementation. For this deeper analysis, three search terms were used: (search term 2: " "Data Governance" AND ("IT Governance" OR "IT Governance"), (search term 3: " "Data Governance" AND ("Information Governance" OR "Information Governance"), (search term 4: " "Data Governance" AND ("Corporate Governance").

The search filter "Computer Science" was used for the Springer Link database. For the remaining databases listed, no further filter options were used. An important limiting factor for the literature search is the time frame. However, there was a deliberate decision not to narrow down the time frame because there is no need to limit the time frame in the context of data governance. Based on this literature base, a selection was performed using the criteria of duplicates, review of abstracts, scientific suitability, and relevance to the content. Subsequently, forward and backward searches according to Webster and Watson (2002) were used to locate an additional 30 sources.

4   Results

The basis for the following peer review of the literature analysis has already been established in Sect. 3. In order to answer the research question, this section evaluates the literature reviewed and provides further hypotheses for explicit, future research. Here, data can be classified as "raw material", whereas information is referred to as "data in context" [21].

4.1   Characteristics of Data Governance

In general terms, the focus of data governance is on data and information. Here, data can be classified as "raw material", whereas information is referred to as "data in context" [21]. Wang and Otto take similar approaches with respect to data and quality. Wang considers data quality as the usability of data, while Otto specifies the statement and states that data has value only if it is used [4, 22]. Against this background, data governance aims to maximize the value of data in organizations, which at the same time highlights the importance of data quality management [4]. Wende refers to a clear distinction between the two terms. Data governance complements data management but cannot replace it [23]. In the following, the characteristics are described in more detail based on the design-oriented approaches of role allocation, tasks and responsibilities. Organizational aspects, such as strategy, funding, metadata management, data standards, guidelines, and metrics are not discussed further [24].

Personnel Structures and Responsibilities in Data Governance
An important area of data governance is the distribution of roles and responsibilities for tasks. The diagram below illustrates the distribution of roles within data quality management.

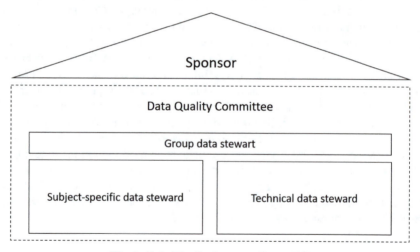

Fig. 1. Role Distribution according to [10]

Here, senior management must exemplify and approve the data governance guidelines. The sponsor role represents the strategic direction of data quality management and ensures executive support [10, 23]. The data quality committee acts as a link between strategic and operational levels and ensures that policies and standards are set. Within the framework of the Data Quality Committee, various data quality improvement projects are carried out under the direction of the Group Data Steward with the help of functional and technical data stewards. The Group Data Steward is mainly responsible for implementing and monitoring the resolutions and decisions. Subject-specific data stewards are employees of the individual departments and are responsible for company-wide data standards. The technical data steward deals with all issues relating to data architecture and system support for data quality management [10].

[25] name further essential roles in the course of data governance. Data custodians must be deployed to ensure the quality of inventory data and to answer questions regarding data quality. They also act as an interface between different groups of people to communicate with the data governance council as needed. Furthermore, Data Custodians can be considered as a leader for data stewards. The roles within data governance are rounded off with user groups which are managed by data stewards, consisting of people from various departments who deal with data or its associated infrastructure. In addition to the data stewards, the authors [26] and [27] list the process owners, the data governance office and the data governance board in order to establish data governance with the necessary roles within the company. [5] take up the mentioned personnel structures and assign them to corresponding domains in data governance. These are categorized based on the domains data principles, data quality, metadata, data accessibility and data lifecycle. Further roles, such as data quality manager, data quality analyst, data architect or the data security officer can be derived from this.

[28] takes up the roles already mentioned and reflects them with regard to data quality in a data ownership concept. This concept is to be regarded as a design framework for subareas of corporate data and the persons responsible for their quality and availability. The advantage of this concept is the clear distinction of responsibilities in order to initiate positive measures with regard to data quality. Within the concept, there are three ideal-typical role distributions. On the one hand, the data collector is responsible for the extraction, processing and storage of data; on the other hand, the data user defines requirements and processes the forwarded data. The data processor, on the other hand, is responsible for modifying and forwarding data based on company processes. In addition, according to [28], other roles exist in the course of data governance. Data owners are responsible for providing high-quality data, while data auditors monitor the results and identify risks. Appropriate countermeasures can be initiated from this, which are also supported by data risk managers to ensure that standards, guidelines and norms are adhered to, in order to evaluate data processes for new potential risks on the basis of this.

Fields of Activity of Data Governance

The responsibility of data governance is divided between management and all employees of the organization. On the other hand, data quality is everyone's responsibility and contributes significantly to the company's performance and success [27]. In order to be able to classify the possible areas of data governance, Weber identified diverse objects of consideration that are included and addressed by data governance. These include data quality management, master data management, information management, and business intelligence [24].

According to [4], data governance deals with the following questions: "Which decisions in the context of data have to be made in the company?", "Which roles exist in the decision-making process?", "To what extent are these roles involved in the decisions?". Furthermore, data governance deals with the main tasks regarding the management of data quality, data architecture, data protection, metadata and the information lifecycle.

In addition, data governance deals with the documentation of legal components related to data [4]. Based on a survey conducted by [29] with 190 companies, the authors were able to identify the following data governance tasks using a qualitative analysis. Based on the survey, the core tasks of data governance are the company-wide standardization of definitions regarding data, as well as the definition of standards, guidelines, processes and strategies regarding information. In addition, the support of departments in the area of data warehousing and business intelligence, the general definition and establishment of rules, and the selection and support of projects with regard to data quality are among the main tasks of data governance.

Responsibilities

Within responsibilities, links are drawn between the identified roles and tasks. The extent to which the responsibilities of the respective roles are designed in the context of tasks depends on the company and the context [10]. Roles and their associated responsibilities are essential. This ensures that there is clear management and accountability of data. To the extent that individuals can be held accountable, it can be assumed that fewer errors will enter the system, and that errors will be detected and resolved earlier, leading to more efficient processes [30].

This is taken up further by [23], who created a concept matrix for this purpose, which can be seen in the following figure. While the technical data steward is responsible for operational activities, the data governance council or the chief steward is responsible for strategic tasks. The business data steward provides support in a wide variety of tasks. The role of the sponsor represents the strategic direction and ensures the support of the management [10, 23].

Roles / Decision Areas	Executive Sponsor	Data Governance Council	Chief Steward	Business Data Steward	Technical Data Steward	...
Plan data quality initiatives	A	R	C	I	I	
Establish a data quality review process	I	A	R	C	C	
Define data producing processes		A	R	C	C	
Define roles and responsibilities	A	R	C	I	I	
Establish policies, procedures and standards for data quality	A	R	R	C	C	
Create a business data dictionary		A	C	C	R	
Define information systems support		I	A	C	R	
...						

R – Responsible; A – Accountable; C – Consulted; I – Informed

Fig. 2. Concept matrix of responsibilities according to [23]

The authors [31] take up the distribution of responsibilities and instead relate them to the areas of activity of the data quality strategy, the data maintenance processes, and the data quality target variables or the help desk. In addition, the role of "Shared Service

Center" is introduced, which is predominantly responsible for the mentioned tasks. In this context, a Data Quality Board is used for monitoring, whereby the technical data steward is predominantly informed, in contrast to the model before.

4.2   Objectives and Challenges of Data Governance

Data governance aims to enable more effective decision making in organizations and reduce operational friction. In addition, data governance aims to maintain the interests, values, and rights of stakeholders [32]. Furthermore, data governance objectives should firmly incorporate training opportunities for management and staff to adopt common approaches to data problems, build standardized, repeatable processes, reduce costs and increase effectiveness by pooling synergies, and ensure process transparency [33–35]. To achieve the goals, some challenges must be overcome in the context of data governance, such as data quality. Here, the dimensions of data quality, such as accuracy, timeliness, and consistency, play a significant role in terms of evaluation. Moreover, the dimensions should be improved by activities that directly affect data or processes regarding data exchange and data preparation [36]. Another challenge is data modelling, as well as data and schema integration. Regarding modelling, the focus is on the representation of data classes in terms of a conceptual model, i.e., a model whose linguistic categories highlight the aspects related to the meaning of data. For data integration, technologies must be available to query and access different independent databases. The schema integration is a challenge regarding the process of harmonizing conceptual descriptions of data across heterogeneous databases. Another challenge relates to data governance management. Here, the consideration is directed to the set of responsibilities and activities and their arrangement in the organization that enable to manage, monitor, control and improve the quality and integration level of the data [37]. Furthermore, the support of top management and change management is needed to be able to realize the goals of data governance. This can be achieved by adopting a uniform approach across the company and harmonizing processes across the company [24].

4.3   Interdependencies with Neighbouring Governance Areas

With the emergence of new governance types and areas, there is an increasing need for clear distinctions and definitions to avoid misunderstandings. In addition to corporate governance, information governance, IT governance and data governance, cloud computing governance has recently become another domain. The latter will not be discussed in detail in the following article. It is therefore important to distinguish between these domains and to define how they are interconnected, especially with regard to data governance. Figure 3 illustrates the interdependencies of the various governance domains [32].

The term governance generally refers to the way an organization ensures that strategies are set, monitored, and achieved [38]. Corporate governance sets the guidelines based on chains of links for the neighbouring governance types. In this respect, corporate governance essentially influences IT governance, which in turn has influences on data governance [39]. Moreover, [12] confirm that corporate governance has a strong

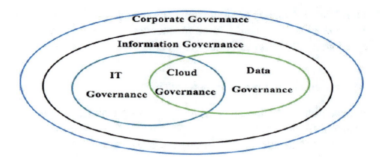

Fig. 3. The interdependencies of Governance-Domains [32]

influence on IT governance in terms of a centralized or decentralized orientation. Furthermore, [23] and [40] argue in the same way that data governance and IT governance follow the principles of corporate governance.

In this context, data governance develops and implements company-wide data policies, guidelines and standards that are consistent with the organization's mission, strategy, values, norms and culture and are anchored in corporate governance [32]. Besides size and competitive strategy, corporate governance is among the most important factors influencing data governance [10]. As IT has become the backbone of any organization, IT-Governance is an integral part of any business strategy and falls under corporate governance. The complexity and volume of data is growing, due to data-driven business decisions and processes, at the same rate as the need for clear data governance policies and guidelines [41, 42]. Attempts to manage data previously failed because they were driven by IT and influenced by rigid processes and fragmented activities [43]. However, essential differences also exist between data and IT governance [23, 44]. While data governance is designed to manage data assets, IT-Governance makes decisions about IT-Investments, the IT application portfolio, and the IT project portfolio. In practice, IT-Governance is primarily focused on an organization's hardware and applications, not its data. Information governance seems to fill a gap that has still not been filled by existing governance structures [45]. The core idea of information governance aims at minimizing problems regarding information asymmetry by forming linkage points to IT-Governance [46]. [38] pick up the idea, pointing out the use of IT-Governance mechanisms in information governance. [47] continue that essential practices of IT-Governance can be considered for information governance in terms of how information is governed. Furthermore, data governance is a component of information governance. While information governance concerns all types of unstructured and structured information, data governance has a more limited scope, focusing only on structured data [48].

5   Conclusion and Outlook

In this scientific contribution, based on a clear delimitation of the technical terms data governance, as well as the adjacent governance types: Corporate-, Information-, and IT- Governance, important contributions about the current, scientific state of research on the topic of Data Governance could be determined by means of literature research according to [19], and a forward/backward research according to [20]. On this basis, an in-depth literature review provided important insights. The characteristics provide a better understanding on the topic of data governance. The distribution of roles, as well as tasks and responsibilities, are elementary components of successful data governance. In addition, data governance has strong points of contact with data quality management.

Furthermore, important challenges and goals were identified. The evaluation of the literature research showed that there is no clear distinction between the individual governance domains. A few articles were able to describe the interdependencies and interfaces of individual types of governance. Derived from this, it became apparent that there is no generally accepted opinion on the classification of the interdependencies of the different governance types. Corporate governance essentially influences the adjacent governance types, especially IT governance. In addition, it was found that information, IT and data governance have cross-references to each other. In this contribution, the interdependencies of corporate, information, IT and data governance were identified and presented.

As a result of the findings of this paper, new areas of research were uncovered. On the one hand, further types of governance, such as cloud governance or security governance, were identified but not explained in detail. On the other hand, the influence, design and success factors of data governance offer further interesting approaches for future research work, since only isolated contributions could be identified on the basis of the literature search and no in-depth consideration was carried out in this regard. For future research work, the following hypotheses should be investigated:

- Which influencing, shaping and success factors are decisive for data governance?
- Which models and frameworks exist for the implementation of data governance?

References

1. Ransbotham, S., Kiron, D., Prentice, P.: Beyond the hype: the hard work behind analytics success (2016)
2. Thompson, N., Ravindran, R., Nicosia, S.: Government data does not mean data governance: lessons learned from a public sector application audit. Gov. Inf. Q. **32**, 316–322 (2015)
3. Brous, P., Janssen, M., Vilminko-Heikkinen, R.: Coordinating Decision-Making in Data Management Activities: A Systematic Review of Data Governance Principles. In: Scholl, H.J., et al. (eds.) EGOVIS 2016. LNCS, vol. 9820, pp. 115–125. Springer, Cham (2016). https://doi.org/10.1007/978-3-319-44421-5_9
4. Otto, B.: Data governance. WIRTSCHAFTSINFORMATIK **53**, 235–238 (2011)
5. Khatri, V., Brown, C.V.: Designing data governance. Commun. ACM **53**, 148–152 (2010)
6. Abraham, R., Schneider, J., vom Brocke, J.: Data governance: a conceptual framework, structured review, and research agenda. Int. J. Inf. Manage. **49**, 424–438 (2019)
7. Tiwana, A., Konsynski, B., Venkatraman, N.: Special issue: information technology and organizational governance: the IT governance cube. J. Manage. Inf. Syst. **30**, 7–12 (2013)
8. Johannsen, W., Goeken, M.: IT-Governance - neue Aufgaben des IT-Managements. HMD - Praxis Wirtschaftsinform **250** (2006)
9. Korhonen, J., Melleri, I., Hiekkanen, K., Helenius, M.: Designing data governance: an organizational perspective. GSTF J. Comput. **2** (2012)

10. Otto, B., Weber, K.: Data Governance. In: Hildebrand, K., Gebauer, M., Hinrichs, H., Mielke, M. (eds.) Daten- und Informationsqualität, pp. 269–286. Springer, Wiesbaden (2015). https://doi.org/10.1007/978-3-658-09214-6_16
11. Thammaboosadee, S., Dumthanasarn, N.: Proposed amendments of public information act towards data governance framework for open government data: context of Thailand. In: 2018 3rd Technology Innovation Management and Engineering Science International Conference (TIMES-iCON), pp. 1–5 (2018)
12. Sharma, D., Stone, M., Ekinci, Y.: IT governance and project management: a qualitative study. J. Database Mark Cust. Strategy Manag. **16**, 29–50 (2009)
13. Weill, P., Ross, J.W.: IT governance. Harvard Business School Press, Boston, Mass, How top performers manage IT decision rights for superior results (2004)
14. van Grembergen, W., Haes, S., de Guldentops, E.: Structures, processes and relational mechanisms for IT governance. In: van Grembergen, W. (ed.) Strategies for information technology governance. IGI Global (701 E. Chocolate Avenue Hershey Pennsylvania 17033 USA), Hershey, Pa (2004)
15. Smallwood, R.F.: Information governance: concepts, strategies, and best practices (2014)
16. Kooper, M.N., Maes, R., Lindgreen, E.E.O.R.: On the governance of information: introducing a new concept of governance to support the management of information. Int. J. Inf. Manage. **31**, 195–200 (2011)
17. de Oliveira, C., Behr, A., Maçada, A.C.G.: Establishing the main mechanisms for the accounting information governance: a delphi study with accountants. AMCIS 2019 Proc. (2019)
18. Wrobel, A., Komnata, K., Rudek, K.: IBM data governance solutions. In: Demazeau, Y., Gao, J., Xu, G. (eds.) 2017 International Conference on Behavioral, Economic Advance in Behavioral, Economic, Sociocultural Computing (BESC). Proceedings of 4th International Conference on Behavioral, Economic, and Socio-Cultural Computing (BESC 2017), Krakow, Poland, 16–18 October 2017, pp. 1–3. IEEE, Piscataway, NJ (2017)
19. Fettke, P.: State-of-the-Art des State-of-the-Art. Wirtsch. Inform **48**, 257–266 (2006)
20. Webster, J., Watson, R.T.: Analyzing the past to prepare for the future: writing a literature review. MIS Q. **26** (2002)
21. Boisot, M., Canals, A.: Data, information and knowledge: have we got it right? J. Evol. Econ. **14**, 43–67 (2004)
22. Wang, R.Y.: A product perspective on total data quality management. Commun. ACM **41**, 58–65 (1998)
23. Wende, K.: A model for data governance – organising accountabilities for data quality management. ACIS 2007 Proc. (2007)
24. Weber, K.: Data Governance-Referenzmodell – Organisatorische Gestaltung des unternehmensweiten Datenqualitätsmanagements (2009)
25. Cheong, L., Chang, V.: The need for data governance: a case study. ACIS 2007 Proc. (2007)
26. Fürber, C., Sobota, J.: Eine Datenqualitätsstrategie für große Organisationen am Beispiel der Bundeswehr. HMD Praxis der Wirtschaftsinformatik **48**(3), 36–45 (2011). https://doi.org/10.1007/BF03340585
27. Yulfitri, A.: Modeling operational model of data governance in government: case study: government agency X in Jakarta. In: 2016 International Conference on Information Technology Systems and Innovation (ICITSI), pp. 1–5 (2016)
28. Harrach, H.: Datenqualitätsmanagement. In: Harrach, H. (ed.) Risiko-Assessments für Datenqualität. Konzept und Realisierung, pp. 41–54. Vieweg+Teubner Verlag / GWV Fachverlage GmbH Wiesbaden, Wiesbaden (2010)
29. Pierce, E., Dismute, W.S., Yonke, C.L.: The state of information and data governance. understanding how organizations govern their information and data assets. IAIDQ and UALR-IQ (2008)

30. Martijn, N., Hulstijn, J., de Bruijne, M., Tan, Y.-H.: Determining the effects of data governance on the performance and compliance of enterprises in the logistics and retail sector. In: Janssen, M., et al. (eds.) I3E 2015. LNCS, vol. 9373, pp. 454–466. Springer, Cham (2015). https://doi.org/10.1007/978-3-319-25013-7_37

31. Weber, K., Otto, B., Österle, H.: Data Governance: Organisationskonzept für das konzernweite Datenqualitätsmanagement. 589–598 (2009)

32. Al-Ruithe, M., Benkhelifa, E., Hameed, K.: Data governance taxonomy: cloud versus non-cloud. Sustainability **10**, 95 (2018)

33. Kamioka, T., Luo, X., Tapanainen, T.: An empirical investigation of data governance: the role of accountabilities. PACIS 2016 Proc. (2016)

34. Poor, M.: Applying aspects of data governance from the private sector to public higher education (2011)

35. Otto, B.: A morphology of the organisation of data governance. In: 19th European Conference on Information Systems, ECIS 2011 (2011)

36. Wang, R.Y., Strong, D.M.: Beyond accuracy: what data quality means to data consumers. J. Manag. Inf. Syst. **12**, 5–33 (1996)

37. Viscusi, G., Batini, C., Mecella, M.: Information Systems for eGovernment. A Quality-of-Service Perspective. Springer-Verlag, Berlin Heidelberg, Berlin, Heidelberg (2010)

38. Weber, K., Otto, B., Österle, H.: One size does not fit all—a contingency approach to data governance. J. Data Inf. Qual. **1**, 1–27 (2009)

39. Tepandi, J., et al.: The data quality framework for the estonian public sector and its evaluation. In: Hameurlain, A., Küng, J., Wagner, R., Sakr, S., Razzak, I., Riyad, A. (eds.) Transactions on Large-Scale Data- and Knowledge-Centered Systems XXXV, 10680, pp. 1–26. Springer, Berlin Heidelberg, Berlin, Heidelberg (2017)

40. Chao, L.: Cloud computing for teaching and learning. Strategies for design and implementation. IGI Global (701 E. Chocolate Avenue Hershey Pennsylvania 17033 USA), Hershey, Pa (2012)

41. Begg, C., Caira, T.: Exploring the SME quandary: data governance in practise in the small to medium-sized enterprise sector. EJISE **15**, 3–13 (2012)

42. Niemi, E.: Working paper: designing a data governance framework (2011)

43. Al-Ruithe, M., Benkhelifa, E., Hameed, K.: Key dimensions for cloud data governance. In: Younas, M., Awan, I., Seah, W. (eds.) 2016 IEEE 4th International Conference on Future Internet of Things and Cloud. FiCloud 2016 : 22–24 August 2016, Vienna, Austria: proceedings, pp. 379–386. IEEE, Piscataway, NJ (2016)

44. Al-Ruithe, M., Benkhelifa, E., Hameed, K.: A conceptual framework for designing data governance for cloud computing. Procedia Comput. Sci. **94**, 160–167 (2016)

45. Faria, F., Maçada, A.C., Kumar, K.: Modelo Estrutural De Governança Da Informação Para Bancos. Rev. adm. empres. **57**, 79–95 (2017)

46. Lajara, T.T., Maçada, A.C.: Information governance framework: the defense manufacturing case study. In: 19th Americas Conference on Information Systems, AMCIS 2013 - Hyperconnected World: Anything, Anywhere, Anytime 3, 1984–1993 (2013)

47. Tallon, P.P., Ramirez, R.V., Short, J.E.: The information artifact in IT governance: toward a theory of information governance. J. Manag. Inf. Syst. **30**, 141–178 (2013)

48. Fleckenstein, M., Fellows, L.: Records management. In: Fleckenstein, M., Fellows, L. (eds.) Modern data strategy, pp. 195–207. Springer, Cham (2018).https://doi.org/10.1007/978-1-4842-2244-7_10

Scenarios for the Use of Master Data Management in the Context of the Internet of Things (IoT)

Rhena Krause[(⊠)] and Cornelia Becker

Department of Business Information Systems, M. Sc. Business Information Systems - Information Management and Data Science, Heilbronn University, Heilbronn, Germany
{rkrause,czeiler}@stud.hs-heilbronn.de

Abstract. The Internet of Things (IoT) connects humans and machines by means of intelligent technology such as sensors or actuators. This makes it possible to network everyday objects or machines in an industrial environment via the internet. The data generated in this way is also known as Big Data. Master data management (MDM) can offer great potential in dealing with data and data quality by providing a set of guidelines for data management and thus enabling a common view of it. In this paper, different approaches for the use of master data management in the context of IoT are analysed. For this purpose, a classification of the possible uses in the different design or functional areas is given in order to highlight areas of master data management with particular potential for use. The analysed results show that of the three design areas of enterprise-wide MDM, the system level is most frequently represented.

Keywords: Master data management · Internet of Things · IoT

1 Introduction

The Internet of Things is a large virtual network in which physical objects are equipped with sensors, actuators and computing power and linked to the Internet. This creates the basis for new types of interactions between companies, individuals and things, which are based on an ever stronger fusion of the physical and digital worlds, extensive availability of data and constant networking [1]. Studies assume that in the next few years several hundred billion "things" will be available on the internet, which can either be used for services or offer them themselves [2, 3]. The driving force of the Internet of Things is the resulting amount of data, also known as Big Data. This term is characterised by high data volume, high speed as well as a large variety of data formats [4]. The huge network and the associated rapidly growing data volume require an intelligent and effective data management model [2]. In addition to the data volume, the management of the The Internet of Things is challenged by the multitude of sensors and objects. According to the Manufacturing Vision Study [5], 62% of global industrial manufacturers still use spreadsheets to manage their assets. The use of intelligent solutions here is expected

© The Author(s), under exclusive license to Springer Nature Switzerland AG 2021
F. Ahlemann et al. (Eds.): WI 2021, LNISO 47, pp. 700–713, 2021.
https://doi.org/10.1007/978-3-030-86797-3_46

to reduce this figure by 20 % till 2022. Efficient master data management can address this by providing a set of guidelines for handling data and data quality, thus enabling a common view of them [6–9]. In detail, master data management describes a process that represents and manages the most important business data entities [9].

This paper investigates the extent to which the potential of master data management can be transferred to the Internet of Things. The research work provides an answer to the following research question:

- Which approaches exist for the use of master data management in the context of the Internet of Things?

The next step is to examine which design areas or specific functions of master data management are particularly suitable for use in the Internet of Things. The following sub-question will be answered:

- How can design areas or functions of master data management be applied to the Internet of Things?

The aim is to identify and compare scenarios for the use of master data management in the context of the Internet of Things on the basis of a systematic scientific literature research. This is to investigate the extent to which master data management can contribute to the Internet of Things and whether certain areas of master data management have a special significance. After defining the basics and terms for a uniform understanding in Sect. 2, the methodological approach is presented in Sect. 3. Section 4 deals with the insights gained from the systematically conducted literature analysis. Finally, a summary is drawn in Sect. 5 and possibilities for further research needs are identified.

2 Basics and Terms

The following section lists relevant definitions for master data management and the Internet of Things. The term Big Data is used in the context of both IoT and MDM and is therefore defined separately.

2.1 Master Data and Master Data Management

Master data describes fundamental business objects in a company that are used in value-adding processes [10]. They represent essential characteristics of real-world objects [11]. Typically, master data is used across several business processes [10] and is only changed in exceptional cases [12]. Examples are customer, supplier, employee, product and material master data [6, 10–12].

Many works emphasise different aspects of master data management (MDM) [7, 11, 13]. Smith and McKeen [9] examine the aspects of master data management in various works and, based on this, define MDM as follows: MDM is an application-independent process that describes, owns and manages the basic business data entities. It also ensures the consistency and accuracy of this data by providing a set of policies for managing it, thus creating a common view of key enterprise data [9]. MDM thus describes an enterprise function that encompasses all planning, monitoring and provisioning activities for master data. In the context of MDM, particular emphasis is placed on ensuring the quality of master data, as this is a prerequisite for being able to fulfil various strategic requirements of a company [6, 7]. The potential benefits of MDM resulting from high data quality include cost savings and improved customer relations [9].

2.2 Design Areas of Master Data Management

Otto and Hüner [11] emphasise that the management of master data should be regarded as an independent management task. For the most part, master data is used everywhere in the company. The relationship of the individual master data classes to different company divisions, business processes and different locations creates a network of relationships. Understanding this network is complex and requires experience within the organisation. MDM can neither be operated by the information technology department nor by the specialist departments alone, since technical expertise is required in addition to information technology training.

The core message of enterprise-wide MDM is, that business transformations based on the strategic use of information technologies can be applied at three different levels: at the strategic level, at the organisational level and at the system level [11]. At the top level, the strategy level, is the master data strategy. The organisational and business process level includes the master data management systems, the master data organisation and the master data processes and methods. At the system level are the application systems for master data and the information architecture. If one takes a closer look at the system level, it becomes clear that different functional areas are needed to categorise the application systems. Otto and Hüner [11] arrange these in the form of a functional architecture, which is divided into functional categories and areas (see Fig. 1). The first level thus describes the six functional categories life cycle management for master data (A), metadata management and master data modelling (B), quality management for master data (C), Master data integration (D), cross-sectional functions (E) and administration (F). These functional categories comprise a total of 19 functional areas as a second level. A third level, which is no longer visible in Fig. 1, distinguishes 72 further functions. These functions represent a function grid that can be used for the detailed analysis of MDM products and serves as the basis for the presentation of results in the form of a concept matrix in Sect. 4 (cf. [11]).

2.3 Internet of Things (IoT)

Internet of Things (IoT) refers to the next logical stage of the internet and its connection to the physical world, where uniquely addressable physical objects or assets interact with each other and pass generated data to a larger network for sharing and processing [14]. This is also evident in Gartner's definition [15]: IoT is a "network of physical objects that contain embedded technology to communicate and sense or interact with their internal states or the external environment". Many of these devices, also known as smart devices, exist as components in buildings or vehicles or are distributed in the environment. In the industrial environment (IIoT), sensors enable the continuous collection of data directly

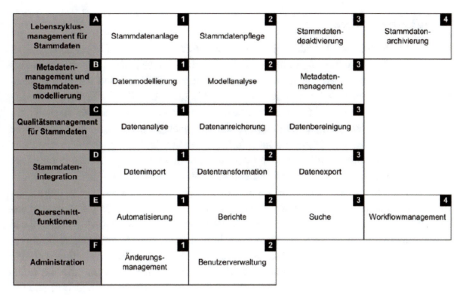

Fig. 1. Functional categories and areas of MDM at system level [11].

in production for the automated control of manufacturing processes [16] or also for condition-based predictive maintenance to minimise downtime [4].

2.4 Big Data

Following Gartner analyst Laney [17], the term Big Data refers to the extreme volume of data ("Volume"), the great variety of data ("Variety") and the high speed ("Velocity") for processing data sets. In recent years, these "3 Vs" have been supplemented by additional factors, depending on the source, including veracity and value [18]. Due to these characteristics, Big Data places special demands on electronic data processing and requires innovative techniques and technologies for storage and further processing [19].

Volume refers to the huge amount of data that is continuously generated by devices in the IoT network (e.g. sensors, actuators, smart devices) [14]. *Variety* refers to the different types of data. In an IoT network, this can be e.g. sensor data, weblogs or streamed video and audio data, which are either collected in a structured or unstructured way. *Veracity* refers to the correctness and accuracy of information that is necessary when processing and analysing Big Data. The proven data management principles such as data quality, data cleansing, master data management and data governance are more important here than ever. *Velocity* describes the high speed at which data is generated and processed. Data processing in the IoT environment can take place either as long-term or real-time analysis [20]. This distinction results in different requirements for the data and its processing. *Value* is the most important aspect of Big Data in terms of data value creation, as it relates to data analysis and the associated gain in knowledge [18].

2.5 IoT Architectures

An IoT architecture is generally represented as a four-layer model [21]. The first layer forms the physical layer and contains the sensors and devices. Here, the sensor data is fed into the transport layer. The transport layer transmits the sensed data using communication technologies, such as RFID, NFC, Bluetooth or WLAN. In the processing layer, the data is stored and further processed using Big Data frameworks. In the application layer, the data is made available to the end user [21]. Building on this layered architecture, further architectural concepts are available depending on the application. In the industrial context, reference architectures are developed by various committees that offer a wide range of standardised concepts and serve as a template to cover different requirements [20]. Essential aspects of architecture concepts are the collection, structuring and integration of the life cycle data of objects, such as machines, plants and products, as well as the mapping of processes on how the information obtained can be made available to humans and machines in real time. An IT architecture therefore requires concepts for real-time processing, decision-making processes and knowledge processing [20]. The most well-known IoT reference architectures include the reference architecture model Industrie 4.0 (RAMI4.0) of the Industrie 4.0 platform and the Industrial Internet Reference Architecture (IIRA) of the Industrial Internet Consortium [20].

3   Research Methodology

The methodological procedure is carried out as a structured literature review according to Fettke [22]. According to this procedure, the methodology is divided into the steps of problem definition (Sect. 1), literature search, literature review, analysis, interpretation and presentation of the identified literature. The methodological approach is supplemented with a concept matrix according to Webster and Watson [23].

3.1   Literature Search

The Springer Link, IEEE, AiSel and Google Scholar databases are used for the literature search in order to retrieve both German-language and English-language scientific publications. The time period was limited to the last five years (2016 to 2020), as the topics of IoT and master data are still a relatively young discipline. The search was limited to the search fields *Abstract*, *Title* and *Keywords* (if possible or available) as well as to the type *Journals* ("Article") and *Conference Papers* ("Conference Paper") in order to obtain hits that reflect the current state of research.

3.2   Literature Review

For the literature evaluation, a search term was defined from German and English search terms containing both the terms on the topic of MDM and terms on the topic of IoT. An initially unstructured rough review of the literature showed that the term "data management" was too unspecific and produced many irrelevant hits. Accordingly, the search term was formulated as follows:

- ("Master Data Management" OR "Master Data" OR Stammdatenmanagement OR Stammdaten) AND ("Internet of Things" OR "Internet der Dinge" OR "Industrie 4.0" OR IoT OR IIoT)

The aim was to map the current state of research in this apparently still very young discipline and to conduct a content analysis of all identified contributions. The results are presented and interpreted in a concept matrix modelled on Webster and Watson [23] in Sect. 4.

4 Results

24 relevant contributions for the use of MDM in the context of the IoT were identified. The central aspect of the investigation was to identify design areas of the enterprise-wide MDM in the respective publication that supports the IoT. It is clear to see that the system level with the functional categories of the functional architecture is most frequently represented with 20 of 24 contributions (Table 1). The organisation level (2 contributions) and the strategy level (1 contribution), on the other hand, were strongly underrepresented. It can be concluded from this that MDM in the IoT context takes place primarily at the system level. The general management of data and the management of assets and devices are identified as further possible uses. The possible uses of MDM in the IoT are based on the functional architecture [A-D] from Fig. 1.

4.1 Strategy Level

Master Data Strategy. MDM is generally of strategic importance, as it needs to be perceived across the company due to different business drivers (compliance, risk management, etc.) [11].

Areas of application: Ng et al. [8] refer to the development of an MDM strategy analogous to the strategy or policy of an organisation or city to optimise the management of urban infrastructures towards smart cities.

4.2 Organisational Level

Master data processes and methods. At the organisational level, the "Master data processes and methods" of the company-wide MDM. This scope emphasises the importance of establishing standards and specifications in the daily handling of master data in the company. This applies to both project business and the execution of business processes. These standards are intended to ensure high data quality.

Areas of application: To meet the needs of smart cities, Indrajit et al. [30] propose an MDM approach. Among other things, this should implement policies, procedures and guidelines that should be used to support the collection, integration and sharing of accurate, timely and consistent master data. Wang and Wang [38] discuss in their paper the data collection of all energy assets using the IoT. Here, the MDM should act as part

Table 1. Concept matrix (own representation)

| Reference | Possible uses of MDM in the IoT | | | | | | | | |
| | Strategy level | Organisational level | System level | | | | | Further areas of application | |
	Master data strategy	Master data processes and methods	Life cycle management	Metadata management and data modelling	Master data integration	Quality management	Information architecture	General data management	Asset/Device Management
[2]					x	x			x
[4]				x					
[8]	x			x		x		x	
[14]						x			
[16]				x					x
[19]							x		
[20]			x	x	x	x	x		x
[24]								x	
[25]				x					x
[26]						x			
[27]				x	x	x			
[28]									x
[29]			x						
[30]		x				x		x	
[31]				x					
[32]				x					
[33]								x	
[34]				x			x		
[35]							x		
[36]							x		
[37]			x			x		x	
[38]		x							
[39]							x		
[40]							x	x	

of an integrated cloud platform and enable data management based on a unified data model and master data management system at the enterprise level, for example through the introduction of standards.

4.3   System Level

The system level comprises the functional architecture with the functional areas of life cycle management, metadata management and data modelling, quality management and data integration as well as the area of information architecture.

Life Cycle Management [A]. The life cycle of a master data starts with its creation in the operational business and ends with its deactivation or archiving. The life cycle management of the MDM covers all activities that the data user carries out during the existence of the master data. This includes the creation, maintenance, deactivation and archiving of master data [11].

Areas of application: Ng et al. [8] present an MDM solution to unlock the value of big infrastructure data in the context of smart city planning. Among other things, the MDM lifecycle management component is used.

Potential areas of application: Hildebrand [29] and Sathi [36] state that technical and organisational challenges of the IoT imperatively require a clear process for the creation, maintenance and deactivation or deletion of master data. Weber et al. [20] also pick up on the importance of lifecycle management as a basis for further data processing in the context of IoT architecture. Potential uses for MDM can be derived from this.

Metadata Management and Data Modelling [B]. Metadata describes the meaning and properties of data that are different from master data or streaming data. Metadata can describe the structure of the data itself and on the one hand unambiguously define the correct use of it. Metadata management in MDM enables efficient management and effective use of master data. The modelling describes the creation of the metadata and for example takes up the support of professional standards [11].

Areas of application: In their paper, Burdack and Rössle [25] propose an MDM solution for managing the metadata of all machines in an IIoT network. This manages the metadata and maps the hierarchical and logical relationships between the machines, the manufacturable components and the materials. Ng et al. [8] use MDM data modelling for their MDM solution in the context of smart city planning. Dagnaw and Tsigie [27] take up master data management in the context of Big Data architectures resulting from the IoT. Here they mention, among other things, the potential of enforcing standard terminologies through the MDM (cf. "Supporting domain-oriented standards" of data modelling [11]). Lassnig et al. [31] emphasise the importance of introducing a reliable MDM, as it makes available a uniform language necessary for the IIoT, like for example through a glossary or dictionary [11]. Ning et al. [34] and Giebler et al. [16] use metadata to describe and manage their master data in more detail.

Potential areas of application: Jesse [4] describes that metadata is essential for the IoT as it annotates sensor data to provide context. The challenge for the IoT in this case is to develop a coordinated metadata system. The metadata management of the MDM can also show possible applications here. Lempert and Pflaum [32] describe a reference architecture for an IoT platform and address the importance of data modelling and visualisation. Weber et al. [20] also address data modelling in their remarks on IoT architecture. Both areas can potentially be supported by MDM, as metadata management also deals with the graphical modelling of data models [11].

Quality Management [C]. Quality management includes all preventive as well as reactive functions to maintain and improve the quality of data. Functional areas for this are data analysis, which contains functions for identifying master data problems, data enhancement with functions for improving the quality of the data (for example, by adding external reference data) and data cleansing, which includes functions to remove detected data problems (e.g. duplicate detection) [11].

Areas of application: Indrajit et al. [30] and Ng et al. [8] propose an MDM approach in the context of smart cities, which among other things should be able to minimise the confusion, including data redundancies and gaps of urban information datasets. Firouzi et al. [14] talk about data preservation possibilities in the field of Big Data and IoT and mention MDM as a method to achieve data quality. Cheng et al. [26] recommend MDM to enable cloud data management in IoT and specifically mention the functionality of data quality management as an application example: they describe it as a complete set of techniques and specifications to ensure integrity, consistency and accuracy of master data. AlSuwaidan [2] emphasises the importance of data management in IoT and sees, among other things, the potential of MDM in data cleansing of different data types. Dagnaw and Tsigie [27] see potentials of MDM in dealing with duplicates, incomplete and erroneous data.

Potential areas of application: Lempert and Pflaum [32] pick up on the importance of data analysis for their reference architecture of the IoT platform; Sathi [37] emphasises the importance of data quality. Both can potentially be supported by the MDM quality management function.

Master Data Integration [D]. The function category master data integration contains supporting functions for the transport (data import and data export) as well as the structural transformation of the master data [11].

Areas of application: Dagnaw and Tsigie [27] emphasise that master data management should provide a systematic approach to data integration that ensures consistent use and reuse of data. The paper by AlSuwaidan [2] describes a data-driven management model for the "Internet of Everything". The model contains an MDM layer that includes data integration as the last component; this mainly refers to data unification (data transformation).

Potential areas of application: In their study on the use of IT architectures for industrial IoT, Weber et al. [20] describe the RAMI4.0 reference architecture. Here, a separate integration level is provided that makes information about assets, events, etc. available for further processing in the corresponding IT systems.

Information Architecture. In addition to the functional architecture, the information architecture for master data is found at the system level [11]. Architectures are of central importance in the implementation of use cases in the IoT environment. Weber et al. [20] examine the reference architectures IIRA and RAMI4.0 in the industrial environment for architecture concepts that support data processing in IoT scenarios. They come to the conclusion that different layers for data processing are necessary for the creation of an IoT architecture: In addition to a speed layer for event-oriented data processing for real-time applications with low latency, a batch layer is needed to support the analysis of historical data for long time analysis (Fig. 2). MDM is applied here because historical data (e.g. customer or device data) is mostly master data.

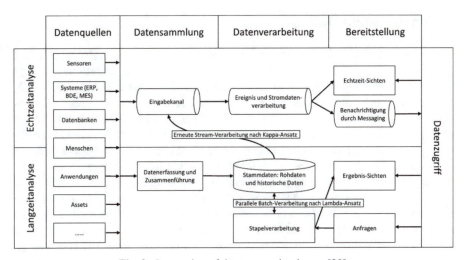

Fig. 2. Integration of data processing layers [20].

Areas of application: Other contributions do not explicitly distinguish between batch and speed layers when examining application areas of MDM, but recommend, for example, a repository for the long-term storage of master data e. g. for IoT specific supply chain management applications [39], a multi-layer master data management architecture in the context of cloud manufacturing [36] or a data-oriented analysis and design method for intelligent, complex software systems (Smart CSS) [34]. For data management in MDM, graph databases are recommended by Petrenko et al. [35] and Storey and Song [19] to represent complex relationships.

4.4 Further Areas of Application

General Data Management. In addition to the specifically explained categories, some of the identified contributions also address the general support of MDM in IoT. Here it is mentioned that MDM offers great potential for overcoming the challenges in dealing with data [8, 24, 26, 29, 30, 33, 37].

Asset-/Device Management. Assets in the context of IoT are physical objects, machines, facilities, field devices or other sensors [41]. In the area of asset/device management, MDM can support the unique identification of devices [2, 16, 25, 28]. Weber et al. [20] see asset management in the RAMI4.0 reference architecture on a so-called management shell, which enables interaction with devices that also have a management shell. In the IIRA reference architecture, asset management is located on the function domain "Control".

5   Summary and Outlook

The analysed results clearly show that of the three design areas of enterprise-wide MDM, the system level, with the functional categories of the functional architecture, is most frequently represented with 80% of all contributions. The organisational level and the strategy level are hardly represented. This could be due to the fact that research into the relationship between MDM and IoT is only just beginning and not many publications have been published in this area. Another conclusion may be that MDM does not actually make a significant contribution to IoT in this area. Furthermore, the articles often do not explicitly distinguish between master data and transaction data, but only talk about "data" or "data processing". However, as shown e.g. by Weber et al. [20], the consideration of historical data and master data, especially for long-term analyses, is also of great importance for the IoT. In other works, such as Petrenko et al. [35], master data analyses are used to improve IoT security concepts. Here, again, the great potential of MDM in the IoT context becomes clear. Furthermore, Burdack and Rössel [25] or Dremel and Herterich [28] recommend using MDM to support asset management. Due to the widespread applications of the IoT, more and more unstructured data in different formats are generated directly in the cloud, without local storage. In this area, MDM can be used to support data management in the cloud (e.g. through functions for managing unstructured data). However, master data (for long-term analysis) and IoT sensor data (for real-time processing) place different demands on a data processing system. Here, it should be critically considered that the MDM is traditionally not designed to process IoT data, which is often generated in real time [4]. In general, it can be said that proven data management principles such as data cleansing, data quality and master data management play an important role in the processing and analysis of Big Data. This is also reflected in the distribution of the results in the concept matrix (Table 1): At the system level, the two functional areas of quality management (8 mentions) and metadata management (9 mentions) are most frequently represented.

During the analysis of the identified contributions, it was observed that the term Big Data was often used in relation to MDM. As already mentioned, it is mainly the variety of data that can be handled by MDM. There is still room for future research here. One starting point could be the investigation of other Big Data areas or "V's" in order to identify further areas of application for MDM. Further research on the topics of MDM and IoT is recommended, as this study shows potential in this area.

References

1. Püschel, L., Röglinger, M., Schlott, H.: Smart things im Internet der Dinge—ein Klassifikationsansatz. Wirtschaftsinformatik Manag. **9**(2), 54–61 (2017). https://doi.org/10.1007/s35 764-017-0042-1
2. AlSuwaidan, L.: Data management model for internet of everything. In: Awan, I., Younas, M., Ünal, P., Aleksy, M. (eds.) MobiWIS. LNCS, vol. 11673, pp. 331–341. Springer, Cham (2019). https://doi.org/10.1007/978-3-030-27192-3_26
3. Tenzer, F.: Prognose zur Anzahl der vernetzten Geräte im Internet der Dinge (IoT) weltweit in den Jahren 2016 by 2020. https://de.statista.com/statistik/daten/studie/537093/umfrage/ anzahl-der-vernetzten-geraete-on-the-internet-of-things-iot-worldwide/#statisticContainer. Accessed on 18 July 2020
4. Jesse, N.: Internet of Things and Big Data: the disruption of the value chain and the rise of new software ecosystems. AI Soc. **33**, 229–239 (2018). https://doi.org/10.1007/s00146-018-0807-y
5. Zebra: Manufacturing Vision Study, http://online.zebra.com/mfgvisionstudy_DE, accessed 2020/04/14.
6. Otto, B., Kokemüller, J., Weisbecker, A., Gizanis, D.: Master data management: data quality for business processes. HMD Prax. Inf. Syst. **48**, 5–16 (2011). https://doi.org/10.1007/BF0 3340582
7. Scheuch, R., Gansor, T., Ziller, C.: Master Data Management: Strategie, Organisation. Architektur. dpunkt.verlag, Heidelberg (2012)
8. Ng, S.T., Xu, F.J., Yang, Y., Lu, M.: A master data management solution to unlock the value of big infrastructure data for smart, sustainable and resilient city planning. Procedia Eng. **196**, 939–947 (2017). https://doi.org/10.1016/j.proeng.2017.08.034
9. Smith, H.A., McKeen, J.D.: Developments in practice XXX: master data management: salvation or snake oil? Commun. Assoc. Inf. Syst. **23** (2008). https://doi.org/10.17705/1CAIS. 02304
10. Otto, B., Ebner, V.: Measuring master data quality: findings from an expert survey. In: Schumann, M., Kolbe, L., Breitner, M.H., Frerichs, A. (eds.) Multikonferenz Wirtschaftsinformatik (MKWI) 2010, pp. 221–222. Universitätsverlag Göttingen, Göttingen (2010)
11. Otto, B., Hüner, K.M.: Funktionsarchitektur für unternehmensweites Stammdatenmanagement. Inst. for Business Informatics St. Gall. Report No, 68 (2009)
12. Mertens, P.: Integrierte Informationsverarbeitung 1 - Operative Systeme in der Industrie. Gabler, Wiesbaden (2013). https://doi.org/10.1007/978-3-8349-8231-5
13. Berson, A., Dubov, L.: Master Data Management and Customer Data Integration for a Global Enterprise. Mcgraw-hill (2007)
14. Firouzi, F., Farahani, B., Weinberger, M., DePace, G., Aliee, F.S.: IoT fundamentals: definitions, architectures, challenges, and promises. In: Firouzi, F., Chakrabarty, K., Nassif, S. (eds.) Intelligent Internet of Things, pp. 3–50. Springer, Cham (2020). https://doi.org/10.1007/978-3-030-30367-9_1
15. Gartner: Internet of Things (IoT). https://www.gartner.com/en/information-technology/glo ssary/internet-of-things. Accessed on 18 July 2020
16. Giebler, C., Gröger, C., Hoos, E., Eichler, R., Schwarz, H., Mitschang, B.: Data Lakes auf den Grund gegangen. Datenbank-Spektrum **20**(1), 57–69 (2020). https://doi.org/10.1007/s13 222-020-00332-0
17. Diebold, F.X.: On the origin(s) and development of the term "Big Data." SSRN Electron. J. (2012). https://doi.org/10.2139/ssrn.2152421
18. Karagiorgos, N., Siozios, K.: Data analytic for improving operations and maintenance in smart-grid environment. In: Siozios, K., Anagnostos, D., Soudris, D., Kosmatopoulos, E.

(eds.) IoT for Smart Grids. PS, pp. 147–161. Springer, Cham (2019). https://doi.org/10.1007/
978-3-030-03640-9_8

19. Storey, V.C., Song, I.-Y.: Big data technologies and management: what conceptual modeling
can do. Data Knowl. Eng. **108**, 50–67 (2017). https://doi.org/10.1016/j.datak.2017.01.001

20. Weber, C., Wieland, M., Reimann, P.: Konzepte zur Datenverarbeitung in Referenzarchitek-
turen für Industrie 4.0. Datenbank-Spektrum **18**(1), 39–50 (2018). https://doi.org/10.1007/
s13222-018-0275-z

21. Knittl, S., Neuberger, V., Dieterle, S.: HMD Praxis der Wirtschaftsinformatik **57**(3), 558–570
(2020). https://doi.org/10.1365/s40702-020-00623-w

22. Fettke, P.: State-of-the-Art of the State-of-the-Art An investigation of the research method
"Review" within business informatics. WIRTSCHAFTSINFORMATIK. **48**, 257–266 (2006)

23. Webster, J., Watson, R.T.: Analyzing the past to prepare for the future : writing a literature
review. Manag. Inf. Syst. Res. Cent. **26**, xiii–xxiii (2002)

24. Ahlers, D., Wienhofen, L.W.M., Petersen, S.A., Anvaari, M.: A smart city ecosystem enabling
open innovation. In: Lüke, K.-H., Eichler, G., Erfurth, C., Fahrnberger, G. (eds.) I4CS 2019.
CCIS, vol. 1041, pp. 109–122. Springer, Cham (2019). https://doi.org/10.1007/978-3-030-
22482-0_9

25. Burdack, M., Rössle, M.: A concept of an interactive web-based machine learning tool for
individual machine and production monitoring. In: Czarnowski, I., Howlett, R.J., Jain, L.C.
(Hrsg.) Intelligent Decision Technologies 2019. S. 183–193. Springer Singapore, Singapore
(2019). https://doi.org/10.1007/978-981-13-8303-8_16

26. Cheng, G., Li, Y., Gao, Z., Liu, X.: Cloud data governance maturity model. In: 2017 8th
IEEE International Conference on Software Engineering and Service Science (ICSESS). S.
517–520. IEEE (2017). https://doi.org/10.1109/ICSESS.2017.8342968

27. Dagnaw, G.A., Tsigie, S.E.: Data management practice in 21st century: systematic review.
Int. Res. J. Multidiscip. Stud. **5**, 1–10 (2019)

28. Dremel, C., Herterich, M.: HMD Praxis der Wirtschaftsinformatik **53**(5), 646–661 (2016).
https://doi.org/10.1365/s40702-016-0250-9

29. Hildebrand, K.: Master Data Life Cycle – Management der Materialstammdaten in SAP®. In:
Hildebrand, K., Gebauer, M., Hinrichs, H., Mielke, M. (eds.) Daten- und Informationsqualität,
pp. 299–310. Springer, Wiesbaden (2018). https://doi.org/10.1007/978-3-658-21994-9_18

30. Indrajit, A., van Loenen, B., van Oosterom, P.: Multi-Domain Master Spatial Information
Management for Open SDI in Indonesian Smart Cities. (2017)

31. Lassnig, M., Schön, S., Stabauer, P., Selhofer, H.: Transformation verschiedener
Wirtschaftssektoren durch Industrie 4.0: Wie sich ausgewählte Branchenprofile im Industrial
Internet verändern. Books on Demand, Norderstedt (2017)

32. Lempert, S., Pflaum, A.: HMD Praxis der Wirtschaftsinformatik **56**(6), 1178–1203 (2019).
https://doi.org/10.1365/s40702-019-00562-1

33. Müller, D., Schumacher, C., Zeidler, F.: Intelligent adaption process in cyber-physical production systems. In: Margaria, T., Steffen, B. (eds.) ISoLA. LNCS, vol. 11246, pp. 411–428.
Springer, Cham (2018). https://doi.org/10.1007/978-3-030-03424-5_28

34. Ning, D.J., Wang, Y., Guo, J.: A data oriented analysis and design method for smart complex
software systems of IoT. In: 2018 International Symposium in Sensing and Instrumentation
in IoT Era (ISSI). S. 1–6. IEEE (2018). https://doi.org/10.1109/ISSI.2018.8538199

35. Petrenko, S., Makoveichuk, K., Olifirov, A.: New methods of the cybersecurity knowledge
management analytics. In: Sukhomlin, V., Zubareva, E. (eds.) Convergent 2018. CCIS, vol.
1140, pp. 296–310. Springer, Cham (2020). https://doi.org/10.1007/978-3-030-37436-5_27

36. Ren, L., Zhang, Z., Zhao, C., Zhang, G.: Cloud-based master data platform for smart manufacturing process. In: Zhang, X., Liu, G., Qiu, M., Xiang, W., Huang, T. (eds.) CloudComp.
LNICSSITE, vol. 322, pp. 163–170. Springer, Cham (2020). https://doi.org/10.1007/978-3-
030-48513-9_13

37. Sathi, A.: Machine-to-Machine Interfaces. In: Cognitive (Internet of) Things. S. 125–136. Palgrave Macmillan, New York (2016). https://doi.org/10.1057/978-1-137-59466-2

38. Wang, Q., Wang, Y.G.: Research on power internet of things architecture for smart grid demand. In: 2018 2nd IEEE Conference on Energy Internet and Energy System Integration (EI2). S. 1–9. IEEE (2018). https://doi.org/10.1109/EI2.2018.8582132

39. Woo, S., et al.: Secure-EPCIS: addressing security issues in EPCIS for IoT applications. In: 2017 IEEE World Congress on Services (SERVICES). S. 40–43. IEEE (2017). https://doi.org/10.1109/SERVICES.2017.16

40. Zhao, C., Ren, L., Zhang, Z., Meng, Z.: Master data management for manufacturing big data: a method of evaluation for data network. World Wide Web 23(2), 1407–1421 (2019). https://doi.org/10.1007/s11280-019-00707-8

41. Kaufmann, T., Servatius, H.-G.: IoT- und KI-Architektur. In: Das Internet der Dinge und Künstliche Intelligenz als Game Changer, pp. 113–149. Springer, Wiesbaden (2020). https://doi.org/10.1007/978-3-658-28400-8_8

A Framework of Business Process Monitoring and Prediction Techniques

Frederik Wolf[(✉)], Jens Brunk, and Jörg Becker

University of Münster – ERCIS, Münster, Germany
{f_wolk09,jens.brunk,becker}@ercis.uni-muenster.de

Abstract. The digitization of businesses provides huge amounts of data that can be leveraged by modern Business Process Management methods. Predictive Business Process Monitoring (PBPM) represents techniques which deal with real-time analysis of currently running process instances and also with the prediction of their future behavior. While many different prediction techniques have been developed, most of the early techniques base their predictions solely on the controlfow characteristic of a business process. More recently, researchers attempt to incorporate additional process-related information, also known as the process context, into their predictive models. In 2018, Di Francescomarino et al. published a framework of existing prediction techniques. Since the young field has evolved greatly since then and context information continue to play a greater role in predictive techniques, this paper describes the process and outcome of updating and extending the framework to include process context dimensions by replicating the literature review of the initial authors.

Keywords: Business process · Prediction · Techniques · Predictive Business Process Monitoring

1 Introduction

Today's economy is highly volatile and uncertain developments, such as the current COVID-19 crisis, pressure organizations to be able to adapt and improve their business processes immediately [1]. Consequently, the domain of predictive business process monitoring (PBPM) gained momentum in business process management (BPM) in the last few years [2]. PBPM leverages prediction techniques to predict and improve operational business processes. PBPM techniques predict the future behavior of a business process during its execution [3, 4] based on predictive models, which were constructed from the historical process event logs [5, 6]. PBPM techniques can address a variety of goals, such as next activity [7], process outcome [8], remaining processing time [9] or pre-determined risks, and apply several different technologies [10]. Due to the complex nature of the often Machine Learning-based (ML) PBPM techniques, their different goals and input requirements, [10] developed a value-adding framework in 2018, which classifies PBPM techniques and supports researchers and practitioners in selecting appropriate PBPM techniques for their endeavor.

© The Author(s), under exclusive license to Springer Nature Switzerland AG 2021
F. Ahlemann et al. (Eds.): WI 2021, LNISO 47, pp. 714–724, 2021.
https://doi.org/10.1007/978-3-030-86797-3_47

Most of the (early) PPM techniques base their analyzes and predictions solely on the control-flow characteristic of a business process, i.e., the process events [10]. Since then, researchers continuously attempt to conceptualize and incorporate additional process-related information, also known as the process context, into their predictive models. The context can be defined as the "minimum set of variables containing all relevant information that impact the design [, implementation] and execution of a business process" [11, p.154]. Context information, originating from sources external [12, 13] or internal (e.g. [14, 15]) to the business process, can improve process predictions since it adds valuable information to the predictive models [5].

For example, [16] confirm a significant relationship between the representation of an event log's context attributes and a DNN's predictive quality in a next activity prediction task. [15] and [17] additionally use a resource attribute of a process log as context information. [14] improve their prediction results by incorporating multiple additional context attributes. [18] explore the effect of different previously used context attributes on a deep learning neural network and compare as well as benchmark their results with previous publications.

Since the initial publication of the above-mentioned Process Prediction Technique Framework (PPTF) by Di Francescomarino et al. in 2018, many new techniques have been developed and existing techniques might have been enhanced. Additionally, the trend of incorporating additional context attributes into the predictive techniques adds another layer of complexity to the task of selecting an appropriate technique for a PBPM endeavor. Therefore, a gap exists for an updated PPTF that also includes detailed information about the capability of incorporating context information. Our research goal (RG) therefore states: *Update the Process Prediction Technique Framework by Di Francescomarino et al. (2018) and extend it by a dimension on context information.*

Section 2 introduces the initial PPTF and other related work. Section 3describes the applied literature search process to update and extend the PPTF, before the new PPTF is presented in Sect. 4. Section 5 then concludes our work and gives an outlook on future work.

2 Background

The PPTF is based on a literature review and classifies existing PBPM techniques in the dimensions prediction type, input data, tool availability, domain, and family of algorithm [10]. The dimension prediction type includes the prediction goal of the PBPM technique. Prediction goals were identified to be time prediction, categorical outcome(s), sequence of next outcomes/values, risk, inter-case metrics or cost. The inputs required by a technique are captured in the input dimension. Generally, techniques take an event log as input that must contain certain information. Some techniques require additional inputs, like a labeling function. If a tool was developed to support a PBPM technique, it is captured in the dimension tool support. A developed tool facilitates using, evaluating and understanding the technique. A technique can be implemented in a standalone tool or as a plugin for an existing tool. PBPM techniques are generally evaluated using event logs, which can either be synthetic or recorded from a real-life process. When selecting a technique for implementation, it is better if the technique is validated with an event log from a similar domain as the domain it will be implemented in. Therefore, the domain of the event log used for validation is captured in the domain dimension. PBPM techniques are usually based on a specific algorithm. For some applications, certain types of algorithms might have benefits over others. Therefore, the family of algorithm is captured in the respective dimension. The framework can be used by both practitioners and researchers. For practitioners, the structure of the framework allows identifying the most suitable PBPM technique for a given scenario. For researchers, it offers a clear classification and characterization of existing PBPM techniques [10].

Many current PBPM techniques incorporate additional process information into their predictive models. Additional process information is also known as the context of a process [19]. It can either be contained in the event log as data elements, or stem from external sources. The context information of a process can consist of several context attributes, which are the specific entities for which information is available. To understand the meaning of context, which types of values a context attribute can have and which technical implications the characteristics of context have, [19] developed a Taxonomy for Business Process Context Information. The taxonomy characterizes context attributes in the dimensions time, structure, origin, relevance, process relation, and runtime behavior. Values of context attributes of a process can either be known at the beginning of a process instance, become known during runtime or be predicted. These characteristics are contained in the time dimension. The structure dimension refers to the format of the context attribute. Information can either be available in a structured, semi-structured, or unstructured format. The origin dimension captures, from which source a context attribute stems. Immediate context attributes are required to execute a process. Information about the internal environment of the organization is stored in internal attributes. Context attributes that have an indirect influence on a process but are within the business network of the organization are external attributes. Any context from outside the business network of the organization is the environment. Some context attributes have a stronger influence on a process than others. The extent of the influence of a context attribute is captured in the relevance dimension. A context attribute can influence various elements of a process. In that sense, context attributes can influence activities, events, the control flow, or artefacts of a process. Which element(s) are influenced by a context attribute is captured in the Process Relation dimension. Some context attributes change their values during the execution of a process, meaning they are dynamic. Context attributes maintaining their value are referred to as being static. Whether a context attribute is static, or dynamic is contained in the Runtime Behavior dimension.

3   Research Method

The review protocol applied by the authors in the literature review of the original PPTF followed the guidelines given by [20]. Towards achieving our RG, we adapt and replicate their literature review process. First, we design the research protocol including the definition of guiding questions, electronic databases used, the search string, and the processing of results. In the second step, we conduct the literature search, identify the final list of papers and extract relevant information from them [10]. Di Francescomarino et al. defined four guiding questions (referred to as GQ1, GQ2, GQ4 and GQ5 in our work) to lead the development of the original framework. For the extension of the framework we add GQ3 to the set of questions because we anticipate that more recent techniques can process contextual inputs beyond the traditional event log:

- GQ1: What aspect do techniques for PPM predict?
- GQ2: What input data do they require?
- GQ3: Which additional input data do they use?
- GQ4: What are their main families of algorithms?
- GQ5: What are the tools supporting them?

The databases used for the literature review are *Scopus, SpringerLink, IEEE Xplore, ScienceDirect, ACM Digital Library* and *Web of Science*. These databases are the same as in the original literature review and were selected as they cover publications in the research field of Computer Science [10]. The original authors used the search string *("predictive" OR "prediction") AND ("business process" OR "process mining")* for running their queries in October 2017. They state that, after removing duplicates, the search in all the databases named above resulted in 779 papers [10]. However, running the same search string in the same databases in February 2020, yielded over 90.000 results. We could not identify the reasons for this discrepancy either on our own or together with the original authors. In our literature review, we added the term *("method" OR "algorithm" OR "technique")* with an AND connector to the search string to focus the results on those studies presenting a PBPM technique and exclude high-level studies on the general topic. Therefore, the final search string is: *("predictive" OR "prediction") AND ("business process" OR "process mining") AND ("method" OR "algorithm" OR "technique")*. To further narrow down the results of the search, we apply selected filters. First, we exclude all papers published before 2017, as these should already be contained in the original framework. Second, the subject area is narrowed down to "Computer Science", the sub-discipline is selected to be "Data Mining and Knowledge". Lastly, all non-English papers are excluded. However, it is not possible to apply all filters in all databases. We executed the queries on February 8th, 2020. Since the high number of results, we assume that in each database, no further valuable sources can be expected after the first 500 results, sorted by relevance. Table 1 gives an overview of the filters applied, the number of results and the number of results considered for each database.

For the processing of the results, we again proceed very similar to the process of the original authors, which includes seven steps [10]. Since we expect that some papers, which we find in our literature review, are already contained in the original framework (namely those which were published between January and October in 2017), we added step 3 to the process to filter those papers. In the first step, duplicates are removed. Duplicates are defined as papers with the same title and the same authors. Second, results are filtered by the title of the study. All documents that are not proper research papers (e.g. white papers, editorials) and all studies that relate to a different research area are excluded. Third, all studies that are already contained in the original framework are excluded. In the next step, position papers and workshop papers were excluded because results in these studies are often less mature as those in conference papers or journals. Fifth, results are filtered by their abstract, assessing their relevance. In the sixth step, the full texts of the results are accessed and filtered by whether the study proposes a novel technique to the field of PBPM. Finally, additional papers are added via a backward search. Table 2 shows the number of results remaining after each step in the literature review process.

Table 1. Literature review: applied filters, Number of results and Number of results considered

Database	Applied filters	Number of results	Results considered
Springer	Discipline "computer science", subdiscipline "Data Mining and Knowledge Discovery", Language "English", Date 2017 - 2020	2114	First 500 by relevance
ScienceDirect	Date 2017- 2020	2704	First 500 by relevance
Web of Science	Date 2017 – 2020	26	26
Scopus	Subject Area "Computer Science", Language "English", Date 2017 – 2020	206	206
IEEE Xplore	Date 2017 – 2020	1327	First 500 by relevance
ACM Digital Library	Date 2017 – 2020	204	204
Total		6581	1936

Table 2. Literature review: processing steps and number of resulting papers

Processing step		Number of results remaining
0	None	1936
1	Remove duplicates	1840
2	Filter by title of studies	77
3	Remove papers existing in original framework (incl. original framework study)	67
4	Remove workshop papers, position papers	60
5	Filter by abstract	28
6	Filter by full text	25
7	Add papers via backward search	29

4   Process Prediction Technique Framework

The results of our literature review confirm that the majority of more recent techniques incorporate context information (at least partially). In total, 19 of the 27 identified techniques use context information. Most of these approaches leverage context information which is contained within the applied event logs. One technique stands out and aims to incorporate information from outside of the event log. The technique provided by [12] analyses data on the sentiment of the news media at the time of process execution to add it to the prediction. Feeding the context information into the prediction model is typically done with one-hot encoding, assigning each value of a context attribute a new column in the input vector [e.g. 9, 21]. In addition, [14] use a min-max normalization to encode continuous data features. The authors state, that in the future the approach might even take images as an input. [22] compare predictions with one-hot encoding and predictions with encoding via entity embedding to predictions without adding context information. They find that entity embedding results in more accurate predictions than one-hot encoding. Both approaches outperform the prediction without context information.

Context Information
Context information was already superficially incorporated in the original PPTF. The *Input* dimension is used to shortly describe the inputs needed for a technique. If the technique takes context information as an input, an attribute like event log (with context information) or similar is contained in this dimension. However, this kind of information is not sufficient to select the correct technique if a PBPM project plans on incorporating context information, as the kind of context information supported vary from technique to technique. It is necessary to incorporate a classification of the type of context information into the PPTF.

Therefore, we combine the framework with the Taxonomy of Business Process Context Information [19] as an addition to the *Input* dimension. The taxonomy enables a classification of context information of business processes in the six dimensions *Time, Structure, Origin, Relevance, Process Relation,* and *Runtime Behavior.* The *Time* dimension relates to the point in time at which the context information is known. *Structure* describes the data model of the context information. The source of the context information is contained in *Origin. Relevance* classifies the importance of the context information to the business process. In the *Process Relation* dimension, the part of a process to which the context information is connected, is captured. Finally, *Runtime Behavior* states whether the context information changes throughout a process instance execution or not [19]. Some of the PBPM techniques assume that context information is stored for an entire case (e.g. the loan amount in a credit granting process) instead of storing it on activity or event level. None of the characteristics in the dimension *Process Relation* fits this assumption. To overcome this, the additional characteristic *Instance* is introduced to the dimension *Process Relation* for the combination of the PPTF and the taxonomy.

In the PPTF, the taxonomy dimensions describe which context information a technique supports. Most approaches work based on machine learning and implicitly or explicitly assign weights to each piece of information. Therefore, the *Relevance* dimension is of little value and is thus neglected in the framework.

Extension of the Technique Framework
Towards the construction of the extended PPMF, the techniques contained in the original framework and the newly identified techniques are inserted. Information on techniques already contained in the original framework is adopted and enriched with more details on context information. For all new techniques, the characteristics of all dimensions of the extended framework are extracted and inserted into the framework. In the literature search, we identified four techniques that are extended versions of techniques that were already contained in the original framework ([9, 23–25]). In these cases, we removed the older techniques in favor of the new and extended ones. In total, the extended PPTF now contains 77 PBPM techniques. Analogous to Di Francescomarino et al., the framework can be read from left to right. The techniques in the framework are sorted hierarchically by their *Prediction Type, Detailed Prediction Type, Inputs* and *Tool Support*. These dimensions can be used to identify candidate techniques with given characteristics. Afterward, the dimensions *Context Information, Domain, Family of Algorithm* and *Comment* can be inspected separately to further narrow down the list of candidate techniques. In the first step of identifying candidate techniques, a user can filter the complete list by the type of prediction. The second column *Detailed Prediction Type* contains information on the concrete type of prediction a technique is performing. Second, techniques can be filtered by their *Input* (columns three to five). Usually, the techniques take an event log including timestamps as input. Some techniques however require additional inputs, like a process model or a labeling function. If these inputs are not available or should not be integrated into the prediction, the respective techniques can be excluded. Third, candidate techniques can be identified by the type of *Tool Support* they offer, which is described in the sixth column of the PPTF. Some techniques offer code for implementation, or plugins for software like ProM, YAWL or Camunda. On the other hand, some techniques do not offer any tool support. Techniques offering tool support require less implementation effort, as at least parts of the implementation are already available. After these three steps for identifying candidate techniques, the PPTF offers further dimensions for assessing each technique individually. *Context Information* is included in columns seven to eleven of the framework. These columns reflect the dimensions of the Taxonomy of Business Process Context Information (i.e., *Time, Structure, Origin, Process Relation* and *Runtime Behavior*) and contain the characteristics of the context information that a technique supports. If a certain context information needs to be included into the prediction, the techniques that do not support it can be excluded. All of the techniques in the framework are usually evaluated by using an event log from a real-life process. In column twelve of the framework, the *Domain* from which the event log stems is referenced. If a technique was validated in the same domain as the process that should be predicted, for example automotive, it could be an indicator that the technique is suitable for that kind of domain. All techniques in the framework are based on a specific type of algorithm, which is contained in the dimension *Family of Algorithm*. Examples are neural networks [e.g. 15], clustering [e.g. 26] and regression [e.g. 12]. This is included in the framework because the relative performance of algorithm families varies depending on the specific PBPM project. Table 3 views several exemplary entries of the extended PPTF with its

dimensions. The entire PPTF is available as a digital appendix in a GitLab repository[1], since including as well as viewing all entries as part of this paper is not feasible.

Demonstration

In the following, we demonstrate the PPTF at the example of one of the techniques that is listed in Table 3 in more detail. Specifically, we explain why the technique shows the respective values of the framework dimension. As exemplary technique, we select [21], which is the sixth line in Table 3 and highlighted for readers convenience. The authors state that the goal of their technique is to efficiently produce a prediction model for any case-level prediction tasks. The authors specifically name next activity prediction and remaining time prediction as examples. Therefore, the technique can be found twice in the framework. First, with Prediction Type *time* and Detailed Prediction Type *remaining time* (as displayed in the framework below) and second with Prediction Type *categorical outcome* and Detailed Prediction Type *Next Activity* (not contained in the exemplary entries). The technique takes an event log as input. The event log should also contain timestamps and event attribute data. Therefore, the Input dimension is set to *Event log with timestamps with context information* (shortened to *event log* for readability purposes in the framework below). The authors of the technique made the source code of the prediction engine publicly available on GitHub. It does not represent a plugin for an existing tool. Therefore, the Tool dimension is set to *Y (impl.)*. Regarding the context information, the technique uses one-hot encoding to encode event attributes. As event attributes are used, the process relation dimension of the context is *event*. An event attribute can only be known once the event took place, not before. Therefore, the Time dimension is set to *runtime*. The fact that context information is processed on the event-level also tells us that the Runtime Behavior of the context information processed can either be *static* or *dynamic*. This is because the value of each can change from event to event and does not have to stay static over the whole instance. As described above, the technique takes an event log as input. No further inputs are needed. This means that all the context information that can be processed need to be contained in the event log. Following this, the Origin of the data has to be either *immediate*, meaning it is the information needed to carry out the process, or *internal* which is information directly related to the process. External or environmental context information would stem from outside the process and are therefore usually not contained in an event log. One-hot encoding maps key: attribute value pairs into vectors. The fact that the context information has a given structure, key:attribute pairs, but not a limited set of attributes of values leads to the Structure dimension being *semi-structured* for this technique. To test the technique, the authors used data sets of BPI challenges from the years 2012, 2013, 2014 and 2018. These data sets represent processes from the financial, automotive, customer support and public administration domains. Therefore, these values are written into the domain dimension. The technique exploits event attributes into recurrent neural network (RNN) prediction models by clustering events by their attribute values and using the cluster labels in the RNN input vectors. Therefore, the families of algorithm used in this technique are clustering and neural networks which concludes the dimensions of the PPTF.

---

[1] https://wiwi-gitlab.uni-muenster.de/j_brun17/process-prediction-technique-framework/.

Table 3. Exemplary entries of the process prediction technique framework

Prediction Type		Input			Tool	Context Time	Structure	Origin	Process Relation	Runtime Behavior	Domain	Family of Algorithm
Overall	Detailed	#1	#2	#3								
time	timestamp of next activity	event log	-	-	ProM Plugin	-	-	-	-	-	logistics	stochastic petri net
time	timestamp of next activity	event log	-	-	N	runtime	semi-structured	immediate	activity	static, dynamic	finance, customer sup-port automotive	probabilistic model
time	maintenance time	event log	-	-	N	-	-	-	-	-	automotive	time series, probabilistic model regression
time	remaining time	event log	-	-	ProM Plugin	a priori, runtime	semi-structured	immediate, internal	activity	state	public administration	regression
time	remaining time	event log	-	-	Y	runtime	structured	immediate, internal	activity	static	healthcare	stochastic petri net
time	remaining time	event log	-	-	Y (impl.)	runtime	semi-structured	immediate, internal	event	static, dynamic	financial, automotive, customer, support, healthcare, financial, public administration	neural network, clustering
time	average sojourn time of activities	event log	-	-	Y	-	-	-	event	-	healthcare, financial, customer support	neural network
...	...	...	...	...	...	...	...	...	...	...	...	...
categorical	next activity	event log	-	-	Y (impl.)	runtime	structured, semi-structured	immediate	event, instance	static, dynamic	financial, automotive	neural network
categorical	next activity	event log	labeling function	process model	ProM Plugin	a priori, runtime, future	structured, semi-structured	immedia, internal, external, environment	event, artefact	static	no validation	classification
categorical	violation of process constraints	event log	context data	-	N	runtime	semi-structured	immediate, internal, external, environment	event, instance	static, dynamic	automotive, logistics	clustering, time-series
...	...	...	...	...	...	...	...	...	...	...	...	...
sequences of outcomes	sequences of outcomes	event log	...	...	N	...	...	...	event	static, dynamic	financial	probabilistic model, regression
risk	risk	event log	labeling function	-	Camunda Plugin	-	-	-	-	-	financial	similarity process graphs, analysis weighted instance statistical
...	...	...	...	...	...	...	...	...	...	...	...	...
inter-case metrics	inter-case metrics	event log	-	...	N	runtime	structured	immediate	event	static, dynamic	no validation	classification, regression, time series
...	...	...	...	...	...	...	...	...	...	...	...	...
cost	cost	event log	threshold(s)	-	N	-	-	-	-	-	transport, logistics	neural network
...	...	...	...	...	...	...	...	...	...	...	...	...

5   Conclusion

This paper addressed the RG to update the PPTF, which was originally developed by in 2018, and extend its dimensions with context information. We reached this goal through a new literature review that builds upon the already existing review results of the initial authors. We integrated the original results with our own and extended the PPTF by context information dimensions, as proposed by [19]. Section 4 describes the updated PPTF and its dimensions. Table 3 shows some exemplary entries of the entire PPTF, which is available as a digital appendix[2], due to its large size.

We believe that this updated PPTF will support researchers and practitioners, who intend to use or develop business process prediction and monitoring techniques. Since the selection of an appropriate prediction technique is not only dependent on the given dimensions of the PPTF but is also strongly influenced by other project-dependent factors, we plan to address this limitation in future work. For example, the PPTF could be leveraged in the development of a PBPM implementation reference process that supports practitioners and researchers in the introduction and implementation of PBPM (e.g. [6]).

References

1. Poll, R., Polyvyanyy, A., Rosemann, M., Röglinger, M., Rupprecht, L.: Process forecasting: towards proactive business process management. In: Weske, M., Montali, M., Weber, I., vom Brocke, J. (eds.) BPM 2018. LNCS, vol. 11080, pp. 496–512. Springer, Cham (2018). https://doi.org/10.1007/978-3-319-98648-7_29
2. Breuker, D., Matzner, M., Delfmann, P., Becker, J.: Comprehensible predictive models for business processes. MIS Q. **40**(4), 1009–1034 (2016)
3. Maggi, F.M., Di Francescomarino, C., Dumas, M., Ghidini, C.: Predictive monitoring of business processes. In: Proceedings of the 26th International Conference on Advanced Information Systems Engineering, pp. 457–472. Springer (2014). https://doi.org/10.1007/978-3-319-07881-6_31
4. Schwegmann, B., Matzner, M., Janiesch, C.: A method and tool for predictive event-driven process analytics. In: Proceedings of the 11th International Conference on Wirtschaftsinformatik, pp. 721–735. AISeL (2013)
5. Márquez-Chamorro, A.E., Resinas, M., Ruiz-Cortés, A.: Predictive monitoring of business processes: a survey. IEEE Trans. Serv. Comput. **11**(6), 962–977 (2017)
6. Becker, J., Brunk, J., Ding, W., Niemann, M.: Conceptualization of an integrated procedure model for business process monitoring and prediction. In: 22nd IEEE Conference on Business Informatics, CBI 2020, Antwerp, Belgium. IEEE (2020)
7. Tama, B.A., Comuzzi, M.: An empirical comparison of classification techniques for next event prediction using business process event logs. Expert Syst. Appl. **129**, 233–245 (2019)
8. Teinemaa, I., Dumas, M., Rosa, M.L., Maggi, F.M.: Outcome-oriented predictive process monitoring: review and benchmark. ACM Trans. Knowl. Discov. Data **13**(2), 1–57 (2019)
9. Verenich, I., Dumas, M., Rosa, M.L., Maggi, F.M., Teinemaa, I.: Survey and cross- benchmark comparison of remaining time prediction methods in business process monitoring. ACM Trans. Intell. Syst. Technol. **10**(4), 1–34 (2019)
10. Di Francescomarino, C., Ghidini, C., Maggi, F.M., Milani, F.: Predictive process monitoring methods: which one suits me best? In: Weske, M., Montali, M., Weber, I., vom Brocke, J. (eds) Business Process Management. BPM 2018. LNCS, vol. 11080, pp. 462–479. Springer International Publishing (2018) https://doi.org/10.1007/978-3-319-98648-7_27

11. Rosemann, M., Recker, J.C.: Context-aware process design: exploring the extrinsic drivers for process flexibility. In: Proceedings of the 18th International Conference on Advanced Information Systems Engineering, pp. 149–158. Namur University Press (2006)

12. Yeshchenko, A., Durier, F., Revoredo, K., Mendling, J., Santoro, F.: Context-aware predictive process monitoring: the impact of news sentiment. In: Panetto, H., Debruyne, C., Proper, H.A., Ardagna, C.A., Roman, D., Meersman, R. (eds.) OTM 2018. LNCS, vol. 11229, pp. 586–603. Springer, Cham (2018). https://doi.org/10.1007/978-3-030-02610-3_33

13. Weinzierl, S., Revoredo, K.C., Matzner, M.: Predictive business process monitoring with context information from documents. In: Proceedings of the 27th European Conference on Information Systems, pp. 1–10. AISeL (2019)

14. Schönig, S., Jasinski, R., Ackermann, L., Jablonski, S.: Deep learning process prediction with discrete and continuous data features. In: Proceedings of the 13th In- ternational Conference on Evaluation of Novel Approaches to Software Engineering, pp. 314–319. Science and Technology Publications (2018)

15. Evermann, J., Rehse, J.R., Fettke, P.: Predicting process behaviour using deep learning. Decis. Support Syst. **100**, 129–140 (2017)

16. Weinzierl, S., Stierle, M., Zilker, S., Matzner, M.: A next click recommender system for web-based service analytics with context-aware LSTMs. In: Proceedings of the 53rd Hawaii International Conference on System Sciences, pp. 1542–1551. IEEE (2020)

17. Camargo, M., Dumas, M., González-Rojas, O.: Learning accurate LSTM models of business processes. In: Hildebrandt, T., van Dongen, B.F., Röglinger, M., Mendling, J. (eds.) BPM 2019. LNCS, vol. 11675, pp. 286–302. Springer, Cham (2019). https://doi.org/10.1007/978-3-030-26619-6_19

18. Brunk, J., Stottmeister, J., Weinzierl, S., Matzner, M., Becker, J.: Exploring the effect of context information on deep learning business process predictions. J. Decis. Syst. 1–16 (2020)

19. Brunk, J.: Structuring business process context information for process monitoring and prediction. In: Proceedings of the Conference on Business Informatics 2020. Antwerp, Belgium (2020)

20. Kitchenham, B.: Procedures for performing systematic reviews. Keele, UK, Keele University **33**(2004), 1–26 (2004)

21. Hinkka, M., Lehto, T., Heljanko, K.: Exploiting event log event attributes in RNN based prediction. In: Welzer, T. et al. (eds) New Trends in Databases and Information Systems. ADBIS 2019. Communications in Computer and Information Science, vol 1064, pp. 67–85. Springer, Cham (2018). https://doi.org/10.1007/978-3-030-30278-8_40

22. Wahid, N.A., Adi, T.N., Bae, H., Choi, Y.: Predictive business process monitoring– remaining time prediction using deep neural network with entity embedding. Procedia Comput. Sci. **161**, 1080–1088 (2019)

23. Mehdiyev, N., Evermann, J., Fettke, P.: A novel business process prediction model using a deep learning method. Bus. Inf. Syst. Eng. **62**(2), 143–157 (2020)

24. Senderovich, A., Di Francescomarino, C., Maggi, F.M.: From knowledge-driven to data-driven inter-case feature encoding in predictive process monitoring. Inf. Syst. **84**, 255–264 (2019)

25. Ceci, M., Spagnoletta, M., Lanotte, P.F., Malerba, D.: Distributed learning of process models for next activity prediction. In: Proceedings of the 22nd International Database Engineering & Applications Symposium, pp. 278–282 (2018)

26. Bernard, G., Andritsos, P.: Accurate and transparent path prediction using process mining. In: Welzer, T., Eder, J., Podgorelec, V., Kamišalić Latifić, A. (eds) Advances in Databases and Information Systems. ADBIS 2019. Lecture Notes in Computer Science, vol. 11695, pp. 235–250. Springer, Cham (2019). https://doi.org/10.1007/978-3-030-28730-6_15

Process Digitalization in Dental Practices – Status Quo and Directions for the German Health Care System

Karolin Bosch[✉], Linda Mosenthin, and Christian Schieder

Weiden Business School,
Technical University of Applied Sciences Amberg-Weiden, Weiden, Germany
{k.bosch,l.mosenthin,c.schieder}@oth-aw.com

Abstract. Process digitalization in health care systems can help to increase treatment quality and foster cost-efficiency at the same time. Several studies have already shown how digitalization can change and automate processes, but do not address the specific needs of dentists. This paper investigates the status quo and the possibilities of process digitalization for dental practices and their interfaces. Based on the assessment of 101 participants of an empirical study and semi-structured interviews with four dentists and four professionals of statutory health insurance we provide insights into the current situation. The analysis reveals that most organizations are in an early stage of digital transformation but are actively working on enhancing the digitalization of their processes. To meet this need, our results deliver a detailed description of prevailing challenges and starting points for process digitalization and optimization in the field of dentistry.

Keywords: German healthcare system · Dental practice · Administrative processes · Business process automation · Process digitalization

1 Introduction

Healthcare systems today are struggling with a variety of different and growing challenges. Limited financial resources, an aging society, and increasing multimorbidity within the population are the limiting factors pressuring resource allocation. New and sophisticated technologies bring new possibilities but frequently put even more stress on financial resources due to their cost intensity. At the same time, medical care of the patient needs to be guaranteed at the highest possible standard [1–3]. Therefore, continuous improvement is necessary. To tackle the tension between efficiency and quality, the digitalization of health care processes has become increasingly important in recent years. With digital process management, it is easier to locate bottlenecks, redundancy, and inefficiency and to initiate countermeasures against them. As a prerequisite, all participants in the health care system need to be highly process-oriented. They need to know and analyze their processes to realize the right potential for optimization [4].

These challenges affect not only the health system in general but also all specialized areas such as dentistry. Dental health affects the whole human body and is therefore a

F. Ahlemann et al. (Eds.): WI 2021, LNISO 47, pp. 725–737, 2021.
https://doi.org/10.1007/978-3-030-86797-3_48

vital part of holistic human medicine. Whereas several studies have already shown how digitalization can improve and automate processes, they do not specifically address dentists and their interfaces [5–10]. This paper investigates the status quo and the directions of process digitalization in dental practices and their interfaces in the German health care system. Therefore, dentists' and statutory health insurance employees' perception of the current state of process digitalization was examined using semi-structured interviews. Furthermore, we conducted an online survey to understand patients' perceptions of actual processes and digitization in the field of dentistry. We aimed to gain the most comprehensive insight possible into the status quo of processes digitalization and to extract starting points for further process optimization.

The remainder of this paper is organized as follows: Sect. 2 lays out the theoretical background and Sect. 3 describes the methodology of the research. The results are presented in Sect. 4 and discussed in Sect. 5 before we conclude the paper in Sect. 6 indicating the limitations of our research and providing an outlook to future work.

2 Theoretical Background

Quality improvement in healthcare stands for improved patient health, better medical care, and targeted professional development. To achieve this, targeted interdisciplinary cooperation between all those involved, such as the health care professions, payers, and managers, is required. This cooperation requires precise knowledge of the processes and procedures in the healthcare system [3]. The term business process can be defined as a series of logically related tasks that are performed to achieve a defined result. The definition of processes in healthcare is the same, except that they achieve a specific clinical outcome. Healthcare processes can be divided into two different types. On the one hand, there are the organizational, administrative processes and on the other hand the medical treatment processes [4, 5]. Processes can map all work and behavioral steps of the various parties along with the treatment of a specific patient or along the entire value chain of the system. Attributes of processes, such as capacity, efficiency, and reliability, illustrate important performance dimensions of healthcare, such as lead time and patient safety. Finally, they have a significant influence on patient satisfaction, costs, and the quality of medical care [6].

By using the right technology, such as modeling systems, process management can be more effective. Technological process management supports the various possibilities of digitization. The optimal management of administrative processes with data-based workflows and the simultaneous use of the right software can advance the digital transformation [11].

The complexity of the German healthcare system is shaped by different actors, institutions, and levels. All organizations and their roles in health care concerning dentists are summarized in the chart below [12–17].

The German Ministry of Health has recognized the need to digitize the system and has therefore drafted several laws for comprehensive reform. The basis for this is the telematics infrastructure (TI), which as digital platform networks all players in the statutory health insurance system. On this platform, all information can be securely exchanged across all sectors of the system. The connection to the TI is mandatory for all

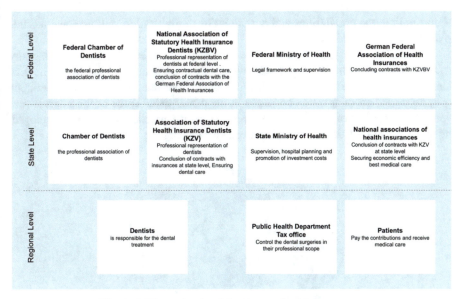

Fig. 1. Different levels of the German healthcare system

health care providers. For patients, participation is voluntary. Patients have sovereignty over their data and decide who receives what data and which applications they want to activate. In principle, the secure and digital exchange of treatment and medication data is intended to increase treatment safety and efficiency. Since the beginning of 2019, all dentists must be connected to the TI. The first implemented application is the online comparison of the master data of the insured persons. Other applications, such as the electronic medication plan, the standard case data management, and the electronic patient record (ePA) are currently under development [18, 19].

3 Methodical Approach

To obtain the most comprehensive picture possible of the status quo, a qualitative and quantitative approach was chosen. On the one hand, expert interviews were conducted with relevant actors in the healthcare system. On the other hand, an online survey was conducted. This approach is intended to examine the current situation from different perspectives. For a holistic view, the respective results are combined.

The conducted expert interviews were semi-structured and based on an interview guideline that was adapted to the specific expert groups. Each interview was scheduled for one hour and was held online via video or telephone. The goal of these interviews was to clearly define the administrative processes in dental practices and their interfaces as well as the possibilities of optimization and automation through digitalization. In order to obtain all the information required, the interview guide was set up accordingly. Priority was to understand the role and task of the interviewee and his or her organization and to capture all administrative processes in the organization and the interfaces to the dentists. In addition, personal wishes regarding work and process optimization, the current status of digitization, the possibilities and opportunities of digitization, and personal attitude to digitization were also to be surveyed [20–22].

A total of four participants (two women; two men; no miscellaneous) of a statutory health insurance company were interviewed, one participant working in the field of telematics and the other three in the dental domain. Four interviews (three women; one man; no miscellaneous) were conducted in the dental field. Three of the interviewees work as dentists, two of them have a leading position in a practice and are self-employed, the fourth person is a dental administrative assistant (Fig. 2).

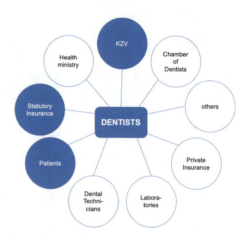

Fig. 2. Possible and investigated interfaces to dentists (blue)

An online survey was carried out online without target groups to survey a representative cross-section of the society. Before the survey began, the participants had to agree to the respective consent and data processing declaration. First, sociographic data and the insurance status were queried. The survey aimed to find out the opinion of the population on digitization in everyday life in cooperation with dentists and insurance companies [23, 24]. A total of 101 persons (58 women; 43 men; no miscellaneous) aged over 18 years participated in the online survey.

4   Results

In the following section, the results of the interviews and the survey are presented in detail one by one. All results were measured on the gradual ten-point response scale in Likert format.

4.1   Interview with Experts from a Health Insurance Company

First, a comprehensive analysis and evaluation of the results of the semi-structured interview with the health insurance company are presented. Due to the open questions that were asked during the entire interview, no significance and correlation between the individual results can be calculated. It was not relevant which gender or age the participants had, it was only about the professional experience and their field of application. On average, the interviewees have a work experience of 26.25 years. They feel that digitization is very helpful in their everyday lives (9.125 out of 10), although the current level of digitization in their field of work is only in the middle of the range (5.875 of 10). The desire and the existing potential to make the daily work more digital became clear from the results. Cooperation with all interfaces is rated as quite good (7.25 out of 10), but there are still some areas where process optimization is necessary (Table 1).

Table 1. Administrative processes

Processes	Current status of digitalization	Comment
1. Performance audit	○	For performance auditing, all billing reports are sent to the health insurance company via PDF
2. Approval process	◐	In this process, there is an automatic mail dispatch via ePost
3. Settlement process	●	The entire settlement process works on the digital level as long as it is not interrupted by errors
3.1 Process of correction loop for settlements	○	Starting at the point where a review of the process is necessary, the system switches from online to analog

The tasks of the health insurance company include the admission of dentists, invoicing, taking over remuneration negotiations, and answering questions relevant to the profession. Direct contacts with dentists are very rare and only take place when problems arise or wishes and innovations are to be discussed at a strategic level. On the administrative level, there is contact with the Association of Statutory Health Insurance Dentists (KZV). Digitalization has already progressed. For example, mails are scanned and automatically distributed as an eFile to the relevant departments. Between 1500 and 2000 applications are received daily by mail and are digitized. Invoicing is also already digital, as the software, checks the billing applications, and only conspicuous cases are forwarded to the clerks. Overall, less than 10% are classified as conspicuous and over 90% are processed directly by the system in digital form. The reports for the performance audits are sent to the health insurance company as PDF files and analyzed by them. The three administrative processes are shown in the table below.

Deficits of Digitization. Despite optical character recognition (OCR), the allocation and appropriate distribution of incoming mails are relatively difficult. Here, the technology and the entire process should be more mature and advanced. The compatibility of the different organizations as well as technical systems of health insurance companies, dentists, and the KZV is not given and therefore there are many barriers. Besides, due to existing political barriers, cooperation with the KZV on a strategic level is often problematic. The data flow and all communication between the health insurance companies and the KZV are not transparent and therefore important information is sometimes lost. Currently, dentists and the KZV only pass on data that is helpful for the assessment to a limited extent. A lot of collected data is withheld because the KZV does not consider it necessary for the billing process of the insurance company. This means that the health insurance company often lacks information for a precise examination of the treatment provided.

Possibilities of Digitization. In general, paperless collaboration and the automation of mass business would mean more time for customer care and thus increased customer satisfaction. Greater transparency through digitization means that fraud is less possible. A bonus app could also help to digitize the current analog bonus system to simplify the calculation of the subsidy for dental prostheses. In the future, admissions, assessment procedures, and court proceedings should have to be digitized. TI and ePA will increase efficiency and save costs. This means that once approved, patient data can be digitally transferred from doctor to doctor and from health insurance company to doctor. However, communication with patients will continue to take place by post. One of the risks of the electronic patient file is "dental stalking".

4.2 Interview with Dental Practices

In the following, the results of the interviews with dental practices are explained. For the evaluation of the results, the same conditions apply to the health insurance company. The average number of professional experiences in years is very high with a value of 19.5 years.

The interviewee finds digitization helpful in their everyday life (7.25 out of 10), the current status in their practice is slightly better than average (6.5 out of 10) and cooperation with all interfaces is also rated as above average (7.75 out of 10).

The entire health care system, external laboratories, and also tax consultants are seen as interfaces. In total five different administrative processes are relevant in a dental practice. These processes are appointment management, accounting, material and quality management, and personnel administration (Table 2).

Currently, there are great differences between individual practices, especially in the area of billing and licensing. Due to different levels of competence of the contact persons at the health insurance companies, but also within the practice, the contact to health insurance companies, insurances, and KZV is very different.

Many dentists have been converting their systems from paper to digital for some time now, resulting in performance, transmission, and control problems. There are software products such as DAMPSOFT or synMedico that are designed to help with digitization. However, these are not adapted to the individual needs of a single practice and are relatively expensive. Due to the high costs associated with the introduction of such software products, the decision is often made not to use such programs. Moreover, the transition to digitization also means that a large number of new and different problems will arise in practice. Therefore, a permanent restructuring of practice often requires an

Table 2. Current status of the administrative processes in dental surgeries

Administrative processes	Current status of digitalization	Examples
Appointment	◑	A scheduling tool, where experience shows that online implementation is difficult to achieve
Accounting	◑	An interface between the tax office and finance office is needed, preferably digital, to be able to act more flexibly
Material planning	◐	Online tools for material planning and procurement would enable automated ordering and would save time for all employees
Quality management	◐	Online quality management and the completion of the required documents could be designed online and immediately checked by the respective office
Personal administration	◕	Time and vacation planning online for all employees to have a simple and quickly customizable overview

external consultant and the help of IT specialists. Thus, in addition to software costs, long-term support costs are also incurred. Also, the digitization of various processes is not conducive to achieving the desired results. This is the case, for example, when making appointments online. The correct coordination of appointments is not conducive from a business point of view, as it could lead to overbooking or idle time in the practices.

Deficits of Digitalization. Digitization brings with it a high degree of trust, and the misuse of data poses a very great danger. In addition, the conversion and training effort is immense and only makes the current situation even more difficult. Technology providers have often digitized their customer service. This makes it difficult to find simple help and quick support for technical questions. The number of possible evaluations is increasing, which provides more transparency, but logically also increases control by interfaces such as health insurance companies, health authorities, and tax authorities. The compulsory participation in TI is perceived as uncomfortable by all dentists surveyed.

Possibilities of Digitization. Digitization can facilitate the billing process with partners and patient data can be used in a simple and encrypted form for research purposes. TI has been very active in the field of data protection and is very securely established in this area. The step of patient education could be simplified by digital media. The software can be expanded to include role-based ticket and inbox systems so that the workflow can be completely digital.

4.3 Online Questionnaire with Customers

In addition to the interviews just mentioned, the results of the online survey were analyzed in detail (all results with $p < .05$ are shown as statistically significant). In the first step, negatively coded items were undone. Within the measurements, sum values and necessary calculations were formed according to the corresponding specifications.

In principle, it was not relevant for the conduct of the study whether female, male, or diverse persons participated. The age of the test persons was also irrelevant. Nevertheless, it can be stated that with the number of 58 women out of a total of 101 participants and 43 men, a broad spectrum of genders was reached and therefore all generated results are representative.

The average participant in the survey is 28.64 years old and insured by the AOK (42.6%), and has no supplementary dental insurance. The participant goes to the dentist 1.6 times a year and finds the processes in the dental practice and the cooperation between health insurance and dental practice relatively simple. In addition, the average participant generally finds digitalization very important and uses it in everyday life.

A total of 26 health insurance companies were counted, of which 2 account for the majority with 60.4% (AOK: 42.6%, Techniker Krankenkasse 17.8%). Otherwise, a large number of small health insurance companies such as Barmer GEK, IKK, Allianz, DAK-Gesundheit, DaBeKa were mentioned.

Of all participants, 18 had private and 83 statutory insurance, which corresponds to a total of 82.2%. It should be noted that in the case of privately insured persons, there is no need for cooperation between the practice and the health insurance company, as the latter must handle the billing itself. On average, there is a very small difference between the assessment of the simplicity of the procedures in the dental practice and the simplicity of these procedures in the cooperation with the health insurance companies in the case of privately and legally insured persons. The concerns expressed by the participants relate to cybersecurity, transparency, and cooperation. The following table shows all relevant correlations and their significance in terms of how customers perceive process optimization in dental practice.

There is a significant connection between the feeling of simplicity of the processes as a patient in the dental practice and the feeling of cooperation between health insurance companies and dentists ($r(101) = .41$; $p = .00$). The general perception of the importance of digitization in everyday life also influences the perception of the sense of digitalization in dental practices ($r(101) = .52$; $p = .00$). In addition, the general perception of digitization also influences the importance of cooperation between practices and insurance companies ($r(101) = .32$; $p = .001$). The current degree of digitization in dental practices is perceived as well as the degree of cooperation between dentists and health insurance companies ($r(101) = .48$; $p = .00$). Those who consider digitization in dental practices to be useful also find it useful in the cooperation between health insurance companies and practices ($r(101) = .38$; $p = .00$). People who find digitization important also use it in everyday life ($r(101) = .49$; $p = .00$). The described and other significant findings are summarized in Table 3.

Table 3. Summary of the significant findings of the online survey

Expression 1	Expression 2	r (101)	P
The simplicity of the processes as a patient in the dental practice	Cooperation between health insurance companies and dentists	.41**	.000
The general perception of the importance of digitization in everyday life	the perception of the sense of digitalization in dental practices	.52**	.000
The general perception of digitization	Importance of cooperation between practices and insurance companies	.32**	.001
The current degree of digitization in dental practices	Degree of cooperation between dentists and health insurance companies	.48**	.000
The use of digitalization in dental practices	Importance of the digitalization of cooperation between dental practices and insurance companies	.38**	.00
Digitization in everyday life is important	Use of digitization	.49**	.00

* The correlation is significant at the 0.05 level (two-sided)
** The correlation is significant at the 0.01 level (two-sided)

5   Discussion

In the following, the presented results are discussed. Digitization in the healthcare sector is becoming increasingly relevant for all parties involved. This is shown by the results collected by health insurance companies, dentists, and patients. Each of these target groups considers the expansion of digitization and general process optimization in the dental sector to be target-oriented.

On the part of health insurance companies, this affects both the increased digitalization and automation of their internal processes and the cooperation with dentists. This is reflected in the various projects on which the health insurance companies are working. A large number of projects concern the general digitalization of internal approval and billing processes, but also the digitalization of the cooperation with the KZV, dentists, and the insured. The future automatic transmission of authorization from the health insurance company to the dentist carries the risk of jeopardizing the sovereignty of the patient. The authorization should always be transmitted via the patient to the dentist. An automated process should be designed accordingly.

There are different degrees of digitization among dentists. This is probably related to the size and entrepreneurial competence of the practices. In particular, the competence of the management to correctly interact with the interfaces to other companies and to recognize the limits and interfaces of processes is a key factor [25].

The digital transformation of processes is associated with major barriers and obstacles. First of all, additional efforts are required to convert to and familiarize themselves with the new technology. The introduction of standard software is only partially possible.

The software must be adapted to the individual needs of a particular practice. There are also efforts to familiarize dental staff, dentists, and customers with digitization. For the dental staff, the changeover to digital solutions means that, in addition to familiarization, permanent training and troubleshooting is required. In addition, at the beginning of the changeover, double management of all files is necessary to avoid errors due to duplication of work. For these reasons, digitization is hardly economically viable and profitable for individual practices in the first step.

Despite the many disadvantages and the additional work involved in the changeover from analog to digital, long-term advantages in process optimization and workload reduction are possible. In the long term, dental practices hope to have more time for patient treatment and thus better care. Besides, the practices will benefit in the long term from easier customer information, documentation, and appointment management. They will thus support digitalization in the field of dentistry. Possible starting points for reducing the obstacles and efforts involved in digitization are the exchange of information between the various practices. By creating networks, practices can share knowledge and experience on how to switch over and use the software. In addition to knowledge, cloud-based process management enables them to work together on optimizing and digitizing their processes [11]. This exchange and standardization allow synergy effects to be leveraged.

From the collected results it is clear that there are general interfaces that should be digitized. These interfaces are more generally valid since they also affect other organizations. On the one hand, the digitization of the billing of dental practices, from bank data to tax consultants and tax offices, would make daily work easier. On the other hand, the digitization of the judiciary and its interfaces to dentists would also be a matter of the same importance. Another general wish is the development of video conference portals for larger conferences to enable a more personalized exchange.

Especially for dental practices, various approaches have emerged that could be designed and implemented. For example, the digitalization of the continuing education process, through information sheets and information platforms for patients, would simplify patient education and thus significantly simplify the daily routine of every dentist, since times are becoming shorter and education has already taken place in advance. A further example would be the possible extension of the existing software solutions by a role-based ticket and inbox system, to demonstrate a secure and simple administration of patients, files, and important tasks. An artificial intelligence, which queries all relevant factors, could be a solution for the future but would have to be further developed and include many factors. The technology thus offers a wide range of possibilities. It only needs to be adapted to the respective needs.

In general, all processes that affect the patient are more difficult to automate. The reason for this lies in the treatment plan, which is adapted to the patient. Each treatment plan spans different interfaces and organizations. Thus, each interface affects the flow of information and the timing component of the process. Patient behavior is difficult to predict and schedule into a process in a standardized way. One example of this is the dental information provided to the patient and its legally compliant digital documentation. In principle, all respondents to the online survey support digitization in the dental field and its interfaces.

The Ministry of Health has recognized the opportunities provided by digitization and is driving it forward with legislation. The aim is to force all players in the system to use a uniform digital procedure wherever possible. For example, all dentists must be connected to the TI. Some dental practices have already switched over to other digital technologies, on their own initiative.

Despite the efforts of the German government to create a uniform approach to digitization, there are many small-scale solutions and different approaches. The different perspectives of the various parties inevitably create barriers that make easy digitization difficult. These barriers would have to be disclosed to define a targeted approach to process digitization for all parties. This step is probably the most difficult step for targeted, successful, and patient-centered digitization of the entire dental sector across the different organizations.

In addition, there is generally little know-how in process management. Many potentials are seen in the development of necessary competencies and the correct application of digital process management. For targeted modeling and digitization of the process, a stakeholder analysis is an opportunity to unite the different intentions and perspectives of the interfaces. It is important to permanently include the voice of the patients. A patient-centric approach is essential for achieving this. The response to the TI will show whether it is already sufficiently user-centric or whether it needs to be developed further in this sense.

6 Conclusion and Future Work

This work is subject to some restrictions. For example, the healthcare system in Germany was examined with a focus on dentists. Therefore, no conclusions can be drawn about other healthcare systems. Likewise, the lack of patient insight into the processes in dental practices and their interfaces can lead to distortions. In addition, more interviews should be conducted for a more precise listing of all administrative processes. The number of interviews and the type of actors interviewed should be expanded.

This work can provide a basis for collecting more and deeper information about the individual parties involved and their processes in the future. It is the first step to explore to what extent processes in this sector can be digitized and which processes are most important in this context. It also serves to find out where there are gaps in digitization in the daily routine of dental practices and which daily tasks could be simplified through process optimization.

This thesis aimed to get a first impression of the processes and the possibilities for optimization and automation, as there is generally little research on this topic so far.

For a specific process analysis, more intensive research is necessary. For this purpose, research should specialize in all interfaces and their processes (see Fig. 1). To get a detailed result, each organization involved in the system should be considered separately. Differentiation of the processes between public and private health insurance companies is also useful. This is where the statutory health insurance companies should have the most interfaces since the private health insurance companies only have contact with the patients.

The presented general and dental approaches can be concretized and investigated in further work. The field of dentistry, like many areas of daily life, is undergoing digital change. All affected organizations are trying to optimize and automate processes with the help of digitization. Often, however, they do this without consideration for each other and without involving the other parties involved. The results of the survey and interviews confirm this. They also show different starting points for future process optimization. These optimizations should be used comprehensively and purposefully in future work. In this way, the possibilities of digitalization can be used in the best possible way for dentistry. For an active and goal-oriented digital design of the healthcare system, the starting points shown should be taken up and deepened in future work. Digitization affects us all and should also have an impact on all areas of life. Therefore, dentistry should not stop it and should increasingly rely on the digitalization of analog procedures.

References

1. Marsilio, M., Prenestini, A.: Making it happen: Challenges and transformations in health care processes, people management, and decision-making. Heal. Serv. Manag. Res. 33, 53–54 (2020). https://doi.org/10.1177/0951484820906314
2. Porter, M.E., Lee, T.H.: The strategy that will fix health care. Harv. Bus. Rev. 91, 50–70 (2013)
3. McCullough, J., Economics, E.S.-J.H.: Undefined: Monitoring Technology and Firm Boundaries: Physician–Hospital Integration and Technology Utilization. Elsevier (2010)
4. Buttigieg, S., Dey, P.K., Gauci, D.: Business process management in health care: current challenges and future prospects. Innov. Entrep. Heal. 1 (2016). https://doi.org/10.2147/ieh.s68183
5. de Koning, H., Verver, J.P.S., van den Heuvel, J., Bisgaard, S., Does, R.J.M.M.: Lean six sigma in healthcare. J. Healthc. Qual. 28, 4–11 (2006). https://doi.org/10.1111/j.1945-1474.2006.tb00596.x
6. Müller, R., Rogge-Solti, A.: BPMN for Healthcare Processes (2011)
7. Mens, J., Ahlers, B., van Hattem, B., Ravesteyn, P.: Value-based healthcare through a standardised process management model. ECMLG 2015 Proc. 8 (2015)
8. Rolón, E., Chavira, G., Orozco, J., Soto, J.P.: Towards a framework for evaluating usability of business process models with BPMN in health sector. Procedia Manuf. 3, 5603–5610 (2015). https://doi.org/10.1016/j.promfg.2015.07.748
9. De Ramón Fernández, A., Ruiz Fernández, D., Sabuco García, Y.: Business Process Management for optimizing clinical processes: a systematic literature review. Health Inf. J. (2019). https://doi.org/10.1177/1460458219877092
10. Gastaldi, L., Appio, F.P., Corso, M., Pistorio, A.: Managing the exploration-exploitation paradox in healthcare: three complementary paths to leverage on the digital transformation. Bus. Process Manag. J. 24, 1200–1234 (2018). https://doi.org/10.1108/BPMJ-04-2017-0092
11. Lederer, M., Knapp, J., International, P.S.: Undefined: The digital future has many names—How business process management drives the digital transformation. ieeexplore.ieee.org (2017)
12. Maier, C., Juschkat, T.: Digitization in the German health care system - an analysis of the status quo using the example of the dental sector. Eur. J. Bus. Manag. Res. 5 (2020). https://doi.org/10.24018/ejbmr.2020.5.3.331
13. Gesundheitswesen in Deutschland. https://vbw-zukunftsrat.de/Gesundheit-und-Medizin/Analyse?box=56&box_56=Gesundheitswesen-in-Deutschland. Accessed on 10 Aug 2020
14. Was macht ein angestellter Zahnarzt? https://www.deutscher-zahnarzt-service.de/blog/was-macht-ein-angestellter-zahnarzt. Accessed on 08 Aug 2020
15. KZBV - Kassenzahnärztliche Bundesvereinigung – Startseite. https://www.kzbv.de/. Accessed on 08 Aug 2020

16. Startseite: Bundeszahnärztekammer - Arbeitsgemeinschaft der Deutschen Zahnärztekammern e.V. (BZÄK), https://www.bzaek.de/. Accessed on 08 Aug 2020

17. Aufgaben und Organisation der GKV I BMG. https://www.bundesgesundheitsministerium.de/themen/krankenversicherung/grundprinzipien/aufgaben-und-organisation-der-gkv.html. Accessed on 10 Aug 2020

18. Telematikinfrastruktur. https://www.gematik.de/telematikinfrastruktur/. Accessed on 10 Aug 2020

19. E-Health – Digitalisierung im Gesundheitswesen. https://www.bundesgesundheitsministerium.de/e-health-initiative.html. Accessed on 09 Aug 2020

20. Louise Barriball, K., While, A.: Collecting data using a semi-structured interview: a discussion paper. J. Adv. Nurs. **19**(2), 328–335 (1994). https://doi.org/10.1111/j.1365-2648.1994.tb01088.x

21. McIntosh, M.J., Morse, J.M.: Situating and constructing diversity in semi-structured interviews. Glob. Qual. Nurs. Res. **2** (2015). https://doi.org/10.1177/2333393615597674

22. Flick, U., von Kardorff, E., Steinke, I.: Wolff in Flick et a, pp. 178–183 (2004)

23. Evans, J.R., Mathur, A.: The value of online surveys. Internet Res. **15**, 195–219 (2005). https://doi.org/10.1108/10662240510590360

24. Sue, V., Ritter, L.: Conducting Online Surveys. SAGE Publications, Inc. (2015) https://doi.org/10.4135/9781506335186

25. Caputo, A., Fiorentino, R., Garzella, S.: From the boundaries of management to the management of boundaries: business processes, capabilities and negotiations. Bus. Process Manag. J. **25**, 391–413 (2019). https://doi.org/10.1108/BPMJ-11-2017-0334

Watch This! The Influence of Recommender Systems and Social Factors on the Content Choices of Streaming Video on Demand Consumers

Raphael Weidhaas[1]([✉]), Stephan Schlögl[1], Veikko Halttunen[2], and Teresa Spieß[1]

[1] Management Center Innsbruck, Management, Communication and IT, Innsbruck, Austria
{raphael.weidhaas,stephan.schloegl,teresa.spiess}@mci.edu
[2] Faculty of Information Technology, University of Jyväskylä, Jyväskylä, Finland
veikko.halttunen@jyu.fi

Abstract. Streaming Video-on-demand (SVOD) services are getting increasingly popular. Current research, however, lacks knowledge about consumers' content decision processes and their respective influencing factors. Thus, the work reported on in this paper explores socio-technical interrelations of factors impacting content choices in SVOD, examining the social factors WOM, eWOM and peer mediation, as well as the technological influence of recommender systems. A research model based on the Theory of Reasoned Action and the Technology Acceptance Model was created and tested by an n = 186 study sample. Results show that the quality of a recommender system and not the social mapping functionality is the strongest influencing factor on its perceived usefulness. The influence of the recommender system and the influence of the social factors on the behavioral intention to watch certain content is nearly the same. The strongest social influencing factor was found to be peer mediation.

Keywords: Streaming Video on Demand · Social influence · (e)Word of mouth · Peer mediation · Technology influence · Recommender systems

1 Introduction

Subscription Video on Demand (SVOD) services are booming. A survey by Deloitte[1] showed that 69 % of respondents have subscribed to at least one video streaming provider, a number climbing to 80% in the age group 22-35. SVOD consumers particularly value the possibility to choose from an extensive number of available movies, shows and documentaries without thinking about their individual cost. Consequently, the price for a single content unit is taken out of the selection process, increasing the influence other factors may have on people's consumption choices. While there is previous work investigating content choice behavior in cinema and television (e.g. [1, 2]), only few researchers

---

[1] https://www2.deloitte.com/content/dam/Deloitte/lt/Documents/technology-media-telecommu nications/LT_DI_Digital-media-trends-13th-edition.pdf [accessed: 25.10.2020].

© The Author(s), under exclusive license to Springer Nature Switzerland AG 2021
F. Ahlemann et al. (Eds.): WI 2021, LNISO 47, pp. 738–753, 2021.
https://doi.org/10.1007/978-3-030-86797-3_49

have so far studied the behavior of SVOD consumers (e.g. [3]). Focusing on well-known influencing factors, such as Word of Mouth, electronic Word of Mouth and peer mediation, as well as the role modern recommender systems may play, the work presented in this paper aims to help close this research gap. To do this, the Theory of Reasoned Action [4] and the Technology Acceptance model [5] served as theoretical underpinning for a survey collecting data on people's content choice. The subsequent analysis used structural equation modeling to investigate respective effects. The paper is organized as follows: First, we provide a brief introduction to the influencing factors relevant for the statistical analysis. Next, we proceed with the description of the methodological approach, the data analysis and result discussion. Finally, we reflect on some limitations of the presented work and propose topics for further investigation.

2 Factors Influencing Content Choice

While overall, aspects influencing people's content consumption behavior are certainly manifold, one may subdivide them into social and technical factors. With respect to the former, previous research has shown that informal and non-commercial face-to-face interaction between consumers, i.e. so-called Word of Mouth (WOM), has a significant influence on people's product and service choices [6]. Although this type of communication is usually rather subjective, happening coincidentally in private conversations, and thus difficult to observe [7], it was found that with respect to the field of video consumption both positive (e.g. [8]) as well as negative viewing experiences (e.g. [9]) increase the presence of WOM. It was further shown that high box office revenues, which are usually considered a sign of high quality, may trigger 'me too' behavior [1] and consequently lead to positive WOM [2].

In addition, it may be argued that the continuing popularity of social media platforms and other Internet-based information channels has eased the sharing of people's opinions and experiences. Thus, today we find many different forms of online communication, leading to a great number of opinions that are available at all times, helping content consumers choose [10, p. 1]. With this so-called electronic WOM (eWOM), Marchand et al. [11] highlight product reviews, such as Amazon's customer reviews, and microblogs, such as Twitter, as particularly important types of informal information exchange, and thus influencial for people's choices. Similar to traditional WOM, it was shown that also eWOM (no matter whether it has a positive or negative connotation) preceding movies and during their first week after release, triggers 'imitation behavior' [12]. An empirical analysis of revenue data has furthermore revealed that there seems to be a direct association between the number of pre-release 'Likes' on a movie's Facebook-page and its opening week box office sales [13].

While WOM and eWOM communication are defined as forms of informal communication in non-commercial, and therefore private contexts, they do not necessarily happen with peers; i.e. communication partners may not always stand in a closer relationship to each other. Peer relations emerge from a sense of equality and lead to the reciprocation of behaviors of other peer group members (i.e., peer mediation). This requires the reflection of others' ideas and opinions, which eventually leads to a peer group's mutually constructed world view [14, p. 3]. Discussions about consuchoice of content, leadingto the following med media content are, of course, also part of peer relationships, often leading to pressure situations in cases where content is missing or could not be consumed by parts of the group [15, p. 530]. To this end, Nathanson [14] has shown that in adolescent media use, peer mediation has a higher influence than parent mediation, and that peers with similar academic or social problems may be drawn together by their media consumption patterns. A qualitative long-term study carried out among teenage girls in different US middle schools led to similar results. Most girls in peer groups agreed to watch the same shows, read the same magazines and listen to the same music. Their behavioral patterns, as well as clothing choices, were highly influenced by their choice of media, and very similar within the individual peer groups [16]. While most of these peer mediation studies are carried out with children or teenagers, as peer influences are usually stronger and more important during adolescence [14], we see an increasing demand for the investigation of adult peer groups. Although later in life peers may be less influential with respect to defining one's worldview, they are likely to affect media and content consumption behavior. A recent study has for example pointed to an influence of peer mediation on the attitude towards and consequent use of health apps on mobile phones [17].

2.1 Technical Influence

A recommender system tries to predict the probability for a user to consume or buy a product. In order to do this, the system analyzes usage behavior and presents suggestions to help users find the right content, product or service [18]. In general, recommender systems can be divided into two categories: Content-based systems and collaborative filtering systems. The former focus on previous user behavior, while collaborative filtering systems involve preferences of others in their analytical process. Thus, they try to incorporate the previously mentioned social influencing factors (i.e., WOM, eWOM and peer mediation) in their recommendation decision [19]. The aim is to provide the user with a sense of socialization that never happened [20]. Streaming platforms usually use a mix of content-based and collaborative filtering systems. Additionally, online behavior and browser cookies are consistently tracked and analyzed, while users are logged into their media account (e.g., Netflix [3]). This allows the inclusion of data that was generated even before the account was created (e.g., social media and shopping behavior) [21]. Most literature on recommender systems focuses on technical aspects and improvements [22]. Only few studies try to shed light on the influence these systems have on users' decision processes. Pittman and Eanes [3], for example, found that the amount of available content on streaming platforms leaves too many choices for viewers, impeding rational decision making and leading to unsatisfied outcomes. The use of recommender systems, on the other hand, makes them consume content they would not have consumed otherwise. Another study examined the persuasive nature of recommender systems and found that users tend to rely on the system's recommendation when preceding recommendations were satisfactory [23]. Although this persuasive power may also lead to potential negative psychological effects such as excessive use and addictive behavior (e.g. [24]), it is said that the constant technological improvement of recommender systems makes them ever more efficient in helping users choose desired content. Hosanagar et al. [25], for example, discovered that collaborative filtering lets users widen their interests and find more similarities with others. These similarities may also create more WOM and/or eWOM and thus in turn should be considered as a recurring factor influencing content choice.

2.2 Socio-Technical Interrelations as a Research Gap

The above shows that most research on content choice focuses on single influencing factors. However, it may be argued that content choice is not only influenced by a single factor, but rather by a multitude of factors. And these factors not only influence viewers in their choice, but also themselves reciprocally. That is, the emergence and success of WOM leads to 'imitation behavior', particularly in peer groups [1]. Also, WOM and eWOM communication are difficult to separate, as pure face-to-face WOM is difficult to observe and measure (e.g. [2, 7]). In other words, influencing factors are often examined individually but their synergies are seldom taken into consideration. In addition, most of the extant literature about media content choice is focusing on television or cinema. Choice and decision processes in SVOD, which so heavily pushes the use of recommender systems, is less researched. Also, most literature on recommender systems focuses on technological improvements [22]. While, according to Pittman and Eanes [3], the improvements of these recommender systems will eventually dominate all other influencing factors, it is unlikely that consumers will stop discussing their experiences and impressions via WOM or eWOM. Thus, it seems important to investigate the interrelation between these factors and how they, as a group, eventually influence the consumers' choice of content, leading to the following research question:

To what extent does the mapping of social influencing factors (WOM, eWOM and peer mediation), imitated by recommender systems, affect the content choice of subscription video-on-demand users?

3 Methodology

Given that the above stated research question investigates a socio-technical problem space, we require a research model which integrates social/personal, as well as technical influencing factors. To this end, the Theory of Reasoned Action (TRA) aims to explain one's behavior based on attitudinal and social factors [4]. That is, an individual's attitude towards a specific behavior and its subjective norms determine the behavioral intention which, eventually, leads to the actual behavior. According to this framework, the attitude towards a specific behavior is influenced by the beliefs about the outcome of said behavior and the evaluations of this outcome [26]. The subjective norms are influenced by normative beliefs about the behavior and the motivation to comply with these norms [14]. Thus, the TRA may serve as a solid basis for our socio-technical research model as it combines both attitudinal and social factors. Social factors are reflected by one's subjective norms, formed by normative beliefs and the motivation to comply with those beliefs. These normative beliefs are a standard that is set by a person's social environment and thus may be represented by the previously discussed social influencing factors WOM, eWOM and peer mediation. The attitudinal factors, on the other hand, are described as one's attitude towards a specific behavior. In our case, attitude towards the behavior of watching content recommended by a streaming platform's recommender system. As this does not entirely align with the TRA's representation of an attitude towards a behavior, given that the behavior is influenced by a technology, we need to further expand our model. To this end, Davis [5] developed the so-called Technology Acceptance Model (TAM), which states that a user's intention to use a technological system is determined by its perceived usefulness, its perceived ease of use, and the user's attitude towards using the system. Both perceived usefulness and perceived ease of use are further influenced by external factors. While previous work has shown that TAM may be used to study the acceptance of recommender systems (e.g. [27]), it should be highlighted that here the attitude towards use serves as the counterpart to the attitude towards behavior in TRA, eventually reflecting the acceptance of using the technology. This is supported by the fact that TAM in its original form neglects subjective norms and focuses entirely on the user as a single person – an aspect which was often criticized (e.g. [28]). Hence, similar to more recent TAM studies (e.g. [29]), we find it necessary to also include these social constructs and consequent influence on the use of the technology, eventually leading to our proposed research model illustrated in Fig. 1.

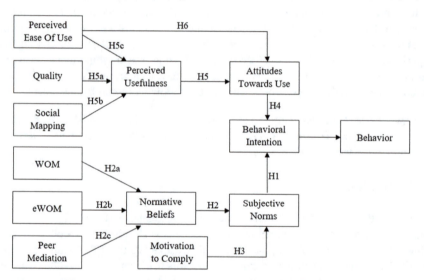

Fig. 1. Proposed research model derived from TAM and TRA

4   Hypotheses

Based on the research model described above, we developed a set of 13 hypotheses, focusing on the influence social and technological factors have on consumers' content choice in SVOD. The goal was to better understand how the intention to watch certain content is formed. The analysis thus compares the influences of an individual's social environment and the influences of a technology which tries to imitate this social environment, i.e. the recommender system (cf. Table 1).

5   Research Model and Survey Design

In accordance with the above stated hypotheses we developed a 44-item questionnairee[2]. The first questionnaire section asked participants about the type, number and frequency of use, connected to certain streaming services (Q01-03). Next, we investigated people's intention to consume streaming content in general and after hearing about it (Q04-05). Subsequently, the influence of the social environment was measured with 14 question-naire items based on the TRA [4]. The first three of these items (Q06-08) assessed the respondents' subjective norms, inspired by the work of Chin et al. [30]. Individual nor-mative beliefs were reflected by items connected to the social influencing factors WOM, eWOM and peer mediation. This is, two WOM items (Q09-10) evaluated individuals' likeliness to watch a movie or show after positive [2] as well as negative WOM com-munication [8, 9]. Three eWOM items (Q11-13) were phrased similarly to the WOM items, but modified so as to reflect a social media context [12, 13]. A fourth eWOM item (Q14) assessed the respondents interest to actively search for user generated informa-tion on cinematic rating platforms, such as IMDB or Rotten Tomatoes [11]. Next, peer mediation was assessed based on four items (Q15-18) which evaluated the respondents in conversing about movies and shows with their peers [14, 31]. Finally, the last item of this block (Q19) assessed the motivation with which people would comply with these subjective norms [4].

Next, a block of 21 question items was used to measure the influence of recommender systems. This question set was mainly based on the TAM literature by Davis [5]. The first three items (Q20-22) evaluated the respondents' attitudes towards recommender systems, where the questions were modified according to the work of Pittman and Eanes [3]. Next, we used four items (Q23-26) from a previous TAM study conducted by Armentano and Christensen [27] assessing the overall perceived usefulness of a recommender system and four items (Q27-30) about its perceived quality with respect to diversity, novelty and match with people's interests [32]. Following, we included items on the recommender systems' mapping of social influencing factors (Q31-36). Here, the items which were used to evaluate the normative beliefs (WOM, eWOM and peer mediation) were aligned with the functionality of recommender systems. These items were taken from the original TAM by Davis [5] and the already mentioned work by Armentano and Christensen [27]. The block concluded with four items inspired by Armentano and Christensen [27], Pu et al. [32] and the System Usability Scale [33], assessing perceived ease of use (Q37-40). The last four questionnaire items of the survey (Q41-44) collected demographic data on age, gender, current occupation and country of origin.

Building upon previous work [34], our target group of the questionnaire was focus-ing on university students. Young people between the age of 22 and 35 are considered as the most regular users of streaming services[3]. Therefore, the questionnaire was dis-tributed online via different social media channels (e.g. Facebook, LinkedIn, Instagram) as well as through direct contact in Universities in three European countries, i.e. Austria, Finland and Germany (note: countries were determined by the origins of the research

---

[2] https://doi.org/10.13140/RG.2.2.26579.60966.

[3] https://www2.deloitte.com/content/dam/Deloitte/lt/Documents/technology-media-telecommu nications/LT_DI_Digital-media-trends-13th-edition.pdf [accessed: 25.10.2020].

team members). In order to translate the English source questionnaire into German and Finnish the translation-back-translation procedure was applied [35, p. 39]. In addition, we conducted pre-tests in all three of the countries. Copies of the final questionnaire in English and German are available here: (anonymized). They were launched in May 2019 and stayed available for a timeframe of 20 days, during which a total of 253 people participated, 212 of whom completed all questions. Incomplete questionnaires were excluded from further analysis.

Table 1. Hypotheses and their Evaluation

1	Individuals' subjective norms regarding the choice of content towatch will be positively related to their intention to watch contenton SVOD platforms	D	Influence 24.0% (t-value = 2.244)
2	Individuals' normative beliefs regarding the choice of content to watch will be positively related to their subjective norms	D	Influence 38.5% (t-value = 4.731)
2a	eWOM in individuals' social environment will be positively related to their normative beliefs regarding the choice of content to watch	–	Non-significant Influence 2.4% (t-value = 0.153)
2b	eWOM in individuals' online environment will be positivelyrelated to their normative beliefs regarding the choice of contentto watch	D	Influence 38.9% (t-value = 2.570)
2c	Peer mediation in individuals' social environment will bepositively related to their normative beliefs regarding the choice of content to watch	D	Influence 74.8% (t-value = 6.021) Strongest Influence
3	Individuals' motivation to comply to subjective norms about content on SVOD platforms will be positively related to their subjective norms regarding the choice of content to watch	D	Influence 19.2% (t-value = 2.155)
4	Individuals' attitude towards the usage of recommender systemsr egarding the choice of content to watch will be positively related to their intentions to watch content on SVOD platforms	D	Influence 20.3% (t-value = 2.194)

(continued)

Table 1. (*continued*)

5	Individuals' perceived usefulness of recommender systems willbe positively related to their attitude towards the usage of recommender systems	D	Influence 49.8% (t-value = 8.602)
5a	A recommender system's perceived quality will be positively related to its perceived usefulness	D	Influence 67.7% (t-value = 14.823)
5b	A recommender system's mapping of social influencing factors will be positively related to its perceived usefulness	D	Influence 16.8% (t-value = 3.432)
5c	A recommender system's perceived ease of use will be positively related to its perceived usefulness	–	Non-Significant Influence 4.6% (t-value = 1.050)
6	Individuals' perceived ease of use of recommender systems willbe positively related to their attitude towards the usage of recommender systems	–	Non-significant Influence 7.2% (t-value = 0.812)
7	Individual's subjective norms regarding the choice of content tocontent on SVOD platforms, than their attitudes towards the use f recommender systems	D	Influence of sub norms (24.0%) higher than influence of att. towards use (20.3%)

6 Results

The statistical analyses on the questionnaire data were conducted using R, R-Studio and SmartPLS 3.0 for structural equation modeling (SEM). In order to compute accurate SEM results, a minimum sample size of ten times the number of structural paths in a model is required [36, p. 47]. As our research model has twelve structural paths and we received 186 complete and applicable responses (note: 26 of the complete 212 responses had to be excluded from analysis as participants declared to not use video streaming services), the required minimum of 120 data sets was fulfilled, for which result accuracy may be assumed. Also, we were able to set the confidence level to 95%, the minimum R^2 level to 0:10 and the statistical power to 80%. Table 2 provides some descriptive summary of the collected data.

Table 2. Descriptive statistics

Age	<20 years	2	1.08%
	20 to 29 years	149	80.11%
	30 to 39 years	24	12.90%
	>40	11	5.91%
Occupation	In School	3	1.61%
	Training/Apprenticeship	3	1.61%
	University Student	121	65.05%
	Employee	47	25.27%
	Civil Servant	3	1.61%
	Self-Employed	3	1.61%
	Unemployed/Seeking	2	1.08%
	Others	4	2.15%
Nationality	Austria	66	35.48%
	Germany	62	33.33%
	Finland	43	23.12%
	Others	15	8.06%

6.1   Measurement Model

With respect to the measurement model, latent variables were measured in a reflective manner [36, p. 38]. Only the normative beliefs construct differs from the rest of the latent variables as it is defined by three other latent variables (i.e. WOM, eWOM and peer mediation) for which a different assessment was required. Becker, Klein, & Wetzels [37] suggest a reflective-formative approach, since the underlying latent constructs are not similar to each other, but belong to the same higher concept. Figure 2 illustrates the resulting measurement model.

Investigating the resulting relations, it can be seen that R^2 for the target endogenous variable BEH_INT is 15:2%, which means that the two latent variables SUB_NORMS and ATT_USE explain 15:2% of the variance of BEH_INT. Furthermore, the constructs NORM_BELIEFS and MOTIV_COMPLY explain 27:4% of the variance of SUBJ_NORMS and the R^2 value of the reflective-formative concept NORM_BELIEFS is at 99:3%, showing that the reflective concepts WOM, EWOM and PEERS explain 99:3% of the variance of NORM_BELIEFS. Also, the variance of ATT_USE is explained by the PERC_USEF and PERC_EASE, with an R2 value of 0:277. Finally, PERC_USEF has an R2 value of 61:3%, which means that the latent variables QUALITY, SOCIAL_MAP and PERC_EASE explain 61; 3% of its variance.

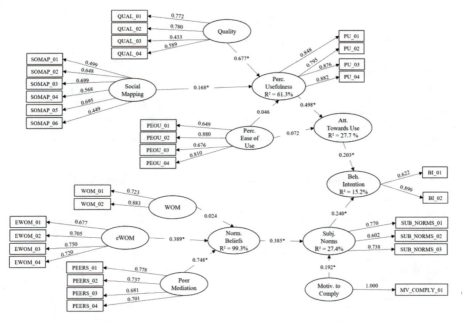

Fig. 2. SEM Results (* = significant with p < 0.05)

6.2 Inner Model Path Coefficient Sizes and Significance

The inner path coefficients of the model explain the effect strength between latent constructs. Usually, effects close to 0 are not significant. In order to validate significance, t-values were calculated through a bootstrapping algorithm (5000 sub-samples). Table 3 lists the respective results. As the significance level was set to 5%, t-values above 1:96 define a significant relationship [36].

Table 3. Inner model path coefficient sizes and significance

	Path coefficient	t-value
ATT_USE - BEH_INT	0.203	2.194
EWOM - NORM_BELIEFS	0.389	2.570
MOTIV_COMPLY - SUBJ_NORMS	0.192	2.155
NORM_BELIEFS - SUBJ_NORMS	0.385	4.731
PEERS - NORM_BELIEFS	0.748	6.021
PERC_EASE - ATT_USE	0.072	0.812
PERC_EASE - PERC_USEF	0.046	1.050
PERC_USEF - ATT_USE	0.498	8.602

(*continued*)

Table 3. (*continued*)

	Path coefficient	t-value
QUALITY - PERC_USEF	0.677	14.823
SOCIAL_MAP - PERC_USEF	0.168	3.432
SUBJ_NORMS - BEH_INT	0.240	2.244
WOM - NORM_BELIEFS	0.024	0.153

Table 4. Lower outer loadings

Measure	Latent Construct	Outer Loading
BI_01	BEH_INT	0.622
SUB_NORMS_02	SUBJ_NORMS	0.602
EWOM_01	EWOM	0.677
PEERS_03	PEERS	0.681
QUAL_03	QUALITY	0.433
SOMAP_01	SOCIAL_MAP	0.499
SOMAP_02	SOCIAL_MAP	0.648
SOMAP_03	SOCIAL_MAP	0.699
SOMAP_04	SOCIAL_MAP	0.568
SOMAP_05	SOCIAL_MAP	0.695
SOMAP_06	SOCIAL_MAP	0.449
PEOU_01	PERC_EASE	0.649
PEOU_03	PERC_EASE	0.676

Table 5. AVE

Latent Variable	AVE
ATT_USE	0.713
BEH_INT	0.590
EWOM	0.509
PEERS	0.526
PERC_EASE	0.577
PERC_USEF	0.724
QUALITY	0.435 ara>
SOCIAL_MAP	0.361
SUBJ_NORMS	0.500
WOM	0.651

6.3 Convergent Validity

The convergent validity explains the extent to which a concept's indicator correlates positively with the other indicators of the same concept. Two measures are commonly used to evaluate the convergent validity: The outer model loadings and the average variance extracted (AVE) [36]. The outer loadings are the relationships between reflective constructs and their indicator variables. They show how good a measure reflects the actual latent construct. Hair et al. [36] recommend values of 0.7 or higher for reliable indicators. However, they argue that it is common to obtain weaker indicators in social science studies, especially with newly developed scales. Given the exploratory nature of our study, some of our questionnaire items did not have a validated research background. Thus, indicator loadings between 0.4 and 0.7 should be accepted. Additionally, the bootstrapping procedure highlighted statistical significance for all outer loadings. Table 4 shows the indicators with outer loadings between 0.4 and 0.7.

The lower outer loadings of BI_01 and SUBJ_NORMS_02 are rather unexpected, since both constructs are derived from the TRA standard items by Fishbein and Ajzen [4]. Additionally, SUB_NORMS_02 is the exact counterpart to SUB_NORMS_01. The lower outer loadings may be explained by questionnaire items which were either derived from different research papers, and thus have no similar validated concept or lack a clearly validated research background. Especially the measures of SOMAP_01-06 were newly developed from extant literature. However, since there are no similar studies available and this research is exploratory, it was decided to keep all indicators in the construct. Such should not only provide initial data, but also appeal to future research to develop novel research constructs, especially with respect to the social mapping context. As a second measure one should consider the Average Variance Extracted (AVE), which is the mean of the squared loadings of the indicators associated to a certain latent construct. An AVE of 0.5 or higher shows that the construct explains more than half of its indicator's variance. Therefore, AVE below 0.5 indicates that more variance remains on the (measurement) error than on the construct [36]. Table 5 shows the AVE of our constructs. Single item constructs have been removed, since AVE is irrelevant for them. For the constructs QUALITY and SOMAP the AVE is smaller than 0.5, while all the other concepts seem rather stable, for which one may argue that the lower outer loading of some measures seems compensated in the whole picture. Additionally, the stop criterion was reached after 64 of 300 iterations of the PLS algorithm, which further underlines the reliability of the values [38].

6.4   Internal Consistency Reliability

In order to assess the internal consistency reliability of a PLS-SEM model, two measures are recommended. The first measure is Cronbach's α, which represents the reliability through computing the intercorrelations of the observed indicator variables. In general, a Cronbach α of 0.7 or higher is considered satisfactory. However, in exploratory research such as ours, values between 0.6 and 0.7 may be accepted as well. Cronbach's α is considered a rather conservative approach, since it tends to underestimate the internal consistency reliability [36, p. 135]. Additionally, Cortina [39] argues that it is very dependent on the number of measured items, resulting in lower values with smaller item numbers. The results should thus be treated cautiously and the composite reliability should be observed as an additional verification. This measure takes the different outer loadings into account and can be examined in the same way as Cronbach's α. Values above 0.95 are not desired, since it would imply that the indicators of a certain construct are redundant. The composite reliability is known to overestimate the values, and therefore it is always recommended to observe both values [36, p. 136]. Table 6 shows our Cronbach α values as well as the composite reliability of the model's underlying latent constructs. Single item constructs were again removed, as the measures are not applicable for them. It can be seen that constructs with low Cronbach α measures have rather low values, but in contrast, acceptable or high composite reliability values. The comparison of both show the internal consistency reliability of the underlying latent constructs.

6.5 Discriminant Validity

The discriminant validity evaluates how constructs are distinct to each other; i.e. whether they are unique and not covered by other constructs in the model. It is recommended to assess the discriminant validity with two measures. The first approach is to examine the cross-loadings, which means to compare any construct outer loadings with their cross loadings with other constructs. The outer loadings of a construct should always be higher than its cross loadings [36, p. 138]. To this end, our data did not show any problematic cross-loadings. The second measure of discriminant validity is the Fornell-Larcker Criterion. This method compares the square roots of the AVE values with the correlations of latent variables. Each construct AVE square root should be higher than its correlations with any other constructs [36, p. 139]. Results show one problematic value, i.e. QUALITY – PERC_USEF. Since it is only one problematic case, which does not appear in the cross-loadings, it was decided to not remove any indicators. The problematic value may be explained by the rather similar wordings of the PU and QUAL questions; e.g. PU_01 "I think the movies and shows that are suggested to me are attractive" and QUAL_02 "The recommended movies or shows that I already knew before (e.g. from the cinema or television) are usually movies that I like". Given the rather complex distinction between the concepts quality and usefulness, especially in an entertainment context, the wordings are quite similar.

Table 6. Cronbach's α and composite reliability

Construct	Cronbach's α	Composite reliability
ATT_USE	0.658	0.829
BEH_INT	0.329	0.736
EWOM	0.679	0.806
PEERS	0.698	0.816
PERC_EASE	0.750	0.843
PERC_USEF	0.873	0.913
QUALITY	0.561	0.745
SOCIAL_MAP	0.662	0.767
SUBJ_NORMS	0.522	0.748
WOM	0.478	0.787

7 Conclusions, Limitations and Potential Future Research

The objective of the presented work was to examine the influences of recommender systems and social influencing factors on consumers' SVOD content choices. Especially the recommender systems functionality that tries to map these social influencing factors was examined. This was approached by examining the influence of the social mapping functionality on consumers' perceived usefulness of a recommender system. Results show that the social mapping functionality has a moderate influence on the perceived usefulness. The strongest influence derived from the recommender system's quality. The attitude towards the use of a recommender system and the subjective norms had a relatively similar moderate influence on the behavioral intention. This shows that both factors are important and considerable. The strongest influencing factor on the formation of subjective norms seems to be peer mediation. This supports the assumption that people rely highly on the opinion of close friends and family members regarding their content choices. Surprisingly, WOM communication had no significant influence on normative beliefs at all. Since the influence of WOM on movie choices is reported by a wide range of studies, this result may be caused by a mistake in the research design. Perceived ease of use had neither a significant influence on the perceived usefulness, nor on the attitude towards use. The reasons for this are quite obvious, since there is practically no complexity in using a video streaming platform. This raises the question whether the concept of perceived ease of use may not become obsolete in leisure contexts, where user interfaces are fairly simple to use. Regarding subjective norm, it can be underlined that the opinion and influence of peers is the most trusted factor in content choice. Regarding the attitude towards the usage of a recommender system, it is the quality of the system's functionality, followed by the social mapping functionality, which are most influential.

With respect to the limitations of our work, it was already highlighted that some question blocks lacked validity, as they were derived from different sources. Especially the examination of social mapping resulted in a low validity. Additionally, our approach to combine two research frameworks was new and not previously validated. However, as already mentioned before, most literature studies recommender systems from a technological point of view. There is a lack of critical analysis of their actual influences and therefore, our approach was meant to be rather exploratory. Furthermore, despite all methodical limitations, the model gained solid results and has shown reliability and validity. It is a first step to enable and support further research. To this end, as recommender systems and social factors are not alone influencing the content choice of video streaming users, future research should examine different factors, such as for example 'binge behavior'. Also, further studies aiming to validate our research model are necessary, especially regarding the influences of the recommender system's social mapping functionalities.

It should also be highlighted that the frameworks used as a basis for our research model were developed for other contexts. For example, TAM was developed for business contexts and thus does neither account for today's omnipresence of social media nor other social influence factors [28]. Our attempt to overcome this lack by pairing the model with the TRA may be seen as a first step but requires additional exploration and validation.

In times of the COVID-19 pandemic, it might also be argued that streaming behaviour changes in the context of personal contact restriction. Since peer mediation and personal communication are not very apparent in this setting, there could be a stronger shift to influences from recommender systems and online communication. Future studies are needed to shed light on these special circumstances and their impact on future behavior after the pandemic.

References

1. Kim, E., Kim, S.: Online movie success in sequential markets: determinants of video-on-demand film success in Korea. Telematics Inform. **34**(7), 987–995 (2017)
2. Liu, Y.: Word of mouth for movies: its dynamics and impact on box office revenue. J. Mark. **70**(3), 74–89 (2006)
3. Pittman, M., Eanes, R.S.: Streaming media, algorithmic efficiency, and the illusion of control. In: MacDougal, R. (ed.) Communication and Control: Tools, Systems, and New Dimensions, pp. 133–145 (2015)
4. Fishbein, M., Ajzen, I.: Belief, attitude, intention, and behavior: an introduction to theory and research (1975)
5. Davis, F.D.: Perceived usefulness, perceived ease of use, and user acceptance of information technology. MIS Q. 319–340 (1989)
6. Westbrook, R.A.: Product/consumption-based affective responses and postpurchase processes. J. Mark. Res. **24**(3), 258–270 (1987)
7. Godes, D., Mayzlin, D.: Using online conversations to study word-of-mouth communication. Mark. Sci. **23**(4), 545–560 (2004)
8. Mishra, P., Bakshi, M., Singh, R.: Impact of consumption emotions on wom in movie consumption: Empirical evidence from emerging markets. Australasian Mark. J. **24**(1), 59–67 (2016)
9. Ladhari, R.: The effect of consumption emotions on satisfaction and word-of-mouth communications. Psychol. Mark. **24**(12), 1085–1108 (2007)
10. Hennig-Thurau, T., Gwinner, K.P., Walsh, G., Gremler, D.D.: Electronic word-of- mouth via consumer-opinion platforms: what motivates consumers to articulate themselves on the internet? J. Interact. Mark. **18**(1), 38–52 (2004)
11. Marchand, A., Hennig-Thurau, T., Wiertz, C.: Not all digital word of mouth is created equal: Understanding the respective impact of consumer reviews and microblogs on new product success. Int. J. Res. Mark. **34**(2), 336–354 (2017)
12. Wang, F., Zhang, Y., Li, X., Zhu, H.: Why do moviegoers go to the theater? the role of prerelease media publicity and online word of mouth in driving movie going behavior. J. Interact. Advert. **11**(1), 50–62 (2010)
13. Ding, C., Cheng, H.K., Duan, Y., Jin, Y.: The power of the "like" button: the impact of social media on box office. Decis. Support Syst. **94**, 77–84 (2017)
14. Nathanson, A.I.: Parents versus peers: exploring the significance of peer mediation of antisocial television. Commun. Res. **28**(3), 251–274 (2001)
15. Suess, D., Suoninen, A., Garitaonandia, C., Juaristi, P., Koikkalainen, R., Oleaga, J.A.: Media use and the relationships of children and teenagers with their peer groups: a study of finnish, spanish and swiss cases. Eur. J. Commun. **13**(4), 521–538 (1998)
16. Durham, M.G.: Girls, media, and the negotiation of sexuality: a study of race, class, and gender in adolescent peer groups. J. Mass Commun. Q. **76**(2), 193–216 (1999)
17. Kwon, M.W., Mun, K., Lee, J.K., McLeod, D.M., D'Angelo, J.: Is mobile health all peer pressure? the influence of mass media exposure on the motivation to use mobile health apps. Convergence **23**(6), 565–586 (2017)
18. Park, D.H., Kim, H.K., Choi, I.Y., Kim, J.K.: A literature review and classification of recommender systems research. Expert Syst. Appl. **39**(11), 10059–10072 (2012)
19. Wang, Y.Y., Luse, A., Townsend, A.M., Mennecke, B.E.: Understanding the moderating roles of types of recommender systems and products on customer behavioral intention to use recommender systems. Inf. Syst. e-Bus. Manage. **13**(4), 769–799 (2015)
20. Pittman, M., Sheehan, K.: Sprinting a media marathon: Uses and gratifications of binge-watching television through netflix. First Monday **20**(10) (2015)

21. Martin, F.J., Donaldson, J., Ashenfelter, A., Torrens, M., Hangartner, R.: The big promise of recommender systems. AI Mag. **32**(3), 19–27 (2011)
22. Alharthi, H., Inkpen, D., Szpakowicz, S.: A survey of book recommender systems. J. Intell. Inf. Syst. **51**(1), 139–160 (2017). https://doi.org/10.1007/s10844-017-0489-9
23. Nanou, T., Lekakos, G., Fouskas, K.: The effects of recommendations' presentation on persuasion and satisfaction in a movie recommender system. Multimedia Syst. **16**(4–5), 219–230 (2010)
24. Hasan, M.R., Jha, A.K., Liu, Y.: Excessive use of online video streaming services: impact of recommender system use, psychological factors, and motives. Comput. Hum. Behav. **80**, 220–228 (2018)
25. Hosanagar, K., Fleder, D., Lee, D., Buja, A.: Will the global village fracture into tribes? recommender systems and their effects on consumer fragmentation. Manage. Sci. **60**(4), 805–823 (2013)
26. Kim, S., Lee, J., Yoon, D.: Norms in social media: the application of theory of reasoned action and personal norms in predicting interactions with Facebook page like ads. Commun. Res. Rep. **32**(4), 322–331 (2015)
27. Armentano, M.G., Christensen, I., Schiaffino, S.: Applying the technology acceptance model to evaluation of recommender systems. Polibits **51**, 73–79 (2015)
28. Bagozzi, R.P.: The legacy of the technology acceptance model and a proposal for a paradigm shift. J. Assoc. Inf. Syst. **8**(4), 3 (2007)
29. Youn, S.y., Lee, K.H.: Proposing value-based technology acceptance model: testing on paid mobile media service. Fash. Text. **6**(1), 13 (2019)
30. Chin, C.Y., Lu, H.P., Wu, C.M.: Facebook users' motivation for clicking the "like" button. Soc. Behav. Person.: Int. J. **43**(4), 579–592 (2015)
31. Hu, M., Zhang, M., Wang, Y.: Why do audiences choose to keep watching on live video streaming platforms? an explanation of dual identification framework. Comput. Hum. Behav. **75**, 594–606 (2017)
32. Pu, P., Chen, L., Hu, R.: A user-centric evaluation framework for recommender systems. In: Proceedings of the Fifth ACM Conference on Recommender Systems, pp. 157–164. ACM (2011)
33. Brooke, J., et al.: Sus-a quick and dirty usability scale. Usability Eval. Indust. **189**(194), 4–7 (1996)
34. Halttunen, V., Schlögl, S., Weidhaas, R.: Digital content consumption: a finnish-Austrian cross-country analysis. In: Proceeding of the MCIS Mediterranean Conference on Information Systems (2019)
35. Van de Vijver, F.J., Leung, K., Leung, K.: Methods and Data Analysis for Cross-Cultural Research, vol. 1. Sage (1997)
36. Hair Jr., J.F., Hult, G.T.M., Ringle, C., Sarstedt, M.: A Primer on Partial Least Squares Structural Equation Modeling (PLS-SEM). Sage publications (2016)
37. Becker, J.M., Klein, K., Wetzels, M.: Hierarchical latent variable models in PLS-SEM: Guidelines for using reflective-formative type models. Long Range Plan. **45**, 359–394 (10 2012)
38. Wong, K.K.K.: Partial least squares structural equation modeling (PLS-SEM) techniques using smartpls. Mark. Bull. **24**(1), 1–32 (2013)
39. Cortina, J.M.: What is coefficient alpha? an examination of theory and applications. J. Appl. Psychol. **78**(1), 98 (1993)

Predicting Hourly Bitcoin Prices Based on Long Short-Term Memory Neural Networks

Maximilian Schulte[(✉)] and Mathias Eggert

Department of Economics, Fachhochschule Aachen, Aachen, Germany
maxschulte@mailbox.org, eggert@fh-aachen.de

Abstract. Bitcoin is a cryptocurrency and is considered a high-risk asset class whose price changes are difficult to predict. Current research focusses on daily price movements with a limited number of predictors. The paper at hand aims at identifying measurable indicators for Bitcoin price movements and the development of a suitable forecasting model for hourly changes. The paper provides three research contributions. First, a set of significant indicators for predicting the Bitcoin price is identified. Second, the results of a trained Long Short-term Memory (LSTM) neural network that predicts price changes on an hourly basis is presented and compared with other algorithms. Third, the results foster discussions of the applicability of neural nets for stock price predictions. In total, 47 input features for a period of over 10 months could be retrieved to train a neural net that predicts the Bitcoin price movements with an error rate of 3.52%.

Keywords: Bitcoin · Neural nets · LSTM · Data analysis · Price prediction

1 Introduction

In the past few years, the concept of cryptocurrencies made its way to the public with an open debate whether digital, decentralized currencies should be taken seriously or not. While many perceive Bitcoin and other cryptocurrencies as a pure speculative bubble, others see similarities with the early age of the internet, because of its underlying technology called Blockchain [1]. Certainly, Bitcoin is a highly volatile asset class. Solely in 2017, the price of Bitcoin rose by 2000% from under $1.000 in January, to almost $20.000 by the end of the year. In the following months of 2018, the price plummeted rapidly to under $7.000 in early February [1]. In December 2020, Bitcoin reached a new high of $23.000 and a renewed rapid increase is indicated[1]. These Bitcoin price changes are hard to predict due to the underlying high volatility. The general objective of this paper is to address this difficult task. Several researchers worked on predicting Bitcoin price changes based on twitter sentiments and blockchain information [e.g., 2, 3]. The majority of them focuses on Support Vector Machine (SVM) and regression models. So far, only Guo et. Al. [4] and Mohanty et al. [5] present results of an advanced neural network with a variety of input features as a predictive model for Bitcoin price changes. Against this background, the paper at hand answers the following research questions:

---

[1] https://www.nytimes.com/2020/11/30/technology/bitcoin-record-price.html.

F. Ahlemann et al. (Eds.): WI 2021, LNISO 47, pp. 754–769, 2021.
https://doi.org/10.1007/978-3-030-86797-3_50

- What are significant indicators of Bitcoin price performance? (RQ1)
- How applicable are neural networks for predicting hourly Bitcoin prices? (RQ2)

The structure of the paper at hand is as follows. First, we provide related work on neural nets and a literature review about research works on the prediction of bitcoin price movements. Section 3 comprises the research design and a detailed description of the data collection, adjustment, and analysis. In Sect. 4, we present the results of our analysis, which contains the predictors found and the performance of the developed neural net. Section 5 contains the discussion of the results. The paper ends with a summary and an outlook on further research in the field of bitcoin price prediction.

2 Preliminary Study on Bitcoin Price Prediction

At the time of writing this paper, 26 research works investigating Bitcoin prediction models were found by using the IEEE Xplore Digital Library, the AIS eLibrary (AISEL), Google Scholar and the following search terms: *prediction, predict, bitcoin, stock market, time-series, regression, neural net, recurrent neural net, machine learning and LSTM*. We classify these papers by applying two dimensions: input features and applied analysis method. The results are depicted in Fig. 1. Historical data on price or trade volumes as basic input parameters in time-series forecasting can be complemented by more indicators. For example, public interest or public opinions in a certain subject are influencing factors for the performance of a stock [6]. Data from Twitter, Facebook, Reddit, and popular News-Sites arguably represent a portion of the public opinion, while google search trends for example represent the public interest. Researchers and practitioners used such data of the past to address regression problems [e.g., 7, 8].

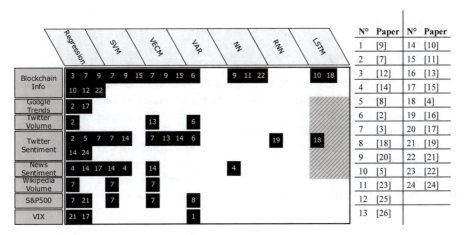

Fig. 1. Bitcoin price prediction approaches

In the reviewed papers, Blockchain information (e.g., blocks mined, number of transactions, total mining revenue, and cost per transaction or hash rates) is the most commonly used input parameter, supplementary to price data. The second mostly applied input feature is the Twitter sentiment. Nine research teams applied Twitter sentiments. Surprisingly, only three teams used Twitter volume data. Abraham et al. found out that Twitter volume and Google search trends are highly correlated with daily price changes [7]. Mc Wharter [15] found Google trends data to be the best predictor out of eight studied variables. Lamon et al. [10] used news headlines as text input feature. This method provides promising results for predicting general price trends, but struggles in accurate price predictions [10].

Out of the 26 considered works, 14 papers used regression models, either to forecast or to complement their approach by comparing it to other models. Their focus is on multivariate linear regression, logistic regression, and vector auto regression. The five works on SVM models are either early works in the field or showed that SVM performs worse than other approaches. Madan et al. [11] showed a decrease in accuracy when applying a SVM algorithm in contrast to binominal generalized linear models. In the reviewed papers, three approaches apply *Vector Autoregression* (VAR) [2, 9, 18]. *Vector error correction models* (VECM) are applied in an event study in order to find a connection between Twitter sentiment, Twitter volume and price reactions [26]. Three approaches that apply simple feedforward *neural networks* (NN) train the model solely with price data. Three out of six papers presenting *recurrent neural networks* (RNN) or LSTM models apply solely historical data on prices and trade volume [13, 27, 28]. Mc Nally et al. [13] for example build both a RNN and a LSTM network on daily price data. At the time of writing this paper and to our best knowledge, no investigations of applying neural networks, as predictive models of hourly Bitcoin price movements are available, which motivates the work at hand.

3   Research Design

3.1   Research Planning

In order to identify relevant predictors (RQ1) and to evaluate the performance of neural networks for hourly Bitcoin price predictions (RQ2), we conduct a four-step procedure (Fig. 2). As the collection of the required data comes from different sources, we describe the *Data Collection* individually for each data source. The step *Data Adjustment* comprises data cleansing. *Sentiment Scoring* comprises the finding of sentiment polarity in both the collected tweets and news headlines. Afterwards, we merge the separate data sets and remove duplicates. Finally, *Model Development and Validation* comprises the development and validation of four different forecasting models.

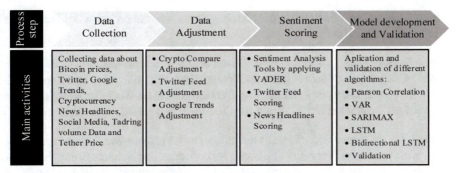

Fig. 2. Data preparation and analysis process

3.2 Data Collection

We list all data collected for the analysis in Table 1. Every data set is collected between September 2nd 2018 and July 26th 2019. In the following, we briefly describe all data sources and the retrieved data sets.

Table 1. Data sources

Data	Source	Method	Details
Price Data	Crypto Compare API	Python REST API	Bitcoin and Tether prices
Twitter Feed	Twitter API + kaggle.com	Python library "tweepy"	Represents public opinion
Google Trends	Google API	Python library "PyTrends"	Represents public interest
News Headlines	Crypto Compare API	Python REST API	Represents public opinion
Reddit/ Facebook/ GitHub Data	Crypto Compare API	Python REST API	Represents public opinion

Bitcoin Price Data: Deviating from all related works, we did not collect the price changes of Bitcoin daily, but on hourly basis instead. A site, which provides global price data, is *cryptocompare.com*, which offers a free-to-use API to collect hourly aggregated price and volume data of over 70 cryptocurrency exchanges.

Twitter Data: To collect every tweet regarding Bitcoin, we apply the Python library *tweepy*. 2.8 million Tweets regarding Bitcoin have been collected in the period of 7th of May to 26th of July in 2019. We extracted the timestamp, the text, the number of likes and retweets and complement it by historical tweets regarding Bitcoin, uploaded by a user on Kaggle.com, which led to over 6 million tweets in the period of 2nd September 2018 to 26th July 2019.

Google Trends Data: In addition to sentiment scores as a representation of the public opinion, Google Trends data is going to represent overall public interest. To pull trend data from Google's API, the Python library *PyTrends* was used. We pulled Google Trends data between September 2nd 2018 and July 26th 2019 and scaled the results.

Cryptocurrency News Data: To study the influence of cryptocurrency-related news sites on price movement and volatility of Bitcoin, we collect related headlines through Crypto Compare's API. Crypto Compare tracks the 40 biggest cryptocurrency-related news sites including: *CoinDesk, TodayOnChain, CoinTelegraph, CCN* and *NullTx*. According to crypto compare, headlines regarding Bitcoin include the phrases *"BTC", "BITCOIN"* and *"SATOSHI"*, while headlines with the phrase *"BITCOIN CASH"* are excluded. In total, 35.000 headlines for the timespan of 2nd of September 2018 to 26th of July 2019 were retrieved.

Social Media Volume Data: Besides providing data on price changes and news feed, Crypto Compare also offers hourly data on social media platforms regarding certain cryptocurrencies. For Reddit, the *subreddit "r/Bitcoin"* is tracked on the number of subscribers, active users, posts, and comments per hour, as well as posts and comments per day. For Facebook, the page *"@Bitcoin"* is tracked on the number of likes and the total number of users that are talking about the page. The Twitter account *"@Bitcoin"* is tracked on the number of followers, favorites, statuses, the number of users who are followed and the number of lists that the account is part of. The data set also contains seven data points on Bitcoins repository on *GitHub*. The platform offers the number of repository stars, forks, open and closed pulls, as well as open and closed bugs.

Tether Price Data: Tether is a special form of cryptocurrency, a so-called *stable coin*. The increasing amount of trading in Tether has a big impact on Bitcoin prices and according to Griffin and Shams [29] should be investigated for price manipulation. In order to receive hourly price and volume data on Tether, we apply the Crypto Compare API once again.

3.3 Data Adjustment

Crypto Compare Data: By applying the python library pandas, we convert the column containing the hourly timestamp from a regular string object into a *datetime object*, in order to sort it in chronological order. The datetime object was then reduced to hours, by strafing the datetime object to format "%y-%m-%d %H", in order to merge it with other data sets later on.

Twitter Data: To obtain a clean data set, we drop all duplicates and all data sets containing no data (empty containers). Finally, we reduce the original data to keep the timestamp and the text rows for the sentiment analysis.

Google Trends Data: To get the correct scaling of the Google Trends data, we apply a Python script to overlap the weekly data points and calculate a ratio, in which the scales are adjusted. The script takes a start- and endpoint as a datetime object and a keyword input as a string object. Afterwards, we create a list, in which a datetime object of the starting point represents every new week. A for-loop now iterates over the range of the weekly list, starts downloading data, creates a Pandas data frame out of it and appends the data frames to another list. We fill the data frames with hourly timestamps of the weekly timeframe and obtain the weekly scaling between 0 and 100. By overlapping the weekly timeframes with one datapoint, a recalling of the weekly data would be possible. For that purpose, we use a third list to store the ratio between the score of the last hour of week 1 and the first hour of week 2 and so on. A second for-loop now iterates through all weekly data and applies this ratio as a correction parameter to the list of weekly Pandas data frames, except the first element (because there is no last hour of week zero). The weekly data frames are now merged into a single data frame representing the complete time period requested. Even though the correction parameter led to accurate values, the overall scaling needs to be fixed once again, since it is not in a range between 0 and 100.

3.4 Sentiment Scoring

In order to receive sentiment scores, we apply the python library VADER on both the collected tweets and collected news headlines. All hyperlinks included in the tweets were deleted. Due to the optimization of VADER to social media texts including emojis and special characters, we decided to keep them, as they probably provide more accurate results regarding the polarization of the given text. Since every tweet with the hashtag Bitcoin were collected, no additional filtering on languages was done. In order to handle non-english tweets, we apply the *Google Translate* Python library. The Google Translate script checks whether the given text is written in English and thus translates the text if necessary.

VADER delivers a score that indicates the polatization of the text (positive: 1, neutral: 0, negative: -1) We solely append a score of a text if it is either above 0.3 or below -0.3, otherwise a 0 is added in the final data set. Applying this approach brings 3.648.079 individual scored tweets for the timespan of 2nd of September 2018 to 26th of July 2019. The final Twitter dataset consists of hourly timestamps with the average of the sentiment values for the respective hour. We apply the same approach on the data set of 35.000 collected news headlines.

3.5 Model Development

In order to find linear relationships between input features and the Bitcoin close price, we apply the *Pearson correlation* analysis. In addition, we compare the results and the predictive power of four approaches: VAR, SARIMAX, LSTM and BiLSTM. A Vector auto regression (VAR) model is a multivariate linear time-series model and is considered as a simple and flexible alternative to the traditional multiple-equations models. VAR uses linear relations between variables, a trend component, constant intercepts and uncorrelated errors (Garcia and Schweitzer 2015). The definition of a lagging parameter and a minimum of two endogenous variables are needed, in order to fit the model. We train the VAR on Bitcoin close, low and high prices as exogenous variables and since VAR models do not have any hyperparameters, we do not need to tune these models.

A Seasonal Autoregressive Integrated Moving-Average with Exogenous Regressors (SARIMAX) model is an ARIMA model that can also handle seasonal components (S) and includes the modeling of exogenous variables (X). We configure the Bitcoin close price as endogenous variable and the collected input features as exogenous variables.

A *Neural Network* (NN) is an information-processing mechanism that is inspired by the human brain. NN learn from "observational data, figuring out its own solution to the problem at hand" [30]. By receiving a set of inputs (also called features) and performing increasingly complex calculations, the network outputs a predictive value or class assignment. A NN consists of a web of nodes called *neurons*, which are grouped up in layers and linked to each other through connectors.

Unlike conventional NN, also called feed forward networks, Recurrent Neural Networks (RNN) can receive a sequence of values as input. To make predictions on statistical data, a time series can be implemented as a sequence, where an output can be the next value in that sequence. In a RNN, the output of the layer is added to the next input and fed back into the same layer, which is typically the only layer in the entire network [31]. The problem of *vanishing gradient*, already known from feedforward networks, is further reinforced by the architecture of RNNs, because each time step is the equivalent of an entire layer of a feed-forward network. This leads to even smaller gradients and to a loss of information over time [32]. To address that problem, so-called gates were introduced to RNNs to forget or remember the current input, if the network decides the information is required for future time steps [31] (Chung et al. 2014). An often-used gate architecture today is called Long Short-Term Memory (LSTM). LSTM Networks were proposed in 1997 by Hochreiter and Schmidhuber and were designed to soften the vanishing or exploding gradient problem [33].

We build the LSTM models with the Python libraries *TensorFlow* and *Keras* [34], while the training was done with a GPU (GeForce GTX 1660Ti). We prepare the data set by framing it as a supervised learning problem and normalizing the input variables. Next, we split the given data into a training set and a test set, in order to test the model on data that is unknown. Therefore, we use a ratio of 90% training data and 10% test data.

We improve the training of the model by changing the hyperparameters, such as the number of layers or neurons or Epochs. For implementing a *Bidirectional LSTM* (BiLSTM) network, which is an advanced version of a regular (or unidirectional) LSTM, we use the same procedure as for the regular LSTM.

A commonly used technique for validating prediction models is cross-validation, which tests how the results of a model generalize to an independent data set, by estimating how accurate a predictive model performs outside the training set [35]. Therefore, the data set must be split into a training set and test set. Cross-validation also works for tuning hyperparameters. To use hyperparameter tuning, the training set needs to be split again into a validation set and a training subset. The model is trained on the training subset, while the parameters are chosen in a way that minimizes the error for the validation set. By using the selected parameters, we train the model on the full training set and test it on the test data set. In order to validate the performance of the VAR and SARIMAX models, a 5-fold cross-validation was performed. In order to tune the hyperparameters and validate the performance of the LSTM and BiLSTM, we apply a 5-fold nested cross-validation.

The final step comprises the tuning of hyper parameters. SARIMAX models have two sets of parameters, the order parameters (p, q, d) and the seasonal parameters (P, Q, D). We evaluate the performance of the model by the Akaike Information Criteria (AIC) score. While the number of layers is fixed to one and the number of epochs to 30, the nested cross-validation process tries to find the best combination of an Optimizer (Adam, RMSprop or SGD), 64 or 128 neurons and a batch size of either 32 or 72. We evaluate the results by applying the loss functions Mean Square Error (MSE) and Mean Absolute Percentage Error (MAPE). The used Python script reveals the best working combination of parameters for every test set in the cross-validation process. The BiLSTM and LSTM parameters are also tuned by nested cross-validation. The number of layers is fixed to three and the number of epochs to 30. Due to unconvincing results of our factor analysis, we decided to integrate all collected features into our training. In order to compare the performance of the five models, we use the results of 5-fold cross-validation for all models for the same time span. To quantify the results, we calculate a MAPE score for each model and for each fold, as well as an average of the MAPE for the complete time span.

4 Results

4.1 Influencing Factors

In total, we analyze the power of 47 influencing factors to predict the Bitcoin price movements. Table 2 provides the results of the Pearson correlation analysis. 2 out of 47 possible factors are statistically non-significant (News sentiment score and Tether price high). In contrast to the non-significant factors, we identify eight factors that strongly correlate with the Bitcoin price development, i.e. these factors have a correlation coefficient above 0.7 or less than −0.7. In line with other studies about the predictive power of Twitter sentiment [e.g. 7, 26], we also identify a strong correlation for the hourly Bitcoin price movements. In addition, we confirm the close relationship between the cryptocurrencies Bitcoin and Tether. All Tether prices that are measured in Bitcoin provide a correlation coefficient above −0.9. Thus, the data reveals that the higher the Tether price, the lower the Bitcoin price and vice versa. All Bitcoin price data have a significant influence on the Bitcoin hourly price, which is not surprising because these values (BTC price high, low, and open) relate to the hourly price directly. Besides factors that have a strong correlation with the Bitcoin price, we also identify factors with a medium correlation. Among others, the page views of Crypto Compare receive correlation coefficients between 0.4 and 0.5. Less important indicators are Facebook likes as well as GitHub code pulls.

Table 2. Bitcoin price correlation coefficients

Variable	Coefficient	Variable	Coefficient
Twitter Sentiment Score	0.7534131***	CryptoC. Forum Page Views	0.4774623***
News Sentiment Score	−0.0038534	CryptoC. Influence Page Views	0.4720214***
Google Trends	0.3141094***	CryptoC. Markets Page Views	0.4587880***
Reddit Subscribers	0.3656004***	CryptoC. Overview Page Views	0.5380816***
Reddit Comments per Hour	0.2833215***	CryptoC. Points	0.4829218***
Reddit Comments per Day	0.2833221***	CryptoC. Posts	0.4701490***
Reddit Active Users	0.0502295**	Bitcoin Price High	0.9998439***
Reddit Posts per Day	0.2574809***	Bitcoin Price Low	0.9998195***
Reddit Posts per Hour	0.2574877***	Bitcoin Price Open	0.9996947***
Facebook likes	0.1302711***	Bitcoin Volume from	0.0634226***
Facebook talked about	−0.0401814**	Bitcoin Volume to	0.4098491***
GitHub Rep. Open Pull Issues	0.3614214***	Tether Price Close (BTC)	−0.9380909***
GitHub Rep. Closed Issues	0.2054122***	Tether Price High (BTC)	−0.9375232***
GitHub Rep. Closed Pull Issues	0.2345545***	Tether Price Low (BTC)	−0.9384082***
GitHub Rep. Forks	0.2298345***	Tether Price Open (BTC)	−0.9378622***
GitHub Rep. Open Issues	0.2407842***	Tether Volume from (BTC)	0.6001629***
GitHub Rep. Stars	0.1874888***	Tether Volume to (BTC)	0.0765503***
GitHub Rep. Subscribers	-0.0261862*	Tether Price Close (USD)	0.0562241***
CryptoC. Total Page Views	0.5044371***	Tether Price High (USD)	0.0117722
CryptoC. Trades Page Views	0.5120901***	Tether Price Low (USD)	0.0909971***
CryptoC. Forum Comments	0.4724169***	Tether Price Open (USD)	0.0564081***
CryptoC. Analysis Page Views	0.4554351***	Tether Volume from (USD)	0.2937562***
CryptoC. Charts Page Views	0.4373161***	Tether Volume to (USD)	0.2944756***
CryptoC. Followers	0.5362737***	*** $p \leq 0.001$, ** $p \leq 0.01$, * $p \leq 0.05$	

4.2 Model Results

The SARIMAX model showed the best results with an order of (2, 1, 0) and a seasonal order of (0, 0, 0) 6000. The best working hyperparameters for LSTM and the Bidirectional LSTM network, found in nested cross-validation, are listed in Table 3. The comparison of the predictive power of the models for the fifth cross-validation is depicted in Fig. 3.

The regular LSTM seems to deliver the best results judging by the graphical comparison. The BiLSTM shows a curve with big spikes. The SARIMAX model shows a good coverage of the original curve, but does not react to the price drop in mid-July. The VAR model curve appears to be a relatively solid representation of the original curve but is for most of the time below the real price level.

The corresponding MAPE scores of all five validations and averages are compared in Table 4. It should be noted that both LSTM and BiLSTM achieve their best performance in CV2, as the market was not very volatile at the time. The 3.52% error in CV5 of LSTM Network is particularly good as the market was volatile at that time and can be viewed as the best performance of all models and validations. The VAR receives a MAPE of 6.36% in CV5 although its average error rate is much higher. However, the average value is increased heavily by the outlier value of the second cross-validation. Apparently, the VAR model needs more data to function properly in comparison to the neural networks. Similarly, the SARIMAX model behaves worse in CV2 than in CV1, but improves significantly.

Table 3. Best BiLSTM and LSTM hyperparameters

Network	Loss function	Cross-Validation	Optimizer	Learn rate	Batch Size	Neurons	Layers
LSTM	MSE	CV1	SGD	0.2	72	64	2
		CV2	SGD	0.2	32	64	2
		CV3	SGD	0.2	32	128	2
		CV4	Adam	0.2	72	128	2
		CV5	RMSProp	0.2	72	128	2
	MAPE	CV1	Adam	0.2	32	64	2
		CV2	RMSprop	0.2	32	64	2
		CV3	RMSprop	0.2	32	64	2
		CV4	Adam	0.2	32	64	2
		CV5	Adam	0.2	72	64	2
BiLSTM	MSE	CV1	Adam	0.2	72	64	3
		CV2	Adam	0.2	72	128	2
		CV3	Adam	0.2	72	128	3

(*continued*)

Table 3. (*continued*)

Network	Loss function	Cross-Validation	Optimizer	Learn rate	Batch Size	Neurons	Layers
		CV4	SGD	0.2	72	128	2
		CV5	SGD	0.2	72	64	2
	MAPE	CV1	Adam	0.2	72	64	3
		CV2	RMSprop	0.2	72	128	2
		CV3	RMSprop	0.2	72	64	3
		CV4	Adam	0.2	72	64	2
		CV5	RMSProp	0.2	72	64	2

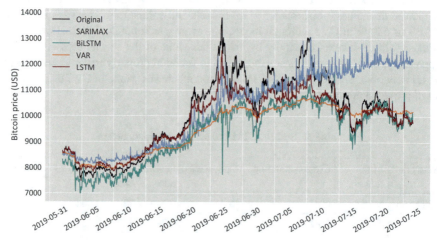

Fig. 3. Result comparison of the fifth cross-validation prediction

Table 4. Error comparison

Model	Cross-Validation	Percentage of absolute error CV5	Error average for all CV
LSTM	CV1	27.29%	8.93%
	CV2	1.18%	
	CV3	3.73%	
	CV4	8.95%	
	CV5	3.52%	

(*continued*)

Table 4. (*continued*)

Model	Cross-Validation	Percentage of absolute error CV5	Error average for all CV
VAR	CV1	63.39%	104.20%
	CV2	407.7%	
	CV3	31.86%	
	CV4	11.55%	
	CV5	6.36%	
BiLSTM	CV1	31.68%	13.03%
	CV2	1.93%	
	CV3	7.55%	
	CV4	16.93%	
	CV5	7.05%	
SARIMAX	CV1	37.61%	26.06%
	CV2	69.24%	
	CV3	9.68%	
	CV4	5.66%	
	CV5	8.10%	

5   Discussion and Outlook

The results of the Pearson Correlation Analysis suggest that the public opinion is a measurable indicator of Bitcoin price changes. On the one hand, the very high correlation between Twitter sentiment scores and the close price shows the importance of the public opinion for the price change of Bitcoin and supports earlier work on daily data. Cryptocurrency news headlines on the other hand do not show any correlation. This is surprising since news outlets specialized on cryptocurrency have arguably a more direct contact to the industry than Twitter. This finding could implicate that the Twitter sentiment score also represents the Twitter community's reaction to certain price changes in the respective time span, rather than Bitcoin's price changing according to the general Twitter polarity. Nevertheless, the results confirm the influence of public opinion on Bitcoin's hourly closing prices.

Measurements of public interest in Bitcoin show a similar picture. The Google Trends scale data correlates moderately and therefore shows a relationship between the amount of Google search queries and the price trend. While the active users on Reddit per hour do not correlate with close prices, the track of Bitcoin's Subreddit shows a weak correlation. However, the values for Facebook activities do not seem to be associated with close prices, since Facebook's *likes* and Facebook's *talked about* show no linear relationship. In summary, public interest in Bitcoin has a measurable impact on hourly price movements.

Surprisingly, every data point of the internal data pulled from Crypto Compare correlates with the Bitcoin hourly close prices. The data points are a track of the usage of their site and forum. Even though not directly related to Bitcoin, the total page views of cryptocompare.com show a high correlation with close prices. This could be due to the fact, that Bitcoin remains a pseudonym for cryptocurrencies and people possibly get involved by hearing of Bitcoin first. Another surprising medium correlated input data point is the number of open pull issues on GitHub, which is the notification on changes being pushed to a repository, which is then being discussed and reviewed by collaborators. This predictor may represent the disagreement of the mining community about changes in the underlying Blockchain implementation of the Bitcoin network. Supporting the paper of Griffin and Shams, the hourly data of all Tether price measurements are very negatively correlated with Bitcoin close prices, as well as the volume of traded tether coins [29].

The comparison of the forecasting results reveals that Long Short-Term Memory networks are best suited for Bitcoin price prediction out of the five models that we considered in the analysis. We cannot identify a particular optimizer to work better than another since the three optimizers are distributed equally in the best performing combinations of hyperparameters. The error rate of 3.52 percent on unseen data in the last validation process is a good result, since it outperforms the second-best models by 40 percent in the forecasting error. Even when comparing the average error rates, LSTM receives the best average error rate with a value of 8.993 percent, which outperforms the second-best model by 30%. Guo et. al. achieved comparable results, as they stated that their study showed a 50% more accurate performance of LSTM networks compared to foundational statistical indicators [5].

In each validation process, the regular Long Short-Term Memory network outperforms the bidirectional LSTM, which is surprising since BiLSTM is a more advanced version of neural net models. Perhaps the network architecture does not fit this particular forecasting problem. The VAR model performs much better if it gets all input features than if it gets only a few. It also reaches the highest average error rate of the five models, but adapts convincingly over the course of the cross-validation, scoring the second lowest error on the last test set. The SARIMAX performance is the second worst performing model, according to the average error rate and the error rate of the fifth cross-validation.

Against the background of these results, the paper at hand contributes to research in three ways. First, 45 significant indicators on the Bitcoin price are identified and discussed. Second, we confirm that the usage of a trained long short-term memory (LSTM) neural network produces the best Bitcoin price predictions on an hourly basis. Third, the results provide a basis for a fruitful discussion of the applicability of neural nets for stock price predictions.

From a practical perspective, the tracking of hourly data points might be used as a trading strategy, as the model performs well on unknown data. The results could encourage asset managers to test the model in practice. All input features that the model was trained on could be streamed live for the respective hour and fed into a trading bot system. Another application is the use as a forecasting model for the highest price of the next hour, in order to follow the trading strategy of selling at the highest price in the respective hour.

A general limitation of this work is the restraint in data availability. This paper has no claim to completeness, as there could exist more predictors. Hourly data on Blockchain information, the Standard & Poor's 500 and the CBOE Volatility Index are not included in the data set due to missing data availability. The inclusion of such data or the increase of the analyzed time period might improve the forecasting model. Furthermore, solely Twitter feeds and news headlines represent the relationship between public opinion and Bitcoin prices. Even though these are arguably solid measurements, the public opinion on certain topics is obviously represented by more than just two data points and suggest integrating other data points. The same applies to Google Trends as a representation of public interest. Applying more advanced tuning techniques such as grid-search, especially for the SARIMAX model might improve the hyperparameter tuning of the considered models.

The developed models in this paper are a starting point for a more precise Bitcoin price forecasting and lead to more research on hourly forecasting with different models and different input variables. Further research should focus on the application and evaluation of such models in practice. We suggest conducting a case study together with asset managers in order to verify the applicability of LSTM for Bitcoin price prediction in asset management.

References

1. Popper, N.: After the Bust, Are Bitcoins More Like Tulip Mania or the Internet? New York Times (2019)
2. Garcia, D., Schweitzer, F.: Social signals and algorithmic trading of Bitcoin. Royal Soc. Open Sci. **2**, 1–13 (2015)
3. Georgoula, I., Pournarakis, D., Bilanakos, C., Sotiropoulos, D.N., Giaglis, G.M.: Using time-series and sentiment analysis to detect the determinants of Bitcoin prices. SSRN J. (2015). https://doi.org/10.2139/ssrn.2607167
4. Mohanty, P., Patel, D., Patel, P., Roy, S.: Predicting fluctuations in cryptocurrencies' price using users' comments and real-time prices. In: 2018 7th International Conference on Reliability, Infocom Technologies and Optimization (Trends and Future Directions) (ICRITO), pp. 477–482. IEEE (2018)
5. Guo, T., Bifet, A., Antulov-Fantulin, N.: Bitcoin volatility forecasting with a glimpse into buy and sell orders. In: 2018 IEEE International Conference on Data Mining Workshops (ICDMW), pp. 989–994. IEEE (2018)
6. Tetlock, P.C.: giving content to investor sentiment: the role of media in the stock market. J. Finan. (2007). https://doi.org/10.1111/j.1540-6261.2007.01232.x
7. Abraham, J., Higdon, D., Nelson, J., Ibarra, J.: Cryptocurrency price prediction using tweet volumes and sentiment analysis. SMU Data Sci. Rev. **1** (2018)
8. Galeshchuk, S., Vasylchyshyn, O., Krysovatyy, A.: Bitcoin response to twitter sentiments. In: 6th International Workshop on Information Technologies in Economic Research (ITER 2018) (2018)
9. Aalborg, H.A., Molnár, P., de Vries, J.E.: What can explain the price, volatility and trading volume of Bitcoin? Financ. Res. Lett. **29**, 255–265 (2019)
10. Lamon, C., Nielsen, E. and Redondo, E.: Cryptocurrency Price Prediction Using News and Social Media Sentiment. https://www.semanticscholar.org/paper/Cryptocurrency-Price-Prediction-Using-News-and-Lamon-Nielsen/c3b80de058596cee95beb20a2d087dbcf8be01ea. Accessed on 22 Nov 22

11. Madan, I., Saluja, S. and Zhao, A.: Automated Bitcoin Trading via Machine Learning Algorithms. https://www.semanticscholar.org/paper/Automated-Bitcoin-Trading-via-Machine-Learning-Madan/e0653631b4a476abf5276a264f6bbff40b132061. Accessed on 22 Nov 2019
12. Akcora, C.G., Dey, A.K., Gel, Y.R., Kantarcioglu, M.: Forecasting Bitcoin price with graph chainlets. In: Phung, D., Tseng, V.S., Webb, G.I., Ho, B., Ganji, M., Rashidi, L. (eds.) PAKDD 2018. LNCS (LNAI), vol. 10939, pp. 765–776. Springer, Cham (2018). https://doi.org/10.1007/978-3-319-93040-4_60
13. McNally, S., Roche, J., Caton, S.: Predicting the price of bitcoin using machine learning. In: 2018 26th Euromicro International Conference on Parallel, Distributed and Network-based Processing (PDP), pp. 339–343. IEEE (2018)
14. Ceyhan, K., Kurtulmaz, E., Sert, O.C., Ozyer, T.: Bitcoin movement prediction with text mining. In: 2018 26th Signal Processing and Communications Applications Conference (SIU), pp. 1–4. IEEE (2018)
15. McWharter, N.: Bitcoin and Volatility: Does the Media Play a Role?. https://creativematter.skidmore.edu/econ_studt_schol/82
16. Pant, D.R., Neupane, P., Poudel, A., Pokhrel, A.K., Lama, B.K.: Proceedings on 2018 IEEE 3rd International Conference on Computing, Communication and Security (ICCCS). October 25th - 27th, 2018, Kathmandu, Nepal: an IEEE Nepal Sub Section Conference. IEEE, Piscataway, NJ (2018)
17. Radityo, A., Munajat, Q., Budi, I.: Prediction of Bitcoin exchange rate to american dollar using artifical neural network methods. In: 2017 International Conference on Advanced Computer Science and Information Systems (ICACSIS) (2017)
18. Giudici, P., Abu-Hashish, I.: What determines bitcoin exchange prices? a network VAR approach. Financ. Res. Lett. **28**, 309–318 (2019)
19. Rodricks, Matthew, R.: Statistical Determinants of Bitcoin. http://www.wpi.edu/Pubs/E-project/Available/E-project-042518-122138/unrestricted/MQP_Final.pdf. Accessed on 22 Nov 2019
20. Greaves, A. and Au, B.: Using the Bitcoin Transaction Graph to Predict the Price of Bitcoin. https://www.semanticscholar.org/paper/Using-the-Bitcoin-Transaction-Graph-to-Predict-the-Greaves-Au/a0ce864663c100582805ffa88918910da89add47. Accessed on 22 Nov 2019
21. Saad, M., Mohaisen, A.: Towards Characterizing Blockchain-based cryptocurrencies for highly-accurate predictions. In: IEEE INFOCOM 2018 - IEEE Conference on Computer Communications Workshops (INFOCOM WKSHPS), pp. 704–709. IEEE (2018)
22. Shah, D., Zhang, K.: Bayesian regression and Bitcoin. In: 2014 52nd Annual Allerton Conference on Communication, Control, and Computing (Allerton), pp. 409–414. IEEE (2014)
23. Indera, N.I., Yassin, I.M., Zabidi, A., Rizman, Z.I.: Non-linear Autoregressive with Exogeneous input (narx) Bitcoin price prediction model using PSO-optimized parameters and moving average technical indicators. J. Fundam. Appl. Sci. **9**, 791 (2018)
24. Stenqvist, E. and Lönnö, J.: Predicting Bitcoin price fluctuation with Twitter sentiment analysis. https://www.semanticscholar.org/paper/Predicting-Bitcoin-price-fluctuation-with-Twitter-Stenqvist-L%C3%B6nn%C3%B6/0954565aebae3590e6ef654fd03410c3bdd7d15a. Accessed on 22 Nov 2019
25. Jang, H., Lee, J.: An empirical study on modeling and prediction of Bitcoin prices with Bayesian neural networks based on blockchain information. IEEE Access **6**, 5427–5437 (2018)
26. Kremser, T., Radszuwill, S., Schweizer, A., Steffek, B.: How do large stakes influence Bitcoin performance? evidence from the Mt.Gox Liquidation Case. In: 27th European Conference on Information Systems (2019)

27. Wu, C.-H., Lu, C.-C., Ma, Y.-F., Lu, R.-S.: A new forecasting framework for Bitcoin price with LSTM. In: 2018 IEEE International Conference on Data Mining Workshops (ICDMW), pp. 168–175. IEEE (2018)
28. Yiying, W., Yeze, Z.: Cryptocurrency price analysis with artificial intelligence. In: 5th International Conference on Information Management (2019)
29. Griffin, J.M., Shams, A.: Is Bitcoin Really Un-Tethered? SSRN J. (2018). https://doi.org/10.2139/ssrn.3195066
30. Nielsen, M.: Neural Networks and Deep Learning. http://neuralnetworksanddeeplearning.com. Accessed on 22 Nov 2019
31. Chung, J., Gulcehre, C., Cho, K., Bengio, Y.: Empirical evaluation of gated recurrent neural networks on sequence modeling. In: NIPS 2014 Deep Learning and Representation Learning Workshop (2014)
32. Hochreiter, S.: The vanishing gradient problem during learning recurrent neural nets and problem solutions. Int. J. Unc. Fuzz. Knowl. Based Syst. **06**, 107–116 (1998)
33. Hochreiter, S., Schmidhuber, J.: Long short-term memory. Neural Comput. **9**, 1735–1780 (1997)
34. Abadi, M., Agarwal, A., et al.: TensorFlow: Large-Scale Machine Learning on Heterogeneous Distributed Systems. http://arxiv.org/pdf/1603.04467v2
35. Vanderplas, J.T.: Python Data Science Handbook. O'Reilly (2017)

Author Index

F. Ahlemann et al. (Eds.): WI 2021, LNISO 47, pp. 771–773, 2021.
https://doi.org/10.1007/978-3-030-86797-3

Printed in the United States
by Baker & Taylor Publisher Services